Caffeine-Related Disorders

Cannabis-Related Disorders

Cocaine-Related Disorders

Hallucinogen-Related Disorders

Inhalant-Related Disorders

Nicotine-Related Disorders

Opioid-Related Disorders

Phencyclidine-Related Disorders

Sedative-, Hypnotic-, or Anxiolytic-
Related Disorders

Polysubstance-Related Disorder

Schizophrenia and Other Psychotic Disorders

Schizophrenia

    Paranoid Type

    Disorganized Type

    Catatonic Type

    Undifferentiated Type

    Residual Type

Schizophreniform Disorder

Schizoaffective Disorder

Delusional Disorder

Brief Psychotic Disorder

Shared Psychotic Disorder

Psychotic Disorder Due to a General Medical Condition

    With Delusions

    With Hallucinations

Substance-Induced Psychotic Disorder

Mood Disorders

Depressive Disorders

    Major Depressive Disorder

    Dysthymic Disorder

Bipolar Disorders

    Bipolar I Disorder

    Bipolar II Disorder (Recurrent
      Major Depressive Episodes With
      Hypomania)

    Cyclothymic Disorder

Mood Disorder Due to a General Medical Condition

Substance-Induced Mood Disorder

Anxiety Disorders

Panic Disorder

    Without Agoraphobia

    With Agoraphobia

Agoraphobia Without History of Panic Disorder

Specific Phobia

Social Phobia (Social Anxiety Disorder)

Obsessive-Compulsive Disorder

Posttraumatic Stress Disorder

Acute Stress Disorder

Generalized Anxiety Disorder

Anxiety Disorder Due to a General Medical Condition

Substance-Induced Anxiety Disorder

Somatoform Disorders

Somatization Disorder

Conversion Disorder

Pain Disorder

Hypochondriasis

Body Dysmorphic Disorder

Factitious Disorders

With Predominantly Psychological Signs and Symptoms

With Predominantly Physical Signs and Symptoms

With Combined Psychological and Physical Signs and Symptoms

(continued on inside back cover)

Abnormal Psychology

Abnormal
Psychology

Fourth Edition

David S. Holmes
University of Kansas

Allyn and Bacon

Boston   London   Toronto   Sydney   Tokyo   Singapore

Executive Editor, Psychology: Rebecca Pascal
Development Editor: Lisa Ziccardi
Series Editorial Assistant: Whitney Brown
Senior Marketing Manager: Caroline Croley
Editorial Production Supervisor: Susan McIntyre
Editorial Production Service: Jane Hoover/Lifland et al., Bookmakers
Composition Buyer: Linda Cox
Manufacturing Buyer: Megan Cochran
Cover Administrator: Linda Knowles
Design and Electronic Composition: Glenna Collett

Copyright © 2001, 1997 by Allyn & Bacon
A Pearson Education Company
160 Gould Street
Needham Heights, MA 02494

Internet: www.abacon.com

Library of Congress Cataloging-in-Publication Data

Holmes, David S., (David Sheridan)
    Abnormal psychology / David S. Holmes.—4th ed.
        p. cm.
    Includes bibliographical references and index.
    ISBN 0-321-05681-7
    1. Psychology, Pathological.   2. Psychology, Pathological—Case studies.   3. Mental illness—Treatment.   I. Title.

RC454.H62 2000
616.89—dc21
                                                    00-040131

All chapter-opening art is the work of Gail Perazzini (perazzini@att.net).

Text and photo credits appear on page 665, which should be considered an extension of the copyright page.

Printed in the United States of America
10 9 8 7 6 5 4 3 2 1   05 04 03 02 01 00

Contents

Each chapter concludes with **Summary, Questions for Making Connections,** and **Key Terms and People.**

PART II   Anxiety, Somatoform, and Dissociative Disorders

5 Anxiety Disorders: Phobias, Generalized Anxiety, and Panic   *122*

PART III   Mood Disorders and Suicide

PART IV   Schizophrenia

10 Schizophrenia: Symptoms and Issues *278*

Preface

Choosing a textbook is an important and difficult task—important because a textbook is a crucial aspect of your course, and difficult because there are so many books from which to choose and each has many facets. I'm very excited about this new edition of my book, and in this preface I'll try to give you a brief overview of what I've done and why.

Goals

Three goals guided the preparation of this edition. The first is to *teach and involve students.* Regardless of how up-to-date or sophisticated a book may be, if it does not teach, it is essentially useless. To help students learn I have organized the material so that ideas build on one another in a systematic fashion. I have also tried to communicate a sense of excitement about the progress occurring in the area of abnormal psychology. Finally, I continue to use numerous case studies to illustrate symptoms, causes, and treatments.

My second goal is to *incorporate the many new findings* about the causes and treatments of abnormal behavior. The field of abnormal psychology is evolving very rapidly, and almost every section of the book has new material—much of it intriguing and some of it surprising. For example, there is a discussion of the use of *magnetism* (transcranial magnetic stimulation) for treating depression. Magnetism? That sounds like a throwback to Mesmer 200 years ago, but in fact the results of a recently published series of double-blind placebo-controlled experiments consistently indicate that the application of an electromagnetic field to the left frontal lobe (via magnets on the forehead) can dramatically reduce depression in otherwise treatment-resistant patients (see Chapter 8).

My third goal is to provide students with a *platform for future learning.* The necessity of understanding abnormal behavior does not end with the final examination in the course. Our students are going to continue to be exposed to many new ideas about abnormal behavior through sources such as television, and to prepare them for those ideas I have attempted to *teach critical thinking by modeling.* That is, I consistently raise the tough questions that must be asked when considering new ideas. Furthermore, I try to provide *a framework into which future ideas can be integrated.* In other words, I attempt to provide students with

current answers but also with perspectives for evaluating and understanding future answers.

Organization

A few comments about the organization of the book may be helpful.

Overall Organization. As the Contents indicates, the overall organization is fairly traditional. However, the material need not be assigned in the order in which it appears in the Contents. The six parts and the chapters within each part are designed to be largely freestanding; thus, they can be reordered, and some can even be omitted, thereby allowing you to "customize" the book.

Organization within Chapters (Topics). An important change in this edition is the division of each chapter into a number of Topics. In most of the chapters the Topics are focused on specific disorders. For example, Chapter 5 contains Topics devoted to phobias, generalized anxiety disorder, and panic disorders. However, when a chapter is devoted to a single disorder such as depression, Topics are focused on the symptoms, explanations, and treatments of the disorder. Each Topic is a complete and freestanding unit. Each begins with one or more vignettes illustrating the human side of psychological disorders and raising questions to be considered, and each ends with a Thinking Critically section. In these Thinking Critically sections I review tough issues and attempt to draw conclusions. I have experimented with this Topic approach for a number of years and find that it works well; students like the manageable "chunks" of material, and the organization facilitates learning. Furthermore, the use of stand-alone Topics that can easily be reordered or omitted provides you with another opportunity to "customize" the book.

Disorders as "Packages" (Symptoms, Explanations, and Treatments). In this edition each disorder is presented as a "package" consisting of *symptoms, explanations,* and *treatments.* In other words, for each disorder I first describe the symptoms, then I indicate how the symptoms can be explained, and finally I describe the treatments that derive from the explanations. I use this approach because even though disorders may be grouped together because they share a common symptom, such as anxiety, the disorders in a group may have very different causes and require different treatments. For example, phobias are very different from panic attacks, and both of those disorders are distinct from obsessive-compulsive disorder.

When discussing each disorder, I use a consistent outline for presenting material:

Symptoms
    Mood, Cognitive, Physical, Motor
Issues
    History, Prevalence, Gender/Sociocultural Factors, Diagnostic Problems
Explanations
    Psychodynamic, Learning, Cognitive, Physiological
Treatments
    Psychodynamic, Learning, Cognitive, Physiological
Thinking Critically

This approach provides students with a template within which to organize material. That template facilitates teaching, aids recall, and enhances the ability to compare ideas and disorders.

Writing Style

There are two things I should point out about my writing style: First, in most cases *I write in the first person.* My goal is to talk with and engage students, not to write a "textbook." In our lectures we "bring students in" by talking and interacting with them, and that is what I have tried to do with this book. Furthermore, I talk about "*your* brain" rather than "*the* brain." When this approach was class-tested, students reported that this "voice" made the material more relevant and gave the information a greater impact.

The second point is that I have placed a very high priority on organization, clarity, and simplicity. Every section follows an outline, each paragraph begins with a thesis sentence or question, and my writing has a simple, direct style. As a professor you already know the material and how the pieces fit together, but that's not the case for students—for them most of the ideas are new. The clarity of the writing was one of the features students appreciated most in earlier editions, and I hope I have enhanced that strength in this edition.

Orientation

Whether they admit it or not, authors have points of view that influence their books. What is my orientation? I can probably answer that general question by answering four specific questions related to abnormal behavior.

Do Different Disorders Have Different Causes? Many authors favor a particular point of view, and implicitly or explicitly they explain virtually every disorder from that point of view. In contrast, it is my belief that *different disorders have different causes* and *no single theory can account for all disorders.* For instance, some disorders, such as phobias, appear to be learned, whereas others, such as schizophrenia, may be caused by physiological problems in the brain. Furthermore, some disorders may stem from more than one cause; for example, depression may be the result of stress, incorrect beliefs, or physiology. Therefore, for each disorder I first present all of the explanations for which there is some empirical support, and then in the Thinking Critically section I step back, evaluate the evidence and suggest conclusions. In other words, in this book I approach each disorder as a mystery; we collect the clues and then try to identify the "villain."

Do Different Disorders Require Different Treatments? If different disorders have different causes, then it follows that different disorders require different treatments. Therefore, after describing how a particular disorder can be explained, I discuss the various treatments that follow from the different explanations. Linking treatments to causes provides another means of understanding the causes, and the cause–treatment links provide a "package" for the reader.

What Role Does Physiology Play in Abnormal Behavior? For many students and mental health professionals, the role of physiology in abnormal psychology is controversial and troublesome, but this need not be the case. There is no doubt that in the past few years physiology has provided the basis for many impressive breakthroughs in our understanding and treatment of abnormal behavior. However, it is not necessarily the case that physiology is taking over and eliminating psychology; rather, the best explanations and treatments come from an integration of physiology and psychology. For example, there is no doubt that schizophrenia is due to biochemical and structural problems in the brain, but the symptoms are often triggered or exacerbated by psychological stress.

Physiology influences abnormal behavior in two ways: First, in some disorders physiology is the *primary cause.* Schizophrenia is a good example of this. Second, even when physiology is not the cause of a disorder, it plays a role because ultimately *all behaviors are the result of physiological processes in the brain.* In other words, physiology is the final step in the pathway to behavior. For example, stress leads to depression because it changes the levels of neurotransmitters in the brain, and those changes in neurotransmitters lead to depression. (That is an example of the integration of physiology and psychology.) The fact that physiology is the final common step explains why drugs can sometimes be effective treatments even when physiology is not the primary cause of the disorder. For instance, antidepressants can be used to adjust neurotransmitter levels until the stress can be overcome. Recognizing this is important because it disabuses students of the notion that because disorders can be treated with drugs, the disorders must necessarily have a physiological cause. Because of the many interconnections between the psychological and physiological causes of abnormal behavior, discussions of psychological and physiological factors are interwoven throughout this book.

What Roles Do Gender and Culture Play in Abnormal Behavior? Differences in gender and culture are associated with a wide variety of factors that are linked to abnormal behaviors, including stress levels, role models, and physiology. We cannot have a complete explanation of abnormal behavior without considering these factors; therefore, in the discussion of each disorder I have included comments on the roles of gender and sociocultural factors. The comments are woven into the discussions and become parts of the overall pictures. Below is a guide to some of the gender and sociocultural coverage found in this edition:

- Chapter 1 includes a section titled "What Roles Do Gender and Culture Play in Abnormal Behavior?" which gives an overview of gender and cultural influences on abnormal behavior.
- Chapter 4 contains a discussion of the sociocultural factors involved in diagnostic techniques.
- Chapter 6 includes a major Topic section entitled "Gender and Sociocultural Factors in Anxiety Disorders," which covers the important issues of gender, age, social class, ethnicity, and culture.
- Chapter 7 includes a discussion of the role gender and sociocultural factors play in the explanation for and diagnosis of somatoform disorders.
- Chapter 8 includes a section on the role of gender and socioeconomic factors in the explanation for and diagnosis of major depressive disorder.
- Chapter 9 contains a discussion of the gender and socioeconomic factors that are involved in the diagnosis of bipolar disorder and also a section on gender, age, and culture as these factors relate to suicide.
- Chapter 10 includes a section on sociocultural factors—including age, gender, ethnicity, and social class—related to schizophrenia.
- Chapter 13 discusses sociocultural factors that are related to autism.
- Chapter 14 includes material on the role sociocultural factors such as gender and age play in eating disorders.
- Chapter 15 discusses sociocultural factors related to drug use.
- Chapter 17 discusses the problems of measuring intelligence and the role of sociocultural factors with

regard to this issue. There is also material on retardation due to psychosocial factors.

Pedagogical Features

The most important pedagogical feature of any book is the quality of the writing—if that's not good, the book just won't teach. However, there are some additional features that can be added to enhance the degree to which students can learn from a book, and this book has a number of such features. Two of these features (Thinking Critically and Questions for Making Connections) are new to this edition.

- *Chapter Outlines.* Each chapter begins with a detailed outline that can be used to guide reading and facilitate reviewing.
- *Vignettes.* Each Topic is preceded by one or more vignettes that illustrate the problem to be considered, raise important questions, and "bring the student in."
- *Case Studies.* There are over 60 major case studies and many more examples that illustrate symptoms, causes, and treatments.
- *Thinking Critically: Questions about [Topic].* New in this edition is a section at the end of each Topic entitled "Thinking Critically: Questions about [topic]." In these sections I examine tough issues, evaluate evidence, and suggest conclusions. For example, in Chapter 8 I ask, what do we really mean when we say we have "effective" treatments for depression? The answer may be somewhat surprising.
- *Summaries.* At the end of each chapter there is a "bullet" summary that can be used for reviewing.
- *Questions for Making Connections.* Also new in this edition is a set of questions at the end of each chapter. Although answering these questions requires knowledge of the material, most of them also require that the student make connections across Topics, explanations, and disorders. The goal here is to facilitate active processing of information.
- *Lists of Key Terms and People.* At the end of each chapter there is an alphabetical list of the key (boldfaced) terms and people discussed in that chapter. Students use these to test their recall.
- *Running Glossary.* I have discovered that end-of-book glossaries go largely unused and that what students want and use is a running glossary in which new terms are defined at the bottom of the page on which the terms first appear. Students use this as a study device, and when they need more information they can conveniently find it on the page. Running glossaries have been used effectively in introductory psychology texts, but I originally hesitated to use one in this book because I was afraid it would be viewed as "dumbing down." However, class testing revealed that

students really liked this feature and found it to be effective, so I have included it.

What's New in This Edition?

In preparing this edition, I did an extensive amount of rewriting to incorporate new information and make the material more accessible to students. To give you a sense of the changes and additions, below I list a few of them:

- In Chapter 1 I have expanded the coverage of the history of abnormal psychology as well as coverage of today's mental health professionals. In particular, there is more information on counselors and social workers than in previous editions.
- In this edition I have divided the introductory discussion of the explanations for abnormal behavior into two chapters (Chapters 2 and 3). The information about treatment approaches is directly linked to the explanations for abnormal behavior from which those approaches grew.
- In Chapter 4 I have expanded the section on psychological interviews
- In this edition I cover anxiety disorders in two chapters (Chapters 5 and 6) rather than three, and I have integrated discussion of explanations and treatments for each anxiety disorder. I have also updated the coverage of physiological treatments and expanded the discussion of the relationship between gender and anxiety disorders.
- In Chapter 7 I have added a new section on the link between somatoform and obsessive-compulsive disorder, a new section on recent legal cases and the diagnosis of dissociative personality disorder, and a new case study on somatoform versus physical disorders and the implications for insurance coverage.
- In this edition I cover mood disorders in two chapters (Chapters 8 and 9) rather than three, and I have integrated discussion of explanations and treatments for each mood disorder. There is also an explanation of the use of repetitive magnetic stimulation for the treatment of depression.
- In Chapter 9 I have added a new section on diagnostic criteria for bipolar and cyclothymic disorders and a new section on "unawareness of mania," and I have expanded coverage of drugs in treating bipolar disorder. I have also added a new section on psychoeducation as a treatment for bipolar disorder, a new case study detailing a student's account of depression and mania, and a new case study featuring Dr. Kay Redfield Jamison talking about mania, depression, and treatment.
- In this edition I've consolidated the coverage of schizophrenia into two chapters instead of three: one on symptoms and issues (Chapter 10) and the other on explanations and treatments (Chapter 11). I've added a new case study highlighting the importance of ruling out other explanations before a diagnosis of schizophrenia is made.
- I have reorganized Chapter 12 so that it follows the *DSM* clusters of personality disorders. I have also added coverage of adjustment disorders and several new case studies to this chapter.
- I have extensively updated the research and references in Chapter 13. There is also some new information linking the symptoms of autism to problems with specific areas of the brain.
- In Chapter 14 I have expanded the coverage of sociocultural factors and eating disorders. I have also added a new section on the relationship between cancer and stress and a new case study about a high school student's battle with anorexia.
- In Chapter 15 I have expanded the coverage of explanations and treatments for drug abuse—including new material on Naltrexone, Antabuse, Alcoholics Anonymous, and D.A.R.E. There is also a new case study.
- I have added two new case studies to Chapter 16: one that includes a note from a man with gender identity disorder and another about a boy who was raised as a girl.
- I have updated the coverage of Alzheimer's disease in Chapter 17 and included new material on Turner's syndrome and savant syndrome.

Supplements for Instructors

Instructor's Manual. Written by Thomas Joiner of Florida State University, this manual includes detailed chapter overviews, learning objectives, and chapter outlines; key terms and concepts; lecture enhancements, including teaching notes, discussion questions, additional lecture ideas, and class activities; and suggestions for readings and film/video resources.

Test Bank. Completely revised for the 4th edition, this tool, written by Rebecca and R. James Walker-Sands, includes between 125 and 150 questions per chapter, in multiple choice, true-false, and short answer/essay formats. For ease of use each test question includes an answer, page reference, difficulty rating, and question type (applied, conceptual, factual, etc.). This collection of test questions can also be edited using Allyn and Bacon's state-of-the-art computerized testing system.

Computerized Testing System. Allyn and Bacon Test Manager is an integrated suite of testing and assessment tools for Windows and Macintosh. You can use Test Manager to create professional-looking exams in just minutes by building tests from the existing database of questions, editing questions, or writing your own. Course management features include a class roster, gradebook, and item analysis. Test Manager also has everything you need to create and administer online tests.

Patient Videos. Because I believe there is no better way for a student to learn about disorders than from people who are affected by them, adopters of this textbook will receive two videos in which I interview patients diagnosed with various disorders, from attention-deficit/hyperactivity disorder to schizophrenia. These patients believe that speaking out about their disorders will remove much of the stigma that society places on them. Some of those interviewed are also featured in case studies in the text.

APPI Video Series and Guide. A series of seven videos on diagnostic issues and treatments for a variety of disorders is available from American Psychiatric Press, Inc. A text-specific video guide correlates the content of the videos with the textbook and provides test questions on video content.

Transparencies. A new collection of four-color transparencies, which extend visual learning beyond the textbook, is available on adoption. This collection includes images from the text, as well as additional ones, to help further enhance teaching and learning.

PowerPoint CD-ROM. A collection of PowerPoint slides highlighting key concepts in each chapter is available for easy use in your lectures. This presentation tool is available in CD-ROM and Web formats and includes integrated images from the text to further enhance your presentations.

Supplements for Students

Study Guide. Developed by Pamela Brouillard at Texas A&M University, Corpus Christi, this student resource includes questions on key issues from the chapters, chapter outlines and key terms, chapter learning objectives and summaries, multiple-choice self-tests, sample case studies, and answer keys for each chapter.

Practice Tests. This manual of self-tests, created by Grant Rich of Antioch College, provides students with 25 multiple-choice questions per chapter, complete with answer justifications for the incorrect choices. Students will be able to test their knowledge before taking the classroom test.

Case Studies in Abnormal Behavior by Robert G. Meyer. Now in its 5th edition, this rich collection of case studies, including contemporary and classic cases, illustrates a wide range of clinical and legal issues related to abnormal psychology.

Casebook of Psychological Disorders: The Human Face of Emotional Distress by Steven S. Schwartzburg. This casebook offers 15 lively cases illustrating a wide range of specific *DSM-IV* diagnoses. Issues relating to gender and cultural diversity are integrated, highlighting how psychological distress is experienced and treated in real life.

Quick Guide to the Internet for Abnormal Psychology. This helpful resource provides direct routes to research on particular mental disorders, contacts with support services and Web locations of mental health professional organizations. This guide makes searches on the Internet more efficient and provides helpful information for doing research on the Internet, such as how to cite Internet sources. It also directly links you and your students with the extensive Web site that accompanies this textbook.

Online Supplements

Companion Web Site with Online Practice Tests. This companion Web site, which can be accessed at *www.abacon. com/holmes,* offers a wide range of resources to both the instructors and students. Students will find learning objectives, practice tests, and links to stable URLs with brief descriptions of what will be found at the site, who the author is, and how it is relevant to the chapter material. Also available on the Web site are interactive case studies and news updates to help further apply psychology to students' everyday lives and to provide applied examples for lectures. Students can also download patient video clips for selected chapters.

Acknowledgments

Writing and revising this book was a huge task, and its completion was made possible by the help of many individuals. First, recognition should go to the thousands of researchers whose work provided the basis for this book. Without their efforts we would still think that abnormal behavior was caused by demons.

Second, and very important, is the large number of colleagues (especially LSW), friends, and family members (especially ESH) who provided information, advice, and support throughout this exciting but sometimes difficult period of revision. These people were invaluable—thanks!

Third, thanks are due to my students, who kept asking tough questions, and to the clients who shared their painful experiences. Insofar as this book is dedicated to anyone, it is dedicated to my students and to the many individuals who suffer from mental disorders. I hope that this book will take us one step further in the process of understanding abnormal behavior.

Fourth, this revision would still be a pile of manuscript pages if it had not been for the staff at Allyn and Bacon. Most notable in that group are Rebecca Pascal, Executive

Editor for Psychology; Lisa Ziccardi, Development Editor; Susan McIntyre, Editorial Production Supervisor; and Caroline Croley, Marketing Manager. Thanks are also due to Jane Hoover and her group at Lifland et al., Bookmakers, to designer and graphic illustrator Glenna Collett, to photo researcher Helane Prottas, and to anatomical artist Jay Alexander.

Finally, it is important to acknowledge the contributions of the reviewers who have carefully read the manuscript and offered helpful suggestions on this and the three previous editions. I would like to thank them all:

James Backlund, Kirtland Community College

Marilyn Blumenthal, State University of New York at Farmingdale

Thomas Bradbury, University of California, Los Angeles

Linda Bosmajian, Hood College

James F. Calhoun, University of Georgia

Michael Cline, J. Sargeant Reynolds Community College

James Clopton, Texas Tech University

Eric Cooley, Western Oregon State University

Laurie Corey, Westchester Community College

Robert D. Coursey, University of Maryland at College Park

William Curtis, Camden County College

Linda K. Davis, Mt. Hood Community College

Richard Downs, Boise State University

Donna K. Duffy, Middlesex Community College

Sally Foster, Mira Costa College

Stan Friedman, Southwest Texas State University

William Rick Fry, Youngstown State University

Steve Funk, Northern Arizona University at Flagstaff

Herb Goldberg, licensed psychologist, Los Angeles

Bernard S. Gorman, Nassau Community College

Pryor Hale, Piedmont Valley Community College

James E. Hart, Edison State Community College

Stephen Hinshaw, University of California, Berkeley

William G. Iacono, University of Minnesota

Rick Ingram, San Diego State University

James Reid Jones, Delta State University

Boaz Kahana, Cleveland State University

Stephen R. Kahoe, El Paso Community College

Carolin Keutzer, University of Oregon

Alan King, University of North Dakota

Herbert H. Krauss, Hunter College

Marvin Lee, Shenandoah University

Stephen Lopez, University of California, Los Angeles

Joseph Lowman, University of North Carolina, Chapel Hill

David Lowy, Oakland University

Janet R. Matthews, Loyola University

Paul Mazeroff, Catonsville Community College

Gary McClure, Georgia Southern University

Joseph Newman, University of Wisconsin–Madison

Dimitri Papageorgis, University of British Columbia

Rebecca Rogers, University of Augusta

Karen Saenz, Houston Community College—Eastside Campus

George W. Shardlow, City College of San Francisco

Steven S. Smith, University of Wisconsin–Madison

Brian Stagner, Texas A & M University

Genevieve D. Stevens, Houston Community College System

Yolanda Suarez-Crowe, Jackson State University

R. Bruce Tallon, Niagra College

Carol Thompson, Muskegon Community College

David Wittrock, North Dakota State University

Continuing Support and Feedback

Helping students develop an understanding of abnormal psychology is an exciting but demanding task, and *if there is anything I can do to help you with that task, please do not hesitate to contact me.* My e-mail address is: Dholmes@ ukans.edu; my office phone is: (785) 864-9823; my home phone is: (913) 722-6907; and my office address is: Psychology Department, Fraser Hall, University of Kansas, Lawrence, KS 66045. *Good luck with your course. I will look forward to hearing from you.*

David S. Holmes

David Holmes is currently on the faculty at the University of Kansas, where he holds a Chancellor's Club Distinguished Professorship. He received his PhD in clinical psychology from Northwestern University and did his clinical internship at the Harvard Medical School (Massachusetts Mental Health Center). He has been on the faculty at Northwestern University, the University of Texas, the New School for Social Research, and the University of Kansas. He was also a Visiting Research Scholar in the Personality and Social Psychology "think tank" at the Educational Testing Service, Princeton.

Professor Holmes focuses most of his attention on the areas of psychopathology, personality, and health psychology. He has published more than 130 articles in leading scientific journals and received numerous awards for teaching. For example, he received the Award for Distinguished Teaching in Psychology from the American Psychological Foundation. The citation for that award called attention to his "*writing accessible textbooks with impeccable scholarship.*" He was also named the Outstanding Teacher in a Four-Year College or University by the Division of Teaching of the American Psychological Association, received the Standard Oil Foundation Award for Excellence in Teaching, was twice named as an Outstanding Professor by the Mortar Board Society, received a Kemper Fellowship for Distinguished Teaching, and was named as one of the Outstanding Educators in America. His Distinguished Professorship at the University of Kansas is unique in that it was designed to recognize an individual who has made national contributions in both research and teaching.

Within the American Psychological Association, Professor Holmes served on the Board of Scientific Affairs (chair), the Board of Educational Affairs, the Committee on Membership and Fellowship (chair), and the Board of Convention Affairs (chair). He has been elected a Fellow in the Divisions of Clinical Psychology, Personality and Social

Psychology, Health Psychology, Teaching of Psychology, and General Psychology. He was also elected a Fellow of the American Psychopathological Association. For six years Professor Holmes served on the Advanced Psychology Test committee for the Graduate Record Examination.

1

Introduction:
History and Issues

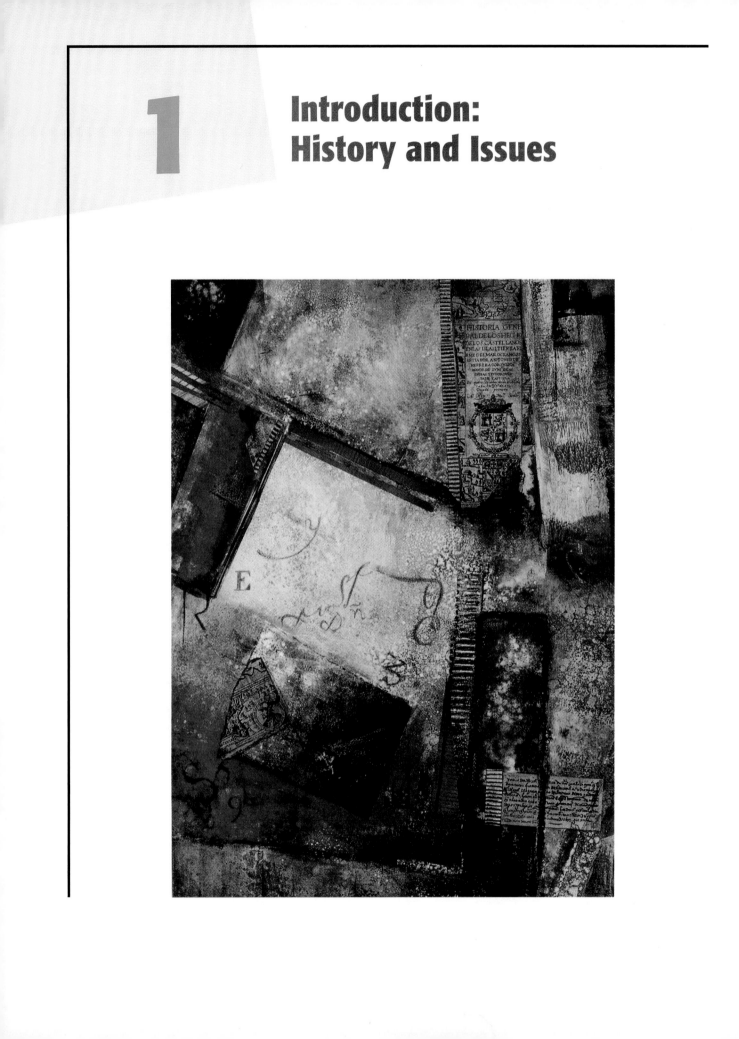

MENTAL DISORDERS CONSTITUTE one of the most serious and perplexing problems you may ever face. For example, consider the following e-mail message I received recently from one of my students, a National Merit Scholar who is on a major scholarship. She is exceptionally bright, but because of her severe depression and fear of people, she is miserable and unable to function and may eventually be forced to drop out of school.

Dear Dr. Holmes,

Your syllabus says that we should talk to you if we have physical or psychological problems that might influence our class work, and I'd like to take you up on that offer. My problems are primarily psychological. I've struggled with depression for as long as I can remember. It comes and goes, but it's pretty bad right now. I've skipped all of my classes for the past three days because I was too depressed to get out of bed. When I'm like that, I can't do anything but sleep or just sit there and stare at the walls. I had really bad spells like this when I was in the sixth and tenth grades, and my grades suffered because of it. I'm afraid the same thing is going to happen now.

I have really sudden mood swings. Like last Wednesday, I was completely depressed in the morning, then in the afternoon I cleaned my entire dorm room from top to bottom and wrote a three page paper and went to a friend's party and came home and still wasn't tired. That doesn't happen too often, though. Most of the time I'm somewhere between depressed and really, really depressed. I feel better at some times than others. (At the moment, I'm only slightly depressed, or I wouldn't be able to sit here and write this to you.) But I'm never, ever happy for more than a few minutes at a time.

That isn't my only problem. I used to think I was just shy, but now that I'm in college it's becoming a huge problem. I'm terrified of big groups of people, and I can't go to a crowded place, or to a place I haven't been before, by myself. Sometimes even when I'm with someone else, I still can't go to crowded places. A guy that I like asked me to the movies the other day, and I had to make up some excuse not to go because I couldn't stand the thought of a crowded movie theater. I get really nervous getting off the elevator in my dorm if there are people in the lobby. I don't know how I'm ever going to get my research paper done, because I can't go to the library. Some days I don't eat, because I can't go to the dining hall alone. I get panicky just thinking about things like that.

My mother has all the symptoms of manic depression. She made my life a living hell, and I don't ever want to do that to anyone else. I know I need help. I'm sorry for bothering you with this, but I thought you'd probably be able to give me better advice than anyone else could. I also wanted you to know that I didn't miss your class because I was too lazy to come or because I didn't care. I want to do well, but when you feel like you're living in a dark little hole, it's hard to concentrate on anything else.

When I start feeling a little better, I'll sort of regret telling you this, because when I'm not as depressed I feel stupid for ever being depressed at all. But I know I really need to do something. I'm tired of being miserable all the time. Thanks for your help.

A few weeks later, after she had left school, I received the following note from the student:

dear professor holmes,
i was on 10 mg a day of Prozac for two weeks, then i started taking 20 mg a day . . . and i just want to die . . . i don't even believe in God, but i keep praying that if there is one, he'll let me die, because i can't take this anymore. . . .

This student gave me permission to publish her messages in the hope that they would help others. We'll return to her later.

Unfortunately, this student is not an isolated example; many people suffer from even more serious and bizarre symptoms. For example, later in this book you will learn about a man who has hallucinations (hears voices), so that when he is with other people he does not know whether the voices he hears are actually the voices of other people talking to him or are hallucinations. This makes it very difficult for him to function. You will also meet a friend of mine named Betty who sees "monks" in her apartment who tell her she should slash her wrists. Sometimes Betty also has difficulty talking to people because her thoughts get scrambled and her sentences don't make sense. Other people are plagued with eating disorders, substance abuse disorders, and gender identity disorders.

To put the problem of abnormal behavior into perspective, consider the following:

▶ More than 30% of Americans will suffer from at least one major psychological disorder during their lifetimes.

▶ About 15% of the U.S. population suffers from major depression, and the rate is increasing.

▶ Antidepressants are among the most frequently prescribed drugs in the United States.

▶ Alcoholism and alcohol abuse cost the U.S. economy about $125 billion a year.

▶ Psychiatric disorders account for 14.2% of high school dropouts and 4.7% of college dropouts; it is estimated that every year more than 7 million people terminate their education prematurely because of these disorders (Kessler, Foster, Saunder, & Stang, 1995).

While these figures are staggering, they do little to convey the intensely personal aspects of the problem:

▶ The confusion and terror felt by an individual with schizophrenia when suddenly the world just does not make sense anymore

▶ The agony and despair of the depressed individual who feels unreachable, "in a dark little hole"

▶ The conflict of the individual who suffers from bulimia and who binges and purges every day until her teeth and throat rot from the gastric acid

▶ The shock of the mother whose unresponsive infant is labeled "autistic"

▶ The terrible feeling of helplessness experienced by a mentally ill patient when the heavy door to the "closed ward" swings shut and locks

This book is not about the problems of other people. Mental illness touches all of us at some point during our lives; if you are not the one afflicted, then it will be a family member, loved one, or close friend. Although the problem of abnormal behavior is personally relevant and emotionally charged, in this book we will be exploring it from an

Mental illness touches all of us, regardless of our age, gender, race, cultural background, or socioeconomic status. It is important to remember that the psychological disorders you will learn about in this book have significant personal ramifications for those people who are afflicted, as well as their family members and their friends.

objective and scientific point of view. Nevertheless, it is important that we keep in mind the intense and significant personal ramifications of what we are studying.

We now know a great deal about the causes and treatment of abnormal behavior. However, there is still a gap between what we know and what we need to know. In this book I will tell you about what we know, but I will also be honest in telling you about the gaps in our knowledge.

To establish a foundation for our study of abnormal behavior, in this chapter we will consider four basic questions: (1) What behaviors are abnormal? (2) How did our explanations for abnormal behavior develop? (3) Who are today's mental health professionals? (4) What are the "hot button" questions about abnormal behavior?

TOPIC I

What Behaviors Are Abnormal?

> Michael often hears a voice talking to him when no one else is around; in other words, he has hallucinations. In most European cultures, this would result in his being defined as having a psychiatric disorder. But would Michael necessarily be defined as having a psychiatric disorder if he lived in another culture? That is, are hallucinations always considered abnormal?
>
> Nicole believes that she is God and has returned to earth to save civilization. Is she suffering from a psychiatric disorder, or might she really be God? Even if we agree that Nicole is wrong about who she is, does that mean she has a psychiatric disorder? In other words, is simply being wrong a symptom of a psychiatric disorder?

As many as 30% of us will show abnormal behaviors that are serious enough to justify our being diagnosed as suffering from a psychiatric disorder, but what behaviors are "abnormal"? If we are going to study the causes and treatments of abnormal behaviors, we had better begin by deciding what is abnormal.

 ## Distress, Disability, and Deviance

Arriving at a generally acceptable definition of abnormal behavior is difficult because some people prefer to define such behavior from the point of view of the *individual whose behavior is being considered*, whereas others prefer to define it from the point of view of the *culture in which the individual is living*. Both viewpoints have something to contribute to an overall definition, so let's consider both of them.

The Individual's Perspective

In defining abnormal behavior from the point of view of the individual, attention is focused first on the individual's **distress.** For example, emotions such as anxiety and depression can cause psychological pain for individuals, and so those feelings are defined as abnormal. In other words, just as physical pain is a sign of a physical abnormality, so psychological pain is an indicator of a psychological abnormality.

Second, attention is focused on the individual's **disability.** Specifically, behavior that interferes with an individual's ability to function personally, socially, or occupationally can be defined as abnormal. For example, if an individual is so depressed that he or she cannot study, work, or interact with others effectively, the depression can be defined as abnormal behavior. From the personal point of view, then, abnormality is defined primarily in terms of the individual's *happiness* and *effectiveness;* what others think about the behavior is irrelevant.

The Culture's Perspective

In defining abnormal behavior from the cultural point of view, attention is focused on **deviance,** that is, the degree to which an individual's behavior differs, or *deviates,* from cultural norms. For example, an individual who hallucinates will be viewed as abnormal because most people do not hallucinate. However, it is relevant to note that what is abnormal in one culture may be normal in another culture. Indeed, in some cultures hallucinations are taken as a sign of schizophrenia and the individual is hospitalized, whereas in other cultures hallucinations are believed to be the voice of a god and the individual is made a priest (Murphy, 1976). It should also be noted that only deviant behaviors that a culture considers "bad" are defined as abnormal. Having an IQ of 140 or being exceptionally well adjusted is also deviant, but such "good" deviance is not customarily thought of as "abnormal." From the cultural point of view, then, abnormality is defined in terms of societal norms, and the feelings of the individual are disregarded.

> **distress** Emotions such as anxiety and depression that upset an individual; a factor used to define abnormal behavior from an individual's point of view.
>
> **disability** Disruptions in the ability to function personally, occupationally, or socially; a factor used to define abnormal behavior from an individual's point of view.
>
> **deviance** The degree to which an individual's behaviors differ from others'; a factor used to define abnormal behavior from a cultural point of view.

Comment

From the preceding discussion it is clear that distress, disability, and deviance (the "three Ds") all play a role in defining abnormal behavior and that no one factor is sufficient to account for all abnormal behavior. For example, if we ignore distress and look only at deviance, a depressed individual will be ignored until he or she attempts suicide, whereas if we ignore deviance and rely only on distress, the happy but hallucinating individual with schizophrenia will not be treated.

Sometimes the personal and cultural points of view concerning what is abnormal come into conflict. Such a conflict occurred with respect to homosexuality. The practice of homosexuality deviates from our cultural norm, and thus for many years it was defined as abnormal and considered a disorder. However, in 1980 the panel of experts that makes the decisions concerning what behaviors are abnormal (see discussion below) reconsidered the issue and decided that homosexuality would be considered a disorder only if the individual was anxious or depressed because of his or her homosexuality (American Psychiatric Association, 1980). In other words, the cultural perspective was abandoned, and attention was shifted to the personal point of view. The issue was considered again in 1987, and at that time the decision was made to completely eliminate homosexuality as a disorder (American Psychiatric Association, 1987). The notion is that if a homosexual individual suffers from anxiety or depression, attention should be focused on the abnormal behaviors, not on the individual's sexual orientation.

In summary, both personal and cultural aspects of behavior are taken into consideration in determining what is abnormal. It is therefore possible for the definition of abnormality to differ from individual to individual, from culture to culture, and from time to time. It is hazardous to attempt a specific definition, but it might be said that *abnormal behavior is behavior that is personally distressful or personally disabling or is so culturally deviant that other individuals judge the behavior to be inappropriate or maladaptive.*

It is certainly helpful to have a general conception of what is abnormal, but we must recognize that the decisions have already been made concerning what behaviors constitute disorders. Specifically, an "official" list of disorders and the behaviors that go with each disorder are published in the *Diagnostic and Statistical Manual of Mental Disorders–* Fourth Edition (American Psychiatric Association, 1994). Some controversy exists about what behaviors are and are

myth of mental illness   The notion that rather than reflecting mental illness, abnormal behavior is simply different or wrong or a reasonable response to an unreasonable situation.

not included in this manual. From a practical perspective, however, the manual is definitive: If a behavior is listed, it is abnormal; if it is not listed, it is not abnormal. I will discuss this diagnostic manual in greater detail in Chapter 4.

Finally, one more very important point must be made: *Behaviors are abnormal, not people.* Stated in another way, *people may behave abnormally, but they themselves are not abnormal.* This distinction is important because saying that a person is abnormal implies that there is something wrong with the entire person, when that is not the case. Indeed, even when an individual suffers from a serious disorder such as schizophrenia, the disorder involves only a part of the person's being. Therefore, throughout this book, rather than talking about depressives, schizophrenics, and alcoholics, I will talk about *persons who suffer from* various disorders. With this as background, let's go on to the question of whether mental illness really exists.

The Myth of Mental Illness

Is there really such a thing as mental illness, or is it all just a myth? I just pointed out that there is an official list of mental disorders, and it is usually assumed that those disorders are due to an underlying "mental illness"; that is, something is "wrong" with an individual, and therefore that individual needs to be "treated." However, some critics have argued that the behaviors listed as "disorders" are just different— not wrong, not sick, *just different.* In other words, it has been suggested that *mental illness is a myth* (Szasz, 1961, 1970). Let's consider this radical departure from the usual point of view.

The **myth of mental illness** is based on three notions. First, it is argued that abnormal behavior is simply *different* behavior and not necessarily a reflection of an illness. For instance, some individuals feel more comfortable dressing and behaving like members of the opposite sex. Is that the result of a mental illness, or are they just behaving differently? In considering your answer, take into account how modes of dress and acceptable behavior for men and women have changed lately.

Second, an individual may have an unusual belief, but this does not mean that the individual is *wrong.* Indeed, many leaders and inventors were originally thought to be "crazy." Furthermore, even if an individual is wrong, that does not mean that he or she is sick. For example, if you are wrong about your solution of a math problem, it does not mean that you are sick. Might an individual with a delusion simply be mistaken rather than sick?

Third, theorists who believe that mental illness is a myth argue that abnormal behavior is due to something wrong with *society* rather than with the individual. For example, if an individual breaks down in the face of an overwhelming stress such as a war, the problem lies in the society that started the war, not in the individual. Furthermore, if society does not provide the individual with the support necessary to survive the stress, the problem is again in the society rather than in the individual. Withdrawing or becoming depressed may be a *rational response to an irrational situation* rather than a sickness. In summary, then, these theorists argue that being different, being wrong, or responding strongly to negative events should not be the basis for labeling an individual as having a "disorder" and being "sick."

If the concept of mental illness is wrong, why is it such a popular explanation for abnormal behavior? Proponents of the point of view that mental illness is a myth argue that the notion of mental illness is popular because it is a convenient way for us to deal with people who disturb us. For example, if we label as "sick" people whose behavior we find disturbing, we can see them as different from us, which makes us feel better about ourselves. Also, if we label them as sick, we can justify locking them up so that they can no longer disturb us. In short, we label individuals as mentally ill because they are *disturbing,* not because they are *disturbed.* As support for this notion, proponents of the myth of mental illness cite cases of individuals who were institutionalized for many years simply because they were annoying other people. These individuals may not have been "out of their minds," but by locking them up we put them out of *our* sight and out of *our* minds. Finally, by using mental illness as an explanation for deviant behavior, we avoid responsibility for the social problems that underlie the deviant behavior. That is, if we say the individual is sick and should be treated, we do not have to undertake the difficult task of changing society.

Is mental illness a myth or a reality? The myth notion is a radical departure from the traditional point of view, but it does have some merit. There are some serious forms of abnormal behavior that do result from environmental factors rather than from disease. For example, *brief psychotic disorder* involves hallucinations, delusions, and a disruption of thought processes, but that disorder is a *reaction* to an overwhelming stress, and the symptoms clear up when the stress is reduced, regardless of whether the individual gets treatment (see Chapter 10). It is also true that the definition of mental illness may have been stretched a little. For example, if a child has difficulty with arithmetic, he or she can be diagnosed as suffering from *mathematics disorder* (see Chapter 13). Similarly, if you are unduly concerned about your physical appearance, you could be diagnosed as suffering from *dysmorphic disorder* (see Chapter 7). But are these really psychiatric illnesses?

There is no doubt that sometimes the psychiatric system is abused and individuals are mistakenly labeled as mentally ill, sometimes even incarcerated in hospitals. However, there are also individuals who experience serious symptoms in the absence of environmental stress and whose symptoms can only be relieved with some form of therapy. Consider the student whose e-mail message you read at the beginning of this chapter; her periods of depression are very upsetting for her, make her unable to function, and occur independently of what is happening around her. Furthermore, as other case studies will illustrate, some individuals suffer terribly from their bizarre symptoms—symptoms that cannot be written off simply as rational responses to an irrational society. Clearly, *some individuals do suffer from serious disorders, and they are ill.*

The notion that mental illness is a myth is less popular today than it was 20 years ago, a change that is probably a reflection of our increased understanding of abnormal behavior. Although it is now generally agreed that mental illness exists, it is important that we not ignore the voice of dissent on this issue. In other words, we must be careful not to simply dismiss disagreeable behavior as being due to illness; nor should we permit the system to be misused in order to remove disagreeable persons from sight, regardless of whether such removal occurs by accident or by intent. Mental illness is not a myth, but the possibility raises important issues we must keep in mind.

TOPIC II
How Did Our Explanations for Abnormal Behavior Develop?

It was originally believed that abnormal behavior was caused by evil spirits or the Devil. Even today, some religious groups use prayer and exorcism to treat abnormal behavior. Do some people still believe that the Devil causes abnormal behavior?

In Paris in the 1770s, a physician named Mesmer treated patients by running a wand over their bodies to correct imbalances in their "magnetic fluids." The treatment was effective for many people. Could psychiatric disorders be due to imbalances in magnetic fluids? What did we learn about abnormal behavior from Mesmer's method of treatment?

When Pavlov's dogs heard a bell, they salivated. When some people go up in tall buildings, they become frightened. What do Pavlov's salivating dogs have to do with people who become frightened in tall buildings?

One of my major goals in this book is to explain what causes abnormal behavior and how it is treated. However, before beginning that discussion, let's briefly look back to see how abnormal behavior has been explained and treated in the past. This history of "madness" is interesting, but it also has important implications because some of the mistakes of the past are being repeated today. Looking back may help us avoid or correct those mistakes. Indeed, sometimes it is easier to see the foolishness of ideas in the context of the past rather than the present. Finally, I should point out that early explanations and treatments for abnormal behaviors were usually a function of the prevailing philosophical beliefs of the time rather than the state of objective knowledge. For example, when society was dominated by religion, abnormal behavior was thought to be caused by evil spirits or the Devil. Therefore, this discussion will be organized in terms of major historical periods that differed in terms of the prevailing world view. As you get through each section, ask yourself whether the ideas presented are still influencing us today. A flow chart of the evolution of the ideas about and treatments for abnormal behavior is presented in Figure 1.1.

The Beginning: Evil Spirits

The earliest explanation of abnormal behavior revolved around evil spirits, and there is reason to believe that this explanation goes all the way back to prehistoric times. Specifically, archaeologists have found human skulls from the Stone Age in which neat circular holes were chipped. It has been speculated that these were the skulls of disturbed individuals and the holes were made to release the evil spirits thought to cause abnormal behavior. The procedure of chipping or drilling holes in the skull is called **trephination** (tref-e-NA-shun). Although the idea that trephination was an early treatment for abnormal behavior is widely held, it is only speculation because there are no written records indicating exactly why the holes were chipped; it is possible that trephination was used to treat headaches or wounds from battles (Maher & Maher, 1985).

However, we do have written records from the early Chinese, Babylonians, Egyptians, Greeks, and Hebrews that make it clear that these peoples believed that abnormal behavior was caused by evil spirits and that the treatment involved driving the spirits out. For example, in the Bible there is a description of how, by pretending to be "mad," David convinced his enemies that he was possessed by an evil spirit and thereby frightened them away. In another biblical case Christ is reported to have cured a man of abnormal behavior by casting out his "devils" and hurling them into a herd of swine, who then began to behave strangely. The process of curing mental illness by driving out evil spirits or the Devil is called **exorcism** (EK-sor-siz-uhm). There was nothing unusual about early peoples' attributing abnormal behavior to evil spirits because in their cultures it was believed that many other phenomena, such as fires and floods, were caused by supernatural forces.

Greek and Roman Civilizations: Physiology

As the Greek and Roman civilizations developed, religion was largely replaced by reason, and the explanation for abnormal behavior shifted from evil spirits to physical prob-

FIGURE 1.1

Beliefs about the causes of abnormal behavior and its treatment have changed over time.

Prehistoric Times and Earliest History
Evil spirits are thought to cause abnormal behavior. The mentally ill are tortured to drive spirits out.

↓

Greek and Roman Civilizations
Physiological problems (humors in the body) are thought to cause abnormal behavior. The mentally ill are viewed as patients and treated with diet and lifestyle changes.

↓

The Dark Ages
The Devil is thought to cause abnormal behavior. The mentally ill are persecuted or killed as witches.

↓

The Age of Enlightenment
The mentally ill are protected in asylums and later in hospitals. It is proposed that mental illness is due to emotional stress and strain. Moral treatment (patients are released from their chains and treated more humanely) is introduced and then abandoned. It is also believed that mental illness is due to physiological problems. Treatments include bleeding, spinning, and drugs.

↓

The Modern Era

Psychological Explanations	*Physiological Explanations*
Suggestibility	Chemical imbalances in the brain
Unconscious conflicts	
Learning	Structural problems in the brain
Incorrect beliefs	

lems in the body. Specifically, around 400 B.C. a Greek physician named **Hippocrates** (hip-POK-ruh-tez; c. 460–c. 377 B.C.) suggested that behavior was controlled by four fluids in the body called **humors** and imbalances in the levels of these humors led to abnormal behaviors. Hippocrates argued that an excess of the black humor caused depression, too much yellow humor led to anxiety, high levels of phlegm resulted in a dull or sluggish ("phlegmatic") temperament, and too much blood caused rapid mood swings. You've probably heard someone described as being in a good or bad *humor;* that term comes from Hippocrates' humoral theory of behavior.

Because it was assumed that abnormal behavior was the result of high levels of particular humors, treatment was

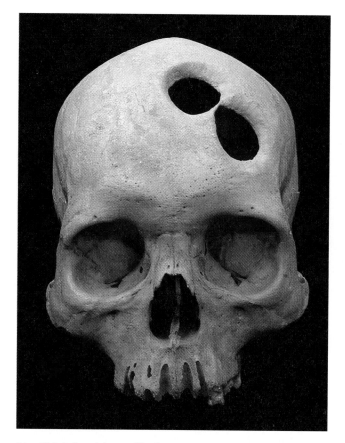

It is widely believed that trephination was an early treatment for abnormal behavior, but it is only speculation since there are no written records that indicate exactly why the holes were chipped in the skull.

focused on restoring the appropriate balance among the humors. This was usually done by bleeding the individual, altering diet, increasing exercise, reducing alcohol intake, or making general lifestyle changes. Furthermore, because disturbed individuals were considered to be suffering from illnesses, they were cared for like other sick people.

The Dark Ages: The Devil

After about a thousand years the Greek and Roman civilizations began to decline, and the period commonly called the Dark Ages (c. A.D. 500–1500) began. During this period religion again became the dominant force in virtually all aspects of life, and life was perceived as a struggle between the forces of good and evil. The forces of evil were led by the Devil who, among other wicked deeds, caused abnormal behaviors. Not only were disturbed individuals thought to be victims of the Devil, some were suspected of being agents of the Devil, sent to corrupt others. These individuals were labeled as *witches,* and witches had to be identified and stopped. To aid in this task, in 1486 two

monks published a manual titled *Malleus Maleficarum (The Witch Hammer),* which contained numerous tests that could be used to determine whether an individual was a witch. One particularly interesting test involved holding individuals under water for a long period of time; if they did not drown, it was concluded that they must be witches and therefore had to be killed. On the other hand, if the individuals did not survive, they were acquitted of being witches. Unfortunately for the mentally ill, the manual listed abnormal behaviors as signs of being a witch, so the mentally ill were often pursued and killed. In America witch-hunts reached their peak in the 1690s with the famous Salem witchcraft trials, which involved a twist. It has been assumed that disturbed individuals were labeled as witches and persecuted in the Salem trials, but we now know that in many cases it was the accusers, not the accused, who were disturbed. Specifically, young girls who had vivid imaginations (or possibly delusions) or who were involved in family feuds accused perfectly normal individuals of being witches. Persecution of individuals labeled as witches abated in most areas of Europe as early as 1610, and it was legally brought to a halt in America around 1700.

Another popular supernatural explanation of abnormal behavior that arose during this period revolved around the effects of the moon. Specifically, it was thought that the phases of the moon, particularly the full moon, could lead to abnormal behavior. This belief is not completely unreasonable; if the moon can influence the tides of the oceans, why not the tides of behavior? Belief in lunar influences on abnormal behavior led to the terms *lunatic, loony,* and *moonstruck,* which are still used today.

The Age of Enlightenment: Asylums and Moral and Physiological Treatments

The Dark Ages were followed by the Age of Enlightenment, a period in which the guiding philosophy incorporated both religion and science. From religion came a strong con-

trephination   A procedure in which holes are drilled in the skull; thought to be used by Stone Age people to release the evil spirits that cause abnormal behavior. (The term is based on the Latin word *trephine,* which is a small circular saw used for removing a circular disk of bone.)

exorcism   A treatment for mental illness that involves driving out the Devil or evil spirits thought to cause the disorder.

Hippocrates   An early Greek physician who proposed that abnormal behaviors resulted from the imbalance of humors (fluids) in the body.

humors   Fluids in the body, whose imbalance was thought by early Greeks to cause abnormal behavior.

In their 1486 manual *Malleus Maleficarum,* two monks described a test for determining whether an individual was a witch—holding the individual under water for a long period of time to see if he or she drowned. Those who survived were considered witches and therefore had to be killed, while those who did not survive were acquitted of being witches.

cern about the welfare of others, and from science came an interest in finding natural rather than supernatural explanations. This combination led to an interesting and important evolution in how mentally ill persons were regarded and treated.

Asylums and Hospitals

The first phase of this evolution was driven primarily by humanitarianism and involved the establishment of **asylums** (a-SI-lumz), where mentally ill individuals could be given refuge and care. (*Asylum* means "a place of refuge or protection.") Actually, asylums were not built exclusively for the mentally ill but were also intended for other groups, including beggars and the physically ill. The inclusion of the mentally ill with the other groups receiving care represented an important philosophical shift; specifically, rather than being seen as *problem people* who needed to be persecuted or punished, the mentally ill were now viewed as *people with problems* who needed help.

Recognition that the problems of the mentally ill were different eventually led to the development of separate institutions to care for them. The first of these was the **Hospital of St. Mary of Bethlehem,** established in London in 1547 for the care of disturbed individuals. However, the word *care* is hardly appropriate to describe the treatment of patients in these early hospitals. In fact, nothing was done for them other than to confine them under horrible conditions. For example, they were often chained to the wall, sometimes in a way that prevented them from lying down to sleep. In other cases violent individuals were secured in small cage-like structures. Furthermore, large numbers of extremely disturbed individuals were confined in close quarters, resulting in dreadful chaos and confusion. Indeed, the word *bedlam,* which means "a scene of uproar and confusion," was derived from the name of the Bethlehem hos-

pital. Unfortunately, the public had little concern for the conditions in these early hospitals. On the contrary, the screaming and ranting patients in these institutions were considered a source of amusement, and tickets were sold to watch them. During this period the Bethlehem hospital became one of the major tourist attractions in London! In summary, while confining patients in such hospitals was an improvement over actively torturing and executing them, it was a long way from truly humanitarian treatment.

Moral Treatment

These dreadful conditions persisted for more than 200 years. However, late in the 16th century changes started to occur. Some physicians who were overseeing the mentally ill began to speculate that mental illness might be the result

The word *bedlam,* which means uproar and confusion, originates from the name of the Hospital of St. Mary of Bethlehem, where patients were confined under generally awful conditions.

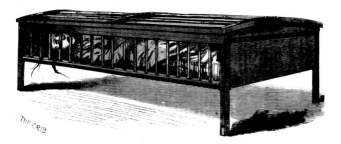

Cagelike structures such as the one in this illustration were used at the Bethlehem hospital to confine violent patients.

Parties and dances and other aspects of "moral treatment" were meant to make patients feel like normal, respectable individuals.

of emotional stress and strain. Although this is a common notion today, it was completely new at that time and considered extremely radical; indeed, until that point only supernatural forces (evil spirits, the Devil) and physiological problems (levels of humors) had been considered as causes of abnormal behavior.

The notion that emotional stress and strain might be the cause of abnormal behavior had two important effects. First, if abnormal behavior was the result of stress, it meant that patients needed to be cared for in less stressful environments, which led to more humane treatment of the patients. The physician who is usually credited with introducing truly humane care of patients was a Frenchman named **Philippe Pinel** (fi-LEP pe-NEL; 1745–1826), who in 1792 directed that the chains be removed from the patients in his hospital in Paris and that the hospital be renovated to make it more pleasant. However, Pinel was not the only or even the first one to make such changes. For example, at about the same time in England, **William Tuke** (tyook; 1732–1822) and other Quakers opened a "retreat" for patients on a country estate, where patients could get rest, fresh air, and exposure to nature. Furthermore, almost 10 years earlier in the United States, **Benjamin Rush** (1745–1813) had introduced the notion of humane care of patients at Pennsylvania Hospital. A woman who played an important role in this regard was **Dorothea Dix** (1802–1887). Dix was a New England schoolteacher who became concerned about the terrible living conditions and harsh treatments forced on mentally ill patients. Between 1841 and 1881 she conducted an effective campaign to inform the public about the problem and raise money for new hospitals. In fact, she is credited with establishing 32 mental hospitals throughout the United States.

The second effect of this new view of abnormal behavior revolved around how patients were treated once their chains were removed. Specifically, every attempt was made to treat the patients as normal, respectable individuals—for example, by taking them on pleasant walks, reading to them, having the staff give them small gifts, and having parties and dances for them. This approach is generally referred to as **moral treatment** because many of the activities had an undercurrent of moral or religious guidance.

Freeing patients from their chains, building better hospitals, and using moral treatment were widely acclaimed as effective ways to cure mental illness, and paintings of the time depicted patients becoming calm and normal when their chains were removed. While this may have been true for a few patients, it seems unlikely that these changes produced significant improvement in most cases. Indeed, if freedom, fresh air, and dances were sufficient to cure mental illness, it would not be the serious problem it is today.

asylums   Institutions developed primarily during the Age of Enlightenment in which the mentally ill could take refuge. (*Asylum* means "a place of refuge or protection.")

Hospital of St. Mary of Bethlehem   The first hospital specifically for the mentally ill; established in London in 1547.

Philippe Pinel   A physician who began improving the conditions and care of mentally ill patients in Paris in 1792.

William Tuke   An English Quaker who founded a retreat for the mentally ill in England in the 1790s.

Benjamin Rush   A physician who introduced humane care of mental patients in the United States in the 1780s.

Dorothea Dix   A New England schoolteacher who waged an active campaign to build mental hospitals in the United States.

moral treatment   One of the first psychological treatments to be used for mental patients; it involved providing better living conditions for patients and treating them as normal individuals.

This painting shows patients being unchained at the Salpêtrière Hospital in Paris in 1792. The movement toward more humane treatment of mental patients marked an important turning point in society's attitude toward the mentally ill. However, it did not lead to significant improvement for most patients because effective treatments were not yet available.

Physiological Treatment

Although moral treatment attracted most of the attention, a variety of physiological treatments were also employed during this period. One such treatment, used by Benjamin Rush and others, involved *bleeding* patients, a procedure based on the notion that mental illness was due to excessive blood in the brain. Two things are notable about the use of bleeding as a treatment: First, it had been used by Hippocrates more than 2,000 years earlier (see the earlier discussion of his humoral theory); second, it was also widely used for various physical disorders. For example, when George Washington, the first President of the United States, became sick with what was probably a throat infection, two-thirds of his blood was drained out and he died within hours (Morens, 1999). (Interestingly, on the day Washington died at Mount Vernon, Rush was being tried for malpractice in Philadelphia because of his use of bleeding.) Another physiological treatment used by Rush involved spinning patients around, often until they passed out. Rush was quoted as saying that every institution should have one of these spinning devices. Rush also used fear as a treatment, a strategy he apparently thought would shock a patient's system back to normality. To induce the fear, Rush would put the patient in a coffinlike box and then submerge the box under water until bubbles from the patient's breathing ceased to come to the surface, at which point the patient was brought up and revived (hopefully). Rather than frightening individuals *out* of their wits, apparently Rush was trying to frighten them back *into* their wits.

The use of drugs such as alcohol, opium, and marijuana (*cannabis*) to calm or sedate patients was also introduced during this period (Renvoise & Beveridge, 1989). These drugs

certainly did not provide cures, but they probably made the patients easier to manage so that they could be cared for in more humane ways (i.e., they did not need to be strapped down during manic or violent periods).

Overall, what emerged during the Age of Enlightenment were two parallel approaches to abnormal behavior: One was based on psychological explanations and led to moral treatment, whereas the other was based on physiological explanations and led to physiological treatments. However, before this age came to an end, the psychological explanation and moral treatment had been largely abandoned; patients were still hospitalized in relatively humane conditions, but treatments were primarily physiological in nature. Why was moral treatment abandoned? One widely held explanation is that it became so popular and so many hospitals were opened that there were simply not enough funds to support the large staffs necessary to implement it. In other words, moral treatment died because of its own success. Indeed, although Dorothea Dix is widely praised for working to open many hospitals, it is also suggested that the movement she started resulted in an overexpansion that caused the collapse of moral treatment. However, it is also possible that moral treatment was abandoned because it simply didn't work for the vast majority of seriously disturbed patients who were hospitalized at the time. The idea that releasing patients from their chains and having them attend dances in the country can lead to lasting cures makes a great story, but as you will learn later, effective treatment of the more serious forms of abnormal behavior requires more than compassion. In any event, as the Age of Enlight-

One early treatment consisted of spinning patients. Benjamin Rush, the "father of American psychiatry," is quoted as saying that "no well-regulated institution should be unprovided with the circulation swing."

enment came to a close, moral treatment had come and gone, individuals who behaved abnormally were hospitalized in relatively humane conditions, and the treatments they received were usually physiological in nature. That set the stage for the beginning of the modern era.

The Modern Era: Psychology and Physiology

Moral treatment may have died with the end of the Age of Enlightenment, but a number of interesting new psychological explanations and treatments were about to emerge.

Psychological Processes

Suggestion and Hypnotism. To find the beginnings of modern psychological explanations, we must go back to about 1770 in Paris where a physician named **Franz Mesmer** (MEZ-mur; 1734–1815) was treating patients who were suffering from a variety of symptoms such as paralysis, blindness, pain, seizures, and deafness. Mesmer believed that the symptoms were the result of imbalances in the "magnetic fluids" in his patients' bodies. To correct the imbalances Mesmer had the patients sit around a large tub filled with a "magnetic fluid." While music played in the background, the patients took iron rods from the tub and applied them to those parts of their bodies in which they were having symptoms. Mesmer also touched the patients with his magnetized wand. As the treatment session progressed, some of the patients would start to tremble; their limbs would twitch convulsively; they would groan, choke, laugh, and scream; and, finally, some of them would dance wildly or faint. This "crisis" would continue for some time, but when it finally subsided, many of the patients were apparently cured.

Mesmer's successes attracted considerable attention, and his patients included such notables as King Louis XVI, Queen Marie Antoinette, and the Marquis de Lafayette. Although Mesmer became very popular with his patients, his professional colleagues thought he was a quack, and in 1784 they convened a panel of experts to examine his practices. (The members of the panel included Benjamin Franklin, who was the U.S. ambassador to France; Joseph Guillotin, who invented the decapitating machine; and Antoine-Laurent Lavoisier, who discovered oxygen.) The panel failed to find any support for the effects of magnetism on physical disorders; instead they concluded that the effects of Mesmer's treatment were due to *suggestion* (Bromberg, 1959). Furthermore, Mesmer was labeled a charlatan and barred from further medical practice. Ironically, although Mesmer believed that abnormal behavior was due to a *physical* factor (imbalances in magnetic fluids), his work led others to the conclusion that a *psychological* factor (suggestion) played an important role in many

Mesmer's work led others to the conclusion that a psychological factor played an important role in many disorders. This engraving shows one of Mesmer's treatment sessons.

disorders. Here's a footnote to Mesmer's career: Although he died in obscurity in Switzerland in 1815, he has had a lasting influence on psychology because he is considered the father of hypnotism, originally known as **mesmerism** (MEZ-mur-iz-um).

Let's now jump ahead about 100 years to Paris, where a physician named **Jean-Martin Charcot** (shar-KO; 1825–1893) was treating patients suffering from physical symptoms for which no physical cause could be found. For example, an individual might have a paralyzed arm, but no muscle or nerve damage could be found to account for the paralysis. At the time such problems were referred to as **hysterical disorders.** Charcot discovered that patients with hysterical disorders were very susceptible to hypnosis and that he could effectively treat their symptoms with hypnosis. Indeed, Charcot became famous for demonstrations in which he hypnotized patients and then dramatically eliminated or induced symptoms. To explain the link between hysterical disorders and susceptibility to hypnosis, Charcot suggested that both hypnotizability and hysterical symptoms resulted from a neurological weakness. However, while Charcot was away on a trip, some of his students tried to hypnotize people who were not suffering from hysterical disorders, and they discovered that these normal individuals could be hypnotized and could have symptoms induced. Upon his return Charcot was forced to revise his explanation and conclude that hypnotizability and hysterical disorders

Franz Mesmer A French physician who believed that disorders were due to imbalances of magnetic fluids and who is considered to be the father of hypnosis.

mesmerism The original term for hypnosis.

Jean-Martin Charcot A French physician who thought that illnesses were due to a weak nervous system and treated them with hypnosis.

hysterical disorders Physical disorders for which a physical cause cannot be found.

did not result from neurological weakness (a physiological cause) but were instead the effects of suggestion (a psychological cause).

It is noteworthy that both Mesmer and Charcot began with physiological theories of abnormal behavior (magnetic fluids and neurological weaknesses), but the work of both led to the conclusion that abnormal behavior was the result of psychological factors. That set the stage for the entrance of Sigmund Freud.

Unconscious Conflicts. At about the time that Charcot was working in Paris, a young neurologist named **Sigmund Freud** (Froyd; 1856-1939) began treating patients with hysterical disorders in Vienna. Freud was at a loss to explain his patients' symptoms and come up with an effective treatment, but a breakthrough came when a colleague told him about an interesting patient called **Anna O.** Anna had been suffering from a variety of hysterical symptoms that included paralyses of her arms and legs, problems with her vision and speech, lapses in memory, difficulty with eating, and a persistent cough. What was particularly interesting about Anna was that her symptoms appeared to be related to stressful experiences from earlier in her life. For example, sometimes Anna was unable to drink water, and while talking one day she reported that some years earlier she had been disgusted by the fact that a friend had allowed her dog to drink out of a pitcher that Anna later used herself. Anna had not consciously made the connection between the earlier experience and her present symptom, but apparently the event had been so repulsive to her that later she began to gag when she started to drink water.

The story of Anna O. led Freud to begin thinking about hysterical disorders in terms of psychological causes, and over time he developed the idea that abnormal behaviors are caused by unconscious stresses that stem from early experiences. Specifically, Freud suggested that if an experience was especially anxiety-provoking, the individual would banish the memory of the experience to an area of the mind that Freud called the **unconscious.** Doing so had two implications: First, after the memory was in the unconscious, the individual was no longer able to remember the

experience, and therefore the experience could no longer cause the individual anxiety. Second, although the individual no longer remembered the experience, the experience would continue to influence the individual's behavior from the unconscious. For example, an unconscious concern about being abandoned might lead an individual to be depressed and cling to others for no apparent reason.

If abnormal behaviors were due to stressful experiences stored in the unconscious, the question Freud faced was, what treatment could be used to expose the experiences, reduce the stress associated with them, and thereby reduce the symptoms? In response Freud developed a treatment called **psychoanalysis,** in which the patient went progressively back through his or her life experiences and examined each experience from a more mature and objective standpoint. Once an experience was understood and the anxiety associated with it was reduced, the individual could go deeper to find the next experience. Eventually the individual would come to the crucial experience that provided the basis for the symptoms, and after the anxiety associated with that experience was eliminated, the symptoms would disappear. Freud likened the process to an archaeological dig in which the patient unearthed layer after layer of his or her earlier life and, in so doing, got a better understanding of earlier experiences and how they were affecting him or her in the present. Of course, the problem was that the important early experiences were buried in the unconscious, so Freud had to develop techniques to get to that material. One technique he developed was *dream interpretation.* The notion was that during sleep people were less careful about keeping material in the unconscious, and so the material slipped out in the form of dreams; by interpreting the dreams Freud could determine what was in the unconscious (Freud, 1900/1957). Another technique was *free association.* During therapy Freud would have a patient lie comfortably on a couch and say whatever came to his or her mind without any restrictions or censorship. For example, at the beginning of a session a patient might comment that while driving earlier in the day he had been cut off by a man in another car. This might lead the patient to talk about earlier instances in which he had been frustrated or threatened by other men. The string of associations might ultimately lead to memories about feeling threatened by his father—experiences that might still be influencing him but of which he was unaware. The notion underlying free association was that if patients do not defensively censor what they are thinking and saying, important ideas will come to awareness. Freud's notions about unconscious material offered a completely new explanation for abnormal behavior, and psychoanalysis provided a new means of treating it.

Sigmund Freud   An early neurologist who suggested that abnormal behaviors were the result of stressful experiences that were stored in the unconscious and continued to influence the individual.

Anna O.   A patient who played an important role in Freud's thinking about the causes and treatments of abnormal behavior.

unconscious   According to Freud, a portion of the mind in which anxiety-provoking memories are stored.

psychoanalysis   A treatment developed by Freud in which the patient goes back over earlier experiences to find and understand the one that is causing current symptoms.

Learning.   Freud's theory quickly became the dominant explanation for abnormal behavior, but even as its popularity was spreading, the seeds of a competing explanation were being planted. Specifically, a Russian physiologist named **Ivan Pavlov** (1849–1936) was working with dogs in his laboratory and making some very unusual discoveries about behavior. Pavlov discovered that if he repeatedly paired the sound of a bell with the presentation of meat, which caused the dog to salivate, eventually simply ringing the bell without presenting any meat would cause the dog to salivate. Today we call this process *classical conditioning*. Through classical conditioning a wide variety of physiological responses, such as salivation, can be controlled by external stimuli, such as bells. What does this have to do with abnormal behavior? We'll come to that shortly.

While Pavlov was working with dogs in Russia, an American psychologist named **Edward L. Thorndike** (1874–1949) was studying how cats solved problems. He noticed that if a cat was given a reward (a bit of food) after turning a wheel to escape from a box, the cat was likely to use the wheel-turning behavior again in the future. In other words, Thorndike pointed out that the behavior of animals could be controlled by rewards and punishments, a process that he called *operant conditioning*. (The term *operant* comes from the fact that the animal acts, or *operates*, to get rewards or avoid punishments.)

The work of Pavlov and Thorndike suggested that conditioning (learning) could influence behavior, but their work was limited to animals and they were not interested in the abnormal behaviors of humans. However, a brash young American psychologist named **John B. Watson** (1878–1958) seized the notion of conditioning and actively promoted the idea that conditioning could be used to explain abnormal behavior in humans. For example, Watson suggested that fears (phobias) are the result of classical conditioning. He demonstrated this in a simple experiment in which each time a young child was shown a white rat, a loud noise was sounded that frightened the child. Although the child was not initially afraid of the rat, after the rat had been paired with the noise a number of times, simply seeing the rat caused the child to become frightened. Watson also argued that operant conditioning could lead to abnormal behaviors. For example, if having a temper tantrum led to being given what he or she wanted, a child would be more likely to continue to have tantrums.

The notion that conditioning could be used to explain abnormal behaviors was quickly extended to the possibility that conditioning could be used to treat abnormal behaviors. For example, if an elevator phobia was due to the pairing of an elevator with fear (classical conditioning), then the phobia could be treated by repeatedly exposing the individual to elevators in a nonstressful way, thus breaking the link between elevators and fear. Similarly, if temper tantrums were due to the fact that they resulted in rewards (operant conditioning), then the tantrums could be treated by no longer rewarding the tantrums. This approach to treatment was called **behavior therapy.** The learning approach to abnormal behavior quickly became popular because of its scientific basis and because it provided a fast and inexpensive alternative to Freud's psychoanalysis.

Incorrect Beliefs. By the 1970s there were two competing explanations for abnormal behavior, unconscious conflicts and conditioning. However, some psychologists thought that both of these explanations missed the most important factor in behavior—beliefs. Specifically, it was suggested that incorrect beliefs lead to abnormal behaviors. For example, an individual holding the belief "I am not a worthwhile person" could become depressed, and the individual who believes that all snakes are dangerous could develop a phobia for snakes. This explanation gained support in the 1980s when psychologists began to understand more about how thinking works and how problems with the thought process can lead to incorrect beliefs. For example, once an individual has a particular belief, information that is contrary to the belief is ignored; therefore, an incorrect belief does not get corrected. This means that individuals who think they are worthless will notice only their failures and thus spiral down into depression.

The research of many psychologists contributed to what has come to be known as the "cognitive revolution" in psychology. A psychiatrist named **Aaron Beck** (b. 1921) used their findings to build a treatment approach called **cognitive therapy,** in which patients learn to correct the incorrect beliefs that led to their abnormal behavior. For example, individuals who are depressed because they believe that they are no good are taught to replace their incorrect beliefs about themselves with more realistic beliefs.

Physiological Processes

Although the physiological explanation got off to an early start with the Greeks (see the humoral theory of Hippocrates), two factors slowed its development: First, during the Dark Ages religion pushed science aside; second, early investigators lacked the techniques necessary to study brain functioning. However, in the 1950s an interesting accident opened the door to new physiological explanations and

Ivan Pavlov   A Russian physiologist who discovered classical conditioning.

Edward L. Thorndike   An American psychologist who identified operant conditioning.

John B. Watson   An American psychologist who applied the principle of conditioning to the understanding and treatment of abnormal behavior in humans.

behavior therapy   An approach to treatment in which patients unlearn abnormal behaviors.

Aaron Beck   A psychiatrist who played a major role in developing cognitive therapy.

cognitive therapy   An approach to treatment in which patients learn to replace incorrect beliefs with more accurate beliefs.

treatments. Specifically, a group of French chemists was working on a powerful new antihistamine designed to treat allergies. When they tested it on the patients in a local mental hospital who were suffering from schizophrenia, the chemists discovered that the drug not only cleared up the patient's congestion but also reduced some of the symptoms of schizophrenia! That is, after taking the drug that was designed to clear up nasal congestion, patients who had previously been uncontrollable became calm, their cognitive confusion and hallucinations were reduced, and their behaviors became much more normal. You might say that the antihistamine cleared up the patients' heads in more ways than one!

The discovery that an antihistamine reduced the symptoms of schizophrenia was important for two reasons: First, more powerful forms of the antihistamine were quickly adapted for use as antipsychotic drugs, and these drugs revolutionized the care and treatment of highly disturbed patients. Almost overnight hospital wards went from confusion and chaos to calm and control. Furthermore, many patients who had previously needed to be institutionalized could be given medication and released, so the number of hospitalized patients began dropping sharply. These drugs did not offer a complete solution to patients' problems, and they had some serious side effects, but they represented a very important step forward in treatment. The second important effect of the antipsychotic drugs was that they opened up a new way of studying the causes of abnormal behavior. That is, if researchers could determine what these drugs altered or affected in the brain, it might be possible to determine what had caused the abnormal behavior. The search was on for chemical causes of abnormal behavior and new drugs to treat it.

More recently, the physiological explanations for abnormal behaviors have advanced even further because of the development of new techniques for imaging the brain, such as CT scans and MRIs. These techniques have enabled investigators to identify structural problems in the brain that are linked to abnormal behavior. For example, we now know that disorders ranging from schizophrenia to obsessive-compulsive disorder are associated with certain structural problems in the brain. These findings are helping to round out our understanding of abnormal behavior.

THINKING CRITICALLY

Questions about the History of Abnormal Behavior

1. *Have early views of abnormal behavior been abandoned?* Over the past 3,000 years explanations for abnormal behavior have ranged from evil spirits to biochemistry, but people have not completely given up many of the early explanations. For example, you may have been amused when you read that the Devil was used to explain abnormal behavior and that treatment involved driving the Devil out. However, you should recognize that in some religious and cultural groups, abnormal behaviors are still blamed on the Devil and exorcism is still condoned as a treatment. Clinging to notions that lack scientific support is unfortunate because doing so may deprive some individuals of effective treatment. In other cases early explanations have been modernized and refined. For instance, the humoral theory introduced by Hippocrates over 2,500 years ago may have been a bit simplistic, but if humors are thought of as hormones or neurotransmitters, the theory is as modern as tomorrow's research findings. The point here is that a variety of interesting ideas have been offered in the past, and what we need to do is refine those that have merit and move beyond those that lack scientific support.

2. *Is the inhumane treatment of the mentally ill a thing of the past?* There is no doubt that mentally ill persons were treated terribly in the past; they were tortured, driven out of towns and cities, left in deplorable conditions, and sometimes killed. Unfortunately, despite our more modern views of abnormal behavior, the mentally ill are still often treated in ways that are not all that dissimilar from how they were treated hundreds of years ago. For example, when governments face budget problems or conflicting priorities, funds for the care of the mentally ill are often the first to be cut. As a consequence, state hospitals are often little more than warehouses. Furthermore, many such hospitals have simply been closed, the patients have been turned out onto the streets, and others seeking help have no place to go. Indeed, it is estimated that one-third of homeless people are former mental patients, and they are the ones who are least able to take care of themselves and who live in the worst conditions. Also, irrational fears of disturbed individuals still persist among the general public. Consider the case of a city in New York where such fears led the residents to pass a law prohibiting disturbed individuals from living within city limits. We often shake our heads in dismay when we think how terribly disturbed individuals were treated in the past, but we tend to look away so that we do not see how they are treated today.

TOPIC III

Who Are Today's Mental Health Professionals?

Lorie is depressed and wants to see someone for therapy, but whom should she see—a psychologist, a counselor, a psychiatrist, or a social worker? What are the differences among these professionals, and how does someone like Lorie decide which one to see?

Debra's goal is to work with girls who have eating disorders, but she is confused about whether she should study to become a psychologist, a psychiatrist, or a social worker. What types of training are required for these professions?

Now that you have an understanding of how our views of abnormal behavior have developed, we can go on to consider the training and activities of those professionals who are most directly involved in the mental health area. Questions like "What is the difference between a psychiatrist and a psychologist?" are often asked, and it is important for you to understand the differences and the similarities.

Psychiatrists

Psychiatrists are individuals who attended *medical school* for 4 years and then completed a 1-year medical internship. At that point they received an **MD degree** (Doctor of Medicine) and were qualified to practice general medicine. They then entered a *residency program* in which they spent about 3 years studying psychiatry. Residency programs are based in hospitals and are focused on the clinical practice of psychiatry, that is, on the treatment of individuals with psychiatric disorders. At the end of the residency, psychiatrists took an examination and became *board-certified,* or qualified to practice psychiatry.

Clinical Psychologists

There are two routes to becoming a **clinical psychologist.** Traditionally, clinical psychologists are individuals who went to *graduate school* for 4 to 6 years, during which they studied abnormal behavior (e.g., diagnosis, treatment) and research techniques (e.g., design of experiments, statistics). During their time in graduate school, they wrote a master's thesis and a doctoral dissertation, both of which involved original research. After completing their graduate studies, they went on to complete a 1-year clinical psychology internship in a hospital or clinic, where they refined their clinical skills. Upon completion of their internship, they received a **PhD degree.** (*PhD* stands for Doctor of Philosophy, and the degree reflects the scholarly heritage of clinical psychology as opposed to a more narrow training for clinical practice.) After earning the PhD degree, individuals in most states took an examination to become licensed or certified to practice clinical psychology.

It's important to note that the training of psychiatrists is focused almost exclusively on clinical practice, whereas the training of clinical psychologists in PhD programs involves a blend of research and clinical practice. In other words, the training of PhD psychologists is designed to produce individuals who are *scientists,* able to conduct research to advance our understanding of abnormal behavior, but who are also *practitioners,* able to work with disturbed individuals. This approach to training is referred to as the **scientist-practitioner model.**

In an alternative model for training clinical psychologists, research training in graduate school is greatly reduced or even eliminated, and attention is focused primarily on the development of clinical skills. This model was developed because it was argued that many clinical psychologists spend their entire careers in clinical practice and do not do any research after they get their degrees; therefore, the time they spend in graduate school learning research methodology is not productive and can be better spent developing clinical skills. This graduate school program and the usual 1-year clinical psychology internship lead to the **PsyD degree** (Doctor of Psychology). Like the MD degree program, the PsyD degree program prepares individuals for clinical practice.

Today's clinical psychologists may have either a PhD or a PsyD degree, and there is some controversy over which type of training is more appropriate. However, when evaluating the qualifications of a psychologist, rather than arguing about which approach to training is best, it is more important to ask whether the quality of the individual's training is *sufficiently high* and whether the training is *relevant to the work he or she is doing.*

The most notable difference in the professional activities of psychiatrists and clinical psychologists is that psychiatrists can prescribe drugs and perform other medical procedures such as electroconvulsive therapy, whereas clinical psychologists cannot. That is, psychiatrists are licensed to practice medicine, and psychologists are not. In the future, however, this difference may become blurred because there is a movement to give clinical psychologists the option of getting additional training so that they will be able to prescribe drugs to treat psychiatric disorders (DeLeon & Wiggins, 1996; DeNelsky, 1996; Hayes & Heibly, 1996; Klein, 1996; Lorion, 1996; Pachman, 1996; Plante, Boccaccini, & Andersen, 1998; Sammons, Sexton, & Meredith, 1996). The

psychiatrists   Mental health professionals who are physicians with additional training in the practice of psychiatry and are able to prescribe drugs and carry out other medical procedures.

MD degree   The degree (Doctor of Medicine) earned after completing medical school.

clinical psychologists   Mental health professionals who have gone to graduate school in psychology, completed a clinical internship, and earned either a PhD or a PsyD degree.

PhD degree   The degree (Doctor of Philosophy) earned by clinical psychologists, which reflects training in both clinical practice and research.

scientist-practitioner model   The approach to training clinical psychologists that emphasizes both clinical practice and research.

PsyD degree   The degree (Doctor of Psychology) earned by clinical psychologists trained primarily in clinical practice.

argument is that the need for individuals who can prescribe drugs far outstrips the number of available psychiatrists and that, with some additional training, clinical psychologists can fill that need. Advocates for prescription privileges for psychologists also argue that there are already numerous nonphysician professionals, such as nurse-practitioners and dentists, who have limited prescription privileges, so precedents exist for extending similar privileges to clinical psychologists. Furthermore, psychologists in some hospitals have been prescribing drugs informally for years, under the supervision of psychiatrists. To evaluate the ability of psychologists to prescribe psychiatric drugs, the National Institute of Mental Health has been conducting an experiment in which a number of psychologists are receiving additional training in physiology, pharmacology, and the prescription of drugs, and their prescriptions are being monitored by a panel of experts. Some psychologists have already completed the program and are prescribing drugs within the military system. If this program is found to be generally successful, laws may be passed to extend limited prescription privileges to clinical psychologists. However, even if the results of the experiment indicate that properly trained psychologists can effectively prescribe psychiatric drugs, the granting of prescription privileges to psychologists will probably not occur in the near future because there is strong opposition from the American Medical Association. There are also some psychologists who argue that the traditional distinction between psychiatrists and psychologists should be maintained (Plante et al., 1998). Nevertheless, the fact that prescription privileges for psychologists are being given serious consideration reflects a basic and important change and is a development to watch.

Social workers and counselors are playing an increasingly important role in the treatment of individuals with psychiatric disorders. Many of the day-to-day decisions concerning the care and welfare of patients are managed by these professionals.

 ## Counselors and Social Workers

Two other professional groups that are playing an increasingly important role in the treatment of individuals with psychiatric disorders are psychological counselors and clinical social workers. **Counselors** usually have an **MA degree** (Master of Arts) in either psychology or counseling psychology, whereas **social workers** usually have an **MSW degree** (Master of Social Work). Both of these degree programs typically take 2 years of graduate school, are focused primarily on the skills necessary for clinical practice, and involve "hands-on" clinical training. There are three reasons why counselors and social workers are now taking on many of the responsibilities that were once the domain of psychologists and psychiatrists: First, many of the day-to-day decisions concerning the care and welfare of patients do not have to be made by psychologists and psychiatrists (see the discussion of case management later in this section). Second, there is no evidence that individuals with advanced training in psychotherapy are more effective than individuals with less training at treating clients with psy-

chiatric disorders (Dawes, 1994). Third, having counselors and social workers treat patients has a definite economic advantage because they are less highly compensated than psychiatrists and psychologists. (I will discuss the economics of health care in the next section.) There is some resistance on the part of some psychologists and psychiatrists to the increasing role of counselors and social workers, but the trend is likely to continue.

 ## Other Professionals

Other professionals who work in the mental health area include *psychiatric nurses, occupational therapists, recreation therapists, art therapists,* and *music therapists.* In Chapter 19 I will discuss the specific roles these individuals play, but in most cases their effectiveness is related to the fact that they provide additional normal contacts and role models from whom disturbed individuals can receive feedback and guidance. That is, sports, art, and music are mediums through which people can interact rather than treatments per se.

Finally, a comment should be made about **case managers** (sometimes called *case workers*). Today many individuals with serious psychiatric disorders live in the community rather than in hospitals (see Chapter 19), and it is essential that someone keep in touch with them; that is the role of case managers. They visit patients regularly in their homes and help them with daily tasks such as bill paying and shopping. Case managers also provide patients with social contact, which is very helpful because individuals with serious disorders are often rejected by their families and friends and become isolated. Finally, case managers make sure that patients are taking their medications, and they monitor patients' symptoms so that changes in medications can be made if necessary. For patients in the community, case managers are crucial for survival. Case managers may be social workers or, in some cases, *paraprofessionals,* that is, individuals who have had some training but are not highly trained professionals. In the war against mental illness, case managers are the foot soldiers in the trenches, fighting the battles on a daily basis.

THINKING CRITICALLY

Questions about Today's Mental Health Professionals

1. *What changes have taken place in terms of who provides treatment for individuals with psychiatric disorders?* Over the last 50 years major changes have taken place in terms of the types of mental health professionals who provide treatment for individuals with psychiatric problems, and this evolution is continuing today. Until the early 1950s only psychiatrists were permitted to provide psychotherapy; psychologists were limited to doing diagnostic testing, and social workers focused on helping the families of disturbed individuals. However, laws were changed in the 1950s and 1960s, and psychologists joined psychiatrists as providers of psychotherapy. During the 1990s growing numbers of social workers began providing psychotherapy. In other words, psychologists initially supplanted psychiatrists, and social workers are now supplanting psychologists. Earlier I pointed out that in the future psychologists may be able to prescribe drugs for psychiatric disorders, which will be another step in the evolution of who provides treatment.

2. *Why are these changes occurring?* This evolution in who provides treatment is driven primarily by two factors, the first of which is the *need for treatment.* As the number of patients needing treatment exceeds the capacity of one professional group, other professional groups are brought in. A second and very important factor is the *cost of treatment.* As costs rise and resources dwindle, the insurance companies that pay for treatment seek out professional groups that require less compensation; psychologists are less expensive than psychiatrists, and social workers are less expensive than psychologists. (I will discuss the economics of treatment in the next section.) Overall, the evolution of who provides treatment can have positive effects, such as providing more treatment at less cost. However, it is important that the professionals who provide treatment, whoever they may be, are appropriately trained and that a high standard of care is maintained.

3. *If you or someone you know needs help, how do you go about selecting a mental health professional?* This is an extraordinarily difficult question to answer, but two points

should be recognized: First, a cautionary note should be sounded. Current laws regulate only the use of the labels *psychiatrist, psychologist,* and *social worker;* this means that *anyone* can "hang out a shingle" and offer services as a *psychotherapist, counselor,* or any other title that implies expertise in the area of mental health. Therefore, when selecting someone as a source of help, it is essential that you carefully check their qualifications.

Second, different kinds of problems require different kinds of treatment (social support, counseling, psychotherapy, drugs), so you must select someone who is qualified to provide the kind of treatment needed. The problem lies in the fact that you or your relative or friend probably will not know exactly what type of treatment is needed. One strategy is to see someone who is a member of a group of professionals with different areas of expertise so that colleagues are available for assistance and different professionals can participate in the treatment. Hopefully, what you will learn in this book about abnormal behavior and its treatment will help you understand the problem and select the correct mental health professional.

TOPIC IV

What Are the "Hot Button" Questions about Abnormal Behavior?

Michelle is constantly anxious, tense, and worried. She was interviewed by three mental health experts, and they came up with three different explanations for her anxiety. One suggested that her anxiety is caused by unconscious conflicts, another argued that she is anxious because she views the world as a hostile place, and the third contended that her anxiety is the result of high levels of neurological activity in her brain. What

counselors Mental health professionals who usually have an MA degree in either psychology or counseling and who are trained primarily for clinical practice.

MA degree The degree (Master of Arts) earned in graduate school by some mental health professionals; it involves less time and training than a PhD or PsyD degree.

social workers Mental health professionals who usually have an MSW degree and are trained primarily for clinical practice.

MSW degree The graduate degree (Master of Social Work) earned by social workers.

case managers Social workers or paraprofessionals who do much of the day-to-day work in managing the lives and treatment of mentally ill individuals; also known as case workers.

is the cause of Michelle's anxiety, and why don't the experts agree?

After his father died, Mike was very depressed and was given antidepressant medication. The medication helped, but why? His depression was caused by a psychological problem, so why did pills that change brain chemistry help him?

Sarah is suffering from her second bout of serious depression. The first bout occurred 10 years ago, and after a year of therapy, which was paid for by her insurance company, she felt fine. However, this time her psychologist told her that her insurance company has approved payment for only six treatment sessions. Will that be enough to overcome her depression? Why is her treatment being limited to six sessions?

Before concluding this chapter I want to discuss six "hot button" questions that arise with regard to the causes and treatments of abnormal behavior. These questions are often a source of controversy and misunderstanding, so discussing them here will provide you with a background for understanding much of what will be covered later in this book.

What Causes Abnormal Behavior?

The question of what causes abnormal behavior is hotly and often bitterly debated. It's not that we don't have an answer; rather, we have a number of different answers, and mental health professionals do not agree on which one is correct. For example, some argue that abnormal behavior is due to *stress,* others believe that it is *learned* or caused by *incorrect beliefs,* and still others contend that it is due to *physiological problems in the brain.* In Table 1.1 I have used anxiety to illustrate the different explanations, and later I'll describe these explanations in greater detail (see Chapters 2 and 3).

Some textbook authors gloss over differences of opinion concerning what causes abnormal behavior and argue that

---

TABLE 1.1

Four possible explanations for anxiety

- *Stress:* Overwhelming stress, such as serious financial problems, leads to anxiety.

- *Learning:* If anxiety is repeatedly paired with an object such as a dog, the process of classical conditioning causes the object to take on the ability to elicit anxiety whenever it is present.

- *Incorrect beliefs:* Incorrect beliefs, such as "the world is a hostile place," lead to anxiety.

- *Physiology:* Abnormally high levels of activity in the brain lead to anxiety.

---

a consensus has been found, but that is not the case. In fact, important differences of opinion remain, and those authors are simply ignoring points of view with which they disagree. Unfortunately, to ignore competing points of view is not a solution; instead we need to have an understanding of *all* points of view so that we can select among them as we try to explain a particular disorder. Therefore, in this book I will present a number of explanations, and one of your tasks will be to examine and evaluate each explanation before drawing any conclusions. In developing an understanding of abnormal behavior, you need to understand why one explanation works for a particular disorder and other explanations do not.

Debates over which explanation is correct are motivated by two factors: First, many of these debates are motivated by honest attempts to find the correct answer, and they continue because finding the cause of abnormal behavior is not always simple or fast. Second, some of the debates are motivated by "turf battles." That is, professionals who were originally trained in terms of one explanation may feel threatened by new, alternative explanations, causing them to "dig in their heels," so to speak. The world of abnormal psychology is changing rapidly, and it is important for you to understand the changes. In this book we will put aside the issues of professional turf and focus on the evidence. Doing that will not pose a threat to any one group of theorists because, as you will soon see, no one group has the "whole truth," and each group may have a piece of it.

Do Different Disorders Have Different Causes?

I just pointed out that one of our tasks will be to identify the correct explanation for each disorder, but I did not mean to imply that there is *one* correct explanation for all disorders. In fact, quite the opposite is the case; it is now clear that *different disorders have different causes.* For instance, phobias are apparently learned, whereas schizophrenia is due primarily to physiological problems in the brain. Furthermore, in some cases *there is more than one cause for a particular disorder.* For example, depression may be caused by stress or by physiological problems in the brain. In other words, the correct explanation for abnormal behavior depends on which disorder we are considering.

The notion that different disorders have different causes is contrary to the position taken by some theorists who assert that their explanation can account for virtually *all* disorders. The proponents of a particular explanation may gain confidence when their explanation accurately explains one or more disorders, but then they go on to assume that it is also correct for other disorders. This is like assuming that because germs cause infections, they also cause broken legs. The fact that phobias may be learned does not necessarily mean that schizophrenia is learned.

In this book one of our goals is to determine which explanation (or set of explanations) is best for *each* disorder. Doing this will be like trying to solve a mystery: For each disorder we will have a different set of clues (symptoms), and our challenge will be to see what explanation best accounts for those clues.

Do Different Disorders Require Different Treatments?

If different disorders have different causes, it follows that *different disorders require different treatments.* For example, disorders caused by psychological stress can be best treated with some form of psychological therapy, whereas those caused by physiological problems in the brain are better treated with drugs. Therefore, after determining the cause (or causes) of a particular disorder, we will go on to determine which cause-related treatment is most effective for that disorder. Overall, then, we will be identifying "packages" that consist of *symptoms, causes, and treatments.*

What Role Does Physiology Play in Abnormal Behavior?

Is physiology an important factor in psychological disorders? Some mental health professionals argue that psychological disorders are due to psychological problems and physiology is irrelevant, whereas others claim that physiology plays an important role in many disorders. When considering this difference of opinion, it is essential to recognize that there are really two issues. The first revolves around the question of whether physiology causes abnormal behavior; for instance, is schizophrenia due to problems with child-rearing or problems in brain functioning? The question of cause is a real "hot button" issue, and we'll examine it in depth when we consider each of the disorders.

The second issue revolves around the fact that even when physiology is not the cause of a disorder, it plays a role in the disorder because ultimately *all behaviors are the result of physiological processes in the brain.* For example, your thoughts are made possible by electrical activity in specific sets of cells (neurons) in your brain. Indeed, later you will learn that stimulation of specific cells in the brain with a very fine electrode "calls up" previous thoughts, images, and feelings. The point here is that disorders can be triggered by any one of a number of different factors such as stress, learning, thoughts, or genes, but those factors ultimately cause physiological changes in the brain, and those changes then lead to specific abnormal behaviors. In other words, *physiology is the common final step in the pathway to abnormal behavior.* This point is illustrated in Figure 1.2. The fact that physiology is the last step in any pathway to abnormal behavior is important because it enables us to

FIGURE 1.2

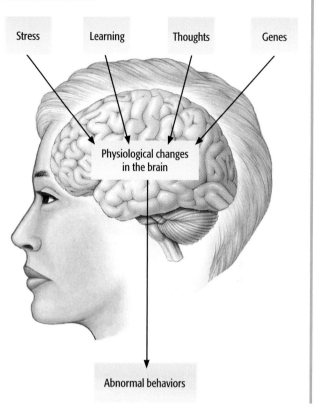

Physiology is the common final step in the pathway to abnormal behavior.

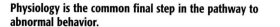

understand how the various factors cause abnormal behaviors. That is, rather than just saying that stress causes depression, we can understand that stress causes changes in the brain, which then cause depression.

The fact that physiology is the last step in the path to abnormal behavior is also very important because it can influence how some disorders are treated. Consider the following case: A young man's family is killed in a terrible automobile crash, and as a consequence he becomes deeply depressed and suicidal. The cause of his depression is clearly psychological (the stress of the loss of his family), and psychotherapy may help, but it may take years to overcome the feelings of loss and stress. Because something must be done to help the young man until the stress can be brought under control, he may have to take drugs, at least temporarily, to correct his brain chemistry, which was disrupted by the stress. In other words, in some cases it may not be immediately possible to treat the real cause of a problem, so practitioners must do the next best thing and intervene at the physiological level. In other cases a disorder may be caused by a genetic problem, and it may be necessary to use drugs (or even surgery) to change the physiological process triggered by the genes. Overall, then, understanding physiology is crucial for understanding and treating abnormal behavior.

What Roles Do Economic Factors Play in Treatment?

Until recently the cost of health care, which includes psychiatric treatment, was increasing at a rate two or three times faster than other costs, so something had to be done to control those costs. One approach involves what is called **managed health care.** With this approach *decisions concerning treatment are managed by a panel hired by the insurance company that is paying for the treatment.* The notion is that some treatments that are provided are not really necessary or are not the most effective ones. By having a panel of experts oversee the treatments, those problems can be avoided and costs can be reduced.

The changes introduced by managed care can be illustrated with the following example: Before managed care was introduced, an individual who felt that he or she had a problem would go to a therapist, and if the therapist believed that treatment was necessary, it was begun and it continued until the client and therapist agreed that the problem was solved. The client's insurance company paid for the treatment with almost no questions asked. In contrast, with managed care when an individual goes to a therapist, the therapist must prepare a proposal for the individual's insurance company in which the therapist describes the client's problem, proposes a specific type of treatment, and indicates how many treatment sessions will be required. That proposal is then evaluated by a panel of professionals hired by the insurance company, and the panel makes a decision concerning whether the treatment plan is appropriate and whether the insurance company will pay for it. If the plan is approved, the treatment is begun. However, if the therapeutic goals are not reached by the end of the prescribed number of treatment sessions, the therapist may request additional sessions. The panel overseeing the treatment may grant the request, or it may prescribe an alternative treatment. For example, if a depressed individual has not responded to psychotherapy, he or she may be switched to drug treatment. Alternatively, it is possible that no further treatment will be approved.

The key to managed care is that the decisions concerning treatment are taken out of the hands of the therapist and given to an independent panel. Many therapists argue

managed health care   An approach to health care in which a panel of experts hired by a patient's insurance company makes decisions about whether proposed treatment is reasonable and will be paid for by the insurance company.

HMO   Abbreviation for health maintenance organization, which is the term used for an insurance program that employs the managed care approach.

that this approach is inappropriate. They believe that they are in a better position to make judgments about treatment than are panel members who have never seen the client, and they also contend that the panel members who make decisions are more concerned with reducing costs than with reducing clients' problems. A term frequently heard in the debate over the merits of managed care is **HMO,** which stands for *health maintenance organization* and refers to an insurance program that employs the managed care approach.

The debate over managed care continues, but whether we like it or not, managed care is here for the foreseeable future, and it is having a profound influence on treatment. Specifically, it is (1) limiting the amount of treatment that is available, (2) requiring therapists to offer proof that their treatments are effective, and (3) forcing therapists to develop treatments that can be effective in a relatively short period of time. We will take these issues into account in our discussions of treatments.

Another effect of managed care is that insurance companies are more likely to contract with less costly mental health professionals for the treatment of clients. Whereas treatment was once provided primarily by psychiatrists and psychologists, it is now likely to be provided by social workers or psychological counselors. Similar changes occurred in the area of medicine; services once provided by physicians are now the responsibility of nurse-practitioners.

Drastic changes in psychiatric care have also occurred because of reductions in government funding of care. Specifically, in attempting to reduce costs and taxes, many states have simply closed their state mental hospitals (see Chapter 19). Therefore, in times of crisis an individual's only option may be a private hospital. However, the costs of those facilities usually amount to more than $1,000 a day, which puts them well beyond the means of most people. What would you do if you suffered from a psychiatric disorder that required long-term hospitalization and the costs were over $1,000 a day? Many former and would-be patients are now homeless, living on the streets, under bridges, and in shelters.

Overall, economic factors are playing an increasingly important role in treatment, and if we are to develop a realistic view of treatment, we must take these factors into account. Therefore, in this book we will consider not only the question of *what treatments are effective,* but also *what treatments are cost-effective.*

What Roles Do Gender and Culture Play in Abnormal Behavior?

For many years the roles of gender and culture in abnormal behavior were largely ignored. However, that era has come to an end, and today we are aware of numerous links between gender, culture, and abnormal behavior. Consider the following:

- Women are at least twice as likely as men to suffer from depression, but when women suffer from schizophrenia, they often have a less serious form and are more likely to improve than men.
- Schizophrenia is much more prevalent in the lower than in the upper socioeconomic classes.
- Some disorders are specific to certain cultures and do not occur in other cultures.
- Language differences, variations in willingness to admit to symptoms, and cultural stereotypes often result in inaccurate diagnoses.

In addition to recognizing that gender and cultural differences are important, it is essential that we develop an understanding of *why* these factors are important. For example, are women more likely to suffer from depression because society places more stress on them, or is their higher level of depression due to a physiological difference between women and men? Is schizophrenia more prevalent in the lower classes because of greater stress or poorer health care, or is it because people with the disorder cannot function effectively and therefore drift downward? Are disorders that once occurred only in a few cultures crossing borders and occurring more widely? For instance, in some Asian and African cultures there is a disorder known as *amok,* in which an individual (usually a male) who has experienced a personal setback, such as a failure or breakup of a relationship, withdraws for a few days and then emerges with a weapon and begins killing people indiscriminately. Is this disorder spreading? What about the instances in the United States and Europe in which upset adolescents go to school and begin shooting their classmates? Has amok come to Western cultures, and if so, why? Obviously, understanding the links between gender and culture and abnormal behavior will enhance our understanding of many disorders.

The roles of gender and culture in abnormal behavior pose important and complex questions. Therefore, in this

Women are more than twice as likely as men to suffer from depression. What do you think causes such a difference? Are women more likely to suffer from depression because of societal stressors, or is their higher level of depression due to a physiological difference between women and men?

book issues of gender and culture will be considered in the context of specific disorders. For example, when I discuss schizophrenia, I will explain why it occurs more frequently in the lower classes, and I will discuss some of the reasons why women with the disorder do better than men. Similarly, when discussing how diagnoses are made, I will describe some of the problems posed by cultural differences. In other words, I will weave discussion of these factors throughout the book.

With this material as background, we can go on to examine the explanations that have been offered for abnormal behavior.

Summary

Topic I: What Behaviors Are Abnormal?

- Abnormal behavior can be defined in terms of the individual or the culture in which the individual functions. When abnormal behavior is viewed from the point of view of the individual, the crucial factors are distress and disability, whereas from the culture's perspective, deviance is the important factor. There are wide differences across cultures in what is defined as abnormal behavior.
- Some critics argue that mental illness is a myth: Rather than reflecting an illness, abnormal behavior is simply different behavior, wrong behavior, or behavior that

reflects problems in society. This notion is popular because it enables us to label as "sick" and institutionalize people who are different from us and thus disturbing to us.

Topic II: How Did Our Explanations for Abnormal Behavior Develop?

- Initially it was believed that abnormal behavior was caused by evil spirits, and treatment focused on driving them out with a procedure called exorcism.
- During the height of the Greek and Roman civilizations, abnormal behavior was attributed to physiological causes,

such as an imbalance of the humors in the body, and treatment focused on restoring a balance.

▶ During the Dark Ages it was believed that abnormal behavior was caused by the Devil, and attention was focused on identifying witches and driving the Devil out, often through torture.

▶ During the Age of Enlightenment disturbed individuals were cared for in asylums and later in hospitals. When it was proposed that abnormal behavior stemmed from psychological stress, moral treatment was introduced by such people as Pinel, Tuke, and Rush. Dix worked to establish hospitals for the mentally ill. A variety of physiological explanations and treatments (e.g., bleeding, spinning, drugs) were also introduced at this time. By the end of this era, moral treatment had been largely abandoned because it was too expensive or ineffective. Physiological treatments became the primary interventions.

▶ The modern era introduced a number of new explanations and related treatments: Mesmer and Charcot brought attention to the role of suggestion, and hypnosis was sometimes used to relieve symptoms. Freud explored the influence of unconscious conflicts and developed psychoanalysis as a means of uncovering and dealing with them. Pavlov and Thorndike demonstrated that the behavior of animals can be influenced by classical and operant conditioning, and Watson used those procedures to explain normal and abnormal behavior in humans. Furthermore, it was suggested that the principles of conditioning could be used to treat abnormal behavior, an approach called behavior therapy.

▶ Many psychologists objected to the fact that behaviorism ignored the role of cognitions (thoughts), and in the 1970s it was suggested that incorrect beliefs led to abnormal behaviors. As a treatment procedure, Beck and others developed cognitive therapy, in which clients learn to replace incorrect beliefs with more accurate beliefs.

▶ The discovery that drugs could reduce abnormal behaviors led to increased interest in physiological explanations for abnormal behavior, and breakthroughs in medical technology refined our understanding of how problems in the brain can lead to abnormal behavior.

Topic III: Who Are Today's Mental Health Professionals?

▶ Psychiatrists first go to medical school and earn an MD degree; they then complete a psychiatric residency in which they develop the skills necessary for clinical practice. They are qualified to prescribe drugs and perform other medical procedures.

▶ Psychologists first go to graduate school in psychology and then complete a clinical psychology internship. Those who earn a PhD degree are trained for both clinical practice and research, whereas those who earn a PsyD degree are trained primarily for clinical practice. There is now a movement to provide some psychologists with additional training so that they can prescribe drugs.

▶ Counselors have gone to graduate school and usually have an MA degree in psychology or counseling, whereas social workers have gone to graduate school and have an MSW degree. These individuals are trained primarily for clinical practice, and they are taking over many of the responsibilities previously assumed by psychologists and psychiatrists.

▶ Other mental health professionals include psychiatric nurses, occupational therapists, recreation therapists, art therapists, music therapists, and case managers.

▶ The roles of mental health professionals are changing. For example, whereas once only psychiatrists were allowed to practice psychotherapy, today many psychologists, counselors, and social workers also provide psychotherapy. This evolution is driven by increasing demand for treatment and the need for less expensive treatment.

Topic IV: What Are the "Hot Button" Questions about Abnormal Behavior?

▶ Abnormal behavior can be caused by a number of factors, including stress, learning, incorrect beliefs, and physiological problems in the brain.

▶ Different disorders can stem from different causes. For example, phobias may be learned, whereas schizophrenia is due to physiological problems in the brain. Furthermore, some disorders may have more than one cause. For instance, depression may be caused by incorrect beliefs or by physiological problems in the brain.

▶ Because different disorders can have different causes, they often require different treatments.

▶ Physiological factors play two roles in abnormal behavior: First, they are the cause of some disorders; second, they are the final common pathway for the symptoms of all disorders. Because physiology is the last step in the pathway to symptoms, in cases in which the primary cause of a disorder, such as an overwhelming stressor, cannot be treated immediately, it is often possible to intervene with drugs at the physiological level and thereby treat the symptoms.

▶ There are two reasons why economic factors are playing an increasingly important role in the treatment of abnormal behavior: First, the introduction of managed health care limits the amount of treatment that is available, requires therapists to prove that their treatment techniques are effective, forces therapists to use treatments that are effective in a short period of time, and takes the decisions concerning treatment out of the hands of therapists. Second, cutbacks in federal and state support for psychiatric hospitals have resulted in the closing of many hospitals, thus reducing the treatment options for many individuals.

▶ Gender and culture play important roles in abnormal behavior; for example, women are more likely to suffer from depression than men, and schizophrenia occurs more frequently in lower socioeconomic classes. Recognizing these differences is important, and to thoroughly understand abnormal behavior we must understand how gender and culture influence it.

Questions for Making Connections

1. Imagine yourself in another culture. What behaviors might be considered normal in that culture but considered abnormal in Western European culture? Are there behaviors labeled "abnormal" in that culture that are considered normal in Western European culture?

2. Your answer to this question may change as you learn more about abnormal behavior, but at this point do you think that abnormal behavior is due to "illness," or is it behavior that is simply wrong or different, or is it due to problems in society? Justify your position.

3. Mental illness has been explained differently at different times in history. Explain how some early explanations are still used today. What early explanations have been abandoned?

4. Describe the training and roles of the various mental health professionals. How is managed care changing the treatment of abnormal behaviors? If you developed some form of abnormal behavior, to whom would you go for help? What provisions does your health insurance make for the treatment of abnormal behavior?

Key Terms and People

In reviewing and testing yourself, you should be able to discuss each of the following:

Anna O., p. 14
asylums, p. 10
Beck, Aaron, p. 15
behavior therapy, p. 15
case managers, p. 18
Charcot, Jean-Martin, p. 13
clinical psychologists, p. 17
cognitive therapy, p. 15
counselors, p. 18
deviance, p. 5
disability, p. 5
distress, p. 5
Dix, Dorothea, p. 11
exorcism, p. 8
Freud, Sigmund, p. 14

Hippocrates, p. 8
HMO, p. 22
Hospital of St. Mary of Bethlehem, p. 10
humors, p. 8
hysterical disorders, p. 13
MA degree, p. 18
managed health care, p. 22
MD degree, p. 17
Mesmer, Franz, p. 13
mesmerism, p. 13
moral treatment, p. 11
MSW degree, p. 18
myth of mental illness, p. 6
Pavlov, Ivan, p. 15

PhD degree, p. 17
Pinel, Philippe, p. 11
psychoanalysis, p. 14
psychiatrists, p. 17
PsyD degree, p. 17
Rush, Benjamin, p. 11
scientist-practitioner model, p. 17
social workers, p. 18
Thorndike, Edward L., p. 15
trephination, p. 8
Tuke, William, p. 11
unconscious, p. 14
Watson, John B., p. 15

2 Overview of Explanations and Treatments: Psychodynamic and Learning Approaches

IMAGINE FOR A MOMENT that you are about to take a trip to a country you've never visited before; what would you do? You would probably get a map so that you would not get lost, and you might also get a guide book to help you understand what you would be seeing. This chapter and the next one are the maps and guides for your study of abnormal behavior, and as such are very important. Specifically, in these chapters I will discuss the various explanations for abnormal behavior and describe the treatments associated with each explanation. Before doing that, however, it will be helpful if we briefly consider the topic of stress, because in one way or another stress plays a role in each of the explanations we will examine.

 ## An Overview of Stress

The word *stress* is often used to refer both to a cause of stress (e.g., a test is sometimes called a stress) and to a *response* (e.g., you experience stress when you take a test). However, to be more precise it is helpful to use the word **stressor** when talking about a *cause of stress* and the word **stress** when talking about the *response to a stressor*.

Having made that distinction, we must define what a stressor is. Actually, it's difficult to define stressors because what may be a stressor for one individual may not be a stressor for another. For instance, standing in a cage with 10 hungry lions would undoubtedly be a stressor for many of us, but it is not a stressor for an experienced lion tamer. Therefore, rather than attempting to define stressors by describing what they are, it's more effective to define them operationally in terms of what they cause us to do: *Stressors are situations that require major adjustments that overtax us.* Facing the lions would be a stressor for you or me because we would be overtaxed by having to fight or run, but the lion tamer would simply go through his or her well-practiced routine. It's also noteworthy that both negative and positive situations can be stressful because both can require major adjustments. For example, getting married is generally a positive experience, but because it can require major adjustments, it can be a stressor.

Components of Stress

The stress response has two components: *psychological* and *physiological.* The psychological component involves our *emotions,* such as anxiety and emotional tension. The physiological component of the stress response involves our *bodily changes,* such as increased heart rate, blood pressure,

stressor A situation that requires a major adjustment, which overtaxes us and therefore leads to stress.

stress A negative emotion that occurs when a problem (stressor) taxes us beyond our normal limits.

Even a joyous life event, such as getting married, can be considered a stressor because it can require major adjustments in a person's lifestyle.

and muscle tension. Those changes prepare us for physical action—*fight* or *flight.* Both the psychological and physiological effects can be unpleasant.

An interesting question that arises is, which comes first—the psychological response or the physiological response? In other words, do your emotions lead to physiological responses, or do your physiological responses lead to emotions? On the one hand, it is widely assumed that *stressors trigger psychological responses (emotions) that in turn lead to physiological responses.* That is, because you are frightened, your heart rate increases. In this case the individual reasons, "I see someone who might be a mugger; I am frightened, and because of my fear my heart is beginning to beat faster." On the other hand, it is also possible that *stressors trigger physiological responses that in turn lead to psychological responses.* That is, your heart rate increases, and therefore you begin experiencing fear. In this case the individual reasons, "I see someone who might be a mugger; my heart is beating faster, so I must be afraid." That possibility may sound backwards, but evidence for it comes from research in which college students were given drugs that increased their heart rates, and when that occurred, the students experienced fear despite the fact that there was nothing in the situation to frighten them (Schachter & Singer, 1962). The fact that physiological responses can trigger emotions is important because in some cases individuals may become physiologically aroused by some *nonemotional* stimulus, such as exercise or a chemical imbalance in the brain, and the arousal leads to a false emotional response. For instance, male college students who had just ridden a bicycle and therefore were physiologically aroused were more likely to respond with aggression when they were mildly annoyed than were male college students who had not exercised (Zillmann & Bryant, 1974). In this case it appears that the students said to themselves something like "This guy provoked me and I'm aroused, so I must be very angry; I'm going to really let him have it!"

From Stressors to Abnormal Behavior

Now that you understand the concepts of stressors and stress, we can move on to discuss the process that leads from stressors to stress and then to abnormal behavior. The steps in that process are discussed in the following paragraphs and summarized in Figure 2.1.

1. *Awareness and appraisal.* The first step involves becoming *aware* that a stressor exists and *appraising* the danger it poses (Lazarus, 1999; Lazarus & Folkman, 1984). An individual who is not aware of a tumor developing in his or her body or is not aware of an impending examination does not get anxious. Indeed, in a study of adolescents who had cancer, it was found that those who were less aware of the seriousness of their disease showed fewer signs of psychological distress than those who were more aware (Burgess & Haaga, 1998). It appears then that there is some truth in the old sayings that ignorance is bliss and if you are calm while everyone around you is upset, you probably don't understand what's going on. Clearly, awareness and appraisal make up the essential first step leading to stress and abnormal behavior.

2. *Coping.* Once you are aware of the potential stressor, you may begin coping—that is, solving the problem or

FIGURE 2.1

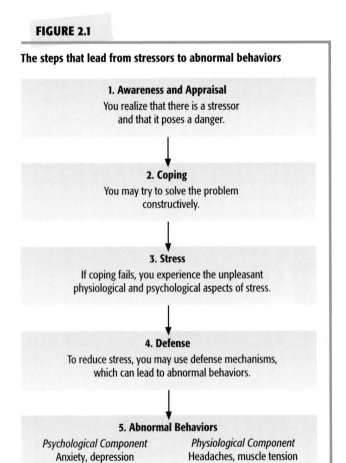

The steps that lead from stressors to abnormal behaviors

1. Awareness and Appraisal
You realize that there is a stressor and that it poses a danger.

2. Coping
You may try to solve the problem constructively.

3. Stress
If coping fails, you experience the unpleasant physiological and psychological aspects of stress.

4. Defense
To reduce stress, you may use defense mechanisms, which can lead to abnormal behaviors.

5. Abnormal Behaviors

Psychological Component	*Physiological Component*
Anxiety, depression	Headaches, muscle tension

adjusting to it. For instance, the individual who discovers a tumor can go in for treatment, and the student facing an exam can reduce social activities and spend more time studying. If the coping is effective, it will slow down or stop the process that leads to stress. For instance, cancer patients who were actively involved in coping with their disease, such as by getting treatment, were less anxious than other patients who were not actively involved in coping (Osowiecki & Compas, 1998).

3. *Stress.* If you don't try to cope or if you are unable to cope effectively, the situation will overtax you, and then the unpleasant psychological and physiological effects of stress will be triggered.

4. *Defense.* When faced with stress, you may begin using *defense mechanisms* to reduce the stress. Defense differs from coping in that coping involves *constructive problem solving,* whereas defense *involves reducing stress without solving the problem.* For example, one defensive strategy involves redefining the stressor so that it is no longer viewed with alarm: A tumor could be called a "bump," or an exam could be thought of as a "quiz." In one experiment conducted in my laboratory, two groups of students were told that they were going to receive a series of painful shocks, but the students in one group were told to think of the shocks as "vibrating sensations" rather than painful shocks. The students who redefined the shocks as vibrating sensations subsequently had lower heart rates, perspired less, and reported less anxiety while waiting for the shocks than did the students who did not use redefinition (Bennett & Holmes, 1975; Holmes & Houston, 1974; Houston & Holmes, 1974). Clearly, redefining the shock as something less frightening reduced stress.

Another defensive strategy is *avoidant thinking,* which involves intentionally distracting oneself from thinking about upsetting things (Bloom et al., 1977). Dentists may use music to distract their patients from the stressful sound of the drill, and students often watch television as a means of distracting themselves from unpleasant tasks on which they should be working. The students may not be particularly interested in what is on the TV, but watching it blocks thoughts about studying and tests. (I will discuss defenses in greater detail later in this chapter; see the section on defense mechanisms.)

A defense may reduce stress in the short run, but the individual may postpone action to solve the problem because the stress has been reduced. In the long run, then, the defense can bring on more serious consequences and higher stress. For example, to avoid stress some individuals avoid seeking medical attention for symptoms such as persistent headaches or a lump in the breast; by the time they are finally forced to get attention, it is too late for effective treatment.

5. *Abnormal behavior.* The final step in the process involves the emergence of abnormal behavior. This can

Watching TV even though you really should be studying for an exam is an example of avoidant thinking, which is a technique that involves intentionally distracting oneself from thinking about unpleasant tasks or upsetting events.

occur in three ways: First, the defenses may reduce the stress, but *the behavior involved in the defenses may be abnormal.* For example, an individual who is afraid that something bad might happen if he or she goes out of the house might defend against the fear by staying in the house; however, staying in the house for months at a time is abnormal (it is known as *agoraphobia*). Second, if the defenses are not effective, *the psychological component of stress will persist,* resulting in high levels of anxiety or depression. Third, if the defenses are not effective, *the physiological component of stress will persist,* and the chronic high level of arousal can lead to physical problems such as coronary artery disease and to biochemical changes in the brain that can result in other symptoms. The ways in which stress is related to specific disorders will be discussed throughout the rest of this book.

With this explanation of stress as background, we can go on to consider the various explanations and treatments for abnormal behavior. Before doing that, however, two points should be noted: First, in presenting each explanation I will initially take the role of an advocate and argue on behalf of the explanation. After arguing for each explanation, I will then step back and raise the tough questions the critics have asked about it. Maintaining a critical attitude is important because theories that appear correct when first presented may not actually be correct. For example, when we simply look at the horizon, the theory that the world is flat appears accurate, but we know that's not the case. Because good scientific evidence is required to support a theory, in this book we'll look for the evidence. Your job will be to evaluate that evidence and draw a conclusion.

Second, in this and the following chapter I will give you only general introductions to the explanations and treatments; in later chapters we will consider how the explanations and treatments are used in dealing with specific disorders. In other words, these overviews are designed simply to introduce you to the concepts and provide you with templates you can use to organize what you will learn later. With those points in mind, let's begin by considering Freud's psychodynamic explanation for abnormal behavior.

When Martha was an infant, her mother was scrupulous about keeping her clean and neat. Indeed, during Martha's toilet training her mother became very upset when Martha soiled her diapers. Now, as an adult, Martha is extremely neat and orderly. In fact, her ability to function is impaired because she is always cleaning and organizing rather than doing other things that must be done. Is Martha's current behavior a result of her experiences during toilet training? Do you remember your toilet training, and if not, why not?

Mark is not doing well in calculus. He has a very important examination next week, and he is "stressed out" about it. In attempts to reduce his stress he is watching a lot of television, and he is trying to convince himself that the exam won't really count for that much of his final grade. Will these defense mechanisms work? What other defenses do people use?

psychodynamic approach The view that abnormal behaviors are the result of unconscious conflicts; developed primarily by Freud. (*Psycho* means *mind,* and *dynamic* means *force,* so psychodynamic explanations refer to the interplay of forces in the mind.)

Sigmund Freud An early neurologist who was primarily responsible for developing the psychodynamic approach to abnormal behavior.

Josef Breuer An early colleague of Freud's, who is best known for treating Anna O.

Anna O. A patient of Josef Breuer whose case led to the identification of the "talking cure," the discovery that symptoms are the result of previous experiences, and much of Freud's explanation of abnormal behavior.

catharsis The notion that talking about negative feelings can make an individual feel better (from a Greek word meaning "to cleanse or purge").

stages of psychosexual development The oral, anal, phallic, latency, and genital stages described by Freud, during which conflicts must be resolved.

oral stage The first stage of psychosexual development identified by Freud, in which pleasure is associated with the mouth.

Anna O. suffered from a wide variety of symptoms, including paralyses, occasional inability to speak or eat, depression, and hallucinations. Freud reported that those symptoms were the result of stressful early experiences and, furthermore, that when Anna became aware of the links between her experiences and her symptoms, the symptoms disappeared. Freud's theory of abnormal behavior and treatment is based in large part on the famous case of Anna O., but was Freud's report of the case accurate?

Luis is in psychotherapy, but what exactly does that mean? Is he lying on a couch talking about his childhood, and will these sessions go on for years? Exactly what is psychotherapy, and why does it work?

To understand the development of the **psychodynamic approach,** we have to go back to the beginning of the 20th century, when a young neurologist named **Sigmund Freud** (1856–1939) was struggling with a problem: Many of his patients suffered from physical symptoms such as paralyses, but Freud could not find any physiological causes for the symptoms. Freud was stumped, but **Josef Breuer,** one of his colleagues, told him about a patient known as **Anna O.,** who provided the explanation. In Case Study 2.1 you will find a description of Anna O. and her treatment.

Freud learned three important things from the case of Anna O: First, from Anna's "talking cure," he realized that *talking about a problem can relieve stress and thereby temporarily relieve symptoms.* Today we refer to this as **catharsis** (ka-THAR-ses), a word derived from a Greek word meaning "to cleanse or purge." The notion is that purging negative feelings makes an individual feel better, something you've probably experienced after talking about a bad experience. Second, Freud discovered that *symptoms are the result of previous experiences.* More specifically, *stress* created by early experiences leads to abnormal behavior. In other words, just as extreme physical stress can cause a steel girder to twist out of shape and eventually break, so psychological stress can cause a distortion or breakdown of the personality. Third, Freud realized that *by eliminating the conflicts associated with the previous experiences that led to the stress, the related symptoms could be eliminated.* That is, rather than just straightening out the girder, it is necessary to eliminate the force that is causing it to bend out of shape. In general, then, the case of Anna O. provided the foundation for Freud's theory, which we will consider in greater detail in the following sections.

 **Freudian Theory**

For Freud, the most important cause of stress is *the conflict between what we want to do to satisfy our needs and the restraints imposed on us by society* (Fenichel, 1945; Freud,

1955). In other words, conflict exists between what we want to do and what our conscience or society tells us is all right to do. That conflict results in stress, and the stress leads to abnormal behaviors. According to Freud, the conflicts are originally encountered during early childhood, and how we resolve the conflicts during childhood determines whether we develop abnormal behaviors later in life. In view of the significance Freud placed on childhood experiences, it is important for us to consider some of the experiences that Freud thought were crucial.

Stages of Psychosexual Development

Freud suggested that we all go through a series of **stages of psychosexual development,** during which we must deal with various conflicts. Those stages are summarized in Table 2.1 (on p. 32), and here I will comment briefly on the major features of each stage.

First is the **oral stage** (birth to about 18 months), during which an infant's attention is focused primarily on the *mouth and feeding.* Some infants are fed whenever they want, thus leading them to believe that the world is a giving, caring, responsive place. These individuals may go through life expecting that others will be good and will always take care of them (feed them). In contrast, other infants are fed on a rigid schedule or only after they have cried vigorously for a long period of time, thus leading them to believe that the world is a hostile place in which you must yell, kick, and scream to get what you want. They might go through life being demanding and tyrannical and overreacting when they do not immediately get what they want.

The Famous Case of Anna O.

CASE STUDY 2.1

ANNA O. WAS an exceptionally bright, imaginative, energetic, and attractive 21-year-old woman living in Vienna early in the 20th century. Although she was "bubbling over with intellectual vitality," she lived a somewhat restricted life and spent much of her time daydreaming, or in what she called her "private theatre."

Unfortunately, Anna became very ill. Her symptoms included problems with vision, paralyses in her right arm and leg, a severe cough, left-sided headaches, an occasional inability to talk, times when her sentences were almost unintelligible because she intermixed words from four or five different languages, and intervals when she was unable to eat or drink. She also suffered from serious depressions, was suicidal, and was plagued with hallucinations (she saw black snakes that weren't there). In addition, there were dramatic changes in her personality: At times she was depressed and anxious but otherwise normal; at other times she hallucinated and was abusive or "naughty" (for example, she threw things at people).

Clearly, Anna was severely disturbed, and eventually a distinguished neurologist named Josef Breuer was called in to treat her. Because the cause of her symptoms was not clear, Breuer spent a great deal of time talking with

Anna about them. In doing so he discovered something remarkable: After talking about her symptoms while hypnotized, "she would wake up clear in mind, calm and cheerful." Anna referred to this as her "talking cure." Unfortunately, the effects of her talking cure were short-lived and the symptoms soon returned, so she had to go through the hypnosis and talking again.

A second interesting discovery made by Breuer was that Anna's symptoms were linked to her previous experiences. A simple example of this involved her inability to drink during one particularly hot summer: "She would take up the glass of water she longed for, but as soon as it touched her lips she would push it away." This lasted for about 6 weeks, during which she relied on fruits to lessen her tormenting thirst. However, during hypnosis one day she complained about an English lady whom she disliked and then, with great disgust, recounted an experience she had when she visited the woman; specifically, she was repulsed by the fact that the woman's little dog—"a horrid creature!"—drank out of a glass from which she might drink. Surprisingly, after describing the incident and her anger, she asked for something to drink and drank it without difficulty. When she

awoke from her hypnotic state, her inability to drink had disappeared completely, "never to return." This strategy of finding the experience that provided the basis for a symptom allowed all of Anna's symptoms to be eventually "talked away." Indeed, with this approach "the whole illness was brought to a close."

The case of Anna O. was seen as a stunning success for two reasons: First, it was a scientific success because it revealed that previously unexplainable symptoms could be accounted for with past experiences; second, it was a therapeutic success in that Anna O. was apparently completely cured. Indeed, when Breuer and Freud wrote about Anna O. in their famous book entitled *Studies in Hysteria,* they reported that after a time "she regained her mental balance entirely. Since then she has enjoyed complete health."

As a footnote to this case, I should mention that Anna O. (whose real name was Bertha Pappenheim) later became the first social worker in Germany and founded a number of homes for orphaned children. (Later in this chapter we will consider a controversy that arose over the case of Anna O.)

Source: Breuer & Freud (1895).

TABLE 2.1

Stages of psychosexual development

Stage	Issues and conflicts
Oral	Pleasure associated with oral stimulation (sucking, eating). Infants learn that others will satisfy their needs willingly or that they must fight for everything. Age: birth to about 18 months.
Anal	Toilet training is important, and attitudes toward cleanliness and control are developed. Age: 18 months to 3 years.
Phallic	Conflicts over sexuality (Oedipus and Electra complexes). The superego develops through identification with parents. Age: 3 years to 6 years.
Latency	Nothing much happens. Age: 6 years to puberty.
Genital	Individual achieves maturity and struggles with the conflicts and roles that were developed in earlier stages. Age: puberty to death.

During the **anal stage** (18 months to 3 years), which comes next, the child goes through toilet training; how this training is handled can influence the individual's personality. For instance, if a parent reacts with anxiety and disgust to the "mess" a child makes, the child may learn to be overly concerned about cleanliness and orderliness, possibly even becoming obsessive and compulsive about them. Indeed, the many TV advertisements for toilet bowl cleaners may be evidence of the traumatic and lasting effects of the American approach to toilet training. Furthermore, if the parent is strict and demanding in the process of toilet train-

Freud suggested that a child's experience with toilet training may lead to future conflicts and problems.

ing (remember the toilet seat you were strapped into until you "performed"?), the child may rebel and refuse to "go" when instructed to do so. As a consequence, as an adult the individual may be stingy, withholding, or obstinate. These traits are being referred to when a person is described as "anal" or "anal retentive." By contrast, if the parent encourages the child and praises the child when a bowel movement is produced, the child may grow up to be generous, productive, and creative.

Following the anal stage is the **phallic stage** (3 years to 6 years), during which the child supposedly becomes sexually attracted to the parent of the opposite sex, thereby setting up a conflict with the parent of the same sex. For instance, the little boy apparently becomes sexually attracted to his mother but then finds he must compete with his father for his mother's attention. During this conflict, the little boy notices that some of his peers—little girls—do not have a penis, and he concludes that they have been castrated by a vengeful father. That leads to the belief that if he continues to compete with his father, his father will castrate him. This belief causes him to stop competing with his father. However, he is still attracted to his mother, so he attempts to possess his mother vicariously by *identifying* with his father; that is, he acts like his father and thereby becomes his father symbolically and wins his mother in his imagination. That resolves the conflict, and by acting like his father, the little boy takes on the culturally approved male role. If the little boy fails to resolve the conflict by identifying with his father, he will not internalize the male role and may never develop a conscience (i.e., the culture's rules of right and wrong). Freud called this the **Oedipus** (ED-i-pus) **complex,** named for a character in a Greek tragedy who unknowingly murdered his father and married his mother.

With regard to the little girl, Freud suggested that she becomes attracted to her father because of her "penis envy"; that is, she realizes that she does not have a penis, feels incomplete, and is attracted to her father because he has one. However, to get her father the little girl must compete with her mother, but she is frightened by what her mother might do to her because of that competition; after all, apparently her mother already castrated her. Therefore, the little girl identifies with her mother so that she can have her father vicariously. By identifying with her mother, the little girl takes on the cultural role, standards, and mores for females. Freud referred to this as the **Electra** (e-LEK-tra) **complex.** He suggested that women's continuing penis envy leads to what he believed were their feelings of inferiority and their dependent role in society.

Having gotten through the turmoil of the phallic stage, children enter a psychologically quiet period that Freud called the **latency stage** (6 years to puberty). During this period things are essentially "on hold" until puberty. However, with the onset of puberty and the increases in sexual urges that come with it, individuals enter the **genital stage** (puberty to death). The genital stage does not involve any new development of personality; rather, the individual plays out the role that was developed in earlier stages. In other words, the plot of life has been written, the individual has learned his or her lines, and like a Greek tragedy, the story grinds on to its inevitable conclusion.

Today many psychologists agree with Freud's general notion that childhood experiences provide the foundation for later personality, but they often reject the importance Freud placed on some factors, particularly the suggestion that children are sexually attracted to their parents.

Structure of Personality

For Freud conflicts are at the heart of abnormal behavior. To describe how conflicts develop and are resolved, he offered his **structural approach to personality,** in which he divided the personality into three components: the *id,* the *ego,* and the *superego.* The **id** is the *source of all our innate biological needs,* and the id's goal is to satisfy those needs as rapidly as possible. Because the id seeks to satisfy needs and provide pleasure, it is governed by what Freud called the **pleasure principle;** that is, *the id simply seeks immediate pleasure.* However, the id is very ineffective in satisfying our needs. For instance, when we are hungry, rather than taking constructive action such as preparing a meal, the id might have us simply think about food. Have you ever daydreamed about something, such as a good meal or a satisfying relationship? If so, Freud would say that is the effect of your id at work.

In sharp contrast to the id is the **superego,** which embodies the *restraints imposed on us by societal rules and moral values.* We learn the dos and don'ts of society as children by identifying with our parents, but eventually those rules become part of us (the superego) rather than external forces. However, those restraints can result in conflicts with the id; for example, the id wants sex now, but the superego says wait. In other words, your id tries to push you forward while your superego tries to hold you back.

To resolve the conflicts between the id and the superego, Freud introduced the notion of the **ego,** which supposedly *mediates between the id and the superego.* To accomplish that the ego tries to find realistic and effective ways of satisfying the needs of the id while not violating the rules of the superego. For example, when we get hungry, the ego tries to find appropriate ways of getting food rather than leaving the id simply to fantasize about it. If the ego is functioning properly, we work for our food rather than fantasizing about it or stealing it. The roles of the id, ego, and superego are illustrated in Figure 2.2.

The interactions of the id, ego, and superego can result in abnormal behavior in a variety of ways. For example, if the ego is not effective in satisfying the needs of the id, the id will revert to the use of fantasies to satisfy its needs, thereby possibly leading to hallucinations or delusions (seeing or thinking things that we experience as true but

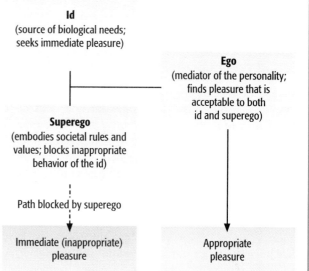

FIGURE 2.2

The ego resolves conflicts between the id and the superego.

Id
(source of biological needs; seeks immediate pleasure)

Ego
(mediator of the personality; finds pleasure that is acceptable to both id and superego)

Superego
(embodies societal rules and values; blocks inappropriate behavior of the id)

Path blocked by superego

Immediate (inappropriate) pleasure

Appropriate pleasure

anal stage   The second of Freud's stages of psychosexual development; important for the development of needs for cleanliness and order, as well as other habits.

phallic stage   The third stage of psychosexual development described by Freud; most notable during this phase is the Oedipal or Electra complex.

Oedipus complex   Freud's term for the attraction a young boy feels toward his mother.

Electra complex   Freud's term for the attraction a young girl feels toward her father.

latency stage   The fourth of Freud's stages of psychosexual development; little is thought to occur during this stage.

genital stage   The last of Freud's stages of psychosexual development, in which the individual plays out the role developed in earlier stages.

structural approach to personality   Freud's theory that the personality consists of id, superego, and ego.

id   According to Freud, the component of the personality that is the source of our innate biological needs.

pleasure principle   Concept controlling the id, which seeks immediate pleasure.

superego   According to Freud, the component of the personality that embodies the restraints imposed on us by societal rules and moral restraints.

ego   According to Freud, the component of personality that mediates between the id and the superego.

that are not true). By contrast, if the superego somehow gains most of the power, the individual may become overly restricted and rigid, possibly even obsessive about doing things "right." It's important to recognize that Freud did not suggest that the id, ego, and superego are little people in the personality; rather, they are the concepts he used to illustrate how conflicts are developed and resolved.

Levels of Consciousness

Freud also described personality in terms of three levels. At the top level is the **conscious mind,** which contains *all of the thoughts and feelings we are aware of at any one time;* it is what we are thinking and feeling *right now.* At the middle level is the **preconscious,** which is where we store *memories of such things as phone numbers and past events. We can recall them if we try.* At the bottom level, and most important for Freud, is the **unconscious,** which is where *we store anxiety-provoking memories and feelings.* Because these memories and feelings are psychologically painful, we have locked them away in our unconscious and *cannot bring them up for recall.* Although we are not able to remember what is in our unconscious, it continues to influence our behavior. Indeed, Freud suggested that many of our "unexplainable" behaviors are in fact caused by unconscious memories, conflicts, and feelings. For example, excessive cleanliness may be due to an unconscious concern about "messing" developed when one was a child. Similarly, Freud suggested that some individuals date people who are like their fathers or mothers because they still have an unconscious lust for their parents (recall the Oedipus and Electra complexes).

Although we are usually not aware of what is in our unconscious, sometimes material slips out. For example, at night when our defenses are down, unconscious material may come out in the form of dreams. In other cases, slips of the tongue may reveal unconscious thoughts. Consider the case of the man who, when ordering dinner number six

from a menu, accidentally says to the attractive waitress, "I'll have sex, please." Was that a meaningless slip of the tongue, or did it reflect an unconscious desire? Suggesting that there is an unconscious is a handy theoretical device because any behavior that cannot be explained by observable factors can be attributed to the influence of the unconscious.

With regard to its levels, Freud likened personality to an iceberg: A small part of it appears above the surface (the conscious), part of it occasionally bobs into view (the preconscious), but the major portion is below the surface and invisible (the unconscious); see Figure 2.3. Just as the submerged portion of an iceberg can be dangerous for a ship at sea, the unconscious can be dangerous to you as you navigate through life. That is, you may run afoul of things in your unconscious that will wreck you. As you will learn later, a major goal of some forms of psychotherapy is to bring unconscious material to consciousness so that the individual becomes aware of it and can deal with it in an appropriate way.

Defense Mechanisms

Because stress is an unpleasant experience, Freud suggested that we may use defense mechanisms to avoid it. Specifically, **defense mechanisms** are *psychological maneuvers in which we distort reality to avoid stress and reduce anxiety.* For example, we may avoid the stress of an impending exam by ignoring it or telling ourselves that it isn't really important. There are numerous defense mechanisms, the most important of which are discussed here (for a review, see Holmes, 2000).

1. *Repression.* One way of dealing with anxiety-provoking conflicts or thoughts is to *force them into the unconscious so that we will no longer be aware of them.* Of course, if you are not aware of a problem, the problem can't make you anxious. The process by which we send upsetting material to the unconscious is called **repression.** Repressed material is not lost like forgotten material; instead, it is *stored* in the unconscious, where it continues to influence our behavior without our awareness. For example, Freud suggests that we are unlikely to remember anything about our toilet training because we have repressed those "dirty" experiences, but they continue to influence our behavior through unconscious processes, possibly making us compulsively neat. Repression is the most important defense mechanism because it is through repression that material gets into the unconscious, and the unconscious plays a crucial role in Freud's explanation of abnormal behavior.

2. *Suppression.* Another way to deal with anxiety-provoking material is to *intentionally avoid thinking about it,* a process called **suppression.** The most common method of suppressing material is to think about something else. For instance, you may watch television to distract yourself from thinking about the fact that you just got turned down for a

---

conscious mind The top level of personality, which contains the thoughts and feelings of which we are aware at any time.

preconscious The middle level of personality, where we have stored memories that can be recalled.

unconscious The bottom level of personality, where we have stored anxiety-provoking memories or feelings that cannot be recalled but that continue to influence us.

defense mechanisms Psychological maneuvers through which we distort reality to avoid stress and reduce anxiety.

repression A defense mechanism through which we force anxiety-provoking thoughts and feelings into the unconscious.

suppression A defense mechanism through which we intentionally avoid thinking about anxiety-provoking material.

FIGURE 2.3

Freud suggested that the mind is like an iceberg, with three levels of consciousness.

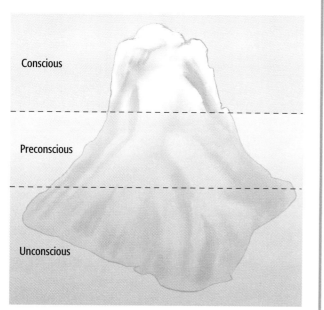

Conscious

Preconscious

Unconscious

job you really wanted. Note that suppression differs from repression in that with suppression you are *aware* of the problem but try to avoid thinking about it ("I'm just not going to think about that problem"), whereas with repression you are *no longer aware* of the problem ("What problem?").

3. *Denial.* **Denial** involves *reinterpreting anxiety-provoking material to make it less threatening.* For instance, if you just failed an important exam, you might reinterpret the exam as "just an unimportant quiz" and thereby reduce your anxiety.

4. *Projection.* **Projection** is the process whereby we *attribute our own personality characteristics to other people.* For example, if you are frightened, you might see other people as frightened, too. Projection serves as a defense mechanism in the following way: If you project an unacceptable personality trait onto another person whom you respect, your belief that the other person has the trait might reduce your concern about having the trait. For instance, if you are hostile and believe that a respected friend is also hostile, you may conclude that being hostile is not such a bad thing after all.

5. *Displacement.* There are two kinds of displacement: **Object displacement** occurs when we *express a feeling toward one individual (object) that should be expressed toward another.* For example, a man may be angry with his boss, but because it could be threatening to express the anger against his boss, he expresses it against his wife, who may be less able to retaliate. In contrast, **drive displacement** occurs when we *transfer the energy from one feeling*

(drive) that cannot be expressed to another feeling that can be expressed. Freud suggested that sexual feelings, which often must be inhibited, may be displaced and expressed as aggression, which may be more acceptable. You may have experienced or seen in a film an instance in which aggression was suddenly replaced by passion; that was an instance of drive displacement.

6. *Regression.* During stress we may use **regression** to *return to an earlier stage of life in which we were more secure and successful.* This explains why some people when frustrated go back to using previously successful strategies for solving problems, such as crying and temper tantrums. Do you chew your pencil when you are tense? Freud suggested that the pencil is a breast substitute, and chewing on it is a regression to the oral stage, when you gained pleasure from nursing. Could it also be that those plastic water bottles so many people carry these days are breast substitutes?

7. *Identification.* When using **identification,** we *take on the personal characteristics of another individual* and thereby symbolically become the other individual, which may help us satisfy our needs vicariously. For instance, dressing like someone you admire is a form of identification and may make you feel better about yourself. Alternatively, when you identify with someone of whom you are afraid, you may feel as though you have taken on some of that person's power and thereby reduced your fear. Indeed, some prisoners in the Nazi concentration camps walked, dressed, and acted like their feared Gestapo captors in attempts to deal with that fear.

8. *Rationalization.* **Rationalization** involves *giving a good reason instead of the real reason for some behavior;* in so doing we can disguise our actual, but unacceptable, motivations. For example, an individual who punishes another person severely for some minor transgression may claim that he or she is trying to help the other person, but what

denial   A defense mechanism through which we reinterpret anxiety-provoking material to make it less threatening.

projection   A defense mechanism through which we attribute our personality characteristics to other people.

object displacement   A defense mechanism through which we express a feeling toward one individual (or object) that should be expressed toward another.

drive displacement   A defense mechanism through which we express one feeling (drive) instead of another one that is threatening.

regression   A defense mechanism through which we return to an earlier stage in life in which we were more secure and successful.

identification   A defense mechanism through which we take on the personal characteristics of another person.

rationalization   A defense mechanism through which we give a good reason instead of the real reason for a behavior.

the individual may really be expressing is aggression against a disliked person.

9. *Compensation.* If we feel threatened in some area, we may *work extra hard to overcome the real or imagined weakness,* a process referred to as **compensation.** It is interesting to note that many athletes suffer from physical problems such as asthma, and Freud might have suggested that their athletic training is a means of overcoming their concerns about their physical problems. This is where the notion of overcompensation for inferiority comes from.

10. *Intellectualization.* To avoid threatening emotions, we may *focus on the objective, nonemotional details of an otherwise emotional situation.* This is called **intellectualization.** For example, a terminally ill individual may focus his or her attention on the technical aspects of a disease rather than the fact that he or she is facing death.

Although defense mechanisms can help us avoid anxiety, they usually do so at a cost. When your anxiety is reduced, you become less likely to use realistic ways of overcoming the problem that caused the anxiety. For example, if you use denial to reduce the anxiety associated with a forthcoming exam, you may not study hard enough and may fail the exam. Furthermore, defense mechanisms typically involve distortions of reality, and these distortions can reduce the effectiveness of your behaviors. For instance, if you project your hostility onto other people, you may become fearful of them, which will interfere with your ability to interact effectively with them.

Some neo-Freudians believe that anxiety stems from feelings of inferiority for which individuals then attempt to compensate. Pictured here is Jim Abbott, who became a major league pitcher despite the fact that he has only one hand.

 Neo-Freudian Theories

Freud's theory was widely accepted at first, and Freud attracted many followers. However, some of Freud's followers soon began to disagree with some of his ideas, and one by one they broke with Freud and began building their own theories. These theorists introduced new ideas, but because they retained many of Freud's ideas, such as the notions of the unconscious and the importance of early experiences, we refer to them as **neo-Freudians,** that is, *new Freudians.*

> **compensation** A defense mechanism through which we work extra hard to overcome some real or imagined weakness.
>
> **intellectualization** A defense mechanism through which we focus on the objective, nonemotional details of an otherwise emotional situation.
>
> **neo-Freudians** Theorists who accepted many of Freud's basic ideas but differed with him over the question of what causes anxiety.
>
> **Alfred Adler** A neo-Freudian who believed that we are influenced by our feelings of inferiority.

The most important departures from Freud's theory are those that revolve around the question of what causes stress. Whereas Freud emphasized conflicts over biological needs such as sex, the neo-Freudians focused on *personal or interpersonal conflicts.* In the following sections I'll describe the ideas of three prominent neo-Freudians: Alfred Adler, Karen Horney, and Carl Jung.

Alfred Adler: Feelings of Inferiority

Alfred Adler (1870–1937) was an early dissenter from the Freudian group who suggested that individuals are influenced by their *feelings of inferiority* rather than by sexual conflicts (Ansbacher & Ansbacher, 1956). Adler argued that we begin life as weak, helpless, and dependent and then spend much of our lives trying to overcome or compensate for our real or imagined inferiorities. As an example, Adler disclosed that his own feelings of inferiority stemmed from the fact that as a child he was diagnosed as being terminally ill. He eventually recovered, but the experience left an indelible impression on him. He claimed that he became a physician in an attempt to compensate for his concerns about his own physical vulnerability. Because Adler had a much more down-to-earth approach than Freud did, his ideas became very popular in counseling centers, where it seemed to make more sense to help people overcome their feelings of inferiority than to resolve their incestuous wishes about their parents.

Karen Horney: Interpersonal Conflicts

Another prominent neo-Freudian was **Karen Horney** (HORN-i; 1885–1952), who argued that stress and anxiety are due to *interpersonal conflicts* over issues such as dominance and inconsistencies in love (Horney, 1937, 1939, 1945). Specifically, she suggested that because some parents are overly dominant and inconsistent in providing love, their children have problems relating to them, and these troubled relationships provide the models for later relationships. To cope with these problems, Horney suggested, people use one of three interpersonal styles (Horney, 1945). One style involves *moving toward people*; individuals with this style deal with their anxiety by becoming dependent upon others and by seeking excessive love and support from them. Unfortunately, these relationships are one-sided and short-lived because the individuals want, but can't give, support and love. A second style involves *moving against people*; by fighting and overcoming others, individuals briefly overcome their feelings of insecurity and gain a sense of power and respect from others. However, gains based on winning battles don't lead to good relationships, and soon the individuals are left alone and vulnerable. The third style involves *moving away from people*; individuals who adopt this style attempt to avoid anxiety by becoming self-sufficient and independent. Their notion seems to be "If I don't love or need anyone, I can't get hurt by anyone." This reduces anxiety in the short run, but it ultimately leads to isolation and loneliness. Do any of these patterns fit with how you relate to others?

Another aspect of Freud's theory that Horney rejected was his belief that women are inferior because they have penis envy (Horney, 1967). Horney argued that insofar as women feel inferior to men, it is because of their cultural role; furthermore, when women strive to be like men, it is because they want the power given to men by society, not because they want a penis. Indeed, Horney went on to suggest that men envy women's ability to give birth, and may even have *breast envy*. Why else, she asked, would men spend so much time looking at women's breasts? These ideas made Karen Horney the first major psychologist with a feminist point of view.

Carl Jung: The Collective Unconscious

Carl Jung (yoong; 1875–1961) broke with Freud in a bitter dispute over the nature of the unconscious. Jung agreed with Freud that we have an unconscious in which we store all of our anxiety-provoking personal experiences, but Jung went on to argue that we also have a **collective unconscious** in which *we have stored the memories of all of the experiences*

that occurred to our ancestors over the entire course of evolution (Jung, 1963, 1964). Furthermore, Jung suggested that these collected experiences influence our current behaviors. For example, snakes were a serious threat early in our evolutionary history, and because that memory is stored in our collective unconscious, we have irrational fears of snakes (snake phobias) today. In general, it was Jung's position that understanding an individual does not require acting like a detective who examines the individual's *personal* history, but instead acting like an anthropologist who digs through the individual's *evolutionary* history. Because Jung's approach is rather mystical (e.g., we are influenced by all of our dead ancestors, going back to amoebas), it is popular with some groups but has few fans among scientists.

Overall, then, the neo-Freudians offer some interesting alternatives to Freud's position concerning the causes of stress, but they do so without abandoning some of his most popular notions such as the role of early experiences, defense mechanisms, and the unconscious.

 ## Treatment: Psychotherapy

If abnormal behavior is the result of conflict and stress, then the goal of treatment is to reduce those problems. That brings us to the topic of psychotherapy. In general, **psychotherapy** is a process in which *by talking with a therapist, a client (patient) resolves conflicts and reduces stress and thereby overcomes abnormal behaviors* (Levenson & Butler, 1999; Ursano & Silberman, 1999). However, there are substantial differences among therapists in how they conduct psychotherapy. Let's consider some of those differences.

Many psychotherapists play a rather passive role and simply make observations or ask questions about the client's behaviors. For instance, a therapist might say, "It seems you're most likely to become upset and even angry when you're dealing with women, particularly women in positions of authority. I wonder why that is?" The therapist might also use the client's behavior in therapy to illustrate how the client reacts inappropriately. For example, the therapist might comment, "I've noticed that every time we

Karen Horney   A neo-Freudian who believed that anxiety is due to interpersonal conflicts.

Carl Jung   A neo-Freudian who believed that we are influenced by a collective unconscious.

collective unconscious   Jung's concept of an unconscious in which we have stored all of the experiences that occurred to our ancestors over the entire course of evolution.

psychotherapy   A process in which, by talking with a therapist, a client (patient) resolves conflicts and reduces stress and thereby overcomes abnormal behaviors.

disagree about something, you come late to our next session. Is this a passive way of expressing your annoyance? Do you do that to other people? Might that be why your relationships go bad?" In general, the goal of these therapists is to lead their clients to develop their own insights about their problems and potential solutions. In contrast, other therapists take a more active role and simply tell the client what the problem is and what should be done.

There are also wide differences in what therapists focus on during therapy. First, some therapists believe that symptoms stem from problems *within the client,* such as unresolved conflicts, whereas others believe that symptoms arise because of *external problems,* such as financial difficulties, interpersonal conflicts, the need to care for others, or the failure to achieve goals. Second, what therapists focus on is also influenced by their *theoretical orientation.* For instance, those who subscribe to Freud's theory concentrate primarily on sexual conflicts, whereas followers of Adler are concerned with feelings of inferiority. Finally, therapists differ in terms of whether they focus on the *past* or the *present.* Specifically, many therapists take the position that current symptoms are the result of past problems, which must be resolved to overcome the symptoms. In contrast, other therapists acknowledge that symptoms may have their roots in the past, but they argue that "the past is past" and what is important is to determine what to do now. Consider this analogy: If you were lost, one individual might try to help you by taking you back to the point at which you made your wrong turn and then have you start over; another person might simply determine where you are now and figure out how you can get to your destination. In other words, one therapist might ask, "Where did you go wrong?" while another therapist might ask, "How can we get you from here to where you want to be?"

In most cases psychotherapy involves one-to-one interactions between the therapist and the client. At times, however, there may be more than one client in the session; indeed, the number of clients may range from three or four to eight or more, and the group may include more than one therapist. This **group psychotherapy** has a number of advantages (Bednar & Kaul, 1994; Vinogradov, Cox, & Yalom, 1999). For example, although some individuals may find talking about problems in front of others threatening at first, the group can become a source of support; it can be comforting to realize that other people have similar prob-

lems and that they are making progress in overcoming them. One woman in group therapy for married couples commented, "For me, it's very instructive to see how other couples deal with conflicts over money, sex, in-laws, whether to have children, infidelity, careers, and so on. It's valuable to see that other people can cry and that men can be intimidated." The other members of the group can also aid in the therapeutic process by helping the client explore problems and come up with solutions. Probably most important is the fact that the group provides a microcosm of life outside of therapy. While they are in the group, individuals can see how they respond to others and how others respond to them, and they can practice new ways of relating. An interesting extension of group psychotherapy is **family therapy,** in which a family works on shared problems as a group (Alexander, Holtzworth-Monroe, & Jameson, 1994; Kadis & McClendon, 1999). Having family members come together with a therapist who can exert some control and facilitate interactions can enhance communication among them.

The most recent innovation in psychotherapy involves the computer; there are now hundreds of therapists providing online therapy via chat rooms or e-mail (Murphy & Mitchell, 1998; Rothchild, 1997; Shapiro & Schulman, 1996). Proponents of this approach point out that therapy via computer is much less expensive than traditional therapy and that it makes treatment available to people who would have difficulty getting to a therapist's office. Also, some clients report that they are less inhibited when communicating via computer than talking face-to-face. However, skeptics argue that important elements of therapy are interpersonal cues and "chemistry," and they question whether therapy that doesn't involve face-to-face contact can be effective. On the other hand, proponents point out that intense relationships can be developed and maintained for years through letters and that the computer simply provides a very fast mail delivery system. Furthermore, a large body of evidence indicates that simply writing about one's problems and potential solutions can lead to improvements even if no one reads what is written, which suggests that e-mail therapy might work (Pennebaker, 1997). It's too early to know if therapy via computer is effective, but it is a development to watch.

Finally, a comment should be made concerning how long psychotherapy lasts. Traditionally, client and therapist worked together until the problem was solved; in other words, therapy was an open-ended process that might go on for years. However, it is becoming increasingly common for the client and therapist to agree in advance that the treatment will be limited to a relatively few number of sessions, such as 10 or 15. In this **time-limited psychotherapy,** the number of sessions is limited in an attempt to make the client work harder, make more efficient use of the time available, and thereby speed up the process. Just as students sometimes put off working on a tough term paper until just

group psychotherapy   Psychotherapy in which one or more therapists meet with a group of clients.

family therapy   A form of group therapy in which a therapist works with a family.

time-limited psychotherapy   A way of conducting psychotherapy in which the number of sessions is agreed upon at the outset.

Psychotherapy has joined the ranks of important services now available online. Hundreds of therapists provide online therapy via chat rooms or e-mail, providing a less expensive and more accessible alternative to traditional therapy. However, skeptics argue that online therapy lacks the interpersonal connection that is so important to psychotherapy.

before it is due, clients sometimes avoid the difficult issues in therapy if they think they can put them off until later sessions. Time-limited therapy does not allow for that. Note that time-limited psychotherapy is not a type of therapy but rather a way of packaging or streamlining traditional forms of psychotherapy. The only difference may be that with the time-limited approach the therapist may have to be somewhat more active to keep the client and the process moving along. Surprisingly, research indicates that time-limited therapy is usually at least as effective as unlimited-time therapy (Koss & Shiang, 1994). Finally, it's noteworthy that whereas the time-limited strategy was once an option, it is now often required by insurance companies in an effort to reduce costs (see the discussion of the role of economics in treatment in Chapter 1).

From this discussion it should be clear that psychotherapy encompasses a wide variety of strategies and styles. Therefore, when someone uses the term *psychotherapy*, you should seek additional information concerning exactly what they are referring to. Also, knowing about the differences in psychotherapy may help you select a therapist if the need ever arises. In Case Study 2.2 (on p. 40) you'll find one person's account of her therapeutic experience.

The psychodynamic approach is summarized in Figure 2.4, and with this as background we can consider some of the questions that have been raised by critics of this approach.

FIGURE 2.4

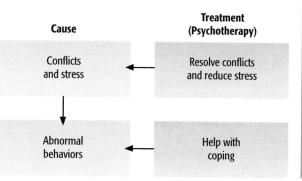

The psychodynamic approach: Conflict and stress cause abnormal behaviors; psychotherapy is focused on resolving conflicts and coping.

THINKING CRITICALLY

Questions about the Psychodynamic Approach

1. *What is the scientific evidence for Freud's theory?* You may be surprised to learn that by today's standards of scientific evidence, there is very little support for many of the major aspects of Freud's theory. Most of the empirical investigations conducted to test Freud's major ideas simply do not offer any support for them. The concept of repression is an interesting case in point. Despite over 80 years of research there is no consistent clinical or laboratory evidence for the notion of repression (see Chapter 7). Indeed, rather than forcing anxiety-provoking memories into the unconscious, individuals are often unable to get those memories out of consciousness and are, in fact, continually bothered by them. For example, memories of terrible experiences such as rapes and wartime attacks are not repressed but instead persist and torment individuals (see the discussion of posttraumatic stress disorder in Chapter 6). The failure to find evidence for repression is particularly noteworthy because repression is the cornerstone of Freud's explanation of abnormal behavior; that is, it is through repression that memories supposedly get into the unconscious, from which they lead to abnormal behaviors. With regard to the absence of evidence, it is interesting to note that when psychiatrists were surveyed recently concerning multiple personality disorder, a disorder based on the notion that some personalities are repressed, three-quarters reported that they no longer believed that there was evidence to support the existence of that disorder (Pope et al., 1999). Clearly, the absence of evidence for some of Freud's most basic ideas is causing mental health professionals to rethink their earlier acceptance of his ideas.

One Client's Experience in Psychotherapy

"I'VE BEEN GOING TO A THERAPIST for a little over a year now, and usually I go once a week. I started because I was, well, I just wasn't happy. I was always tense, and that seemed to be wrecking all of my friendships, and I was a loner. I didn't know what to do about it until one day a friend of mine suggested that I might 'see someone for some professional advice.' My first reaction was, 'That's not for *me*. I'm not crazy!' But then I discovered that a lot of my friends were in or had been in therapy, so I thought I'd give it a try.

"I didn't know quite what to expect at first; I thought I'd lay on a couch and talk about my mother and father a lot, but that's not what happened. My therapist is a woman about 40 years old, but I don't know for sure because she never talks about herself. A couple of times I got up enough courage to ask her something about herself, but each time she just said something like 'We're here to talk about you, and I think it would be better if we kept focused on that.' She was very nice about it, but she drew a clear line.

> ". . . If I think everyone else has problems, maybe the problem is in the way I think about other people."

"During my sessions I sit in a comfortable chair and my therapist sits across from me. There's a desk in the office, but she doesn't sit behind it. The office is quiet and very comfortable.

"Originally, we spent time talking about my being tense and the problems I was having with people—we sort of had to get the issues on the table so that we'd know what we were working on. After that, we spent time talking about other things, like my family, experiences in school, and my job. It seemed like she was trying to get to know me in general, but often when we were talking about what seemed to be 'side issues,' examples would come up of people or situations that upset me. In talking about it, I came to realize that my problem was really pretty pervasive and I'd had it for a long

time. At first I thought, 'Gee, I've been around problem people for a long time.' We spent a lot of time talking about my interactions with other people, and then a pattern started to emerge, a pattern that went way back. It seemed that I never really had any close relationships, and instead I was always fighting people. My therapist called it 'moving against or away from others rather than with or toward them.' When I realized that, I was faced with a tough question: *Did I move against other people because they had a problem, or did I have a problem?* I didn't want to think the problem was with me, so I struggled with the question for a long time. Usually, I was pretty defensive and came up with long lists of problems with other people. My therapist never disagreed, but she asked gentle, prodding questions that forced me to question myself. She never pushed or argued with me; she would just pose questions or suggest alternatives. She was gentle, but some of her observations opened up some pretty painful possibilities. It isn't always fun to look at yourself from the outside and turn things upside down. The bottom line came to be, 'If I think everyone else has problems, *maybe the problem is in the way I think about other people*. Maybe I need to change the way I think about other people.' That was a real change in perspective for me, and to be perfectly honest, I haven't completely accepted it yet. I can buy it intellectually (it makes sense), but buying it emotionally is a little different. What I'm doing now is experimenting a little; when a conflict starts to emerge, I ask myself, 'Is this problem out there or in me?' I think I'm doing better, but you don't change 20 years of experience overnight.

"Even if it's true that my problems are due to me, that doesn't explain why I developed them in the first place. One day, my therapist sort of suggested that maybe I was very sensitive—insecure?—and that by finding fault or running away from other people I avoid the risk of being rejected. That

led to a long discussion about security, and the issue is still hanging there. Even if I am insecure, why am I that way? Objectively, I've got a lot going for me, but subjectively, I'm not sure. You see, the answer to one question just leads to another question, and therapy goes on and on.

"The talking has been good, but I've had ups and downs with my therapist. There were times when she really got on my nerves. For a while I almost stopped going. In fact, I skipped a number of sessions without telling her that I wasn't coming because I was convinced that she didn't like me and that the only reason she was seeing me and being nice to me was that I was paying her. I remember that there used to be a man who had an appointment before me, and my therapist would always be smiling at him when he left her office, and then she'd turn to me in a very businesslike way. When I came to the conclusion that I was just a paying customer, I really felt hurt—but I didn't say anything. The first two times I cut sessions, she made some comment about my missing, and I said that an emergency had come up, and she let it pass. The third time I did it, she told me I would have to pay for missed sessions, and she asked why I had missed. I fumbled around and came up with some dumb excuse—and she just sat there. I talked around in circles, and after letting me hang for a while, she asked whether I was upset with her and whether I was dealing with the feeling by running away—or at least by not coming in. In other words, was I dealing with her like I dealt with everyone else? I said, 'Of course not; why should I be upset with you? You haven't done anything to me.' I know now that I was using denial and playing word games. I didn't realize it at the time, but I was doing with her what I do—or did—with everyone.

"Therapy is tough to explain, but this is what I have been going through."

We also have to consider the case studies that provide the foundation for Freud's theory. For Freud's followers the lack of empirical evidence for his ideas did not pose a problem because they believed that his case studies proved his points. However, there are two serious problems with the use of Freud's case studies to support his theory: First, *with case studies it is virtually impossible to prove causal relationships,* and therefore they cannot be used as evidence. In other words, the fact that an individual with a disorder had a particular experience as a child does not necessarily mean that the experience caused the disorder; it could have been caused by any one of a number of other factors, such as another experience or genes. (For a more detailed discussion of the problems with case studies, see Chapter 4.)

The second problem concerning Freud's case studies is that *he did not report them accurately;* indeed, it is not an overstatement to say that Freud lied about them (Crews, 1998; Gray, 1988). For years there were suspicions that Freud's reports were not accurate because the biographies and autobiographies of his clients often told stories that were very different from those told by Freud. Freud and his defenders dismissed the differences by suggesting that former clients were trying to cover up their previous problems. However, recently discovered letters and hospital files make it clear that Freud was not truthful about some of his most important cases.

Because this is an important and controversial issue, I'll illustrate it with two classic examples. The first is the famous case of Anna O., the woman who provided the foundation for Freud's theory. You will recall from Case Study 2.1 that Freud and Breuer reported that as a consequence of her talking cure, Anna *"regained her mental balance entirely"* and *"since then she has enjoyed complete health"* (Breuer & Freud, 1895; emphasis added). However, we now know that within a month of the end of her treatment Anna was so ill that Breuer and her family had to hospitalize her. In fact, in a letter to his fiancée, Freud explained that Anna was so ill that Breuer "wishes she were dead so that the poor woman could be free of her suffering. He says she will never be well again, that she is completely shattered" (Borch-Jacobsen, 1998, p. 16). Also important are Anna's hospital records, which indicate that when she was admitted she was seriously addicted to morphine. This suggests that if she experienced any relief from her symptoms while she was being treated, it was because she was being heavily sedated with drugs, not because of her talking cure, as alleged by Freud. (It's also noteworthy that Freud never mentioned the medication in his account of Anna's treatment.) Clearly, the case of Anna O. was not as Freud reported it.

Another dramatic case involves a patient named Emma Eckstein; that case is summarized in Case Study 2.3 (on p. 42).

Freud's lack of honesty in reporting his cases certainly disqualifies them as evidence for his theory and raises questions about his character. Of course, the fact that Freud did not report the cases accurately does not necessarily mean that the underlying principles are not correct, but his lack of truthfulness in combination with the absence of laboratory evidence certainly raises serious questions.

2. *Are early experiences as important as Freud suggested?* A basic tenet of Freud's theory is that early experiences play the major role in shaping our personalities, and you've probably heard stories about people whose problems in adulthood could be traced to problems during childhood, such as physical or emotional abuse. The notion that early experiences are important is widely accepted, but what's the evidence? You may be surprised to learn that, contrary to what is generally believed, a growing body of evidence indicates that *early negative experiences do not necessarily lead to abnormal behaviors* (Clarke & Clarke, 1976; Emery & Forehand, 1994; Kagan, 1996, 1999; Kessler et al., 1997; Masten & Coatsworth, 1998; Seligman, 1995; Weinberg et al., 1992). For example, after being adopted into a good home, most children who were originally exposed to serious problems such as violence and abuse show normal and even excellent levels of adjustment. Similarly, children who lived through the disruption of divorce, prolonged periods of isolation, or even *torture in concentration camps* often show normal personalities later in life. Indeed, when Freud examined children who survived the Nazi concentration camps, he was unable to find serious lasting effects (Freud & Dann, 1951).

Could it be that the effects of early negative experiences can be reversed by subsequent positive experiences, or that individuals learn to cope with or overcome the early experiences? Actually, the notion that we can overcome experiences is not completely foreign to psychology; after all, psychotherapy is based on the premise that understanding previous problems and learning to cope with them allow people to overcome the effects of earlier traumatic experiences. In other words, a river may start flowing in one direction because of the slope of the land, but if it encounters a dam or the land begins to slope in another direction, its path and direction may change dramatically. Similarly, our early experiences may start us in one direction, but their importance may be diminished, if not eliminated, by subsequent experiences.

So why have mental health professionals clung to the importance of early experiences? The answer seems to be that they work with clients who have problems, and they find negative experiences in those clients' backgrounds. Although people without current problems may also have had early negative experiences, mental health professionals don't work with those people so they can't disconfirm their belief about the long-term effects of early experiences. Because the role of early experiences is crucial not only to Freud's theory, but also to much of the general thinking in psychology today, it is a topic to which we will give careful attention throughout this book.

Freud and the Case of the Bleeding Nose

ONE OF FREUD'S FIRST PATIENTS was an attractive 27-year-old woman named Emma Eckstein. Emma was suffering from stomach ailments and menstrual problems that Freud thought were due to psychological conflicts over masturbation. Early in the treatment a colleague of Freud's named Wilhelm Fliess performed an operation on Emma's nose. The operation was done because Freud and Fliess believed there was a connection between the nose and sexual organs. Indeed, Fliess argued that in addition to the psychosexual stages listed by Freud, there was also a *nasal stage* of psychosexual development.

The operation did not reveal anything unusual, but a couple of days after the operation Emma began experiencing nose bleeds that became progressively more serious and painful. Because of

> **What we see here is malpractice, a cover-up, and a blatant deception. . . .**

the continued bleeding and pain, another physician examined Emma's nose and made an interesting discovery. As he removed some of the blood clots from around Emma's nose, he found a thread coming from one of her nostrils, and when he began pulling on the thread, it led to a strip of gauze, and by the time he stopped pulling on the gauze, *he had removed about a foot and a half of gauze from her nasal cavity!* Fliess had apparently used the gauze to stop the bleeding during the operation, and then he had forgotten to take it out of Emma's nose before closing the operation. Emma's bleeding was due to the seriously bungled operation.

In a letter to Fliess, Freud originally pointed out that Emma's bleeding nose was due to a botched operation, but later he changed the story. Specifically, Freud dismissed the operation as the cause of Emma's problem and declared instead that "her episodes of bleeding were hysterical [psychologically

caused], were occasioned by [sexual] longing, and probably occurred at the sexually relevant times [menstruation]" (Masson, 1984, p. 100). Indeed, later he wrote that Emma "became restless during the night because of an unconscious wish to entice me to go there [to her bedside], and since I did not come during the night, she renewed the bleedings, as an unfailing means of rearousing my affection" (p. 101).

It's noteworthy that the letters concerning the real cause of Emma's bleeding were hidden by Freud's daughter, Anna, and we would never have known the truth if the letters had not been discovered accidentally years later in a bureau drawer in Freud's home. What we see here is malpractice, a cover-up, and a blatant deception to make Emma's symptoms fit with Freud's theory.

Source: Masson (1984).

---

3. *Why is it important to understand Freud today?* If there is so little evidence for Freud's theory and if we know that he was not honest in reporting his cases, you may be wondering why I and other authors spend so much time discussing Freud and his theory. There are three good reasons: First, regardless of whether or not he was correct, *Freud had, and continues to have, a very important influence on Western thinking about the causes of behavior.* Indeed, Freud's books are on virtually every list of the great books of Western culture, and when *Time* magazine selected the most influential thinkers of the 20th century, Freud was named first and given more attention than others, such as Albert Einstein (Gray, 1999). Because Freud's theory is so prominent and because terms such as *id, superego, ego, repression,* and *Oedipus complex* are so widely used, it is important that you understand the theory and some of its terminology.

Second, it is also important that you understand Freud's theory so that you will be aware of its limitations and the fact that many of its most important features lack scientific support. In other words, sometimes we have to spend time learning what is known to be incorrect so that we will not blindly accept those earlier ideas and repeat the mistakes of the past. To paraphrase an old saying, those who do not

understand the mistakes of the past may repeat them. Thus, it's important that you are inoculated against that possibility.

Third and finally, I hasten to add that not all of Freud's ideas have been discredited. For example, his notions concerning defense mechanisms and the role of stress in abnormal behavior are widely accepted, so it is essential for you to understand those ideas and their origin. Certainly we should not overreact and dismiss all of Freud's ideas.

4. *Why does psychotherapy work?* Some years ago there was a controversy over whether psychotherapy was really effective for reducing abnormal behavior. Critics argued that people in psychotherapy showed the same rate of improvement as people who were not; the notion seemed to be "Time heals all wounds." Today, however, the results of more sophisticated research indicate that psychotherapy can be effective, and the question has been changed to "*Why* is it effective?" At first the answer appears clear: Psychotherapy works because skilled therapists can help clients resolve conflicts or at least learn to cope with problems effectively. But consider these two findings: First, a wide variety of research indicates that the training of psychotherapists does not enhance the success of their therapy; that is, highly trained therapists are not more effective than untrained individuals (see reviews by Dawes, 1994; Lambert & Bergin, 1994). For example, in one investigation hospitalized patients were treated either by psychiatrists or by medical students who had no training in psychiatry (Miles, McLean, & Maurice, 1976). The patients who were treated by the students showed the same rate of improvement as those treated by the psychiatrists. Second, although therapists who have different theoretical orientations focus on entirely different causes when treating clients with any one disorder, all forms of psychotherapy appear to be equally effective (Lambert & Bergin, 1994; Wampold et al., 1997). These findings pose an awkward problem: We have evidence that psychotherapy is more effective than no treatment, but *we do not have evidence indicating what makes psychotherapy effective*. In response to this dilemma it was suggested that the effects of psychotherapy are due simply to *social support*. The role of social support has received considerable attention lately, and we now know that such support is important for both avoiding the effects of stress and recovering from stress. That is, individuals who have close friends in whom they can confide and from whom they receive emotional support are less influenced by stress and recover from stress more quickly (Winefield, 1987; see also Chapter 9). The argument is that friendship, or social support, is the crucial factor in the improvement seen in psychotherapy and that psychotherapy is simply the "purchase of friendship" (Schofield, 1964). We will consider this issue in greater detail when we discuss the role of psychotherapy in treating various disorders.

With this material as background we can go on to consider the learning approach to understanding and treating abnormal behavior, an approach that provides a sharp contrast and an interesting alternative to the psychodynamic approach.

Social support is important for avoiding the effects of stress and recovering from stress. Having close friends in whom we can confide and who can provide us with emotional support helps to guard against the influence of stress.

TOPIC II
The Learning Approach

Albert is a young child who cries with fear when he is shown a ball of cotton. Albert appears to have a phobia for cotton, but how did this phobia develop? Interestingly, Albert also becomes frightened when he is shown a small white rabbit. Are the two fears connected somehow, and if so, how?

Carlos is participating in a psychological experiment and has developed a rather strange response; each time he is shown a woman's shoe, he has an erection. In a similar experiment Anthony also developed an interesting response; he has an erection each time he is shown a triangle. How were these responses developed, and what implications do they have for understanding abnormal behaviors?

Latisha is 4 years old, and she is very difficult to deal with because she has a temper tantrum if she does not immediately get what she wants. She screams, kicks, throws things, and sometimes even bangs her head. Because her tantrums are so disruptive and in some cases potentially dangerous, her parents often give in to her demands. However, in an attempt to teach Latisha that tantrums will not always get her what she wants, her parents have sometimes not given in, but that strategy did not work. What is causing these tantrums, and why have the attempts to eliminate them by ignoring her demands failed?

In the 1950s many psychologists became dissatisfied with Freud's psychodynamic explanation for abnormal behavior because it was not supported by empirical evidence and because psychotherapy appeared to be a slow and sometimes ineffective process. Seeking an alternative, some psychologists developed a new approach based on *learning;* in essence, these psychologists asked, "If learning can be used to explain and change *normal* behaviors, why not use it to explain and change *abnormal* behaviors?" Because psychologists had been studying learning in the laboratory for many years, there was a broad base of scientific evidence for how learning worked, making the move to learning a logical step. The basic tenets of the **learning approach** to abnormal behavior are that *abnormal behavior is learned* and that *treatment should be based on unlearning inappropriate behaviors and learning appropriate behaviors.*

learning approach   The theory that abnormal behavior is learned and treatment should be based on unlearning inappropriate behaviors and learning appropriate behaviors.

Ivan Pavlov and his assistants accidentally discovered classical conditioning while collecting saliva from dogs.

At the outset we need to acknowledge two general points concerning this approach: First, *advocates of this explanation do not make any assumptions about internal processes, such as thinking, that they cannot directly observe.* Instead, they take the position that explanations for abnormal behaviors should be based only on *observable* variables. Therefore, they limit their attention to external factors such as stimuli and rewards, avoiding all of the unverifiable notions used in the psychodynamic approach, such as the unconscious. Because of their strict reliance on observable behaviors, psychologists who espouse the learning explanation are referred to as **behaviorists,** and their approach to psychology is called **behaviorism.**

The second point is that the learning explanation encompasses two distinctly different types of learning, *classical conditioning* and *operant conditioning,* which lead to different types of abnormal behaviors. In the following sections I'll explain the two types of conditioning and describe the abnormal behaviors to which they can lead.

Classical Conditioning

The year is about 1915, and a Russian physiologist named **Ivan Pavlov** (1849–1936) is studying the role of saliva in digestion. He is doing his research with dogs, and to collect

saliva for analysis his assistant rings a bell to get the dog's attention. Pavlov then blows a small amount of powdered meat into the dog's mouth to make the dog salivate, and the saliva is collected from a tube fitted into the dog's mouth. As the story goes, one day Pavlov's assistant accidentally rang the bell before Pavlov was ready to blow the powdered meat into the dog's mouth. Much to Pavlov's surprise the dog salivated when it heard the bell, even though it had not been given any powdered meat. What Pavlov accidentally discovered with his salivating dogs is what we now call **classical conditioning.** Specifically, he discovered that if a neutral stimulus (e.g., a bell) is consistently *paired* with a stimulus (e.g., food) that elicits a particular response (e.g., salivation), eventually the neutral stimulus will take on the ability to elicit the response. In other words, after the bell was paired with the powdered meat, the bell alone caused salivation. The neutral stimulus (e.g., the bell) that takes on the ability to elicit the **conditioned response** is called the **conditioned stimulus,** and the stimulus that originally elicited the **unconditioned response** (e.g., the food) is called the **unconditioned stimulus.** This process is diagrammed in Figure 2.5.

Let's now jump to the United States in about 1920, where a brash young psychologist named **John B. Watson** (1878–1958) and his colleague **Rosalie Rayner** (1900–1935) are trying to show that fears are learned rather than innate. To do that they conduct what is now a famous study on an 11-month-old boy called **Little Albert** (Watson & Rayner, 1920). They first present a white rat to Little Albert, who shows no fear of the rat and even enjoys playing with it. Next, they present the white rat again, but this time they also make a loud noise that frightens the little boy. This procedure of pairing the rat with a frightening noise is repeated a number of times. Finally, they present the white rat to Albert without the frightening noise, but despite the absence of the noise, *Albert responds with fear to the white*

behaviorists   Psychologists who espouse the learning explanation for behavior.

behaviorism   The notion that the study of behavior should focus only on observable behaviors.

Ivan Pavlov   A Russian physiologist who discovered classical conditioning.

FIGURE 2.5

Steps and terms in the classical conditioning process

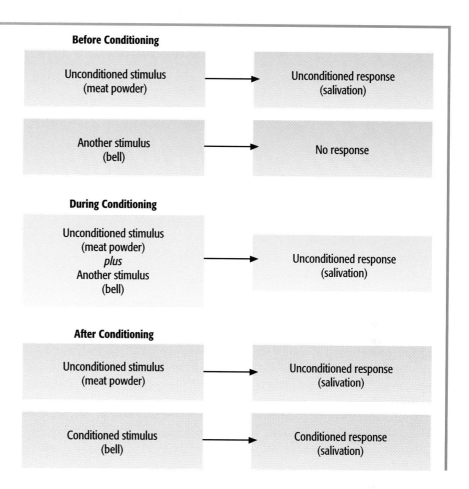

Before Conditioning

| Unconditioned stimulus (meat powder) | → | Unconditioned response (salivation) |

| Another stimulus (bell) | → | No response |

During Conditioning

| Unconditioned stimulus (meat powder) *plus* Another stimulus (bell) | → | Unconditioned response (salivation) |

After Conditioning

| Unconditioned stimulus (meat powder) | → | Unconditioned response (salivation) |

| Conditioned stimulus (bell) | → | Conditioned response (salivation) |

rat. What we see here is a clear example of the classical conditioning of fear in a human. (The procedures Watson and Rayner used have been criticized for a variety of technical reasons [Harris, 1979]. However, the principles suggested by this original demonstration were subsequently confirmed by a substantial amount of well-controlled research [Hilgard & Marquis, 1961].)

Here's a story of how I once developed an unusual (abnormal?) classically conditioned response: One day after cooking a meal, I began scrubbing a frying pan with Comet cleanser, and suddenly I became nauseated and sick to my stomach. I assumed that it was something I had eaten that was causing the nausea (I wasn't the world's greatest cook at the time), so I lay down on the couch for a few minutes, hoping that the nausea would soon pass. While lying there, for reasons I did not understand at the time, I began thinking about a course in psychology I had taken as an undergraduate student several years earlier. I thought about the instructor, about some of the class projects, about my experiences in the laboratory—and then suddenly I realized why I was sick! In that class it was my job to clean the monkey cages, a task that was particularly unpleasant because I had to spend hours scrubbing feces-encrusted surfaces with

Comet cleanser. While doing that I was often on the verge of getting sick to my stomach. What happened was that the smell of the Comet cleanser was repeatedly paired with my

classical conditioning   The pairing of a neutral stimulus with a stimulus that elicits a response so that eventually the once-neutral stimulus elicits the response.

conditioned response   A response that is elicited by a conditioned stimulus.

conditioned stimulus   A once neutral stimulus that takes on the ability to elicit a conditioned response.

unconditioned response   A response that is elicited by an unconditioned stimulus.

unconditioned stimulus   A stimulus that originally elicits a response in classical conditioning.

John B. Watson   An American psychologist who demonstrated that fears could be conditioned in humans.

Rosalie Rayner   A colleague of Watson's in the research on the conditioning of fear.

Little Albert   An 11-month-old boy in whom Watson and Rayner conditioned fear.

nausea, and I developed a classically conditioned nausea response to the smell. Two years later, when I was confronted with the smell, the nausea response was elicited and I became sick to my stomach.

Classical conditioning is usually associated with negative responses such as fear and nausea, but it can also be used to develop *positive* responses such as sexual arousal. Consider the following interesting experiment: Men were first shown a slide of a pair of woman's black boots, and their sexual arousal (erections) was measured. As you might expect, the men did not become aroused. Next, the men were put through a series of conditioning trials in which they were shown the slide of the boots quickly followed by a slide of a scantily dressed woman that caused them to become sexually aroused. In other words, on each trial the boots were paired with sexual arousal. After the conditioning trials the men were shown the slide of the boots *but not the slide of the woman,* and their sexual arousal was assessed. On that occasion *every one of the men in the experiment had an erection when shown the slide of the boots* (Rackman, 1966; Rackman & Hodgson, 1968). Clearly, the positive emotion of sexual arousal had been classically conditioned. This experiment was repeated recently with other stimuli, resulting in conditioned sexual arousal to geometric figures such as squares and triangles (Langevin & Martin, 1975; Plaud & Martini, 1999).

How is classical conditioning relevant for understanding abnormal behavior? *Through classical conditioning inappropriate emotional and physiological responses can be developed,* such as Little Albert's fear, my nausea, and the men's sexual arousal. Little Albert's fear of the rat would certainly be considered abnormal. Indeed, if he had been brought to a clinic, he would probably have been diagnosed as suffering from a *phobia* (an irrational fear). My getting sick to my stomach every time I used Comet cleanser would be considered strange if not abnormal, and sexual responses to shoes or geometric forms are certainly not normal.

Generalization of Responses

Importantly, once a response is linked to a particular stimulus through classical conditioning, *the conditioned response can also be elicited by other stimuli that are similar to the conditioned stimulus.* For example, although Little Albert was conditioned to be afraid of a white rat, he also became fearful when he was shown a rabbit, a dog, and even a ball of cotton (all furry objects). Similarly, men who were conditioned to have erections when shown a black boot also had erections when shown a pair of gold sandals. This process is called **generalization.** The degree to which generalization occurs is a function of the *similarity between the conditioned stimulus and the new stimulus;* that is, the greater the similarity between a conditioned stimulus (e.g., a white rat) and a new stimulus (e.g., a ball of cotton), the more likely it is that the new stimulus will elicit the condi-

tioned response. Stimuli that are very dissimilar will not elicit the conditioned response. For example, Little Albert did not show an increase in his fear response to a set of wooden blocks.

Generalization greatly increases the number of stimuli that can elicit a particular conditioned response, which can sometimes make it difficult to understand someone's responses. For example, if you did not understand the concept of generalization, you would not be able to explain Little Albert's fear of cotton. The generalization of a conditioned response is illustrated in Figure 2.6.

Vicarious Classical Conditioning

It is clear that in many cases classical conditioning can be used to explain the development of emotional responses, such as the fears that underlie phobias. But what about cases in which a particular stimulus elicits a fear with which it was never actually paired? For example, it is unlikely that an individual who has a fear of flying or a fear of elevators was ever in an airplane or an elevator that crashed. To explain those cases learning theorists point out that individuals can develop classically conditioned fear responses simply by *seeing or hearing about another individual who expressed fear in response to the conditioned stimulus.* For instance, another child who only watched while Little Albert was conditioned to be afraid of the white rat could also develop the fear response. This type of classical conditioning of a response is called **vicarious** (vi-KER-e-us) **conditioning.**

The development of fears through vicarious conditioning was demonstrated in an interesting series of experiments with monkeys (Cook et al., 1985; Mineka et al., 1984). In these experiments *observer monkeys* that were not afraid of snakes were first put into a cage with a real snake, a toy snake, or a black cord. As expected, they showed no fear. The observer monkeys were then moved to another

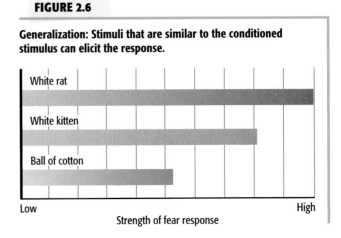

FIGURE 2.6

Generalization: Stimuli that are similar to the conditioned stimulus can elicit the response.

	Low	High
White rat		
White kitten		
Ball of cotton		

Strength of fear response

FIGURE 2.7

Monkeys showed fear of a snake and related objects after seeing another monkey show fear of a snake.

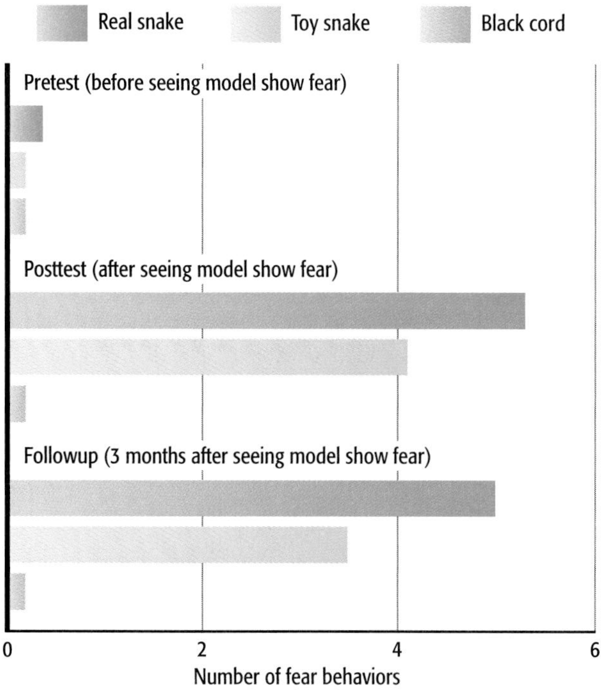

Real snake   Toy snake   Black cord

Pretest (before seeing model show fear)

Posttest (after seeing model show fear)

Followup (3 months after seeing model show fear)

Number of fear behaviors

Source: Adapted from Cook et al. (1985), Figure 8, p. 603.

cage from which they could watch a *model monkey* interact with the snake and the other objects. The model monkey was afraid of snakes, and as the observer monkeys watched, the model screeched in fear and ran from the snake. Following that the observer monkeys were again put in the cage with the real snake, the toy snake, or the black cord, and this time they reacted with fear. Indeed, not only were they afraid of the real snake, but because of generalization (recall the earlier discussion) they also showed fear of the toy snake. The conditioned fear persisted and was almost as strong 3 months later when the monkeys were tested again. These results are presented in Figure 2.7. Vicarious conditioning can easily result in inappropriate fears. For example, a child who simply sees a parent's fear response to a harmless spider can develop a fear of spiders. It could even be that hearing stories, such as the one about Miss Muffett's response to the spider that sat down beside her, might lead to a vicariously conditioned fear of spiders.

Endurance of Responses

Once a classically conditioned response is established, *it can last indefinitely.* For example, my conditioned response to the scrubbing with Comet lasted for over 2 years before it popped up unexpectedly when I was again exposed to the

cleanser. A more dramatic demonstration of the endurance of classically conditioned responses is provided by an experiment on sheep. In this experiment a red light was paired with a shock to the hooves of the sheep so that they became classically conditioned to experience fear and lift their front hooves whenever they saw a red light (J. Bescherat, personal communication, 1963). When the conditioning was completed, the sheep were turned out to pasture for 9 years. However, when they were brought back into the laboratory and the red light was turned on, they immediately lifted their front hooves. That is, after 9 years away from the laboratory, the sheep still showed the conditioned response.

The fact that classically conditioned responses can last for a very long time is important because in some cases individuals may forget the experiences that led to their conditioning and therefore not understand why they are giving a particular response. Indeed, if individuals do not remember how a response was conditioned, they may come up with a different but erroneous explanation for that response. That was the case with my nausea response to the Comet cleanser; at first I didn't remember the conditioning and so attributed my nausea to bad food.

Extinction and Spontaneous Recovery

If classical conditioning can lead to abnormal emotional responses and if the responses can last for a long time, the next question is, can anything be done to eliminate the responses? Fortunately, yes: If the conditioned stimulus (e.g., the bell) is presented repeatedly *without being paired with the unconditioned stimulus* (e.g., the meat powder), eventually the conditioned response will cease to be elicited. For example, when Pavlov's dogs repeatedly heard the bell but were not given any meat, they eventually stopped salivating in response to the bell. Similarly, I've now scrubbed many pans with Comet cleanser, but I haven't scrubbed any more nauseating monkey cages, so I no longer respond with nausea to the cleanser. This process of eliminating classically conditioned responses is called **extinction.**

Sometimes, after extinction seems to have eliminated the conditioned response, the response will recur. For

---

generalization   The process by which a conditioned response comes to be elicited by stimuli that are similar to the conditioned stimulus.

vicarious conditioning   Development of a classically conditioned response (emotion) by an individual who has simply seen or heard another individual being conditioned.

extinction   Elimination of a classically conditioned response by repeated presentation of the conditioned stimulus without the unconditioned stimulus.

instance, following the extinction trials Pavlov's dogs stopped salivating to the sound of the bell. Then, after a period of time went by, the bell was rung again and the dogs salivated, though to a lesser degree than they did before extinction. The return of a classically conditioned response after extinction occurs is called **spontaneous recovery.** The recovered response will be weaker than the original response, and over time it can be extinguished. The cycle of extinction, spontaneous recovery, and extinction may have to be repeated a number of times until the response is completely eliminated. Spontaneous recovery can be discouraging to an individual who is trying to extinguish an inappropriate fear (a phobia) because the fear will keep coming back, though in a progressively weaker form. In other words, spontaneous recovery can result in "relapses."

Involuntary Nature of Responses

One final and important point is that *classically conditioned responses do not appear to be under voluntary control.* That is, once the conditioning has been completed, the conditioned response occurs whenever the stimulus is presented, regardless of whether or not the animal or person wants to give it. For instance, Pavlov's dogs had no choice but to salivate when they heard the bell, Little Albert had no choice but to be fearful when he saw the rat, and I could not inhibit my feelings of nausea when I smelled the cleanser. The involuntary nature of classically conditioned responses leads to feelings of being out of control, and this can add to the problem. For example, if later in life Albert was given a ball of cotton, he would have no choice but to become very fearful, regardless of how irrational he realized it was and how hard he tried not to be afraid; it is understandable how such an experience could cause him to question his sanity. Overall, then, classical conditioning can lead to serious, prolonged, confusing, and uncontrollable abnormal emotional and physiological responses.

---

spontaneous recovery   Return of a classically conditioned response after it has apparently been extinguished.

operant conditioning   The process by which rewards are used to increase the use of a response or punishments are used to decrease the use of a response.

B. F. Skinner   Psychologist who refined the principles of operant conditioning by working with rats and pigeons.

vicarious conditioning   Development of an operantly conditioned response (behavior) by an individual who has only seen or heard about another individual using the response; also known as observational learning or modeling.

extinction   Elimination of an operantly conditioned response by withholding the reward following the response.

Operant Conditioning

Up to this point I have discussed the development of inappropriate *emotional* responses such as fear, but what about the development of inappropriate behaviors? For example, how can learning be used to account for the fact that some people are inappropriately aggressive or withdrawn or have temper tantrums? For that we must turn to **operant conditioning,** which is the process by which *rewards are used to increase the use of a response or punishments are used to decrease the use of a response* (Skinner, 1953).

The principles of operant conditioning were refined by **B. F. Skinner** (1904–1990) in his research with rats and pigeons. In the simplest of these experiments, rats were placed in a small cage called a *Skinner box,* which contained a lever. When the rats pushed the lever, food was dropped into a cup in the cage, and because the rats were hungry, they quickly learned the response of pushing the lever to get the food. In other experiments the rats were placed in a Skinner box that had a grid on the floor through which painful electrical shocks could be administered to the rats, but by pushing the lever the rats could turn off the shocks. The rats in these experiments learned to reduce their pain by pushing the lever to stop the shocks. In all of these experiments the rats learned the lever-pushing response because it resulted either in a reward or in the elimination or avoidance of something negative. Learning theorists then used the Skinner box and the behavior of the rats as models of our world and our behaviors. That is, they argued that much of our daily behavior can be understood in terms of our attempts to gain rewards or to avoid punishments. For instance, you may be reading this book to obtain the reward of getting a good grade or to avoid the punishment associated with getting a bad grade.

Operant conditioning can readily be used to explain the development of abnormal behaviors; that is, *abnormal behaviors develop when they lead to rewards or avoid punishments.* For example, a child may have temper tantrums to gain attention, you may withdraw into a fantasy world because it is more pleasant than the real world, and an individual who is claustrophobic may stay out of small rooms to avoid the anxiety triggered by being in a confined space.

Unlike classical conditioning, operant conditioning is not due to the pairing of two stimuli; instead it is due to the fact that a *response leads to a reward or avoids a punishment.* However, I should also point out that behaviorists do not use the term *reward* because that term implies an internal process that cannot be observed, such as the reduction of a drive like hunger, and behaviorists believe that scientists should confine themselves to *observable* events. To avoid the problems posed by using the term *reward,* behaviorists use the term *reinforcement,* which describes *what happens* (the response is strengthened) but does not imply any particular underlying process. However, for the sake of convenience, in this discussion I will take a more liberal position and use the word *reward.*

Individual Differences in Rewards and Punishments

Sometimes it is difficult to understand what is rewarding a particular response because what is a reward for one person may not be a reward for another. For example, some individuals find the aches, pains, sweat, and exhaustion associated with strenuous exercise rewarding; others find it punishing. If those who find it punishing do not take the perspective of those who find it rewarding, they may find it difficult to understand why others exercise. In general, however, *rewards are things we work to get,* and *punishments are things we work to reduce or avoid.* Because individuals vary in what they find rewarding and punishing, it is crucial for us to analyze behavior in terms of *what the individual involved* considers rewarding or punishing, not what *we* think is rewarding or punishing.

Vicarious Operant Conditioning

In each of the examples I have used so far, the individual who learned the response received a reward for the response. However, it is also possible for individuals to learn responses simply by seeing another person use the response and get a reward. A famous example of this is the experiment in which some children watched an adult act aggressively toward a large, inflated plastic doll. Specifically, the adult picked the doll up and threw it or hit it with a hammer, behaviors the children apparently enjoyed. In contrast, in another condition of the experiment other children watched as the adult simply sat passively and did not show any aggression toward the doll. Later all of the children were mildly frustrated (they were not allowed to play with a toy they wanted), and then they were allowed to interact with the doll. What happened was that the children who had observed the aggressive adult used more than twice as many aggressive responses as the children who had observed the passive adult. Furthermore, the types of aggressive responses used by the children were very similar to the types of aggressive responses used by the adult (Bandura & Walters, 1963). In other words, if the children saw the adult throw the doll, they threw the doll; if they saw the adult hit the doll, they hit the doll. It's also possible to learn a response simply by hearing about another person using the response. Indeed, the rate of suicide goes up dramatically after a nationally publicized suicide (see Chapter 9). This indirect form of operant conditioning is referred to as **vicarious** (vi-KER-e-us) **conditioning,** but it is also sometimes called *observational learning* or *modeling* (Bandura, 1969; Bandura & Walters, 1963). The fact that operant conditioning can take place vicariously greatly increases the possibilities for developing abnormal behaviors. (Note that

What is rewarding for one person may not be rewarding for another. While some individuals are rewarded by the sweat and exhaustion associated with strenuous exercise, others find it punishing.

earlier I discussed vicarious *classical* conditioning, which leads to *emotions.* The vicarious *operant* conditioning discussed here leads to *behaviors.*)

Extinction

Just as rewards will strengthen a response, so *the absence of rewards following a response will cause the individual to stop using the response;* this process is called **extinction.** The extinction of *appropriate* responses can lead to abnormal behaviors; for example, if you are consistently ignored (not rewarded) when you make appropriate interpersonal responses, such as greeting and talking with other people, you might give up those behaviors and withdraw into a world of fantasy that is more rewarding. On the other hand, extinction can also be used to eliminate *inappropriate* behaviors such as temper tantrums (see the later discussion of behavior therapy).

Schedules of Reward

We now come to an important question: How frequently should people be rewarded for behavior that is to be strengthened and maintained? Should they be rewarded each time they use the response or only sometimes? There are two answers to this question: First, when developing a new response it is important that individuals receive a

Children (bottom rows) used aggressive responses similar to those they saw an adult model (top row) use.

reward *each time they use the response*. This is necessary to strengthen the response and also because during the early phases of conditioning rewards provide feedback and guidance about what behavior is wanted. Second, once a response is learned, if we want to reduce the likelihood that it will be extinguished, the response should be rewarded *some of the time but not every time it is used;* that is, the response should be rewarded on a **variable schedule.** For example, an individual on a variable schedule of reward might be rewarded after three responses, then after ten, and then after five. A variable schedule reduces the likelihood of extinction because with a variable schedule individuals never know when they will be rewarded. Thus, if for some reason they don't always get a reward after using a response, rather than beginning extinction they assume that they will get rewarded sometime in the future, and they continue responding. Gambling provides an excellent example of the effects of a variable schedule of reward: People who play slot machines never know when the machines will pay off, so they continue putting money in them even though many times they get no reward. They keep playing because they think, "Maybe next time. . . ." Contrast this with what you

do if you put money in a Coke machine and nothing happens. Because the machine always paid off in the past, when it doesn't pay off, you assume something is wrong and you don't put in more money (your response to that machine is extinguished).

Variable schedules of reward are great for protecting appropriate behaviors from extinction, but they pose two problems when it comes to inappropriate (abnormal) behaviors: First, an individual on a variable schedule often makes responses that are not rewarded, and therefore it can sometimes be difficult to determine what is maintaining the responses. Second, and more important, because variable schedules increase resistance to extinction, they make it difficult to use extinction to eliminate inappropriate responses. For example, children who occasionally get what they want when they have a temper tantrum are on variable schedules, so it can be very difficult to extinguish the tantrums (see the later discussion of behavior therapy). Indeed, a parent who only sometimes gives in to a child's temper tantrums will actually be strengthening the response by putting the child on a variable schedule of reward.

Voluntary Nature of Responses

Unlike classically conditioned responses, *operantly conditioned responses are under voluntary control;* that is, Skinner's rats could decide whether or not to press the lever to

variable schedule (of reward)   A procedure in which not every operantly conditioned response is rewarded; this reduces extinction.

The intermittent schedule of reward used in slot machines keeps people responding, even though they are seldom rewarded.

get the food, you can choose whether or not you are going to read this book in preparation for the examination, a child can voluntarily stop having temper tantrums, and a gambler can decide to stop putting quarters in the slot machine. Although operant responses are voluntary, at some point the motivation to perform a response may be so high that the individual has very little choice except to use the response. For instance, a student who is terrified of small places may have little option but to flee in uncontrollable fear when the instructor closes the door of a small classroom. With this information as background, let's go on to consider how the principles of learning are used in treatment.

 ## Treatment: Behavior Therapy

If abnormal behavior is learned, then it follows that treatment simply involves *unlearning* the abnormal behavior. To emphasize the fact that the learning approach focuses on *changing behavior* rather than on changing underlying factors (as favored by Freud and his colleagues), advocates of the learning approach refer to their treatment as **behavior therapy** rather than psychotherapy. In general, the unlearning of abnormal behaviors is accomplished through *extinction,* but different extinction procedures must be used depending on whether the behavior is the result of classical or operant conditioning (Agras & Berkowitz, 1999). We'll consider the extinction of classically conditioned emotional responses first.

Extinction of Classically Conditioned Emotional Responses

As I explained earlier, the extinction of classically conditioned responses involves breaking the link between the conditioned stimulus and the conditioned response by repeatedly presenting the conditioned stimulus by itself—that is, without the unconditioned response such as salivation or fear. For example, in the case of Little Albert, extinction of his fear of the white rat would involve repeatedly showing him the white rat without pairing it with the frightening noise. Similarly, in the case of an individual with a phobia for heights, the individual might be taken to the top of a tall building without letting anything bad happen. This procedure is generally referred to as **exposure** because the individual is simply *exposed* to the conditioned stimulus. It is also sometimes referred to as **flooding** because being exposed to the conditioned stimulus may initially flood the individual with anxiety (Emmelkamp, 1994). We'll examine this approach to treatment in greater detail in Chapter 5, when we consider the treatment of phobias.

Extinction of Operantly Conditioned Behavioral Responses

The extinction of operantly conditioned responses simply involves *not rewarding the unwanted response.* When the response no longer leads to rewards, the individual stops using the response. This can be illustrated with the research on the treatment of temper tantrums (Derby et al., 1998; Williams, 1959). In that research the number of tantrums children had during a baseline period was counted, and then the mothers of the children were instructed to consistently ignore the children whenever they had a tantrum. In other words, after the baseline period the children were not given attention or anything else they wanted that might reward a tantrum. The effects of such treatment are illustrated in the case of a little boy who used tantrums (crying) to avoid being put to bed. As you can see in Figure 2.8 (on p. 52), at first he cried for 45 minutes, but the next night, when he realized that he was not going to get attention or be allowed to stay up longer, he didn't cry at all. On the third through the sixth nights, he usually cried less than 5 minutes, and after that he simply gave up crying and went

behavior therapy The approach to changing behavior that is based on learning.

exposure A strategy used for extinguishing fear responses, in which the individual is exposed to the feared stimulus but nothing bad is allowed to happen.

flooding Another term for exposure, arising from the fact that with exposure the individual can be flooded with anxiety.

FIGURE 2.8

Extinction was effective for reducing tantrums (crying) at bedtime.

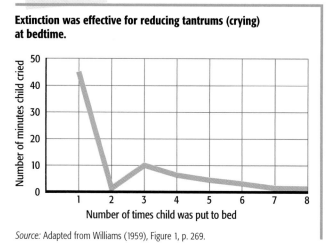

Source: Adapted from Williams (1959), Figure 1, p. 269.

to bed. With this approach it's important that individuals *never* be rewarded for the unwanted behavior because occasional rewards will result in a *variable schedule of reward,* which makes responses very difficult to extinguish (see the earlier discussion of schedules of reward).

At the outset of this discussion I said that treatment was based on extinction, but in some cases it may also be necessary to *teach the individual a new response to replace the inappropriate response being extinguished.* For example, a child whose temper tantrums were being extinguished might need to be taught to ask appropriately for things he or she wants. In other words, in addition to teaching an individual not to use one response, it may be helpful to teach him or her another response to use. The learning approach to explaining and treating abnormal behavior is summarized in Figure 2.9.

FIGURE 2.9

The learning approach: Conditioning leads to abnormal emotional responses and behaviors; behavior therapy focuses on extinction and learning new responses.

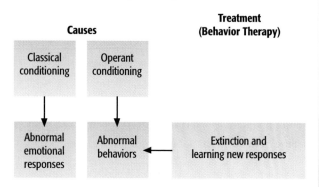

Note: Behavior therapy focuses on symptoms rather than underlying causes.

Questions about the Learning Approach

1. *Can learning account for complex abnormal behaviors?* It's clear that conditioning can be used to explain simple behaviors such as fears (phobias), but can learning also be used to account for highly complex abnormal behaviors such as hallucinations (i.e., hearing voices when no one is really there)? Probably not, but that is not sufficient justification for rejecting the learning explanation completely. Different disorders can have different causes, and it may be that learning can only be used to account for relatively simple disorders such as phobias.

2. *Is conditioning an automatic process, or does it involve thinking?* For many years it was generally assumed that conditioning was an *automatic* process that did not involve thinking. The implication was that insofar as our behaviors are conditioned, we are not much more than robots who are controlled by external factors such as rewards and punishments. Are you an externally controlled robot, or is your behavior determined by what you *think* and *want* to do? Are abnormal behaviors automatic? Some psychologists have challenged the notion that conditioning is an automatic process and have suggested that it actually involves thinking. That notion, if correct, provides a very different slant on the nature of conditioned behaviors. So let's consider the possible role of thinking first in classical conditioning and then in operant conditioning.

The traditional view of classical conditioning is that when a neutral stimulus, such as a white rat, is consistently paired with a response, such as fear caused by a loud noise, *the neutral stimulus and the response become somehow connected in the brain.* Thus, when the neutral stimulus is presented, the response is *elicited automatically;* that is, seeing the white rat leads to an automatic fear response. However, it may be that what really happens in classical conditioning is that the individual realizes that a certain stimulus, such as a white rat, *predicts the occurrence of an event,* such as a loud noise, and so when the stimulus occurs, the individual *prepares for the event,* such as by becoming fearful (Davey, 1987, 1992; Rescorla, 1988). In other words, when Little Albert responded with fear to the white rat, it was because he had figured out that the appearance of the rat signaled that a loud and frightening noise would follow. In the case of Pavlov's dogs, they salivated when they heard the bell because they expected that food was coming. In general, this is referred to as the **expectancy theory of classical conditioning.**

This explanation makes intuitive sense, but what's the evidence? To test the expectancy explanation, an experiment was conducted that involved the conditioning of fear in rats; the procedures and the results of that investigation are summarized in Table 2.2 (Kamin, 1969). In the first

TABLE 2.2

TABLE 2.2

Procedures and results of an experiment indicating that classical conditioning is due to expectations rather than to the simple pairing of a stimulus with a response

	Phase one	Phase two	Phase three (test)
Group one	Tone $\rightarrow$ Shock	Tone + Light $\rightarrow$ Shock	Tone $\rightarrow$ Fear Light $\rightarrow$ No fear
Group two		Tone + Light $\rightarrow$ Shock	Tone $\rightarrow$ Fear Light $\rightarrow$ Fear

Note: In this experiment the measure of fear was the reduction of a bar-pressing response that led to the presentation of food.

Source: Kamin (1969).

phase of the experiment the rats in Group One participated in a conditioning procedure in which a *tone* was paired with a shock so that the rats developed a fear response to the tone. In contrast, the rats in Group Two did not participate in any conditioning procedure during the first phase. In the second phase of the experiment the rats in both groups participated in a conditioning procedure in which *the tone and a light together* were paired with the shock so that the rats showed a fear response to that *combination* of stimuli. Finally, in the third (test) phase of the experiment the rats in both groups were presented with the tone and the light *separately.* The question was, which stimulus would elicit the conditioned response—the tone, the light, or both? If conditioning is due simply to the *pairing of stimuli with responses,* the rats in *both* groups would respond with fear to *both* the tone and the light because *both* stimuli had been paired with the response in the second phase. On the other hand, if conditioning is due to the development of *expectancies,* the rats in Group One would respond with fear only to the tone because in the first phase they had learned that the tone led to the shock; therefore, the later pairing of the light and tone together with the shock was irrelevant. That is, the rats already knew that the tone signaled the coming of the shock, so the information about the light was irrelevant.The results supported the notion that conditioning is due to expectations; that is, the rats in Group One that were first conditioned to respond to the *tone alone* showed conditioned fear responses *to the tone but not to the light,* whereas the rats in Group Two that were first conditioned to respond to *the tone and the light together* showed conditioned fear responses to *both the tone and the light.* In summary, then, it was not simply the pairing of a stimulus with a response that led to conditioning; rather it was the *information* provided by the pairing that led to conditioning. Similar results have been found with humans (Jones et al., 1990, 1992).

Overall, it appears that classical conditioning is due to expectations rather than simple automatic connections in the brain, but there's still one problem: If classically conditioned responses are due to expectations, why aren't they under voluntary control? One answer appears to be that in most cases individuals appear to give a response "automatically" because they are convinced that the stimulus will lead to a particular event; for example, individuals with phobias for dogs will "automatically" become fearful when they see a dog because they are sure the dog will bite them. This explanation changes our view of classical conditioning, and we will examine it in greater detail later when we consider anxiety disorders (see Chapters 5 and 6).

Now let's consider the role of thinking in operant conditioning. It was traditionally believed that when a reward followed the use of a particular response, the use of the response was automatically strengthened (reinforced) by the reward. However, it now appears that operant conditioning can be thought of as an instance of *problem solving and cooperation.* That is, it seems that conditioning occurs when an individual *figures out that a response leads to a reward* (i.e., solves the problem) and then *decides to give the response to get the reward* (i.e., cooperates).

Let me illustrate this with some early research on *verbal conditioning,* a process in which rewards are used to change an individual's verbal behavior. Specifically, in experiments on verbal conditioning, an individual is given a stack of 60 cards; printed on each card is one verb (e.g., *ran*) and six pronouns (*I, he, she, we, they, it*). The individual's task with each card is to make up a sentence using the verb and any one of the pronouns (e.g., "I ran to class" or "They ran over the hill"). While the individual makes up the first twenty sentences, the experimenter sits passively and says nothing. This provides a baseline measure of pronoun use. After that, every time an individual in the experimental condition uses a specific pronoun selected at random by the experimenter, such as *I,* the experimenter responds by saying, "good" or "hmm hmm." In other words, the individual is rewarded for using a specific pronoun. In contrast, indi-

expectancy theory of classical conditioning The notion that in the process of classical conditioning individuals come to realize that a stimulus predicts the occurrence of an event.

FIGURE 2.10

Students increased their use of a specific pronoun when they were rewarded for using it.

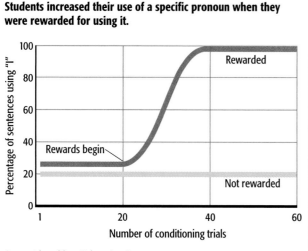

Source: Adapted from Holmes (1967).

viduals in the control condition are never rewarded, no matter what pronouns they use. The results of these experiments indicate that after individuals began receiving rewards for using a specific pronoun, they usually showed an increase in the use of that pronoun. The results of one experiment are summarized in Figure 2.10.

The finding that individuals use rewarded pronouns more than nonrewarded pronouns clearly illustrates operant conditioning, but is the conditioning an automatic process or is the individual thinking? The answer came from an investigation in which I asked students who had just participated in a verbal conditioning experiment whether they were aware that the experimenter had said "good" after they used a particular pronoun (Holmes, 1967). What I learned was that *only those students who were aware of the fact that the experimenter said "good" after they used a particular pronoun showed the conditioning effect.* In other words, conditioning was not an automatic process; instead it only occurred if the students solved the problem of what they had to do to get rewards. If they did not solve that problem, they did not show any conditioning (their use of pronouns did not change).

However, not all of the students who solved the problem of how to get rewards showed an increase in the use of the rewarded pronoun. That fact led me to ask the students what they did after they became aware that the use of a particular pronoun led to a reward. The answers were clear: Some students decided to cooperate and give the responses that led to the rewards, whereas others decided they would not cooperate (a reaction later dubbed the "screw you effect"). These results are summarized in Figure 2.11. Overall, then, verbal conditioning is not an automatic process in which the learner is passive; instead it is a result of active

problem solving ("What do I have to do to get the reward?") and a conscious decision concerning cooperation ("I will go along with what this experimenter wants me to do to get the reward"). Findings like these clearly indicate that operant conditioning involves thinking.

Why is it important that conditioning may be due to thoughts rather than to automatic connections in the brain? The importance lies in the fact that it changes our view of ourselves: We are not simply robots who respond automatically to conditioned stimuli, rewards, and punishments. Instead, we are thinking organisms that understand, plan, and decide what to do. The finding that we think rather than simply respond has implications for treatment, and we will consider that next.

3. *Why is extinction effective for reducing phobias?* At first the answer seems obvious: Extinction works because it breaks the link between a conditioned stimulus and a conditioned response. However, I just pointed out that classical conditioning can involve thinking (expectations about what will happen) rather than just simple connections. Thus, it may be that extinction actually works because it changes people's expectations about what will happen after the conditioned stimulus occurs. For example, after extinction Little Albert may have caught on to the fact that the appearance of the white rat would not be followed by a frightening noise. This suggests that treatment should be focused on changing expectations. Does this also mean that the learning approach to explaining and treating abnormal behavior is useless and wrong? No, it suggests that conditioning procedures may simply be one of the ways that people get information (i.e., the pairing of stimuli leads them to realize that the presence of a particular stimulus predicts

FIGURE 2.11

Students showed conditioning only if they were aware of the reward and decided to cooperate.

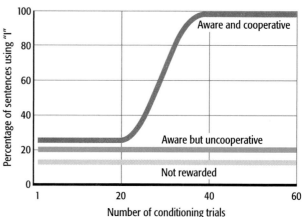

Source: Adapted from Holmes (1967).

that something will happen) and that extinction procedures can be used to change beliefs (e.g., if people who are afraid of dogs are around dogs and don't get bitten, they may realize that dogs are not dangerous). In the next chapter we will expand on this when we consider the cognitive approach to explaining and treating abnormal behavior.

Summary

Overview of Stress

▶ Stressors require adjustments that overtax us, thereby leading to stress, and the stress then leads to abnormal behaviors.

▶ Stress has psychological (emotional) and physiological (bodily change) components. There is a question as to whether psychological responses lead to physiological responses or physiological responses lead to psychological responses; both explanations appear to be correct.

▶ The steps leading from a stressor to abnormal behavior are (1) awareness and appraisal of the stressor, (2) attempts to cope with the stressor, (3) the onset of stress, (4) the use of defense mechanisms, and (5) the emergence of abnormal behavior that results from the defensive behaviors or the failure of the defense.

Topic I: The Psychodynamic Approach

▶ The psychodynamic explanation was developed by Freud, and its major tenet is that abnormal behavior is the result of conflicts between what we want to do to satisfy our needs and the restraints that are imposed on us by society. Furthermore, Freud suggested that such conflicts were originally encountered in childhood and that how we resolve them influences the rest of our lives.

▶ Freud suggested that individuals go through five stages of psychosexual development (oral, anal, phallic, latency, and genital) and that the conflicts encountered in these stages influence later development. Two notable problems are the Oedipus complex for males and the Electra complex for females.

▶ In his structural approach to personality, Freud described the personality as having three components: (1) the id, which is the source of biological needs; (2) the superego, which embodies the moral arm of society; and (3) the ego, which mediates between the id and the superego.

▶ Freud also proposed that there are three levels of consciousness: (1) the conscious mind contains what we are aware of at any one time, (2) the preconscious contains material we can recall when necessary, and (3) the unconscious contains material that is anxiety-provoking and cannot be recalled.

▶ To defend against anxiety individuals may use defense mechanisms, which are psychological maneuvers by which we distort reality in ways that will help us avoid stress and reduce anxiety. Examples are repression, suppression, denial, projection, displacement, regression, identification, rationalization, compensation, and intellectualization. Defense mechanisms can reduce anxiety, but they do so at a cost: If they are effective, the individual does not take constructive action to solve the problem, and they distort reality.

▶ Neo-Freudians accepted many of Freud's ideas but argued that stress and anxiety stemmed from personal and interpersonal problems rather than conflicts over biological needs such as sex. Notable among the neo-Freudians are Adler, Horney, and Jung.

▶ For advocates of the psychodynamic explanation, the treatment of choice is psychotherapy. The goal of psychotherapy is to eliminate conflicts and stress, or at least to help the client learn how to cope with them, but there are wide differences in the nature of psychotherapy.

▶ Concerns about the psychodynamic approach revolve around the facts that there is very little evidence for many of Freud's most important concepts, that Freud was not truthful in reporting his case studies, that early experiences may not be as important as Freud suggested, and that no one understands exactly why psychotherapy works.

Topic II: The Learning Approach

▶ The basic tenet of the learning explanation is that abnormal behavior is learned through classical conditioning and operant conditioning.

▶ Classical conditioning was first identified by Pavlov, and it involves the pairing of a stimulus that elicits a particular response (e.g., a noise that elicits fear) with a neutral stimulus that does not elicit the response. After the pairing, the neutral stimulus will elicit the response. Classical conditioning provides the basis for emotional and physiological responses; for example, Watson and Rayner conditioned a fear (phobia) for white rats in Little Albert by pairing a frightening noise with a white rat. Classical conditioning can also play a role in positive emotions such as sexual arousal.

▶ Stimuli that are similar to the conditioned stimulus can also elicit the conditioned response, a process called generalization.

▶ Classically conditioned responses can be developed by hearing about or seeing others being conditioned, a process called vicarious conditioning.

▶ Classically conditioned responses can last a long time, but they can be extinguished if the conditioned stimulus is presented consistently without being paired with the unconditioned stimulus. However, the response may later recur in a weaker form, which is called spontaneous recovery.

▶ Classically conditioned responses do not appear to be under voluntary control.

▶ Operant conditioning is the process by which rewards (reinforcements) are used to increase the use of a response and punishments are used to decrease the use of a response. For example, children may learn to have tantrums to get what they want. The principles of operant conditioning were refined by Skinner.

▶ What is a reward for one individual may not be a reward for another individual. Operant conditioning can take place vicariously, a process that is sometimes called observational learning, or modeling.

▶ If an operantly conditioned response is no longer followed by a reward, the response will be extinguished. Variable schedules of reward make responses more resistant to extinction.

▶ Operantly conditioned responses are under voluntary control.

▶ Treatment based on learning is focused on extinguishing abnormal behaviors and learning appropriate behaviors. This type of treatment is referred to as behavior therapy.

▶ Critics question whether conditioning can be used to explain complex symptoms such as hallucinations and delusions; it probably can't. Some theorists also question whether conditioning is an automatic process or involves thinking. It appears that classical conditioning may be due to expectations and that operant conditioning is due to problem solving and cooperation.

Questions for Making Connections

1. Alicia has a phobia for snakes, even snakes she knows are harmless, and simply cannot control her fear. Furthermore, she does not understand why she has this fear because she does not remember ever being hurt by a snake. How would psychodynamic theorists such as Freud explain and treat Alicia's phobia? In contrast, how would learning theorists explain and treat it?

2. You probably have a "conscience" that leads you to behave in ways that are approved within your culture. How does Freud explain the development of your conscience and what is his term for it? In contrast, how would learning theorists explain the development of a conscience?

3. Freud suggested that there are three levels of consciousness. What are those levels? What role does repression supposedly play with respect to the unconscious? How do psychodynamic theorists use the unconscious to explain abnormal behaviors? What importance do behaviorists ascribe to the unconscious?

4. If an early experience leads to a current abnormal behavior, how would psychodynamic therapists go about changing the behavior? How would a therapist who subscribed to the learning approach go about changing the behavior?

5. You will probably be tested on the material in this chapter in the near future, and thinking about the test and its implications for your grade may make you anxious. What defense mechanisms might you use in an attempt to reduce that anxiety? Will they work? What might be their long-term consequences? Compare defending to coping.

6. Describe the famous case of Anna O. and her treatment. What impact did that case have on the development of Freud's theory, and what concerns does it raise today?

7. The psychodynamic and learning approaches lead to very different explanations and treatments for abnormal behavior. Based on what you know now, if you had to subscribe to one of those two approaches, which one would you elect and why?

Key Terms and People

In reviewing and testing yourself, you should be able to discuss each of the following:

Adler, Alfred, p. 36

anal stage, p. 32

Anna O., p. 30

behavior therapy, p. 51

behaviorism, p. 44

behaviorists, p. 44

Breuer, Josef, p. 30

catharsis, p. 30

classical conditioning, p. 44

3

Overview of Explanations and Treatments: Cognitive, Physiological, and Other Approaches

IN THE PRECEDING CHAPTER I explained the *psychodynamic* and *learning approaches* to abnormal behavior. Those explanations have much to offer, but they also have some limitations. So in this chapter we will consider two other approaches: the *cognitive approach* and the *physiological approach*. We will also briefly examine three offshoots of the major approaches: the *sociocultural, family systems*, and *humanistic approaches*. We will pick up our discussion in the 1970s when interest in the learning approach was beginning to wane.

TOPIC I
The Cognitive Approach

José has a phobia for dogs, and when he is asked why he is afraid of dogs, he says, "Simple. Dogs can bite you, and, in fact, some dogs have rabies–they're dangerous!" Nicki is very depressed and explains her mood by pointing out that no one likes her and she doesn't think things will get better. Do your thoughts influence your feelings and behaviors? Might psychiatric disorders be the result of incorrect beliefs, such as the generalization that all dogs are dangerous?

Have you ever noticed that one thought often leads you to another on the same topic, or that one thought involving a particular mood leads you to another involving the same mood? For example, one depressing thought may lead to another depressing thought. How does memory work? Can problems with memory contribute to abnormal behaviors?

Lisa thinks she is a failure, and she is very depressed. It appears that her negative beliefs about herself caused her depression. However, when Lisa takes an antidepressant drug her depression lifts and her views of herself become positive. From this it might be concluded that, rather than her thoughts causing her depression, her depression influences her thoughts. Do thoughts influence mood, or does mood influence thoughts?

The learning explanation for abnormal behavior was very popular because it was based on solid scientific evidence. However, in the 1970s some psychologists became dissatisfied with this approach because it portrays people as little more than laboratory rats or robots whose behaviors are controlled by external factors such as rewards and punishments. Furthermore, in the 1970s psychologists were discovering a lot about how thought processes work, so it was a natural step to link problems with thinking to abnormal behavior. The result was the **cognitive approach** to abnormal behavior, the major tenet of which is that *abnormal behaviors result from incorrect beliefs.* Advocates of this position argue, for example, that phobias for dogs occur because people have incorrect beliefs that all dogs are dangerous and that depressions occur because people incorrectly believe they are no good, the world is an awful place, and things won't get better.

The notion that incorrect beliefs cause abnormal behaviors makes intuitive sense, but *why* do people have those beliefs and *why* do they maintain them when faced with evidence to the contrary? For instance, why does an individual with a phobia for dogs continue to believe that dogs are dangerous despite the fact that most dogs are not dangerous? To answer these questions we must turn our attention to how we process and retrieve the memories we use to form our beliefs.

 ## Stages of Memory Processing

Memory plays a major role in determining your behavior. After all, your memories of past experiences provide you with the information you use to form your beliefs and guide your behavior. For instance, if you remember many failures from your past, you may conclude that you're incompetent, give up, and become depressed. Because memories play an important role in normal and abnormal behavior, I'll begin this discussion with an overview of how memory works.

The most widely accepted explanation of memory is the **three-stage theory of memory.** The stages are (1) the entry of information into the *sensory memory,* where important information is selected for attention; (2) the passage of that information into the *short-term memory,* where it is used in thinking and processed for storage; and (3) the storage of

---

cognitive approach   The view that abnormal behaviors are caused primarily by incorrect beliefs.

three-stage theory of memory   The theory that information goes through the sensory memory and the short-term memory before being stored in the long-term memory.

sensory memory   The first stage of memory, in which information is held briefly and then selected information is sent on to the short-term memory for greater attention.

short-term memory   The second stage of memory, in which thinking is done and information is processed for storage.

long-term memory   The third stage of memory, in which information that has been processed in the short-term memory is stored.

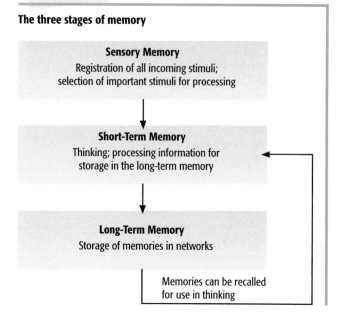

FIGURE 3.1

The three stages of memory

Sensory Memory
Registration of all incoming stimuli; selection of important stimuli for processing

Short-Term Memory
Thinking; processing information for storage in the long-term memory

Long-Term Memory
Storage of memories in networks

Memories can be recalled for use in thinking

---

memories in the *long-term memory.* These stages of memory processing are summarized in Figure 3.1 and discussed in the following sections.

Sensory Memory

Everything you see, hear, feel, and smell goes first to your **sensory memory.** It's like a videotape recording of everything that is happening. However, the sensory memory can only hold the information for a second or two at most; after that the memory fades and is lost. Consequently, you must quickly select from your sensory memory the information that is most important and send it on to your short-term memory for processing. The fact that you have to select information quickly is relevant for understanding behavior in two ways: First, in the selection process you may *focus too much attention on some things* and thereby get a distorted view of the world. For example, you might focus on airplane crashes and therefore develop an unrealistic view of how dangerous it is to fly, which could result in a phobia for flying. Second, you may *ignore things that are important.* For instance, if you ignore your achievements, you may develop an unrealistic view of yourself that can lead to depression.

Short-Term Memory

The information that is selected from your sensory memory is next sent to your **short-term memory,** which is where you *think* and *process information for storage* in the long-term memory. When you process information for storage, you *establish links between the new information and* *other pieces of information that are already in storage.* By establishing those links you *develop networks of related memories.* Making those links and building the networks is crucial because later, when you want to recall something, recalling anything in the relevant network will eventually lead you to the memory for which you are searching. Furthermore, recalling one memory in a network can lead you to "automatically" recall other memories in the same network. For example, if you recall your elementary school classroom, memories of your classmates will probably jump to mind. (I'll discuss this in greater detail when I discuss how memories are retrieved.)

Long-Term Memory

Your **long-term memory** is where you store all of the information that was processed in your short-term memory. You are not conscious of the information stored in your long-term memory; if the information is needed, however, it can be activated and brought back to your short-term memory for use. There is a constant interplay between the short- and long-term memories in that information is continually being brought up from the long-term memory, used for thinking, and then sent back to the long-term memory. Let's now consider how you recall memories.

How Memories Are Recalled

How do you retrieve memories from that huge file we call the long-term memory? There are three things you need to know to answer that question: First, *each memory is made up of a cluster of components, such as images, feelings, and physiological responses, and the activation of any one of the components will lead to the activation of the overall memory.* For example, your memory of a particular individual could involve his or her name, likeness, the scent of his aftershave or her perfume, and your emotional response to the individual. However, the activation of any one of those components will result in the memory of the individual; that is, the individual's name will bring the individual to mind, but so will his or her scent. Indeed, years ago when a woman was going to be separated from a man for a long time, she would give him her handkerchief on which she had put some of her perfume, so that her scent would keep his memory of her alive while they were separated.

Second, *the activation of one memory in a network can activate other memories in that network* (Bower, 1981; Collins & Loftus, 1975; Estes, 1991; Ingram, 1984). Have you ever noticed that when you revisit a place from your childhood, you are suddenly flooded with old memories? In this case the physical stimuli of the setting triggers the network that contains the memories, and the memories come back. Importantly, there are networks made up of

memories that all share a common *mood;* when you are in a particular mood, it will activate the related network and you will recall memories involving that mood (Rusting, 1998). The effect of mood on recall was cleverly demonstrated in an experiment in which students who were in a neutral mood learned a group of *pleasant* and *unpleasant* personality-related words: *considerate, helpful, thoughtful, pleasant, kind, friendly, rude, cruel, hostile, ungrateful, impolite, mean* (Clark & Teasdale, 1985). The students then were made to feel happy or depressed and finally were asked to recall the words. The results indicated that students who were made to feel happy recalled more pleasant words and students who were made to feel depressed recalled more unpleasant words. In another experiment conducted with anxious and nonanxious individuals, it was found that after learning lists of words that were *neutral* (e.g., *bookcase, stereo*), *positive* (e.g., *brilliant, triumph*) and *threat-related* (e.g., *assault, tornado*), the anxious individuals were more likely to recall threat-related words than other words, whereas the nonanxious individuals did not differ in their recall of different types of words (McCabe, 1999). With regard to abnormal behavior, the activation of one depressing memory or one anxiety-provoking memory could lead to the activation of an entire network of depressing or anxiety-related memories, and recalling all of those could lead to depression or anxiety.

Third, *memories or networks used recently or frequently can be activated more easily and become stronger than those used less recently or frequently.* In other words, the use of a memory or network *primes* it for future use. Of course, priming becomes circular; a primed network is more likely to be used, and using it primes it for use again. For example, once you think a depressing thought, you are likely to continue to think about that and other depressing memories. This is apparently why depressed individuals tend to recall what's bad in their lives and rarely remember the good. Furthermore, if you are not actively thinking about something else, a primed network will be activated automatically. This accounts for why you tend to drift back to a particular topic unless you are focusing your attention elsewhere. A friend of mine who tends to be depressed uses a computer analogy to describe his depressing thoughts as his "default option." In other words, whenever he is not thinking about something else, he begins thinking depressing thoughts. To avoid that default option he tries to distract himself with television, radio, or reading.

A diagram of a simplified set of memory networks is presented in Figure 3.2 (on p. 62). The overall network is made up of three networks: one involving negative memories (in blue), one involving memories of people (in green), and one involving positive memories (in pink). There are strong associations or connections within networks (solid lines) and weaker associations or connections among networks (broken lines). An individual with this set of networks who experienced a failure or thought about one would go on to recall other failures, rejections, missed opportunities, and possibly the death of a loved one. If activation of the negative network is prolonged, the individual might become depressed. In contrast, when this individual experienced a success or thought about a successful experience, he or she would go on to recall praise from others, good relationships, and possibly a pleasant vacation. The individual might become more positive and upbeat if the positive network is activated frequently.

 ## Problems with Memory

In most cases our memories work well, but in some instances problems arise that distort what we recall. Such distortions can lead us to see the world incorrectly, so let's consider some of the problems.

Selective Attention and Selective Recall

One important problem revolves around the fact that we are more likely to select some memories for recall than others. Specifically, only a fraction of the information that enters the sensory memory gets moved to the short-term memory, and only a limited amount of information that comes to the short-term memory is processed for storage in the long-term memory. Because of this **selective attention,** we simply do not store all of the information to which we are exposed. Furthermore, **selective recall** of stored information occurs because some networks are more likely to be activated than others. Importantly, the selectivity in what we attend to, store, and recall is not random; instead, it is guided by *the information we think is important and the information we have used in the past.*

How is all this related to abnormal behavior? Selective attention and recall are relevant for understanding abnormal behavior because *focusing on particular types of experiences can lead to the development of incorrect beliefs, and those beliefs can lead to abnormal behaviors.* For example, if you believe that you are socially inadequate, you will notice and recall every minor social slight and blunder, which could cause you to become withdrawn and isolated. Furthermore, if you believe that others are rejecting you, you may begin avoiding other people or start behaving toward them in a hostile manner—even if that belief is incorrect. These actions can bring on the rejection you had incorrectly perceived earlier. This sequence of events is an example of a phenomenon called a **self-fulfilling prophecy.**

The next question is, when and why do we start selectively attending to and recalling specific types of information? These processes usually begin as the result of some important event, often one that occurs early in life (Beck & Emery, 1985; Chorpita & Barlow, 1998; Randolph & Dykman, 1998). Consider this possibility: A woman who as a

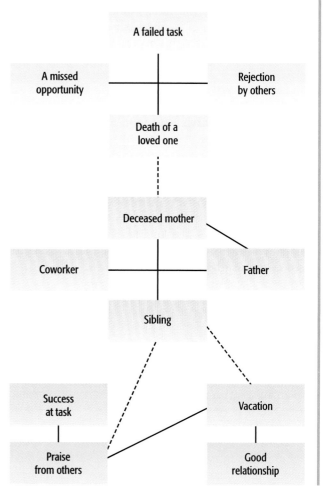

FIGURE 3.2

A hypothetical set of three connected memory networks
This overall network is made up of three networks: one involving negative memories (blue), one involving memories of people (green), and one involving positive memories (pink). Strong associations are indicated with solid lines, and weaker associations are indicated with broken lines.

child was very ill now focuses her attention on minor physical sensations that might be new symptoms. Because of her excessive attention to these sensations (symptoms?), she often incorrectly believes that she is ill, a disorder called *somatization* (see Chapter 7). In other cases early experiences with failure predispose individuals to focus on and recall failures, leading to low self-esteem and depression.

Distortions of Memories

So far we have assumed that our memories are accurate and that problems arise only because we focus on some memories more than others. However, this is not a complete picture because memories can be *distorted,* and, of course, dis-

Selective attention and recall can cause erroneous thoughts that may, in turn, lead to inappropriate or abnormal behavior. If you incorrectly think that others are rejecting you, you may, in fact, bring on that rejection by avoiding people or by behaving in a hostile way.

torted memories can lead to incorrect beliefs and inappropriate behaviors. The ease with which memories can be distorted was clearly demonstrated in an experiment in which college students were shown a movie of a traffic accident. One group was later asked to recall how fast the cars were going when they *contacted* each other, whereas another group was asked to recall how fast the cars were going when they *smashed*. The students with whom the word *smashed* was used estimated the speed to be 28% faster than the students with whom the word *contacted* was used (Loftus & Palmer, 1974). Clearly, memories can be distorted rather easily, and distorted memories can distort our behavior.

False Memories

There is also evidence that **false memories** can be "implanted" and, once implanted, be very resistant to correction. Specifically, if someone suggests to you that you had a particular experience, and if you do not have strong evidence to the contrary, you may accept the suggested experience as real. This was demonstrated in an experiment in which reports of parents were used to identify college students who as children had *never stayed overnight in a hospital* (Hyman, Husband, & Billings, 1995). These students then participated in an interview in which they were asked to recall the details of a number of childhood experiences. Most of these experiences were events that had really happened to the students (parents' reports were used to identify the true events), but one was a *false* event about staying overnight in a hospital. If a student did not recall a particular experience, the experimenter went on to the next experience. At the end of the interview the students were encouraged to think more about the events and try to

remember more details before the next interview, which occurred a few days later. In the second interview the students were again asked to recall the events. The results indicated that although none of the students "recalled" the false event in the first interview, 20% of them did so in the second interview! In fact, not only did they "remember" the event, they elaborated on it and provided a variety of details concerning it. Furthermore, when the students were told at the end of the second interview that one of the events they had been asked to describe was false and were asked to indicate which one it was, most of the students who had "recalled" the false event were unable to say which one it was. A variety of other experiments have yielded similar findings, clearly indicating that false memories can be easily induced (e.g., Ceci, Huffman, & Smith, 1995; Hyman et al., 1995; Loftus, 1992; Loftus & Coan, 1995).

A more dramatic example of an implanted memory occurred in the case of a man who, after prolonged questioning, pleaded guilty to sexually molesting his daughters (Ofshe & Watters, 1994). To test the possibility that the confession was due to a suggestion made during the interrogation process, an experiment was conducted in which the man was told a *totally false* story that two of his other children had now accused him of forcing them to have sex while he watched. When he denied it, he was told to think about it and was returned to his jail cell. The next day the man reported "remembering" the event, and he added vivid details of what had happened. (It is noteworthy that the man had nothing to gain by his admission; indeed, because of it he could have faced an additional prison sentence.) Faced with the overwhelming (but false) evidence of his children's testimony and without any proof to the contrary, he accepted the accusations as true and then embellished the suggestion.

Relatedly, there is now a considerable body of evidence that some "confessions" given by alleged criminals in the course of interrogation are completely false (Bedau & Radelet, 1987; Kassin & Kiechel, 1996; Kassin & Wrightsman, 1993; Wrightsman, Nietzel, & Fortune, 1998). For example, in one case an 18-year-old man named Peter Reilly who was suspected of killing his mother was given a polygraph (lie detector) test and was interrogated for a 25-

selective attention   The process that causes only a limited amount of the incoming sensory information to be processed in memory.

selective recall   The process that makes us more likely to recall information that is in activated memory networks.

self-fulfilling prophecy   A result that occurs largely because the individual expects it (e.g., failure because of the expectancy of failure).

false memories   Implanted memories that are not real but that the individual believes to be accurate.

Paul R. Ingram (left) confessed to molesting his daughters after he "recalled" false memories suggested by his interrogators. Here he is shown at his sentencing in Tacoma, Washington.

hour period. Reilly initially denied that he had committed the crime, but confusion and self-doubt were introduced during the long interrogation, especially when he was told that the results of the polygraph test proved that he was guilty. Eventually he said, "Well, it really looks like I did it," and he confessed. However, after Reilly had spent two years in prison, it was discovered that he had been in another state at the time of the murder and could not possibly have done it. What happened in this case is that law enforcement officials lied to the suspect about the evidence they had and, in so doing, implanted the memory that he had committed the crime. Needless to say, false memories can lead to highly distorted views of the world and to inappropriate behaviors. Furthermore, false memories can lead to incorrect explanations for current behaviors.

To sum up, the cognitive explanation suggests that (1) our early experiences lead to the initial development of

cognitive therapy A treatment method designed to change the incorrect beliefs that lead to abnormal behaviors.

cognitive restructuring The process of rebuilding a client's beliefs that occurs in cognitive therapy.

memory networks; (2) those networks lead to selective attention and selective recall; (3) memories can be distorted, and false memories can be implanted; (4) selective attention, selective recall, distorted memories, and false memories can lead to incorrect beliefs; and (5) incorrect beliefs can lead to abnormal behaviors. It should also be noted that *the cognitive explanation does not rely on unconscious beliefs or conflicts* and thus avoids many of the problems associated with the psychodynamic explanation. Individuals may not be aware of how their memory works and may not know why they recall what they recall, but according to the cognitive approach, it is what individuals *consciously think and believe* that guides their normal and abnormal behaviors. Because of that, individuals can tell us why they behave as they do. A classic example of how incorrect beliefs can lead to a disorder is presented in Case Study 3.1.

Finally, in most cases cognitive theories have focused on negative results. For example, selective attention to stressful things in the environment can lead to anxiety, and selective attention to depressing experiences can lead to depression. However, the flip side of this has also been proposed; that is, *selective attention to positive things can lead to illusions of well-being and good mental health* (Colvin & Block, 1994; Taylor & Brown, 1988, 1994). By focusing on positive things, individuals see their positive traits as special and their poor abilities as normal and dismiss their problems as inconsequential. This can make the individuals feel good about themselves and enable them to get on with life. The notion that cognitive distortions of reality can lead to good mental health is a dramatic departure from the usual idea that good mental health involves being "in contact with reality." However, it is an interesting possibility that deserves attention.

 ## Treatment: Cognitive Therapy

If it is true that incorrect beliefs cause abnormal behaviors, then it follows that *treatment should involve correcting the incorrect beliefs,* and, indeed, a method called **cognitive therapy** was developed for changing incorrect beliefs (Beck & Emery, 1985; Wright & Beck, 1996). Cognitive therapy involves a process often called **cognitive restructuring,** which is the rebuilding of a client's beliefs. This is how it is done: First, to determine what beliefs are causing the symptoms, clients are asked to keep records of the thoughts they have when they are experiencing their symptoms. A depressed client may discover that she thinks she's no good or the world is a terrible place, whereas a client with a dog phobia may find that he thinks dogs are dangerous. Second, clients are asked to consider their beliefs as *hypotheses* rather than facts, and they are asked to *test* their hypothe-

Incorrect Beliefs and the Development of an Anxiety Attack

WHILE SKIING HIGH in the Rocky Mountains, a 40-year-old man began to perspire heavily. In addition, he felt short of breath, weak, cold, unstable, and as though he were going to faint. He became extremely anxious, fearing that he was having a heart attack and that he was going to die. Because he was on the verge of collapse, he was taken from the slopes on a stretcher and rushed to a hospital. A thorough examination did not reveal any physical abnormalities, so it was concluded that he had suffered a panic attack—an acute *anxiety attack.*

This man had skied many times before, and on those occasions the altitude, exertion, and weather conditions had caused him to experience the same physical symptoms of shortness of breath, chest pains, fatigue, sweating, and cold. The question then is, why did the symptoms lead to a panic attack on this occasion?

To answer that question, cognitive theorists suggested that the man misinterpreted his normal physiological responses to exercise and altitude as the symptoms of a heart attack because several weeks earlier his brother, who was only a few years older, had died of a heart attack. That is, the cognitive theorists suggested that the man's thinking went something like this: "If my brother could die of a heart attack after exercising, so could I. These symptoms must mean that I am having a heart attack; *I'm about to die!*"

In other words, because of the recent death of his brother, the man had an active memory network associated with that death. That network resulted in selective attention to the physical symptoms of altitude and fatigue because the symptoms were like those of a heart attack. The active network also caused the symptoms to be misinterpreted as signs of a heart attack; thus the man erroneously expected to have a heart attack, and this perception gave rise to his anxiety.

Source: Adapted from Beck & Emery (1985).

CASE STUDY 3.1

> ... it was concluded that he had suffered a panic attack— an acute *anxiety attack.*

---

ses. For example, a person with a phobia for dogs might be asked to spend some time with friendly dogs to see if they really are dangerous, whereas a depressed person who believes that he or she is disliked by others might be asked to go to a party and observe how others respond. The goal is for the client to discover that the beliefs that led to the problems are incorrect. Once this occurs, the client can replace the incorrect beliefs with correct ones and thereby eliminate the symptoms. Because *behaviors,* such as spending time with dogs or going to parties, are often used to change beliefs, this approach is sometimes called *cognitive-behavioral therapy.*

There is a good deal of evidence to support the effectiveness of cognitive therapy. For instance, in one experiment depressed individuals who received cognitive therapy to help them develop more accurate beliefs about themselves and the world showed greater reductions in depression than did individuals in a control condition who received a placebo pill that they thought was an antidepressant drug (Jarrett et al., 1999). Furthermore, the cognitive therapy was as effective as an antidepressant drug for reducing depression. These results are summarized in Figure 3.3.

In a variation on cognitive therapy some therapists force clients to develop more accurate beliefs by actively cross-examining them and challenging their beliefs. For example,

FIGURE 3.3

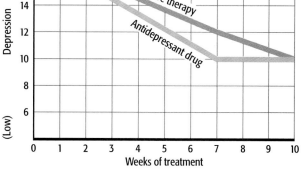

Cognitive therapy was more effective than a placebo pill for reducing depression.

Note: Scores are Hamilton Ratings of Depression. The antidepressant drug used was Nardil (phenelzine).

Source: Jarrett et al. (1999); adapted from Table 2 and Figure 1, p. 435.

FIGURE 3.4

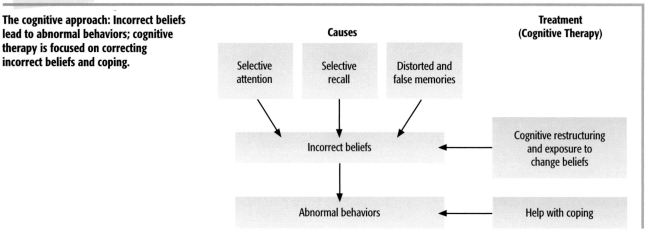

FIGURE 3.4

The cognitive approach: Incorrect beliefs lead to abnormal behaviors; cognitive therapy is focused on correcting incorrect beliefs and coping.

when working with an individual who has a phobia for high places, the therapist might ask, "How many tall buildings have ever fallen over?" "Have you ever heard of anyone accidentally falling out of a tall building?" or "Isn't it really safer to be up in a tall building than on the ground trying to cross a busy street?" Such questions force clients to reexamine their beliefs, recognize the errors in their logic, and develop more accurate beliefs. This approach is called **rational-emotive therapy,** a term derived from the fact that therapists try to compel clients to be more *rational* about the beliefs that lead to the clients' emotions (Ellis, 1962; Ellis & Grieger, 1977, 1986).

The cognitive approach is very popular today because it portrays people as thinking human beings rather than robots who are controlled by rewards and punishments, because its basic notions are supported by solid evidence from modern research in cognitive psychology, and because it has been shown to be effective for a variety of disorders. The cognitive approach for explaining and treating abnormal behaviors is summarized in Figure 3.4.

THINKING CRITICALLY

Questions about the Cognitive Approach

1. *Are incorrect beliefs causes or effects of abnormal behaviors?* The cognitive explanation is based on the assumption that incorrect beliefs cause abnormal behaviors, but it is possible that *the reverse may be the case;* that is, *abnormal behaviors may lead to incorrect beliefs.* Consider this possibility: A chemical imbalance in the brain causes an individual to become depressed, and because the individual is unaware of the imbalance, he or she looks for an explanation in the environment and incorrectly concludes that the

depression stems from the fact that the world is a terrible place that is not going to get any better. In this case the depression led to the incorrect beliefs. It is also possible that a depressed mood will trigger memories of depressing experiences; the individual then incorrectly concludes that recalling the negative experiences caused the depression. In other words, rather than memories triggering mood, mood may trigger memories. Evidence supporting this possibility comes from an experiment in which depressed individuals who had negative memories and beliefs were given an antidepressant drug that eliminated their depression; when the depression was eliminated, so were the negative memories and beliefs (e.g., Simons et al., 1984). Does that mean that the cognitive explanation is wrong? No, it simply means that beliefs may not *always* be causes. It is therefore important to ask, *when* are beliefs causes and *when* are they effects?

2. *Can incorrect beliefs explain all abnormal behaviors?* Cognitive theorists often argue that their approach can account for all of the major abnormal behaviors, but that is not the case. For example, later we'll consider *generalized anxiety disorder,* in which individuals constantly feel anxious but do not know why they are anxious; that is, the anxiety seems to "come out of the blue." It is difficult for cognitive theorists to account for this disorder because the cognitive explanation assumes that incorrect beliefs lead to abnormal behavior, but one of the major characteristics of generalized anxiety disorder is that the individual *does not have an explanation for the anxiety.* Does this mean that the cognitive explanation is wrong? No, it simply means that, like other explanations, it may not account for all disorders.

Overall, then, the cognitive explanation adds to our understanding of abnormal behavior; like the other explanations, however, it does not provide *the* explanation for *all* disorders.

TOPIC II
The Physiological Approach

All day Ben felt tense and "wired," but he didn't know why. It felt like he had had too much caffeine, even though he hadn't had any. Was there something brewing in his unconscious that was bothering him, or was his brain overactive for some reason?

Rochelle goes though occasional periods of depression. During those periods her sleep pattern is thrown off, she eats more, and she isn't particularly interested in sex. Why is she depressed, and why are her sleep, appetite, and sexual drive influenced?

Kevin suffers from schizophrenia. If he does not take his medication, he has hallucinations and his thought processes are disrupted. The medication clears up the symptoms, but it also sometimes causes his muscles to jerk uncontrollably. Why does a drug that influences hallucinations and thought processes also influence muscle activity?

Many people take antidepressants such as Prozac, Zoloft, and Paxil. Why do those drugs work?

The notion that abnormal behaviors are due to physiological problems was introduced more than 2,000 years ago by the Greek physician Hippocrates, who suggested that abnormal behaviors were caused by imbalances of the *humors* (fluids) in the body (see Chapter 1). However, for many years the role of physiological factors remained largely unexplored because scientists lacked the necessary techniques for studying problems in the brain. That began to change in the early 1960s as a consequence of two developments: First, scientists discovered drugs that reduced some of the symptoms of abnormal behaviors and, by determining what the drugs did in the brain, were able to identify some of the causes of those behaviors. Second, the development of sophisticated techniques for studying the brain enabled investigators to see actual images of brain structures and processes that are associated with abnormal behaviors (Grisom et al., 1999). This combination of new drugs and new methods for imaging the brain led to a flood of important findings and to the **physiological approach** to abnormal behavior. The basic tenets of this approach are that abnormal behavior is due to *chemical imbalances that cause problems in how the brain's neurons communicate with each other* and to *problems with brain structures.*

The Brain

We begin this section with a brief discussion of brain physiology and then go on to consider how problems in the brain can lead to abnormal behaviors.

Levels of the Brain

The first thing to note about the brain is that it contains *three major levels, each of which controls different behaviors.* Let's start at the bottom and work our way up. At the bottom of the brain is the **brain stem.** The brain stem is responsible for *controlling basic physiological functions,* such as breathing and heart rate. It also plays a role in *generating arousal* (electrical activity), which serves to keep us awake and alert. The arousal that is generated in the brain stem is carried to the higher levels of the brain by a set of nerve tracts called the **reticular** (ri-TIC-yu-ler) **formation.** (*Recticular* means "network.")In essence, the brain stem can be thought of as a power generating plant, and the reticular formation can be thought of as the network of lines that carry the power to where it is needed. The brain stem, the other levels of the brain, and the reticular formation are illustrated in Figure 3.5 (on p. 68).

The middle level of the brain is called the **midbrain.** The structures in the midbrain have three major responsibilities: First, they *maintain homeostasis;* that is, they preserve an equilibrium by controlling things such as the length of time we sleep, the amount of food we eat, and our level of sexual activity. Second, structures in the midbrain are responsible for *processing memories for storage;* problems in the midbrain can therefore lead to disorders such as Alzheimer's disease, in which the individual cannot save new experiences in memory. Third, structures in the midbrain play a role in *controlling emotions;* so problems in the midbrain can also lead to depression, mania, and anger. It's interesting to note that one structure in the midbrain—the *hypothalamus*—controls *both* homeostasis and emotions, which explains why a person who is depressed because of a problem in the hypothalamus may also have problems with sleeping, eating, and sex.

rational-emotive therapy   A form of cognitive therapy in which therapists try to force clients to develop more accurate beliefs by cross-examining the clients and challenging their beliefs.

physiological approach   The notion that abnormal behavior is due to chemical imbalances that cause problems with synaptic transmission and to brain damage.

brain stem   The lowest level of the brain, which is primarily responsible for controlling basic physiological functions and generating arousal.

reticular formation   A set of nerve tracts that carry arousal (electrical activity) from the brain stem to higher levels of the brain.

midbrain   The middle level of the brain, which is responsible for maintaining homeostasis, processing memories for storage, and controlling emotions.

FIGURE 3.5

Levels of the brain and their functions

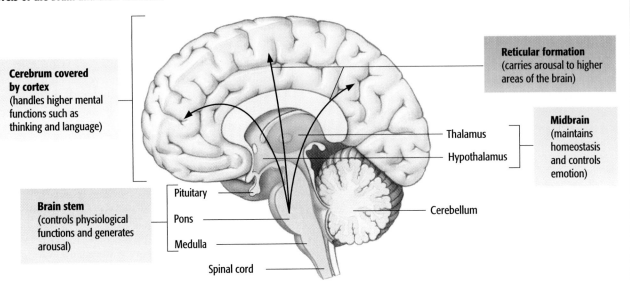

Cerebrum covered by cortex
(handles higher mental functions such as thinking and language)

Reticular formation
(carries arousal to higher areas of the brain)

Midbrain
(maintains homeostasis and controls emotion)

Thalamus

Hypothalamus

Brain stem
(controls physiological functions and generates arousal)

Pituitary

Pons

Medulla

Cerebellum

Spinal cord

The third level of the brain is the **cerebral cortex** (suh-REE-brel KOR-teks), which is a thin layer of cells called *neurons* that covers the outside of the brain. *The higher mental functions* such as thinking and language are located in the cortex, and so problems there can disrupt those functions. For example, individuals who have too much activity in the area of the cortex that is responsible for thinking can become very confused, a condition that can lead to the serious disorder known as *schizophrenia.*

Types of Problems in the Brain

In general, there are two types of problems in the brain that can lead to abnormal behavior. The first type revolves around *chemical imbalances* that influence how the neurons (cells) in the brain communicate with one another. Those imbalances usually cause the neurons to be overactive or underactive. For example, if the neurons in the hypothalamus are underactive, the individual may become depressed; whereas if they are overactive, the individual may become overly excited. The second type of problem affects the *structures* of the brain; that is, parts of the brain may be malformed or damaged. Of course, if structures in the brain are damaged, they will not function well and that can lead to abnormal behavior. For example, some depressed individuals have structural problems in their cortex, which can slow down their thought processes and may cause them to make poor judgments. Problems with brain functioning are responsible for many disorders. In the next section I'll explain how the brain functions, how the functions can be

disrupted, and how the disruptions can lead to abnormal behavior.

Neuroanatomy and Neuronal Functioning

Now that you have an overview of the major structures in the brain, we can consider the cells that make up the structures.

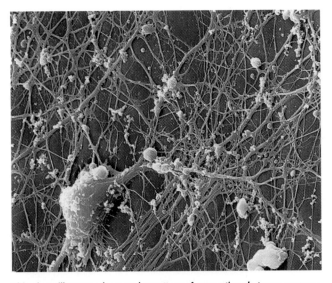

This photo illustrates the complex pattern of connections between neurons.

FIGURE 3.6

A neuron (nerve cell)

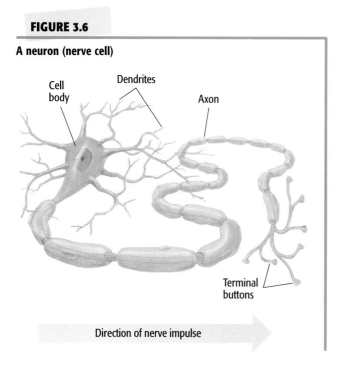

Direction of nerve impulse

The Neuron and the Nerve Impulse

The brain consists of between 10 and 12 billion cells called **neurons** (NOOR-ahns), and chains of neurons make up **nerve tracts.** Neurons differ greatly in size and shape depending on their function, but they all share a number of structural characteristics; see Figure 3.6. Specifically, each neuron has (1) a set of **dendrites** (DEN-drytz), which are branchlike structures that *receive stimulation from other neurons;* (2) a **cell body,** which can also *receive stimulation from other neurons;* and (3) an **axon** (AK-sahn), which is an armlike structure that *carries stimulation to other neurons.* The important thing about neurons is that they carry *electrical signals* called **nerve impulses** that are essential for the functioning of the brain. Indeed, the brain is largely an electrical system. A nerve impulse starts when one neuron stimulates the dendrite or cell body of another neuron; the impulse then travels from that dendrite or cell body down to the end of the axon, where it is transmitted to the next neuron in the nerve tract.

Neurotransmitters and Synaptic Transmission

When a nerve impulse reaches the end of an axon, it must "jump" the small gap that separates one neuron from another; jumping that gap is necessary if the impulse is going to stimulate the next neuron and continue down the chain. The gap between two neurons is called the **synapse** (SIN-aps). The neuron *from which* the impulse is jumping is called the **presynaptic** (pre-sin-AP-tik) **neuron,** and the neuron *to which* it is jumping is called the **postsynaptic**

(post-sin-AP-tik) **neuron.** To make the jump possible, the presynaptic neuron releases a chemical called a **neurotransmitter** that flows across the synapse and stimulates the postsynaptic neuron. The neurotransmitter stimulates the postsynaptic neuron by entering **receptor sites** on the dendrites or the cell body of the postsynaptic neuron. Figure 3.7 (on p. 70) illustrates a neurotransmitter being released, flowing across the synapse, fitting into a receptor site on the postsynaptic neuron, and causing it to fire. Note that the process by which the nerve impulse travels down the axon is *electrical,* whereas the process by which it crosses the synapse is *chemical.*

When a neuron is stimulated, it *either fires or does not fire.* If it does fire, it does so with a given amount of energy, regardless of the strength of the stimulation that triggered the firing. This is known as the **all-or-none principle** of neuron activity. Because neurons always fire with the same amount of energy, the intensity of overall neuron activity is a function of the *frequency* with which neurons fire or the *number* of neurons that fire. When there is not enough neurotransmitter at the synapses in an area of the brain, the neurons in that area will not fire or too few of them will fire, and that area of the brain will be underactive. In contrast, if there is too much neurotransmitter, there may be excessive neurological activity, caused by neurons firing too many times or by too many neurons firing. In either case

cerebral cortex   The highest level of the brain, which consists of a thin layer of neurons that covers the outside of the brain and carries out the higher mental functions.

neurons   Cells in the nervous system.

nerve tract   A chain of neurons.

dendrites   Branchlike structures on a neuron that receive stimulation from other neurons.

cell body   The body of a neuron, which can receive stimulation from other neurons.

axon   An armlike structure extending out from the body of a neuron, which carries stimulation to other neurons.

nerve impulse   The electrical signal carried by a neuron.

synapse   The small gap between two neurons.

presynaptic neuron   The neuron from which a nerve impulse is leaving.

postsynaptic neuron   The neuron to which a nerve impulse is going.

neurotransmitter   A chemical that is released by a presynaptic neuron and flows across the synapse and stimulates the postsynaptic neuron.

receptor sites   Openings on a neuron into which a neurotransmitter fits, thereby stimulating the neuron.

all-or-none principle   The fact that when a neuron is stimulated, it either fires or does not fire but always fires with the same amount of energy.

FIGURE 3.7

Neurotransmitters are released by the presynaptic neuron, cross the synapse, and stimulate the postsynaptic neuron.

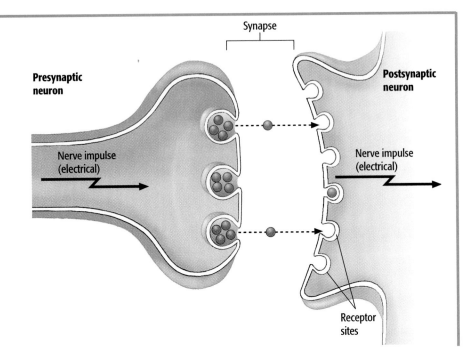

abnormal behavior may result. For example, low levels of neurotransmitters in the area of the brain that controls mood can result in depression, whereas high levels can result in mania.

There are many neurotransmitters, and because *any one neurotransmitter can operate in more than one area of the brain,* a particular neurotransmitter can influence more than one behavior. This explains why otherwise unrelated sets of symptoms sometimes occur together. For instance, the neurotransmitter that is responsible for some depression also plays a role in appetite, which is why depressed individuals often show changes in appetite. The fact that a particular neurotransmitter can act in more than one area of the brain also explains why some drugs have *side effects.* Consider the following example: Schizophrenia can be due to high levels of a neurotransmitter called *dopamine,* which operates in the area of the brain that is responsible for

thought processes. To alleviate the effects of high levels of dopamine, individuals with schizophrenia are given drugs to block the action of that neurotransmitter (they block the receptor sites so that dopamine cannot stimulate the neurons). However, dopamine also operates in the area of the brain that is responsible for motor behavior; therefore, some drugs used to treat schizophrenia can also influence motor behavior, leading to such side effects as difficulty in walking and twitching.

Factors That Influence Synaptic Transmission

Transmission of nerve impulses across the synapses often plays an important role in abnormal behavior, so we must give some attention to the factors that influence synaptic transmission.

Levels of Neurotransmitters

The level of a neurotransmitter at a synapse is crucial because if it is too low, the next neuron will not receive enough stimulation to fire, and if it is too high, the neuron will be overstimulated. Three processes influence the level of the neurotransmitter at the synapse:

1. *Production.* The presynaptic neuron may produce too much or too little of the neurotransmitter.

---

catabolism   The process of chemically breaking down neurotransmitters at the synapse.

reuptake   The process by which a neurotransmitter is reabsorbed by the presynaptic neuron.

blocking agents   Chemical that fit into receptor sites on neurons and thereby block the entry of neurotransmitters.

inhibitory neuron   A neuron that makes a connection with either a presynaptic or a postsynaptic neuron, whose firing inhibits the transmission of nerve impulses by that neuron.

FIGURE 3.8

Synaptic transmission is reduced by low production of neurotransmitters, reuptake, catabolism, and blocking of receptor sites.

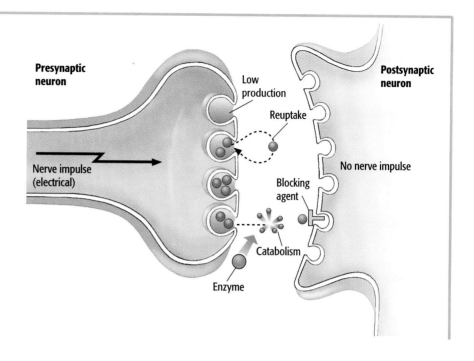

2. *Catabolism.* Substances that are present in the synapse may break down the neurotransmitter molecules, and too much or too little of a neurotransmitter may be destroyed. This process of chemically breaking down neurotransmitters at the synapse is called **catabolism** (ka-TAB-o-liz-em).

3. *Reuptake.* The presynaptic neuron may reabsorb (or "take up") the neurotransmitter before it can stimulate the next neuron. In other words, the presynaptic neuron can be thought of as a sponge that reabsorbs liquid that was originally squeezed out of it. This process is called **reuptake** (re-UP-tayk). Excessive reuptake reduces the level of the neurotransmitter below the level needed for synaptic transmission to occur.

A malfunction of any one of these processes can alter the level of a neurotransmitter, which can affect synaptic transmission and result in abnormal behavior. These processes are illustrated in Figure 3.8.

Blocking Agents

A neurotransmitter stimulates a postsynaptic neuron by fitting into receptor sites on the neuron, much as a key fits into and opens a lock. Other chemicals that are structurally similar to a particular neurotransmitter can also fit into the receptor sites, but these chemicals do not cause the neuron to fire because they do not fit the receptor sites perfectly. These chemicals are called **blocking agents** because their

presence *blocks the neurotransmitter from getting into the receptor sites,* thus preventing stimulation of the postsynaptic neuron. It's like putting the wrong key in a lock: the key does not open the lock, and it prevents you from inserting the right key. Some drugs used to treat psychological disorders are blocking agents. For example, the drugs used to treat schizophrenia block the neurotransmitter dopamine from entering neurons' receptor sites, thus reducing the excessive levels of synaptic transmission and decreasing the disruption of thought processes. The blocking of receptor sites is illustrated in Figure 3.8.

Inhibitory Neurons

Another factor that affects synaptic transmission is the activity of inhibitory neurons. An **inhibitory neuron** is a neuron that makes a connection with either a presynaptic or a postsynaptic neuron; see Figure 3.9 (on p. 72). *When the inhibitory neuron fires, it inhibits the transmission of the nerve impulse between the pre- and postsynaptic neurons.* Specifically, when the inhibitory neuron releases its neurotransmitter and stimulates the *presynaptic* neuron, the presynaptic neuron releases less of its neurotransmitter, thereby reducing the likelihood that the postsynaptic neuron will be stimulated and fire. In contrast, when the inhibitory neuron stimulates the *postsynaptic* neuron, the sensitivity of the postsynaptic neuron is decreased, thus making it less likely to fire if it is stimulated by the presynaptic neuron.

FIGURE 3.9

When an inhibitory neuron fires, it can inhibit the activity of the presynaptic or postsynaptic neuron with which it makes a connection.

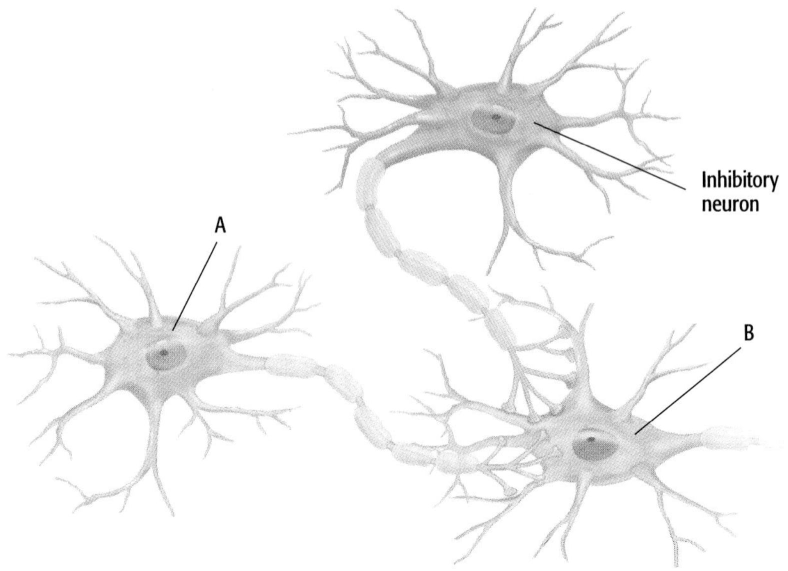

Inhibitory
neuron

A

B

Inhibitory neurons play important roles in a number of disorders. For example, some forms of anxiety occur because inhibitory neurons in the areas of the brain that are responsible for emotional arousal are not active enough, which leads to excessive synaptic transmission and to what we experience as anxiety. Have you ever been tense and uptight but unable to put your finger on the problem? It might have been that your inhibitory neurons were not active enough.

Neuron Sensitivity

A fourth factor influencing synaptic transmission is the level of sensitivity of the postsynaptic neuron; more sensitive neurons are more likely to fire when stimulated than those that are less sensitive. One explanation for depression is that the neurons associated with pleasure have become less sensitive and so less likely to fire, making the individual less likely to experience pleasure.

Number of Receptor Sites

Finally, the level of synaptic transmission can be influenced by the number of receptor sites on the postsynaptic neuron. Specifically, if the postsynaptic neuron has many receptor sites, it is more likely that a neurotransmitter will find its way into one of them and thus more likely that the neuron will be stimulated than if the neuron had fewer receptor sites. With regard to abnormal behavior, some individuals with schizophrenia have an excessively high number of receptor sites, leading to high levels of synaptic transmis-

sion, high levels of neurological activity, and a disruption of thought processes.

Hormones

Hormones are *substances that are secreted by glands directly into the bloodstream* and, once there, serve to *stimulate* activity. Indeed, the word *hormone* is derived from a Greek verb meaning "to stir up." Depending on which hormones are involved, abnormal levels of hormones can stir up different types of behaviors, such as behaviors involving aggression (see Chapter 12). It is important to note that our behaviors can be influenced by our current levels of hormones and also by the levels of hormones to which we were exposed during our prenatal development. For instance, high levels of cross-sex hormones during the prenatal period can alter brain structures and in extreme cases cause an individual of one sex to feel and behave like a member of the opposite sex, a condition known as *gender identity disorder* (see Chapter 16).

Genetics and Biological Traumas

It's clear that problems in the brain can cause abnormal behaviors, but the next question is, what causes the problems in the brain? There are two answers to that question, the first of which is genetics (Knowles, Kaufmann, & Rieder,

1999). **Genetics** is the set of biological factors (genes) that determine each individual's inherited characteristics. It has been known for years that genes play an important role in determining physical characteristics such as height and physical disorders such as heart disease, but it is now also known that genes play important roles in personality and abnormal behavior. In fact, it is now widely agreed that about 50% of the differences in personality among normal individuals are due to genetics and that many forms of abnormal behavior have a genetic basis (Carey & Di Lalla, 1994; Kendler, Neale, et al., 1993a, 1993b, 1993c; Lander & Schork, 1994; Nigg & Goldsmith, 1994; Reiss, Plomin, & Hetherington, 1991; Rieder, Kaufmann, & Knowles, 1994). However, the fact that there is a genetic basis for traits and disorders does not mean that you inherit a specific trait or disorder; what you may inherit is a high or low level of a particular neurotransmitter or a structural problem in the brain, which can lead you to have a particular trait or disorder. For example, if you inherit a high level of the neurotransmitter dopamine, you may have high levels of neurological activity in areas of the brain where thinking occurs, and that can disrupt your thought processes and lead to symptoms of schizophrenia (e.g., confusion, hallucinations). Evidence for the role of genes in abnormal behavior comes from the finding that one of the best predictors of whether you will suffer from a particular disorder is whether you have *biological relatives* who suffer from that disorder, even if you've had little or no contact with those relatives.

Two qualifications should be noted with regard to the effects of genes: First, in many cases *genes interact with environmental factors to result in disorders.* Just as some individuals carry the genes for freckles but do not develop freckles until they go out in the sun, so do some individuals carry the genes for a particular disorder but do not develop it until they are exposed to stress, which then triggers the disorder. This is often referred to as the **diathesis-stress** (dy-ATH-thee-sis) **model** for explaining abnormal behavior. *Diathesis* means "predisposition," and the notion is that genes establish a predisposition for a disorder and then the disorder is triggered by stress.

Second, because most disorders arise from a *combination* of genes and because your genes come from both of your parents, you may get all, some, or none of the genes that are necessary to develop a particular disorder. That is, if you have biological relatives with a disorder, you may get the disorder, you may get a mild form of it or you may not get it at all. For example, the children of parents with schizophrenia may develop that disorder or they may develop mild problems with thought processes that are not serious enough to qualify for the diagnosis of schizophrenia. In other words, it all depends on which or how many of the genes you get.

Genes can lead to various psychiatric disorders, but not all disorders are due to genes. Some disorders are instead

We've known for years that genetics can influence physical characteristics such as height and weight, hair and eye color. But today we know that genetics can also play an important role in personality and abnormal behavior.

caused by **biological traumas,** which are *physical injuries or diseases.* Consider the following interesting finding: About 20 years after a major flu epidemic there will be an increase in the occurrence of schizophrenia (Bradbury & Miller, 1985; Torrey et al., 1997). Why? If a woman has a serious case of the flu while she is pregnant, the fever associated with flu can influence the development of the brain of her unborn child in ways that can lead to schizophrenia in the child 20 years later (Barr, Mednick, & Munk-Jorgensen, 1990; Chen et al., 1996; Kirkpatrick et al., 1998; Wright et al., 1995). Problems during birth, such as a prolonged delivery during which the infant is deprived of oxygen, can

hormones   Substances secreted by glands into the bloodstream, where they stimulate activity.

genetics   The set of biological factors (genes) that determine each individual's inherited characteristics.

diathesis-stress model   The notion that physiological factors such as genes can establish a predisposition to a disorder, which can then be triggered by stress.

biological traumas   Physical injuries or diseases, which often influence brain development or functioning.

also result in schizophrenia years later (Cantor et al., 1997; Dalman et al., 1999; Geddes & Lawrie, 1995).

Overall, then, the point is that genetic factors and biological traumas can cause physiological problems in the brain, which can lead to abnormal behaviors.

Treatment: Medication and Surgery

If abnormal behavior is caused by physiological problems in the brain, is there anything that can be done to overcome those problems? The answer to that question depends on whether the problem arises in synaptic transmission or brain structures.

If the problem is in synaptic transmission, *drugs can be used to normalize the transmission.* Consider this scenario: A man is depressed because his level of a neurotransmitter that is responsible for mood is too low. To overcome the problem he is given a drug that *blocks the reuptake* of the

Antidepressants such as Prozac block the reuptake of the neurotransmitter that is responsible for mood. Blocking the reuptake makes the neurotransmitter available at the synapse, which increases neurological activity and improves mood.

neurotransmitter (recall that reuptake is the process by which the presynaptic neuron reabsorbs the neurotransmitter). Blocking reuptake makes more of the neurotransmitter available at the synapse, which increases neurological activity and improves mood. In fact, this is what antidepressants such as Prozac, Zoloft, and Paxil do. Here's another example: A woman is suffering from schizophrenia because she has high levels of the neurotransmitter dopamine; those high levels cause an excessively high level of activity in her brain, which results in confusion and hallucinations. She is given a drug that blocks the receptor sites for dopamine so that the activity in her brain and her symptoms are reduced.

However, there are cases in which the levels of synaptic transmission are too high and cannot be reduced with medication. In some of those cases *surgery* may reduce the transmission. For example, some serious cases of obsessive-compulsive disorder can be treated by making small lesions (cuts) in a particular nerve tract (Hollander, Simeon, & Gorman, 1999; Jenike, 1998). The lesions apparently reduce the flow of nerve impulses through the tract and effectively lessen the symptoms. It is important to note, however, that surgical procedures are only appropriate for a *very limited set of disorders* and even then are used only in *extreme cases* in which other treatments have not been successful. Furthermore, you should not confuse modern surgical procedures with the *lobotomies* performed from the 1930s through the 1950s, in which large portions of the brain were removed or cut off from the rest of the brain (see Chapter 11). Today's procedures are much more specific and refined.

Unfortunately, it is more difficult, sometimes even impossible, to correct structural problems in the brain that lead to abnormal behavior. That is because the structural problems are often due to the *deterioration and death* of neurons. Once neurons in the central nervous system are damaged or die, nothing can be done for them; they are simply lost. However, although the structural problems cannot be "fixed," drugs can sometimes be used to increase the activity of undamaged portions of the structures, thereby allowing them to compensate for the damaged portions.

Because strong evidence for the physiological approach has been accumulating at a rapid rate, this explanation is gaining widespread acceptance. It is noteworthy that although for many years psychologists generally opposed the physiological explanation and the use of drugs for the treatment of abnormal behaviors, today the American Psychological Association is *lobbying to get psychologists the right to prescribe drugs.* Indeed, it is likely that within 5–10 years psychologists will win that right, reflecting a major change in the treatment of psychiatric disorders. The physiological approach to explaining and treating abnormal behavior is summarized in Figure 3.10.

FIGURE 3.10

The physiological approach: Chemical imbalances and structural problems lead to abnormal behaviors; treatment is focused on correcting the imbalances.

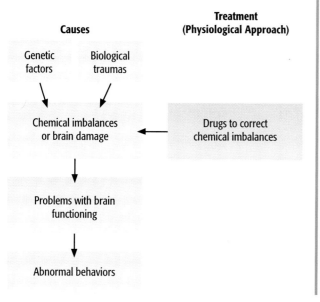

THINKING CRITICALLY

Questions about the Physiological Approach

1. *Are we controlled by our chemistry?* There is strong evidence for the physiological approach, but many people simply don't like the notion that their behaviors and emotions can be controlled by chemistry and modified with medication. That concern is clearly reflected in the comments made by a student of mine who had been depressed. When psychotherapy didn't help, she began taking an antidepressant drug. The drug was effective, but that bothered her. She wrote:

I know that when I'm not on my medication I'm depressed, unhappy, negative, and impossible to live with. I'm just a bitch, and no one likes to be around me. On the other hand, when I take my medication, I'm happy, upbeat, relaxed, and fun to be with. Then I like myself, and everyone else likes me. Obviously those little pills make a big difference in my personality, and I like the difference they make. The problem is that it bothers me that I'm not in control of myself. My depression seems to be "in the wiring" and not under my control. It's clear that those pills make a real difference in me, but it's frightening to realize that some chemical in my brain determines whether or not I'm a nice person. *Am I a person, or am I a biochemical reaction taking place in a*

test tube called a body? From my experience, it is clear that my personality is determined by chemicals in my brain, but *I'm very uncomfortable about that.*

Wondering whether one's personality is "a biochemical reaction taking place in a test tube called a body" may be an overreaction, but concerns about this issue are common. Three points should be noted: First, personality and abnormal behavior are not completely "locked in" by physiological factors. Indeed, it is now generally agreed that physiological factors account for about 50% of the differences in personality, which leaves 50% of the differences due to environmental/personal factors (Zuckerman, 1995). Second, although physiological factors may play a role in our behaviors, we can do a variety of things to change or compensate for those physiological factors. For example, exercise, diet, stress management, and medication can all have an influence. In other words, we are not helpless in the face of physiology. Third, regardless of whether we like it or not, physiology is a powerful force, and denying it is as foolish as ignoring gravity. The key is not to ignore it but to understand it and work with it.

2. *Do physiological factors work alone in causing disorders?* The answer to this question is sometimes yes, as when genetic factors cause serious problems with neurotransmitters or with structures in the brain. However, it is important to recognize that in other cases physiological factors may result only in a *predisposition* to a disorder; then the disorder may be triggered by a psychological factor. For instance, an individual might inherit a somewhat low level of the neurotransmitter linked to depression, and although the inherited level is not low enough to cause depression, psychological stress could lower it even more and thus push the individual into depression. In such a case the disorder is the result of the combination of physiological and psychological factors.

3. *Can physiology be used to explain all disorders?* No. Although many disorders once thought to be caused by psychological factors are now known to be due at least in part to physiological factors, physiology cannot be used to explain all disorders. For instance, many phobias (fears) appear to be learned.

4. *If a drug is effective for treating a disorder, does that mean the disorder is due to physiological factors?* Possibly, but not necessarily. A drug may correct a chemical imbalance in the brain that is indeed the cause of a disorder, but it is also possible for a drug to correct an imbalance that is being caused by a psychological factor. Recall that physiology is not always the cause of a disorder, but it is the final common step in the pathway to symptoms (see Chapter 2); thus a drug may simply correct the problem in that pathway rather than addressing the cause. For instance, psychological stress can change the level of a neurotransmitter, which results in depression; in such a case a drug can correct the

TABLE 3.1

Causes and treatments of abnormal behavior as suggested by the psychodynamic, learning, cognitive, and physiological approaches

Cause	Process	Treatment	Process
Psychodynamic approach			
Stress	Stress leads to symptoms. Defenses lead to symptoms.	Psychotherapy	Resolve conflicts Aid coping
Learning approach			
Classical conditioning (anxiety)	Inappropriate behaviors are conditioned.	Behavior modification	Extinguish unwanted responses
Operant conditioning (behaviors)	Inappropriate behaviors are conditioned.	Behavior modification	Extinguish unwanted behaviors Teach new behaviors
Cognitive approach			
Incorrect beliefs	Selective attention Selective recall Distorted memories False memories	Cognitive therapy	Develop accurate beliefs Aid coping
Physiological approach			
Problems with neurotransmitters	Genetics	Drugs	Adjust levels of neurotransmitters
Structural problems in the brain	Biological traumas		

level of the neurotransmitter without correcting its cause (the stress).

5. *Do drugs cure abnormal behaviors?* No. A drug can correct a problem with a neurotransmitter, but the problem will return if the drug is withdrawn. In other words, *drugs are treatments, not cures;* therefore, individuals may have to continue taking drugs for a long time. Some people are critical of the use of drugs to treat psychiatric problems because the drugs only provide treatment, but this fact is not unique to psychiatric disorders. For example, insulin is effective for treating but not curing diabetes, and many individuals with diabetes may have to take insulin for the rest of their lives, but no one suggests that these individuals should not take insulin because it is only a treatment.

6. *Do psychiatric drugs have bad side effects?* Some drugs can have serious side effects, and I'll describe those effects later, when I discuss various drug treatments. However, three general points should be noted here: First, many newer drugs have fewer side effects than earlier ones; today's drugs often act more like a bullet that knocks out the symptoms than like a shotgun blast that knocks out the whole person. Second, people differ in their responses to

various drugs, so if one drug is causing serious side effects, another drug should be tried. Third, and most important, although a drug may have side effects, those may be seen as a reasonable trade-off for the symptoms. Indeed, many people are more than happy to trade a miserable depression for a dry mouth (a side effect of some antidepressants).

Overall, the physiological approach is one of the oldest explanations for abnormal behavior, and it is rapidly expanding as new techniques for studying the brain become available. This does not necessarily mean, however, that the physiological explanation is replacing other explanations. Although that may occur with some disorders, the physiological approach often complements the other approaches and helps us understand why they are effective. Throughout this book, then, I will explain the new physiological findings and integrate them with psychological findings.

This concludes our discussion of the four major approaches to abnormal behavior. The major points of these approaches are summarized in Table 3.1, and you may want to review those points before we go on to briefly consider three offshoots of these approaches.

In some cultures, spirit possession is thought to be a cause of abnormal behavior. In this photo, a Candomble priestess in Brazil holds a woman possessed by a saint in order to control the spirit.

TOPIC III
Sociocultural, Family System, and Humanistic Approaches

Schizophrenia is a very serious disorder that involves symptoms such as hearing and seeing things that do not exist (hallucinations). One consistent finding about schizophrenia is that it occurs more frequently in the lower socioeconomic classes. Are the effects of class strong enough to cause symptoms such as hallucinations?

Some years ago a psychologist who was counseling college students concluded that the students' abnormal behaviors did not come from within them but rather were caused by a blocking of their growth toward personal development and fulfillment. That explanation is very different from the other notions we have considered, such as conditioning and physiology. Can the failure to achieve personal fulfillment lead to serious disorders?

Today the understanding of abnormal behavior is dominated by the psychodynamic, learning, cognitive, and physiological approaches. However, there are three other explanations that deserve mention here. They are the sociocultural, family system, and humanistic approaches. These explanations can be important but they can be subsumed under the other explanations we have already discussed. For example, cultural factors certainly influence the development of abnormal behaviors but do so because they influence the level of stress or the behaviors taught in a particular culture. The following discussion will help you understand how these three explanations fit in with the other explanations and allow you to be familiar with them in case you encounter them elsewhere.

Sociocultural Approach

The **sociocultural approach** focuses on the fact that *social and cultural factors can play important roles in abnormal behavior,* reflected in the differences in abnormal behaviors across cultures (Griffith & Gonzales, 1994; Junko-Tanaka-Matsumi, 1997). For example, in Asia there is a disorder known as **koro** that involves anxiety stemming from the belief that the genitalia are retracting into the abdomen and that the process will result in death. A less dramatic but possibly more important culturally based difference in abnormal behavior is the higher prevalence of schizophrenia in the lower socioeconomic classes than in the higher ones.

Sociocultural factors influence abnormal behavior in three ways:

1. They can determine *what behaviors are labeled as abnormal.* For example, in most societies hearing a voice that other people do not hear (i.e., a hallucination) is defined as abnormal, but in some cultures it is assumed that the voice is the voice of God, and the individual is regarded as a religious leader rather than a patient.

2. Sociocultural factors can influence the *level of abnormal behavior* because one culture or group may have more

sociocultural approach   The notion that social and cultural factors can play important roles in abnormal behavior.

koro   A disorder that involves anxiety stemming from the belief that the genitalia are retracting into the abdomen and that the process will result in death.

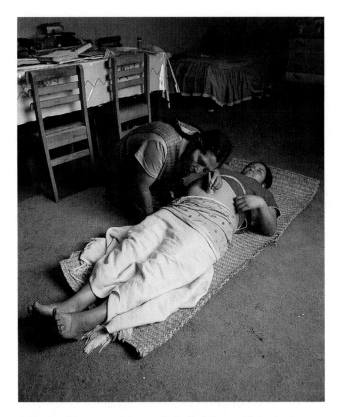

Sociocultural factors can influence the level of abnormal behavior. For example, in some cultures or socioeconomic classes women sometimes receive inadequate medical care while they are pregnant, and that can lead to problems in the prenatal brain development of their children.

or less of a factor that contributes to abnormal behavior. For example, there may be more stress in one culture or social class than another, and because stress leads to abnormal behavior, there may be a relationship between culture or class and the level of abnormal behavior. Also, in some cultures or classes women receive poor medical care while they are pregnant, which can lead to problems in the prenatal brain development of their children, which can, in turn, lead to disorders.

3. Differences in the role models across cultures or classes can influence *what symptoms develop.* For example, in Malaysia and Africa there is a disorder called **amok** (a-MOK), in which an individual (usually a male) broods for a brief period after a humiliating experience and then begins indiscriminately killing people, finally often killing himself. (This disorder is related to the phrase *running amok,* which is used to describe an individual who is out of control and causing trouble.) Although amok is not approved of in the Malaysian and African cultures, it is recognized as a means of responding to stress, and there are role models for it. It is interesting to note that a similar pat-

tern of behavior has begun appearing in Western societies. For example, a depressed former employee returns to the place of employment in a rage and begins randomly shooting people and then often commits suicide (Gaw & Bernstein, 1992). Other dramatic examples involve adolescents who feel depressed or "put down" and begin shooting their classmates (Cohen, 1999). These incidents follow a pattern and tend to cluster in time, thus reflecting the effects of role models (Cloud, 1999).

We can see the effects of culture on abnormal behavior by noting how some cultural changes lead to changes in abnormal behavior (Shorter, 1992; Spanos, 1994). For instance, at one time stress frequently led to paralyses of the arms and legs, but today such paralyses almost never occur. That change probably reflects the fact that people have increasing medical sophistication and so fewer believe that stress can cause paralysis; therefore they are less likely to use paralysis as a response to stress.

Sociocultural factors clearly play important roles in abnormal behavior, and we must be sensitive to their effects. However, it is essential to recognize that these factors alone do not explain abnormal behaviors; instead, they act as part of the explanations we have already discussed. That is, sociocultural factors influence abnormal behaviors because they influence (1) levels of stress, (2) what behaviors can be learned, (3) what beliefs can be developed, and (4) physiological factors. Looked at in another way, each of the major explanations for abnormal behavior can be thought of as an equation for predicting behavior, and sociocultural factors are some of the values that can be plugged into those equations (e.g., high or low stress, models or no models for a particular behavior). Therefore, rather than explicitly discussing the sociocultural explanation for a disorder, I will discuss the role played by sociocultural factors in each of the other explanations.

Family System Approach

The **family system approach** focuses on *the role of the family in the development of abnormal behavior.* For example, family members can generate conflict and stress for one another and provide models of abnormal behavior for one another. In these ways the family can be the source of abnormal behavior. In fact, from this position the abnormal behavior of an individual is seen as a result of an abnormal, or dysfunctional, family. For this reason psychologists who subscribe to the family system explanation do not treat a disturbed individual in isolation but instead treat the entire family.

According to the family system approach, abnormal behavior of an individual is a result of an abnormal or dysfunctional family. This approach suggests that family members can provide models of abnormal behavior for one another, by generating conflict and stress.

tion of the situation. Second, human behavior is motivated by a desire to *achieve enhanced levels of personal fulfillment* rather than simply to avoid negative consequences.

The emphasis on the conscious control of behavior surfaced in the 1960s and early 1970s as a reaction against the psychodynamic, learning, and physiological explanations, in which human beings are seen as simply the product of unconscious drives, conditioning, and physiology—as pawns of uncontrollable forces. When the humanistic position was first offered, it seemed somewhat radical. However, the notion that our behaviors are controlled by conscious thoughts is now encompassed in the cognitive explanation, and therefore that element of the humanistic position is no longer unique. On the other hand, the notion that behavior is motivated by a desire for positive personal development and fulfillment remains distinctive. That is, the psychodynamic and learning explanations assume that our behaviors are driven by a desire to reduce stress or gain rewards, and the cognitive and physiological explanations do not make any assumptions about what motivates us.

The leading proponent of the humanistic position was **Abraham Maslow** (1908–1970), who suggested that we have five levels of needs that range from basic physiological needs to higher needs, and after we satisfy the needs at one level, we move on to the next level. Figure 3.11 (on p. 80) shows the needs, from bottom to top: *physiological needs, safety needs, belongingness and love needs, esteem needs,* and the *need for self-actualization.* **Self-actualization** is the highest level of fulfillment, and people who achieve it are able to rise above their own needs and freely experience and give of themselves.

From the humanistic perspective anxiety and abnormal behaviors occur when we are blocked as we try to move up

The family system is important, but I will not use it as a separate explanation because the effects that family members have on one another, such as creating stress and providing role models, are dealt with by the other explanations. In other words, the family system does not provide a unique explanation for abnormal behavior; rather it provides a *context* (the family) in which other factors, such as stress and learning, can lead to the development of abnormal behavior.

 ## Humanistic Approach

The **humanistic approach** to abnormal behavior is based on two notions: First, the behavior of human beings is due to *conscious choices that are based on the individual's percep-*

amok   A disorder found primarily in Malaysia and Africa in which, after a humiliating experience and a period of brooding, an individual begins indiscriminately killing people.

family system approach   The notion that the family plays a key role in the development of abnormal behavior.

humanistic approach   An explanation for abnormal behavior based on the notions that the behavior of human beings is due to conscious choices and that this behavior is motivated by a desire to achieve enhanced levels of personal fulfillment rather than simply to avoid negative consequences.

Abraham Maslow   A leader of the humanistic movement.

self-actualization   The highest level of fulfillment, which allows people who achieve it to rise above their own needs and freely experience and give of themselves.

FIGURE 3.11

Maslow organized human needs from basic physiological needs to the need for self-actualization.

Need for Self-Actualization
(fulfill one's potential, be creative)

Esteem Needs
(self-esteem, accomplishment, respect)

Belongingness and Love Needs
(acceptance by others, love and be loved)

Safety Needs
(security, safety)

Physiological Needs
(oxygen, water, food, comfortable temperature)

Source: Adapted from Maslow (1970).

the ladder of needs to fulfillment—that is, when there is a difference between where we are and where we think we ought to be. The problem becomes circular: Although we

originally become anxious because we are not moving up, being anxious then serves to block our moving up.

In this approach therapy is focused on helping individuals overcome obstacles and close the gap between where they are now (the *current self*) and where they want to be (the *ideal self*). A well-known form of therapy designed to help clients attain personal fulfillment was developed by a psychologist named **Carl Rogers** (1902–1987); he called it **client-centered therapy** (Rogers, 1951). In this type of therapy the therapist assumes that clients are competent and that the therapist's major task is to reflect back to the clients what they are saying so that the clients can clarify for themselves what it is they want and what they need to do to achieve it. To establish an environment in which clients can explore and grow freely, the therapist provides them with *unconditional positive regard* and *sincere empathic understanding*. In other words, the therapist accepts each client uncritically as a basically good person and attempts to understand what the client is experiencing. Furthermore, the therapist often shares his or her own personal reactions, feelings, and experiences, thereby becoming more of a "real" person for the client. This is in sharp contrast to the detached and unrevealing behavior of most traditional psychotherapists. The atmosphere of acceptance and understanding established by the therapist allows the client's inner strength and qualities to surface so that personal growth can occur and anxiety can be left behind. Use of this type of therapy is much less common today than it was in the 1970s, but the notions of uncritical acceptance and empathic understanding have been adopted by many therapists. Some of the principles and techniques of client-centered psychotherapy are illustrated in Case Study 3.2.

There are two reasons why the humanistic explanation is largely ignored today. The first is that many of its most

These Habitat for Humanity workers could be described as *self-actualized,* meaning that they have risen above their own needs in order to freely experience and give of themselves.

A Client-Centered Psychotherapist and a Client

THE FOLLOWING EXCHANGE took place between a therapist and a client during a client-centered psychotherapy session. The client felt hopeless about herself and spent most of the hour discussing her feelings of inadequacy and lack of personal worth.

Client: (Long pause.) I've never said this before to anyone—but I've thought for such a long time—This is a terrible thing to say, but if I could just—well, if I could just find some glorious cause that I could give my life for, I would be happy. I cannot be the kind of a person I want to be. I guess maybe I haven't the guts—or the strength—to kill myself—and if someone else would relieve me of the responsibility—or I would be in an accident—I—I—just don't want to live.

Therapist: At the present time things look so black to you that you can't see much point in living—

Client: Yes—I wish I'd never started this therapy. I was happy when I was living in my dream world. There I could be the kind of person I want to be—But now—There is such a wide, wide gap—between my ideal—and what I am. I wish people hated me. I try to make them hate me. Because then I could turn away from them and could blame them—but no—It is all in my hands—Here is my life—and I either accept the fact that I am absolutely worthless—or I fight whatever it is that holds me in this terrible conflict. And I suppose if I accepted the fact that I am worthless, then I could go away someplace—and get a little room someplace—get a mechanical job someplace—and retreat clear back to the security of my dream world where I could do things, have clever friends, be a pretty wonderful sort of person—

Therapist: It's really a tough struggle—digging into this like you are—and at times the shelter of your dream world looks more attractive and comfortable.

Client: My dream world or suicide.

Therapist: Your dream world or something more permanent than dreams—

Client: Yes. So I don't see why I should waste your time—coming in twice a week—I'm not worth it—What do you think?

Therapist: It's up to you. . . . It isn't wasting my time—I'd be glad to see you—whenever you come—but it's how you feel about it—if you don't want to come twice a week—or if you want to come twice a week?—once a week?—It's up to you.

Client: You're not going to suggest that I come in oftener? You're not alarmed and think I ought to come in—every day—until I get out of this?

Therapist: I believe you are able to make your own decision. I'll see you whenever you want to come.

Client: I don't believe you are alarmed about—I see—I may be afraid of myself—but you aren't afraid of me—

Therapist: You say you may be afraid of yourself—and are wondering why I don't seem to be afraid for you?

Client: You have more confidence in me than I have. I'll see you next week—maybe.

In this exchange the client expresses her feelings that her growth has been stifled (the gap between her ideal and what she is), and the therapist does not attempt to find or solve an underlying problem but instead accepts her uncritically (even her thoughts of suicide), expresses interest in seeing her, and indicates that he believes she can make good decisions herself.

> . . . if I could just find some glorious cause that I could give my life for, I would be happy.

Source: Excerpt from *Client-Centered Therapy* by Carl R. Rogers. Copyright by Houghton Mifflin Company. Reprinted with permission.

important concepts, such as self-actualization, are poorly defined and impossible to measure. This impression makes the theory impossible to test, and an untestable theory is of little value.

The second problem is that the humanistic theorists have not developed a comprehensive theory of abnormal behavior. They have focused most of their attention on the mild anxiety and depression that relatively normal individuals experience, but they have not systematically addressed more serious disorders. However, it might be noted that in one attempt to explain schizophrenia a leading proponent of the humanistic position suggested that schizophrenia was not a disorder but simply an alternative form of adjustment, and that "normal" individuals were the ones who suffered from a problem because they allowed themselves to be unduly restricted by cultural restraints (Laing, 1964). Obviously, that position is not widely accepted today.

You should be aware of the humanistic explanation because it provides an interesting counterpoint to the other explanations. However, because the humanistic approach has not been applied to a broad range of abnormal behav-

Carl Rogers   A psychologist who developed client-centered therapy.

client-centered therapy   A form of psychotherapy in which therapists provide uncritical acceptance of clients and help them identify what they want and how they need to grow to achieve it.

FIGURE 3.12

The sociocultural, family system, and humanistic approaches

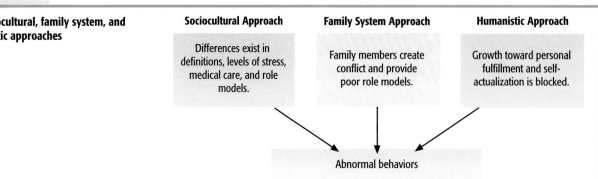

iors or subjected to many empirical tests, it will not be used systematically in this book.

The sociocultural, family system, and humanistic approaches highlight important issues, such as the role of culture and the family, to which we must be sensitive in considering explanations for abnormal behavior. These three approaches are summarized in Figure 3.12.

THINKING CRITICALLY

Questions about the Sociocultural, Family System, and Humanistic Approaches

1. *Are there disorders that are unique to one culture?* Because culture can play a role in influencing abnormal behavior, it is often assumed that there are "culture-bound" disorders (American Psychiatric Association, 1994). We will consider that possibility in greater detail later, but I should point out here that what are sometimes thought to be different disorders are simply the same disorder explained differently. For example, in some cultures gods or ghosts are used to explain symptoms, resulting in a disorder called *ghost sickness;* in other cultures the same symptoms are accounted for by physiologically based factors and called *schizophrenia*. The use of different explanations does not necessarily mean that the disorders are different. Consider the following: In European American cultures schizophrenia is now thought to be caused by problems with neurotransmitters and brain structures. Does that mean that schizophrenia is now a different disorder than it was 300 years ago when it was thought to be caused by the Devil? Of course not. Furthermore, identification of "culture-bound"

disorders sometimes appears to reflect ethnocentrism on the part of those defining the behaviors as "disorders." For example, in some countries individuals openly express extreme levels of grief following the death of a family member, but in the United States that behavior is defined as a disorder (*ataque de nervois;* American Psychiatric Association, 1994). Why is it seen as a disorder? It could be argued that the restrained emotional response to death valued in European-American cultures may be less appropriate and less helpful in the long run than an open expression of grief. Clearly, we must be careful not to label as a "culture-bound" disorder behavior that is simply different.

2. *When various members of a family show abnormal behaviors, does that mean that the behaviors are the result of dysfunctional family interactions?* Possibly, but not necessarily, because the shared abnormal behaviors may be due to shared genes. Indeed, later you will learn that when the children of parents who suffer from various disorders are adopted and raised by nonbiological parents who do not have the disorders, the children often have the same disorders as their biological parents, despite the fact that they were not raised by those parents. The failure to recognize that some abnormal behaviors are the result of physiological factors (e.g., genes) can have unfortunate consequences. Indeed, for many years psychologists put a heavy burden of guilt on mothers because it was thought that schizophrenia was the result of "bad parenting"; we now know that parenting has virtually nothing to do with the development of schizophrenia. A similar situation existed with the disruptive childhood behavior pattern known as attention-deficit/hyperactivity disorder. I do not mean to imply that parents and family interactions are not important; I only want to point out that we must be careful in assigning causes for abnormal behaviors.

Summary

Topic I: The Cognitive Approach

▶ The cognitive approach suggests that abnormal behavior is caused primarily by incorrect beliefs.

▶ Information goes through three stages of memory: (1) In the sensory memory information is registered, and important information is selected for attention; (2) in the short-term memory information is used for thinking and processed for storage; and (3) in the long-term memory information is stored.

▶ Memories are made up of components and the activation of any component will result in activation of the entire memory. Memories are stored in networks of related memories, and the activation of one memory will activate the entire network. The recall of a memory primes it for easier recall later.

▶ Problems with information processing occur because of selective attention and selective recall of information. Problems also occur because memories become distorted, and false memories can be implanted.

▶ Cognitive therapy involves changing incorrect beliefs. Clients may be asked to consider their beliefs as hypotheses and then test those hypotheses. The process of changing beliefs is sometimes called cognitive restructuring. In rational-emotive therapy, a type of cognitive therapy, therapists actively challenge clients' beliefs.

▶ A major question concerning the cognitive explanation is whether beliefs are a cause or an effect of abnormal behaviors.

Topic II: The Physiological Approach

▶ The physiological approach is that abnormal behavior is due to chemical imbalances that cause problems with how neurons in the brain communicate with each other (i.e., problems with synaptic transmission) and to problems with brain structures (i.e., brain damage).

▶ The brain has three levels. The brain stem controls basic physiological functions (breathing, heart rate) and generates arousal (electrical activity) that affects other areas of the brain. The midbrain maintains homeostasis (i.e., controls how much we eat, sleep, and desire sex), processes memories for storage, and is responsible for emotion. The third level is the cerebral cortex, which is where higher mental functions such as thinking and language are located.

▶ The brain is composed of cells called neurons. When the dendrites or body of a neuron are stimulated, an electrical impulse is generated that travels to the end of the neuron's axon. There it stimulates the release of a neuro-transmitter that flows across the synapse (gap) that separates one neuron from another. The neurotransmitter enters a receptor site on the next neuron, causing that neuron to fire. A neuron fires on the all-or-none principle, so the intensity of neural activity is due to the frequency of firing or the number of neurons that fire.

▶ Neurotransmission is crucial because too little or too much can lead to problems (e.g., depression or mania, respectively). Neurotransmission can be influenced by (1) levels of neurotransmitters (production, catabolism, reuptake), (2) blocking agents, (3) inhibitory neurons, (4) sensitivity of postsynaptic neurons, and (5) the number of postsynaptic receptor sites for neurotransmitters.

▶ Hormones are substances that are secreted into the bloodstream, where they travel to various parts of the body and stimulate activity; in some extreme cases this can lead to abnormal behaviors. During prenatal development hormones can influence brain development, which can result in abnormal behaviors.

▶ Genetics can influence factors such as the level of neurotransmitters, which can in turn influence behavior. Biological traumas occurring during fetal development or birth can also lead to problems in the brain, which can later cause abnormal behavior.

▶ In most cases the treatment of the physiological factors that contribute to abnormal behavior involves drugs that normalize the levels of neurotransmission. Although some new forms of surgery can be used to correct problems in the brain, those cases are very rare.

▶ There is a good deal of evidence to support the physiological explanation, but (1) people object to the notion that they are controlled by brain chemistry, (2) physiological factors do not necessarily work alone in causing abnormal behavior, (3) the fact that drugs are effective treatments does not necessarily mean that disorders are caused by physiological factors, (4) drugs are treatments rather than cures, and (5) drugs can have side effects.

Topic III: Sociocultural, Family System, and Humanistic Approaches

▶ The sociocultural approach focuses on the fact that social and cultural factors can influence behavior because they can (1) determine what is labeled abnormal, (2) influence the level of abnormal behavior (e.g., one class or culture may have more stress), and (3) influence the symptoms of abnormal behavior (models may lead to different behaviors). However, sociocultural factors have their effects through processes that are embodied in other explanations; for example, they influence the level of stress (psychodynamic approach), what behaviors are learned (learning approach), and what beliefs are developed (cognitive approach).

▶ The family system approach focuses on the role of the family in abnormal behavior. Family influences can be important, but they have their effects through processes that are central to other explanations; for example, families can increase stress (psychodynamic), teach abnormal behavior (learning), or foster erroneous beliefs (cognitive).

▶ Within the humanistic approach behavior is seen as due to conscious choices that individuals make and their desire to achieve enhanced levels of personal fulfillment (self-actualization). However, the notion that conscious choices influence behavior has been taken over by the cognitive approach. Apart from that, the humanistic explanation has been largely abandoned because many of its central concepts were not adequately defined or measurable and because it was never used to develop a comprehensive theory of abnormal behavior.

▶ When considering disorders across cultures, we must be careful not to assume that disorders are different simply because different explanations are used for them. We must also be cautious about labeling behavior as a disorder because it differs from what commonly occurs in our own culture. And we must be careful about assuming that dysfunctional family interactions are responsible for the occurrence of disorders within a family, because the disorders might be due to shared genes.

Questions for Making Connections

1. Track a specific experience through the stages of memory. As you go through each stage, point out how problems might arise that could distort the memory of the experience and possibly result in abnormal behavior.

2. In Chapter 2 you learned about the learning approach, which involves classical and operant conditioning. What are the similarities and differences between that approach and the cognitive approach, which we discussed in this chapter?

3. Imagine two neurons in a nerve tract. The first neuron is stimulated and a nerve impulse is produced. Follow that impulse down the neuron to the synapse, and explain how the impulse "jumps" across the synapse. What factors can increase the likelihood that the second (postsynaptic) neuron will be activated? What factors can decrease the likelihood that it will be activated?

4. From a physiological perspective abnormal behavior is the result of biochemical and structural problems in the brain. What causes those problems, and what, if anything, can be done to correct them?

5. Give examples of how the sociocultural, family system, and humanistic approaches can be used to explain abnormal behavior. Using those examples, explain how these three explanations can be subsumed under the other approaches we have discussed.

6. From your perspective what is the major strength and the major weakness of each of the approaches we have discussed (psychodynamic, learning, cognitive, physiological)?

7. What connections do you see among the various approaches to abnormal behavior? Do they overlap or complement each other?

8. At this point which two explanations do you think are most helpful for explaining abnormal behavior?

Key Terms and People

In reviewing and testing yourself, you should be able to discuss each of the following:

all-or-none principle, p. 69
amok, p. 78
axon, p. 69
biological traumas, p. 73
blocking agents, p. 71
brain stem, p. 67
catabolism, p. 71
cell body, p. 69
cerebral cortex, p. 68

client-centered therapy, p. 80
cognitive approach, p. 60
cognitive restructuring, p. 64
cognitive therapy, p. 64
dendrites, p. 69
diathesis-stress model, p. 73
false memories, p. 63
family system approach, p. 78
genetics, p. 73

hormones, p. 72
humanistic approach, p. 79
inhibitory neuron, p. 71
koro, p. 77
long-term memory, p. 61
Maslow, Abraham, p. 79
midbrain, p. 67
nerve impulse, p. 69
nerve tract, p. 69

4

Diagnostic Techniques and Research Methods

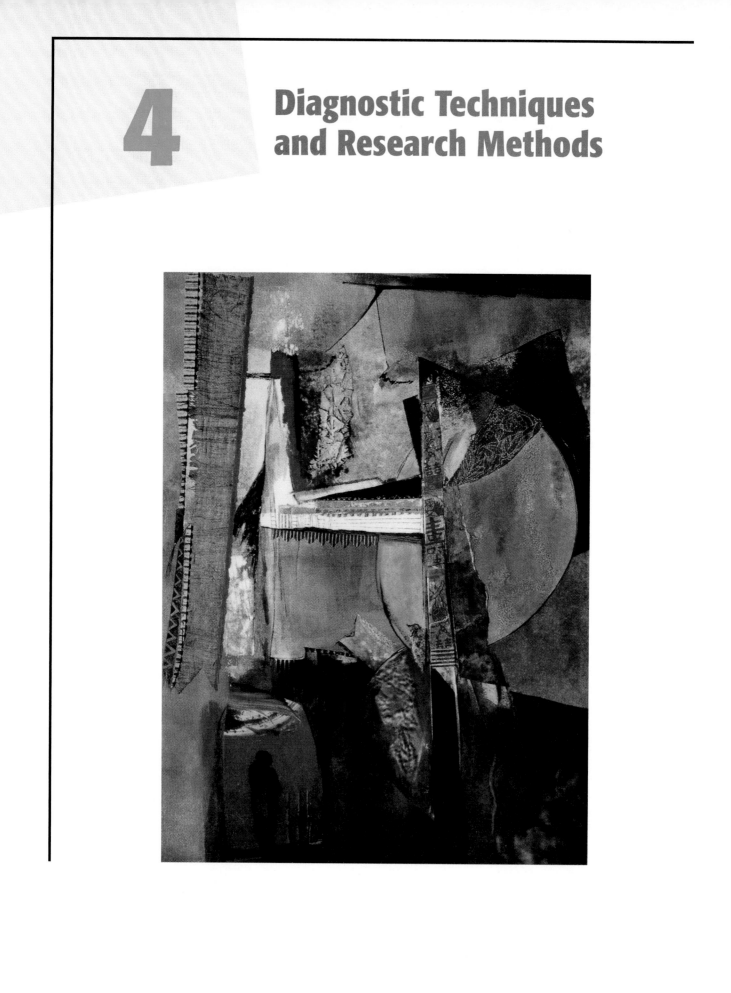

In this chapter I am going to discuss two topics. First, I will describe the techniques used to *diagnose* abnormal behavior. Understanding the diagnostic process is important because we must accurately diagnose a problem before we can treat it. The second topic is research methodology. I will describe the methods used to *study* abnormal behavior. Understanding research procedures is important because research findings provide the foundation for our understanding and treatment of abnormal behavior.

TOPIC I

Diagnostic Techniques

Jeffery is taking a test called the MMPI that includes over 500 true–false items, such as "I feel sad most of the time," "I never put off until tomorrow what I should do today," and "I hear voices when no one else is around." Because he wants to "look good" on the test, Jeffery is going to lie on some of his responses. Will Jeffery be able to fake the results without getting caught? What can we learn about personality and abnormal behavior from the MMPI?

Caroline is undergoing a diagnostic evaluation. As part of the procedure she is given a test in which she is shown a series of inkblots and asked to tell what she sees in the inkblots. How is what she sees in the inkblots related to her personality? Is this a good measure of Caroline's personality?

When Ricardo came to the psychological clinic, he was given an MMPI, which was originally developed for use with individuals who are European American. Will the MMPI provide an accurate picture of Ricardo, who is Hispanic American?

Labeling an individual as "abnormal" tells us little because the label is too broad. For example, it does not tell us whether the individual is anxious, depressed, having physical problems, hallucinating, delusional, addicted to drugs, or suffering from any of hundreds of other symptoms. The need for better descriptions led to the development of **diagnostic systems,** which are used to group sets of symptoms into various disorders.

diagnostic systems Systems used to group sets of symptoms into various disorders.

A diagnostic system serves two major purposes: First, it enables us to *describe* individuals who suffer from abnormalities. For example, the diagnostic label "major depression" tells us much more about an individual's symptoms than does the label "abnormal." Second, a diagnostic system helps us decide how to *treat* individuals. A diagnostic system itself does not include treatments, but once a set of symptoms (a diagnosis) is linked to a particular cause or an effective treatment, the diagnosis helps us determine how an individual with that diagnosis should be treated.

Two diagnostic systems are currently in use. The system used in the United States is presented in the 4th edition of the **Diagnostic and Statistical Manual of Mental Disorders,** generally referred to as **DSM-IV** (American Psychiatric Association, 1994). The system used throughout the rest of the world is set forth in the 10th edition of the **International Classification of Diseases,** better known as **ICD-10.** The two systems are similar but do have some differences (American Psychiatric Association, 1994, apps. G and H). Because it would be helpful if everyone used the same system, the two systems are in the process of being merged. In this book *DSM-IV* will be used as the basis for identifying the symptoms that are necessary to make a diagnosis.

Diagnostic Systems for Abnormal Behavior

Before discussing the techniques used to make diagnoses, let's get an overview of the diagnostic process.

Background

The *Diagnostic and Statistical Manual of Mental Disorders* was introduced by the American Psychiatric Association in 1952 and has undergone extensive revisions since then (Williams, 1999). In its early editions the manual consisted simply of brief descriptions of the symptoms of various disorders, along with short discussions of what was thought to cause them. When making a diagnosis, a clinician selected either the description or the cause that best fit the patient.

Unfortunately, this early system suffered from two serious deficiencies: First, the descriptions of the disorders were rather vague. Second, there was no consistent basis for diagnoses because a diagnosis could be based either on the patient's *symptoms* or on what was thought to *cause* the symptoms. The vagueness of the descriptions and the inconsistent basis for making diagnoses led to two practical problems. The first one was that the system was *unreliable.* (The **reliability** of a diagnostic system refers to the degree to which an individual with a given set of symptoms will receive the *same* diagnosis when examined by different individuals or by the same individual at different times.) For example, when a number of individuals worked independently to diagnose a patient, there was often less than 50% agreement among them concerning the proper diagnosis (Beck et al., 1962; Ward et al., 1962; Zigler & Phillips, 1961). The second practical problem was that diagnoses made using the system were often *invalid;* in other words, patients often got incorrect diagnoses. (The **validity** of a diagnostic system refers to the degree to which an individual will receive the *correct* diagnosis.) The invalidity of the diagnoses stemmed from their unreliability; that is, because different clinicians came up with different diagnoses for the same patient, some of those diagnoses had to be wrong. Obviously, a system that yielded so many unreliable and invalid diagnoses was not very useful, so a radically new system was developed.

The Current System

The current system incorporates four important advances:

1. *The specific symptoms for each diagnosis are clearly listed.* Earlier manuals simply contained a short, vague description of each disorder, but *DSM-IV* lists the precise symptoms of each disorder and specifies how many symptoms must be present before the diagnosis can be made. For example, in Table 10.1, you will find a list of the symptoms that are necessary for a diagnosis of schizophrenia.

In an attempt to make the system even more objective and uniform, *DSM-IV* also contains decision trees for making diagnoses. **Decision trees** are sets of questions that lead the clinician through a series of branches based on the patient's symptoms, with the branches eventually leading to a diagnosis. A decision tree for diagnosing mood disorders is presented in Figure 4.1. With the symptoms clearly listed and the steps in the decision process specified, the diagnostic process has become more objective and more uniform in its application and therefore more reliable. The only place for subjectivity is in deciding what symptoms the patient has.

Diagnostic and Statistical Manual of Mental Disorders (*DSM-IV*)   The manual containing the diagnostic system currently used in the United States (4th edition).

International Classification of Diseases (ICD-10)   A publication containing the diagnostic system currently used in countries other than the United States (10th edition).

reliability (of a diagnostic system)   The degree to which an individual with a given set of symptoms will receive the *same* diagnosis when examined by different individuals or by the same individual at different times.

validity (of a diagnostic system)   The degree to which an individual will receive the *correct* diagnosis.

decision trees   Sets of questions about symptoms that eventually lead to diagnoses.

FIGURE 4.1

A decision tree for diagnosing mood disorders

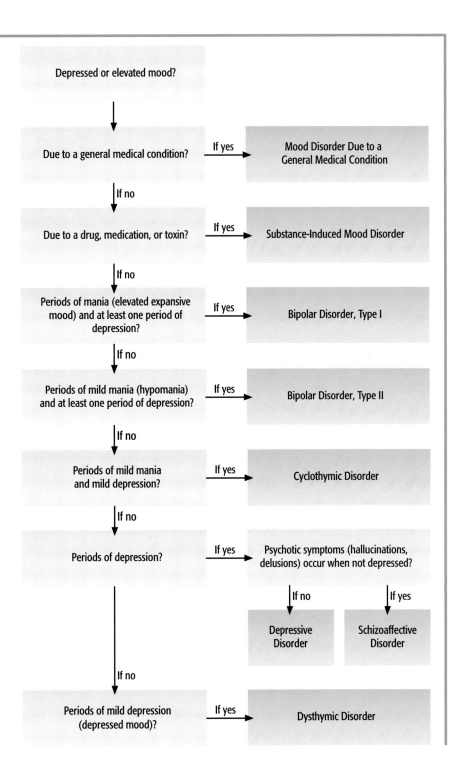

2. *Assumptions about the suspected causes of disorders are not used in making diagnoses.* With the current system diagnoses are based on observable behaviors rather than on what is thought to have caused the disorder. The elimination of assumptions about causes resulted in the elimination of some popular diagnostic labels because the labels implicitly suggested an underlying cause. For example, for many years the term *neurotic* was used to refer to disorders involving the symptoms of anxiety. However, because *neurotic* implies that anxiety stems from unconscious conflicts, the term was eliminated from *DSM-IV*. What were previously called *anxiety neuroses* are now called *anxiety disorders*.

The new diagnostic label simply describes the symptoms and does not imply any assumptions about their cause. In general, *DSM-IV* is atheoretical; that is, it is not based on any theory.

However, attention to the causes of symptoms has not been completely eliminated because *objective evidence* concerning certain causes can influence a diagnosis. For example, if an individual is hearing the voice of Joan of Arc (i.e., hallucinating) or believes that he or she is God (i.e., delusional) and if an examination reveals organic brain damage, the diagnosis will be changed from "schizophrenia" to "psychotic disorder due to a general medical condition." Similarly, if there is evidence that the individual recently took a hallucinogenic drug such as LSD, the diagnosis will be changed to a "substance-induced psychotic disorder." However, it should be recognized that the use of objective evidence about brain damage or previous drug use is very different from the previous use of assumptions about ill-defined causes such as "conflict with mother."

3. *The number of disorders listed has been greatly increased.* The first edition of the manual listed only 66 disorders, but *DSM-IV* lists more than 397—more than a 500% increase. Some critics have suggested that too many problems are now listed as disorders, thereby overextending the boundaries of "abnormal." For example, it may be pushing the limits a bit to diagnose a child who is having difficulty with arithmetic as having a "mathematics disorder." The increase over time in the number of disorders listed in the *DSM* is illustrated in Figure 4.2.

4. *Individuals are given diagnoses on five separate axes.* Until the publication of *DSM-III*, individuals were given one diagnostic label, such as "depression," which described their major clinical problem. However, individuals are now given diagnoses on five *axes* (dimensions) so that their diagnoses contain more information. These axes are as follows:

Axis I: Clinical Syndromes. This axis contains all of the *major serious disorders* such as anxiety, depression, schizophrenia, substance abuse, sexual disorders, sleep disorders, and eating disorders.

Axis II: Personality Disorders and Mental Retardation. This axis contains two categories; the first is *personality disorders,* and the second is *mental retardation. Personality disorders* include obsessive-compulsive personality disorder, dependent personality disorder, and antisocial personality disorder (see Chapter 12). Individuals can have diagnoses on both Axes I and II. For example, an individual could suffer from major depression (Axis I) and also show compulsive personality traits (Axis II). Personality disorders were placed on a separate axis because their symptoms are usually less serious and dramatic than those of clinical syndromes (Axis I), and the developers of the diagnostic system wanted to make sure that personality disorders were not overshadowed or ignored.

FIGURE 4.2

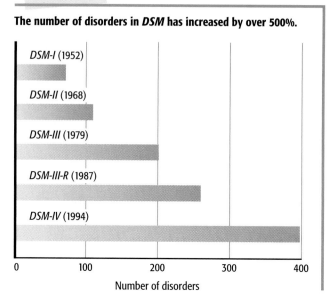

The number of disorders in *DSM* has increased by over 500%.

Axis III: General Medical Conditions. This axis allows a diagnostician to indicate whether there are any medical conditions that are relevant to the diagnosis or treatment of the disorder. For example, evidence of organic brain damage is probably relevant for diagnosing an individual with impaired cognitive abilities, and the presence of diabetes might influence the treatment of a patient with depression.

Axis IV: Psychosocial and Environmental Problems. This axis provides the diagnostician with an opportunity to indicate whether there are any psychosocial or environmental problems that might affect an individual's diagnosis, treatment, or prognosis. Examples of potential problems include the loss of social support, death of a loved one, discrimination, educational problems, economic problems, legal problems, and other sources of stress.

Axis V: Global Assessment of Functioning. This axis permits the diagnostician to rate an individual's present psychological, social, and occupational functioning and his or her highest level of functioning during the past year. The rating of present functioning reflects the degree to which the individual needs treatment. The rating of previous functioning indicates the level of adjustment the individual can be expected to achieve after the disorder has been eliminated. For example, a therapist who knows that an individual had only a marginal level of functioning during the best of times will not have unrealistic expectations regarding treatment outcome. Level of functioning is rated on a scale from 1 to 100, with endpoints labeled "persistent inability to function" and "superior functioning."

The introduction of the multidimensional approach greatly expanded the information provided by a diagnosis. For example, instead of simply labeling an individual "depressed" as was done before, a mental health professional might now specify that the individual (1) is depressed; (2) tends to be obsessive-compulsive in personality style, which may make psychotherapy difficult; (3) suffers from a serious heart disorder, which may contribute to the depression; (4) is experiencing moderate psychosocial stress, which may also contribute to the depression; and (5) has functioned very well within the past year, which suggests that he or she has the potential to do well again.

Although *DSM-IV* certainly embodies improvements, many mental health professionals have raised objections to it. Specifically, there is controversy over what disorders should be included, what disorders should be omitted, how disorders are organized, and whether *DSM-IV* is biased in favor of medicine over psychology (Nathan & Langenbucher, 1999; Regier et al., 1998). Because *DSM-IV* is the official listing of disorders, I will follow it in our discussion of abnormal behaviors, but I will also point out where there are problems.

Problems with Diagnostic Systems in General

The *DSM* and *ICD* systems are generally effective, but there are three fundamental problems with any diagnostic system. The first is that whenever an individual is put into a category, some of the individual's *uniqueness will be lost,* and as a result something very important about that individual may be missed. Here is a simple example to illustrate this point: You can be categorized (diagnosed) in terms of your sex, age, and ethnic background, but describing you as, for example, female, young, and Hispanic undoubtedly leaves out some of the most important things about you. The various axes in *DSM-IV* may help capture certain of the relevant differences among individuals, but whenever we use a label or even a number of labels, we always lose some important information about a particular individual.

The second problem is that diagnostic systems can lead us to *attribute characteristics to individuals that they do not possess.* For example, the diagnosis of "schizophrenia" is often associated with hallucinations and delusions, and therefore it is often assumed that a patient with schizophrenia will have hallucinations and delusions. However, the diagnosis of "schizophrenia" does not necessarily require that an individual have hallucinations or delusions because other symptoms can lead to this diagnosis. Unfortunately, the implicit link between hallucinations and delusions and schizophrenia can lead to the erroneous assumption that all individuals with schizophrenia have hallucinations and delusions. Then an individual who does not report having these symptoms may be viewed as being defensive and denying or hiding the symptoms. What is worse is that assumptions about symptoms can actually lead to the creation of the symptoms through the process of suggestion. For example, if a mental health professional assumes that a patient with schizophrenia has hallucinations and repeatedly asks the patient about them, the patient may begin to think that he or she *should* have them. Because the line between thoughts and "voices in my head" can become blurred, it is only a short jump for the patient to start to interpret thoughts as voices—and *voilà,* the patient reports that he or she has hallucinations!

The third problem with diagnoses is that we often use them to refer to the *whole individual* when, in fact, they refer only to *one particular aspect of the individual.* For example, sometimes we refer to individuals as "schizophrenics" rather than as "individuals with schizophrenia." This is the equivalent of referring to an individual with cancer as "cancerous." Using a diagnostic label to refer to an entire individual is inappropriate because it implies that the disorder influences all aspects of the individual's life, which is often not the case. For example, some individuals with serious disorders such as schizophrenia live relatively normal and productive lives, and other people are not aware of their symptoms (see Case Study 10.4). To avoid attributing a disorder to the whole individual, *DSM-IV* does not use expressions such as "a schizophrenic" or "an alcoholic" but instead recommends the phrases "an individual with Schizophrenia" and "an individual with Alcohol Dependence." I will follow this approach in this book.

There are clearly problems with any diagnostic system, but three things on the positive side should be noted. First, the current system is a great improvement over previous versions. Second, by recognizing the problems inherent in any system, we may be able to avoid some of those problems by keeping in mind that individuals are unique and

Axis I: Clinical Syndromes   A category in *DSM-IV* that includes the major serious disorders (e.g., anxiety, depression, schizophrenia).

Axis II: Personality Disorders and Mental Retardation   A category in *DSM-IV* that includes both personality disorders and mental retardation.

Axis III: General Medical Conditions   A category in *DSM-IV* that indicates whether there are any medical conditions that might influence diagnosis or treatment of an individual.

Axis IV: Psychosocial and Environmental Problems   A category in *DSM-IV* that indicates whether there are any psychosocial or environmental problems that might influence diagnosis, treatment, or prognosis.

Axis V: Global Assessment of Functioning   A category in *DSM-IV* that rates an individual's current level of functioning and highest level of functioning in the past year so that potential levels of improvement can be estimated.

not just like others in their diagnostic group, being careful not to assume that individuals have symptoms for which there is no direct evidence, and focusing on disorders rather than on people. Third, we must be flexible and ready to change the system as new information becomes available. For example, a firm understanding of what causes disorders would allow them to be grouped by causes rather than symptoms, which would help in making decisions about treatment.

Checklists as an Alternative

Because of the problems associated with diagnostic labels, it might be useful to replace diagnoses with **checklists of symptoms.** We could use such checklists to rate an individual on a variety of dimensions, such as the degree to which the individual has symptoms such as hallucinations, delusions, depression and anxiety, the degree to which the individual is suicidal, verbally responsive, able to sleep, motivated to improve, able to interact effectively with others, bothered by feelings of guilt, physically active, able to organize, able to concentrate, reliable, and honest; and the degree to which support is available to the individual from family and friends. With ratings on dimensions like these we would know, for example, that an individual is depressed but also that he or she is suicidal, willing to talk (which is certainly important in dealing with suicidal individuals), and honest and that there is a social support system in place that could care for the individual outside of the hospital.

In some respects the use of checklists is the next step beyond the use of multiple axes for making diagnoses, but there are some important differences between the two

A diagnostic interview can reveal a lot about a person, from both what the person says and how the person behaves.

methods. The checklist has many more dimensions, so we get much more information. Also, a checklist can be completed by a variety of people, such as nurses, social workers, ward attendants, friends, and family members, in addition to psychologists and psychiatrists, thereby giving a broader perspective on the individual being rated. This might be helpful because the traditional interview from which diagnostic impressions are obtained is usually brief and may not yield a very representative picture of the person. Multiple judgments from a variety of raters can give a much better idea of an individual's problems, as well as when and where the problems are most likely to occur. With a checklist, the individual could even provide a self-rating, and the inconsistencies between this self-report and the reports of others might help a great deal in understanding the individual. Checklists have been tried and found to be very effective (Derogatis, 1993; DuPaul et al., 1997; Wittenborn, 1951, 1962). However, probably because they involve a radical departure from the traditional way of thinking about and describing patients, they have not yet gained widespread acceptance.

With this material as background, in the next section I will discuss the techniques used to assess the symptoms that lead to diagnoses.

Techniques for Diagnosing Abnormal Behavior

Four techniques are used to assess symptoms: *interviews, observations, psychological tests,* and *physiological tests.* More than one technique is usually used because the different techniques provide different types of information, and the strengths of one technique can compensate for the weaknesses of another.

Interviews

Interviews are important because they are usually the first contact individuals have with a mental health professional, and the decisions made on the basis of the initial interview can have long-term implications. For example, a screening interview may be used to decide whether the person really has a disorder, what tests might be necessary, whether the person needs treatment immediately or can wait, and what type of treatment may be most appropriate (e.g., social support, counseling, psychotherapy, or drugs).

The first part of an initial interview is usually focused on determining an individual's major complaints ("What problems caused you to come in today?") and what is happening in the individual's life that might be causing the symptoms or might be being disrupted by the symptoms. Once these questions are answered, an attempt is made to round out the picture of the individual as a person. Specifically, questions are asked about the individual's family, occupation, education, typical day, social history, medical history, psychiatric history, and family history (Scheiber, 1999). In addition to considering the content of the individual's verbal responses to questions, the interviewer also makes observations concerning the individual's appearance (appropriately dressed or disheveled), motor behavior (agitated or motionless), emotion (crying or manic), contact with reality (hearing voices), and thought processes (confused, problems with attention, nonsense responses to questions), among other things. Overall, then, the goals are to (1) assess the nature and severity of the presenting symptoms, (2) collect information that might be helpful in determining the cause of the symptoms, and (3) evaluate the individual's strengths and social support. All of that will be used for making a diagnosis using the five axes in the *DSM-IV* and formulating a treatment plan.

There are two types of interviews. In a **structured interview** the interviewer asks a specific list of questions (Bryant et al., 1998; Butler et al., 1998; Trull et al., 1998); in an **unstructured interview** the interviewer "goes with the flow," pursuing topics of interest and avoiding dead ends. Structured interviews have the advantage of ensuring that all relevant topics are covered, at least superficially. Unstructured interviews may miss something relevant, but they allow for deeper probing when an important point is revealed. The best approach may be to do a structured interview followed by an unstructured interview in which important points are followed up.

One of the most frequently used structured interviews is the *mental status exam* in which the individual is asked to (1) give the date (year, season, date, day), (2) indicate his or her present location (country, city, clinic/hospital), and (3) start with 100 and repeatedly subtract 7 (100, 93, 86, . . .) (Wise, Gray, & Seltzer, 1999). Other questions sometimes assess long-term memory, such as by asking the individual to name the last five presidents. The mental status exam is used to assess gross problems with orientation, and if the individual is found to be "in touch," more refined questions can follow (see earlier examples).

An interview also provides an opportunity to observe an individual's behavior. Indeed, an individual's style of responding may be more important than the content of what he or she is saying. In some interviews the interviewer may actually behave in a particular way to see how the individual reacts. For example, in an interview designed to measure the *Type A behavior pattern,* which involves aggressive and competitive behaviors, the interviewer will occasionally pause and fumble briefly as if searching for the right word to use. What the interviewer is really doing is waiting to see if the individual will jump in and finish the sentence (Rosenman, 1978).

In other situations the combination of verbal content and behavioral style may be informative. For example, when asked about hallucinations, a patient might respond harshly, saying, "No! I don't hear voices! Only crazy people hear voices, and I'm not crazy!" In that case the inappropriate vehemence of the patient's denial of hallucinations may lead the interviewer to conclude that in fact the patient does experience them.

In sum, an interview can be of value because it provides both information about the individual and an opportunity to observe the individual. However, the interview does have a number of weaknesses. First, patients may not be good or honest reporters concerning their behavior. Second, sometimes the interviewer's interpretation of what a patient says or does may be based on an inference, and the inference may be wrong. For example, I just suggested that a patient's particularly vehement denial that he was hearing voices could be interpreted as suggesting that in fact he was hearing voices, but it is also possible that the strength of the denial was due to the fact that the patient was offended by the question, exasperated by being repeatedly asked about hallucinations, or just tired and cranky. Finally, an interview situation may not be particularly good for observing behavior because it is time-limited and not representative of more relevant life situations. In other words, the way an individual responds in a formal interview in the office of a social worker, psychologist, or psychiatrist may not be the way the individual responds in the "real world."

Observations

Observation of an individual in his or her natural environment enables us to assess behavior directly and to evaluate the effects of situational factors on behavior. However, direct observation usually plays a relatively minor role in the assessment of abnormal behavior because it is simply not practical to have trained observers "in the field" recording behavior. In addition, serious ethical questions are associated with observing individuals without getting their permission. Even if a patient does give permission for observation, the behaviors that can be observed through one-way windows in a hospital are probably not typical because the individual is aware of being observed.

In contrast to adults, young children are frequently observed as part of assessment. With children it is often possible to arrange situations in which they can be observed while they interact with peers or parents, and in

---

checklists of symptoms   An alternative to diagnostic labels for rating individuals on various dimensions.

structured interview   An interview in which the interviewer follows a specific set of questions. (Contrast with *unstructured interview.*)

unstructured interview   An interview in which the interviewer does not use a specific set of questions but instead follows leads as they come up. (Contrast with *structured interview.*)

In order to assess behavior directly, psychologists use techniques such as observing children in their natural environment.

these situations the children often ignore or are unaware of the observers. Teachers can also be excellent observers of behavior, and their reports are especially helpful in diagnosing disorders such as attention-deficit/hyperactivity disorder (DuPaul et al., 1997; Power et al., 1998). Other children can also provide reliable reports concerning symptoms such as anxiety and depression in their peers (Cole et al., 1998). The fact that observation can be used with young children is important because sometimes their self-reports differ greatly from the reports of their behavior given by adults (Handwerk et al., 1999).

Psychological Tests

Psychological tests can be divided into four types: *objective personality tests, projective personality tests, intelligence tests,* and *neuropsychological tests.* In the following sections I will briefly consider each type.

Objective Personality Tests. In some respects **objective personality tests** are an extension of the interview method of collecting information because these tests consist of lists of questions to which the individual responds. Numerous objective tests are used to measure a wide variety of abnormal behaviors, ranging from brief periods of anxiety to chronic schizophrenia.

The most widely used objective test of abnormal behavior is the **Minnesota Multiphasic Personality Inventory,** usually referred to as the **MMPI.** The MMPI was originally published in 1942, and a revision, the **MMPI-2,** was published in 1989. The MMPI-2 contains 567 questions grouped to form scales that measure nine types of abnormal behavior, ranging from depression to schizophrenia. There is also a scale that measures masculinity–femininity. Each item is answered by checking "True," "False," or "Can-

not Say." Table 4.1 contains items similar to those found on some of the MMPI-2 scales. An individual gets a score on each scale, and the scores are plotted on a graph to yield a personality profile. Figure 4.3 is an MMPI-2 personality profile for an individual who has elevated scores on the Depression and Schizophrenia scales.

In addition to the "clinical" scales that measure problems such as depression and schizophrenia, there are also three "control" scales that are used to identify individuals for whom the test scores may not be valid. For example, a Lie scale identifies individuals who are trying to fake good

TABLE 4.1

True/false items similar to those found on MMPI clinical scales

Hypochondriasis (HS; Scale 1)
I have trouble with my bowel movements. (T)
I experience chest pains several times each week. (T)

Depression (D; Scale 2)
I generally feel that life is worth living. (F)
I do not sleep well. (T)

Conversion Hysteria (Hy; Scale 3)
Often I feel weak all over. (T)
It is easy for me to keep my balance when I walk. (F)

Psychopathic Deviate (PD; Scale 4)
I have many fewer fears than other people. (T)
In school, I was frequently in trouble for acting up. (T)

Masculinity-Femininity (Mf; Scale 5)
I enjoy raising houseplants. (T)
I like to cook. (T)

Paranoia (Pa; Scale 6)
A lot of people have it in for me. (T)
I have frequently been punished for things that were not my fault. (T)

Psychasthenia (Pt; Scale 7)
I am anxious most of the time. (T)
I usually wake up feeling rested and fresh. (F)

Schizophrenia (Scale 8)
I cannot keep my attention focused on one thought. (T)
I hear strange things that others do not hear. (T)

Mania (Scale 9)
I am a very important person. (T)
I like to stir up activity. (T)

Social Introversion (Scale 0)
I like to talk to members of the opposite sex. (F)
At parties I sit by myself or with one other person. (T)

Note: The answer in parentheses after each item—T for true or F for false—is the one that contributes to a score that indicates the disorder.

FIGURE 4.3

An MMPI-2 profile for an individual with symptoms of depression and schizophrenia

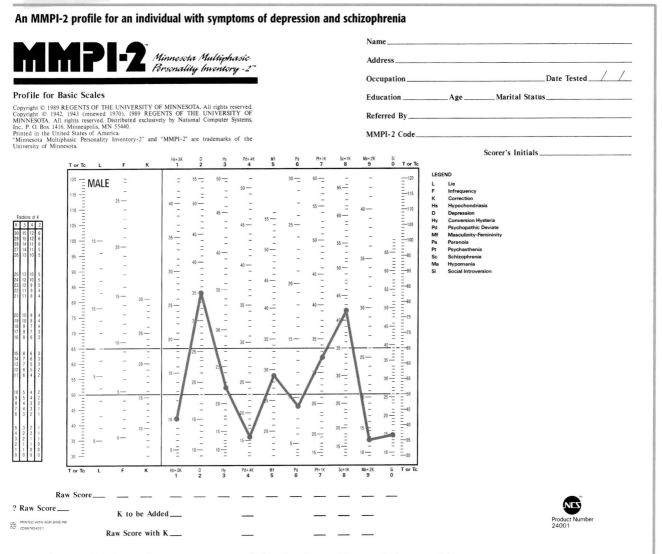

Source: Minnesota Multiphasic Personality Inventory-2 (MMPI-2) Profile for Basic Scales. Copyright © 1989 by the Regents of the University of Minnesota. All rights reserved. "MMPI-2" and "Minnesota Multiphasic Personality Inventory-2" are trademarks.

scores. The Lie scale contains items like "I never put off until tomorrow things that should be done today." Because it is unlikely that there are many people who can honestly mark "True" for items like these, the assumption is that an individual who consistently does mark them "True" is lying. Although a high score on the Lie scale provides some potentially interesting information about the individual, it causes the scores on the other scales of the test to be ignored as invalid (Arbisi & Ben-Porath, 1998; Bagby et al., 1997; Wetter et al., 1994).

Interpretations of the MMPI-2 can be based on simple inspection of the personality profile (see Figure 4.3), but it is also possible to use a computer program to compare an individual's profile with the profiles of thousands of other people who have completed the test. The program then prints out a description of those with similar profiles (Bloom, 1992; Duckworth & Anderson, 1995; Matarazzo,

objective personality tests Tests of personality that consist of objective items or questions (e.g., true or false, multiple choice) that individuals respond to. (Contrast with *projective personality tests.*)

Minnesota Multiphasic Personality Inventory (MMPI-2) The revised version of a widely used objective test for assessing psychiatric disorders and personality.

1986). The MMPI-2 can also be scored for a variety of newer scales that measure characteristics such as dominance, social responsibility, college maladjustment, and posttraumatic stress disorder (Arita & Baer, 1998; Barthlow et al., 1999; Graham, 1990). By using the new scales along with the traditional ones, a mental health professional can develop a very comprehensive description of an individual.

A version of the MMPI has also been designed specifically for use with adolescents. This test is known as the **MMPI-A.** It has somewhat fewer items, the items are written at a lower reading level (6th grade), and the test measures topics such as family problems that are particularly relevant for understanding adolescents.

There are many objective tests, and they are one of the most efficient and effective means of collecting data about individuals. However, the quality of a test rests on the adequacy of the norms used in building it. For example, when the MMPI-2 was being developed, did the items on the Schizophrenia scale consistently differentiate between individuals who did and did not have schizophrenia? Unfortunately, many tests are published in which the items look good (i.e., they have *face validity*), but they do not actually do what they are supposed to do (i.e., they do not have *empirical validity*). The MMPI-2 is not a perfect test, but as you will see later, it is one of the most helpful measures for describing and diagnosing individuals (Garb, Florio, & Grove, 1998; Helmes & Reddon, 1993).

Projective Personality Tests. In psychology the term **projection** refers to the fact that we often attribute our own personality characteristics and feelings to other people or to inanimate stimuli such as inkblots; that is, we project our traits much like a motion picture projector projects images on a screen. For example, an angry individual might see other people as angry or might interpret an inkblot as an enraged monster. We may also project the *cause* of our feelings; for example, a frightened individual may see others as frightening (i.e., hostile).

Projective personality tests aim to assess what an individual projects onto others. In theory, if we know what the individual projects, we will know what the individual is like and how he or she sees the world. When taking a projective test, the individual is shown various stimuli, such as inkblots or pictures of people, and is then asked to tell what the inkblots look like or what is going on in the picture. Because the inkblots are really only inkblots and because the pictures do not tell a particular story, what the individual sees in the inkblots and pictures supposedly derives from the projection of the individual's own traits, needs, and conflicts. It is also believed that because there are no clearly right or wrong answers, it is difficult to fake answers on projective tests.

The best-known projective test is the **Rorschach** (ROR-shok) **test,** which was developed by Herman Rorschach after he noticed that his children saw different things when they looked at the same clouds (Rorschach, 1942). The Rorschach consists of 10 cards, each with one inkblot printed on it. Two inkblots like those in the Rorschach are presented in Figure 4.4. Five of the cards have inkblots done in shades of black and gray, and five have inkblots done with different colored inks. An individual being tested is given one card at a time and asked to tell the test administrator what he or she sees in that inkblot or what the inkblot represents.

Responses to the Rorschach are scored in two ways. First, attention is given to the content of what the individual saw in the inkblot. For example, responses involving snarling monsters or squashed bugs might be interpreted as suggesting that the individual is hostile or sees the world as a hostile place, whereas responses involving a smiling cat or

FIGURE 4.4

Two inkblots like those on the Rorschach

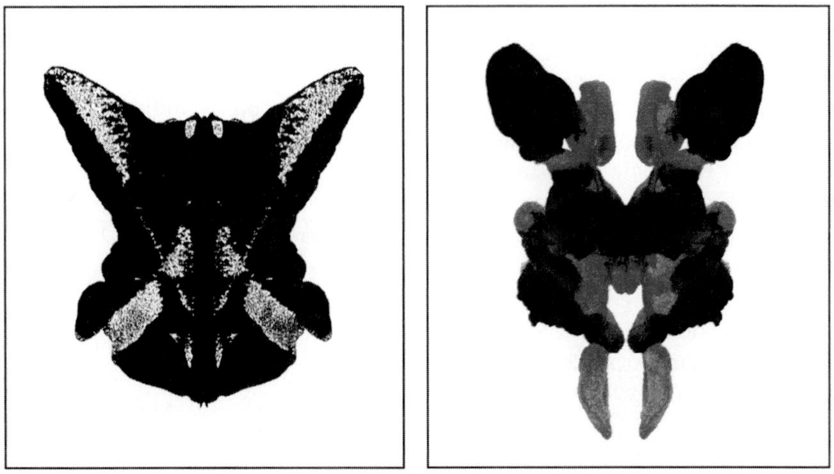

flowers could be interpreted as suggesting that the individual is friendly and sees the world as a pleasant place.

Second, attention is given to what aspect of the inkblot led the individual to see what he or she saw. For example, does the actual shape of the inkblot justify what was seen? (Can you see a lobster in the blot on the right side of Figure 4.4?) If the shape justifies the response, the response is considered to be an appropriate or healthy one, and it is scored F+ (F stands for the form, or shape, of the object). However, if the response cannot be justified by the shape of the inkblot, it suggests that the individual does not perceive the world accurately and is not in touch with reality. In that case the response is scored F–. There are lists of acceptable responses for each card, but the judgment concerning whether a response can be justified is usually made by the test administrator; that is, if the test administrator can see what the client sees the response is justified, but if the administrator cannot see what the client sees, the response is not justified. We do not expect any individual to give all F+ responses, but if the proportion of F+ responses falls below 60%, there is reason for concern over the degree to which the individual is in contact with reality.

The use of color in making responses is believed to be important because it supposedly reflects the amount of emotion the individual has. For example, an individual who sees brightly colored flowers in Figure 4.4 supposedly has more emotion than an individual who sees only the shape of the flowers. It is also believed that how an individual uses color reflects how the individual deals with emotion. For example, if an individual gives appropriate responses (F+) to cards that are black and white but poor responses (F–) to cards that contain color, it is suspected that when confronted with emotions (color), the individual is overwhelmed and no longer functions well. Furthermore, if an individual takes longer to respond to a colored card or cannot think of a response for a colored card, that reaction is called "color shock," and it is interpreted as meaning that the individual is overwhelmed by emotion and cannot function when faced with emotion.

Numerous other factors are also taken into consideration when scoring responses to the Rorschach. For example, using the shades of gray in interpreting the inkblots supposedly reflects depression, and seeing motion, such as "a person running," is interpreted as reflecting a rich fantasy life. (For more information on scoring, see Beck et al., 1961; Exner, 1993; Exner & Weiner, 1994; Klopfer, 1962.)

The Rorschach test is widely used, but serious questions have been raised about its validity and value (Garb et al., 1998; Hunsley & Bailey, 1999; Sechrest, Stickle, & Stewart, 1998; Wood, Nezworski, & Stejskal, 1996a, 1996b, 1997). One problem is that the interpretations of the responses are based on assumptions that may not be true. For example, the scoring assumes that the use of color in a response reflects emotion, but there is little evidence for this assump-tion. Critics also point out that if the test has value, using it in combination with other tests should increase the accuracy of the assessments made, but this is not what happens. On the contrary, when the Rorschach test is used in combination with demographic information such as age, sex, social class, and personal history, assessments are less accurate than when they are based only on the demographic information (see, for example, Garb, 1985). In other words, the Rorschach test appears to introduce errors into assessment, errors that apparently stem from the incorrect assumptions on which the scoring of the Rorschach is based.

Another widely used projective test is the **Thematic Apperception Test,** usually referred to simply as the **TAT** (Murray, 1943). The TAT consists of a series of pictures about which individuals are asked to make up stories. Figure 4.5 is a picture from the TAT. Theoretically, the stories an individual tells reflect the themes, problems, conflicts, and characters that are important in the individual's life.

Like the Rorschach, the TAT has a number of problems that undermine its usefulness. The most serious problem is that the TAT only measures traits that individuals know they have; that is, there is no evidence that the TAT measures traits of which individuals are unaware (Holmes, 1968, 1981). For example, a hostile individual who believes that he or she is hostile will project hostility on the TAT, but a hostile individual who is not aware that he or she is hostile will not project hostility on the TAT at a rate any greater than individuals who are not hostile. The fact that the TAT measures only conscious characteristics greatly limits its usefulness, and the results of a variety of investigations have revealed that simple self-reports are usually more effective than TAT stories for measuring personality (e.g., Holmes, 1971; Holmes & Tyler, 1968). For example, freshmen students' self-ratings of their levels of motivation were better predictors of their subsequent grades than were ratings of their motivation based on their TAT responses.

MMPI-A A form of the Minnesota Multiphasic Personality Inventory designed for use with adolescents.

projection An individual's attribution of his or her own personality characteristics and feelings to other people or to inanimate stimuli, such as inkblots.

projective personality tests Tests in which individuals are shown ambiguous stimuli (e.g., inkblots, pictures of people, incomplete sentences) and asked to talk about them or complete them. (Contrast with *objective personality tests*.)

Rorschach test A projective personality test in which the individual tells what he or she sees in a series of inkblots.

Thematic Apperception Test (TAT) A projective personality test in which the individual makes up stories about what is going on in a series of pictures.

FIGURE 4.5

A picture from the Thematic Apperception Test (TAT)

Source: Reprinted by permission of the publishers from Henry A. Murray, *Thematic Apperception Test,* Cambridge, Mass.: Harvard University Press, Copyright © 1943 by the President and Fellows of Harvard College, © 1971 by Henry A. Murray.

Another problem with the TAT is that individuals can fake their responses (Holmes, 1971). For example, in one investigation students took the TAT twice, once responding honestly and once trying to hide their real personalities. Both sets of stories were then read by psychologists who came up with completely different personality interpretations for the two sets. Furthermore, the psychologists could not identify which stories were the honest ones and which were the fakes!

Finally, even when an individual is not faking, there is a problem with interpreting the stories because it is difficult to determine whether individuals are projecting *their traits* or the *causes of their traits.* For example, if an individual describes people in the stories as hostile, does it mean that the individual *is hostile,* or does it mean that the individual *is afraid* because he or she sees other people as hostile?

Another projective test is the **Incomplete Sentences Test** (Rotter & Rafferty, 1950), in which the individual is given a sheet with incomplete sentences such as "My mother . . . ," "What bothers me is that . . . ," and "Other people . . . ." The individual then completes the sentence with whatever comes to mind first. In another projective test, the **Draw-A-**

Person Test, the individual is asked to draw a person (Machover, 1949), and the **House-Tree-Person Test** asks the individual to draw a house, a tree, and a person (Buck, 1948). There is also a children's version of the TAT known as the **Children's Apperception Test** or **CAT** (Bellak, 1954). Most of these tests do not have formal scoring procedures. Instead, interpretations are dependent on the subjective judgments and clinical intuition of the tester.

For years a hot debate has raged over the value of projective tests. On the one hand, critics have argued that research has revealed very little evidence that these tests help in making clinical judgments but has instead shown that the tests may actually lead to errors (as I mentioned with regard to the Rorschach). On the other hand, advocates have argued that clinical experience with the tests suggests that they are revealing and helpful, and that lack of empirical evidence for their usefulness is the result of the insensitivity of the research methods used to assess them. An alternative position is taken by some users of the tests who agree with the critics that the tests are without empirical support but continue to use them as a means of facilitating the interview process, much as "icebreakers" are used at parties. The debate over the value of projective personality tests has been going on for years, and although these tests are still widely used, they are considered much less important now than they were some years ago.

Intelligence Tests. Intelligence tests often play an important role in determining a diagnosis and developing a treatment plan; for example, they can be used to help decide whether an individual's problems are due to mental retardation. The results of intelligence tests can also be used to determine what type of therapy will be most effective; for example, if testing reveals that an individual has poor reasoning skills, it might be concluded that traditional psychotherapy will not be an effective treatment approach.

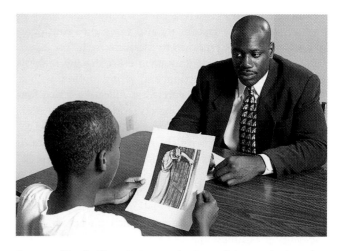

A person taking the Thematic Apperception Test makes up stories that reflect underlying themes and problems from his or her life.

Intelligence tests are used to help determine a diagnosis and develop a treatment plan.

FIGURE 4.6

Block design is one subtest used to measure intelligence.

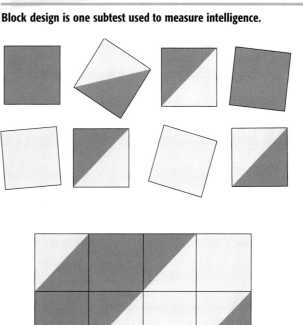

The intelligence tests used in clinical settings usually involve one-on-one interactions between an individual and an examiner during which the individual performs a series of tasks such as math problems and puzzles. These tests may take 2 hours or more to complete. They allow for the assessment of various abilities and provide the examiner with an opportunity to watch the individual work so that the examiner can determine the reasons for poor performance and take them into consideration. For example, individuals who are excessively anxious or depressed may perform at levels below their actual ability, and this can be taken into consideration when interpreting the results and predicting future performance.

Most intelligence tests contain subscales designed to measure **verbal intelligence** and **performance intelligence.** With the **Wechsler Adult Intelligence Scale, Revised edition (WAIS-R),** verbal intelligence is measured with six subtests:

1. Information (e.g., "How far is it from New York to San Francisco?")
2. Comprehension (e.g., "Why do we have laws?")
3. Arithmetic (e.g., "A shirt that usually sells for $30 is reduced in price by 15% during a sale. What does the shirt cost during the sale?")
4. Similarities (e.g., "How are a pound and an inch alike?")
5. Digit Span (e.g., "Repeat the following list of numbers from memory: 2, 7, 9, 4, 8.")
6. Vocabulary (e.g., "What does the word *overture* mean?")

Performance intelligence is measured with five subtests:

1. Picture Completion (looking at pictures of objects and determining what parts are missing)
2. Block Design (arranging blocks to form designs; see Figure 4.6)
3. Picture Arrangement (arranging a set of pictures to make a story)
4. Object Assembly (putting puzzles together)
5. Digit Symbol (learning to associate numbers with various symbols)

The WAIS-R is the most widely used test for individuals over 16 years of age. For school-age children there is the

Incomplete Sentences Test A projective personality test in which an individual completes sentences such as "What makes me most angry is . . . ."

Draw-A-Person Test A projective personality test in which an individual draws a person.

House-Tree-Person Test A projective personality test in which an individual draws a house, a tree, and a person.

Children's Apperception Test (CAT) A children's version of the Thematic Apperception Test.

verbal intelligence A person's ability to define words, provide information, explain similarities, do arithmetic and remember lists of numbers.

performance intelligence Intelligence based on a person's ability to perform tasks such as putting a puzzle together and arranging colored blocks to make a design.

Wechsler Adult Intelligence Scale, Revised edition (WAIS-R) A widely used individual intelligence test for people over 16 years of age.

Wechsler Intelligence Scale for Children, Third edition, known as the **WISC-III,** and for preschoolers there is the **Wechsler Preschool-Primary Scale of Intelligence,** known as the **WPPSI.** The **Stanford-Binet test** can also be used with children. Because of the importance of measuring intelligence and because of the necessity that intelligence tests be unbiased with regard to culture or social class, new tests of intelligence are being developed constantly.

Individual intelligence tests are very reliable and effective for predicting school performance (e.g., Canivez & Watkins, 1998). Because they involve reasoning and problem solving, they can also be helpful for predicting performance in the real world.

Neuropsychological Tests. When it is suspected that an individual is suffering from some sort of organic brain damage, **neuropsychological tests** may be used to identify the location and nature of the damage (Nelson & Adams, 1997). Such testing is based on the fact that different abilities are located in different areas in the brain. Therefore, by measuring the pattern of an individual's abilities and disabilities, it is possible to make inferences about the location and extent of the brain damage. Some neuropsychological tests measure as many as 14 different abilities and may require a day to complete. The tests include such activities as puzzles that must be done while blindfolded, verbal tasks involving naming objects and concepts, and reaction-time tasks. The two most frequently used neuropsychological tests are the

---

Wechsler Intelligence Scale for Children, Third edition (WISC-III)   A widely used individual intelligence test for children.

Wechsler Preschool-Primary Scale of Intelligence (WPPSI) A widely used individual intelligence test for preschoolers.

Stanford-Binet test   An early but still widely used individual intelligence test for children.

neuropsychological tests   Tests that are used to determine the location and nature of brain damage.

Halstead-Reitan Neuropsychology Battery   A neuropsychological test for assessing brain damage.

Luria-Nebraska Battery   A neuropsychological test for assessing brain damage.

computerized axial tomography (CT scan)   A technique that produces images of very thin "slices" of internal body parts, particularly the brain.

magnetic resonance imaging (MRI)   A technique that yields images of very thin "slices" of internal body parts, particularly the brain.

electroencephalograph (EEG)   A technique used to record electrical activity in the brain.

positron emission tomography (PET scan)   A technique that measures brain activity by recording the location of radioactive isotopes that have bound to chemicals found in the brain.

sphygmomanometer   A device used to measure blood pressure.

Halstead-Reitan Neuropsychology Battery and the **Luria-Nebraska Battery.**

What may be a more important function than locating the site of the damage is identifying the nature of the resulting disability, such as memory loss, loss of ability to form concepts, or problems with motor coordination. Identifying the disability is important in terms of designing a treatment program (i.e., deciding what abilities need to be retrained or compensated for) and making plans for the individual's future functioning (i.e., deciding how much help this individual will need in daily living).

Physiological Tests

As you learned in Chapter 3, many abnormal behaviors are due to problems with structures in the brain or to problems with the levels of activity in various areas of the brain. For example, some symptoms of schizophrenia are attributable to the fact that certain parts of the brain have not developed properly, whereas other symptoms occur because some areas of the brain are overactive. For many years it was not possible to see the structures of the live brain or to measure its activity, but there are now a variety of techniques for doing so. These techniques have greatly enhanced the diagnosis of some types of abnormal behavior.

Measuring Brain Structures. The first technique used to assess the structures in the brain was the X-ray. Today X-rays have been largely replaced by **computerized axial tomography** (to-MOG-ruh-fee), better known as the **CT scan,** and by **magnetic resonance imaging,** better known as **MRI.** These techniques are similar to X-rays in that they produce images of internal organs, such as the brain. However, they differ from X-rays in that rather than producing an image that shows all of the overlapping parts of the brain, CT and MRI techniques produce pictures of very thin "slices" of the brain; therefore one part of the brain cannot hide other parts behind it. An MRI of the human brain is presented in Figure 4.7.

Measuring Brain Activity. The first technique used to measure electrical activity in the brain was the **electroencephalograph** (e-lek-tro-en-SEF-uh-lo-graf), which is usually called an **EEG.** With this technique electrodes are placed at numerous locations on the skull, and they detect underlying electrical activity in the brain. The procedure is analogous to putting your ear to the outside wall of a factory and listening to the sounds coming from inside in an attempt to determine which machines are running and how fast they are running; it works, but it is a rather primitive method.

A more recent and more sophisticated technique for measuring brain activity is **positron emission tomography,** which is usually referred to as a **PET scan.** With this technique an *isotope* (radioactive agent) that binds to a particular chemical in the brain, such as glucose (blood sugar) or a neurotransmitter, is administered to the patient. Then recording where the isotope goes reveals the location and

FIGURE 4.7

An MRI scan of the brain
MRI scans, such as the one shown here, and CT scans have largely replaced X-rays as the best techniques to assess the structures in the brain.

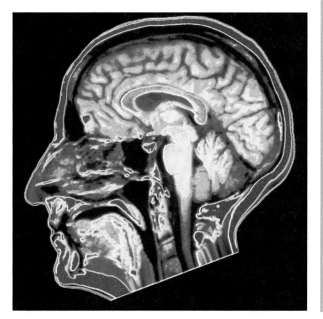

activity of the relevant chemical. For example, if more glucose is detected in a particular area of the brain, more activity must be going on in that area because glucose is what fuels activity. The location of the isotope can be recorded because isotopes emit positrons, which can be detected with equipment sensitive to radioactivity—hence the name *positron emission tomography*. The PET scan results in diagrams of activity in the brain, taken *one slice at a time;* indeed, the word *tomography* comes from a Greek word

meaning "section." PET scans reflecting glucose metabolism (energy use) in the brain of a patient during manic and depressed periods are presented in Figure 9.1. As you can see in that figure, certain areas of the brain are more active during the manic period than during the depressed period.

Measuring Physiological Reactions. It is sometimes important to measure physiological reactions; for example, high blood pressure can be an indicator of stress or anxiety. Blood pressure is measured with a **sphygmomanometer** (sfig-mo-muh-NOM-uh-tur). The principle on which the sphygmomanometer is based is quite simple. An inflatable cuff is wrapped around the person's arm just above the elbow and is inflated until the pressure in the cuff is high enough to pinch off the arteries that carry blood down the arm to the hand. Then the pressure in the cuff is slowly reduced while the technician monitors the pressure and listens for a pulse in the artery just below the cuff. When the first pulse is able to get through, it means that the blood pressure is about the same as the pressure in the cuff, so the pressure in the cuff is noted and used as the measure of the systolic (sis-TOL-ik) blood pressure.

Another frequently used measure of anxiety is the amount of moisture produced by the skin; arousal causes the hands to become damp. *Skin conductance* is measured by putting electrodes on two fingers and passing a tiny electrical current (too small to be felt) from one electrode to the other. If the hands are moist, more of the current can get from one electrode to the other, and the amount of current that gets to the second electrode can be used as a measure of moisture and arousal. The bottom (smooth) line in Figure 4.8 shows the sudden change in the skin's conduction of current when a "dirty" word made the individual anxious (see point 1). When the individual heard a neutral word, there was no increase (see point 2). The top line in Figure 4.8 is a measure of the blood flowing into the finger

FIGURE 4.8

Increases in anxiety lead to increases in skin moisture and increases in skin conductance.
At point 1 the individual heard a "dirty" word; at point 2 the individual heard a neutral word. Increases in anxiety also reduce blood flow to the hands (see the decrease in the size of pulse spikes in the top line).

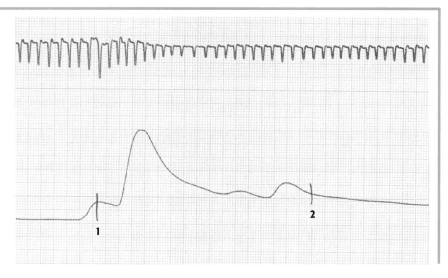

with each pulse, and as you can see, the amount of blood decreases when the individual becomes anxious. It is this decrease in blood that may make your hands feel cold when you are anxious. (Note that unlike skin conductance, blood flow does not return to its baseline quickly, and therefore it is a less useful measure.) With this discussion as background, we can next consider some interesting and sometimes controversial issues associated with diagnostic testing.

Issues Concerning Diagnostic Methods

Considerable progress has been made in the development of diagnostic methods, but a number of basic issues that remain problematic deserve comment.

Measurement of Transient versus Enduring Traits

Assume that you administer the same personality test to the same individual on two separate occasions one month apart and that the test yields very different results on the two occasions. The difference in results poses a problem because it appears to make the results of the first administration of the test useless for predicting the individual's future behavior (e.g., his or her test scores on the second occasion). Is there something wrong with the test? Possibly, but possibly not. A paradox associated with personality testing is that even if a test is exceptionally effective for assessing thoughts and feelings at the time it is given, it may not be effective for explaining past behavior or predicting future behavior. This is because some aspects of personality (and abnormality) can change over time, and therefore what is measured today may not have existed earlier or may not exist later. Some clinicians defend projective tests that are criticized for being unreliable (yielding different results at different times) by suggesting that the tests are reliable but that the individuals being tested have changed and the tests have picked that up. However, even if it were true that the tests are sensitive to such changes and this is why they appear to be unreliable, the fact remains that the tests do not help with understanding past behavior or predicting future behavior.

Traits versus Situations for Predicting Behavior

Our diagnostic procedures are designed to assess personality traits such as hostility, anxiety, and sociability so we can

---

use those traits to explain past behavior and predict future behavior. However, it has been argued that behavior is determined by *situational factors* rather than personality traits (Mischel, 1990). For example, your professor may be reserved and constrained in class but may be outgoing and uninhibited at a social gathering. Similarly, your friend may be relaxed and confident when alone but extremely anxious and fearful when in groups. In these cases the individuals' behaviors are strongly influenced by the social context; we could not use their behavior in one context to predict their behavior in another context.

There has been considerable controversy over the question of whether traits or situations are more important for determining behavior, but it now appears that both factors influence behavior. Specifically, it appears that the *level* of the trait and the *level* of the situational demands determine which will be the controlling factor. For example, an individual with a high level of hostility will probably behave in a hostile manner regardless of the situation (i.e., he or she will not be influenced by the situation), whereas an individual with a low level of hostility will behave in a hostile manner only in situations that call for hostility (i.e., he or she will be influenced by the situation). Obviously, traits *and* situations as well as the interactions between them must be considered in attempting to understand behavior.

Unfortunately, most diagnostic tests do not take the situation in which the test is being administered into account. Furthermore, most diagnoses are made in professional offices, and because those offices are generally very different from the settings in which persons live, behaviors observed and measured there may not be particularly helpful for predicting real-life behaviors.

Comorbidity

An individual can suffer from two or more psychological disorders (e.g., depression and schizophrenia) at the same time, just as an individual may suffer from two or more physical disorders (e.g., diabetes and pneumonia) at the same time. The co-occurrence of two or more disorders is called **comorbidity.** (The word *morbid* refers to disease, and *morbidity* refers to the occurrence of disease, so *comorbidity* means the co-occurrence of two or more diseases.) Rates of comorbidity among some psychological disorders can be as high as 70%, so you should not be surprised if an individual's symptoms fit more than one diagnosis (Barsky, 1992; Brady & Kendall, 1992; Kendall, 1992; Sanderson et al., 1990).

There are three explanations for comorbidity, and each has different implications. First, it is possible that some individuals suffer from two disorders simply *by chance* and there is no connection between the two disorders. Second, it is possible that *one disorder leads to another.* For example, having an eating disorder may cause an individual to

---

comorbidity   The co-occurrence of two or more disorders in a single individual.

become depressed. Third, it may be that the *two disorders stem from a common cause.* For example, mood and appetite are both controlled by the same area of the brain, so a problem in that area could result in the comorbidity of depression and an eating disorder. Thus, we must recognize that comorbidity occurs and must be familiar with patterns of comorbidity because they may provide clues to the causes of some disorders.

Comorbidity also has important implications for treatment. If you assume that two disorders co-occurred by chance, you will treat them separately; if you assume that one led to another, you will treat the primary disorder; and if you assume that the disorders stem from a common cause, you will treat the cause. Finally, comorbidity may influence prognosis because the existence of one disorder may make the treatment of another disorder more or less difficult. For example, personality disorders may hinder the treatment of depression (Shea, Widiger, & Klein, 1992).

Subjectivity, Suggestion, and Diagnostic Fads

Despite all the attempts to make the diagnostic system objective, it still embodies a great deal of subjectivity, and this leads to errors in diagnoses. The subjectivity is not in what symptoms are necessary for a particular diagnosis, because the symptoms have been clearly laid out in *DSM-IV* and *ICD-10.* Rather the subjectivity lies in the degree to which the mental health professionals who are making the diagnoses look for particular symptoms, interpret ambiguous behaviors as symptoms, or even suggest symptoms to the individual. For example, one colleague of mine sees the symptoms of multiple personality disorder in virtually every patient he sees, whereas most mental health professionals never see one patient with a multiple personality disorder in their entire careers (see Chapter 7). Do individuals with multiple personality disorders somehow seek out my colleague, are other therapists missing the diagnosis, or is my colleague biased in his probing for and interpretation of symptoms? I suspect that my colleague is biased. Similarly, the staff in one hospital in which I worked was very interested in schizophrenia, whereas in a nearby hospital bipolar disorder (manic depression) was of most interest. Each time patients were transferred between the two hospitals, their diagnoses were changed. Did the patients' symptoms and disorders change on the trip between the two hospitals? I doubt it.

It should also be noted that there are diagnostic fads, which cause a particular diagnosis to be popular and widely used for a time, only to taper off later. Obsessive-compulsive disorder provides a good case in point. In a recent 20-year period there was an increase of more than 500% in the number of publications on that disorder, and in the same period the use of that diagnosis in one leading hospital increased by 400% (Stoll, Tohen, & Baldessarini, 1992).

FIGURE 4.9

Publications on obsessive-compulsive disorder and diagnoses of the disorder increased rapidly during the 1980s.

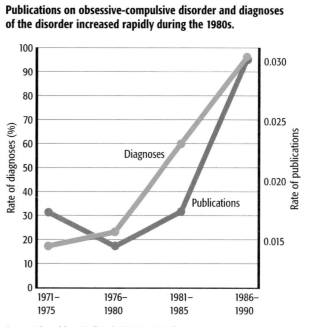

Source: Adapted from Stoll et al. (1992), p. 639, Figure 1.

Those findings are reflected in Figure 4.9. Clearly diagnoses can be influenced by the specific interests of an individual who makes a diagnosis and by general fads that occasionally sweep through the profession. Unfortunately, both of those factors can reduce the validity of diagnoses.

Sociocultural Factors

It is important to realize that individuals from lower socioeconomic classes or ethnic minority groups are often less likely to get into the mental health system than other individuals; see Figure 4.10 (on p. 104) (Mason & Gibbs, 1992; Paradis, Hatch, & Friedman 1994). That is the case despite the fact that individuals from these groups sometimes have high rates of psychiatric disorders. Why is that? Let's consider some possibilities.

Limited Access or Use. One reason poor and ethnic minority individuals are underrepresented in the mental health system is that they are often less likely to come in for help. That occurs because they may (1) be less aware of the services that are available, (2) be less able to afford the services, (3) be more concerned about the stigma associated with seeking psychiatric help, (4) be more likely to view problems as physical rather than psychological, (5) have cultural backgrounds that provide nonpsychological explanations for their symptoms (e.g., possession by a spirit), or (6) use

FIGURE 4.10

Members of minority groups are underrepresented in the mental health care system.

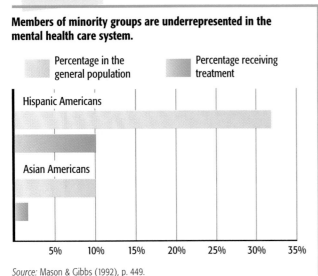

■ Percentage in the general population   ■ Percentage receiving treatment

Hispanic Americans

Asian Americans

5%   10%   15%   20%   25%   30%   35%

Source: Mason & Gibbs (1992), p. 449.

folk healers and culturally based remedies such as exorcism instead of psychological treatments. To overcome these obstacles programs are being introduced to educate individuals about psychological problems and treatments. Attempts are also being made to make affordable services available in the communities in which the individuals live (see the discussion of community mental health centers in Chapter 19). A federal program begun some years ago has made most public buildings in the United States accessible to individuals with physical disabilities by eliminating physical obstacles and constructing wheelchair ramps; now we must focus on eliminating cultural obstacles and constructing "psychological ramps" to the treatment system.

Bias in Diagnostic Procedures. Unfortunately, getting poor individuals and members of ethnic minority groups "into the building" is only half the problem, because they may still face a problem—bias in diagnostic procedures. That bias can come in numerous forms, but the most obvious is *language.* Describing psychiatric symptoms is always difficult, but doing so in an unfamiliar language is almost impossible. (Imagine trying to explain your anxieties, depression, or hallucinations to someone in a foreign language you barely know!) Thus, it is essential that individuals who conduct diagnostic evaluations be able to speak the language of the individuals they are evaluating. Similarly, it is necessary to have tests that are printed in the language of the individuals who are being evaluated (Barbee, 1992). Fortunately, progress is being made in this area; for example, the MMPI is now available in different languages, and these new forms appear to be effective (Cheung & Ho,

1997; Lucio, Reyes-Lagunes, & Scott, 1994; Timbrook & Graham, 1994). Furthermore, a review of 25 studies over a period of 31 years indicated that the MMPI does not unfairly portray African Americans or Hispanic Americans as suffering from more disorders than their European American counterparts (Hall, Bansal, & Lopez, 1999).

A more subtle bias occurs when the individual who is conducting the evaluation does not thoroughly understand the culture of the person being evaluated, because this lack of understanding can lead to misdiagnoses (Cueller, 1998; Garb, 1997; Garretson, 1993; Good, 1992; Malgady & Constantino, 1998; Whaley, 1997). This was illustrated by the case of a Guyanese woman who was suffering from panic attacks and agoraphobia. (*Panic attacks* are brief but very intense feelings of anxiety that are associated with rapid heart rates, dizziness, and feelings that one is about to die; *agoraphobia* is a fear of going outside because something embarrassing might happen, such as a panic attack.) In describing her symptoms the woman said:

> I feel like I'm going to die. . . . I worry it's not natural . . . not natural causes, evil like someone put a curse on me. . . . I'm afraid people might look at me and ridicule me because of how I look, people might talk about me."
> (Paradis et al., 1994, p. 611)

The woman's mention of a curse, which was consistent with her cultural beliefs, led the clinician to conclude, "The patient's bizarre delusion of an evil spirit inside her body [and] her paranoid delusions of people thinking she is ugly and laughing at her . . . all speak for the diagnosis of schizophrenia" (p. 611). In this case, then, what would ordinarily be diagnosed as a pair of anxiety disorders (panic and

For a variety of reasons, including limited access and bias in diagnostic procedures, individuals from racial and ethnic minority groups are often less likely than other individuals to get into the mental health system. To overcome these obstacles programs are being introduced to educate individuals about psychological problems and treatment.

agoraphobia) was erroneously diagnosed as a very serious psychotic disorder (schizophrenia) because of the cultural insensitivity of the interviewer. Similarly, an Indian psychiatrist misdiagnosed a man as psychotic because in the interview the man talked about a woman who flew through the sky holding an umbrella. Of course, the woman was Mary Poppins, but because the psychiatrist was not familiar with the story, he assumed that the man was psychotic! The problem is that different cultures have different "realities," and mental health professionals must be sensitive to those differences before diagnosing an individual as being "out of touch."

In other cases an interviewer may be biased against seeing psychological problems in minority group members. For example, in one study it was found that African Americans who washed their hands frequently because they suffered from obsessive-compulsive disorder were not diagnosed as having a psychiatric disorder but instead were diagnosed as having skin conditions and were sent to dermatologists for treatment (Friedman et al., 1993). Problems such as these will be overcome when mental health professionals receive more training in cross-cultural and minority issues and when the profession attains more ethnic diversity.

THINKING CRITICALLY
Questions about Diagnostic Techniques

1. *What type of information is most helpful in making diagnoses?* In this section you learned that information for making diagnoses can be obtained with a variety of strategies including interviews, observations, objective personality tests, projective personality tests, and physiological measures. But what information is most helpful in making diagnoses? To answer this question researchers have given clinicians different types of information about individuals and then asked them to make judgments about the individuals. These investigations revealed some surprising findings (Garb, 1985). For example, you might assume that watching the videotape of an interview with an individual would yield better judgments and predictions than simply reading a transcript of the interview because the clinicians could take into account the individual's gestures, vocal quality, and demeanor. However, that was not the case. Clinicians who only read the transcript made more accurate predictions than did clinicians who only watched the videotape. Similarly, clinicians were more accurate in making judgments when they were given only demographic information than when they were given both demographic information and projective test (Rorschach, TAT) responses. These findings suggest that the visual and auditory cues

gained in interviews may distract the interviewer from the content of the interview that is most important, and this may lead to inaccurate interpretations of interview behavior and projective test responses and, in turn, to errors in diagnoses.

In sharp contrast to these findings are results indicating that the addition of MMPI responses to demographic data consistently led to more valid personality assessments. Furthermore, the addition of neuropsychological test results (Halstead-Reitan battery) to scores from general IQ tests greatly increased the validity of clinical judgments concerning brain damage. These results suggest that the most helpful information is information that is directly relevant and that does not require much interpretation, thus leaving little room for erroneous assumptions. The fact that the MMPI has consistently been found to add to the accuracy of predictions is particularly interesting because the MMPI is the least expensive and least time-consuming means of collecting information; the patient simply fills out a questionnaire, and the responses can be quickly and inexpensively scored by computer.

This point is clearly illustrated by an experience I had in a diagnostic case conference some years ago, in which a group of psychiatrists, psychologists, nurses, and social workers were discussing the question of whether a particular patient was homosexual. (At the time homosexuality was against the law, and it was assumed that the patient might be hiding his sexual orientation and that his orientation might have some bearing on his current problems.) Many scholarly theories and observations were offered, during which one psychologist got bored and fell asleep. The chief of staff became somewhat annoyed with the sleeper and in a loud voice said, "And Doctor Roberts, what do *you* think?" The psychologist jerked back to wakefulness and replied, "I, er, oh, he is a homosexual." The chief of staff challenged him by saying, "And what makes you think so?" To which the psychologist calmly replied, "I gave him an MMPI, and on every question that asked about homosexuality, he answered yes." Case closed! The point here is that it is best to use information *directly relevant* to the diagnosis and that direct measures such as self-reports or observations are often better than responses to projective tests, which require inferences or theories to connect them to the behaviors in question.

2. *Are highly trained mental health professionals more accurate than statistical formulas in making predictions about people?* Missing in our discussion to this point is a consideration of the individual who uses test results to make diagnoses or predictions about people. The question to be asked here is, are highly trained professionals more effective in making predictions from test results than relatively simple statistical formulas into which the test results are simply inserted? You might be surprised that I am even asking this question, because it is widely assumed that diagnostic decisions must be made by trained professionals, but you may be even more surprised at the answer.

In the research on the effectiveness of clinical versus statistical prediction, information about individuals is collected and then either given to a group of professionals who use it to make predictions about the individuals or inserted into formulas that are used to make predictions (the formulas generate scores that determine decisions, much like your test scores determine your grade in a course). The effectiveness of using clinical as opposed to statistical procedures to make predictions has been evaluated for a wide variety of research areas, including what diagnoses individuals will receive; how well individuals will perform in college, in medical school, or in the military; the likelihood that individuals will commit violent acts; the likelihood that individuals will commit other crimes after being paroled; and the intellectual performance of individuals following brain damage. The information that has been used to make those predictions has included such data as the results of psychological tests, the results of IQ tests, school records, history of drug use, and demographic factors such as age, gender, and social class.

Approximately 150 studies have been completed on the question of the accuracy of clinical versus statistical prediction, and the surprising finding is that in almost every study the *statistical formulas resulted in more accurate predictions than the clinical judgments* (Dawes, 1994; Dawes, Faust, & Meehl, 1989; Meehl, 1997). In some studies the clinicians had the same information that was used in the formulas; in other studies the clinicians had *more* information, but the results were the same—the formulas resulted in more accurate predictions. Furthermore, in some studies the clinicians were even given the results of the statistical predictions to use in making their own judgments, but whenever the clinicians attempted to "improve" on the statistical predictions, the accuracy of their predictions went down. It is also interesting to note that the poor performance of the clinicians was not due to the inclusion of some inept clinicians who brought the overall performance level down. Indeed, when individual performances were examined, even the clinicians who did *best* did not do better than the statistical formulas.

Why don't the professionals do better? There seem to be two answers to this. The first is that statistical formulas can handle *more information* at one time than a human can. Specifically, humans can deal with only about seven pieces of information at one time. However, predictions often require the consideration of many more pieces of information, and formulas do not have a limit in terms of the amount of information they can handle. The second reason why formulas perform better is that some pieces of information are more important to a given prediction than other pieces and so various pieces must be given different

weights. While humans are not particularly good at doing that, it can be done easily with formulas.

Many professionals attempt to deny or ignore the evidence concerning the effectiveness of statistical prediction because they find it threatening, but that should not be the case. What is important is that humans have been able to build statistical formulas that can do certain things better than we can do them ourselves. Not only do the formulas serve as effective tools, but they also free us up to do other things that formulas cannot do. Analogously, the fact that computers can do computations faster and better than we can in our heads does not threaten or diminish us; rather we accept computers as tools that help us work more effectively. (Do you calculate square roots in your head, or do you do them quickly on a calculator so that you can get on to the more important aspects of the problem?) The statistical approach to prediction is slow in coming, but it is undoubtedly the way of the future.

From the foregoing discussion it should be clear that diagnoses are essential for describing individuals and treating psychiatric disorders but that the process of arriving at valid diagnoses is difficult and fraught with problems. With this material as background, we can now consider the methods used for studying abnormal behavior.

TOPIC II
Research Methods

To test the effects of a new antidepressant drug, an investigator first asked 100 depressed patients whether they were interested in trying the drug. The 60 patients who said they were interested were then given the new drug, whereas the other 40 patients continued taking an older drug that they had been using for some time. Three months later the investigator rated the degree to which the patients were depressed, and those who took the new drug got lower scores. The investigator concluded that the new drug was more effective than the older drug in reducing depression. Was that conclusion justified? If not, why not?

Professor Simpson wants to know whether long-term stress causes depression. Because it is not possible to create long-term stress in a laboratory, the professor compared the levels of depression in individuals who were either employed or unemployed and under a lot of financial stress. She found that the unemployed individuals were more depressed. Can she definitely conclude that the stress of unemployment causes depression? If not, why not?

Professor Wright collected data on intelligence and height from 1,000 students and then computed a correlation coefficient to see if intelligence was related to height. The correlation was

+.10, which was statistically significant. Given this finding, what can the professor conclude about the relationship between intelligence and height, and is the relationship important? What do we mean when we say that a finding is "significant"?

Finding the cause of a particular type of abnormal behavior is like solving a complex mystery, and research methods are the strategies we use to evaluate the clues in the mystery. Understanding research methods will help you evaluate the information about abnormal behavior contained in this book, but it will also help you evaluate the findings that you will read or hear about in the future. Unfortunately, many of the "breakthrough" findings that receive a lot of attention in the media are not based on adequate research. An understanding of research methods will make you a more sophisticated consumer of reported findings.

Methods for Studying Abnormal Behavior

Research methods can be divided into four types: *case study, correlational, controlled experimental,* and *multiple-baseline experimental.* In the following sections I will discuss the strengths and weaknesses of each type and illustrate how each type can be used in an attempt to answer one question: Does bad parenting lead to abnormal behavior?

Case Study Research

The first thing that many people do when looking for the cause of a disorder is to consider the personal history of an individual who has the disorder. This is called **case study research.** In studying an individual (a case), you might find that the individual's parents were hostile and rejecting when the individual was a child and then conclude that the individual's problems result from "bad parenting." Having observed this relationship in the one person in your case study, you might then conclude that bad parenting leads to abnormal behavior in general. (Indeed, it was through a series of case studies that Freud developed his theory of abnormal behavior.) Unfortunately, although case studies provide an excellent source of hypotheses (potential explanations) about the causes of abnormal behavior, *they cannot be used to prove that a particular hypothesis is correct* because it is impossible to rule out other potential hypotheses. For example, an individual may have received bad parenting, but he or she may also have seen high levels of violence on television, been frustrated in school, inhaled high levels of lead from automobile exhaust, grown up during a period of rapid cultural change, or inherited genes that lead

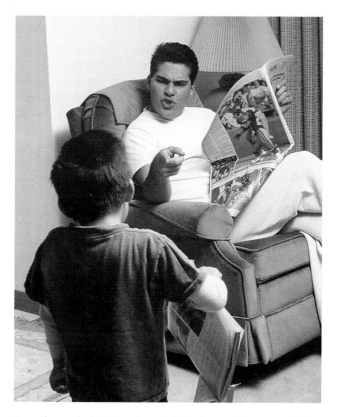

Researchers and scientists use case studies to document the personal history of an individual with a psychological disorder. For example, if a researcher found that an individual being studied had hostile and rejecting parents, the researcher might conclude that the individual's problems were a result of "bad parenting." But why can't case studies be used to prove that a hypothesis such as this is correct?

to abnormal behavior. All of these factors have been used to account for abnormal behavior, but a case study cannot show which of these factors, if any, are responsible for the behavior. Furthermore, it is hazardous to form a general hypothesis on the basis of a case study because *it cannot predict whether a relationship that occurs in one individual will also occur in others.*

In summary, case studies can provide excellent descriptions of abnormal behavior and can suggest potential explanations for the behavior, but they cannot be used to *prove* the explanations. I have included numerous case studies in this book, but I did so to illustrate points that are backed up by research; the case studies themselves do not prove anything. Having noted the problems with case studies, let's go on to consider another strategy.

case study research Research based on the intensive study of one individual, which does not allow conclusions concerning cause and effect or generalizations to other individuals.

Correlational Research

A second research method involves collecting data on a number of people and then testing to determine whether individuals who have high scores on one variable, such as abnormal behavior, also have high scores on another variable, such as bad parenting. For example, you could collect data on the degree to which 100 people show a particular type of abnormal behavior and the degree to which they were exposed to bad parenting, and then you could see whether those with the highest levels of abnormal behavior had received the worst parenting. Called **correlational research,** this type of study is like case study research in that observations are made about the co-occurrence of two variables (e.g., bad parenting and abnormal behavior). However, in correlational research observations are made of many individuals instead of just one, allowing the researchers to determine whether the relationship between the two variables holds for most of those people. For example, if we examined 100 individuals and consistently found that those who showed the most abnormal behavior had received the worst parenting and those who showed the least abnormal behavior had received the best parenting, we could conclude that there was a reliable correlation between quality of parenting and abnormal behavior. Such a relationship is presented graphically in Figure 4.11(a). By contrast, if the relationship between quality of parenting and abnormal behavior was found in only a few of the people we studied, we could not conclude that there was a reliable correlation between parenting and behavior. Such a nonrelationship is presented graphically in Figure 4.11(b).

The nature and strength of the relationship between two variables is expressed by a statistic called a **correlation coefficient** (represented by r). Correlation coefficients range between +1.00 and −1.00. A *positive* correlation (e.g., +.40) indicates that individuals with *high* scores on one variable have *high* scores on the other variable (e.g., high levels of abnormal behavior are associated with high levels of bad parenting). In contrast, a *negative* correlation (e.g., −.40) indicates that individuals who have *high* scores on one variable have *low* scores on the other variable (e.g., high levels of abnormal behavior are associated with low levels of bad parenting).

Importantly, the fact that two variables are correlated does not mean that we can draw conclusions concerning cause and effect. For instance, if there is a positive correla-

---

correlational research   Research that is based on correlations and that does not allow conclusions concerning cause and effect to be drawn.

correlation coefficient (r)   A statistic that reflects the degree to which two variables covary (e.g., increase or decrease together).

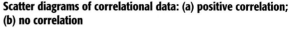

FIGURE 4.11

Scatter diagrams of correlational data: (a) positive correlation; (b) no correlation

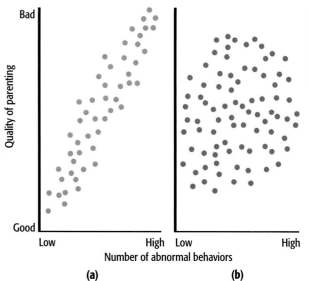

---

tion between bad parenting and abnormal behavior, it might be that bad parenting causes abnormal behavior, but it could also be that abnormal behavior causes bad parenting. That is, children's abnormal behavior might frustrate their parents and cause them to use bad parenting techniques.

Furthermore, a correlation between two variables does not mean that there is any causal relationship between the two variables. Instead the correlation may be due to the influence of a *third* variable. For example, in the case of the correlation between bad parenting and abnormal behavior, it is possible that genetic factors caused both the parents and their offspring to behave in abnormal ways. Similarly, socioeconomic stresses may have caused the parents to behave badly, and the same stresses may also have caused the children to behave badly. In these cases, then, the relationship between parenting and abnormal behavior is actually due to the influence of a third variable. Here's another example: In the *New England Journal of Medicine,* it was reported that older men who walked 2 or more miles a day lived longer than men who walked less, and from that finding many people concluded that walking prolongs life (Hakim et al., 1998). What's wrong with that conclusion? Might it be that men who were healthier were able to walk more and also lived longer? That is, rather than walking prolonging life, might good health lead to both walking and a long life? In other words, the connection between walking and life span may have been due to a third variable, general health.

In summary, correlational research shows whether reliable relationships exist between variables, but it does not allow us to conclude that a difference in one variable *causes* a difference in another variable. Establishing causal relationships requires the use of experimental approaches I'll describe next.

Controlled Experimental Research

Imagine this: An investigator interested in the causes of abnormal behavior first divides a large group of children into two groups. A test indicates that the children in both groups are well adjusted, with no differences between the groups in the level of abnormal behavior. Next the investigator instructs the parents of the children in one group to use bad parenting techniques when raising their children and the parents of the children in the other group to use good parenting techniques. Finally, 10 years later the investigator measures the levels of abnormal behavior in the two groups and finds that the children who were given bad parenting have higher levels of abnormal behavior than those in the other group (see Figure 4.12). From these results the investigator concludes that bad parenting causes the abnormal behavior.

This is an example of **controlled experimental research.** Specifically, with this method investigators manipulate (change) one variable, such as type of parenting, in one group but not in another group and then measure a second variable, such as abnormal behavior, in both groups. If there is a difference between the groups in the level of the second variable (abnormal behavior), it can be concluded that the manipulation of first variable (type of parenting) caused the difference. The variable whose effects are being studied (e.g., parenting) is called the **independent variable,** and the variable that is influenced (e.g., children's behavior) is called the **dependent variable.** (An easy way to remember the names for the variables is to recall that the dependent variable is *dependent* on—or influenced

by—the independent variable.) Let's consider the procedures of experimental research in a little more detail.

The first step in experimental research is the **random assignment** of participants to **experimental** and **control conditions.** For example, the first individual to arrive for the experiment might be assigned to the experimental condition, the second to the control condition, the third to the experimental condition, and so forth. Random assignment is used in an attempt to make the participants in the two conditions initially comparable. If participants have been randomly assigned, it is assumed that the participants in the two conditions are comparable, but investigators sometimes test this assumption by comparing the two groups on a **pretest** of the dependent variable.

The second step involves altering the independent variable in the experimental condition but not in the control condition, a procedure known as **experimental manipulation.**

Finally, we use a **posttest** to measure the dependent variable in the two conditions. If a difference in the dependent variable is found between individuals in the experimental and control conditions, the manipulation of the independent variable is assumed to have caused the difference.

---

controlled experimental research   Research involving the use of variables and experimental and control conditions.

independent variable   The variable whose effects are being studied in an experiment; the variable that is manipulated.

dependent variable   The variable that is influenced by the independent variable in an experiment; the variable whose change is measured.

random assignment   A procedure by which participants in research are assigned to conditions in a nonsystematic fashion in an attempt to make the participants in the conditions initially comparable.

experimental condition   The condition in an experiment in which the independent variable is manipulated.

control condition   The condition in an experiment in which the independent variable is not manipulated.

pretest   A measurement of the dependent variable before the independent variable is manipulated in an experiment in order to be sure that the participants in the various conditions are initially comparable.

experimental manipulation   The changing of the independent variable to see whether it influences the dependent variable.

posttest   A measurement of the dependent variable after the independent variable has been manipulated in an experiment in order to determine whether the manipulation had an effect on the dependent variable.

FIGURE 4.12

Results of a hypothetical experiment on good versus bad parenting

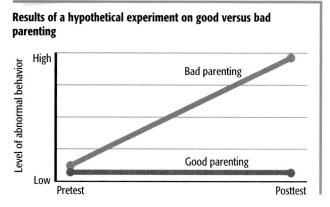

In any experiment *it is essential that the participants in the experimental and control conditions be alike and be treated alike, except with respect to the independent variable.* If there are other differences between the groups, it will be impossible to determine which variable is responsible for the change that is observed in the dependent variable. For example, if we manipulated type of parenting but the participants in the bad parenting condition also happened to go to poorer schools, we could not determine whether their levels of abnormal behavior were due to bad parenting, poor schooling, or the combination of bad parenting and poor schooling. If there is more than one difference between the conditions, the experiment is said to be **confounded.** (The word *confound* comes from a Latin word meaning "to pour together, confuse, ruin.") In the example experiment I just described, bad parenting and schooling were "poured together," and so the experiment was confounded. Thus the results are confused—and useless.

Multiple-Baseline Experimental Research

Another way of experimentally testing the effects of an independent variable is to use **multiple-baseline experimental research,** in which the participants are observed over a series of time periods in which the independent variable is and is not manipulated. For example, in trying to determine whether hostility on the part of parents leads to social withdrawal in children, the social behavior of children would be observed for periods in which the parents (1) behaved in a normal way toward the children (first baseline period), (2) acted in a hostile manner toward the children (experimental period), and (3) again behaved in a normal way toward the children (second baseline period). If the children showed more social withdrawal during the experimental period than during the baseline periods, it could be concluded that hostility on the part of parents causes social withdrawal in children. An example of results obtained for a multiple-baseline experiment is presented in Figure 4.13. In that experiment the effects of a drug on the symptoms of schizophrenia were tested, and the periods in which the patient was given the drug were interspersed with periods in which the patient was not given the drug. The results show that symptom levels were low during the

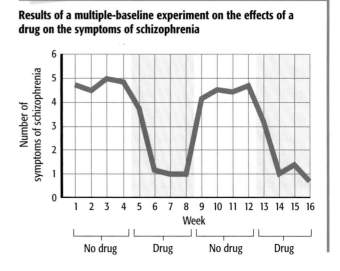

Results of a multiple-baseline experiment on the effects of a drug on the symptoms of schizophrenia

drug periods and high during the no-drug (baseline) periods, therefore indicating that the drug is effective.

Strategies for Avoiding Practical and Ethical Problems

Experiments are the best means of establishing causal relationships, but it is often impossible to conduct experiments because of practical problems. For example, in a study of the effects of bad parenting, it would not be feasible to get the parents in the experimental condition to behave badly toward their children for 10 years. Similarly, when studying the effects of prolonged stress, researchers cannot experimentally manipulate events such as wars, earthquakes, and deaths of family members.

It is also sometimes impossible to conduct experiments because the manipulations would be unethical. For instance, we could not do the experiment on the effects of bad parenting that I described earlier because it would be unethical to intentionally expose children to bad parenting that we suspect will result in abnormal behavior. Similarly, we could not study the effects of brain damage on behavior by cutting out parts of the brains of individuals in an experimental condition. Because of such practical and ethical problems, researchers must sometimes rely on alternative strategies, such as animal research, analogue research, quasi-experimental research, delayed treatment, and placebo and double-blind procedures.

Animal Research

One strategy used to avoid practical and ethical problems is to do experiments on animals. For example, when investi-

---

confounded experiment   An experiment in which more than one independent variable is changed, making it impossible to determine which variable influenced the dependent variable.

multiple-baseline experimental research   A research strategy in which participants are observed over a series of time periods in which the independent variable is and is not manipulated.

Animals are used in research when it is impractical or unethical to use humans. For example, to study the relative importance of contact and feeding in forming attachments, this rhesus monkey was raised with a cloth "mother" and a wire "mother" that had a feeding bottle. The study showed that the monkey preferred the cloth mother (contact) and went to the wire mother only for nourishment. Such a study could not have been conducted with a human infant.

gators were interested in determining the effects of extreme social isolation on the emotional development of infants, they raised monkeys in complete isolation (Harlow, 1959). In research on the effects of brain damage on abnormal behavior, parts of the brains of rats and monkeys were destroyed, and the effects on the animals' behavior were studied. However, research on animals also poses some problems. First, there is always the question of whether the results obtained with animals can be generalized to humans. Is a monkey's emotional response comparable to a human's emotional response? Can a monkey develop schizophrenia? Second, ethical standards also place limitations on what can be done with animals. Whereas once animals were treated as objects, today they are accorded many of the rights formerly reserved for humans, such as protection from undue pain (American Psychological Association, 1994).

Analogue Research

A second means of overcoming practical and ethical problems is to do **analogue** (AN-uh-log) **research.** An *analogue* is something that is *similar* to something else, and analogue research studies the effects of experimental manipulations similar to but not as extreme as those in which the researchers are really interested. For example, we could not expose children to years of bad parenting, but we could bring children into a laboratory for an hour and have them interact with an individual who acted either in a mildly hostile manner (experimental condition) or in a neutral manner (control condition). We would not expect the brief experience with the mildly hostile individual to result in long-term serious abnormal behavior, but it could cause moderate and brief tension, anxiety, or withdrawal. From this we might assume that if children were exposed to a more hostile individual for a longer period, more serious abnormal behavior might result. The problem with analogue research is that researchers can never be certain of the degree to which they can generalize from the analogous situation to the situation they are actually interested in.

Quasi-Experimental Research

A third means of avoiding some of the practical and ethical problems of experimental research is to use **quasi-experimental research** (Cook & Campbell, 1979). Quasi-experimental research does not actually manipulate the independent variable but instead takes advantage of naturally occurring situations in which there are differences in that variable. For example, if we were studying the effects of chronic stress on the development of depression, we might compare people who live near a potentially dangerous nuclear power plant to those who live near a coal-fired power plant with an excellent safety record (Baum & Fleming, 1993). If the groups of people living near the two different types of power plants are the same on all other variables (age, sex, race, intelligence, socioeconomic status, ethnic background), but those who lived near the nuclear power plant are more depressed, we might conclude that the chronic stress of living near a dangerous power plant

analogue research   A research strategy in which variables or participants similar but not identical to those of interest are studied (e.g., lower levels of stress or animals); often used to avoid practical or ethical problems in research.

quasi-experimental research   A research strategy in which the investigator uses naturally occurring situations in which there are differences in the independent variable (e.g., studying persons in stressful jobs rather than creating stress for persons); often used to avoid practical or ethical problems in research.

leads to depression. The important thing to recognize about quasi-experimental research is that *participants are not randomly assigned to conditions,* and therefore participants in the different conditions may not be comparable on all variables except the independent variable. It is possible that the individuals living near the nuclear power plant were more depressed before moving to that community or that some factor in the community other than the stress of living in the shadow of the nuclear power plant led to the depression.

Delayed Treatment

When an experiment is conducted to test the effects of a particular treatment such as psychotherapy or drugs, the participants in the control condition are not given any treatment. This raises an ethical problem because the experimenters are intentionally withholding a potentially effective treatment from individuals who need it. Some researchers try to overcome this problem by arguing that when the experiment is being conducted, they do not yet know for sure that the treatment is effective, and therefore they are not knowingly withholding an effective treatment. However, this argument is weakened by the fact that if they did not strongly believe that the treatment would be effective, they would not be testing it. The ethical problem posed by withholding treatment may be avoided to some extent by providing the treatment to the participants in the control condition after the experiment is over. With this procedure, called **delayed treatment,** everyone gets the treatment, but the individuals in the control condition get it later (Ackerson et al., 1998; Davidson & Horvath, 1997; Schmidt et al., 1997). Giving the participants in the control condition delayed treatment can also add to the research findings because if those individuals do not improve during the control (delay) period but then do improve when the treatment is begun, this provides additional evidence from which to conclude that the treatment is effective.

---

delayed treatment A research strategy in which individuals in the control condition are given the treatment later; used to avoid ethical problems of denying treatment to some participants.

placebo effect A phenomenon whereby the expectation that a treatment will have an effect may produce the effect, even though the treatment has no therapeutic effect.

demand characteristics The pressures to behave in a specific way in a given situation (e.g., to behave like a patient while in a hospital), which can cause participants in an experiment to do what they thing the experimenter expects.

Placebo and Double-Blind Procedures

Finally, two practical problems can arise in research, especially in research on treatments for abnormal behavior. One of these problems is the **placebo** (plu-SE-bo) **effect.** A placebo (e.g., a pill with no active ingredients), by definition, has no *therapeutic effect.* However, some patients who are given placebos and who believe they are getting an effective treatment may show improvement in their conditions (Quitkin, 1999; Shapiro & Shapiro, 1997). For example, if patients are given colored water labeled "powerful pain reliever," they may actually experience some relief from their pain. Furthermore, there is evidence that clients in treatment for depression show their greatest improvements during the first few sessions of therapy, despite the fact that strategies on which the treatment is based have not yet been introduced (Ilardi & Craighead, 1994). It appears that just getting into therapy may have an effect that is as strong or stronger than the therapy itself. Clearly, if we are to understand the effects of therapy, we must be able to separate the various influences.

The second practical problem involves what are called **demand characteristics.** Individuals in experiments will sometimes intentionally do what they think the experimenter wants them to do, regardless of whether the experimental manipulation was actually effective in changing their behavior (Orne, 1962). For example, patients in a treatment condition may report feeling better and may act better because they think they *should* rather than because they actually *do.* Obviously, both the placebo effect and demand characteristics can influence the results of experiments and lead to conclusions that treatments were effective when they were not.

To avoid the problems associated with the placebo effect and demand characteristics, researchers find that it is essential to include a placebo treatment condition in which patients think that they are getting the treatment but the crucial element of the treatment is missing. In a study of the effects of drugs, there might be (1) a *treatment condition,* in which patients receive pills containing active ingredients, (2) a *placebo condition,* in which patients receive pills that do not contain active ingredients, and (3) a *no-treatment condition,* in which patients do not receive any pills. The degree to which patients in the placebo condition show greater improvement than patients in the no-treatment condition reflects the placebo effect, and the degree to which the patients in the treatment condition show greater improvement than the patients in the placebo condition reflects the actual effect of the treatment. This effect is illustrated in Figure 4.14. Note that placebo effects are not limited to drugs; they also occur with psychological interventions such as psychotherapy. Unfortunately, it is much more difficult to design a placebo condition for an experiment involving psychotherapy, but one is essential nevertheless.

FIGURE 4.14

Results of an experiment comparing the effects of drug treatment, a placebo, and no treatment on the symptoms of depression

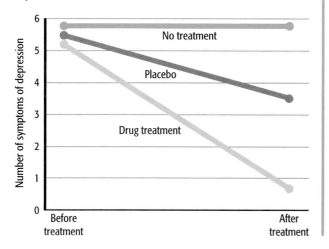

The effects of suggestion influence not only the participants in experiments but also raters who are evaluating the participants. For example, if a depressed patient is given a treatment that the therapist thinks will help, the therapist may selectively notice improvements in the patient (e.g., smiles) and ignore behaviors that suggest a lack of improvement (e.g., lack of activity). The effects of suggestion on both participants and raters can be avoided by using a **double-blind procedure,** in which neither the participants nor the raters know which partipants are receiving the treatment and which participants are receiving the placebo. That is, both patients and raters are *blind* to the conditions. In double-blind experiments on the effects of drugs, patients in the experimental condition are given pills containing active ingredients, while those in the placebo condition are given pills with no active ingredients, but neither the patients nor the raters know which patients are receiving the drugs and which are receiving the placebo. Some double-blind experiments can be more difficult to pull off than you might at first think because some treatments produce side effects, and patients who experience no side effects may catch on to the fact that they are not getting the real treatment (Bystritsky & Waikar, 1994). In such experiments it is sometimes necessary to give the patients in the placebo condition a drug that causes the side effects but not the treatment effect.

 **Genetic Research**

Genetic factors are playing an increasingly important role in our understanding of many physical and psychological disorders, and therefore we need to consider the procedures

used in this area of research (Plomin, De Fries, & McClearn, 1990; Reiss et al., 1991). Genetic research is not a type of research, like correlational and experimental research; rather it is a *topic* of research. Because it involves some unique procedures and problems, it deserves special attention in this discussion of research methods.

Procedures

The effects of genes are usually studied indirectly through the use of three procedures. The first of these is the **family study,** in which investigators determine whether a particular disorder is more likely to occur in the *biological relatives* of an individual with the disorder than it is in people in general. In other words, the question is, do disorders run in families? This method is based on the fact that members of a biological family share more genes with one another than they share with nonfamily members. If abnormal behavior is due to genetic factors, it would be expected that the biological relatives of individuals with a particular disorder would be more likely to have the disorder. However, even if it were found that a disorder did run in families, we could not necessarily conclude that the disorder was due to genetic factors because family members usually share the same environment as well as some of the same genes.

The second method is the **twin study. Monozygotic** (mon-o-zi-GOT-ik), **MZ** or identical, **twins** have *identical* genes, and **dizygotic** (di-zi-GOT-ik), **DZ,** or fraternal, **twins** do not. So, if a disorder is due to genetic factors, the disorder will be more likely to co-occur in MZ than in DZ twin pairs. The rate of co-occurrence of a disorder is called the **concordance** (kun-KOR-dens) **rate.** (The word *concordance* is based on *concord,* which means "agreement.")

---

double-blind procedure   A procedure used in experimental research to avoid the effects of suggestion—neither the participants nor the raters know which participants are receiving the treatment or the placebo.

family study (in genetics)   A procedure for determining the genetic contribution to a disorder by studying the degree to which biological relatives (as contrasted with nonbiological) have the disorder.

twin study (in genetics)   A research procedure in which the concordance rate of a disorder is compared in monozygotic and dizygotic twin pairs in an effort to determine the degree to which the disorder is due to genetic factors.

monozygotic (MZ) twins   Twins who have identical sets of genes; sometimes called identical twins.

dizygotic (DZ) twins   Twins who do not have identical sets of genes; sometimes called nonidentical or fraternal twins.

concordance rate   The rate of co-occurrence of a disorder in specific pairs of persons, usually monozygotic or dizygotic twins.

Genetic research, often involving the study of identical twins, has become an increasingly important method of research.

With data obtained from monozygotic and dizygotic twins, we can estimate the degree to which a particular characteristic, such as depression, is due to genetic factors. The simplest way to do this is to compute correlations that reflect the concordance rates in DZ and MZ twin pairs, then subtract the correlation for DZ twin pairs from the correlation for MZ twin pairs, and finally multiply the difference by 2. For example, if depression is correlated .15 in DZ twin pairs and .40 in MZ twin pairs, we could conclude that about 50% of the variability in depression is due to genetic factors: $.40 - .15 = .25 \times 2 = .50$ (Falconer, 1960). This formula provides only a rough estimate (and sometimes an overestimate) of the effects of genes; more complicated and sophisticated formulas have been developed that provide more accurate estimates.

adoptee study (in genetics)   A procedure for studying the role of genetic factors by comparing adopted children to their biological and adoptive parents; greater similarity to biological parents reflects a greater influence of genetic factors.

One potential problem in studying twins is the possibility that pairs of MZ twins share more personal experiences than pairs of DZ twins (e.g., greater overlap of friends, similar dressing). If this were the case, part of the higher concordance rate among MZ twins could be due to their shared experiences rather than to their shared genes (Loehlin & Nichols, 1976). Although there is strong evidence that the overlap in experiences is not an important factor, we should keep that potential in mind (Kendler, 1993; Plomin et al., 1990).

The third method for studying genetic factors is the **adoptee study.** With this procedure investigators examine the rates of a disorder in children who were born to parents either having or not having the disorder and then raised by adoptive parents not having the disorder. In other words, the children have the genes of their biological parents who either did or did not have the disorder, but they are raised by normal parents. Therefore, if the offspring of parents who had the disorder show a higher rate of the disorder than the offspring of parents who did not have the disorder, it can be concluded that genetic factors contributed to the development of the disorder. For example, in the case of schizophrenia there is strong evidence that the biological children of parents with schizophrenia have higher rates of schizophrenia than the biological children of normal parents, even when all of the children are raised by adoptive parents. Adoptee studies can provide very convincing evidence for the effects of genes.

A fourth approach involves studying genes themselves, a strategy that has been made possible by recent technological advances. Although a variety of studies have been based on this approach, the findings have been very inconsistent and therefore this approach has not yet yielded many firm conclusions. The weakness of the findings probably stems from the fact that most disorders are due to more than one gene, and researchers do not yet have techniques that enable them to consider the roles of multiple genes.

The Role of Environmental Factors

Two things should be noted with regard to the roles of genetic and environmental factors in abnormal behavior. First, environmental variables are not limited to *social* variables, such as economic class, interpersonal relations, and situational conflicts, although these are what people usually think of when the concept of environment is mentioned. Instead, environmental factors also include a host of *physiological* variables, such as the hormones to which a fetus is exposed during the prenatal period, maternal illness during the prenatal period, complications during the birth process, and exposure later in life to physical traumas and toxins such as lead. Nonsocial environmental factors such as these are very important in a variety of disorders.

Second, it should be noted that one way to calculate the extent to which environmental factors contribute to a disorder is by subtracting from 100 the degree to which genes influence the disorder. In other words, if we assume that the total causes of a disorder equal 100 and take away the proportion of the total that is due to genes, what is left is the proportion due to environmental factors. For example, with the earlier example of depression it was concluded that 50% of the variability among individuals in depression is due to genes, so it can be concluded that the remaining 50% of the variability is due to environmental factors. However, using this subtraction approach may lead us to *overestimate* the degree to which environmental factors contribute to a disorder. The problem is that other factors such as errors in measurement are also included in the variability remaining after the variability due to genetic factors has been subtracted, thus artificially inflating the amount of variability attributed to environmental factors. Indeed, it has been estimated that errors in measurement of personality and abnormal behavior may contribute between 15% and 30% of the variability that is not accounted for by genetic factors (Tellegen et al., 1988). This was illustrated by a study in which the investigators measured the abnormality in twins twice—rather than only once as is usually done—figuring that if they missed a problem on one occasion, they might pick it up on the second occasion (Kendler, Neale, et al., 1993a). The results indicated that when this more sensitive double measurement procedure was used, the amount of variability that could be attributed to genetic factors went up by about 20%. This clearly demonstrates that the variability that remains after the variability attributable to genetics has been subtracted is due to a combination of environmental factors and other factors such as errors—and *not* to environmental factors alone.

A Few Words about Statistics

After data have been collected, it is essential that they be evaluated objectively, and to do that we use a wide variety of **statistical tests.** A thorough discussion of these tests is beyond the scope of this book, but a few general comments about them are necessary so that you will be better able to put test results into perspective.

Most statistical tests are used to assess the *reliability* of the findings of an investigation. For example, if we collect data and then compute a correlation between scores measuring "bad parenting" and scores measuring "maladjustment in children," we may find that the scores are correlated +.30. Once we have the correlation, we have to determine whether it reflects a *real* relationship that will be found again if we collect a new set of data or whether it is due to *chance*—a one-time fluke. To make this determination we use a statistical test designed to indicate how many

times out of 100 we can expect that particular correlation to occur by chance. If the results of the test indicate that the correlation can be expected to occur *by chance fewer than 5 times in 100,* we can conclude that the correlation is **statistically significant.** Stated in another way, a statistically significant result is one that is expected to occur in at least 95% of investigations (i.e., 95 times out of 100). Similarly, if we conduct an experiment and find that children who were treated badly have a mean maladjustment score of 40, whereas children who were treated well have a mean maladjustment score of 10, we have to determine whether the difference in means is due to the way the children were treated or to chance. If a statistical test indicates that the difference in means is expected to occur fewer than 5 times in 100 by chance, we can conclude that the difference in means is statistically significant.

Statistical testing for reliability is fairly straightforward, but there are two conceptual problems you should keep in mind. The first is that even if results are statistically significant, *if the experiment is confounded, the results are meaningless* (see the earlier discussion of confounded experiments). In other words, the fact that the results are statistically significant does not necessarily mean that they are valid. In evaluating any finding we must determine whether the investigation was methodologically sound.

The second problem stems from the use of the word *significant.* Most people assume that *significant* means "important," but to statisticians it means "reliable." Therefore, you must not misinterpret a statistically significant (reliable) effect as necessarily important, because a great many statistically significant findings are in fact *trivial.* For example, we may find that a particular treatment has a statistically significant effect on patients' depression scores, but the treatment may change the scores by only 2 points on a scale that runs from 1 to 100. The 2-point change may be statistically significant (reliable) but trivial in terms of its practical effect on patients' lives. Here's another example: There was a great deal of excitement when it was reported that a new drug (Orlistat) was significantly more effective than a placebo for reducing weight in people who were obese (Davidson et al., 1999). However, careful inspection of the data indicated that the individuals taking the drug lost only $6\frac{1}{2}$ pounds more than those taking the placebo; that difference was reliable but probably not "significant" for people who weighed over 220 pounds.

The problem of differentiating between statistically significant and important findings can be illustrated with a

statistical tests Tests used to determine whether research findings are significant (reliable).

statistically significant Reliable (i.e., likely to occur fewer than 5 times in 100 by chance). (Contrast with *clinical significance.*)

Research on Exercise and Depression: An Example of the Process

IN MY LABORATORY at the university, my students and I study stress and the physiological processes associated with stress. One day, while we were working on a particularly difficult problem, I became frustrated and grumpy, so I took a break and went for a run. (I usually run about 6 miles a day.) When I returned from the run, I felt much better, and later my students and I talked about how running often helps me reduce stress. During that discussion one of my students suggested that we study the effects of running on stress and possibly on depression. She joked that I provided a good *case study,* but we needed to study the effects of exercise on "real people." Everyone thought it was an interesting idea, so that day a new research program was launched.

The first thing we did was to conduct a simple *correlational study.* Specifically, we asked a group of students to fill out questionnaires concerning their levels of exercise and their levels of depression. When we computed a correlation between their exercise scores and their depression scores, we found a *statistically significant negative correlation* of −.27; that is, we found that higher levels of exercise were reliably associated with lower lev-

els of depression. This correlation suggested that there was a relationship between exercise and depression, but, of course, it did not allow us to answer the question of whether exercise led to lower levels of depression or whether depressed individuals were less likely to exercise.

We then conducted an *experiment* designed to answer the question, do individuals who exercise show greater reductions in depression than individuals who do not exercise? First, we administered a questionnaire that measured depression to a large number of women students. We then invited the 45 women who were most depressed to participate in the experiment (they all agreed). Next, these 45 women were *randomly assigned* to three conditions. The first condition was the *exercise condition;* the women in that condition went to the gym twice a week for 10 weeks for a strenuous aerobic exercise class. They were also asked to work out on their own at least twice during each week. The second condition was a *placebo condition;* the women in that condition were taught relaxation exercises, and they were asked to use those exercises 4 days per week for 10 weeks. It is important to note that the women in both the exercise and the placebo conditions

were told that there was evidence that the treatments they were receiving were effective for reducing depression; therefore the women in both conditions expected improvements in their depression. However, we had no reason to believe that relaxation exercises would reduce depression. The third condition was a *no-treatment condition;* the women in that condition were told that there were no longer any openings in the treatment conditions, and therefore their treatment would be temporarily postponed. All of the women completed self-report measures of depression at the beginning of the project (the *pretest*), after 5 weeks (the *midtreatment test*), and after 10 weeks (the *posttest*). The results are presented in the accompanying figure.

The statistical tests conducted on the data revealed that the women in the exercise condition showed significantly greater declines in depression than did the women in the placebo or no-treatment conditions. More specifically, there was no significant difference among the scores for the three conditions on the pretest. However, on both the midtreatment test and the posttest, the women in the exercise condition reported significantly lower levels of depression than the women in the placebo and no-treatment condi-

correlation. To determine the strength of a correlation we *square* it, and the resulting value indicates the percentage of variability in one variable that can be accounted for by the other variable. For example, correlations of .30 are typical in the behavioral sciences and are often reliable, but a correlation of .30 accounts for only 9% of the variability! That is, if parenting and abnormal behavior were correlated .30, knowing how bad the parenting had been would allow us to account for only 9% of the differences in abnormal behavior.

clinical significance The practical importance of a research finding. (Contrast with *statistical significance.*)

Because statistical tests assess only statistical significance, we must also gauge the **clinical significance,** or practical importance, of our findings. Many attempts have been made to develop a quantitative approach to determining clinical significance, but they have been largely unsuccessful; in most cases clinical significance is assessed by a *subjective* judgment (Jacobson, 1988; Jacobson & Truax, 1991; Speer, 1992). However, one rule of thumb for deciding whether an effect is important is to determine whether it causes patients to move from one category to another, such as from "depressed" to "normal" (Ogles, Lambert, & Sawyer, 1995).

Finally, it is important to recognize that there is often a bias in the publishing of findings; specifically, findings that

tions. On the midtreatment test and the posttest, the women in the placebo condition reported slightly lower levels of depression than the women in the no-treatment condition, but those differences were not statistically significant, indicating that expectancies alone were not sufficient to reduce depression. Overall, then, these findings indicated that exercise was effective for reducing depression and that the effect was not due to a placebo (expectancy) effect.

In this experiment the results were statistically significant, but the question is, were they also *clinically significant?* The answer is probably yes. As I pointed out earlier, one measure of clinical significance is whether the treatment is effective for moving individuals from one category to another, and that did happen in this experiment. Specifically, the women began the experiment with depression scores of about 12, which are thought to reflect "clinical" levels of depression, but by the end of the treatment period, the women in the exercise condition had scores of about 3, which are considered to be in the "normal" range. In contrast, the women in the placebo and no-treatment conditions did not move into the normal range. It could there-

fore be concluded that exercise was effective for achieving reductions in depression that were reliable (statistically significant) and practically important (clinically significant).

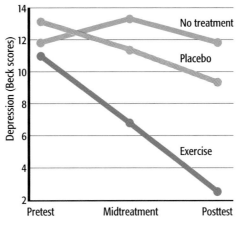

Source: McCann & Holmes (1984).

You might have noted that there was a potential ethical problem with this experiment in that we withheld what we thought was an effective treatment (exercise) from some seriously depressed individuals who needed treatment. To some extent this problem was overcome by giving the exercise treatment to the women in the

placebo and no-treatment conditions after the experiment was over. However, this was not a perfect solution because the women in the placebo and no-treatment conditions had to endure their depressions for 10 weeks longer than necessary. (What if one of the women from whom we had temporarily withheld treatment had committed suicide during that 10-week period?)

This experiment answered an interesting and important question concerning the relationship between exercise and depression, but it also raised other questions. For example, what is it about exercise that reduces depression? Is exercise as effective as psychotherapy for reducing depression? Does depression return when the exercise is stopped? Would the same effects be found with men? Those questions led to other experiments, but as the saying goes, that's another story. The process of research almost always yields answers that lead to more questions.

Sources: Holmes (1993); McCann & Holmes (1984).

are statistically significant are published, whereas those that are not significant are not published. This poses a problem because one investigator may find a statistically significant result and it will be published, but when other investigators who conduct similar investigations do not find statistically significant results, their results are not published. When that happens, the erroneous finding remains uncorrected in the literature and may mislead researchers and practitioners. This publication bias was illustrated in a comparison of the results of published and unpublished studies on the effectiveness of family therapy for treating abnormal behavior (Shadish et al., 1993). The published and unpublished studies were equally good in terms of design, but the published studies indicated stronger effects for family ther-

apy, thus distorting the conclusions that readers drew from the reports. Unfortunately, there is no simple solution to this problem.

In summary, just as all that glitters is not gold, all results that are statistically significant and published are not necessarily important or reliable. All of the research findings reported in this book are statistically significant (reliable), and I have attempted to select findings that are clinically or theoretically significant as well.

In the foregoing discussion I have summarized the basic elements of research design and statistics. In Case Study 4.1 I briefly describe a research program that was conducted in my laboratory. In that description you can see how the elements of research fit together in the "real world."

Questions about Research Methods

1. *What is the best research strategy?* In general, the best strategy is controlled experimental research because if this type of research is done correctly, it is the most likely type to lead to clear-cut conclusions concerning cause and effect. However, when we use the word "best," we must also take the well-being of research participants into account; if the research procedures place the participants at risk, the research is unethical and certainly cannot be considered to be the best strategy. Overall, then, we must always look out for the good of the individuals who participate in research and if necessary make compromises, such as using analogue or quasi-experimental research, so that we do not harm participants.

2. *How can you decide whether you can draw meaningful conclusions concerning cause and effect from a particular investigation?* First, you must determine whether *any* conclusions concerning cause and effect can be drawn from the research. Remember, you can't draw cause-and-effect conclusions from case studies, from correlations, or from con-trolled experiments that are confounded. Second, even if you can draw a conclusion, you must still determine whether the conclusion can be generalized to the situation in which you are interested. Therefore, you must ask whether the participants in the investigation are like those in whom you are interested: Results with chimpanzees might not be generalizable to humans. Next you must ask whether the independent and dependent variables are like those in which you are interested: Is the stress of unem-ployment similar to the stress in which you are interested? Is hitting an inflated plastic doll the type of aggression in which you are interested? Third, if you can draw conclu-sions and generalize them to the situation in which you are interested, you have to determine whether the effects are strong enough to be practically meaningful. Unfortunately, although we can determine whether effects are reliable (sta-tistically significant), we do not have an objective means of determining whether effects are strong enough to be important in "the real world." Overall, then, the process of scientific research is objective, but decisions as to whether the findings are important for the real world are often sub-jective.

Summary

Topic I: Diagnostic Techniques

▶ A diagnostic system helps us describe individuals who suffer from abnormalities and decide how to treat them. The diagnostic system used in the United States is pre-sented in the *Diagnostic and Statistical Manual of Mental Disorders,* 4th edition, known as *DSM-IV;* the system used elsewhere in the world is covered by the *Interna-tional Classification of Diseases,* 10th edition, known as *ICD-10.*

▶ In *DSM-IV* the symptoms for each disorder are listed, but assumptions about causes are not made. Five axes (di-mensions) are used in making diagnoses:

1. *Clinical Syndromes,* which includes the major serious disorders, such as anxiety, depression, and schizophre-nia
2. *Personality Disorders and Mental Retardation,* which consists of personality disorders, such as obsessive-compulsive personality disorder and dependent per-sonality disorder, and mental retardation
3. *General Medical Conditions,* which indicates medical problems that might be relevant for diagnosing and treating the individual
4. *Psychosocial and Environmental Problems,* which in-cludes factors that might influence an individual's diag-nosis, treatment, or prognosis

5. *Global Assessment of Functioning,* which allows a rating of the individual's current and previous levels of func-tioning

▶ Any diagnostic system has inherent problems: (1) Unique aspects of individuals may be lost; (2) characteristics may be incorrectly attributed to individuals as a function of their diagnoses; and (3) a diagnosis may be used to refer to an entire individual (e.g., a "schizophrenic") when it only applies to a particular aspect of the individual.

▶ Interviews enable individuals to tell us about their prob-lems and the factors that might contribute to them. Inter-views also enable us to observe the behavior that occurs during the interview. Interviews can be structured or unstructured. Problems with interviews stem from the honesty or accuracy of the reports and the validity of the inferences that interviewers draw.

▶ Observations can be used to assess behavior and the effects of situational factors, but observations are often impractical to carry out and sometimes raise ethical questions.

▶ Psychological tests can be divided into four types:

1. Objective personality tests are like interviews in that individuals can report on how they feel and how they react, but these tests are generally more comprehensive

and time-efficient than interviews. The most widely used objective personality test is the MMPI.

2. Projective personality tests are those in which individuals project their personal characteristics and feelings onto ambiguous stimuli such as inkblots or meaningless pictures. The best-known projective tests are the Rorschach and the TAT. Problems with these tests include the subjective nature of the interpretation of the responses, the possibility that responses may be faked, and the fact that the tests measure only characteristics of which the test takers are aware.

3. Intelligence tests are used to measure individuals' abilities in different areas (e.g., information, comprehension, arithmetic, vocabulary). With an individually administered test the administrator can observe the test taker's performance and make judgments about when and why problems with functioning arise. One very widely used intelligence test is the WAIS-R.

4. Neuropsychological tests are used to identify the nature, location, and effects of brain damage. The best-known tests of this type are the Halstead-Reitan Neuropsychology Battery and the Luria-Nebraska Battery.

▶ Physiological tests can be used to assess the structures in the brain; techniques used today are CT scans and MRI. Brain activity is measured with EEGs and PET scans. Physiological reactivity is measured with tests of blood pressure and skin conductance.

▶ Several issues or problems are associated with diagnostic methods:

1. We may be able to assess what an individual is like at the time of the assessment, but because individuals change, the results may not be helpful in understanding how the individual was in the past or will be in the future.

2. Our ability to understand and predict behavior from personality assessments may be limited because to some extent behavior is determined by situational factors.

3. Comorbidity refers to the fact that an individual can suffer from two or more disorders at one time. The comorbidity of disorders may be due to (a) the chance occurrence of two disorders at the same time, (b) the fact that one disorder leads to another disorder, or (c) the fact that both disorders stem from a common cause.

4. The diagnostic process can be improperly influenced because diagnosticians may (a) subjectively focus on one symptom or disorder, thereby ignoring others, (b) implicitly suggest symptoms to clients, and (c) be influenced by current diagnostic fads.

5. Sociocultural factors can influence who receives diagnoses because individuals who are poor or from ethnic minority groups are often less likely to use mental health services. Furthermore, when those individuals do use the services, their diagnoses may be biased by language differences or by misinterpretation of behaviors by diagnosticians who are unaware of cultural differences.

▶ Objective information, such as demographic information and self-reports, that is directly related to the behavior in question is more helpful for making diagnoses than are inferences based on observations made in interviews or on projective test responses.

▶ Statistical formulas have consistently been found to be more effective than subjective judgments made by diagnosticians for making predictions. This is probably because the formulas can handle more information and they are more effective at assigning relative importance (weight) to different pieces of information.

Topic II: Research Methods

▶ Case studies are based on observations of particular individuals. Although case studies can be a good source of hypotheses, they cannot be used to determine cause-and-effect relationships or to predict whether similar relationships would hold for other individuals. Also, the observations are often biased.

▶ Correlational research is used to determine whether relationships are reliable over many individuals, but conclusions about causation cannot be based on correlations.

▶ Controlled experimental research involves manipulating an independent variable in the experimental condition but not in the control condition, and then noting changes in the dependent variable between the two conditions.

▶ Multiple-baseline experimental research involves the repeated introduction and withdrawal of an independent variable over a series of trials, while changes in the dependent variable are measured.

▶ There are five research strategies for avoiding practical and ethical problems:

1. Animals may be substituted for humans in some research, but care must be taken not to violate the rights of the animals.

2. Analogue research involves using experimental manipulations that are similar to those in which the researchers are actually interested but that cannot be used because they are not practical or ethical. The problem with this approach is that results may not be generalizable to what the researchers are actually interested in.

3. Quasi-experimental research takes advantage of naturally occurring situations in which there are differences in the independent variable. Confidence in the findings is limited by the fact that individuals are not randomly assigned to conditions.

4. Delayed treatment can be used to overcome the problem of withholding potentially helpful treatments from individuals in a control condition.

5. A placebo condition is used to avoid the practical problems arising from the placebo effect and demand characteristics. Double-blind procedures are used to avoid the effects of suggestion on participants and raters.

▶ The effects of genes are studied indirectly by (1) determining the degree to which disorders run in families, (2) comparing the concordance rates in monozygotic and dizygotic twin pairs, and (3) comparing siblings who were adopted and raised separately. Variability that is not accounted for by genes may be due to physiological or social factors in the environment or to errors in measurement.

▶ Statistical results indicating that a finding is significant mean that the finding is reliable; that is, it will usually occur by chance fewer than 5 out of 100 times. The clinical (or practical) significance of findings is based on subjective judgments, such as whether a treatment moves an individual from one category to another (e.g., from clinically depressed to normal).

Questions for Making Connections

1. If you had to diagnose an individual who might be suffering from a psychiatric disorder, what types of tests would you use and why? What types of tests would you be less likely to use and why?

2. A friend of yours knows an individual who was sexually abused as a child and who is now depressed. Based on that person's experience, your friend concludes that childhood sexual abuse causes depression. On what kind of evidence is your friend basing this conclusion? Why or why not is a conclusion based on this kind of evidence justified?

3. An investigator measures strength and aggression in 100 young men and finds a correlation of +.40 that is statistically significant. What can you conclude about the relationship between strength and aggression? How much of the variability in aggression (differences in aggression) can be accounted for by the data on strength?

4. Design an experiment to determine whether taking PCP ("angel dust") causes schizophrenia. Are there ethical problems with the experiment?

5. Assume that you want to test the effects of a new drug on anxiety but you have only four individuals with high anxiety on which to test the drug. Could you conduct a test of the drug's effectiveness? If so, how would you do the test?

6. Design an experiment on the effects of psychotherapy that would involve a control condition for the placebo effect. Is it ethical to include a no-treatment condition? If not, how might you minimize that problem?

7. Assume that you want to determine whether genetic factors play a role in schizophrenia. What three procedures could you use to determine whether there is a link between genes and schizophrenia? What are the strengths and weakness of the different approaches?

Key Terms and People

In reviewing and testing yourself, you should be able to discuss each of the following:

adoptee study, p. 114
analogue research, p. 111
Axis I: Clinical Syndromes, p. 90
Axis II: Personality Disorders and Mental Retardation, p. 90
Axis III: General Medical Conditions, p. 90
Axis IV: Psychosocial and Environmental Problems, p. 90
Axis V: Global Assessment of Functioning, p. 90
case study research, p. 107
checklists of symptoms, p. 92

Children's Apperception Test (CAT), p. 98
clinical significance, p. 116
comorbidity, p. 102
computerized axial tomography (CT scan), p. 100
concordance rate, p. 113
confounded experiment, p. 110
control condition, p. 109
controlled experimental research, p. 109
correlation coefficient (*r*), p. 108
correlational research, p. 108

decision tree, p. 88
delayed treatment, p. 112
demand characteristics, p. 112
dependent variable, p. 109
Diagnostic and Statistical Manual of Mental Disorders (DSM-IV), p. 88
diagnostic systems, p. 87
dizygotic (DZ) twins, p. 113
double-blind procedure, p. 113
Draw-A-Person Test, p. 98
electroencephalograph (EEG), p. 100
experimental condition, p. 109
experimental manipulation, p. 109

5 Anxiety Disorders: Phobias, Generalized Anxiety, and Panic

IN THIS AND THE FOLLOWING CHAPTER we are going to examine the symptoms, causes, and treatments of six disorders that are generally referred to as anxiety disorders. **Anxiety** is an emotional state that involves fear, worry, and physiological arousal. In **anxiety disorders** *anxiety is the major symptom,* but what you must recognize is that *anxiety takes different forms in different disorders.* For instance, anxiety may (1) be linked to specific objects like snakes, (2) be general and seem to "come out of the blue," (3) occur in sudden bursts that are so overwhelming they may lead to

panic, (4) appear only when the individual does not perform a compulsive act, such as not stepping on cracks in the sidewalk, or (5) be a remnant of a traumatic event that occurred years ago. The symptoms of the six anxiety disor-

anxiety An emotional state that involves fear, worry, and physiological arousal.

anxiety disorders Disorders in which anxiety is the major symptom.

TABLE 5.1

Symptoms of the anxiety disorders

Phobic disorders	Persistent and irrational fears of a specific object, activity, or situation
Generalized anxiety disorder	Anxiety that occurs across many situations and persists for at least 6 months
Panic disorder	Brief periods of exceptionally intense anxiety accompanied by physical symptoms that include shortness of breath and chest pain
Obsessive-compulsive disorder	Persistent ideas, thoughts, or impulses that cause anxiety (obsessions) and irrational behaviors that an individual feels driven to perform over and over (compulsion)
Posttraumatic stress disorder	Anxiety associated with the reexperiencing of an extremely traumatic event that occurred some time in the past
Acute stress disorder	Anxiety that occurs within 4 days of an extremely traumatic event and lasts less than 4 weeks

Note: To qualify as a disorder in *DSM-IV,* an anxiety disorder must cause clinically significant distress or impair social, occupational, or other important areas of functioning.

Source: Adapted from American Psychiatric Association, 1994.

ders are summarized in Table 5.1. Clearly, anxiety has many faces that you need to be able to recognize and understand.

It is also important to note that anxiety can be a symptom of many other disorders, such as depression and schizophrenia, but in those disorders anxiety is a *secondary symptom* because it is the *result of other problems.* For example, a woman who is suffering from depression may be anxious because she believes she is a useless failure and doomed to a life of misery. Similarly, a man with schizophrenia may be anxious because he has a delusion that his brain is being destroyed by gamma waves from the planet Egregious. The distinction between primary and secondary anxiety is important to keep in mind when making diagnoses and planning treatments. In this chapter we will first consider the symptoms and issues associated with anxiety in general and then go on to examine three of the anxiety disorders.

hyperventilation Rapid breathing whereby oxygen intake is reduced, resulting in symptoms such as light-headedness, headache, tingling of the extremities, heart palpitations, chest pain, and breathlessness, and often occurring because of anxiety.

Symptoms and Issues of Anxiety

You have probably been anxious at some time, so you know what it's like: You're tense and worried, your heart pounds, your stomach is upset, and you may pace back and forth. Does the fact that you've been anxious mean you have an anxiety disorder? When does anxiety become abnormal?

Melanie is terrified by small, crawling bugs; she has a phobia. Doug is constantly anxious with no apparent cause; he suffers from generalized anxiety disorder. When Alicia comes into a room, she must touch all four walls or she becomes very anxious; she has obsessive-compulsive disorder. Toshio has brief bursts of anxiety that are so intense he thinks he is having a heart attack and will die; he suffers from panic disorder. Anxiety is the major symptom in all of these disorders. Do they all have a common cause and treatment, or do they have different causes and require different treatments?

Symptoms of Anxiety

Anxiety involves a variety of symptoms such as fear, distractibility, muscle tension, and restlessness. Because all of these play important roles, let's begin with a discussion of exactly what makes up anxiety.

Mood Symptoms

Mood symptoms in anxiety disorders consist primarily of anxiety, tension, panic, and apprehension. An individual suffering from anxiety experiences feelings of impending doom and disaster. Secondary mood symptoms caused by anxiety may include depression and irritability. The depression stems from the fact that the individual does not see a solution for his or her problems and is ready to give up and "throw in the towel." Loss of sleep due to anxiety can lead to irritability.

Cognitive Symptoms

Cognitive symptoms in anxiety disorders revolve around the doom-and-disaster scenarios anticipated by the individual. For example, an individual with a fear of being out in public (agoraphobia) will spend a great deal of time worrying about all the terrible things that can happen out there and planning how to avoid those disasters. Furthermore, because the individual's attention is focused on potential disasters, the individual ignores the real problems at hand and is therefore inattentive and distractible. As a consequence, the individual often does not work or study effectively, which can increase his or her anxiety.

Physical Symptoms

The physical symptoms of anxiety can be divided into two groups. The first group consists of the *immediate symptoms,* including sweating, dry mouth, shallow breathing, rapid pulse, increased blood pressure, throbbing sensations in the head, and feelings of muscular tension. These symptoms reflect a high level of arousal of the autonomic nervous system, and they are the same responses we see in fear. Other immediate symptoms can occur because the individual begins breathing too rapidly, a process known as **hyperventilation.** Hyperventilation can result in light-headedness, headache, tingling of the extremities, heart palpitations, chest pain, and breathlessness. These primary physical symptoms are what you would experience if your professor suddenly announced a pop quiz worth half your grade!

If the anxiety is prolonged, the second group of physical symptoms may set in. These *delayed symptoms* include chronic headaches, muscular weakness, gastrointestinal distress, and cardiovascular disorders, including high blood pressure and heart attacks. These symptoms reflect the *fatigue* or *breakdown* of the physiological system caused by the prolonged arousal. You might experience these symptoms if you failed the quiz referred to earlier and then worried about getting a failing grade for the entire semester.

Not everyone who suffers from anxiety experiences the same physical symptoms. That's because there are individual differences in the patterning of autonomic reactivity (Lacey, 1950, 1967). For example, when I am anxious, I tend to experience muscular tenseness, particularly in my throat (a response that, if prolonged, results in a change in or loss of my voice). Someone else may be more likely to respond with an increase in blood pressure (which, if prolonged, can result in hypertension).

Motor Symptoms

Because of their high levels of arousal, anxious individuals often exhibit restlessness, fidgeting, pointless motor activity such as toe tapping, and exaggerated startle responses to sudden noises. Because these activities are not goal-directed, they are unproductive and often interfere with effective functioning. For example, if you are anxious before a test, you may pace around in your room, but the pacing does not make you feel better and will even prevent you from doing some useful last-minute studying.

 ## Normal versus Abnormal Anxiety

When considering anxiety, we need to distinguish between *normal* and *abnormal* anxiety. You've probably experienced anxiety at some time, but does that mean you suffered from

The anxiety you feel when preparing for or taking a tough exam is usually a normal, adaptive, and positive response that makes you study and work harder.

an anxiety disorder? Probably not. Indeed, in many instances anxiety is a normal, adaptive, and positive response that serves to motivate us and increase our productive efforts. For example, anxiety often makes students study harder for exams, and psychotherapists actually prefer their clients to have some anxiety because it causes them to work harder on their problems. The question is, when is anxiety abnormal?

There are three factors to consider when making a distinction between normal and abnormal anxiety:

1. *The level of the anxiety.* In many situations some level of anxiety is appropriate, but if the anxiety goes above that level, it can be considered abnormal. For example, it is normal to be somewhat anxious about flying, but it is abnormal to have such high anxiety that you faint when you get on a plane or refuse to get on.

2. *The justification for the anxiety.* Anxiety for which there is not a realistic justification is considered abnormal. For instance, an individual may be anxious in elevators because he or she thinks they will crash, but that is not a realistic reason for the anxiety because elevators hardly ever crash.

3. *The consequences of the anxiety.* Anxiety that leads to negative consequences can be considered abnormal. Examples of negative consequences include poor performance at school or on the job, social withdrawal, high blood pressure, and personal discomfort. Indeed, in *DSM-IV* anxiety is considered a symptom if it "interferes significantly with the person's normal routine, occupational (academic) functioning, or social activities or relationships, or there is a marked distress about having [the anxiety symptoms]" (American Psychiatric Association, 1994, p. 417).

Overall, then, we must consider the level, justification, and consequences of anxiety in making the distinction between normal and abnormal anxiety. However, in the final analysis there is no simple rule or cutoff point, and ultimately the decision concerning the normalcy of anxiety is a subjective one.

One Disorder or Different Disorders?

Because anxiety is a major symptom in all of the anxiety disorders, for many years it was assumed that all of the anxiety disorders had a common cause and could be treated similarly; that is, it was assumed that the various disorders were simply variations on the common symptom of anxiety. However, it is now clear that even though they all involve anxiety, *the various anxiety disorders are different disorders that stem from different causes and must be treated differently.* Similarly, just because colds and brain cancer can both involve headaches, we should not conclude that colds and brain cancer are different forms of the same disorder and should be treated the same. Therefore, we will consider each anxiety disorder separately, and our task will be to determine what cause and what treatment are most appropriate for each disorder. In other words, each disorder can be considered a mystery in which the symptoms are the clues to the cause. The challenge is to find an explanation that fits the symptoms and a treatment that fits the explanation. For some disorders we may find that there is more than one culprit in the mystery. Let's begin with phobic disorders.

THINKING CRITICALLY

Questions about Symptoms and Issues of Anxiety

What connections are there among the mood symptoms, cognitive symptoms, and physical symptoms of anxiety? The various symptoms of anxiety are related, but there are differences of opinion about how they are related. On the one hand, some theorists believe that cognitive symptoms, such as excessive worrying, cause anxiety as well as physical symptoms such as high blood pressure. That is, people are anxious and physically tense because they worry. On the other hand, other theorists argue that anxiety causes cognitive and physical symptoms. In other words, people feel anxious, so they worry and become physically tense. Are the feelings of anxiety a cause or an effect? I'll discuss this question later when I explain specific anxiety disorders, but here it is important to recognize that the various symptoms of

anxiety are connected and that you need to keep in mind the question of cause and effect.

TOPIC II

Phobic Disorders

Nicole is afraid of spiders; in fact, she is terrified of them. She has never been hurt by a spider, she knows that most spiders are not dangerous, and she knows that there are no dangerous spiders where she lives, but she is still afraid of them. Nicole has a phobia. How did her phobia develop? Why can't she control her fear?

Kevin is afraid to go out of the house because he is afraid something bad will happen and that it will be difficult or embarrassing for him to escape the situation. He doesn't know what it is that might happen, but he doesn't want to take any chances and so he stays home. Kevin is suffering from agoraphobia. How did this develop, and can it be treated?

Ramon has a phobia for high places. In an attempt to help him overcome this phobia, his therapist has been taking him to higher and higher floors in a tall building. Will this work, and if it does, why?

The first disorder we will discuss is phobias, which can range from mildly annoying to serious and debilitating.

Symptoms and Issues

Phobias are *persistent and irrational fears of specific objects, activities, or situations* (American Psychiatric Association, 1994). For example, individuals may be afraid of bugs, elevators, going out in public, or high places. Importantly, phobias involve fears that have *no justification in reality* (e.g., fear of harmless animals) or fears that are *greater than what is justified* (e.g., extreme fear of flying), and the individual with a phobia is *aware of the irrationality of his or her fear.* In other words, people with phobias know that their fear is not really justified, but they cannot stop being afraid. For example, an individual with a phobia for elevators *knows* there are hundreds of thousands of elevators, knows these elevators each make hundreds of trips every day of the year without anyone getting hurt, and *knows* that the probability of getting hurt in an elevator is very low (maybe even lower than using the stairs). However, despite this knowledge the individual is still afraid to ride in an elevator. In phobic disorders, then, we see an inappropriate separation of the cognitive and emotional aspects of psychological functioning.

In some cases a phobia can seriously interfere with an individual's ability to function. The degree to which a phobia will be disruptive is determined in part by the likelihood that the individual will encounter the feared object or situation in daily life. For example, *claustrophobia* (klos-truh-FO-be-uh), a fear of small enclosed places, would not be particularly disruptive for a Kansas wheat farmer, but it could pose a serious problem for an office worker living in New York City, who must frequently spend time in cramped elevators, small windowless offices, and crowded subway cars. Many people have phobias for harmless insects, but because they do not encounter the insects on a regular basis, those fears do not have a major effect on their lives.

Phobias can lead to disruptive behavior in two ways: First, avoiding the phobic object or situation can have unfortunate consequences. For example, if an individual with an elevator phobia were offered a good job on the 15th floor, he or she might have to decline the offer in order to avoid taking the elevator. I have had a number of students who could not take classes that met in small rooms because they had phobias for small spaces. Second, if the feared object or situation cannot be easily avoided, the individual may experience uncontrollable and overwhelming fear and panic. When this occurs, the individual may have very embarrassing emotional outbursts, including fainting and frantic attempts to escape. Consider what a person with a spider phobia might do if he or she suddenly saw a spider while in an elevator with his or her boss.

The case of the sportscaster John Madden illustrates the inconvenience caused by a phobia. Rather than taking a few hours to fly from New York to San Francisco to broadcast a football game, he must spend 3 or 4 days on his bus to get to his destination. His symptoms are described in Case Study 5.1 (on p. 128).

Phobic disorders are probably more common than you think because people with phobias often conceal their problems quite effectively. I was completely unaware of a colleague's elevator phobia because each time we went to our offices on the 4th floor, he would say something like, "Let's take the stairs. The exercise will be good for us." I finally became aware of his phobia one day when we had to move some heavy boxes to the 6th floor, and after the boxes were loaded into the elevator, he told me he would take the stairs and meet me at the top.

Phobic disorders are divided into three types based on the kind of situation that elicits the fear. In the following sections we'll consider these three types: agoraphobia, social phobia, and specific phobias.

Individuals with agoraphobia often confine themselves to their homes, in order to avoid situations from which it would be difficult to escape if they were overcome with fear or experienced paniclike symptoms.

the individuals are afraid of panicking and embarrassing themselves, so they avoid public situations.

Because of their fear of embarrassing themselves, people with agoraphobia may confine themselves to their homes and venture out as little as possible, and when they do go out, they may only do so with someone they believe will be able to help them if they become anxious. Note that individuals with agoraphobia do not avoid people because of any fear of people; instead they avoid people because "something" might happen that they cannot control and then they will embarrass themselves.

Agoraphobia is diagnosed in about 7% of women and in about 3.5% of men (Kessler et al., 1998); the reasons for the gender difference will be discussed in Chapter 6. However,

 ## Agoraphobia

Individuals who suffer from **agoraphobia** (ag-uh-ruh-FO-be-uh) are *afraid of being in situations in which escape would be difficult or embarrassing if paniclike symptoms occurred* (American Psychiatric Association, 1994). In other words,

phobias   Persistent and irrational fears of specific objects, activities, or situations.

agoraphobia   An anxiety disorder in which an individual avoids being away from home because of a fear of being in situations in which escape might be difficult or embarrassing if paniclike symptoms occurred.

John Madden—A 260-Pound "Fraidy Cat"?

JOHN MADDEN IS 6 feet 4 inches tall and weighs 260 pounds. As a football player, he was an offensive and defensive tackle, and following his playing career, he was the coach of the Oakland Raiders for 10 years. Madden is not the sort of fellow you would expect to be afraid of much, but guess again. Madden suffers from a variety of fears, most of which seem to revolve around small spaces.

Madden's fear of being hemmed in is very general. He is afraid of planes, elevators, crowds, and even tight-fitting clothing. The anxiety that keeps him out of planes causes him considerable inconvenience as a sportscaster because he must make frequent trips from coast to coast to broadcast football games. Rather than making the trip in a matter of a few hours by plane, it takes him 3 or 4 days to make the trip on his bus.

Madden originally misdiagnosed his symptoms of anxiety as the effects of an inner-ear infection. Whenever he flew, he became tense, but he thought the tension was just a physiological reaction to the altitude. He soon realized, however, that the symptoms started as soon as the stewardess closed the door—before the plane was off the ground. One day Madden had a flight from Tampa to California with a stop in Houston. He got off in Houston, checked into a hotel, and never flew again. Madden reports that at first he was embarrassed by his phobia, but now he publicly jokes about it.

As is often the case with individuals who suffer from one phobia, Madden appears to have a variety of other anxieties. His more general anxiety is reflected in the fact that he is a chronic worrier. He points out that he gave up a very successful coaching career with the Raiders because his constant worrying made his life miserable, and he just "burned out."

Sportscaster John Madden (right) suffers from a fear of flying that greatly interferes with his professional life. He must take a train or bus from coast to coast to broadcast football games.

we are often unaware that people we know have the disorder. That's because they successfully conceal it by declining social invitations; they are always "too busy" or have "something else to do" at home. Furthermore, because they avoid social gatherings, we have less contact with them, and therefore we are less likely to realize they have a problem. An interesting example of a woman with agoraphobia is described in Case Study 5.2.

social phobia   An anxiety disorder in which an individual avoids others because of an irrational fear of behaving in an embarrassing way.

specific phobias   All phobias other than agoraphobia and social phobia; irrational and persistent fears about specific objects or situations.

Social Phobia

The major symptom shown by individuals with **social phobia** is an *irrational fear that they will behave in an embarrassing way,* and as a consequence these individuals show high levels of anxiety in social situations and/or they avoid social situations (American Psychiatric Association, 1994). Social phobia is very similar to agoraphobia in that both involve fear of embarrassment, but the difference lies in the fact that social phobia is limited to those situations in which *scrutiny by others is likely.* For example, an individual with social phobia would be uncomfortable going to a crowded meeting only *if he or she were going to have to make a speech,* whereas an individual with agoraphobia would be uncomfortable going to a crowded meeting because he or she might develop paniclike symptoms and leaving the

The Woman Who Went to Bed Dressed: A Case of Agoraphobia

ANN IS A 34-YEAR-OLD, college-educated woman who is married and has two children. When I first met her, she impressed me as being mature, attractive, and personally outgoing. Ann had a normal childhood and adolescence, and her early adult life had gone smoothly. However, about 3 years ago she began to feel somewhat "tense, nervous, and upset" whenever she left the house to shop, go to a party, or carpool the children.

At first the anxiety was relatively mild, and she described it as a "vague tension that sort of came from nowhere." As time went by, however, the level of anxiety became progressively greater. Within a year her anxiety when out of the house was so high that she was unable to go more than a few blocks from home unless her husband or her sister was with her "for protection." Sometimes, even when she was out with her husband, she would begin to tremble, have "hot flashes," and start sweating, and she would have to leave wherever she was and go home as quickly as possible. This resulted in a variety of embarrassing situations. For example, she left parties abruptly, fled from crowded stores, and once ran out of church in the middle of the service. When friends noticed her unusual behavior, she would explain it by saying that she was "tired" or "not feeling well" or had a lot of work at home that needed to be done.

It got to the point where Ann rarely ventured out of the house. When she did, it was only for very brief periods, and she never went far. If Ann thought about going out of the house, she would become so anxious by the time she was supposed to leave that she would not be able to do so. To get around this problem whenever it was necessary for her to shop, Ann would go to bed the night before fully dressed and made up. When she awoke the next morning, she would immediately jump out of bed and run out of the house, hoping to get to the store before her anxiety got so high that she would have to stop and return home. This worked about half of the time, but sometimes she would get "trapped in the checkout line" and have to leave her basket and rush home in a panic.

Ann could not explain why she became anxious when she left the house. She could only say that there might be "an emergency," but she could not remember an emergency ever occurring or name a specific emergency that might occur other than her getting sick. She recognized the irrationality of her fear. She also realized that her fear was disrupting her life and her family, but no matter how hard she tried, she could not suppress or overcome it.

> . . . her anxiety while out of the house was so high that she was unable to go more than a few blocks from home . . . .

meeting might be difficult or embarrassing. Social phobia might be thought of as extreme introversion or shyness. Obviously, social phobia can severely constrict an individual's life. This disorder afflicts about 15% of women and about 11% of men at some point in their lives (Davidson et al., 1994; Kessler et al., 1994). An example of a relatively minor social phobia is presented in Case Study 5.3 (on p. 130).

Specific Phobias

The third type of phobic disorders consists of **specific phobias,** which are *all of the phobias other than agoraphobia and social phobia.* In other words, specific phobias are *irrational and persistent fears about specific objects or situations* (e.g., animals, flying, heights, injections, seeing blood). It is not clear exactly why agoraphobia and social phobia were singled out as separate diagnoses, but that is the convention followed in *DSM-IV.* Specific phobias are quite common, occurring in about 16% of women and almost 7% of men (Kessler et al., 1994). See Chapter 6 for a discussion of the gender differences.

This playground scene made a woman with a spider phobia very anxious because it reminded her of spiders in a web.

"Phone Phobia": A Case of a Social Phobia

THE FOLLOWING ACCOUNT was written by an intelligent professional woman who describes herself as suffering from "phone phobia." That label is something of a misnomer because she is not anxious about the telephone itself but rather about the social interactions that take place on the phone.

When I'm on the phone, I am extremely tense–it's as if I'm "on the line"....

"When I'm on the phone, I am extremely tense—it's as if I'm 'on the line,' and I am almost paralyzed with fear. I feel as though I have to justify making the call so that I don't 'bother' the other person, and I feel that I have to explain what I want clearly and briefly so as not to take up too much of the other person's time. I am always sure that I am going to make an ass of myself when I call someone.

"Over the years, I have developed certain strategies for dealing with my phone phobia. For any call, I establish a day and a time for making the call—it's on my calendar. However, I often postpone important calls if my level of tension is too high when they come up on my calendar. If I make the call and the other person is out, I am always relieved.

"I also feel threatened, tense, and anxious when I receive calls. I feel as if I'm being put on the spot, and I won't be able to think fast enough to come up with intelligent answers to the other person's questions. When the phone rings, I may start to tremble badly. To deal with my fear, I have established a firm rule for myself: I always pick up the phone after the second ring. With that rule, I give myself a little time to build up my courage, but I can't avoid the fear by not answering the phone. This phone phobia makes my professional and personal life really difficult. It's all rather crazy, but I can't get over it, so I just try to get around it."

It's interesting to note that this woman was once my editor, and we always had to have our conference calls at *7 in the morning* because after that her anxiety about the call got too high.

Explanations for Phobias

We now come to our first challenge, which is to determine what causes phobias. To meet that challenge we will examine the strengths and weaknesses of the psychodynamic, learning, cognitive, and physiological explanations for phobias.

The Psychodynamic Explanation: Symbolically Expressed Conflicts and Stress

Freud argued that anxiety is caused by conflicts and stress and that if the conflicts and stress are too threatening to be expressed directly, they *are expressed symbolically in the form of phobias.* For example, conflict and stress about castration might be expressed as a phobia for snakes, because snakes can be viewed as phallic symbols. Similarly, a trauma associated with birth might lead to a phobia for elevators, because a trip in an elevator symbolizes the individual's trip through the birth canal. Freud used the fact that individuals are unable to explain their phobic fears as evidence for the unconscious (repressed) nature of the stressful conflict. In other words, the cause of the fear is so threatening that the individuals cannot allow it to reach consciousness. Although such symbolic interpretations are still widely used in literature, there is no scientific evidence to support them and this approach is now generally ignored by most mental health professionals. Therefore, let's go on to consider more viable explanations.

The Learning Explanation: Classically Conditioned Fears

The learning explanation is simply that *phobias are classically conditioned fear responses.* In other words, at some time fear was paired with a stimulus, such as a snake, and now that stimulus can elicit the fear in the same way the ringing of the bell caused Pavlov's dogs to salivate. The classic example of the conditioning of a phobia is the case of Little Albert. You will recall that initially Albert was not afraid of a white rat, but after a frightening noise was sounded each time he was shown the white rat, he became afraid when he was shown the rat even if the noise was not sounded (see Chapter 2). Clearly, if you saw Albert's reaction to a harmless white rat, you would conclude that he had a phobia. Furthermore, because of the process of *generalization,* stimuli that are *similar* to the stimulus with which the fear was originally paired can also elicit the response. Recall, for example, that after being conditioned to fear the white rat, Albert also showed fear responses to other furry animals and to a ball of white cotton. Therefore, the process of generalization can be used to explain why people become fearful (phobic) of objects and situations other than the specific ones with which the fear was originally paired.

The conditioning explanation for agoraphobia is particularly interesting because the frightening experience that often provides the basis for the conditioning is a *panic attack.* Panic attacks are a symptom of another anxiety disorder (panic disorder) I'll discuss later; here I'll just point out that panic attacks involve the sudden onset of ex-

For most people this would be a beautiful view, but for a person with a fear of heights, it would be terrifying.

tremely high levels of anxiety and physical symptoms such as a very high heart rate and shortness of breath. These attacks are so severe that individuals often think they are having a heart attack and will die. When panic attacks occur in public, the fear is paired with being in public, and agoraphobia develops. The link between panic attacks and agoraphobia is so common that there is a specific diagnosis for it, *panic disorder with agoraphobia* (American Psychiatric Association, 1994).

Conditioning seems to be a good explanation for the development of phobias, but two questions must be answered: First, why do phobias persist even when there is no longer reason to believe that the stimulus will lead to a frightening experience? In other words, why aren't phobias *extinguished?* To answer that question we must consider the role of *operant conditioning,* the procedure by which we learn behaviors that enable us to obtain rewards or avoid punishments (see Chapter 2). What happens in the case of phobias is that individuals *avoid the phobic stimuli as a means of avoiding the fear they think it will provoke, and therefore they do not discover that the stimuli are not dangerous.* Therefore, the phobia does not have an opportunity to be extinguished. For example, individuals with a phobia for dogs will not play with dogs and so do not come to realize that most dogs are not dangerous and do not overcome their fear.

Second, why is it that people sometimes develop phobias for objects or situations with which fear was never directly paired? For instance, how can an individual develop a classically conditioned fear response to elevators if he or she has never been in an elevator that crashed? The answer is that the fear can be conditioned *vicariously;* that is, the individual only needs to see or hear about someone else experiencing fear of the object for the conditioning to take place. Recall, for example, that monkeys developed fears of snakes after simply watching another monkey show fear in the presence of a snake (see Chapter 2).

Overall, then, the classical conditioning of fear responses fits well with what we know about phobias, and therefore it provides a good explanation for this disorder. However, before drawing any conclusion about the cause of phobias, we must go on to consider other explanations.

The Cognitive Explanation: Incorrect Beliefs

From the cognitive perspective it is assumed that phobias are the result of *incorrect beliefs about the danger posed by the phobic objects or situations* (Beck & Emery, 1985; Williams, 1990). In other words, people with phobias simply have incorrect information, which leads to incorrect beliefs. For example, people with a phobia for snakes are simply *wrong* in their belief that snakes are dangerous, and people with a phobia for elevators are just *wrong* in their belief that elevators are likely to crash. In addition to holding incorrect beliefs about the danger posed by the stimuli, individuals with phobias also have incorrect beliefs about their ability to deal with the situation; they just don't think they can handle the situation.

You might ask, if phobias are caused by incorrect beliefs, why can't phobias be overcome by correcting the incorrect beliefs? Why not just convince an individual with a phobia for elevators that elevators almost never crash and therefore are not dangerous? Actually, as you will learn later, this is exactly what cognitive therapists try to do with their clients during therapy, but the therapists argue that the process is not simple because the incorrect thoughts are *automatic—* they pop into the individual's head without conscious control.

Both the learning and the cognitive explanations make sense, so which explanation is correct? Actually, both are probably correct in the sense that the cause of a phobia may sometimes be best explained by a combination of the two. Consider the following: First, the explanations may work together because *conditioning may simply be one of the ways we form beliefs.* You will recall that it was originally assumed that classical conditioning *did not involve thinking;* specifically, classical conditioning was thought to occur when a stimulus was simply *paired* with a response so that a link was made (e.g., in the case of Little Albert a white rat was paired with a loud noise; see Chapter 2). However, later research indicated that in many cases the pairing of a stimulus with the response is not enough; instead classically conditioned responses develop when an individual comes to *expect* (think) that the stimulus will lead to a particular consequence (e.g., Little Albert realized that the presence of the white rat signaled that a frightening noise would follow). If it's true that classical conditioning involves thinking and developing expectations, then conditioning is simply a means through which we develop beliefs about what stimuli will have frightening consequences.

A second reason why both explanations may be correct is that there are *two pathways in the brain that lead to the area responsible for fear* (Le Doux, 1992, 1994, 1998). One of those pathways begins at one of your sense organs, either your eyes or your ears; then it leads to a structure in your brain called the *thalamus,* where a rough identification of incoming stimuli is made; and finally it goes to a structure called the *amygdala* that generates emotion. This pathway does not involve much thinking. The second pathway also begins at your sense organs and goes to your thalamus, but from there it leads to higher areas of your brain that are associated with thinking, and only then does it go to the amygdala. This pathway involves cognitive activity, and although it may take a while, it can override the other pathway. The existence of the two pathways explains why when you first see something that could be dangerous, such as a coiled object, you feel a sudden surge of fear—the coiled object could be a snake, and the first pathway has activated the amygdala. However, after you think about it briefly and evaluate the stimulus more carefully, you conclude that the coiled object is just a piece of rope, and the fear subsides; the second pathway has arrested the activity in the amygdala. Clearly, the classical conditioning of fear involves a relatively automatic process (the first pathway) as well as a cognitive process (the second pathway), so neither explanation should be abandoned. The two pathways are illustrated in Figure 5.1.

Overall, then, the conditioning and cognitive explanations, taken singly or together, provide a good explanation for phobias. However, two questions remain unanswered: Why are some people more likely to develop phobias than others, and why do phobias tend to run in families? To answer these questions we turn to the physiological explanation.

The Physiological Explanation: Neurological Arousal and Genetics

Although there is no physiological explanation for why people develop a *particular* phobia, physiology can explain why some people are more likely than others to develop phobias and why a person who has one phobia is likely to have other phobias. The notion is simply that *higher levels of neurological arousal increase the likelihood that conditioning will take place, so individuals with higher levels of arousal will be more likely to develop classically conditioned phobias*

(Chaney et al., 1993; Gerardi et al., 1994; Southwick et al., 1993). In other words, neurological arousal and conditioning work together to lead to phobias.

There are three ways in which high arousal can contribute to the conditioning of phobias. First, higher levels of arousal can enhance the conditioning process. Indeed, later you will learn that drugs that increase neurological arousal increase the possibility of conditioning (see Chapter 12). Second, when confronted with a potentially fear-provoking stimulus, highly aroused individuals are more likely to respond with fear, making it more likely that for them fear will get paired with that stimulus. (Think about how, when you are aroused and tense, any little noise will cause you to jump.) Third, fearful experiences are more likely to get stored in memory than are other experiences, so individuals are more likely to recall frightening experiences associated with particular stimuli, and this can lead to phobias (McGaugh, 1989, 1990; Pitman, 1989; Squire, 1986). In summary, it appears that high levels of arousal play an important role in determining whether conditioning will occur and what individuals will remember. In other words, high physiological arousal sets up a *predisposition* to develop phobias, and then experiences determine what objects or situations will lead to phobias.

Given that arousal facilitates the development of phobias, the next question is, why do some people have higher levels of arousal than others? Arousal levels are due in large part to genetic factors, thereby suggesting a genetic basis for phobias (Basoglu et al., 1994). Indeed, there is strong support for a genetic basis (Hollander et al., 1999; Knowles et al., 1999). For example, in a comparison of the rates of phobias in identical (monozygotic) and nonidentical (dizygotic) female twins, it was found that the rates were higher in the identical twins. Indeed, it was estimated that the heritability for phobias was as high as 40% (Kendler, Neale, et al., 1992b).

Overall, then, from a physiological perspective it appears that (1) some individuals inherit high levels of neurological arousal, (2) the high levels of arousal lead to better classical conditioning, and (3) the enhanced classical conditioning increases the likelihood that the individuals will develop phobias. However, which phobia an individual develops depends on his or her experiences, so in this explanation the interaction between physiological and experiential factors is crucial.

Finally, specific attention needs to be focused on social phobia. As I noted earlier, this disorder can be conceptualized as extreme *introversion* or *shyness.* If that is the case, physiology may play an important role because introversion and shyness are known to be influenced strongly by genes (Bouchard & Hur, 1998; Kagan, Resnick, & Snidman, 1999). For example, identical (monozygotic) twins are more likely to be similar in terms of introversion than are nonidentical (dizygotic) twins, leading to the conclusion that the heritability of introversion is about 60%. The

FIGURE 5.1

There are two pathways to fear in the brain.

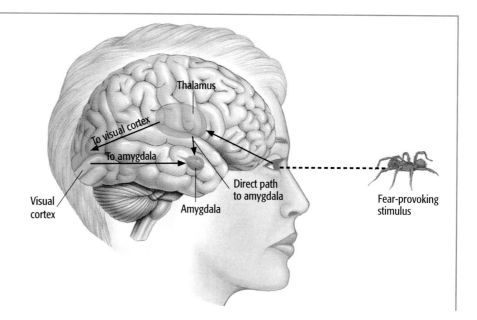

notion is that individuals inherit a low threshold for arousal and therefore overreact to social stressors, causing them to withdraw to avoid the stress (Kagan et al., 1999).

 ## Treatments for Phobias

Now that we have developed an understanding of what causes phobias, we can go on to consider the procedures that are usually used to treat them. We will consider treatments based on the learning, cognitive, and physiological explanations, because the psychodynamic explanation no longer seems viable (see earlier discussion).

The Learning Approach: Using Extinction

At the outset I should remind you that treatments based on learning are usually referred to as "*behavior* therapy" rather than "psychotherapy." That's because with the learning approach the emphasis is on *changing behaviors directly* rather than changing underlying factors, such as unconscious conflicts or beliefs, which supposedly influence the behaviors.

If phobias are classically conditioned fear responses, then the treatment of choice is **extinction.** As you learned in Chapter 2, extinction involves repeatedly exposing the individual to the stimulus that ordinarily elicits fear, but the situation is controlled so that in fact nothing frightening happens after the stimulus is presented. An example of the extinction of a phobia for dogs is presented in Case Study 5.4 (on p. 134).

Unfortunately, being exposed to a frightening stimulus as part of extinction can sometimes result in very high levels of fear; indeed, the exposure procedure is sometimes called *flooding* because the individual is "flooded" with fear. This can have two negative consequences: First, it can be stressful and unpleasant. Second, because the fear is present at the same time as the stimulus, the fear may again be paired with the stimulus, and therefore the experience may wind up being a conditioning trial rather than an extinction trial. To avoid these problems a procedure was developed in which an individual could be exposed to the stimulus without the fear being elicited. This is how it works: The individual begins by compiling a list of feared stimuli in which the stimuli are arranged in order from least feared to most feared. For example, an individual with a phobia for dogs might list the following situations: (1) watching a small puppy in a cage 10 feet away, (2) sitting next to a small dog, and (3) petting a large German shepherd. Second, the individual is taught how to relax deeply. This is usually done by teaching the individual how to relax his or her muscles (Jacobson, 1938; see the description in this chapter). Third, the individual is told to begin relaxing and is then asked to imagine the least-feared stimulus. The process is started with the least-feared stimulus because it is

extinction   A procedure used to treat phobias in which the stimulus that ordinarily elicits the fear is presented repeatedly without anything frightening being allowed to happen, so that eventually the link between the stimulus and the fear response is eliminated.

Treatment of a Dog Phobia with Extinction

CASE STUDY 5.4

NED WAS A COLLEGE SENIOR majoring in mathematics. He was well adjusted in all respects except that he had an extreme fear of dogs. So far as he could remember, he had never been hurt or bitten by a dog.

I decided to use exposure to dogs as a means of extinguishing Ned's fear. To do this, Ned and I first went to a local pet shop that had a large number of puppies for sale. The puppies were small and very friendly, and each was in a cage. At first we simply walked around the shop looking at other things but staying away from the dogs. When Ned was relaxed and comfortable, he and I walked slowly over to a cage containing a small cocker spaniel puppy that looked somewhat sleepy. This did not bother Ned much, and I asked him to put his finger through the bars of the cage and scratch the puppy's head. He was a little tentative, thinking that the puppy might snap, but he did it, and nothing much happened. Next we went to a cage with three or four wide-awake and active puppies in it, and I asked Ned to put his hand in and play with the puppies. Again he was tentative, but he did it. After he was comfortable with that, I encouraged him to roughhouse with the puppies a little and let them chew on his finger a bit. Again he started out somewhat tentatively, but he did it, and after a few

> ... Ned ... felt exhilarated; he had played with dogs and enjoyed it.

minutes he was enjoying playing with the pups. From there we went from cage to cage, playing with the various puppies.

After about 40 minutes Ned smiled somewhat sheepishly and said, "Once you get used to them, they're kinda fun. Their little teeth can be sharp, but if you're careful, it's all right." However, he then added, "But they're only puppies—not full-grown dogs." I told him we would take it one step at a time and that his "homework" before our next session was to go to three or four different pet stores and play with the puppies. The homework was designed to expose him to as many puppies as possible and have him deal with the puppies without me there for support.

At the beginning of our next session Ned reported that he had gone to five different pet shops to play with puppies, that two or three times he had picked puppies up to hold them, and that he was comfortable doing that, but he hastened to add, "But those are only puppies. Dogs are a different thing." After talking for a few minutes, we went to a nearby park where a canine obedience class was being held. The dogs in the class were full-grown, on leashes, and generally well behaved because this was one of the final sessions. We watched the class for a while, noting specifically that the dogs were controllable. After the class we talked to the owners, and Ned very tentatively petted the dogs while their owners held them on a short leash. Ned then

worked with the owners to put two dogs through their exercises ("sit," "stay," "come," etc.). At first he was really nervous when a dog would come, but in time, he got used to it. When the session was over, Ned was exhausted (it had been a strain), but he also felt exhilarated; he had played with dogs and enjoyed it.

At our next session Ned and I developed a list of training exercises that would expose him to more dogs, different kinds of dogs, and dogs in different circumstances. He went to more pet stores and obedience classes as well as to dog shows and veterinarians' offices. He also sought out friends who had dogs and spent time with them and their dogs. If a fear is to be extinguished, it is important that the feared stimulus be experienced over and over in the absence of fear. Also, because Ned's fear had generalized, it was important that all of the fear-related stimuli be experienced over and over. During the next couple of weeks, I pushed Ned really hard to increase the amount and types of exposure. Over time the fear slowly diminished, and Ned could play easily with relatively big dogs. At the end of the treatment period Ned commented, "Well, the fear is gone. There is really no reason to be afraid; dogs are like people—most of them are friendly and the only problem is to separate the friendly ones from the others. After this treatment I'm not afraid of dogs—I'm sick of them!"

least likely to result in a strong fear response. Once the individual is able to remain relaxed while thinking of the first stimulus, he or she is asked to begin thinking about the

systematic desensitization A treatment for reducing fear responses (phobias) in which an individual is first taught to relax and then, while relaxed, is presented with fear-related stimuli, beginning with those that produce the least fear.

modeling A treatment strategy for phobias in which the fearful individual watches another person who does not show fear of the object or situation, resulting in vicarious extinction of the fear response.

next least feared stimulus. This procedure is repeated until the individual is relaxing while thinking about the most-feared stimulus—that is, until the fear is extinguished. If the individual becomes anxious during the procedure, he or she is asked to go back to imagining a previous stimulus with which relaxation was possible. In this example the individual simply imagines the feared stimuli, but it is also possible to have the individual actually experience progressively more frightening stimuli. For example, an individual who is phobic for high places might be taken to higher and higher floors of a tall building. This treatment is called **systematic desensitization** (Wolpe, 1958) because the individual's *sensitivity* to the feared stimuli is *systematically*

If an individual who has a classically conditioned fear of dogs is repeatedly exposed to friendly dogs, his or her fear of dogs will eventually be extinguished.

reduced (lowest to highest fear). To some extent I used a form of systematic desensitization when I worked with Ned, who was afraid of dogs (see Case Study 5.4). A classic example of systematic desensitization is described in Case Study 5.5.

In the examples I have used so far, extinction was achieved by exposing the individuals to the objects they feared while not allowing the individuals to experience fear. However, it is also possible to extinguish a fear response by having an individual observe another person deal with the feared object while not experiencing fear. For example, watching another person play with dogs can reduce the fear of dogs. In other words, just as fears can be developed vicariously through observation (see Chapter 2), they can also be extinguished vicariously. This approach to treatment is often referred to as **modeling;** that is, watching a non-frightened model can reduce fears.

Finally, a comment should be made concerning a high tech approach to extinction—the use of computers and *virtual reality.* Virtual reality consists of lifelike, computer-generated simulations of scenes or objects. In therapy such simulations can be used to expose individuals to stimuli for which they have phobias (Bullinger et al., 1999; Glantz et al., 1996). For instance, an individual with a phobia for flying can participate in a computer-generated flight simulation. Virtual reality simulations can seem more "real" than imagined scenarios, and it is often more convenient to use a computer simulation than to have a client go to the actual situation or confront the actual object. It appears then that what started as a computer toy may become a therapeutic tool. Thus far, however, the use of virtual reality is limited to objects and situations that do not involve social interactions because social interactions cannot yet be programmed. Unfortunately, there is not yet enough evidence to draw conclusions concerning the effectiveness of therapy employing virtual reality, but it should work at least as well as therapy involving imagination.

Are treatments based on extinction effective? The answer is generally yes; indeed, there are literally hundreds of experiments in which various treatments involving extinction were compared to no treatment, placebos, or other

Systematic Desensitization: The Case of Little Peter

A FORM OF SYSTEMATIC DESENSITIZATION was reported as early as 1924 in the case of Peter, a young boy, who, like Little Albert, had become afraid of furry objects such as rabbits and fur coats. To overcome this fear, a rabbit was presented to Peter, but it was initially presented far enough away so that Peter did not become afraid. A laboratory assistant then began feeding Peter his favorite food, as the rabbit was slowly brought closer and closer. Feeding was used to elicit relaxation and pleasure because relaxation training would not be effective with a child as young as Peter. The hope was that the pleasure associated with eating would overwhelm and inhibit the fear, thus allowing extinction to take place. In fact, the procedure was effective in eliminating Peter's fear. Within a short period of time, Peter was sitting calmly and eating with the rabbit right next to him.

This case is often cited as an example of the effectiveness of systematic desensitization, but it should be recognized that other processes were going on as well. Most noteworthy is the fact that on most days during the treatment period, other children who were not afraid of the rabbit were brought in to play with Peter and the rabbit, and it appears that some of Peter's fear was reduced by observing the fearlessness of the other children. In other words, Peter may have experienced some vicarious extinction.

Sources: Based on Jones (1924) and Kornfeld (1989).

CASE STUDY 5.5

types of treatment, and the individuals who received the extinction-based treatments usually showed greater and faster improvements than the individuals in the other conditions (Agras & Berkowitz, 1999; Carlin, Hoffman, & Weghorst, 1997; Mavissakalian & Perel, 1996). However, despite this evidence treatments based on extinction are used less today than they were some years ago. This is largely because of a shift in interest to cognitive-based therapy, which we consider in the next section.

The Cognitive Approach: Changing Beliefs

If the cognitive explanation is correct and phobias are due to incorrect beliefs, then therapy should be focused on changing the incorrect beliefs, and indeed this strategy has proven to be effective (Barlow, Esler, & Vitali, 1998; Kurtman et al., 1998; Wright & Beck, 1999). For example, in an experiment with individuals who had social phobias, the individuals in a cognitive-behavioral treatment condition were *exposed to groups of people* and *given cognitive training to change their incorrect beliefs.* Among other things they were told to think, "Nothing bad will happen to me in a group of people." In contrast, the individuals in a placebo condition received lectures on phobias and group support. Anxiety was measured before treatment began, immediately after treatment ended, and 3 and 6 months later. The results indicate that the individuals who received the cognitive-behavioral treatment showed greater improvements than the individuals in the placebo condition (Heimberg et al., 1990). Those findings are illustrated in Figure 5.2.

Although the results of this experiment demonstrate that cognitive-behavioral treatment led to improvement, a question remains as to whether the improvement was due to the *cognitive strategies* used for changing beliefs or to the fact that the individuals were *exposed* to groups and nothing bad happened. That exposure could have led to extinction or it could have led the individuals to realize that there was no reason for fear. To examine the separate effects of cognitive and behavioral components of treatments, researchers conducted an experiment in which in one condition individuals with severe driving phobias received a treatment that consisted of *both* the cognitive and the behavioral components (Williams & Rappoport, 1983). Specifically, the cognitive component involved (1) training in relabeling feelings (e.g., "These anxious feelings won't harm me; they're just uncomfortable"), (2) developing pos-

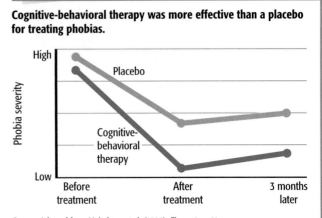

FIGURE 5.2

Cognitive-behavioral therapy was more effective than a placebo for treating phobias.

Source: Adapted from Heimberg et al. (1990), Figure 1, p. 11.

itive expectations (e.g., "I will be able to manage regardless of how I feel"), (3) focusing on task-relevant thoughts (e.g., "I need to keep my mind on my driving"), and (4) using self-distraction (e.g., planning recreational activities). The behavioral component of the treatment consisted of 11 hours of driving practice—that is, *exposure* to the feared situation. In contrast, individuals in another condition of the experiment received only the behavioral component of the treatment (i.e., 11 hours of driving practice). The results revealed that the individuals who received only the behavioral treatment (driving practice) showed anxiety reductions that were as great as those who received the combined treatment. From these results it was concluded that the best way to rectify incorrect beliefs that lead to fears is to give clients firsthand demonstrations that their beliefs are incorrect and that they can function effectively. In other words, demonstrations via exposure are more effective for changing beliefs than cognitive retraining. These findings do not mean that changing beliefs is not effective for reducing fears; instead they simply indicate that behavioral strategies such as exposure to the feared stimulus may be the most effective means for changing incorrect beliefs. Thus cognitive therapy involving exposure remains an important strategy for combating phobias (Salaberria & Echeburua, 1998; Shear et al., 1998).

The Physiological Approach: Using Drugs to Reduce Arousal

Phobias are fear responses, and because fear is based on physiological arousal, it might be possible to treat phobias with drugs that *block physiological arousal and thereby block fear* (Roy-Byrne & Cowley, 1998). In other words, if an individual is given a drug that inhibits physiological arousal, the individual cannot become fearful and therefore

benzodiazepines A class of drugs used to reduce anxiety by increasing the activity of inhibitory neurons; well-known examples are Valium and Xanax.

beta blockers A class of drugs that limit the degree to which the heart rate can increase; sometimes used to treat anxiety disorders.

cannot have a phobic response. In fact, phobias are sometimes treated with drugs called **benzodiazepines** (ben-zo-di-AZ-uh-pinz), which are often referred to as "tranquilizers." Commonly used benzodiazepines include Valium (diazepam) and Xanax (alprazolam). (Table 5.2, later in this chapter, provides a more complete list of benzodiazepines.)

Early evidence that benzodiazepines can reduce phobias was provided by an interesting experiment on pigeons. The pigeons were first taught to peck at a disk to receive food. Once that response was learned, the pigeons were given electrical shocks when they pecked the disk. After receiving the shocks they ceased pecking the disk. In human terms a phobia had been induced in the pigeons (fear of pecking the disk). In the next phase of the experiment the pigeons either were or were not given benzodiazepines, and it was found that when they were given the drug their pecking of the disk returned almost to the normal (preshock) level, whereas when they were not given the drugs they continued to avoid pecking the disk (Houser, 1978; Sanger & Blackman, 1981). In this experiment benzodiazepines were effective for overcoming the phobia. A number of experiments with humans also showed benzodiazepines to be effective for reducing phobias (Conner et al., 1998; Davidson et al., 1994; Hollander et al., 1999; Levin, Schneier, & Liebowitz, 1989).

A good friend of mine has a severe phobia for flying, and before getting on a plane she has two strong martinis. Alcohol is a strong *depressant* (as are benzodiazepines, see Chapter 15), so after taking the drinks my friend is so relaxed that she is simply unable to have a fear response. *This form of "self-medication" is certainly not recommended,* but it illustrates the point.

Another type of drug that can be effective for treating phobias is a class called **beta blockers.** Beta blockers *limit the degree to which the heart rate can increase* and are widely used by individuals with heart problems who have to avoid cardiac stress. However, beta blockers can also be used to treat individuals with phobias because if the heart rate does not increase, the fear response will be limited, which helps to suppress the phobia (Hollander, Simeon, & Gorman, 1994; Levin et al., 1989).

When individuals first begin taking drugs to treat phobias, the drugs are only effective because they *suppress* the phobic fears; that is, the drugs just hold the fears in check. However, as the treatment progresses, the drugs can help to *eliminate* the phobias because if the fears are suppressed, individuals are more likely to put themselves in situations in which they will experience the phobic stimuli and discover that nothing terrible will happen. As a result, the phobic fear may very well be extinguished or the individuals may correct their beliefs regarding the fearful nature of the stimuli. In other words, the drugs can facilitate the processes of extinction and belief change, which reduce the phobias.

THINKING CRITICALLY
Questions about Phobic Disorders

1. What causes phobias? There are actually two good explanations for phobias. The first is that they are classically conditioned fear responses. The second is that they are the result of incorrect beliefs about what is dangerous. The conclusion that both of these explanations are correct is supported by the fact that there are two pathways in the brain for fear responses, one of which involves more thinking than the other. Furthermore, in some cases the explanations may overlap; that is, conditioning may be one of the ways people develop the incorrect beliefs that underlie some phobias. In other words, the pairing of a stimulus (e.g., a white rat) with a frightening consequence (e.g., a loud noise) leads to the expectation (belief) that the stimulus always predicts the frightening consequence.

2. What is the most effective strategy for treating phobias? It appears that procedures that involve exposure to the frightening stimulus are most effective for treating phobias. Exposure is effective because it can lead to extinction and because it can change beliefs. In other words, exposure is the treatment of choice regardless of whether phobias are due to conditioning or incorrect beliefs. Other strategies used in cognitive therapy to change beliefs may also be helpful. Drugs (benzodiazepines or beta blockers) can also be used to treat phobias because they suppress fear responses, which can lead to extinction of the conditioned fear response or to changed beliefs about the danger posed by phobic stimuli. Overall, then, it appears that we have a good understanding of phobias and of effective strategies for treating them.

TOPIC III
Generalized Anxiety Disorder

Rondell is constantly tense and anxious, but he can't put his finger on exactly what's upsetting him; he just knows that something terrible will probably happen. If nothing really bad happened in his past and he doesn't know of anything bad that will happen in the future, how can we explain his anxiety? Could it be that there is something in his unconscious that is upsetting him, or is his anxiety caused by a biochemical imbalance in his brain?

Jessica suffers from high anxiety, and she is taking a tranquilizer to help reduce it. The drug is effective, but is it treating the cause of her anxiety or just controlling her symptoms? Will she have to stay on the drug the rest of her life?

In this section we will consider generalized anxiety disorder, which, although it revolves around anxiety, is very different from the phobic disorders.

Symptoms and Issues

Generalized anxiety disorder (GAD) involves anxiety that is *persistent across many situations and lasts for at least 6 months* (American Psychiatric Association, 1994). In other words, unlike phobias, in which anxiety is a response to a specific stimulus such as a dog or an elevator, generalized anxiety disorder has as its main symptom anxiety that is not linked to any particular stimuli but instead is constantly present. It is as though the individual were constantly enveloped in an electrified cloud of anxiety with no way to escape from it. To get an idea of what generalized anxiety disorder is like, think about how you may have felt just before taking an exceptionally important examination for which you were not prepared. Then imagine that feeling persisting for months without your knowing why you were upset.

The fact that individuals with GAD are plagued with uncontrollable worries was demonstrated in an interesting experiment in which individuals who did and did not have GAD were first asked to spend 5 minutes thinking about anything they wished but told *not to think about white bears* (an irrelevant thought). If they thought about white bears, they pushed a button to indicate the thought intrusion. They were then asked again to think about anything they wished for 5 minutes, but this time they were instructed *not to think about things that worried them* and to push the button if a worry-related thought intruded. The results were clear: (1) both groups were effective in suppressing irrelevant thoughts about white bears, (2) individuals who did not have GAD were effective in suppressing worry-related thoughts, but (3) individuals with GAD were very ineffective in suppressing worry-related thoughts (Becker et al., 1998). Indeed, the average individual with GAD had about two worry-related thoughts every minute—despite attempting to suppress them. These findings are illustrated in Figure 5.3. Because individuals with GAD are constantly worried, they are distractible and suffer from fatigue, muscle tension, and sleep disturbances (Wittchen et al., 1994).

Generalized anxiety disorder appears to afflict about 6.6% of women and about 3.6% of men, so it is a fairly widespread problem (Kessler et al., 1994; Wittchen et al., 1994).

Explanations for Generalized Anxiety Disorder

The key aspect of GAD is that the anxiety is general in nature and often difficult for the individual to explain. So how can we explain the disorder? Freud proposed that individuals suffering from this disorder were not aware of why

FIGURE 5.3

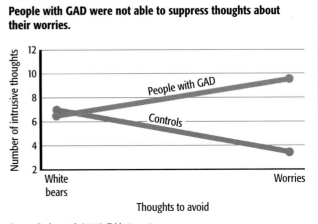

People with GAD were not able to suppress thoughts about their worries.

Source: Becker et al. (1998), Table 3, p. 48.

they were anxious because they had *repressed* the cause of the anxiety. However, there is no sound evidence for this proposition, and mental health professionals have generally abandoned it. Learning theorists argued that anxiety is the result of *classical conditioning*. Although classical conditioning does provide a good explanation for phobias (see Topic II), it does not explain GAD because the anxiety of GAD is not linked to specific stimuli. In view of these problems, let's go on to look at the cognitive and physiological explanations.

The Cognitive Explanation: Incorrect Beliefs

Explaining GAD poses a problem for cognitive theorists because cognitive explanations for disorders usually revolve around incorrect beliefs, but individuals with GAD often cannot explain exactly why they are anxious. In other words, their anxiety "comes out of the blue" and they cannot give specific reasons for it. In fact, one study of the reasons individuals with GAD gave for being anxious reported that the main concern was the social embarrassments the individuals feared they would experience *because of their anxiety* (Breitholtz, Westling, & Oest, 1998). In other words, their anxiety-related beliefs were associated not with the *causes* of their anxiety but instead with the *consequences* of their anxiety.

However, some cognitive theorists argue that although individuals with GAD do not have precise fears, they do have vague concerns that lead to general anxiety. In a test of this notion, individuals with GAD were compared to individuals with other disorders in terms of their reported worries about a variety of topics, such as current relationships, work, finances, physical threat, and the future (Dugas et al., 1998). It turned out that the only thing the individuals with GAD worried about more than the other individuals was some unspecified problem *in the future.*

Individuals with GAD apparently have vague concerns about what might happen in the future, but those concerns might be an *effect* of their anxiety rather than the *cause* of their anxiety. For example, might it be that individuals with GAD are anxious because of a biochemical imbalance in the brain *of which they are not aware,* so they use vague concerns about problems in the future to *explain* or *justify* their anxiety. Support for this possibility comes from an experiment conducted during the Cold War when Russia was considered an enemy of the United States. In this experiment American college students either were or were not made to feel anxious; the students were then shown pictures of Russians and were asked to describe the Russians. The results revealed that students who had been made to feel anxious saw the Russians as hostile warmongers and as providing a reason to be anxious, whereas the students who had not been made anxious saw the Russians as nice people (Bramel, Bell, & Margulis, 1965). For instance, when judging a picture of a smiling Russian standing in a wheat field, anxious students thought he was probably hiding a guided missile silo under his field. In this case anxiety determined beliefs. Other experiments have yielded similar findings (e.g., Schachter & Singer, 1962; White, Fishbein, & Rutstein, 1981).

The finding that anxiety can influence beliefs is exactly what we would expect based on what we know about how memory works. That is, the presence of anxiety leads us to focus on anxiety related material and recall that material, both of which can lead us to incorrect beliefs about the amount of danger that actually exists (see Chapter 3). The influence of anxiety on recall was demonstrated in an experiment in which anxious and nonanxious individuals first learned lists of words that were *neutral* (e.g., *armchair, refrigerator*), *positive* (e.g., *optimistic, successful*), or *threat-related* (e.g., *cancer, weapon*) and then were tested for their recall of the words (McCabe, 1999). The results were simple: Anxious individuals recalled more threat-related words, whereas nonanxious individuals did not differ in their recall of different types of words; see Figure 5.4. Clearly, there is evidence that at least in some cases *anxiety influences beliefs rather than the other way around.*

Overall, then, general worries about the future could lead to GAD, but we must be cautious in making that connection because there is good reason to believe that at least in some cases the anxiety exists prior to the worries about the future, and this preexisting anxiety leads to the worries. Furthermore, the cognitive approach does not explain why individuals with GAD often have biological relatives who also have the disorder (Hollander et al., 1999; Knowles et al., 1999). These limitations do not mean that the cognitive explanation is wrong, only that it may not account for all cases of GAD. Therefore, we must go on to consider another explanation.

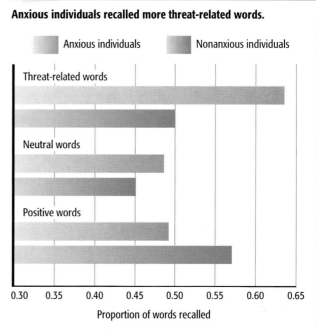

FIGURE 5.4

Anxious individuals recalled more threat-related words.

Source: McCabe (1999), Table 4, p. 33.

The Physiological Explanation: Neurological Arousal and Genetics

The physiological explanation posits that GAD is caused by *excessive neurological activity in the area of the brain that is responsible for anxiety* (Brawman-Mintzer & Lydiard, 1997). In particular, it is believed that the high levels of brain activity are the result of the *underactivity* of the **inhibitory neurons** that ordinarily reduce neurological activity. You will recall that inhibitory neurons make connections with excitatory neurons at the synapses between the excitatory neurons, and when the inhibitory neurons release a neurotransmitter, the neurotransmitter inhibits the transmission of nerve impulses across the synapses, which reduces brain activity (see Chapter 3). However, if the inhibitory neurons do not release enough neurotransmitter, the activity of the excitatory neurons to which they are connected will go unchecked and can become too high.

generalized anxiety disorder (GAD) A disorder in which anxiety is persistent across many situations and lasts for at least 6 months.

inhibitory neurons Neurons that reduce neurological activity and thus anxiety by releasing a neurotransmitter that inhibits the transmission of nerve impulses across the synapses.

The neurotransmitter from inhibitory neurons that is crucial for inhibiting anxiety-related activity is known as **GABA** (*gamma-aminobutyric acid*). In short, then, (1) when low levels of GABA are released by the inhibitory neurons, the activity of excitatory neurons is not inhibited, (2) the failure to inhibit the activity of the excitatory neurons results in a high level of activity of the neurons in the areas of the brain that are responsible for arousal, and (3) this high level of activity is experienced as anxiety. The fact that the anxiety of GAD is not linked to any specific objects such as animals or elevators is exactly what we would expect from low levels of GABA because GABA levels are not influenced by environmental stimuli.

Evidence for the GABA explanation for anxiety is based on our understanding of the effects of the benzodiazepines, drugs that can reduce anxiety (Marangell, Silver, & Yudofsky, 1999; Roy-Byrne & Cowley, 1998). Specifically, the benzodiazepines reduce anxiety because they increase the likelihood that GABA will bind to (fit into) the receptors on the neurons, thereby reducing the activity of those neurons and reducing anxiety. The fact that increasing the levels of GABA is an effective way to reduce anxiety that otherwise appears to come "out of the blue" provides strong evidence for the physiological explanation for GAD.

The physiological explanation for GAD can also be used to explain why individuals with GAD have anxious or worrisome thoughts. Specifically, the presence of physiologically generated anxiety activates the networks in which anxiety-related thoughts and memories are stored (McCabe, 1999; see Chapter 3). Furthermore, when these networks are activated and individuals begin thinking about anxiety related topics, the individuals are likely to erroneously attribute their anxiety to the thoughts because they are unaware of the biochemical cause of the anxiety. In other words, the physiologically caused anxiety triggers anxiety-related memories and worries, which individuals then use to explain their anxiety. Overall, then, the physiological explanation is the reverse of the cognitive explanation; that is, the physiological explanation suggests that anxiety leads to anxiety-related thoughts, whereas the cognitive explanation suggests that anxiety-related thoughts lead to anxiety.

If GAD is caused by high levels of neurological arousal, then we must ask why some individuals have high arousal levels and others do not. In most cases the answer lies in genetics (Hollander et al., 1999; Knowles et al., 1999). Evidence for the role of genes comes from two sources: First, there is consistent evidence that individuals who have GAD have more biological relatives with the disorder than do individuals who do not have GAD. Indeed, in one study it was found that the rate of GAD among the biological relatives of persons with GAD was almost 20%, whereas among the nonbiological relatives of persons with GAD it was only 3.5% (Noyes et al., 1987). Second, even more persuasive evidence comes from studies in which it was found that identical (monozygotic) twins were more likely to both have the disorder than were nonidentical (dizygotic) twins (Kendler, Neale, et al., 1992a). In other words, the degree to which individuals share genes is related to the degree to which they share the disorder, thus offering strong support for the role of genetics. However, we cannot use genetics to account for all cases of GAD because twin studies have indicated that the heritability of GAD is only about 30%. This means that other factors also contribute to the disorder. These could be psychological in nature, such as incorrect beliefs about negative events in the future, or they could be other physiological factors, such as biological traumas (disease and injury) that influence brain development.

Before concluding this discussion I should comment briefly on a physiological disorder that is often mentioned as a cause of GAD is probably not a cause. Since as early as 1871 there have been reports that patients who suffer from anxiety also tend to have a heart disorder known as **mitral valve prolapse** (Da Costa, 1871; Gorman, 1984; Singh, 1996). The physical symptom of this disorder is a heart murmur (i.e., an odd sound that occurs when the heart beats). The murmur occurs because the *mitral valve* in the heart (the valve that normally stops blood from flowing back from the left ventricle into the left atrium) is *prolapsed* (pushed back too far) so that there is some backflow of blood. In other words, when the ventricle contracts, some of the blood flows back into the heart rather than out of the heart, and the sound of the blood flowing back into the heart is the heart murmur.

Mitral valve prolapse is diagnosed in 40–50% of anxious individuals but in only 5–20% of the nonanxious population. There is a relationship between the diagnosis of mitral valve prolapse and anxiety, but the relationship is probably *correlational* rather than *causal*. That is, although the heart

---

GABA (*gamma-aminobutyric acid*)   A neurotransmitter that is released by inhibitory neurons and is crucial for the control of anxiety; low levels of GABA lead to high neurological activity and anxiety.

mitral valve prolapse   A heart disorder that is correlated with anxiety but is probably not a cause of anxiety; the valve between the left ventricle and atrium does not close completely and, when the ventricle contracts, there is a backflow of blood into the atrium.

progressive muscle relaxation training   A strategy for treating anxiety by teaching the individual to relax all of the major muscle groups.

biofeedback training   A procedure in which an individual is taught to relax by being given feedback about changes in physiological responses (e.g., heart rate, blood pressure, muscle tension) so that the individual can learn to reduce those associated with anxiety.

palpitations, chest pains, and shortness of breath sometimes associated with mitral valve prolapse may contribute to anxiety, it is more likely that highly anxious individuals get more thorough physical examinations and therefore a mitral valve prolapse is more likely to be diagnosed in them than in other people (Dager et al., 1988; Gorman et al., 1988; Margraf, Ehlers, & Roth, 1988).

Treatments for Generalized Anxiety Disorder

The preceding discussion has provided us with some explanations for GAD. The next question is, how can GAD be treated?

The Learning Approach: Learning to Relax

When I discussed the explanations for GAD, I pointed out that there was not a viable explanation based on learning; that is, GAD is not a classically conditioned response. However, two treatments based on learning have been developed for GAD. The notion is that although conditioning did not cause the anxiety, individuals can learn to relax, and the relaxation response will *block* or eventually *replace* the anxiety response.

Muscle Relaxation Training. One strategy for learning to relax involves **progressive muscle relaxation training** (Jacobson, 1938). In a typical muscle relaxation training session the individual reclines in a comfortable chair and is put through relaxation exercises by a trainer, who speaks in a slow and soothing manner. The trainer gives instructions like the following:

> Settle back as comfortably as you can. Close your eyes, take a deep breath, hold it, and then let it out. Now take another deep breath, holding it deeply and then letting it out. And another. Still another. As you continue to breathe deeply, let yourself relax—more and more. Relax more and more with each breath. I am now going to make you aware of certain sensations in your body and then show you how you can reduce these sensations. First, direct your attention to your arms—to your hands in particular. Clench both fists. Clench them tightly, and notice the tension in the hands and in the forearms. Notice this tension as it spreads from your fingers through your hands and through your wrists. As you continue to focus on this tension, I want you to count to yourself slowly along with me. When you reach 3, gradually relax the tension in these muscles. Gradually unclench your fists, and let your hands hang loose. Ready? Now count with me: 1, 2, 3. Gradually relax. Note the difference between the tension and the relaxation. Concentrate now on the sensation of relaxation as it comes to replace the tension. Try to make this process continue. Focus on the relaxation as it spreads throughout

Many people use meditation as a stress-reducing technique. However, evidence from controlled experiments indicates that meditation is no more effective than simply sitting quietly.

> your fingers, your hands, your wrists, and your lower arms. Once again, now, clench your hands into fists tightly, noticing the tension in your hands and forearms. Tighten. Again, count slowly with me, and when you reach 3, gradually reduce the tension in your hands and arms: 1, 2, 3. Now relax. Let your fingers spread out, relaxed, and note the difference once again between tension and relaxation.

This procedure is repeated a number of times, and then the trainer moves on to different sets of muscles (upper arms, shoulders, back, legs, neck, forehead) until the individual has learned how to relax all of the major muscle groups. The notion is that once individuals have learned how to relax, they can apply what they have learned to overcome general anxiety.

Biofeedback Training. A more "high tech" approach to teaching relaxation involves **biofeedback training.** In biofeedback training electrodes that detect physiological responses such as heart rate, blood pressure, or muscle tension are attached to the individual. The individual then watches a computer display or listens to a tone that provides feedback about changes in the responses. For instance, the individual might listen to a tone that goes up and down as heart rate goes up and down. Using this feedback the individual tries to learn to reduce anxiety-related physiological responses and thereby lower anxiety. I will discuss the effects of biofeedback training in greater detail in Chapter 14, but two points should be made here. First, contrary to what is usually assumed, most of the evidence indicates that *biofeedback is no more effective for reducing responses such as heart rate and blood pressure than simply sitting quietly and resting* (e.g., Holmes, 1985; Roberts, 1985). In other words, biofeedback training is associated with reduced levels of arousal, but sitting quietly has the same effect. Thus effects of biofeedback training are probably due to sitting quietly. The one exception to this is muscle tension, but muscle tension can be reduced just as effectively with muscle relaxation training, which is much less expensive than biofeedback training (see previous discussion and Chapter 14). Second, *there does not appear to be any evidence that biofeedback training generalizes beyond the treatment setting.* That is, biofeedback training (or sitting quietly) may reduce arousal during the training session, but it does not reduce arousal in subsequent stressful situations (Bennett, Holmes, & Frost, 1978). Because of these problems, biofeedback training does not appear to be an effective means for treating GAD.

The Cognitive Approach: Changing Beliefs and Distraction

There are two interesting cognitive strategies for treating GAD: (1) cognitive therapy, which involves changing beliefs related to anxiety and (2) meditation, which involves distraction.

Cognitive Therapy. Earlier, when I discussed the causes of GAD, I pointed out that the anxiety typically seems to "come out of the blue" and that the incorrect beliefs associated with the disorder often revolve around concerns about the consequences of the anxiety and vague worries about the future (Breitholtz & Westling, 1998; Dugas et al., 1998). Because incorrect beliefs may play less of a role in GAD than in some other disorders, it is not surprising that research on the effects of cognitive therapy for treating GAD is relatively scarce and the effects are often found to be "modest" (Barlow et al., 1998, p. 307). However, this does not mean that the treatment is not effective, because help-

ing clients develop more realistic views of their ability to *cope with their anxiety* and whatever might happen in the future can reduce anxiety. In this regard it is noteworthy that there is evidence that cognitive therapy for GAD can be more effective than traditional psychotherapy, in which the focus is on "underlying causes," and that it is particularly helpful for preventing relapses after the termination of drug treatment (Bruce, Spiegel, & Hegel, 1999; Durham et al., 1999; Gould et al., 1997; Stanley, Beck, & Glassco, 1996).

Meditation. Some attention should also be given to the use of **meditation** to reduce general anxiety (D. H. Shapiro, 1980; West, 1987). Although meditation is not part of traditional cognitive therapy, it is a cognitive strategy because it involves focusing thoughts "inward," which diverts attention from anxiety-related thoughts. The crucial factor in most forms of meditation is the use of a **mantra,** which is a meaningless word such as "abna" that an individual repeats over and over while meditating. The mantra is used to "clear the mind"; that is, using it keeps the individual from thinking about anything that might be arousing. In short, the mantra provides *distraction.* It has also been suggested that meditation serves to refresh individuals and replenish their energy so that they can cope better, but exactly how this is accomplished has never been explained scientifically.

Meditation has been practiced for centuries in the Far East, and a form called *transcendental meditation* was popularized in the West during the 1960s and 1970s (Mahesh Yogi, 1963). Another meditative technique that has gained widespread acceptance involves simply counting rather than repeating a mantra; this technique is known as the *relaxation response* (Benson, 1975).

Most of the attention given to meditation revolves around the possibility that it can reduce the physiological arousal related to anxiety. There is no doubt that arousal levels drop during meditation, but the important point that is often overlooked is that *meditation does not result in greater reductions in physiological arousal than simply resting without meditating* (Holmes, 1983, 1984b, 1987). That has been consistently demonstrated in more than 20 experiments. The results of one such experiment are illustrated in Figure 5.5. In that experiment individuals who were either highly trained or untrained in meditation had their physiological arousal measured during three periods: (1) while they simply sat quietly, (2) while they either meditated or rested, and (3) while they again simply sat quietly. As you can see in Figure 5.5, the meditators showed declines in arousal while they meditated, but the individuals who simply rested showed equally great declines in arousal. At present, then, it cannot be concluded that meditating is more effective than resting for reducing the physiological causes or effects of anxiety.

Although meditation does not reduce physiological arousal more than sitting quietly, it is possible that it might reduce subjective feelings of anxiety. This possibility was

---

meditation   A strategy for reducing physiological arousal that involves focusing thoughts "inward," thereby diverting attention from anxiety-related thoughts; the process is often aided by the use of a mantra.

mantra   A meaningless word that is repeated over and over during meditation, and whose effectiveness for reducing arousal is probably due to the distraction it provides.

anxiolytics   A class of drugs used to treat anxiety; sometimes also called *minor tranquilizers.*

FIGURE 5.5

Persons who meditated did not show greater reduction in physiological arousal than persons who rested.

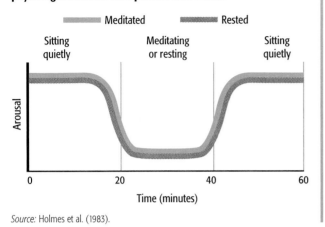

Source: Holmes et al. (1983).

tested in an interesting series of experiments in which individuals were randomly assigned to conditions in which they participated in (1) *real meditation,* (2) *bogus meditation* (sitting quietly with eyes closed but not using a mantra), or (3) *antimeditation* (engaging in deliberate, active cognitive activity designed to be the opposite of meditation) (Smith, 1976). The individuals in all three conditions were led to believe that the "meditation" they were performing would reduce their anxiety. The results indicated that the individuals in *all three* conditions reported decreases in anxiety and that there were no differences in the degree to which the various "meditation" procedures reduced anxiety. Because bogus meditation and antimeditation were as effective as real meditation, it must be concluded that the anxiety reductions were due to *expectations* about the effects of the "meditation" rather than to the meditation per se. In summary, the existing evidence indicates that meditating may reduce arousal and anxiety, but sitting quietly and one's expectations about what will happen are responsible for these effects. In other words, there is no evidence that meditation per se is effective for reducing anxiety (Hollander, Simeon, et al., 1994).

The Physiological Approach: Using Drugs to Reduce Arousal

The physiological explanation for GAD is that the anxiety stems from high levels of activity in the brain, so it follows that the physiological approach to treatment uses *drugs that lower the activity.*

Treatment with Drugs. The drugs that are used to treat anxiety are often referred to as "minor tranquilizers," but they are technically called **anxiolytics** (an-zi-o-LIT-iks). This term is made up of *anxiety* and *lytic,* which comes from a Greek word meaning "able to loose," so it literally means "able to loose anxiety." The most commonly used drugs for treating GAD work by *increasing the activity of the inhibitory neurons* so that the excitatory neurons will be less active. You will recall from our earlier discussion that GABA is the neurotransmitter that is responsible for the activity of the inhibitory neurons, that antianxiety drugs work by facilitating the entrance of GABA into the receptor sites on the excitatory neurons, which are then less likely to fire (Marangell et al., 1999). The drugs work primarily in the limbic system, which plays an important role in generating emotional arousal, and in the reticular formation, which carries the arousal to higher levels of the brain (see Chapter 3). The drugs that increase GABA activity are the benzodiazepines, including Valium (diazepam) and Xanax (alprazolom). Valium is a relatively fast-acting drug that reaches its peak concentration in the brain within 1 hour. It is then transported out of the brain rather quickly, but its *metabolites* (substances produced during its chemical breakdown) remain, and because these metabolites are effective for reducing anxiety, the clinical effects of Valium are prolonged. Valium is a very safe drug, and no deaths due to overdose have been reported. This is because there is an upper limit to Valium's ability to reduce neurological activity, and this limit is below the point at which respiratory activity and other vital functions are inhibited. However, it is important to recognize that the combination of high levels of benzodiazepines with other drugs that reduce neurological activity can be lethal. For example, alcohol also reduces neurological activity, and when it is taken along with a benzodiazepine, the combined effects may be enough to stop respiration and kill the individual. Frequently used benzodiazepines are listed in Table 5.2.

A substantial amount of evidence indicates that benzodiazepines are effective for reducing general anxiety (Greenblatt & Shader, 1974, 1978; Kellner, Uhlenhuth, & Glass, 1978; Marangell et al., 1999; Roy-Byrne & Cowley, 1998). For example, benzodiazepines were found to be

TABLE 5.2

Frequently used benzodiazepines

Trade name	Generic name	Typical daily dose
Ativan	lorazepam	2–6 mg
Klonopin	clonazepam	1–4 mg
Librium	chlordiazepoxide	15–100 mg
Valium	diazepam	4–40 mg
Xanax	alprazolam	1–6 mg

FIGURE 5.6

Valium was more effective than a placebo for reducing anxiety.

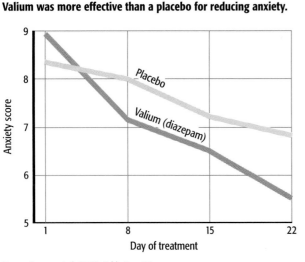

Source: Burrows et al. (1976), Table 4, p. 178.

more effective than placebos in 22 of 25 experiments conducted in one 5-year period. The results of one experiment in which Valium was compared to a placebo are presented in Figure 5.6. Furthermore, in double-blind experiments in which groups of participants received either benzodiazepines or placebos and then the treatments were reversed, anxiety went down when individuals were taking the benzodiazepines and up when they were taking the placebos. Overall, then, it can be concluded that benzodiazepines are effective for treating general anxiety.

Another type of antianxiety drug has been developed, and although we do not yet understand exactly how it works, it has been found to be very effective and to have fewer side effects than the benzodiazepines (Casacalenda & Boulenger, 1998; Lader & Scotto, 1998; Pollack et al., 1997). A widely used drug of this type is BuSpar (buspirone), which provides an excellent alternative to the benzodiazepines.

Concerns about Drug Treatment. Drugs can be effective for treating generalized anxiety disorder, but we must give some attention to the concerns that have been raised about their use. First, there is no doubt that benzodiazepines have side effects, including drowsiness, light-headedness, dry mouth, nausea, blurred vision, constipation, and problems with memory. As many as 30% of the individuals who take these drugs may experience side effects. However, individu-

---

drug dependence A condition that occurs when an individual experiences physical symptoms after use of a drug is reduced or terminated; commonly called *addiction.*

---

als who take placebos also experience many of the same side effects, suggesting that some of them are due to suggestions or expectations rather than the drugs per se (Evans, 1981). However, that does not reduce their unpleasantness. Given that benzodiazepines do have side effects, the question is, do the side effects outweigh the treatment effects? The answer is generally no; in most cases individuals would rather put up with the side effects than suffer from the symptoms the drugs relieve. In cases in which the side effects are worse than the symptoms, a good strategy is to try a lower dose or a different drug because different drugs often have different patterns of side effects.

Three points should be noted concerning the side effects of benzodiazepines:

1. The side effects are usually *not severe enough to disrupt normal living.* For example, abut 10% of individuals who take Valium experience a dry mouth, but at worst this is only a minor annoyance and does not generally interfere with normal daily living.

2. Some people report that the drugs cause drowsiness or confusion, but there is evidence that the proper dosages of benzodiazepines can actually *enhance mental functioning* (Bond et al., 1974). This enhancement occurs because without the drugs anxiety levels are so high that they interfere with performance, but the drugs reduce the anxiety, and consequently performance improves. For most individuals the net effect seems to be positive.

3. Over time many of the *side effects disappear* or become relatively unimportant. This may occur because the body adjusts to the effects of the medication.

A second concern revolves around the fact that *drugs are treatments, not cures;* when a drug is withdrawn, the individual's symptoms may return. This is certainly a limitation, but it is not necessarily a reason to forgo use of the drugs, especially in cases for which a cure is not available. Consider this: If you have a bad headache, you may take an aspirin to relieve the pain. The aspirin will not cure the headache, but it will relieve the pain and let you get on with your activities. Should you not take aspirin just because it is not a cure? Perhaps a better analogy is to diabetes, a disorder that stems from the insufficient production of insulin, which is very similar to the underproduction of GABA. Diabetes can be treated effectively with insulin injections on a regular basis, but the insulin does not cure the problem of underproduction of insulin by the body. Should individuals with diabetes stop taking insulin because it does not cure the disorder? Perhaps some day cures will be identified for headaches, diabetes, and anxiety, but until then we may have to be content with symptom relief.

Because benzodiazepines provide treatments rather than cures, individuals often ask whether they will have to take the drugs the rest of their lives. Possibly, but probably not, because most anxiety disorders diminish with age (Christensen et al., 1999; Costello, 1982; Krasucki et al., 1998; Magee et al., 1996; see also Chapter 6). One strategy for determining whether a drug is still necessary is to occasionally reduce the dosage and see whether the symptoms return. Of course, this needs to be done under careful supervision.

Finally, we must address the question of whether prolonged use of benzodiazepines results in **drug dependence,** or what is commonly called *addiction.* Dependence is said to occur if *physical symptoms appear when an individual stops using a drug* (see Chapter 15). Some years ago concerns were raised because physicians were prescribing benzodiazepines very widely, and anecdotal evidence suggested that some individuals had become addicted. Research on the addictive quality of benzodiazepines is difficult to do because some of the symptoms that occur when individuals stop taking the drugs may be the symptoms for which the drugs were originally taken. For instance, if individuals become tense and anxious, that may simply be due to fact that they are no longer taking their antianxiety medication, and these symptoms should not be mistaken for symptoms of dependence. However, there is some evidence that drug dependence can develop after *prolonged use at high levels.* For example, when patients who had been on high daily doses of benzodiazepines for at least 3 months were switched to a placebo, they showed symptoms such as muscle tremors and cognitive confusion that were not part of their original symptom pattern (Busto et al., 1986). Clearly, some dependence can develop, but the symptoms can be minimized by slowly reducing the dosage levels (Rickels et al., 1991). Overall, then, drugs can be effective for treating GAD, but they are not necessarily a quick and easy fix.

Questions about Generalized Anxiety Disorder

1. *How does GAD differ from phobic disorders, and do the differences require different explanations?* GAD provides a sharp contrast with phobias in that in phobias the anxiety is associated with specific stimuli and is due to classical conditioning or incorrect beliefs, whereas in GAD the anxiety is general in nature and apparently caused in large part by high levels of activity in the brain. That overactivity in the brain appears to occur because the inhibitory neurons are not releasing enough of the neurotransmitter GABA. However, it also appears that in some cases GAD may be caused or exacerbated by concerns about the future and worries about the consequences of the anxiety. With regard to the anxiety-related thoughts that are associated with GAD, it is important not to confuse cause and effect. That is, some of the beliefs about future problems may be a result rather than a cause of anxiety.

2. *What strategies seem to be most useful in treating GAD?* There are a number of viable treatments available for GAD. Specifically, progressive muscle relaxation can be used to reduce tension, and cognitive therapy can be used to aid individuals in coping (i.e., help them realize they can deal with the anxiety) and possibly change vague incorrect beliefs about impending problems. When these approaches are not effective, drugs (primarily benzodiazepines) can be used to reduce neurological activity and anxiety. Although the drugs are effective, it is important to recognize that they are treatments rather than cures and that they can have annoying side effects. Overall, then, we are developing a better understanding of GAD and effective treatments. With the discussion of phobias and GAD behind us, we can go on to consider panic disorder, which involves a completely different set of symptoms, causes, and treatments.

One evening Yoko was sitting quietly watching television when suddenly she felt short of breath, her heart began beating very fast, everything turned gray, and she thought she was going to pass out. Her first thought was, "I'm having a heart attack, and I'm going to die!" She went to the emergency room, but by the time she got there, the symptoms were gone and the physician couldn't find any evidence of damage to her heart. Did she have a minor heart attack, or did she have some type of anxiety attack?

Chad has frequent panic attacks in which his heart races, and he has difficulty breathing. Sometimes an attack will begin in the middle of the night when he is deeply asleep. As part of a research project at a nearby hospital, Chad was given a mixture of regular room air and carbon dioxide to breath, and that also caused a panic attack. Why would a panic attack occur when he was deeply asleep, and why would carbon dioxide cause panic attacks?

To treat Tyrell's panic attacks his physician prescribed an antidepressant drug (Prozac). The drug was effective for controlling the panic attacks, but Tyrell wondered why a drug that is usually used to treat depression is effective with an anxiety disorder. Recently Tyrell stopped taking the drug, and now when the symptoms occur, he sits down, breathes deeply, and says to himself, "Hey, this is not a heart attack, and I'm not dying. This is just an anxiety attack, and I'll be all right in a few minutes." This strategy is working, and Tyrell no longer needs to take the medication. What is the most effective treatment for panic disorder?

The last disorder we will consider in this chapter is panic disorder, which, as the name implies, can be terrifying.

Symptoms and Issues

Panic disorder involves *brief periods of exceptionally intense spontaneous anxiety*. During a panic attack an individual may experience physical symptoms that include shortness of breath, heart palpitations, chest pains, sensations of choking or smothering, dizziness, numbness or tingling of the extremities, hot and cold flashes, sweating, faintness, trembling, and shaking. These periods come and go suddenly, usually last about 10 minutes, and occur unpredictably. Indeed, they seem to come "out of the blue."

An example of the changes in heart rate that are associated with a panic attack is shown in Figure 5.7. These data were collected quite by chance when a woman happened to have a panic attack while she was receiving relaxation training and having her physiological responses monitored. Note that the attack occurred while she was relaxing in a nonstressful situation and that in less than 2 minutes her heart rate increased by 52 beats per minute, an increase of 81%. The fact that the attack occurred when the woman was deeply relaxed is particularly interesting, and something we will have to account for later.

Because of the physical symptoms, individuals who have panic attacks sometimes misinterpret them as heart attacks. One patient who suffered from panic attacks said, "Most people only face dying once; I do it a couple of times a week! It's scary." Furthermore, individuals who experience panic attacks become concerned about losing control and often think that they are "going crazy"; therefore, they sometimes begin avoiding public places in favor of staying home where they feel safe. If the avoidance becomes extreme, the individual may be diagnosed as suffering from

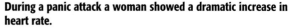
FIGURE 5.7

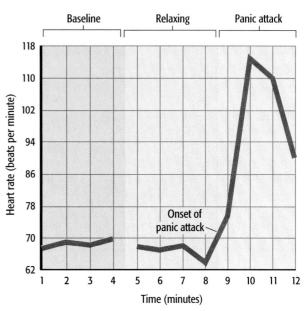

During a panic attack a woman showed a dramatic increase in heart rate.

Source: Adapted from Cohen, Barlow, & Blanchard (1985), Figure 2, p. 98.

---

panic disorder An anxiety disorder in which the major symptom is brief periods of exceptionally intense spontaneous anxiety.

panic disorder with agoraphobia A disorder in which an individual develops agoraphobia as a result of having experienced panic attacks outside the home.

sodium lactate A salt that can cause panic attacks if injected into people who have had spontaneous panic attacks or who have a family history of such attacks.

carbon dioxide A colorless, odorless gas that can cause panic attacks in people who have a personal or family history of such attacks.

Stage 4 sleep The deepest stage of sleep, in which physiological activities such as respiration slow down and dreams do not occur.

nocturnal panic attacks Panic attacks that occur during Stage 4 sleep.

---

panic disorder with agoraphobia rather than just panic disorder (see the earlier discussion of agoraphobia). Between attacks the individual is often anxious about possible impending attacks, causing an elevated general level of anxiety.

Panic disorder is thought to be rather common, occurring in 5% of women and 2% of men (Kessler et al., 1994, 1998). It's also noteworthy that individuals who have panic disorder are also very likely to suffer from depression. Indeed, about half of the individuals with panic disorder in one sample also met the diagnostic criterion for major depression (Kessler et al., 1998). A description of a rather mild panic attack in an undergraduate student of mine is presented in Case Study 5.6.

Apart from the symptoms I have just described, there are a number of unusual features of panic disorder that merit attention. I will describe these features here, and later we will try to account for them, using the various explanations.

Injections of Sodium Lactate Can Cause Panic Attacks

The first interesting finding is that *injections of* **sodium lactate** *(a salt) can bring on panic attacks* (Appleby et al., 1981; Gorman et al., 1988; Guttmacher, Murphy, & Insel, 1983). In the research on the effects of sodium lactate, individuals

A Panic Attack in Class

AN UNDERGRADUATE STUDENT recently gave me the following account of one of her panic attacks.

"It was around 10:00 a.m., and I was taking notes in an introductory philosophy class. As I was writing, my hand started to tremble, and I began having difficulty writing. My handwriting became steadily worse, and I started getting very dizzy. This had never happened to me in a class before, and I didn't know what to do. I thought about trying to leave the room, but I was afraid that I wouldn't make it to the door. I tried to get rid of the dizziness by laying my head down, but it only got worse. I was trembling so badly that I could not take notes, and in an attempt to hold on, I tried to focus all of my attention on the profes-

sor. It didn't work. I could barely see him, I couldn't hear him, and the room looked like a black-and-white photo negative. I became extremely frightened and thought that I was going to black out. The girl next to me saw that I was having trouble and suggested that I leave the room, but I couldn't understand what she was saying—it was all a distant blur. Eventually I got up and stumbled out of the room— right in the middle of the lecture. I knew that if I didn't walk out, I would be carried out. I sat down outside the classroom and put my head between my knees to get rid of the dizziness and blackness. It was several minutes before the symptoms went away, and I could return to the classroom.

"Since that first attack, I have had five or six similar attacks. They are always extremely frightening, but now that I understand what's happening and know that I'll get over it and won't die or something, it's not quite as bad. Having the attacks can be very embarrassing, and I worry that sometime I am really going to make a fool out of myself somewhere. Fortunately, most times people just think I am getting sick, and they are very sympathetic."

CASE STUDY   5.6

. . . now that I understand what's happening . . . it's not quite as bad.

---

who did or did not suffer from panic attacks and individuals who did or did not have a family history of them were brought into a laboratory and given sodium lactate intravenously for approximately 20 minutes. Within about 10 minutes most of the individuals who had a personal or family history of panic attacks began experiencing severe attacks. They became tense and then terrified, and they showed elevated heart rate and blood pressure. When the injections were terminated, the panic attacks subsided and the individuals returned to their normal states. It's noteworthy that the panic attacks that were induced with sodium lactate were indistinguishable from those that occur spontaneously outside of the laboratory. Furthermore, the panic attacks were not due to the stress of the injections because the individuals did not have attacks when they were given placebo injections, which they thought were sodium lactate. Finally, it should be noted that sodium lactate only triggers panic attacks in people who regularly suffer from such attacks or who have biological relatives who suffer from them. Why would sodium lactate lead to panic attacks? We'll come to that later.

Inhalation of Carbon Dioxide or Hyperventilation Can Cause Panic Attacks

It is also known that *inhaling air that contains small amounts of* **carbon dioxide** *can trigger panic attacks in individuals who have a personal or family history of panic attacks*

(Biber & Alkin, 1999; Dager et al., 1995; Gorman et al., 1994; Klein, 1994; Perna, Bertani, et al., 1995; Perna, Cocchi, et al., 1995; Verburg et al., 1998). For example, if individuals breathe an air mixture that contains as little as 5% carbon dioxide, those who have a personal or family history of panic attacks will have an attack. Similarly, *if individuals hyperventilate, those who have a personal or family history of panic attacks will have a panic attack.* (Hyperventilation involves rapid, shallow breathing. When individuals hyperventilate, they get less oxygen and feel "short of breath.")

Panic Attacks Can Occur during Stage 4 Sleep

Third, it's important to note that *panic attacks can occur during sleep.* Specifically, they occur during **Stage 4 sleep,** which is *very deep sleep during which dreams do not occur* (Craske & Barlow, 1989; Mellman & Uhde, 1989). (See Chapter 14 for a discussion of stages of sleep and dreaming.) The panic attacks that occur during Stage 4 sleep are called **nocturnal panic attacks,** and their occurrence raises an interesting question: Why should someone suddenly panic when soundly asleep and not thinking or dreaming?

Antidepressant Drugs Can Inhibit Panic Attacks

We will discuss the treatment of panic attacks later in this chapter, but here it should be noted that *antidepressant drugs such as Prozac can inhibit panic attacks.* Indeed, not

Panic attacks can occur during Stage 4 sleep, when an individual is in a deep, dreamless sleep.

only can antidepressant drugs inhibit the natural occurrence of panic attacks, but they can also block panic attacks caused by injecting sodium lactate or by inhaling carbon dioxide (Bocola et al., 1998; Klein, 1982; Nardi et al., 1997; Rifkin et al., 1981). That is, if individuals who ordinarily have panic attacks in response to sodium lactate or carbon dioxide are given an antidepressant before being given the sodium lactate or carbon dioxide, they will not have a panic attack. Why does an antidepressant drug suppress an anxiety disorder? That will become clear shortly.

Explanations for Panic Disorder

As you learned in the preceding section, panic disorder has some unique characteristics, such as the fact that in some people it can be triggered by sodium lactate. These characteristics are important in our discussion of what causes panic disorder because to be complete, an explanation must be able to account for all of these characteristics. That is, the explanation must be able to answer four questions: (1) Why do panic attacks occur in general? (2) Why do panic attacks occur during Stage 4 sleep? (3) Why are panic attacks triggered in some people by injections of sodium lactate? (4) Why can panic attacks be eliminated with antidepressant drugs? Answering these questions posed a serious challenge, and for many years panic disorder could not be adequately explained. As you will see, however, the mystery may have been solved fairly recently in a unique way.

The Psychodynamic Explanation: Breaking Out of Threatening Material

The psychodynamic explanation suggested that *panic attacks occur when threatening material that is stored in the unconscious threatens to break out* (Vuksic-Mihaljevic et al., 1998). For example, if incestuous wishes about a parent began slipping into consciousness, the individual might panic. Although interesting, this idea has no empirical support, and today it is generally ignored.

The Learning Explanation: Classical Conditioning of Extreme Fear

Learning theorists originally argued that *panic attacks were classically conditioned anxiety responses.* In other words, anxiety had been paired with the situation sometime in the past, so when the individual again experienced the situation, he or she experienced the anxiety and panicked. That explanation conceptualized panic attacks as severe phobias. However, the explanation was soon abandoned because panic attacks are not linked to specific stimuli. Furthermore, the notion of conditioning could not explain why panic attacks occur during nondreaming sleep, why they can be triggered by sodium lactate, and why they can be reduced with antidepressant drugs.

The Cognitive Explanation: Misinterpretation of Physical Arousal

The most popular psychological theory of panic attacks has been offered by cognitive theorists who propose that panic attacks occur when for some reason an individual experiences a *normal* increase in physiological arousal, for example, when exercising, but *misinterprets that increase in arousal as a symptom of a serious medical problem,* such as a heart attack (Beck & Emery, 1985; Clark et al., 1994). This situation was illustrated in Case Study 3.1. As you may recall, a man became short of breath while skiing, interpreted his physical sensations as the symptoms of a heart attack, and panicked. Of course, panicking further increases arousal, which provides more reason for concern; the panic increases, and a vicious cycle ensues. In other words, from the cognitive perspective *panic attacks are the result of misinterpretations and exaggerations of normal physical symptoms.*

The cognitive explanation is widely accepted, but it has a number of limitations. For example, it cannot account for the fact that panic attacks sometimes occur during Stage 4 sleep, during which there is no thinking or dreaming. That's a problem—if individuals are soundly asleep and not thinking or even dreaming, how could they misinterpret physical arousal as symptoms? Furthermore, the cognitive explanation cannot explain why sodium lactate triggers panic attacks or why antidepressant drugs reduce panic attacks. These are important limitations, which raise questions about the viability of the cognitive explanation.

The Physiological Explanation: An Overly Sensitive Respiratory Control Center and Genetics

An interesting physiological explanation is that panic disorder is caused by an *overly sensitive respiratory control center in the brain stem* (Hollander et al., 1999; Klein, 1993; Stein et al., 1995; Taylor, 1994). That may sound a little strange at first, so let me begin by discussing the role of the respiratory control center. At the base of your brain is a structure called the *brain stem*, and one of its functions is to monitor and control basic physiological activities, such as heart rate and respiration (see Chapter 2). Of most interest here is the **respiratory control center,** an area in the brain

The sensation of suffocation may cause a panic attack in an individual whose respiratory control center is overly sensitive to minor increases in the level of carbon dioxide in the blood.

stem that monitors the level of oxygen in the blood. If you are receiving too little oxygen, the respiratory control center sends signals to higher levels in your brain indicating that you need more oxygen, and you will begin breathing more deeply. For example, I suspect that there have been times when you were sitting comfortably, possibly watching television or reading, and then for no immediately apparent reason you took a deep breath and let it out as a sigh. What probably happened was that because you were so relaxed or possibly because you were slumped in the chair, you weren't breathing deeply enough and the oxygen level in your blood dropped. That drop was detected by your respiratory control center, which then caused you to take a deep breath to restore your oxygen level to normal. Important in this explanation is that one of the factors that is used by the respiratory control center to assess the level of oxygen in the blood is the level of carbon dioxide. Carbon dioxide is a by-product of the respiratory process, and if the level of carbon dioxide gets high relative to the level of oxygen, that signifies the need for more oxygen. In other words, a high level of carbon dioxide in the blood indicates that more carbon dioxide is being produced than oxygen is coming in. Sensing and correcting that imbalance is a normal process that is necessary for survival. However, it appears that some people have an overly sensitive respiratory control center, and when that center detects very minor increases in the level of carbon dioxide, it sends false alarms indicating suffocation to higher structures in the brain. Those alarms are false because there really is no crisis; the individual only needs to take a few deep breaths to correct the imbalance. The next question is, how is this related to panic attacks? The notion is that when individuals receive the information that they are suffocating, they panic, and it's the panic about suffocation that we see in panic attacks. In other words, panic attacks occur when an individual with an overly sensitive respiratory control center for some reason gets less oxygen.

Let's now see if this explanation fits with the other things we know about panic attacks. First, unlike any of the other explanations, this explanation can easily account for the fact that panic attacks can be triggered by injections of sodium lactate. As it turns out, when sodium lactate is in the bloodstream, it is converted into carbon dioxide, which is monitored by the respiratory control center in the brain stem. Of course, if the control center is overly sensitive, the increase in carbon dioxide causes it to signal the onset of suffocation, and the individual panics. In other words, sodium lactate triggers panic attacks because it increases

respiratory control center An area in the brain stem that monitors the levels of oxygen in the blood; its overreaction to low levels of oxygen can lead to a panic attack.

carbon dioxide in the blood, thereby causing a sensitive respiratory control center to warn of suffocation.

An overly sensitive control center also explains why hyperventilation and inhaling carbon dioxide can result in panic attacks; both increase carbon dioxide levels, which trigger false alarms about suffocation. The physiological explanation can also account for why panic attacks occur during Stage 4 sleep. Specifically, during deep sleep respiration is greatly reduced, thus increasing the likelihood that oxygen levels in the blood will be reduced, and therefore triggering a false alarm of suffocation.

Finally, the physiological approach also provides an explanation for why antidepressant drugs can be effective for treating panic attacks. Those drugs block the reuptake of serotonin, thus making more serotonin available at the synapses. This is relevant for panic attacks because it appears that serotonin acts to *inhibit* activity in the respiratory control center (Eriksson & Humble, 1990). In other words, higher levels of serotonin reduce the tendency of the respiratory control center to overreact and send false alarms when the individual experiences a minor oxygen deficit. Lowering the sensitivity of the respiratory control center reduces the panic attacks.

Before concluding our discussion of the role of the respiratory control center, a brief comment should be made concerning a disorder known as **Ondine's curse,** in which an individual has an *insensitivity to the lack of oxygen* (Haddad et al., 1978). Individuals with this disorder do not sense low blood levels of oxygen; so when they are deprived of oxygen, they do not take corrective action and may even die. (*Sudden infant death syndrome* may have a similar cause; an infant may roll face down and smother rather than awakening.) The existence of this disorder illustrates that the respiratory control center can be undersensitive as well as oversensitive, and it provides an interesting counterpoint for panic disorder.

If it is true that panic attacks are due to an overly sensitive respiratory control center, another question arises, why is the center overly sensitive? To answer that question, we must turn to genetics. There is consistent evidence for a genetic basis for panic disorder; for example, about 25% of the biological relatives of persons with panic disorder also have the disorder, whereas only about 2% of nonbiological relatives share the disorder (Crowe et al., 1983). Even

more impressive are the findings that identical (monozygotic) twins are *five times* more likely to share the disorder than nonidentical (dizygotic) twins (Torgersen, 1983; see also Hollander et al., 1999; Kendler, Pedersen, et al., 1993; Knowles et al., 1999; Perna et al., 1997). It is also the case that successive generations of individuals with the disorder show earlier onsets and more severe disturbances, which also reflect the influence of genes (Battaglia et al., 1999). Clearly, the degree to which individuals share genes influences the degree to which they will share panic disorder. Furthermore, an oversensitivity to carbon dioxide, which appears to provide the basis for panic attacks, has also been shown to be inherited (Perna et al., 1995, 1996). One qualification should be noted, however: Genetic factors do not account for all of the cases of panic disorder. The remaining cases may be due to biological traumas, such as difficulties during birth, that influence brain development (see the discussion of biological traumas in Chapter 11). Overall, then, these findings provide additional strong evidence for the biological basis of panic disorder and specifically for the explanation concerning oversensitivity to carbon dioxide.

Clearly, the physiological explanation for panic attacks can account for findings that the other explanations cannot; thus it appears to be the best overall explanation.

Treatments for Panic Disorder

Because there is no evidence that panic disorder is due to the breakthrough of threatening material from the unconscious or to classical conditioning of fear, we need not discuss treatments that might be used to overcome those causes. We can simply consider the two most widely used treatments: cognitive therapy and medication.

The Cognitive Approach: Correcting Misinterpretations and Coping

Cognitive theorists assume that panic attacks occur because individuals misinterpret and overreact to minor physiological changes. Therefore, in treating panic attacks, cognitive therapists help their clients avoid those misinterpretations, by (1) teaching clients to interpret the physiological changes more realistically ("This chest pain is not a heart attack"), (2) convincing clients that they can cope with the situation and there is no need to panic ("You can handle this situation"), and (3) teaching clients how to relax instead of panicking ("Breathe deeply and slowly").

There is evidence that this cognitive treatment can reduce the severity of panic attacks (Barlow et al., 1998; Clum, Clum, & Surls, 1993; Goldberg, 1998; Hecker et al.,

---

Ondine's curse A disorder in which the respiratory control center is insensitive to low levels of oxygen in the blood and, as a consequence, may cause the individual to die from suffocation.

serotonin A neurotransmitter that has a number of functions, one of which is the inhibition of activity of the respiratory control center.

1998; Klosko et al., 1990; Margraf et al., 1993; Michelson et al., 1990; Penava et al., 1998; Shear et al., 1991). There is even evidence that simply providing clients with written information or a videotape about how to use cognitive techniques for dealing with panic attacks can help, so this is a very cost-effective approach (Lidren et al., 1994; Parry & Killick, 1998).

Although cognitive therapy is effective, there are questions about whether the effects are really due to changes in the basic misinterpretations that are suspected of causing panic attacks. It may be that cognitive therapy is effective because it helps individuals realize that they can *cope with the situation* (Mattick et al., 1990; Michelson & Marchione, 1991). For example, if individuals come to realize that they are not going to die, when an attack comes on, they simply sit quietly, breathe deeply in an attempt to relax as much as possible, and wait for the attack to pass. When individuals realize they are not going to die, that realization reduces their anxiety and reduces some of their symptoms. This does not mean that the treatment is not effective, only that the effects are due to *coping* rather than to *changing the cause* of the disorder. Consistent with the coping explanation is the finding that simply informing clients that "panic is not dangerous" is as effective as the more traditional complete cognitive therapy (Shear et al., 1994). Similarly, merely having a "safe person" present during a panic attack greatly reduces the symptoms of panic (Carter et al., 1995).

Another explanation for why cognitive therapy is effective is that in most cases the treatment involves having the client try to relax by *breathing deeply,* and the deep breathing may help overcome the oxygen deficit, which triggered the false alarm about suffocation (Barlow et al., 1998; Klein, 1993; Stein et al., 1995; Taylor, 1994).

Overall, then, it's clear that the cognitive approach to treating panic attacks is effective, but its effectiveness may be due to coping and deep breathing rather than to the development of more accurate interpretations of the arousal that supposedly caused the panic.

The Physiological Approach: Using Drugs to Reduce Sensitivity

From the physiological perspective panic disorder is caused by an overly sensitive respiratory control center in the brain stem. How can that be treated? It turns out that the activity of the respiratory control center is controlled at least in part by the neurotransmitter **serotonin.** Specifically, it appears that *serotonin serves to inhibit the activity of the respiratory control center,* and therefore *increases in serotonin activity may decrease the sensitivity of the center.* Fortunately, some antidepressant drugs are very effective for increasing serotonin activity, and there is a large body of evidence indicating that those drugs are effective for treating panic attacks (e.g., Bakker, van Balkom, & Spinhoven, 1998; Clum et al.,

1993; de Beurs et al., 1995; den Boer & Slaap, 1998; Hiemke & Benkert, 1998; Hollander, DeCaria, et al., 1994; Londborg et al., 1998; Lydiard et al., 1998; Mattick et al., 1990; Mavissakalian & Perel, 1989, 1992a, 1992b; Pohl, Wolkow, & Clary, 1998; Spiegel, 1998). Most of the investigations were double-blind experiments, in which patients were randomly assigned to drug or placebo conditions, and the antidepressants were consistently found to be more effective for reducing panic attacks than the placebos. Furthermore, symptom relief lasted as long as the individuals stayed on the antidepressants, but when the antidepressants were discontinued, the panic attacks returned. In other experiments it was found that progressively higher levels of an antidepressant were progressively more effective for reducing the severity of panic disorder, thus offering more evidence of their utility (Mavissakalian & Perel, 1995). Those results are summarized in Figure 5.8.

As an aside, it might be noted that the effects of these drugs provide additional support for the notion that panic attacks are triggered by physiological factors rather than by misinterpretations of normal changes in arousal. Specifically, the antidepressants do not eliminate normal increases in arousal (indeed, in the early stages they may even make the individual jittery) and do not influence cognitive interpretations. Despite the continued presence of those factors, however, individuals taking the drugs do not have panic attacks.

Antidepressants are effective for controlling panic attacks, but what about the side effects? For most people the side effects diminish with time, are minimal, and are judged to be reasonable trade-offs for the relief in symptoms (Baldwin & Birtwistle, 1998; Davidson, 1998; Labbate,

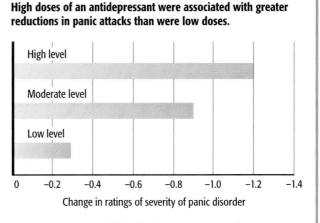

FIGURE 5.8

High doses of an antidepressant were associated with greater reductions in panic attacks than were low doses.

Note: Scores are based on clinicians' judgments on a 5-point scale.

Source: Mavissakalian & Perel (1995), Table 2, p. 676.

Grimes, & Arana, 1998; Londborg et al., 1998). Should everyone who has panic attacks take antidepressants, and will they have to stay on the drugs forever? The answer to both questions is no. I'll discuss those issues in the next section.

Finally, I should comment on an interesting alternative treatment—aerobic exercise. Aerobic exercise consists of activities such as running, swimming, and cycling that increase the heart rate to about 80% of its maximum rate for at least 30 minutes. In an interesting experiment individuals with panic disorders were randomly assigned to three conditions in which for 10 weeks they took an antidepressant drug (Anafranil/clomipramine) or exercised daily (running) or took a placebo pill (Broocks et al., 1998). The drug worked faster than the exercise, but each of those treatments was more effective than the placebo. Why does aerobic exercise help with panic attacks? Two reasons: First, aerobic exercise increases the production of serotonin, so its effect is similar to that of an antidepressant; second, aerobic exercise enhances cardiovascular fitness, allowing individuals to process oxygen more efficiently and avoid the build-up of carbon dioxide, which triggers panic attacks.

THINKING CRITICALLY

Questions about Panic Disorder

1. *What causes panic disorder?* Both physiological and cognitive factors contribute to panic disorder. On the one hand, an overly sensitive respiratory control center is probably the primary cause of the disorder. That conclusion seems valid because the physiological explanation can account for findings that other explanations cannot (e.g., the roles of sodium lactate and carbon dioxide and the effects of antidepressants). On the other hand, cognitive factors do play a role in that, when faced with the onset of

a panic attack, an individual can become frightened and that can increase arousal and the sense of panic. For example, one of my students who has severe panic attacks knows that they are due to a physiological problem and that she is not going to die, but she still worries about what's happening to her and whether, for example, she'll be able to get home, which contributes to the panic. The important point, however, is that the cognitively driven element of her panic only kicks in after an attack has been triggered by an overresponse of her respiratory control center.

2. *What about the treatments for panic disorder?* There is little doubt that antidepressant drugs are effective for treating panic attacks; they can reduce "naturally occurring" attacks and even inhibit attacks arising from injections of sodium lactate and inhalation of carbon dioxide. However, it also appears clear that cognitive therapy can be effective in helping individuals cope with the disorder, thus making the disorder less disruptive.

With the findings concerning drugs and cognitive therapy as background, the question is, are drugs always necessary? The answer to that question is definitely no. In most cases individuals can learn to cope with the symptoms and even reduce them using strategies such as deep breathing. In other words, for most cases cognitive therapy is the treatment of choice. Unfortunately, however, there are individuals who have frequent panic attacks that are beyond coping, and there are also individuals whose attacks can have dangerous consequences—for example, when the attacks occur while the individuals are driving. In those cases medication may be necessary.

This concludes the discussion of the first set of anxiety disorders. In the next chapter we will consider three other anxiety disorders: obsessive-compulsive disorder, posttraumatic stress disorder, and acute stress disorder. We will also examine some of the gender and sociocultural factors that are associated with anxiety disorders.

Summary

Topic I: Symptoms and Issues of Anxiety

▶ The major mood symptoms of anxiety disorders are anxiety, tension, panic, and apprehension, but depression and irritability may also be seen. Cognitive symptoms revolve around worries about doom and disaster, and individuals may be distracted and inattentive. The immediate physical symptoms include sweating, rapid heart rate, muscular tension, and high blood pressure. If anxiety is prolonged, delayed physical symptoms such as muscular weakness, high blood pressure, and heart attacks can occur. Motor symptoms include unproductive activities such as restlessness and pacing.

▶ Anxiety can be considered abnormal if its level is too high, it is not justified by the situation, or it leads to negative consequences.

▶ Anxiety takes different forms in the various anxiety disorders, and rather than simply being variations on a theme, these disorders have different causes and require different treatments.

Topic II: Phobic Disorders

▶ Phobias are persistent and irrational fears of specific objects, activities, or situations.

▶ Avoiding phobic objects or situations can disrupt behavior, and if the phobic objects or situations cannot be avoided, exposure to them can result in overwhelming fear and inappropriate behaviors.

▶ Agoraphobia involves fear of being in situations in which escape would be difficult or embarrassing if paniclike symptoms occurred. People with agoraphobia often confine themselves to their homes.

▶ Social phobia involves an irrational fear that the individual will behave in an embarrassing way, causing the individual to have high levels of anxiety in social situations, and even to avoid them.

▶ Specific phobias are all of the phobias other than agoraphobia and social phobia.

▶ The psychodynamic explanation for phobias is that they are symbolic expressions of unconscious conflicts and stress. From the learning perspective phobias are thought to be classically conditioned fear responses. Cognitive theorists assert that phobias are the result of incorrect beliefs about the danger posed by the phobic objects or situations. Physiology cannot be used to explain particular phobias, but high levels of neurological arousal can predispose individuals to develop phobias in general because the arousal facilitates conditioning.

▶ The learning approach to the treatment of phobias (behavior therapy) is based on extinction. One extinction-based treatment, known as systematic desensitization, involves exposing the individual to the feared stimuli in controlled steps so that the individual's sensitivity to it is gradually reduced. Modeling can also be used to extinguish fears vicariously.

▶ Cognitive therapy is focused on changing incorrect beliefs. A particularly effective means of doing that is to expose the individual to the feared stimulus without letting anything bad happen. There are differences of opinion over whether the fear reduction that results from such exposure is due to changed beliefs or extinction, and it appears that both processes may be involved.

▶ The physiological treatment of phobias involves the use of drugs, usually benzodiazepines or beta blockers, that block physiological arousal and thereby block fear. Initially the drugs only suppress the phobias. As treatment progresses, however, they may eliminate the phobias because in the absence of the fear the individual may expose himself or herself to the phobic stimuli, which can result in extinction or changed beliefs.

Topic III: Generalized Anxiety Disorder

▶ The major symptom in generalized anxiety disorder (GAD) is persistent anxiety that occurs across many situations and lasts for at least 6 months.

▶ The psychodynamic explanation that GAD stems from repressed conflicts has been generally abandoned. Classical conditioning cannot be used as an explanation because the anxiety of GAD is not linked to specific stimuli.

▶ The cognitive explanation is that individuals with GAD have incorrect beliefs about the general level of danger they face. However, that explanation encounters a problem in that the individuals often cannot point to specific reasons for their anxiety but instead attribute it to vague concerns about the future. It is possible, however, that those concerns are the result rather than the cause of the anxiety. Furthermore, the cognitive explanation cannot explain why individuals with GAD have biological relatives with the disorder.

▶ The physiological explanation is that GAD arises because the inhibitory neurons are underactive and do not adequately reduce the activity of the excitatory neurons; the overactivity of the excitatory neurons causes anxiety. More specifically, it is proposed that the inhibitory neurons produce low levels of a neurotransmitter called GABA, which is crucial for inhibiting the activity of the excitatory neurons. Evidence for this explanation comes primarily from the fact that drugs (benzodiazepines) that increase GABA activity are effective for decreasing anxiety. There is evidence for a genetic basis for GAD, and it is probably the case that individuals inherit the tendency to produce low levels of GABA. The physiologically caused anxiety can activate networks of anxiety-related thoughts, and this activation can result in the worries that accompany GAD.

▶ One treatment for GAD involves progressive muscle relaxation training. The notion is that a learned relaxation response can overcome and replace anxiety. It has also been proposed that biofeedback training can be used to reduce anxiety-related physiological responses, but except for muscle tension, biofeedback training does not have any greater effects on such responses than does sitting quietly.

▶ The effects of cognitive therapy appear to be somewhat limited, probably because GAD is not due primarily to incorrect beliefs. However, cognitive therapy can be effective for helping individuals develop positive beliefs about their ability to cope with their anxiety. Meditation has been proposed as a treatment, but its effects are due to simply resting (which reduces physiological responses) and expectations that it will reduce anxiety.

▶ Drugs can be used to reduce the neurological activity that leads to general anxiety. Specifically, benzodiazepines increase GABA activity. The drugs have side effects, but most of these are relatively minor, do not interfere with functioning, and diminish with time. Drugs are treatments rather than cures, and high dosage levels for prolonged periods can result in drug dependence.

Topic IV: Panic Disorder

▶ Panic disorder involves brief periods of exceptionally intense spontaneous anxiety. The anxiety is so intense that individuals often believe they are having a heart attack.

▶ In persons who have panic attacks or who have a family history of them, panic attacks can be brought on by injections of sodium lactate, inhalation of carbon dioxide, or hyperventilation. Panic attacks can occur during deep sleep and can be treated with antidepressant drugs. Explanations must be able to account for all of these facts.

▶ The psychodynamic explanation, which is focused on the breakthrough of anxiety-provoking material, and the learning explanation, which is focused on classical conditioning of anxiety, have been abandoned because they cannot account for such aspects of the disorder as the effect of sodium lactate.

▶ The cognitive explanation for panic disorder is that individuals misinterpret normal increases in arousal as signs of a serious medical problem and therefore panic. However, the cognitive explanation cannot account for other aspects of the disorder, such as the occurrence of panic attacks during deep sleep, when the individual is not thinking or dreaming.

▶ The physiological explanation is that individuals with panic disorder have an overly sensitive respiratory control center in the brain stem, and when the blood oxygen level gets low (relative to the carbon dioxide level), false alarms about suffocation are triggered, and the individuals panic. This explanation accounts for all of the aspects of the disorder.

▶ Cognitive therapy can be effective in treating panic disorder, probably because it helps individuals cope with the disorder (i.e., realize that they are not having a heart attack) and because it involves deep breathing, which replenishes the blood oxygen.

▶ Antidepressants that increase serotonin activity can inhibit panic attacks, apparently because serotonin is the neurotransmitter associated with inhibitory neurons in the respiratory control center. Increased activity of these inhibitory neurons can decrease the oversensitivity and reduce false alarms about suffocation. However, in many cases learning to cope via cognitive therapy seems to be sufficient.

Questions for Making Connections

1. Describe the learning and cognitive explanations for phobic disorders. Explain how those explanations may be two ways of looking at the same process.

2. What is the major difference between the symptoms of phobic disorders and those of generalized anxiety disorder? Do you think that difference means that the two types of disorders have different causes? What explanation or explanations do you think best account for each type of disorder?

3. Explain why phobias can differ across cultures.

4. Learning and cognitive approaches to the treatment of phobias appear to be effective. Why are both of these effective? Is there a common element that makes them both effective? If you were going to treat a phobia, how would you do it?

5. Panic attacks can be triggered by sodium lactate, be triggered by inhaling carbon dioxide, occur during deep sleep, and be treated with antidepressants. How does the physiological explanation account for all of these factors? Can other explanations account for any of them?

6. Explain why cognitive therapy can be effective for treating phobic, generalized anxiety, and panic disorders. Why are drugs effective for treating them?

Key Terms and People

In reviewing and testing yourself, you should be able to discuss each of the following:

agoraphobia, p. 127
anxiety, p. 123
anxiety disorders, p. 123
anxiolytics, p. 143
benzodiazepines, p. 137
beta blockers, p. 137
biofeedback training, p. 141

carbon dioxide, p. 147
drug dependence, p. 145
extinction, p. 133
GABA (gamma-aminobutyric acid), p. 140
generalized anxiety disorder (GAD), p. 138

hyperventilation, p. 125
inhibitory neurons, p. 139
mantra, p. 142
meditation, p. 142
mitral valve prolapse, p. 140
modeling, p. 135
nocturnal panic attacks, p. 147

6 Anxiety Disorders: Obsessive-Compulsive, Posttraumatic Stress, and Acute Stress

IN THIS CHAPTER we will continue our consideration of anxiety disorders; specifically, we will examine *obsessive-compulsive disorder, posttraumatic stress disorder,* and *acute stress disorder.* As I did with the other disorders, I will describe the symptoms, explanations, and treatments for each disorder, and again our goal will be to determine what explanations and treatments are most effective for each disorder. At the end of this chapter I will step back and discuss some of the broad issues associated with anxiety disorders, such as the roles played by gender, age, class, and culture.

TOPIC I
Obsessive-Compulsive Disorder

Whenever Marilyn touches herself on one side of her body, she must also touch herself at the same spot on the other side of her body. When Eric goes up a flight of stairs, he must always reach the top step on his right foot. Monique is very concerned about germs, so she washes her hands repeatedly. She does it so frequently she has literally washed the skin off, and now her hands are always bleeding. Bill cannot simply walk through a door once; instead he must go back and forth through the door two, three, or sometimes seven times before he can go on. All of these behaviors are compulsions, but are they all signs of a disorder? Why do some people feel compelled to perform compulsive acts?

To treat Monique's hand-washing compulsion, dirt is put on her hands, and she is not allowed to wash them. The hope is that she will realize that the washing is not necessary. The treatment is working for Monique, but it is not effective for some individuals. Those people are treated with antidepressant medication. The medication often helps, but why should an antidepressant help with a disorder that involves anxiety?

Mike suffers from epilepsy and shortly before having a seizure, he will sometimes begin having obsessive thoughts. Why is there a link between seizures and obsessions?

The first disorder we will consider in this chapter is obsessive-compulsive disorder. As the preceding examples indicate, obsessions and compulsions can be mild annoyances or major symptoms that seriously disrupt an individual's life.

An Interview with a Man Who Suffers from Obsessive-Compulsive Disorder

CASE STUDY 6.1

HERE IS AN EXCERPT from an interview I had with a man named Bill, who suffers from obsessive-compulsive disorder. He is a college graduate who had a successful career; because his disorder interfered with his work, however, at the time of the interview he was working at a lower-level position.

Holmes: Could you begin by telling me how the problem began?

Bill: I can't tell you what the specific events were, but for a while I felt like something wasn't right in my life. I even talked to my wife about going to a marriage counselor. One of the behaviors I noticed first was that when it was time to eat, I would always reach into the cabinet and take the second dinner plate, not the top plate. The thought was that there might be germs on the top plate, but that plate would protect the second one. That's how it all started. I can't tell you what the second ritual was, but it didn't take long before I developed a lot of rituals.

There seemed to be two basic rituals. Anytime I was going anywhere, whether it was going from one part of the house to another or leaving the house, I would always walk out backward. For example, I would always back out of the house. The other thing was that I would always do things over and over. For example, I would open and close the car door twice and open and close the house door twice. If I was going through a door, I would do it twice. I would walk through and then turn around and do it again. A circular pattern developed in which I did things over and over. Numbers became very important in this whole pattern. I had to do things a certain number of times. It wasn't always the same number. It depended on how high my anxiety was. Two was a common number, so was four, five, seven, or nine, but never would I go above eleven or twelve. Thirteen was a terribly unlucky number. The more anxious I was, the more times I had to do things.

Holmes: What was it you had to do seven times?

Bill: Any of the things. Opening and closing the car door or going through a door.

Holmes: And what did you think would happen if you didn't do this?

Bill: I think that when I first started doing rituals, I saw it more as a protection. When I took the second plate, I wouldn't get germs, and that would keep me from getting sick. Very quickly it took a negative twist, where if I didn't do one of these things, something terrible would happen. Always I had a fear of a heart attack, a fear of a stroke, and a fear of dying. Those were the three major fears. In a short time I had a full-blown set of rituals. And the rituals covered every part of my life. For example, I'd wake up in the morning and I'd have to throw the sheets off of me, cover myself up again, and then throw the sheets off again. From that point everything I did was controlled by the rituals. They controlled how I brushed my teeth—right down to how I picked up the toothbrush. I would pick it up, put it down, and then pick it up again. I'd put my socks on, take them off, and then put them on again. Shirt on and off and on again. Again the number two. It would take me 3½ hours to get dressed and out in the morning!

It got to the point that I couldn't go by graveyards and couldn't go by hospitals—they reminded me of death. Then it got to where I couldn't

Symptoms and Issues

Obsessive-compulsive disorder, which we usually refer to simply as **OCD,** involves *recurrent obsessions or compulsions or both.* An **obsession** is a *persistent idea, thought, image, or impulse that an individual cannot get out of his or her mind and that causes anxiety.* Common clinical obsessions involve thoughts of violence (killing or harming someone), contamination (becoming infected with germs), and doubt (persistently wondering whether one has done something like hurting another individual). We all occasionally go through periods when we cannot get a thought out of our heads (e.g., "Did I lock the door?"), but because those episodes do not last long and are not particularly upsetting, they are not classified as obsessions.

Obsessions can interfere with normal thoughts and thus can impair an individual's ability to function. For instance, it would be hard to study if you were constantly thinking about killing someone or worrying about whether you were picking up germs from the book you were reading. Obsessions can also limit behavior; for example, obsessions about infections cause individuals not to go out in public where they might be exposed to germs.

In contrast, a **compulsion** is a *behavior that an individual feels driven to perform over and over.* For instance, Case Study 6.1 reveals some of the compulsions of a man named Bill who cannot simply walk through a door; instead he must walk through it backwards or walk back and forth through the door two, three, or even seven times. Acts like that are called "rituals," and individuals feel compelled to perform them because they believe that if they don't, *something terrible will happen.* For example, an individual may feel that it is necessary to wash his or her hands repeatedly in order to avoid contamination from germs that will result in serious illness or death. However, in many cases the individuals are not sure exactly what terrible thing will happen

even go by signs, like hospital signs. If I came to stop signs—"Stop" meant my heart might stop—so I had to do everything to avoid these. It got to the point—let's say I came to a stop sign. I'd say, "Is it all right if I go by the stop sign?" and whoever I was with had to say, "Yes." They couldn't say "hm-mm" or "OK." I would keep badgering them until they said the word *yes.* When they said the word *yes,* it would be all right.

You can't imagine how degrading this was for me, so I'd say to myself, "By God, I'm not going to do it this time," and I'd get by the stop sign without asking permission. Maybe I'd get half a block down the street—and I'd break out in a sweat and have to make a U-turn and go back through the stop sign again. I became a real U-turn artist. There have been times I've made five or six U-turns on a busy street in the space of ten blocks—just so I could go back through stop signs again. God, it was insane! If I didn't do one of my rituals, I'd really panic. I remember that when I left work, I would have to drive around the building twice before going home. On a bad day I'd have to do it eleven times. Well, one day I said, "The hell with this, I'm not going to do it—bingo.

I'm going to drive straight home." So I didn't drive around the building and started home, but as soon as I got about a block away, I could sense some shallow breathing, heart starting to race a little bit, all the signs. To make a long story short, about midway home I thought, "I blew it, I blew it, I've got to go back!" I just froze. Then the panic started. All the physical symptoms came, and I thought, "I'm losing it. I've got to get back to get around the building!" Then I thought, "No, I'll never make it. I'll have to get home." So I drove 70 and 80 miles an hour down city streets—my foot just shaking on the pedal. Once I got to the top of a hill where I could see the house, I could feel the tension drop. By the time I got home, I was real shaky, but it was over.

Holmes: Your family must have become upset about this.

Bill: My youngest daughter literally hated my guts. No one understood it—I didn't understand it. Gee, anyone ought to be able to walk through a damn door without doing it twice. What do you mean you can't do that! It was very difficult.

Holmes: Earlier you said that you did your rituals to avoid possibly dying.

How did you connect something like picking up a toothbrush with dying? Why did picking up a toothbrush twice protect you from possibly dying?

Bill: Well, everything is connected to living. You put the toothbrush in your mouth, but you have to breathe through your mouth. Anything that had to do with my mouth or nose was … Putting a shirt on over my head—put a shirt on my chest … What's in your chest? Your heart. All these things, ha!—there's an insane logic to it all. It all had its purpose. It's kind of like the guy sitting in a field in Kansas snapping his fingers over and over, and when another guy asks him why he is snapping his fingers, he says, "It keeps the elephants away." The other guy then says, "Hell, there aren't any elephants in Kansas." The first guy responds, "See, it works!"

> **Always I had a fear of a heart attack, a fear of a stroke, and a fear of dying.**

if they don't perform the ritual. Bill, in Case Study 6.1, for example, does not know what will happen if he doesn't walk through the door backwards, but he's sure *something* bad will happen. This uncertainty makes the acts even more irrational. As you can see from the case study, OCD can be very serious and disruptive of the daily life of someone who suffers from it.

Performance of the compulsive act may temporarily relieve some anxiety because the terrible expected consequence is avoided, but compulsions do not lead to feelings of pleasure. In fact, because individuals know that their compulsions are irrational, the performance of the compulsions often causes them to experience anxiety. Behaviors such as excessive eating, drinking, and gambling are sometimes referred to as "compulsive," but that use of the term is incorrect. Pleasure is derived from those activities, whereas true compulsions are not pleasurable. Indeed, there does not appear to be a link between OCD and gambling (Black et al., 1994).

Explanations for Obsessive-Compulsive Disorder

Explaining obsessive-compulsive disorder poses a challenge because the symptoms are often very bizarre, but they occur in individuals who are otherwise normal. Why, for example, does an intelligent and well-educated man believe

obsessive-compulsive disorder (OCD)   A disorder that involves recurrent obsessions, compulsions, or both.

obsession   A persistent idea, thought, image, or impulse that an individual cannot get out of his or her mind and that causes anxiety.

compulsion   A behavior that an individual feels driven to perform repeatedly to avoid some negative consequence; often referred to as a ritual.

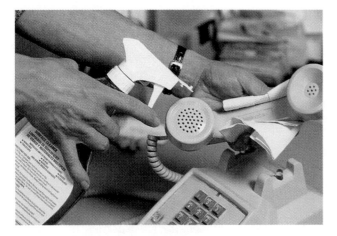

Individuals with obsessive-compulsive disorder may be driven to clean their surroundings frequently in order to prevent germ contamination.

that he must walk through a door five times to prevent some unknown terrible consequence? A number of initially popular explanations for OCD fell apart on close examination, but a true explanation may be imminent. In this discussion I will first comment briefly on the explanations that have been discarded. Because these occasionally reappear, you should know why they are now generally ignored.

The Psychodynamic and Learning Explanations: Defenses against Anxiety

Psychodynamic theorists originally argued that obsessions and compulsions were used to control the anxiety that stemmed from unconscious conflicts. For instance, these theorists contended that individuals who focused on irrelevant thoughts (obsessions) were doing so to avoid thinking about anxiety-provoking material that was slipping out of the unconscious and posing a threat. Similarly, compulsive performance of rituals might be used by individuals to keep themselves from actually doing something inappropriate. For example, if individuals are constantly washing their hands, they cannot be masturbating.

Learning theorists offered a similar explanation, although they framed it in terms of *operant conditioning* (Dollard & Miller, 1950). Specifically, they suggested that (1) individuals with OCD have high levels of anxiety, (2) individuals use their obsessions and compulsions to reduce the anxiety (e.g., hand washing reduces fear of contamination), and (3) the reduction in anxiety is rewarding, so the obsessions and compulsions will be used again and again.

These explanations based on anxiety reduction are interesting, but there is a problem: When individuals with OCD are given anxiety management training or drugs that reduce their anxiety, they generally continue to have their obsessions and perform their compulsions—they are just less anxious about doing so. That is, the symptoms persist

in the *absence* of anxiety, and therefore the symptoms apparently are not used to reduce anxiety. In view of the problems with the psychodynamic and learning explanations, it appears that we must seek another explanation.

The Cognitive Explanation: Incorrect Beliefs

The cognitive explanation for compulsions is that they are the result of *incorrect beliefs* that something terrible will happen if the compulsion is not performed (Summerfeldt & Endler, 1998). Compulsions do appear to be the product of incorrect beliefs, but the more important question is, how do the incorrect beliefs develop? It is usually assumed that the beliefs result from previous experiences or from problems with information processing, such as selective attention and selective recall of information that supports the need for the compulsion. While this may be possible in some cases, (e.g., when individuals who have learned that germs are dangerous compulsively wash their hands), in other cases it is difficult to see how the beliefs develop simply from misinformation. For instance, how could previous experiences, selective attention, and selective recall lead to the belief that to avoid some terrible consequence you must touch all four walls of a room or walk through a door backwards five times? Beliefs like this border on being *delusions* (incorrect beliefs that are held despite strong evidence to the contrary) of the kind that occur in more serious disorders such as schizophrenia (see Chapter 10). Although it seems likely that some people could be persuaded to believe that the world is a dangerous place and this belief could lead them to be anxious, it seems very unlikely that otherwise normal, intelligent, and well-educated people could be convinced that if they don't walk through a door backwards, something terrible will happen to them. Furthermore, as you will remember from Case Study 6.1, the individual often knows the belief is irrational. Because the cognitive explanation cannot provide a reasonable scenario for how bizarre incorrect beliefs develop, the viability of the explanation is weakened.

Overall, then, the cognitive explanation seems to have part of the answer (i.e., incorrect beliefs guide behaviors), but it lacks a convincing explanation for how highly incredible incorrect beliefs develop. For another perspective on this disorder, which may help explain the development of those beliefs, let's consider the physiological explanation.

The Physiological Explanation: Brain Dysfunctions and Genetics

Recent research has revealed three interesting problems in the brains of individuals with OCD. At first the problems seem unrelated to one another and to the symptoms, but in fact there is a common thread. I will discuss the problems in the brain in the following sections, and then we'll try to put the pieces of the OCD puzzle together.

Low Levels of Serotonin. The first finding is that in many cases *low levels of the neurotransmitter* **serotonin** *are related to OCD.* The link between serotonin and OCD was discovered quite by accident when individuals who suffered from both depression and OCD were prescribed antidepressants to improve their moods. The antidepressants, which *increase the levels of serotonin,* reduced the depression and also reduced the symptoms of OCD, so investigators speculated that serotonin must be involved in OCD. Well-known antidepressants that are effective for reducing OCD symptoms include Prozac (fluoxetine), Zoloft (sertraline), Paxil (paroxetine), and Anafranil (clomipramine) (Greist et al., 1995). (In Chapter 2 I explained how these drugs increase levels of serotonin; see also Chapter 8.)

Strong experimental support for the link between serotonin and OCD came from an investigation in which individuals with OCD were given either a drug that *reduced serotonin activity* (it blocked the serotonin receptors at the synapse) or a placebo. Of those who took the drug, 55% showed a substantial *increase* in their OCD symptoms, whereas none of those who took the placebo showed an increase in symptoms (Hollander, DeCaria, et al., 1994). In other words, decreasing serotonin levels increased symptom levels. These findings are presented in Figure 6.1.

The connection between levels of serotonin and OCD was also demonstrated in two interesting experiments with dogs that showed severe chronic licking of their paws or flanks, behaviors that can be seen as comparable to the hand washing of humans with OCD (Rapoport, Ryland, & Kriete, 1992; Wynchank & Berk, 1998). In one of those experiments the dogs were given either (1) an antidepressant drug that increased serotonin levels (Prozac/fluoxetine), (2) an antidepressant drug that did not influence serotonin, or (3) a placebo. The results were clear: Dogs that received the drug that increased serotonin levels showed substantial reductions in licking, whereas the dogs who received the other drug or the placebo did not. (As an aside, I might mention that I know of more than one family in which both the human and the canine members take antidepressants for their obsessive-compulsive symptoms!)

It's clear that many cases of OCD are due to low levels of serotonin, but there are two reasons to believe that some cases are not. The first reason is that reducing serotonin levels increases symptoms in only about half of the patients (Hollander et al., 1992; see also earlier discussion). The second reason is that drugs that increase serotonin levels are effective for treating only about half of the clients with OCD (Clomipramine Collaborative Study Group, 1991). It therefore appears that we must look for additional explanations.

High Levels of Brain Activity. The second important physiological finding with regard to OCD is that some individuals with the disorder have *abnormally high levels of activity in*

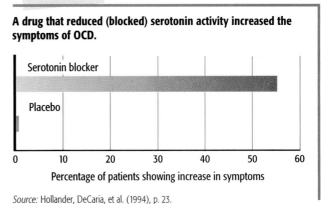

FIGURE 6.1

A drug that reduced (blocked) serotonin activity increased the symptoms of OCD.

Percentage of patients showing increase in symptoms

Source: Hollander, DeCaria, et al. (1994), p. 23.

certain structures of the brain (Baxter et al., 1987, 1992; Insel, 1993; Robinson et al., 1995; Saxena et al., 1998; Wilson, 1998). Most notably, by using PET scans investigators have found that individuals with OCD have high levels of activity in the **orbitalfrontal** (or-bet-el-FRENT-l) **area** of the cortex. The orbitalfrontal area is at the *side and rear of the frontal lobes.* It is an important area because the nerve tracts that link other areas of the brain to the frontal lobes pass through it (Damasio, 1994; Zald & Kim, 1996). In other words, the orbitalfrontal area can be thought of as the "interface board" between the rest of the brain and the frontal lobes, where thinking is done. The other structures that show high levels of activity (the *caudate nucleus* and *basal ganglia*) are lower in the brain, and there is also high activity in the the **cingulate gyrus,** which is the nerve tract that connects those structures to the orbitalfrontal area. Overall, then, there is a network of connected brain structures that is overactive in persons with OCD, and this overactivity may influence thought processes (see the later discussion).

Related to the issue of brain overactivity is the finding that individuals who develop disorders such as epilepsy and Parkinson's disease, which involve increased levels of brain activity, sometimes show the simultaneous development of obsessive-compulsive symptoms (Insel, 1993). Indeed, in some individuals the onset of an epileptic seizure, which is

serotonin A neurotransmitter that is present in low levels in individuals with OCD.

orbitalfrontal area An area at the side and rear of the frontal lobes through which pass the nerve tracts that connect lower areas of the brain to the frontal lobes; individuals with OCD have high levels of activity in this area.

cingulate gyrus A nerve tract that connects lower areas of the brain to the orbitalfrontal area; individuals with OCD have high levels of activity in this tract.

caused by an erratic increase in brain activity, is preceded by obsessive thoughts. This provides additional evidence that abnormalities in brain activity are linked to OCD.

It's clear that people with OCD have excessively high activity in certain structures of the brain, but why? We do not as yet have a complete answer, but it appears that serotonin may be the neurotransmitter for inhibitory neurons in these structures. Thus, if serotonin levels are low, the inhibitory neurons will be underactive and thereby allow other neurons to be overactive (Blier & Montigny, 1998). This provides an interesting connection between the findings concerning low levels of serotonin and high brain activity. Later I will explain how this overactivity may be related to symptoms.

Damaged Brain Structures. The third interesting finding is that brain imaging studies have revealed damaged structures in the brains of individuals with OCD, particularly the *orbitalfrontal* area (Robinson et al., 1995; Wilson, 1998). In some cases the damage (malformation) may be due to genetic factors, but in other cases OCD developed after a brain tumor or surgery damaged the brain (Berthier et al.,

1996; Damasio, 1994). An example of this is presented in Case Study 6.2.

Other evidence linking brain damage to OCD comes from the finding that individuals with OCD show many **soft signs of brain damage** (Bihari et al., 1991; Hollander et al., 1990; Purcell et al., 1998b). These soft signs include minor problems with motor coordination, such as the inability to bring together the index fingers of the two hands when the arms are stretched in front of the body and the eyes are closed. (These are called "soft" signs because they are based on *indirect* measures of neurological problems rather than on direct measures such as CT scans.) Indeed, individuals who have OCD show almost four times as many soft signs of brain dysfunction as individuals who do not have OCD. Moreover, among individuals who have OCD, those showing more soft signs of brain damage have more severe obsessions ($r = .37$). Clearly, there is a substantial and growing body of evidence that individuals with OCD suffer from a number of physiological problems in the brain.

Finally, we must give some attention to the question of what causes the various problems in the brain. At this point

The Man Whose Brain Tumor Led to Obsessive-Compulsive Disorder

CASE STUDY 6.2

Mr. Ervin (not his real name) was a 35-year-old accountant and the comptroller of a moderate-sized construction company. He was generally conservative in style, effective in business and personal matters, and respected as a leader. He did not have any history of obsessive-compulsive symptoms or any other psychiatric disorder. However, over a couple of months Mr. Ervin began having problems with his vision, and he also began showing changes in his personality. In an attempt to diagnose the visual problems, Mr. Ervin was given a neurological examination. That examination revealed that Mr. Ervin had a slow-growing brain tumor located in the orbitalfrontal area (on one side of the rear of his frontal lobes). The tumor was apparently causing the visual problems and the personality changes.

Surgery was used to eliminate the tumor, and following an uneventful 2-week stay in the hospital and a 3-month recovery period at home, Mr.

Ervin returned to work. Although Mr. Ervin recovered well from the surgery, the changes in his personality persisted and got worse. Of most interest is the development of severe obsessive-compulsive symptoms. For example, if Mr. Ervin was planning to eat out, he would spend hours considering each restaurant's seating arrangements, menu, atmosphere, and management. Having done that, he would drive to each of the restaurants to see how busy they were, but even then he would not be able to make a decision concerning where to eat. He had similar problems when he had to make any sort of minor purchase. He also had great difficulty making decisions to get rid of useless possessions. For example, at one point he had a collection of dead houseplants, old phone books, broken fans, and broken television sets, along with three bags of empty orange juice cans, 15 cigarette lighters, and countless stacks of old newspapers. His compulsions also extended to personal grooming; it usually took him 2 hours

to get ready to leave the house in the morning, and sometimes he would spend the entire day shaving and washing his hair.

Mr. Ervin had an IQ of about 125. He did not show any other behavioral evidence of brain damage or dysfunction, but brain scans revealed that there were localized lesions in the area of the brain where the surgery had been done (orbitalfrontal area). All of the other parts of his brain were normal in both structure and function.

What caused the onset of Mr. Ervin's obsessive-compulsive disorder? It is impossible to answer that question definitively, but it is relevant to note that his symptoms began to develop at the same time that his tumor began to develop and that his tumor and the subsequent surgery were in the area of the brain that has been linked to OCD.

Source: Based on Eslinger & Damasio (1985).

we know of two causes, the first of which is genetics. For example, in one study the biological relatives of individuals who had OCD were 12 times more likely to have the disorder than were the biological relatives of individuals who did not have the disorder (14.2% versus 1.2%) (Goldstein et al., 1994). The other cause for the problems in the brain is biological traumas, such as tumors or surgery (Berthier et al., 1996; Damasio, 1994). As you might expect, individuals for whom brain damage and OCD are due to a known biological trauma do not have family histories of OCD; that is, in those cases the cause is not genetic.

Brain-Behavior Links

The question now is, how do brain overactivity and brain damage lead to the symptoms of OCD? This question is difficult to answer because the areas of the brain that are overactive or damaged are involved in a variety of complex processes. In general, however, they are associated with *assessing the environment* ("What's happening?") and *making decisions about how to respond* ("What should I do?") (Delgado & Moreno, 1998; Miguel, Rauch, & Jenike, 1997; Zald & Kim, 1996a, 1996b). For example, portions of the orbitalfrontal cortex are responsible for detecting errors, so it may be that high activity there leads individuals to be excessively concerned about errors and thereby causes the individuals to try to do things "just right" or to do things repeatedly until they get them right. We also know that individuals who have their orbitalfrontal area destroyed become impulsive and disregard risks, so it appears that high activity in that area might have the reverse effect; that is, it may make the individuals restrained and inhibited, which is what we see in individuals with OCD.

Overall, then, it appears that the brain dysfunctions seen in individuals with OCD disrupt information processing, and this disruption may lead to incorrect beliefs and compulsions. The chain of events is illustrated in Figure 6.2.

Treatments for Obsessive-Compulsive Disorder

A 40-year followup of individuals with OCD revealed that almost half eventually recovered (Skoog & Skoog, 1999). It is encouraging that the disorder may "burn out" over time, but 40 years is a long time to wait, and even then only half of the patients recovered. Thus, because OCD can be long-lasting and debilitating, it is essential that it be treated. Fortunately, there are a number of effective treatments.

The Cognitive Approach: Exposure and Response Prevention

One interesting strategy for changing the beliefs of individuals who suffer from OCD is to expose them to a situation

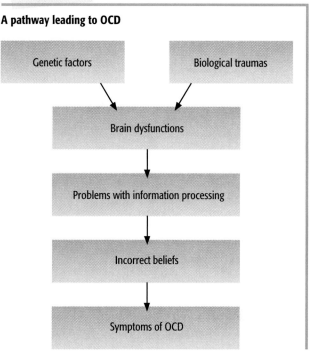

FIGURE 6.2

A pathway leading to OCD

in which they believe they must perform a ritual to avoid some calamity, but then prevent them from using the ritual. For example, an individual with a hand-washing compulsion may be exposed to dirt and then not allowed to wash his or her hands. If the person does not perform the ritual and nothing terrible happens, his or her beliefs about the necessity of the ritual may be changed. This procedure is called **exposure and response prevention,** and it has been found to be very effective for treating OCD (Abramowitz, 1996, 1997; Hartl & Frost, 1999; Franklin & Foa, 1998; Lindsay, Crino, & Andrews, 1997; McKay, 1997). In one experiment individuals with OCD were randomly assigned to conditions in which they received either exposure with response prevention or training in anxiety management over a 3-week treatment period. As indicated in Figure 6.3 (on p. 164), exposure and response prevention resulted in

soft signs of brain damage   Symptoms such as minor problems with motor coordination that are indirect measures of neurological problems.

exposure and response prevention   A treatment for compulsions in which the individual is exposed to a situation in which the compulsion would ordinarily be used but is prevented from using it; the notion is that when the compulsion is not used and nothing terrible happens, the individual will change the incorrect belief that the compulsion must be used.

FIGURE 6.3

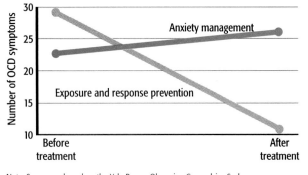

Individuals treated with exposure and response prevention showed greater decreases in symptoms of OCD than did those treated with anxiety management.

Note: Scores are based on the Yale-Brown Obsessive-Compulsive Scale.

Source: Lindsay et al. (1997), Table 2, p. 137.

substantial decreases in both obsessions and compulsions, whereas anxiety management had little or no effect (Lindsay et al., 1997).

Not only is exposure and response prevention effective for treating OCD, but there is evidence that it can be as effective as drugs (e.g., Abramowitz, 1997; Franklin & Foa, 1998; Hohagen et al., 1998; van Balkom et al., 1998). We will return to this issue after considering drug therapy.

Finally, it is interesting to note that in two studies it was found that exposure and response prevention resulted in lower levels of activity in the caudate nucleus, one of the areas of the brain that are known to be overactive in individuals with OCD (Baxter et al., 1992; Schwartz et al., 1996) This is a very interesting finding, but its meaning is not yet clear. It could be that the activity in that part of the brain is a *result* of the disorder; so when the disorder is treated, the activity subsides. Or it could be that the activity is a *cause* of the disorder, which is overcome with the treatment (Schwartz, 1998). However, the treatment does not reduce activity in the orbitalfrontal cortex, which is the area higher in the brain on which most of the attention has been focused.

The Physiological Approach: Drugs and Surgery

In recent years there has been an increasing use of drugs and even surgery to treat serious cases of OCD. Let's consider why and how well these treatment strategies work.

Drugs to Increase Levels of Serotonin. Because low levels of serotonin are implicated in many cases of OCD (see the earlier discussion), it would seem that drugs that increase levels of serotonin would benefit those cases. In fact, a large body of evidence indicates that *antidepressant* drugs that

make more serotonin available at the synapses are effective for treating OCD (Fallon et al., 1998; Greist et al., 1995; Greist & Jefferson, 1998; Hollander, 1998; Hollander, De Caria, et al., 1994; Hollander et al., 1988; Rauch & Jenike, 1998). (See Chapters 2 and 8 for a more detailed discussion of how these drugs work.)

The effectiveness of antidepressants for treating OCD was demonstrated in an experiment in which a large number of individuals with OCD were given one of three dosage levels of Prozac (20, 40, or 60 mg per day) or a placebo, and then their symptoms of OCD were assessed over a 13-week period (Pigott et al., 1990; Tollefson et al., 1994). The results indicated that all of the dosage levels of Prozac were more effective than the placebo and that higher levels of Prozac produced better results than lower levels. The fact that there was a dose-dependent relationship (higher doses were more effective) is particularly interesting and persuasive. These findings are illustrated in Figure 6.4. It is also noteworthy that studies of brain activity have revealed that individuals whose symptoms of OCD are reduced by antidepressants also show decreased activity in the areas of the brain that are overactive in people with OCD (Baxter et al., 1992; Benkelfat et al., 1994; Rubin et al., 1995; Swedo et al., 1992). Overall, then, antidepressants increase levels of serotonin, which then reduce levels of brain activity, which in turn reduce the symptoms of OCD.

Case Study 6.3 provides an interesting illustration of the effects of an antidepressant on a young woman's compulsions.

While the findings concerning the effectiveness of the antidepressants for treating OCD are impressive, the bad news is that antidepressants may be an effective treatment

FIGURE 6.4

Higher dosage levels of Prozac (fluoxetine) led to greater reductions in the symptoms of OCD.

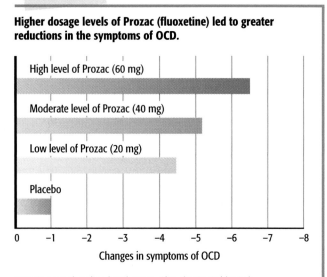

Note: Scores are based on the Yale-Brown Obsessive-Compulsive Scale.

Source: Adapted from Tollefson et al. (1994), Figure 2, p. 564.

An Unexpected and Helpful Side Effect in the Treatment of Depression

A STUDENT OF MINE had a long history of depression, and because psychotherapy was not effective, her psychiatrist prescribed a moderate level of an antidepressant (Prozac, 20 mg per day). (Depression and its treatment will be discussed in Chapter 8.)

Initially her depression improved, but about two months later it got worse; she became suicidal and called me. We arranged for her to stay with a friend for the night, and the next day her psychiatrist increased the level of the antidepressant (to 40 mg). The dose was increased on a Friday, and when I saw the student on the following Tuesday, she surprised me with a big hug and said, "It's great—it's *great!* The rituals are gone!" I was somewhat taken aback and said, "I don't understand. What rituals?" She smiled a bit

sheepishly and explained that she had not told her psychiatrist or me that for years she had been suffering from a variety of compulsions. For example, every morning in the shower she had to wash the parts of her body in a very specific order. Then, after getting out of the shower, she had to dry herself in the same order, and she had to put on her clothes in a very specific order. If she did anything out of order, she would become extremely anxious and would have to undress, reshower, re-dry, and redress.

She then went on to explain that what was "great" was the fact that two days after taking the higher dose of the antidepressant, she had showered, dried, dressed, and left her apartment—only then did she realize that she had not followed her ritual and she

was not upset about it! She did not understand why the ritual was no longer necessary, but she thought it was great; she was relieved and happy.

What appears to have happened with this young woman is that when the dosage of the antidepressant was increased, it increased the levels of serotonin enough to clear up the compulsions. The effect was surprising to the young woman because she did not know that antidepressants could influence compulsions. Clearly, this was an unexpected and distinctly positive side effect!

> . . . when the level of the antidepressant was increased, it increased the levels of serotonin enough to clear up the compulsions.

---

for only about half of the individuals who suffer from OCD. Consider the following experiment: For a 10-week period over 500 patients were given either an antidepressant (Anafranil/clomipramine) or a placebo, and their symptoms were assessed (Clomipramine Collaborative Study Group, 1991). As indicated in Figure 6.5, the antidepressant was clearly more effective than the placebo. In general, the patients taking the antidepressant drug showed a 36% decline in symptoms, whereas the patients taking the placebo showed only a 2% decline in symptoms.

These results are positive, but the limitation of the drug treatment shows up when the data are looked at in a different way. The results in Figure 6.5 are based on overall means, but when improvements in individual patients are considered, it turns out that by the end of the treatment only *half* of the patients who were taking the drug had scores in the normal range. This means that some of the patients showed large improvements, whereas others showed small or no improvements, suggesting that the drug was working for only a subgroup of patients. This result is consistent with the notion that OCD may stem from more than one cause.

In the preceding section I pointed out that exposure and response prevention can be as effective for treating OCD as antidepressant drugs. This leads to the question of whether a *combination* of the two treatments might be more effective than either one alone. Unfortunately, the answer to this

question is no: Combinations of cognitive therapy and drug treatment have not been found to be more helpful than either treatment alone (Hohagen et al., 1998; van Balkom et al., 1998). It might also be asked whether the two

FIGURE 6.5

An antidepressant (Anafranil/clomipramine) was more effective than a placebo for reducing the symptoms of OCD.

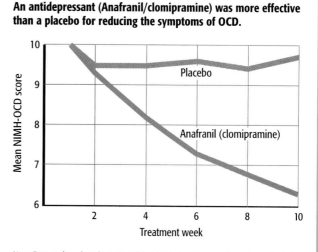

Note: Data are based on the NIMH Global OC Scale. Data are collapsed over Study 1 (patients who had been ill for at least 2 years) and Study 2 (patients who had been ill for at least 1 year).

Source: Clomipramine Collaborative Study Group (1991), Table 3, p. 734.

treatments are effective for different groups of clients. For example, do individuals who are not helped by cognitive therapy respond to drugs, and vice versa? Unfortunately, we do not have an answer to this question as yet.

Surgery on Connecting Nerve Tracts. You may be surprised to learn that with some severe cases of OCD for which other treatments are ineffective, surgery may be a viable alternative (Baer et al., 1995; Greist & Jefferson, 1998; Hay et al., 1993; Jenike, 1998; Jenike et al., 1991). The procedure that is used most often and appears to be most effective involves making small lesions (cuts) in the nerve tract that connects lower structures in the brain, such as the basal ganglia and thalamus, to the orbitalfrontal area in the cortex of the frontal lobes. As you will recall, this nerve tract is called the *cingulate gyrus*. The operation is known as a **cingulotomy** (sin-gu-LOT-o-me; *tomy* means "to cut," so *cingulotomy* means "to cut the cingulate"). The cingulate gyrus is only partially cut, so communication with the orbitalfrontal area is reduced but not stopped. The notion is that breaking some of the connections between the lower structures of the brain and the orbitalfrontal area will reduce the excessive levels of activity in the orbitalfrontal area, and this reduction in activity will reduce the symptoms. This explanation is consistent with the findings discussed earlier that individuals with OCD have abnormally high levels of activity in the orbitalfrontal area, in some other structures lower in the brain, and in the nerve tract that connects those structures to the orbitalfrontal area. The surgical procedure seems to be effective with about 50% of the patients on whom it is used. That rate is impressive because the procedure is used only with individuals whose symptoms are very severe and who have not been helped by other treatments. Side effects have not been reported.

Overall, then, it appears that both psychological and physiological treatments are effective for OCD.

THINKING CRITICALLY

Questions about Obsessive-Compulsive Disorder

1. *What causes obsessive-compulsive disorder?* It is clear that the explanation for OCD is more complicated than was once thought. Indeed, rather than being a simple strategy for avoiding anxiety, OCD appears to be more complex. The explanation that is emerging is that (a) the disorder originates from dysfunctions in the brain that impair reasoning, (b) those impairments in reasoning lead to incorrect beliefs about the necessity of using certain behaviors, and (c) those incorrect beliefs lead to compulsions. What we see in this explanation is a melding of physiological and cognitive explanations; that is, brain physiology influences thought processes, and then thoughts (beliefs) influence behavior.

Although an important part of our understanding of OCD is based on a cognitive explanation, that explanation involves a noteworthy departure from the traditional cognitive explanation in that the incorrect beliefs are not considered to stem from strictly psychological processes, such as selective attention and selective recall. Instead, the incorrect beliefs are considered to be due in large part to problems in the brain that disrupt the processing of information. The notion that problems with brain physiology can influence thoughts is not new and is supported by other findings. For instance, later you will learn that the disturbed thoughts of individuals with schizophrenia are also due to excessive arousal in the brain (see Chapter 11). Most interesting in that regard is the fact that the delusions (i.e., incorrect beliefs held despite overwhelming evidence to the contrary) seen in schizophrenia bear a striking resemblance to some of the extreme incorrect beliefs that lead to compulsions.

2. *What strategies seem to be most effective for treating obsessive-compulsive disorder?* If incorrect beliefs and compulsions have their origins in physiological problems in the brain, does this mean that compulsions must be treated with drugs or surgery? No; there is strong evidence that exposure and response prevention can be effective for treating many cases of OCD. What seems to happen is that when individuals are confronted with strong evidence that their beliefs are wrong and their compulsions are not necessary (e.g., when they are not allowed to wash their hands, and they discover that nothing terrible happens), they correct their mistaken beliefs. That is, they use the evidence to override the mistaken conclusion that stemmed from their problems with brain functioning. However, it is important to recognize that exposure and response prevention is not effective for all individuals; in those cases for which it is not effective, it may be that the brain dysfunctions are too serious to be overcome by reasoning. In other words, demonstrations that compulsions are not necessary may not be sufficient to overcome incorrect beliefs that stem from severe brain dysfunctions. If so, it may be necessary to use medication (antidepressant drugs) or, in very extreme cases, even surgery.

Overall, then, we find that a combination of explanations is most effective for understanding OCD and that there are several effective strategies for treating the disorder.

TOPIC II
Posttraumatic and Acute Stress Disorders

Five years ago a man tried to rape Carlita one night while she was walking home. Now Carlita is often anxious when she sees men she doesn't know, and because of her fears she has become withdrawn and doesn't go out much. Furthermore, when she is alone at night, the memory of the attack and her fear sometimes come flooding back; it's like the attack is happening all over again, and it's terrifying. Carlita suffers from posttraumatic stress disorder. Why do the memories and fear keep coming back?

While he was driving through a terrible storm about 10 years ago, Colin's car was swept off the road and into a river. His car tumbled over and over, and Colin almost drowned before he got out. Today Colin is still a little tense about driving, and he becomes so fearful when it rains even a little that he is unable to drive. Even when he is not driving, rain brings the whole experience back. Colin suffers from posttraumatic stress disorder. Is there a treatment for this disorder?

In this section we will focus on posttraumatic stress disorder, but at the end of the section I will also comment on acute stress disorder. Both disorders involve high levels of anxiety following a stressful (traumatic) experience, but they differ in how long the anxiety lasts.

Symptoms and Issues

Posttraumatic stress disorder, usually referred to simply as **PTSD,** involves a variety of anxiety-related symptoms that start after a particularly traumatic event and then continue for a long time (Lyons & Adams, 1999; Paige, 1997; Southwick et al., 1995). Five factors are necessary for a diagnosis of PTSD (American Psychiatric Association, 1994):

1. *The individual must have experienced or witnessed a traumatic event* in which physical injury or life was threatened. Traumatic events include natural disasters (floods, earthquakes), accidental disasters (plane crashes, fires), and deliberate disasters (wars, torture, death camps, rape, assaults).

2. *The event is persistently reexperienced.* For example, the individual frequently recalls the event, has disturbing dreams about it, experiences "flashbacks" to the event, or feels the intense anxiety that was felt during the original event. As one woman described it, "It's as though the experience keeps echoing through my brain." This reexperiencing persists for many years after the event (Falk, Hersen, & Van Hasselt, 1994). A good friend of mine survived savage combat as a 19-year-old GI in the Battle of the Bulge during World War II, and today, more than 50 years later, he still wakes up two or three nights a week with terrifying nightmares about the fighting.

3. *The individual avoids stimuli associated with the trauma and shows a general numbing of responsiveness.* In other words, the individual tries not to think or talk about

Victims of traumatic events, such as the earthquake that devastated western Turkey in the summer of 1999, are at risk for posttraumatic stress disorder.

the traumatic event and avoids activities related to the event. That can lead to psychological "numbing," in which individuals have less interest in usual activities, feelings of detachment from others, and blunted emotional responses when they are not reexperiencing the traumatic experience (Litz, 1992). In short, individuals with PTSD have limited and emotionally flattened lives that are punctuated with periods of intense anxiety stemming from the earlier trauma.

4. *The individual may show a generally heightened arousal* that stems from the anxiety. This high arousal can

cingulotomy   An operation in which the cingulate gyrus is partially cut; used for severe cases of OCD in which other treatments have not been effective.

posttraumatic stress disorder (PTSD)   An anxiety disorder in which an individual who has experienced a traumatic event persistently reexperiences the event (has "flashbacks"), avoids stimuli associated with the event, shows psychological numbing, and shows generally heightened arousal; these symptoms must persist for longer than a month.

result in problems with sleep, irritability, difficulty in concentrating, and an exaggerated startle response.

5. *The symptoms must last for more than a month.*

PTSD has undoubtedly existed throughout history, but it gained widespread attention when it was observed in veterans of the Vietnam War. An example of PTSD in a Vietnam veteran is presented in Case Study 6.4.

Posttraumatic Stress Disorder: A Vietnam Veteran Talks about His Life

CASE STUDY 6.4

"MY MARRIAGE IS falling apart. We just don't talk anymore. Hell, I guess we've never really talked about anything, ever. I spend most of my time at home alone . . . she's upstairs, and I'm downstairs. Sure we'll talk about the groceries and who will get gas for the car, but that's about it. She's tried to tell me she cares for me, but I get real uncomfortable talking about things like that, and I get up and leave.

"I really don't have any friends, and I'm pretty particular about who I want as a friend. The world is pretty much dog eat dog, and no one seems to care much for anyone else. As far as I'm concerned, I'm really not a part of this messed-up society. What I'd really like to do is have a home in the mountains, somewhere far away from everyone.

Sometimes I get so angry with the way things are being run, I think about placing a few blocks of C-4 [military explosive] under some of the sons-of-bitches.

"I usually feel depressed. I've felt this way for years. There have been times I've been so depressed that I won't even leave the basement. I'll usually start drinking pretty heavily around these times. I've also thought about committing suicide when I've been depressed. I've got an old .38 that I snuck back from Nam. A couple of times I've sat with it loaded, once I even had the barrel in my mouth and the hammer pulled back. I couldn't do it. I see Smitty back in Nam with his brains smeared all over the bunker. Hell, I fought too hard then to make it back to the world [United States]; I can't waste it now. How come I survived, and he didn't? There has to be some reason.

"Sometimes my head starts to replay some of my experiences in Nam. Regardless of what I'd like to think about, it comes creeping in. It's so hard to push it back out again. It's old friends, their faces, the ambush, the screams, their faces . . . . You know, every time I hear a chopper [helicopter] or see a clear unobstructed green treeline, a chill goes down my back; I remember. When I go hiking now, I avoid green areas. I usually stay above the timber line. When I walk down the street, I get real uncomfortable with people behind me that I can't see. When I sit, I always try to find a chair with something big and solid directly behind me. I feel most comfortable in the corner of a room, with walls on both sides of me. Loud noises irritate me, and sudden movements or noise will make me jump.

"Night is the hardest for me. I go to sleep long after my wife has gone to bed. It seems like hours before I finally drop off. I think of so many of my Nam experiences at night. Sometimes my wife awakens me with a wild look in her eye. I'm all sweaty and tense. Sometimes I grab for her neck before I realize where I am. Sometimes I remember the dream; sometimes it's Nam, other times it's just people after me, and I can't run anymore.

"I don't know, this has been going on for so long; it seems to be getting gradually worse. My wife is talking about leaving. I guess it's no big deal. But I'm lonely. I really don't have anyone else. Why am I the only one like this? What the hell is wrong with me?"

Source: Goodwin (1980), pp. 1–2.

The atrocities of war can take a considerable toll on the mental health of those who experience the horrors firsthand. Posttraumatic stress disorder gained widespread attention when it was observed in veterans of the Vietnam War.

Three points should be noted before going on: First, although PTSD first gained attention and prominence from cases associated with military combat, *PTSD can result from many types of stressors.* Indeed, victims of natural disasters, accidents, child abuse, rape, and other crimes also suffer from PTSD (North et al., 1999). One woman I know who lived through a fierce hurricane becomes very anxious and has flashbacks each time there is a heavy rain. In another case a student was attacked while walking to her car one night, and now she experiences severe anxiety and a flashback whenever she is walking alone at night. Additionally, the frequent anxiety and memories of the attack have led her to be withdrawn and depressed. Clearly, we must be sensitive to a wide variety of stressors when evaluating the possibility of a PTSD.

Second, *when making a diagnosis of PTSD, we must have strong evidence linking the stressor to the symptoms.* When faced with symptoms such as anxiety and depression, individuals often look to their past experiences for explanations. Although past experiences may provide convenient explanations, they may not be correct explanations. Indeed, anxiety and depression may stem from many factors other than past experiences, and we must ask why an experience is supposedly causing symptoms now when it did not do so earlier. For example, if an individual becomes anxious or depressed in his or her 30s, does a traumatic event in childhood or adolescence provide the best explanation? More importantly, a growing body of evidence indicates that the memories of previous stressful experiences that are blamed for the symptoms are often simply inaccurate. This was illustrated in an interesting study of a group of GIs who served in the war known as Desert Storm (Southwick et al., 1997). During the war the GIs were exposed to missile attacks, the deaths of their comrades, and the badly disfigured bodies of enemy soldiers. One month after the war and again two years later, the men completed questionnaires that measured their memories of their combat experiences and were also tested to determine whether they were suffering from PTSD. The results revealed two interesting findings: First, almost 90% of the men *changed their reports of their combat experiences over the 2-year recall period* (some recalled more stressful experiences, some fewer), thus indicating that their recall of their experiences was often inaccurate. Second and more important, the men who were diagnosed as suffering from PTSD were most likely to be those who *changed their memories to include more traumatic events.* In other words, it appears that the men who experienced symptoms of anxiety and depression changed their memories as a way of explaining their symptoms. Other investigators have found similar effects in other groups, such as those involved in fires and natural disasters (Roemer et al., 1998; Spiegel, 1998). These findings clearly indicate that in at least some individuals the symptoms of PTSD are not linked to actual stressful experiences and that PTSD is a misdiagnosis in those cases. Finally, in some cases therapists use PTSD as a diagnosis when the cause of the symptoms is not immediately apparent, the notion being that there must have been a preceding traumatic event and it has been repressed. Of course, all of these problems with the use of the PTSD diagnosis does not mean that traumatic experiences do not lead to PTSD; rather it suggests that we must be careful in making the diagnosis of PTSD and should not simply use it as a "default option" to explain symptoms.

Third, *when making a diagnosis of PTSD, we must rule out the effects of physiological problems that are associated with the traumatic event.* That is, we must be sure that the symptoms are due to a psychological stressor rather than a related physiological problem. Most noteworthy in this regard are **concussions,** which are *minor brain injuries that can be caused by a blow to the head.* Concussions are likely to occur during traumatic experiences such as attacks and accidents, and they can result in symptoms that are very similar to those of PTSD, such as problems with concentration, lack of feelings or emotions, depression, and anxiety. Because concussions are often associated with traumatic events and lead to many of the same symptoms seen with PTSD, it is easy to misdiagnose the effects of a concussion as a case of PTSD (Trudeau et al., 1998). With these cautions in mind, let's go on to consider the explanations for PTSD.

The essential role that traumatic experiences play in PTSD is illustrated by a pair of identical (monozygotic) twins who were raised, educated, and trained to be combat pilots together; the only difference between them was that one was shot down and spent time as a prisoner of war (Sutker, Allain, & Johnson, 1993). When the twins were given psychological evaluations, only the twin who had been a prisoner of war showed the symptoms of PTSD. Obviously, experiencing a traumatic event is crucial to developing PTSD. However, not everyone who experiences a traumatic event develops the disorder, and that leads to the question of why only some people develop it. There appear to be two primary reasons: First, individuals who develop the disorder seem to have a history of other stressful or traumatic experiences (Bremner et al., 1993; Zaidi & Foy, 1994). A history of traumatic experiences may lead the individual to expect traumas again in the future ("Oh, no; here we go again . . ."), or the experiences may have long-term effects on the nervous system that lead to higher levels of arousal (see Chapters 2 and 3). Second, genetics plays a role in who will develop the disorder (Davidson, Tupler, et al., 1998; True et al., 1993). With these factors in mind,

concussion A minor brain injury that can be caused by a blow to the head.

let's go on to consider the explanations for PTSD and see how these predisposing factors fit the explanations.

Explanations for Posttraumatic Stress Disorder

The original speculations concerning the cause of PTSD revolved around the notion that the traumatic event had been so threatening that it had been repressed and that symptoms such as anxiety and depression were the result of unconscious conflicts associated with the repressed material. Furthermore, the reexperiencing of the event was thought to occur when defenses were lowered and the experience, or at least parts of it, slipped back into consciousness. Although this psychodynamic explanation is interesting, it lacks empirical support (see later discussion of repression in Chapter 7) and has been generally abandoned. In view of that, let's go on to consider the learning, cognitive, and physiological explanations. Because the learning and cognitive explanations are really very similar, I'll discuss them together.

The Learning and Cognitive Explanations: Classical Conditioning and Incorrect Beliefs

PTSD can be conceptualized best as a *classically conditioned fear response* (Mineka & Zinbarg, 1998; Pynoos et al., 1996; Rasmusson & Charney, 1997). In other words, it appears that during the traumatic event the fear that the individual experiences is paired with the stimuli in the situation; therefore when the individual later encounters those stimuli, the fear response is elicited, and the individual reexperiences the feelings and the memories ("flashbacks"). Consider the case of a soldier in Vietnam who was walking across an open field with his comrades when suddenly the enemy opened fire from hiding places in a line of trees on the other side of the field. For hours the air was filled with gunfire, helicopters came roaring in to join the battle, and there were screams of men who were being killed or terribly wounded. For hours he fought for his life and was terrified. Now, years later, the sight of a tree line or the sound of a helicopter can trigger the fear; emotionally he's back fighting for his life, terrified. Similar effects can be seen in students who are in class when one of their classmates begins shooting; long after the shooting incident, whenever the students are in a classroom similar to the one in which the shooting took place, the memories come back and the students become anxious and depressed. In that regard it is interesting to note that after the shooting at Colombine High School in Colorado, where 17 students and a teacher were killed, the students specifically asked that the school alarm be changed because the original one, which sounded throughout the shooting, triggered anxiety and terrible

memories of the shooting. Clearly, stimuli associated with the traumatic event activate the PTSD symptoms. In attempts to avoid the stimuli and their frightening consequences, individuals often withdraw from people or situations that involve those stimuli. In essence, then, PTSD can be thought of as a phobia.

Classical conditioning provides a very good explanation for PTSD, but could the disorder also be explained in terms of incorrect beliefs? Yes; recall that classical conditioning can be interpreted as a procedure by which individuals develop expectations (beliefs). In view of that notion it can be argued that a combat veteran with PTSD becomes highly anxious when he hears the sound of a helicopter because he is responding to his incorrect belief that the sound of a helicopter signals a threat, as it did in the past. Similarly, when the students at Columbine High School heard the school alarm, they thought another shooting was starting.

Overall, then, the pairing of fear with stimuli leads to either conditioning or incorrect beliefs, depending on how you interpret the process. In either case conditioning of a fear response provides a good explanation for PTSD.

The Physiological Explanation: Arousal Enhances Conditioning

PTSD appears to be an instance of the classical conditioning of fear. However, if that's the case, why do some individuals develop the classically conditioned fear response while others who experience the same stressor do not? For example, many of the men and women who served in the Vietnam War underwent similar stress, so why didn't all of them develop PTSD? Similarly, why do some, but not all, of the people who live through a serious earthquake develop PTSD? The answer seems to be that individuals who develop PTSD have *higher levels of neurological arousal* than individuals who do not develop the disorder, and the higher levels of arousal *enhance the likelihood that conditioning will occur* (Armony & LeDoux, 1997; Charney et al., 1993; Gerardi et al., 1994; Southwick et al., 1993; see also the discussion of arousal and the conditioning of phobias in Chapter 5). In other words, higher levels of neurological arousal lead to better conditioning, so individuals with higher levels of neurological arousal are more likely to develop the responses that lead to a diagnosis of PTSD. This explanation is consistent with the growing body of evidence suggesting that genetics plays a role in PTSD (Davidson, Tupler, et al., 1998; True & Pitman, 1999; Yehuda, 1999). That is, individuals with PTSD inherited high levels of arousal from their parents, whose high arousal levels made them also more likely to suffer from PTSD.

It may also be that the prolonged stress (anxiety) associated with PTSD leads to chemical changes in the brain, which can cause new symptoms or exacerbate existing symptoms (Yehuda, 1998). For instance, stress can reduce the levels of the neurotransmitter serotonin, and low levels of serotonin can result in depression (see Chapter 8). Therefore, having PTSD could lead to other symptoms. These new symptoms would be "secondary" symptoms, but they would be difficult to distinguish from the primary symptoms of the disorder. In summary, stress, classical conditioning (or incorrect beliefs), and physiological arousal interact to result in PTSD.

Treatments for Posttraumatic Stress Disorder

There are two approaches to the treatment of PTSD: One involves psychological strategies for extinguishing the conditioned responses or changing the incorrect beliefs that cause the disorder, and the other involves using drugs to control the symptoms.

The Learning and Cognitive Approaches: Exposure and Coping

It now appears that the most effective psychological strategies for treating PTSD involve *exposure* to the stimuli that elicit the anxiety and flashbacks (Bryant et al., 1998; Carlson, 1996; Keane, 1998; Marks et al., 1998). The exposure may take a symbolic form, as when individuals talk about their experiences in a relaxed environment, or it may involve the actual stimuli but take place in circumstances in which nothing bad happens. Learning theorists attribute the effects of exposure to *extinction*. In other words, for them the key to treating PTSD lies in breaking the links between classically conditioned stimuli and fear. In that regard it is noteworthy that many Vietnam veterans reported improvements in their symptoms when they returned to Vietnam for visits after the war was long over and the country was at peace. Initially, they became anxious when they visited the sites where they had fought terrifying battles, but once they spent time there in an atmosphere of peace, the old conditioned responses were slowly extinguished. This does not mean that conditioned fear responses are gone forever, because *spontaneous recovery* of such responses can occur (see Chapter 2). Instances of spontaneous recovery should not be considered as treatment failures but simply as expected short-term setbacks in treatment. When spontaneous recovery occurs, additional extinction trials will further reduce the frequency and intensity of the conditioned responses.

Cognitive theorists agree that exposure is crucial, but they argue that the underlying process is the *changing of incorrect beliefs*. That is, when individuals are exposed to the stimuli that trigger the anxiety and flashbacks and nothing bad happens, their beliefs change, and they no

In an interesting illustration of the fact that PTSD can be conceptualized as a classically conditioned fear response, survivors of the Columbine High School shooting asked that the school alarm be changed. The original alarm, which sounded throughout the shooting, triggered anxiety and awful memories.

longer expect something bad to happen (Tarrier et al., 1999).

Regardless of whether the underlying process is extinction or the changing of beliefs, there is evidence that cognitive therapy that involves exposure is effective for treating PTSD (Keane, 1998). For instance, in one experiment women who had been raped and were suffering from PTSD were randomly assigned to one of four conditions (Foa et al., 1991):

1. *Prolonged exposure* involved repeatedly imagining the assault as vividly as possible and describing it aloud in the present tense. In addition, the descriptions were tape-recorded, and the women listened to their tapes at least once a day as homework. The therapy also involved going to the site where the assault had taken place.
2. *Stress inoculation training* consisted of instruction and practice in a variety of stress-reducing strategies, including muscle relaxation, controlled breathing, cognitive restructuring, and role playing.
3. *Supportive counseling* involved unconditional emotional support and help with problem solving but no exposure or anxiety management training.

FIGURE 6.6

Prolonged exposure and stress inoculation training were more effective than supportive counseling or a wait-list control condition for reducing the symptoms of PTSD.

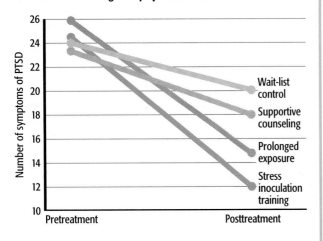

Note: Data based on ratings of an independent clinical judge who was not aware of the conditions in which the women were placed.

Source: Foa et al. (1991), Table 3, p. 719.

4. Women in the *wait-list control* condition were told that they would be treated in 5 weeks.

As indicated in Figure 6.6, the women who received exposure therapy showed greater reductions in the symptoms of PTSD than did the women who received supportive counseling or no treatment (wait-list control).

However, it is noteworthy that the stress inoculation training was also effective for reducing the symptoms of PTSD. Stress inoculation training probably reduced symptoms because the women learned how to control their anxiety, and that control gave them confidence that they would be able to deal with the symptoms in the future. Thus the training may have reduced anxiety directly, and if anxiety was reduced, extinction may have occurred or the women may have changed their beliefs about the stress.

Importantly, cognitive therapy that involves exposure and stress inoculation can also be effective for reducing acute stress and preventing the development of PTSD (Foa et al., 1995). That was demonstrated in an experiment in which women who had been recently raped were randomly assigned either to a treatment condition, in which they learned strategies for controlling anxiety and imagined the assault "as if it is happening now," or to a control condition, in which they were not given any therapy. Symptoms of PTSD were assessed at the beginning of the 4-week treatment/no-treatment period, at the end of that period, and again 4½ months later. The results are presented in Figure 6.7, and they indicate that women who received treatment showed a 73% reduction in symptoms at the end of therapy, whereas the women in the control condition showed a 35% reduction at the same time. The reductions in symptoms at the followup assessment were 85% and 68%, respectively. These results, especially the immediate effects of the treatment, are encouraging.

Exposure and learning to cope with the symptoms of PTSD often occur in the context of behavioral or cognitive therapy but can also occur less formally in "drop-in centers" for veterans, crisis intervention centers, various support groups, and rape counseling programs.

Rape counseling programs, such as this one, can help rape survivors learn to cope with the symptoms of PTSD.

FIGURE 6.7

Cognitive therapy (prolonged exposure and stress inoculation training) was effective for reducing acute stress disorder and preventing the development of PTSD.

Note: Scores indicate severity of PTSD (PTSD Symptom Scale).

Source: Foa et al. (1995), Table 2, p. 951.

The Physiological Approach: Drugs to Reduce Anxiety and Depression

The physiological approach to the treatment of PTSD involves using antianxiety drugs such as Valium and Xanax to control the symptoms of anxiety and antidepressants to reduce depression (Davidson et al., 1998; Ratna & Barbenel, 1997; Yehuda, Marshall, & Giller, 1998). However, it can be argued that because the disorder appears to be due to classical conditioning or incorrect beliefs, the drugs are only reducing the symptoms and not treating the cause of the disorder (van der Kolk et al., 1994). That may be true, but it is also possible that if individuals are less anxious, they will be more likely to put themselves in situations that would have triggered anxiety prior to taking the drugs; then, when they do not become anxious, their conditioned responses will be extinguished or their beliefs will change (see the discussion of drug treatment of phobias in Chapter 5). Indeed, drug treatment can be used as an adjunct to psychological interventions (Yehuda et al., 1998).

Acute Stress Disorder

The symptoms of acute stress disorder are essentially identical to those of PTSD with one important exception: **Acute stress disorder** *occurs within 4 weeks of the traumatic event and only lasts between 2 days and 4 weeks,* whereas PTSD can appear later than 4 weeks after the traumatic event and

lasts longer than 4 weeks (American Psychiatric Association, 1994). In other words, acute stress disorder is an intense reaction that *ends within a month of the event that triggered it.* The similarity between the symptoms of acute stress disorder and those of PTSD is reflected in the fact that individuals may initially be diagnosed as suffering from acute stress disorder, but if the symptoms last more than a month, the diagnosis will be changed to PTSD. Consider this example: Shortly after an incident in which a gunman shot 14 people in an office building, 12 of the 32 other people in the building were diagnosed as having acute stress disorder. When the people were examined again about 10 months later, most of them received a diagnosis of PTSD, indicating that acute stress disorder can be a good predictor of PTSD (Classen et al., 1998). The causes and treatments for acute stress disorder also appear to be similar to those for PTSD.

Questions about Posttraumatic and Acute Stress Disorders

1. *What seem to be the best explanations for posttraumatic and acute stress disorders?* After some controversy it now appears that PTSD and acute stress disorder can best be understood as being due to the classical conditioning of fear (anxiety). In other words, intense fear is paired with stimuli that are present during a traumatic event, and later those stimuli elicit the fear and memories associated with the event. Of course, from a cognitive perspective the "conditioning" can be interpreted as a process by which incorrect beliefs are developed. That is, because certain stimuli were associated with the traumatic event, individuals come to believe that those stimuli are signals that the traumatic event is going to occur again. However, regardless of whether we use a conditioning or cognitive interpretation, the process and results are the same.

2. *How can these disorders be treated?* The key to successful treatment seems to be exposure to the fear-provoking stimuli so that the fear is extinguished (learning explanation) or the incorrect beliefs are changed (cognitive explanation).

This concludes our discussion of specific anxiety disorders. In the final section we will review the evidence concerning the influence of gender, age, and sociocultural factors on anxiety.

acute stress disorder   An anxiety disorder that involves the same symptoms as PTSD, but the symptoms last less than 1 month.

TOPIC III

Gender, Age, and Sociocultural Factors in Anxiety Disorders

LouAnne is a social worker in a psychological clinic where she sees many clients who have anxiety disorders. Will her clients with anxiety disorders be more likely to be males or females, and will they be more likely to come from one ethnic group than another?

David has a severe phobia for snakes. He is not seeking treatment for his phobia because he lives in a city where there aren't any snakes; thus, the phobia doesn't pose a problem. If his phobia is not treated, will it simply remain constant in the background, will it get worse, or will it diminish as he gets older?

Now that you understand the symptoms, causes, and treatments associated with the various anxiety disorders, we can examine the roles played by gender, age, social class, ethnicity, and culture.

Gender

One of the strongest findings associated with anxiety disorders is that *they occur more frequently among women than men* (Breslau et al., 1997; Fredrikson et al., 1996; Gallagher & Millar, 1998; Kessler et al., 1994; Krasucki, Howard, & Mann, 1998; Yonkers et al., 1998). For example, women are more likely than men to suffer from phobias and from multiple phobias (5.4% versus 1.5%; Fredrikson et al., 1996). The incidence of anxiety disorders in women and men is presented in Figure 6.8.

There are some interesting differences between women and men in terms of the stressors they point to as the causes of their anxiety (Alonso et al., 1998). Specifically, women report being most stressed by a change in the health or behavior of a relative, an argument with a partner, a change in occupational responsibilities, a problem with colleagues, and a change in eating habits. In contrast, men report being most stressed by a change in place of residence, a change in personal habits, a change in working conditions, and the beginning of an intimate relationship. These reports suggest that interpersonal problems are more likely to lead to anxiety in women than men.

One explanation for the gender difference is that women are faced with more stressors than men (e.g., they earn less and take on more responsibilities for others; Rosenfield, 1999). Alternatively, women may be more predisposed to anxiety disorders because of physiological factors such as

FIGURE 6.8

Anxiety disorders occur more frequently in women than in men.

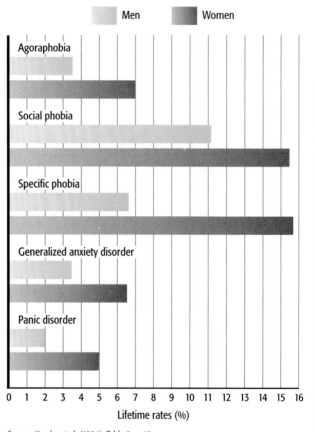

Source: Kessler et al. (1994), Table 2, p. 12.

hormonal levels (Hendrick et al., 1996; Walsh, 1998). There are not yet sufficient data to point clearly to either of these explanations, and it may be that both play a role.

Age

There is also strong evidence that anxiety disorders *decline with age* (Christensen et al., 1999; Costello, 1982; Krasucki et al., 1998; Magee et al., 1996). For instance, the prevalence of intense fears among women between 56 and 65 years of age is only about half of what it is among women between 18 and 25. Interestingly, one study revealed that anxiety disorders that did occur in older people were not particularly disruptive to the individuals and did not interfere with their activities (Manela, Katona, & Livingston, 1996). This suggests that even if anxiety disorders do not disappear completely, they diminish in strength.

Research shows that women are more likely than men to suffer from anxiety disorders. A possible explanation for this finding is the fact that women tend to be faced with more stressors than their male counterparts, particularly as they struggle to balance the demands of a job or career with their responsibilities to their families.

Why do anxiety disorders decrease with age? There are three possibilities: (1) Over time the classically conditioned anxiety responses extinguish; (2) "age brings wisdom," and older individuals abandon the incorrect beliefs that provided the basis for their earlier anxieties; (3) older individuals are less physiologically responsive and therefore less prone to anxiety responses. Unfortunately, we are not yet in a position to choose among these explanations.

Socioeconomic Class

Some data suggest that phobias are more prevalent among individuals with less education (Robins et al., 1984). It may be that less educated individuals may be more likely to have incorrect beliefs about dangers around them. Also noteworthy is the finding that the rate of some anxiety disorders is linked to where individuals live. For instance, the rate of PTSD among young, lower-class individuals in the inner

city is almost 40% (Breslau et al., 1991). That high rate was attributed to the fact that the individuals had high rates of sudden injuries, physical assaults, seeing someone hurt or killed, and rape. It is also the case that anxiety disorders are more prevalent among poor individuals, for whom simply getting by financially is a source of stress and anxiety (Muntaner et al., 1998).

Ethnicity and Culture

In contrast to the findings with regard to gender, age, and social class, there is virtually no evidence that the incidence of anxiety disorders differs across ethnic groups within a particular country (Brown et al., 1999; Ginsburg et al., 1996; McNeil, Kee, & Zvolensky, 1999; Thorson, Powell, & Samuel, 1998). Indeed, one group of researchers concluded that in the United States "Hispanics and Caucasians were *remarkably* similar" in terms of their rates, ages of onset, and gender differences in anxiety disorders (Ginsberg et al., 1996, p. 517, emphasis added). It could be argued that the similarity in rates among ethnic groups within any one country occurs because the groups have all been acculturated to the same beliefs. However, this seems unlikely, and there is evidence from Navaho Native Americans that the degree to which they identify with their culture is unrelated to the incidence of anxiety disorders (McNeil et al., 1999).

There is also no reliable evidence that the incidence of anxiety disorders is different across groups in different countries (Junko-Tanaka-Matsumi, 1997). Furthermore, when differences are found, they can often be attributed to problems with the research. For instance, rather than objectively studying the presence of symptoms in samples from various countries, investigators often simply determine the rates of disorders by counting the numbers of individuals who came for treatment. However, the numbers of individuals seeking treatment can be influenced by differences in the definition of a disorder and differences in the availability of treatment. Overall, then, there is presently no compelling evidence that anxiety disorders are linked to ethnic or cultural background.

A Concluding Comment about Anxiety Disorders

This concludes our discussion of anxiety disorders. In looking back, there are two important points you should recognize: First, it should be clear that although all of these disorders involve anxiety, *anxiety takes very different forms in the different disorders*. For example, the anxiety may (1)

Socioeconomic class appears to be a factor associated with anxiety disorders. Lower-class individuals, such as those who live in this slum in Montana, deal with the daily stress of simply getting by financially and thus are more susceptible to anxiety disorders.

be linked to specific objects such as elevators, (2) be general and seem to "come out of the blue," (3) occur in sudden bursts that are so overwhelming they may lead to panic, (4) appear only when the individual does not perform a compulsive act, such as not walking through a door backwards, or (5) be a remnant of a traumatic event

that occurred years ago (see the summary of symptoms in Table 5.1). Second, it should also be clear that *anxiety disorders often have different causes and require different treatments.* In other words, unlike what was once thought, one theory or treatment does not fit all of the anxiety disorders.

TABLE 6.1

Explanations and treatments for anxiety disorders

Disorder	Explanation(s)	Treatments
Phobic disorder	1. Classical conditioning 2. Incorrect beliefs 3. Physiological arousal, which enhances conditioning	1. Extinction (exposure) 2. Cognitive therapy to change beliefs (via exposure) 3. Drugs to block anxiety
Generalized anxiety disorder	1. High levels of arousal in the brain 2. Incorrect beliefs	1. Drugs to reduce brain activity 2. Cognitive therapy to change beliefs (aid coping) 3. Muscle relaxation training
Panic disorder	1. Overly sensitive respiratory control center 2. Incorrect beliefs	1. Antidepressants to suppress reactivity of the respiratory control center 2. Cognitive therapy to change beliefs (aid coping)
Obsessive-compulsive disorder	Brain dysfunctions that influence reasoning, leading to incorrect beliefs	1. Exposure and response prevention (results in extinction or change in beliefs) 2. Antidepressants that increase serotonin activity 3. Surgery (cingulotomy)
Posttraumatic stress and acute stress disorders	1. Classical conditioning 2. Incorrect beliefs 3. Physiological arousal, which enhances conditioning	1. Extinction (exposure) 2. Cognitive therapy to change beliefs (via exposure) 3. Drugs to block anxiety or depression

Of course, you should also know what the explanations and treatments for the various anxiety disorders are, and to help you with that I have summarized them in Table 6.1. In using Table 6.1 it is important to recall that depending on what approach you use, classical conditioning can be considered to be a process by which links are established between stimuli and responses (the learning approach) or a process by which individuals develop beliefs that stimuli provide signals concerning a forthcoming event (the cognitive approach).

Questions about Gender, Age, and Sociocultural Factors in Anxiety Disorders

1. *If cultural factors cause high levels of anxiety, are the resulting problems really psychiatric disorders?* It seems clear that living in a lower-class area in which there are high rates of injury and crime is associated with high rates of anxiety disorders. Certainly those environmental factors are realistic reasons to be anxious. So, if individuals do become anxious under those circumstances, is it appropriate to label them as suffering from a psychiatric disorder? Here's a more extreme example: If a soldier becomes anxious during a battle in which his or her life is threatened, does the individual have an anxiety disorder? In other words, in those circumstances isn't anxiety a normal response to a realistic threat? Stated yet another way, do these cases show a "sick environment" or a "sick person"? The answer to the question of whether an individual has an anxiety disorder

does not depend simply on the presence of anxiety. Instead it depends on what the individual *does about the anxiety* and *whether the anxiety disrupts the individual's life.* So, anxiety that makes you more careful in potentially dangerous situations would not be characterized as a disorder, but anxiety that causes you to stay at home so that you can't go to work or participate in normal social activities might lead to a diagnosis of an anxiety disorder. This analysis leads to two approaches to the treatment and prevention of anxiety disorders: First, some professionals such as sociologists suggest correcting environmental factors such as crime and poverty that lead to anxiety, thereby forestalling its development. Second, mental health professionals propose helping individuals learn to cope with the stressors in their lives. Taken together, these approaches suggest this strategy: Fix the problems you can, and learn to cope effectively with those you can't.

2. *Do gender, age, and sociocultural factors provide good explanations for anxiety disorders?* These factors can certainly lead to some disorders, but as I have repeatedly shown in this chapter, different anxiety disorders can stem from different causes. Therefore it would be incorrect to attribute all anxiety disorders to these factors. Furthermore, although these factors are linked to some anxiety disorders, the links do not necessarily indicate causation. For example, younger individuals are more likely to suffer from phobias, but this link with age probably simply reflects differences in physiological arousal, which influence conditionability, which influences the development of phobias. In other words, age is simply a "marker" for conditionability. In summary, we must be flexible in considering causes for anxiety disorders, and we must be careful to distinguish between factors that are correlated with disorders and those that cause disorders.

Summary

Topic I: Obsessive-Compulsive Disorder

▶ Obsessive-compulsive disorder (OCD) involves recurrent obsessions or compulsions or both. An obsession is a persistent idea, thought, image, or impulse that an individual cannot get out of his or her mind and that causes anxiety. A compulsion is a behavior (sometimes called a ritual) that an individual feels driven to perform over and over because of a fear that something terrible will happen if the behavior is not performed.

▶ OCD was once thought to reflect unconscious conflicts or defenses against them, but those explanations have been generally abandoned.

▶ Obsessions appear to be driven by incorrect beliefs (e.g., "If I don't do this something terrible will happen"). In some cases the beliefs are bizarre (similar to delusions), and it does not appear that normal psychological processes can be used to account for them.

▶ OCD is associated with (1) low levels of serotonin; (2) high levels of activity in the orbitalfrontal area of the brain, areas lower in the brain (the caudate nucleus, basal ganglia), and the nerve tract (the cingulate gyrus) connecting those areas to the orbitalfrontal area; and (3) brain damage (particularly in the orbitalfrontal area).

▶ It appears that the physiological problems in the brain disrupt information processing and may lead to the incorrect beliefs that drive compulsions.

▶ Some compulsions can be treated effectively with exposure and response prevention, a procedure in which an individual is not permitted to use a compulsion.

▶ Some compulsions can be treated effectively with antidepressants that increase the levels of serotonin (the drugs block the reuptake of serotonin).

▶ In extreme cases in which other treatments have not worked, a cingulatomy may be used. In that procedure the cingulate gyrus is partially cut to reduce brain activity.

▶ Overall, OCD appears to be due to physiological and cognitive factors; brain dysfunctions impair reasoning and lead to incorrect beliefs that cause compulsions.

Topic II: Posttraumatic and Acute Stress Disorder

▶ The symptoms of posttraumatic stress disorder (PTSD) involve the persistent reexperiencing of a traumatic event, the avoidance of stimuli associated with the event, emotional blunting, and heightened arousal. The symptoms must last for more than a month.

▶ PTSD can stem from any traumatic event. A diagnosis of PTSD requires strong evidence for the link between the event and the symptoms, and other explanations (e.g., concussions) for the symptoms must be ruled out.

▶ PTSD is now generally conceptualized as a classically conditioned fear response, but cognitive theorists frame the process as involving the development of incorrect beliefs about the danger in situations. Heightened physiological arousal appears to enhance conditionability and predispose individuals to the disorder.

▶ Exposure to the anxiety-provoking stimuli can be an effective treatment, because it leads either to extinction or to changed beliefs. Drugs can also be used to control the symptoms of anxiety and depression.

▶ Acute stress disorder involves the same symptoms as PTSD, but it occurs within a month of the traumatic event and lasts only between 2 days and 4 weeks. The explanations and treatments are the same as those for PTSD.

Topic III: Gender, Age, and Sociocultural Factors in Anxiety Disorders

▶ Anxiety disorders occur more frequently among women than men, but it is not clear to what extent that difference is due to psychological versus physiological factors.

▶ The frequency and intensity of anxiety disorders declines with age, but the reasons are not yet clear.

▶ Some anxiety disorders (e.g., PTSD) are more common in the lower socioeconomic classes, probably because life is more stressful for individuals in those classes.

▶ There is no reliable evidence that the incidence of anxiety disorders differs markedly across ethnic or cultural groups.

Questions for Making Connections

1. How can incorrect beliefs be used to explain compulsions? How can the notion that incorrect beliefs cause compulsions be integrated with the findings that people with OCD have abnormally high levels of activity in their brains and/or damaged areas in their brains?

2. Describe the treatment known as exposure and response prevention. Explain the effects of that treatment in terms of the learning and cognitive approaches.

3. Mike is depressed and is having trouble concentrating. He thinks that he might have PTSD, because some years ago he was in a serious automobile accident in which his best friend was killed. What questions or cautions would you consider before making that diagnosis?

4. Biological relatives of individuals with PTSD are more likely to suffer from the disorder than are members of the general population. How can that be explained?

5. Are the various anxiety disorders simply "variations on a theme," or are they really different disorders? Answer this question by describing the symptoms and apparent cause or causes of the phobic, generalized anxiety, panic, obsessive-compulsive, posttraumatic stress, and acute stress disorders.

6. Given what you know about the relationships of gender, age, socioeconomic class, and ethnicity and culture to anxiety disorders, describe what might be the typical person with PTSD.

Key Terms and People

In reviewing and testing yourself, you should be able to discuss each of the following:

acute stress disorder, p. 173

cingulate gyrus, p. 161

cingulotomy, p. 166

compulsion, p. 158

concussion, p. 169

exposure and response prevention, p. 163

obsession, p. 158

obsessive-compulsive disorder (OCD), p. 158

orbitalfrontal area, p. 161

posttraumatic stress disorder (PTSD), p. 167

serotonin, p. 161

soft signs of brain damage, p. 162

7

Somatoform and Dissociative Disorders

IN THIS CHAPTER I will discuss two groups of disorders. First, I will explain *somatoform disorders*. These disorders involve physical symptoms for which no physical cause can be found. For example, an individual may suffer from paralyses, pains, or digestive problems, but because no physical cause can be found, it is assumed that the cause is psychological. Second, I will review *dissociative disorders*. These disorders occur when an individual loses contact with parts of his or her experience or personality. For instance, the individual may suffer from amnesia or, in the case of "multiple personalities," the individual may be unaware of parts of his or her personality. As you will see, there is a great deal of controversy about some of these disorders.

TOPIC I
Somatoform Disorders

Alice sees her doctor frequently about a wide variety of physical symptoms, including pains, lumps, dizziness, blurred vision, digestive problems, and numbness. In most cases a cause cannot be found, so she is sent to specialists, who do additional workups. Even they have difficulty making a firm diagnosis. Alice's case is made more complex by the fact that after a short period of treatment her symptoms usually change, and then additional medical consultations are necessary. Alice's ill-

nesses cause her considerable anxiety and depression and result in huge medical bills. If physical causes for Alice's symptoms cannot be found, what does cause them?

William does not have a lot of physical symptoms, but when a minor one occurs, he thinks it is an early sign of some very serious disorder and becomes extremely worried. For example, he recently developed a minor rash on his arm and immediately concluded that he had advanced skin cancer. Why does William overreact? Is such a reaction a symptom of a psychiatric disorder?

The clerical staff of a research institute was under pressure to get a large amount of data entered into the computer. The employees worked long hours at their terminals, and on Wednesday two of them went home early complaining of headaches, dizziness, and nausea. Around 11 o'clock the next morning, four others began vomiting uncontrollably, three reported that their vision was so blurred that they could not see across the room, one fainted, and others reported lesser forms of physiological distress. At first it was thought that the computer screens were giving off excessive radiation or that chemical pollutants had gotten into the air-conditioning system, but environmental engineers were unable to confirm either of those possibilities. After 2 days of rest the staff went back to work in the same environment with no ill effects. The staff probably suffered from *mass psychogenic illness*. Are psychological disorders like this "catching"?

The dominant feature of most **somatoform disorders** is the presence of *physical symptoms,* such as pain, paralysis, blindness, or deafness, *for which there is no demonstrable physical cause.* In the absence of a physical cause, it is assumed that the symptoms stem from psychological causes.

At the outset we must distinguish between somatoform disorders and **psychosomatic disorders,** such as tension headaches and certain cardiovascular disorders. In both somatoform and psychosomatic disorders, the causes are psychological and the symptoms are physical. However, the difference between the two is that with somatoform disorders *there is no physical damage* (e.g., an individual may complain about chest pain and shortness of breath, but there is nothing wrong with the cardiovascular system), whereas with psychosomatic disorders *there is physical damage* (e.g., stress may have resulted in actual damage to the cardiovascular system). The term *somatoform* is used because the symptoms take the *form* of a *somatic* (physical) disorder. Somatoform disorders are important because they disrupt the lives of individuals just as real physical illnesses do and also because they place a heavy and unnecessary burden on the health care system (Martin & Yutzy, 1999).

Somatoform Disorders

There are five somatoform disorders: *somatization disorder, hypochondriasis, conversion disorder, pain disorder,* and *body dysmorphic disorder.* The major symptoms of these disorders are summarized in Table 7.1.

Somatization Disorder

The diagnosis of **somatization** (so-mat-uh-ZA-shun) **disorder** is used for individuals who have *numerous, recurrent,* *and long-lasting complaints of physical symptoms that are apparently not due to any actual physical cause.* To be diagnosed as suffering from somatization disorder, an individual must have reported at least (1) two gastrointestinal symptoms (e.g., nausea, vomiting, intolerance for several foods), (2) one sexual symptom (e.g., indifference, erectile dysfunction, irregular menses), (3) one neurological symptom (e.g., paralysis, weakness, difficulty in swallowing), and (4) pain in four locations (e.g., head, abdomen, joints).

Individuals with this disorder reject the notion that their symptoms are caused by psychological factors, and they persist in seeking a medical solution. By middle adulthood they have complained about almost every symptom pattern imaginable, have consulted every specialist available, and have stocked a medicine cabinet that rivals the shelves of a pharmacy. Their medical concerns often take over and dominate their lives.

Somatization is usually a lifelong disorder in which individuals seriously overuse the health care system (Bell, 1994; Smith, 1994; Williams & House, 1994). For example, during one 25-year period, a 48-year-old woman had 77 admissions to 10 different hospitals, underwent 11 operations, and spent 856 days in the hospital (the equivalent of almost 2½ years!), yet no physical disorder was ever found that could explain her symptoms. It is also common for individuals with somatization disorder to suffer from depression and anxiety (Noyes et al., 1994). It is usually thought that the depression and anxiety are consequences of the individual's belief that a serious medical problem exists. In everyday terms, an individual with somatization disorder is often referred to as a "hypochondriac," but as you will learn next, that diagnosis is reserved for a somewhat different set of symptoms.

Hypochondriasis

The dominant feature of **hypochondriasis** (hi-po-kon-DRI-uh-sis) is the *unrealistic belief that a minor symptom*

TABLE 7.1

Predominant symptoms of somatoform disorders		
	Disorder	*Symptoms*
	Somatization disorder	Numerous, recurrent, and long-lasting physical complaints for which a physical cause cannot be found
	Hypochondriasis	An unrealistic belief that a minor symptom reflects a serious disease
	Conversion disorder	One or more major physical symptoms involving voluntary motor or sensory functions for which a physical cause cannot be found
	Pain disorder	Pain for which a physical cause cannot be found
	Body dysmorphic disorder	Preoccupation with some imagined or minor defect in one's physical appearance

Note: Symptoms must be serious enough to result in impairment in social, occupational, or other important areas of functioning.

reflects a serious disease. That is, individuals with this disorder interpret minor physical sensations as signs of abnormalities that will inevitably lead to serious diseases; consequently, they become very anxious and upset about what they think are serious impending disorders. For example, a headache is interpreted as a symptom of a developing brain tumor, or a slight skin irritation is seen as an early sign of skin cancer. Medical examinations and reassurances that there is nothing wrong may temporarily allay the concern, but soon a new sign of impending physical disease will be found, and the cycle starts over again.

Hypochondriasis is similar to somatization in that both disorders involve concerns about physical symptoms. However, the two disorders differ in that individuals with somatization disorder are concerned with *a wide variety of current symptoms and diseases,* whereas individuals with hypochondriasis show *excessive anxiety about one or two symptoms and the implications those symptoms could have for potential future diseases.* Hypochondriasis is a long-term disorder, is more likely to be diagnosed in women than in men, and is likely to be accompanied by depression and anxiety (Barsky et al., 1998; Gureje, Uestuen, & Simon, 1997). Indeed, even after 5 years of treatment, most of the patients in one group still had enough symptoms to justify a diagnosis of hypochondriasis. The prolonged nature of the disorder is important because the individuals affected by it spend much of their lives suffering and run up extremely high medical bills with little or no benefit.

Conversion Disorder

A diagnosis of **conversion disorder** is made when an individual has *one or more major physical symptoms involving voluntary motor or sensory functions for which a physical cause cannot be found.* Frequently cited conversion symptoms include paralysis, seizures, blindness, deafness, tunnel vision, anesthesia (loss of feeling or sensation), and paresthesia (pricking or tingling sensations of the skin). In many cases the symptoms are closely related to the individual's activities or occupation. For example, pilots who fly at night develop night blindness, whereas pilots who fly during the day develop day blindness (Ironside & Batchelor, 1945). Violinists develop paralysis or cramps in the hands.

Certain features of conversion disorder help us distinguish between it and an actual physical disorder. The most conclusive of such clues is the occurrence of a symptom pattern that could not possibly be the result of a physical cause. An example of this is the classic glove anesthesia, in which the individual loses feeling in the hand up to the point at which a glove would stop. Given the actual nerve pathways in the arm and hand, such a pattern of insensitivity is impossible. The distinction between glove anesthesia and the actual nerve pathways is illustrated in Figure 7.1. However, as the level of medical sophistication in the general public increases, individuals are less likely to exhibit

FIGURE 7.1

The lack of feeling in glove anesthesia does not follow the nerve pathways in the hand.

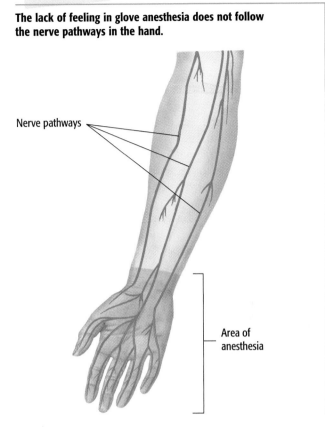

Nerve pathways

Area of anesthesia

symptom patterns that are blatantly impossible; hence it is becoming more difficult to distinguish conversion disorder from actual physical disorders on the basis of the inappropriateness of the symptom patterns (Binzer, Anderson, & Kullgren, 1997).

somatoform disorders   A class of disorders that involve physical symptoms for which physical causes cannot be found and that include somatization disorder, hypochondriasis, conversion disorder, pain disorder, and body dysmorphic disorder.

psychosomatic disorders   Disorders that have psychological causes but have symptoms that involve physical damage.

somatization disorder   A somatoform disorder involving numerous, recurrent, and long-lasting complaints of physical symptoms for which no physical cause can be found.

hypochondriasis   A somatoform disorder characterized by an unrealistic belief that minor symptoms reflect serious diseases.

conversion disorder   A disorder in which an individual has one or more major physical symptoms that impair motor or sensory functioning and for which a physical cause cannot be found.

Another clue pointing to conversion disorder is the absence of the negative consequences that would inevitably result from a physical disorder. For example, individuals with conversion disorder who suffer from epileptic-like seizures may not hurt themselves during the "seizures," and psychogenically blind individuals may not bump into things.

A final clue leading to a diagnosis of conversion disorder is inconsistency of the symptom pattern. Specifically, in an individual with conversion disorder, the symptoms may change with changes in the stressor (a paralyzed leg before a track meet and a paralyzed hand before an examination), whereas there will be greater consistency in symptoms that stem from an actual physical disorder. Unfortunately, in many cases all of these clues are lacking, making the differential diagnosis of this disorder very difficult.

A dramatic example of an alleged conversion disorder that I observed occurred in a sophomore woman who came to the university hospital about midway through the fall semester with "intermittent blindness." This woman's vision would begin dimming on Sunday evening, and she would be blind by Monday morning. The "blindness" lasted until Friday evening, but her vision was completely restored by Saturday morning. This cycle persisted for 3 weeks. The student showed no surprise at the unusual nature of her disorder and expressed no concern about her condition. Indeed, she observed cheerily that she was sure we would be able to take care of the problem and, after all, it was not interfering with the important social activities associated with football weekends! After 3 weeks the symptoms remitted. It is not clear why they remitted at that point, but the change may be associated with the fact that the midterm examination period was over. The student stayed in school (but did not go to many of her classes because she was "too far behind") until the last week of the semester, when she withdrew "for medical reasons."

Pain Disorder

Pain disorder involves the *complaint of pain in the absence of an identifiable physical cause,* in which case the pain is thought to have a psychological origin. Individuals with pain disorder are very concerned about their problem, and they may make frequent visits to physicians for treatment. The extent of the impairment caused by this disorder ranges from slight inconvenience to total incapacity and need for hospitalization. Pain disorder could be loosely considered a subtype of somatization disorder; the only difference between the two is that pain is the only symptom reported with pain disorder.

Body Dysmorphic Disorder

Body dysmorphic (dis-MOR-fik) **disorder** involves a *preoccupation with some imagined or minor defect in one's physical appearance.* Examples include excessive concern about a mole or the shape of one's nose. Not included in this diagnosis is anorexia, which involves unjustifiable concern about body weight (see Chapter 14). Body dysmorphic disorder is the most recent addition to the group of somatoform disorders, added with the publication of *DSM-III-R* in 1987. In some cases body dysmorphic disorder can lead to social withdrawal, occupational dysfunction, and even suicide. The disorder occurs more often in women than in men, and the parts of the body about which individuals are concerned differ between women and men. Specifically, women report more concerns about breasts and legs, whereas men have more preoccupations with genitals, height, and body hair (Perugi et al., 1997). The symptoms are often accompanied by depression and anxiety disorders, particularly social phobias and obsessive-compulsive disorder (Albertini & Phillips, 1999; Biby, 1998; Phillips et al., 1998; Wilhelm et al., 1997).

Before concluding our discussion of somatoform disorders, we should give some attention to a related phenomenon called **mass psychogenic illness** (Jones et al., 2000). Mass psychogenic illness involves *an epidemic of a particular manifestation of a somatoform disorder.* The best known of these epidemics are the dancing manias that erupted in the 15th and 16th centuries. In those epidemics large groups of people danced, hopped, and jerked uncontrollably for hours or days until they finally fell down, exhausted (Martin, 1923).

Contrary to what is often assumed, mass psychogenic illness did not stop with the Middle Ages. In fact, numerous epidemics have been reported in recent years, but these are less extreme than the medieval dancing manias (Sirois, 1982). For example, a sudden outbreak of a peculiar illness spread quickly among Boston grade school children who were gathered at an assembly (Small & Nicholi, 1982). The children reported experiencing dizziness, hyperventilation, weakness, headache, nausea, and abdominal pain. Among the 224 children who attended the assembly, almost 50 required some type of treatment on the scene and 34 had to be hospitalized. However, no physical basis could be found for any of the symptoms. Other instances of mass psychogenic illness involved 84 women in a television assembly plant in Singapore who began screaming, fainting, and

---

pain disorder   A somatoform disorder whose major symptom is the complaint of pain for which a physical cause cannot be found.

body dysmorphic disorder   A somatoform disorder in which an individual is preoccupied with some imagined defect in her or his physical appearance.

mass psychogenic illness   Manifestation of a somatoform disorder (e.g., fainting, nausea) in a large number of people at one time.

The dancing manias of the 15th and 16th centuries were early examples of mass psychogenic illness. In these manias groups of people hopped and jerked uncontrollably.

going into trances (Chew, Phoon, & Mae-Lim, 1976); 85 women and 59 men working in a factory in the Southeastern United States who developed dizziness, nausea, difficulty in breathing, headaches, and a bad taste in the mouth (Folland, 1975); 35 women working in an office of a Midwestern university who experienced nausea, vomiting, dizziness, and fainting (Stahl & Lebedun, 1974); over 900 persons (mostly schoolgirls) who developed blindness, headache, stomachache, and discoloration of the skin (Hefez, 1985); and 45 schoolchildren in Bali who experienced sudden periods of fainting, visual hallucinations, and uncontrollable dancing (Suryani & Jensen, 1992). In one case of an unexplained outbreak of "allergy" among plastics workers, it was found that those workers who developed the illness had a higher rate of anxiety or depressive disorders (54% vs. 4%) and somatization (69% vs. 13%) than those who did not develop the illness, thereby suggesting a psychological predisposition or cause (Simon, Katon, & Sparks, 1990).

It is interesting to note that there have been changes in the purported causes of mass psychogenic illness over the past 500 years, and those changes reflect changes in the culture. For instance, in the 15th century the illness was often attributed to curses, whereas now it is attributed to factors such as radiation from computer screens. An example of mass psychogenic illness is presented in Case Study 7.1.

Mass Psychogenic Illness in Junior High and High School Students

CASE STUDY 7.1

ON APRIL 13, 1989, approximately 600 student performers gathered at the Santa Monica Civic Auditorium for the 40th annual "Stairway to the Stars" concert. This was the major classical music performance for the year for students in the 6th through 12th grades. The performance started at 7:30 p.m., but shortly thereafter it was interrupted when symptoms such as headaches, dizziness, weakness, abdominal pain, shortness of breath, chills, chest pain, and nausea began spreading through the student performers. Eleven students found themselves unable to open their eyes, and 18 fainted. The problem became so bad that the concert had to be stopped, and the students, along with the 2,000 spectators, were forced to evacuate the auditorium.

The fire department set up a treatment area outside the auditorium. The ill students were placed on stretchers lined up on the lawn, and eight ambulances were used to rush the most severely ill students to local hospitals.

Physical examinations and laboratory tests performed on the students did not reveal any abnormalities. Furthermore, there was no evidence of toxic fumes or materials in the area. Because there were no confirmed physical illnesses and no evidence of environmental threats, the school officials rescheduled the concert for the next evening, but many parents were unconvinced of the safety of the situation and therefore kept their children at home.

A followup study of the students who did and did not develop symptoms revealed some interesting differences. For example, when compared to students who did not show symptoms, those who did show symptoms were more likely to have had a chronic illness (25% vs. 10%), more likely to have had a recent acute illness (17% vs. 11%), more likely to have experienced the death of a relative or friend (70% vs. 55%), and, most important, more likely to have observed a friend get sick at the concert (71% vs. 41%).

The affected students truly believed that they were sick and showed signs of illness such as vomiting or fainting, but no underlying physical causes could be identified. The absence of underlying causes, in combination with the data concerning the influence of suggestion (e.g., previous experience with illness and seeing others become sick), supports the diagnosis of mass psychogenic illness.

> **The affected students truly believed that they were sick and showed signs of illness such as vomiting or fainting . . . .**

Source: Small et al. (1991).

Issues

Before going on to discuss the causes of somatoform disorders, we need to discuss a few issues that will help put these disorders into perspective.

Historical Background and Prevalence

Descriptions of what appear to be somatoform disorders (particularly conversion disorder) date back to as early as 1500 B.C. In most instances the early patients were women (Veith, 1965). The ancient Greeks attributed the disorders to sexual problems. Specifically, they suggested that when the womb was not sexually satisfied, it went wandering through the body in search of satisfaction and disrupted the body's functioning. For example, if a woman had a paralyzed arm, it was assumed that the womb had become stuck in her shoulder or elbow. As a treatment for the wandering womb, the early Greek physicians recommended more sex. The belief that sex played a role in somatoform disorders is reflected in the fact that they were called "hysterical" until 1980—the term *hysteria* comes from the Greek word for "womb."

Increased attention was focused on somatoform disorders in the 19th century, when **Jean-Martin Charcot** (shar-KO; 1825–1893), a famous French physician, dramatically demonstrated that he could use suggestion to induce and eliminate many of the symptoms of "hysteria." His notion was that individuals who were prone to the disorders had "weak nervous systems" and therefore were susceptible to suggestion. Sigmund Freud also worked with patients suffering from somatoform disorders and, like the Greeks a few centuries earlier, concluded that the basis of the disorders was sexual—specifically, conflicts over sexuality (see the later discussion). Interestingly, Freud did not believe that the disorder was limited to women. Early in his career he presented a paper at a meeting of the Vienna Medical Society on "male hysteria." His suggestion that males suffer from hysteria was met with disbelief and laughter, and he was literally laughed off the stage and almost banished from the medical society.

The diagnostic label "hysteria" was eliminated in 1980 with the publication of *DSM-III*, when the term *somatoform* was substituted. This was done to avoid the connotations of a sexual cause associated with the word "hysteria." It is estimated that about 2% of the population experiences various somatoform disorders, a rate that has held steady since shortly after the turn of the 20th century (American Psychiatric Association, 1994; Stephens & Kamp, 1962).

Gender and Sociocultural Factors

Women are more likely than men to be diagnosed as suffering from somatoform disorders (Golding, Smith, & Kashner, 1991). Unfortunately, we do not know why this is the case. It may be that for historical reasons diagnosticians are biased in favor of diagnosing the disorder in women,

In the 19th century French physician Jean-Martin Charcot demonstrated that somatoform symptoms could be introduced and eliminated by means of suggestions. Freud was so impressed with Charcot's work that he kept a copy of this etching in his office.

that women are more likely to seek help for the types of complaints associated with somatoform disorders, or that there is something about the causes of the disorders (e.g., particular stresses or physiological factors) that predisposes women to them.

Somatoform disorders occur throughout the world, but there are differences across cultures in what symptoms occur and what explanations are used for the symptoms (Janca et al., 1995; Kirmayer & Young, 1998). For example, in Asia there is a disorder called **koro** that involves anxiety stemming from the belief that the genitals are withdrawing into the body and that death will follow. Similarly, in India a disorder called **dhat** involves depression, numerous physical complaints (such as a decline in semen production, weakness, fatigue), and the belief that the symptoms are due to a decline in a vital fluid (sukra) in the body (Paris, 1992).

It appears that somatoform disorders that occur in different cultures are probably due to a common underlying cause, but the symptoms and explanations take different forms as a function of the role models and belief systems of the cultures (Chaturvedi, 1993; Janca et al., 1995). Koro provides a good illustration of this. Specifically, we now know that koro can be successfully treated with the same antidepressant drug (clomipramine) that is effective for treating disorders in Western culture that involve bodily concerns, such as body dysmorphic disorder, thus suggesting that a common cause is responsible for the disorders in both cultures (Goetz & Price, 1994). It is also noteworthy that with the general merging of cultures, koro is occurring in Western cultures and proposals have been made to include this disorder in the next edition of *DSM* (Fishbain, 1991). With regard to dhat it is relevant to recall that years ago in the United States, bodily complaints were often attributed to low levels of various bodily fluids, and popular traveling "medicine shows" sold assorted "elixirs of life" that were claimed to replenish the fluids and relieve the complaints.

Are Somatoform Symptoms Real or Faked?

Are the symptoms seen in somatoform disorders real or faked? Certainly there are individuals who fake physical illnesses in deliberate attempts to *avoid responsibility* or to *obtain economic benefits* such as insurance payments. Faking illness for those reasons is called **malingering** (ma-LIN-ger-ring). In contrast, some individuals fake symptoms to get the *attention* or *sympathy* that comes with being sick. Individuals who do that are diagnosed as having **factitious** (fak-TISH-us) **disorders.** (The term *factitious* is based on a Latin word meaning "to make," and it means "not natural" or "sham.") Unfortunately, in many cases individuals with factitious disorders go beyond simply reporting symptoms that do not exist and may artificially induce serious symptoms that could be life-threatening. For example, an indi-

vidual may fake *hemophilia* (a physical disorder in which blood does not clot) by taking high doses of *anticoagulants* (drugs that inhibit the clotting of blood). Doing that is very dangerous because if injured, the individual can bleed to death.

Persons with factitious disorders are sometimes referred to as "hospital hobos" or "hospital addicts," and individuals with dramatic cases of these disorders are often referred to in the media as suffering from *Munchausen syndrome,* a term derived from the name of a German baron who achieved notoriety because of his exaggerated stories about his exploits (Leamon & Plewes, 1999). Other individuals may suffer from **factitious disorders by proxy** (often called *Munchausen syndrome by proxy*). A *proxy* (PRAK-se) is a person who acts for another person, and persons with factitious disorders by proxy fake serious symptoms in someone close to them, often a child, and thereby gain attention and sympathy. Using hidden video cameras, investigators have documented mothers intentionally harming their children (e.g., giving them medication, smothering them) in order to create medical emergencies that will attract notice and concern. Obviously, factitious disorders can have very serious medical implications and can needlessly run up huge costs.

So, yes, faking of symptoms does occur, but not all somatoform disorders are faked. The best evidence for the reality of somatoform symptoms comes from research on the **placebo** (pla-CE-bo) **effect** (Quitkin, 1999; A. Shapiro,

---

Jean-Martin Charcot A 19th-century physician who thought that somatoform (hysterical) disorders were due to a weak nervous system and who treated them with suggestion (hypnosis).

koro A disorder occurring primarily in Asia that involves panic-like symptoms stemming from the belief that the genitalia are retracting into the abdomen and that the process will result in death.

dhat A disorder occurring primarily in India that involves depression, numerous somatic complaints (such as a decline in semen production, weakness, and fatigue), and the belief that the symptoms are due to a decline of a vital fluid (*sukra*) in the body.

malingering Faking illness to avoid responsibility or obtain economic gain.

factitious disorders Disorders that involve faking symptoms to gain attention or sympathy; extreme cases are called *Munchausen syndrome.*

factitious disorders by proxy disorders that involve faking symptoms in another person, such as a child, in order to gain attention or sympathy for self; often called *Munchausen syndrome by proxy.*

placebo effect A phenomenon whereby the expectation that a treatment will have a specific effect may produce the effect, even if the treatment has no therapeutic value.

1980). The placebo effect occurs when an individual is given a treatment that has no therapeutic value (e.g., a pill that does not contain any active ingredients), but the individual believes that the treatment should help and subsequently shows the expected change (see Chapter 4). Many studies document the positive effects of placebos on physical symptoms (e.g., reductions in pain), and it is generally agreed that the placebo effect is due to suggestion. The placebo (suggestion) effect is relevant for understanding somatoform symptoms because placebos can be used to induce symptoms as well as reduce them. Overall, then, although the symptoms do not have physiological causes, individuals can really believe they have the symptoms and are not necessarily faking.

Differential Diagnoses, Medical Costs, and Medical Progress

A serious problem stems from the difficulty of separating somatoform disorders from real physical disorders. That is, in some cases somatoform disorders are mistaken for real physical disorders, and in other cases real physical disorders are misdiagnosed as somatoform disorders. For example, in one series of cases individuals who had difficulty talking and showed unusual motor movements were diagnosed as suffering from conversion disorder, but later it was discovered that in fact they were suffering from Tourette's syndrome (Kulisevsky et al., 1998). In another interesting case a woman had two experiences in which she became upset but was unable to talk and had some temporary paralyses. When taken to an emergency room, CT scans and examinations by a neurologist failed to reveal a physiological cause, so she was diagnosed as suffering from *hysteria,* the

original term for somatoform disorders. The reasoning apparently was that the woman was upset about something but conflicted over whether she should say anything, so she became unable to talk, thereby resolving the conflict. However, the next time she had an attack, an MRI revealed a weakened blood vessel (a *cerebral aneurysm*) that had broken. In other words, her "hysterical" symptoms were in fact due to brief disruptions in blood flow in the brain (*transient ischemic attacks;* see Chapter 17). There are even cases in which individuals were diagnosed as suffering from a somatoform disorder but later died from a medical disorder for which they did not get treatment (Gross, 1979; Slater & Glithero, 1965; Whitlock, 1967). Fortunately, this appears to be happening less frequently today because of the increased sophistication of medical technology, such as PET and MRI scans, used for making diagnoses (Binzer & Kullgren, 1998).

Because patients with somatoform disorders often have rather vague complaints or because a physical cause for their complaints cannot be found immediately, they are frequently given extensive medical tests in attempts to diagnose the problem. These diagnostic tests, along with the unnecessary treatments that may be tried, can lead to extremely high medical bills. Indeed, it has been estimated that somatoform disorders add between $20 billion and $30 billion to the cost of health care in the United States.

To solve the problem of costs, programs have been put into place to identify and then screen out individuals who have somatoform disorders so that they do not proceed further in the medical system. These programs can be very effective in cutting costs. For example, in one program individuals who somatized were identified, and their physicians either were or were not sent a letter informing them of the possible psychological nature of their patients' symptoms (Smith, Rost, & Kashner, 1995). Simply informing the physicians resulted in a 33% reduction in their patients' medical costs as compared to those of patients whose physicians were not informed. Surprisingly, the patients whose physicians were informed also reported an improvement in physical functioning that was almost 10% greater than that reported by the other patients. It appears that when additional testing was not pursued, the patients felt comforted and assured that they were not suffering from a serious disorder.

However, a problem can arise when a patient who usually has a somatoform disorder develops a real medical problem; if the new symptom is "written off" as another somatoform symptom, the individual will not get the treatment he or she needs. Therefore, mental health professionals and psychologists and physicians who screen individuals must be careful not to dismiss a legitimate medical problem in an individual who ordinarily comes in with somatoform complaints. Of course, such caution leads back to more testing and higher costs. Obviously, this is a thorny problem for which there is no simple solution.

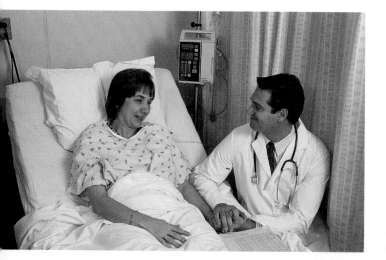

The nonspecific symptoms of which patients with somatoform disorders often complain can lead to serious overuse of the health care system, particularly when expensive diagnostic tests are used in an attempt to diagnose the problem.

Finally, you should recognize that as medical science progresses, some of what we currently think are somatoform disorders may someday be found to be actual physical disorders. Somatoform disorders consist of physical symptoms for which there is no *demonstrable* cause, but the failure to demonstrate a physical cause can be due simply to the fact that one has not yet been identified. For example, some years ago women who showed the physical symptoms of pregnancy but who were not pregnant were diagnosed as having a conversion disorder known as **pseudocyesis** (syoo-do-si-E-sis), which means "sham pregnancy." Indeed, Freud described this problem and referred to it as *hysterical pregnancy*. However, with an increased understanding of hormone imbalances, these individuals are now known to be suffering from a physical disorder. In other words, once the disorder was better understood, it was converted from a psychological disorder to a physical disorder. Clearly, the problem of identifying somatoform disorders is complex and continuing, and we will return to this issue later.

Explanations

Now let's go on to consider the explanations for somatoform disorders.

Psychodynamic Explanations

Freud's explanation for somatoform disorders was that when wishes or drives are not expressed, *the pent-up emotional energy associated with the wishes or drives is converted into physical symptoms* (Freud, 1920/1955). That notion provided the basis for the term *conversion disorder*. Freud also suggested that the expression of emotions that have been pent up will reduce symptoms because the "charge" associated with the emotions is reduced. Today this kind of emotional release is called **catharsis** (ka-THAR-ses). You may have experienced catharsis when you finally talked about a problem that you had kept "bottled up inside." The notion that bottled-up tension leads to somatoform disorders is interesting, but perhaps a bit too simplistic. Let's consider some other possibilities and return to it later.

Learning Explanations

The basic tenet of the learning explanation is that symptoms are learned and used because they *result in rewards.* The reward can occur in three ways: First, somatoform symptoms may enable an individual to *avoid some unpleasant or threatening situation.* For example, a form of conversion disorder involving a paralyzed hand may enable a student to skip an examination for which he or she is not prepared. I once worked with an athlete who always "pulled a muscle" before any track meet in which the competition

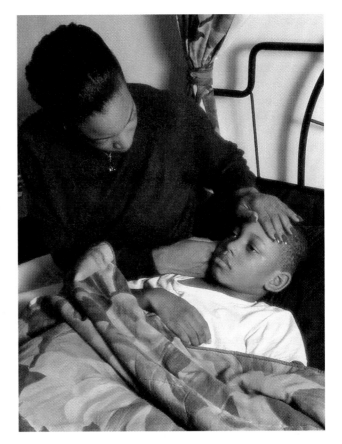

Children who gain attention for sick behavior are more likely to develop somatoform disorders. This child is learning that being ill can result in concern, sympathy, and care.

was particularly good and might threaten his unbeaten record. His "pulled muscle" was rewarding because it protected his unbeaten record. Second, somatoform symptoms can *provide an explanation of or justification for failure,* thereby relieving the individual of personal responsibility. The student who comes home at the end of the semester wearing an eye patch because of "eye trouble" is less likely to be blamed for his failing grades. Third, somatoform symptoms can *attract concern, sympathy, and care* for the individual, and that attention can be very rewarding.

Rewards can maintain the use of the symptoms, but how do the symptoms develop in the first place? One possibility is that individuals learn to play the role of a sick individual either by observation or through personal experience with illness. We each play many roles, and we must learn the

pseudocyesis A conversion disorder involving symptoms of pregnancy; formerly called *hysterical pregnancy* (means "sham pregnancy").

catharsis A release of emotional tension, often achieved by talking about a problem.

behaviors for each role. When we first try out a new role, it requires effort and seems unreal; we are "playing" the role. However, as time goes by, the role becomes second nature, and the distinction between role and self becomes blurred. We are no longer playing the role—we have internalized the role, and the role is us.

In the case of somatoform disorders, an individual may have learned the role of a sick individual while actually being sick or by observing another individual who was sick (Schwartz, Gramling, & Mancini, 1994). Later, when facing stress or in need of attention, the individual might shift to the "sick" role just as someone might change from a "party-goer" role to a "student" role, as the situation required. This change to the sick role is not done with any more conscious intent than you used when you changed to your student role by picking up this book and beginning to study. The situation demanded it, you were accustomed to the role, and you used it. Furthermore, the individual with a somatoform disorder is not faking a role any more than you are now faking a student role. Just as you have internalized the role of student and are not faking it, the individual with a somatoform disorder has internalized the role of sick individual and is not faking that role.

Consistent with the notion that role models contribute to the development of somatoform disorders, there is clear evidence that individuals who suffer from somatoform disorders do indeed have *role models for sick behavior*. In one investigation it was found that children with somatization disorder were more likely to have parents with the disorder than were children with verified medical disorders (Livingston, 1993). Similarly, patients with pseudoepileptic seizures were more likely to know someone, such as a parent, who had seizures than were individuals who had real epileptic seizures (Eisendrath & Valan, 1994). Finally, information from patients revealed that two variables associated with hypochondriasis are a high level of life defeats and a high level of family illness (Bianchi, 1973). It appears that when dealing with stress (defeat), individuals with a family history of illness (models) may complain of illnesses.

Cognitive Explanations

From a cognitive perspective somatoform disorders occur because individuals focus too much attention on physical sensations or characteristics and misinterpret them. For example, if you focus attention on the sensations in your head, after a while you may notice what seems to be a pain; then, to explain the pain, you may interpret it as a symptom of some disorder.

Is there evidence for this? In one study students in one condition listened to a tape recording in which they were asked to concentrate on various bodily sites and the sensations at those sites, whereas students in a control condition listened to music (Schmidt et al., 1994). Later, when the

students used a checklist to indicate what symptoms they were experiencing, those who focused their attention on bodily sites and sensations reported almost twice as many physical symptoms as those who listened to the music. Similarly, when students walked on a treadmill and listened to their own breathing or to a tape recording of city sounds, those who listened to their breathing later reported more headaches, cardiovascular problems, and other symptoms of overexertion (Pennebaker, 1982). This effect is apparently stronger in individuals who suffer from somatoform disorders. For example, in a study in which individuals who were already suffering from hypochondriasis were asked to focus their attention on ambiguous physical sensations, those with hypochondriasis were more likely to interpret the sensations as symptoms of serious illnesses rather than as temporary unimportant sensations (Hitchcock & Mathews, 1992). In other words, thinking about sensations can lead some individuals to interpret the sensations as symptoms, and individuals with somatoform disorders are very likely to do that.

Attention to sensations can lead to a report of "symptoms," but why do some people focus their attention on sensations? Role models and previous experiences with real illnesses can influence what we attend to and how we interpret what we feel. Furthermore, at one time or another when there was something we didn't want to do, most of us have looked for an excuse and maybe noticed some minor physical complaint (a little headache) that enabled us to avoid a disagreeable event. We were not necessarily lying or faking the problem; after thinking about it for a while, we came up with a symptom that had some minimal basis in reality. If focusing on the physical complaint was successful in getting us out of the disagreeable event or getting us some sympathy, we might do it again and again, until it became a frequent and seemingly natural means of solving problems.

In summary, learning and cognitive factors may work together to result in somatoform disorders. Specifically, (1) role models or actually being sick leads an individual to learn the role of a sick person and/or to focus attention on bodily sensations; (2) the role and the attention to physical sensations lead to the acting or noticing of "symptoms"; and (3) the "symptoms" result in rewards (attention) or enable the individual to avoid stressful situations, so they are used repeatedly. Let's now turn to the physiological explanations.

Physiological Explanations

We generally assume that individuals who suffer from somatization disorder or hypochondriasis are complaining about symptoms that are not really there. However, it may be that these individuals are *more physiologically aroused* and their arousal provides the basis for what they interpret as physical symptoms (Barsky et al., 1998; Bell, 1994). In other words, individuals who experience bodily sensations that others do not may be more likely to conclude that they are suffering from some disease. I am not suggesting that these individuals have more actual *symptoms,* only that they may have more *sensations* that they *interpret* as symptoms.

Support for the connection between physiological arousal and somatoform disorders comes from findings that individuals with somatoform disorders have unusually high levels of physiological arousal as measured by heart rate, muscle tension, blood chemistry, and skin conductance (perspiration on the skin) (Hanback & Revelle, 1978; Rief, Shaw, & Fichter, 1998; Sanyal, Chattopadhyay, & Bishwas, 1998). Furthermore, individuals with somatoform disorders show higher levels of arousal during stress. The high levels of arousal could result in more physical sensations, which could be misinterpreted as "symptoms," and this could be more likely to occur if the individual had a personal or family history of real disorders (see the preceding section).

We should also give some attention to the interesting finding that conversion symptoms are more likely to occur on the left side of the body (Galin, Diamond, & Braff, 1977; Min & Lee, 1997; Stern, 1977). This is of interest because the left side of the body is controlled primarily by the right side of the brain, and the right side of the brain is primarily responsible for emotions. On the basis of these two facts, researchers have speculated that a high level of emotional arousal on the right side of the brain disrupts other functioning on that side of the brain and produces unusual physiological symptoms on the left side of the body. This notion is referred to as the *hemispheric dominance explanation* for somatoform disorders. This explanation is strikingly similar to Freud's suggestion that an emotional "charge" is converted into "unusual bodily innervations."

Link to Obsessive-Compulsive Disorder

Thus far we have implicitly assumed that somatoform disorders are different and separate from other types of psychiatric disorders. That may be true, but there is a growing belief that somatoform disorders are actually a *subtype of obsessive-compulsive disorder* (Biby, 1998; Black, 1998; Brown, 1998; Hollander, 1998; Hollander & Benzaquen, 1997). There are two reasons for this belief: First, the symptoms seen in somatoform disorders are often "obsessive" in nature. That is, individuals with somatoform disorders seem obsessed with their health, and individuals with body dysmorphic disorder appear to be obsessed with some minor or imagined deformity. Moreover, these concerns about health and appearance are not based in reality but are delusional, just like many of the beliefs that occur in obsessions (see Chapter 6). For example, the erroneous beliefs that people with body dysmorphic disorder have about

their physical "deformities" could qualify as delusions. The second reason for suspecting an overlap between the disorders is that the drugs (antidepressants) that are effective for treating OCD can also be effective for treating somatoform disorders (see the following section on treatments). This *suggests* (but does not necessarily *prove*) that the same underlying mechanism may be operating in both sets of disorders. The possibility that there is a link between somatoform and obsessive-compulsive disorders is consistent with the notion I discussed earlier that, rather than being distinct groups, psychiatric disorders can be organized along *continuums* or *spectrums* based on similar symptoms or underlying causes (see Chapter 4). In this case we might be dealing with an *obsessive-compulsive spectrum* or a *serotonin spectrum.*

However, if somatoform disorders are part of a larger group of disorders, we must be able to explain why some individuals obsess about health problems and are diagnosed as suffering from somatoform disorders, whereas others obsess about cleanliness and are diagnosed as suffering from OCD. The difference in the form the symptoms take seems to lie in the experiences the individuals had that led them to focus their attention on one particular topic or another. In the case of somatoform disorders, individuals who have predispositions to obsessions may have been ill or known someone who was ill, so they focus their obsessions on health-related topics. In this scenario, then, whether a person develops a somatoform or obsessive-compulsive disorder is simply a function of the experiences that guide that person's obsessions. Overall, then, to understand somatoform disorders it may be helpful to understand obsessive-compulsive disorder (low serotonin, high activity or damage in the orbitalfrontal area of the brain; see Chapter 6) and recognize the role of experience in directing attention.

 ## Treatments

Somatoform disorders are usually considered very difficult to treat (Martin & Yutzy, 1999). Indeed, most specialists use the word *management* rather than *treatment* when discussing interventions for somatoform disorders (Nathan & Gorman, 1998; Simon, 1998). However, our ability to treat these disorders may be improving as we develop a better understanding of them.

In general, five strategies are used to treat or manage these disorders:

1. *Change beliefs about "symptoms."* With this strategy the goal is to teach patients to stop focusing on the sensations that provide the basis for their "symptoms" (Martin & Yutzy, 1994; Visser & Bouman, 1992). Furthermore, when they do notice the sensations, patients are instructed not to interpret them as symptoms of some serious disorder. Unfortunately, attempts to change patients' attention and beliefs are often counteracted by the media's constant barrage of "medical news" in which new symptoms and disorders are discussed, thus increasing attention and creating potentially erroneous beliefs.

2. *Reduce depression and obsessions.* Second, rather than treating somatoform disorders per se, some investigators advocate treating the depression that often accompanies disorders (Fallon, Klein, & Liebowitz, 1993; Goetz & Price, 1994; Noyes et al., 1998). The notion underlying this approach is that depression causes somatoform disorders because depressed individuals focus their attention on bodily complaints and assume that the worst will happen (see Chapter 8), thus leading to a somatoform disorder. Similarly, it has been suggested that individuals should be treated for the obsessive-compulsive symptoms that provide the basis for somatoform disorders (see the earlier discussion; Hollander, 1998). For example, in one study individuals with body dysmorphic disorder who were treated with Prozac showed declines in the symptoms of both body dysmorphic disorder and OCD (Phillips, Dwight, & McElroy, 1998; see also Escobar, 1996; Perugi et al., 1996; Hollander, Allen, et al., 1999).

3. *Reduce arousal.* A third approach involves reducing stress and thereby reducing the arousal that provides the basis for physical sensations that lead to the symptoms. In this regard it is interesting to note that "opening up" and talking about stressful experiences can reduce physical complaints, some of which are probably somatoform (Pennebaker, 1990, 1993). Specifically, students who came to a laboratory and simply wrote for 20 minutes about previous traumatic events showed a 50% lower rate of visits to the university health center than did students who wrote about trivial events. The catharsis associated with talking about the stress reduced physiological arousal, which in turn reduced the sensations that probably provide the basis for somatoform complaints.

4. *Reduce pain.* Antidepressant drugs are often effective for reducing pain, and there have been numerous placebo-controlled experiments in which it was found that antidepressants were effective for reducing pain in patients with pain disorder (Fishbain et al., 1998; Wilson & Gil, 1996).

5. *Provide reassurance.* Finally, in cases in which other approaches are ineffective, the emphasis may have to be on providing emotional support and reassurance for patients so that they can cope with and endure their "symptoms" without constantly seeking medical attention (Barsky, 1993; Kellner, 1992). Part of providing reassurance involves convincing the patients that they are not "crazy" and that their symptoms will not lead to a chronic mental or physical illness or death (Martin & Yutzy, 1999).

THINKING CRITICALLY

Questions about Somatoform Disorders

1. *What causes somatoform disorders?* The first question we have to address is whether the group of somatoform disorders is a unique set of disorders or occurs as part of a larger group of disorders. That is a tough question, but the weight of evidence seems to be tipping the scale in the direction of concluding that somatoform disorders are a subset of a larger group of disorders that can be referred to as the *obsessive-compulsive spectrum,* or possibly the *serotonin spectrum,* of disorders. (Whether you elect to use the obsessive-compulsive or serotonin label is determined by whether you focus on similarities in symptoms [obsessions] or in suspected causes [low levels of serotonin].) The notion that somatoform disorders are part of a larger set of disorders is derived from the similarity in symptoms (bodily concerns seem obsessional) and the possible similarity in cause (low levels of serotonin). Individuals with somatoform disorders may focus on bodily concerns rather than other things, such as cleanliness, because of their experiences with medical problems. This approach provides an interesting way to conceptualize somatoform disorders and may suggest useful treatment strategies. If you reject this notion, somatoform disorders can be explained with a combination of physiological, learning, and cognitive explanations. Specifically, sensations associated with high levels of physiological arousal may attract an individual's attention, and then because of previous experiences or role models, the individual misinterprets the sensations as symptoms.

2. *When is a somatoform disorder not a somatoform disorder?* The answer, of course, is when the symptoms have a real physiological cause. However, the problem is that we have not yet identified the causes of all physiological disorders, and insofar as a physiological cause for a symptom remains unknown, the symptom produced by the unknown cause will be incorrectly labeled as a somatoform symptom. As the science of medicine advances, the number of somatoform disorders recedes. For example, earlier I pointed out that the pains and paralyses in the hands of people such as violinists were once assumed to be the result of conversion disorder, but today we know the symptoms are due to *carpal tunnel syndrome,* a physiological disorder that results from pressure on a nerve in the wrist. How many mistaken diagnoses of somatoform disorders are made because of an incomplete understanding of medicine?

The distinction between a somatoform and a physical disorder has important implications in terms of insurance coverage for treatment and disability; specifically, many insurance policies have much lower limits on what they will pay for the treatment of a somatoform disorder versus an

Somatoform or Physical? Implications for Insurance Coverage

Ms. KELLY WAS a 56-year-old woman who had worked her way up to a relatively high managerial position in a large corporation. At about age 50 she began experiencing daily "episodes" in which she was temporarily paralyzed. Following each episode she would experience symptoms like those of a "mini-stroke"; for example, she would have serious problems with memory. As a result, Ms. Kelly became unable to work, and she applied for disability payments from her medical insurance company. However, those payments were stopped after 6 months because of a mental illness limitation/exclusion in her insurance policy. (It is common for insurance policies to place stricter limitations on the time for which payments will be made for psychiatric disorders than for physical disorders.) The first question here is, did Ms. Kelly have a psychiatric (somatoform) disorder or a physical disorder that could not be diagnosed? The answer to that question is important because it determines whether she will continue to receive insurance payments.

To ascertain whether the illness was psychological or physical, Ms. Kelly underwent a thorough examination at a prestigious hospital. The examining physician concluded that Ms. Kelly had "*either* a major psychiatric disorder (somatoform) or a physical disorder that had evaded diagnosis so far." The physician went on to conclude that (1) there was no doubt that Ms. Kelly was totally disabled by her disorder, (2) there was no stressor in her life that could be used to account for a psychiatric disorder, and (3) he was convinced that she was not faking the disorder. So what did she have? In this case, as in others, because a cause for a physical disorder could not be found, it was *assumed* that Ms. Kelly had a psychiatric disorder, and her insurance payments were terminated. Was it fair to conclude that Ms. Kelly had a psychiatric disorder and to terminate her coverage simply because physicians could not find a physical cause for her disorder? After all, remember that a cause for her alleged psychiatric disorder could not be found either!

Apart from the question of whether or not Ms. Kelly had a psychiatric disorder, is it appropriate for insurance companies to provide fewer benefits for a psychiatric disorder than a physical disorder, even when the two have exactly the same symptoms? Is this discrimination against individuals with psychiatric disorders? In Chapter 11 you will read about a case in which the U.S. government's Medicaid program would not pay for a drug that is effective for treating schizophrenia because it was expensive (about $9,000 a year). However, a suit was filed alleging discrimination because Medicaid would pay $50,000 dollars a year for patients to receive dialysis for kidney disease. The plaintiffs won that case, and the drug is now paid for by Medicaid. Should a suit be filed on behalf of patients who suffer from somatoform disorders?

> **Should a suit be filed on behalf of patients who suffer from somatoform disorders?**

Note: It is likely that Ms. Kelly was having *transcient ischemic attacks* (TIAs), which are brief interruptions of blood supply to the brain (see Chapter 17). Depending on what part of the brain is affected, symptoms can include weakness, problems with vision or hearing, dizziness, slurred speech, and loss of memory. Because the brain damage is minor and diffuse, it is difficult or impossible to detect.

---

actual physical disorder. A problem of this type is illustrated by the woman described in Case Study 7.2.

Having developed an understanding of somatoform disorders, we can go on to consider the controversial dissociative disorders.

Dissociative Disorders

In a famous case portrayed in the movie *The Three Faces of Eve,* Eve had three personalities that were very different from one another. For example, Eve Black was wild and promiscuous, whereas Eve White was quiet and demure. Furthermore, Eve White was completely unaware of the existence of Eve Black. Eve had what was once called *multiple personality disorder* but is now called *dissociative identity disorder.* We frequently hear about this disorder, but does it really exist? What is the evidence for this disorder?

There is the case of a man whose plane was shot down during World War II but who, because of the trauma associated with the crash, was unable to recall the crash until he was in psychotherapy. This man's repression of the stressful event led to a disorder known as *dissociative amnesia.* What is the evidence for repression? Do people really become amnesic for stressful events?

Sometimes Kent feels as though he is out of his body and looking down on himself. This sensation is referred to as *depersonalization.* Have you ever had an experience like that? Is depersonalization a serious disorder?

The major symptom in **dissociative disorders** is that individuals are *not aware of or lose contact with important aspects of their personalities or environments*. For example, individuals with dissociative amnesia cannot remember important events, and those with dissociative identity (multiple personality) disorder are unaware of aspects of their personalities. The term *dissociative disorder* is used because it is assumed that individuals with symptoms like amnesia are *dissociating* themselves (escaping) from parts of their experience that give rise to stress. In other words, the individuals are *repressing* experiences or parts of themselves that are stressful, and the **repression** results in gaps or holes in their awareness (e.g., amnesia).

Dissociative Disorders

Four dissociative disorders are identified in *DSM-IV.* Each disorder involves dissociation, but the nature of the dissociation differs from disorder to disorder. That is, an individual may forget some stressful experience (dissociative amnesia), leave a stressful situation and develop a new identity (dissociative fugue), develop alternative personalities (dissociative identity disorder), or feel detached from bodily or mental processes (depersonalization disorder). The major symptoms of dissociative disorders as they are described in *DSM-IV* are summarized in Table 7.2. After reviewing the symptoms, we will go on to consider the controversial question of whether these disorders actually exist.

Dissociative Amnesia

Dissociative amnesia is characterized by a *sudden inability to remember important personal information or events* to an extent greater than ordinary forgetfulness. This type of amnesia usually occurs immediately following some type of severe stress, and it is the stressful event or information associated with it that is forgotten. The classic examples of dissociative amnesia occur in soldiers who, after fighting in a terrible and traumatic battle, are unable to recall the battle but later, with the aid of psychotherapy, are able to recover the memories (Henderson & Moore, 1944). More recently some mental health professionals have reported instances of individuals who are amnesic for stressful experiences of sexual abuse during childhood but are later able to recover those memories (e.g., Terr, 1994). It has also been suggested that dissociative amnesia can be triggered by unacceptable impulses or acts such as an extramarital affair; the individual simply does not remember doing the unspeakable—or the unthinkable!

Obviously, there are many reasons why we are sometimes unable to recall things, and it is important not to confuse dissociative amnesia with failure to recall because of (1) ordinary forgetting, (2) disorders such as Alzheimer's disease, (3) the use of drugs such as alcohol, or (4) the amnesia that occurs following a concussion. The factor that distinguishes between those memory losses and dissociative amnesia is that in dissociative amnesia the individual is *motivated not to remember something as a way of reducing stress.*

Dissociative Fugue

An individual who is experiencing **dissociative fugue** (fyoog) suddenly and unexpectedly *moves to a new locale, is amnesic for his or her previous identity, and may assume a new identity.* This flight from present reality typically follows a severe stress such as a marital quarrel, personal rejection, military conflict, or natural disaster. The fugue state may last only a few hours, but generally it lasts months. During the fugue the individual behaves appropriately and

---

TABLE 7.2

Predominant symptoms of dissociative disorders

Disorder	Symptoms
Dissociative amnesia	Sudden inability to remember important personal information or events, to an extent greater than can be explained by ordinary forgetfulness
Dissociative fugue	Sudden travel to a new locale, with amnesia for previous identity and the possible assumption of a new identity
Dissociative identity disorder	Two or more distinctly different personalities, each in control of the individual at different times, and the inability to recall important personal information (e.g., the existence of other personalities)
Depersonalization disorder	Feeling detached from one's body or mental processes

Note: Symptoms must be serious enough to result in impairment in social, occupational, or other important areas of functioning.

Dissociative amnesia can occur immediately following an unusually stressful event, such as after an individual loses his or her home or loved ones in an earthquake.

does not show any signs of suffering from a psychological disorder; the person simply starts a new life and does fine. When the fugue ends, the individual returns to his or her original identity and has no memory of what took place during the fugue. The feature of fugue that distinguishes it from amnesia is that the individual in the fugue is unaware that he or she has lost memories and substitutes new memories and a new identity.

One interesting case that was diagnosed as fugue involved a man who was having serious financial and marital problems. The day following a particularly heated argument with his wife about their impending bankruptcy, the man went fishing and did not return. When his empty boat was found on the lake, it was presumed that he had fallen overboard and drowned. However, about a year later the man's "widow" was on an automobile trip in a nearby state and stopped for lunch at a roadside restaurant. She was surprised at the quality of the food but even more surprised when on her way out she discovered her "late" husband sitting in one of the booths and learned that he was now married to the woman who owned the restaurant. When confronted, he appeared not to know her.

Dissociative Identity Disorder (Multiple Personality)

The term **multiple personality disorder** has been used for many years, but in *DSM-IV* that term was replaced with **dissociative identity disorder.** An individual diagnosed as having dissociative identity disorder appears to have *two or more distinctly different personalities,* each of which is in control of the individual at different times, and the individual is *unable to recall important personal information.*

More specifically, some of the personalities are not aware of the other personalities (Fahy, 1988; Putnam, 1989; Ross, 1989). Although the disorder is usually conceptualized in terms of the individual's having more than one personality, it may be more accurate to say that instead of having multiple personalities, the individual has *one personality with multiple parts that are not integrated and not always acknowledged as existing.*

Dissociative identity disorder has received a great deal of attention in the popular press, films, and television. Some of the best-known accounts of dissociative identity are *The Three Faces of Eve* (Thigpen & Cleckley, 1957), *Sybil* (Schreiber, 1973), *The Five of Me* (Hanksworth & Schwarz, 1977), and *The Minds of Billy Mulligan* (Keyes, 1981).

In dissociative identity disorder there is usually a sharp contrast between at least two of the personalities. One personality is usually "good," while the other is of more questionable character. The contrast is apparent in the book and movie *The Three Faces of Eve.* Eve White was a quiet, demure, and somewhat inhibited young woman who had been in psychotherapy for the treatment of headaches and blackouts. While talking to her physician one day, Eve White put her hands to her head as if she had been seized by a sudden pain. After a moment she seemed to shake herself loose and looked up with a reckless smile and a bright voice and said, "Hi there, Doc!" When asked her name, she immediately replied, "Oh, I'm Eve Black" (Thigpen & Cleckley, 1954, p. 137). In contrast to Eve White, Eve Black was a wild, promiscuous, devil-may-care woman. As you might have guessed, the "good" personality is usually not

dissociative disorders   A group of disorders involving a loss of awareness of or contact with important aspects of one's personality or environment; examples are dissociative amnesia, dissociative fugue, dissociative identity disorder, and depersonalization disorder, but questions have been raised about the existence of these disorders as they are traditionally described.

repression   A defense mechanism whereby threatening memories are stored in the unconscious.

dissociative amnesia   A dissociative disorder characterized by a sudden loss of memory, due to a psychological stress.

dissociative fugue   A dissociative disorder in which an individual suddenly moves to a new locale, does not recall his or her previous identity, and assumes a new identity.

multiple personality disorder   The term that was previously used for what is now called *dissociative identity disorder.*

dissociative identity disorder   A dissociative disorder in which an individual appears to have two or more distinctly different personalities and while in one personality may not be able to recall other personalities; this diagnostic label replaced *multiple personality disorder.*

Chris Sizemore is the woman on whom *The Three Faces of Eve* was based. She claimed that she had 21 separate personalities.

aware of the "bad" personality, but the "bad" personality is usually aware of (and bored with) the "good" personality.

The case of Eve appears to have been more complex than originally portrayed. In a book published 23 years later, the woman known as Eve (actually Chris Sizemore) explained that she had actually had 21 separate personalities or, as she put it, "strangers who came to inhabit my body" (Sizemore & Pittillo, 1977). Surveys reveal that individuals with dissociative identity disorder report having from 2 to 60 different personalities, the average being 13 to 16 (Putnam et al., 1986; Ross, Norton, & Wozney, 1989; Ross, Miller, et al., 1990; Schultz, Braun, & Kluft, 1989). The results of these surveys also indicate that about 90% of the individuals diagnosed as having dissociative identity disorder are women.

Some comment should be made to clear up the confusion that sometimes arises over the terms *dissociative identity, schizophrenia,* and *split personality. Dissociative identity* refers to a disorder in which an individual develops a number of distinctly different and separate personalities. In contrast, the term *schizophrenia* refers to a disorder in which the individual has one personality but that personality has split off from reality (Bleuler, 1950) (see Chapter 11). An individual with dissociative identity disorder does not necessarily have schizophrenia, and an individual with schizophrenia does not necessarily have multiple personalities. The term *split personality* is not a diagnostic label; it is slang, without any clinical meaning.

depersonalization disorder A dissociative disorder that involves persistent or recurrent experiences of feeling detached from one's body or mental processes.

Depersonalization Disorder

Depersonalization disorder involves persistent or recurrent experiences of *feeling detached from one's body or mental processes.* Individuals feel as if they are outside of their bodies, looking down on themselves, or as if they are in a dream. It is important to note that during the experience the individuals are still in touch with reality; for example, they know that they are not really out of their bodies, but it just feels *as if* they are. In fact, depersonalization occurs in as many as 30% of normal individuals at some time, and the symptoms do not constitute a disorder unless they impair the individual's functioning (Ross, Joshi, & Currie, 1990). The symptoms are most common in early adulthood (ages 25 to 44), and then they begin to drop off dramatically.

The depersonalization experience can probably be best described as an "as if" sensation with regard to the self: Individuals with this disorder feel *as if* they are acting mechanically, *as if* they are in a dream, *as if* parts of their bodies have changed in size, or *as if* they were out of their bodies and viewing themselves from a distance. In talking about depersonalization experiences, one person explained, "It was like I somehow drifted out of my body and floated way above it, and I could look down on me like I was someone else on a stage." Another said, "My body seemed to be made of rubber that could stretch. . . . I really didn't have any definite form. Sometimes my head would become huge, or my arms would become extremely long and I'd have big hands. It was really kind of crazy."

The "as if" nature of depersonalization disorder is important because it distinguishes this disorder from schizophrenia, in which an individual may have the same symptoms but believes them to be true. Because the feelings in depersonalization disorder are perceived as unnatural (e.g., looking down at oneself from above), individuals with this disorder are often concerned that they might be "going crazy," and therefore the symptom pattern is often accompanied by anxiety.

Depersonalization disorder is different from the other dissociative disorders in that *it does not involve a loss of memory or identity, as the others do.* In contrast to the other dissociative disorders, depersonalization disorder causes the individuals to simply experience a temporary change in the way they view themselves. Depersonalization is a less extreme and less dramatic response to stress.

The occurrence of depersonalization was documented in an interesting study of journalists who witnessed the execution of a prisoner in the gas chamber of the San Quentin Prison (Freinkel, Koopman, & Spiegel, 1994). When questioned later, the journalists reported a high rate of symptoms of depersonalization. For example, 60% reported that they felt "estranged or detached from other people." Some years ago I was with a woman who had just been hit by a car and whose leg was badly broken; indeed, it was bent at a 90° angle to the side at the knee! Despite the fact that the woman had not been given any medication, she was very calm, and as the medical personnel prepared to put her in the ambulance, she said rather quizzically, "You know, it's like this isn't happening to me. It's like I'm sitting up on top of the ambulance watching all of this from a distance—it's like a movie. It's really fascinating to see how the leg is bent and what everyone is doing." Clearly, in the face of stress the woman depersonalized the situation. However, in cases like that the depersonalization is not considered a disorder because it does not impair the individual's functioning; indeed, the depersonalization may actually aid functioning by permitting the person to perceive and act objectively.

 ## Issues

In the preceding sections I presented dissociative disorders as they are described in *DSM-IV* and as they are traditionally thought to occur. However, it is important to recognize that there is now good reason to question the accuracy of those portrayals and even question the existence of some dissociative disorders. In the following sections I will review the evidence concerning dissociative disorders in general and dissociative identity disorder in particular.

Evidence for Repression

When I introduced dissociative disorders at the beginning of this chapter, I pointed out that they are based on the psychological process called *repression*. For example, individuals with dissociative amnesia supposedly repress their memories of stressful events, and those with dissociative identity disorder supposedly repress stressful aspects of their personalities. Indeed, in these examples *dissociation* is simply a synonym for *repression*. However, the fact that most dissociative disorders are based on repression leads to a serious problem: *We have no objective evidence that repression actually occurs.* Obviously, if there is no evidence for repression, we face an awkward problem in explaining dissociative disorders. Actually, the concept of repression is widely used in psychology, and thus the question of its existence has broad implications. Because of the importance of repression, in the following paragraphs I will first review the ways in which repression has been studied, and then I will discuss the implications of the findings as they relate to dissociative disorders.

Laboratory Research. For more than 70 years investigators have tried to demonstrate repression in the laboratory. In this research individuals either were or were not exposed to stressors such as electric shocks or being told that they suffered from serious psychiatric disorders, and then their memories for information related to the stressors were

tested. None of this research yielded any evidence for repression; instead the individuals were temporarily *distracted* by the stressors, which briefly reduced some of their memories, but they did not lose their memories about the stressors (see Holmes, 1974, 1990). In fact, the reverse happened; individuals reported that they were *focusing on the stressors* rather than repressing them. Consider this: If you had just been told that you were developing a serious psychiatric disorder, I suspect you'd worry about that rather than push it from memory. The fact that the laboratory research did not produce evidence for repression was surprising, but it was not a source of concern because psychologists simply assumed that the stressors that were used in the laboratory were too "artificial" or not strong enough. Furthermore, the absence of laboratory evidence was not seen as particularly important because psychologists also assumed that there were good case studies that supported the existence of repression. We will consider that evidence next.

Classic Case Studies. The classic case studies to which psychologists turned for evidence for repression involved soldiers who could not remember anything about terribly stressful battles they had just fought but who were later able to remember the battles when they were given therapy to reduce the stress (Henderson & Moore, 1944; van der Hart, Brown, & Graafland, 1999). The notion was that the stress of the battles was so great that the soldiers had repressed the entire experience. For many years those cases were accepted as evidence for repression, but a careful examination of them revealed two crucial problems. The first problem is that in no case was the possibility of physically caused amnesia ruled out. That is a serious omission because we know that concussions can cause amnesia (e.g., football players sometimes cannot remember plays in which they were tackled very hard and hit their heads), and in battlefield conditions in which bombs and grenades were going off, it is very likely that the soldiers experienced concussions. In other words, if there were losses in memory, they were probably due to physiological rather than psychological causes.

The second problem is that in the cases in which the memories were later "recovered" in therapy, the recovery was accomplished with techniques such as role playing, hypnosis, or interviews conducted while the client was under the influence of sodium amytal (a sedative that relaxes individuals and is commonly referred to as "truth serum." However, all of those techniques increase the possibility of suggestion and thus invalidate the reports given by clients. Indeed, various professional organizations in psychology and psychiatry have explicitly warned against using those techniques in therapy because they are likely to *introduce* rather than *recover* "memories." It appears then that the "repressed memories" that were supposedly "recovered" by the soldiers were actually suggested to them by

Before careful examination revealed several problems with the case study research technique, psychologists looked to case studies of war veterans for evidence of repression. Researchers studied soldiers who could not remember anything about traumatic battles they had fought in until they were given therapy to reduce the stress.

their therapists. (For a more detailed discussion of the implanting of false memories, see Chapter 3; see also Ceci et al., 1995; Hyman et al., 1995.)

Despite these problems some mental health professionals have persisted in using war-related case studies as evidence for repression, but the most recent attempt to do so had a surprise ending. In a 1997 article a case was reported of a tail gunner whose plane had been shot down over England and whose memory of the crash had been repressed until it was recovered in psychotherapy. Specifically, in therapy he remembered how the plane had crashed in a farm field and how he, despite a broken arm, had pulled the pilot from the burning wreck. This dramatic case attracted a lot of attention; indeed, a bold headline in the newsletter of the American Psychological Association read "WWII Veterans Provide Evidence of Repressed Memories" (*APA Monitor*, 1997, p. 8). However, that conclusion was premature. A check of military records revealed that no airplane matching the description given by the patient was ever flown in the European theater of action during World War II (Giglio, 1998; see also Piper, 1999; Roediger & Bergman, 1998). In other words, in therapy he remembered crashing in an airplane that never existed! This not only demonstrates again the problems with case studies, but it raises a question: If repression is responsible for so many disorders, why must supporters of the notion rely on case studies from long ago or about dead people? Shouldn't we be able to find verifiable evidence in recent experiences of live people? Let's go on to consider another approach to studying repression.

Followups with Trauma Victims. In order to avoid the problems with case studies, investigators next turned to the strategy of identifying individuals who were known to have

undergone serious traumatic experiences and then testing the individuals' memories about their experiences. Examples included children who had been kidnapped and then buried alive (Terr, 1979, 1983), children who had witnessed a parent's murder (Malmquist, 1986), and individuals who had been brutalized in Nazi concentration camps (Strom et al., 1962), among many others. These individuals had certainly undergone the types of experiences we would expect them to repress. However, the surprising finding was that *in every case the individual was able to recall the traumatic experience!* Indeed, rather than being repressed, the memories were recalled very vividly, and in many cases the individuals could not get the memories out of their minds. In other words, rather than being repressed and leading to dissociative disorders, the traumatic experiences were recalled in great detail and often led to *posttraumatic stress disorder* (see Chapter 6). This is exactly the opposite of what you would expect to occur based on the theory of repression, and hence, once again, the research does not provide evidence for repression.

However, before concluding this discussion of studies of trauma victims, there is one study that requires some additional comment because it initially appeared to provide evidence for repression. In this study the investigator identified female children who had been brought to a hospital because of sexual abuse. Seventeen years later the individuals were then interviewed about the traumatic experiences of their lives (Williams, 1992, 1994). The results indicated that *38% of the women did not report the instance of abuse* that had been documented in the hospital records. This finding was widely interpreted as evidence for repression. However, there is a serious problem with the investigation that originally went unnoticed: Individuals who did not report sexual abuse *were never explicitly asked about the abuse.* That is, if a woman did not spontaneously report the abuse, the assumption was that she had repressed the memory. However, this ignores the possibility that some women had simply chosen not to report the experience. Strong evidence for that possibly is provided by a similar study in which investigators followed up and interviewed individuals who had been abused as children (Femina, Yeager, & Lewis, 1990). Like those of the earlier study, the results indicated that 38% of the individuals did not report the abuse. Importantly, however, in contrast to the other study, the individuals were then asked about the possibility of abuse, and when that was done, *all of them immediately acknowledged it.* Furthermore, when they were asked why they had not initially reported the abuse, they said things like "I try to block this out of my mind" and "My father is doing well now. If I told now, I think he would kill himself." Similarly, in a review of numerous reports of dissociative amnesia following traumatic events, it was found that amnesia (nonreporting of the event) occurred only in studies in which individuals were not directly asked about the experience (Pope et al., 1998).

The important point here is that although individuals may try to put stressful memories out of their minds (i.e., repress them), they are unable to do so, and the follow-up studies of trauma victims do not provide any evidence for repression. Indeed, these studies provide strong evidence that *stressful memories persist.* (Parenthetically, it might be noted that there is also a large body of laboratory evidence that emotion, particularly negative emotion, enhances recall; e.g., McGaugh, 1990).

Clinical Observations. Many therapists argue that they see evidence for repression while treating clients in psychotherapy; that is, the therapists see clients block out memories that they should have. Unfortunately, it is difficult to confirm these observations because of the practical and ethical problems of having independent observers watch what is going on in therapy. However, these problems were overcome a few years ago when many of the "world's leading experts" on repression were brought together for a conference at Yale University (Singer, 1990). At the conference videotapes were shown of psychotherapy sessions in which it was believed that repression was occurring. The experts watched the tapes, took notes about when they thought repression was occurring, and then began discussing the instances of repression. The interesting finding was that when the experts began discussing the instances of repression, there was no agreement among any of them concerning when or whether repression had occurred (Holmes, 1990). Obviously, if a phenomenon cannot be reliably identified, the observations cannot have validity. Thus no reliance can be placed on observations of repression during psychotherapy. (As an aside, it might be noted that when an expert assumed that repression was occurring it was usually because he or she thought the patient should

be remembering something. However, because different experts worked from different theories, they were expecting different memories, which led to the unreliability of the judgments.)

Despite over 80 years of research there is still no evidence for repression. This lack of evidence takes many mental health professionals by surprise because repression is an important and widely accepted notion in psychology. The question that then arises is, where does the absence of repression leave us? That is, how can we account for the disorders that supposedly depend on repression? First, the fact that there is no evidence does not necessarily mean that repression does not exist because it is impossible to prove that something does not exist; new evidence may be found tomorrow. However, after 80 years of research it would seem prudent to consider alternative explanations rather than simply to assume that evidence will be found someday. Second, it may be that the disorders that supposedly stem from repression are due to other processes, most notably mistaken interpretations by clinicians, suggestibility, outright faking, or physiological problems. For example, what appear to be losses of memory resulting from repression may be due instead to such things as concussions, deterioration of the brain, normal forgetting, or the fact that the individual never knew what the therapist assumed was known. It may also be that some individuals fake a lack of memory to avoid responsibility. Indeed, some of these possibilities are explicitly mentioned as viable alternative explanations in *DSM-IV.* Therefore, in the following section I will discuss the evidence suggesting that dissociative identity disorder is due to suggestion rather than repression (dissociation).

Evidence for Dissociative Identity Disorder

Dissociative identity disorder has been accepted as a diagnosis since 1980 when it first appeared in *DSM-III* as multiple personality disorder, but there is an interesting controversy over whether individuals actually have multiple personalities as they are described in *DSM* or whether the disorders are due to role playing or faking (Lilienfeld et al., 1999; Reisner, 1994; Sarbin, 1997; Spanos, 1994). This question is of theoretical interest but it also has important legal implications because an individual may not be held responsible for wrongful acts committed by an alternative personality, especially if the individual was unaware that the other personality existed. Indeed, dissociative identity disorder has been used in many criminal cases as part of the insanity defense (James, 1998; James & Schramm, 1998; Slovenko, 1997; Steinberg, Bancroft, & Buchanan, 1993). For example, Kenneth Bianchi, known as the "Hillside Strangler" and alleged to have raped and strangled at least 12 young women, claimed that he was not legally responsible for the crimes because his other personality committed the acts (see Case Study 7.3 on p. 200). A somewhat differ-

The Hillside Strangler: A Case of Dissociative Identity Disorder?

CASE STUDY 7.3

IN THE FALL AND WINTER of 1977–1978, 10 young women were raped and strangled, and their nude bodies were left on various hillsides in Los Angeles County. The killer became known as the "Hillside Strangler." In January 1979 two women were raped and strangled in Bellingham, Washington. Shortly thereafter a good-looking, 27-year-old man named Kenneth Bianchi was arrested and charged with those murders. Later he was also charged with some of the murders in Los Angeles. As part of his criminal and psychiatric evaluation, Bianchi participated in a series of interviews that were videotaped. Those tapes provide a fascinating objective record of what some experts believe is dissociative identity disorder and others believe is a scam that Bianchi used in an attempt to be declared insane so that he would not be punished for his crimes.

The presence of the second alleged personality originally came out when Bianchi participated in an interview under hypnosis conducted by a psychologist named Watkins, a specialist in multiple personalities who was working for the defense.

Watkins: I've talked a bit to Ken, but I think that perhaps there might be another part of Ken that I haven't talked to, another part that maybe feels somewhat differently from the part that I've talked to. And I would like to communicate with that other part. And I would like that other part to come to talk to me. . . . Part, would you please come to communicate with me? . . . Would you please come, Part, so I can talk to you? Another part, it is not just the same as the part of Ken I've been talking to. . . . All right, Part, I would like for you and I to talk together, we don't even have to—we don't have to talk to Ken unless you and Ken want to. . . .

Bianchi: Yes.

Watkins: Part, are you the same thing as Ken, or are you different in any way? . . .

Bianchi: I'm not him.

Watkins: You're not him. Who are you? Do you have a name?

Bianchi: I'm not Ken.

Watkins: You're not Ken. OK. Who are you? Tell me about yourself.

Bianchi: I don't know.

Watkins: Do you have a name I can call you by?

Bianchi: Steve.

Watkins: Huh?

Bianchi: You can call me Steve.

Bianchi then went on to talk about how he (Steve) had strangled and killed "all these girls," pointing out that "I fixed him [Ken] up good. He doesn't even have any idea." At the end of the interview, the psychologist asked to speak to Ken, who then promptly returned. When Ken was asked about Steve, he replied, "Who's Steve?"

In a later interview, after Ken was told about the existence of Steve, Ken talked about his "readiness for the fight" for dominance with Steve. Ken also began complaining of headaches, a symptom that Watkins attributed to the conflict and struggle over the emergence of Steve against Ken's will. When Watkins asked Ken why he was feeling bad, there was an angry snarl, and then Steve emerged, complaining about the difficulty of getting out now that Ken knew about him. He said:

All these f— years I had it made. I could come and go as I pleased. He never knew about me. But now he does. I have some feeling it's partly your fault. You started this whole f— thing. . . . I try to come out. Instead I stay where I'm at, and he complains about f— headaches. . . . I'd like to give him a big f— headache.

Investigations of Bianchi's past revealed that he had participated in numerous scams. In one case he stole a psychologist's diploma, inserted a new name, and began a practice as a psychologist. He was also involved with a teenage prostitution ring. Despite clear evidence that those things occurred, Ken denied them and claimed to have had amnesic episodes during the periods in question. Watkins concluded that the illegal acts had been perpetrated by another personality of which Ken was not aware, and Watkins suggested that this was additional evidence for the diagnosis of dissociative identity disorder. In contrast, the prosecution considered these to be instances of conscious misrepresentation.

ent legal complication arose in a case in which a woman apparently consented to have sex with a man and then later accused him of rape when one of her other personalities emerged and objected (Smolowe, 1990). In an interesting divorce case a man filed for divorce because his wife had had an affair. However, his wife's defense and her basis for a large alimony settlement was that she had remained faithful; it was Andrea, one of her 13 personalities, who had cheated on him. Because of widespread interest in this disorder and the numerous legal and psychological implica-

tions it has, it is important for us to carefully evaluate the evidence concerning it.

Famous Case Studies. When discussing dissociative identity disorder, many people cite famous case studies, particularly the case of Sybil, so we will begin with an examination of that case. Sybil (who we now know to be Shirley Ardell Mason) was alleged to have 16 personalities, including 2 who were males (Schreiber, 1973). The case of Sybil attracted national attention in 1973 when it provided the basis

The expert witnesses for the prosecution were led by a psychologist-psychiatrist named Martin Orne, who argued that rather than suffering from dissociative identity disorder, Bianchi suffered from antisocial personality disorder and that he was faking the multiple personalities to avoid punishment. (Major symptoms of antisocial personality disorder include repeated criminal behavior, lying, and a lack of anxiety; it will be discussed in Chapter 12.) A number of points were made to discredit the diagnosis of dissociative identity disorder. First, it was suggested that the disorder had not appeared spontaneously but had been suggested to Bianchi by Watkins. Some support for that is found in the transcript of the interview in which Steve originally emerged.

Second, Orne laid a small trap for Bianchi by suggesting that if he really did have dissociative identity disorder, he would have a third personality. The idea behind this was that if Bianchi was faking and if he were led to believe that having another personality would give his diagnosis more credibility, he would begin showing one. After the suggestion was made, Bianchi was hypnotized. Steve appeared first, followed shortly by a third personality, Billy.

The prosecution also pointed to a history of crime and lying. With regard to lying it is interesting to note that although Bianchi claimed to know nothing about dissociative identity disorder, a search of his room revealed

numerous textbooks on psychology. He had also been a psychology major in college, thus making it unlikely that he was unfamiliar with the disorder. It was also discovered that Bianchi had made a number of other conscious attempts to mislead the prosecution (e.g., he had asked others to lie about where he was at various crucial times).

Facing overwhelming evidence and serious questions about the validity of his multiple personality defense, Bianchi withdrew his plea of not guilty by reason of insanity and entered into a plea bargain. (The demand for the death penalty was dropped in exchange for Bianchi's pleading guilty and testifying against another individual who had been involved in the murders.)

Despite his plea bargain, Bianchi steadfastly maintained that he had dissociative identity disorder. When given an opportunity to address the court before the sentence was passed, Bianchi gave an impassioned and tearful speech in which he said that he would have to devote his entire life to seeing that no one would follow in his footsteps. However, in sharp contrast to that display of emotion and regret, a detective assigned to the case reported that within 3 minutes of leaving the courtroom, Bianchi was sitting with his feet up on a desk, smoking a cigarette, and laughing.

In his concluding comments before sentencing Kenneth Bianchi, the judge observed, "Mr. Bianchi caused confusion and delay in the proceedings. In

When Kenneth Bianchi was accused of being the "Hillside Strangler," he claimed that he had multiple personalities and that one of them, Steve, had committed the crimes. It was ultimately determined that Bianchi did not have dissociative identity disorder, and he was sentenced to life in prison.

this Mr. Bianchi was unwittingly aided and abetted by most of the psychiatrists, who naively swallowed Mr. Bianchi's story, hook, line, and sinker, almost confounding the criminal justice system."

Kenneth Bianchi was sentenced to life in prison.

Sources: Allison (1984); Orne et al. (1984); *People* v. *Buono* (1983); Watkins (1984).

for a best-selling book and later when it was turned into a popular movie. At the time the case was presented, dissociative identity disorder was not listed in *DSM,* and interest in the case apparently played a large role in the formal acceptance of dissociative identity disorder in *DSM-III* in 1980. The case of Sybil is fascinating, but a couple of things should be noted before accepting it as evidence for dissociative identity disorder: First, the only report we have of the case is the popularized version written by a professional author, not by Sybil's therapist. Second, there is now strong

evidence that the facts of the case were not as they were presented in the book (Miller & Kantrowitz, 1999). For example, one of the physicians involved in Sybil's treatment has stated that Sybil did not suffer from dissociative identity disorder but instead was simply a highly suggestible woman in whom the symptoms were planted (Associated Press, 1998). Indeed, in audiotapes of a discussion between Sybil's therapist (Cornelia Wilbur) and the author of *Sybil* (Flora Schreiber), it becomes clear that during therapy the therapist was planting personalities and related memories rather than discovering them (Rieber, 1999; Borch-Jacobsen, 1997). Other classic case studies of dissociative identity disorder, such as *The Three Faces of Eve,* have been similarly debunked as fiction or instances of suggestion. (For a fascinating and highly readable discussion of those cases, see Acocella, 1998.)

Overall, then, cases such as those of Sybil and Eve may be interesting reading, but they are unacceptable as science; indeed, the reports of Sybil's other personalities do not have much more credibility than the recent reports of sightings of Elvis Presley. However, the fact that these cases do not provide evidence for dissociative identity disorder does not necessarily mean that the disorder does not exist, so let's go on to consider the other evidence.

Differences on Personality and Intelligence Tests.
Those who believe in the existence of dissociative identity disorder cite numerous reports indicating that personality and intelligence tests reveal large differences among the various personalities of any one patient (Brandsma & Ludwig, 1974; Congdon, Hain, & Stevenson, 1961; Jeans, 1976; Keyes, 1981; Larmore, Ludwig, & Cain, 1977; Luria & Osgood, 1976; Osgood & Luria, 1954; Osgood, Luria, & Smith, 1976; Prince, 1908; Thigpen & Cleckley, 1954; Wagner & Heise, 1974). For example, tests may reveal that one personality is hostile and not particularly bright, while another personality is loving and smart. However, those findings are not persuasive because it is easy to give false responses to tests and because the individuals who interpreted the patients' responses to projective tests were not blind to the conditions and thus may easily have been biased in their scoring. Clearly, we need better evidence.

Physiological Differences.
Believers in dissociative identity disorder also point to research indicating that different patterns of brain wave activity (EEGs) are associated with the different personalities of any one individual (Braun, 1983b; Coons, Milstein, & Marley, 1982; Larmore et al., 1977; Ludwig et al., 1972). Indeed, in the case of one individual with four personalities, it was reported that it was "as if four different people had been tested" (Larmore et al., 1977, p. 40). These findings initially provided support for the validity of dissociative identity disorder. However, the value of the findings was greatly diminished by the results of a study in which EEG activity was recorded in two individuals diagnosed as having multiple personalities and one normal individual who role-played different personalities (Coons et al., 1982). It was found that the EEG differences between the personalities that were role-played by the normal individual were actually *greater* than the EEG differences between the personalities of the individuals diagnosed as having dissociative identity disorder. Because simple differences in concentration or mood can influence brain wave activity, differences in brain wave activity cannot be used to

verify the existence of multiple personalities (Coons, 1988; Coons et al., 1982; Miller & Triggiano, 1992). Differences among personalities on a wide variety of other physiological measures such as heart rate, respiration, skin conductance, and cerebral blood flow have also been examined, but as with brain waves, the differences among the multiple personalities of one individual were no greater than the differences among the roles played by normal individuals (Miller & Triggiano, 1992). The point here is that because we all show differences in physiological responses when we are in different roles or moods, such differences cannot be used to demonstrate separate personalities.

Therapists have also reported case studies in which one personality had a toothache, was color-blind, or had an allergy, but the individual's other personality did not suffer from those problems (Braun, 1983a; Wilson, 1903). However, while those are interesting stories, *there is no objective evidence to support them.* For example, a frequently cited case of an individual with diabetes who supposedly required different amounts of insulin while in different personalities can be traced back to one unsubstantiated "observation" that has simply been reported over and over. Furthermore, even if it were true that an individual used different amounts of insulin in "different personalities," that would not provide evidence for multiple personalities because we know that people require different amounts of insulin during different emotional states, so taking different amounts would reflect differences in emotion, not in personality. Clearly, the evidence does not provide any support for the existence of dissociative identity disorder as it is described in *DSM*.

Suggestion.
There are two alternative explanations for the behavior of individuals who appear to have dissociative identity disorder. The first is that it is possible that the symptoms are *suggested to the individual by a therapist.* This possibility gains indirect support from the fact that most therapists never see one case of dissociative identity disorder in their entire careers (Gruenewald, 1971; Rosenbaum, 1980), whereas some therapists report seeing as many as 100 or more such cases (Allison & Schwartz, 1980; Bliss, 1980, 1984; Braun, 1984; Kluft, 1982; Watkins, 1984). The implication is that therapists who are particularly interested in this disorder subtly suggest the symptom pattern to their patients. In that regard it is noteworthy that individuals with dissociative identity disorder are generally regarded as being highly suggestible and that the disorder is often discovered while the client is under hypnosis (a state of heightened suggestibility). Disorders produced as a result of treatment (e.g., suggestions of the therapist) are called **iatrogenic** (yat-ro-GEN-ik) **disorders.**

Evidence concerning the role that therapists' suggestions play in the development of dissociative identity disorder comes from the records of interactions between therapists and patients during therapy (Spanos, Weekes, & Bertrand, 1985; Sutcliffe & Jones, 1962). This is illustrated in the following quotation from an interview with Kenneth Bianchi, the Hillside Strangler, who later reported dissociative identity disorder (see Case Study 7.3). Before Bianchi made any comments reflecting the possibility of multiple personalities, the interviewer said:

> I think that perhaps there might be another part of Ken that I haven't talked to. . . . I would like to communicate with that other part. . . . I would like that other part to come to talk to me. . . . Part, would you please come to communicate with me? . . . Would you please come, Part, so I can talk to you? (Orne, Dinges, & Orne, 1984, p. 128)

Not only did the interviewer suggest the possibility of another personality, but he actually gave the other personality a name ("Part") and repeatedly pleaded with it to come out and talk to him!

This case led to an interesting study in which three groups of college students were asked to role-play Bianchi in an interview situation (Spanos et al., 1985). Students in one condition participated in an interview that closely followed the one used with Bianchi in that the interviewer (1) suggested that they might have another "part," (2) said he would like to communicate with that part, and (3) talked directly to "Part." Students in the second condition participated in a similar interview, but the interviewer (1) suggested that we sometimes have thoughts and feelings that are "walled off" and (2) said that he would like to be in contact with "another part of you," but (3) did not address "Part" directly. In the control condition the interviewer did not talk about a part or walled-off thoughts and feelings. When the students were then asked who they were and to talk about themselves, those in the first two conditions enacted another personality (used a different name, feigned amnesia for their real personality, and admitted to a crime their real personality denied). Furthermore, in a later session in which the students were asked to take personality tests as themselves and again as another part of themselves, the students in the first two conditions gave very different test responses on the two administrations, whereas there was no difference in the control condition. In other words, when the interviewer suggested the possibility of multiple personalities, the students' behavior and personality test scores were consistent with multiple personalities, but when the interviewer did not suggest that possibility, the students did not behave as though they had multiple personalities. These results clearly indicate that the way an interview is conducted can suggest the possibility of a multiple personality (Spanos, 1986).

Suggestions made to patients could lead them to fake dissociative identity disorder deliberately or to believe that they actually had the disorder; in either case they would

act in accordance with the diagnosis. In view of the publicity the disorder gets, if an authority suggests that someone has the disorder and if having the disorder explains or justifies the person's behavior, he or she may very well yield to the suggestion.

Faking. The second explanation is that at least in some cases the individual is consciously *faking* the disorder to avoid responsibility or to get attention. The husband of a student of mine claimed to have multiple personalities when one day his wife came home unexpectedly and discovered him dressed in her clothes. He had a transvestic fetishism (see Chapter 16), but he tried to convince his wife that she was married to his "normal personality," who knew nothing about his "transvestite personality," who came out only when she was not home. However, during a thorough examination he admitted the attempted deception.

The problems surrounding the diagnosis of dissociative identity disorder are highlighted in the case of the Hillside Strangler, who is discussed in Case Study 7.3. While reading the case study, ask yourself the following questions: (1) Was Kenneth Bianchi suffering from dissociative identity disorder, or was he feigning it in an attempt to escape punishment? (2) Did the interviewer suggest the disorder to him? (3) Should he have been treated for his disorder or punished for his crimes? (4) Do people really suffer from dissociative identity disorder?

Recent Legal Cases. Because of the questions that have been raised concerning the existence of dissociative personality disorder, former patients who were treated for the disorder have questioned whether their treatment was necessary and ethical. Indeed, a variety of malpractice suits were filed, and in one high visibility case the patient won a judgment of over $10 million. In considering these cases, it is important to note that using the diagnosis of dissociative identity disorder is not necessarily malpractice (after all, the diagnosis is in the *DSM*), but the issue of malpractice arises in how the individual is then treated.

Where does all this leave us? What do mental health professionals think about dissociative identity disorder? A recent survey of American psychiatrists revealed that only about 25% now believe that there is strong support for either dissociative amnesia or dissociative identity disorder (Pope et al., 1999). Clearly, the tide has turned with regard to this set of disorders; they simply may not exist as they are traditionally described.

---

iatrogenic disorders   Disorders that are inadvertently produced as a result of treatment for other disorders.

Explanations

Discussing the explanations for dissociative disorders puts us in a somewhat awkward position because I have just pointed out that serious questions have been raised over whether these disorders really exist. However, because some mental health professionals do believe these disorders exist and do treat them, it is important that you know what is traditionally thought about their causes.

Psychodynamic Explanations

Psychodynamic theory suggests that dissociative disorders result from individuals' attempts to dissociate themselves from stressful events or to obliterate their memories of the events. In other words, dissociative disorders involve what can be considered as massive uses of repression (see Chapter 2 and the earlier discussion). More specifically, many theorists assume that early childhood sexual abuse is at the root of dissociative disorders (Maldonado & Spiegel, 1999). For example, it has been suggested that an individual defends against the memory of abuse by breaking off part of the personality linked to the abuse. Although that explanation is widely accepted, the fact that there is no reliable evidence for repression makes its acceptance hazardous at best. Furthermore, the evidence linking childhood sexual abuse to dissociation is weak at best (Mulder et al., 1998; Rind, Tromovitch, & Bauserman 1998).

Learning, Cognitive, and Physiological Explanations

Learning and cognitive theorists have had relatively little to say about the development of dissociative disorders, probably because of the skepticism over whether they actually exist. However, it is possible that role playing could be used to explain at least an approximation of dissociative identity disorder. In that regard it should be recognized that many of us have multiple personalities in that we play different roles in different situations. Sometimes those roles are quite different, even conflicting. To avoid conflict we may keep our different roles completely separate and may not attend to the conflicts. For example, when I was an undergraduate, there was some conflict between my "jock" role and my "student" role. I behaved very differently in the two roles: I usually dressed differently in the two roles and had different sets of friends, and although I did not realize it at first, when I was a senior, a friend pointed out that my different sets of friends even called me by different names (Dave vs. David). The trouble with this explanation is that with multiple roles we are *aware* of the "other personality" (I knew I was a student *and* an athlete), but that is not the case with

individuals who have dissociative identity disorder. Therefore, the development of different and conflicting multiple roles can be used to explain an *approximation* of dissociative identity disorder, but whether multiple roles can account for what is technically referred to as dissociative identity disorder has not yet been resolved.

Finally, it is relevant to note that dissociative amnesia, dissociative fugue, and dissociative identity disorder could be used to avoid responsibility, and thus they could be *rewarding*. For example, if an individual behaved inappropriately, he or she could simply say, "I don't remember doing that" or "Oh, it was my other personality" and thus no longer be accountable or blamed. That would be an extension of the excuse many of us have used when we said, "I'm sorry. *I just wasn't myself* today." One woman I know uses an extreme response; whenever she is faced with a problem, she reverts to her "infant" personality and goes to bed, demanding that others take care of her.

Treatments

Just as there is controversy over whether dissociative disorders exist, there is also controversy over how the disorders should be treated, with possibilities including psychotherapy, hypnosis, and even exorcism to eliminate multiple personalities (Boyd, 1997; Bull, Ellason, & Ross, 1998; Spiegel & Maldonado, 1999). However, traditionally it has been assumed that first there must be a resolution of the conflict that made it necessary to dissociate from (or repress) the experiences that led to the disorders (Kluft, 1993; Loewenstein, 1994; Spiegel, 1994). In cases of dissociative identity disorder, the conflicts among personalities must be resolved, and then each of the personalities must be reconciled and melded into the core personality. In many cases that can take years because one personality may object or new ones may develop. In that regard it is interesting to note that when I made the videotape that accompanies this book, I interviewed a woman who was diagnosed as having dissociative identity disorder. It took a long time to get her consent to make the tape because permission had to be negotiated with each of her many personalities. In therapy each personality must accept the solution and then agree to go away, and for that there is great resistance. Because of this, psychotherapy with individuals with dissociative identity disorder can go on for years and cost hundreds of thousands of dollars. Serious questions have been raised over whether insurance companies should pay for the therapy, especially when there is growing doubt that the disorder exists as it is described. In fact, in recent years the treatment of individuals with dissociative identity disorder has resulted in many malpractice lawsuits, and former patients have been awarded millions of dollars in damages (Acocella, 1998). Furthermore, faced with dwindling evidence for the disorder and serious questions about malpractice, the prestigious Rush-Presbyterian Hospital in Chicago simply closed the clinic it had established for the treatment of dissociative identity disorder.

However, even if one takes the position that these disorders do not exist as they are traditionally described and explained, individuals who display the symptoms probably do need some form of treatment because they obviously have a problem that led them to use the behaviors; that is, the behaviors are solving some problem (e.g., helping the individual escape responsibility) or satisfying some need (e.g., getting attention). Therefore, rather than treating the disorder per se, a therapist might ask why a patient has selected the role of a person with the disorder and then work to resolve that problem.

THINKING CRITICALLY

Questions about Dissociative Disorders

Do the disorders known as dissociative amnesia, dissociative fugue, and dissociative identity disorder really exist? This is the fundamental question in this section, and there are two answers to it. The first answer is no—there is no objective evidence that these disorders exist as they are traditionally described (e.g., Piper et al., 2000). Furthermore, there is no evidence for the existence of repression, which supposedly provides the basis for the disorders. Five or ten years ago it would have been heresy to question the existence of these disorders, but as I pointed out earlier, a survey of psychiatrists indicated that three-quarters of them do not think there is sufficient evidence to justify belief in these disorders (Pope et al., 1999). Of course, it is always possible that new evidence will be found in the future, but at present there is simply no evidence for these disorders.

However, the second answer is yes—these disorders do exist. How can I say that after I just said they don't exist? Here we have to make a distinction between the *objective* existence and the *phenomenological* existence of the disorders. We cannot prove objectively that the disorders exist, but if individuals believe the disorders exist, they will behave as though they exist. Therefore *for them* the disorders do exist. However, that type of existence requires a very different conceptualization and treatment strategy than have traditionally been used. In essence, dissociative identity disorder is based on *delusion* rather than *dissociation,* and treatment is focused on correcting the incorrect belief that is the delusion rather than trying to resolve conflicts between the personalities and then integrate them.

Summary

Topic I: Somatoform Disorders

▶ Somatoform disorders involve physical symptoms for which there is no demonstrable physical cause; so it is assumed that there is a psychological cause. In contrast, psychosomatic disorders also have psychological causes, but they involve actual physical damage.

▶ There are five somatoform disorders: (1) somatization disorder, which involves numerous physical complaints; (2) hypochondriasis, which involves excessive concern over any minor symptom; (3) conversion disorder, which involves a major motor or sensory symptom; (4) pain disorder, which involves pain without any discernible physical cause; and (5) body dysmorphic disorder, which involves a preoccupation with a minor or imagined physical defect. Mass psychogenic illness is an epidemic of a particular somatoform disorder.

▶ Somatoform disorders occur in about 2% of the population and are more common among women than among men. The early Greeks described these disorders, and they were later studied by Charcot and Freud. These disorders occur in all cultures, but the form they take and the explanation offered differ as a function of what role models are available and the prevailing beliefs of the culture.

▶ Evidence for the existence of these disorders comes from the placebo effect, in which symptoms can be induced or eliminated through suggestion. Somatoform disorders can lead to high medical bills because of attempts to identify a physiological cause. Problems can arise if real medical problems are erroneously attributed to somatoform disorders. With new findings in medicine, some of what were once thought to be somatoform disorders have been identified as medical problems.

▶ From a psychodynamic viewpoint somatoform disorders are thought to stem from pent-up emotional energy, which is converted into physical symptoms.

▶ Learning theorists assume that somatoform symptoms are learned and are rewarding in that they help the individual avoid stress or lead to sympathy.

▶ The cognitive explanation for somatoform disorders is that individuals focus attention on normal bodily sensations and misinterpret them as symptoms.

▶ The physiological explanation holds that individuals with somatoform disorders are highly aroused and misinterpret the arousal as symptoms.

▶ It may also be that somatoform disorders are a subtype of obsessive-compulsive disorder or possibly a part of the serotonin spectrum of disorders.

▶ Treatment of somatoform disorders revolves around (1) moving patients' attention away from bodily sensations and changing their beliefs about the meaning of bodily sensations, (2) reducing depression that might lead to focusing on bodily sensations and interpreting them pessimistically, (3) reducing arousal that leads to bodily sensations that might be misinterpreted, and (4) providing emotional support so that individuals can cope more effectively.

Topic II: Dissociative Disorders

▶ Individuals with dissociative disorders lose contact with important elements of their personality or environment.

▶ There are four dissociative disorders: (1) Dissociative amnesia is an inability to remember important personal information or events that is not due to physiological causes. (2) Dissociative fugue is a disorder in which an individual has amnesia for his or her previous identity and moves to a new location to assume a new identity. (3)

Dissociative identity disorder (multiple personality disorder) is a disorder in which an individual's personality is fragmented so that he or she appears to have two or more personalities. (4) Depersonalization disorder involves the feeling of being detached from one's body.

▶ Serious questions must be raised concerning the existence of most dissociative disorders because they are based on the concept of repression, for which no reliable evidence has been found.

▶ There is no objective evidence for the existence of dissociative identity disorder as it is traditionally described and explained, and instances of this disorder appear to be due to suggestion.

▶ The psychodynamic explanation for dissociative disorders holds that individuals are attempting to separate themselves from stressful events or from stressful parts of themselves.

▶ Learning, cognitive, and physiological theorists have had little to say about dissociative disorders, probably because of the skepticism over their existence.

▶ Treatment for individuals with these disorders is probably best focused on determining why the individual is using the symptoms (e.g., to gain attention, to avoid responsibility) and then helping the individual find better ways to achieve the goal.

Questions for Making Connections

1. What problems are posed by the fact that individuals are diagnosed with somatization and pain disorders only when a physiological cause for their symptoms cannot be found? Will these disorders cease to exist when we have a better understanding of physiological disorders and better diagnostic techniques?

2. Suppose you were a mental health professional and a client was referred to you because he had physical symptoms for which a physiological cause could not be found. What would you do? If you decided to treat the individual, what treatment would you use and why?

3. Are somatization and body dysmorphic disorders subtypes of obsessive-compulsive disorder? Why or why not? Do somatization and body dysmorphic disorders involve delusions?

4. Do you believe that repression occurs? What evidence do you have for your position? If repression does not exist, what implications does that have for our understanding of dissociative disorders?

5. If someone came to you with the symptoms of dissociative identity disorder, what would you do?

Key Terms and People

In reviewing and testing yourself, you should be able to discuss each of the following:

body dysmorphic disorder, p. 184
catharsis, p. 189
Charcot, Jean-Martin, p. 186
conversion disorder, p. 183

depersonalization disorder, p. 196
dhat, p. 187
dissociative amnesia, p. 194
dissociative disorders, p. 194

dissociative fugue, p. 194
dissociative identity disorder, p. 195
factitious disorders, p. 187
factitious disorders by proxy, p. 187

8 Mood Disorders: Major Depressive Disorder

In this and the following chapter, we will examine the fascinating topic of **mood disorders.** These disorders involve symptoms that range from deep depression to wild mania. Understanding these disorders is important because at least 15% of the population will suffer from a mood disorder at some time, and the disorders can be very serious.

At the outset it is essential to recognize that there are two major types of mood disorders. One is **major depressive disorder,** in which *depression is the primary symptom.* (Major depressive disorder is sometimes referred to as *unipolar depression.*) The other major mood disorder is **bipolar disorder,** in which *depression alternates with mania.* The term *bipolar* refers to the fact that mania and depression are two "poles" between which the mood swings. (This disorder was originally called *manic-depressive disorder.*)

There are also milder forms of these disorders. The milder form of major depressive disorder is known as **dysthymic** (dis-THI-mik) **disorder,** and the less severe form of bipolar disorder is called **cyclothymic** (si-klo-THI-mik) **disorder.** The organization of these mood disorders along with their symptoms is shown in Figure 8.1 (on p. 210). A decision tree for diagnosing mood disorders can be found in Figure 4.1.

Depression is a primary symptom in both major depressive disorder and bipolar disorder, but it is very important

to recognize that *these are two different disorders.* Therefore, I will discuss major depressive disorder in this chapter and bipolar disorder in the next chapter. I will also discuss suicide in the next chapter because, although suicide is not a mood disorder, it is often related to problems with mood.

Before discussing the symptoms of depression, we should take note of five things that dramatically demonstrate why depression is such a serious problem:

1. Depression is widespread. In fact, estimates of the prevalence of serious depression in the general population range from 12% to 17% (Coryell, Endicott, & Keller, 1991; Kessler et al., 1994). Actually, the prob-

---

mood disorders   Disorders in which depression and mania are the major symptoms.

major depressive disorder   A mood disorder in which the primary symptom is depression; sometimes referred to as *unipolar depression.*

bipolar disorder   A mood disorder in which depression alternates with mania; originally called *manic-depressive disorder.*

dysthymic disorder   A milder form of major depressive disorder; also referred to as *dysthymia.*

cyclothymic disorder   A milder form of bipolar disorder.

lem is even greater than these estimates suggest because the large number of individuals who suffer from dysthymic disorder are not included in the estimates. Indeed, depression occurs so frequently that it is sometimes referred to as the "common cold of psychiatry." Unfortunately, it is much more serious than the common cold.

2. Depression is a persistent problem that is likely to recur (Coyne, Pepper, & Flynn, 1999; Muller et al., 1999). For example, the rate of recurrence (relapse) for serious depression is about 90%.

3. Apart from feeling bad, people who are depressed suffer from slowed thought processes and impairments in memory that can interfere with their functioning (Austin et al., 1999; Burt, Zembar, & Niedershe, 1995).

4. Women are twice as likely to suffer from depression as men (Kessler et al., 1994; Smith & Weissman, 1992). This has been found to be the case in 30 countries over a period of 40 years.

5. It is alarming to note that the prevalence of depression is increasing worldwide (Lewinsohn et al., 1993). This may represent a serious trend, and concerns have been raised about the coming "age of melancholy."

Overall, then, depression is a widespread, chronic, and serious problem with many ramifications; thus it is essential that we understand its causes and treatments.

TOPIC I
Symptoms and Issues

Lois is a 36-year-old woman who spends most of the day slumped in a chair staring blankly at the floor. Her face is slack and expressionless. She is unkempt and rarely moves or speaks. Occasionally, she weeps quietly to herself. Lois has difficulty getting to sleep at night, and she usually awakens at about 2:30 a.m. and cannot get back to sleep. She does not care about eating and has lost 12 pounds in the past 3 months. When asked what was wrong, she slowly gave the following answer in a voice that was almost inaudible: "Everything is wrong; everything has gone wrong. It's just too much. (Long pause) I'm a complete failure. (long pause) I just don't think things will get better—and I just don't care anymore. (begins crying) I wish I were dead. Then I'd have it over with. . . . Everyone would be better off without me around. I just can't make it anymore." Lois has been like this for about 3 months. She suffers from major depressive disorder. Where do we draw the line between the "normal" depression many of us experience occasionally and "abnormal" depression? What other symptoms tend to go along with depression?

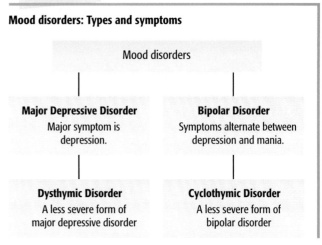

FIGURE 8.1

Mood disorders: Types and symptoms

Mood disorders

Major Depressive Disorder
Major symptom is depression.

Bipolar Disorder
Symptoms alternate between depression and mania.

Dysthymic Disorder
A less severe form of major depressive disorder

Cyclothymic Disorder
A less severe form of bipolar disorder

Depression involves many symptoms other than depression, and we must be aware of these symptoms when making diagnoses. So let's begin by examining the symptoms of major depression.

Mood Symptoms

Obviously, the primary symptom of depression is a lowering of mood; individuals feel depressed, "blue," sad, hopeless, discouraged, and "down." Frequently, depressed individuals also feel isolated, rejected, and unloved. They sometimes describe themselves as being alone in a deep, dark hole, where they cannot be reached and from which they cannot climb out.

Cognitive Symptoms

There are three types of cognitive symptoms in depression:

1. *Negative beliefs about self, the world, and the future.* A major characteristic of depressed individuals is that they view everything negatively. Specifically, they think they are inadequate, inferior, and simply no good. (This feeling is sometimes referred to as low self-esteem.) Depressed individuals also tend to think that the world is a rotten place, that no one likes them, and that the problems they are facing are insurmountable. Finally, depressed individuals are pessimistic about the future. Not only do they see themselves and the world as bad, they don't believe that things will improve. Indeed, a common thought of depressed individuals is "Why go on?" (The negative beliefs about self,

Individuals suffering from depression often feel hopeless and sad and have a sense of being isolated, unwanted, or rejected. It is interesting to note that women are twice as likely as men to suffer from depression.

at least some situations depressed individuals are "sadder but wiser" about themselves.

2. *Low motivation.* Because depressed individuals do not believe that they will be able to solve their problems, they have little motivation to work on the problems or even seek help in overcoming them. For them all seems hopeless, so there is no point in trying. Of course, if they do not work on and overcome their problems, the accumulation of unsolved problems provides an additional reason for depression. Consider the case of a student who failed a midterm examination and became depressed. The failure and depression led the student to think, "I guess I'm just not smart enough to get through this course. I'll certainly flunk the final, so there is no point in going to class or working on this course anymore." Obviously, the student's low self-esteem, pessimism, and lack of motivation will result in another failure that will provide more reasons for depression and will confirm his beliefs about his inadequacy; a vicious circle has started.

3. *Impaired thinking.* An important cognitive problem associated with depression is impaired thinking; that is, during periods of depression individuals are less effective at solving intellectual and social problems, and the impairment is not due simply to a lack of motivation (Marx, Williams, & Claridge, 1992; Schotte, Cools, & Payvar, 1990). In particular, depressed individuals have difficulty with problems involving memory (Backman & Forsell, 1994; Burt et al., 1995). You may have noticed that when you are depressed you are less effective at studying and solving problems. Of course, difficulty with problem solving will lead to more failures, poorer self-esteem, and greater depression.

Motor Symptoms

Two different types of motor symptoms are evident with depression:

1. *Psychomotor retardation.* The most common motor symptom in depression is **psychomotor retardation,** which involves a *reduction or slowing of motor behavior.* Individuals with psychomotor retardation have a great deal of difficulty "getting started" and may simply want to stay in bed. When they do get up, they are likely to sit with a drooping posture and a blank, expressionless gaze. When they move, they move very slowly, as though they are dragging a 10-ton weight. They may even report feeling like they have the weight of the world on their shoulders and simply cannot

psychomotor retardation The most common motor symptom in depression, which involves a reduction or slowing of motor behavior.

world, and future are often referred to as the *negative triad of depression.*) Negative beliefs are important symptoms of depression, but they may also be a cause of depression. That is, thinking that you're no good, the world is a bad place, and the future is bleak could be depressing.

Although depressed individuals usually do see themselves as being less good than other people, one qualification should be noted: In some cases depressed individuals are actually *more accurate* than nondepressed individuals in their self-perceptions. Specifically, rather than depressed individuals distorting their perceptions downward, *nondepressed individuals may distort their perceptions upward.* For example, when college students were asked to estimate how well they performed on a task, depressed students gave lower estimates than nondepressed students, but the estimates of the depressed students were closer to their actual performance than were the higher estimates of the nondepressed students. Furthermore, when college students were asked to rate their social skills, the lower estimates of depressed students were closer to the ratings made by independent judges than were the higher estimates of nondepressed students (Alloy & Abramson, 1979; Lewinsohn et al., 1980). This prompted the investigators to suggest that in move under this burden. Speech patterns are also affected by psychomotor retardation: Individuals talk very little; when they do talk, it is in a quiet monotone, and they often break off talking in midsentence because they do not have the energy to finish the sentence. It is noteworthy that individuals who show psychomotor retardation also have more problems with thinking and memory and a low rate of recovery from depression (Lemelin & Baruch, 1998; Steffens et al., 1999; Van Loden et al., 1998).

2. *Psychomotor agitation.* In contrast, some depressed persons show **psychomotor agitation**—they are unable to sit still, are restless, and are constantly fidgeting or pacing. Because their activities are random rather than focused on achieving any particular goal, their high levels of activity do not gain them anything. These individuals may also have sudden outbursts of complaining, in which they shout or talk rapidly. One woman with psychomotor agitation spent her days walking in circles around her bedroom, wringing her hands and weeping, and she cried through most of the night. On the surface psychomotor agitation involves many of the symptoms of anxiety, and it is sometimes difficult to differentiate between agitation and anxiety. Psychomotor agitation in depression can also be confused with mania because both involve a high level of activity. However, an individual with an agitated depression is *sad*, whereas an individual with mania is *happy*.

Psychomotor agitation is a symptom of depression. Individuals who show psychomotor agitation are restless and may spend a lot of time crying, pacing, or wringing their hands.

 Physical Symptoms

Finally, there are four physical symptoms that are often associated with depression:

1. *Disturbed sleep.* Depressed individuals frequently have difficulty getting to sleep. They may also experience *early morning awakening;* that is, they may wake up early in the morning (around 2:00 a.m., for example) and be unable to get back to sleep. Early awakening appears to be associated with more severe depression, and as the depression begins to lift, the time of awakening becomes later and later. In some cases of depression, however, individuals begin sleeping more than usual. One way or another, then, sleep patterns are disrupted in depression.

2. *Disturbed eating patterns.* It is also common for depressed persons to have disturbed eating patterns; some lose their appetites and reduce the amount they eat, whereas others have increased appetites and consume large amounts of food. As with sleep, there is a disruption, but it can go in either direction.

3. *Decreased sexual drive.* Another physical symptom often associated with depression is decreased sexual drive. This is sometimes referred to as a loss of **libido** (li-BE-do) because *libido* is the psychodynamic term for "sexual drive." Although depression can lead to a decrease in sexual drive, you should note that some of the drugs used to treat depression also reduce sexual drive (see the later discussion of treatments), so when considering this symptom, it is essential to distinguish between the effects of the depression and the effects of the drugs.

4. *Increased physical illnesses.* Finally, apart from the problems with sleep, appetite, and sex, depressed individuals are more susceptible to a variety of diseases. This occurs because with depression there is a decline in the functioning of the immune system (Herbert & Cohen, 1993). Specifically, there is evidence that depressed individuals produce fewer white blood cells, technically called *lymphocytes* (LIM-fo-sits), which play an important role in combating foreign substances, such as germs (see Chapter 14). The reduction in the activity of the immune system in depressed individuals probably stems from the fact that the stress associated with depression retards the functioning of the system. There is growing evidence that depression is linked to cardiovascular disease, but the exact relationship is not yet clear (Glassman & Shapiro, 1998; Musselman, Evans, & Nemeroff, 1998; Panzarino, 1998; Severus et al., 1999; Takemura et al., 1998; Wulsin, Vaillant, & Wells, 1999).

When seeking treatment, many individuals focus on their physical symptoms and tend to ignore their psychological symptoms. That is, they come in complaining of

There are several physical symptoms associated with depression. Decreased sexual drive is one of them, although some drugs used to treat depression can also result in a loss of libido.

poor appetite, fatigue, lack of sleep, and lack of sexual interest rather than depression. This results in what is called **masked depression;** that is, the depression is concealed by a "mask" of physical symptoms. Unfortunately, if individuals only complain about physical symptoms, their disorder may be misdiagnosed.

The question of why the cognitive, motor, and physical symptoms occur in depression is one we will consider in the next section when we examine the explanations for depression. Certainly, any comprehensive explanation will have to account for these symptoms as well as the depression. An example of an individual suffering from major depression is presented in Case Study 8.1 (on p. 214).

 ## Diagnostic Criteria

Feelings of sadness, disappointment, grief, and depression are part of the human condition and are experienced by almost everyone at some time. In view of that fact the questions we must ask are, what distinguishes normal depression from abnormal depression, and what symptoms must be present for an individual to be diagnosed as having major depressive disorder?

Normal versus Abnormal Depression

The boundary between normal and abnormal depression is not clear, but two factors should be considered in making the distinction. The first factor is the *depth* of the depression. It is normal to feel somewhat "down," "blue," or mildly depressed occasionally or when something bad happens, but we must be concerned if the depression is so deep that

the individual cannot function adequately. The second factor is the *duration* of the depression. Regardless of the depth of the depression, there is cause for concern if the depression is prolonged and the individual does not "snap out of it." In circumstances such as the death of a loved one, it is justifiable to be depressed for a while, but if the depression is more prolonged than what is justified by the original cause, the possibility of abnormal depression must be considered.

DSM-IV Criteria for Major Depressive Disorder

The three diagnostic criteria for major depressive disorder are listed in Part A of Table 8.1 (on p. 215).

In diagnosing depression it is important to distinguish between **primary depression,** which is a symptom *in and of itself,* and **secondary depression,** which is depression that

psychomotor agitation   A motor symptom in depression that involves constant movement, such as fidgeting or pacing.

libido   A psychodynamic term for sex drive; there is a loss of libido in depression.

masked depression   Depression that is concealed by complaints revolving around physical symptoms rather than mood.

primary depression   Depression that is a symptom of major depressive disorder in and of itself. (Compare with secondary depression.)

secondary depression   Depression that is the result of some other disorder or a side effect of medication, rather than a symptom of a mood disorder. (Compare with primary depression.)

Major Depression in a Young Woman

> **Life is an absurd waste of time....**

DIANE IS A 28-YEAR-OLD single woman who has suffered from severe depression since she was 16. Her first period of depression culminated in an almost fatal drug overdose. After her suicide attempt she was hospitalized on and off for several years. When not in the hospital, she was treated regularly in the outpatient clinic. Treatment consisted of psychotherapy and antidepressant drugs. Her adjustment during this period was only marginal, but she was able to complete high school.

Diane has now remained out of the hospital for about 7 years, but her depression has persisted. In describing her feelings, she says, "I wish someone would give me a spoon and tell me to move a mountain. Then my sense of hopeless futility would be more tangible. . . . Life is an absurd waste of time. . . . My existence is a freak accident of nature. . . . It seems that I can only handle short, sweet episodes of positive momentum."

Her overwhelming sense of worthlessness and inadequacy has prevented her from establishing any meaningful friendships that could challenge her negative self-image and provide support. Not surprisingly, her ruminations concerning her "emotional hellishness" interfere with her capacity to concentrate, think clearly, and make decisions. She spends much of her time staring into space, looking, but seeing only gray, negative images of life.

Diane is a bright young woman, and although plagued by almost ceaseless depression, she has managed to complete college and hold several part-time jobs. However, consistent with her unrealistic self-devaluation, she minimizes these accomplishments, saying, "It took so long to finish college, my degree is useless, and the work is mindless." She seems to lack any foundation on which to build a positive self-evaluation. Despite the severity of her depression and her sense of hopelessness, Diane has not attempted suicide again. She credits therapy with providing her with at least one supportive and nurturing relationship that helps her get through the "rough spots of life." She views the possibility of long-term meaningful change skeptically: "I've been miserable all my life, and I don't know if I know how to live differently. I'm not sure I know what it is like to be happy. I probably wouldn't recognize it if I was."

---

is the *result of some other disorder,* such as anxiety, alcoholism, schizophrenia, or cancer (Becker et al., 1997; Paradiso & Robinson, 1998; Rackman & Garfield, 1998; Roy, 1996). For example, depression is a symptom of many

Many events can trigger feelings of sadness and grief. Unless the feeling is very severe or lasts a long time, the sadness these parents might feel after the departure of their daughter would not be classified as clinical depression.

physical disorders, such as Parkinson's disease. For individuals for whom depression is the result of a physical disease, there is a specific diagnosis of **mood disorder due to a general medical condition** (American Psychiatric Association, 1994). The distinction between primary and secondary depression is crucial in terms of treatment; specifically, with primary depression we must focus on the depression, whereas with secondary depression we must treat the other disorder.

DSM-IV Criteria for Dysthymic Disorder

Earlier I pointed out that there is a less severe depressive disorder known as dysthymic disorder (see Figure 8.1). The diagnostic criteria for that disorder are listed in Part B of Table 8.1. Because the symptoms of dysthymia are less severe than those of major depressive disorder, many individuals with dysthymia are not diagnosed as having a disorder. Therefore, they do not get treatment, and they go through life feeling miserable and missing much that is positive. In other words, this disorder can be a long-term, chronic problem. In addition, because these individuals do not know that they have a psychiatric disorder, they assume that they are "bad people" or "the world is a terrible place." The presence of dysthymia early in life can also be serious because it is predictive of major depressive disorder later. Indeed, in a followup of children who suffered from dysthymia, it was found that almost 50% had developed major

Diagnostic criteria for depressive disorders

A. Major depressive disorder

1. The individual must have experienced two or more major depressive episodes. A depressive episode is defined as a period of at least 2 weeks during which nearly every day the individual experiences five or more of the following symptoms:

    (a) depressed mood,
    (b) diminished interest or pleasure in activities,
    (c) a 5% weight loss or a dramatic change in appetite,
    (d) insomnia or hypersomnia,
    (e) psychomotor retardation or agitation,
    (f) fatigue or loss of energy,
    (g) feelings of worthlessness or guilt,
    (h) diminished ability to concentrate or indecisiveness, and
    (i) recurrent thoughts about death and suicide.

    These symptoms result in clinically significant distress or impairment in social, occupational, or other important areas of functioning.

2. The symptoms cannot be accounted for by other disorders such as schizophrenia in which depression is a symptom.

3. The individual must not have had a period of mania. This restriction excludes people who are actually suffering from bipolar disorder (see Chapter 9).

B. Dysthymic disorder

1. Depressed mood for most of the day on more days than not for 2 years (1 year for children and adolescents).

2. Presence of at least two of the following symptoms while depressed:

    (a) poor appetite or overeating,
    (b) insomnia or hypersomnia,
    (c) low energy or fatigue,
    (d) low self-esteem,
    (e) poor concentration or difficulty making decisions, and
    (f) feelings of hopelessness.

3. No major depressive disorder.

Source: American Psychiatric Association (1994).

depressive disorder (Kovacs et al., 1994: Lewinsohn et al., 1991). Clearly, dysthymia is a problem in itself and may be predictive of more serious problems to come. Case Study 8.2 (on p. 216) is based on an essay written by a student of mine who appears to have had dysthymic disorder, which developed into more serious depression.

 ## Types of Depression

At one time it was assumed that different types of experiences, such as giving birth or getting older, resulted in different types of depression and that the different types had to be treated differently. So that the types of depression could be distinguished, they were given different diagnostic labels. In contrast, today it is agreed that although the situations in which depression arises can be different, the underlying factors are the same in most cases; therefore, many of the differing labels have been dropped. However, *DSM-IV* uses "specifiers" to describe a few types of depression. For

example, a woman who becomes depressed after giving birth will be diagnosed as suffering from depression, but the specifier "with postpartum onset" will be added. In the following sections I will describe two types of depression that are identified with specifiers.

Depression with Postpartum Onset

Women who suffer from *severe and persistent depression that sets in within 1 month of giving birth* are diagnosed as suffering from **depression with postpartum onset** (American Psychiatric Association, 1994). Disturbances of mood associated with childbirth are widespread, but they do not

mood disorder due to a general medical condition   A diagnosis that is used when depression (or mania) stems from physical disease.

depression with postpartum onset   Severe and persistent depression in a woman that sets in within 1 month after she gives birth.

A Student's Struggle with Depression

It angered me that people were so damn happy and all I could do was watch.

"I FEEL AS THOUGH I have spent my whole life trapped inside a glass bottle. I could look out and view the world, but it always seemed dulled and distorted by the thick, scratched glass. If anyone would shake me up the slightest bit, I felt as though I was going to crack and shatter in a million pieces. Perhaps that was precisely what I wanted so that I could cut people with the millions of jagged edges. My anger was enormous. It angered me that people were so damn happy and all I could do was watch.

"After experiencing these feelings for as much of my life as I could remember, I entered psychotherapy at the age of 17 because my parents thought I was 'depressed.' I agreed to go for therapy because in the pit of my stomach I really did not want to go on feeling the way I did. When the time came to enter college, I quit my therapy and concluded that my feelings of entrapment and isolation must just be a major character flaw.

My first year of college was filled with ups and downs. I couldn't seem to keep any relationships intact, with males or females. It seemed that everyone was always tired of being around me and accused me of being perpetually pessimistic. Sometimes I would spend days secluded by myself. When people would ask if something was wrong, I would reply with a philosophical answer about how some people need more time to themselves than others and that I had accepted that fact about myself. I rationalized my seclusion by telling myself that people who aren't comfortable by themselves are actually more insecure than those who can be alone. As I was never happy with what I was doing in the present, I tended to move around a lot in a ploy to 'experience different things' and 'get in touch with myself.' As time went by, my depression was pushed to an all-time low, and I found myself incapacitated. I began spending more and more time in my bed, huddled under my blankets with my door closed. Most of the time, I didn't feel particularly bad about not accomplishing anything because I knew that I physically couldn't get out of bed and I had lost faith that I had any academic prowess whatsoever. All of my relationships deteriorated because nobody wanted or knew how to deal with me. This only served to substantiate what I had decided about myself—that I was a worthless person who could never accomplish anything."

We will return to this student's experiences later when we consider the treatment of depression.

---

all qualify as disorders. At the low end of severity of such mood disturbances are some degree of depression, anxiety, irritability, loss of appetite, sleep disturbance, tearfulness, and emotional instability that is normal and to be expected after giving birth. Those responses are not considered to constitute a disorder, and they probably occur because of the physical discomfort and stress associated with labor and delivery, the hormonal changes that occur with childbirth, the onset of lactation, the side effects of medication, and the hospital environment.

At an intermediate level of severity is what is often referred to as the "maternity blues." Those blues involve changes in mood and crying, but because the depression is not particularly deep and usually lasts only between 2 and 4 days, the blues are not considered to be a disorder (O'Hara, Schlechte, Lewis, & Varner, 1991; O'Hara,

seasonal affective disorder (SAD)   The original term for what is now called *depression with seasonal pattern.*

depression with seasonal pattern   A mood disorder characterized by depression during winter when less light is available and sometimes hypomania during spring when light levels increase; originally called *seasonal affective disorder (SAD).*

Schlechte, Lewis, & Wright, 1991). Between 50% and 80% of new mothers have this reaction.

In contrast, about 0.5% of new mothers suffer from a serious and prolonged depression and are diagnosed as suffering from depression with postpartum onset. This depression is (1) not related to the age of the mother, (2) not related to the number or order of pregnancies, (3) more likely to recur in women who have a history of depression, (4) more likely to occur in women who have a history of other psychiatric disorders, (5) more likely to occur in women with a family history of other psychiatric disorders, and (6) predictive of future depression (Abou-Saleh & Ghubash, 1997; Bagedahl-Strindlund & Rupert, 1998; Cox, 1992; Hopkins, Marcus, & Campbell, 1984; Nonace & Cohen, 1998; O'Hara & Swain, 1996). In other words, women who suffer from depression with postpartum onset appear to be generally predisposed to depression.

Postpartum depression is serious by itself, but it can also lead to other tragic consequences. For example, women who suffer from this disorder are at increased risk for suicide (Appleby et al., 1998). In addition, some depressed mothers have persistent thoughts of killing their babies, and there is a growing number of cases in which depressed mothers did kill their infants (Jennings et al., 1999; Toufexis, 1988). Furthermore, the mother's depression can lead to depression in the father (Ballard, 1996; Boath et al., 1998;

Soliday et al., 1999; Zelkowitz & Milet, 1997). Finally, there is evidence that the children of depressed mothers are at increased risk for emotional and cognitive problems during infancy and the early school years (Beck, 1998; Murray & Cooper, 1996; Sinclair & Murray, 1998). Despite the fact that postpartum depression can be serious and is relatively common, many women are not aware of it and are caught by surprise when it happens to them. Also, many women try to hide their depression because they feel guilty about having such feelings at a time when they should be feeling joyful. Clearly, this is a type of depression of which expectant mothers and fathers should be aware.

The cause of postpartum depression is complex and not yet clearly understood, but two factors merit attention. On the one hand, physiological factors such as hormonal fluctuations probably play a role in postpartum depression because it is known that massive hormonal changes take place after delivery and during the 2-day "latency period" that usually occurs before the onset of the depression (Abou-Saleh et al., 1998; Hendrick, Altshuler, & Suri, 1998; Hendrick & Altshuler, 1999). On the other hand, the psychological stress associated with increased responsibilities, personal and physical limitations due to child care, changes in the family, lack of social support, and additional financial obligations could trigger the depression (Bergant et al., 1999; Righetti-Veltema et al., 1998). This notion is consistent with findings linking stress to depression (see Topic II) and leads to the view that in at least some cases there is nothing unique about postpartum depression (Gotlib et al., 1991; O'Hara, Schlechte, Lewis, & Varner, 1991; O'Hara, Schlechte, Lewis, & Wright, 1991; Whiffen, 1992). A mild case of postpartum depression is described in Case Study 8.3.

Depression with Seasonal Pattern

Some individuals, particularly women, are likely to experience depression during the winter months and may show a slight "high" (hypomania) in the spring (Blazer, Kessler, & Schwartz, 1998; Sher et al., 1999; Suhail & Cochrane, 1998; Vera, 1998). Indeed, there is an increase in hospital admissions for depression during the winter. For many years this was referred to as **seasonal affective disorder (SAD),** but now it is officially called **depression with seasonal pattern** (American Psychiatric Association, 1994). The changes in mood are linked to the number of hours of sunlight per day; that relationship is illustrated in Figure 8.2 (on p. 218), where amount of sunlight and levels of depression are plotted for the months of the year. As you might expect, the relationship between depression and months of the year is reversed in the Southern Hemisphere, where winter comes in July and August. Although levels of sunlight are involved in this disorder, it is not yet how reduced levels of sunlight trigger depression.

A First-Person Account of a Mild Postpartum Depression

CASE STUDY 8.3

"A FEW DAYS after delivering our second child, I started to feel very anxious, guilty, and depressed. Although we had a happy, healthy 4-year-old son, I now felt utterly helpless in taking care of this new infant. I felt very guilty, thinking that I should have prepared myself better by reading books or something. I couldn't remember what to do for specific problems, and I was generally anxious about everything. I felt hopelessly inadequate.

"I wasn't even slightly hungry, and when I did eat, I either vomited or had diarrhea. This made me worry that my baby wasn't getting proper nutrition because I was breastfeeding. I would awake an hour or two before the alarm went off at 6:00 a.m., and I would start worrying that I wouldn't be able to get everything done on time or that I wouldn't be a good wife and mother. It was terrible.

"I was extremely tired and exhausted all of the time, and I cried at the drop of a hat. I couldn't concentrate on anything very long, and I felt entirely overwhelmed with my predicament. I couldn't imagine how my mother had coped with six children and maintained her sanity. I remember that I did a great deal of complaining that I simply couldn't handle all of this, but somehow I kept going enough to get by.

"Meanwhile, the baby picked up on my unhappiness and anxiety and became extremely fussy, which made me feel even less capable as a mother. I recall very clearly a day when a friend stopped in, and although the baby wouldn't stop crying for me, she stopped immediately when my friend took her. My friend persuaded me to call my physician, who prescribed some antidepressants for a couple of weeks. Before long, the symptoms went away, and I was more like my normal self, even after I stopped taking the pills. Soon I was enjoying life again as I had before, and at our 6-week checkup, both the baby and I were in excellent condition and fine spirits."

Note: Although they appeared to be effective in this case, antidepressant drugs are not necessarily effective, nor are they the treatment of choice in all cases of depression with postpartum onset; see Topic III.

> ... I now felt utterly helpless in taking care of this new infant.

FIGURE 8.2

For some individuals there is a relationship between the amount of daily sunlight and depression.

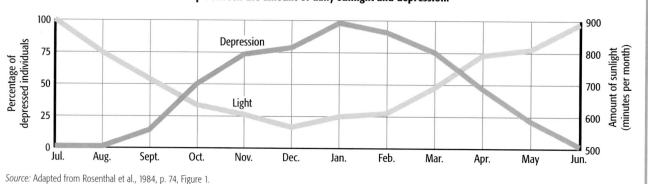

Source: Adapted from Rosenthal et al., 1984, p. 74, Figure 1.

Gender and Socioeconomic Factors

One of the most striking things about depression is that it occurs at least twice as often in women as it does in men (Culbertson, 1997; Kessler et al., 1994; Nolen-Hoeksema, 1990). As I mentioned earlier, this has been found in more than 30 countries over the past 40 years. Furthermore, repeated episodes of depression are more likely to occur in women than in men (Lewinsohn et al., 1994). The question is, why? Four general explanations have been offered:

1. *Women are simply more likely than men to report depression or seek help, so it just appears that they are more likely to suffer from depression.* This does not appear to be the case because the difference in rates of depression between women and men are found in community studies in which everyone in a community is thoroughly examined (Agency for Health Care Policy and Research, 1993).

2. *Women are exposed to more stressors or higher levels of stressors than men are.* We know that stress can cause depression (see the later discussion), and women experience more stress as a consequence of factors such as poverty, child-care responsibilities, and sexual abuse (McGrath et al., 1990). This is a popular explanation that might account for some of the difference, but in studies of men and women who were under comparable levels of stress, the women still had higher levels of depression (Amenson & Lewinsohn, 1981; Breslau et al., 1997; Radloff & Rae, 1979).

3. *Women have personality traits that predispose them to develop depression.* Some theorists have speculated that it is not the level of stress to which women are exposed but rather how they deal with the stress that leads to depression

(McGrath et al., 1990; Nolen-Hoeksema, 1990). Specifically, many women use more passive approaches to problem solving than men typically do, and the passive strategies may exacerbate their problems. Those findings led to a call for a more "feminist" approach to treatment that emphasized assertiveness for women (McGrath et al., 1990).

4. *Physiological factors predispose women to depression.* Advocates of this explanation point out that the difference in rates of depression between women and men does not appear until adolescence when differences in hormones develop, but critics respond by saying that adolescence is more stressful for women than men (Brooks-Gunn & Petersen, 1991; Buchanan, Becker, & Eccles, 1992; Nolen-Hoeksema & Girgus, 1994). The role of physiology in depression is complex, and we will explore it in greater detail later.

Overall, then, there is strong evidence that depression is more common among women than men, but at present we simply do not know why. There may be multiple reasons, and we will return to this issue later.

There is also a striking age-related difference in depression—depression is much more prevalent among older individuals than among younger ones (Murphy & MacDonald, 1992). It is often assumed that this increase is the result of the stress associated with failing health, the death of friends and loved ones, and the fact that older individuals are often less valued. However, we now know that many cases of depression are the result of structural problems in the brain (see the later discussion), and at least some of the depression we see in older people may be the result of changes in the brain that occur late in life.

It is also the case that individuals in the lower socioeconomic classes suffer from more depression than those in higher classes, and the reason seems to be that individuals in the lower classes are exposed to more stressors, such as

The incidence of depression increases substantially after about age 64. The proportion of individuals who commit suicide also rises for this age group.

unemployment, divorce, lack of education, and poor health (Brown et al., 1995; Leff, 1992; Paykel & Cooper, 1992; Smith & Weissman, 1992).

In sharp contrast to the preceding findings, at present there is no reliable evidence that ethnic background per se is related to levels of depression (Weissman et al., 1991). Indeed, two researchers commented that what is most striking are the "similarities rather than the differences among racial groups in rates of major depression" (Smith & Weissman, 1992, p. 121). However, because members of ethnic minority groups may be overrepresented in the lower classes, where there are more stressors, there may be an indirect relationship between ethnicity and depression (Brown et al., 1995). The important point here is that the differences in depression are due to differences in stressors, not differences in ethnicity per se.

Now that you understand the symptoms and issues associated with depression, we can go on to consider the important question of what causes depression.

THINKING CRITICALLY
Questions about Symptoms and Issues

Should DSM include a disorder called premenstrual dysphoric disorder? There is currently an "unofficial" disorder known as **premenstrual dysphoric disorder,** which involves *depression and related symptoms that precede a woman's monthly menstruation.* (*Dysphoria* refers to a state of feeling unwell or unhappy.) Critics of the diagnosis argue that it makes "abnormal" a normal part of the female expe-

rience and that the existence of this diagnosis says, in essence, that *some women have a psychiatric disorder every month.* Obviously, that would have wide-ranging economic, professional, and political ramifications. Critics also charge that the diagnosis was introduced simply to increase the pool of patients who qualify for treatment, thereby increasing the income of mental health professionals.

In contrast, proponents of the diagnosis point out that there are some women who suffer from serious symptoms that are associated with menstruation, and establishing the diagnosis will recognize their suffering as real and give them the opportunity to obtain treatment that can be paid for by insurance. (A patient cannot be reimbursed for treatment for a disorder that is not listed in *DSM-IV.*) The proponents have even gone so far as to suggest that this diagnosis will enhance the women's movement because with proper treatment more women will be able to compete more effectively. Finally, proponents of the diagnosis point out that the fact that some women suffer from the disorder does not mean that all women do. They draw an analogy to schizophrenia: The fact that schizophrenia exists does not mean that everyone suffers from it. Because of the controversy, in *DSM-IV* the premenstrual dysphoric disorder is included in an appendix of disorders that require "further study."

At present, to be diagnosed as suffering from premenstrual dysphoric disorder, a woman must experience at least five of the following symptoms shortly before each menstruation over the course of a year, the symptoms must remit within a few days after menstruation, and the symptoms must be severe enough that they interfere with the woman's normal functioning: (1) depression, (2) anxiety, (3) sudden mood swings, (4) anger or irritability, (5) decreased interest in things such as work, school, friends, and hobbies, (6) difficulty concentrating, (7) lethargy, (8) appetite changes, (9) sleep disturbances, (10) feeling overwhelmed or out of control, and (11) physical symptoms associated with the menstrual cycle (e.g., breast tenderness, headaches, weight gain). Note that this diagnosis does *not* refer to what is generally called *premenstrual syndrome (PMS),* which many women experience; premenstrual dysphoric syndrome is a much more extreme and serious pattern of symptoms. Accurate figures are not yet available, but it is estimated that this disorder might afflict between 3% and 5% of the female population. Do you think this disorder should be included in *DSM?*

premenstrual dysphoric disorder   A disorder that has been proposed for inclusion in *DSM* and that is characterized by depression and related symptoms that precede a woman's monthly menstruation.

Explanations for Depression

Charles is a 26-year-old salesman who has been admitted to a psychiatric hospital because he is very depressed and talking about "ending it all." The mental health professionals in the hospital have differing views about what caused his depression. Some point out that Charles has been under a lot of stress on his job and argue that the stress caused his depression. Others take the position that Charles thinks he is a failure and his low self-esteem led to the depression. Finally, some argue that his depression is the result of low levels of neurotransmitters in his brain. What caused Charles's depression?

It should now be clear that depression can be a very serious and chronic disorder, so it is crucial that we understand it. In this section we will consider three popular explanations for depression: psychodynamic, cognitive, and physiological.

Psychodynamic Explanation

The key factor in the psychodynamic explanation for depression is *stress,* and in this section we will seek to answer three questions: Does stress cause depression, how does stress cause depression, and why don't all people who are exposed to stress become depressed?

Stress

There is consistent evidence that *stress can lead to depression* (Kendler et al., 1999). Indeed, the presence of a stressor such as a physical illness, a geographic move, interpersonal problems, or a natural disaster (e.g., hurricane, tornado, earthquake) is one of the best predictors of depression (Brown et al., 1995; Mazure, 1998; Sattler et al., 1995; Schafer, Wickrama, & Keith, 1998; Williamson et al., 1998; Zipfel et al., 1998). For example, in one investigation it was found that almost 30% of the individuals who experienced a catastrophic financial loss when a bank failed developed severe depression, whereas only 2% of individuals who did not experience that loss developed depression (Ganzini, McFarland, & Cutler, 1990). Similarly, the rate of depression among older people whose spouses have died is almost ten times higher than the rate among those whose spouses have not died (Turvey et al., 1999).

The effects of chronic stress were documented in individuals who lived near a nuclear power plant at which an accident occurred and deadly radiation was almost released. Living near the power plant after the accident was a source of constant stress because there was always the possibility of another accident. To test the effects of the

stress, researchers compared people who lived near the power plant where the accident occurred to people who lived near an undamaged nuclear plant, people who lived near an undamaged coal-fired plant, and people who did not live anywhere near an energy plant (Baum, Gatchel, & Schaeffer, 1983; Baum & Fleming, 1993). These comparisons revealed two interesting findings: First, the individuals living near the damaged plant reported higher levels of depression than the others. Second, when given a series of problems on which to work, those who lived near the damaged plant made fewer attempts to solve the problems and did not perform as well as the others. In other words, the chronic stress of living under the threat of deadly radiation resulted in depression and depression-related problems such as low motivation and impaired thinking. These results are presented in Figure 8.3.

The Link between Stress and Depression

Stress can cause depression, but how does it do it? To answer this question I must jump ahead a bit and point out that low levels of certain neurotransmitters in the brain can cause depression (those neurotransmitters are *serotonin* and *norepinephrine;* see the section on physiological explanations in Topic II). That fact is relevant for understanding the link between stress and depression because *prolonged stress can lower the levels of the neurotransmitters that are related to mood.* In other words, the chain of events is:

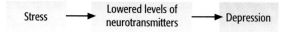

Evidence for the link between stress and lowered levels of neurotransmitters comes from research in which ani-

The emotional stress that surrounds the loss of a spouse or parent can increase an individual's risk for developing depression.

FIGURE 8.3

Individuals living near a damaged nuclear power plant (a) were more depressed and (b) made fewer attempts to solve problems than did other people.

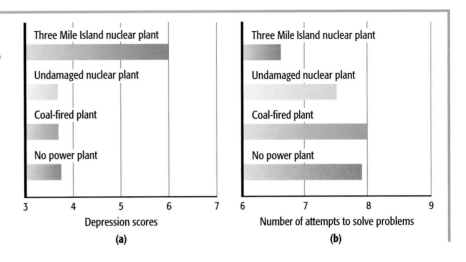

Source: Data from Baum et al. (1983), pp. 568–569, Tables 2 and 3.

mals were or were not exposed to stressors, and then the levels of the neurotransmitters in their brains were assessed (E. A. Stone, 1975). The stressors used included electric shocks, heat, noise, conflict, social separation, fighting, and observing other animals fighting. In almost every case exposure to the stressor led to reduced levels of neurotransmitters, sometimes by as much as 40% or 50%. The exact process by which stress reduces neurotransmitter levels is not yet understood, but it may be that the high level of neurological activity associated with stress somehow "uses up" the neurotransmitters.

In a particularly interesting study that is relevant for understanding depression in humans, investigators studied the changes in a mood-related neurotransmitter (serotonin) in monkeys that were moved from one social group to another (Raleigh et al., 1984). In the first group the monkeys were leaders and enjoyed high social status, but in the new group the monkeys were isolated at the bottom of the social hierarchy. When the monkeys' status dropped and they were isolated, their neurotransmitter levels dropped, and they appeared to be depressed. There is a striking parallel between what happened in this experiment and what happens when individuals go away to school, move to a new location, are forced to take job demotions, or are forced into retirement. The next time you are under stress and you become depressed, it may be because the stress lowered your levels of mood-related neurotransmitters.

Factors That Reduce the Stress–Depression Relationship

Stress can trigger depression, but not everyone who is exposed to stress becomes depressed. Therefore, we must ask, what factors protect individuals from the effects of stress?

Social Support. One factor that can block the stress-depression connection is the amount of *social support* an individual has available when facing stress. Specifically, individuals who have a close friend are less likely to become depressed when under stress (e.g., Mathiesen, Tambs, & Dalgard, 1999; Monroe et al., 1983; Stevenson, Maton, & Teti, 1999; Winterowd, Street, & Boswell, 1998). For example, in one study college students reported on the number of "close friends" they had, and later their levels of depression were measured after the stress of final examinations (Monroe et al., 1983). The results revealed that students who had the most close friends were the least likely to become depressed. Apparently, the presence of friends helped the students through the stress of finals.

However, it is not simply the *number* of friends but rather the *quality* of the relationships that is important (Billings, Cronkite, & Moos, 1983). One friend with whom you can be really close is more important than several superficial relationships. Furthermore, having a close friend does not necessarily mean that you will get social support from that individual. Indeed, in one study it was found that friends sometimes simply echoed what the depressed individual was saying (i.e., agreed with their negative views) and in so doing actually strengthened the depression in the other person (Belsher & Costello, 1991).

We know that individuals who have social support are less likely to be depressed, but we do not yet understand the process by which social support offers protection from depression. One possibility is that stressful events are simply less stressful when the burden can be shared with others. In that regard it is interesting to note that when people are waiting for a stressful event (a painful electric shock), most prefer to wait with others (Schachter, 1964). In other words, misery likes company—or more likely, company reduces misery.

Individual Differences. There are also some individual difference factors that can reduce the stress–depression relationship. One of those factors is the type of *coping strategy* individuals use to deal with stressors (Billings & Moos, 1981; Billings et al., 1983; Coyne & Whiffen, 1995; Coyne, Aldwin, & Lazarus, 1981; Folkman & Lazarus, 1980; Pearlin & Schooler, 1978). In general, depressed individuals are likely to use *passive* strategies such as avoidance, acceptance, wishful thinking, eating, and smoking, whereas nondepressed individuals are likely to use *active* strategies that are focused on overcoming the problem. Unfortunately, it is not clear whether the use of passive strategies is a cause or an effect of depression; that is, using passive strategies could lead to depression, or depressed persons might use passive strategies. However, regardless of what caused what, passive strategies serve to maintain depression because they are often ineffective for solving problems and reducing stress.

Another important individual difference factor is **aerobic** (a-RO-bik) **fitness.** Aerobic fitness refers to the effectiveness with which an individual can process oxygen, and it is improved by exercises such as jogging, swimming, and cycling, in which the heart rate is elevated for prolonged periods of time. There is a substantial amount of evidence that individuals who are in better aerobic condition show smaller physiological responses to stress (e.g., smaller increases in heart rate), and the lessened responses to stress may serve to reduce the possibility of depression (Holmes & McGilley, 1987; Holmes & Roth, 1985; McGilley & Holmes, 1988; Sinyor et al., 1983). In one investigation we identified a group of students who were experiencing a high degree of life stress (e.g., divorce of parents, geographic moves, broken relationships) that might be expected to lead to depression (Roth & Holmes, 1987). We then gave the students either 10 weeks of aerobic training, 10 weeks of relaxation training, or no treatment. When the students were later tested for fitness and depression, we found that those who received the aerobic training showed higher levels of fitness and lower levels of depression than students in the other conditions (see also Roth & Holmes, 1985). Apparently, improvements in aerobic fitness helped to protect these students from the effects of stress that might otherwise have caused depression.

Yet another individual difference factor is the *prestress level of mood-related neurotransmitters.* Earlier I pointed out that stress can lower the levels of mood-related neurotransmitters, and lowering these neurotransmitters can

Individuals who are in better aerobic condition show lowered physiological responses to stress.

lead to depression. However, if an individual begins with a high level of these neurotransmitters, stress is less likely to lower the level to the point at which depression sets in. In contrast, individuals who begin with a low level are at greater risk for stress-related depression because it takes less stress to reduce their neurotransmitters below the critical level. In other words, high prestress levels of neurotransmitters offer protection from stress, whereas low prestress levels create a predisposition to stress-related depression (Monroe & Simons, 1991).

It's clear that stress can lead to depression, but before drawing any overall conclusions concerning the cause of depression, we must consider two other explanations. Next we will examine the cognitive explanations.

 **Cognitive Explanations**

Cognitive explanations suggest that people become depressed because they *have negative (depressing) beliefs* or because they *feel helpless* in controlling the stressful events in their lives.

Incorrect Negative Beliefs and Depression

What do depressed individuals think about themselves and the world around them? That's easy to answer: They think they are worthless, no one likes them, the world is a rotten place, and things are not going to get any better (Hamilton & Abramson, 1983). Negative beliefs like these are often thought to be *symptoms* of depression, but cognitive theorists turn this around and argue that *negative beliefs are the cause of depression* (Beck, 1967, 1976).

aerobic fitness The effectiveness with which an individual can process oxygen, which is improved by exercise in which the heart rate is elevated for prolonged periods of time; it can be an antidote for depression because it reduces the response to stress.

Problems with Information Processing. It seems reasonable to conclude that incorrect negative beliefs lead to depression, but why do some individuals develop those incorrect beliefs, while others do not? The answer offered by cognitive theorists is that (1) some individuals have negative early experiences, such as failures or rejections, (2) those experiences lead the individuals to develop networks of negative memories, and (3) these networks then cause the individuals to *selectively attend to negative information* and *selectively recall negative experiences*. This selective attention and selective recall then result in the individuals having distorted information with which to form beliefs, so they develop incorrect negative beliefs that lead to depression.

Do depressed individuals selectively attend to negative information? Yes (Gotlib & Krasnoperova, 1998). Consider this finding: When depressed and nondepressed individuals were shown "happy" and "sad" faces, the depressed individuals looked more at the sad parts of faces than did the nondepressed individuals, suggesting that the depressed individuals focused more on the negative aspects of life (Matthews & Antes, 1992). In a related study in which depressed and nondepressed individuals were asked to rate the happiness of persons whose pictures they were shown, the depressed individuals were more likely to rate the pictured individuals as depressed, again suggesting that depressed individuals tend to see the world negatively (George et al., 1998; see other findings concerning selective attention in Chapter 3).

Are depressed individuals also more likely than nondepressed individuals to recall negative events? Again the answer is yes (Murray, Whitehouse, & Alloy, 1999). For example, depressed persons are more likely than nondepressed persons to recall things such as failures, being left out of peer groups, or being criticized by teachers or employers (Blaney, 1986; Bower, 1981, 1987; Gotlib & Krasnoperova, 1998; Johnson & Magaro, 1987; Matt et al., 1992). However, it could be that depressed individuals actually have more negative experiences than other people and therefore have more negative things to remember. To get around this possibility, experiments were conducted in which positive and negative moods were artificially induced in people and then their recall was assessed. The results consistently indicated that whether people recall positive or negative things is a function of their current mood. Figure 8.4 summarizes the findings of many studies of selective recall; as you can see, whether people recall negative or positive things is related to their mood, regardless of whether the mood occurred naturally or was induced.

Negative Beliefs as a Cause of Depression. It is apparent that depressed individuals are more likely to think about negative things and have more negative beliefs than nondepressed individuals. However, the crucial question remains, *does focusing on the negative aspects of life and having nega-*

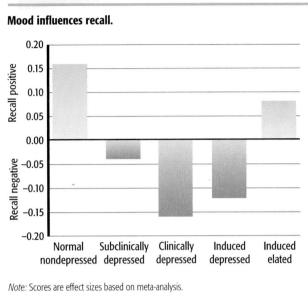

FIGURE 8.4

Mood influences recall.

Note: Scores are effect sizes based on meta-analysis.

Source: Matt et al. (1992), p. 248, Figure 1.

tive beliefs cause depression? Three approaches have been used to answer this question:

1. *Reading negative material to cause depression.* In the first approach nondepressed individuals read either negative or positive statements, and then their levels of depression and related behaviors were measured. The negative statements were similar to the following: "I'm discouraged and unhappy about myself," "I feel worn out," and "My health might not be as good as it's supposed to be." The results revealed that individuals who read negative statements reported higher levels of depression and showed more depression-related behaviors, such as wanting to be alone, poorer performance on an intelligence test, and slower talking and writing (Blaney, 1986; Bower, 1981; Goodwin & Williams, 1982). These findings would seem to support the cognitive explanation, except for the following: The depressions were not particularly deep, they did not last more than a few minutes, and they could be completely eliminated by a simple distraction such as working briefly on another task (Frost & Green, 1982; Isen & Gorgoglione, 1983). In other words, thinking negative thoughts resulted in feelings that were like the sadness we feel while watching a "depressing" movie, but the thoughts did not result in "clinical" depression of the kind we are discussing here. In view of this, let's consider the second approach to the problem.

2. *Measuring negative beliefs before depression occurs.* In the second approach investigators measured the levels of negative beliefs held by nondepressed individuals and then did followup examinations to determine whether individuals with high levels of negative beliefs were more likely to become depressed than those with low levels of negative beliefs. This approach provided a crucial test of the theory. However, in virtually every investigation the results indicated that individuals with high levels of negative beliefs were no more likely to become depressed than those with low levels (see reviews by Alloy et al., 1999; Barnett & Gotlib, 1988; Persons & Miranda, 1992; Segal & Ingram, 1994). The consistent failure to show that negative beliefs cause depression led some of the strongest supporters of the cognitive explanation to question whether negative beliefs result in depression.

3. *Activating latent negative beliefs in depression-prone individuals.* The finding that people who report high levels of negative beliefs are not at increased risk for depression posed a serious threat to the cognitive theory. In an attempt to solve this problem, some theorists proposed that individuals who are prone to depression have "latent" negative beliefs of which they are not aware (that's why they don't report them before they become depressed), but these negative beliefs can be activated by a sad mood or a negative experience, and then the activated beliefs lead to depression (Beck et al., 1979; Persons & Miranda, 1992). This is an interesting explanation because it gets around the finding that people who suffer from depression do not report negative beliefs before they become depressed but do report them after they become depressed. If such latent beliefs exist, they should occur primarily in individuals who are prone to depression because it is the existence of the beliefs that leads to depression.

In a crucial test of this latent beliefs explanation, investigators measured negative beliefs in two groups of individuals before and after a sad mood was induced by having them watch a sad movie (Brosse, Craighead, & Craighead, 1999). One group had a history of depression, so it was expected that they had latent negative beliefs; the other group did not have a history of depression, so it was assumed that they did not have latent negative beliefs. Contrary to the prediction that the sad movie would trigger negative beliefs in only the depression-prone individuals, *both* groups reported increases in negative beliefs after the sad movie. This was a blow to the theory but was exactly what would be expected based on what we know about the activation of memory; that is, we all undoubtedly have a network that includes some negative memories and beliefs, and a sad mood can activate this network (see Chapter 3).

In summary, despite a substantial amount of research, at the present time there is no reliable evidence that negative beliefs cause depression. However, this does not necessarily mean that negative beliefs do not contribute to depression, and in the next two sections, we will examine ways in which this can happen.

Negative Beliefs as a Predisposing Factor in Depression. Although negative beliefs do not cause depression by themselves, it may be that they *predispose individuals to become depressed when the individuals are exposed to stress.* In other words, depression may result when stress is added to negative beliefs. To test this possibility, a number of investigators collected data on negative beliefs, life stress, and symptoms of depression (Kwon & Oel, 1992; Olinger, Kuiper, & Shaw, 1987; Robins & Block, 1989; Segal et al., 1992). Their results revealed that *some* depressed individuals had experienced stressful life events, but *most* depressed individuals reported *both* negative beliefs *and* stressful life events. It appears that if individuals view themselves as ineffective and worthless and the world as bad, these beliefs may heighten the stress and thereby result in depression.

The predisposing effect of negative beliefs was nicely demonstrated in a study of college students who failed an examination (Metalsky et al., 1993). First the students were tested to determine the degree to which they had negative views of themselves, then they were given their grades on the examination, and finally their levels of depression were assessed every day for 5 days after they received their grades. The results indicated that there was a general increase in depression immediately after the students received their failing grades, but only the students who had negative views of themselves were still depressed 5 days later; those who had more positive views "bounced back" from the initial depression. These findings are illustrated in Figure 8.5.

Negative Beliefs as a Prolonging Factor in Depression. It is also possible that negative beliefs may help *prolong depression after it sets in.* If individuals believe that they are no good and the future is bleak, they may be less likely to work actively to overcome the stressors that triggered their depression (Eaves & Rehm, 1984). This possibility is supported by the results of a study in which it was found that depressed individuals who had more negative beliefs were *less likely to improve* than those who had fewer negative beliefs (Lewinsohn et al., 1981).

To sum up, it is clear that (1) depressed individuals have more negative beliefs than nondepressed individuals; (2) depressed individuals are more likely than nondepressed individuals to focus on and recall negative things; (3) there is no consistent evidence that negative beliefs per se cause clinical levels of depression; (4) negative beliefs can predispose individuals to depression when the individuals are exposed to stress, and (5) negative beliefs may prolong depression.

Learned Helplessness and Depression

The second major cognitive explanation for depression is that *individuals learn that they cannot control future nega-*

FIGURE 8.5

After failing an examination, students who had negative views of themselves remained depressed, whereas students with more positive views "bounced back."

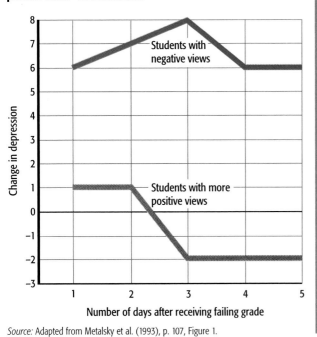

Source: Adapted from Metalsky et al. (1993), p. 107, Figure 1.

tive events, so they feel helpless, and the feelings of helplessness lead to depression. This is referred to as the **learned helplessness explanation** (Abramson, Seligman, & Teasdale, 1978; Miller & Norman, 1979; Peterson & Seligman, 1984; Roth, 1979; Seligman, 1975). The major difference between the negative beliefs explanation and the learned helplessness explanation is that individuals with negative beliefs believe that they are *responsible* for the negative things that happen in their lives ("I'm no good"), whereas individuals who have learned helplessness believe that they are *helpless* in controlling the negative things ("Everything is falling in on me, and there's nothing I can do"). The difference, then, is one of self-blame (negative beliefs) versus lack of control (learned helplessness).

Early Laboratory Research. The learned helplessness explanation was discovered accidentally in a series of experiments with dogs (see Maier & Seligman, 1976). In one of those experiments the dogs were exposed to one of three conditions. In one condition the dogs were placed in a cage and given a series of *inescapable* (uncontrollable) shocks. When the shocks first occurred, the dogs jumped, barked, scratched, and generally thrashed around, but their responses were ineffective, and the dogs simply had to

endure the shocks. In a second condition the dogs were placed in a cage and given a series of *escapable* (controllable) shocks. Specifically, the dogs could escape the shocks by jumping over a small barrier and going to the other side of the cage. These dogs quickly learned to escape the shocks. In the third condition the dogs were placed in the cage but were never shocked, so they had no reason to learn an escape response.

Twenty-four hours later all of the dogs were returned to the cage and given shocks that they could escape if they jumped over a low barrier. The results indicated that on the first trial the dogs that had learned to escape the shocks on the previous day jumped over the barrier very quickly to avoid the shocks. This was expected. The dogs that had not been shocked before required a little more time to jump over the barrier because they had not had any experience with it before, but by the third or fourth trial they were also quickly avoiding the shocks. This was also expected. However, the unexpected finding was that the dogs that received the inescapable shocks on the previous day made little attempt to avoid the shocks (they did not jump the barrier) and eventually simply lied down and endured them. Apparently, because of their previous experience in which they had been unable to do anything about the shocks, these dogs simply gave up in the new situation. The investigators pointed out the similarities between the responses of the dogs and the responses of depressed humans and suggested that the experience with inescapable stress (learned helplessness) caused depression in the dogs. The responses of the three groups of dogs are presented in Figure 8.6 (on p. 226).

After learned helplessness was discovered in animals, similar experiments were conducted with humans. For example, in one experiment students were exposed to a loud noise that they either could or could not avoid by pushing a button; later they were exposed to a loud noise that they could avoid by moving a lever. In that new situation the students who had earlier learned that they were helpless to control the noise were less likely to use the lever to terminate the noise (Hiroto, 1974). The fact that those students made fewer attempts to avoid the loud noise was interpreted as evidence for depression, and it was concluded that learned helplessness led to depression in humans (Hiroto & Seligman, 1975).

Helplessness and Stress. Learned helplessness quickly became a popular explanation for depression, but there is a

> **learned helplessness explanation**   A cognitive explanation for depression that holds that learning that one is helpless to control negative events in life will lead to depression, probably because feelings of helplessness lead to more stress.

FIGURE 8.6

Dogs exposed to inescapable shocks did not jump the barrier to avoid shocks in a new situation.

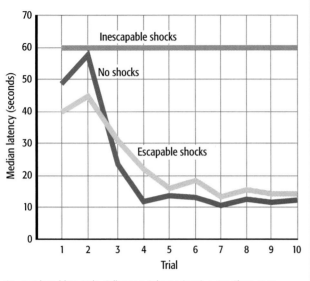

Source: Adapted from Maier, Seligman, & Solomon (1969), p. 328, Figure 10-13.

problem with the explanation: Individuals who are helpless in controlling (escaping from) stressors must endure more stress than individuals who can control stressors, so it is probably not helplessness per se that causes depression, but instead *it is the increased stress that occurs because of the helplessness.* For instance, the dogs in the original experiment that were in the uncontrollable shock condition experienced many more painful shocks than the dogs in the controllable shock condition, and it was probably the high level of resulting stress that led to their depression. In other words, the learned helplessness effect is really due to *increased stress.*

Support for the notion that stress is the crucial factor in learned helplessness comes from research in which it was found that animals in helpless situations showed physiological changes in their brains that were *stress-related* and

serotonin   A neurotransmitter whose low levels have been linked to depression.

norepinephrine   A neurotransmitter whose low levels have been linked to depression.

metabolites   Substances that result when neurotransmitters are broken down in the brain; levels of metabolites can be used as indirect measures of levels of neurotransmitters.

tryptophan   An amino acid found in proteins, particularly in dairy products and turkey, which is converted into serotonin in the body; low levels of tryptophan can trigger depression in some individuals.

known to cause depression (Anisman, 1978; Glazer & Weiss, 1976; Weiss, Glazer, & Pohoresky, 1976; see the later discussion of brain chemistry and depression). Furthermore, drugs that correct those changes in the brain eliminated the effects of the helplessness (Nankai et al., 1995; Semba et al., 1998; Sherman, Sacquitne, & Petty, 1982).

Overall, then, it appears that learning to feel helpless can lead to depression, but the learned helplessness is not the direct cause of the depression; the helplessness simply leads to more stress, and we already know that stress can cause depression (see the earlier discussion). We can now go on to the last set of explanations for depression—the physiological explanations.

Physiological Explanations

The physiological explanations suggest that *depression is caused by problems in the areas of the brain that are responsible for mood.* More specifically, it is believed that problems with neurotransmitters, low levels of brain activity, and structural problems in the brain disrupt brain functioning and lead to depression. Let's consider these possibilities.

Low Levels of Neurotransmitters

The first physiological factor in depression is *low levels of neurotransmitters in the areas of the brain that are responsible for positive mood.* The notion is that if those levels are too low, the areas of the brain responsible for positive mood will be underactive, which will lead to depression (Delgado et al., 1992; George et al., 1995). The two neurotransmitters that are implicated in depression are **serotonin** (seh-ruh-TOW-nin) and **norepinephrine** (nor-ep-i-NEF-rin). What's the evidence?

Evidence Based on Metabolites. One way to determine whether levels of neurotransmitters are linked to depression is to compare the levels in individuals before, during, and after depression to see whether changes in the levels precede changes in mood. Unfortunately, neurotransmitters cannot be measured in live brains, so instead investigators compare levels of **metabolites** (ma-TA-bow-lyts), which are *substances that result when neurotransmitters are broken down naturally in the brain.* After metabolites are passed out of the brain, they can be found in urine and cerebral spinal fluid. By measuring metabolite levels in these fluids, we can indirectly measure levels of neurotransmitters.

The relationship between the level of the metabolite of norepinephrine (MHPG) and mood is illustrated in Figure 8.7. In that figure daily levels of the metabolite are plotted for one patient, along with an indication of whether that patient's mood was depressed, normal, or manic. As you

A patient showed lower levels of the metabolite of norepinephrine (MHPG) just before and during depression and higher levels just before and during mania.

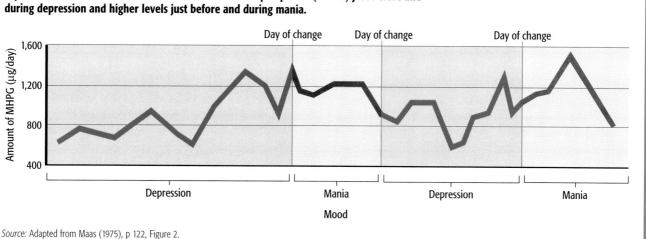

Source: Adapted from Maas (1975), p 122, Figure 2.

can see in the figure, metabolite levels were generally lower during depression than during mania (Agren, 1982; Beckman & Goodwin, 1980; Bond, Jenner, & Sampson, 1972; De Leon-Jones et al., 1975; Jones et al., 1973; Maas, 1975; Maas, Fawcett, & DeKirmenjian, 1972; Muscettola et al., 1984; Schildkraut et al., 1973; Schildkraut et al., 1978). Furthermore, it's important to note that metabolite levels started to rise a few days *before* the patient's mood changed from depression to mania and started to fall *before* the patient's mood changed from mania to depression. This is relevant because it suggests that the change in neurotransmitter level caused the mood change, rather than vice versa. What we see in these findings, then, is that naturally occurring changes in neurotransmitter levels are linked to changes in mood.

Evidence Based on Lowering Levels of Neurotransmitters. A more powerful way to test the relationship between neurotransmitter levels and depression is to experimentally lower the neurotransmitter levels in nondepressed individuals and then determine whether the individuals become depressed. In one such experiment depression was measured before and after individuals were given either a placebo or a drug that lowered serotonin and norepinephrine levels (Berman et al., 1999). The results were clear: Individuals who took the drug that lowered the neurotransmitter levels showed a dramatic increase in depression, whereas those who took the placebo showed a much smaller increase in depression. These findings are illustrated in Figure 8.8.

A second approach to studying the role of neurotransmitters in depression revolves around diet. If depression is due to low levels of neurotransmitters, and if neurotransmitters are influenced by diet, then diet should influence

depression. Although there is no consistent evidence that normal variations in diet influence clinical levels of depression, there is evidence that extreme changes in the intake of foods containing **tryptophan** (TRIP-tuh-fan) can influence mood in some individuals (Finn et al., 1998; Markus et al., 1998; Price et al., 1998). Tryptophan is an amino acid found in proteins, and there are particularly high levels of it in dairy products and turkey. Tryptophan is relevant for depression because it is converted into serotonin in the body. It follows, then, that if individuals eat a diet low in

Individuals who took a drug that reduced levels of serotonin and norepinephrine showed greater increases in depression than did individuals who took a placebo.

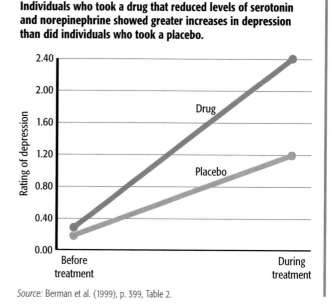

Source: Berman et al. (1999), p. 399, Table 2.

tryptophan, levels of serotonin will drop and depression may result.

In one test of the tryptophan–depression relationship, individuals who either did or did not have a family history of depression were put on a 1-day diet that had either low or normal levels of tryptophan, and their moods were monitored (Benkelfat et al., 1994). The results indicated that within the first 5 hours 30% of the individuals who had a family history of depression and who were on the low-tryptophan diet entered a mild depression, whereas none of the individuals who were on a normal tryptophan diet became depressed. The fact that the effect of a low tryptophan level was limited to individuals who had a family history of depression suggests that those individuals already had genetically determined low levels of serotonin. Thus, it was more likely that the low-tryptophan diet would reduce those levels to the point at which depression would be triggered. In another experiment it was found that individuals who were already depressed became more depressed when they were given a low-tryptophan diet (Delgado et al., 1994). Overall, then, it is apparent that lowering serotonin and norepinephrine can bring on depression.

Neurotransmitters and the Symptoms Associated with Depression. Earlier, when I discussed the symptoms of depression, I pointed out that depressed individuals also experience problems with sleep, appetite, and sex. Interestingly, the physiological explanation can account for why these symptoms occur with depression. Specifically, low levels of neurotransmitters are thought to influence the functioning of the **hypothalamus** (hy-poh-THAL-uh-muhs), which is a structure in the midbrain that is responsible for four things: mood, sleep, appetite, and sexual arousal. If the functioning of the hypothalamus is disrupted because of low levels of neurotransmitters, all of those behaviors will be influenced. It has also been found that reducing serotonin levels results in impaired memory (Riedel et al., 1999). Overall, then, problems with neurotransmitters account for depression and its related symptoms, thus increasing the credibility of this explanation.

All of these findings support the notion that depression results from low levels of neurotransmitters, but there is a problem with this explanation: The drugs used to treat depression increase levels of neurotransmitters within a couple of *hours,* but the depression does not lift for *weeks*

(see the later discussion of treatments). Clearly, levels of neurotransmitters provide a link in the chain that leads to depression, but there must be another link as well. In other words, low levels of neurotransmitters must influence some other factor that then triggers the depression, but we do not yet know what that other factor is.

Low Levels of Brain Activity

In the preceding section I suggested that low levels of neurotransmitters lead to depression because they reduce the activity of the hypothalamus. However, investigators have recently discovered that a number of other areas in the brain are also underactive in individuals who suffer from depression. For example, by measuring electrical activity, metabolism, and blood flow, investigators discovered that the **left prefrontal cortex** is underactive in depressed persons (Elliott et al., 1998; Gotlib, Ranganath, & Rosenfeld, 1998; see reviews by Soares & Mann, 1997a, 1997b; Tomarken & Keener, 1998). Where is the left prefrontal cortex, and why is it important? The prefrontal area is the *most forward portion of the frontal lobes,* and the cortex is the *thin layer of neurons covering the lobes;* see Figure 8.9. This area is important because it has connections with many other parts of the brain and because it is where information from the other parts of the brain is brought together and integrated. In other words, the prefrontal cortex is where you do much of your thinking and where you decide what to do and feel (George et al., 1994, 1996; Teasdale et al., 1999;

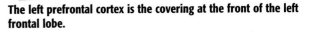

FIGURE 8.9

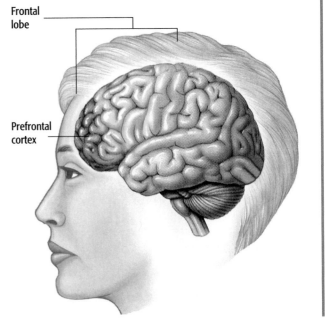

The left prefrontal cortex is the covering at the front of the left frontal lobe.

Frontal lobe

Prefrontal cortex

---

hypothalamus   A structure in the midbrain that is responsible for mood, sleep, appetite, and sexual arousal; problems here cause depression and related symptoms (changes in sleep, appetite, and sexual drive).

left prefrontal cortex   The thin layer of neurons (cortex) covering the most forward portion of the left frontal lobe; damage here is related to depression.

Weinberger, 1993). The *left* prefrontal cortex is particularly important because analytical thinking is done primarily in the left hemisphere of the brain.

Overall, then, low activity in the left prefrontal cortex could lead to the impaired thought processes and problems with memory that occur in depression. In fact, when depressed and nondepressed persons work on complex intellectual tasks, the depressed persons show less activity in the prefrontal cortex (Elliott et al., 1997). The low activity could also lead to depression because emotional material is not being effectively integrated with other material.

Another part of the brain that is underactive in depressed persons is the **cingulate** (sometimes called the *cingulate gyrus;* SIN-gu-let JI-res). The cingulate is a band of nerve tracts that encircles a number of structures in the midbrain and then leads to the frontal lobes. This band of nerve tracts carries information back and forth between the midbrain and the prefrontal cortex. To use an analogy to a highway, think of the cingulate as a "beltway" around a city (the midbrain), which picks up traffic from that city and carries it to and from another location (the prefrontal cortex). The connection between the midbrain and the prefrontal cortex is important because some structures in the midbrain are responsible for emotion, and information from them must be integrated in the prefrontal cortex. The low level of activity in the cingulate indicates that there is a reduced flow of information between the prefrontal cortex and other areas of the brain, which in turn suggests that mood is not being effectively integrated with other information.

Finally, it is noteworthy that some of the structures in the midbrain are also underactive in depression. For example, a structure known as the **basal ganglia** (BAY-suhl GANG-glee-uh) is underactive. That is relevant because the basal ganglia plays a role in motor activity; so underactivity there explains why many depressed individuals show psychomotor retardation (Goffinet et al., 1997; Sobin & Sackeim, 1997). Indeed, individuals with psychomotor retardation are more likely to show low levels of activity in the basal ganglia than other persons. Again, then, physiology can be used to explain depression and its related symptoms.

Structural Problems in the Brain

Consider this finding: People who have strokes are likely to suffer from depression. That's not surprising because a stroke is a serious problem and a reason for depression. However, it turns out depression is more likely to occur in individuals whose strokes occurred in the *left* prefrontal cortex than in individuals who suffered a stroke in the right prefrontal cortex (Morris et al., 1996; Paradiso & Robinson, 1998; Singh, Herrmann, & Black, 1998). Why? The answer appears to be that the strokes damage the left prefrontal cortex and the damage there leads to depression. Let's consider the evidence for the role of the left prefrontal cortex in depression.

Evidence linking structural problems in the left prefrontal cortex to depression comes from MRI (magnetic resonance imaging) scans of the brains of individuals who are and are not depressed. Specifically, there is an area in the left prefrontal cortex that is about 45% *smaller* in depressed individuals than it is in nondepressed individuals (Damasio, 1997; Drevets et al., 1997). This area is about the size of a thimble, and it is located about $2\frac{1}{2}$ inches behind the bridge of the nose on the left side. It is also interesting to note that in addition to being smaller, this area is about 8% less active in depressed individuals than it is in nondepressed individuals. The finding that this area is smaller and less active in depressed individuals is consistent with other findings that damage to the left prefrontal cortex can disrupt emotional reactions (Bechara et al., 1997; Damasio, 1994, 1995). Structural problems in the brain can also be used to account for the slowed thinking and difficulty with problem-solving that are sometimes associated with depression. Indeed, it is the depressed individuals who have structural problems in the brain who are most likely to show cognitive impairments (Soares & Mann, 1997).

In summary, then, there is solid evidence that depression is associated with (1) low levels of specific neurotransmitters, (2) low levels of activity in the left prefrontal cortex, the cingulate, and structures in the midbrain, and (3) structural problems in the left prefrontal cortex. These findings fit together and appear to account for the depression and the related symptoms. That is, low levels of neurotransmitters and structural problems can lead to low activity in the brain, and the areas of the brain that are affected are those associated with the regulation of mood. Furthermore, reduced brain activity can also be used to explain the symptoms that are often associated with depression, such as slowed thought processes, impaired reasoning, and psychomotor retardation.

Genetic and Prenatal Factors

If depression stems from low levels of neurotransmitters and structural problems in the brain, the next question is, what causes those problems? There are two possible answers: genetics and illness of the mother during pregnancy that can influence brain development in the fetus. Let's consider the evidence.

Genetics and Depression. One of the best predictors of depression is a family history of depression. Indeed, individuals who have biological relatives who suffer from de-

---

cingulate   A band of nerve tracts that carries information between the midbrain and the prefrontal cortex.

basal ganglia   A structure in the midbrain that is responsible for motor activity, so low levels of activity here are related to psychomotor retardation.

pression are more than twice as likely as other individuals to suffer from depression (Nurnberger & Gershon, 1992). Even stronger evidence for the role of genetics comes from studies of twins in which it is consistently found that both twins of identical (monozygotic) pairs are more likely to suffer from depression than are both twins of nonidentical (dizygotic) pairs. Indeed, in one study 70% of the identical twins shared depression, whereas only 30% of the nonidentical twins did so (Kendler, McGuire, et al., 1993b). It is also the case that twins have levels of depression similar to the levels of their parents (Kendler, Walters, et al., 1994).

The most convincing evidence of a genetic basis for depression comes from studies of individuals who either did or did not have depressed biological parents and who were raised by nondepressed adoptive parents. In one study of this type almost 40% of the adopted biological offspring of depressed parents were later found to be depressed, whereas only 0.07% of the adopted biological offspring of nondepressed parents were found to be depressed (Cadoret, 1978a). The overall heritability of depression appears to be between 33% and 45% (Kendler, Neale, et al., 1992b).

Finally, an interesting experiment with monkeys provides evidence concerning the mechanism by which genetic factors lead to depression. In that experiment investigators examined the levels of serotonin and norepinephrine in (1) biological monkey parents, (2) "adoptive" monkey parents, and (3) offspring raised by biological or adoptive monkey parents (Higley et al., 1993). The results revealed that the levels of serotonin and norepinephrine in the biological parents were related to the levels of those neurotransmitters in their offspring, regardless of whether the offspring were raised by the biological or adoptive parents. In other words, genetic factors influenced levels of serotonin and norepinephrine. That finding is important because, as you learned earlier, depression is related to levels of serotonin and norepinephrine in the brain.

Genetics and Stress. Genes can lead to depression because they influence neurotransmitter levels and brain structures, but there is another mechanism by which genes can contribute to depression: *Genes can lead to stressful life events that in turn lead to depression* (Kendler et al., 1999). The fact that genes can lead to stressful life events may seem surprising, so let me explain how this works.

It is often assumed that stressful life events are random and due to chance; that is, stressful life events are due to "bad luck." However, have you ever noticed that some people have more bad things happen to them or are involved in more personal crises than others? In fact, there is now evidence that some individuals are more likely than others to have automobile accidents, suffer industrial injuries, experience financial crises, and be victims of criminal attacks (Kendler, Neale, et al., 1993c). The fact that stressful events are not random suggests that there is an underlying explanation for their occurrence, and part of the explanation is genes. No, you do not inherit stressful life events per se; rather, you inherit levels of various neurotransmitters that influence your personality, and then your personality influences the stress in your life. For example, a low level of serotonin, which can be determined in part by genetics, is related to impulsivity, and impulsivity can easily lead an individual to make foolish decisions that result in stressful life events (see Chapters 9 and 12).

Evidence for the role of genetic factors in stressful life events comes from studies of twins. For instance, in one study it was found that identical twins had a higher rate of shared stressful life events than nonidentical twins (Plomin, Lichtenstein, et al., 1990). Furthermore, the effect was the same regardless of whether the pairs of twins were raised together or apart, thus indicating that a common family environment did not account for the effect. It was also found that identical twins were more likely to share stressful events in which the individual was *directly involved,* such as illnesses, injuries, criminal assaults, and interpersonal conflicts, than to share stressful events that caused stress for the individual but that occurred to other people, such as deaths, illnesses, and injuries of someone else (Kendler, Neale, et al., 1993c).

Clearly, many of the stressful events in which individuals are directly involved are not random events or bad luck; they are due to behaviors that are influenced by genetic factors. The link between genes and stressful life events increases the role that genetic factors play in the development of depression. The two pathways by which genes can lead to depression are illustrated in Figure 8.10. Note, how-

Psychologists have found that genetic factors can play a role in stressful life events. One particular study found that identical twins had a higher rate of shared stressful life events than did nonidentical twins.

FIGURE 8.10

Two pathways between genetics and depression

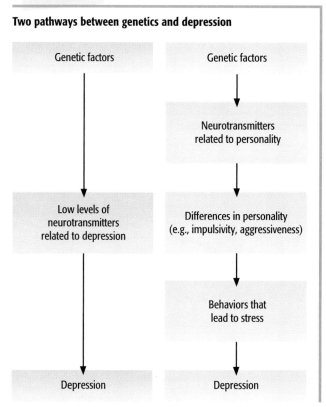

---

ever, that I do not mean to imply that stress and depression are always due to genetic factors; those factors are important, but environmental factors must also be considered (see the earlier discussion).

Prenatal Illness. Here is an interesting finding: Individuals who were born in Finland between October and November of 1957 were more likely to suffer from depression later in life than individuals born between October and November in the preceding years (Machon, Mednick, & Huttunen, 1997). Why? In 1957 there was a severe influenza epidemic 3 to 6 months before the children were born (i.e., during the second trimester of their prenatal development). There is growing evidence that when a pregnant woman is ill, her illness can disrupt brain development in the fetus, and the resulting problems in the brain can lead to psychiatric disorders (Torrey et al., 1997; see also Chapters 11, 12, and 14). It appears that the increased risk of depression in Finnish children born during those 2 months in 1957 was due to the fact that their mothers were more likely to have had the flu during the crucial second trimester than were the mothers of children born in preceding years. Overall, then, we must consider prenatal factors as well as genetic factors as causes of the physiological problems that lead to depression.

Questions about the Explanations for Depression

1. *Does stress cause depression?* Yes, there is strong evidence that stress can cause depression. Furthermore, we understand the process by which stress causes depression: It lowers the levels of mood-related neurotransmitters in the brain, and those lower levels trigger depression. Stress is a good explanation for depression, but three qualifications should be noted: The first is that stress does not lead to depression in all individuals. Some individuals appear to be protected from stress because they have a lot of social support, they use active problem-solving strategies for overcoming the problems causing the stress, they are in good aerobic condition, or they have high levels of mood-related neurotransmitters. The second qualification is that the events used to explain depression must be truly stressful. Many people who are depressed report being annoyed by many "daily hassles," such as misplacing or losing things, social obligations, and too many responsibilities, and often those hassles are cited as causes of the depression (Fry, 1989; Holahan, Holahan, & Belk, 1984; Kanner et al., 1981; Wolf, Elston, & Kissling, 1989). However, it appears that getting upset by those little things may be more a *result* of an existing depression than a *cause* of depression (Johnson & Bornstein, 1991). In other words, the same level of hassles do not bother the people when they are not depressed. Recognizing this is important when looking for the cause of depression. The third qualification is that some individuals become depressed in the absence of stress, which means that depression can be caused by factors other than stress. In general, then, stress is a good explanation but not a complete explanation for depression.

2. *Do incorrect negative beliefs cause depression?* Probably not, at least not in and of themselves. Although the notion that negative beliefs cause depression is very popular and widely researched, the preponderance of evidence simply does not support it. If the effect were as strong as many people believe it to be, evidence certainly would have appeared in the research, and, to date, it has not. However, negative beliefs do play a role in depression. Specifically, there is evidence that individuals who have negative beliefs are more likely to become depressed when they encounter stress, probably because their negative views of themselves and the world heighten the stress. Furthermore, the presence of negative beliefs can prolong depression once it sets in.

3. *If negative beliefs do not cause depression, why do depressed individuals have so many negative beliefs?* To answer this question we must go back to what we know about how mood and memory interact. We know that mood can activate mood-related memories and beliefs by activating the networks in which the mood-related material is stored.

It appears, then, that depressed individuals have negative memories and beliefs *because they are depressed.* Strong evidence for this explanation comes from experiments in which mood was changed with drugs and there was a subsequent change in memories and beliefs. For instance, when nondepressed individuals who did not have negative beliefs were given a drug that caused depression, the individuals became depressed, and *they were also suddenly flooded with negative thoughts* (Berman et al., 1999; also refer back to Figure 8.8). In contrast, when depressed individuals who already had negative beliefs were given a drug that reduced their depression, their depression went away *and so did their negative beliefs* (Simons, Garfield, & Murphy, 1984). The fact that increasing and decreasing depression can increase and decrease negative beliefs provides good evidence that mood influences beliefs, rather than the other way around.

4. *Does learned helplessness cause depression?* Simply learning that you are helpless in controlling stressful events is probably not sufficient to cause clinical depression, but individuals who are helpless in controlling (avoiding) stressful events will experience more stress, and the resulting high level of stress can cause depression. In a sense helplessness causes depression, but it is the increased stress that comes from being unable to avoid stressors that is the key factor.

5. *Do physiological factors cause depression?* Yes, low levels of neurotransmitters (serotonin and norepinephrine), low levels of activity in particular areas of the brain (left prefrontal cortex, cingulate, and some structures in the midbrain), and damage in particular areas of the brain (particularly the left prefrontal cortex) are all linked to depression. Critics once argued that these problems were the result of depression rather than its cause, but that position is no longer tenable because we now know that experimentally lowering neurotransmitter levels can bring on depression. Furthermore, procedures that result in lesions in the crucial areas of the brain can result in depression. It is also noteworthy that physiological factors can also account for the symptoms associated with depression; for example, structural problems in the brain are linked to the impaired thinking that often accompanies depression, and low levels of neurotransmitters are related to problems with appetite, sleep, and sex. Finally, low levels of neurotransmitters provide the pathway between stress and depression. That is, stress lowers the levels of the neurotransmitters, and those low levels then trigger depression.

The findings concerning physiology are persuasive, but two limitations should be recognized: First, low levels of neurotransmitters are linked to depression, but some other factor must also be involved. That is the case because although the drugs that increase the levels of neurotransmitters do so immediately, there is usually a delay of 3 weeks or more before the depression lifts. Obviously, there is a link in the chain we don't yet know about. Second, problems in various areas of the brain can cause depression, but again we do not completely understand the process that leads to depression. We can say things such as, "The areas of the brain that are underactive in depressed individuals are responsible for integrating emotional information," but this is too simplistic. Unfortunately, a detailed understanding of the physiological processes that lead to depression is a long way off because the functioning of the brain is incredibly complex.

6. *What is the best explanation for depression?* There is no one best explanation for depression; instead, as indicated in Figure 8.11, there are a number of pathways to depression.

TOPIC III
Treatments for Depression

Joan was depressed. She kept thinking, "I'm no good. I'll always fail, and I'll never be happy or successful. On top of that no one likes me—what's the use." To overcome these negative self-defeating beliefs, she and her therapist conducted several experiments to see whether she really was incompetent and disliked. For example, she went to parties where she discovered that people were interested in what she had to say and liked her. Following that she and her therapist began a program of replacing her incorrect negative beliefs with more accurate ones. Now, whenever she thinks a negative thought, she stops and asks herself whether the thought is realistic. This approach has changed her view of herself and her future. Will the changes reduce her depression?

When Andre became depressed, his physician prescribed an antidepressant drug. It took 4 weeks for the drug to reduce his depression, but after that he felt normal again. How do antidepressants work? Will Andre have to stay on the drug for the rest of his life?

Last year Fred became very depressed. Neither psychotherapy nor antidepressants helped, so he was started on a course of electroconvulsive therapy in which an electrical shock was administered to his brain three times each week. Each shock caused a brief convulsion. After six shocks, his depression lifted. Why did shocks to his brain reduce his depression? Did the shocks cause brain damage?

Depression is a serious disorder that afflicts many people and that can last for years, so it is essential for it to be treated. Fortunately, today we have a number of effective treatments, and in this section we will consider psychotherapy, cognitive therapy, and a variety of physiological treatments, including drugs, electrical shocks, magnetism, and bright light.

FIGURE 8.11

Pathways to depression

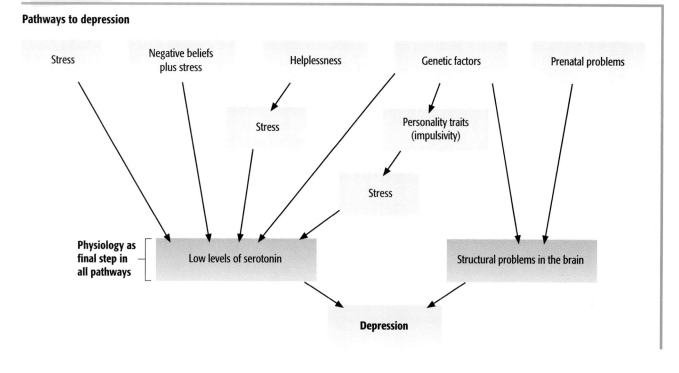

Psychodynamic Approaches

From the psychodynamic perspective depression stems from stress, and it therefore follows that the psychodynamic approach to treatment is focused on helping individuals overcome stress and develop ways of avoiding stress in the future. The traditional technique for treating individuals who are depressed because of stress is *psychotherapy,* and there is evidence that psychotherapy can be effective (Craighead et al., 1998; Frank & Spanier, 1995; Levenson & Butler, 1999). Fairly recently, attention has been focused on the effects of a form of psychotherapy called **interpersonal psychotherapy,** in which therapists first help clients identify interpersonal problems (stress) that cause depression and then work with the clients to resolve those problems (Weissman & Markowitz, 1998). This form of therapy has been used in research because its goals and procedures are clearer than those of most other forms of psychotherapy. In the most important test of the effects of interpersonal psychotherapy, it was compared to the effects of cognitive therapy, antidepressants, and a placebo pill (Elkin et al., 1989). The results revealed that after 16 weeks of treatment 43% of the individuals who received interpersonal psychotherapy were judged to be recovered, a recovery rate that was similar to that of cognitive therapy (36%) and antidepressants (42%) and greater than that of the placebo pill (21%).

The finding that interpersonal psychotherapy is more effective than a placebo pill is certainly encouraging, but the fact that other forms of psychotherapy that differ greatly in focus and technique have also been found to be effective raises a question about what it is that makes psychotherapy effective. In other words, if all of the techniques (long-term psychoanalysis, individual therapy, group therapy, attention from a social worker, etc.) are effective, it is difficult to determine what the crucial factor is that makes psychotherapy effective (Lambert & Bergin, 1994; Weinberger, 1995). In fact, if people improve almost regardless of what is done for them, we are put in the awkward position of concluding that the differences among psychotherapeutic techniques may be irrelevant. The only element that is common to all of the approaches is *social support,* and that may be the crucial element in the psychotherapeutic treatment of depression. That speculation is consistent with the evidence described earlier indicating that social support is important for minimizing the effects of stress. (We will return to this issue later.)

interpersonal psychotherapy (for depression)   A form of psychotherapy in which therapists first help clients identify interpersonal problems (stress) that cause depression and then work with the clients to resolve those problems.

Psychotherapy is frequently used to treat individuals suffering from depression. It is effective in both reducing the relapse rate for depression and helping individuals improve their social adjustments and interpersonal relationships.

Cognitive Approaches

The goal of **cognitive therapy** is to *replace the inaccurate negative beliefs that are thought to cause depression with more accurate positive beliefs* (Beck et al., 1979; Wright & Beck, 1994). This approach is often called *cognitive-behavioral therapy* because therapists have their clients use both cognitive strategies such as reasoning to change beliefs and activities to test beliefs.

Replacing Negative Beliefs

In cognitive therapy the therapist tries to replace negative beliefs through a three-step process. The first step is to *identify the negative beliefs* that are influencing the patient's mood and behavior (e.g., "I am depressed and withdrawn because others don't like me, and I'll always be rejected by

---

cognitive therapy (for depression)   A psychological treatment in which the goals are to replace the inaccurate negative beliefs that are thought to cause depression with more accurate positive beliefs; sometimes called cognitive-behavior therapy.

tricyclics   A group of antidepressants that reduce the reuptake of serotonin and norepinephrine, thereby making more of the neurotransmitters available at the synapses.

bicyclics   A group of antidepressants that reduce the reuptake of serotonin, thereby making more of this neurotransmitter available at the synapses; also known as selective serotonin reuptake inhibitors (SSRIs).

---

others in the future"). Rather than letting the patient accept the negative beliefs as true, the therapist tells the patient to consider them as *hypotheses* to be tested. In other words, the therapist does not agree or disagree with the patient's views but takes a "let's see if you are correct" approach.

The second step involves helping the patient *test to determine whether the hypotheses are valid.* For example, if a patient is depressed because of the belief that he or she is disliked, the therapist and patient might conduct a little experiment in which the patient asks someone for a date to see if others actually do dislike and reject the patient.

Third, once the patient tests his or her negative beliefs and finds that that many of them are false, the therapist helps the client *replace the incorrect negative beliefs* with more accurate beliefs. For example, a patient will be instructed to replace negative beliefs with thoughts like "I may not be perfect, but I am not a bad person, and others do like me." This is not a simple step, and it takes practice to get the positive thoughts to be as automatic as the negative ones were. An important part of this phase of therapy involves activity planning. Rather than just thinking more accurate thoughts, the patient works with the therapist to plan activities consistent with the new accurate thoughts. In the case of a patient who feels rejected, the therapist may help the patient plan a variety of social activities such as dates and parties. This is important because the patient needs consistent confirmation of the new beliefs concerning social acceptability. It is essential that the scheduled activities be carefully graded in terms of difficulty. For instance, a young man who has felt depressed and rejected and who has isolated himself socially for 2 years before therapy should probably start with a casual coffee date rather than attempt a weekend with the homecoming queen! It is assumed that this process will take between 16 and 20 treatment sessions over a period of 12 to 16 weeks (Craighead et al., 1998).

Because improvements in cognitive therapy occur when the patient collects data that actually disprove his or her negative beliefs, the individual will not be dependent on the therapist in the future. If negative beliefs crop up again, the patient will have learned to check and eliminate them. Indeed, the long-term success of cognitive therapy depends on the patient's careful monitoring of thoughts so as to avoid slipping back into the habit of using negative beliefs. Whenever such a belief crops up, the patient is taught to ask three questions (Hollon & Beck, 1979):

1. What is my evidence for this belief?
2. Is there another way of looking at this situation?
3. Even if this belief is true, is it as bad as it seems?

Effectiveness of Cognitive Therapy

There is a substantial amount of evidence that cognitive therapy can be effective for treating depression (Craighead et al., 1998; Wright & Beck, 1999). Indeed, the evidence

FIGURE 8.12

Cognitive therapy was as effective as drug therapy, and the combination of cognitive and drug therapy was most effective.

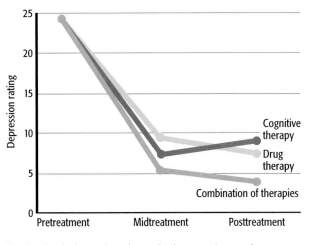

Note: Data based only on patients who completed treatment. Scores are from Hamilton Rating Scale for Depression (adjusted).

Source: Hollon et al. (1992), p. 777, Table 2.

FIGURE 8.13

Cognitive therapy was effective for reducing the likelihood of relapsing after drug therapy was terminated.

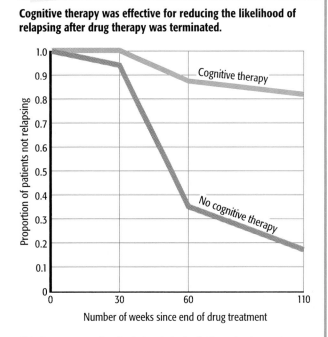

Note: Scores are proportion of patients not relapsing (not becoming depressed again).

Source: Adapted from Fava et al. (1998), p. 819.

indicates that cognitive therapy is as effective for treating moderate depression as are antidepressant drugs (Elkin et al., 1989; Hollon et al., 1992; Rush et al., 1977; Simons et al., 1984). The results of an experiment in which moderately depressed clients received either cognitive therapy, drug therapy, or a combination of cognitive therapy and drug therapy are presented in Figure 8.12 (Hollon et al., 1992). As you can see, cognitive therapy and drug therapy were equally effective, but the combination was somewhat more effective than either of the treatments separately. The fact that cognitive therapy is as effective as drug therapy was also illustrated earlier in Figure 3.3 (Jarrett et al., 1999).

Cognitive therapy can also be effective for preventing relapses after depression is reduced with drugs (Bower, 1990; Fava et al., 1998; Miller et al., 1989). Specifically, in one experiment individuals who had been successfully treated with antidepressants were randomly assigned to conditions in which they either did or did not receive cognitive therapy, and in both conditions the drugs were tapered off over a 20-week period. Followup measures of depressive symptoms over the next 2 years revealed that those who received cognitive therapy were much less likely to relapse. Those findings are illustrated in Figure 8.13.

Physiological Approaches

In this section we will examine four physiological approaches to the treatment of depression: drugs, electroconvulsive shocks, magnetic stimulation of the brain, and bright light. We will spend somewhat more time on these treatments than we have on other treatments because there are many misconceptions about them and some are very controversial. It's important that you understand these treatments because they are playing increasingly important roles in the treatment of depression.

Drug Treatment

Because depression is linked to low levels of mood-related neurotransmitters, drug treatment is focused on *increasing the levels of these neurotransmitters.* In the following sections I will (1) explain how different types of drugs increase neurotransmitter levels, (2) discuss the effectiveness of the drugs for reducing depression, and (3) describe their side effects.

Types of Antidepressants. There are a number of different types of antidepressant drugs, and each type increases neurotransmitter levels in a different way. In Table 8.2 (on p. 236) you will find a list of the most widely used antidepressant drugs, and in this section I will explain how the drugs work.

1. *Tricyclics and bicyclics: Drugs to reduce reuptake.* The drugs most widely used in the treatment of depression are the **tricyclics** and the newer **bicyclics**. The terms *tricyclic* and *bicyclic* are derived from the chemical structures of the

TABLE 8.2

Frequently used antidepressants

Trade name	Generic name	Typical dosage range (mm/day)
Tricyclics		
Tofranil	Imipramine	150–300
Elavil	Amitriptline	150–300
Anafranil	Clomipramine	75–200
Bicyclics (SSRIs)		
Prozac	Fluoxetine	20–80
Paxil	Paroxetine	20–50
Zoloft	Sertraline	50–200
MAOIs		
Nardil	Phenelzine	45–90
Parnate	Tranylcpromine	10–30
Marplan	Isccarboxizid	10–30
Atypical		
Desyrel	Trazadone	400–600
Wellbutrin	Bupropion	150–450
Effexor	Vanlafaxine	

Source: Nemeroff & Schatzberg (1998).

drugs, which involve three (tri-) or two (bi-) rings (circles). These drugs work by *reducing the reuptake* (reabsorption) of serotonin or norepinephrine by the presynaptic neurons (see Chapter 2). Of course, if the reuptake is blocked, more of the neurotransmitters are available at the synapses. The bicyclics that have attracted the most attention are Prozac, Zoloft, Paxil, and Celexa.

The bicyclic antidepressants differ from the tricyclics in two important ways: First, whereas tricyclics block the

selective serotonin reuptake inhibitors (SSRIs) A group of antidepressants that inhibit the reuptake of serotonin; also known as *bicyclics.*

MAOIs A class of drugs that inhibit the effects of the enzyme that destroys the neurotransmitter at the synapse, thereby making more of the neurotransmitter available; these drugs can have very serious side effects when taken in conjunction with food or drugs that contain tyramine.

tyramine A substance in many foods and drugs that can interact with an MAOI to cause a severe increase in blood pressure.

lithium A drug (technically a salt) primarily used to treat bipolar disorder but sometimes used to treat depression.

psychomotor stimulants A group of drugs that includes amphetamines and cocaine and that increase the production of neurotransmitters by the presynaptic neurons and thus decrease depression; rarely used because the depression becomes worse when the drugs are no longer taken.

reuptake of serotonin and norepinephrine, *bicyclics block primarily the reuptake of serotonin.* Indeed, bicyclics are referred to as **selective serotonin reuptake inhibitors (SSRIs).** Second, *most bicyclics have fewer or less serious side effects than tricyclics.* For example, whereas tricyclics can cause a considerable weight gain, bicyclics do not result in a weight gain and may even result in a small loss in weight. (I will discuss side effects in greater detail later.)

When Prozac was introduced, a controversy arose because there were reports that it could lead to suicide and murder. This controversy is discussed in Case Study 8.4.

2. *MAOIs: Drugs to reduce catabolism.* Neurotransmitters are *catabolized* (destroyed) at the synapse by other chemicals known as *enzymes.* This is a normal process, which is necessary for keeping the synapse "clean." However, one way to increase the level of a neurotransmitter at the synapse is to reduce its catabolism. In other words, if less is destroyed, more will be available to make transmission possible. Therefore, a class of drugs was developed that works by *inhibiting the effects of the enzyme that destroys the neurotransmitter.* These drugs are called **MAOIs** because the enzyme that breaks down the neurotransmitter is known as *monoamine oxidase* (MON-o-uh-mean OK-si-days, which is abbreviated *MAO*), and the drugs inhibit (*I*) that enzyme.

MAOIs can be effective for treating depression, but there is a serious problem with their use (Marangell et al., 1999; Nemeroff & Schatzberg, 1998): If MAOIs are taken in combination with foods or drugs that contain a substance called **tyramine** (TI-ruh-mean), a severe increase in blood pressure can occur; this increase can cause strokes, which may be fatal. Tyramine is present in foods such as unpasteurized cheese, aged meats, yeast extract, wines, some beers, and avocados, and it occurs in drugs such as stimulants, decongestants, antihypertensives, and tricyclic antidepressants. Because so many common foods and drugs can cause negative reactions to MAOIs, some authorities believe that MAOIs should only be taken by patients who are in a hospital where their diet can be carefully supervised and where help is available in the event of complications. At present MAOIs are usually used only after other antidepressant medications have been found to be ineffective.

3. *Lithium: A drug to stabilize neurotransmission.* **Lithium** is a drug (technically a salt) that is primarily used to treat bipolar disorder (see Chapter 9), but it is sometimes used to treat depression that is separate from bipolar disorder (Joffe et al., 1993; Price & Heninger, 1994). Specifically, lithium is used alone or in combination with tricyclics or bicyclics when those other drugs are not completely effective. In other words, lithium is a "second line of defense." For example, in one experiment depressed patients who had not shown improvement with a bicyclic (Prozac) were put on a combination of the bicyclic and lithium, and the

Prozac—Panacea or Paradox?

PROZAC (fluoxetine) was introduced in 1987 and immediately became one of the most widely used drugs in the United States. Indeed, it was heralded as a panacea for depression, and more than a million prescriptions were being filled every month. However, the view of Prozac changed suddenly when it was reported that six patients became suicidal after taking it (Teicher, Gold, & Cole, 1990). Shortly after this report appeared, TV talk shows were filled with people telling horror stories about the alleged effects of Prozac, and Prozac "survivor" groups were formed around the country to provide support for those who had gone through the "perils of Prozac."

Possibly the most dramatic aspect of the Prozac story involved the allegation that Prozac led people to commit murder. For example, it was alleged that Joseph Wesbecker was under the influence of Prozac when he stormed into a building with an AK-47 assault rifle and shot 20 people (8 fatally) before killing himself. Many defendants in murder cases began using what came to be known as the "Prozac defense"—using Prozac to explain their violent acts, thereby relieving themselves of criminal responsibility and opening up the manufacturer to huge lawsuits.

The alleged increase in violent behavior associated with taking Prozac was particularly surprising in view of the drug's biochemical effects. We know that *low* levels of serotonin are associated with aggressive behavior and suicide (see Chapters 9 and 12),

but Prozac results in *higher* levels of serotonin because it blocks the reuptake of serotonin. In other words, from a biochemical standpoint, if Prozac has any effect on aggression, it should reduce it. However, it is hypothetically possible that Prozac has some paradoxical effect on behavior. Is Prozac a dangerous drug? Should it be withdrawn from the market?

Case studies can provide a signal that a problem may exist, but we should not draw conclusions from them because the reported effects may be due to other factors. For example, in some of these cases the individuals were on several medications in addition to Prozac and were suffering from several psychiatric disorders. Consequently, it may have been those factors rather than the Prozac that led to the disturbed behavior. So case studies aside, what results have been generated by controlled research?

First, there is some evidence that, compared to a placebo, antidepressant drugs in general may lead to a *slight* increase in suicide of about 1% (Gardner & Cowdry, 1985; Mann & Kapur, 1991; Rouillon et al., 1989; Soloff et al., 1987; see Chapter 9). If such an effect occurs, it is probably due to the fact that as the depression begins to lift, individuals have more energy and are more active and are thus more likely to act on their lingering suicidal thoughts. In any event, if this effect occurs, it does not appear to be anything like the effect attributed to Prozac.

Second, the results of large-scale controlled experiments did *not* reveal

any evidence that Prozac resulted in an increase in suicidal thoughts or behavior (Altamura et al., 1989; Leon et al., 1999; Muijen et al., 1988; Sacchetti et al., 1991; see review by Mann & Kapur, 1991). Instead Prozac was found to be generally more effective than other drugs and placebos in reducing suicidal urges and depression (Beasley et al., 1991; Fava & Rosenbaum, 1991).

If the controlled research does not support the initial claims that Prozac leads to increased rates of suicidal thoughts, how do we account for the case studies? First, it is possible that the behaviors were the result of the other medications the patients were taking or the other disorders from which they suffered. Second, it is also possible that in some instances the behavior was indeed an abnormal reaction to the Prozac. With virtually every drug there are some individuals who have abnormal reactions to it (e.g., some people cannot take aspirin), so there may be people who cannot tolerate Prozac. However, if that is the case, the solution is not to withdraw Prozac from the market but to monitor patients carefully and prescribe a different drug for those who cannot tolerate Prozac.

And what about the "Prozac defense"? Juries generally rejected this defense, and it is no longer used.

> With virtually every drug there are some individuals who have abnormal reactions to it . . . .

---

results indicated that the combination was more effective than the bicyclic alone (Fava et al., 1994). It is not clear exactly why lithium works, but it probably stabilizes the release of neurotransmitters or stabilizes the sensitivity of the receptors on the postsynaptic neurons. (I will discuss lithium in more detail in Chapter 9.)

4. *Psychomotor stimulants: Drugs to increase neurotransmitter production.* A group of drugs known as **psychomotor stimulants,** which includes drugs such as am-phetamines and cocaine, can decrease depression because they *increase*

the production of neurotransmitters by the presynaptic neurons. Unfortunately, most psychomotor stimulants are addicting and have only short-term effects. Furthermore, when individuals stop taking stimulants, their depression is often worse than it was before the stimulants were taken. That effect occurs because the neurons adjust to the assistance provided by the stimulants; so when the stimulants are no longer present, the neurons produce even less of the neurotransmitter than they did before the drugs were used. Because of the problems posed by the use of psychomotor stimulants, they are rarely used to treat depression, and their use for self-treatment is definitely not recommended.

5. *Atypical antidepressants.* Finally, there is a newer group of drugs called **atypical antidepressants,** which do not fit into any of the above groups and which cannot be easily characterized because they differ widely among themselves. These drugs can be effective for reducing depression and do not have some of the side effects of some of the other drugs (see the later discussion).

Effectiveness of Antidepressants. There is no doubt that antidepressant drugs can be effective for reducing depression (e.g., Marangell et al., 1999; Nemeroff & Schatzberg, 1998). For example, in one study over 200 patients were randomly assigned to conditions in which they received either Prozac or Paxil, and their levels of depression were monitored weekly for 12 weeks (Chouinard et al., 1999). As indicated in Figure 8.14, both drugs were effective, and almost 90% of the patients reported a decrease in depression of 50% or greater.

A comment should be made here concerning **Saint John's wort** (*Hypericum perforatum*), an herbal medicine that has been reported to be effective for treating depression (Linde et al., 1996). Those results are encouraging, but it's important to recognize that the experiments on which the conclusions were based suffer from a variety of methodological problems; for example, it is not clear how depression was measured, and only persons with very mild levels of depression were studied (DeSmet & Nolen, 1996). The effectiveness of Saint John's wort for treating depression is an interesting possibility, but at present its effects are unproven.

As a footnote to the discussion of the effects of antidepressants, I will quote from the student who wrote about her depression in Case Study 8.2. You may recall that in her essay she described her feelings of living inside a glass bottle and how she huddled under the covers in her bed. At the end of her paper she described her experience with Prozac this way:

> As I sit at my computer successfully completing the first major term paper I've been able to tackle this semester, I am thankful for the development of Prozac, and I am

atypical antidepressants A relatively new group of drugs that can be effective in reducing depression.

Saint John's wort (*Hypericum perforatum*) An herbal medicine that has been reported to be effective for treating depression, but more research is needed to confirm its effects.

electroconvulsive therapy (ECT) The application of electrical shocks to the brain to reduce depression; commonly called *shock therapy*.

FIGURE 8.14

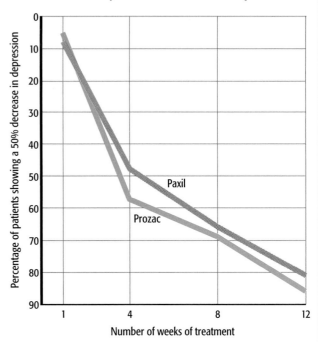

Patients who took bicyclics showed decreases in depression.

Note: The 50% decrease in depression was as measured on the Hamilton Rating Scale.

Source: Chouinard et al. (1999), p. 44, Table 4.

willing to risk the possible side effects. I am now able to experience everyday joys that I once could only envy in other people. I still have days when I feel "blue," but that is perfectly normal, and *Prozac is no panacea.* It has not been determined how long I will remain on Prozac, but as for now, I am just enjoying life. I like people, I'm proud of what I'm accomplishing, and I love myself.

Prozac helped this woman, but she was correct in pointing out that it isn't a panacea, so let's go on to consider some of the limitations of antidepressants.

Limitations of Antidepressants. Antidepressant drugs can be effective, but two important qualifications should be noted: First, *the drugs are a treatment, not a cure.* This means that many individuals may have to stay on the drugs for long periods of time. That was clearly demonstrated in three experiments in which depressed patients were first successfully treated with antidepressants and then were assigned to conditions in which they either continued to take the drug or began taking a placebo (Doogan & Caillard, 1992; Montgomery & Dunbar, 1993; Montgomery et al., 1988). The results revealed that relapse rates were up to three-and-a-half times higher in patients who were switched to the placebos. Those results are summarized in Figure 8.15. The

FIGURE 8.15

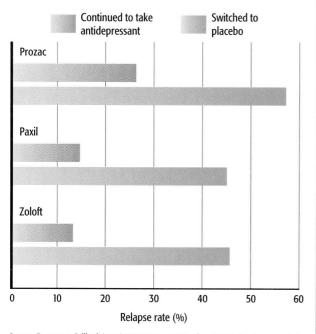

Patients who were switched to a placebo showed greater relapse rates than those who remained on antidepressants.

Legend: Continued to take antidepressant / Switched to placebo

Categories: Prozac, Paxil, Zoloft

Relapse rate (%) — 0, 10, 20, 30, 40, 50, 60

Source: Doogan & Caillard (1992); Montgomery & Dunbar (1993); Montgomery et al. (1988).

fact that antidepressants do not provide cures is unfortunate, but the same is true of drugs used for other disorders, such as insulin for diabetes (see the discussion of this issue in Chapter 5).

The second limitation is that there is usually *a delay of about 4 weeks before the drugs have an effect.* We do not yet understand the reason for this delay, and patients should be warned about it so that they do not become disappointed and stop taking the drugs when they do not work immediately. The delayed effect of the antidepressant drugs has implications for individuals who are suicidal and for whom immediate relief is necessary. For these individuals hospitalization might be necessary until they are no longer a danger to themselves, or it might be necessary initially to use some other, faster-acting treatment, such as electroconvulsive therapy (to be discussed shortly), to break the depression.

Side Effects. The question that always arises with regard to antidepressants is, do they have side effects? I have already mentioned that MAOIs can have lethal side effects and that psychomotor stimulants can lead to deeper depression, but the widely used bicyclics and tricyclics can also result in side effects such as dryness of the mouth, blurring of vision, difficulty in urination, constipation, palpitations of the heart, low blood pressure, and drowsiness (Post, 1994; Silver, Yudofsky, & Hurowitz, 1994). However, these side effects can be minimized by using the lowest dose of the

drug that is effective. Furthermore, in many cases the side effects diminish over time as the body adjusts to the drug and the individual learns to cope with the side effects. It is essential that individuals be aware of possible side effects so that they can deal with them and not misinterpret them as additional symptoms of their disorder. Unfortunately, mental health professionals are often insensitive to the serious problems side effects can pose for their clients.

A notable side effect that occurs with many of the bicyclic drugs, such as Prozac, Zoloft, and Paxil, is difficulty in sexual functioning; specifically, the drugs increase time to orgasm or may even eliminate the possibility of having an orgasm (Nafziger et al., 1999; Piazza et al., 1997; Rosen et al., 1999; Waldinger et al., 1998). This does not occur in all individuals, and the strength of the effect is strongly related to the dosage level of the drug that is taken. Also some of the atypical antidepressants do not have this side effect. Indeed, there is some evidence that one of the atypical antidepressants called Welbutrin (bupropion) may actually increase sexual arousal, and it has been suggested that individuals may switch to that drug on days when sexual activity is likely.

One side effect was made dramatically clear to me when I participated in a study of the effects of Prozac. I describe that experience in Case Study 8.5 (on p. 240).

It is important to consider the trade-off between side effects and symptom relief. Regrettably, sometimes the side effects are intolerable, and the use of the drug has to be terminated and another drug tried. In other cases there may be side effects, but they are an acceptable price to pay for the relief from the misery the individual has to endure without the drug. As with most things, then, drug treatment for depression is a matter of balances, compromises, risks, and benefits. The important thing is for both therapist and client to be informed about the options and the consequences.

As a brief footnote to this discussion of side effects, I should point out something that many people worry about but that does not appear to be a side effect—taking tricyclics during pregnancy does not have negative effects on the fetus (Wisner et al., 1999). This information is especially important because many women experience depression during pregnancy.

Electroconvulsive Therapy

A second physiological treatment for depression involves stimulating the brain with electrical shocks; this technique is called **electroconvulsive therapy (ECT),** or commonly "shock therapy" (Fink, 1999). ECT is used widely for the treatment of depression, and it is estimated that more than 10,000 patients in the United States receive ECT each day. However, ECT is frequently misunderstood and is often the focus of public and professional outcries, so it is essential that we give it careful attention.

"I Can't Sit Still!"—A Potential Side Effect of Prozac

CASE STUDY 8.5

. . . I felt as though there was a huge motor in my chest that was running at top speed, and *I simply could not sit still.*

THERE IS EVIDENCE that Prozac can relieve depression, but some individuals claim that it does more than that—it makes them "better than well." Specifically, after relieving their depression it makes them more outgoing, more assertive, and generally more effective personally and professionally (Kramer, 1993). To test that possibility, I participated in a project in which I first monitored my mood for a period of 1 month and then began taking Prozac to see if my mood improved. The project was planned as a multiple-baseline study (see Chapter 4) in which I would or would not take Prozac at different times to see if my mood went up and down between "normal" and "better than normal." Unfortunately, I never got beyond the first "on-drug" period. Within a day of beginning the drug, I developed a serious side effect. Specifically, I felt as though there was a huge motor in my chest that was running at top speed, and *I simply could not sit still.* At the time I was writing a chapter for this book, and prior to taking the drug I was able to sit and work at my computer for hours at a time. However, after taking the drug I would sit and work for about 5 minutes, and then I would have to get up and walk around. I would then go to another room, where I would try to read, but that would last for only about 5 minutes. Then I would take my portable computer and try to work in another room, but I was able to work for only a few minutes. I kept moving from room to room, trying one thing and then another but never getting much done. By the end of the day I had tried to work in every chair in every room and probably walked miles, but I had not gotten anything done.

It is important to note that I did not go into a manic state; that is, I did not feel elated or more motivated. Furthermore, I did not feel anxious, except about the fact that I was not getting any work done—*I just could not sit still!*

For 2 days I kept telling myself, "David, these side effects will go away; just hang in there." (How many times in the past had I heard myself say that to other people!) After 3 days there was no improvement and I wasn't getting any work done, so I stopped taking the drug. In less than 12 hours, I was back to normal.

The side effect from which I suffered is called **akathisia** (ak-uh-THIZH-yuh), which means "restlessness," and it is a relatively common side effect of Prozac (Lipinski et al., 1989; Silver et al., 1994). I am one of the people who cannot take Prozac, and my experience made me much more sensitive to the problems some people have with side effects.

Background and Procedures. ECT was originally developed as a treatment for schizophrenia when it was observed that patients who suffered from both schizophrenia and epilepsy showed reductions in their symptoms of schizophrenia immediately following an epileptic convulsion. Clinicians speculated that if epilepticlike convulsions could be artificially induced, they might be effective in treating schizophrenia. Originally the convulsions were produced with drugs such as insulin (Meduna, 1935), but it was quickly learned that greater control over the convulsions could be achieved if they were brought on with an electrical shock to the brain. Thus, electroconvulsive therapy was born (Cerletti & Bini, 1938). Since then we have learned that ECT is not effective for treating schizophrenia per se, but it can be effective for treating depression.

In the typical portrayal of shock therapy in horror movies, a screaming patient is held down on an operating table by brutish attendants while a physician holds large electrodes to the patient's temples, a flash of lightninglike electrical current arcs between the electrodes, and the patient shudders in pain and falls unconscious, brain-damaged and changed for life. The early use of ECT may have involved some elements of that scenario, but it bears no resemblance to the procedures in use today.

Today the patient is first given a strong sedative and a muscle relaxant. The sedative induces sleep, so the patient is not conscious when the convulsion is induced, and the relaxant reduces muscular contractions during the convulsion. (Before muscle relaxants were used, patients often broke bones during the convulsions.) Once the patient is unconscious and relaxed, electrodes are placed on the skull, and an electrical current of between 70 and 150 volts is passed between the electrodes for $1/10$ second to 1 second to induce the convulsion. As the convulsion runs its course (usually in 45–60 seconds), the patient shows some minor muscle contractions, which are usually limited to small movements of the arms or a slight movement of the toes. The degree to which muscle contractions occur depends on the amount of muscle relaxant that is administered. During the convulsion it is necessary to put something in the patient's mouth to prevent swallowing of the tongue. The patient's breathing is reduced during the convulsion, so he or she is usually given oxygen during and for a brief time following the convulsion. A few minutes after the convulsion, the patient regains consciousness. The entire procedure can take less than 15 minutes, and after having been through it once, most patients do not report any greater concern than would be expected for any other minor med-

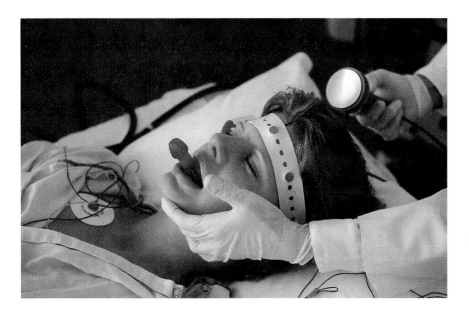

Modern procedures used to administer electroconvulsive therapy (ECT) bear little resemblance to those of the past. Today the patient is unconscious during treatment and is given a muscle relaxant to reduce muscle contractions during the seizure.

ical procedure (Bernstein et al., 1998). Indeed, many patients I know say that they would rather undergo ECT than go to the dentist to have a cavity filled!

ECT is generally given three times per week (e.g., Monday, Wednesday, and Friday). The number of treatments necessary to obtain results differs widely from patient to patient. Many respond after 5 to 8 treatments. If 8 or 10 treatments have not resulted in improvement, it is usually concluded that the treatment will not be effective, and it is stopped. ECT can be given on either an outpatient or an inpatient basis, but it is usually used for inpatients because they are more severely depressed.

Effectiveness of ECT. The first question we must ask is, is ECT more effective than antidepressant drugs? Yes, ECT is generally more beneficial than those drugs. For instance, in one experiment patients who had not responded well to antidepressants were assigned to either of two conditions; in one they received an SSRI (Paxil/paroxetine), and in the other they received ECT (Folkerts et al., 1997). About 30% of the patients in the drug group improved, whereas 60% of those who received ECT improved, which indicates that ECT can help patients who are not responding well to medication.

In addition to being more effective, ECT has the advantage of producing its effects faster than drugs. Antidepressants can take up to 4 weeks to reduce depression, but ECT can begin showing its benefits within 3 or 4 days. The speed with which ECT works makes it very helpful in treating suicidal patients who may be a danger to themselves as long as they are depressed, and its use may decrease the length of time that depressed patients must be hospitalized. Indeed, in one study it was found that patients who received ECT spent 13 fewer days in the hospital than did patients who

received drugs (Markowitz et al., 1987). Thus ECT not only saved the patients time, but it saved each patient well over $13,000 in hospital costs.

Next we must ask, is ECT a long-lasting treatment, or are patients treated with ECT likely to relapse? Unfortunately, like drugs, ECT is a *treatment, not a cure,* and therefore individuals will relapse. However, rather than simply stopping treatment after the depression lifts, most patients are put on a maintenance dose of an antidepressant drug to reduce relapses, a procedure that usually appears to be effective. In other words, the strategy is to break the back of serious depression with ECT and then maintain the improvement with medication.

However, in some cases drug maintenance is not effective and patients slip back into deep depression. To overcome that problem, there has been a movement in recent years to use what is called **maintenance ECT.** With this procedure traditional ECT treatment is used until the depression is reduced, and then, in addition to drugs, the individual is given followup shocks on a regular basis, such as one per month, to maintain the effects that were achieved with the initial treatment. There is a growing body of evidence that maintenance ECT can be effective, and because only one shock is used at each followup treatment, this procedure does not trigger the negative side effects that are associated with more extensive use of ECT (Beale, Bernstein, &

akathisia Restlessness, or the inability to sit still for long, a common side effect of Prozac.

maintenance ECT The regular use of shocks (i.e., one per month) to maintain reduced levels of depression first achieved with ECT.

Kellner, 1996; Petrides, 1998; Rabheru & Persad, 1997). Furthermore, this is a very cost-effective strategy because it can be done on an outpatient basis (or at most with one overnight stay in the hospital) and because it reduces the need for rehospitalization by preventing relapses.

Despite substantial evidence that ECT is effective for treating depression, we still do not know why it works. In fact, more than 50 theories have been advanced to account for the effects of ECT, but we have not reached any conclusions concerning the mechanism by which it works (Lerer, Weiner, & Belmaker, 1984; Silver et al., 1994). It is interesting to note, however, that following ECT there is increased blood flow in the brain, which reflects increased brain activity (Nobler et al., 1994). That observation is relevant because, as you learned earlier, depression is caused in part by decreased brain activity.

Side Effects. Is ECT safe? Definitely yes. In followup studies of over 20,000 patients who received an average of more than five shocks, not one fracture or death was found (Kramer, 1985; Reid et al., 1998). In fact, it is even safe for elderly individuals who have heart problems (Gormley et al., 1998; Rice et al., 1994).

One occasional side effect of ECT is **retrograde amnesia** (RET-ro-grad am-NE-zha), which is the *loss of memory for past events.* In other words, patients receiving ECT may lose their memories of some events that occurred prior to the treatment, and as the number of treatments increases, the memory loss extends farther back in time. However, in most cases the loss is minimal and little more than a minor annoyance. Although an event or a name may be forgotten, it can be relearned and there is no permanent impairment. Furthermore, there is now evidence that the memories that were lost can be regained as time goes by (Calev et al., 1991). That was demonstrated in a study in which the memory of depressed patients was measured before and immediately after receiving ECT and then again 1 month and 6 months later. The results indicated that there was a considerable loss in memory immediately after the treatment. However, 1 month later memory was back to the pretreatment level, and 6 months later it was actually a little higher than the preshock level, probably because the patients were generally functioning better after the depression lifted. In some cases the effects of shock on memory may be exaggerated by patients who blame the treatment for the normal forgetting that we all experience.

One question that is often asked with regard to ECT is, does it cause brain damage? Of course, the application of

150 volts of electrical current to the delicate neurons in the brain will result in some damage. However, with modern techniques that use lower-level shocks and provide oxygen to the patient during the convulsion to prevent anoxia, it is impossible to detect any brain damage even with highly sensitive CT and MRI scans (Devanand et al., 1994).

A more important question is, does ECT result in impaired cognitive functioning? You may be surprised to learn that ECT can actually *improve* cognitive functioning (Sackeim, 1985). The improvement stems from the fact that depression reduces cognitive functioning; so when the depression is eliminated by the shock, functioning improves. There are even data indicating that patients who received more than 100 ECT treatments over their lifetimes did not differ from nonshocked patients on measures of cognitive functioning (Devanand et al., 1991, 1994). Because of the effectiveness of ECT and the fact that it can be given in such a way that side effects are minimized, the use of ECT is increasing dramatically (Rosenbach, Herrmann, & Dorwart, 1997; Thompson, Weiner, & Myers, 1994). However, it is important to note that ECT is a treatment of last resort for individuals for whom drugs have not been effective and whose depression is serious.

Overall, then, modern ECT is a safe and effective way of dealing with severe depression that does not respond to medication.

Transcranial Magnetic Stimulation

A new strategy for treating depression involves the use of *magnetism.* That may sound a little strange, so let me begin by giving you a little background. About 10 years ago it was discovered that if a small electromagnet is placed on the scalp and used to create a brief but powerful electromagnetic field, the neurons in the field directly beneath the electrode will be stimulated and they will fire. Furthermore, if a high frequency of magnetic pulses is used, the neurons will fire at a high frequency, but they will not stimulate other nearby neurons. The rapid firing of the neurons disrupts their normal functioning, so whatever role they played is temporarily "knocked out." For example, if the magnetic stimulation is applied to the temporal lobe, where language is controlled, the individual will temporarily lose the ability to speak; if the stimulation is applied to the occipital lobe, where vision is located, the individual will experience temporary blindness (Pascual-Leone et al., 1992, 1994).

These findings are interesting, but how are they related to the treatment of depression? Some investigators speculated that repeated electromagnetic stimulation of neurons in the frontal lobes might have effects similar to those of ECT, and that led to development of a treatment known as **repetitive transcranial magnetic stimulation.** With this treatment the patient is conscious, sits up, and wears a skullcap that contains the electromagnets that provide the

---

retrograde amnesia The loss of memories for past events that can occur, probably on a temporary basis, with ECT.

repetitive transcranial magnetic stimulation The use of an electromagnetic field to stimulate activity in neurons in the frontal lobes as a treatment for depression.

stimulation. The procedure takes only a few minutes, is painless, does not involve the use of any medication, is safe, and generally does not have any side effects (Figiel et al., 1998; Wasserman, 1996).

Although this treatment is still in the development stage, the results of controlled research consistently indicate that it is effective for reducing depression (George, 1998; George et al., 1995; George, Wassermann, et al., 1997; George, Lisanby, et al., 1999; Klein et al., 1999; Pascual-Leone, Catala, et al., 1996; Pascual-Leone, Rubio, et al., 1996; Reid et al., 1998; Stoudemire et al., 1998). For example, in one experiment depressed patients who had not responded well to antidepressants were given either transcranial magnetic stimulation to the left prefrontal cortex on each of 5 days or sham treatments in which other areas of the brain were stimulated or the electromagnets were not actually turned on (Pascual-Leone et al., 1996). The results were dramatic: The patients who received the real treatment showed an immediate 50% reduction in their symptoms, whereas the sham treatments had virtually no effects on depression. These results are illustrated in Figure 8.16. However, what is also apparent in that figure is that the effects of the treatment lasted less than a month. The fact that the effects did not last longer is disappointing, but this treatment might be used to break depression that does not respond to drugs. Once the depression is broken, the improvement can be maintained with drugs, as it is following ECT. Compared to ECT, transcranial magnetic stimulation has the advantage of being easier and faster. Also, as with ECT, we do not understand exactly why it works. It may be that the stimulation rejuvenates the activity in the left frontal lobes, which is reduced in depression (see the earlier discussion).

Light Therapy for Depression with Seasonal Pattern

Earlier I pointed out that in a subset of individuals depression appears to be triggered by reduced levels of light (see the discussion in Topic I of depression with seasonal pattern). If reduced light leads to depression in some individuals, then exposing them to more light should relieve their depression. That prescription was initially offered more than 2,000 years ago when Aretaeus said, "Lethargics [depressed individuals] are to be laid in the light and exposed to the rays of the sun." Despite the amount of time that has elapsed since light therapy was suggested, there is still controversy over this treatment and it is still being refined (Bauer, Kurtz, Rubin, & Marcus, 1994; Lam, 1994; Murphy et al., 1993; Oren et al., 1994; Teicher et al., 1995; Termal et al., 1989; Wirz-Justice et al., 1993). However, it does appear that the treatment is effective for at least some individuals and that bright light (at least 2,500 lux and as high as 10,000 lux) is more effective than dim light (Wehr & Rosenthal, 1989). Some investigators have also found that light is more effective in the *morning* than in the evening, but the data are not consistent (e.g., Avery et al., 1993; Saeed et al., 1998; Wirz-Justice et al., 1993).

Regardless of when the light is used, the crucial factor seems to be to extend the time during the day that the individual gets light—that is, to create an earlier morning or a later night. Although light therapy can reduce depression, it is not effective with all individuals, and in some cases it

FIGURE 8.16

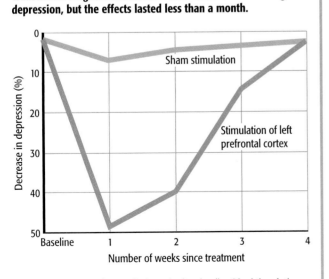

Transcranial magnetic stimulation was effective for reducing depression, but the effects lasted less than a month.

Note: Scores are percent decreases in depression from baseline. Stimulation of other sites yielded results similar to those of sham stimulation.

Source: Adapted from Pascual-Leone et al. (1996), Figure 3, p. 236.

Exposure to bright light has been shown to be effective for some individuals who suffer from depression with seasonal pattern. Why light therapy works, however, is still unclear.

must be supplemented with antidepressant drugs (Saeed et al., 1998). Furthermore, light therapy is not as effective for reducing depression as is the return of summer with its natural high level of light (Lamberg, 1998).

The process underlying the use of light therapy to treat depression with seasonal pattern is not clear (Avery et al., 1998). One hypothesis revolves around the production of *melatonin* (mel-uh-TO-nin), a hormone that regulates sleep activity cycles and at high levels may depress mood. Melatonin production is increased when periods of light are shorter, as they are in the winter. When the individual is exposed to light in the morning or at night, thereby increasing the total period of light, the production of melatonin may be suppressed. This explanation is still under investigation, and it is too early to draw a conclusion.

THINKING CRITICALLY

Questions about the Treatments for Depression

1. *Do we have effective treatments for depression?* Earlier I concluded that psychotherapy, cognitive therapy, and various physiological treatments were all "effective" for reducing depression, but what do I mean by "effective"? To answer that question, let's consider the results with cognitive therapy. It is generally agreed that about 60% of depressed individuals who complete cognitive therapy recover (Craighead et al., 1998). However, about 25% of those who recover relapse within the first year after treatment. Therefore, if we started with 100 moderately depressed clients, at the end of therapy about 60 would be recovered, but during the first year about 15 of them would relapse (25% of 60); so at the end of 1 year, only about 45 of our 100 clients would be considered recovered. Unfortunately, the success rate may even be less than that because about 30% of individuals who begin treatment drop out. If we excluded 30 who are likely to drop out from our original group of 100, the number of successfully treated clients after 1 year would be about 31. Importantly, psychotherapy and drug therapy have rates of dropout, recovery, and relapse that are similar to those of cognitive therapy, so moderately depressed clients who are treated with those

---

nonspecific factors (in therapy) Elements of the therapeutic situation, such as the relationship with the therapist, an explanation for the symptoms, and a treatment procedure that the patient believes will reduce the symptoms, that occur in all therapies and may account for the fact that very different types of therapies are often found to be equally effective.

---

strategies do not fare any better. This analysis puts the word "effective" in a different light; the *treatments are effective, but only for between 30% and 45% of clients*. We should be encouraged that these treatments can help some individuals, but the fact that we will be able to help fewer than half of the people who are treated is a source of concern. Recognizing the limitations of the treatments is also important in terms of how we view people who remain depressed despite treatment. In other words, rather than being critical of such individuals and asking, in essence, "What's wrong with you?" we should ask, "What's wrong with our treatments?" Overall, then, the picture that emerges is a lot less bright than what is usually implied when we say our treatments are effective.

2. *Is one type of treatment more effective for treating depression than the others?* This is an important question from a practical standpoint, and it is also a "hot button" question because the proponents of each treatment want theirs to be "the winner." Actually, there are two answers to this question. First, when considering mildly or moderately depressed individuals, it appears that psychotherapy, cognitive therapy, and antidepressants are equally effective (e.g., Elkin et al., 1989; Hollon et al., 1992; Rush et al., 1977; Simons et al., 1986). Second, with severe depression it appears that physiological treatments such as antidepressants and ECT are more effective than psychotherapy or cognitive therapy (Jacobson & Hollon, 1996; Klein, 1996; Thase & Howland, 1994; Thase et al., 1991, 1997; but see also DeRubeis et al., 1999). Indeed, as cases of depression progress from moderate to severe, the treatment of choice changes from psychotherapy, cognitive therapy, or antidepressants to antidepressants and ECT.

3. *Are combinations of treatments more effective than any one treatment by itself?* Yes, there is consistent evidence that combinations of psychological and physiological treatments are more effective for reducing depression and preventing relapse than either type of treatment by itself (Di Mascio et al., 1979; Fava et al., 1998; Frank, 1991; Frank, Kupfer, & Perel, 1989; Frank et al., 1990; Frank et al., 1991; Hollon et al., 1992; Klerman, 1990; Klerman et al., 1974; Weissman et al., 1979). There appear to be two reasons for this. First, with combinations of treatments clients benefit from a number of different treatment factors (e.g., social support, stress reduction, changing beliefs, changing neurotransmitter levels) rather than just one. Second, different treatment factors appear to influence different aspects of major depressive disorder. Specifically, psychological treatment is more effective than drug treatment for helping patients deal with problems of living, social functioning, and interpersonal relations, whereas drug treatment is more effective for reducing the feelings of depression (see reviews by Klerman & Schechter, 1982; Weissman, 1979). In other words, psychological treatments have major influences on *behavior,* whereas drugs influence *mood.* This does not mean that psychological treatments do not influence depression and that drugs do not influence the problems of daily living. It means only that the different approaches are relatively more effective with different sets of symptoms.

4. *Why are the treatments effective for treating depression?* It may surprise you to learn that in many cases we are not really sure exactly why treatments for depression work. Earlier, when I discussed physiological treatments, I pointed out that we do not know why ECT works and that the fact that antidepressants increase neurotransmitter levels does not provide a complete explanation for why antidepressants work. There are also gaps in our understanding of why psychological treatments work. For example, it is generally assumed that the effects of cognitive therapy are due to changing negative beliefs, but serious questions about that were raised when investigators examined four major studies and plotted improvements in depression over weeks of therapy. They found that most of the improvement occurred in the first few weeks of therapy, *before attention was focused on actually changing beliefs* (Ilardi & Craighead, 1994). In other words, improvement occurred before the major element of the cognitive therapy was introduced. But if the improvements were not related to the changing of beliefs, what caused them? The investigators suggest that they may have been due to what are called **nonspecific factors** in therapy, which are elements such as the relationship with the therapist (e.g., empathy and support), a rational concept (or "myth") that provides an explanation for the symptoms, and a treatment procedure (or "ritual") that the patient believes will reduce the symptoms (Frank, 1982; Imber et al., 1990; Weinberger, 1993, 1995). All of these factors can contribute to the effects of therapy, and they are called *nonspecific* factors because they occur in all therapies. Indeed, the fact that very different types of therapies are often found to be equally effective in reducing depression can be attributed to their sharing of these nonspecific factors. This fact clearly raises questions about why cognitive therapy works.

In summary, we have come a long way in our treatment of depression, and we now have a variety of treatments that can be effective for some people. However, we must not become complacent and conclude that we have "the answer" or "the treatment." There are still many questions to be answered, and our treatments must be improved so that we can be more effective with more people who suffer from depression.

Summary

▶ There are two major mood disorders: major depressive disorder and bipolar disorder. Dysthymic disorder is a less severe form of major depressive disorder, and cyclothymic disorder is the less severe form of bipolar disorder.

Topic I: Symptoms and Issues

▶ Mood symptoms of depression revolve around the lowering of mood; persons feel depressed, "blue," and "down."

▶ Cognitive symptoms involve negative thoughts, low motivation, and impaired thinking.

▶ Motor symptoms include psychomotor retardation and psychomotor agitation.

▶ Four physical symptoms often accompany depression: disturbed sleep patterns (difficulty getting to sleep, early morning awakening), disturbed eating patterns (increased or decreased appetite), decreased sexual drive, and increased physical illnesses. Focusing on physical symptoms can result in masked depression.

▶ Clinical depression is different from normal depression in that it is deeper and of longer duration. To be diagnosed as having major depressive disorder, an individual must experience at least two major depressive episodes. We must be careful to distinguish between primary depression and secondary depression, the latter of which stems from some other disorder.

▶ Some types of depression are identified in *DSM* with specifiers. Two of these are depression with postpartum onset (which is depression after childbirth) and depression with seasonal pattern (which is depression associated with less daylight).

▶ Women are at least twice as likely to suffer from depression as men, but exactly why that is so is not yet clear. Depression increases with old age, an effect that might be due to increased stress or changes in the brain. Individuals in lower socioeconomic classes suffer from more depression, probably because of increased stress. Ethnicity per se is not linked to incidence of depression, but there may be an indirect link because members of some ethnic groups are more likely to be in the lower socioeconomic classes.

Topic II: Explanations for Depression

▶ The psychodynamic explanation revolves around stress. There is good evidence that stress can cause depression. It does so because it reduces levels of mood-related neuro-transmitters.

▶ The depressing effects of stress can be reduced by social support, active coping strategies, aerobic fitness, and relatively high prestress levels of mood-related neurotransmitters. Annoyance with daily hassles is more an effect than a cause of depression.

▶ There are two cognitive explanations for depression: (1) People become depressed because they have incorrect negative beliefs about themselves, the world in general, and the future. (2) Learned helplessness causes depression.

▶ There is evidence that depressed individuals focus on negative information, are likely to recall negative material, and hold negative beliefs. However, there is no reliable evidence that negative beliefs by themselves cause depression. Specifically, reading negative material does not lead to clinical levels of depression, persons with negative beliefs are not at increased risk for depression, and depression-prone persons are not more likely than other persons to have "latent" negative beliefs. It appears that negative beliefs are primarily an effect rather than a cause of depression. However, having negative beliefs can enhance the likelihood that individuals will become depressed if they are exposed to stress, and negative beliefs can prolong depression.

▶ Learned helplessness may lead to depression, but the effect is due to the fact that people who are helpless in avoiding stressful events will experience more stress. It is increased stress rather than helplessness per se that leads to the depression.

▶ There are three physiological reasons for depression: (1) Low levels of serotonin and norepinephrine can cause depression. Evidence for that conclusion comes from the study of metabolites of these neurotransmitters and from experiments in which levels of these neurotransmitters were lowered with drugs or diet. (2) Low levels of activity in the brain are related to depression. Areas or structures of particular importance are the left prefrontal cortex, where information is integrated, the cingulate, which carries information between the frontal lobes and midbrain, and structures in the midbrain, such as the basal ganglia, which is responsible for motor activity. (3) Structural problems in the brain, particularly in the left prefrontal cortex, can cause depression. It is also noteworthy that physiological factors can also account for symptoms associated with depression, such as problems with sleep, appetite, sex, and thinking.

▶ Genetic factors can result in low levels of neurotransmitters and structural problems in the brain that then cause depression. Genetic factors can also lead to personality characteristics, such as impulsivity, that lead to increased stress, which can then cause depression. Finally, illnesses such as influenza in pregnant women can cause problems with brain development in fetuses, and the resulting problems in the brain can lead to depression.

Topic III: Treatments for Depression

▶ Psychotherapy in general and interpersonal psychotherapy in particular can be effective for treating depression.

▶ Cognitive therapy can be effective for treating depression and for reducing the number of relapses following drug treatment.

▶ Tricyclic, bicyclic, and atypical antidepressants can be effective for treating depression, but their effects often do not appear for 3 or 4 weeks, they are treatments rather than cures, and they can have side effects. MAOIs can reduce depression, but they can also result in dangerously high blood pressure if taken with foods or drugs that contain tyramine. Psychomotor stimulants (amphetamines, cocaine) can reduce depression, but depression levels will be higher than predrug levels when the drugs are no longer taken.

▶ Electroconvulsive therapy (ECT) can quickly reduce severe depression that cannot be controlled with other treatments. However, to prevent relapse, patients must then be given antidepressants or maintenance ECT. Although it can cause temporary retrograde amnesia, ECT is safe, and there is no evidence that it impairs cognitive abilities. A new treatment known as repetitive transcranial magnetic stimulation appears to have positive short-term effects on depression. Finally, light therapy can be effective for individuals who suffer from depression with seasonal pattern.

▶ Currently available treatments for depression can be effective, but recovery lasting 1 year may be limited to as few as 50% of the individuals who begin treatment. For mild or moderate levels of depression, psychotherapy, cognitive therapy, and antidepressants appear to be equally effective. For severe depression, a combination of antidepressants and ECT is more effective than psychotherapy or cognitive therapy.

▶ In general, combinations of different types of therapy (e.g., psychotherapy or cognitive therapy plus antidepressants) are more effective than any one therapy by itself. Unfortunately, we do not completely understand why many treatments work: (1) The effects of cognitive therapy may be due to changed beliefs or nonspecific factors, (2) increased levels of neurotransmitters are not sufficient to explain the effects of antidepressants, and (3) we do not know why ECT works beyond the fact that it increases brain activity.

Questions for Making Connections

1. Earlier I pointed out that physiology can be the final common step in the pathway to symptoms. Explain how physiology is the final common step in the pathway by which stress and learned helplessness lead to depression.

2. Treatments for depression should be related to the causes of depression. What are the psychodynamic, cognitive, and physiological explanations for depression, and how are the respective treatments designed to overcome the causes?

3. Stress, negative beliefs, levels of neurotransmitters, problems with brain structures, genes, and prenatal problems all contribute to depression. Explain how these factors can interact to result in depression.

4. Depression can range from mild to very severe. What treatments seem to be most effective for depression at different levels of severity?

5. We often say that we have effective treatments for depression. What qualifications should we attach to that claim?

6. Negative beliefs are linked to depression. Explain how the causal relationship can work in both directions.

Key Terms and People

In reviewing and testing yourself, you should be able to discuss each of the following:

aerobic fitness, p. 222
akathisia, p. 240
atypical antidepressants, p. 238
basal ganglia, p. 229
bicyclic, p. 235
bipolar disorder, p. 209
cingulate, p. 229
cognitive therapy, p. 234
cyclothymic disorder, p. 209
depression with postpartum onset, p. 215
depression with seasonal pattern, p. 217
dysthymic disorder, p. 209
electroconvulsive therapy (ECT), p. 239
hypothalamus, p. 228
interpersonal psychotherapy, p. 233

learned helplessness explanation, p. 225
left prefrontal cortex, p. 228
libido, p. 212
lithium, p. 236
maintenance ECT, p. 241
major depressive disorder, p. 209
MAOIs (antidepressants), p. 236
masked depression, p. 213
metabolites, p. 226
mood disorder due to a general medical condition, p. 214
mood disorders, p. 209
nonspecific factors, p. 245
norepinephrine, p. 226
premenstrual dysphoric disorder, p. 219
primary depression, p. 213

psychomotor agitation, p. 212
psychomotor retardation, p. 211
psychomotor stimulants (as antidepressants), p. 237
repetitive transcranial magnetic stimulation, p. 242
retrograde amnesia, p. 242
Saint John's wort, p. 238
seasonal affective disorder (SAD), p. 217
secondary depression, p. 213
selective serotonin reuptake inhibitors (SSRIs), p. 236
serotonin, p. 226
tricyclic, p. 235
tryptophan, p. 227
tyramine, p. 236

9

Mood Disorders: Bipolar Disorder and Suicide

IN THIS CHAPTER we will first consider bipolar disorder, and then we will turn our attention to the topic of suicide. Although suicide is not a mood disorder, it is included here because it is a problem that is closely linked to mood disorders.

TOPIC I

Bipolar Disorder

Carl was a happily married man of 28 who had always been very stable. However, 2 years ago he went through a period in which he became noticeably more active and extravagant. He slept less, had an unusual amount of energy, and made many unrealistic plans for his small business. He also went on buying sprees during which he spent large amounts of money on clothes and things for the house. He seemed to be going off in five or six directions at once, without giving any one much thought. After about a month Carl slowly became his "old self" again, much to his wife's relief. Everything was normal for about a year, but then he began slipping into a depression. He

stopped making business calls, at home he sat alone in his study, and he was convinced that he was a "rotten failure." He just wanted to be left alone. This depression lifted after a while, and Carl returned once again to his normal behavior. A week ago, however, he again started becoming very active, even agitated. He made plans for a vacation in the South Pacific as a celebration of a big business deal that he thought he would close, when in fact the deal was only in the idea stage. He also signed a contract to have an addition put on the house, but then put the house up for sale and started negotiating to buy another one that was completely out of his price range. Emotionally he was "on top of the world" and felt as though he could achieve anything he tried. He slept very little and called people in the middle of the night to set up business appointments he never kept. After about a week of this, his wife realized that he was completely out of control. She called the family physician, who admitted Carl to the psychiatric ward of the local hospital. Carl was diagnosed as suffering from bipolar disorder. What causes major mood swings like Carl's? Can they be treated, or does the individual have to "ride them out"?

Bipolar disorder is the second of the two major mood disorders. It differs from major depressive disorder in that it involves *swings of mood between mania and depression.* Because this disorder involves both mania and depression, it was once called *manic-depressive disorder.* There are two types of bipolar disorder: *Type I* involves mania and depression, whereas *Type II* involves *hypomania* and depression. Hypomania is simply a milder form of mania, so Type II is less serious. There is also a generally less severe form of bipolar disorder called **cyclothymic** (si-klo-THI-mik) **disorder,** in which both the mania and the depression are less extreme. Bipolar disorder occurs in about 1.5% of the population (Kessler et al., 1994). If individuals who have cyclothymic disorder are included, the percentage of occurrence is considerably higher—perhaps twice as high.

Symptoms

Bipolar disorder involves a variety of symptoms other than depression and mania. Mania involves a number of mood, cognitive, and motor symptoms, and understanding them is essential for making a diagnosis (Serretti et al., 1999). Because we examined depression and its related symptoms in Chapter 8, here I will focus on mania.

Mood Symptoms

During manic episodes the predominant mood is *euphoria.* The individual is excited, excessively happy, emotionally expansive, and generally "flying high." *DSM-IV* suggests that irritability can also be present during a manic episode, but irritability probably occurs only when people try to restrain the individual's inappropriate behavior. For example, a 200-pound manic patient became irritated and hostile when I objected to the fact that he had torn down my office drapes. He did not like the way the office was decorated, and in his expansive mood he had decided to redo it for me!

In its early stages mania may not be recognized as a symptom because the individual simply appears to be happy, carefree, unconcerned about potential problems, self-reliant, apparently productive, and festive.

---

bipolar disorder   A mood disorder that involves swings of mood between mania and depression; previously known as *manic-depressive disorder.*

cyclothymic disorder   A less severe form of bipolar disorder.

secondary mania   Mania that is the side effect of a drug or the result of a disorder other than bipolar disorder.

Cognitive Symptoms

Important cognitive symptoms in mania include *inflated self-esteem* and *grandiosity.* Patients with mania have completely unrealistic beliefs about themselves and what they can accomplish. One manic person I knew thought he had single-handedly saved the world from an energy crisis by inventing an automobile engine that would run on water ("Hey, water contains hydrogen which is combustible"), and he spent much of his time flying around the country looking for financial backers for his new company. When problems with his idea were pointed out, he brushed them aside as "minor details" that would be "worked out later."

Another cognitive symptom often seen in mania is *distractibility;* manic individuals are continually shifting their attention or getting distracted by other ideas or plans. This is often referred to as a *manic flight of ideas.* In some cases the flight of ideas is so rapid that it is difficult to follow the individual's train of thought and even the individual cannot evaluate what he or she is thinking. The thoughts of the inventor I just mentioned were jumping around so fast that he was unable to think his idea through carefully enough to realize that it could never work. Because of their inability to focus attention and because they keep shifting from task to task, most manic patients are ineffective and do not accomplish much.

Some patients with bipolar disorder also have *delusions* similar to those seen in schizophrenia. One patient told me in rapid succession that she was married to Burt Reynolds, she was the first woman President of the United States, and her three daughters had been murdered in the hospital. Delusions such as these are not always a component of bipolar disorder, but when they do occur, the individual is given a diagnosis of bipolar disorder *with psychotic features.*

Motor Symptoms

Bipolar patients literally run from one project to the next. During a particularly severe manic episode, one person drove through the downtown area of a large city at breakneck speed, sideswiping cars and driving wildly down sidewalks to get around cars at intersections. He had "important business deals to close" and was in a great hurry. Because individuals with mania are involved in so many things and because their confidence in their ultimate success is so exaggerated, they often spend very large amounts of money in very short periods of time. In some cases they quickly go through their life savings and run themselves deep into debt.

However, mania does not always result in ineffective behavior. I once knew a very creative patient who was an interior decorator. Whenever she had a severe manic episode (about once a year), she would completely redecorate her home by herself. Almost without stopping to sleep, she would repaint and repaper her entire home in less than a week. She would use bright, cheery colors and do very creative things. I often envied her energy and the results.

Physical Symptoms

The only consistent physical symptom seen in mania is a *decreased need for sleep.* Individuals suffering from mania are constantly "fired up" and "on the move," and they sleep very little. These individuals ignore fatigue, aches, pains, and other physical problems that may exist.

Case Study 9.1 (on p. 252) presents a student's description of her experience with bipolar disorder.

Diagnostic Criteria

The diagnostic criteria for bipolar and cyclothymic disorders are listed in Table 9.1.

In making a diagnosis we must be careful to distinguish between mania that is part of bipolar disorder and **secondary mania,** which is the *side effect of a drug or the result of some other disorder* (Silverstone & Hunt, 1992). For example, secondary mania can be a side effect of high levels of some antidepressant drugs. In those cases it appears that the drug "overshoots the mark" and brings the patient out of depression, past a normal mood state, and into mania.

 **Issues**

Before going on to discuss the causes of bipolar disorder, we need to consider a few issues, such as whether bipolar and major depressive disorders are different disorders and how long it takes to go through a manic-depressive cycle.

Bipolar and Major Depressive Disorders as Different Disorders

Because depression is a major symptom in both bipolar and major depressive disorders, it is tempting to assume that these are actually one disorder and that bipolar individuals simply have the additional symptom of mania. However, as indicated in Table 9.2 (on p. 253), the two disorders show a variety of other differences, and these differences suggest that the two are separate disorders. If they

---

TABLE 9.1

Diagnostic criteria for bipolar and cyclothymic disorders	**A. Bipolar Disorder**

A. Bipolar Disorder

1. The presence or history of a manic episode. A manic episode involves three or more of the following:

    (a) inflated self-esteem or grandiosity
    (b) decreased need for sleep
    (c) more talkative than usual or pressure to keep talking
    (d) flight of ideas or racing thoughts
    (e) distractibility
    (f) increase in goal-directed activity or psychomotor agitation
    (g) excessive involvement in pleasurable activities that have a high potential for painful consequences (e.g., engaging in unrestricted buying sprees, sexual indiscretions, or foolish investments).

The symptoms cause clinically significant distress or impairment in social, occupational, or other important areas of functioning.

2. The presence or history of a major depressive episode (see Table 8.1 for the criteria for a major depressive episode).

3. The mood episodes are not better accounted for by other disorders.

B. Cyclothymic Disorder

1. For at least 2 years the individual has had numerous periods with hypomanic symptoms (see Note) and numerous periods with depressive symptoms that do not meet the criteria for major depressive disorder (see Table 8.1).

2. During the 2-year period the individual has not been without the symptoms for more than 2 months at a time.

Note: Different qualifiers are used depending on whether the most recent episode was mania or depression. There are two types of bipolar disorder. Type I involves mania and depression, whereas Type II involves *hypomania* and depression. Hypomania is a mild form of mania. The criteria for hypomania are the same as those for mania, but the symptoms result in impairments in social or occupational functioning that are less serious than those seen in mania.

Source: American Psychiatric Association (1994).

"I'm Okay, You're Okay!"—A Student Slips into Depression and Mania

CASE STUDY 9.1

THE FOLLOWING ACCOUNT was written by a sophomore student of mine.

"I began thinking I might be slightly emotionally unstable my freshman year. I had frequent fights with my boyfriend in which I would fly off the handle and blow everything out of proportion, and I cried all of the time. I also became extremely irritable and lashed out at everyone I knew, especially my roommate. I noticed that I was very tired most of the time and slept for huge amounts of the day. It got more and more difficult to get out of bed in the morning, and my appetite all but disappeared. I dropped 13 pounds virtually overnight. For some reason I didn't understand, Princess Diana's death upset me greatly. I cried nonstop for days after her funeral. It was at that point that I realized something was wrong, and I went to the mental health clinic. They determined that I was suffering from severe clinical depression and put me on Paxil (an antidepressant). I responded to the Paxil, and I started to think I was cured.

"But my behavior was still abnormal. One day I would be pretty happy, while the next I would be either extremely sad or full of rage. It was nearly impossible to be around me. I started acting very impulsively. One day I wondered what it would be like to have my nose pierced, and within 30 minutes I had it done! I then proceeded to a shoe store and bought a very expensive pair of shoes that I could barely afford. It seemed like I was on a steep incline, like at the beginning of a roller coaster.

"Then, as if by magic, I suddenly didn't feel sad anymore at all. I was ecstatic most of the time. I enjoyed going to class and became very vocal, answering questions and offering comments frequently. I stopped sleeping altogether; I simply didn't need it. I

> **One day I would be pretty happy, while the next I would be either extremely sad or full of rage.**

was having ideas and theorizing and philosophizing all the time. I thought I was figuring everything out. But it got worse. I thought my boyfriend was Jesus. I thought God had sent him to me from Heaven. I thought every sign and billboard was a personal message to me. The day before my complete breakdown I went to my philosophy class in a strangely altered mood. I talked nonstop throughout class, adding to whatever anyone said. I also announced to the class that I was gay, though I'm not. At the end of class I stood up on my chair and tried to get everyone to chant with me, 'I'm okay, you're okay! I'm okay, you're okay!' My friends thought I was on some drug and were very concerned about me. I was behaving very inappropriately, but my actions had no impact on me whatsoever. I thought I was great and everyone loved me. My actions became vulgar, and I behaved in a very sexual way, making comments that were not typical of me.

"That night the resident assistant in the dorm got worried about me and called me into her room. I started screaming and crying that I didn't want to die. I was sure that I had figured out every mystery in the world, and I must therefore die. She called an ambulance, and the police came. When they were trying to strap me down on the gurney, I punched one of them out. Everyone gasped, but I thought it was hilarious. They sedated me a little in the ambulance, and once I got to the hospital, I was further sedated with Haldol (an antipsychotic). I must have slept for days.

"Being in the hospital was a positive experience, once I got past the shock of being in a 'loony bin.' I mean I thought I had reached absolute perfection and had discovered and solved every mystery in the world, and there they were telling me I was crazy. I met lots of people who were bipolar or depressed, and I met a woman with schizophrenia. They were friendly and taught me that it was okay to need help, and the

faster I got help, the faster I could start my new life. I was in the hospital for 2 weeks, and the nurses let my friends throw a big Christmas party for me in the hospital.

"In the hospital I started taking high levels of Depakote (a drug for mania), Paxil (an antidepressant), and Zyprexa (an antipsychotic), and I continued taking those after I was released. For a while it seemed to work, but after a few months I started skipping my medication, got depressed, and attempted to commit suicide. This caused me to go back into another hospital for 2 weeks, and it was there that I truly began to understand my illness. I had an excellent doctor and social worker, and they made sure I got the correct combination of drugs. For me the best combination is Depakote, Zoloft (an antidepressant), and Stelazine (an antipsychotic).

"Since then I have accepted my illness and have stopped fighting my medication. At first I thought the euphoric episode I went through was worth all the crushing pain that came with the depressions. But now I know that even the mania is bad because it causes me so much embarrassment. I have put my life back together, and my medicine has leveled me. The only problem I have is frequent insomnia, but I take Ativan (an antianxiety drug) for that. I am happy to talk about my disorder because it gives me an opportunity to show others what it is like to have a mental disorder. We don't all run around in straitjackets counting in fractions. I do take offense when people refer to the mentally ill as 'crazy' or 'psycho.' There are a lot of misconceptions and stigmas involved with mental illness, but in most cases, if medication is administered properly, we are just as 'normal' as everyone else."

Note: Because this student suffered from serious delusions as well as mania and depression, she would be diagnosed as suffering from bipolar disorder *with psychotic symptoms.*

TABLE 9.2

Differences between bipolar and major depressive disorders

	Bipolar disorder	*Major depressive disorder*
Symptoms	Depression and mania	Depression
Incidence	About 1.5%	12% or more
Gender ratio	Equal	Twice as many women
Genetics	Relatives have bipolar disorder.	Relatives have major depressive disorder.

were the same disorder, it would be difficult to understand why, for example, major depressive disorder occurs more often in women than in men, whereas bipolar disorder is equally likely to occur in women and men. It should also be noted that some cases of major depressive disorder appear to "convert" to bipolar disorder. What is really going on is that the individuals had bipolar disorder all along but before the "conversion" had shown only the depressive symptoms (Akiskal et al., 1995; Coryell et al., 1995).

Cycle Time

A frequently asked question is, how long does it take individuals with bipolar disorder to go through one cycle of mania and depression? There is no simple answer because there is great variability in cycle time. For instance, one study found that about 35% of individuals with bipolar disorder went through only one cycle in a 5-year period, whereas about 1% of such individuals went through 22 cycles—about one cycle every 3 months (Coryell, Endicott, & Keller 1992).

In recent years some interest has been focused on individuals who show **rapid cycling,** which consists of four or more cycles per year (Avasthi et al., 1999; Bauer, Calabrese, Dunner, & Post, 1994; Coryell et al., 1992; Robb et al., 1998; Tondo & Baldessarini, 1998; Wolpert, Goldberg, & Harrow, 1990). In general, rapid cycling is more likely to occur in women and initially at least is more difficult to treat than slower cycling. Rapid cycling probably reflects a more severe form of the disorder.

Creativity

Are individuals who suffer from mental disorders more creative than other individuals? It has often been assumed that they are, and the reasoning runs like this: Individuals with mental disorders often view the world differently, and creativity often involves putting things or ideas together in

Why is there such a strong relationship between bipolar disorder and creativity? Psychologists are not certain about the reason, but they do recognize that such bipolar symptoms as grandiosity and expansive thoughts can contribute to the creative process. Vincent Van Gogh suffered from bipolar disorder and produced more paintings during his manic periods.

a different way; so abnormality may lead to creativity. One problem encountered in studying the potential link between abnormality and creativity involved the difficulty of defining and measuring creativity. However, researchers got around this problem by identifying as "creative" those individuals, such as famous artists and writers, who other people generally agreed were "creative" (whatever that might mean). The investigators then compared the rates of various disorders in these creative individuals to the rates in noncreative individuals. These comparisons revealed that the creative individuals were more likely to suffer from mood disorders in general and bipolar disorder in particular (Andreasen, 1987; Jamison, 1993, 1996; Ludwig, 1994; Post, 1996; Schildkraut, Hirshfeld, & Murphy, 1994). For

rapid cycling   Four or more cycles of mania and depression per year, probably reflecting a more severe form of bipolar disorder.

example, in one study of creative writers, 80% had experienced at least one depressive episode, and 43% had a history of mania. Because the incidence of mania in the general population is only about 1.5%, the incidence among creative writers was almost 30 times higher than what it is in the general population.

Given that there is a strong relationship between bipolar disorder and creativity, the question is, why? The answer is not completely clear, but it has been argued that symptoms of bipolar disorder such as grandiosity, expansive thoughts, high activity level, and the ability to function on limited amounts of sleep all contribute to the production of creative works. That is, the individual ignores the restraints regarding what "should" be done and also produces more of everything, thus increasing the likelihood of producing something unique (creative). The link between mania and creative productivity is illustrated by the findings that, for example, Robert Schumann produced more musical compositions during his manic moods and Vincent van Gogh produced more paintings during his manic periods (Jamison, 1994).

The link between creativity and bipolar disorder raises an interesting question with regard to treatment: If treatment can eliminate mania, is it appropriate to treat individuals with bipolar disorder, thereby eliminating their mania and possibly their creativity (Jamison, 1995a, 1995b)? How much great art, literature, and music would have been lost if all people with bipolar disorder had been effectively treated for their mania?

Gender and Socioeconomic Factors

Bipolar disorder occurs about equally in men and women (Kessler et al., 1994). This pattern is very different from that for major depressive disorder, in which women outnumber men 2 to 1. It was once thought that bipolar disorder did not appear until adolescence, but there is now some evidence that some children who appear to be suffering from attention-deficit/hyperactivity disorder (see Chapter 13) may actually be suffering from hypomania. Also unlike major depressive disorder, which is most likely to occur in lower classes, bipolar disorder occurs equally across classes.

Unawareness of Mania

Earlier I pointed out that we sometimes do not recognize mania in its early stages because the individuals merely seem to be in exceptionally good moods. What is more serious, however, is that even when mania becomes severe and the individuals are out of control, *they do not recognize that they have a problem;* thus it becomes exceptionally difficult to get them to accept treatment (Pallanti et al., 1999). This problem is dramatically illustrated by the personal experiences of Kay Redfield Jamison, who is a professor of psychiatry at Johns Hopkins School of Medicine and one of

the world's leading authorities on bipolar disorder. Professor Jamison suffers from bipolar disorder herself, and despite her expertise, when she slips into a manic episode, she does not realize it—she just thinks she's feeling great and will not listen to those around her who express concern. In an interesting attempt to solve this problem, she wrote a letter to herself while in a normal state reminding herself that she is unable to recognize it when she is manic. She then gave the letter to her husband with instructions to show it to her when she became manic and refused treatment.

Explanations

Now let's turn to the question of what causes bipolar disorder. At present there are no widely held psychodynamic, learning, or cognitive explanations for bipolar disorder; in general, most attention is focused on physiological explanations for the disorder. The decline in interest in psychological explanations occurred primarily because those that were offered were not particularly persuasive and treatments based on them were ineffective. Furthermore, drugs were found to be very effective for treating the disorder, which reduced interest in finding psychological explanations. However, to provide you with some historical background, I will briefly describe a once-popular psychodynamic explanation for bipolar disorder. Following this description, I will explain how stress can trigger mania, and then I will discuss the physiological explanations.

Psychodynamic Explanations

Manic Flight from Depression. The basic tenet of one psychodynamic explanation was that individuals with bipolar disorder are basically very depressed (which they show during their depressive phase), but when the depression becomes too great, they attempt to *escape the depression* with manic behavior (Freeman, 1971; Lewin, 1951). During the manic phase patients were said to be in a "manic flight from depression." In other words, the manic behavior was seen as a defense against overwhelming depression. The flight-from-depression explanation had a good deal of intuitive appeal because a commonly suggested remedy for depression is to "go out and do something wild" or to "put on a happy face."

There were also numerous case studies that could be interpreted as supporting the flight-from-depression explanation. For example, I knew one patient with bipolar disorder whose husband was having affairs with other women, and in her manic phase she would dance around the hospital ward singing, "I'm going to wash that man right out of my hair"—on a number of occasions, she dumped washbasins of water over her head! Her singing and dancing were interpreted as an attempt to distract herself from her "underlying depression" about her husband. Her therapist also pointed out that her "real concern" about her husband came out in the content of what she sang; that is, she wanted that unfaithful man "out of her hair." Anecdotal reports such as this are interesting, but there is no evidence that mania is a flight from depression.

Stress. It was also once thought that stress caused bipolar disorder, the notion being that when faced with stress some individuals go into an uncontrollable frenzy of activity. However, we now know that stress by itself *does not cause* bipolar disorder, but stress can bring on mania or cause a relapse in *individuals who are physiologically predisposed to bipolar disorder* (Hammen & Gitlin, 1997; Johnson & Roberts, 1995; Malkoff-Schwartz et al., 1998). For example, in one study individuals with bipolar disorder who experienced a high number of stressful life events were found to be almost five times more likely to relapse than those who experienced a low number of stressful life events (Ellicott et al., 1990). Overall, then, it appears that stress can contribute to some cases of bipolar disorder, probably because it exacerbates an underlying physiological problem. With this as background, let's consider the physiological explanations.

Physiological Explanations

From the physiological perspective bipolar disorder is generally thought to stem from some form of *instability in brain activity and structural problems in the brain* (Dubovsky & Buzan, 1999; Perez et al., 1999; Soares et al., 1999; Strakowski et al., 1999). Specifically, it appears that changing levels of synaptic transmission in the areas of the brain responsible for emotion may lead to swings between mania and depression. It may also be that those areas of the brain responsible for emotional arousal are enlarged in individuals with the disorder and that this contributes to mania. Let's consider these possibilities.

Changes in Synaptic Transmission and Brain Activity. First, it should be pointed out that mania is associated with high levels of brain activity, whereas depression is associated with low levels of activity. This is illustrated in Figure 9.1, which shows PET scans of the brain of a patient with bipolar disorder. PET scans reflect glucose metabolism, which is a measure of brain activity. The three scans in the top row in the figure were taken during a depressed phase; the three scans in the bottom row were taken during a manic phase. We are looking down on the patient's brain from above; the three scans in each row represent three cross sections (planes) of the brain. The colors indicate different amounts of glucose metabolism: Red and yellow indicate higher metabolism, and blue and purple indicate lower metabolism. In the manic phase the patient had a much higher rate of cerebral glucose metabolism than in the depressed

phase; in fact, the rate of glucose metabolism was 36% higher on the manic day than on the depressed day (Baxter et al., 1985).

The question is, what causes these changes in brain activity? One factor is *changes in the levels of neurotransmitters.* Numerous investigations have revealed that mania is associated with high levels of neurotransmitters, whereas depression is associated with low levels (Agren, 1982; Beckman & Goodwin, 1980; Bond et al., 1972; De Leon-Jones et al., 1975; Jones et al., 1973; Maas, 1975; Maas et al., 1972; Muscettola et al., 1984; Schildkraut et al., 1973; Schildkraut et al., 1978). High and low levels of a neurotransmitter and their links to mania and depression were illustrated in Figure 8.7.

Changes in brain activity are also thought to be due to changes in the *sensitivity to stimulation of the postsynaptic neurons* (Dubovsky & Buzan, 1999). In other words, at certain times the receptor sites may be very sensitive to stimulation, which leads to high brain activity and mania, but at other times the receptor sites may be less sensitive to stimulation, which results in low brain activity and depression.

Changes in neurotransmitter levels and in neuron sensitivity appear to be important for explaining the mood swings that occur in bipolar disorder, but the question then becomes, what causes the changes in neurotransmitter levels and neuron sensitivity? Two factors seem to be important: First, it appears that genetic factors provide the basis for the instability (see the later discussion). Second, however, evidence suggests that stress can stimulate a cycle of instability. In one study it was found that after rats had been injected with a strong stimulant (cocaine), which resulted in arousal similar to that which occurs during stress, they showed a cycling of brain activity similar to that

FIGURE 9.1

PET scans reveal high levels of brain activity during mania.

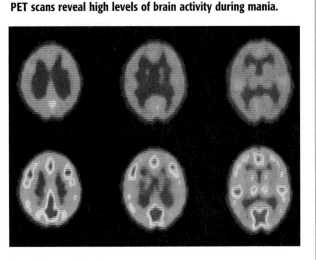

Source: Baxter et al. (1985).

seen in bipolar disorder (Antelman et al., 1998). Importantly, this cycling of brain activity and related behavior could be prevented by giving the rats injections of lithium, which is used to control bipolar disorder in humans (see the next section on treatments). In general, then, the process that leads to bipolar disorder appears to be as follows: (1) Genetic factors establish a predisposition to instability in synaptic transmission (varying levels of neurotransmitters and neuron sensitivity), (2) stress may trigger a cycle of instability, (3) changes in synaptic transmission cause changes in the levels of brain activity, and (4) the changes in brain activity lead to changes in mood.

Problems with Brain Structures. Investigators have also found that many individuals with bipolar disorder have a substantially *larger amygdala* and somewhat *larger nerve tracts and other structures in the brain related to emotion* (Altshuler et al., 1998; Strakowski et al., 1999). The **amygdala** (uh-MIG-da-la) is a structure in the midbrain, and its enlargement is particularly interesting because it plays a major role in emotional arousal (see Chapter 3). The enlargement of the nerve tracts that conduct emotion-related information suggests that an excessive amount of emotion-related material could be carried along those "highways," which might lead to mania. The findings concerning brain structures in individuals with bipolar disorder are different in two ways from the findings associated with individuals who suffer only from depression: First, with bipolar disorder *larger* brain structures were found, whereas with major depressive disorder *smaller* brain structures were found. Second, somewhat *different sets of brain structures* were involved. These differences are consistent with the point made earlier that bipolar and major depressive disorders are different disorders.

Genetic Factors. Initial evidence for the role of genetics in the development of bipolar disorder comes from the finding that individuals who have a first-degree relative (i.e., parent or sibling) with bipolar disorder have a risk of developing the disorder that is almost 10 times higher than that of individuals who do not have a first-degree relative with the disorder (Nurnberger & Gershon, 1992). Even stronger evidence can be found in studies of identical and nonidentical twins. For instance, it was found that among identical twins the concordance rate for bipolar disorder was almost 60%, whereas among nonidentical twins the concordance rate was less than 20% (Bertelsen, Havald, & Hauge, 1977). Finally, a study of the biological and adoptive parents of individuals who developed bipolar disorder revealed that 31% of the biological parents of the patients had bipolar disorder, but only 2% of the adoptive parents had the disorder (Mendlewicz & Rainer, 1977). Overall, it is clear that genetics plays an important role in bipolar disorder; indeed, it is estimated that the heritability of bipolar disorder is about 80%, which is substantially higher than the

heritability for most other psychiatric disorders and for normal personality traits (Rutter et al., 1999).

Prenatal and Perinatal Factors. A heritability of about 80% is high, but it also means that about 20% of the cases cannot be explained with genetic factors. How can we account for the remaining cases? One possibility is illnesses or traumas during the prenatal (pregnancy) and perinatal (birth) periods cause problems with brain development, which in turn lead to the disorder. Investigators tested this possibility by finding families in which one child had bipolar disorder but another child did not. The investigators then compared the medical records of the mother during each pregnancy. They also examined the medical records related to the birth of each child. The results revealed two things: First, the mothers were more likely to have been ill or exposed to toxins when pregnant with the child who developed bipolar disorder than when pregnant with the child who did not. Second, the children who developed bipolar disorder experienced many more complications at the time of birth than did their siblings who did not develop the disorder. The birth complications included prolonged labor, the use of forceps in delivery, skull fractures, delayed respiration, excess bleeding following birth, and jaundice following birth (Kinney et al., 1993, 1998). It appears, then, that prenatal and perinatal problems may have caused disruptions in brain development, which later led to bipolar disorder, and that prenatal and perinatal problems can account for cases of bipolar disorder that cannot be linked to genetic factors.

The pieces of the puzzle of bipolar disorder are beginning to come together. The important question remaining is, can the disorder be treated? I will answer that next.

Treatments

For many years we did not have an effective treatment for bipolar disorder; during periods of mania patients were simply restrained in straitjackets, "knocked out" with heavy doses of sedatives, or locked in seclusion rooms. Fortunately, this picture has changed dramatically, and today most cases of bipolar disorder can be effectively treated. In this section I will describe a number of strategies that can be used to treat bipolar disorder, ranging from drugs to education.

Lithium

In 1949 it was discovered that **lithium,** a naturally occurring salt, was effective for controlling both the mania and the depression seen in bipolar disorder (Cade, 1949). Although lithium was used extensively in Europe to treat bipolar disorder as early as 1950, it is poisonous and can be lethal at high levels, and therefore it was not approved for use in the United States until 1970. Since its approval, however, it has been used widely as a defense against the symptoms of bipolar disorder.

Lithium is effective for treating between 60% and 70% of the adults and children who suffer from bipolar disorder (Greil et al., 1998; Keck & McElroy, 1998; Kulhara et al., 1999; Marangell et al., 1999; Schou, 1998). In one series of studies in which patients with bipolar disorder were given either lithium or a placebo, 62% of the patients who received lithium remitted their symptoms, whereas only 5% of the patients who were given the placebo did so. In another study it was found that when individuals stopped taking lithium, almost 70% relapsed within the first year (Baldessarini, Tondo, & Hennen, 1999). Although lithium is effective, it is not yet clear why. It appears that lithium stabilizes the levels of neurotransmitters and/or stabilizes neuron sensitivity, but exactly how it does this has not yet been established (Antelman et al., 1998; Dubovsky & Buzan, 1999).

Despite lithium's effectiveness for treating bipolar disorder, there are three problems with its use: First, between 30% and 40% of patients are not helped by lithium. Second, even among those whom lithium helps, it is often not a complete treatment. Specifically, some individuals relapse, and even if they do not relapse, as many as 20% will continue to show some symptoms and may have problems with social or occupational functioning (Coryell et al., 1998; Gitlin et al., 1995; Goldberg, Harrow, & Grossman, 1995; Kulhara et al., 1999; Strakowski, DelBello, et al. 1999). The third problem revolves around lithium's side effects. As I mentioned earlier, at high levels lithium is poisonous, so it is essential to monitor lithium levels in the bloodstream. During the first week, while levels are being established, it is necessary to take blood samples every day. Following that, weekly samples are necessary, and eventually checkups can be reduced to about one a month. However, even when the blood levels are within a safe range, lithium can have troublesome side effects, the most common of which are thirst and frequent urination (to eliminate the fluids taken in to quench the thirst). At somewhat higher levels lithium can cause difficulty with concentration, memory, and motor coordination (Shaw et al., 1987). At even higher levels muscle tremors, gastric distress, and dizziness may set in (Herrington & Lader, 1981).

Anticonvulsants, Antipsychotics, and Antidepressants

Because lithium is not always effective and can produce unpleasant side effects, in recent years there has been a trend toward the use of **anticonvulsant drugs** to treat bipolar disorder (Calabrese et al., 1999; Keck & McElroy, 1998; Marangell et al., 1999; Marcotte, 1998). These drugs were originally developed to treat epilepsy. We know that epilep-

tic seizures are caused by the excessive firing of neurons in the brain, and anticonvulsant drugs are effective for controlling that firing and the seizures. Thus, it appears that anticonvulsants are effective for treating mania because they control the excessive firing of neurons that underlies mania. The anticonvulsive drugs that are used most widely to treat mania are Tegretol (carbamazepine), Klonopin (clonazepam), and Depakote (valproic acid).

Another approach to the control of mania involves the use of **antipsychotic drugs,** which are *drugs that are usually used to treat schizophrenia* (Barbini et al., 1997; Frye et al., 1998; Ghaemi & Sachs, 1997; Segal, Berk, & Brook, 1998; Tohen & Grundy, 1999; Tohen et al., 1999; Vieta et al., 1998). As you will learn later, schizophrenia is due to excessively high levels of arousal in the brain, and these drugs reduce the symptoms of schizophrenia by reducing the arousal (see Chapters 10 and 11). Fortunately, antipsychotics can also reduce the arousal that leads to mania. These drugs have the additional advantage of reducing the psychotic (schizophrenic) symptoms, such as delusions, that sometimes occur in mania.

Anticonvulsants and antipsychotics provide additional treatment options, but unfortunately there is no way to predict ahead of time which type of drug will be most effective and have the fewest side effects for any one individual. Indeed, when students with bipolar disorder gather in my office and talk about their medications, I am always amazed at the differing reactions they report: One will swear by a drug, whereas another will report having terrible side effects with that drug. At present finding the right drug is usually a matter of trial and error.

Finally, although lithium, antipsychotics, and anticonvulsants are effective for controlling mania, for some individuals they are somewhat less effective for reducing depression, so those individuals are often prescribed antidepressants as well (Amsterdam et al., 1998). You will recall that the student who wrote about her bipolar disorder in Case Study 9.1 said that her symptoms could only be controlled with a combination of an anticonvulsant, an antipsychotic, and an antidepressant.

amygdala   A structure in the midbrain that plays a major role in emotional arousal.

lithium   A naturally occurring salt that is effective for controlling both the mania and the depression of bipolar disorder but that can be lethal at high levels.

anticonvulsant drugs   Drugs that control excessive firing of neurons in the brain and were originally developed to treat epilepsy but are now also used to treat bipolar disorder (primarily mania).

antipsychotic drugs   Drugs that reduce high levels of arousal in the brain and are usually used to treat schizophrenia but are also used to treat bipolar disorder (primarily mania).

Before leaving the topic of drugs, I must point out that many patients simply stop taking their drugs after their moods have been stabilized. This usually occurs because (1) when the symptoms are gone, the patients do not think they need the drugs anymore, (2) the patients become annoyed with the side effects, or (3) the patients miss the fun of the manic highs and go off the medication in the hope of experiencing those highs again (Jamison & Akiskal, 1983; Van Putten, 1975). It is interesting to note that patients with bipolar disorder are more likely to discontinue taking their drugs than patients with major depressive disorder, who experience only depression if they stop taking their medication (Kocsis & Stokes, 1979).

An individual who goes off lithium is 28 times more likely to have a manic episode than an individual who stays on the medication (Suppes et al., 1991). However, in some cases the patient is foiled in the attempt to bring on mania because depression sets in instead. The experience of one patient who voluntarily discontinued his medication is presented in Case Study 9.2.

Electroconvulsive Therapy and Transcranial Magnetic Stimulation

Unfortunately, drugs are not effective for some individuals, but for them electroconvulsive therapy (ECT) can be an option. Indeed, ECT can be effective for bringing about a quick recovery for about 60% of individuals with mania for whom drugs did not work (Janicak & Levy, 1998; Mukherjee, Sackeim, & Schnur, 1994). (ECT appears to be effective for about 80% of manic patients in general.) Interestingly, individuals with mania appear to have lower thresholds for seizures than depressed individuals do, and therefore lower voltage levels can be used in the treatment, which can reduce the side effects of the shocks. As in the treatment of severe depression, the most effective strategy for severe cases of bipolar disorder involves the use of ECT in combination with medication (Mukherjee, 1993).

Finally, there is also some evidence that transcranial magnetic stimulation is effective in reducing mania (Grisaru et al., 1998). Interestingly, stimulation in the right prefrontal lobe is more effective than stimulation in the left lobe, which is the opposite of what happens with depression. Once again we have evidence that mania is not simply the flip side of depression.

psychoeducation A psychological treatment for bipolar disorder in which patients and family members learn about the disorder, how to cope with it, and how to treat it.

Psychoeducation

Finally, we come to the very important topic of psychological treatment. In the preceding sections I explained how drugs and ECT are often effective for controlling the symptoms of bipolar disorder, but I also pointed out that for most individuals those treatments are not enough; that is, in many cases not all symptoms are eliminated, and some patients continue to have trouble functioning, they can relapse, and they might stop taking their medication. That is where psychological interventions come in (Basco & Rush, 1996; Craighead et al., 1998; Miklowitz, 1996; Scott, 1996). In general, psychological treatment is focused on two factors, the first of which is *stress reduction*. Reducing stress is crucial because stress can trigger mania or make it worse. If stress is reduced, not only will the symptoms be lessened, but in some cases the individual may be able to get along with less medication. To reduce stress therapists teach the patient how to recognize and avoid stressors and how to cope with stress that cannot be avoided. Importantly, therapists also help family members accept the fact that the patient suffers from a potentially serious disorder that requires some adjustment on their part in order to reduce stress for the patient. That is, just as family members must make accommodations for a person with a heart condition or a broken leg, so must they make adjustments in order to reduce the demands and stress on someone with bipolar disorder.

The second factor in psychological treatment involves helping the patient and family recognize when there is a change in symptoms that might require a change in medication. Earlier I pointed out that patients often cannot recognize when they are entering a period of mania and need more medication. Therefore, it is essential that they be taught to watch for the signs that they are getting out of control and that people around them become sensitive to the symptoms as well. Catching a mood swing early can avoid a lot of problems, including a major increase in medication and possible hospitalization. Finally, psychological treatment is also focused on assuring that patients continue to take their medication. Patients must be made aware of the importance of taking their medication, and sometimes the people around them must help monitor medication usage.

From this description it should be clear that the psychological treatment of bipolar disorder is not "therapy" in the traditional sense; instead it can be best conceptualized as **psychoeducation.** In other words, patients and family members learn about the disorder, how to cope with it, and how to treat it. Fortunately, psychoeducation for bipolar disorder can be provided by a wide variety of mental health professionals at relatively little cost, and this type of intervention has been found to be very effective (Clarkin et al., 1998).

A Student with Bipolar Disorder Who Stopped Taking His Lithium

"AFTER BEING 'NORMALIZED' on lithium, I began to wonder whether I could exercise any conscious control over my moods. Having been through both extremes of bipolar illness, I believed that I would be able to detect the warning signals that would tell me when a mood swing was coming on. An inability to sleep and lack of appetite signaled a high coming on, and unwarranted depression and listlessness signaled a low. I rationalized that during my level period I was medicating myself needlessly. Also, various aspects of taking lithium carbonate bothered me. The side effects of stomach discomfort, dry mouth, and the need to urinate frequently were very annoying, as was the simple hindrance of having to carry and take pills three times a day.

"I also missed the wonderful feeling involved in the manic high. I believed that if I were to stay off lithium long enough to notice the first signs of mania coming on, I could then medicate myself to the point of holding my mood at a mild 'hypomanic' state. This would let me feel happier and more energetic than usual, and I thought that with 'a little medication,' I could keep from climbing too high.

"The problem, as I found out, is that it is very difficult to detect those first signals—especially those of depression. When I went off my medication, I found myself so depressed that I didn't even care enough to start the lithium again. Lithium does not have a fast-acting antidepression effect, and it took a long time for me to benefit when I did resume taking the medication.

"My attempt to keep track of my high and control it was also unsuccessful. When I was feeling better (higher), I thought, 'I can handle this—I'm sure I can handle a little more.' Unfortunately, during the manic state it is very hard to be objective, and I lost control. In the end the expression 'letting it get away from you' seems a very apt way to describe what generally happened when I went off my medication.

"After a couple of disastrous experiences (I had to drop out of school and go back into the hospital until I was again normalized on lithium), I am now back on the medication for good, or at least until we have established that I am no longer at risk for bipolar mood swings. I now take my lithium in timed-release capsules, and the side effects are no longer noticeable."

> I also missed the wonderful feeling involved in the manic high.

I want to conclude our discussion of bipolar disorder with Case Study 9.3 (on p. 260), which presents some comments from Professor Kay Redfield Jamison, who has battled this disorder for years.

THINKING CRITICALLY

Questions about Bipolar Disorder

1. *Why do individuals with bipolar disorder swing between mania and depression?* The swings between mania and depression are the result of changes in brain activity that appear to be due primarily to changes in the levels of neurotransmitters and in the sensitivity of postsynaptic neurons. Mania may also be facilitated by the increased size of certain brain structures, most notably the amygdala. These differences are in turn probably caused by genetic factors, as well as by prenatal and perinatal problems that have long-term influences on brain development and functioning. Although a shift in mood often appears to occur spontaneously, in many cases the cycling of mania and depression is set off by stress. Stress by itself will not result in mania, but it leads to mania in those individuals who have a physiological predisposition to bipolar disorder.

2. *Do we have effective treatments for bipolar disorder?* Yes and no. On the positive side lithium, anticonvulsants, antipsychotics, antidepressants, ECT, transcranial magnetic stimulation, and stress reduction can all reduce the symptoms of bipolar disorder. There are two reasons why physiological and psychological treatments must go hand in hand: First, to achieve maximal treatment effects and avoid relapses, the individuals and their families need to learn how to reduce stress and cope with the disorder. Second, the individuals must learn the importance of continuing to take their medication, even if they are not in a manic or depressed state. Being symptom-free is a result of taking the medication, not a reason to stop taking it.

On the negative side the treatments are simply not enough for many individuals. That is, the treatments are able to greatly reduce symptoms, but low levels of symptoms often persist and interfere with daily functioning. Furthermore, relapses do occur, even when the treatments are continued. We have come a long way in our ability to treat bipolar disorder, but we do not yet have treatments that are completely effective for everyone.

Kay Redfield Jamison Talks about Mania, Depression, and Treatment

CASE STUDY 9.3

DR. KAY REDFIELD JAMISON is a leading expert on bipolar disorder. She also suffers from the disorder and has written a sensitive and fascinating autobiography entitled *An Unquiet Mind*, in which she describes her experiences. It is a book I highly recommend. Here she talks about mania, depression, and treatment.

On Becoming Manic

"When you're high, it's tremendous. The ideas and feelings are fast and frequent like shooting stars, and you follow them until you find better and brighter ones. Shyness goes, the right words and gestures are suddenly there, the power to captivate others a felt certainty. There are interests found in uninteresting people. Sensuality is pervasive, and the desire to seduce and be seduced irresistible. Feelings of ease, intensity, power, well-being, financial omnipotence, and euphoria pervade one's marrow. But, somewhere, this changes. The fast ideas are far too fast, and there are far too many; overwhelming confusion replaces clarity. Memory goes. Humor and absorption on friends' faces are replaced by fear and concern. Everything previously moving with the grain is now against—you are irritable, angry, frightened, uncontrollable, and enmeshed totally in the blackest caves of the mind. You never knew those caves were there." (p. 67)

On the Change to Depression

"A floridly psychotic mania was followed, inevitably, by a long and lacerating, black, suicidal depression; it lasted more than a year and a half. From the time I woke up in the morning until the time I went to bed at night, I was unbearably miserable and seemingly incapable of any kind of joy or enthusiasm. Everything—every thought, word, movement—was an effort. Everything that once was sparkling now was flat. I seemed to myself to be dull, boring, inadequate, thick brained, unlit, unresponsive, chill skinned, bloodless, and sparrow drab. I doubted, completely, my ability to do anything well. It seemed as though my mind had slowed down and burned out to the point of being virtually useless. . . . Washing my hair took hours to do, and it drained me for hours afterward; filling the ice-cube tray was beyond my capacity, and I occasionally slept in the same clothes I had worn during the day because I was too exhausted to undress. . . . Suicidal depression, I decided in the midst of my indescribably awful, 18-month bout of it, is God's way of keeping manics in their place. It works. Profound [depression] is a day-in, day-out, night-in, night-out, almost arterial level of agony. It is a pitiless, unrelenting pain that affords no window of hope, no alternative to a grim and brackish existence. . . ." (pp. 110, 111, 114)

On Treatment

"At this point in my existence, I cannot imagine leading a normal life without both taking lithium and having had the benefits of psychotherapy. Lithium prevents my seductive but disastrous highs, diminishes my depressions, clears out the wool and webbing from my disordered thinking, slows me down, gentles me out, keeps me from ruining my career and relationships, keeps me out of a hospital, alive, and makes psychotherapy possible. But, ineffably, psychotherapy heals. It makes some sense of the confusion, reins in the terrifying thoughts and feelings, returns some control and hope and possibility of learning from it all. . . . Psychotherapy is a sanctuary; it is a battleground; it is a place I have been psychotic, neurotic, elated, confused, and despairing beyond belief. But, always, it is where I have believed—or learned to believe—that I might someday be able to contend with all of this." (pp. 88–89)

Source: Jamison (1995).

Dr. Kay Redfield Jamison, a world-renowned expert on bipolar disorder, has struggled with the disorder for years.

3. *How do the treatments for mania work?* It seems clear that anticonvulsants, antipsychotics, and stress reduction inhibit mania because they reduce the brain activity that leads to mania. In contrast, it is suspected that lithium works by stabilizing neurotransmitter levels and/or neuron sensitivity, but how that happens is not clear. Finally, the effects of ECT on bipolar disorder are simply not understood, and furthermore they are paradoxical, in that ECT can stop both mania and depression. ECT must somehow "reset" the system, but how it works is a mystery. Obviously, we still have much to learn about the treatment of bipolar disorder.

TOPIC II
Suicide

Kate was a 23-year-old fashion assistant buyer for a large department store. Over a 2-year period she became somewhat depressed. She attributed her poor mood to exhaustion brought on by the constant strain of her job. She began going to a psychotherapist but stopped after only a few sessions because she didn't think she could be helped. Feeling hopeless, she occasionally gave some thought to suicide; it would provide a release from the constant strain she was under—and why not? She had nothing to live for. On a number of occasions Kate made comments to her friends like "Nothing seems to be going right; sometimes I feel like stepping in front of a truck" or "Probably the best thing for me to do tonight is to take all the pills in my medicine cabinet and just not wake up tomorrow morning." Her friends knew that Kate was depressed, but they thought she would snap out of it, and they didn't take her comments about suicide seriously. When Kate did not come in for work for 2 days and did not answer her phone, a friend went to her apartment. She found Kate dead in her bed with a variety of empty pill bottles next to her. Kate had left a short note in which she simply apologized for not being a better person. Why do people commit suicide? Are there reasons other than depression and stress? Can suicide be prevented?

Suicide is a very serious problem. Consider the following facts:

- Suicide is one of the ten leading causes of death in the United States.
- Suicide is the second leading cause of death among young males.
- Well over 30,000 people in the United States will commit suicide this year.
- In 1997 the U.S. Senate passed a resolution declaring suicide prevention to be "a national priority."

The magnitude of the problem is actually much greater than the statistics suggest because many "accidents" are in fact disguised suicides. Furthermore, it is estimated that there are at least 15 attempted suicides for each one that is successful (Jamison & Baldessarini, 1999). The seriousness of the problem is clearly reflected in the findings of a study of college students: 26% of the students had considered suicide in the preceding 12 months, 2% had attempted suicide in the preceding 12 months, and 10% had attempted suicide at some time in the past (Meehan et al., 1992; see also Crosby, Cheltenham, & Sacks, 1999; Kessler, Borges, & Walters, 1999). In view of the pervasiveness and seriousness of the problem, it is important that we give suicide careful consideration.

Issues

Before considering the causes of suicide, we need to examine some of the issues associated with suicide. These may provide some clues to the causes.

Gender and Age

Women are three times more likely to *attempt* suicide than men, but men are three times more likely to *succeed* in committing suicide. The higher success rate among men reflects the fact that they use more violent techniques (shooting themselves, jumping from buildings) than women (overdosing, wrist slashing), and those more violent techniques are more likely to be successful (Isometsae & Loennqvist, 1998). Indeed, in one study it was found that men were more than 20 times more likely to use guns, whereas women were 3 times more likely to use drugs. Why are women more likely to attempt suicide? The answer to that question is not completely clear, but it may be that they are more likely to suffer from depression, which plays a major role in suicide (see the later discussion). It has also been suggested that suicide is a more acceptable behavior for women than it is for men (Langhinrichsen-Rohling et al., 1998). It is also the case that physical abuse, often from a spouse, is linked to suicide among women in many cultures (Fischbach & Herbert, 1997). Finally, there appear to be some differences between women and men in why they commit suicide; depression seems to be a more important motive for women, whereas aggression may be more important for men (Prigerson & Slimack, 1999).

In almost all cultures suicide rates increase with age (Lester, 1991b; Purcell, Thrush, & Blanchette, 1999). In the United States the greatest increase comes between the ages of 65 and 84; in fact, for individuals over the age of 65 the suicide rate is twice the national average. The generally high rate of suicide among older adults is due primarily to the very high rate of suicide among white males over 65 (McIntosh, 1992). Those findings are reflected in Figure 9.2 (on p. 262). Older individuals are more likely to be successful in their suicide attempts than their younger counterparts, probably because they use more lethal means and are more likely to be resolute about what they are doing.

Culture

There are dramatic differences in suicide rates among cultures, ranging from a high of about 45 suicides per 100,000 persons in Hungary and Germany to a low of less than 1 per 100,000 persons in Nicaragua and Egypt (Diekstra, 1990). The cultural differences appear to be primarily due to three factors, the first of which is the degree to which suicide is an acceptable act. Indeed, in Japan and some other

FIGURE 9.2

Men have a higher rate of suicide than women, and the difference increases with age.

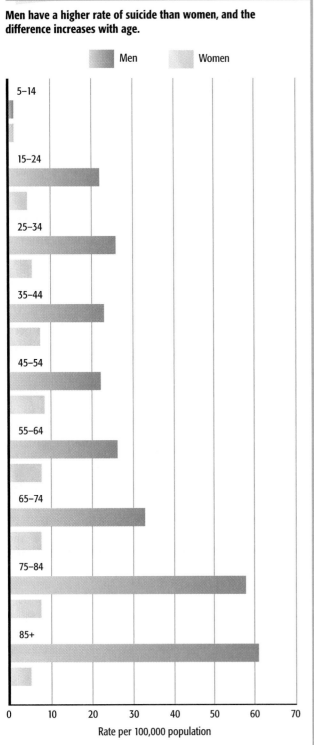

Source: Adapted from McIntosh (1992), Figure 3, p. 20.

whereas in Buddhism it is an acceptable way to resolve serious personal problems (Iga, 1993). Among African Americans church attendance is associated with a reduced acceptability of suicide as a solution for problems (Stack, 1998). The role of culture is strong and lasting; indeed, the rate of suicide among immigrants mirrors the rate of suicide in the country from which they immigrated rather than the country in which they currently live (Lester, 1997b).

The second reason for cultural differences in suicide rates is differences in stress (Hawton, 1992). Support for this comes from studies documenting that suicide rates go up and down with levels of stress within a country. For example, during the period immediately following the breakup of the Soviet Union, suicide rates in the former Soviet bloc countries were low because a great Western-type economic expansion was expected, and there was a high level of optimism. However, when the expansion failed to materialize and unemployment soared, so did suicide rates (Vaernik, 1998). In contrast, in other countries the rates of suicide remained relatively stable at that time.

The third contributor to differences in suicide rates among cultures is the difference in the degree to which depression is successfully identified and treated. Because suicide often stems from depression, effective treatment of depression reduces the rate of suicide.

Suicide Rates

Some reports have suggested that the rate of suicide among the general population in the United States is increasing and that the rate among adolescents has tripled over the past 30 years. Indeed, the problem has been labeled an *epidemic* (Centers for Disease Control, 1986). However, what at first appears to be an increase in suicide is probably due to the increased willingness of medical examiners to label a suicide as a suicide, rather than to cover it up by calling it an accident (Gist & Welch, 1989; Madge & Harvey, 1999; Males, 1991a, 1991b). This conclusion is based on the following facts and reasoning: The overall death rate (accidents plus suicides) has remained flat among people in the 19–44 age range, so if the suicide rate were increasing, the accident rate would have to be decreasing; however, there is no evidence that the accident rate has decreased. Overall, then, what appears to be a change in the suicide rate may actually reflect a change in attitudes toward suicide reporting.

Suicides, Covert Suicides, and Suicide Gestures

Many suicides are disguised and hence are not recognized as suicides. For example, when people do not want others to know that they have committed suicide because they are ashamed or because their life insurance policy will not pay off for suicide, they may commit **covert** (ko-VURT) **suicide,** or suicide disguised to appear as an accident. Auto-

countries suicide is considered an honorable thing to do (Domino & Takahashi, 1991). The differences in acceptability of suicide are often determined by religious differences. For example, in Catholicism suicide is a mortal sin,

For some people, suicide gestures are cries for help. In other cases suicide gestures represent attempts to manipulate or control others.

mobile accidents are one method of covert suicide (Bollen & Phillips, 1981; Phillips, 1977, 1979). Individuals who use cars when attempting suicide will intentionally drive into the paths of other cars, trucks, or trains. On two occasions a depressed woman I knew drove her car at high speed into a bridge support in an attempt to kill herself, but both times the incidents were listed as accidents rather than suicide attempts. It also appears that some individuals try to provoke the police into shooting them as a means of committing suicide (Wilson et al., 1998).

In sharp contrast to covert suicides are **suicide gestures,** behaviors that are designed to appear as suicide attempts but are not really meant to be lethal. That is, individuals engage in suicidal behavior but do not really want to kill themselves. For example, they may take an overdose of pills but not enough to kill themselves, or they may slash their wrists but not deeply enough to bleed to death. Individuals who make suicide gestures generally make them in such a way that other people will find out. For instance, they may leave the empty pill bottle out or allow others to notice their bandaged wrists. In some cases suicide gestures are *cries for help* (Farberow & Shneidman, 1961; Lester & Akande, 1998). The individuals are desperate but do not

know how to ask for help, are too ashamed to ask for help directly, or have asked for help and were ignored because others did not realize how upset they were. In those cases the suicide gestures are a way of dramatizing the seriousness of the problem and asking for help indirectly.

For other individuals, suicide gestures are attempts to *manipulate or control the people around them.* For instance, after the breakup of a relationship an individual may make a suicide gesture in an attempt to get the other person to come back. In general, individuals who make suicide gestures tend to be female, younger, less mature, and less depressed than individuals who actually intend to die, and their suicide gestures tend to be more impulsive and less lethal than actual attempts (McHugh & Goodell, 1971; Weissman, 1974). Nevertheless, it is often difficult to distinguish between a suicide gesture and an attempted suicide. Moreover, even when it is clear that the individual is only making a gesture, the behavior should be taken very seriously because the gesture is a sign of a problem. Furthermore, *in making the gesture, the individual might accidentally kill himself or herself.*

Some suicide attempts that fail nevertheless have serious consequences. For example, taking an overdose of certain drugs can lead to long-term problems such as liver or brain damage. A particularly distressing example of such a consequence is presented in Case Study 9.4 (on p. 264). This case also illustrates the difficulty of determining who will and will not commit suicide and the problem of what to do with individuals who are only suspected of suicidal intentions.

Warnings and Notes

In many cases individuals who are contemplating suicide will give some warning. Indeed, interviews with friends and relatives of individuals who committed suicide indicated that between 60% and 70% of the victims had openly said that they wanted to commit suicide and another 20% to 25% had talked about the topic of suicide, thereby indirectly signaling their intentions (Farberow & Simon, 1975; Rudestam, 1971). These suicide signals can be indications of what the individuals plan to do, or they can be a means of letting others know how upset the individuals are, in an indirect attempt to get help. *Remarks about committing suicide should always be taken seriously.* Ignoring a plea for help can further convince the individual of the hopelessness of the situation. In one investigation it was found that

---

covert suicide Suicide disguised to appear as an accident.

suicide gestures Behaviors that are designed to appear as suicide attempts but are not really meant to be lethal; the gestures may be cries for help or attempts to manipulate others.

An Unsuccessful Suicide Attempt

ANN WAS A VERY BRIGHT, attractive, personable, and energetic single woman who was 52 years old. She was an avid jogger and swimmer and was in excellent physical condition. As a physical therapist at a large metropolitan hospital, Ann specialized in working with patients who were severely disabled by strokes or spinal cord injuries. She worked with patients whom others despairingly referred to as "almost vegetables."

One spring Ann checked into a general hospital for a complete head-to-toe medical checkup. She did not complain of any particular problem; she just told the physician that it was time for a checkup. Early in the morning of Ann's second day in the hospital, a nurse who was walking by saw Ann standing on the narrow sill outside her 15th-floor window. As she stood there, she was lifting herself up and down on her toes "like you do just before you take a dive." The nurse walked quietly up behind Ann, grabbed her, and pulled her back into the room. Ann was subsequently sent to a psychiatric hospital for evaluation.

> **Ann was annoyed that she was suspected of attempting to commit suicide.**

Ann was annoyed that she was suspected of attempting to commit suicide. She said that she had been "trying to get some fresh air" and was simply doing her "breathing exercises" on the sill. She denied any thoughts of suicide and pointed out that because of her excellent condition and balance, there was no chance of her falling. The evaluation did not reveal any signs of psychopathology, and Ann, knowing hospital routines, was helpful and compliant—a model patient.

One aspect of Ann's record that concerned the hospital staff was that both her mother and her older sister had died of heart attacks in their mid-50s, an age that Ann was quickly approaching. It was suggested that Ann believed that she was also going to have a premature heart attack that would leave her in a condition like that of the patients with whom she worked every day. When Ann was questioned about this, she adamantly denied any such concerns and pointed out that if there was a potential problem, she had done the right thing by going into the hospital for a thorough checkup.

There was considerable debate among the hospital staff over whether or not Ann was in fact suicidal and what to do about it. Some argued that she had "too much ego strength" to commit suicide, others argued that "it takes a lot of ego strength to commit suicide," and others questioned how long this otherwise healthy patient could be kept in the hospital, even if there was a consensus that she was suicidal. She was not willing to participate in therapy ("Why should I? I don't have a problem!"), and it did not seem reasonable to keep her locked up for the rest of her life.

While being evaluated, Ann had been assigned to an open ward, the door of which was watched by an attendant so that only patients with passes could leave. Three days after Ann's case conference, the attendant was briefly drawn away from the door by a scuffle between two adolescent patients. During his brief absence Ann walked quietly off the ward. She went directly to the center of the hospital, where there was a large circular staircase that went up four floors. She went up to the top floor, climbed up on the banister, and threw herself headfirst down the stairwell. Ann landed on her back and broke her neck. She survived but was paralyzed from the neck down. Today Ann is a complete invalid, existing in the very state she sought to avoid through her suicide attempt.

---

about half of people who heard suicide threats simply denied the importance of what they were hearing and did nothing (Rudestam, 1971). In some cases the individuals who heard the threats actually *avoided* the suicidal individuals thereafter.

The notes left by individuals who commit suicide have attracted a lot of interest, and hundreds of such notes have been collected and analyzed (Cohen & Fiedler, 1974; Farberow & Simon, 1975; Lester, 1997a, 1997b, 1998; Wilkinson, 1999). Unfortunately, these notes add little to our understanding of suicide. For the most part they are rather matter-of-fact statements apologizing for the suicide, explaining why the suicide was necessary, saying good-bye to loved ones, and indicating the desired disposition of personal property.

Timing of Suicides

During what season of the year do you suppose people are most likely to commit suicide? Many people think that suicides are most likely to occur during the cold, dark, depressing days of winter, but exactly the opposite is true (Jessen et al., 1999). In fact, it was discovered more than 100 years ago that the suicide rate was higher in the six warmest months of the year (April through September) than in the six coldest months (Durkheim, 1897/1951). The rate was found to rise slowly from January to a peak in June, and this pattern still holds today (Jessen et al., 1999). The reason for the pattern is not clear, but it may be that the feelings of depression and hopelessness felt by suicidal individuals contrast sharply with the optimism felt by other people in spring, and this contrast increases their feelings of dispair and leads to their suicides. However, this explanation is only speculation.

Twenty years ago suicides were not more likely to occur on any particular day, but now they are most likely to occur on Mondays (Jessen et al., 1999; Maldonado & Kraus, 1991). The stress of "facing the workweek" may be responsible for this effect, and the change over time may be due to the increasing number of women in the workforce. That is, because more women are now working, a greater proportion of people start working on Mondays; thus more people are likely to be stressed on Mondays.

Myths about Suicide

Table 9.3 presents a number of popular myths about suicide. Recognizing that these statements are myths is important because believing them can lead you to misinterpret or ignore the warning signs given by a person contemplating suicide, perhaps with tragic consequences.

Suicide as a Positive, Rational Act

Throughout this discussion suicide has been viewed, implicitly if not explicitly, as a negative act, as abnormal behavior, and as something that should be prevented. In many instances this is certainly the case, but we should at least consider the possibility that for some persons suicide may be a positive act reflecting a reasonable and rational decision (Werth, 1999).

Probably the clearest examples of suicide as a positive act occur when individuals are experiencing excruciating pain while dying of a terminal illness (Hendin, 1999). For them there is terrible pain but no hope, and an earlier painless death might seem a reasonable alternative. Many states now legally sanction what might be called "passive suicide" in that they respect *living wills,* which are documents in which individuals request that medical procedures not be used to prolong life in hopeless circumstances. In those cases death comes because treatment is withheld, but in some cases simply withholding treatment may not result in death. In such cases, as well as in cases where individuals are not able to commit suicide without help, groups such as the Hemlock Society advocate "assisted suicide," in which someone, possibly a physician, provides the individual with the means to commit suicide and may even actively help. Assisted suicide is illegal in many places, but it is practiced in various European countries, where, contrary to the concerns of its opponents, it has not come into widespread use. It is interesting to note that Freud died by means of physician-assisted suicide (McCue & Cohen, 1999). When he was first diagnosed as suffering from throat cancer, Freud asked his physician to promise not to let him die in extreme pain. Sixteen years later, when the pain became unbearable and Freud could barely eat or talk, he reminded his physician of their earlier agreement. The physician then gave Freud an injection of morphine, which put him into a peaceful sleep. A second injection a few hours later caused a coma from which Freud did not awaken.

The situation becomes less clear in cases in which the individual is not terminally ill or in great pain but for some

TABLE 9.3

Myths about suicide

Myth	Reality
People who talk about suicide won't commit suicide.	Untrue. Between 60% and 80% of persons who commit suicide have communicated their intent ahead of time.
All suicidal behaviors are designed to end life.	Untrue. Some people are trying to kill themselves, but others may be making suicide gestures that are calls for help or attempts to communicate the depth of their despair.
Only very depressed persons commit suicide.	Untrue. Many people who commit suicide are depressed. However, very depressed people generally do not have enough energy to commit suicide, although they may do so as they start to get better. Also, reaching the decision to commit suicide can relieve stress and depression, so people may appear less depressed just before committing suicide. Finally, suicide can be the result of a delusion, or it can even be a well-thought-out solution to a problem unrelated to depression.
Protestants are more likely to commit suicide than Catholics.	Untrue. The evidence concerning this is mixed, but there does not appear to be an overall difference in suicide rates between these two religious groups.
Suicide rates are higher in winter than in summer.	Untrue. There is actually evidence that suicide rates increase as spring arrives.

Some people see suicide as an act that reflects a rational decision. Groups such as the Hemlock Society advocate assisted suicide, which involves providing individuals with the means to commit suicide. Pictured here is Janet Good, founder and past president of the Michigan chapter of the Hemlock Society, shaking hands with Dr. Jack Kevorkian, a retired pathologist who has assisted several suicides.

rational reason decides that the time for death has come. This is most likely to occur in older adults who realize that their health and ability to function are beginning to decline. Not wanting to go through the decline, dependence, and degradation that may come with old age and deteriorating health, they elect to end their lives. In those cases the decision to die is based on a risk–benefit analysis: The individuals weigh the risk of losing some remaining good years against the benefit of ensuring that they will not have to go through the suffering that can come with old age. Is suicide a rational act in those cases?

Case Study 9.5 was written by the son of a woman who elected to die, despite the fact that her life could have been saved by heart surgery and she might have had some productive years ahead of her. This case falls in the large gray area between the definition of what behavior is appropriate and the definition of what constitutes suicide. Did this woman commit suicide? Did she make a rational and reasonable decision? Should she have been diagnosed as a danger to herself, committed to a hospital as a psychiatric patient, and treated against her will (part of which treatment would have been the surgery)? Or was she a strong woman with strong beliefs about having personal control of her own destiny, who simply took control of the situation—*her* situation? Is signing a living will a suicidal act? Are there situations in which suicide is a reasonable, rational, positive act? These questions have far-reaching philosophical, theological, and legal implications that are beyond resolution here. They are also questions you may have to face someday—for a client, for someone you love, or for yourself.

Explanations

It is often assumed that people commit suicide simply because they are depressed. However, for many individuals it is more complicated than that, and in this section we will examine the many reasons for suicide.

Psychodynamic Explanations

Depression. Depression certainly plays an important role in many suicides. Indeed, it has been estimated that at least 80% of suicidal patients are depressed, and the rate of suicide among depressed individuals is 22 to 36 times higher than that among nondepressed individuals (Angst, Angst, & Stassen, 1999; DeMan, 1999; Lesage et al., 1994; Simpson & Jamison, 1999). Depressed individuals commit suicide because they don't think life is worth living. A frequent comment made by depressed individuals is "I wish I were dead."

The rate of suicide among depressed individuals would probably be even higher if it were not for the fact that many severely depressed individuals simply do not have the energy to commit suicide. Because of this, many suicides occur after the individuals begin to get better. The individuals are still depressed, but as they start to improve, their energy begins to return and they are better able to carry out the suicidal act. For example, during the worst of her depression, one woman sat motionless, stared into space, and wept quietly. However, when her depression began to lift and she started to move around, one of her first actions was to go to the bathroom and take an overdose of medication, which killed her.

Stress. Another explanation is that people commit suicide to escape stress. Indeed, a variety of investigations have indicated that people who attempt suicide experience up to four times as many negative life events (e.g., separations, abuse, financial problems, diagnoses of serious illnesses) just prior to their attempts than do nonsuicidal people over a comparable period of time (Cochrane & Robertson, 1975; Huff, 1999; Lecomte & Fornes, 1998; Paykel, Prusoff, & Myers, 1975; Slater & Depue, 1981; Thompson et al., 1999; Westrin, Ekman, & Traeskman-Bendz, 1999).

Other evidence for the influence of stress on suicide comes from the finding that the suicide rate increases during economic recessions. Indeed, it almost doubled during the Great Depression of the early 1930s, and it went up again during the recession of the 1970s (National Institute of Mental Health, 1976; Wekstein, 1979). More recently the economic turmoil in Japan and the countries of the former Soviet Union have led to dramatic increases in suicide rates in those countries (Lester & Saito, 1998; Vaernik, 1998).

"It's Been a Great Life. Good-bye, World."

"MOTHER WAS A SMALL, ACTIVE woman of 72 who could pass for much younger. She exercised regularly, took classes at the university each semester, did volunteer work reading books onto tapes for visually impaired persons, and had a part-time job in the student union. (She took the job because she liked to be as independent as possible and because she liked the contact with the young students.) She was happy and described her current life as 'the best years of my life.'

"One day, while at the union, Mother experienced severe pains in her chest and left arm. She immediately recognized the pains as signs of a heart attack. Thinking she was going to die, she looked up and said, 'It's been a great life. Good-bye, World.' Mother was rushed to the hospital, and as she was wheeled into the emergency room, she admonished the nurse, 'I have a living will! Don't do anything extraordinary for me. I don't want some machine keeping me alive!'

"Mother recovered from the heart attack, but all was not well. An angiogram revealed that she had 90% blockages in five major coronary arteries. Her physician came to her hospital room and explained the problem to her, went on to point out that the problem could be overcome with major bypass surgery, and told her that he had already made arrangements for the surgery. Mother listened attentively, and when he was through, she said quietly but firmly, 'Thank you, but I don't think I'll have the operation.'

"'But Margaret, you don't understand. If you don't have the operation, you'll die.'

"'I understand,' she replied, 'but I am ready to die, and there are three reasons I don't want the operation. First, all I would be buying with the operation is time—time to wait to die of something else that might be more painful and difficult. I've seen too many of my friends struggle with things like cancer. . . . I've started to decline, and I am going to stop it here. I'm going to die, and a heart attack

seems like the best of the alternatives. Second, I've lived my life, and it's been a good life. I've done most of the things I wanted to do, my children and grandchildren are grown, and this is a good time to go. Oh, sure, there are some things I'd like to do, but on balance, I'm ready. Third, I don't want to become a burden to anyone. The operation, the recuperation in a nursing home, and the limitations on my activities after that will put a strain on everyone, and I don't want that. Also, this whole thing will wind up costing a lot of money. I know that insurance will pay for most of it, but why spend that kind of money on me at this point in time? It just doesn't make sense; others need those resources more than I do.'

"The physician argued with her, and finally Mother took his hand as if to console him and said, 'No, Doctor, you don't understand because you're not where I am. You're 50 years old; you're healthy; you have many important things to do—you have lots of living left. I'm 72; life is good and I am happy, but my health is obviously failing, I'm going to begin to decline, and this is a good time to wind it up. I really don't have much in front of me, and I'd rather go now while I'm ahead. No, Doctor, I'm going to check out of the hospital and go home. For years I've been very careful about my diet and I've denied myself what I've wanted, but tonight if I want butter on my potato, I'll put *real butter* on it, and if I want chocolate cake for desert, I'll have *two* pieces.'

"Mother checked out of the hospital that evening, went home, and continued doing 'her thing.' She wasn't happy about this turn of events, and in letters to friends she mused over things that she would have to leave undone, but she concluded that on balance she was making the right decision.

"About 5 days after Mother left the hospital, she had another attack. She sat and waited to die, but the pain became unbearable, so she finally had to call the hospital and go to the emer-

gency room. The physician and I met her there, and he explained that if we acted quickly, the bypass surgery could still be done. Mother declined and asked how much time 'the process' would take and whether the pain could be controlled. Shaking his head with dismay, the physician told her that without the operation she would probably live only another day or so and that, yes, the pain could be controlled with morphine. Mother quipped with a grin, 'Morphine—gee, I get to be a junkie before I go—another new experience!'

"Mother was taken to the intensive care unit, where she was hooked to a morphine pump and a vital signs monitor. We spent that evening and the next day talking and reminiscing. As the time went by, the level of morphine had to be increased, and consequently Mother would occasionally drift off to sleep. When a nurse would come in to check on her, she would wake up, we would talk some more, and then she would drift off again. Late that night, I sat by Mother's bed holding her hand and watching the heart rate monitor. Finally, her heart began to slow, gave a few erratic beats, and then stopped. Mother had died. As I looked at her and wept, I thought of how much I loved her, how much I would miss her, and how *proud* I was of her. Mother had been a positive woman who had remained in control. She had died with as little pain and as much dignity as possible. She arranged her death so that she was not a burden to others, and by saving resources, she contributed to others who she thought needed them more.

"As I said earlier, I was very proud of Mother, and it did not occur to me until sometime later that in a technical sense, *Mother had committed suicide.* Suicide—we usually think of that as a desperate act of a hopeless person. Maybe we need to rethink our conception of suicide and death with dignity."

CASE STUDY 9.5

> . . . I've lived my life, and it's been a good life.

Economic turmoil in Japan and the former Soviet Union in the late 1990s led to a dramatic increase in suicide rates in those countries, highlighting the influence of extreme stress on suicide.

Fantasies. Another interesting factor in suicides are the fantasies about what suicide will accomplish (Furst & Ostow, 1979). Four fantasies have been singled out as most common:

1. *Reuniting with a deceased person.* The death of a loved one often leads to suicide, and some theorists suggest that by committing suicide individuals are attempting to join the dead person in an afterlife. Indeed, in many religious funeral ceremonies it is explicitly stated that we will all be reunited after death.

2. *Rebirth.* Another fantasy about what suicide will accomplish is that after death the individual will be reborn in heaven, free of his or her current problems. Consistent with this notion, in many religious funeral services the deceased individuals are described as having been relieved of their worldly burdens and having gone to a new life in a better place.

3. *Self-punishment.* When we do things of which we do not approve, we often punish ourselves in a variety of

little ways, such as depriving ourselves of some pleasure or treat. Of course, killing oneself is the ultimate punishment that guilty individuals may seek.

4. *Revenge.* Finally, some individuals commit suicide to "get back at" others and make them feel guilty. This motivation is often reflected in suicide notes that say, in effect, "This would not have happened if you had been nicer to me." Children may be more likely to use this because they are powerless to attack adults, so they commit suicide in an attempt to get back at the adults. It is not unusual for a child to think or say, "When I'm dead, you'll be sorry you weren't nicer to me!"

Learning Explanations

Rather than considering the factors that cause an individual to want to commit suicide, learning theorists have focused their attention on the processes that facilitate committing suicide once the decision has been made to do so.

Imitation. One of the important factors in the learning explanation for suicide is *imitation.* That is, when depressed or facing stress, an individual may hear about a person who committed suicide, and this may suggest suicide as a solution (Maris, 1997). The other individual's act may also suggest an effective way of committing suicide.

Evidence for the effects of imitation come from the fact that suicide rates increase dramatically following reports of suicides on television or in newspapers (Stack, 1990). Examples of this are provided in Table 9.4, where you will find the dates of seven suicides that were reported on nationally televised evening news programs. With each date is the number of individuals who committed suicide in the United States during the following week and during a comparable control week that was not preceded by the report of a suicide. These data indicate that the number of suicides increased by 7% following a nationally publicized suicide. The effect of imitation on suicide is probably stronger than the data in Table 9.4 suggest because those data reflect only overt cases of suicide. Data from other investigations indicate that motor vehicle fatalities also increase following well-publicized suicides, and it is likely that some of those deaths are actually covert suicides (Bollen & Phillips, 1981; Phillips, 1977, 1979). Imitation even influences rates of physician-assisted suicide (Phillips et al., 1999). Specifically, in the month following a nationally publicized case in which a physician admitted prescribing a lethal dose of barbiturates for a woman with leukemia, there was an 11% increase in deaths of female leukemia patients, and the rate jumped to almost 40% for patients who were very similar to the patient in the report. Because the deaths involved prescription drugs, it was assumed that physicians had assisted.

TABLE 9.4

Increases in suicides following stories about suicide on TV evening news programs

Date of story	Number of suicides after story	Number of suicides during control period	Difference
April 25, 1972	554	444	110
June 4, 1973	528	435	93
September 11, 1973	487	514	–27
July 15, 1974	482	462	20
April 11, 1975	593	572	21
September 3, 1975	553	501	52
May 13, 1976	550	575	–25
Totals	**3,747**	**3,503**	**244**

Source: Adapted from Bollen and Phillips (1982), Table 1, p. 804.

An interesting but unfortunate example of the effects of imitation on suicide can be seen in the "epidemics," or clusters, of suicides that occur among adolescents (Gould, Wallenstein, & Davidson, 1989; Yoder, 1999). In these cases an adolescent commits suicide, and then a number of his or her friends also commit suicide. For example, 2 days after a boy was killed in an automobile accident, his closest friend said he would see him again "some sunny day" and then committed suicide by running his car engine in a closed garage. Six days later another young friend committed suicide in the same way. That was followed by the suicide of a third boy who did not know the others, but who had newspaper articles about their suicides on his bulletin board at home. In addition to these three successful suicides, there were 12 unsuccessful suicide attempts in the following 8 weeks. Another example of imitation occurred in a very small town in Connecticut where *eight* young girls were brought to the hospital during one 5-day period because of suicide attempts (Rosenberg & Leland, 1995). With regard to these findings, it is interesting to note that one study revealed that the best predictors of suicide among adolescents are a history of attempts and a recent attempt by a friend (Lewinsohn et al., 1994). In other words, depressed individuals can be led to suicide by the example of others.

Finally, the effects of imitation on the strategies that individuals use to commit suicide is illustrated by the number of people who kill themselves by jumping off the Golden Gate Bridge in San Francisco. More than 1,000 people have committed suicide by jumping off that bridge, but fewer than 200 have committed suicide by jumping off the San Francisco–Oakland Bay Bridge only a short distance away. Indeed, some individuals drive over the Bay Bridge to get to the Golden Gate Bridge so that they can jump from it. Given its history, the Golden Gate Bridge is apparently "the place to do it." Similarly, in Trinidad over 80% of the suicides are due to the use of a particular poison that is rarely used elsewhere, despite the fact that it is widely available (Hutchinson et al., 1999).

Given that suicide can be due at least in part to imitation, could we reduce suicide by reducing the publicity it gets? Yes. For example, in an attempt to end a rash of sensational suicides in which individuals threw themselves in front of subway trains, news reporters agreed to stop publicizing the suicides. The reduction of publicity led to a sharp reduction in that particular type of suicide (Etzersdorfer, Sonneck, & Nagel-Fuess, 1992).

Behavioral Contagion. Simply getting the idea to commit suicide is usually not enough to result in the act. Even if an individual wants very much to commit suicide, there are usually restraints against it (e.g., "It is wrong to commit suicide," and "Nice people don't commit suicide"). However, these restraints can be overcome through the process of behavioral contagion (Wheeler, 1966). **Behavioral contagion** occurs when (1) an individual wants to do something, (2) is restrained from doing it because society says that the behavior is wrong, (3) sees someone else do it and "get away with it," and then (4) thinks that he or she can get away with it also. Examples of behavioral contagion include crossing the street against the traffic light and smoking in no-smoking areas when others do so first. Contagion differs from imitation in that *contagion reduces restraints against performing a known behavior,* whereas *imitation introduces a new behavior.*

The concept of behavioral contagion is useful in understanding suicide because it explains why it is suddenly "all right" to take one's own life. Behavioral contagion can reduce *external restraints* that stem from cultural rules ("You can't do that") because the individuals see that they *can* get away with it. However, contagion does not reduce *internal restraints* that stem from one's own beliefs ("I don't think I should do that") (Ritter & Holmes, 1968). Therefore, suicide will be "contagious" if the individual is only restrained by the fact that society says that suicide is wrong; it will not be contagious if the individual is restrained by the personal belief that suicide is wrong.

Rewards. Suicide threats and gestures are sometimes calls for help, but they may also be used to manipulate others, often to get rewarding attention (Bostock & Williams, 1975). In one case a man began threatening to kill himself

behavioral contagion The process by which observing someone perform a prohibited act such as suicide reduces external restraints against performing the act.

when a woman he had been dating broke off the relationship and refused to see him. He wrote to her saying, "Without you there is nothing in life for me. Unless there is a chance that you will see me, I will end it all." At first the woman gave in because the threats frightened her. However, such threats are not a basis for a relationship, so she eventually told the police about the threats and stopped seeing him. Individuals who use suicide threats to manipulate others pose difficult problems because if we attempt to extinguish the behavior by ignoring it, we run the risk that the individual will actually attempt suicide and possibly succeed, either accidentally or intentionally.

Cognitive Explanations

The cognitive explanation suggests that people who commit suicide do not have good problem-solving skills, so they are unable to solve the problems facing them. This inability leads to a feeling of hopelessness, and eventually they commit suicide because they see no other alternative.

Poor Problem Solving Skills. Many suicidal individuals do in fact have poor problem-solving skills (Biggam & Power, 1999; D'Zurilla et al., 1998; Orbach, Bar-Joseph, & Dror, 1990; Pollock & Williams, 1998; Schotte & Clum, 1987). Specifically, suicidal individuals suffer from *cognitive rigidity,* which means that they lack the flexibility to see alternative solutions for their problems. In one study suicidal and nonsuicidal psychiatric patients were asked to list alternative uses for a number of common items such as pencils and paper clips. The suicidal patients came up with only 40% as many uses as the nonsuicidal patients. Furthermore, when each patient was reminded of an interpersonal problem from real life and was asked to generate solutions for it, the suicidal patients generated fewer than half as many solutions as the nonsuicidal patients did.

The inability to solve problems can have a number of serious implications. First, people who are unable to solve problems will experience more failures, thereby increasing their stress levels. Second, the inability to solve problems leads to feelings of hopelessness, which, as you will see next, are closely related to suicide. Third, once cognitively rigid individuals decide on suicide as a solution for their problems, they tend to pursue only that "solution." For example, a poor problem solver who faces financial difficulties may not be able to come up with an effective solution for the difficulties, and this may cause increased stress and feelings of hopelessness. Also, with no solution in sight suicide may seem to be the only option for this individual.

Hopelessness. *Hopelessness* is the belief that "things won't get better," and the degree to which an individual feels hopeless is a powerful predictor of suicide (Beautrais, Joyce, & Mulder, 1999; Beck, Weissman, et al., 1974; Beck, Steer, et al., 1985, 1990; Hewitt et al., 1998; Ivanoff & Jang, 1991;

TABLE 9.5

Sample items from the Hopelessness Scale (agreement with a statement is related to suicide)

- ▶ I might as well give up because I can't make things better for myself.
- ▶ My future seems dark to me.
- ▶ I just don't get the breaks, and there's no reason to believe I will in the future.
- ▶ All I can see ahead of me is unpleasantness rather than pleasantness.
- ▶ Things just won't work out the way I want them to.
- ▶ It is very unlikely that I will get any real satisfaction in the future.
- ▶ There's no use in really trying to get something I want because I probably won't get it.

Source: Beck et al. (1974), Table 1, p. 862.

Mazza & Reynolds, 1998; Rifai et al., 1994). Table 9.5 contains some of the items from a scale frequently used to measure feelings of hopelessness. These items will give you some understanding of what is meant by hopelessness and why individuals who agree with the statements are more likely to commit suicide.

The important role of hopelessness in suicide was demonstrated in a study in which more than 200 inpatients who had taken the Hopelessness Scale were followed up 5 to 10 years later to determine which ones had committed suicide (Beck et al., 1985). Of the 14 patients who had committed suicide, 13 had had high scores on the Hopelessness Scale.

Delusions and Hallucinations. The rate of suicide among individuals who suffer from schizophrenia is relatively high (Westermeyer, Harrow, & Marengo, 1991). Why? One reason is that individuals with schizophrenia may have delusions that lead them to kill themselves. For example, they may believe that they are the Devil and do not deserve to live or that they are cornered by foreign agents and must escape by poisoning themselves. Alternatively, they may have auditory hallucinations (voices) telling them to kill themselves. Finally, despair over their condition may lead to suicide.

Reasons for Not Committing Suicide. From the previous discussion it is clear that there are numerous cognitive factors that contribute to suicide, but there are also cognitive factors that make suicide less likely. Table 9.6 (on p. 270) lists six cognitive factors that have been shown to reduce suicidal intent.

Finally, one other reason why some individuals do not commit suicide is that they *lack an effective means by which*

TABLE 9.6

Cognitive factors that reduce suicidal intent

1. *Survival and coping beliefs:* "I still have many things left to do." "No matter how badly I feel, I know that it will not last."

2. *Responsibility to family:* "It would hurt my family too much, and I would not want them to suffer." "My family depends on me and needs me."

3. *Child-related concerns:* "The effect on my children would be harmful." "It would not be fair to leave the children for others to take care of."

4. *Fear of suicide:* "I am a coward and do not have the guts to do it." "I am afraid that my method of killing myself would fail."

5. *Fear of social disapproval:* "I would not want other people to think I did not have control over my life." "I am concerned about what others would think of me."

6. *Moral objections:* "My religious beliefs forbid it." "I am afraid of going to hell."

Source: Based on Dyck (1991), Jobes & Mann (1999), Linehan et al. (1983).

to do it. For example, accessibility of guns is related to the suicide rate; if guns are not available, suicide rates are lower (Carrington & Moyer, 1994; Clarke & Lester, 1989; Kellermann et al., 1992). Other factors that have been linked to reductions in suicide include the introduction of exhaust emission controls that reduced the amount of poisonous carbon monoxide that comes from automobiles (Clarke & Lester, 1989), the detoxification of home heating gas (Lester, 1990), and lower heights of buildings (Marzuk et al., 1992; Shioiri et al., 1999). An elderly and very ill man in a hospital commented to me, "I want to die and I would commit suicide, but locked up in here, *I can't find a way to do it.*"

Overall, then, it appears that some individuals feel hopeless and consider suicide but do not attempt it because of the offsetting effects of various cognitive factors or because of a lack of effective means. The presence of these cognitions and options helps us understand why not everyone who feels hopeless commits suicide.

Many of the psychological factors that have been shown to contribute to suicide are reflected in the background and experiences of the young man discussed in Case Study 9.6 (on p. 272).

Physiological Explanations

Here's an interesting finding: Identical twins are almost 15 times more likely than nonidentical twins to both commit suicide. Is there a gene for suicide? Let's look at some of the physiological explanations for suicide.

Low Levels of Serotonin. We now know that low levels of the neurotransmitter **serotonin** are related to suicide (Les-

ter, 1995; see reviews by Korn et al., 1990; Mann et al., 1999; Rifai, Reynolds, & Mann, 1992). Why? At first you might recall that low levels of serotonin lead to depression (see Chapter 8) and assume that the depression leads to the suicide. This can certainly be the case, but something else must be going on as well. Low levels of norepinephrine can also lead to depression but are less likely to be related to suicide. Furthermore, when patients were given drugs that increased levels of serotonin or norepinephrine, the drugs that increased serotonin were more effective for reducing suicide than those that increased norepinephrine (Sacchetti et al., 1991).

Why is it that low levels of serotonin are particularly likely to lead to suicide? To answer this question you first need to know that low levels of serotonin are related to *aggression* as well as depression. Indeed, numerous studies have revealed that men with long histories of aggressive behavior have lower levels of serotonin than nonaggressive men (Coccaro et al., 1996; Lahey et al., 1993; Rogeness, Javors, & Pliszka, 1992; Virkkunen et al., 1989; Virkkunen et al., 1994; Zubieta & Alessi, 1993). Furthermore, drugs such as Prozac that increase serotonin levels reduce aggression (Coccaro & Kavoussi, 1997; Heiligenstein et al., 1992; Kruesi et al., 1992; Saltzman et al., 1995). However, low levels of serotonin do not cause aggression directly. Instead, normal levels of serotonin *inhibit* aggressive responses that were punished in the past; so, when the levels of serotonin drop, the inhibition lifts and the aggressive responses are used.

The role of serotonin in inhibition was neatly demonstrated in an experiment in which rats first learned to run to the end of a simple straight maze, where they found food (Soubie, 1986; Spoont, 1992). Once that response was learned, an electrical shock grid was placed on the floor of the maze just before the place at which the rats got the food. After getting shocked a few times when they crossed the grid, the rats learned to stop before getting to the grid. However, when the rats were then injected with a drug that lowered their levels of serotonin, they ignored the possibility of shock and ran across the grid to get the food. That is, low levels of serotonin reduced the inhibition of punished responses. In view of that finding, the process linking serotonin to suicide appears to be as follows: A low level of serotonin leads to depression and to a decrease in the inhibition of inappropriate responses. Thus, when the depressed individual thinks of suicide, there is not enough inhibition to restrain the behavior and the individual attempts suicide.

Having established that low levels of serotonin are linked to suicide, we must next ask, what causes low levels

serotonin   A neurotransmitter that at low levels leads to depression and reduces inhibition of aggression, both of which can lead to suicide.

The Suicide of a 27-Year-Old Male Graduate Student

I'm not crazy. I just don't know what I want to do.

CHUCK WAS A MATURE, upper-middle-class, 27-year-old graduate student in chemistry. After graduating from college, he married a woman he had dated for 2 years and took a job with a large chemical company. Although he did very well at his job, he became dissatisfied. He attributed his unhappiness to the fact that, without more education, he could not move up in the company. With his wife's support he quit his job and returned to graduate school to get a master's degree.

Graduate school was demanding and often stressful. Although his grades were excellent and his professors cited him as one of the most promising students, Chuck began to wonder whether he had what it took to "make it." More important, he began to wonder whether he wanted to make it. He frequently asked himself, "Is it all worth it?" He continued to do well in his coursework, but he seemed to lose his sense of direction and found it increasingly difficult to enjoy himself. His worry about keeping up in school, in combination with his self-doubts about his future, led him to become anxious, moody, and

depressed, and he became increasingly difficult to live with. After about a year he and his wife separated. She was opposed to the separation and wanted to stay together to work on the problem and help him. However, as his depression deepened, Chuck easily became angry and wanted to be left alone. Figuratively, he pushed her away. His wife moved back to her parents' home in a distant city, and Chuck moved into a small apartment, where he lived alone.

When Chuck started missing many of his classes and stopped going to the laboratory, his professors insisted that he "see someone for help." Chuck saw no point in it ("I'm not crazy. I just don't know what I want to do. I'm behind and unhappy, not crazy!"), but under pressure from his professors, he finally went to a psychiatrist.

During the first few sessions with the psychiatrist, Chuck admitted that he sometimes got quite depressed and that he was having difficulty sleeping through the night. He also acknowledged that sometimes he would spontaneously say to himself, "I wish I were dead" or "Life is terrible." Chuck occasionally talked about suicide in the abstract, but he denied that he was seriously considering suicide. In dis-

cussing suicide, it came out that his mother had once attempted suicide when he was about 12. He knew that she had subsequently received some psychiatric help, but he was too young at the time to know what had been done for her, and she had been killed about 4 years later, when a car she was driving ran off the road.

The psychiatrist prescribed a tricyclic antidepressant for Chuck, but after 2 weeks of taking it, his depression had not improved. Chuck stopped taking the drug against the advice of the psychiatrist, who felt that not enough time had elapsed to give the drug a chance to have an effect. With the depression getting worse, the psychiatrist became concerned and recommended that Chuck voluntarily check into a psychiatric hospital where other treatments could be tried and where he could be more closely supervised. Chuck objected but agreed that he would think about hospitalization over the next couple of days and that they would discuss it again at their meeting the following Thursday.

Sitting on his bed that night, Chuck placed the barrel of a shotgun in his mouth and pulled the trigger.

---

of serotonin? There are two explanations: First, *stress* can cause a reduction in the levels of serotonin (see Chapter 8), and we already know that suicidal individuals experience as many as four times as many stressful life events as nonsuicidal individuals. Thus, in some cases the relationship is

Second, low levels of serotonin can be *inherited* (see Chapter 8). In those cases the relationship is

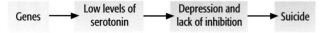

We will consider the role of genetics later.

Low Levels of Cholesterol. It may surprise you, but low cholesterol can lead to suicide. Indeed, in one study it was

found that men with very low cholesterol levels were twice as likely to make a serious suicide attempt as their counterparts with higher cholesterol levels (Boston, Dursun, & Reveley, 1996; Kunugi et al., 1997; Maes et al., 1997; Muldoon, Manuck, & Mann, 1992; Papassotiropoulos et al., 1999). Why should low cholesterol lead to suicide? A clue to the answer came from studies of people who changed to a very low cholesterol diet because they were suffering from heart disease. Following the change in diet, deaths due to heart disease went down, but the overall death rate remained unchanged because there was an increase in deaths due to suicide, violence, and accidents. Such deaths are known to be associated with low levels of serotonin; that is, low serotonin causes people to be less inhibited and less careful, which leads to violence and accidents. Therefore, investigators speculated that the low levels of cholesterol led to low levels of serotonin. To test this possibility they fed monkeys a low cholesterol diet and found that the monkeys' levels of serotonin went down and their levels of aggression went up (Kaplan, Manuck, & Shively, 1991; Muldoon et al., 1992).

Overall, then, we know that low levels of serotonin can lead to suicide and that a number of factors, such as stress, low cholesterol, and genetics can cause low serotonin. We will consider genetics next.

Genetic Factors. The possibility that genetics plays a role in suicide comes from the finding that almost 50% of the individuals who attempted suicide had a family history of suicide (Roy, 1983; Roy et al., 1999). Of course, that could be due to social modeling, so we must turn to studies of twins and adoptees. There is evidence that identical twins are almost 15 times more likely to both commit suicide than are nonidentical twins, a difference illustrated in Figure 9.3 (Roy, Centerwall, & Robinette, 1991; Roy, Segal, & Sarchiapone, 1995; Statham et al., 1998). Studies of adoptees also provide evidence for a genetic link. For example, in one study it was found that the biological parents of adoptees who committed suicide had a 4.5% suicide rate, whereas the adoptive parents had a 0% suicide rate (Schulsinger et al., 1979; see also Wender et al., 1986).

The notion underlying these findings is that individuals inherit genes that cause low levels of serotonin, which can then lead to suicide. Support for this comes from the fact that investigators have identified a specific gene that is linked to lower levels of serotonin (it is called the *TPH gene*), and individuals who attempted suicide were more likely than nonsuicidal individuals to have that gene and lower levels of serotonin (Nielsen et al., 1994).

In summary, numerous factors contribute to suicide, including depression, stress, fantasies, imitation, behavioral contagion, rewards, poor problem-solving skills, hopeless-

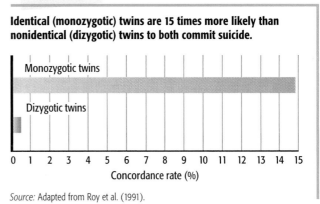

FIGURE 9.3

Identical (monozygotic) twins are 15 times more likely than nonidentical (dizygotic) twins to both commit suicide.

Source: Adapted from Roy et al. (1991).

ness, delusions, hallucinations, and low levels of serotonin. We know a lot about suicide; the remaining question is, can we prevent it?

Suicide Prevention

Earlier I pointed out that suicide is a leading cause of death, so an important question is, can suicide be prevented? Let's examine three lines of defense that can be used to prevent suicide.

Education

The first line of defense is to educate people about suicide (Kalafat & Ryerson, 1999). Specifically, this means teaching people (1) how to recognize the signs of suicidal behavior in themselves and others, (2) why it is important to get help, and (3) where to get the help. Educational programs are run for individuals of all ages, but they are often focused on schoolchildren or young adults, who are just entering or going through a high-risk period for suicide.

The evidence concerning the effectiveness of educational programs is mixed. On the one hand, participants in some of these programs do become more knowledgeable about the signs of suicide and where they can go for help (Goldney, 1998). However, other programs do not have any measurable effects, and some actually increase the risk of suicide (Callahan, 1996; Garland & Zigler, 1993; Lester, 1992; Metha, Weber, & Webb, 1998). The increase may occur because the programs stigmatize suicidal individuals and therefore discourage them from seeking help. In this regard it is interesting to note that prevention programs appear to be more effective for females than for males, possibly because seeking help may be more consistent with the traditional female role (Overholser, Evans, & Spirito, 1990).

One research finding was that almost 50% of individuals who attempted suicide had a family history of suicide, indicating that genetics may play a role. Pictured here are Ernest Hemingway and his granddaughter Margaux, who both committed suicide. Hemingway's brother also took his own life.

In other cases it appears that the attention these programs give to individuals who have committed suicide glorifies their deaths (e.g., as "romantic tragedy"), which can lead others to follow (Callahan, 1996).

Therapy, Medication, and ECT

For those suicidal individuals who do seek help, the second line of defense involves treating the depression, stress, hopelessness, poor problem-solving skills, and low levels of serotonin that can lead to suicide. Fortunately, psychotherapy and cognitive therapy can be used to help suicidal individuals overcome many of those problems and decrease their thoughts about suicide (Evans et al., 1999; MacLeod et al., 1998; Mueller-Oerlinghausen & Berghoefer, 1999; Spirito, 1997). Furthermore, antidepressants, lithium, antipsychotic drugs, and ECT have been found to be effective in reducing depression and suicide in suicidal individuals (Coppen & Farmer, 1998; Goodwin, 1999; Jamison & Baldessarini, 1999; Nilsson, 1999; Palmer, Henter, & Wyatt, 1999; Prudic & Sackeim, 1999; Reid, 1999). For instance, individuals with bipolar disorder who took lithium showed reduced rates of suicide, but when they stopped taking the lithium, they showed a 20-fold increase in suicide attempts, and fatalities were 14 times more frequent (Baldessarini et al., 1999). Concerns are sometimes raised about the possibility that suicidal individuals will use the drugs that have been prescribed to treat their depression to commit suicide, but in fact fewer than 5% try, and in most cases the overdoses are not lethal.

Crisis Management

Unfortunately, some individuals do not seek help, or the treatments they receive are not effective, leaving these individuals on the brink of suicide. For them the last line of defense is *crisis management.* Specifically, at that point we must do something to stop or at least slow down the behaviors that are leading to suicide so that we can find an alternative solution for the individual. This is often done by the staff of *suicide prevention centers,* which are walk-in clinics where individuals can go for help during a crisis. These centers are usually located in community mental health centers, hospital emergency rooms, and general crisis centers. There are also telephone "hot lines" that individuals can use to call for help when they are contemplating suicide. These hot lines are particularly useful because it is easier to pick up a phone than to travel to a clinic, and the individual may feel more comfortable talking over the phone than face to face with a counselor. A key feature of all of these programs is *easy accessibility.* If an individual is contemplating suicide, we want to make it as easy as possible for that person to get help as soon as possible. Unlike other services whose motto often appears to be something like "Take an aspirin and see me next week," suicide pre-

vention centers have as their motto "Tell us about the problem, and let's see what we can do about it *now.*" (For a fascinating description of one student's experience working in a crisis center, see Case Study 19.5 in Chapter 19.)

In most cases crisis management programs are staffed by *paraprofessionals*—individuals who are not professional mental health workers but have some training in counseling. For example, many of my undergraduate students spend time volunteering in crisis centers. Of course, the paraprofessionals have professionals on whom they can rely for advice and backup when necessary.

There are differences in the strategies used for suicide crisis management, but in most cases a counselor has five general goals:

1. *Establish a relationship.* First the counselor must establish a positive relationship with the individual who has come in or called for help. A trusting relationship is important so that the individual will be honest about the seriousness of his or her suicidal intent and so that later the individual will have confidence in what the counselor suggests. One crucial factor in developing the trusting relationship is that the counselor *not be judgmental.* The counselor should not agree with the decision to commit suicide, but he or she must accept the individual's concerns so that together they can begin seeking an alternative solution.

2. *Assess the risk of suicide.* Early in the discussion the counselor must determine whether (a) a suicidal act has already been started (e.g., have pills already been taken?), (b) the individual is on the brink of a suicidal act, or (c) the individual is just thinking about committing suicide. This assessment has serious implications for what must be done: Do we send the police and an ambulance, or do we try to talk the person out of going further?

3. *Clarify the problem.* If it is determined that the individual is not in imminent danger, the counselor can go on to identify what led to the crisis. That clarification is essential if a solution other than suicide is going to be found.

4. *Activate the individual's strengths.* Next it is important to give the individual support, encouragement, and reasons for living. To do this the counselor can point to the strengths and contributions of the individual as well as to the important role he or she has in the lives of others.

5. *Develop a plan.* Once the problem has been identified and the individual has been stabilized, a plan for solving the problem that led the individual to consider or attempt suicide must be developed. In most cases the counselor has to play a major role in developing the plan because if the individual could do it, there would not be a crisis. However, it is important to keep the individual involved; it has to be "our" plan so that the individual gets a sense of control and support. Often the plan involves a "contract" between the counselor and the suicidal individual, in which the individual agrees not to attempt suicide before contacting the counselor (Drew, 1999). This serves as a protection, but it

Suicide prevention counseling is often done by paraprofessionals. Here a young volunteer tries to help a young man who is contemplating suicide.

also reinforces the sense of the counselor's concern for and commitment to the individual.

There are many suicide prevention programs, but it is not clear how effective they are. One factor that limits their effectiveness is that as few as 2% of suicidal individuals contact the programs for help, and those who do are usually not the individuals who are at the greatest risk for suicide (Lester, 1989). This is not surprising because individuals who recognize that there is help for their problems probably wouldn't be planning suicide. Obviously, if the programs are not used much or are not used by individuals who are at high risk, their effectiveness will be limited.

Do the programs reduce suicide rates for the individuals who contact them? The evidence suggests that the programs can be effective in those cases, but there is no hard evidence from which we can draw firm conclusions (Neimeyer & Pfeiffer, 1994; Shaffer & Craft, 1999). For example, one investigator compared the change in suicide rates in communities that did or did not introduce prevention programs and found that the rate of increase was lower in the communities in which the programs were introduced (Lester, 1991a, 1991b, 1993). This result is encouraging. Because programs were not randomly assigned to communities, however, it is possible that those communities that elected to have the centers were somehow different from the ones that did not, and that it was this difference in the communities, rather than the presence of the programs, that influenced suicide rates. For instance, might it be that the communities that elected to have the programs were more affluent or more "psychologically minded"?

I began this section with a question: Can suicide be prevented? The answer is yes and no. We have treatments that can work, but they do not work for everyone and many people do not come for help. We've made a start toward suicide prevention, but it is still one of the major causes of death.

THINKING CRITICALLY
Questions about Suicide

1. *Why do people commit suicide?* If there is anything you take from this section, it should be that suicide is a complex behavior. Yes, depression, hopelessness, and stress are major causes of suicide, but many people who feel depressed and hopeless or are exposed to stress do not commit suicide. In view of that fact we must consider other factors such as imitation, behavioral contagion, and the cognitive reasons for not committing suicide (e.g., family responsibilities, moral objections). It is also essential to realize that suicide has a strong physiological component— low levels of serotonin lead to depression and reduce inhibitions. Those low levels of serotonin can stem from stress, low levels of cholesterol, or genetics. Finally, cultural values and religion can contribute to or limit suicides. Clearly, there is much more to suicide than an individual's simply wanting to "end it all."

2. *What should be done when someone talks about suicide or makes a suicide attempt?* The most important thing is that you *should not ignore the real or implied threat.* Talk to the person, find out what's going on, suggest that he or she get help, or get help for the person. Of course, some people talk about suicide or make suicide gestures to manipulate other people, but it is very difficult to distinguish between gestures and attempts, and it can be tragic when an attempt is misinterpreted as a gesture and nothing is done.

3. *Can we prevent suicides?* There is not a simple or particularly encouraging answer to that question. First, education can be useful in helping people recognize the signs of suicide and know where to go for help, but educational programs must be designed very carefully so that they do not romanticize suicide and thereby instigate it. Second, for those who come in for help, we have treatments that can be effective for reducing the depression, stress, and hopelessness that often lead to suicide. However, those treatments do not work for everyone and even among those who are originally helped, the relapse rate is high (Oquendo et al., 1999; see also Chapter 8). Third, for those who do not seek help initially, crisis management by suicide prevention centers may be useful in defusing the situation, but few people who are serious about suicide make use of crisis management services. In summary, we have some "filters" that can catch some people as they progress toward suicide, but many people slip through or go around those filters and kill themselves. Can we prevent suicides? Often yes, but in many cases no, either because our treatments do not work or because people do not come in for treatment. Unfortunately, then, suicide prevention remains an unmet challenge.

Summary

Topic I: Bipolar Disorder

▶ Bipolar disorder involves shifts in mood between depression and mania. Type I bipolar disorder involves depression and mania, whereas Type II involves depression and hypomania. The milder form of bipolar disorder is called cyclothymic disorder. Bipolar disorder occurs in about 1.5% of the population and occurs with equal frequency in women and men.

▶ In mania the mood is characterized by euphoria. Cognitive symptoms include inflated self-esteem, grandiosity, distractibility, and in some cases delusions; motor symptoms involve excessive activity; and the primary physical symptom is a decreased need for sleep.

▶ Major depressive disorder and bipolar disorder share the symptom of depression, but they appear to be different disorders. There are individual differences in cycle time, with rapid cycling being more frequent in women and probably indicating a more severe disorder. There is a link between bipolar disorder and creativity, and it may be that the grandiosity and high activity levels lead to creative productions. Individuals are often unaware that they are having a manic episode, which makes it difficult to get them to accept treatment.

▶ Contrary to what was once thought, mania is not a flight from depression. Although stress per se is not a cause of mania, stress can trigger mania or lead to a relapse in individuals who are predisposed to bipolar disorder.

▶ Mania and depression are associated with increased and decreased activity in the brain, respectively. The differences in brain activity are linked to high and low levels of neurotransmitters and to differences in the sensitivity of postsynaptic neurons.

▶ Individuals with mania have been found to have enlargement of particular brain structures, most notably the amygdala (which plays a role in emotional arousal) and the nerve tract that carries emotion-related information to the frontal lobes.

▶ Genetics plays a very important role in bipolar disorder (heritability is estimated to be about 80%). There is also research linking prenatal and perinatal problems to bipolar disorder. Genetic, prenatal, and perinatal problems appear to cause the problems in the brain that lead to bipolar disorder.

▶ Lithium is effective for treating between 60% and 70% of the cases of bipolar disorder, but care must be taken in using lithium because it is poisonous. It can also lead to serious side effects. Anticonvulsants and antipsychotics are also used to treat mania. These drugs appear to reduce mania because they reduce brain activity. Sometimes antidepressants are taken to help treat the depression in bipolar disorder. Many patients cease taking their medication for mania because they think they no longer need it, don't like the side effects, or want to experience a manic "high."

▶ When drugs are not effective, bipolar disorder can be treated with ECT or transcranial magnetic stimulation. Such treatments must be followed up with drugs.

▶ The psychological treatment for bipolar disorder involves psychoeducation. Patients and their families learn how to avoid or cope with stress, recognize changes in symptoms that require changes in medication, and monitor medication use. This is effective for reducing symptoms and relapses.

Topic II: Suicide

▶ Women are more likely to attempt suicide, but men are more likely to succeed. Thus the rate of suicide is higher in men than in women. Individuals over 65 have the highest suicide rate.

▶ Suicide rates differ across cultures, owing primarily to differences in the degree to which suicide is an acceptable act, in levels of stress, and in the effectiveness with which depression is treated.

▶ Reports of a rapidly increasing suicide rate are probably due to an increasing willingness to record a death as a suicide rather than hide it as an "accident."

▶ Covert suicides are suicides disguised as accidents. Suicide gestures are behaviors that are designed to look like suicide attempts but in fact are not and are probably used to communicate a level of despair, attract attention, or manipulate others.

▶ Warnings about interest in committing suicide should always be taken seriously. Notes left by individuals who commit suicide are usually only apologies, explanations, or good-byes and tell us little about the act.

▶ Suicide rates rise as winter turns to spring and then decrease, and suicides are more likely to occur on Mondays than other days.

▶ There are numerous myths about suicide, including "People who talk about suicide won't commit suicide" and "Only depressed individuals commit suicide."

▶ It can be argued that in some circumstances (e.g., when facing a terribly painful death), suicide might be a rational and positive act rather than an abnormal behavior.

▶ There is strong evidence that depression and stress are important causes of suicide. It also appears that fantasies about what might be accomplished by suicide play a role.

▶ Learning about another person's suicide may suggest suicide as a solution or suggest a particular means of committing suicide. Behavioral contagion can reduce external restraints against committing suicide. In some cases suicide gestures are used to attract rewarding attention.

▶ Poor problem-solving skills and hopelessness can also lead to suicide. The rate of suicide is high among individuals with schizophrenia, owing to their delusions, hallucinations, and depression.

▶ Cognitive factors that reduce suicidal intent include coping beliefs, responsibilities to family, concerns about children, fear of suicide, fear of social disapproval, and moral objections. Suicides can also be reduced by the unavailability of a means of performing the act.

▶ Low levels of serotonin contribute to suicide because they cause depression and reduce inhibitions against committing suicide. Low levels of cholesterol are also linked to suicide because they lead to low levels of serotonin.

▶ Genetics plays an important role in suicide, primarily because it influences serotonin levels.

▶ The strategies for suicide prevention involve (1) educating people about the signs of suicide and where to get help; (2) treating depression, hopelessness, poor problem-solving skills, and low serotonin levels, and (3) crisis management for individuals who are about to commit suicide.

▶ The effectiveness of suicide prevention programs is limited because treatments do not work for everyone and many suicidal individuals do not come in for help.

Questions for Making Connections

1. Compare the causes of depression with the causes of mania. (Consider beliefs, stress, neurotransmitters, and brain structures.) What are the similarities and differences?

2. Each disorder has a "package" of symptoms, causes, and treatments. How are the symptoms, causes, and treatments of bipolar disorder related?

3. Describe the various strategies for treating bipolar disorder. How do physiological and psychological strategies work together?

4. How do genetics and prenatal and perinatal problems complement each other in helping explain mood disorders?

5. Are drugs, ECT, and transcranial magnetic stimulation treatments or cures for mood disorders? What is the evidence for your answer?

6. Describe the characteristics of an individual and a situation that would maximize the likelihood that the individual will commit suicide.

7. Assume you receive a call from a friend who is very suicidal. Your friend wants to talk with you and will not call anyone else. What steps would you take to help prevent your friend from committing suicide?

Key Terms and People

In reviewing and testing yourself, you should be able to discuss each of the following:

amygdala, p. 256
anticonvulsant drugs, p. 257
antipsychotic drugs, p. 257
behavioral contagion, p. 269
bipolar disorder, p. 250

covert suicide, p. 262
cyclothymic disorder, p. 250
lithium, p. 256
psychoeducation, p. 258
rapid cycling, p. 253

secondary mania, p. 251
serotonin, p. 271
suicide gestures, p. 263

10 Schizophrenia: Symptoms and Issues

THE TERM **schizophrenia** (skit-zo-FRE-ne-uh) refers to a set of serious disorders that involve what are undoubtedly among the most complex and frightening symptoms we will encounter. For example, individuals suffering from schizophrenia may hear voices, think other people or machines are controlling them, feel bugs crawling through passages in their bodies, believe other people are plotting against them, and use sentences that sound like pure nonsense. Such symptoms are difficult to understand and sometimes frightening because they are totally beyond the realm of experience of most people. That is, many of us may be able to understand disorders involving anxiety and depression because we have experienced those symptoms, but few of us have had hallucinations and delusions. Furthermore, until recently the fear of schizophrenia was intensified by the fact that the disorder was considered to be untreatable, and therefore a diagnosis of schizophrenia meant a life of misery and hopelessness on a back ward of a mental hospital. However, as you progress through this chapter and the next, you will learn that our understanding of schizophrenia is changing rapidly and that many of our earlier conceptions and fears of the disorder may no longer be appropriate.

Before discussing the symptoms of schizophrenia, I want to make a brief comment about the labels that are used when talking about individuals who suffer from schiz-

ophrenia. Many people talk about individuals with schizophrenia as "schizophrenics," but this is not appropriate. Just as we do not talk about people with cancer as "cancers," we should not talk about people with schizophrenia as "schizophrenics." In doing so we are implying that the disorder encompasses the individual's entire being, but that is not the case. In other words, having schizophrenia can be very serious, but there is more to an individual than the disorder, and therefore it is not appropriate to write off a whole individual as "schizophrenic." Many people have mild cases of schizophrenia and learn to cope with the symptoms (e.g., they may hear voices, but they ignore them), or their symptoms do not interfere with their lives. Indeed, many individuals with schizophrenia function effectively in society, and their friends and acquaintances may not even be aware they have the disorder.

Instead of talking about "schizophrenics," in this book I will talk about "individuals with schizophrenia" or "individuals who suffer from schizophrenia." In some cases this will seem awkward and wordy, but the way we label people

---

schizophrenia A set of serious disorders that involve a decline in functioning, along with such symptoms as hallucinations, delusions, and/or disturbed thought processes, which must persist for at least 6 months.

is important because labels can influence our perceptions. For example, the use of nonsexist language has reduced some of the stereotypes associated with gender. When I originally wrote the chapters on schizophrenia, I used the traditional approach and talked about "schizophrenics," but when I revised the chapters using the phrase "individuals with schizophrenia," a subtle but important change emerged: The people I talked about became *people with a problem* rather than *problem people*. With this clarified, let's go on to discuss the symptoms of schizophrenia.

TOPIC I

Symptoms of Schizophrenia

Over the past few weeks Lauren began behaving strangely. For example, when talking with friends she would jump from topic to topic, and sometimes she would laugh uncontrollably for no apparent reason. She also began attributing her personal problems to "cosmic radiation." Finally, when she began arguing with people who were not present, her friends became very concerned and took her to a hospital where she was admitted to the psychiatric unit with a diagnosis of schizophrenia. What does it mean to be diagnosed as suffering from schizophrenia? Will Lauren get better?

Barkley has hallucinations in which voices tell him what to do, and because he follows those directions, he often behaves very inappropriately and can no longer function in his job as a salesman. In contrast, Morgan has a delusion that she is a member of the British royal family and demands that others pay her the respect she believes she is due. She was also having a hard time in school, and because her grades fell so much, she dropped out. Barkley and Morgan have very different symptoms, but both have been diagnosed as suffering from schizophrenia. How can they have different symptoms but the same disorder?

Allan had always been a loner and had just never "gotten his act together." He drifted through high school without ever really getting involved or having any friends. After high school he tried working in a couple of fast-food places, but he could not seem to "keep things straight," and he lost those jobs. Allan was brought to a psychiatric hospital when the police found him on the street only half-dressed. During his admission interview he could give his name but did not know the day of the week, the month of the year, or where he was. It was difficult to talk with him because his sentences were gibberish. Sometimes he talked about "them," but it was not clear who "they" were. Allan was admitted to the hospital with a diagnosis of schizophrenia. What is Allan's prognosis?

In this section I will describe the cognitive, mood, physical, and motor symptoms of schizophrenia as well as the different types of schizophrenia.

Cognitive Symptoms

The cognitive symptoms of schizophrenia include *hallucinations, delusions, disturbed thought processes,* and *cognitive flooding.*

Hallucinations

Hallucinations are *perceptual experiences that do not have a basis in reality.* An individual who hears, feels, smells, or sees things that are not really there is said to be hallucinating. *Auditory* hallucinations are the most common type. They frequently involve hearing voices that comment on the individual's behavior, criticize the behavior, or give commands. For example, a woman named Betty, whom we will discuss later (in Case Study 10.3), hears monks chanting, "Cut yourself and die. Cut yourself and die." Less frequently, auditory hallucinations involve other sounds, such as motors running. It is also common for individuals with schizophrenia to have *tactile* hallucinations, in which the individual imagines tingling or burning sensations of the skin or various kinds of internal sensations. Finally, *visual* and *olfactory* hallucinations (seeing or smelling things that are not there) also occur in schizophrenia. For example, Betty sees monks who parade through her apartment or gather around her desk to criticize her while she is trying to work. Visual and olfactory hallucinations are somewhat less common than the other types of hallucinations.

It is important to realize that for an individual who is having them, *hallucinations appear to be real perceptions,* so real that they are completely indistinguishable from real perceptions. For example, Betty knows that there are no monks in her apartment, but they appear so real that sometimes she has to call me so that I can reassure her that in fact there are no monks in her apartment.

Delusions

Delusions are *erroneous beliefs that are held despite strong evidence to the contrary.* Some delusions are bizarre and patently absurd, whereas others are possible but unlikely. For example, the belief that a machine in the state capitol building is sending out waves that make you constantly think about sex is a bizarre delusion, whereas the belief that there are FBI agents hiding behind the trees in your backyard to spy on your sexual behavior is a nonbizarre delusion. The more bizarre the delusion, the more likely it is that the individual is suffering from schizophrenia.

The most common delusions are **delusions of persecution,** in which individuals think that others are spying on them or planning to harm them in some way. Also common are **delusions of reference,** in which objects, events, or other people are seen as having some particular significance to the person. For example, one male patient believed that when a woman across the room folded a newspaper in a certain way, it was a sign that he was being followed by spies. Similarly, whenever another patient saw a TV commercial for Coca-Cola, she interpreted it as a warning that the people she was with at the time could not be trusted. Individuals who suffer from schizophrenia may also experience **delusions of identity,** in which they believe that they are someone else. Common examples of this include delusions about being Jesus, Joan of Arc, the president of the United States, Michael Jackson, or some other famous person. In many cases individuals with schizophrenia develop extremely elaborate delusional systems involving numerous interrelated delusions, and their hallucinations are incorporated into their delusions. One woman who thought she was the Virgin Mary (delusion of identity) heard voices (auditory hallucinations) that she thought were the voices of sinners crying out to her for mercy. Similarly, the stomach pains (physical hallucinations) felt by another individual with schizophrenia were taken as evidence that he had been poisoned (delusion of persecution). Finally, many people who suffer from schizophrenia have **delusions of grandiosity,** which lead them to believe that they are very special in some way (e.g., exceptionally talented or prestigious). One man thought he had a new explanation for the universe, that his theory would discredit Einstein's theory, and that he was destined to become world-famous.

Most normal individuals also have some beliefs that are inconsistent with reality. For example, we are sometimes incorrect in our assumptions about the motives of others, or we see ourselves or others as better or worse than is actually the case. However, the delusional beliefs in schizophrenia are more bizarre, more pervasive, and more resistant to change in the face of contrary evidence than are the distortions that most of us live with from day to day (Oltmanns & Maher, 1988).

Disturbed Thought Processes

In addition to the problems concerning *what* individuals with schizophrenia think (e.g., delusions), there are also problems with the *way* they think. Specifically, the thought processes of these individuals are characterized by a "loosening" of the associative links between thoughts so that the individuals frequently spin off into irrelevancies (Bleuler, 1936). For example, a patient may be talking about his coat and then with no apparent transition will begin talking about medieval castles in Spain.

Disturbances in thought processes are illustrated by the following response of a person with schizophrenia to the question "Who is the president of the United States?":

I am the president, I am the ex-president of the United States, I have been a recent president. Just at present I was present, president of many towns in China, Japan and Europe and Pennsylvania. When you are president,

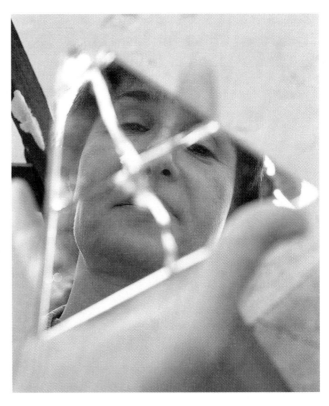

Shattered and distorted thought patterns are characteristic of patients suffering from schizophrenia.

you are the head of all, you are the head of every one of those, you have a big head, you are the smartest man in the world. I do testory and all scientist of the whole world. The highest court of doctoring, of practicing, I am a titled lady by birth of royal blood, [pointing to another patient] he has black blood, yellow blood, he is no man, a woman, a woe-man. . . . (Bleuler, 1936, pp. 72–73)

hallucinations   Perceptual experiences (i.e., sounds, feelings, sights, or smells) that do not have a basis in reality.

delusions   Erroneous beliefs that are held despite strong evidence to the contrary; often a symptom of schizophrenia.

delusions of persecution   Delusions in which individuals incorrectly believe that others are spying on them or planning to harm them in some way.

delusions of reference   Delusions in which individuals incorrectly believe that objects, events, or other people have some particular significance for them.

delusions of identity   Delusions in which individuals incorrectly believe that they are someone else.

delusions of grandiosity   Delusions in which individuals incorrectly believe that they are very special in some way (e.g., exceptionally talented or prestigious).

The Three Christs of Ypsilanti: A Confrontation of Delusions

CASE STUDY 10.1

Some years ago in a hospital in Ypsilanti, Michigan, a psychologist brought together three patients, each of whom believed that he was Christ. The goal was to see how—or if—these three men could resolve their conflict over who was Christ. Although each believed that he was Christ, they went by the names of Joseph, Clyde, and Leon. What follows is a summary of some of their interactions with one another and the psychologist. The first day each man was asked to introduce himself:

Joseph: My name is Joseph Cassel.

Psychologist: Joseph, is there anything else you want to tell us?

Joseph: Yes, I'm God.

Clyde: My name is Clyde Benson. That's my name straight.

Psychologist: Do you have any other names?

Clyde: Well, I have other names, but that's my vital side, and I made God five and Jesus six.

Psychologist: Does that mean you're God?

Clyde: I made God, yes. I made it 70 years old a year ago. Hell! I passed 70 years old.

Leon: Sir, it so happens that my birth certificate says that I am Dr. Domino Dominorum et Rex Rexarum, Simplis Christanus Pueris Mentalis Doktor. [In Latin this means "Lord of Lords and King of Kings, Simple Christian Boy Psychiatrist."] It also states on my birth certificate that I am the reincarnation of Jesus Christ of Nazareth, and I also salute, and I want to add

> **I know who I am. I'm God, Christ, the Holy Ghost. . . .**

this. I do salute the manliness in Jesus Christ also, because the vine is Jesus and the rock is Christ, pertaining to the penis and testicles, and it so happens that I was railroaded into this place because of prejudice and jealousy and duping that started before I was born, and that is the main issue why I am here. I want to be myself. I do not consent to their misuse of the frequency of my life.

Psychologist: Who are "they" that you are talking about?

Leon: Those unsound individuals who practice the electronic imposition and duping. . . . I want to be myself; I don't want this electronic imposition and duping to abuse me and misuse me, make a robot out of me. I don't care for it.

Joseph: He says he is the reincarnation of Jesus Christ. I can't get it. I know who I am. I'm God, Christ, the Holy Ghost, and if I wasn't, by gosh, I wouldn't lay claim to anything of the sort. I'm Christ. . . . I know this is an insane house and you have to be very careful.

And so it went, each patient asserting that he was God and often rambling off into other associations and delusions. One day, when Leon was holding his head as if in pain, the psychologist asked, "Do you have a headache?"

Leon: No, I don't, sir, I was "shaking it off," sir, cosmic energy, refreshing my brain. When I grab cosmic energy from the bottom of my feet to my brain, it refreshes my brain. The doctor told me that's the way I'm feeling, and that it is the proper attitude. Oh!

Pertaining to the question that you asked these two gentlemen [a question about why they were here], each one is a little institution and a house—a little world in which some stand in a clockwise direction and some in a counterclockwise, and I believe in a clockwise rotation.

Sometimes the men developed other delusions to explain the conflicts brought on by their original delusions. For example, when Clyde was asked to explain the fact that Joseph and Leon both also claimed to be God, he explained, "They are really not alive. The machines in them are talking. Take the machines out of them and they won't talk anything. You can't kill the ones with machines in them. They're dead already."

When asked where the machines were located, Clyde pointed to the right side of Joseph's stomach. The psychologist then asked Joseph to unbutton his shirt, and with his permission Clyde tried to feel around for the machine. When he couldn't find it, he said, "That's funny. It isn't there. It must have slipped down where you can't feel it."

After living together constantly for over 2 years and after meeting every day in an attempt to resolve their conflict, each of the three Christs of Ypsilanti still thought that he was Christ. Furthermore, none showed improvement in his schizophrenia.

Source: Adapted from Rokeach (1964).

The phrases used by individuals with schizophrenia are generally grammatically correct, but the thoughts expressed are disjointed and do not make sense when put together. Because of its apparent random nature, the language of individuals with schizophrenia has been described as a **word salad.** Each ingredient (phrase) is separately identifiable, but they have been mixed or tossed so that there is no order to them.

Some of the delusions and disturbed thought processes seen in schizophrenia are illustrated in Case Study 10.1.

If individuals who suffer from schizophrenia have disturbed thought processes, their intellectual functioning is going to be impaired, and therefore in many cases we find that these individuals perform at *reduced intellectual levels* (Danion, Rizzo, & Bruant, 1999; Heaton et al., 1994; Mohamed et al., 1999). For example, it would be difficult to perform well in an interview or on a test if you were giving responses that consisted of random thoughts strung together. Interestingly, the original term for schizophrenia was **dementia praecox** (di-MEN-shuh PRE-koks), which means "premature deterioration." When that term was introduced, it was thought that the patients suffered from the same type of intellectual deterioration that underlies senility but that it had set in prematurely. However, it was later realized that the deterioration in schizophrenia is very different from that in senility. Consequently, the impaired intellectual functioning seen in schizophrenia is now referred to as the **schizophrenic deficit** in order to distinguish it from other forms of intellectual impairment.

Although disturbed thought processes often result in reduced intellectual functioning, some individuals who suffer from schizophrenia continue to function very well. For example, when a new edition of the prestigious *Oxford English Dictionary* was being prepared, a great many new and important entries came from a man whose return address was that of a psychiatric hospital in England. The dictionary's editor assumed that the additions were coming from a physician on the staff of the hospital and was surprised when he learned that they were coming from a long-time patient who was suffering from schizophrenia (Winchester, 1999). Similarly, later (in Case Study 10.5) you will read about a man who earned a PhD in psychology and worked his way up to one of the chief administrative positions in a state mental health department, and whose colleagues were surprised when he announced that he had suffered from a very severe case of paranoid schizophrenia since early adulthood.

Cognitive Flooding (Stimulus Overload)

An important element in the cognitive experience of individuals with schizophrenia is the *inability to screen out irrelevant internal and external stimuli*. It is as though the "filter" that most of us have for eliminating extraneous stimuli is missing or broken in these individuals. As a consequence, individuals with schizophrenia are forced to attend to everything around and within them, and they feel overwhelmed, as though they are being flooded to the point of overload with perceptions, thoughts, and feelings. This experience is called **cognitive flooding,** or **stimulus overload.** The inability to screen out stimulation is reflected in the following quotations from a patient:

> Things are coming in too fast. I lose my grip of it and get lost. I am attending to everything at once and as a result I do not really attend to anything. Noises seem to be louder to me than they were before. . . . I notice it most with background noises. Colors seem to be brighter now almost as if they are luminous. (McGhie & Chapman, 1961, p. 105)

Cognitive flooding can be understood in terms of brain activity. For example, if you present a series of sounds to an individual who is not suffering from schizophrenia, the brain will show a considerable response (increased electrical activity) to the first sound but a greatly reduced response to subsequent sounds. In other words, the individual adapts to the stimulation, "closing the gate" on it, so to speak. However, individuals who suffer from schizophrenia do not show this adaptation, or *gating*. Instead, they show as great a response to subsequent stimuli as they did to the first stimulus (Braff, Grillon, & Geyer, 1992; Judd et al., 1992; Perry, Geyer, & Braff, 1999). This effect is illustrated in Figure 10.1, in which the brain activity in response to two sounds is plotted for individuals who were and were not suffering from schizophrenia. The decline in responsiv-

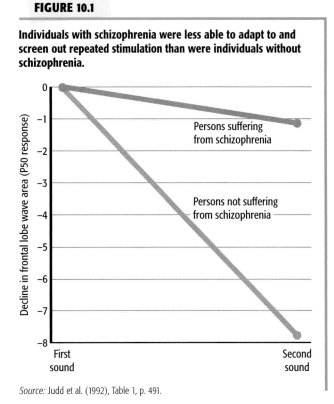

FIGURE 10.1

Individuals with schizophrenia were less able to adapt to and screen out repeated stimulation than were individuals without schizophrenia.

Source: Judd et al. (1992), Table 1, p. 491.

word salad   The language of persons with schizophrenia, in which each phrase is identifiable but the order is random and the thoughts expressed are disjointed.

dementia praecox   A term that refers to early deterioration of cognitive abilities, once used for schizophrenia.

schizophrenic deficit   The impairment in intellectual functioning seen in schizophrenia and due to the disturbance in thought processes.

cognitive flooding   In schizophrenia the experience of being overwhelmed by external and internal stimuli, which contributes to problems with thought processes; also called *stimulus overload.*

stimulus overload   In schizophrenia the experience of being overwhelmed by external and internal stimuli, which contributes to problems with thought processes; also called *cognitive flooding.*

ity shown by individuals who were not suffering from schizophrenia was more than six times greater than the decline shown by individuals who were suffering from schizophrenia. Obviously, the inability to close the gate on incoming stimulation can be very disruptive.

Mood Symptoms

There are two important things to note about the mood symptoms of schizophrenia. The first is that *as many as 60% of individuals with schizophrenia also suffer from serious depression* (Black & Andreasen, 1994). Their moods are often described as "blunted" or "flat." Some of the depression may be a side effect of the drugs used to treat schizophrenia, or it may result from the stress of struggling with the disorder. However, beyond those effects depression may simply be a symptom that co-occurs with schizophrenia; that is, rather than being a reaction, it might be part of the disorder. We will return to this issue later.

The second thing to note concerning mood symptoms is that individuals with schizophrenia often show emotional responses that are *inappropriate.* For example, when hearing of a death in the family or watching a very funny film, an individual who has schizophrenia may remain impassive and show little or no emotional response. Alternatively, when discussing an injury or some other serious topic, the same individual may break into laughter.

One explanation for the inappropriate emotional responses is that individuals with schizophrenia are responding to their hallucinations and delusions rather than to the elements in the actual situation. For example, one day I was having lunch with a friend of mine who suffers from schizophrenia, and although we were talking about a very pleasant topic, she began to appear upset, depressed, and even distraught. I became concerned, and when I asked if something was wrong, she replied, "Oh, I'm sorry; it's just that everyone in the restaurant has blood running down their faces. It's just one of my hallucinations." (My friend describes her symptoms in greater detail in Case Study 10.3.) This situation is analogous to one in which four persons are listening to recordings on headphones. Three of the people are listening to quiet mood music, while unknown to the others the fourth person is listening to a very funny comedy album. To those listening to mood music, the laughing of the fourth person will appear inappropriate. Viewed in this way, the mood disturbances of schizophrenia do not involve a disturbance of mood per se; rather mood is disturbed because of underlying cognitive problems.

To sum up, many individuals with schizophrenia suffer from depression or otherwise inappropriate emotions, and these problems with mood may occur because depression is part of the disorder or because the individuals are responding to their hallucinations or delusions rather than to the

This artwork was done by Betty, a woman who suffers from schizophrenia and who is profiled in Case Studies 10.3, 11.5, and 19.2.

reality of the situation. In some cases, if we knew what the individuals were responding to, their responses might be perfectly appropriate. For example, my friend's response to the bleeding faces was appropriate; I just did not know that she was seeing bleeding faces.

Physical Symptoms

DSM-IV does not list any physical symptoms for schizophrenia. However, many of the drugs that are used to treat schizophrenia have physical side effects such as dryness of the mouth and increased sensitivity to the sun, so we must be careful not to confuse the effects of the treatment with the effects of the disorder.

Motor Symptoms

The range of motor symptoms in schizophrenia is broad. Some individuals with schizophrenia remain immobile for long periods of time, whereas others are very agitated and exhibit a high level of activity. In some cases individuals with schizophrenia have difficulty sitting still, and they repeatedly get up and sit down. Other motor symptoms include unusual facial grimacing and repetitive finger and hand movements.

As with some of the other symptoms, it is important to distinguish between the motor symptoms of schizophrenia and the side effects of the medications that are used to treat it. As you will learn later, many of the drugs that are given to individuals with schizophrenia influence areas of the brain that are responsible for motor behavior, and thus some (but not all) of the tremors, muscular contortions, and stiff gaits exhibited by these individuals are due to the treatment and not the disorder (Fenton, Wyatt, & Mc-Glashan, 1994).

Before concluding this discussion of the symptoms of schizophrenia, I should point out that despite the bizarre nature of the symptoms, individuals with schizophrenia *are not aware of their symptoms* (Xavier et al., 1994). That is, they are completely unaware that they are hallucinating, having delusions, and suffering from a thought disorder. The fact that individuals may not know that they have these serious symptoms is important—if they do not know about the symptoms, they will not seek treatment or compensate for them.

Diagnostic Criteria

From the preceding discussion it should be clear that the clinical picture of schizophrenia encompasses a wide variety of symptoms. However, *an individual does not have to have all or even most of those symptoms to be diagnosed as suffering from schizophrenia.* This means that different individuals may have *very different sets of symptoms* and still be diagnosed as suffering from the *same disorder*—schizophrenia. For example, one individual might have hallucinations and delusions, another might have hallucinations and disorganized behavior, a third might have disorganized speech and flat mood, and a fourth might have bizarre delusions, but they would all receive a diagnosis of schizophrenia. Indeed, to be diagnosed as suffering from schizophrenia, an individual need only show *a decline in social or occupational functioning* (e.g., poor work, interpersonal relationships) and *any two of the following:* (1) delusions, (2) hallucinations, (3) disorganized speech, (4) grossly disorganized behavior, or (5) flat mood or apathy. Actually, only one of these symptoms is necessary if it consists of delusions that are bizarre or hallucinations that involve a voice that talks constantly. Because of these criteria, there are 12 different possible combinations of symptoms that can lead to the diagnosis of schizophrenia, and aside from a decline in functioning, no single symptom is common to all individuals with the diagnosis. The diagnostic criteria for schizophrenia are summarized in Table 10.1.

It is also important to note that the diagnosis of schizophrenia is arrived at by *exclusion.* That is, individuals who suffer from certain medical conditions or are taking particular drugs sometimes show the symptoms of schizophre-

TABLE 10.1

***DSM-IV* diagnostic criteria for schizophrenia**

A diagnosis of schizophrenia is based on the following criteria:

1. Individual has two or more of the following:
   a. Delusions
   b. Hallucinations
   c. Disorganized speech
   d. Grossly disorganized behavior
   e. Flat mood, apathy
   or one of the following:
   a. Bizarre delusions
   b. Constant hallucinations in which a voice talks constantly or two voices converse

2. Individual shows a decline in social or occupational functioning.

3. Symptoms persist for at least 6 months.

4. Other psychotic disorders and medical conditions have been ruled out.

Source: Adapted from American Psychiatric Association (1994).

nia, and therefore an individual is diagnosed as having schizophrenia only after all other possible causes have been ruled out. An interesting example of the problem of separating schizophrenia from other disorders is presented in Case Study 10.2 (on p. 286).

Finally, it is crucial to note that despite all of its strange symptoms, *schizophrenia does not necessarily imply an inability to live effectively outside of a hospital.* The diagnosis requires that there be a deterioration from a previous level of functioning, but if the demands on the individual are low or do not involve areas in which the symptoms will be disruptive, the individual may be able to function effectively in society. Whether or not individuals with schizophrenia are able to function in society depends on factors such as (1) the nature of the symptoms (delusions may be less disruptive for daily functioning than stimulus overload), (2) the context in which the individual must function (hallucinations will be less disruptive for a farmer plowing a field than for a secretary working in a busy office), (3) the degree to which others will tolerate deviance (eccentricities are better tolerated in a university than in a law firm), and (4) the severity of the symptoms. A colleague of mine is widely known as a brilliant scientist, but what most people do not know is that he suffers from schizophrenia. Similarly, I know of a student who graduated from a prestigious medical school and then announced that he had been hallucinating and delusional for the previous 5 years. Indeed, as part of his medical school training, he had done an intensive psychiatric rotation on the ward to which he was later admitted, but no one detected his problem during that rotation!

Many of the symptoms and problems of individuals with schizophrenia are illustrated in Case Study 10.3 (on pp. 287–288).

Schizophrenia or Not Schizophrenia?—That Is the Question

Was Mr. Erickson suffering from schizophrenia?

MR. ERICKSON was 64 years old and lived with his wife in a large old farmhouse in the countryside of New Hampshire. He was very sociable and "sharp as a tack," and there was no history of psychiatric disorders in his family. However, about a year ago he started talking about "the agents" who were out to get him. At first his wife ignored his comments, thinking he was only joking, but then he began putting flour on the stairs leading to the attic so that he could "trace their movements." Furthermore, one night he called 911 and told the operator that "they are in the attic, and I'm afraid they're going to kill us or burn down the house." The operator immediately sent a police SWAT team and engines from the local fire department, but there was no one in the attic or any evidence that anyone had been there.

After that incident Mr. Erickson was given a psychiatric evaluation from which it was concluded that he was suffering from "schizophrenia, probably paranoid type," and he was admitted to a prestigious psychiatric hospital for treatment. After 3 weeks of intensive treatment he was released; he was still vaguely concerned about "them," but he was rather sedated by a high level of antipsychotic medication. A month later he again called 911, telling the operator that "they're up in the attic again, ready to attack." Again the police were sent, but no one was found in the attic.

Mr. Erickson's schizophrenic disorder posed a serious problem; it did not seem to be helped by antipsychotic drugs and it was causing considerable problems. For example, when his wife disconnected the phones so that he could not call the 911 operator, he slipped out of the house in the middle of the night and walked to a neighbor's and called from there.

Was Mr. Erickson suffering from schizophrenia? The three psychiatrists who examined and treated him thought so, but a neuropsychologist came up with a different diagnosis and explanation. She suggested that Mr. Erickson had either a tumor or an inflammation of the brain, specifically in the temporal lobe, which was generating the symptoms. (In the next chapter I will explain how such factors can cause symptoms.) In fact, subsequent brain scans revealed swelling in the left temporal lobe. Furthermore, when Mr. Erickson took antiinflammatory medication (prednizone), his delusions cleared up immediately. This case clearly illustrates the importance of ruling out other explanations before making a diagnosis of schizophrenia. Remember, a diagnosis of schizophrenia is made only by exclusion, after all other explanations for the symptoms have been ruled out.

Phases of Schizophrenia

Individuals who suffer from schizophrenia are thought to go through three phases:

1. Some patients go through a **prodromal phase,** which precedes the onset of the full-blown disorder. (*Prodromal* is from the Greek word for "running before.") In this phase intellectual and interpersonal functioning begins to deteriorate, some peculiar behaviors appear, emotions start to become inappropriate, and unusual perceptual experiences begin to occur. This phase can last anywhere from a few days to many years.

2. Next is the **active phase,** in which the symptom patterns are clear-cut and prominent. Hallucinations, delusions, and disorders of thought and language become identifiable, and behavior may become more severely disorganized.

3. Some patients go through a **residual phase** that is similar to the prodromal phase in that the symptom picture again becomes less clear. Symptoms such as hallucinations and delusions may still exist, but they are less active and less important to the individual. Associated with the muting of symptoms is a general blunting of mood and often a general decline in intellectual performance (Davidson et al., 1995). This combination of symptoms often makes it impossible for individuals to return to the levels of functioning they enjoyed before the onset of the illness.

Although it is not officially recognized as such, there is another phase that some patients enter, often referred to as the **burned-out phase.** This phase is most likely to be seen in patients who have been hospitalized for many years, and the symptoms are probably due in large part to the effects of long-term institutionalization. Burned-out individuals show few, if any, of their original symptoms, but they do

---

prodromal phase The first phase of schizophrenia, which precedes the onset of the full-blown disorder.

active phase The second phase of schizophrenia, in which the symptom patterns are clear-cut and prominent.

residual phase The third phase of schizophrenia, in which the symptoms become less marked.

burned-out phase An unofficial fourth phase of schizophrenia, in which persons who have been hospitalized for many years no longer show the original symptoms but display a very severe deterioration of social skills, probably due in large part to their long-term institutionalization.

A Talk with Betty about Her Symptoms

BETTY IS A GOOD FRIEND of mine who suffers from a severe case of schizophrenia. Betty is a very bright, articulate, and friendly woman who graduated from college with a degree in fine arts and later earned a master's degree in library science. Her father was the president of a large state university, her mother is a teacher and nurse, and her three sisters are successful professionals.

Betty's schizophrenia first appeared when she was in college, and she has now struggled with the symptoms for over 20 years. She has been hospitalized many times and has had just about every treatment imaginable. She is currently on a variety of drugs that we will discuss in Chapter 11. It has been about 3 years since her last hospitalization, and she now lives by herself in an apartment. Betty calls me three or four times a week for brief chats and what she calls "reality checks." Each semester she comes to my class to talk about schizophrenia. Below is an excerpt from an interview in which Betty and I talked about some of her symptoms.

David: Betty, let's talk a little about your symptoms. Could you begin by telling me about your hallucinations?

Betty: Hallucinations have been a major part of my illness. Probably the first hallucination I had was the sound of glass breaking when people walked. You know, that real fine crystal, and it would be kind of crunchy when people walked. It seemed strange, and I couldn't understand it, but I heard it all the time. The next hallucination that developed was electricity coming out of people's bodies, in colors. I could see it, and I didn't want to get radiation.

David: What did it look like?

Betty: Like neon, just coming out of their bodies in different colors. People looked like they had bands of color coming out of their bodies, and it was too hot for me to be close to them, physically, because I could feel the waves, the heat. I don't see the radiation much anymore, but now I see auras around people. Different people have different colors.

David: Do I have an aura now?

Betty: Oh, yes, blue. Blue is good. People with blue auras are good.

David: Have you had other visual hallucinations?

Betty: I think the most awful hallucination I had—and still have—is the blood, blood pouring down people's faces. Sometimes everybody has blood pouring down their foreheads and down their front. When I look at people, they are all bloody. It's really horrible. The first time it happened, I was so scared and nobody believed me. They didn't understand what I was seeing, and they kind of ignored me and sneered. It still happens, usually at night, but sometimes in the afternoon. It's like living in a slaughterhouse, and I don't want to look at anybody, so I just kind of keep to myself.

David: How do you deal with this? What do you do when it happens when you are talking to someone and the person starts bleeding?

Betty: I try and just finish the conversation and get away, but sometimes I can't. I just try to act normal. I have this thing about acting normal; I just say, "Hi, how are you?" and then I get out of there. I see the blood, I can't stop seeing it, so I have to get away from the bloody people.

David: Could you tell me about the demons?

Betty: They started up a long time ago. They used to come and go, but now they are constantly with me—around me all the time. I have two sets. One is my in-head set, and they chant, "Cut yourself and die. Cut yourself and die." And sometimes they come out of my head; that really frightens me, and I want to get armed.

David: Armed?

Betty: Yes, get a knife or something to protect myself.

David: What about the other set?

Betty: Well, they're outside my head; I can see them. They wear black cloaks and hoods over their heads. They're men. I can't see their features, but they are human. They wear those leather pointy shoes, like the ones they wore in the Middle Ages. They don't chant; they talk to me. They tell me I'm stupid and worthless.

David: Where do you see them? Are they here now?

Betty: No, they're in my apartment all of the time, but I don't think I've ever seen them on the street. When I sit at my desk, they line up behind me, and when I go to bed, they stand at the foot of the bed. They say all kinds of horrible things, like I should have been a dead fetus and that I'm useless and I hurt so many people in my life that I could never repay them all. It's terrible.

David: How real do the demons appear?

Betty: How real? *Absolutely real.* I mean, intellectually, I know they are hallucinations, *but they are real to me.* I know they are hallucinations, but sometimes I have my doubts. That's when I have to call you for a "reality check"—to have you assure me that they are hallucinations. Hallucinations are very real, and they can lead you to do some strange things. One night, I had this hallucination that I was covered in blood and dead, and I went into the kitchen and got a knife and cut my arm up. I thought, if I can bleed, I'm not dead, I'm alive.

David: Do you ever have other kinds of hallucinations?

Betty: Yes, I smell things. Rotting flesh. I smell that off and on, not often. I often taste things. Things taste like metal—very unpleasant.

David: Let's shift to delusions. Can you tell me about your delusions?

Betty: Well, there's what I call the "ticker tape" delusion that everyone can read my forehead.

David: I don't understand.

Betty: You know, like in Times Square, where the words go around the front of the building in light bulbs. I thought that my thoughts flashed across my forehead so everyone could read my thoughts. I was convinced that people could read my thoughts that way, and I couldn't figure out how to make it stop, so sometimes I would walk around with my hands over my forehead to keep people from reading my thoughts. I should also tell you about the "shower" delusion. I had a friend, and every morning when I got in the shower, I thought

(continued)

Case Study 10.3 *(cont.)*

he was able to read my mind, so whenever I was in there, I tried to keep thinking good thoughts about him. You know, "Andy is so nice," "Oh, gee, I really like Andy." I wanted him to think that I only thought good things about him.

Shown here is Betty (right) and her case manager, who plays an extremely important role in Betty's life.

David: This happened only in the shower?

Betty: Yep, but I thought that my mother could read my mind anywhere. That's why I made up the code.

David: The code?

Betty: Yes, if Mother said a certain sentence, that meant she was reading my mind but wasn't telling me. And the sentence would be something inane, like "How are you?"

David: So if your mother said "How are you?" that was a signal that she was reading your mind?

Betty: Yes, and I was furious that she was doing it. I confronted her, and she denied it, but I didn't believe her.

David: Have you had any other delusions?

Betty: Oh, yes, lots. Probably my major delusion has been that the police are after me. Whenever I see a patrol car, I am sure they are following me, and they can really frighten me. I am convinced that they can read my mind with their equipment, on their radios, and they are after me. They do it real cleverly; they don't just come out and get me. They watch; they're waiting for a chance. It's really scary.

David: Do you think that now?

Betty: (pauses with a somewhat sheepish smile) Well . . . I know it's a delusion, but . . . well, yes, I still think they are after me. Now I think, well, I'm not going to be paranoid about the police, and then a patrol car goes by and . . . I don't know . . . The funny thing is, I don't know what they would do to me or what I've done. You know, I have this feeling, a profound feeling of guilt. . . . When I see a patrol car, it is a sign of oncoming psychosis.

David: A symbol of oncoming psychosis? I don't understand.

Betty: Well, they zap me with their radar, and eventually it will destroy my brain.

David: Let's talk a little about disturbances of thought processes. What's that like?

Betty: Well, it's like you have roads through your brain. When you think, you travel on them. Mine have detours and barricades. My thoughts get blocked or get detoured, and it

gets all mixed up. I don't know quite when it started, but when I get a thought, I can't always follow it to completion. Sometimes it happens when I am talking. I get confused, or all of a sudden I'll think, "The demons are here," and then I'll start to worry about them or listen to them, so I get distracted.

David: Betty, can you tell me what it's like to function, to get through the day, with all of these symptoms?

Betty: It's hell. I see people doing things, just doing simple things, and it's so hard for me. People get up and eat and read and clean the house, and I have such a hard time just getting into the shower—and then I might have to worry about someone reading my mind. Everyone seems so competent, and I can't do it. . . . I think it's a dirty trick from the demons. . . . I can't always think right, and then there is the paranoia. It makes everything so hard to do. When I am around people, I think they can read my mind, that they know about my illness, that they are making fun of me, so I leave. I remember one day when I was working at the library and I had to alphabetize some cards, and I just couldn't do it. Sometimes when I am really sick, it is like everyone is speaking in Greek to me, and I can't understand it. It is like being in Italy and not speaking Italian, and no one can speak English to you. You just can't understand what is happening. It is just like being out of it. It's *hell*.

---

display a very serious deterioration of social skills. They may eat with their hands, urinate in their clothing, and be completely insensitive to people around them. It is unlikely that a burned-out patient would ever be able to function outside a hospital. These patients are sometimes referred to as "back-ward" patients because they are generally "warehoused" out of sight of other patients and the public. Fortunately, the number of such patients seems to be declining, probably because we now have more effective treatments and so fewer patients deteriorate to this degree. Also, with the new emphasis on community-based treatment, even disturbed patients are less likely to be kept in a hospital for long periods of time, and therefore they avoid

the effects of institutionalization (see Chapter 19). The story of a burned-out patient is presented in Case Study 10.4.

Types of Schizophrenia

So far I have discussed schizophrenia as though it were one disorder, but it is generally agreed that schizophrenia is probably a group of disorders, and it is now common to talk about "schizophrenias" or "schizophrenic disorders." In *DSM-IV* distinctions are made among five types of schizo-

Old Alex: A Case of Burned-Out Schizophrenia

THE WARD STAFF usually calls the patient "Old Alex." When he was hospitalized 36 years ago, he was diagnosed as "schizophrenic." He was described as intelligent and articulate but agitated and suffering from delusions of omnipotence. Then Alex thought he was "the brother of God, sent to free those who were damned by the Devil." Today Alex sits slumped in a metal chair in a lonely corner of Ward G. His mouth twitches frequently, and his head occasionally jerks involuntarily to the left. He is dressed in wrinkled blue pants and a plaid shirt, the laces of his shoes are not tied, and he does not wear socks. There is a large urine stain on his pants just below the belt.

Much of the time Alex seems to be dozing, but when he is awake, he stares blankly at the wall a few feet in front of him. *Wheel of Fortune* is on the television and Vanna White is smiling and turning letters, but he doesn't seem to notice her—or anything else. Old Alex has been sitting there and staring at the wall for as long as any of the ward staff can remember.

At 11:30, when it is time for lunch, a young attendant comes over, shakes Alex's shoulder gently, and says, "Come on, Alex, it's time for lunch. Come on,

Alex, lunch." Alex turns his head and looks up. He looks at the young attendant for a few moments with great effort, as if he were straining to see through a dense fog. Then he gets up and shuffles with a stiff-legged gait toward the door, where the other patients are waiting to be taken to the dining room. Once in the dining room he eats his food with his fingers rather than with a fork, but when scolded by the attendant he wipes his fingers on his shirt and begins using his fork.

Alex never makes any trouble on the ward, and he is liked by the staff. He has to be prodded to dress in the morning, and four or five times a day he has to be reminded about going to the bathroom, but he is compliant and does whatever he is told in a mechanical way. His bad table manners do not reflect symptoms; it is more as though he has simply forgotten to use his fork.

Other people are often around Alex on Ward G, but he seems isolated and not really with them. Alex has an older sister in New Jersey who sent him a small box of cookies at Christmas 2 years ago, but that is the only contact he has had with his family for many years. Once every couple of years the students from an abnormal psychology

class visit the hospital, and Alex is one of the patients they interview. The interview is usually rather disjointed because Alex tends to lose the thread and drift off. When asked whether he still thinks he is the brother of God, he concentrates for a while as if trying to remember the plot of a long-forgotten movie and then responds somewhat distractedly, "Er . . . I don't think so. . . . Maybe. . . ."

Every 6 months Alex is brought up for a routine evaluation at a ward staff meeting. This is strictly routine; his behavior has not changed in years, and there are no new treatments to be tried with him. The entries in his hospital file are repetitive: "No change. Recommend that care on domiciliary ward be continued." Alex will live out his life slumped in the chair, staring at the wall, unaware that the woman on TV has just turned over a winning set of letters. There is a small graveyard behind the hospital, and someday Old Alex will be quietly moved there.

CASE STUDY 10.4

> **Alex will live out his life slumped in the chair, staring at the wall . . . .**

The prognosis for burned-out patients with schizophrenia is very poor. These individuals have been hospitalized for many years and have experienced a serious deterioration in social skills.

phrenia: **paranoid** (PAR-uh-noyd), **disorganized, catatonic** (kat-uh-TON-ik), **undifferentiated,** and **residual.** The symptoms of these types are listed in Table 10.2 (on p. 290).

paranoid schizophrenia   A type of schizophrenia characterized by delusions of persecution.

disorganized schizophrenia   A type of schizophrenia showing the most psychological disorganization and lacking a systematic set of delusions.

catatonic schizophrenia   A rare type of schizophrenia usually characterized by lack of or peculiar motor movements.

undifferentiated schizophrenia   A catchall diagnosis for all persons with schizophrenia who do not fit into the other categories.

residual schizophrenia   A mild disorder that occurs after at least one schizophrenic episode and is characterized by some of the symptoms of schizophrenia, which are generally muted.

TABLE 10.2

Types of schizophrenia listed in *DSM-IV*

Type	Symptoms and comments
Paranoid schizophrenia	Symptoms include delusions or auditory hallucinations. Delusions usually revolve around persecution or grandiosity. None of the other symptoms associated with schizophrenia (e.g., disorganized speech or thought processes, problems with mood) are present. Paranoid schizophrenia is thought to be very different from other forms of schizophrenia.
Disorganized schizophrenia	Symptoms include disorganized speech, disorganized behavior, and flat or inappropriate mood.
Catatonic schizophrenia	Symptoms revolve primarily around motor activity and must include at least two of the following: (1) motoric immobility; (2) excessive motor activity that is purposeless; (3) extreme negativism, such as resistance to instructions or mutism; (4) peculiar voluntary movements, such as bizarre postures, strange mannerisms, grimacing; (5) repeating in parrotlike fashion statements made to them (*echolalia*) or imitation of the movements of others (*echopraxia*). This type is extremely rare today.
Undifferentiated schizophrenia	Individuals with this type have hallucinations and delusions, but they do not qualify for any of the other types. This is essentially a "catchall" diagnosis for individuals who do not fit any of the other types.
Residual schizophrenia	Individuals with this type do not have prominent delusions, hallucinations, disorganized speech, disorganized behavior, or catatonic behavior. However, they show minor evidence of previous symptoms; that is, they may have odd beliefs or unusual perceptual experiences. The fact that individuals who no longer have the symptoms of schizophrenia can be diagnosed as suffering from *residual* schizophrenia appears to be a reflection of the early notion that schizophrenia is not treatable ("once a schizophrenic, always a schizophrenic").

Source: Based on American Psychiatric Association, 1994.

Although the five types of schizophrenia described in Table 10.2 are officially recognized in *DSM-IV*, there are two serious problems with this classification system. First, many individuals who suffer from schizophrenia *do not fit neatly into any one type.* Second, the classification of individuals into these types has *not led to an understanding of what causes schizophrenia or how to treat the disorder.* Because of these problems, the division of schizophrenia into the five types is not of much theoretical or practical value. For diagnostic (descriptive) purposes, in the future it might be better to abandon these official types and instead simply describe an individual as "suffering from schizophrenia with . . ." and list the individual's specific symptoms

positive symptoms (of schizophrenia)   Symptoms such as hallucinations, delusions, disturbances of thought, and bizarre behaviors that are believed to be due to problems with neural transmission. (Contrast with *negative symptoms.*)

negative symptoms (of schizophrenia)   Symptoms such as flat mood, poverty of speech, inability to experience positive feelings, apathy, and inattentiveness that are thought to be due to structural problems in the brain or low levels of activity in the frontal lobes. (Contrast with *positive symptoms.*)

psychoticism   One type of positive symptom of schizophrenia, consisting of hallucinations and delusions.

disorganization   One type of positive symptom of schizophrenia, consisting of thought disorders, bizarre behaviors, and inappropriate mood.

Persons who suffer from catatonic schizophrenia may remain immobile, sometimes in strange positions, for long periods of time. This disorder is relatively rare.

(e.g., "schizophrenia with delusions" or "schizophrenia with thought-process problems"). That format would be more descriptive, and once we link different symptoms to different causes, it would provide a guide to treatment.

The one *DSM-IV* type that does appear to be different from schizophrenia in general is paranoid schizophrenia. The differences lie in the facts that the symptoms are limited to delusions (usually involving persecution) and sometimes hallucinations and that individuals with paranoid schizophrenia do not show the disorganization and deterioration of thought processes characteristic of others with schizophrenia. Indeed, individuals suffering from paranoid schizophrenia are often otherwise bright, competent, and effective. In Case Study 10.5 (on pp. 292–293) a colleague of mine describes his experience with paranoid schizophrenia.

Positive versus Negative Symptoms of Schizophrenia

Because the traditional typology of schizophrenia did not prove to be helpful in understanding or treating the disorder, investigators began searching for an alternative means of classifying symptoms and individuals. The most promising of these alternative classification schemes involves grouping the symptoms of schizophrenia into two types: positive symptoms and negative symptoms (Andreasen, 1982; Andreasen & Olsen, 1982; Easton et al., 1995; McGlashan & Fenton, 1992).

Nature of Positive and Negative Symptoms

Positive symptoms include *hallucinations, delusions, thought disorders,* and *bizarre behaviors.* These are called *positive* symptoms because they are *additions* to normal behavior; that is, normal individuals do not have hallucinations and delusions. In contrast, **negative symptoms** include *flat mood, poverty of speech, inability to experience positive feelings, apathy,* and *inattentiveness.* These are called *negative* symptoms because they reflect the *absence* of normal behaviors; that is, normal individuals have fluent speech and can experience positive feelings.

There are probably two types of positive symptoms (Andreasen et al., 1995). One type, called **psychoticism,** consists of hallucinations and delusions. In other words, psychoticism is characterized by the *production of false stimulation (hallucinations) or ideas (delusions).* The second type of positive symptoms, called **disorganization,** consists of thought disorders (confusion), bizarre behaviors, and inappropriate mood. It is characterized by *disorganization of thinking and behavior.* The positive and negative symptoms of schizophrenia are summarized in Figure 10.2.

The symptoms of schizophrenia clearly fall into the types shown in Figure 10.2, but it is important to recognize that most individuals are not limited to positive symptoms or negative symptoms, but rather they have more symptoms of one type than of the other.

Characteristics Associated with Positive and Negative Symptoms

It seems clear that there is a difference between positive and negative symptoms, but the question is, is it a difference that makes a difference? That is, are positive and negative symptoms related to factors that help us understand and treat schizophrenia? The answer appears to be yes, and in this section I will discuss the characteristics that are associated with the positive and negative symptoms.

Premorbid Adjustment. It is consistently found that negative symptoms are more likely than positive symptoms to

FIGURE 10.2

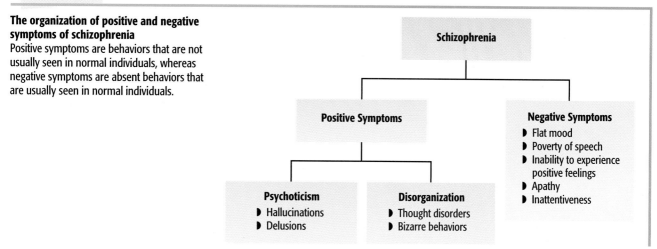

The organization of positive and negative symptoms of schizophrenia
Positive symptoms are behaviors that are not usually seen in normal individuals, whereas negative symptoms are absent behaviors that are usually seen in normal individuals.

A Psychologist Talks about His Own Struggle with Schizophrenia

Frederick J. Frese III was a 26-year-old college graduate when the symptoms of schizophrenia began to develop. At the time he was a lieutenant in the U.S. Marine Corps, where he was responsible for guarding atomic weapons and providing security for the Fleet Intelligence Center for Europe. Fred wrote the following about his symptoms and how he dealt with them.

"Work became very difficult for me, and I could not understand why everything seemed so hard to do in a proper manner. After several months of struggling to understand why things were so difficult, I suddenly figured it all out. It became quite obvious to me that during the Korean War, the Chinese had taken prisoners and given them posthypnotic suggestions. By the use of certain 'key words,' the Chinese were controlling those who had been their prisoners. It was very easy for me now. All I had to do was to find out which Marines and others had served in Korea and avoid them, because if they found out that I knew about them, surely they would take steps to neutralize me. My immediate superior, a certain major, often talked about his experiences in the Korean War. He needed to be helped, and our country needed protection from him and the others under Chinese control. In order to help him, I decided to call the base hospital, where I talked to a psychiatrist about how we might best go about 'deprogramming' the persons who had been hypnotized. The psychiatrist asked me to come to the hospital to talk with him. I did so, but after a brief chat, I was escorted to a small single room in the hospital, where I was told that I was now a psychiatric patient and could not leave. Soon thereafter I learned that I had been given the diagnosis of paranoid schizophrenia. Clearly, in my mind I had made a serious mistake. Obviously, the psychiatrist had been in Korea, too.

"Those whom the Chinese controlled now knew that I had discovered them, and I knew that it was only a matter of time before one of them would be 'activated' to kill me. I started demanding that a priest administer the last rites before they got to me. After about 3 days a kindly priest visited me and administered the sacrament, and I was prepared to die.

"But I was lucky. Before long a plane arrived that took me to Washington, where I became a patient in the Naval Hospital in Bethesda, Maryland. I was promptly escorted to the psychiatric ward. There I would remain for 5 months while I very carefully probed everyone I came in contact with to find out if they had ever been to Korea. I totally resisted the idea that I had a psychiatric problem. I just knew something very important that others did not know, and I did not seem to be able to convince anyone of the great threat that our country was facing. There was nothing wrong with me other than the fact that 'I knew too much.' After 5 months I was released from the hospital and from the Marine Corps.

"Because I had learned to speak some Japanese when I was in the service, I enrolled in a graduate school to study international business. Those who were controlled by the Chinese did not seem to be around the school. Maybe I was safe. Maybe they had forgotten me, and I could quietly live a

---

be associated with *poor premorbid adjustment.* For example, before being diagnosed as suffering from schizophrenia, individuals with primarily negative symptoms (1) showed poorer social and sexual functioning, (2) progressed less far in school, and (3) performed worse in work settings than did individuals with primarily positive symptoms. There also appears to be a tendency for negative symptoms to be associated with lower scores on intelligence tests.

Consistency over Time. It is also noteworthy that *negative symptoms are consistent over time,* whereas positive symptoms tend to wax and wane (Arndt et al., 1995; Davidson et al., 1995; McGlashan & Fenton, 1992). Insofar as negative symptoms change over time, they tend to get worse.

Gender. *Men are more likely than women to suffer from negative symptoms.* The reason for the gender difference is not clear, but it reflects the less optimistic prognosis for males suffering from schizophrenia.

Response to Treatment. Finally, it is important to note that, in general, *positive symptoms respond better to drug treatment* than do negative symptoms. Indeed, until very recently no effective treatments for negative symptoms were known, and even the recently developed treatments for these symptoms are only moderately effective (see Chapter 11).

The findings that, compared to negative symptoms, positive symptoms are associated with better premorbid adjustment, show a more rapid onset, are less consistent over time, and respond better to drug treatment have been used to suggest that positive and negative symptoms have different causes. Specifically, it may be that positive symptoms are due to fluctuations in brain chemistry, whereas negative symptoms are due to progressive brain damage. (I will discuss those possibilities in Chapter 11.) In any event the use of the distinction between positive and negative symptoms is promising and is clearly more valuable than the traditional typology of schizophrenia. The characteris-

regular life. After a year I graduated from business school and secured employment with a *Fortune* 500 company. The company needed my skills in Japanese to deal with Japanese manufacturing firms. It was very exciting to be receiving so much attention. But then, in all the excitement I started behaving very strangely. I suddenly started being controlled by numbers and lights. Red lights stopped me, and green lights started me, and all tasks were translated through numbers. I began stopping everything whenever I saw a red light, no matter where the red light might be, and not starting again until I saw a green light. Finally, after a lot of desperate acts, one Sunday I went to a cathedral in the downtown area, where without invitation I started assisting the priest celebrating the High Mass. Shortly thereafter I began feeling and behaving more strangely. I started grunting, then barking. I began turning into a monkey, then into a doglike animal, then into a reptile, a dragon, then into a wormlike creature. Later I was to 'realize' that what I was experiencing was like going backward through an evolu-

tionary process. Finally, I degenerated totally. I had become only one atom, and it was the atom in the center of an atomic bomb. I was being loaded onto a bomber airplane. The world was going to end in nuclear holocaust, and I had been turned into the mechanism for its destruction. Everything was over. It was only a matter of time. . . .

"Unusual experiences like these happened to me numerous times during the past 23 years. But after the first 10 years, during which I was in nine different hospitals for a total of about 300 days, I have not had to be rehospitalized. I still have breakdowns, but I have learned to sense when they are coming on and to 'cut short' the mechanism of the breakdown. I usually handle these circumstances or attacks by taking time off from work and staying around home singing, dancing, synthesizing the religions of the world, eating raw acorns, or behaving in some other strange manner as I work out my problems.

"During the time between breakdowns, I have earned a PhD in psychology and worked as a psychologist and administrator in a large state hos-

pital, helping other people with schizophrenia who have not learned to cope as well as I have. I very much like being around the patients because I can see a lot of myself in each of them. We have a common experience. Whether the patients might be 'mystic Abyssinian warriors' or hiding from 'the Green Gang,' whether they are hearing voices or cannot button their shirts properly, I remember 'being there' myself, and I know it is possible to return from that 'parallel reality' that one enters through the mechanism of psychosis."

Today Dr. Frese works as a psychologist and mental health administrator in Ohio. His case clearly illustrates the symptoms of schizophrenia and demonstrates that it is possible for some individuals to lead very productive lives while suffering from the disorder.

> **. . . I started behaving very strangely. I suddenly started being controlled by numbers and lights.**

tics associated with positive and negative symptoms are summarized in Table 10.3.

son's disease causes hallucinations like those seen in schizophrenia, and if you did not know about the medication's side effects, you might erroneously diagnose an individual

THINKING CRITICALLY

Questions about the Symptoms of Schizophrenia

1. *What problems are involved in making and interpreting a diagnosis of schizophrenia?* A major problem in making a diagnosis of schizophrenia involves excluding other explanations for the symptoms. Recall that a diagnosis of schizophrenia can only be made when all other potential explanations have been ruled out. Therefore, to make a diagnosis of schizophrenia you must not only know the symptoms of schizophrenia but must also know what other disorders and medications can lead to the same symptoms. For example, one of the medications used to treat Parkin-

TABLE 10.3

Characteristics associated with positive and negative symptoms of schizophrenia

Characteristic	Positive symptoms	Negative symptoms
Onset	Later	Earlier
Stability over time	Symptoms fluctuate	Symptoms consistent over time
Frequency of occurrence	More frequent in women	More frequent in men
Response to treatment	Good	Poor

who is taking the medication as suffering from schizophrenia. Similarly, some individuals brought to emergency rooms suffering from "schizophrenia" are later found to be showing the effects of high levels of amphetamines. Knowing all the side effects and disorders that can lead to symptoms like those of schizophrenia can be very difficult and is often beyond the knowledge of one person. Therefore, it is sometimes advisable to get second opinions from health care specialists in other areas.

The problem with interpreting a diagnosis of schizophrenia lies in the fact that two or three people who are all diagnosed as suffering from schizophrenia may not have any of the same symptoms. In other words, because so many different sets of symptoms can lead to a diagnosis of schizophrenia, such a diagnosis does not tell us much about the person's symptoms. The fact that different sets of symptoms can lead to the same diagnosis leads to the next question of whether schizophrenia is really one disorder.

2. *Is schizophrenia one disorder or a number of different disorders?* A number of types of schizophrenia, such as disorganized and catatonic, have been identified, but as I pointed out earlier, the distinctions among those types have not been useful in terms of understanding schizophrenia or treating it. Therefore, today they are largely ignored. In contrast, however, the distinction between positive symptoms (hallucinations, delusions, disruptions in thought processes) and negative symptoms (flat mood, poverty of thought, inability to experience positive feelings, apathy, inattentiveness) is clear and is related to both the development of schizophrenia (positive symptoms set in later) and its prognosis (positive symptoms are more likely to respond to treatment). These differences certainly suggest that different processes underlie the positive and negative symptoms and that we may be dealing with two different disorders that both result in symptom patterns that lead to the same diagnosis. It will be important to keep the distinction between positive and negative symptoms in mind when we consider the causes and treatments of schizophrenia in the next chapter.

TOPIC II

Issues Associated with Schizophrenia

Ted was trapped for 14 hours in a collapsed building following an earthquake. When they found him, he was hallucinating, delusional, and incoherent. At the hospital he was diagnosed as suffering from brief psychotic disorder. The symptoms seem to be the same as schizophrenia, so how is this disorder different from schizophrenia? Will Ted recover, or is his illness going to be a chronic problem?

Professor Sheridan completed a study of 2,000 patients who were suffering from schizophrenia. One striking finding was that most of the patients tended to be from the lower socio-economic classes. Why is schizophrenia more prevalent in the lower classes? Is it because people in those classes are subject to higher levels of stress? Do people drift down into the lower classes because their disorder makes it difficult for them to function occupationally? Or is there a class bias in making diagnoses?

In this section I will discuss the history of our thinking about schizophrenia and the links between schizophrenia and factors such as age and gender. Finally, I will describe a number of disorders that are related to schizophrenia.

History and Current Views

Now that you understand the symptoms of schizophrenia, it will be helpful to briefly consider how our views of schizophrenia developed, because the early conceptions still influence us today. The history of modern attempts to describe and explain schizophrenia goes back to the beginning of the 20th century when **Emil Kraepelin** (a-MEL KRA-puh-lin; 1856–1926) in Germany and **Eugen Bleuler** (OY-gen BLOY-lur; 1857–1939) in Switzerland focused their attention on the problem. These two men offered very different views of the disorder, and the two views started us on different tracks for understanding it.

Kraepelin's Views: Early Onset, Deterioration, Poor Prognosis

Kraepelin argued that schizophrenia began *early in life* and that the symptoms reflected a *progressive and irreversible intellectual deterioration* that was like that of senility. Indeed, he is the one who labeled the disorder *dementia praecox* (premature deterioration). Consistent with his notion that schizophrenia was like senility and was progressive, Kraepelin believed that the disorder had a *physiological cause* and that the *prognosis was very poor*. Kraepelin had a basically pessimistic view of the disorder.

Bleuler's Views: Variable Onset, Disorganization, Better Prognosis

In sharp contrast to Kraepelin, Bleuler argued that schizophrenia could develop at *any point in life,* and rather than being a senile-like deterioration, the disorder was due to a *disorganization or breakdown of the associative threads that connect words, thoughts, and feelings.* Specifically, he suggested that patients' disordered language patterns stem from their use of misconnected words, their problems in thought processes result from their use of misconnected thoughts, and their inappropriate moods are a result of their emotions being disconnected from their thoughts. To describe that disorganization and breakdown of associations, Bleuler coined the term *schizophrenia,* which literally means "splitting of the mind." With regard to cause Bleuler agreed with Kraepelin that the underlying cause of schizophrenia was *physiological,* but he argued that the symptoms could be brought on by psychological factors such as stress. Finally, Bleuler offered a more optimistic view concerning the prognosis, suggesting that some individuals did get better. The views of Kraepelin and Bleuler are summarized in Table 10.4.

When we look at these two strikingly different views of schizophrenia from today's perspective, several questions arise: How did these two men come up with such different views, which one of them has been proven to be correct, and what view is held today? It appears that Kraepelin and Bleuler came up with different views because they were working with patients who were suffering from different types of schizophrenia; Kraepelin must have been working with patients who suffered primarily from negative symptoms (e.g., early onset, deterioration, poor prognosis), whereas Bleuler seems to have been working with patients who suffered from primarily positive symptoms (e.g., later onset, disorganization, good prognosis). Who was correct? Obviously, we now know that they were both correct, but for different subsets of patients. However, for most of the 20th century Kraepelin's views prevailed, while Bleuler's were largely ignored. This is unfortunate because Kraepelin's emphasis on the negative, largely untreatable symptoms led us to a very pessimistic view of schizophrenia. Today we recognize that schizophrenia involves both positive and negative symptoms. Therefore, our view of schizo-

phrenia is an amalgamation of the views of Kraepelin and Bleuler, but the more pessimistic views of Kraepelin still seem to be dominant.

Prevalence

The results of large-scale community studies in which thousands of individuals were interviewed suggest that about *1.5% of the population suffer from schizophrenia at some time during their lives* (Kendler, Gallagher, et al., 1996; Robins et al., 1984). The seriousness of the problem is further magnified by the fact that schizophrenia is often a long-term disorder. That is, not only do a lot of people suffer from schizophrenia, but they suffer from it for a long period of time.

Sociocultural Factors

There are a number of links between schizophrenia and sociocultural factors such as age, gender, and social class.

Age

Schizophrenia is most frequently diagnosed during *early adulthood;* usually between the ages of 25 and 44 (Robins et al., 1984). In fact, in early editions of the *DSM* it was specified that the onset of schizophrenia must be before the age of 45, but *DSM-IV* does not set an upper age limit for onset.

Gender

The evidence concerning a possible link between gender and schizophrenia is inconsistent: Some studies reveal a higher rate for women, others reveal a higher rate for men, and still others show no difference (e.g., Hambrecht et al., 1994; Iacono & Beiser, 1992; Robins et al., 1984). However, there is consistent evidence that *men are usually first diagnosed as having the disorder at a younger age than women are*

TABLE 10.4

Views of Kraepelin and Bleuler concerning schizophrenia

	Kraepelin	*Bleuler*
Onset	Early	Early or late
Process	Progressive deterioration (like senility)	Disorganization (breaking of associations)
Cause	Physiology	Physiology, but can be triggered by stress
Prognosis	Poor	Poor or good
Name	*Dementia praecox* (premature deterioration)	*Schizophrenia* (splitting of the mind)

Note: Kraepelin seems to have been describing *negative symptoms,* whereas Bleuler seems to have been describing *primarily positive symptoms.*

Emil Kraepelin Theorist who coined the term *dementia praecox* and suggested that schizophrenia had an early onset, consisted of progressive and irreversible intellectual deterioration, and was caused by physiological factors.

Eugen Bleuler Theorist who coined the term *schizophrenia* and suggested that the disorder stemmed from a disorganization or breakdown in mental associations.

(Gorwood et al., 1995; Szymanski et al., 1995). That difference has been found in more than a dozen studies in numerous countries. The relationship between gender and age at the time of diagnosis is illustrated in Figure 10.3.

We do not know exactly why the onset of the disorder is earlier in men than in women, but there are three possibilities: First, it is possible that women are more likely to be at home than men, so their pathology is more likely to remain unidentified for longer than that of men. Another possibility is that biochemical or hormonal differences between men and women play a role by either triggering the disorder earlier or suppressing it until later in one of the sexes. For example, it is thought that estrogen plays a role in suppressing the activity of the neurotransmitter that leads to the symptoms of schizophrenia (see Chapter 11) (Seeman & Lang, 1990). A third explanation is that women are more likely to suffer from positive than negative symptoms, and, as I mentioned earlier, positive symptoms have a later onset than negative symptoms. All of these factors may contribute to the gender difference in the age of onset of schizophrenia.

Ethnicity

It is noteworthy that the rate of schizophrenia is about the same across virtually all of the countries and cultures in which it has been studied, and the differences that are sometimes found appear to be due to differences in how the disorder is defined or explained (Edgerton & Cohen, 1994; Mete et al., 1993). In that regard it might be noted that in some cultures schizophrenia is given a different name, such as "ghost sickness." Such names simply reflect differences in the explanations that cultures have for the disorder (e.g., that it is caused by ghosts). However, schizophrenia by another name is still schizophrenia and we should not assume that it does not occur in other cultures simply because it is given a different name.

Although the rate of schizophrenia is the same across cultures, the content of the delusions may differ as a function of the culture (El-Islam, 1991). For example, in highly industrialized societies delusions may involve beliefs that thoughts are controlled by computer microchips, whereas in less-developed societies delusions may revolve around the effects of spirits or demons. There is evidence that in countries such as Sweden, Japan, England, Germany, and the United States, the rate of schizophrenia is higher in cities than it is in rural areas. However, this is probably due to the effects of social class and migration to cities by disturbed individuals rather than to anything unique to cities per se (Freeman, 1994). I will discuss the variables of social class in the following section.

Socioeconomic Class

One very consistent finding is that individuals in the lower classes are more likely to be diagnosed as suffering from schizophrenia than are individuals in the middle or upper classes. In fact, the rate of schizophrenia has been reported to be as much as *eight times higher* in the lower classes (Black & Andreasen, 1999; Dohrenwend & Dohrenwend, 1974; Kohn, 1973; Strauss et al., 1978). It may be that the link between class and schizophrenia is due to the higher level of stress that is associated with life in the lower classes and that may trigger the disorder. I will explain the role of stress in schizophrenia in Chapter 11; here I will consider five alternative explanations for the relationship between social class and schizophrenia.

Downward Social Drift. One explanation is that suffering from schizophrenia leads individuals to drift downward into the lower socioeconomic classes (Myerson, 1940). Such a drift is to be expected because schizophrenia frequently results in greatly reduced levels of social and intellectual functioning, thus making it difficult for individuals to maintain their position in society. Consider the case of Betty from Case Study 10.3. Betty's father was a university president, her mother is a nurse, and Betty has a master's degree, but her symptoms are so severe that she is unable to work and is supported by disability insurance. If the social drift hypothesis is true, the lower-class status of individuals

FIGURE 10.3

Schizophrenia is diagnosed earlier in males than in females.

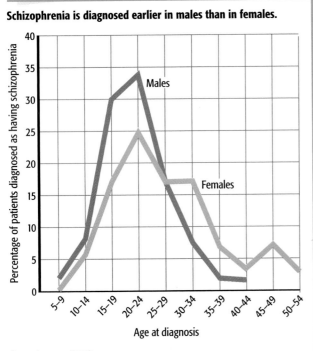

Source: Loranger (1984).

It has been suggested that because schizophrenia involves impaired functioning, it results in a downward drift into the lower socioeconomic classes. In extreme cases, a person with schizophrenia may become homeless.

with schizophrenia would be a result rather than a cause of the disorder.

In one study of the social drift hypothesis the investigators compared the socioeconomic classes of a group of male patients who suffered from schizophrenia to the socioeconomic classes of the patients' fathers (Turner & Wagonfeld, 1967). The results indicated that about 43% of the patients had drifted downward from the classes of their fathers, whereas national census data at the time of the study suggested that only 26% of males in general showed such a drift.

Clearly, schizophrenia can result in a downward social drift. However, by itself that drift does not appear sufficient to account for the strong relationship between class and schizophrenia, so we must consider additional possibilities.

Bias in Diagnosis. Because it is widely believed that schizophrenia is more likely to occur among lower-class individuals, it is possible that socioeconomic class is used as a factor in making the diagnosis. To test that possibility, I once gave two groups of psychiatrists sets of written descriptions

of patients and asked them to make diagnoses based on the descriptions. The descriptions given to the two groups were identical except in one set the patients were described as having an upper-class background, whereas in the other set the patients were described as having a lower-class background. Although both sets of patients had the same symptoms, the lower-class patients were more likely to be diagnosed as suffering from schizophrenia, whereas the upper-class patients were more likely to be diagnosed as suffering from bipolar disorder. It does seem, then, that socioeconomic class influences diagnosis, but by itself the bias effect does not appear strong enough to account for the strong relationship between class and schizophrenia.

Bias in Treatment. If lower-class patients get lower-quality treatment than do upper-class patients (and they probably do, because they cannot afford better treatment), then lower-class individuals with schizophrenia will be in treatment for longer periods of time and their numbers will increase over time. Therefore, when counts are made, more lower- than upper-class individuals would be found with schizophrenia, but the difference would be a reflection of the differences in treatment rather than in the incidence of the disorder among upper- and lower-class patients (Kramer, 1957).

Bias in Self-Presentation. It is also possible that differences in the ways upper- and lower-class individuals present themselves and interact with the hospital staff influence whether or not the individuals are diagnosed as suffering from schizophrenia. For example, given the same set of symptoms, a poorly educated lower-class individual with inadequate social skills may be seen as having schizophrenia, whereas an upper-class individual will be seen as "eccentric" (Hollingshead & Redlich, 1958).

Prenatal and Perinatal Complications. In Chapter 11 you will learn that some cases of schizophrenia can be linked to prenatal complications such as poor diet or diseases of the mother during pregnancy and to perinatal complications such as problems during labor or illness immediately after birth. Because these problems are more likely to occur among poorer individuals, they may account for the higher proportion of schizophrenia in lower classes (Goodman & Emory, 1992).

From this discussion it should be clear that lower-class individuals are more likely to be diagnosed as having schizophrenia than are upper-class individuals and that there is evidence supporting a number of explanations for this relationship. However, the nature of the relationship is not completely clear, and it is probably determined by a combination of several factors.

This concludes the discussion of issues associated with schizophrenia. In the next section I will describe some other psychotic disorders that appear to be related to schizophrenia.

Other Psychotic Disorders

Now that you understand the symptoms of schizophrenia, we can go on to consider what are referred to as "other psychotic disorders" (American Psychiatric Association, 1994). There are five disorders in this group, and their symptoms are described in Table 10.5. It is important to be aware of the similarities and differences between each of these disorders and schizophrenia so that you will not confuse them with schizophrenia.

Brief Psychotic Disorder

Brief psychotic disorder is similar to schizophrenia in that the symptoms involve delusions, hallucinations, disorganized speech, and disorganized behavior, but only *one* of those symptoms is necessary for a diagnosis of brief psychotic disorder. Thus, this disorder can be somewhat less serious than schizophrenia. More important, brief psychotic disorder differs from schizophrenia because it only lasts between 1 day and 1 month; that is, it is a *brief* disorder. Furthermore, in some cases brief psychotic disorder is thought to stem from *overwhelming stress.* Indeed, prior to the publication of *DSM-IV* this disorder was called *brief reactive psychosis;* the term *reactive* was used to reflect the fact that the symptoms were a reaction to stress. We see cases of brief psychotic disorder after disasters such as earthquakes and wars (Susser et al., 1995).

Schizophreniform Disorder

Schizophreniform (skit-zo-FREN-i-form) **disorder** is very much like schizophrenia in that the core symptoms required for a diagnosis are the same (two symptoms from the group that includes delusions, hallucinations, disorganized speech, disorganized behavior, and flat mood). However, schizophreniform disorder differs from schizophrenia

brief psychotic disorder A disorder similar to schizophrenia but involving only one of the symptoms (delusions, hallucinations, disorganized speech, or disorganized behavior), sometimes stemming from overwhelming stress, and lasting only from 1 day to 1 month.

schizophreniform disorder A psychotic disorder involving the symptoms of schizophrenia that does not involve a decline in social or occupational functioning and lasts only between 1 month and 6 months.

TABLE 10.5

Symptoms of other psychotic disorders

Brief psychotic disorder

▶ One or more of the following: delusions, hallucinations, disorganized speech, grossly disorganized behavior.
▶ Symptoms last 1 day to 1 month.

Schizophreniform disorder

▶ Two or more of the following: delusions, hallucinations, disorganized speech, grossly disorganized behavior.
▶ Symptoms last 1 to 6 months.

Schizoaffective disorder

▶ Major mood symptoms (depression or mania).
▶ Two or more of the following that occur with mood symptoms: delusions, hallucinations, disorganized speech, grossly disorganized behavior.
▶ Delusions or hallucinations sometimes occur in the absence of mood symptoms.

Shared psychotic disorder

▶ A delusion develops in the context of a relationship with another person who has an existing related delusion.

Delusional disorder

▶ One or more nonbizarre delusions.
▶ No hallucinations, disorganized speech, or grossly disorganized behavior.
▶ Apart from the effects of the delusions, functioning is not impaired.

Source: American Psychiatric Association (1994).

Brief psychotic disorder—typically lasting anywhere from 1 day to 1 month—has symptoms similar to those of schizophrenia. Brief psychotic disorder is often seen after devastating events such as war. Pictured here are ethnic Albanian refugees from Kosovo.

in two ways: (1) It does not involve a decline in social or occupational functioning, and (2) it lasts only between *1 month and 6 months.* In other words, this disorder has the *form* (core symptoms) of schizophrenia, but because it has a shorter duration and the individual does not deteriorate, it is not considered to *be* schizophrenia.

Viewing the disorders on a continuum beginning with brief psychotic disorder and going on to schizophreniform disorder and then on to schizophrenia reveals two important differences. First, as we move toward schizophrenia, there are *more symptoms.* Brief psychotic disorder involves *one* of the core symptoms (delusions, hallucinations, disorganized speech, disorganized behavior, flat mood), the schizophreniform disorder involves *two* of the core symptoms, and schizophrenia involves *two* of the core symptoms *plus* a decline in social or occupational functioning. Second, as we move toward schizophrenia, the *symptoms last longer.* Specifically, in brief psychotic disorder the symptoms go away within *1 month,* in schizophreniform disorder the symptoms go away within *6 months,* and in schizophrenia the symptoms may persist at one level or another indefinitely, even throughout the individual's life. It is assumed that individuals with brief psychotic disorder or schizophreniform disorder will soon be symptom-free regardless of what is or is not done for them, so the prognoses for individuals with these disorders is very good.

Historically, the diagnoses of brief psychotic disorder and schizophreniform disorder were introduced to provide diagnoses for individuals who had the symptoms of schizophrenia *but who got better.* In other words, the new diagnoses were necessary because it was widely assumed that schizophrenia is a progressive disorder that does not get better, so when it was found that some individuals did get better, new diagnoses were needed. However, it may be that brief psychotic disorder, schizophreniform disorder, and schizophrenia are not three separate disorders but just different levels of severity of one underlying disorder, schizophrenia. For example, schizophreniform disorder might simply be a "mild" form of schizophrenia.

Schizoaffective Disorder

As the name implies, **schizoaffective** (skit-zo-uh-FEC-tiv) **disorder** involves a *combination of schizophrenia and a major mood disorder* (depression or mania). To be diagnosed as having schizoaffective disorder, an individual must at one time have shown the core symptoms of schizophrenia *and* a mood disorder and at another time shown only symptoms of schizophrenia (delusions and hallucinations). This is a somewhat controversial disorder because it can be asked why the individual is not simply diagnosed as suffering from schizophrenia *and* a mood disorder, just as an individual might have a cold and a broken arm.

Shared Psychotic Disorder

The diagnosis of **shared psychotic disorder** is used when an individual develops a *delusion as a consequence of a close relationship with another individual who has a delusion.* For example, a woman who has a delusion that she is a movie star might have a friend who thinks she is an important movie producer.

Delusional Disorder

In **delusional disorder** the major symptom is the *presence of one or more delusions.* However, unlike many of the delusions seen in schizophrenia, the delusions that are present in delusional disorder are *nonbizarre.* In other words, they involve situations that could occur in real life, such as being followed, poisoned, infected, loved from a distance, or deceived by others. It is important to note that individuals with delusional disorder do not show the general decline in social or occupational functioning that is seen in schizophrenia. Indeed, the presence of an unshakable delusion in an individual who otherwise appears normal and functions well is one of the striking things about delusional disorder. Case Study 10.6 (on p. 300) involves a man with very limited delusional disorder, whereas Case Study 10.7 (on p. 301) was written by a young woman who had very pervasive delusional disorder. It is interesting to note that to some extent the young woman may also have suffered from shared psychotic disorder, because her mother "taught" her most of the delusions.

THINKING CRITICALLY

Questions about the Issues Associated with Schizophrenia

Are there connections among schizophrenia and the other psychotic disorders? As we move along a continuum from brief psychotic disorder to schizophreniform disorder and then to schizophrenia, the number of symptoms and the duration of the symptoms increase. That observation has

---

schizoaffective disorder   A psychotic disorder involving a combination of schizophrenia and a major mood disorder (depression or mania).

shared psychotic disorder   A disorder in which an individual develops a delusion as a consequence of a close relationship with another individual who has a delusion.

delusional disorder   A psychotic disorder in which the major symptom is the presence of one or more nonbizarre delusions, usually involving persecution.

A Successful Executive with a Delusional Disorder

. . . Arronson had suffered from a delusion that "others" were plotting against him. . . .

GEORGE ARRONSON WAS a very successful executive in a large corporation. He was intelligent, hardworking, and quietly competitive. Those were the traits he thought were necessary to "keep one step ahead of the competition." Arronson was happily married, the father of two children, and well liked by his friends and colleagues. He had done well, his future was bright, and there was no sign of any problems.

One day Arronson got to the office before his secretary had arrived. At about 9 o'clock a telephone repairman arrived to install a new phone in the office. The secretary did not know that Arronson was already in his office, so she sent the repairman in without announcing him. When the door to his office opened and Arronson saw an unknown man carrying a heavy metal case and wearing a jacket with a phone company emblem on it, he reached into his desk drawer, took out a .38 caliber revolver, and shot the repairman at point-blank range. He then ran from the office but was soon caught.

A psychological examination revealed that for years Arronson had suffered from a delusion that "others" were plotting against him, were trying to steal his ideas, and would eventually try to "eliminate" him. Arronson could not explain who the "others" were, but he believed that "they" got access to his mail and tapped his phone to "track" his ideas. Arronson was in a competitive business in which there was some "corporate espionage," but his beliefs were clearly delusional. The extremity of his delusions was reflected in the fact that he kept vans stocked with cans of food in four parts of the city (north, south, east, and west). The vans and food were to be used to help with his "getaway if they ever closed in." When the repairman entered the office unannounced carrying a black metal case, Arronson thought "they" were coming for him, and he shot in self-defense.

---

led to the speculation that rather than there being a group of distinctly separate disorders, there may be a **spectrum of schizophrenic disorders.** The schizoaffective, delusional, and shared psychotic disorders might also be part of that spectrum, in that they consist of some of the symptoms that make up schizophrenia. An analogy can be drawn to the common cold. In its most severe and complete form a cold involves a runny nose, congested head, cough, and that "ache all over" feeling. Different individuals may have more or fewer of those symptoms to more or less severe degrees, but they all have a cold. Similarly, individuals with other psychotic disorders may have different forms or less severe cases of schizophrenia. We will return to this possibility in the next chapter, when we discuss the causes, explanations, and treatments for schizophrenia. Before going on to those, consider the following whimsical description of schizophrenia by Lynne Morris:

> I
> am
> the
> rear tire
> of a bicycle,

spectrum of schizophrenic disorders   A range of disorders (brief psychotic, schizophreniform, delusional, schizoaffective, and shared psychotic disorders) that share symptoms with schizophrenia but may differ in severity.

> not trusted enough
> to be a
> front tire,
> expected to go
> round and round
> in one narrow rut,
> never going very far,
> ignored
> except
> when I
> break down.
> Then
> I get lots of
> frightening,
> angry
> attention
> and
> I am put into
> a
> garage,
> sometimes for months,
> where
> I forget my function
> and
> I become afraid
> to function
> and all functions seem useless.
> Next time out
> I think I will be
> an off-ramp
> from a
> freeway.

A Serious Delusional Disorder in an Undergraduate Woman

CASE STUDY 10.7

"I WAS RAISED in a very chaotic family. When I was a very young child, my mother taught me a complex fantasy life designed to 'escape all of the people who would like to take advantage of us.' By the age of 5 or 6 I was already having a difficult time distinguishing between fantasy and reality.

"My mother was very concerned about established organizations such as school and government that might learn too much about our family. 'They' might try to lock us up. I was never allowed to fill out any of the typical enrollment forms in grade school, but instead I had to take them home so that Mom could pick and choose what was pertinent for the school records. Often this rigorous screening would end in parent-teacher conferences, after which Mom would tell me, 'They will definitely be watching you now.'

"By age 10 I totally believed my mother. The teacher would send home notes about the fact that I was talking to myself or some other aberrant behavior. Mom would tell me that I shouldn't do these things in public, but that I could be 'normal' at home. And so I often stayed in the closet for hours talking to myself and enjoying the praise from Mom for being such a 'good girl.'

"The punishments my mother gave me for misbehavior were often bizarre. They typically involved cleansing rituals, in which I would be placed in a bathtub full of water and told to pray for purification and forgiveness.

"At 15 I entered high school, and this was the beginning of the serious downhill slide. There were too many people, and they were constantly staring at me, or so I thought. I adopted many strategies for avoiding them. I wouldn't look into their eyes. I wouldn't participate in any school activities. I was an honor student, but I wouldn't attend any of the functions associated with that status. I did attend one academic award ceremony at my mother's insistence. She didn't believe that I was a scholar, but she wanted us to go to

'find out why they are persecuting the family.'

"I always attempted to avoid social contact. I would dress in unusual clothing (often my brother's or my mother's) and use a lot of makeup in an attempt to keep people from recognizing me. For relaxation I sat in front of a strobe light and thought cosmic and mystic thoughts.

"By my sophomore and junior years my paranoia was fairly intense. Other girls I knew had begun to date and establish their femininity, but I was being taught at home that sex was the work of the Devil and that all men are suspect. I began to question the motives of my girlfriends and their relationships with boys. As a consequence they discontinued their friendships with me. Now I was sure it wasn't just the men who were suspect, but that these girls were actually boys who were sent to trick me. I began to keep files on everyone I knew.

"After graduation from high school, I got a job and moved out of the house. To others things seemed relatively calm, but they were anything but calm within my mind. My fears about governmental agencies became so intense that I started checking my apartment for bugs and telephone taps whenever I returned home. Whenever I got a wrong-number call, I was certain that this marked the beginning of some complex eavesdropping scam whereby 'they' could now hear everything going on inside my home. I changed my telephone number so often that finally the phone company refused to change it anymore without a fee. Now, I concluded, the phone company was in on the plot.

"It was at this stage that I began to hear voices. At first they were friendly, and I thought I had been chosen by God for some special mission. I sat in the backyard or in the bedroom closet for hours and waited for messages that never came. After several weeks the theme of the voices changed, and I felt damned and doomed. The voices

would tell me of elaborate traps that were designed to get me, and they often involved the people with whom I worked. Whenever I spent any time with other people, I was sure they could hear my thoughts. . . . In an effort to elude my persecutors, I packed my car one fall evening and escaped in the night to wander around the southeastern United States. The money ran out in about 3 weeks, and 'they' were still following me anyway, so I returned home.

"When I returned, everything was the same. I still checked the apartment, I still sat in the closet, and often I stayed up the entire night roving from room to room so that 'they couldn't get a fix on me.' Finally, I could no longer cope with it all by myself, so I got in my car and drove to my parents' house. I drove in a roundabout fashion to elude my followers. When I arrived at their home, I had my 'breakdown.' I felt as if my limbs were not attached to my body and that my brain and mind were separate entities. I was waving my arms about madly in an attempt to get my mind to return to my brain and the two of them to reestablish themselves in my body. I was incoherent and began to cry. I knew that God was punishing me for all of my sins and that I would surely go crazy and die."

> **The voices would tell me of elaborate traps that were designed to get me. . . .**

Note: This account was written when the woman was a senior in college. I have kept in contact with her over the years, and I can report that after extensive treatment she is now for the most part symptom-free and is doing very well in a professional career. When I recently asked how she was getting along, she commented about how busy she was at work but said that it was a lot easier working now that she did not have to spend time checking every room for bugs. One clear sign of her improvement is her willingness to allow me to print her story.

Summary

Topic I: Symptoms of Schizophrenia

▶ The cognitive symptoms of schizophrenia include hallucinations, which are perceptual experiences that do not have a basis in reality; delusions, which are erroneous beliefs that are held despite strong evidence to the contrary; disturbed thought processes, which can be seen in loose associations and intruding thoughts; and cognitive flooding (stimulus overload), which is the inability to screen out irrelevant stimuli.

▶ The major mood symptom in schizophrenia is depression. Mood is often inappropriate.

▶ There are no physical symptoms of schizophrenia.

▶ Motor symptoms range from immobility to agitation. With all symptoms it is important to distinguish between those that are due to the disorder and those that are side effects of drugs.

▶ To be diagnosed as suffering from schizophrenia, a person must show a decline in social or occupational functioning and present any two of the following symptoms: delusions, hallucinations, disorganized speech, disorganized behavior, and flat mood. As a consequence, there are wide differences among individuals who have been given the diagnosis of schizophrenia. The diagnosis of schizophrenia is made by exclusion.

▶ The phases of schizophrenia are the prodromal phase, when the symptoms develop; the active phase, when symptoms are full-blown; and the residual phase, when symptoms are less active. Unofficially, there also appears to be a burned-out phase, in which patients have very few symptoms but show a serious deterioration of social and personal functioning.

▶ *DSM-IV* lists five types of schizophrenia: disorganized, catatonic, paranoid, undifferentiated, and residual. However, this system is not a useful way to classify patients.

▶ An unofficial but effective way to classify types of schizophrenia involves using positive and negative symptoms. Positive symptoms are additions to normal behaviors and include hallucinations, delusions, thought disorders, and bizarre behaviors. Negative symptoms reflect the absence of normal behaviors and include flat mood, poverty of speech, inability to experience positive feelings, apathy, and inattentiveness.

▶ Relative to positive symptoms, negative symptoms are more likely to be associated with poor premorbid adjustment, to be consistent over time, to occur in men, and to show poorer response to drug treatment.

Topic II: Issues Associated with Schizophrenia

▶ Our conceptions of schizophrenia are influenced by the early work of Kraepelin and Bleuler. Kraepelin believed that the disorder had an early onset and showed progressive deterioration like that in senility; he called it *dementia praecox* ("premature deterioration"). Bleuler believed that the disorder could have an early or late onset, involved a breaking of associations, and might improve with time; he called it *schizophrenia* ("splitting of the mind").

▶ About 1.5% of the population suffer from schizophrenia.

▶ Schizophrenia is most frequently diagnosed in early adulthood. Men are usually diagnosed as suffering from schizophrenia earlier than women are, and the prevalence of the disorder is consistent across cultures.

▶ Schizophrenia is diagnosed more frequently in individuals from the lower socioeconomic classes. Class differences may be due to downward social drift, bias in diagnosis, bias in treatment, bias in self-presentation, or prenatal and perinatal complications that are more common in the lower classes.

▶ Five other psychotic disorders are currently recognized: (1) Brief psychotic disorder involves only one or more of the symptoms of schizophrenia (delusions, hallucinations, disorganized speech, disorganized behavior, negative symptoms) and lasts no longer than 1 month. (2) Schizophreniform disorder involves two or more of the symptoms of schizophrenia and lasts only between 1 and 6 months. (3) Schizoaffective disorder involves major mood symptoms (depression or mania) and two of the symptoms of schizophrenia. (4) Shared psychotic disorder involves a delusion that develops in the context of a relationship with another person who has a related delusion. (5) Delusional disorder involves nonbizarre delusions but no other symptoms of schizophrenia, and apart from the effects of the delusion, the individual's functioning is not impaired.

▶ Schizophrenia and other psychotic disorders may represent different sets of symptoms or levels of severity in a spectrum of schizophrenia disorders.

Questions for Making Connections

1. Give examples of positive and negative symptoms. Do negative symptoms and depression overlap? If you had to have either positive or negative symptoms, which would you prefer and why?

2. What are the problems associated with making a diagnosis of schizophrenia? If an individual was diagnosed as suffering from schizophrenia and then the symptoms disappeared within 2 months of their onset, what would you conclude?

3. The diagnosis of schizophrenia doesn't really tell us much about the individual. Why? Can you suggest a better system for diagnosing schizophrenia?

4. What are the similarities and differences between schizophrenia and each of the following disorders: (a) brief psychotic disorder, (b) schizophreniform disorder, (c) schizoaffective disorder, (d) shared psychotic disorder, and (e) delusional disorder?

Key Terms and People

In reviewing and testing yourself, you should be able to discuss each of the following:

active phase, p. 286
Bleuler, Eugen, p. 294
brief psychotic disorder, p. 298
burned-out phase, p. 286
catatonic schizophrenia, p. 289
cognitive flooding, p. 283
delusional disorder, p. 299
delusions, p. 280
delusions of grandiosity, p. 281
delusions of identity, p. 281
delusions of persecution, p. 280
delusions of reference, p. 280

dementia praecox, p. 282
disorganization, p. 291
disorganized schizophrenia, p. 289
hallucinations, p. 280
Kraepelin, Emil, p. 294
negative symptoms, p. 291
paranoid schizophrenia, p. 289
positive symptoms, p. 291
prodromal phase, p. 286
psychoticism, p. 291
residual phase, p. 286
residual schizophrenia, p. 289

schizoaffective disorder, p. 299
schizophrenia, p. 279
schizophrenic deficit, p. 283
schizophreniform disorder, p. 298
shared psychotic disorder, p. 299
spectrum of schizophrenic disorders, p. 300
stimulus overload, p. 283
undifferentiated schizophrenia, p. 289
word salad, p. 282

11 Schizophrenia: Explanations and Treatments

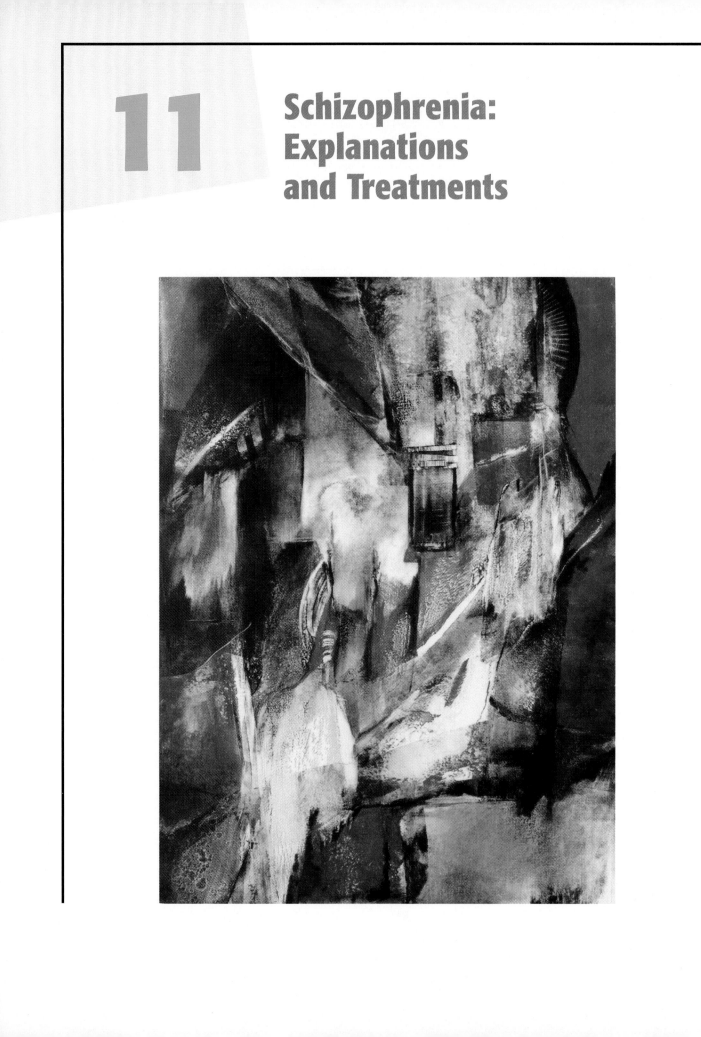

FOR MANY YEARS there was a great deal of controversy over what caused schizophrenia. Some theorists suggested that schizophrenia was due to problems with child-rearing, others believed that it was learned, and still others proposed that it was caused by physiological problems in the brain. Today, however, it is generally agreed that schizophrenia is primarily a *physiological* disorder; that is, schizophrenia is due to problems with brain functioning. This does not mean, however, that psychological factors do not play important roles. Indeed, although stress by itself does not cause schizophrenia, stress can exacerbate the symptoms. There has also been controversy over the treatment of schizophrenia. Because drugs are often not effective in treating all of the symptoms of schizophrenia, it has been argued that psychological treatments must also be used. To provide you with a thorough understanding of the causes and treatments of schizophrenia, in this chapter I will first explain the psychodynamic, learning, and cognitive explanations for schizophrenia. Next, I will explain the physiological bases of schizophrenia. Finally, I will explain how drugs and psychological treatments can be used together to treat schizophrenia.

TOPIC I

Psychodynamic, Learning, and Cognitive Explanations for Schizophrenia

Louise suffers from schizophrenia and often behaves in what seems to be a very immature fashion. Her level of intellectual performance has also declined sharply. Does schizophrenia involve regression to an earlier stage of psychological development?

Yesterday Curtis was hospitalized with schizophrenia. His "schizophrenic break" occurred about a week after he learned that his wife was ill with a disease that is usually fatal. Did the stress associated with her illness cause Curtis to "break"? Does stress cause schizophrenia?

When a waiter asked Carlos how he wanted his steak cooked, Carlos replied, "I'd like it rare; I just don't like common things." The first part of his sentence made sense in terms of the question, but the second part didn't. Why did Carlos, who suffers from schizophrenia, use a sentence that did not make sense?

What causes schizophrenia? In this section we will consider the psychodynamic, learning, and cognitive explanations.

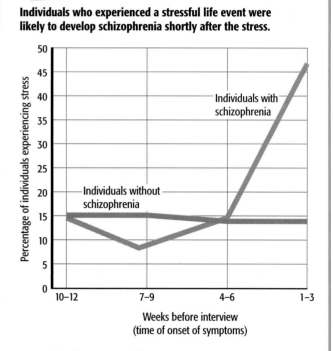

Psychodynamic Explanations

Psychodynamic theorists introduced two explanations for schizophrenia: specifically, problems with child-rearing and stress.

Problems with Child-Rearing

Originally, it was suggested that schizophrenia was due to problems with child-rearing. For example, it was believed that when mothers behaved in inconsistent ways toward their children, such as being overprotective but also rejecting, the children became confused about what was "real" and therefore developed schizophrenia. Although this explanation was once very popular, it has been completely discredited. Recognizing that problems in parenting do not cause schizophrenia is important because for many years the parents of children who developed schizophrenia lived under a cloud of guilt about what they had supposedly done to their children. We don't want to continue imposing that guilt trip.

Stress

Psychodynamic theorists also suggested that schizophrenia is caused by psychological stress. Specifically, it was argued that when exposed to high stress, individuals regress to an earlier stage of psychosexual development at which they feel more secure (see the discussion of regression in Chapter 2). In support of that argument, the theorists pointed out that individuals with schizophrenia often behave in "childlike" ways (e.g., they show reduced levels of intellectual performance) and that those behaviors are the result of regression.

Three things must be noted with regard to this stress explanation for schizophrenia: First, there is no doubt that stress can contribute to schizophrenia. For example, in one study it was found that individuals who developed schizophrenia experienced more stressful events, such as a job loss, a geographic move, or a divorce, just prior to the onset of their symptoms than did other individuals during the same period (Brown & Birley, 1968). Those results are summarized in Figure 11.1. Furthermore, one of the best predictors of whether individuals with schizophrenia will relapse after treatment is whether they return to stressful home environments (Butzlaff & Hooley, 1998).

FIGURE 11.1

Individuals who experienced a stressful life event were likely to develop schizophrenia shortly after the stress.

Source: Adapted from Brown & Birley (1968).

Second, however, there is no evidence that schizophrenia involves regression to an earlier stage of development. It is true that the intellectual performance of individuals with schizophrenia appears to be somewhat childlike, but careful analyses reveal that the errors made by individuals with schizophrenia are different from the errors made by young children (Buss & Lang, 1965). In other words, psychodynamic theorists were correct in their observation that there is a link between stress and schizophrenia, but they were wrong about how stress leads to schizophrenia.

The question of how stress leads to schizophrenia brings us to the third point, which is that although the relationship between stress and schizophrenia was originally suggested by psychodynamic theorists, the role of stress has been incorporated into all of the other major explanations. For example, from a physiological point of view, stress may increase activity in the brain, and high levels of brain activity may disrupt brain functioning and cause schizophrenia. I introduce the role of stress in schizophrenia here because it was first suggested by psychodynamic theorists, but those theorists do not "own" the notion; we will consider the role of stress as we consider other explanations throughout this chapter.

In summary, then, we must not attribute schizophrenia to problems with child-rearing or to regression, but we must develop an understanding of how stress can contribute to schizophrenia. With this as background, let's go on to consider the role of learning in schizophrenia.

Learning Explanations

Could it be that some people *learn* the behaviors we call schizophrenia because the behaviors lead to rewards? Alternatively, if people are labeled as suffering from schizophrenia, does that cause them to behave *as though* they have schizophrenia or cause us to *misinterpret* their behavior as due to schizophrenia? Let's consider these possibilities.

Rewards and Symptoms

Learning theorists suggested that individuals with schizophrenia use abnormal behaviors to get rewards such as attention. On an overcrowded and understaffed hospital ward, a symptom-free patient will not get much attention, and therefore it behooves the patient who wants attention to act a little "crazy." Just as the squeaky wheel gets the grease, so the "weird schizophrenic" gets the attention. Attention is a particularly powerful reward in hospitals where patients are rarely visited and are largely ignored by an overworked staff. Nurses have reported to me that some patients start acting "crazier" when they learn that I am bringing a group of students to the hospital for a tour because the patients want to be picked to visit with the students.

The results of a variety of experiments demonstrate that patients can and will manipulate their symptoms to gain rewards (Braginsky & Braginsky, 1967). For example, if there is a very desirable ward for patients who have serious symptoms, patients will begin displaying more serious symptoms, but if the desirable ward is for patients who are less disturbed, patients will act healthier. In another study it was found that the amount of time patients stayed in the hospital versus in the community was related to the degree to which they liked the hospital versus the community (Drake & Wallach, 1979). Specifically, those in the study who preferred the hospital stayed in the community an average of only about 10 days, whereas those who preferred the community stayed in the community an average of about 230 days. Clearly, the patients manipulated their symptoms to achieve their desired result: hospitalization or life in the community.

Learning theorists also proposed that some individuals who find their social situations unrewarding or punishing will ignore what is going on around them and instead focus on irrelevant things that are rewarding or at least neutral (Ullman & Krasner, 1969). This attention to irrelevant cues results in irrelevant behaviors that are inappropriate to the situation—that is, the symptoms of schizophrenia. This process can be illustrated with a simple, less extreme example. A student who finds a lecture boring (unrewarding) may stop paying attention and begin daydreaming. If the student is then suddenly called on to answer a question, the response will probably miss the point completely and may seem childish, illogical, or inappropriate. In other words, the response will be "schizophrenic."

These explanations for schizophrenia were once very widely accepted, but it is overly simplistic to assume that the symptoms of schizophrenia are the result of rewards. Behaviors can certainly be affected by rewards, but many of the symptoms of schizophrenia seem to be beyond voluntary control and the influence of rewards. Indeed, if rewards were at the heart of symptoms, we could quickly cure schizophrenia by rewarding the individuals for healthy be-

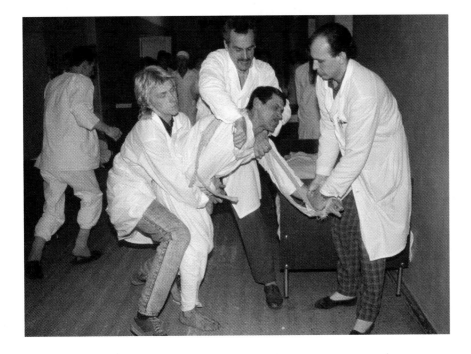

According to learning theorists, patients in mental hospitals may act "crazy" in order to get the attention of overworked staff members.

haviors and punishing them for symptoms; however, the treatment of schizophrenia is more complicated than that. In view of this, let's go on to consider the other explanation offered by learning theorists.

Labels, Roles, and Expectations

Learning theorists have also suggested that some of the symptoms of schizophrenia may develop because individuals are *labeled as "schizophrenic."* Labeling could lead to symptoms in two ways: First, because we expect individuals who are labeled as suffering from schizophrenia to behave abnormally, we may subtly suggest abnormal behaviors to them. Consider the case of a woman who was admitted to a psychiatric hospital with the diagnosis of schizophrenia. Because individuals with schizophrenia often hallucinate, the woman's therapist assumed that she hallucinated and therefore frequently asked her whether she heard voices when no one else was around. The woman did not have hallucinations, but after being asked about it repeatedly, she began to wonder whether she did indeed hallucinate. Given the suggestion that she might (or should?) hallucinate and some time to think about it, she experienced a blurring of the distinction between listening to her thoughts and hearing voices ("Maybe those thoughts in my head are hallucinations"). The next time she was asked, she said, yes, she did hear voices, and thereafter she talked about her thoughts as if they were hallucinations.

Being labeled as suffering from schizophrenia can also lead to symptoms because *the role of being "schizophrenic" permits a wider variety of behaviors than the role of being "normal."* Therefore, an individual who is labeled as suffering from schizophrenia might feel more free to use behaviors that ordinarily would be suppressed. For example, an individual who is diagnosed as suffering from schizophrenia may not be expected to be responsible for his or her behaviors and may therefore be allowed to act more deviantly. One day a patient became very frustrated, and to vent his anger he picked up a chair and began breaking it up by hitting it against the wall. When a ward attendant grabbed him and told him to stop, the patient yelled, "I'm going crazy!" The attendant then yelled back, "You may be crazy, but you can't break up furniture when *I'm* on duty!" Hearing that, the patient stopped, looked thoughtfully at the attendant for a moment, and then said he was sorry and walked away. After that the patient only showed his "obvious deterioration of ego strength" when a more tolerant attendant was on duty.

sensory deprivation The restriction of all sensory inputs (sound, sight, touch, smell), once thought to be a cause of schizophrenia.

The effects of roles and expectations on abnormal behavior were demonstrated in research on **sensory deprivation.** In this research an individual lay in a bed in a sound-proofed and dimly lit chamber with a milk-glass screen over his or her face so that visual and auditory stimulation was greatly reduced. Because the investigators did not know what would happen to people who were deprived of stimulation, the participants were told that if anything unusual began to happen and they wanted to end the session, they could hit a large red "panic button" that was mounted on the wall of the chamber. It turned out that after only a short period in the chamber the individuals began experiencing a variety of symptoms, including hallucinations, disorientation, and an inability to concentrate (Bexton, Heron, & Scott, 1954; Scott, Bexton, & Doane, 1959). Indeed, these findings led some theorists to hypothesize that schizophrenia might be caused by sensory deprivation. However, other investigators speculated that the "symptoms" were being suggested by the procedures (the availability of a "panic button," etc.) (Orne & Scheibe, 1964). To test that possibility researchers conducted an experiment in which one group of individuals was treated in the usual way, while another group was exposed to the same isolation but were told that they were in a "control" condition and were told nothing about symptoms or the panic button. It turned out that the individuals who were warned about symptoms and told about the panic button developed symptoms much like those seen in schizophrenia, whereas individuals in the control condition simply became bored. In other words, taking away the panic button and the implicit suggestion about symptoms eliminated the schizophrenic-like symptoms.

Finally, *an individual's label can also influence your interpretation of what he or she is doing.* For example, if an individual is labeled as "schizophrenic" and is staring off into space, you might assume that he or she is hallucinating rather than just thinking or daydreaming. If the individual misunderstands something you say, you might attribute that to an "underlying thought disorder" rather than to a simple misunderstanding. These interpretations may then influence how you respond to the individual, which may in turn influence how the individual responds to you. The influence of labels on the interpretation of behavior is neatly illustrated in Case Study 11.1.

I had an experience similar to that of the people described in Case Study 11.1 when I was beginning my clinical internship at a large psychiatric hospital. The first day I was instructed to dress informally and "hang out" on one of the wards so that I could "get the feel of the place." Most patients quickly recognized me as "another one of the new trainees," and they spent time talking to me and "showing me the ropes." I spent quite a bit of time talking with one middle-aged man who frequently made religious or biblical references, often called me "son," and once offered to pray for me in my "current time of need."

Normal Individuals in a Mental Hospital: The Effects of Being Labeled as "Schizophrenic"

THIS CASE STUDY does not involve a disturbed individual. It focuses on the experiences of eight *normal* individuals, some of them students, who were admitted to various psychiatric hospitals under the guise of being abnormal. It illustrates what can happen to people when they are simply *labeled* as abnormal.

The people in this study did not have any signs or history of abnormal behavior, but when they presented themselves at the hospitals, they complained of hearing voices. When asked about the voices, they said that the voices were "unclear" but seemed to say words like *empty, hollow,* and *thud.* All of the other information given by the individuals (personal background, frustrations, joys) was true and did not reflect any serious problems. All of the individuals were diagnosed as suffering from schizophrenia and admitted to the hospitals as patients. Once admitted, the pseudopatients *ceased simulating any symptoms and behaved as they ordinarily did.* They talked to other patients, cooperated with all requests from the staff, and when asked how they were feeling, they said that they were fine and were no longer having any symptoms.

The pseudopatients were kept in the hospital and treated for between 7 and 52 days. Despite the extended periods of hospitalization, *none of the hospital staff recognized that the*

patients were, in fact, normal. This was the case despite the fact that once admitted, the patients did not show any symptoms. They were in the hospital and had been labeled as "schizophrenic," so they must be disturbed. In contrast, however, the real patients in the hospital (i.e., individuals who were supposedly out of touch with reality) were often able to recognize the pseudopatients as fakes. They made comments like "You're not crazy. You're a journalist or a professor [referring to the continual note taking]. You're checking up on the hospital."

Not only did the hospital staff not recognize that the pseudopatients were normal, but because the pseudopatients were labeled as "schizophrenic," the staff interpreted their normal behaviors as abnormal. For example, when the pseudopatients were seen sitting outside the cafeteria half an hour before lunch, a psychiatrist interpreted the behavior as reflecting the "oral-acquisitive nature of the syndrome." Apparently, the fact that there was little to do in the hospital other than go to meals was not considered an explanation for their behavior.

The file of one pseudopatient, who experienced the normal ebb and flow in personal relationships, contained the following summary:

> This white 39-year-old male . . . manifests a long history of considerable ambivalence in close relationships,

which begins in early childhood. . . . Affective stability is absent. . . . And while he says that he has several good friends, one senses considerable ambivalence embedded in those relationships.

In other cases, when the pseudopatients became upset, it was always assumed that their behavior was due to schizophrenia rather than to some factor in the environment, such as intentional or unintentional mistreatment by a ward attendant.

Clearly, everything normal about these normal persons was turned around and interpreted as evidence that they were disturbed. There was no way out for these normal persons. Even when they were finally discharged, they were discharged as "schizophrenic in remission." The fact that they were discharged implied that they were behaving normally, but the label implied that the disorder still lurked beneath the surface.

How would your daily behavior be interpreted if you were suddenly labeled as "schizophrenic"?

Source: Adapted from Rosenhan (1973).

CASE STUDY 11.1

> . . . because the pseudo-patients were labeled as "schizo-phrenic," the staff interpreted their normal behaviors as abnormal.

Because I had been instructed not to probe, I did not attempt to identify this man's disorder, but I assumed that he had some delusion revolving around himself as God. Two days later at a staff meeting, the man and I were both a bit red-faced when I discovered that he was the new ward chaplain and he realized that I was the new intern!

The learning approach provides interesting explanations for some of the symptoms of schizophrenia, but before drawing any conclusions about causes, let's look at the cognitive explanation, which to some extent turns our thinking about schizophrenia upside down.

Cognitive Explanation

We usually assume that when people are hallucinating, they are hearing, seeing, or feelings things that really aren't there. However, cognitive theorists turn this around and argue that individuals with schizophrenia actually do hear, see, and feel things that other people do not and that their interpretations of those experiences lead to their hallucinations. In other words, cognitive theorists argue that unusual experiences are the *causes* rather than the *results* of schizophrenia. Let's consider this explanation more closely.

Unusual Sensory Experiences

Hallucinations. To understand the cognitive explanation for hallucinations it is important to recall that many individuals who suffer from schizophrenia cannot screen out sights, sounds, and physical sensations that normal individuals screen out; as a consequence, they are flooded or overloaded with stimulation (see Chapter 10). These perceptions could provide the basis for hallucinations. For example, individuals who are highly sensitive to sounds may hear voices that others do not, and individuals who are sensitive to bodily sensations may report tactile hallucinations, such as gnawing sensations or the feeling that bugs are crawling through their bodies. I do not mean to suggest that the individuals are actually feeling and hearing exactly what they think they are feeling and hearing. Instead, it may be that these individuals are experiencing some vague or irrelevant stimulation, and in an attempt to make sense of it they "fill in the blanks" and come up with a complete and meaningful perception. This filling-in process is not unus-

Persons with schizophrenia may experience stimulus overload; many are aware of sights, sounds, and sensations that normal individuals screen out.

ual or abnormal, and we all do it to make sense of things (Goldstein, 1998).

Delusions. It is generally assumed that we all have the same sensory experiences and therefore all use the same information to draw conclusions about what is going on around us. Consequently, if an individual holds a belief that is contrary to the commonly held evidence, it is assumed that the individual is suffering from a delusion; that is, the belief does not have a basis in reality. However, it may be that some individuals have different sensory experiences (e.g., they hear or feel things that others do not), and those different experiences lead the individuals to reach different conclusions about the world, conclusions that we might refer to as "delusions" (Maher, 1988a, 1988b). Furthermore, if individuals realize that they have sensory experiences that others do not have, they have to come up with explanations for why only they have those experiences, and the explanations could contribute to delusions.

Consider the case of a college student who had a heightened sensitivity to sound and therefore became aware of the buzzing noise made by fluorescent lights and the muffled voices of students talking in the next room. Those sounds seemed very noticeable to her, but when she mentioned them to her roommates, they denied hearing them. The sounds were real to the young woman and had to be explained. However, the denial of those sounds by her roommates also had to be explained. Could it be that the students in the next room were talking about her, that they were causing the light to make noise to annoy her, and that her roommates were now lying to her?

The possible link between unusual sensory experiences and delusions is illustrated in Case Study 11.2 by the man who became sensitive to sights and sounds while driving his car. He had to account for the fact that he was now seeing and hearing things that he had not seen or heard before and that others were not seeing or hearing. Might he assume that he had gained some special powers or that the things he was seeing and hearing were special signs to him?

Finally, consider the case of an elderly woman who was losing her hearing. Because of that loss, it seemed to her as though everyone around her was whispering. Why was everyone whispering? To answer that question she recalled times when she had disagreements with other people, and she concluded that the people around her were now planning to get back at her, perhaps to take her money. Why else would they be whispering? This woman's delusion was rooted in her different sensory experiences, and the delusion was simply given form by the nature of her prior experiences. No amount of psychotherapy concerning her earlier experiences with others could relieve the basis for her delusion—but a hearing aid did it immediately!

There is also laboratory evidence for this link. In one experiment college students were shown pictures of Russians, and while they were looking at the pictures, they were

Sensory Overload and Potential Schizophrenic Symptoms

ONE MORNING I received a telephone call from a friend—a very bright, psychologically sophisticated 34-year-old executive. He was in a state of near panic as he told me that he was afraid that he was "losing his mind" and "going crazy." When I asked what had happened, he told me that while driving to his office that morning, he began having strange experiences. First, he explained that everything he saw was very "intense" and that he could not ignore anything. For example, while driving by billboards, he saw things that he had never noticed before, such as the very small print at the bottom of a billboard that gives the name of the company that owns it. Second, he was having great sensitivity to sounds. He explained that while he was driving on the expressway, he was constantly afraid that he was going to be run over by a huge truck because it sounded to him as though the truck were almost on top of him. However,

when he looked in the rearview mirror, it was obvious that the truck was a long distance away and of no danger to him. Moments later, however, it again sounded like the truck was about to run him down.

One of the most psychologically frightening experiences associated with sound occurred when he pulled up at a stoplight. There were two men in the car in front of him, and as one man turned his head to talk to the other man, my friend suddenly thought that because of his unusual sensitivity to sound, he would be able to hear the man talk despite the fact that he was in another car and the windows were up in both vehicles. Terrified by the possibility of something he knew to be impossible, he looked away, hoping that if he did not see the man speak, he might not hear him.

In his panic over these strange experiences and his loss of control, he called me for help. This was the first

such "attack" that he had experienced, but as I listened to him talk, I recalled a number of related experiences of which I was aware. For example, he had become extremely uncomfortable and disoriented when he had to drive through a long tunnel in which lights flashed by as he drove, he had always disliked loud rock music, and he had complained about movies in which there were sudden and rapid flashes of scenes. Clearly, he was generally sensitive to sensory stimulation, but never before had it been so severe, and in the past he had always been able to cope by avoiding it. For some reason his sensitivity had suddenly been heightened, he was being overwhelmed by stimulation, and he did not know what was happening to him or how to deal with it.

> ...he was generally sensitive to sensory stimulation, but never before had it been so severe....

---

given false physiological feedback concerning their anxiety levels (Bramel et al., 1965). Specifically, the students in one group received feedback indicating that they were very anxious while looking at the pictures, whereas the students in another group received feedback indicating that they were not anxious while looking at the pictures. After getting the feedback, the students were asked to rate the degree to which they thought the Russians were hostile. The results indicated that the students who were led to believe that they were anxious rated the Russians as more hostile than did the students who were not led to believe that they were anxious. It appears that the students who thought they were anxious explained or justified their sensory experiences of anxiety by believing that the Russians posed a threat ("I am anxious because of the threat posed by the Russians"). It might be said that those students developed "delusions of persecution" because of the false information they received about their anxiety.

Distraction

Intellectual Decline. A decline in intellectual functioning is a symptom that must be present for a diagnosis of schizophrenia (see Chapter 10), and cognitive theorists argue that the decline is due to the *intrusion of irrelevant thoughts that*

distract the individuals and disrupt their thought processes (Maher, 1968, 1972, 1983). In other words, if there is a breakdown in the "filter mechanism" that is responsible for screening out irrelevant stimuli, individuals will be flooded with stimulation, which will distract them and interfere with their intellectual performance.

The role of distraction was made clear by Betty, who talked about her symptoms in Case Study 10.3. She described how thinking was like following a road through the brain, but her roads had detours and barricades: "My thoughts get blocked or get detoured, and it gets all mixed up.... When I get a thought, I can't always follow it to completion. Sometimes it happens when I am talking. I get confused."

The distractibility of individuals with schizophrenia was clearly demonstrated in an experiment in which a female researcher read a series of numbers both to individuals who suffered from schizophrenia and to individuals who did not, and then the individuals were asked to recall as many numbers as possible (Lawson, McGhie, & Chapman, 1967). However, on half of the trials a male researcher read irrelevant (distracting) numbers while the female researcher read the test numbers. On the other trials irrelevant numbers were not read. The results revealed that the reading of irrelevant numbers was much more distracting and disrup-

FIGURE 11.2

Distraction resulted in more errors by individuals with schizophrenia than by individuals without schizophrenia.

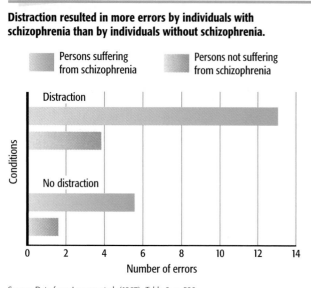

Source: Data from Lawson et al. (1967), Table 2, p. 529.

tive of performance for the individuals with schizophrenia than for the others, suggesting that the individuals with schizophrenia were less able to screen out the irrelevant stimulation. The performance of the individuals who did and did not have schizophrenia is presented graphically in Figure 11.2.

Overall, then, the decline in intellectual functioning seen in schizophrenia can be explained in terms of distraction (see also Lang & Buss, 1965; Neale & Oltmanns, 1980).

Language Problems. Distraction can also be used to explain why some people with schizophrenia use sentences that do not make sense. Specifically, it may be that their language problems stem from the *intrusion of irrelevant and distracting thoughts* (Chapman, Chapman, & Miller, 1964, 1984; Maher, 1983). That is, the uncontrollable intrusion of other thoughts may cause them to "spin off" and begin dealing with new thoughts. These intrusions are due to the individual's *associations* with the words being used, and therefore the problems are called **associative intrusions.** In the following paragraphs I describe four types of associative intrusions that can lead to the strange sentences sometimes used by some people with schizophrenia:

1. *Semantic intrusions.* The first type is the **semantic intrusion,** in which *an alternative meaning for a particular word introduces a new thought.* All of us have more than one association for many of the words we use. Examples of common words with multiple meanings are *rare, diamond, bat, tip, yard,* and *pit.* Each of these words has a *strong association* (the first or most common meaning) and at least one *weak association.* For example, a strong association for

date is "an appointment to go out with someone," whereas a weak association is "a fruit from a palm tree." To explain disordered language it has been suggested that individuals with schizophrenia are likely to use the *strong association, regardless of whether it is the appropriate association.* Consider the following sentence: "When the farmer bought some cattle, he needed a new pen." The word *pen* has two associations: The strong one is "a writing instrument," and the weak one is "a fenced-in enclosure." If you pay attention to the context in which the word *pen* is used in the sentence, you will realize that in this case the weak association ("fenced-in enclosure") is the correct association. However, individuals with schizophrenia are likely to ignore the context and respond using the strong association (Chapman et al., 1964). For example, in response to a person saying, "The cattle were in the pen," an individual who suffers from schizophrenia may say, "Just like the one in my shirt pocket."

2. *Thought content intrusion.* A second type of associative intrusion is the **thought content intrusion,** which occurs when *a word reminds the individual of a different topic, which then intrudes.* For example, an individual with schizophrenia may be telling a story about a particular cat, but mentioning the topic of cats causes the individual to think of another story about another cat and in midsentence to launch off into that story without making the transition clear.

3. *Clang associations.* A third type of associative intrusion, based on the *sound* of a word, is called a **clang association.** Examples of clang associations include *bang* and *fang, dog* and *bog,* and *heed* and *deed.* In the process of constructing the sentence "When I saw the clown, I began to laugh," the individual with schizophrenia might get to the word *clown* and think of the word *down* and then complete the sentence with a phrase involving the word *down,* such as "Jack fell down and broke his crown, and Jill came tumbling after." The resulting sentence might be "When I saw the clown, Jack fell down and broke his crown," which does not make sense.

The disrupting effects of clang associations are obvious in the following statement by a patient suffering from schizophrenia:

> Oh you can have all the keys you want, they broke into the store and found peas, what's the use of keys, policeman, watchman, dogs, dog shows, the spaniel was the best dog this year, he is Spanish you know, Morrow castle what a big key they have Sampson, Schley, he drowned them all in the bay, gay, New York bay, Broadway, the White Way, . . . (Bleuler, 1936)

4. *Habit strength intrusions.* Finally, there are **habit strength intrusions.** Certain words or phrases are frequently used together, and use of one of the words or phrases is likely to make you think of the word or phrase that is habitually associated with it. For example, when using the phrase "when it rains," you are likely to think "it pours." However, you will not use the phrase "it pours" unless it fits with what you are saying. However, individuals with schizophrenia become distracted by the habitual response and use it regardless of whether or not it is appropriate. For example, when answering the question "Who was living at home?" an individual with schizophrenia who had a strong Christian background might say, "The father, the son, and the Holy Ghost." The phrase "the Holy Ghost" intruded because in Christian religious services that phrase often follows "The Father, the Son."

It should be noted that associative intrusions are most likely to occur at transition points in sentences (at commas, the ends of sentences, or other pauses), where attention is most likely to lapse. It is probably because intrusions occur at the ends of phrases that any one phrase in a sentence uttered by a person with schizophrenia makes sense, but the phrases do not fit together.

Overall, the presence of unusual sensory experiences provides an excellent explanation for hallucinations and delusions, and distraction can be used to account for the intellectual and language problems seen in schizophrenia. However, the cognitive theory is incomplete in that it does not explain why some individuals have unusual sensory experiences or are prone to distraction. To explain the unusual sensory experiences and distractibility, we will have to go on to examine the physiological explanation for schizophrenia.

THINKING CRITICALLY

Questions about the Psychodynamic, Learning, and Cognitive Explanations for Schizophrenia

1. *What are the strengths and weaknesses of the psychodynamic explanation?* The notion that problems with child-rearing are largely responsible for schizophrenia developed because therapists who were treating patients with schizophrenia noticed that the mothers of their patients often behaved inappropriately toward their children, such as being inconsistent in their affection, so the therapists assumed those behaviors led to schizophrenia. This once-popular explanation has been completely discredited. The problem was that the therapists were not also seeing mothers of individuals who did *not* have schizophrenia, so therapists didn't realize that those mothers also use many of the behaviors seen in mothers of individuals with schizophrenia. In short, the problem was that these theorists used the *case study method* to arrive at their hypothesis, but as you learned in Chapter 4, case studies cannot be used to

draw conclusions concerning cause and effect. However, it is true that in *some* cases the mothers of individuals with schizophrenia do behave differently and indeed show more symptoms of maladjustment than do other mothers. The problem in drawing conclusions from those cases is that we do not know whether the behaviors of the mothers led to the symptoms in their children or whether the mothers and their children both show symptoms because of a genetic factor. We'll examine that in the next section on the physiology of schizophrenia. Psychodynamic theorists have also suggested that stress causes schizophrenia and have argued that when exposed to a high level of stress, individuals regress to an earlier stage of development in which they feel more secure. While there is no doubt that stress can contribute to schizophrenia, no evidence exists that schizophrenia involves regression to an earlier developmental stage.

2. *What are the strengths and weaknesses of the learning explanation?* It seems clear that labels, roles, and expectations are responsible for some of the symptoms seen in schizophrenia. In other words, just as you behave differently when you are in your "student role" than in your "party person" role, so people labeled as "schizophrenic" may adopt different behaviors. Furthermore, if people are labeled as "schizophrenic," we may also interpret their behaviors incorrectly (e.g., as hallucinating rather than thinking).

However, the learning approach has a number of limitations. First, labels and expectations can have their effects only *after* an individual has been diagnosed (labeled), so the symptoms that result from labels and expectations are only secondary symptoms rather than the core symptoms of schizophrenia. Second, the notion that the symptoms of schizophrenia are due to labels and roles suggests that the symptoms can be changed by simply changing labels and

---

associative intrusions Inappropriate associations that interfere with normal thought processes and are believed to be important in the thought disorders associated with schizophrenia.

semantic intrusions Associative intrusions based on the first or most common meaning of words.

thought content intrusions Associative intrusions based on the inclusion of new and irrelevant thoughts, which occurs when a word reminds an individual of a different topic.

clang associations Associative intrusions based on rhyming words (*bug, dug; clown, frown*), which can result in the intrusion of new thoughts.

habit strength intrusions Associative intrusions based on sets of words that are frequently used together (e.g., "When it rains, it pours"), which may trigger inappropriate new thoughts.

roles, but the treatment of schizophrenia is much more complex and difficult. Overall, then, labels, roles, and expectations can contribute to the symptoms of schizophrenia, but these factors do not provide a convincing or comprehensive explanation for the core symptoms of schizophrenia.

3. *What are the strengths and weaknesses of the cognitive explanation?* The strength of the cognitive approach lies in the fact that it provides excellent explanations for the various symptoms of schizophrenia. Specifically, (a) hallucinations stem from misinterpretations of sensory experiences that people without schizophrenia do not have, (b) delusions occur because the individuals with schizophrenia try to make sense of their unique sensory experiences, (c) declines in intellectual functioning are the result of distraction, and (d) problems with language are due to associative intrusions.

Unfortunately, the cognitive approach has a serious problem in that it does not explain why individuals with schizophrenia have sensory experiences that other people do not have or why individuals with schizophrenia are more distractible and have more associative intrusions. In other words, unusual sensory experiences and distractability lead to symptoms, but the cognitive explanation does not tell us what causes the unusual experiences and distractability. Overall, then, the cognitive explanation has many strengths, but it is not a complete explanation. The physiological explanations that we will consider next may be able to account for the unusual sensory experiences and distractability.

TOPIC II
Physiological Explanations for Schizophrenia

One day, when Arlen shot up on amphetamines, he became disoriented, started hearing voices, and thought his friends were trying to kill him. At the hospital emergency room he was diagnosed as suffering from amphetamine psychosis. Why can

high levels of amphetamines trigger a psychosis? What can we learn about schizophrenia from this?

When Nessa was admitted to a hospital with the diagnosis of schizophrenia, an MRI was done on her brain. The MRI revealed that she had "enlarged ventricles." The ventricles are simply canals in the brain that carry away waste materials. Are enlarged ventricles related to schizophrenia? If so, why is the size of the drainage canals in Nessa's brain related to her schizophrenia?

Amil has Parkinson's disease and is taking a drug called L-dopa. The L-dopa helps control his muscle tremors, but when he takes high doses of the drug, he begins hearing voices. Why does a drug that controls the motor symptoms of Parkinson's disease cause hallucinations? What does this tell us about schizophrenia?

Eric's mother had the flu and a very high fever for a few days during the time she was pregnant with Eric. At age 19 Eric developed schizophrenia. Is there a link between his mother's illness during pregnancy and his schizophrenia 20 years later?

We can now consider the two major physiological explanations for schizophrenia. The first explanation is that *problems with neurotransmitters cause high levels of activity in the brain,* and the high activity levels result in the symptoms. For example, a high level of neurological activity can disrupt thought processes and stimulate hallucinations. The second explanation is that there are *structural problems in the brain.* For instance, damage to the brain can retard cognitive activity and lead to symptoms such as poverty of thought and depression. In other words, schizophrenia is thought to stem from brain overactivity or brain damage. These explanations are not in competition with one another; instead, schizophrenia can stem from problems with either brain overactivity or brain damage, and depending on which one is the cause, different types of symptoms will result.

If problems with brain overactivity and damage cause the symptoms of schizophrenia, the next question is, what causes the overactivity and damage? It now appears that these problems are caused by *genetic factors* and *biological traumas* (illnesses during pregnancy or complications during birth). In other words, there is a two-tiered explanation for schizophrenia: First, genetic factors and biological traumas lead to problems with neurotransmitters (overactivity) and brain development (damage). Second, the problems with overactivity and damage cause the symptoms. This is illustrated in Figure 11.3. In the following sections I will first discuss problems with neurotransmitters and brain development and then consider the evidence linking genetic factors and biological traumas to problems with neurotransmitters and brain development.

dopamine A neurotransmitter in the nerve tracts that carries neurological activity to higher areas of the brain; high levels of dopamine activity are associated with schizophrenia; low levels are associated with Parkinson's disease.

dopamine explanation for schizophrenia The notion that schizophrenia is due to excessive levels of dopamine activity.

FIGURE 11.3

The sequence of causes in the development of schizophrenia

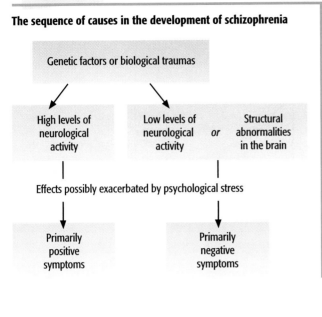

 ## Problems with Neurotransmitters

Problems with neurotransmitters cause high levels of brain activity that lead to some of the symptoms of schizophrenia. In this section we will examine the problems that occur with two neurotransmitters, *dopamine* and *serotonin*.

The Dopamine Explanation

Perhaps the most widely accepted explanation for schizophrenia is that high levels of a neurotransmitter called **dopamine** lead to *high levels of activity in the brain and that high activity then disrupts cognitive functioning and causes symptoms.* Dopamine plays a crucial role in brain activity because it is a major neurotransmitter in the nerve tracts carrying neurological arousal to the higher areas of the brain where thinking occurs. Those nerve tracts are illustrated in Figure 11.4. In other words, if dopamine levels are too high in those tracts, too much arousal is transmitted to the higher areas of the brain, and those areas of the brain become overactive. The overactivity disrupts the brain's function, and that is likely to lead to the *positive symptoms* of schizophrenia, such as disorganized thought processes and hallucinations. This analysis is often referred to as the **dopamine explanation for schizophrenia.** Let's go on to consider three types of evidence for this explanation.

Decreasing Dopamine Activity Reduces Symptoms. The first type of evidence that demonstrates that dopamine activity is related to schizophrenia comes from the finding that *drugs that reduce dopamine activity also reduce the symptoms of schizophrenia, particularly the positive symptoms* (Tamminga, 1998). This evidence will be discussed later in this chapter when we consider the drug treatment for schizophrenia.

Increasing Dopamine Activity Increases Symptoms. Evidence for the role of dopamine also comes from the finding that *drugs that increase dopamine levels increase the positive symptoms of schizophrenia.* For example, amphetamines cause an increase in the release of dopamine, which can cause schizophrenic symptoms in otherwise normal individuals and exacerbate the symptoms in individuals who are suffering from schizophrenia (Baker, 1991; Satel & Edell, 1991; Satel, Southwick, & Gawin, 1991; Snyder, 1976). Indeed, high levels of amphetamines can lead to

FIGURE 11.4

The nerve tracts through which the neurotransmitter dopamine carries activity to higher areas of the brain

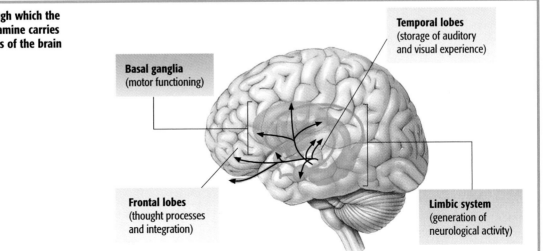

what is called **amphetamine psychosis,** which involves hallucinations, delusions, and disrupted thought processes (Murray, 1998). Fortunately, when dopamine levels return to normal after the amphetamines have left the system, the symptoms disappear.

With regard to the effects of increasing dopamine levels, it is also interesting to note that the drug **L-dopa** (dihydroxyphenylalanine), which is used to treat Parkinson's disease, can produce the symptoms of schizophrenia. Here's how the relationship works: Parkinson's disease involves muscle tremors that stem from *low levels of dopamine* in the area of the brain responsible for motor movements (the basal ganglia). L-dopa is used to treat Parkinson's disease because L-dopa is converted into dopamine in the body, thus increasing the level of dopamine and reducing the muscle tremors. Unfortunately, in addition to increasing the level of dopamine in the area of the brain responsible for motor movements, L-dopa also increases the level of dopamine in other areas of the brain, and this increase results in the symptoms of schizophrenia. Conversely, the use of drugs that reduce schizophrenia by reducing dopamine levels can have the effect of causing the symptoms of Parkinson's disease (see the later discussion of side effects of antipsychotic drugs).

A High Level of Dopamine Receptors Is Related to Symptoms. Finally, there is also evidence that some individuals who suffer from schizophrenia have *more dopamine receptors* than other people (Hietala et al., 1994; Wong et al., 1986). The higher number of dopamine receptors can result in more dopamine activity because when there are more receptors, it is more likely that one of them will get stimulated. Relatedly, it is interesting to note that in men the number of dopamine receptors declines sharply between the ages of 30 and 50, whereas in women the decline is somewhat less dramatic (Wong et al., 1984). The more rapid decline of dopamine receptors in men may account for the fact that men who have positive symptoms of schizophrenia are more likely to show a reduction in their symptoms earlier than women. The relationship between age and number of dopamine receptors is illustrated in Figure 11.5.

In summary, with regard to dopamine, (1) decreasing dopamine activity decreases the symptoms of schizophre-

amphetamine psychosis A disorder involving schizophrenic-like symptoms that result from high levels of amphetamines.

L-dopa (dihydroxyphenylalanine) A drug that increases dopamine levels and is used to treat Parkinson's disease but that can also bring on symptoms of schizophrenia.

serotonin A neurotransmitter that can lead to depression at low levels but can also block the activity of dopamine.

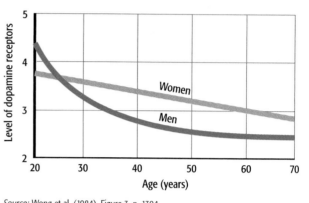

FIGURE 11.5

Dopamine receptors decline more rapidly with age in men than in women.

Source: Wong et al. (1984), Figure 3, p. 1394.

nia, (2) increasing dopamine activity increases the symptoms, and (3) a high number of dopamine receptors (which increases activity) is associated with more symptoms. Increases in brain activity are linked primarily to positive symptoms, such as hallucinations and disordered thought processes, because the high levels of activity stimulate hallucinations and disrupt brain functioning (see the later discussion).

The Serotonin Explanation

I have just described how high levels of dopamine activity play a role in schizophrenia, but there is evidence that *low levels* of **serotonin** are also linked to schizophrenia. Interestingly, low levels of serotonin are linked to both positive and negative symptoms. Let's examine how this occurs.

Low Levels of Serotonin and Positive Symptoms. In some areas of the brain serotonin is the neurotransmitter for the *inhibitory neurons* that reduce the activity of the excitatory neurons that are activated by dopamine. When serotonin levels are low, the inhibitory neurons become underactive and do not reduce the activity of the excitatory neurons. If this occurs, the activity of the excitatory neurons becomes too high and causes the positive symptoms of schizophrenia. In other words, low serotonin may lead to high activity because it does not inhibit that activity. However, by itself a low level of serotonin is not sufficient to cause schizophrenia. Instead, the positive symptoms of schizophrenia are probably due to a low level of serotonin in combination with a high level of dopamine.

Low Levels of Serotonin and Negative Symptoms. Low levels of serotonin can also contribute to the negative symptoms of schizophrenia because low levels of serotonin can cause depression (see Chapter 8), which can provide the basis for negative symptoms such as apathy and poverty of thought. In other words, low levels of serotonin lead to depression, and the depression leads to negative symptoms.

Evidence for the role of serotonin in negative symptoms comes from the fact that antipsychotic drugs that block dopamine and *also increase serotonin levels* are effective for treating both the positive and negative symptoms of schizophrenia, whereas drugs that only block dopamine activity do not influence negative symptoms (see the discussion on drug treatment later in this chapter). There is also evidence that taking antidepressant drugs such as Prozac, which increase serotonin levels, can aid in reducing the negative symptoms of schizophrenia (Brancato et al., 1994; Silver & Shmugliakov, 1998; Zullino, Bondolfi, & Baumann, 1998).

Overall, then, serotonin is linked to both the positive and negative symptoms of schizophrenia: low levels of serotonin do not adequately inhibit neurological activity, so positive symptoms occur, and low levels of serotonin can also lead to depression, which contributes to negative symptoms.

High Neurological Activity and Symptoms

It is clear that high levels of neurological activity lead to the positive symptoms of schizophrenia, so the next question is, *how* does this high activity produce the symptoms? To answer this question we have to consider exactly where the high activity in the brain occurs and then look at what those areas of the brain do. A number of areas are involved, but here I will focus on the two most important ones: the *prefrontal cortex* and the *temporal cortex*.

The Prefrontal Cortex. The **prefrontal cortex** is the thin layer of neurons (*cortex*) that covers the forwardmost part of the frontal lobes; see Figure 11.6. This is a very important part of the brain because it is where *information from different parts of the brain is integrated and where thought processes occur* (Miller & Cummings, 1999). If there is too much activity in the prefrontal cortex, thought processes are disrupted, which can lead to the disturbed cognitive processes we see in schizophrenia (see the earlier discussion of the cognitive explanation).

Evidence linking high brain arousal to schizophrenia comes primarily from two sources: First, PET scans show higher levels of activity in individuals with schizophrenia than in other people (Manoach et al., 1999). Second, evidence comes from the effects of the street drug known as PCP (*phencyclidine*), or "angel dust." The use of PCP results in a dramatic increase in prefrontal activity and sometimes in the development of serious cases of schizophrenia (Abi-Saab et al., 1998; Jentsch & Roth, 1999). Interestingly, when monkeys were injected with PCP, they showed schizophrenic-like behaviors: when they were later given a drug

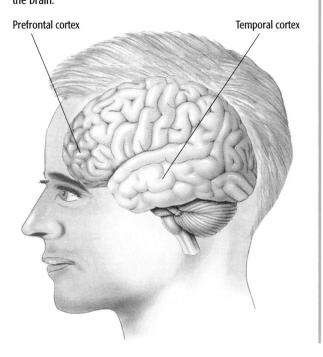

Activity in the prefrontal cortex and the temporal cortex is important in symptoms of schizophrenia.
The cortex is a thin layer of neurons that covers the lobes of the brain.

Prefrontal cortex   Temporal cortex

(clozapine) that is used to treat schizophrenia in humans, their behaviors returned to normal (Jentsch et al., 1997). Overall, then, the research on PCP provides us with both evidence concerning a cause of schizophrenia and an important message concerning the dangers of using PCP.

The Temporal Cortex. Another area of the cortex that is crucial in symptoms of schizophrenia is the **temporal cortex,** which is the thin layer of neurons covering the temporal lobes; see Figure 11.6. The temporal cortex is important because it is where memories for auditory and visual experiences are stored; high levels of activity in the temporal cortex can activate those memories and result in hallucinations. Some background might be helpful to aid you in understanding how this occurs.

prefrontal cortex   The thin layer of neurons covering the forwardmost part of the frontal lobes, where the integration of thoughts and feelings takes place; high and low levels of activity in the prefrontal cortex can lead to symptoms of schizophrenia.

temporal cortex   The thin layer of neurons covering the temporal lobes; high activity in the temporal cortex contributes to hallucinations.

It is generally agreed that memories are stored in groups of neurons and that when a particular group of neurons is stimulated, the memory stored there will be reproduced (Hebb, 1949). This was demonstrated in a fascinating series of studies in which investigators opened up the skulls of humans and then electrically stimulated various areas of the temporal cortex (Penfield, 1955; Penfield & Perot, 1963). The stimulation resulted in immediate, clear, and specific perceptual experiences. For example, when one area of a young man's temporal cortex was stimulated, he said, "Oh, gee, gosh, robbers are coming at me with guns" (Penfield & Perot, 1963, p. 616). In contrast, when the stimulation was applied to another area, he reported hearing his mother talking. For this young man both visual and auditory hallucinations could be produced with simple electrical stimulation. In the case of a young woman, when stimulation was applied at one area, she said, "I hear singing. . . . Yes, it is 'White Christmas,'" and when stimulation was applied at another area, she reported, "That is different, a voice—talking—a man . . . a man's voice—talking" (p. 618). From these findings it is clear that by electrically stimulating areas of the temporal cortex, it is possible to produce hallucinations—that is, perceptual experiences that do not have a basis in reality. It may be then that the excessive stimulation of the temporal cortex by the dopamine-related nerve tracts is responsible for the hallucinations that occur in schizophrenia (Pearlson, 1997).

It is interesting to note that a variety of nonpsychiatric disorders involving high levels of neurological activity in the temporal cortex can also involve hallucinations (Anderson & Rizzo, 1994). For example, individuals who suffer from temporal lobe epilepsy often experience hallucinations just before the onset of their seizures; that is, they have hallucinations at a time when they are experiencing excessive neurological activity in the temporal cortex

(Manford & Andermann, 1998). Similarly, some individuals experience hallucinations when they have migraine headaches (Manford & Andermann, 1998; Schreier, 1998; Spranger et al., 1999). It is noteworthy that because individuals with these disorders know that their hallucinations are due to a neurological disorder, they do not attribute any personal meaning to their hallucinations and generally ignore them; that is, they do not believe that someone is talking to them or that they are hearing the voice of God. Unfortunately, most individuals with schizophrenia do not realize that their hallucinations are neurological artifacts, so, for example, they think that people are really talking to them.

Other support for the notion that high levels of activity in the temporal lobes stimulate hallucinations comes from the fact that PET scans reveal higher levels of activity when patients are hallucinating than when they are not (McCarley et al., 1994; Silbersweig et al., 1995).

In summary, there is strong evidence that high levels of neurological activity in the prefrontal cortex and the temporal cortex are responsible for the positive symptoms of schizophrenia, such as disturbed thought processes and hallucinations. However, to understand the negative symptoms of schizophrenia, we must look to another explanation, involving problems with brain development and activity.

Problems with Brain Development and Activity

The second major physiological explanation for schizophrenia suggests that schizophrenia occurs because specific areas of the brain *do not develop adequately and/or deteriorate faster than what is normal* (Chua & Murray, 1996). In other words, this explanation holds that schizophrenia is due to brain damage. Furthermore, the brain damage can lead to *low levels of brain activity,* which can also contribute to schizophrenia. In general, the notion is that because brain structures are damaged or underactive, the processes they control will be *retarded,* and this retardation can lead to the negative symptoms of schizophrenia, such as poverty of thought and the inability to experience pleasure. This is referred to as the **neurodevelopment theory of schizophrenia.**

Problems with Brain Structures

In the following sections I will describe four structural problems that occur in the brains of individuals with schizophrenia and explain how these problems lead to symptoms.

---

neurodevelopment theory of schizophrenia   The theory that underdeveloped or damaged brain structures and low levels of brain activity lead to schizophrenia.

reversed hemispheric dominance   The fact that in some (right-handed) persons with schizophrenia the right side of the brain is larger than the left side of the brain; the opposite is usually true in persons who do not suffer from schizophrenia.

neural migration   The process by which neurons move from one part of the brain to another and make connections with other neurons. This process is thought to be retarded in schizophrenia.

atrophy   A loss or deterioration of neurons, often seen in the brains of individuals suffering from schizophrenia.

cortical atrophy   Deterioration and death of neurons in the cortex, which is the thin layer of neurons covering the brain.

Reversed Hemispheric Dominance. Your brain is divided into two halves called *hemispheres,* and for most people, especially those who are right-handed, the left hemisphere of the brain is larger than the right hemisphere. However, among many individuals with schizophrenia, *the right hemisphere is larger,* an effect that is referred to as **reversed hemispheric dominance** (Guerguerian & Lewine, 1998; Tiihonen et al., 1998; White, Maher, & Manschreck, 1998). To understand how this occurs you should first know that in infants the right hemisphere is more dominant than the left hemisphere, but at about age 3 the left hemisphere becomes dominant (Chiron et al., 1997). This change from right to left dominance is consistent with the fact that during the early years of life children develop *spatial* abilities (the ability to reach out and grasp objects), which are controlled by the *right* hemisphere, whereas later the emphasis is on *verbal* abilities and *analytical thinking,* which are usually controlled by the *left* hemisphere. The fact that persons who develop schizophrenia do not show the shift in dominance from right to left hemisphere indicates that for some reason their brains did not continue to develop as they should. Indeed, in this respect the structure of the brain in persons with schizophrenia is similar to that in young children (Gilmore, Sikich, & Lieberman, 1997).

It is interesting to note that reversed hemispheric dominance is most likely to be found in individuals for whom schizophrenia started early in life and became progressively worse with time (Guerguerian & Lewine, 1998). That is, problems with brain development in these individuals began early, and as the problems progressed, the symptoms of schizophrenia became worse. Furthermore, reversed hemispheric dominance is more likely to be associated with negative symptoms, such as poverty of thought, than with positive symptoms. That is consistent with the fact that the left hemisphere—where thinking is done—is underdeveloped.

Failure of Neural Migration. You may be surprised to learn that during prenatal development and for a period shortly after birth, some of the neurons in your brain actually moved from one area to another in a process called **neural migration.** Of course, if neural migration fails to occur, there may not be enough of the right neurons in the right places, which can have serious consequences. In fact, there is evidence that *neural migration is retarded* in many individuals who suffer from schizophrenia (Akbarian, Bunney, et al., 1993; Akbarian, Vinuela, et al., 1993; Cannon et al., 1995; Selemon, Rajkowska, & Goldman-Rakic 1995). Specifically, when compared to normal individuals, individuals with schizophrenia have fewer neurons in the gray matter of the cortex than in the white matter that lies beneath the cortex. In other words, individuals suffering from schizophrenia show reduced migration of neurons from the white matter up to the gray matter, an effect that is particularly strong in the prefrontal cortex and temporal cortex. Furthermore, the neurons that have not migrated to the gray matter are sometimes structurally deformed (Lim et al., 1999). What this means is that the prefrontal and temporal cortexes do not have the normal number of neurons, which can reduce brain functioning and contribute to negative symptoms (Bloom, 1993).

Cortical Atrophy. The third structural problem found in the brains of individuals with schizophrenia is **atrophy** (AT-truh-fe), which is a *progressive loss or deterioration of neurons* (Gur, Maany, et al., 1998; Gur, Turetsky, et al., 1999; Kwon et al., 1999; Marsh et al., 1997; Zipursky et al., 1998). When atrophy occurs in the cortex, it is called **cortical atrophy,** and that can have serious implications because the cortex is where higher mental processes such as thinking take place. Most of the attention has been focused on atrophy in two areas of the cortex.

1. *Prefrontal cortex.* Many people who suffer from schizophrenia have a prefrontal cortex that is *smaller and decreasing in size faster* than is the case for people who do not suffer from schizophrenia (Buchanan et al., 1998; Gur, Cowell, et al., 1998; Highley, Esiri, McDonald, Cortina Borja, & Cooper, 1998; Rapoport et al., 1999). For example, in one study of adolescents it was found that over only a 4-year period those with schizophrenia showed an 11% decrease in the size of the prefrontal cortex, whereas those who did not suffer from schizophrenia showed only a 2.5% decrease. Similar declines were also found in the temporal cortex. These dramatic findings are presented graphically in Figure 11.7 (on p. 320). It is normal for the brain to begin shrinking in early adulthood, but the process is much more rapid among individuals with schizophrenia, and this deterioration is linked to an increase in negative symptoms, such as poverty of thought and depression (Strassburger et al., 1997).

2. *Temporal cortex.* The temporal cortex is also important for cognitive functioning because it is where language abilities are primarily located. There is a substantial amount of evidence that individuals with schizophrenia have temporal lobes that are generally smaller, less active, and have less cortex area than those of other people (Coburn et al., 1998; Highley, Esiri, McDonald, Cooper, & Crow, 1998; Hirayasu et al., 1998; Maher et al, 1998; Rapoport et al., 1999). Furthermore, as you might expect, disorganized verbal behavior in schizophrenia has been linked to problems with structures and activity in the temporal cortex (McGuire et al., 1998). Finally, it is interesting to note that in a number of cases individuals who had surgery on their temporal cortex in an attempt to arrest the symptoms of epilepsy developed "schizophrenic-like psychosis" (Kegeles, Humaran, & Mann, 1998; Uesugi et al., 1997).

Overall, then, it is clear that problems in the prefrontal and temporal cortexes can lead to symptoms of schizophrenia, particularly negative symptoms.

Adolescents with schizophrenia showed large reductions in the prefrontal cortex and the temporal cortex.

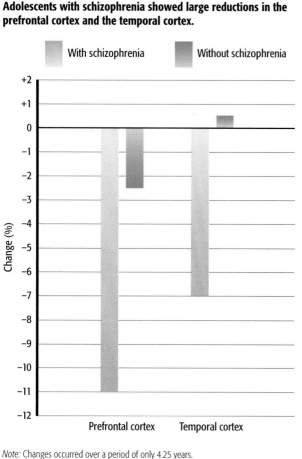

Note: Changes occurred over a period of only 4.25 years.

Source: Adopted from Rapoport et al. (1999), p. 653.

Subcortical Atrophy. Atrophy can also occur in the structures that are beneath the cortex—a problem called **subcortical atrophy.** Thinking does not go on in those structures, but they are crucial for thought because they are responsible for the initial processing of information that is then sent to the cortex and used in thinking. Of course, if the information is not initially processed effectively, thinking can be disrupted. The physical effects of subcortical atrophy are seen most easily in *enlarged ventricles* (DeLisi et al., 1997; Marsh et al., 1999; Staal, Hulshoff, & Kahn, 1999; Wassink et al., 1999). Let me explain: The **ventricles** (VEN-tri-kelz) are *canals that go through the brain* from front to back, and it is through these canals that waste materials from the brain are carried away. Enlargement of the ventricles reflects the fact that the brain is deteriorating; that is, as the brain deteriorates, the ventricles become larger. Enlarged ventricles are not important in themselves, but they indicate a loss of neurons, which is very important. Enlarged and normal ventricles are shown in the MRI scans presented in Figure 11.8. Enlarged ventricles are found in 20–50% of the individuals who suffer from schizophrenia.

Subcortical atrophy can result in the deterioration of a variety of structures in the brain; exactly which structures are affected influences what symptoms develop (Arnold et al., 1995; Bloom, 1993; Breier et al., 1992; Bryant et al., 1999; Flaum et al., 1995; Goldstein et al., 1999; Gur, Maany, et al., 1998; Levitt et al., 1999; McCarley et al., 1999; Nelson et al., 1998; Whitworth et al., 1998; Wright et al., 1999; Zipursky et al., 1992). Although many structures may deteriorate, attention has been focused on three particularly important ones:

1. *Hippocampus.* The **hippocampus** (hip-uh-KAM-puhs) is a small structure that is responsible for the *processing of information for storage in memory;* if the hippocampus is not operating properly, information cannot be saved for later use. For instance, the fact that individuals with *Alzheimer's disease* have difficulty putting new experiences into memory is due to the deterioration of the hippocampus (see Chapter 17). Importantly, there is consistent evidence that the hippocampus is *smaller* in individuals with

Some individuals with schizophrenia have ventricles that are enlarged (left) relative to those of normal individuals (right).

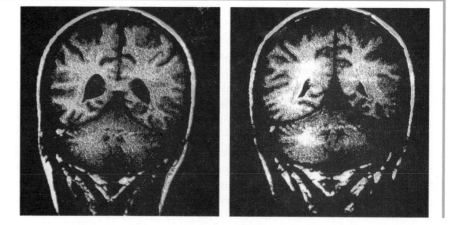

Source: Andreasen (1988).

schizophrenia, most notably in those with negative symptoms (Callicott et al., 1998; Fukuzako et al., 1997; Nelson et al., 1998; Velakoulis et al., 1999). It appears then that the poverty of thought seen in schizophrenia may be due in part to the fact that the necessary information is simply not there because it could not be stored; in other words, there is a poverty of information.

   2. *Thalamus.* The **thalamus** (THAL-uh-mus) is the structure through which most *incoming stimuli, such as sights and sounds, must pass before being sent elsewhere in the brain.* In individuals who suffer from the negative symptoms of schizophrenia, the thalamus is often *smaller* and *less active* than it is in other people (Andreasen, 1997; Buchsbaum et al., 1996; Frazier et al., 1996; Jones, 1997; Portas et al., 1998). Apparently a small and underactive thalamus screens out too much incoming stimulation, thus leading to symptoms such as poverty of thought. In contrast, however, in persons with primarily positive symptoms the thalamus is *enlarged* (Portas et al., 1998). In those cases it appears that the enlarged thalamus does not screen out irrelevant stimulation, and the incoming stimuli interfere with cognitive functioning. In other words, if the thalamus does not "close the gate" on irrelevant stimuli, the individual will be flooded with distracting stimulation (Perry et al., 1999; see also the discussion of cognitive flooding and stimulus overload in Chapter 10).

   3. *Amygdala.* Finally, the **amygdala** (uh-MIG-da-la) is a structure that plays a role in *emotional arousal* and *assertiveness.* Both of these characteristics are lacking in patients with negative symptoms of schizophrenia, which may be attributable to the fact that these persons have an amygdala that is smaller than that of other people (Nelson et al., 1998).

Problems with Brain Underactivity

In addition to the fact that the prefrontal cortex is often smaller and shrinking faster, investigators also found that the prefrontal cortex is *underactive* in persons with schizophrenia, an effect referred to as **hypofrontality** (e.g., Andreasen et al., 1992; Berman et al., 1992; Buchsbaum et al., 1992; Carter et al., 1998; Curtis et al., 1998; Parellada et al., 1998; Ragland et al., 1998; Spence et al., 1998; Volz et al., 1999; Wolkin et al., 1992). (*Hypo* means "less than normal," so *hypofrontality* means "less than normal activity in the frontal lobes.") For example, in one study investigators used PET scans to measure brain activity in individuals who were suffering from schizophrenia and individuals who were not (Buchsbaum et al., 1992). Measurements were made while the individuals were trying to solve a problem. The results revealed that the individuals with schizophrenia had lower levels of activity in the prefrontal cortex. These effects are illustrated in Figure 11.9, where you will notice that the frontal lobes of the individuals with schizophre-

FIGURE 11.9

Some individuals who suffer from schizophrenia (bottom row) show lower levels of neurological activity in their frontal lobes than individuals who do not suffer from schizophrenia (top row).

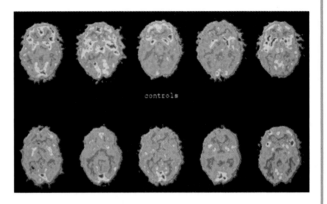

Source: Buchsbaum et al. (1992).

nia (bottom row) are less "lit up" (activity is indicated by brighter colors) than are those of normal individuals (top row).

   Let's pause for a moment to consider what we've learned: It appears that the positive symptoms of schizophrenia are due to high levels of activity in the prefrontal cortex and temporal cortex. The high levels of activity are linked to the neurotransmitters dopamine and serotonin. In contrast, the negative symptoms of schizophrenia are related to structural problems in the prefrontal cortex, the

subcortical atrophy   The deterioration of structures such as the hippocampus beneath the cortex, often seen in patients with schizophrenia, particularly those with negative symptoms.

ventricles   Canals through the brain that carry waste materials away from the brain and that are often enlarged in persons with schizophrenia.

hippocampus   A structure in the brain that is crucial for processing information for storage in memory and that may be damaged in schizophrenia.

thalamus   A structure in the brain where incoming stimuli are initially processed, often smaller and less active in persons with schizophrenia who have negative symptoms than in those who have positive symptoms.

amygdala   A structure in the brain that is responsible for emotional arousal and assertiveness.

hypofrontality   Low levels of activity in the prefrontal cortex that are associated with negative symptoms of schizophrenia.

temporal cortex, and some subcortical structures, particularly the hippocampus, the thalamus, and the amygdala. These structural problems are the result of reversed hemispheric dominance, the failure of neural migration, and atrophy. Negative symptoms are also related to low levels of brain activity. Clearly, we have found links between specific problems in the brain and symptoms of schizophrenia. The question now is, what causes the problems in the brain? To answer this we must consider genetic factors and biological traumas.

 ## Genetic Factors

The first set of evidence for the role of genetic factors in schizophrenia comes from the finding that individuals with biological relatives who suffer from schizophrenia are at increased risk for developing schizophrenia. For example, as indicated in Table 11.1, the concordance rate among siblings is between 8% and 14%, whereas the concordance rate among cousins is only 2% to 6%. (*Concordance* reflects the degree to which two people or groups have a disorder; see Chapter 4.) It is also noteworthy that the prevalence of schizophrenia among individuals who have two parents with schizophrenia (40% to 68%) is substantially higher than that among individuals who have only one parent with schizophrenia (9% to 16%). Furthermore, individuals who have numerous biological relatives with schizophrenia have an earlier onset of the disorder, and the disorder lasts longer than it does in individuals with fewer relatives with schizophrenia (Suvisaari et al., 1999). Clearly, the greater the degree to which an individual shares genes with a person who suffers from schizophrenia, the higher the likelihood that the individual will develop the disorder and the more serious the disorder will be.

It is also interesting to note that the children of individuals with schizophrenia show evidence of the physiological and psychological problems that underlie schizophrenia, even if they do not yet suffer from the disorder (Docherty, 1994; Hans et al., 1999; Hollister et al., 1994; Park, Holzman, & Goldman-Rakic, 1995; Staal et al., 1998). For example, some of the brain structures of these children are smaller, and they have problems with cognitive activities such as concentration, problem solving, and screening out irrelevant stimuli.

Even stronger evidence for the role of genes comes from studies of twins (Black & Andreasen, 1999; Knowles et al., 1999). For example, in 13 studies it has been found that the concordance rate for schizophrenia is higher among identical (monozygotic) twins than among fraternal (dizygotic) twins (see Gottesman, 1991). In addition, the concordance rate is higher if one twin is severely disturbed rather than only moderately disturbed (Gottesman & Shields, 1972).

TABLE 11.1

The risk of developing schizophrenia for individuals with relatives who suffer from the disorder.

	Risk (%)
Children with two parents suffering from schizophrenia	40–68
Children with one parent suffering from schizophrenia	9–16
Parent of a person suffering from schizophrenia	5–10
Nontwin siblings of a person suffering from schizophrenia	8–14
Grandchildren of a person suffering from schizophrenia	2–8
Step-siblings of a person suffering from schizophrenia	1–8
Half-siblings of a person suffering from schizophrenia	1–7
Cousins of a person suffering from schizophrenia	2–6
Nieces and nephews of a person suffering from schizophrenia	1–4

Source: Zerbin-Rudin (1972).

Finally, the strongest evidence for the influence of genes comes from studies of individuals who were adopted and raised by parents other than their biological parents, from whom they received their genes. Consider these three findings:

1. In cases in which individuals who were the biological offspring of *parents with schizophrenia* were adopted and *raised by parents without schizophrenia,* the individuals were just as likely to develop schizophrenia as individuals who were the biological offspring of parents with schizophrenia and were raised by those parents (Heston, 1966; Rosenthal et al., 1968; Rosenthal et al., 1971). In other words, the development of schizophrenia was influenced by individuals' genetic background rather than by who raised them.

2. Individuals who were adopted, raised by parents who did not suffer from schizophrenia, and developed schizophrenia were more likely to have *biological parents* who suffered from schizophrenia than were individuals who were adopted and raised by parents who did not suffer from schizophrenia, but did not develop schizophrenia (Kendler, Gruenberg, & Strauss, 1982; Kety et al., 1975, 1994). This set of findings is similar to those just described, except that in these studies the investigators started with the offspring and then looked at their parents rather than starting with the parents and going on to look at their children. Again, it was the nature of the biological parents rather than the adoptive parents who influenced the development of schizophrenia.

3. In cases in which the biological offspring of *parents without schizophrenia* were adopted and raised by *parents with schizophrenia,* the individuals were *not* more likely to develop schizophrenia than were individuals who were adopted and raised by parents who did not suffer from schizophrenia (Wender et al., 1974). In other words, being raised by disturbed parents did not lead to schizophrenia in individuals who did not have a genetic background of schizophrenia.

Overall, then, the results of the adoption studies clearly and consistently indicate that whether or not individuals develop schizophrenia is determined in large part by whether or not their biological parents suffered from schizophrenia and not by environmental factors, such as who raised them. However, it is important to recognize that *genetic factors do not account for all cases of schizophrenia.* For example, not all of the biological offspring of parents with schizophrenia develop schizophrenia, and there is not a 100% concordance rate for schizophrenia among monozygotic twins. Indeed, genetic factors probably account for less than 10% of the cases of schizophrenia. Does this mean that the genetic explanation is wrong? No, it simply means that genetic factors are only *one* of the primary causes of schizophrenia. In the next section we will consider another primary cause of schizophrenia—biological traumas.

Biological Traumas

The prenatal period and the few months shortly after birth are crucial for brain development because during that time neurons are migrating to their final locations, dendrites and axons are branching out to make more connections, and synapses are being formed (Cannon et al., 1993, 1995; Tamminga, 1999). Unfortunately, **biological traumas** such as diseases, toxins, and lack of oxygen can disrupt brain development; therefore, these traumas may be responsible for cases of schizophrenia that are not due to genetic factors. Let's consider the evidence.

Prenatal Complications

Here is an interesting finding: In the Northern Hemisphere individuals who develop schizophrenia are between 5% and 10% more likely to have been born during the months of January, February, and March than during other months of the year (Bradbury & Miller, 1985; Torrey et al., 1997). Why? Originally, this **season-of-birth effect** puzzled investigators, but we now know it is due to **prenatal complica-**

Studies of families and twins have yielded compelling evidence for a genetic basis for schizophrenia. Shown here are the Genain quadruplets; each of the four developed a schizophrenic disorder.

tions; specifically, it is due to a serious case of the flu in the mother during the second trimester (third to sixth month) of pregnancy (Barr et al., 1990; Chen et al., 1996; Kirkpatrick et al., 1998; Wright et al., 1995). Support for this comes from research in which the investigators first identified periods during which there had been high, medium, and low rates of influenza in the general population. Then the investigators assessed rates of schizophrenia in individuals who had been born shortly after each of those periods. The results revealed that individuals who were born following a period of high influenza rates were more likely to develop schizophrenia than individuals born following periods of medium or low influenza rates. Furthermore, individuals who were in the second trimester of fetal development during the peak of the influenza period were most likely to develop schizophrenia. In other words, people whose mothers were likely to have had the flu during their pregnancy—especially during the second trimester, which

biological traumas   Prenatal and perinatal complications that can lead to abnormal conditions such as schizophrenia.

season-of-birth effect   The fact that individuals who later develop schizophrenia are more likely to have been born in late winter.

prenatal complications   Factors such as a mother's illness during pregnancy that can influence the brain of the fetus and later lead to abnormal conditions, such as schizophrenia.

is crucial for brain development—were at the greatest risk for schizophrenia.

It is clear that a mother's illness influences the brain of her fetus, but we do not understand the underlying process. It is unlikely that the fetus itself becomes infected because the flu virus probably cannot cross the blood-brain barrier between mother and fetus. However, brain damage might result from elevations in temperature, because fever accompanies influenza and we know that an increase of temperature of as little as 2.5°C in the fetus can cause brain damage.

It should be noted that (1) the season-of-birth effect is reversed in the Southern Hemisphere, where winter comes during July, August, and September, (2) the effect is observed during other months if a major influenza epidemic occurs sometime other than during the early winter, and (3) the effect is most likely to be associated with schizophrenia that is characterized by early onset and negative symptoms (Barr et al., 1990; Bradbury & Miller, 1985; Chen et al., 1996; Kirkpatrick et al., 1998; Mednick et al., 1988; Mednick, Machon, & Huttunen, 1990; Torrey, Rawlings, & Waldman, 1988; Watson et al., 1984). The link to early onset and development of negative symptoms rather than positive symptoms is due to the fact that prenatal complications such as the flu result in brain damage rather than problems with neurotransmitters (see the earlier discussion of the causes of positive and negative symptoms).

Finally, it should also be noted that the season-of-birth effect probably accounts for only 5–10% of the individuals who suffer from schizophrenia (Takei et al., 1994; Waddington et al., 1992). However, the important point illustrated by the season-of-birth effect is that *prenatal complications can lead to schizophrenia,* and the mother having the flu is undoubtedly only one of many potential complications (Susser & Lin, 1992; Suvisaari et al., 1999; vanOs & Selten, 1998). Indeed, it has been reported that extreme food deprivation during the first trimester is also linked to schizophrenia later in life. For example, there was a substantial increase in schizophrenia among individuals who were in prenatal development during the terrible Dutch famine of the winter of 1944–1945 (Hoek et al., 1996; Susser et al., 1996). Apparently the inadequate diet of the mothers influenced brain development in the fetuses, which later led to schizophrenia. Schizophrenia has also been linked to exposure to the polio virus during the second trimester (Suvisaari et al., 1999).

> **perinatal complications** Factors such as prolonged labor or oxygen deprivation at the time of birth that can cause brain damage and later lead to abnormal conditions, such as schizophrenia.
>
> **diathesis-stress explanation** The notion that stress can lead to schizophrenia in individuals who have a physiological predisposition to the disorder.

Perinatal Complications

The term *perinatal* refers to the time *immediately around birth,* and **perinatal complications** include problems such as prolonged or difficult labor, oxygen deprivation (*anoxia*), high blood pressure (*preeclampsia*), and the use of forceps in delivery. The notion is that perinatal complications may result in brain damage that can later contribute to the development of schizophrenia.

A substantial amount of evidence now links perinatal complications to schizophrenia (Cantor Graae et al., 1997; Dalman et al., 1999; Geddes & Lawrie, 1995). In one longitudinal study it was found that individuals who developed schizophrenia were almost twice as likely to have experienced perinatal complications as those who did not develop the disorder (Mednick, Parnas, & Schulsinger, 1987). In another investigation of individuals with schizophrenia, it was found that those who had experienced perinatal complications such as bleeding, seizures, and hypertension were more likely to have structural abnormalities in the brain; that is, it appears that perinatal complications led to brain damage, which in turn led to schizophrenia (Kanofsky, Sandyk, & Kay, 1990). Interestingly, in that study the link between perinatal complications and schizophrenia was stronger among individuals who did *not* have a family history of schizophrenia, thus suggesting that perinatal complications accounted for schizophrenia in cases in which genes were not a factor. Finally, it is noteworthy that in a 40-year followup of over 500 individuals with schizophrenia it was found that those who had *not recovered* were more likely to have had perinatal complications than were those who improved (Wilcox & Nasrallah, 1987a, 1987b). This finding is consistent with the notion that perinatal complications lead to brain damage, which in turn leads to the negative symptoms that are more difficult to treat. Clearly, research on prenatal and perinatal complications is providing more of the pieces of the puzzle of schizophrenia.

It is now clear that genetic factors and biological traumas are linked to schizophrenia. However, why don't symptoms develop until adolescence or early adulthood? The answer appears to lie in the fact that some of the areas of the brain that are involved in schizophrenia do not develop fully until adolescence; so problems in their development may not become apparent until adolescence (Weinberger, 1996). It is also noteworthy that a normal process of brain deterioration begins in adolescence and early adulthood, and it may be that the normal decline in combination with the pathological decline results in an overall decrease that triggers the disorder (Hoffman & McGlashan, 1997).

In summary, there is a large and growing body of evidence that schizophrenia is basically a physiological disorder. Specifically, (1) genetics and biological traumas lead to problems with neurotransmitters (neurological activity) and to problems with structures in the brain, and (2) prob-

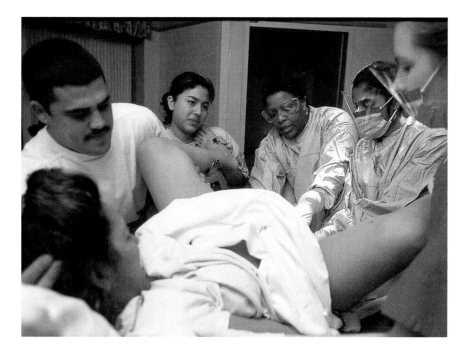

There is ample evidence that suggests that complications that occur during childbirth might result in brain damage that can increase an individual's risk for developing schizophrenia later in life.

lems with neurotransmitters and brain structures result in the positive and negative symptoms.

THINKING CRITICALLY

Questions about the Physiological Explanations for Schizophrenia

1. *If schizophrenia is a physiological disorder, why does psychological stress sometimes trigger the symptoms or make them worse?* In considering this question you should first recognize that for many individuals who suffer from schizophrenia stress does *not* play a role in their disorder; for those individuals the physiological problems by themselves are sufficient to cause schizophrenia. However, in other cases the physiological factors are not enough to cause schizophrenia, but they establish a *predisposition* to the disorder and then stress pushes the individual "over the edge." Consider this possibility: Genetic factors cause an individual to have an abnormally high level of neurological activity, but the level of activity is not high enough to disrupt cognitive functioning and stimulate hallucinations. However, when the individual is exposed to stress, the neurological activity associated with the stress is *added to* the existing high level of activity and results in a level sufficient to cause symptoms. This is the **diathesis-stress explanation** for schizophrenia. (The word *diathesis* means "a constitutional predisposition to a particular state"; see Chapter 2.)

The diathesis-stress explanation can be represented by the following quip: "Humpty Dumpty had a fragile shell, but he didn't break until he fell."

The diathesis-stress explanation brings the findings concerning physiology and psychological stress together nicely and suggests that in treating schizophrenia we must focus on both physiological and psychological factors. However, we must be careful in applying the diathesis-stress explanation because what in some cases appears to be stress leading to a worsening of symptoms may actually be a worsening of symptoms leading to stress. For example, if a fluctuation in dopamine levels causes an individual's symptoms to become worse, the individual's ability to function might decline, and he or she might then lose a job. In that case the stress of the job loss would be associated with the increase in symptoms, but the stress did not increase the symptoms.

2. *Why do women and men with schizophrenia show different symptom patterns?* The best explanation may be that men with schizophrenia have more brain abnormalities than do women with schizophrenia (Nopoulos, Flaum, & Andreasen, 1997). For example, men are more likely to have (a) enlarged ventricles, (b) smaller temporal lobes, (c) a smaller hippocampus, (d) a smaller corpus callosum, (e) a smaller overall brain size, and (f) more abnormalities in the frontal lobes (Nopoulos et al., 1997; Lewine & Seeman, 1995). In other words, earlier and more extensive brain deterioration in men leads to earlier and more serious symptoms.

The next question is, why do men have more brain abnormalities than women? Two answers have been offered: First, males have a *higher rate of injuries during birth* than do females, and these injuries may disrupt brain development. (Note that earlier I pointed out that physical traumas during the perinatal period were related to schizophrenia.) Second, *estrogens (the "female" hormones) may protect the brain from deterioration* (Seeman, 1997). Specifically, just as estrogens appear to protect the brain from the deterioration that leads to Alzheimer's disease, these hormones may also protect the brain from the deterioration that leads to schizophrenia (Toran-Allerand, 1996). Thus, it may be that the increase in estrogens that occurs in women during adolescence protects the neural circuits that develop during adolescence (Lewis, 1997; Riecher-Rossler & Hafner, 1993); this could delay or lessen the development of schizophrenia in women. Interestingly, women who reach puberty early have a later onset of schizophrenia, apparently because the early increase in estrogens protects them longer (Cohen et al., 1999).

There is also evidence that estrogens can have positive short-term effects on symptoms. For instance, women who have a history of acute bouts of schizophrenia are less likely to have a bout when they are pregnant, a time when estrogen levels are steadily rising (Krener et al., 1989). In contrast, immediately following pregnancy when levels of estrogens are falling, the likelihood of schizophrenia increases (Kendell, Chalmers, & Platz, 1987). Finally, the symptoms of schizophrenia tend to be less severe during the time in the menstrual cycle when estrogen levels are high (Gattaz et al., 1994; Riecher-Rossler et al., 1994). Overall, then, estrogens put women at an advantage when it comes to the age of onset and the severity of symptoms of schizophrenia.

3. *Do the physiological explanations for schizophrenia replace the psychological explanations?* No, in fact, the two sets of explanations complement each other and work together. For example, I just pointed out how a physiological predisposition (diathesis) and psychological stress can combine to result in schizophrenia. Furthermore, the physiological explanations complete the cognitive explanation. Specifically, you may recall that the cognitive explanation suggests that distraction is responsible for intellectual decline and language problems in schizophrenia, but it cannot account for why individuals with schizophrenia are more distractable than others. The physiological explanation solves this problem by suggesting that high dopamine activity leads to high levels of neurological arousal, which then lead to distractibility.

4. *What are the strengths and weakness of the physiological approach?* The physiological approach has two strengths: First, it provides a rather comprehensive explanation for schizophrenia, which is based on very sound scientific evidence. For example, problems with dopamine and high neurological arousal account for positive symptoms, whereas problems with brain structures explain neg-

ative symptoms. Second, as you will see in the next section, the physiological approach leads to effective treatment strategies. The weakness of the physiological approach lies in its inability to provide a good explanation for delusions; that is, unlike hallucinations, delusions have not yet been found to have a specific physiological basis. However, that may be because delusions involve complex thought processes and we do not yet understand the neurobiology of thoughts. When neuroscientists discover the basis for normal thought processes, we may then know where to look for the causes of delusions.

TOPIC III
Treatment of Schizophrenia

Some years ago a widely used treatment for schizophrenia involved inserting a knife through the eye socket and into the brain. The knife was then swung up and back to destroy part of the frontal lobes. What was the rationale for this treatment? Are similar treatments used today?

After taking high levels of an antipsychotic drug for about 3 years, Tom began having uncontrollable twitches that were a side effect of the drug. Sometimes his head would jerk to one side, and at other times his tongue would suddenly stick out. This posed a problem: He needed the drug to control his schizophrenia, but the side effect was leading to some very strange behaviors. Can such side effects be controlled? Do all antipsychotic drugs result in side effects like this?

Jessica has positive and negative symptoms of schizophrenia. The drug she is taking reduces her positive symptoms but has almost no effect on her negative symptoms. Why does the drug influence some symptoms and not others? Are there drugs that are effective for treating both positive and negative symptoms?

In the hospital where Mark is being treated for schizophrenia, he is given a poker chip every time he behaves normally, such as dressing appropriately and talking with other people. Mark can then use the poker chips to buy such things as passes to leave the ward or special food treats. As a consequence, Mark is now behaving more normally than he did before. Could this strategy also be used to treat his hallucinations and delusions?

Every week a social worker meets with a group of families, each of which has one member who suffers from schizophrenia. During the sessions they discuss the causes of schizophrenia, the problems it brings to their lives, and how to reduce stress. Since the patients started coming to the meetings, their symptoms have become less serious and they have been able to reduce the amount of medication they take. Why should participation in a group like this help in the treatment of schizophrenia, which is primarily a physiological disorder?

Until quite recently our treatments for schizophrenia were not particularly effective, and a diagnosis of schizophrenia often amounted to a life sentence on a back ward of a state mental hospital. Fortunately, this situation has changed dramatically, and in this section I will explain some of the fascinating breakthroughs we've made in the treatment of schizophrenia. In doing so, however, I am going to take a somewhat different approach than I did when I described the treatment of other disorders. Because for most individuals with schizophrenia the primary intervention involves drugs, which are then backed up with psychological treatments, I am going to begin with the physiological approach and then discuss the cognitive, learning, and psychodynamic approaches. Discussing the drugs first will help you to see how the treatments fit together as a package.

Physiological Treatments

Earlier you learned that the primary causes of schizophrenia are physiological: specifically, high and low levels of neurological activity and structural problems in the brain. The physiological approaches to treatment are designed to correct those problems as much as possible. Although the physiological treatment of schizophrenia now involves drugs, psychosurgery was often used before drugs were available. Therefore, before discussing the drug treatment of schizophrenia, I will comment briefly on the past use of psychosurgery.

Psychosurgery

In the 1930s a report was published in which the authors described how a chimpanzee that was once excitable and violent became docile and friendly after her prefrontal cortex was destroyed (Jacobsen, Wolfe, & Jackson, 1935). Physicians then speculated that the erratic and sometimes violent behavior of individuals with schizophrenia might be brought under control if their frontal lobes were separated from the rest of their brains (Pressman, 1998; Swayze, 1995; Valenstein, 1980). This speculation led to the development of an operation known as a **prefrontal lobotomy** (luh-BOT-uh-me). Specifically, in a prefrontal lobotomy holes were drilled in the top of the skull and then a knife was inserted and pivoted up and back, so that a cut was made separating a portion of the frontal lobes from the rest of the brain. If the operation was not successful in reducing symptoms, it was performed again, but the second time the holes were drilled farther back on the skull so that more of the frontal area would be separated from the rest of the brain.

FIGURE 11.10

A transorbital lobotomy could be performed in a physician's office.

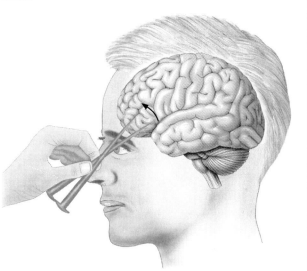

In 1948 the **transorbital lobotomy** was introduced. This procedure involved inserting a knife almost like an icepick through the top of the eye socket and up into the brain. The knife was then moved back and forth to destroy brain tissue. The procedure is illustrated in Figure 11.10. Transorbital lobotomies could be performed as an office procedure and were widely used. (In some cases electroconvulsive shocks were used to induce unconsciousness before the transorbital lobotomy was performed!)

In the years between 1935 and about 1955 thousands of patients received lobotomies. It is difficult to determine how effective the operations were because the nature of the operation differed greatly from hospital to hospital and objective records were not kept on patients' pre- and post-operation symptoms. However, it does appear that in many cases the operations made the patients calmer, more docile, and easier to manage, which increased the likelihood that they would be discharged from the hospital. Needless to say, psychosurgery had a wide variety of serious side effects, such as loss of cognitive abilities and sometimes a complete loss of emotional control. Psychosurgery was also misused

prefrontal lobotomy   An operation once used to treat schizophrenia, in which the frontal lobes are separated from the rest of the brain.

transorbital lobotomy   An operation once used to treat schizophrenia, in which a knife was inserted into the eye socket in order to sever the connections between the frontal lobes and the rest of the brain.

by some physicians. For example, I knew of one who performed transorbital lobotomies on adolescents who had behavior problems in school!

The use of psychosurgery diminished sharply in the mid-1950s, in large part because of the introduction of drugs that were more effective than the surgery and resulted in fewer side effects. (As a footnote to this discussion of psychosurgery, it might be mentioned that the physician who introduced the procedure received the Nobel Prize for his work but was paralyzed later in life when he was shot in the spine by an angry lobotomized patient.) With this as background, let's go on to consider the mainstay of the modern treatment of schizophrenia—drugs.

Drug Treatment

In the early 1950s a group of chemists developed a powerful new antihistamine that they thought would be helpful for clearing up nasal congestion. When they tested the drug on a group of patients in a local mental hospital, they discovered two things. First, the drug did clear up nasal congestion. Second, and much to the surprise of the chemists, the drug also cleared up some of the symptoms of schizophrenia. It wasn't immediately clear why the drug was effective for treating schizophrenia, but it worked and it soon revolutionized the care and condition of mental patients. Almost overnight psychiatric wards were transformed from "hell holes," where patients lived in straitjackets and were largely out of control, to places of relative calm and order. The drugs were not completely effective, and they had some serious side effects, but they provided the first effective treatment for schizophrenia. Let's consider the various drugs used to treat schizophrenia.

Overview of Neuroleptic Drugs. As you learned earlier, one of the physiological causes of schizophrenia is excessively high levels of activity in the areas of the brain where dopamine is the major neurotransmitter. The primary goal of modern drug therapy, therefore, is to *reduce the high level of neurological activity* that leads to schizophrenia. This is done with a group of drugs called **neuroleptics** (noor-uh-LEP-tiks) (Sheitman et al., 1998). The term *neuroleptic* is derived from the Greek *neuro,* which refers to the brain,

and *leptic,* which means "to seize or arrest." In short, neuroleptics relieve the symptoms of schizophrenia by *arresting brain activity.*

Neuroleptics reduce brain activity in three ways. First, they *block the receptors on the postsynaptic neuron* so that the neurotransmitter (dopamine) cannot enter the receptor and cause the neuron to fire. This process is like putting the wrong key in a lock: You cannot open the lock with the wrong key (the neuroleptic), but if the wrong key is in the lock, you cannot get the right key (dopamine) in either.

The second way in which neuroleptics may reduce brain activity is that they *reduce the sensitivity of the postsynaptic receptors.* If the receptors are less sensitive, they will be less likely to fire when stimulated. The belief that neuroleptics reduce receptor sensitivity stems from the fact that sometimes neuroleptics do not begin reducing symptoms for days or even weeks after drug treatment is begun. It appears that over time the presence of the drug changes the sensitivity of the receptors, and this delayed change in sensitivity is responsible for the delay in symptomatic relief.

Third, some newer neuroleptics also increase the levels of the neurotransmitter serotonin. This can help reduce symptoms in a number of ways; for example, the presence of serotonin can *inhibit dopamine activity* (see the later discussion of atypical neuroleptics).

Unfortunately, neuroleptics can have a number of side effects, most of which I will discuss later. However, one serious side effect that I should mention in this overview involves a disturbance in muscle activity. The disturbance can include involuntary tremors, twitches, shaking, and jerking. These occur because dopamine is also a neurotransmitter in the area of the brain that is responsible for motor activity (the basal ganglia). Specifically, dopamine activity inhibits muscle movements, so when the level of dopamine activity is reduced with a neuroleptic, muscle movements go unchecked.

There are numerous neuroleptics available today. I will organize this discussion of them in terms of their biochemical and behavioral effects, and I will refer to them as *low-potency, high-potency,* or *atypical neuroleptics.* In this discussion potency refers to the degree to which a drug blocks the dopamine receptors. Some of the most widely used neuroleptics are listed in Table 11.2.

Low-Potency Neuroleptics. **Low-potency neuroleptics** were the first neuroleptics to be developed, and as the term *low-potency* implies, they are less effective for blocking dopamine receptors than are the high-potency drugs that were developed later. However, they are effective for treating schizophrenia and are still widely used.

The best-known low-potency neuroleptic is **Thorazine** (*chlorpromazine*). Thorazine was first introduced in the mid-1950s, and it immediately became a very popular drug for treating schizophrenia. Indeed, in the 1960s and 1970s

---

neuroleptics   Drugs used to treat psychotic disorders, usually by blocking the receptor sites for dopamine.

low-potency neuroleptics   Drugs such as Thorazine that block relatively few dopamine receptors. (Contrast with *high-potency neuroleptics.*)

Thorazine (chlorpromazine)   An early low-potency neuroleptic that is still widely used in the treatment of schizophrenia.

TABLE 11.2

Widely used neuroleptics

Type	Trade name	Generic name	Typical daily dose
Low-potency neuroleptics	Thorazine	Chlorpromazine	200–600 mg
	Mellaril	Thioridazine	200–600 mg
High-potency neuroleptics	Haldol	Haloperidol	2–12 mg
	Navane	Thiothixene	6–30 mg
Atypical neuroleptics	Clozaril	Clozapine	200–900 mg
	Risperidal	Risperidone	2–6 mg
	Zyprexa	Olanzapine	10–20 mg

the question was not whether patients were on Thorazine but how much were they taking.

The widespread use of Thorazine and other low-potency neuroleptics was justified by their clinical effectiveness. In a classic experiment on their effectiveness, patients who were suffering from schizophrenia were randomly assigned to one of four conditions (Cole, Goldberg, & Davis, 1966; Cole, Goldberg, & Klerman, 1964). Patients in three of the conditions received one of three different neuroleptics (Thorazine, Mellaril, Prolixin), while patients in the fourth condition received a placebo. The patients' psychological functioning was assessed before treatment began and again 6 weeks later.

The results clearly indicated that the three neuroleptics were much more effective for reducing the symptoms of schizophrenia than was the placebo. In fact, as indicated in Figure 11.11, 75% of the patients who received neuroleptics were "much improved," compared to only 25% of the patients who received the placebo. Only 2% of the patients who received neuroleptics got worse, whereas almost 50% of the patients who received the placebo got worse.

It is important to recognize that the neuroleptics did more than just sedate the patients. While it is true that the patients who took the drugs became less hostile, less irritable, and less agitated—changes that could be interpreted as due to a tranquilizing effect of the drugs—it is also true that the patients who received the neuroleptics became more socially active, more coherent in their speech, less disoriented, and better able to take care of themselves, and they had fewer hallucinations and delusions. Obviously, the neuroleptics did a great deal more than simply sedate the patients.

Clearly, low-potency neuroleptics can be effective for treating schizophrenia, but they have a number of important limitations. Specifically, although they can reduce positive symptoms such as disturbed thought processes and hallucinations, *low-potency neuroleptics are ineffective for reducing negative symptoms,* such as poverty of thought and apathy. This ineffectiveness is due to the fact that these drugs reduce the high neurological activity that leads to positive symptoms (see the earlier discussion), but they have no effect on the structural problems in the brain and the low levels of neurological activity that cause negative symptoms. Finally, these neuroleptics can have a number of side effects, such as the involuntary muscle movements I described earlier.

FIGURE 11.11

Patients who took neuroleptics were more likely to improve and less likely to get worse than were patients who took placebos.

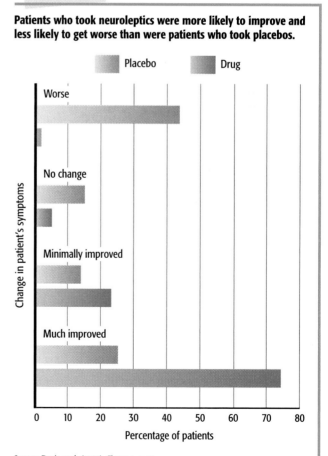

Source: Davis et al. (1980), Figure 1, p. 71.

High-Potency Neuroleptics. Encouraged by the effects of the low-potency drugs, chemists began working to develop drugs that would block more of the dopamine receptors, and in the 1970s a number of **high-potency neuroleptics** were developed. The best known of these drugs is **Haldol** (*haloperidol*). Whereas Thorazine blocks 80% of the dopamine receptors, Haldol blocks about 85% (Farde et al., 1988).

In experiments comparing the effects of Thorazine and Haldol, Haldol was found to be more effective for reducing the symptoms of schizophrenia and therefore became widely used. However, it was quickly discovered that the increased effectiveness of Haldol had a price—an increase in involuntary muscle movements. This is understandable because Haldol blocks more dopamine receptors, and the blocking of certain dopamine receptors leads to muscle problems. Today Haldol continues to be used with many patients, but the dosage levels are kept as low as possible and other drugs are prescribed to reduce the extrapyramidal symptoms. Finally, Haldol and the other high-potency neuroleptics have another limitation: Like the low-potency neuroleptics, *the high-potency neuroleptics do not reduce negative symptoms.* That leaves many patients with untreated symptoms.

Atypical Neuroleptics. The latest development in drug treatment revolves around a group of new drugs called **atypical neuroleptics.** These drugs are called *atypical* neuroleptics because they differ from other neuroleptics in three ways: First, atypical neuroleptics *block fewer dopamine receptors* than do the other neuroleptics. Indeed, whereas Haldol blocks 85% of the receptors, an atypical neuroleptic blocks only 65% (Farde et al., 1988). At first you might think that the lower blocking rate would make atypical neuroleptics less effective for treating schizophrenia, but before drawing this conclusion, consider the second difference.

The second difference is that atypical neuroleptics are *more selective in the sets of dopamine receptors they block.* Specifically, atypical neuroleptics block dopamine recep-

tors in the nerve tracts that lead to the frontal and temporal lobes, as do regular neuroleptics, but atypical neuroleptics block fewer of the dopamine receptors in the nerve tracts associated with muscle movements (Coward et al., 1989; Creese, 1985). This selectivity in blocking reduces the cognitive symptoms of schizophrenia without causing the muscle movement side effects that occur with other neuroleptics. The receptors in the nerve tracts that lead to the frontal and temporal lobes and are blocked by atypical neuroleptics are called **D-2 receptors,** whereas the receptors in the nerve tracts that lead to the muscle area and are not blocked by atypical neuroleptics are called D-1 receptors.

The third difference is that atypical neuroleptics *increase serotonin levels* (Kapur, Zipursky, & Remington, 1999). This can be important for two reasons: First, in some instances serotonin can inhibit dopamine activity (i.e., it serves as an inhibitory neurotransmitter); so by increasing serotonin levels atypical neuroleptics can help reduce the overactivity in the brain associated with dopamine. Second, because low levels of serotonin are related to depression (see Chapter 8), increasing serotonin levels can reduce the depression that often accompanies schizophrenia. Reducing the depression may also help with the negative symptoms of schizophrenia, such as apathy, which may be by-products of depression. With this as background the next question is, how good are the atypical neuroleptics?

The first atypical neuroleptic developed was **Clozaril** (*clozapine*), and it produced some surprising effects in the first major experiment in which it was tested (Kane et al., 1988, 1989). The experiment involved over 300 patients who were chronically ill with schizophrenia and had not responded to previous treatments. These patients were ultimately bound for long-term custodial care in a state hospital unless something dramatic could be done for them. The patients were randomly assigned to two conditions. In one condition the patients received Thorazine (a low-potency neuroleptic) plus medication to relieve the involuntary muscle movements that can be caused by the Thorazine. Patients in the other condition received Clozaril. The patients' symptoms were evaluated each week by raters who did not know which patients were taking which drug.

The results revealed three interesting findings: First, the patients who took Clozaril showed *greater reductions in positive symptoms* (e.g., hallucinations, delusions, thought disorder) than did the patients who took Thorazine. Second, somewhat surprisingly, the patients who took Clozaril also showed *greater reductions in negative symptoms* (e.g., flat mood, poverty of speech, disorientation). Third, the patients who took Clozaril showed *fewer involuntary muscle movements* than the patients who took Thorazine. This was the case despite the fact that the patients who were taking Thorazine were also taking medication to offset such side effects. The results concerning the reductions in positive and negative symptoms by Clozaril are summarized in Figure 11.12. Since that initial experiment was done, nu-

---

high-potency neuroleptics   Drugs such as Haldol that block relatively more dopamine receptors. (Contrast with *low-potency neuroleptics.*)

Haldol (haloperidol)   A widely used high-potency neuroleptic.

atypical neuroleptics   Drugs such as Clozaril that are used to treat schizophrenia and are more selective than other neuroleptics in the blocking of dopamine receptor sites and increase the level of serotonin at synapses.

D-2 receptors   Dopamine receptors in the nerve tracts leading to the higher areas of the brain, which are blocked by atypical neuroleptics.

Clozaril (clozapine)   The first atypical neuroleptic to be developed.

FIGURE 11.12

Clozaril is more effective than a low-potency neuroleptic for reducing both (a) positive and (b) negative symptoms of schizophrenia.

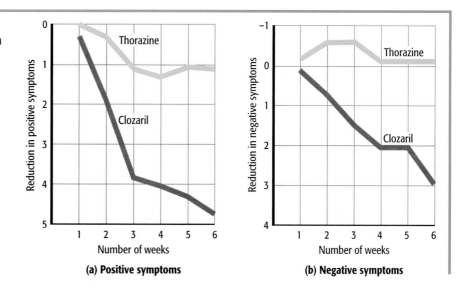

Source: Kane et al. (1988).

(a) Positive symptoms   **(b) Negative symptoms**

merous other investigators have reported similar results, and it appears that Clozaril provides a drug treatment for both positive and negative symptoms that is effective for otherwise hard-to-treat patients (see, for example, Breier et al., 1994; Honigfeld & Patin, 1990; Leppig et al., 1989; Lieberman et al., 1994; Lindstrom, 1989; Meltzer, Bastani, Ramirez, & Matsubara, 1989; Miller et al., 1994; Pickar et al., 1992; Rosenheck, Cramer, et al., 1997; Rosenheck, Dunn, et al.,1999; Soni et al., 1999; Wahlbeck et al., 1999).

Clozaril has two other beneficial effects: First, because it relieves negative symptoms such as apathy and poverty of thought, patients taking Clozaril are more likely to participate in psychological treatment than are patients taking other neuroleptics such as Haldol; by participating in psychological treatment, patients can further enhance their functioning (Rosenheck, Tekell, et al., 1998; see the later discussion of psychoeducation). Second, Clozaril can greatly reduce the rate of suicide attempts among patients with schizophrenia (Meltzer & Okayli, 1995). Specifically, when patients were switched from another neuroleptic to Clozaril, their rate of serious suicide attempts dropped from 6% to zero. This probably occurred because Clozaril reduced feelings of depression and hopelessness (negative symptoms), which often lead to suicide (see Chapter 9 for a discussion of suicide).

Clozaril was an important breakthrough, but there is a potentially serious problem associated with its use. Specifically, up to 2% of the individuals who take Clozaril experience a sudden drop in white blood cells (*leukocytes*). This can be very serious because white blood cells are essential for fighting infection, and if the level of these cells gets too low, an individual may die from infection. Fortunately, this problem can be eliminated within about 2 weeks by simply taking the patient off Clozaril. However, because of the

danger posed by a drop in white blood cells, patients taking Clozaril have to undergo frequent blood tests to assess their white blood cell levels, and this frequent testing adds greatly to the cost of treatment. The cost of treatment has been reduced recently but originally was about $9,000 per year, which put the drug beyond the means of many patients.

Since the introduction of Clozaril, two other atypical neuroleptics have become available: **Riseridal** (*resperidone*) and **Zyprexa** (*olanzapine*). Like Clozaril, these drugs are effective for reducing both positive and negative symptoms, and they have fewer side effects than regular neuroleptics (Beasley, Tollefson, & Tran, 1997; Sanger et al., 1999). In contrast to Clozaril, however, these new drugs do not cause a drop in white blood cells, and they tend to be less expensive (Beasley, 1997; Beasley et al., 1997; Borison et al., 1992; Breier et al., 1999; Kerwin, 1994; Land & Salzman, 1994; Marder & Meibach, 1994; Sanger et al., 1999). These newer atypical neuroleptics, along with others in the research pipeline, greatly increase our options and the effectiveness of drug treatment of schizophrenia. They are truly important developments that have brought substantial improvements in many patients.

Side Effects of Drug Therapy. We now come to the complex issue of the side effects of drug therapy for schizophrenia. Just as there is no denying that neuroleptics can reduce the symptoms of schizophrenia, so there is no denying that these drugs can induce a variety of side effects. In consider-

Riseridal (resperidone)   An atypical neuroleptic.
Zyprexa (olanzapine)   An atypical neuroleptic.

ing drug therapy, then, we must determine what the side effects are, whether they are serious and treatable, and whether they outweigh the benefits of the drugs.

There are two levels of side effects. At the relatively superficial level, patients who are taking neuroleptics often experience symptoms such as dryness of the mouth or excessive salivation, blurred vision, grogginess, constipation, sensitivity to light, reduced sexual arousal, weight gain, and awkward or slowed motor activity. These side effects can be annoying and sometimes embarrassing or disruptive, but they may also be acceptable tradeoffs for dramatic reductions in serious symptoms. For example, Betty, about whom you read earlier (see Case Study 10.3), has gained a considerable amount of weight and often drools because of excessive salivation, but she says she would rather be "fat and relatively free of symptoms than thin and crazy as a loon."

On a more serious level there can be side effects that are very dangerous and can have important long-term implications. Three of those side effects need attention here. First, the most common of the serious side effects involves *involuntary muscle movements,* which I have referred to earlier. The movements are most often associated with the mouth, lips, and tongue, and patients experience involuntary sucking, chewing, lateral jaw movements, smacking and pursing of the lips, thrusting and twisting of the tongue, and ticlike motions of the lips, eyes, and eyebrows. In some cases there are also involuntary movements of the arms and trunk, such as twisting of the body and shrugging of the shoulders. In other cases there can be an involuntary contraction of the diaphragm, which causes the patient to make a noise like a bark. These behaviors are not under voluntary control and go on continually while the patient is awake. This side effect is known as **tardive dyskinesia** (TAR-div dis-ki-NE-zhuh). With low-potency neuroleptics it may be some years before tardive dyskinesia sets in, but with high-potency neuroleptics minor symptoms may begin appearing within days or weeks (Sweet et al., 1995). Note that *tardive* means "late-developing" and reflects the fact that there is a delay between when the individual begins taking the drug and when the side effect begins. *Dys-* means "abnormal," and *kinesia* refers to body movements, so the term

tardive dyskinesia literally means "late-developing abnormal body movements."

Paradoxically, for some patients neuroleptics may be effective in treating schizophrenia but leave the patients acting even more abnormally. For example, when Betty was taking a high-potency neuroleptic, her head would occasionally snap back and her tongue would stick out. Furthermore, because tardive dyskinesia can interfere with speech, coordination, eating, and respiration, it can result in serious disabilities and even death.

There are drugs that can diminish tardive dyskinesia. However, in some cases once tardive dyskinesia is established, it is irreversible, suggesting that some permanent structural alterations of the brain have occurred. Because of this, when the symptoms begin to appear, it is generally advisable to immediately reduce the level of the drug.

A second serious side effect of neuroleptics is the *inability to sit still* (Sachdev & Kruk, 1994). For example, the individual may constantly move from place to place, rock back and forth, or swing a leg. This is called **akathisia** (ak-uh-THIZH-uh), a term that comes from a Greek word meaning "not to sit." Akathisia occurs in about 35% of the individuals who take neuroleptics, and it can be very disruptive because it interferes with other activities. (Note that akathisia can be a side effect of other psychiatric drugs such as Prozac; see Chapter 8 and Case Study 8.5.)

Finally, a relatively rare but very serious side effect is **malignant neuroleptic syndrome,** the symptoms of which include muscular rigidity, a very high temperature that can lead to brain damage, and fluctuating blood pressure that can cause strokes, confusion, agitation, and stupor or coma (Addonizio, 1991; Caroff et al., 1991; Keck, McElroy, & Pope, 1991; Pope et al., 1991). This side effect is more likely to occur with high-potency neuroleptics, is more common in women, and appears to be due to a sudden drop in dopamine activity that causes a general dysregulation of the hypothalamus and other control centers in the brain. Obviously, this is a very serious syndrome, but it occurs in fewer than 1% of the patients taking neuroleptics and can be treated effectively if it is diagnosed early.

It is important that patients be warned about side effects because if the symptoms are not recognized as side effects, they can be very frightening and contribute to the disorder. For example, changes in vision or in sensitivity to light could provide the bases for additional delusions, and an unexplained impairment in sexual performance could be upsetting. However, if these symptoms are initially explained as normal and expected side effects that can be compensated for or treated, their impact will be minimal, especially when compared to the benefits obtained by reduction of the symptoms of schizophrenia.

In summary, some patients are troubled by relatively minor side effects, whereas others suffer considerably from serious side effects. We must be careful not to ignore or grow insensitive to these problems. However, we must also

---

tardive dyskinesia A disorder that involves involuntary muscle movements and is often a side effect of neuroleptic drugs. (See *extrapyramidal symptoms.*)

akathisia A side effect of neuroleptics consisting of the inability to sit still.

malignant neuroleptic syndrome A disorder that involves muscular rigidity, high temperature, and problems with blood pressure, that can be a side effect of high-potency neuroleptics and that is due to a dysregulation of the control centers in the brain.

be cautious in responding to the demands of people who believe that drug therapy should be abandoned because of the side effects. It would be inappropriate to "throw the treatment out with the side effects." Doing so would increase the number of individuals who would have to be confined to hospitals or, more likely, would ultimately be left to wander the streets suffering from hallucinations, delusions, and other symptoms of schizophrenia. That is certainly not an attractive option.

Length of Drug Treatment. A question that always arises is, how long do individuals with schizophrenia have to take medication? Unfortunately, in many cases schizophrenia is a lifelong disorder, and therefore *many individuals will have to take medication for the rest of their lives.* This fact was made clear by the results of an investigation in which more than 4,000 patients were followed up after their neuroleptics either were or were not withdrawn (Gilbert et al., 1995; see also Robinson et al., 1999). The results indicated that within an average of 10 months, 53% of the patients who had their drugs withdrawn had a relapse, whereas only 16% of the patients for whom the drugs were maintained had a relapse. In other words, withdrawal of the drugs resulted in an increase of more than 35% in relapse rates. The relapse rates over a 2-year period are presented in Figure 11.13.

Actually, there is both bad news and good news in the findings linking drug withdrawal to relapse. The bad news is that many patients did relapse when the drugs were withdrawn, which means that many individuals will have to stay on the medication permanently. The good news is that *more than 45% of the patients did not relapse.* This means that after an initial period of treatment, some individuals can go off the drugs without dire consequences (Carpenter & Tamminga, 1995; Greden & Tandon, 1995; Jeste, Gilbert, McAdams, & Harris, 1995; Meltzer, 1995a).

Level of Drug Treatment. Even if it is not possible to withdraw the drug, it may be possible to reduce the dosage level of the drug once the symptoms have been stabilized. In one study of patients who were taking high doses of Haldol, investigators found that for the average patient it was possible to reduce the dosage level by over 60% before the patients' symptoms began to get noticeably worse (Liberman et al., 1994). In fact, some patients even showed *improvements* when the dosage levels were reduced, an effect that can probably be attributed to to the fact that at high levels the drug was sedating these patients, causing a flat mood and slowed thought processes, which had been misinterpreted as symptoms of the disorder.

Of course, if the dosage level is reduced and the symptoms get worse, the dosage level can be increased to head off a complete relapse. Indeed, in one experiment patients were given small "supplements" in dosage levels when their relatives reported the onset of minor symptoms such as trouble concentrating, withdrawal, and depression, and

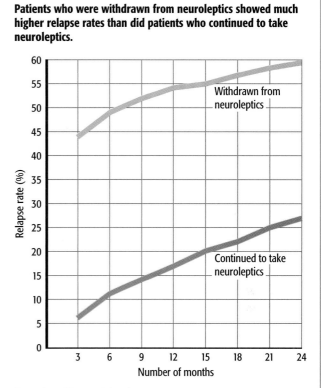

FIGURE 11.13

Patients who were withdrawn from neuroleptics showed much higher relapse rates than did patients who continued to take neuroleptics.

Source: Jeste, Gilbert, et al. (1995), p. 210.

these supplements were effective for reducing relapse rates (Marder et al., 1994).

With regard to dosage levels, it is interesting to note that *women often require lower levels of neuroleptics than do men* (Baldessarini, Kando, & Centorrino, 1995; Szymanski et al., 1995; Yonker et al., 1992). Indeed, in many cases women require only about half as much medication as men to achieve the same therapeutic effects. We do not know exactly why that is the case, but it is not due to differences in body size because the difference in response is found even when women and men of comparable size are studied.

In general, the best overall strategy seems to be to start out using whatever dosage level of the drug is necessary to get the symptoms under control and then to slowly reduce the level. If the symptoms do not get worse, further reductions can be tried, and it may even be possible to withdraw the drug completely. However, if the symptoms get worse, the dose can be increased until the symptoms are again under control. The point is that we must continually test to find the lowest level at which the drug is effective. Of course, the frequent testing of the lower dosage limit requires more attention to the patient than the set-it-and-leave-it approach, but that attention is an important part of effective, humane treatment.

Two last points should be made before concluding this discussion: First, at present we do not have any way to determine which drug will be most effective for a particular patient, so in many cases we must resort to trial and error to find the best drug. The second point is that often the treatment of schizophrenia involves other drugs in addition to neuroleptics. Antidepressants are often necessary because 60% of individuals with schizophrenia also suffer from serious depression and the depression may provide the basis for some of the negative symptoms (Zullino et al., 1998). There is also evidence that antianxiety medication such as Valium (see Chapter 5) may help because it can reduce the effects of stress that can trigger or exacerbate the symptoms of schizophrenia (Carpenter et al., 1999).

Overall, then, it is clear that drugs can be effective for treating schizophrenia, but it is also clear that often drugs are not enough. Therefore, in the following sections I will describe a number of psychological treatments that fill in some of the gaps left by drug treatment.

Cognitive Treatment: Psychoeducation

Although the primary cause of schizophrenia is a malfunction of the brain, the symptoms can be brought on or made worse by psychological stress (see the earlier discussion). Specifically, it appears that stress leads to an increase in neurological activity, which then triggers symptoms. To avoid this individuals with schizophrenia need to learn strategies for avoiding or reducing stress; therefore, programs that involve **psychoeducation** or **social skills training** have been developed (Kopelowicz & Liberman, 1998).

In general, psychoeducation programs consist of three elements (Halford & Hayes, 1991). The first involves *educating the patient and the family* so that they better *understand the disorder*. For example, the patient and the family are taught that schizophrenia, like other disorders such as diabetes and epilepsy, is due to biochemical problems in the brain. In other words, the individual isn't "crazy"—he or she has a neurological disorder. This "normalizes" schizophrenia and makes it less frightening so that everyone can deal with it more realistically.

The second element involves teaching the patient and the family how to *reduce the stress that can lead to symptoms.* Specifically, the individuals and their families are taught strategies for "cooling" the emotional climate in which the individual lives. This may involve placing fewer demands on the individual, being less critical when he or she does not measure up to expectations, and creating a physical environment that is quieter and less brightly lit so as to minimize stimulus overload. After all, because of the disorder the individual may be working under a distinct handicap, so some accommodations must be made. Making many of these accommodations is similar to what is done for individuals with other illnesses or disabilities.

The third goal in this approach is to teach the individual strategies for *coping with the symptoms.* In many cases the drugs do not eliminate all of the symptoms, and therefore it is essential for the individual to learn to cope with the remaining symptoms. Learning to cope with symptoms is not unique to schizophrenia; indeed, individuals with disorders such as diabetes and epilepsy must also learn ways of coping with their symptoms. Coping can take many forms and often requires help from others. For example, Betty (Case Study 10.3) calls me for a "reality check" when she is not sure about what is real and what is a hallucination. In other cases the individual must learn how to avoid stressful interpersonal confrontations. It may also be helpful if an individual learns to avoid overly stimulating physical environments. For example, it would be disastrous for an individual suffering from stimulus overload to attend a rock concert; in some cases even attending a noisy party could be difficult.

The goal of psychoeducation is not to treat the schizophrenia per se but rather to help the individual and the family alter the factors that provoke the underlying processes that lead to the symptoms. In other words, with this approach we attempt to take the stress component out of the diathesis-stress combination and thereby reduce the likelihood of igniting or exacerbating symptoms.

This approach has been shown to be very effective. For example, in one experiment patients were assigned to one of four conditions: (1) drugs only, (2) drugs plus patient social skills training, (3) drugs plus family psychoeducation, or (4) drugs plus patient social skills training and family psychoeducation (Hogarty et al., 1986, 1991; Hogarty, Greenwald, et al., 1997; Hogarty, Kornblith, et al., 1997). All of the patients were returning to family environments that could be characterized as highly emotional, and therefore these patients were at high risk for relapse. The results indicated that 1 year after discharge from the hospital the relapse rates in the conditions were as follows: (1) drugs only, 38%; (2) drugs plus patient social skills training, 20%; (3) drugs plus family psychoeducation, 19%; and (4) drugs plus patient social skills training and family psychoeducation, 0%. These results are summarized in Figure 11.14.

In other research it was found that when both patients and their families received psychoeducation or social skills training, the patients showed fewer symptoms, were less likely to relapse, were more than 12 times less likely to be sent back to a hospital for treatment, and required less medication than other patients; see Figure 11.15 (Falloon et al., 1985; Goldstein, 1980; McFarlane et al., 1995). The fact

---

psychoeducation   A strategy often used in treating schizophrenia, in which the patient and the patient's family are taught about the disorder and how to cope with it.

social skills training   Training designed to help individuals with schizophrenia reduce stress, particularly by managing interpersonal relationships.

Teaching problem-solving skills to patients and their families is more effective for preventing relapse than teaching such skills to patients alone.

that patients did so much better despite having their levels of medication reduced is particularly impressive.

Another important advantage of the psychoeducation approach is that it is relatively inexpensive. The individuals who provide the education and the continuing support need not be expensive mental health professionals such as psychiatrists and psychologists. Indeed, in the city in which I live, psychoeducation is provided by case managers. In some cases the work of the case managers is backed up by volunteers from the community, such as college students, who meet with patients for a couple of hours each week to go for walks, lunch, or coffee. Spending time with normal people provides the patients with role models for appropriate social behavior. Clearly, the psychoeducation and social skills training approach is effective for reducing symptoms and is cost-effective. Case Study 11.3 (on p. 336) focuses on a psychologist who has struggled successfully with his own schizophrenia for over 20 years; he explains how support from others helps him function effectively.

FIGURE 11.14

Patient social skills training and drugs plus family psychoeducation are effective for reducing relapse rates.

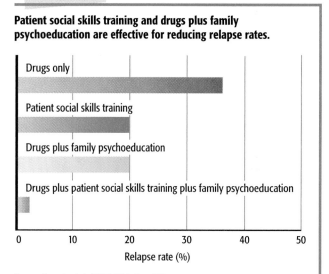

Source: Hogarty et al. (1991), Table 1, p. 342.

FIGURE 11.15

Family management designed to reduce stress was more effective than individual management for reducing the symptoms of schizophrenia.

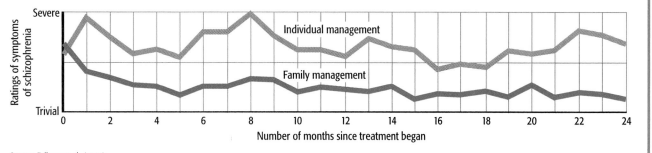

Source: Falloon et al. (1985).

A Psychologist with Schizophrenia Talks about What Helps Him Function Effectively

CASE STUDY 11.3

FREDRICK J. FRESE III is a psychologist who has struggled with schizophrenia for over 20 years. In Case Study 10.5 he described the onset of his symptoms and talked about his occasional "breakdowns." Here he describes some of the things that help him function with his disorder.

"Persons with schizophrenia need to study carefully how they function. Until they can identify their deficits, it is very difficult to start building compensatory mechanisms that will enable them to function better. . . . Persons recovering from schizophrenia should be able to identify, and be on the lookout for, the sorts of persons, places, and things that can cause the type of stress that may precipitate their breakdowns. They should know how to get to environments that are helpful.

> **Persons with schizophrenia need to study carefully how they function.**

"Just as a diabetic must take action to control his or her blood sugar level, persons recovering from schizophrenia must learn to monitor and take measures to counteract an imbalance in subcortical neurochemical activity. But unlike diabetes, schizophrenia seriously interferes with rational processes, and once the irrationality begins, the person may have great difficulty acting in a rational or responsible manner.

"Because of our disability, it is very difficult for us to know what we do that normals do not understand. Therefore, it is very helpful to have a trustworthy normal person around to let us know what it is about our thoughts that perhaps it would be better not to share with everyone else. In my case my wife constantly gives me feedback whenever I am saying or doing things that normal people may consider bizarre or offensive. Some things are rather obvious. If you are hearing voices, it is generally best not to talk back to them while normals are around. If your thoughts are dominated by the importance of the colors or similar sounds in the environment, you probably do not want to reveal too much about this to others.

"With help, other disabled persons learn to compensate for their disabilities and frequently lead dignified, productive lives. The blind learn to use canes and Seeing Eye dogs; people with limited use of their legs learn to use crutches and wheelchairs. For the mentally ill, however, the parameters of our disability are often not easily defined. We need help and feedback so that we can understand exactly the nature of our disability.

"Unfortunately, feedback is not always enough. Sometimes the symptoms overwhelm the person, who then loses the ability to function. When that occurs, some flexibility on the part of other people in the environment is necessary.

"Schizophrenia tends to be an episodic disorder. We are going to have periodic breakdowns. This makes holding employment very difficult because the usual practice is to terminate employees who require frequent periods of leave. Work for us should be structured so that our disabilities are taken into account. Many of us are well educated or have useful skills when we are not having episodes. Why can't jobs be structured for us so that our episodic breakdowns do not automatically result in our loss of employment? Like the general population, we like and need to work, but the world of the chronically well needs to be a little more flexible in understanding that we are going to behave strangely from time to time and there are going to be times when we do not function well at all."

Learning Treatment: Behavior Therapy

Earlier I pointed out that learning theorists believe that individuals with schizophrenia sometimes behave strangely because their behaviors lead to rewards such as attention from others. Based on that assumption, the learning theory approach to treatment involves decreasing rewards for abnormal behaviors and increasing rewards for normal behaviors. Because the focus of the treatment is on *behaviors* rather than on unseen underlying causes, this approach is usually referred to as **behavior therapy** (see Chapter 2). Case Study 11.4 illustrates the use of this approach.

Numerous experiments have demonstrated that many of the symptoms of schizophrenia can be brought under control by manipulating the rewards and punishments that are associated with the symptoms. In those experiments patients were usually given tokens (poker chips) when they behaved appropriately, and the tokens could later be used to buy desired rewards, such as hospital passes, better living conditions, better food, and TV time. In other words, the tokens were used like money, and therefore this approach is often referred to as the **token economy approach** to treatment.

One of the most impressive tests of the token economy approach involved chronic mental patients who were assigned either to a ward on which a token economy approach was used or to a more typical ward (Paul & Lentz, 1977). When patients on either ward behaved appropriately, they were rewarded with positive statements and encouragement. However, the important difference be-

Treatment of Bizarre Symptoms with Techniques Based on Learning

CASE STUDY **11.4**

THE PATIENT WAS a 47-year-old woman who had been hospitalized for 9 years and was diagnosed as suffering from chronic schizophrenia. She had a wide variety of symptoms, but three of them were particularly troublesome. The first was her continual stealing of food and overeating. She always ate everything on her tray and then stole food from the counter and from other patients. Because of her excessive eating, she weighed over 250 pounds, and this was posing a risk to her physical health. Her second troublesome symptom was hoarding hospital towels in her room. Despite the fact that the nurses kept retrieving them, the patient often had as many as 30 towels. The third and most extreme symptom was wearing excessive amounts of clothing. At any one time she might wear six dresses, several pairs of underwear, two dozen pairs of stockings, two or three sweaters, and a shawl or two. In addition, she often draped herself in sheets and wrapped a couple of towels around her head in a turbanlike headdress. These behaviors had persisted for a number of years, and various attempts to change them (therapy, pleading) had been ineffective. Finally, it was decided to try a learning theory approach to treating the symptoms.

The patient's food stealing was treated by punishment (withdrawal of food). Nurses simply removed her from the dining room as soon as she picked up unauthorized food, so she missed a meal whenever she stole food. Within 2 weeks, the patient's food stealing was eliminated, and she ate only the diet prescribed for her. Her weight dropped to 180 pounds in 14 months, a 28% loss.

The hoarding of hospital towels was treated with satiation. Rather than restricting the number of towels the patient had, the staff began giving her more towels. The notion was that if she had more towels than she wanted, the value of the towels would be reduced, and consequently the hoarding would be reduced. (This is like letting workers in a candy factory eat all they want; soon they do not want any more, and they stop eating the product.) At first, when a nurse came into her room with a towel, the patient said, "Oh, you found it for me, thank you." As the number of towels increased rapidly in the second week, the patient responded by saying, "Don't give me no more towels. I've got enough." By the third week of the treatment period, she was being given as many as 60 towels a day, and she said, "Take them towels away. . . . I can't sit here all night and fold towels." Soon her room was overflowing with towels, and in the sixth week, she complained to a nurse, "I can't drag any more of these towels, I just can't do it." When the number of towels in the patient's room reached 625, she started taking towels out of the room, so the staff stopped giving them to her. The patient had apparently had it with towels, and for the next 12 months, the average number of towels found in her room was 1.5 per week.

The patient's wearing of excessive amounts of clothing was treated by punishing overdressing and rewarding reduced dressing. Before each meal the patient was required to get on a scale, and if she exceeded a predetermined weight (her body weight plus a specified number of pounds for clothing), she was simply told, "Sorry, you weigh too much; you'll have to weigh less," and she was not allowed in the dining room for that meal (punishment). The patient quickly learned that if she took some of her clothes off, she could meet the weight requirement and thereby get to eat (reward). Originally she was allowed 23 pounds for clothes, but that was gradually reduced. Within a short period of time, the weight of her clothing dropped from 23 to 3 pounds, and she was dressing normally.

It should be noted that the patient responded with some anger when she was first denied food as part of the treatment for her food stealing and overdressing. When that behavior was not rewarded (it was ignored), it disappeared, and no other inappropriate behaviors were introduced. Finally, it is interesting to note that as the patient's behaviors became less bizarre, patients and staff began interacting with her more, and she began to participate somewhat more actively in social functions.

Source: Adapted from Ayllon (1963).

> . . . as the patient's behaviors became less bizarre, patients and staff began interacting with her more. . . .

---

tween the two wards was that patients on the token economy ward were systematically rewarded with tokens for good behavior, whereas those on the other ward were not. For example, if a patient did a good job of cleaning his room, an attendant would say something like "You did a really good job smoothing the sheets and putting things away this morning, George; here is a token for keeping your room in order." When the patients did not behave well,

behavior therapy An approach to treating schizophrenia in which rewards and punishments are used to change inappropriate behaviors.

token economy approach A treatment approach in which patients with schizophrenia are given tokens for appropriate behaviors, which they can use to buy desired things or privileges.

their poor behavior was pointed out, and they were told that a token was being withheld—for example, "You're not going to get a token this morning because your hair is a mess." The tokens were then used like money to buy meals, rent better sleeping quarters (a four-bed dormitory room cost 10 tokens per week; a furnished one-bed room cost 22 tokens), obtain passes to leave the hospital, purchase time to watch television, buy privileges such as staying up late, and get other miscellaneous things such as use of the phone, laundry service, a haircut, or extra baths.

Two positive findings and two negative findings emerged from this investigation. On the positive side the token economy approach was effective for improving *general behavior,* such as cooperation, social activity, housekeeping, grooming, care of belongings, and appropriate mealtime behaviors. The improvement in interpersonal skills is illustrated in Figure 11.16. Also on the positive side the token economy approach was effective for reducing *disorganized and bizarre motor behaviors,* such as constant rocking, repetitive movements, and blank staring. On the negative side, however, the token economy approach was ineffective for reducing *disorganized and bizarre cognitive behaviors,* such as incoherent speech, hallucinations, and delusions. Nor was it effective for reducing *inappropriate emotional behaviors,* such as aggression, screaming, and cursing.

This pattern of findings indicates that the use of rewards was effective for improving *overt behaviors,* but it was not effective for improving *cognitive processes or emotional responses.* Whether or not behaviors can be influenced by rewards is apparently due to whether or not they are under the voluntary control of the individual; for example, overt motor behaviors are under voluntary control, whereas cognitive processes are not.

The fact that the use of rewards is not effective for controlling the cognitive symptoms of schizophrenia limits the usefulness of this approach. However, despite that limitation it is important to note that more patients from the token economy ward were released from the hospital (96%

vs. 68%) and that more of those patients were able to live independently and support themselves (11% vs. 7%) as opposed to requiring some form of continuing community care. In other words, the token economy approach led to improved behaviors, and the improvements in behaviors were crucial in getting the patients out of the hospital and functioning effectively. To sum up, the token economy approach was not effective for reducing all of the symptoms, but it did reduce some that were important in terms of daily functioning.

Psychodynamic Treatment: Psychotherapy

Finally, we come to the question of whether traditional psychotherapy is effective for treating schizophrenia. A great deal of research has been focused on this question, but as you will see, the results have been very discouraging. For example, in an early classic experiment it was found that the addition of psychotherapy to the usual hospital care did not improve the release rate, length of hospital stay, nurses' assessment of outcome, therapists' assessment of outcome, or patients' intellectual functioning (May, 1968). Furthermore, it was found that the combination of psychotherapy and drug therapy was not more effective than drug therapy alone. In short, the results indicated that psychotherapy did not add to what could be achieved by routine hospital care and drugs.

However, advocates of psychotherapy argued that the results of the early research were limited because the patients were not treated long enough, the therapists were not sufficiently trained, or the treatment programs were not intense enough. Therefore, an investigation was conducted in which a group of 20 patients with chronic schizophrenia were given essentially the best of everything for 2 years (Grinspoon, Ewalt, & Shader, 1968, 1972). The patients lived in a special ward that was designed to provide them with a therapeutically ideal environment. For example, in addition to excellent physical facilities, there was a nursing staff of 25, an occupational therapist, and a social worker. Psychotherapy was provided by senior psychiatrists chosen from among the best in the Boston area. In addition, the patients were involved in an intensive program that included ward meetings, occupational therapy, and frequent outings to the beach, museums, and sports events. If it were available today, such treatment would easily cost in excess of $200,000 per year per patient. Unfortunately, despite the herculean effort at intervention, there was no evidence that the patients showed any improvement over the 2 years of treatment. The fact that the patients did not improve with psychotherapy cannot be attributed to the fact that they were "untreatable" because when they were switched to drug treatment, they improved almost immediately.

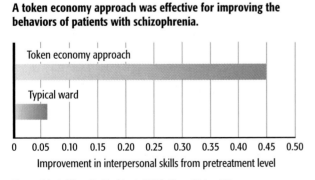

FIGURE 11.16

A token economy approach was effective for improving the behaviors of patients with schizophrenia.

Token economy approach

Typical ward

0 0.05 0.10 0.15 0.20 0.25 0.30 0.35 0.40 0.45 0.50

Improvement in interpersonal skills from pretreatment level

Source: Adapted from Paul and Lentz (1977), Figure 29.4, p. 317.

Overall, then, the well-controlled research has not provided any evidence that traditional psychotherapy is effective for treating schizophrenia, regardless of the outcome measure used (Kopelowicz & Liberman, 1998). Therefore, we must conclude that psychotherapy is not a useful treatment for schizophrenia.

Before concluding our discussion of the treatment of schizophrenia, let's return to Betty about whom I have spoken often in this and the preceding chapter. In Case Study 11.5 Betty describes the treatments she has received over the years, which include psychotherapy, vitamin therapy, shock therapy, atypical neuroleptics, and psychoeducation.

Betty's Therapy—Drugs and More

CASE STUDY **11.5**

CASE STUDY 10.3 focused on my friend Betty, who suffers from a severe case of schizophrenia. Betty has numerous symptoms, in-cluding hallucinations that monks are chanting "Cut yourself and die" and that people dissolve into blobs of blood. Betty has been hospitalized numerous times, but here we will focus on the types of treatment Betty has received over the past 20 years rather than on the experience of hospitalization.

David: Would you tell me what type of therapy you tried first?

Betty: Well, I was living in New York City when I had my first break, and not knowing anything about mental illness at the time, I went to see a psychoanalyst. That was a big and costly mistake. We spent hours talking about things that had nothing to do with any of my symptoms. He just didn't understand. He would ask me about my toilet training, and I would try to talk about that while I was hallucinating his plants marching around the room. It was crazy. I saw him for several years, but we got nowhere. I should have been hospitalized.

David: After analysis where did you go?

Betty: Next was megavitamins; that was hot then. I took 40 different vitamins a day. I carried them around with me in a box along with little cups for water and small bits of food to take with the vitamins. At first I felt better, but it didn't last. I don't really think the vitamins helped; I think I just happened to be going through a period in which the symptoms were less intense. When I started becoming ill again, the vitamins did nothing. Finally I just crashed.

David: OK, the vitamins didn't work. What was next?

Betty: When I crashed, the doctor gave me CO_2 therapy. I'd never heard of it before, but he seemed to think it would help. First, they give you some anticonvulsion medication, and you lay on a table with a mask over your face. You're breathing, but there's no oxygen. You breathe harder and harder, but you can't get your breath, and then all of a sudden, bang, and you're out—unconscious. Oh God, it's terrible; it's like drowning. And while you're out, you are supposed to have these good dreams, but my dreams were hideous. God, they were terrible. I don't know how all of this was supposed to help me, but it didn't. I had the treatment once a week for about a year, and it did nothing. In fact, I got worse.

David: All right, CO_2 therapy didn't work. What did you try next?

Betty: Well, for a while I was on and off a lot of different drugs, mostly antidepressants, but they weren't working, so I went into the hospital for shock therapy, ECT.

David: Did it help?

Betty: When I first woke up—for a few hours after a treatment—I guess I felt a little better, but not much. I wasn't as depressed, but the shocks didn't stop my hallucinations or delusions. My doctors didn't want to give up on shocks, though, so they kept giving me more. They were desperate to find something that would work. After I left the hospital, I kept getting the shocks on an outpatient basis. Three times a week, Mom and I would drive to the hospital in the morning so I could get my shocks. But there really wasn't much improvement—even after about 30 shocks.

David: Well, what was next?

Betty: Then I changed doctors, to a specialist in drugs. He tried a lot of drugs; I was always changing drugs, trying to find the right one or the right combination.

David: Thorazine? Any help from Thorazine?

Betty: Made me drowsy, but didn't stop the symptoms —I was just drugged.

David: Haldol?

Betty: I had the best response to that, although even that wasn't much. Actually, on Haldol I felt so drugged that I didn't care if I was hallucinating.

David: Side effects? Tardive dyskinesia?

Betty: Off and on. I had a lot of facial twitches—my mouth jerked—and I rocked up and back all the time. That drove my mother nuts! For a while I had really bad side effects. I remember that my head would suddenly jerk back, my eyes would roll up, and my tongue would stick out. That was frightening. When that happened, we reduced the dose level, and I started taking more drugs to counteract the side effects. . . . I don't know if this is a typical reaction to taking a lot of drugs, but I just felt like my world was coming apart inside me—coming and going—all very strange. I took Haldol, Stelazine, all of the tricyclics, and all of the MAO inhibitors. I took everything in every combination. Then we tried Clozaril.

David: Tell me about the Clozaril.

Betty: When it first became available, my doctor thought I would be a good candidate. It was very expensive, but I was getting worse and they were getting ready to admit me to the state hospital. I couldn't afford Clozaril, so we went to court to sue Medicaid to pay for it. It was a class-action suit so other patients could get it too. The argument was, it's expensive, but less expensive than going in the hospi-

(continued)

Case Study 11.5 *(cont.)*

tal—which was the direction I was headed. We won, so I could get the drug.

David: Did the Clozaril help?

Betty: Well, first they had to put me in the hospital while I changed drugs. Every 2 weeks they would reduce my other medication and up the level of the Clozaril a little. And when I finally got off the Haldol and onto the Clozaril, I felt really good—almost back to normal. I was feeling like normal people do, and I was thrilled. I was doing so well that when I came back home, the public television station did a special report on me and the effects of the Clozaril. Being on Clozaril was like the patients in the movie *Awakenings:* I was back, I was normal, and it was wonderful! I was really doing great for a few months—(*long pause*)—and then, bam, they were back.

David: "They?"

Betty: The demons, the voices, the monks chanting, the fears about the police—everything. All the symptoms came back. It was terrible, so depressing. But I would never put Clozaril down because it helped a lot for a while, and things are better now than they could be. I'm on the highest dose possible, 900 milligrams a day! I'm just very drug-resistant.

David: You think the Clozaril is helping. Are you having any side effects?

Betty: The weight gain is the worst; I gained more than 20 pounds. I'm becoming a blimp, but I'd rather be fat than mentally ill. Oh, and sometimes the Clozaril makes me drool, but that's not a big deal.

> . . . in most cases, the drugs are not enough.

David: Are you on any other drugs?

Betty: A lot. Zoloft for depression—two 100-milligram tablets twice a day. Klonopin, an antianxiety medication—four 2-milligram tablets at bedtime. That helps me sleep. Next is chloral hydrate. That's a classic old sleeping medication, and I take one before going to bed. Oxybutynin—that is for my bladder problem. The medication makes me incontinent, and this takes care of that. Oh, yes, I also take Ativan for anxiety.

David: That's a lot of medication, but you still have the serious symptoms. How do you handle what can't be controlled with the drugs?

Betty: What people have to understand is that schizophrenia is a physical disease—a problem with the brain—so it has to be treated with drugs. Unfortunately, in most cases the drugs are not enough. People with schizophrenia have to cope with a lot of problems—symptoms that can't be completely controlled with the drugs and problems in daily living that are caused by the symptoms. For those other problems we need social support.

David: Where do you get that social support?

Betty: Well, my case manager is important. She checks with me regularly and helps with all kinds of problems, like taking care of all of the Medicaid forms and things like that. Then I have some very good friends who are also patients. We can support each other because we know what the other person is going through. We can be frank with each other. We know what the symptoms are, so we understand. It makes you feel less

alone. Other patients are important, but it is also very important to have friends who are not sick. The problem is, it is hard to make those connections; we get stuck in a psychiatric clique, a psychiatric ghetto. You have to make contacts in the real world, but that's hard. It's like trying to make integration work. One of the most important things for me is to have someone to call when I get really sick—someone to call when I am depressed or bothered by a delusion and need reassurance. That's when I call you, like last week when I was hallucinating voices from the drain and outside my window that were so real—I called you for reassurance that it was a hallucination. Those "reality checks" and support are important because the drugs can't do it all.

In a recent note to me, Betty summed up the importance of contact with others, and she gave me permission to print part of that note here.

Thank you for talking with me yesterday. I don't understand quite what was wrong, but things weren't adding up. You were most helpful in making things more cohesive for me. Thank you. I usually handle things better when I can identify the source. Most of the time my logic is random. Some things get processed, and others are like black holes. I guess I should be grateful for what I have. I am so much better than when I was on the Haldol. I am slowly coming to accept myself as something more than a broken doll. You have been wonderful to me. You gave me stature and took me seriously. *You saw me as something besides illness.* You have no idea what a gift you gave to me.

THINKING CRITICALLY

Questions about the Treatment of Schizophrenia

1. *Can schizophrenia be treated?* That is not a simple question to answer, but it will be helpful in formulating an answer if we distinguish between our ability to treat positive symptoms and our ability to treat negative symptoms.

With regard to the positive symptoms, there is no doubt that in many cases neuroleptics can reduce hallucinations, delusions, and the disorganization of thoughts. In some cases the drugs are effective for eliminating these symptoms, whereas in other cases, such as Betty's, the drugs only reduce the symptoms. Furthermore, psychoeducation, social skills training, and antianxiety drugs can help in reducing stress for the patient, which then further reduces arousal and positive symptoms. Clearly, although we cannot cure the positive symptoms, we have certainly made important progress in developing treatments for them.

The conclusions concerning the negative symptoms are less clear and less optimistic. On the one hand, the atypical neuroleptics are effective for eliminating or reducing some of these symptoms. That is the case because the negative symptoms are often the result of depression, and atypical neuroleptics increase serotonin levels, which decreases depression. In that regard it is noteworthy that antidepressants also reduce some negative symptoms. On the other hand, however, we seem unable to treat some of the negative symptoms of schizophrenia. That failure occurs because some of these symptoms are due to structural problems in the brain that cannot be changed with drugs. For example, drugs cannot bring back to life neurons that have died (cortical and subcortical atrophy). Similarly, drugs cannot reverse the structural problems in the brain that are the result of the failure of neural migration or the fact that dominance did not shift from the right to the left hemisphere. It is questionable whether the negative symptoms due to brain damage will ever be treatable. However, some of the behavioral problems that tend to occur with the negative symptoms, such as withdrawal and a lack of personal grooming, can be overcome with strategies such as the token economy approach. That is, the underlying problems and symptoms cannot be treated, but some of the inappropriate behaviors can be corrected. Overall, we've come a long way in the treatment of schizophrenia, and as new drugs become available, we are moving even further ahead.

The current and future outlook for many individuals with schizophrenia is becoming increasingly positive.

2. *What about the costs of treating schizophrenia?* There is no doubt that the newer atypical neuroleptics are effective for treating schizophrenia, but there is also no doubt that they can be very expensive, costing $5,000 to $6,000 per year. The cost of the drugs is high, but the cost of alternative treatment is even higher. Indeed, without the drugs individuals would have to be returned to hospitals at a cost of hundreds of thousands of dollars per year!

Because the original cost of Clozaril was high, it was not initially covered by the U.S. government's Medicaid insurance program; therefore, many patients who needed the drug could not get it. (Note that many patients who suffer from schizophrenia are not able to support themselves completely and therefore are dependent on governmental support programs such as Medicaid.) To change the government's policy, my friend Betty filed a class action lawsuit. Betty and her attorney made two points. First, they pointed out that the cost of Clozaril was less than the cost of hospitalization, so providing Clozaril would actually result in a saving. Second, they argued that it was discriminatory for the government to pay $50,000 a year for kidney dialysis for individuals with kidney disease but not to pay $9,000 a year for Clozaril for individuals with schizophrenia. They won the case, and the government now underwrites some of the cost of the drugs used to treat schizophrenia.

Summary

Topic I: Cognitive Explanations for Schizophrenia

▶ Psychodynamic theorists suggested that schizophrenia is due to problems with child-rearing, but there is no evidence for that explanation.

▶ Psychodynamic theorists also proposed that stress leads to schizophrenia, and there is evidence that stress can trigger the onset of symptoms or relapses. However, stress does not lead to schizophrenia in everyone, thus suggesting that it must work along with a physiological predisposition to trigger the disorder. Also, some individuals develop schizophrenia in the absence of stress, thus suggesting that stress is not always necessary for the disorder to develop.

▶ Learning theorists suggested that in some cases the symptoms of schizophrenia are learned because they lead to rewards or reduce unpleasantness. For example, individuals may use symptoms to get attention.

▶ Learning theorists also proposed that schizophrenia develops from labels, roles, and expectations. Specifically,

if individuals are labeled as "schizophrenic," they may feel more free to behave inappropriately, and we may misinterpret normal behaviors as symptoms (e.g., we may see daydreaming as hallucinating).

▶ Cognitive theorists explained hallucinations by suggesting that individuals with schizophrenia have sensory experiences that other people do not have and that those experiences are interpreted as hallucinations. Furthermore, delusions develop because the individuals have to explain their unique sensory experiences.

▶ Cognitive theorists attributed the intellectual decline that occurs in schizophrenia to distraction and the language problems to associative intrusions (a form of distraction).

Topic II: Physiological Explanations for Schizophrenia

▶ The first physiological explanation for schizophrenia is that high levels of dopamine activity in the brain lead to high levels of neurological activity, which disrupt thought processes and stimulate hallucinations (positive symptoms). Evidence for the role of dopamine comes from the findings that (1) decreasing dopamine activity reduces symptoms, (2) increasing dopamine activity increases symptoms, and (3) a high level of dopamine receptors is related to symptoms.

▷ Low levels of serotonin also contribute to positive symptoms because serotonin serves to inhibit the activity of dopamine. It can also lead to the depression seen in schizophrenia, and that depression may contribute to negative symptoms.

▷ High levels of activity in the prefrontal cortex disrupt thought processes, and high levels of activity in the temporal cortex can stimulate hallucinations.

▷ The second physiological explanation is that the brain does not develop normally or deteriorates faster than normal, leading to primarily negative symptoms. Specific brain problems include (1) reversed hemispheric dominance, (2) failure of neural migration, (3) cortical atrophy, and (4) subcortical atrophy. Cortical atrophy is most important in the prefrontal cortex and the temporal cortex. Important sites for subcortical atrophy are the hippocampus, the thalamus, and the amygdala. Low levels of brain activity also contribute to negative symptoms.

▷ Genetic factors play a role in schizophrenia. Evidence comes from studies of families, twins, and adoptees. Furthermore, biological relatives of individuals with schizophrenia have brain characteristics and behaviors that are like those seen in schizophrenia but less severe. However, genetic factors account for only about 10% of the cases of schizophrenia.

▷ Prenatal factors, such as a mother's illness during pregnancy, also contribute to schizophrenia. Similarly, perinatal complications, such as problems during the birth process, can also lead to schizophrenia later in life. Prenatal and perinatal factors disrupt brain development, which then leads to schizophrenia.

▷ The differences in symptom patterns between women and men appear to be due to more problems with brain structures in men and the protective effects of estrogens in women.

▷ The diathesis-stress explanation suggests that psychological stress can trigger the symptoms of schizophrenia in individuals who have a physiological predisposition to the disorder.

▷ The strengths of the physiological approach are that it is based on sound scientific research, it can account for both positive and negative symptoms, and it leads to effective treatments. Physiology does not yet provide a specific explanation of delusions.

Topic III: Treatment of Schizophrenia

▷ Psychosurgery was an early treatment for schizophrenia. Two often-used operations were the prefrontal lobotomy and the transorbital lobotomy. These operations were of questionable value, had serious side effects, and were generally abandoned in the mid-1950s when effective drugs became available.

▷ Drug treatment is focused on reducing neurological arousal. Neuroleptics reduce activity by blocking dopamine receptors, reducing the sensitivity of postsynaptic receptors, and in some cases increasing serotonin activity. Some of these drugs have side effects that involve uncontrollable muscle movements.

▷ Low-potency neuroleptics such as Thorazine block dopamine receptors and reduce positive symptoms but can cause uncontrollable muscle movements. High-potency neuroleptics such as Haldol block more dopamine receptors and are more effective for reducing positive symptoms but cause a high level of uncontrollable muscle movements. Atypical neuroleptics such as Clozaril, Resparodol, and Olanzapine block fewer dopamine receptors than do high-potency neuroleptics, are more selective as to the receptors they block (D-2 receptors related to activity in the cortex rather than D-1 receptors in the motor system), and increase serotonin activity. Atypical neuroleptics reduce positive symptoms, reduce negative symptoms, and do not cause uncontrollable muscle movements.

▷ Psychoeducation reduces stress and thereby can reduce symptoms, relapses, and the need for medication.

▷ Behavioral symptoms associated with schizophrenia can be reduced by not rewarding them or by punishing them, whereas appropriate (normal) behaviors can be increased with rewards. This fact has led to the use of the token economy approach in some mental hospitals.

▷ Traditional psychotherapy is not effective for treating schizophrenia.

Questions for Making Connections

1. Is there a sharp line between normal behaviors and schizophrenia, or is there a continuum of symptoms that runs from normal behaviors to schizophrenia?

2. Explain how the physiological explanation completes the cognitive explanation for schizophrenia.

3. What causes positive and negative symptoms of schizophrenia, and why are the negative symptoms often more difficult to treat?

4. Based on what we know about the causes and treatments of schizophrenia, explain why it is becoming common to

talk about the schizophrenias rather than about schizophrenia.

5. Based on what we know about the causes of schizophrenia, describe an individual who is at a very high risk for developing schizophrenia.

6. Design a treatment for an individual who is suffering from schizophrenia. What drug or drugs would you prescribe and why? What psychological treatments might you try? What side effects should you watch out for? What symptoms will you be able to treat most effectively?

Key Terms and People

In reviewing and testing yourself, you should be able to discuss each of the following:

akathisia, p. 332
amphetamine psychosis, p. 316
amygdala, p. 321
associative intrusions, p. 312
atrophy, p. 319
atypical neuroleptics, p. 330
behavior therapy, p. 336
biological traumas, p. 323
clang associations, p. 312
Clozaril, p. 330
cortical atrophy, p. 319
D-2 receptors, p. 330
diathesis-stress explanation, p. 325
dopamine, p. 315
dopamine explanation for
   schizophrenia, p. 315
habit strength intrusions, p. 312
Haldol, p. 330

high-potency neuroleptics, p. 330
hippocampus, p. 320
hypofrontality, p. 321
L-dopa, p. 316
low-potency neuroleptics, p. 328
malignant neuroleptic syndrome,
   p. 332
neural migration, p. 319
neurodevelopment theory of
   schizophrenia, p. 318
neuroleptics, p. 328
perinatal complications, p. 324
prefrontal cortex, p. 317
prefrontal lobotomy, p. 327
prenatal complications, p. 323
psychoeducation, p. 334
reversed hemispheric dominance,
   p. 319

Riseridal, p. 331
season-of-birth effect, p. 323
semantic intrusions, p. 312
sensory deprivation, p. 308
serotonin, p. 316
social skills training, p. 334
subcortical atrophy, p. 320
tardive dyskinesia, p. 332
temporal cortex, p. 317
thalamus, p. 321
Thorazine, p. 328
thought content intrusions, p. 312
token economy approach, p. 336
transorbital lobotomy, p. 327
ventricles, p. 320
Zyprexa, p. 331

12 Personality, Adjustment, and Impulse-Control Disorders

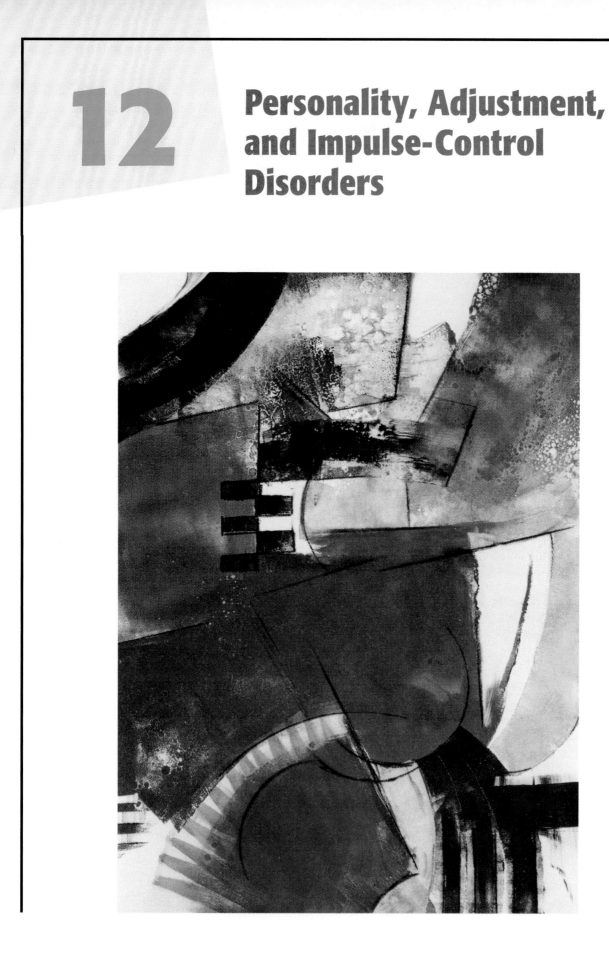

IN THIS CHAPTER we are going to consider three groups of disorders for which many of the symptoms fall in a gray area between normal and abnormal. For example, symptoms include being self-centered, dependent, impulsive, irresponsible, distrustful, aggressive, interpersonally detached, emotionally shallow, overly responsive to stressors, erratic, and "odd." Do you know anyone who has any of those characteristics? If so, the individual might be suffering from a *personality disorder,* an *adjustment disorder,* or an *impulse-control disorder.*

These disorders are often seen as less serious than other disorders, and certainly being dependent, detached, or suspicious is less serious than having hallucinations, delusions, or overwhelming depression. However, these disorders must not be dismissed as trivial or as mere "personality quirks," because over the long haul they can be very debilitating. For example, an individual who cannot get along with others may be unhappy and may make life miserable for other people. Furthermore, individuals who are impulsive and aggressive can cause harm to others and may even become killers.

TOPIC I

Personality Disorders

Constance always wants to be the center of attention, and she'll do just about anything to get attention. One of her strategies is to flirt with all of the guys, and she can be very seductive when she wants to be. However, usually it's "all show"—Constance really doesn't have any feelings for the person she is trying to seduce, and nothing sexual happens. Is Constance just a "flirt," or does she have a personality disorder?

Stan can be a lot of fun to be around because he is charming, bright, articulate, outgoing, and always ready to do something wild. Although Stan is very gregarious, he is actually self-centered and insensitive to the needs of others, and he will often take advantage of others. For example, while living with one woman, he was "sleeping around" and not making much of an attempt to cover his tracks. When confronted, he talked his way out of it, effectively blaming the other women. A careful review of his background reveals that he has been in and out of a lot of scrapes, but in most cases he was able to "con" his way out of trouble. Although he has frequently hurt those around him, he has never shown anxiety or remorse about his behavior. He simply does not seem to have a conscience. Is Stan just irresponsible, or does he have a personality disorder?

In general, *personality* can be defined as the way an individual responds emotionally, cognitively, and behaviorally in various situations, and **personality disorders** revolve around *pervasive and persistent problems with that responding.* For example, individuals may be overly neat, suspicious, irresponsible, self-centered, dependent, socially withdrawn, unstable, or just "strange." These problems begin in adolescence or early adulthood, usually last throughout adulthood, and can seriously interfere with an individual's life (Lenzenweger, 1999; Levy et al., 1999).

Some critics have suggested that many of the behaviors seen in personality disorders are not really symptoms but simply differences in adjustment within the normal range. They argue, for example, that being disinterested in other people or irresponsible does not constitute a psychiatric disorder. On the other hand, because the behaviors can cause distress for the individual and are often disruptive for those around the individual, the behaviors cross the line and are defined as symptoms of disorders. However, it should be noted that because most personality disorders are usually not as serious as the other disorders we have discussed, personality disorders are organized in *DSM-IV* on Axis II (Personality and Mental Retardation) rather than Axis I (Clinical Disorders), on which the other disorders are located. Their location on Axis II also draws special attention to them so that they will not be overlooked.

Before discussing personality disorders, I should point out that at one time or another most of us have shown some of the symptoms of these disorders. For example, we may have been dependent, self-centered, or emotionally detached. However, this does not necessarily mean that we have one of the disorders. Three factors separate people who have personality disorders from those who do not: First, an individual with a personality disorder uses the inappropriate behavior *consistently*, whereas other individuals use it only occasionally. Second, an individual with a personality disorder shows a *more extreme* level of the behavior. For instance, there is a difference between being orderly and being compulsive. Third, in disturbed individuals the behavior results in *serious and prolonged problems with functioning or happiness.* It is important to keep these distinctions in mind so that you will not mistakenly attribute a personality disorder to yourself or someone else.

There are 10 different personality disorders, but they have been organized into three clusters. In *DSM-IV* the clusters are simply labeled as A, B, and C, but they can be described as (1) odd or eccentric, (2) erratic or emotional,

and (3) anxious or fearful, respectively. In the following sections I will briefly describe the disorders in each of the clusters, and later I will discuss their causes and treatments.

Cluster A: Odd or Eccentric

The personality disorders in Cluster A are characterized by behaviors that are odd or eccentric. These disorders are summarized in Table 12.1.

Paranoid Personality Disorder

The dominant feature of **paranoid personality disorder** is an *unwarranted suspicion and mistrust of people* that persists even when there is no evidence for these beliefs. Because these individuals believe people around them pose threats, they tend to be anxious, distant, humorless, and argumentative. Their lack of trust in other people often undermines their interpersonal relationships and interferes with their job performance. However, these individuals often work very hard, probably because they think they must "keep ahead" of others who are "out to get them." This disorder is diagnosed more commonly in men than women (American Psychiatric Association, 1994). Note that although individuals with paranoid personality disorder are suspicious of other people, they do not have well-formed "delusions." That is, they may think other people do not like them and do not help them, but they do not think others are systematically plotting against them.

TABLE 12.1

Cluster A: Personality disorders characterized by odd or eccentric behaviors

Personality disorder	Characteristic behaviors
Paranoid	Is generally distrustful and suspicious of others, despite there being no basis for the concerns. Interprets the motives of others as mean or hostile. Tends to be anxious, distant, humorless, and argumentative.
Schizoid	Is detached from social relationships. Is indifferent to praise or criticism. Has limited range of emotions. Does not experience much pleasure. Is cool and distant.
Schizotypal	Has cognitive or perceptual distortions and eccentricities (ideas of reference, bodily illusions, odd thinking and speech, suspiciousness). Has inappropriate mood. Is ill at ease with others. Has difficulty with close personal relationships.

Source: Adapted from American Psychiatric Association, 1994.

Schizoid Personality Disorder

The primary symptom of individuals with **schizoid** (SKIT-zoyd) **personality disorder** is a *lack of interest in other people or social relationships.* Not only do individuals with this disorder not reach out to others, they rarely respond to others. For example, they are indifferent to praise or criticism from others, and they rarely make reciprocal gestures such as smiling or nodding.

Individuals with schizoid personality disorder also show very little emotion and hence appear aloof, humorless, cold, and emotionally flat. In short, individuals with this disorder are loners—physically, intellectually, and emotionally.

Schizotypal Personality Disorder

Individuals with **schizotypal** (skit-zo-TI-pul) **personality disorder** have many of the symptoms of schizophrenia, but the symptoms are less severe and therefore do not justify a diagnosis of schizophrenia. For example, these individuals often have bizarre beliefs, such as thinking that they are clairvoyant or have mental telepathy. They also engage in eccentric or peculiar behaviors, such as talking to themselves. Furthermore, these individuals are usually socially inept and isolated, and they may not pay any attention to their appearance. However, despite their symptoms they stay just barely on the normal side of the fine line that separates normalcy from schizophrenia. For example, they may say, "I feel *as if* my dead mother were in the room with me," which is subtly different from saying, "My dead mother *is* in the room with me." In other words, individuals with schizotypal personality disorder have *illusions,* whereas individuals with schizophrenia have *delusions.* Similarly, although individuals with schizotypal disorder have odd speech patterns and may ramble, they do not suffer from the serious distortions of speech ("word salads") seen in individuals with schizophrenia. Is schizotypal personality disorder simply a mild form of schizophrenia? We'll consider that possibility later.

Cluster B: Erratic or Emotional

The personality disorders in Cluster B revolve around erratic or emotional behaviors. These disorders are summarized in Table 12.2.

Borderline Personality Disorder

Borderline personality disorder is a serious and confusing disorder that is characterized primarily by *instability.* To get a sense of this disorder, let's consider four areas of instability shown by individuals who suffer from it. First, individ-

---

TABLE 12.2

Cluster B: Personality disorders characterized by erratic or emotional behaviors

Personality disorder	Characteristic behaviors
Borderline	Shows instability in interpersonal relationships (shifts from love to hate), mood (is often depressed or angry), identity (complains of being "empty"), and behaviors (may be impulsive, suicidal, self-mutilating). Has transient disruption of thought processes.
Histrionic	Constantly wants to be the center of attention. Acts in dramatic ways to attract attention. Is sexually seductive. Has shifting and shallow emotions. Is suggestible (easily influenced by others). Usually believes relationships are more intimate then they actually are.
Narcissistic	Has a sense of self-importance. Is preoccupied with success, power, and beauty. Requires attention. Believes that he or she is "special" and should associate with important people. Lacks empathy. Is arrogant and exploits others.
Antisocial	Does not conform to rules. Lies. Acts impulsively. Is aggressive. Disregards the needs of others. Is irresponsible. Lacks anxiety and guilt.

Source: Adapted from American Psychiatric Association, 1994.

---

personality disorders Disorders that involve pervasive and persistent problems with how an individual responds emotionally, cognitively, and behaviorally in various situations; these disorders are less serious than the disorders found on Axis I of *DSM-IV* and are organized on Axis II.

paranoid personality disorder A disorder characterized by an unwarranted suspicion and mistrust of people that persists even when there is no evidence for these beliefs.

schizoid personality disorder A disorder characterized by lack of interest in other people or social relationships.

schizotypal personality disorder A disorder that has many of the symptoms of schizophrenia, but the symptoms are not severe enough to justify the diagnosis of schizophrenia.

borderline personality disorder A disorder that is characterized primarily by instability in interpersonal relationships, mood, identity, and behavior but can also involve intermittent thought disturbances.

uals with borderline personality disorder are very unstable in their *interpersonal relationships* and often vacillate rapidly between passionate love and intense hate. Specifically, at the beginning of a relationship they often over-idealize the other person and want to spend a lot of time with him or her and share the most intimate details of their lives. However, if the other person is not "there for them" as much as they demand, these individuals will suddenly feel that they are being "abandoned" and so will run from the relationship or destroy it. For example, they will change their views of the other person and then become angry over having been misled by the person. On the other hand, they may interpret the abandonment as evidence that they are "bad" and undeserving of love, and that can trigger depression and anxiety. However, a short time later the individuals may again throw themselves completely into the relationship (or possibly another one), only to flee it again over concerns about abandonment. Their relationships are nothing short of chaotic.

Second, individuals with borderline personality disorder are *emotionally* very unstable. Although sometimes they can be positive and upbeat, most of their vacillations in mood are between normal, depression, despair, panic, and anger. Some of the instability results from their chaotic interpersonal relationships, but often their shifts in mood occur without any external justification; they just change.

Third, instability also characterizes their *identity* (self-image); that is, they do not seem to know who they are and are constantly changing, as if searching for a self. The search leads to rapid changes in career plans, values, friends, and personality. In the absence of a stable identity, they often report feeling "empty" or as if they "don't exist."

One of the symptoms of borderline personality disorder is unstable behavior. Individuals with this disorder often act impulsively, such as driving recklessly or becoming extremely agitated on the road.

One woman reported that she felt as though there were a big hole inside of her.

Fourth, individuals with borderline disorder are *behaviorally* unstable. This is notable in three areas. First, they are impulsive; they may gamble, binge eat, take drugs, participate in unsafe sex, spend money irresponsibly, and drive recklessly. Second, they often participate in suicidal behaviors (threats, gestures, and sincere attempts). The third area of behavioral instability involves self-mutilation. For instance, individuals with borderline personality disorder may burn themselves with cigarettes, cut their bodies with knives or razor blades, or scratch or pour acid on their skin (Dulit et al., 1994; Mehlum et al., 1994; Shearer, 1994; Soloff et al., 1994; Winchel & Stanley, 1991). This behavior is not intended to result in death; rather the self-mutilation is often done in an emotionally detached way, and individuals report that they self-mutilate in an attempt to feel or experience themselves as "real." One woman told me, "If I bleed, I know I'm alive. If I cut myself up, I may feel *something*." In other words, self-mutilation can be a means of overcoming feelings of "emptiness" and "not being." Another woman carved the word *slut* into her stomach after having sex with a man. She said she did it to make herself feel bad about what she had done. I will discuss self-mutilation in greater detail later.

Finally, although it is not listed as a symptom in *DSM-IV*, research indicates that some individuals with borderline personality disorder have intermittent periods during which they experience *thought disturbances* (Zanarini, Gunderson, & Frankenburg, 1990b). However, the disturbances are not as extreme as those seen in schizophrenia, so rather than suffering from full-blown hallucinations and delusions, these individuals show only "unusual perceptions" and illusions. For example, one woman told me that sometimes she felt as though she could see through people and other times she felt as though she were dead. Similarly, a student reported that he sometimes felt like he could control events by thinking about them. The important phrases here are "as though" and "like"; that is, the individuals did not completely believe that they were really dead or could control events, but they were approaching those conclusions. These thought disturbances are very similar to those in schizotypal personality disorder (see the earlier discussion). Finally, with regard to thoughts persons with borderline personality disorder are often somewhat paranoid, thinking that others are against them or out to get them.

Because of their fluctuations in interpersonal relationships, mood, identity, and behavior, individuals with borderline personality disorder lead troubled and disorganized lives. In Case Study 12.1 one of my students talks about her struggle with borderline personality disorder.

From the description I've given it is clear that borderline personality disorder shares symptoms with other disorders, particularly major depressive disorder, paranoid personality disorder, schizotypal personality disorder, and possibly

A Student Writes about the Symptoms of Her Borderline Personality Disorder

CASE STUDY **12.1**

LINDA IS A TALL, attractive, and bright young woman. When she was a senior in high school, she received a scholarship to a 6-year combined program for college and dental school that would begin immediately after graduation. However, Linda did not graduate with her classmates. As they marched across the stage, she was confined to a mental hospital with a serious borderline personality disorder. For the next 3 years Linda was in and out of a number of hospitals. She was finally able to enter college, and with support and treatment she was able to graduate. Her symptoms are better but not gone. Here she writes about some of her symptoms.

About Her Feelings and Her Self-Mutilation

"It is very hard for me to explain how I feel and how I felt. Feelings really overwhelm me. There were times when I felt like I would explode or burst because of the feelings. It was like my skin would crawl, and I felt trapped. I felt like screaming or doing something to release the feelings. I usually chose to burn or cut myself. That was a release for me. When I saw the blood coming out, it was like seeing the hurt drip away. Other times when I would hurt myself, it was because of the hatred I felt for myself.

"From the very first time I hurt myself, I loved the feeling. I don't think there are words to explain how it feels. There is so much involved. I felt very 'out of control' with everything in my life, and the cutting and burning gave me a sense of control. The act of mutilating yourself is a very powerful thing. More than control, it gives you a sense of *being*. You *see* the blood or the burnt flesh, and you know *you are real*.

"I remember burning myself one time when I was feeling rejected and very alone. I felt a very intense and overwhelming pain inside, in my gut. The pain was emotional, not physical. I got in my car and just drove. I had tears in my eyes because I hurt so badly. I felt very spaced. That was always how I felt when I hurt myself. I was numb to the point of feeling outside of my body. It is like when you are dreaming. You can see yourself from the outside and all that is going on from that view. I felt very light, as if I were weightless. I drove to a parking lot. I did not go there with the intention of hurting myself, it just happened. I had a cigarette lighter in my car. I lit it and let the flame touch my flesh. I burned a section of my arm that was about 2 inches by 3 inches. The skin blistered and burned. It gave me a warm feeling all over. It didn't hurt, it felt good. I'm not sure what made me stop, but tears came to my eyes after it was all over. Not because it hurt, but because of the release. I felt better when I was done. All of the pain was gone. Maybe the physical mutilation let me focus my attention on the outside, instead of on the internal pain. Whenever I hurt myself, I had a feeling of renewal. It was like starting fresh without all of the emotions.

"The cutting was a lot like the burning, but it seems like I cut myself when I was angry, especially at myself. When I cut myself deeply, I wasn't trying to kill myself, I just wanted to bleed. One time when I cut myself, I dripped the blood all over two pieces of paper and saved it. The blood did something for me. It was a high to see the blood. Maybe it made me feel 'real,' or maybe it was just a release—a release of the pain.

"The release I experienced with the cutting was similar to what I felt with my bulimia. I consider my eating behavior a part of my self-destructive behavior. There was a period of time that I was bingeing and purging five to six times a day. It engulfed my whole life—it *became my life*. The bingeing made me feel kind of high, and I felt like I could start fresh. I never did start fresh. I just kept eating to fill the emptiness and purging to release the emotions. I couldn't stop."

About Her Mood

"I felt depressed most of the time. Sometimes I felt like I couldn't go on in life. It's not that there was something so *wrong* with my life, but there was something *missing*. I still feel like that. It is like there is a huge hole inside of me. Sometimes when I am alone, I can feel it—the emptiness inside of me. There's nothing there. I have tried many things to fill that void—food, alcohol, drugs, sex, relationships—but none of those things make it go away. *I want so badly to feel whole, but I just don't.* I have wanted to kill myself because I don't think I will ever feel whole. More than really wanting to die, I just wanted to be in a coma-like state for a while and then wake up and have everything be better, like I was only having a bad nightmare. I really struggle with finding a meaning in my life—and finding me!"

> **I felt like the whole world was against me.**

About Her Paranoia and Interpersonal Relationships

"I felt like the whole world was against me. I thought people wanted to hurt me. I knew that everyone talked about me and hated me. I knew if 'they' would just leave me alone, I would be OK. I felt like people were hurting me on purpose. I thought if they only knew how much I already hurt inside, they would be sorry for pushing me to hurt more. I grew to hate everyone because of this. It was like a double-edged sword. I felt like no one loved or cared about me, but when they would try to get close, I would push them far away. It was a never-ending circle.

"I have not been able to have any really stable relationships. Most of the men I have gotten involved with are 'safe' in some way. They are really unavailable before I even get involved. I always have an out with these kinds of people. My last relationship was with a drug addict. As long as he had prob-

(continued)

Case Study 12.1 *(cont.)*

lems, I always had a good excuse to get out. When he was clean for 8 months, I got out of the relationship. My biggest fear is rejection, so I do it first.

"One time I jumped into a relationship with a man from out of state. I thought that we would just date for the summer, and then he would go home. Well, he did go home, but I went to visit him one weekend. The very next Friday I dropped out of college and moved into an apartment with him. I had always thought, 'If I could only get to another place, my life will be better.' It was another desperate attempt to fill the emptiness. Well, it was a disaster, and 2 months later I moved back, but

he came with me. Driving back in the U-Haul, I was so desperate that I drove straight through a dangerous ice-storm. I hated him so much that I wanted to have a bad wreck and have him die. I had my seatbelt on so I felt relatively safe. I just wanted so badly for him to die. For 2½ years after that I went through loving him and wanting to marry him one day to hoping he would just overdose and die the next day. I loved him and I hated him.

"I don't understand why I am like this; I wish I did. I think a part of it is that I don't have a grasp of who I am and what I want in life, so I am always changing my mind. One day a man is

the love of my life and I want to marry him, and the next day I hate him. It is a lot like how I feel about *myself*."

Her Treatment

Linda has taken Prozac (a bicyclic antidepressant) for her depression, Haldol (a high-potency neuroleptic) for her psychoticlike symptoms, Tegretal (an anticonvulsant) for controlling her mood swings, and Ativan (a benzodiazepine) for her anxiety. With medication and counseling Linda was able to do well in college and graduate. She has come a long way, but as her comments indicate, she still has a way to go, and this may be a lifelong battle.

schizophrenia. This seems to be the basis for the label "borderline"; that is, individuals with the disorder are on the *borderline* of a number of different disorders, and the instability of their symptoms occurs because the symptoms tend to move up and back across those borders. Indeed, in addition to being given the diagnosis of borderline personality disorder, individuals with this disorder are likely to receive three or four other diagnoses on Axis I of *DSM-IV* "Clinical Disorders" (Zimmerman & Mattia, 1999). This leads to the question of whether borderline personality disorder is *one* disorder or a *combination* of disorders. That is, it might be a combination of a mild case of schizophrenia, a depressive disorder, and an impulse-control disorder (I will discuss impulse-control disorders later).

Histrionic Personality Disorder

The term *histrionic* is based on a Latin word meaning "actor," and individuals with **histrionic** (his-tre-ON-ik) **personality disorder** can be best thought of as actors who insist on being the center of attention on the stage of life. To gain attention they often act in overly dramatic and emotional ways, such as crying, weeping, and threatening to commit suicide. In the dramas and tragedies they generate, they always play the starring role, and others are relegated to supporting roles.

People with this disorder are usually attractive, charming, appealing, and sexually seductive in their roles. However, although they try to charm and seduce everyone, if things start to get serious, they back off quickly. Like moths

to a flame, these individuals flutter around sex, but when things get hot, they back off. That is to be expected because they are only playing a role.

Individuals with histrionic personality disorder are usually quite attractive and sexually appealing. These individuals seek to gain the attention of others by taking center stage and acting overly dramatic or charming. They try to seduce everyone but tend to retreat quickly if things start to get serious.

In addition, despite their great shows of feelings, histrionic individuals are emotionally very shallow, and their emotions may shift quickly from person to person or from positive to negative. Because of their emotional shallowness, their relationships tend to be stormy and short-lived. The changes in these individuals reflect the fact they are acting—as actors, they change roles and partners easily. They are also suggestible, and their behaviors can be easily influenced by those around them, much like an actor's behaviors are influenced by a director. An individual with histrionic personality disorder can be a lot of fun (especially to flirt with) at a party, but the relationship is best ended when the party's over.

Narcissistic Personality Disorder

The model for **narcissistic** (nar-suh-SIS-tik) **personality disorder** is Narcissus, the character in Greek mythology who fell in love with his own reflection in a pond. Individuals with narcissistic personality disorder have an exaggerated sense of their own importance, and they are preoccupied with fantasies about their ultimate success, power, brilliance, or beauty. Because they think they are "special," they demand constant attention and admiration from everyone around them. These individuals see themselves as entitled to favors from others because of their importance, and consequently they take advantage of the people around them. If criticized rather than praised, they may respond with cool indifference, or their overblown egos may collapse like punctured balloons. Also, because they are so self-centered, they have difficulty maintaining relationships. Legend has it that because Narcissus was so absorbed in himself, he spurned the love of Echo, who then went off to die alone in a cave. There may be a moral in that story for people who deal with individuals who have narcissistic personality disorder. The disorder is more prevalent in men than women (Golomb et al., 1995).

Antisocial Personality Disorder

Antisocial personality disorder (abbreviated as **APD**) is particularly interesting because individuals with this disorder are bright, articulate, and socially skilled and often appear to be very well adjusted; the problem is that they simply *lack anxiety or guilt* and therefore engage in antisocial behaviors. That is, without anxiety or guilt to inhibit them, they lie, take advantage of others, commit crimes, are reckless, are sometimes aggressive, and are generally irresponsible. However, because of their well-developed verbal and social skills, they have the ability to explain away their inappropriate behaviors and are usually able to talk themselves out of trouble.

Consider the example of a charming 26-year-old male, who, 3 days before he was to be married, was discovered by

According to Greek mythology, Narcissus fell in love with his own reflection in a pond. Persons with narcissistic personality disorder have a grandiose sense of their own importance and are preoccupied with fantasies about their success, power, brilliance, or beauty.

his fiancée to be having a very active affair with another woman. When confronted with irrefutable evidence of his inappropriate behavior, the young man first professed his

histrionic personality disorder   A disorder in which the individual always wants to be the center of attention, acts in dramatic ways to attract attention, is usually sexually seductive but has shifting and shallow emotions, and is suggestible.

narcissistic personality disorder   A disorder in which the individual has an exaggerated sense of self-importance, is preoccupied with fantasies of success, power, brilliance, or beauty, requires constant attention and admiration, takes advantage of others, and has difficulty maintaining relationships.

antisocial personality disorder (APD)   A disorder characterized by a lack of anxiety or guilt which causes individuals to engage in antisocial behaviors.

unfaltering love for his fiancée and then went on to explain in the most sincere manner imaginable that he had no real feelings for the other woman (which in a sense was probably true) and that he was having the affair only as a means of testing his love for his fiancée. Indeed, he explained that he participated in the affair for the good of his fiancée— once his love had been tested and found to be true, no one else would ever pose a threat to their relationship. He expressed some surprise at her lack of understanding of his affair, but he promised that nothing like that would ever happen again. They were married as planned, but the young man proceeded to engage in a long series of affairs with other women, each of which was "explainable" and was followed by professions of remorse and more promises to reform. Another example of an individual with APD is presented in Case Study 12.2.

As you can see from the cases I have described, individuals with APD are generally self-centered, pleasure seeking, and impulsive. When it serves their purposes, they can profess great love and commitment, but their feelings are actually very shallow. Although individuals with APD frequently cause emotional and financial harm to those around them, they do not usually engage in overt physical aggression. However, there is a subset of individuals with the disorder who may act very aggressively in some situations. These individuals often get attention in the media because their acts of aggression are so extreme and senseless. Examples of widely publicized cases include the two killers who were made famous in Truman Capote's book *In Cold Blood*; Ted Bundy, who was suspected of killing more than 20 women in five states (including two women in a sorority house whom he battered to death); and Kenneth Bianchi, the Hillside Strangler (see Case Study 7.3).

Finally, it is important to recognize that individuals with APD usually do not benefit from punishment. In many situations they avoid punishment by talking their way out of it, but when that is not possible and they are punished, the punishment does not appear to have any effect. I know one individual with APD who was jailed for stealing a car, and when he was released on bail, he stole a car to get home! Because individuals with APD do not learn or benefit from their experiences, they are not deterred and tend to engage in the same inappropriate behavior again and again.

This disorder occurs in about 3% of men but in only about 1% of women (American Psychiatric Association,

1994; Moran, 1999). Interestingly, the rate among male prisoners is estimated to be about 60%. The disorder is at its height during adolescence and early adulthood, and then it seems to "burn out" at around age 40. That burnout is apparent in prison populations; specifically, a large proportion of the inmates between 16 and 40 years of age suffer from APD, but very few inmates over age 40 have the disorder (Hare, McPherson, & Forth, 1988). Apparently, after 40 the disorder has burned out, so individuals are less likely to get into trouble and be imprisoned.

Two terms that are often used for individuals who have APD are **psychopath** and **sociopath**. The term *psychopath* was coined many years ago when it was first thought that APD was caused by physiological problems in the brain— that is, a "pathology of the psyche" (Koch, 1891). In contrast, the label *sociopath* was introduced in the 1940s when it was speculated that the disorder was due to bad parenting—that is, a social problem. The terms *psychopath* and *sociopath* are still widely used, but because *DSM-IV* avoids diagnostic labels that imply a particular cause, we should instead use the strictly descriptive label *antisocial personality disorder*.

Serial killer Ted Bundy could probably be diagnosed as having suffered from antisocial personality disorder. He used his good looks, intelligence, and charm to get close to his victims—all young women—whom he sexually abused and then murdered. Bundy was executed in Florida.

psychopath An early term for a person with antisocial personality disorder; reflects a suspected physiological cause of the disorder.

sociopath A term previously used for a person with antisocial personality disorder; reflects a suspected social (family) cause of the disorder.

An Individual with Antisocial Personality Disorder

CASE
STUDY   **12.2**

As a child Doug was well liked because of his good looks and charming manner. His parents thought he could do no wrong. In fact, however, Doug often disobeyed his parents and teachers, but he usually had a convincing explanation for his actions, or he blamed his friends. Therefore, he was seldom punished for this misbehavior. Once when he was 7, he told all of his friends that he was having a birthday but that he was not going to have a party or get any presents because his father was not working. Hearing that, the neighbors gave him a big party and lots of presents—only to learn that he had lied. His father was working, and it was not even his birthday! His parents thought it was "cute," and he was not punished.

In high school Doug had a series of girlfriends (indeed, he was much sought after) and many casual male buddies, but he never formed close attachments with anyone. His peers looked up to him because he was extroverted and daring, always ready to try something new. The first clear sign of antisocial behavior occurred when Doug was 15. He stole a car that belonged to an older friend and took three buddies on a joyride that lasted several hours. When they were finally caught, Doug lied about his part in the theft, blaming the friends who had accompanied him. His parents believed him, and they convinced the local police that Doug was innocent, so he again went unpunished for his actions.

Doug went to college but never graduated. He had the intelligence to do well, but he just stopped going to class. When he was about to be thrown out of school, he conned a woman in the dean's office into ignoring that last semester's grades (all Fs) by telling her that he had missed class because he had been going home to take care of his parents who had been in a serious accident. Impressed with his devotion to his parents and his "sincere" hope to do better, she gave him an exemption.

One summer, when his parents thought that he was in school taking "extra courses," he was in fact in Aspen tending bar. He got his roommate to forward his checks from home to Colorado.

After college Doug did not hold any job for long. Although he could be hardworking, he usually lost his jobs because he did something foolish. For example, a number of times he simply did not show up for a few days because on the spur of the moment he had decided to go backpacking. Once, while working as an automobile salesman, he drove off one night in a very expensive demonstrator model and did not return. He made no attempt to conceal the car and was caught within a week. When taken to court he claimed that he had intended to return to work the next day and that it was all a "misunderstanding." In exchange for his promise to pay for the use of the car, he was given a suspended sentence. Two days later he left town.

At age 26 Doug married a girl of 18 who worked in one of the bars he frequented. They married almost "as a lark," and neither knew much about the other. He was unemployed, but she believed one of his "lines" in the bar and thought he was a stockbroker.

Without her knowing it they lived for the first couple of months off her savings, which he took from the bank. He also forged checks to pay for a car he leased and numerous items of clothing he bought for himself. Also unknown to his wife, within 2 weeks of the marriage he was having affairs with two other women (his wife thought he was seeing clients). He was eventually caught and convicted for check forgery and served 6 months in jail. A month after he was jailed, his wife discovered that she was pregnant. When she went to pick him up on the day he was scheduled to be released from jail, she discovered that he had been released early "for good behavior" and had left town.

In another state Doug assumed another name and soon met the daughter of a wealthy family and began dating her. She was completely taken in by Doug's good looks, charm, attentive manner, and intelligence. He portrayed himself as a sensitive and lonely man who was rejected by his parents. He told her that he had plans to develop a retirement home, and the woman began giving him substantial amounts of money to lay the groundwork for the project. Doug took the money, opened a lavish office, and started an affair with his secretary.

The problems described here probably constitute only the tip of the iceberg of Doug's inappropriate behavior. Because he was so effective at conning people, much of his misbehavior went undetected or unreported.

> **The first clear sign of antisocial behavior occurred when Doug was 15.**

I will discuss the explanations for most of the personality disorders at the end of this section, but the causes of APD are somewhat unique and require some comment here. The first question we must ask is, why do individuals with APD lack anxiety and guilt? In other words, why don't they have a conscience? To answer that question we should recall that anxiety is the result of classical conditioning; that is, if inappropriate behavior is followed by punishment, thinking about the behavior later will lead to anxiety, and the behavior will not be used. What is important here is that individuals with APD do not classically condition well (Hare, 1965a; Hare & Craigen, 1974; Hare & Quinn, 1971; Lykken, 1957; Schachter & Latané, 1964). For example, in experiments in which a painful electric shock was paired with a tone, individuals with APD were less likely to develop a classically conditioned fear response than were other individuals. The link between problems with classical conditioning and the development of APD was dramatically illustrated in an investigation in which classical conditioning of anxiety was measured in 104 adolescents, and then 10 years later the individuals were followed up to determine which of them engaged in some form of antisocial behavior (Loeb & Mednick, 1976). The results were clear: The individuals who had not been classically conditioned were most likely to get into trouble later. In other words, the absence of classical conditioning meant that these individuals could not develop a conscience that would inhibit inappropriate behavior.

The next question is, why don't individuals with APD classically condition well? The answer seems to lie in low levels of arousal in areas of the brain associated with emotions. That is, if these areas are underactive, anxiety will not be generated, and therefore there can be no pairing of anxiety with inappropriate behaviors in the process of classical conditioning. Evidence for low neurological arousal comes first from EEG recordings that indicate that individuals with APD have unusually slow wave activity in the limbic system of the brain, a system that generates arousal that leads to emotions (see Chapter 4 for a discussion of EEG).

Even more interesting is the finding that by decreasing brain activity we can increase the symptoms of APD. That effect was demonstrated in an experiment in which college students took an important examination and then were administered either a placebo or a drug (chlorpromazine) that decreased their arousal (Schachter & Latané, 1964). Following that, each student was allowed to score the examination that he or she had taken earlier. The results indicated that students who had taken the arousal-decreasing drug cheated more frequently when scoring their examinations than the students who had taken the placebo. Indeed, the difference in cheating between the two conditions was almost 20%. If cheating is taken as an indication of APD, the results of this experiment provide strong evidence that decreasing neurological arousal leads to the symptoms of APD.

Poor classical conditioning of anxiety and low levels of brain activity are clearly linked to APD, but a number of other factors are also involved. Specifically, there is strong evidence that high levels of *testosterone* (the "male" hormone) are linked to the aggressive behavior sometimes seen in individuals with APD (Aromaeki et al., 1999; Raesaenen et al., 1999; Virkkunen et al., 1994). Testosterone appears to energize individuals and guide their energy in the direction of dominance and aggression (see later discussion of aggression). Also important here are the findings that individuals with APD have low levels of *serotonin* (Virkkunen et al., 1989; Virkkunen et al., 1994). That is important because low levels of serotonin are related to impulsivity

(see Topic III). In other words, testosterone motivates aggression, and low serotonin reduces the inhibitions that would ordinarily block the aggressive behaviors.

With regard to serotonin and impulsivity, it is interesting to note that antidepressant drugs that increase levels of serotonin have been shown to be very effective for reducing impulsive behaviors in individuals who have long histories of problems with impulsivity (Coccaro, 1998; Coccaro & Kavoussi, 1997; Heiligenstein et al., 1992; Saltzman et al., 1995). Indeed, in one experiment it was found that individuals who took Prozac showed a decrease in aggression that was 65% greater than the decrease shown by individuals who took a placebo; see Figure 12.1. Those reductions in aggression are particularly impressive because numerous other treatments such as psychotherapy and jail had been ineffective in changing the behavior of the individuals.

The effects of Prozac on impulsivity and aggression were dramatically demonstrated for me by a student of mine who suffered from depression and who had a long history of impulsive and aggressive behaviors that had often gotten him into legal trouble. He began taking Prozac for his depression, which helped, but the Prozac also reduced his impulsive and aggressive behavior, much to the delight of everyone around him. (For discussions of how Prozac and similar drugs increase levels of serotonin, see Chapters 2 and 14.)

Finally, there is evidence that structural problems in the brain can cause APD. The first suggestion of this came from the famous case of Phineas P. Gage, a hard-working and reliable construction worker who supervised the blasting of rock to make way for railroad tracks (Damasio, 1994, 1995). Unfortunately, one day an accidental explosion drove a steel rod into Gage's left cheek and out of the top of his head. Miraculously, Gage lived and showed no physical symptoms of the accident other than the loss of vision in his left eye. However, Gage was changed emotionally: Before the accident he was thoughtful and moderate in his

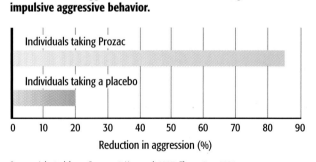

FIGURE 12.1

Prozac reduced aggression in individuals with long histories of impulsive aggressive behavior.

Individuals taking Prozac

Individuals taking a placebo

Reduction in aggression (%)

Source: Adapted from Coccaro & Kavoussi, 1997, Figure 1, p. 1084.

behaviors, but after the accident he became impulsive, and he used such profane language that women were advised to avoid him. Subsequent studies of Gage's skull indicated that when the rod went through his brain, it damaged a large portion of his *prefrontal cortex* (the part of the brain covering the front of the frontal lobes), thus suggesting that the prefrontal cortex is important for impulse control. Other more recent cases have revealed similar changes in personality following damage to the prefrontal cortex, and a study of individuals with APD indicated that they have prefrontal areas that are more than 10% smaller than those of other individuals (Damasio, 2000; Raine et al., 2000).

Overall, then, it is now clear that poor classical conditioning, low levels of brain activity, high levels of testosterone, low levels of serotonin, and damage to the prefrontal cortex can all contribute to antisocial personality disorder. We seem to have found many of the pieces of the puzzle of APD, and now our task is to fit them together and devise treatments.

Cluster C: Anxious or Fearful

The personality disorders in Cluster C are characterized by anxious or fearful behaviors. These disorders are summarized in Table 12.3.

Avoidant Personality Disorder

Individuals with **avoidant personality disorder** are exceptionally sensitive to potential social rejection and the humiliation that goes with it. Because of their concerns about rejection, they avoid relationships unless they are guaranteed uncritical acceptance. They want affection, closeness, and acceptance, but they avoid relationships that might satisfy these needs because of their stronger need to defend against rejection. In other words, avoidance is a defense; if they do not attempt to make friends, they cannot be rejected. The motto of individuals with avoidant personality disorder appears to be "If I don't get close, I can't get rejected and hurt."

One young man with avoidant personality disorder wanted desperately to have close friends with whom he could share experiences, but he was so afraid of rejection that he never attempted to establish friendships. Instead, he focused his efforts on "achieving," with the hope that others would accept him because of his competence; however, acceptance based on his achievements did not satisfy his need for friendship. This very competent young man lived an isolated and unfulfilled existence. Because individuals with avoidant personality disorder cannot satisfy their need for closeness and constantly feel as though they will be

TABLE 12.3	

Cluster C: Personality disorders characterized by anxious or fearful behaviors

Personality disorder	Characteristic behaviors
Avoidant	Avoids interpersonal contact because of fear of criticism and rejection. Is preoccupied with criticism. Views self as inept or inferior. Is reluctant to take personal risks.
Dependent	Has difficulty making decisions without help. Does not assume responsibility. Has difficulty disagreeing or initiating projects. Seeks relationships to get nurturance and support. Is preoccupied with fears of being left alone to take care of himself or herself.
Obsessive-Compulsive	Is preoccupied with details, rules, lists, organization, or schedules. Shows perfectionism. Is devoted to work to the exclusion of leisure and friendships. Is overly conscientious and inflexible. Cannot discard worthless objects. Is reluctant to delegate responsibility. Is rigid and stubborn.

Source: Adapted from American Psychiatric Association, 1994.

rejected, they usually have low self-esteem and suffer from anxiety and depression.

Dependent Personality Disorder

Individuals with **dependent personality disorder** passively allow others to make major decisions for them. In fact, they actively avoid taking responsibility and making decisions. They are often easy to get along with because they will not do anything to jeopardize their relationships with the persons on whom they rely for major decisions. However, their inability to make decisions can result in anxiety and depression, which can interfere with their ability to get anything done. They may feel uncomfortable or helpless when alone, and they will go to great lengths to keep others around them.

avoidant personality disorder   A disorder in which the individual is exceptionally sensitive to potential social rejection and the humiliation that goes with it.

dependent personality disorder   A disorder in which the individual passively allows others to make decisions and actively avoids taking responsibility.

Individuals with avoidant personality disorder are extremely sensitive to the possibility of social rejection. As a result, they protect themselves from the possible humiliation of rejection by avoiding relationships.

One middle-level business manager with dependent personality disorder got along well in his company because he always went along with the group. When votes were taken in meetings, he always looked both ways to see which direction the vote was going before casting his vote. However, he did not advance in the company because he never contributed leadership or unique ideas. He was frustrated and depressed about his position but too afraid to do anything about it. His disorder probably stemmed from a time when, as a newcomer in the company, he offered a new idea and from his perspective got "stepped on."

This disorder is more frequently seen in women, but that may be because the stereotype of women traditionally involves dependence. The cause of this disorder is not clear, but it probably stems from a lack of self-confidence. Overly dependent individuals seem to be saying to themselves, "I am probably going to be wrong, so if I do not initiate anything, I cannot be blamed or criticized."

Obsessive-Compulsive Personality Disorder

Obsessive-compulsive personality disorder involves high needs for perfection, order, and control, and the lives of individuals with this disorder become dominated by the idea that they must get organized and prepared. Problems arise because these individuals get so bogged down with

> **obsessive-compulsive personality disorder**   A disorder in which the individual has high needs for perfection, order, and control and is preoccupied with getting organized and prepared.

organization and details that they do not get started on the projects they have planned. Also their overattention to details prevents them from seeing the "big picture," so they may spend too much time on meaningless or trivial aspects of problems they must solve. A student with obsessive-compulsive personality disorder who has to write a paper may spend endless hours collecting material, organizing it into neat piles, and worrying about tiny details for footnotes but may never clearly define the goal of the paper or actually get around to writing it. In other words, the student spends all the available time preparing and never actually produces anything. Another symptom of obsessive-compulsive personality disorder involves what is frequently called *hoarding;* specifically, individuals are unable to discard worn-out or worthless objects, arguing that they never know when they might need the objects. In other words, these individuals are extreme "pack rats."

Individuals with obsessive-compulsive personality disorder often do not have meaningful interpersonal relations because they are so tied up in getting organized that they do not take time for friendships. Furthermore, because of their need for control, they often insist that others do things *their* way rather than allowing for the give-and-take that is necessary in a friendship. In short, rather than "going with the flow" and being spontaneous in their interpersonal relations, these individuals live behind a dam where everything is controlled and emotionally flat. Finally, individuals with obsessive-compulsive personality disorder are not particularly happy; they do not take time for pleasure or relaxation, and they are constantly worrying about missing some detail and failing.

A question that frequently arises is, how does obsessive-compulsive personality disorder differ from obsessive-compulsive disorder (OCD)? The answer is that the personality disorder revolves around *orderliness and control* and *does not actually involve obsessions and compulsions*, whereas obsessions and compulsions are the major symptoms in OCD. It is odd that the diagnosis of obsessive-compulsive personality disorder is used for individuals who do not have obsessions or compulsions, but that is the convention established in *DSM-IV*. However, *DSM-IV* does point out that if symptoms, especially hoarding, become extreme, a diagnosis of OCD should be considered, or both diagnoses should be used.

 # Explanations and Treatments

Numerous theories have been offered to account for personality disorders, but unfortunately the evidence for most of them is weak, and consequently we are often at a loss to explain these disorders. However, it now appears that some personality disorders are mild forms of more serious disorders, so what we know about the more serious disorders may provide us with an understanding of the related personality disorders. Therefore, in this discussion I will consider the personality disorders in two groups: those that are linked to more serious disorders and those that are not.

Personality Disorders That Are Mild Forms of Other Disorders

Are personality disorders actually less severe forms or early stages of more serious disorders? The answer appears to be yes for schizotypal, schizoid, and borderline personality disorders. As an example, let's consider the four links between schizotypal personality disorder and schizophrenia. First, individuals with schizotypal personality disorder have symptoms such as problems with thought processes that are like those of schizophrenia but less severe (Cadenhead et al., 1999; Cassady et al., 1998; Tompson et al., 1997; Weinstein et al., 1999). Second, individuals with schizotypal disorder show the same problems with brain structures and functioning as individuals with schizophrenia (Buchsbaum et al., 1997; Dickey, McCarley, & Voglmaier, 1999; Hazlett et al., 1999; Niznikiewicz et al., 1999; Trestman et al, 1996; Walker, Lewis, Loewy, & Palyo, 1999; Walker, Logan, & Walder, 1999). Third, individuals who suffer from schizotypal disorder are likely to have biological relatives who suffer from schizophrenia, which suggests a shared genetic cause (Battaglia et al., 1999; Chen et al.,1998; Gladis, Levinson, & Mowry, 1994; Kendler, McGuire, et al., 1993a; Kreman et al., 1998; Maier, Lichtermann, Minges, & Heun, 1994; Siever et al., 1990; Webb & Levinson, 1993). Fourth and finally, prenatal problems such

as nutritional deficiencies that have been linked to schizophrenia are also important in schizotypal disorder (Hoek et al., 1996). Overall, then, similarities in symptoms and causes all point to a connection between schizotypal personality disorder and schizophrenia. Indeed, *typal* means "a type," so the term *schizotypal* literally means "a type of schizophrenia."

Schizoid personality disorder also seems to be related to schizophrenia. Specifically, the interpersonal withdrawal, inability to experience pleasure, and flat mood that characterize schizoid disorder appear to be mild forms of the *negative* symptoms of schizophrenia. As is the case with schizotypal personality disorder, individuals with schizoid personality disorder are likely to have biological relatives who suffer from schizophrenia. It is noteworthy that *oid*, the last syllable in *schizoid*, means "resembling," so *schizoid* literally means "resembling schizophrenia." However, more than just resembling schizophrenia, schizoid personality disorder is probably a mild form of schizophrenia, in which negative symptoms predominate.

Finally, as I described earlier, borderline personality disorder may be a combination of mild forms of schizophrenia, major depressive disorder, and an impulse-control disorder (see the later discussion of impulse-control disorders). In other words, borderline personality disorder is "on the border" of all of those disorders.

The fact that there are links between some of the personality disorders and more serious disorders has two implications for treatment. First, the symptoms of these personality disorders can provide warning signs that the more serious disorders are developing, and therefore the individual can be given treatment to arrest the development of the disorder before it reaches a more severe form. For example, in the case of schizotypal or schizoid personality disorder, stress might be lowered for the individuals so that their symptoms will not be exacerbated (see Chapter 11 for a discussion of how stress can exacerbate the symptoms of schizophrenia). Second, the treatments that are effective for the more serious disorders can be used to treat the personality disorders. For instance, there is a growing body of evidence that the atypical neuroleptics that are effective for treating schizophrenia are also effective for treating the cognitive symptoms seen in schizotypal and borderline personality disorders (Coccaro, 1998; see the discussion of neuroleptics in Chapter 11).

Overall, then, recognizing that some personality disorders are related to more serious disorders provides clues to understanding and treating these personality disorders.

Personality Disorders That Are Exaggerations of Normal Personality Traits

How do we explain personality disorders that are not linked to more serious disorders? There is some controversy over this, but it appears that these disorders are probably *extensions of normal personality* and are best explained in the same way that we explain normal personality—that is, with a combination of genetics and experience. Strong evidence now shows that about 50% of the differences in personalities are due to genetics. That rate has been demonstrated with traits and behaviors as diverse as extroversion, aggression, empathy, altruism, shyness, gambling, interests, drug use, age at first sexual intercourse, talents, job satisfaction, thrill seeking, and the stability of personality over time (Arvey et al., 1989; Benjamin et al., 1996; Bouchard & Hur, 1998; Cadoret et al., 1995; Dunne et al., 1997; Ebstein et al., 1996; Kagan et al., 1999; Loehlin & Nichols, 1976; Lykken et al., 1993; Matthews et al., 1981; McGue et al., 1993; Rushton et al., 1986; Zuckerman, 1995). There is even evidence for genetic influence on the likelihood that an individual will get divorced (Jockin, 1996; McGue & Lykken, 1992). Of course, there are no genes for divorce, but it appears that individuals inherit traits, such as neuroticism, which then contribute to divorce. Importantly, many of the traits and behaviors I have listed are central elements in personality disorders, and the notion is that individuals who have personality disorders have inherited a high level of a disruptive trait, which is interfering with their lives.

Genetics are important, but they account for only about half of the differences in personality; so it is assumed that the remaining portion is due to the unique personal experiences of individuals. For example, individuals with paranoid personality disorder may have experienced or seen persecution early in life, whereas those with dependent personality disorder may have been severely criticized for independent behaviors and taught that they need to look to others for guidance. Exactly what experiences lead to differences in normal personality is still a topic of debate, and our understanding of personality disorders may have to wait for the resolution of that debate. The strength of combining genetics and experiences to explain some personality disorders lies in the fact that it has already been proven to be effective for explaining *personality,* which after all is what personality disorders are all about.

THINKING CRITICALLY

Questions about Personality Disorders

1. *What do we know about self-mutilation?* **Self-mutilation** (sometimes called *deliberate self-harm,* or *DSH* for short) involves directly inflicting physical harm on oneself; common examples include cutting or burning the skin, breaking bones, and self-poisoning. The term *self-mutilation* does *not* include behaviors such as drinking and driving that can indirectly lead to harm. Furthermore, the term does not include behaviors that result from other

problems such as autism, which often involves head banging, or mental retardation, which causes individuals to hurt themselves because they do not know better. It is also important to distinguish between self-mutilation and suicidal attempts or gestures; self-mutilation is *not* designed to kill or gain attention.

Because self-mutilation is often a private behavior, it is difficult to assess how widespread it is, but estimates in the "normal" population range from less than 1% to as high as 12% in college students (Favazza, 1998; Suyemoto, 1998). In psychiatric populations the rate may be as high as 20% . There are suggestions that self-mutilation is increasing, but it is not clear why. It could be that the rate is not really increasing, but people are simply more willing to report it; or it may be that recent publicity in the media about self-mutilation has suggested the behavior to others. Indeed, interest in self-mutilation surged some years ago when Princess Diana of England reported that because of the strain she was under, she had thrown herself down a staircase and cut herself with razors and knives.

Who self-mutilates? The results of most studies suggest that young women are most likely to engage in this type of behavior and that the problem usually begins in adolescence (Wilhelm et al., 1999; Favazza, 1998; Suyemoto, 1998). Self-mutilation is frequently linked to personality disorders, particularly borderline personality disorder, but it often occurs with other disorders such as posttraumatic stress disorder, substance abuse disorder, OCD, and adjustment disorder (see Topic II) (Strain et al., 1999; Wilhelm et al., 1999; Zlotnick et al., 1999). However, it does occur in otherwise normal individuals. In Case Study 12.1 a woman with borderline personality disorder briefly described self-mutilation as one of her symptoms; in Case Study 12.3 a student who shows no other symptoms of a psychiatric disorder discusses her self-mutilation and what she believes leads to it.

The next question is, why do people self-mutilate? There has been much speculation about the cause, but at present we do not have a complete answer. It is clear that impulsivity plays an important role because individuals do not inhibit the inappropriate impulse to self-mutilate, but it is not clear what generates the impulse. (For a discussion of impulsivity, see Topic III.) Finally, it is interesting and encouraging that the atypical neuroleptic Clozaril (clozapine) discussed in Chapter 11 is effective for controlling self-mutilation (Chengappa et al., 1999). Clozaril may be effective because low levels of serotonin are linked to impulsivity, and Clozaril increases levels of serotonin. In sum, we are beginning to get some insights into the causes and treatments for self-mutilation, but we are far from a full understanding of the behavior.

2. *What causes aggression?* By itself aggression is not a personality disorder. However, because aggression contributes to a number of personality disorders and is an

A Student Talks about Her Self-Mutilation

CASE STUDY 12.3

"ONE NIGHT after my mom had done something my father didn't like, he told me, 'You know, your mom isn't too old to get a beating.' I will never forget those words or the sight of my mom's blackened, swollen, and blood-shot eyes the next morning. My dad had beaten my mom and left her un-conscious on the kitchen floor. The day seemed to be the longest of my life. The following Monday my mom filed for divorce. I couldn't believe that my family would ever be broken up. I thought that we would stay together forever as a whole family, even though we lived with a very abusive man. I was young, naive, hurt, and my world was coming apart.

"That night as I sat on the kitchen floor with a butcher knife in front of me, I was ready to take my life; the only problem was that I had unfin-ished business. I knew that if I took my life, I would be leaving behind the most important thing in my life, my family. I knew that my mom needed me to be strong for her and for my younger sister and brother. My mother and I have always been close, for the sheer fact that we both lived a life of hell (caused by my father) and we stood up for each other. . . . This was the start of my self-mutilation. I knew that I couldn't actually take my own life, but the way I was feeling—lost, hurt, angry, betrayed, [with] a sense of no control—I had to cut myself. With 'cutting' I had complete control of what I was doing. I could start and stop at any time and could inflict as much pain as I desired. No one could stop me. That was 6 years ago, and since then I have cut myself 12 differ-ent times for different reasons. I know that my reasons for self-mutilating may not be good reasons, but my rea-sons are very simple. I use it as a form of self-control and an aid for psycho-logical pain; self-mutilation is a relief for me. It calms my anger and pain. I hate feeling that someone else has the upper hand in controlling my emotions, and with 'cutting' I can con-trol the pain that I would be going through, not someone else. I know I have a serious problem. It is something I have been dealing with for the past 6 years. One day, though, I hope to get better and release all of this sup-pressed anger that has been building up for 20 years of my life. One day . . .

"I hope this helps you understand why I do the nasty things that I do. Most people have the percep-tion that self-mutilation is the most disgusting thing in the world. I must agree that it is, but if it helps me get through the hard times, then why not, right?"

> **With "cutting" I had com-plete control of what I was doing.**

important topic generally, some comment about it here is appropriate. There are three major explanations for aggres-sion. The first is that aggression is learned. In a classic demonstration of this explanation, children watched an adult who acted either aggressively or passively toward a large inflated plastic doll (Bandura & Walters, 1963). Specifically, the adult model did one of four things: (1) picked the doll up and threw it, (2) hit it with a hammer, (3) kicked it, or (4) did nothing to it. Later the children were mildly frustrated by being told that they couldn't play with a toy they wanted, and then their behavior with the doll was observed. It turned out that the children behaved toward the doll almost exactly like the adult model they had observed; that is, if the adult model had hit the doll with a hammer, they hit the doll with a hammer, but if the adult model had not acted aggressively, they did not act aggres-sively. Contemporary demonstrations of the modeling of aggression can be found in school or workplace shootings, which almost always occur in clusters; that is, frustrated students or workers see reports of someone else shooting fellow students or coworkers so they do it.

The second explanation is that individuals act aggres-sively because they believe others are hostile; that is, aggres-sion is defensive. For example, in one study boys were shown a videotape in which one child spilled paint on a picture another child was painting; when the boys were asked why the child had spilled the paint, nonaggressive boys said it was an accident, whereas aggressive boys said the boy did it intentionally to ruin the other child's picture (Dodge & Somberg, 1987).

It seems clear that for some individuals learning and beliefs about others can lead to aggression. However, for other individuals something else must be going on, because their aggression seems to come "out of the blue." For these individuals the aggression can be best explained by physio-logical factors, two of which should be considered.

The first important physiological factor is **testosterone** (tes-TAH-tuh-rohn), the "male" hormone. There is a large body of research indicating that moderately high levels of testosterone are related to *dominance* and high levels are

self-mutilation   Engaging in behaviors that directly inflict physical harm on oneself; also known as *deliberate self-harm,* or *DSH.*

testosterone   The "male" hormone that is implicated in aggression.

related to *aggression* (Aromaeki et al., 1999; Banks & Dabbs, 1996; Mazur & Booth, 1998; Pope, Kouri, & Hudson, 2000; Raesaenen et al., 1999; Tremblay et al., 1998). The link between testosterone and aggression in men is widely recognized, but what surprises many people is that testosterone levels also influence aggression in women (Dabbs & Hargrove, 1997; Harris et al., 1996; Harris, Vernon, & Boomsma, 1998). For example, in a study of women in prison it was found that the women's testosterone levels were positively correlated with both the degree to which their crimes had been violent and the degree to which their behavior in prison was aggressive.

The second important physiological factor is low levels of serotonin. As I will explain in greater detail later (see Topic III), low levels of serotonin are related to impulsivity, and if an individual is impulsive, he or she is more likely to act aggressively. The link between low levels of serotonin and aggression became clear in a series of studies in which it was found that men with long histories of aggressive behavior had lower levels of serotonin in their cerebrospinal fluid than did nonaggressive men (Coccaro et al., 1996; Finn et al., 1998; Lahey et al., 1993; Rogeness et al., 1992; Virkkunen et al., 1989, 1994; Zubieta & Alessi, 1993). Furthermore, in one study levels of serotonin were measured in a group of adolescents, and when the adolescents were followed up 2 years later, it was found that those who had had lower levels of serotonin 2 years earlier were much more likely to behave aggressively than were the others (Kruesi et al., 1992). Finally, increasing serotonin levels with drugs is effective for reducing impulsivity and aggression (Coccaro, 1998).

Overall, then, it appears that (1) high levels of testosterone predispose individuals to act aggressively, (2) low levels of serotonin reduce inhibitions against acting aggressively, and (3) social factors such as learning and beliefs about others play a role in determining what aggressive responses will be used and against whom they will be used.

TOPIC II
Adjustment Disorders

Yesterday Shawna did poorly on her physics exam, and next week she has an important paper due in English. She is really "stressed out" and feeling both depressed and anxious. As a consequence she is "snapping" at her friends, not studying well, and not sleeping much. Certainly there are reasons for her to be upset, but she seems to be overreacting. Is Shawna having normal reactions to the presence of a lot of stress, or is she showing symptoms of a disorder?

We now come to a set of disorders known as **adjustment disorders,** in which the symptoms stem from *problems in adjusting to a stressor in the environment.* Common stres-

sors include financial problems, the breakup of a relationship, and problems at school or work. The symptoms revolve around depression and anxiety and related behaviors. For a diagnosis of adjustment disorder the symptoms must set in within 3 months of the occurrence of the stressor. Importantly, the symptoms of adjustment disorders *are not serious enough to justify other diagnoses,* such as major depressive disorder or an anxiety disorder. In other words, the symptoms are in a gray area between normal responses and more serious disorders; see Figure 12.2.

Symptoms and Issues

Adjustment disorders can involve any of three types of symptoms; specifically, they can involve (1) *depression* (depressed mood, tearfulness, feelings of hopelessness), (2) *anxiety* (nervousness, worry, jitteriness), and/or (3) problems with *conduct* (behaviors such as truancy, vandalism, reckless driving, fighting, not fulfilling responsibilities). These three types of symptoms may occur separately or in combination, so when making a diagnosis, we indicate what type or types of symptoms are involved. That is, after indicating a diagnosis of "Adjustment Disorder," we add one of the following qualifiers: "with Depression," "with Anxiety," "with Disturbance of Conduct," "with Anxiety and Depressed Mood," or "with Mixed Disturbance of Emotions and Conduct." You should also note that individuals are diagnosed as suffering from an adjustment disorder only if their emotional and behavioral responses are "in excess of what would be expected from exposure to the stressor" (American Psychiatric Association, 1994, p. 626). In other words, strong responses to *serious* stressors are not considered adjustment disorders.

All of this seems rather straightforward and reasonable, but there is a problem in that *DSM-IV* does not provide guidelines for making the diagnoses. That is, unlike all other disorders, for which there are checklists of symptoms, *DSM-IV* simply says that adjustment disorders involve excessive responses to stressors; exactly what constitutes an excessive response is not specified. The absence of specific criteria for these diagnoses makes them unreliable; that is, what one mental health professional sees as an adjustment disorder may be dismissed by another as simply a normal response.

Explanations and Treatments

The crucial factor in adjustment disorders is the presence of a stressor (Strain et al., 1999). Specifically, in *DSM-IV* it is pointed out that the symptoms occur "in response to an identifiable stressor" and that "once the stressor has termi-

FIGURE 12.2

Adjustment disorders fall between normal responses and other more serious disorders.

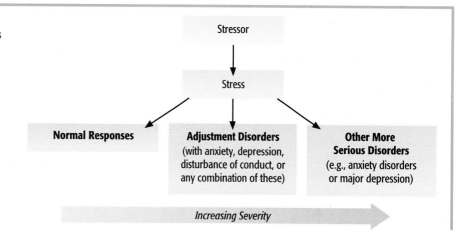

A person with an adjustment disorder has a serious problem adjusting to a particular environmental stressor. Examples of such stressors are financial problems, the end of a relationship, or a work- or school-related problem.

nated, the symptoms do not persist for more than an additional 6 months" (American Psychiatric Association, 1994, p. 626). This means that adjustment disorders are caused primarily by *outside agents* rather than by something within the individual. The situation is similar to infections being

caused by germs. However, when exposed to the same stressors, some individuals overrespond and develop adjustment disorders, whereas others do not. Why the difference in responses? There are two answers to that question: First, people differ in their ability to cope with stressors, and those who are less able to cope will be more likely to develop an adjustment disorder (see Chapter 2 for a discussion of coping). Second, individuals who are predisposed to develop depressive or anxiety disorders may be predisposed to develop adjustment disorders when confronted with stressors. That is, because adjustment disorders appear to be minor forms of depressive and anxiety disorders, the factors that lead to depression and anxiety are probably relevant for the development of adjustment disorders. For example, when individuals who have negative beliefs such as "I'm a lousy person" and "Things aren't going to get better" are exposed to stressors, they are probably more likely to develop "Adjustment Disorder with Depression" than are individuals who do not have negative beliefs. A similar result could occur for individuals who already have somewhat low levels of serotonin, which are then lowered further by prolonged stress (see Chapter 8). Overall, then, what we know about the causes of depression and anxiety can help us understand the development of adjustment disorders.

What treatments are effective for adjustment disorders? Individuals with adjustment disorders constitute a large proportion of the clients seeking help in outpatient clinics and community mental health centers, and most are treated with some form of psychotherapy or counseling

adjustment disorders   Disorders characterized by problems in adjusting to a stressor in the environment, resulting in symptoms such as depression, anxiety, or problems with conduct (behavior).

(Strain et al., 1999). These are the treatments of choice because the individuals need help in dealing with the stressors, and psychotherapy and counseling involve the advice and social support that are crucial for dealing with stress. In some cases individuals might also be given antidepressant or antianxiety drugs to help them through the stressful period; however, in most cases the symptoms are not severe or prolonged enough to justify medication. Indeed, if the symptoms were serious enough for medication, the diagnoses would probably be upgraded to major depressive disorder or an anxiety disorder.

The data concerning the long-term outcomes of adjustment disorders are interesting and raise an important question. The results of one study revealed that for adults the prognosis is fairly good: Five years later 71% were completely well, and only 21% had developed major depression or alcoholism (Andreasen & Hoenk, 1982). In contrast, the picture was less positive for adolescents in that 43% had developed very serious disorders including schizophrenia, schizoaffective disorder, major depressive disorder, and bipolar disorder. These findings raise the question of whether in some cases adjustment disorders that occur *early in life* are *indications of more serious disorders that are developing.* For example, depression generally comes in waves (cycles), and it might be that "Adjustment Disorder with Depression" in childhood or adolescence is the first small wave, to be followed by the larger waves of a major disorder. Also recall that some forms of schizophrenia begin developing early in life, and the symptoms get progressively worse until finally the individuals "cross the line" into schizophrenia. Overall, then, some cases of adjustment disorders may simply be responses to overwhelming stressors and not have any long-term implications, but other cases may reflect developing problems and suggest that the individuals are at risk for developing more serious disorders later. Obviously, adjustment disorders early in life should not be taken lightly or dismissed.

THINKING CRITICALLY

Questions about Adjustment Disorders

1. *Do the symptoms of adjustment disorders really constitute a psychiatric disorder?* The symptoms of an adjustment disorder are certainly a source of concern, particularly since they are sometimes early signs of a more serious disorder that is developing. However, in those cases it might be more appropriate to label the symptoms as "early signs of major depressive disorder" or "early signs of an anxiety disorder" rather than making a diagnosis of adjustment disorder. On the other hand, when the symptoms are not early signs of a more serious disorder, are they really serious enough to jus-

tify designating them a psychiatric disorder? Consider this case: Elaine and Brian dated steadily for almost 2 years but then broke up. The breakup was very upsetting for both of them. Elaine was depressed, cried a lot, didn't think she'd ever find a good relationship, and skipped some classes. Brain was also very upset and got into trouble at his job because he arrived late, antagonized others, and didn't get his work done. These problems lasted about 3 weeks, but now Elaine and Brian are becoming their old selves again and getting on with their lives. Did Elaine and Brian have adjustment disorders, or was what they went though just part of living? In raising this question I am not suggesting that there is no need for the diagnosis of adjustment disorder. Instead I am suggesting that we must be clear about what we mean when we use the diagnosis (is this an adjustment disorder or an early sign of another disorder?) and that we must be sure the symptoms are serious enough to warrant using the diagnosis.

2. *Do some people cause some of their own stressors?* In *DSM-IV* it is clear that adjustment disorders are the result of external stressors, but there is evidence that in some cases individuals actually create external stressors for themselves. For example, there is strong evidence that stressors such as accidents, financial crises, and criminal attacks are not necessarily random and are more likely to occur to some individuals than others (Kendler, Neale, et al., 1993c; see Chapter 8). Indeed, there is a genetic basis for the incidence of stressors; identical twins are more likely to have similar rates of stressors in their lives than are nonidentical twins, and that finding occurs regardless of whether the twins were raised together or apart (Kendler et al., 1993, 1999; Plomin, Lichtenstein, et al., 1990). Of course, there is no gene for stressors. Instead it appears that individuals inherit levels of neurotransmitters or brain structures that influence personality, and then personality traits cause some individuals to behave in ways that lead to stressors. For instance, low levels of serotonin can lead to impulsivity, impulsivity can lead individuals to make bad decisions, and bad decisions can create stressors. The fact that some individuals create some of the stressors that plague them has important implications for treating individuals who suffer from adjustment disorders. Specifically, in cases of individuals who appear to experience "more than their share" of stressors, it might be helpful to determine whether the individuals are contributing to the development of the stressors; if they are, treatment should be focused on helping them to avoid creating new stressors, as well as helping them cope with the stressors they are currently facing. In other words, prevention should be an important element of the treatment. Consider this analogy: If a person keeps falling and breaking his or her leg, should we just keep resetting the broken bone, or should we teach the individual how to walk more carefully?

Impulse-Control Disorders

Debra has just been caught shoplifting. This is the third time she has been caught, but that represents only a fraction of the times she's done it. She doesn't steal because she needs the things she takes, and she can afford to buy the things she steals. When asked about her stealing, she says that when she is in a store, tension builds up, and she just has to steal something. Is she just a thief, or does she have a disorder that causes her to steal?

Calvin is always gambling—playing the lottery, betting on football games, and playing slot machines at a casino. He has lost more money than he can afford to lose. Although he has tried to stop gambling many times, he just can't. After losing, he will often go back the next day to try to break even, a process called "chasing." He is in trouble now because he has very big debts and has even embezzled some money from the company for which he works. Is Calvin addicted to gambling? Is he suffering from a disorder?

Late in the 1790s Philippe Pinel noted that some individuals frequently did things such as set fires or act aggressively for no apparent reason. Because Pinel could not find situational explanations for these behaviors, he assumed that the behaviors were caused by an *instinct for impulsivity*. Over the next 200 years many impulsive behaviors were catalogued, but their cause remained a mystery. Recently, however, an understanding of these behaviors has begun to develop. In the following sections I will describe the symptoms, explanations, and treatments for the five **impulse-control disorders** listed in *DSM-IV*. These disorders and their major symptoms are summarized in Table 12.4.

TABLE 12.4

Impulse-control disorders and their symptoms

Disorder	Symptoms
Intermittent explosive disorder	Recurrent episodes of failure to resist aggressive impulses that result in assaults or destruction of property
Kleptomania	Recurrent failure to resist impulses to steal objects that are not needed
Pyromania	A pattern of setting fires for the relief of tension or because of a fascination with fire
Trichotillomania	Recurrent pulling out of one's own hair
Pathological gambling	Recurrent and persistent maladaptive gambling

Disorders and Symptoms

Aggression, shoplifting, gambling, and hair pulling are common in the general population, and in most cases these behaviors are under voluntary control. However, when the behaviors are *irresistible,* they become symptoms of impulse-control disorders. In general, then, impulse-control disorders are characterized by *an inability to resist an impulse to perform behaviors that are dangerous to others or to the individual.* In some cases the individual may feel an increasing sense of tension before committing the act and then feel pleasure or gratification after completing it. With this as background, let's consider the symptoms of the five impulse-control disorders.

Intermittent Explosive Disorder

An individual can be diagnosed as suffering from **intermittent explosive disorder** if he or she is repeatedly unable to resist acting aggressively and thereby hurts others or destroys property. The degree of the aggression during these outbursts must be grossly out of proportion to any justification in the environment. In other words, the individual "flies off the handle" for little or no reason and as a consequence harms others or destroys property. Individuals with intermittent explosive disorder are also likely to suffer from depression, anxiety, and sometimes eating disorders (American Psychiatric Association, 1994; McElroy et al., 1998).

Kleptomania

Kleptomania (klep-tuh-MA-ne-uh) involves the repeated stealing of objects that are not needed for personal use or for their monetary value. The stealing is often preceded by an increase in tension, and then once the act has been committed, there is a release of tension and feeling of pleasure. (The word *kleptomania* is based on *klep,* which comes from a Greek word meaning "to steal," and *mania,* which comes

impulse-control disorders   Disorders characterized by an inability to resist an impulse to perform behaviors that are dangerous to others or to the individual.

intermittent explosive disorder   An impulse-control disorder that involves repeated failures to resist acting aggressively and thereby causing harm to other people or the destruction of property.

kleptomania   An impulse-control disorder that involves repeated failure to resist the impulse to steal things that are not needed.

from a Greek word meaning "mad," so it means a "stealing madness.") As is the case with intermittent explosive disorder, individuals with kleptomania also tend to suffer from depression, anxiety, and eating disorders (American Psychiatric Association, 1994; Wiedemann, 1998).

Pyromania

The diagnosis of **pyromania** (pi-ruh-MA-ne-uh) is used when an individual deliberately and repeatedly sets fires and does so to reduce tension and/or because of a fascination with fire. An arsonist who sets fires for financial reasons would not be diagnosed as suffering from pyromania. (The term *pyromania* comes from two Greek words: *Pyro*, which means "fire," and *mania*, which refers to madness, so the term means "fire-setting madness.") Very little is known about the cause of this disorder. It has been speculated that people set fires because the excitement associated with fires is pleasurable, but we do not have enough data to draw a conclusion.

Trichotillomania

Many people may play with their hair when they have nothing else to do, but some people intentionally pull hairs out a few at a time, and that leads to the diagnosis of **trichotillomania** (trik-uh-til-uh-MA-ne-uh). (The term is based on three Greek words: *thrix* meaning "hair," *tillein* meaning "to pull out," and *mania* meaning "madness," so it means "madness of pulling hair out.") In some cases the effects can be serious. For example, one woman I know is almost completely bald on the top of her head, so she either wears a wig or combs her hair across the bald spot. A student of mine suffers from trichotillomania, and in Case Study 12.4 she describes her experiences.

Trichotillomania is sometimes seen in young children, and it is equally prevalent among boys and girls. Fortunately, most children "grow out" of the disorder. In cases in which the disorder begins in adolescence/adulthood or persists into adolescence/adulthood, it is more likely to be seen in women than men (Strain et al., 1999). As described in Case Study 12.4, the hair pulling is sometimes preceded by

pyromania An impulse-control disorder that involves deliberate and repeated setting of fires in order to reduce tension and/or because of a fascination with fire.

trichotillomania An impulse-control disorder that involves intentionally pulling out one's hair.

pathological gambling An impulse-control disorder that involves recurrent and persistent maladaptive gambling.

an increase in tension and followed by a feeling of relief or pleasure, but that is not always the case (Hanna, 1997).

Importantly, individuals who suffer from trichotillomania are likely to also suffer from OCD (obsessive-compulsive disorder) and depression (Hanna, 1997; Stanley, Hannay, & Breckenridge, 1997). Furthermore, the drugs that are effective for treating trichotillomania are also effective for treating OCD and depression (Epperson et al., 1999; Ninan et al., 1998; Stanley et al., 1997; Stein et al., 1997; Strain et al., 1999). Specifically, the most effective drugs are the bicyclic antidepressants that increase the level of serotonin at the synapses. The findings that trichotillomania co-occurs with OCD and depression (which are both linked to low levels of serotonin) and that the symptoms of trichotillomania can be reduced with drugs that increase serotonin have led to the speculation that trichotillomania is one of a group of disorders that is caused by low levels of serotonin. More specifically, it has been suggested that trichotillomania may be a type of OCD in which the compulsive behavior happens to be hair pulling (Strain et al., 1999). The notion that trichotillomania is a type of OCD has caused some therapists to treat the disorder with *response prevention,* a strategy found to be effective for OCD (see Chapter 6). For example, when one woman wanted to pull her hair, she was required to pull weeds instead (Salama & Salama, 1999). Successes with behavioral and cognitive therapy have been reported, but because few patients were treated and control conditions were not used, it is impossible to determine whether these approaches are, in fact, effective (Keuthen et al., 1998; Mouton & Stanley, 1996). Overall, then, an understanding of trichotillomania is beginning to emerge, but at present it is premature to draw firm conclusions.

Pathological Gambling

Pathological gambling is different from the other impulse-control disorders in that, whereas no one promotes aggression, stealing, fire setting, or hair pulling, gambling is actively advertised and encouraged by the casino industry and by governments that sponsor lotteries. In other words, gambling is a behavior that is widely encouraged but only up to a point; when that point is passed, the behavior becomes pathological. To be diagnosed as suffering from pathological gambling disorder, an individual must show five or more of the following symptoms:

1. Is preoccupied with gambling
2. Needs to gamble to achieve a desired level of excitement
3. Has been unsuccessful in cutting back or stopping gambling
4. Is restless when trying to cut back or stop gambling
5. Gambles to escape problems or reduce depression

A Student Writes about Her Trichotillomania

"THE 'LOOK': a quick jerk of the head and the squinting of the eyes. Every trichotillomania sufferer knows 'the look' all too well. Imagine meeting a guy for the first time, but he cannot keep his eyes on your face. His eyes keep darting to your head, where an ugly bald spot peers out from its hiding place. Your face feels hot and you want to escape, embarrassed because he has seen your deepest secret. Many people with trichotillomania experience this event too many times in their lifetime; I am one of them.

"When I was about 10 years old, I began to pull out the hair on the crown of my head; however, I do not remember why I started doing it. I continued to do so for about a year, which resulted in a silver-dollar-sized bald spot. My family became concerned, I was extremely humiliated when the students at school made fun of me, and for a while I stopped. Then when I was about 14, I began to pull again, this time at the area near my bangs.

"At age 17 I was also diagnosed as suffering from depression, and I was put on Prozac, but it did not help my depression or my trichotillomania. A number of other drugs were tried, and we finally found that a combination of Depakote and Paxil helped—it reduced my depression, and my trichotillomania went into remission. When I was 18, I was considered to be 'cured,' and my medicine was slowly tapered off. However, without the drugs and with the stress of going away to college, my trichotillomania reappeared.

"My hair pulling usually occurs when I am studying or doing sedentary activities such as talking on the phone or watching TV. However, it increases when I am under stress. I experience a sense of tension before pulling out a hair and sense of relief afterwards, and the pulling of the hair is somewhat pleasure provoking. I do not experience any pain when pulling at the site of my baldness, which is still at my bangs, but it is painful if I pull hairs from other spots.

"I have been fairly successful in covering my bald spot with my bangs, but I hate windy days and avoid swimming because I am afraid that my bald spot will be noticeable. I have often been humiliated when people pointed out my bald spot. I feel as though people look at me with disgust because they do not understand. When asked why I don't just stop pulling my hair out, all I can reply is that it isn't just a bad habit, *it's a disorder.* Believe me, that's not easy to say."

> I experience a sense of tension before pulling out a hair and sense of relief afterwards. . . .

6. Gambles to make up a previous loss
7. Lies to conceal the degree of involvement in gambling
8. Commits crimes such as thefts to finance gambling
9. Has jeopardized or lost an important relationship, job, or educational opportunity because of gambling
10. Relies on others to "bail" him or her out after losing a lot of money gambling

The rate of pathological gambling is relatively high, with most estimates being about 5% of the population (Gupta & Derevensky, 1998; Petry & Armentano, 1999). However, the rate may actually be higher if other "gamblinglike" behaviors such as stock day-trading and video games are included (Fisher, 1994).

Two things characterize individuals who are compulsive gamblers. First, they are impulsive and prone to other risky behaviors that provide quick thrills, such as fast driving, roller coasters, and skydiving (Breen & Zuckerman, 1999; Langewisch & Frisch, 1998; Powell et al., 1999). Second, they tend to suffer from other disorders, most notably depression, OCD, substance abuse, and sometimes antiso-cial personality disorder (Black & Moyer, 1998; Blaszczyn-ski, 1999; DeCaria et al., 1996; Strain et al., 1999). Indeed, among individuals with these disorders, pathological gambling is between two and six times higher than it is in the general population (Strain et al., 1999).

Although the research is limited, it now appears that both genetic and family factors contribute to pathological gambling (Eisen et al., 1998; Winters & Rich, 1998). Exactly how family and genetic factors interact is not yet clear, but it is likely that genetic factors contribute to impulsivity (see the later discussion) and role models in the family lead the individuals to gambling.

Probably the most common treatment for pathological gambling is Gamblers Anonymous, an organization that is modeled after Alcoholics Anonymous. Indeed, there are almost 1,000 chapters in the United States alone. However, research suggests that only about 8% of those who attend the meetings are able to avoid gambling for 1 year (Petry, Armentano, 1999). Cognitive therapy is reported to be of some success, but the research is limited and often plagued with methodological problems that make it difficult to draw firm conclusions concerning its effectiveness (Eche-burua, Baez, & Fernandez-Montalvo, 1996; Sylvain, Ladou-

For some individuals, the impulse to gamble is difficult to control. They are convinced that the next turn of a card or roll of the dice will bring wealth and happiness.

ceur, & Boisvert, 1997; Viets & Miller, 1997). Finally, the results of a few studies suggest that the use of antidepressant drugs that increase serotonin levels might be helpful, probably because they reduce impulsiveness (DeCaria et al., 1996; Hollander, DeCaria, et al., 1998).

Overall, then, although pathological gambling is a pervasive and serious problem, our understanding of its causes and our ability to treat them seem limited.

Explanations and Treatments

It is hazardous to draw conclusions concerning the cause of impulse-control disorders because the research is limited. However, some findings are beginning to emerge that are suggestive of an explanation. One important finding is that impulse control disorders are most likely to co-occur with

OCD and depression. That finding is interesting because both OCD and depression are linked to low levels of serotonin, thus suggesting that impulse-control disorders might also result from low levels of serotonin. Consistent with that notion, a number of studies have revealed that individuals with impulse-control disorders actually have lower levels of serotonin than do persons without these disorders (Carrasco et al., 1994; McElroy et al., 1992; Stein, Hollander, & Liebowitz, 1993). However, the fact that low levels of serotonin co-occur with impulsivity does not necessarily mean that low levels of serotonin *cause* impulsivity; we must ask whether there is experimental evidence linking serotonin to impulsivity. The answer to that question can be found in a series of experiments in which rats first learned to run to the end of a simple straight runway, where they found food. Once that response was learned, an electrical shock grid was placed on the floor of the runway just before the place at which the rats got the food. So, when the rats ran to get the food, they received painful electric shocks. After getting shocked a few times as they crossed the grid, the rats learned to stop before getting to the grid. However, when the rats were then injected with a drug that lowered their levels of serotonin, the rats ignored the possibility of shock and ran across the grid to get the food (Soubie, 1986; Spoont, 1992). In other words, lowering levels of serotonin reduced the inhibition of punished responses and enabled the rats to use impulsively a response that they knew would be punished.

There are numerous human parallels for this finding. For example, criminals who repeat the illegal behaviors for which they were previously sent to prison have low levels of serotonin. Like the rats in the experiment just described, the criminals impulsively ignore the possibility of punishment. In general, then, low levels of serotonin can lead to impulsivity, and models provided by other people may lead the individual to a particular impulsive behavior.

The key to treating impulse-control disorders lies in controlling the impulsivity, and two approaches have been used. First, behavior therapists have tried to restrain the impulsive behavior (Goldman, 1992; McElroy et al., 1989; Murray, 1992). For example, one treatment for kleptomania involved not allowing the individual to go shopping; another for pyromania involved not letting the individual have matches. The effectiveness of this approach is severely limited because it is not possible to restrain individuals from all potential impulsive behaviors. For instance, people have to shop, and it is difficult to keep matches away from them. The second approach involves treating the underlying cause of impulsivity—the low levels of serotonin. That is done with bicyclic antidepressant drugs such as Prozac, Zoloft, and Paxil, which block the reuptake of serotonin, thus making more serotonin available at the synapses (see Chapter 8). A substantial amount of research indicates that this approach can be very effective (Coccaro, 1998; Coccaro

& Kavoussi, 1997; Goldman, 1992; Strain et al., 1999). Indeed, there is evidence that individuals who have long histories of impulsive behavior show rapid and substantial reductions in that behavior when they are given antidepressants (refer back to Figure 12.1). In summary, then, our understanding and ability to treat impulse-control disorders is increasing rapidly, and there is reason for optimism about the future. This is a welcome change for a group of potentially dangerous and destructive disorders that only a few years ago seemed mysterious and untreatable.

THINKING CRITICALLY

Questions about Impulse-Control Disorders

1. *If poor impulse control is caused by low levels of serotonin, why does one individual develop trichotillomania, another intermittent explosive disorder, and a third pathological gambling?* Just as we do not know exactly why individuals develop particular compulsions such as touching walls or walking through doors numerous times (see Chapter 6), so we do not really know why certain individuals develop particular impulse-control disorders. However, it is possible that experiences may channel impulsive behaviors. For example, an individual who gets rewarded for acting aggressively may develop intermittent explosive disorder, whereas an individual who sees parents gamble may develop pathological gambling disorder. In this explanation we see how the integration of physiology and experience can result in a disorder.

2. *Does making it easier to gamble increase the rate of pathological gambling?* To increase tax revenues many state and national governments have legalized gambling in casinos and introduced other forms of gambling such as lotter-

ies. Indeed, the opportunities to gamble are advertised widely, and winning lottery numbers are reported routinely on evening TV news programs. Furthermore, lottery winners are given a great deal of attention and news coverage. Therefore, an important question is, does easy access to gambling and publicity for winning increase pathological gambling? The data on this issue are somewhat mixed and difficult to interpret. On the one hand, the results of a number of studies indicate that areas of the country in which there are more opportunities to gamble have higher rates of pathological gambling (Campbell & Lester, 1999; DeCaria et al., 1996; Petry & Armentano, 1999). However, advocates of gambling point out that these results are based on correlations from which conclusions concerning cause and effect cannot be drawn. For example, it might be that in locations in which there is already a high level of interest in gambling, which could include some pathological gambling, lawmakers are more likely to legalize gambling. That is, interest in gambling may result in more opportunities to gamble rather than vice versa. Advocates of gambling also point to a study done in Windsor, Ontario, Canada, in which 4,000 residents were surveyed by phone before and after a casino was opened, and the responses did not reveal an increase in pathological gambling after the casino opened (Govoni et al., 1998). However, because of the possible risk posed by making gambling easily accessible, casinos and governments that provide gambling opportunities often set aside a portion of their profits to support "hot lines" and treatments for individuals who suffer from pathological gambling. In doing so, they acknowledge the potential risk but argue that the problem can be managed without depriving the rest of the population of the pleasure of gambling and the governments of the revenues. Does government-sanctioned gambling contribute to psychiatric disorders? Are tax revenues for schools and highways a reasonable trade-off for the possibility of increased pathological gambling?

Summary

Topic I: Personality Disorders

▶ Personality disorders involve pervasive and persistent problems in emotional, cognitive, and behavioral responding. The 10 disorders are divided among three clusters:

A. Odd or eccentric: paranoid, schizoid, and schizotypal personality disorders

B. Erratic or emotional: borderline, histrionic, narcissistic, and antisocial personality disorders

C. Anxious or fearful: avoidant, dependent, and obsessive-compulsive personality disorders

▶ Schizotypal, schizoid, and borderline personality disorders appear to be mild forms or early stages of more serious disorders (schizophrenia and major depressive disorder). These personality disorders respond to treatments used for the more serious disorders to which they are related. Most other personality disorders appear to be extensions of normal personality and are caused by a combination of genetics and experiences.

▶ Self-mutilation involves directly inflicting physical harm on oneself. It occurs in otherwise normal individuals but is most common in individuals with various disorders, most notably borderline personality disorder. The cause of self-mutilation is not completely known, but it is related to impulsivity.

▶ A physiological predisposition to aggression is based on high levels of testosterone and low levels of serotonin (which reduce inhibition). The type of aggression and where it is focused can be influenced by learning and beliefs about other people.

Topic II: Adjustment Disorders

▶ Adjustment disorders revolve around problems in adjusting to a stressor in the environment. The stressor can cause depression, anxiety, or problems with conduct (behavior).

▶ Some individuals may be more likely to overrespond to stressors in the environment because they have poor coping skills or because they have negative beliefs or physiological factors that predispose them to develop symptoms. Adjustment disorders are usually treated with psychotherapy or counseling. In some cases adjustment disorders may be early symptoms of more serious disorders that will develop.

▶ Care must be taken not to label normal responses to stressors as adjustment disorders. Some people generate many stressors because of impulsivity or poor judgment, and therefore they are more likely to suffer from adjustment disorders.

Topic III: Impulse-Control Disorders

▶ Impulse-control disorders involve an inability to resist an impulse to perform behaviors that are dangerous to others or the individual.

▶ There are five impulse-control disorders: (1) intermittent explosive, (2) kleptomania, (3) pyromania, (4) trichotillomania, and (5) pathological gambling.

▶ Impulse-control disorders are thought to be caused by low levels of serotonin. Treatment involves trying to restrain the impulsive behaviors or reduce the impulsivity with antidepressants that increase levels of serotonin.

▶ Low levels of serotonin cause the impulsivity that underlies these disorders, but experiences probably determine which disorder will develop. There is concern over the possibility that increased opportunities for gambling and publicity for winners may increase pathological gambling.

Questions for Making Connections

1. Are adjustment disorders, personality disorders, mood disorders, and schizophrenia separate sets of disorders, or are they related to each other on a continuum of mild to severe? What are the implications of your answer for understanding and treating the disorders?

2. Sometimes it is difficult to decide whether an individual who is somewhat dependent, self-centered, shy, difficult to get along with, or "unusual" has a personality disorder. Do you know people whose behaviors might be classified as symptoms of a personality disorder? How could you decide whether an individual has a personality disorder?

3. What might you conclude about an individual who frequently shows the symptoms of an adjustment disorder?

Specifically, what might you consider concerning the cause of the stressors, the characteristics of the individual, the treatments that might be used, and the individual's long-term prognosis?

4. Repeat offenders are a serious problem in the legal system. How can an understanding of personality and impulse-control disorders help us understand those individuals? There is currently a movement toward longer sentences and harsher punishments for repeat offenders. Will that strategy be effective for changing their behavior? Why or why not? What other strategies might be used?

Key Terms and People

In reviewing and testing yourself, you should be able to discuss each of the following:

adjustment disorders, p. 360

antisocial personality disorder, p. 351

avoidant personality disorder, p. 355

borderline personality disorder, p. 347

dependent personality disorder, p. 355

histrionic personality disorder, p. 350

13 Disorders Appearing First in Infancy, Childhood, or Adolescence

WHAT IS THE MOST IMPORTANT thing we do during childhood and adolescence? It's probably that we lay the foundation on which we will build the rest of our lives. If that foundation is weak in any way, we could be in big trouble later. In other words, the disorders that appear during childhood and adolescence are not only serious when they occur, but they can have perilous long-term effects. The disorders we will consider in this chapter range from autism, which can virtually stop an individual's development, to tics, which are simply uncontrollable motor movements.

All of the disorders I will discuss in this chapter are designated in *DSM-IV* as "usually first diagnosed in infancy, childhood, or adolescence." However, two things should be noted about them: First, these disorders are *not limited to early life.* Indeed, almost 30% of children with psychological disorders will carry their disorders into adulthood (Ferdinand & Verhulst, 1995). For that reason it is important that these disorders be detected and treated early. Second, these disorders are *not the only disorders that appear early in life.* In fact, virtually all of the disorders discussed in this book can appear at a young age. For example, depression is often a serious problem in children and adolescents. So why were the disorders discussed in this chapter singled out in *DSM-IV*? They were probably selected because they were the most dramatic or noticeable. For example, a hyperactive child is more noticeable and more of a problem than a depressed child, who sits quietly without the words to describe his or her misery. With this as background, let's begin with disruptive behavior disorders, such as hyperactivity.

TOPIC I
Disruptive Behavior Disorders

Charlie is 6 years old and absolutely out of control. He cannot keep his attention on anything for more than a few seconds. He is constantly squirming, fidgeting, running around, or interrupting people. Furthermore, he does not listen to instructions or ignores those he does hear. When he was younger, his parents thought he was just an "active child," but they now know that he suffers from *attention-deficit/hyperactivity disorder.* Is this disorder caused by poor child-rearing or a physiological problem in the brain? Many children with this disorder take a drug called Ritalin. Does Ritalin help, and does it have any long-term side effects? Should a 6-year-old be taking Ritalin?

Rodney is 15 and always in trouble. At school he frequently bullies other students and often gets into fights. Once he hit a classmate with a baseball bat. He has also been caught stealing a number of times. Last month he stole a car, which he intentionally wrecked "for the hell of it." Rodney also cuts school a lot and has run away from home three times. Obviously, his behavior problems are very serious. Is he just a "bad" kid, or does he have a psychiatric disorder?

In this section we will consider three **disruptive behavior disorders** that involve symptoms such as hyperactivity, violation of rules, and defiant behaviors toward authority figures. These disorders are likely to get children into serious trouble and interfere with the lives of other people.

Attention-Deficit/Hyperactivity Disorder

Did you have a classmate in elementary or middle school who was simply "out of control" much of the time? If so, he or she may have suffered from **attention-deficit/hyperactivity disorder,** which is usually abbreviated as **ADHD.**

Symptoms and Issues

In *DSM-IV* there are two major criteria for a diagnosis of ADHD:

1. *Symptoms of inattention.* The child does not pay attention when spoken to and does not follow through on instructions. Furthermore, the child has difficulty organizing tasks, loses things, is easily distracted, and is often forgetful.
2. *Symptoms of hyperactivity–impulsivity.* The child often fidgets with hands or feet, has difficulty staying in a classroom seat, runs around and climbs on things, and talks excessively; that is, he or she is constantly "on the go" and acts as if "driven by a motor." In addition the child may blurt out answers before questions have been completed, has difficulty waiting for his or her turn, and interrupts or intrudes on others.

These problems with attention and hyperactivity–impulsivity must (1) be present for *at least 6 months,* (2) be present *before the age of 7,* and (3) be serious enough to *interfere with the child's social or academic functioning* (Ameri-

Children with attention-deficit/hyperactivity disorder are unable to focus their attention. They do not listen to directions, are easily distracted, and often fail to complete tasks. They are also often unable to sit still and will run around and climb on things.

can Psychiatric Association, 1994). ADHD is between 5 and 10 times more common among boys than girls and may occur in as many as 5% of elementary school children.

Inattention and hyperactivity–impulsivity are serious symptoms, but what can be even more serious are their long-term effects. Specifically, ADHD can interfere with academic and social development (Popper & West, 1999; Willcutt et al., 1999). Individuals with this disorder quickly fall behind their classmates on tests of academic achievement, and rather than developing close friendships, they become "class clowns" whom others laugh at but do not befriend. Indeed, unless the disorder is treated effectively, individuals with ADHD are at increased risk later in life for dropping out of school, drug abuse, and criminal behavior (Shaffer, 1994).

For many years it was assumed that ADHD was simply a problem of "delayed development" and that the condition was temporary; that is, the child would "grow out of it." However, we now know that between 30% and 80% of children with ADHD continue to show symptoms of the disorder in adolescence and adulthood (Fischer et al., 1990; Lilienfeld & Waldman, 1990; Mannuzza et al., 1991; Mannuzza et al., 1993). Indeed, one of the most important things we have recognized about this disorder in the past few years is that many *adults* suffer from ADHD. Now, rather than thinking that they are bad, stupid, or maladjusted, these individuals recognize that they have a disorder and that it can be treated. Some time ago I met a charming couple in their 60s, and while the husband hugged his wife affectionately, he told me that until recently she had always been "the far side of scatter-brained." His wife grinned and explained that 6 months earlier she had been diagnosed as

disruptive behavior disorders A group of psychiatric disorders that includes attention-deficit/hyperactivity disorder, conduct disorder, and oppositional defiant disorder.

attention-deficit/hyperactivity disorder (ADHD) A disruptive behavior disorder that involves problems with inattention and hyperactivity–impulsivity.

suffering from ADHD and given medication. She said, "It took almost 60 years, but I finally got my act together—or had it put together for me by medication. It's great!"

Case Study 13.1 focuses on a student of mine who suffers from ADHD. She does not have a particularly severe case, but it does interfere with her life, and there is no doubt that her life would have been easier and more productive if she had been diagnosed earlier.

Not all problems with attention and hyperactivity–impulsivity are due to ADHD, so it is essential that care be used in making a diagnosis. Indeed, after reading about ADHD, many students who are not doing well academically immediately assume they have the disorder, and although it is possible, most of these self-diagnoses are not correct. Unfortunately, there is no simple test for the presence of the disorder, so the diagnosis must be based on a clinical judgment. In making that judgment a clinician can rate the child on 12 items in Table 13.1 (on p. 374). However, there is a lot of room for error in these ratings and no specific cut-off score for making a diagnosis, so diagnoses are often unreliable. Some clinicians take a very empirical approach to diagnoses and prescribe Ritalin. If the drug reduces the symptoms, they conclude the child has ADHD; if it doesn't, they withdraw the Ritalin and look for another diagnosis.

With regard to the problem of diagnosis, it is noteworthy that children who are in the manic phase of a bipolar disorder are sometimes incorrectly diagnosed as suffering from ADHD (Nottelmann & Jensen, 1998). Indeed, in one study of adolescents who suffered from bipolar disorder, almost 60% of them met the diagnostic criteria for ADHD when they were in the manic phase of the disorder (West et al., 1995). However, although ADHD and mania share symptoms, they are different disorders, and it is important that they not be confused.

A College Student Writes about Her Attention-Deficit/Hyperactivity Disorder

CASE STUDY 13.1

"I'M NOT YOUR TYPICAL CASE of attention-deficit/hyperactivity disorder because I wasn't diagnosed until my sophomore year in college and because I'm a female, but I've got it and it causes problems. Knowing that I have the disorder helps because now I know what is going on, but knowing does not help the symptoms.

"The best way I can illustrate what it is like to have ADHD is to tell you that focusing on writing this case study is very difficult and frustrating! I've been trying for hours to come up with the next logical thought or sentence. It is taking me forever, and it is still disorganized. I keep drifting off the track. It is no wonder that I was called the 'Space Queen' by one of my high school teachers.

"It's difficult for me to stay on task, whether it's writing a paper, listening to a lecture, or reading a book. Because of this, I'm at an immediate disadvantage academically. It often takes me hours to get through one short textbook chapter, and writing a paper can take forever. My mind just keeps wandering—regardless of how interesting the topic may be.

"Restlessness also contributes to the long length of time it takes me to complete a task. I have to take 'study breaks' very frequently because I simply cannot sit still for long. When I am forced to remain in one place for a period of time, such as in a lecture, I'll generally be swinging my leg or tapping my foot.

"Time is my biggest enemy: The fact that it takes me so long to do anything completely disrupts my life. The amount of time I use to perform anything is the largest disruption in my life. Because my distractions and restlessness make me slower at doing things, I always feel incompetent and rather stupid, which is why I struggle with a bad self-image.

"Low self-esteem is a major component of my disorder. It takes me a long time to do anything, so I feel abnormal and like I'm not intelligent enough to finish assignments as quickly and easily as others. However, some of my problem with self-image is due to my social relationships that get fouled up because of my disorder. I'm typically labeled an 'airhead' because my mind wanders. Frequently I only hear a portion of a conversation and, embarrassingly, I have to ask people to repeat it. That annoys people.

"I've been taking Ritalin for about a year now. It helps, but it's only a treatment, not a cure. It helps me focus and concentrate much better while I study, but it does not completely prevent me from daydreaming. Because Ritalin helps me focus my attention, I'm able to accomplish more in less time than I did before, so I feel a little better about myself. And because it is a stimulant, I feel more motivated to study.

"While on the drug, I am also calmer and not so uptight or agitated in social situations. I don't take sarcastic comments or constructive criticism as personally as I did in the past. I feel that the drug has resulted in some very positive changes. My sister noticed a definite difference and improvement in my personality just days after I began using it. I haven't experienced any negative side effects except for an occasional dry mouth, feeling of thirst, and slight weight loss. But the positive effects far outweigh the negative side effects, and I'm thankful for the difference it has made in my disorder and in my life."

. . . I simply cannot sit still for long.

TABLE 13.1

Items for rating ADHD in schoolchildren

1. Fails to finish things he or she starts
2. Can't concentrate; can't pay attention for long
3. Can't sit still; is restless or hyperactive
4. Fidgets
5. Daydreams or gets lost in his or her thoughts
6. Acts impulsively, without thinking
7. Has difficulty following directions
8. Talks out of turn
9. Does messy work
10. Is inattentive, easily distracted
11. Talks too much
12. Fails to carry out assigned tasks

Source: Adapted from *The Child Attention/Activity Profile* by C. Edelbrock, Pennsylvania State University.

Explanations

Originally it was believed that children with ADHD simply had not yet learned effective strategies for controlling and focusing attention. However, that explanation has been generally abandoned and it is now agreed that ADHD is due to *organic brain dysfunction.* Specifically, there is evidence that the disorder involves *underactivity* in the areas of the brain that are responsible for the control of attention and motor activity (Baving et al., 1999; Biederman & Spencer, 1999; Swanson et al., 1998; Zametkin et al., 1990). For example, as you can see in Figure 13.1, brain scans indicate that individuals with ADHD have lower levels of

FIGURE 13.1

Individuals with ADHD show lower levels of brain activity than do individuals without ADHD.

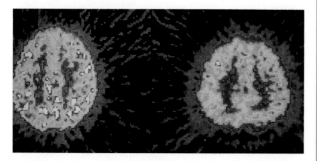

Note: The image on the right is from an individual with ADHD, and the image on the left is from an individual who does not have ADHD. The brighter yellow color indicates more activity (glucose metabolism).

Source: Zametkin et al. (1990).

metabolism in the brain than do individuals who do not have the disorder, and that the greatest differences are in *the prefrontal cortex and the premotor cortex,* areas where attention and motor activity are controlled. But why should low levels of brain activity lead to *high* levels of behavioral activity and rapid shifts in attention? It appears that the areas of the brain that are underactive are responsible for the *inhibition* of motor activity and shifts in attention; that is, low levels of inhibition lead to hyperactivity and rapid shifts in attention. A parallel situation occurs when you drink alcohol: Alcohol is a depressant, and at low levels it depresses the inhibitory areas of the brain, thereby resulting in a "loosening up" of behavior (see Chapter 15). As you will learn later, drugs that stimulate activity in the inhibitory areas of the brain are effective for reducing ADHD.

If ADHD is caused by brain dysfunction, what causes the brain dysfunction? There are two answers to that question, the first of which is *environmental factors,* such as biological traumas and toxins early in life (Levy, Barr, & Sunohara, 1998). For example, infections during the first 12 weeks of pregnancy and lack of oxygen (*anoxia;* uh-NOK-se-uh) during the birth process are linked to ADHD (Gualtieri et al., 1982; Towbin, 1978). Maternal smoking during the prenatal period is also linked to an increased rate of ADHD in children (Millberger et al., 1998; Weissman et al., 1999). Indeed, the rate of ADHD among children of mothers who smoked during pregnancy is twice as high as it is among children of mothers who did not smoke. Another important factor is ingestion of lead, which occurs when children eat chips of paint containing lead or when they inhale air that is polluted with the emissions from automobiles run on gasoline containing lead (David, Clark, & Voeller, 1979; Marlowe et al., 1985; Needleman et al., 1979). The influence of ingesting lead is illustrated in Figure 13.2, which shows that children who had higher lead content in their teeth were more distractible, more impulsive, and more easily frustrated.

Another environmental factor whose role in ADHD was initially overemphasized is food additives, such as colorings, preservatives, and flavorings. It was originally suggested that hyperactivity was an allergic reaction and that as many as 50% of hyperactive children could be returned to normal levels of functioning if they were placed on an additive-free diet (Feingold, 1975, 1976). However, in well-controlled studies in which hyperactive children were given diets containing additives or placebos, it was found that additives accounted for only about 5% of the cases of increased hyperactivity (Conners, 1980; Marshall, 1989). Although the effects of food additives are not as powerful as they were once thought to be, we must not ignore any factor that accounts for even 5% of a disorder as serious as ADHD.

The other factor that contributes to brain dysfunction and ADHD is *genetics* (Biederman & Spencer, 1999; Bieder-

FIGURE 13.2

High levels of lead in children were associated with distractibility, impulsivity, and the tendency to be easily frustrated.

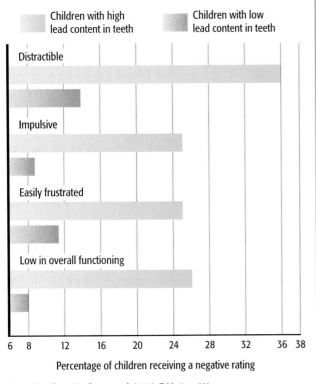

Source: Data from Needleman et al. (1979), Table 3, p. 692.

man et al., 1995; Faraone & Biederman, 1998; Rhee et al., 1999; Rutter et al., 1999; Thapar et al., 1999). Specifically, children with ADHD are more likely to have biological relatives with the disorder than are other children. Furthermore, even if the biological relatives do not have ADHD, they often have mild problems with activity and attention. It is also noteworthy that there is no relationship between the incidence of ADHD among adopted children and the incidence among their adoptive parents. Clearly, the disorder is transmitted biologically, not socially. Overall, then, it appears that environmental factors, such as illness and poisons, and genetic factors lead to brain dysfunctions, which lead to ADHD. How can these problems be treated? We'll consider that next.

Treatments

There are two approaches to treating ADHD, one psychological and one physiological. The psychological approach revolves around teaching children strategies for controlling their hyperactivity and attention. For example, to teach children with ADHD to think through what they are going to do and thereby slow them down, they are given a

"reminder card" with questions like these on it: "What's the problem?" "How can I do it?" "Am I using my plan?" "How did I do?" Children are also given "say it before you do it" exercises, in which they are given a task but must verbalize what they are going to do before doing it.

In contrast, the physiological approach to treatment involves the use of stimulants, the most widely used of which are **Ritalin** (*methylphenidate*) and **Dexedrine** (*dextroamphetamine*). You might think that the last thing a hyperactive child should be given is a *stimulant,* but stimulants are effective for controlling ADHD because they increase activity in the *inhibitory* neurons of the brain, which then reduces motor behavior and distractibility. Students sometimes ask me how it was discovered that a stimulant was effective for treating ADHD. It was an accident: A physician was using stimulants to treat headaches in children, and when he happened to treat children who had both headaches and ADHD, he discovered that the stimulants reduced both sets of symptoms (Gross, 1995). That discovery occurred in 1937, but it was not until relatively recently that the treatment has been generally accepted. (As an aside I should mention that ADHD is also sometimes treated with other drugs that are usually used to treat anxiety, depression, and high blood pressure. Unfortunately, the effects of these drugs on ADHD are generally limited, and they often result in side effects (see Connor, Fletcher, & Swanson, 1999; Greenhill, 1998).

Over the years there has been a great deal of controversy over the question of whether psychological or physiological treatment is more effective for treating ADHD. Based on the results of hundreds of experiments, it now appears that two conclusions can be drawn: First, both psychological and physiological treatments can be effective for controlling ADHD (Greenhill, 1998; Popper & West, 1999). In other words, both treatments are usually more effective than no treatment or a placebo. However, the second conclusion is that the physiological treatment is generally more effective than the psychological treatment. That conclusion can be illustrated with the results of a well-controlled large-scale experiment in which almost 600 children with ADHD were randomly assigned to four conditions: (1) *drug* treatment (Ritalin), (2) intensive *behavior management* at home and school, (3) *combined* drug treatment and behavior management, and (4) *routine community care,* in which parents were told about treatment options available in the community and could take advantage of them if they wished (MTA Cooperative Group, 1999a, 1999b). The ratings of symptoms of ADHD made by parents and teachers over a

Ritalin (methylphenidate)   A stimulant that is effective for treating ADHD.

Dexedrine (dextroamphetamine)   A stimulant that is effective for treating ADHD.

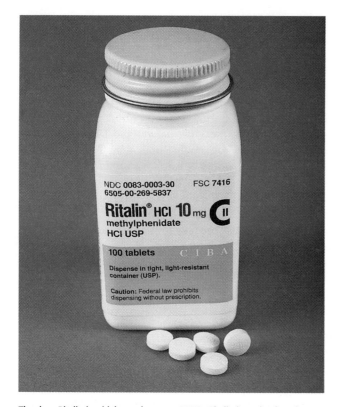

The drug Ritalin is widely used to treat ADHD. Ritalin is a stimulant that reduces motor behavior and distractibility by increasing activity in the inhibitory neurons of the brain.

14-month period consistently indicated that drug treatment was more effective than behavior management or routine care. Furthermore, the combination of drug and behavior management was not more effective than the drug alone, indicating that behavior management did not add to what had been accomplished with the drug treatment; see Figure 13.3. Similar results have been reported in a variety of other investigations, and it appears that drugs are effective for treating almost 90% of the children with ADHD (Greenhill, 1998; Klorman et al., 1994; Mayes et al., 1994). Furthermore, in addition to reducing the problems with attention and hyperactivity, the drugs are also effective for reducing the aggressive and antisocial behavior that often accompanies ADHD (Frederick & Olmi, 1994; Hinshaw, 1991; Hinshaw et al., 1992; Klein et al., 1997).

It is also noteworthy that the drugs have the same beneficial effects on the attention and activity levels of adults with ADHD (Spencer et al., 1995). However, when adults who do not have ADHD take the drug, they get "high" because the stimulant pushes their normal levels of brain activity to higher levels (Volkow et al., 1995; see also Chapter 15). The fact that the drugs can create a "high" poses a problem because some parents take and abuse the drugs that are prescribed for their children.

The drugs begin influencing activity and attention shortly after they are taken, but other effects are usually delayed somewhat. For example, it may take weeks to develop or repair the self-esteem and social relationships that did not develop or were destroyed by the behavior problems associated with ADHD (Frankel et al., 1999). Furthermore, performance on tests of academic achievement will be delayed because children cannot make up in a couple of months of normal behavior what they lost during years of inattention. In other words, the drugs help children control behavior and focus attention, but the drugs cannot overcome the problems that resulted from previous hyperactivity and inattention. To aid in overcoming those problems, counseling or tutoring can be helpful adjuncts.

It is now widely agreed that drugs are effective for overcoming ADHD, but it is important to recognize that drugs are *a treatment not a cure.* Therefore, it is sometimes necessary for individuals to continue taking the drugs for prolonged periods of time, and that necessity leads to the question of whether the drugs have side effects. Initially, the drugs can cause side effects such as problems with sleep and decreased appetite, but those problems are relatively minor and fade with time, and there is no evidence of serious, long-term side effects (e.g., Gadow et al., 1999). However, there is some evidence that Ritalin can slow growth in some children (Klein et al., 1988). Research findings on this side effect are inconsistent, and in cases in which the drug did initially slow growth, the deficit was made up when the children were taken off the drug. Therefore, one treatment strategy involves using Ritalin during the school year but not using it during vacation periods.

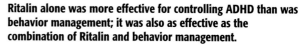

FIGURE 13.3

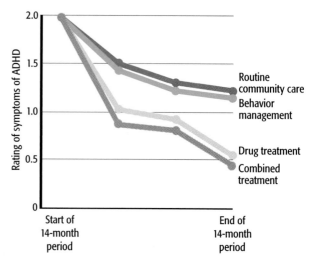

Ritalin alone was more effective for controlling ADHD than was behavior management; it was also as effective as the combination of Ritalin and behavior management.

Note: Scores are based on teachers' reports.

Source: Adapted from MTA Cooperative Group (1999a), Figure A, p. 1084.

One problem with drug treatment of ADHD is that it is sometimes difficult to get children to take the drugs (Stine, 1994). Indeed, rates of noncompliance range between 20% and 70%, and symptoms return within hours if a dose is skipped. Children stop taking the drugs because (1) when they take them, their symptoms go away so they think they no longer need the drugs, (2) they don't like the side effects, or (3) as the effects of one dose wear off, the children become distractible and forget to take the next dose. Fortunately, it is immediately apparent when a child has skipped a dose; the drug can then be given, and within minutes the child is behaving normally again.

Finally, in addition to treating existing cases of ADHD, we must provide better prenatal and perinatal care so that the number of new cases can be reduced (Olds et al., 1998). Reducing smoking during pregnancy would be helpful in that regard. Unfortunately, although the rate of smoking has declined somewhat over the past 10 years, the rate of smoking—particularly heavy smoking—during pregnancy has not (Ebrahim et al., 2000).

In summary, ADHD is known to be due to physiological causes, and we have an effective treatment for it, but more must be done to prevent new cases.

A symptom of conduct disorder is aggression against people, animals, or objects. Many children and adolescents with conduct disorder establish a pattern of criminal activity early in life.

 ## Conduct Disorder

The second disruptive behavior disorder we'll consider is **conduct disorder.** The symptoms of this disorder revolve around a persistent pattern of misbehavior in which the individual is aggressive, destroys property, is deceitful, and breaks rules. Conduct disorder is important not only because it causes problems when individuals are children, but also because it is related to serious behavioral problems later in life. For example, aggression in childhood is the best predictor of aggression in later life, and many children with conduct disorder go on to become serious juvenile offenders and criminals as adults (Quay, 1986; White et al., 1994).

Symptoms and Issues

To be diagnosed as suffering from conduct disorder, an individual must have shown behaviors in at least three of the following four categories *within the preceding year:*

1. *Aggression toward people and animals.* The child or adolescent bullies, threatens, picks fights, and is cruel to people and animals or forces others into sexual activities.
2. *Destruction of property.* The child or adolescent deliberately destroys the property of others, for example, by setting fires.
3. *Deceitfulness or theft.* The child or adolescent breaks into buildings or cars, lies to get what he or she wants, steals, or commits forgery.

4. *Serious violations of rules.* The child or adolescent younger than 13 stays out all night despite rules to the contrary, runs away from home, or is often truant from school.

Conduct disorder usually begins in childhood or adolescence. It occurs in 6–16% of males under the age of 18 and 2–9% of females in the same age group (American Psychiatric Association, 1994). In some individuals the disorder diminishes as the individuals approach adulthood, but in other individuals it persists into adulthood, and the individuals are constantly in trouble. For example, individuals with conduct disorder are at increased risk for drug abuse, criminal behavior, and suicide (Disney et al., 1999; Molina, Smith, & Pelham, 1999). Conduct disorder is also expensive, with costs to parents and authorities running into thousands of dollars a year for each individual treated (Knapp, Scott, & Davies, 1999).

Explanations

A variety of explanations for conduct disorder have been offered. For example, psychodynamic theorists believe that conduct disorder has its origin in the child's relationship with his or her parents. If parents are *overindulgent,* children

conduct disorder   A disruptive behavior disorder that involves a persistent pattern of misbehavior in which the individual is aggressive, destroys property, is deceitful, and breaks rules.

According to learning theorists, the aggressive behavior that characterizes conduct disorder is learned through imitation and rewards. There are numerous findings that individuals who observe aggression in others subsequently perform more acts of aggression.

supposedly grow up believing that they can do anything without fear of punishment, whereas if parents are *overly withholding,* children supposedly grow up believing that they must take what they want, regardless of the consequences. In contrast, learning theorists suggest that the inappropriate behaviors seen in conduct disorder are *learned through imitation and reward* (Bandura, 1983). Consistent with that explanation are numerous findings indicating that individuals who observe aggression in others subsequently perform more acts of aggression (see Chapters 2 and 12). In one classic study it was found that mothers who used aggressive child-rearing methods, such as severe punishment for misbehavior, had children who were more aggressive than those of mothers who used less aggressive methods (Sears, Maccoby, & Levin, 1957). That is, aggression seemed to lead to aggression rather than suppress it. However, it is also possible that the link between aggression in mothers and aggression in children is due to genetic factors or that aggressive and unmanageable behavior in children brought out aggression in parents (Bell, 1968; Frick et al., 1992).

With regard to the learning of conduct disorder, some attention should be given to the link between conduct disorder and sociocultural factors. One of the best predictors of who will develop conduct disorders is socioeconomic status (Lahey et al., 1995). Statistically, African Americans are more likely than other ethnic groups to develop conduct disorder, but analyses have revealed that *ethnicity per se has nothing to do with the development of the disorder.* Instead African Americans were overrepresented among those with conduct disorder only because they were overrepresented in the lower socioeconomic classes. Lower-class membership could contribute to the development of con-

duct disorder in a variety of ways, but one of the strongest is learning. That is, the rewards and role models for antisocial behavior that are available in the lower classes can contribute to the development of the disorder.

Concerns have been raised over the possibility that in some cases a diagnosis of conduct disorder may be misapplied to individuals in high-crime areas, who are using behaviors such as fighting to *protect themselves.* Therefore, *DSM-IV* points out that "the Conduct Disorder diagnosis should be applied only when the behavior in question is symptomatic of an underlying dysfunction within the individual and not simply a reaction to the immediate social context" (American Psychiatric Association, 1994, p. 88). That is, conduct disorder involves behaviors that are generated by the individual, not elicited by a situation.

Recently, attention has been focused on three physiological factors that contribute to conduct disorder, the first of which is *maternal smoking during pregnancy* (Disney et al., 1999; see also Brennan et al., 1999; Raesaenen et al., 1999). Maternal smoking probably affects brain development, and as a consequence it results in substantial increases in conduct problems, particularly aggressive and violent behaviors. Indeed, boys whose mothers had smoked 10 cigarettes (less than half a pack) per day during pregnancy were *four times* more likely to be diagnosed with conduct disorder than were boys whose mothers did not smoke (Weissman et al., 1999). Furthermore, as illustrated in Figure 13.4, the more cigarettes a woman smoked during pregnancy, the more likely it was that her offspring committed a violent crime. This finding is important not only because the effect is strong, but because smoking during pregnancy is a cause of conduct disorder that can be avoided more easily than many of the other causes. Unfortunately, as I noted earlier,

FIGURE 13.4

Smoking during pregnancy is related to offsprings' arrest rate for violent crimes.

Note: Smoking was measured during the third trimester of pregnancy.

Source: Adapted from Brennan et al. (1999), Figure 1, p. 217.

the rate of smoking in general is down, but there has not been a decrease in heavy smoking among pregnant women (Magno Zito et al., 2000).

The second physiological factor of interest is *low levels of serotonin* (Lahey et al., 1993; Rogeness et al., 1992; Zubieta & Alessi, 1993). Serotonin is important because it plays a role in the inhibition of punished responses (Soubie, 1986; Spoont, 1992). For example, if an animal has learned to inhibit a response because the response has been followed by punishment but then the animal's level of serotonin is lowered with a drug, the animal will disregard the possibility of punishment and make the response (see Chapter 12). This disregard for punishment is similar to what we see in the behavior of individuals with conduct disorder. Furthermore, there is a substantial amount of evidence linking low levels of serotonin to conduct disorders and aggression in humans (Coccaro et al., 1996; Finn et al., 1998; Lahey et al., 1993; Rogeness et al., 1992; Zubieta & Alessi, 1993). For example, a study of children and adolescents with conduct disorder found that levels of serotonin measured at one time were correlated −.72 with levels of aggression 2 years later (Kruesi et al., 1992). That is, low levels of serotonin were linked to high levels of subsequent aggression.

The third physiological factor of interest is *high levels of testosterone* in both men and women (Aromaeki et al., 1999; Banks & Dabbs, 1996; Dabbs & Hargrove, 1997; Harris et al., 1996; Harris et al., 1998; Mazur & Booth, 1998; Pope, Khouri, & Hudson, 2000; Raesaenen et al., 1999; Tremblay et al., 1998; Virkkunen et al., 1994). Specifically, in both

men and women, high levels of testosterone are related to high levels of aggression, and the higher the levels of testosterone, the more violent the aggression.

Given that low levels of serotonin and high levels of testosterone are related to the aggression seen in conduct disorder, the question that arises is, what leads to those deviant biochemical levels? Probably the best explanation for chronically low levels of serotonin and high levels of testosterone is genetics. Consistent with that notion are findings indicating that genetic factors play an important role in conduct disorder (Jarey & Stewart, 1985; Lahey et al., 1995; Mednick, Gabrielli, & Hutchings, 1984; Simonoff et al., 1998). Specifically, biological children of parents with conduct disorder have high rates of the disorder even when they are adopted at birth and raised by parents who do not have the disorder. Furthermore, identical twins are more likely to both have conduct disorder than are nonidentical twins.

Each of the explanations just described probably accounts for some cases of conduct disorder, but many cases probably result from the interaction of causes. For example, physiological factors can provide a predisposition to conduct disorder, and then observing others who behave inappropriately may lead to specific symptoms such as aggressive acts.

Treatments

Like other disorders that can stem from different causes, conduct disorder requires different approaches to treatment, depending on the suspected cause. If it is suspected that conduct disorder was learned, the strategy may be to punish the behavior. It might also be effective to reward alternative behaviors that are more appropriate, but unfortunately that is rarely done. Some evidence for the effectiveness of punishment is provided by a study of the arrest records of almost 30,000 males in Denmark (Brennan & Mednick, 1994). The results indicated that among those who were arrested for personal-property offenses such as breaking and entering or car theft, 52% of those who were not punished after their first arrest were arrested in the future, versus only 20% of those who were punished after their first arrest. In other words, punishment resulted in a 32% reduction in future illegal behavior. Furthermore, among individuals who were arrested multiple times, those who were consistently punished were less likely to be arrested in the future than individuals who were punished inconsistently. However, it is important to note that even among individuals who were consistently punished following three or four arrests, there was still a recidivism rate of 67%. In other words, punishment can be effective, but there are individuals for whom punishment does not appear to be effective.

Punishment by itself is often ineffective because it serves to *suppress* the inappropriate behavior only temporarily;

what is needed is to learn and be rewarded for alternative appropriate behavior. That is, it is not enough to say "Don't do that" and punish the behavior; it is also essential to say "Do this instead" and then reward the better behavior. In fact, there is now considerable evidence that early education in combination with social support can be effective for reducing delinquency in children who are at high risk (Yoshikawa, 1994).

For individuals for whom punishment and education are not effective, the problem may be low levels of serotonin that lead to impulsivity, and for those individuals it may be effective to use a drug that increases the levels of serotonin (Ghaziuddin & Alessi, 1992). A drug (fenfluramine) that increases the release of serotonin was found to reduce aggressive and impulsive behavior in men, but the drug had to be withdrawn from the market because it had serious side effects (Cherek & Lane, 1999). However, the bicyclic antidepressant drugs that increase serotonin levels by blocking its reuptake (see Chapter 8) can be effective for reducing impulsivity, aggression, and conduct disorder (Coccaro, 1998; Coccaro & Kavoussi, 1997; Heiligenstein et al., 1992; Saltzman et al., 1995).

Overall, then, although for many years attempts to treat many of the individuals with conduct disorder were relatively ineffective, the addition of drugs to psychological strategies has enhanced the treatment success rate.

Oppositional Defiant Disorder

Finally, a brief comment should be made concerning **oppositional defiant disorder.** Children and adolescents with this disorder often lose their temper, argue with adults, refuse to comply with the requests of adults, deliberately annoy people, are easily annoyed by others, and are frequently angry, resentful, spiteful, or vindictive. Periods of behaviors like these are often normal in children and ado-

oppositional defiant disorder   A disruptive behavior disorder in which children and adolescents often lose their tempers, argue with adults, refuse to comply with the requests of adults, deliberately annoy people, and are frequently angry, resentful, spiteful, or vindictive.

pervasive developmental disorders   A group of psychiatric disorders that includes autistic, Asperger's, childhood disintegrative, and Rett's disorders; virtually all aspects of development are disrupted in these disorders.

autistic disorder   A pervasive developmental disorder that involves extreme problems with social interaction, a greatly reduced ability to communicate, and a very limited range of interests and activities.

lescents, so there is a caution in *DSM-IV* about using this diagnosis unless the behavior pattern is very persistent. It is also important to distinguish the negative behaviors seen in oppositional defiant disorder from the negative behaviors seen in other disorders such as depression. Although oppositional defiant disorder is thought to occur in between 2% and 16% of children and adolescents, little is known about it, and most mental health professionals do not seem particularly concerned about it.

THINKING CRITICALLY

Questions about Disruptive Behavior Disorders

1. *Is ADHD a psychiatric disorder, or is it just misbehavior?* Some critics argue that rather than considering problems with attention and hyperactivity–impulsivity as a *disorder* and treating children with psychotherapy or medication, the behaviors should be thought of as *misbehaviors,* and treatment should be focused on improving child-rearing methods. However, the evidence is now clear that ADHD results from specific brain dysfunctions. To argue otherwise is comparable to arguing that the hands of persons with Parkinson's disease shake because these individuals have not learned to control the shaking. We may still argue about the best way to treat ADHD (see the next question), but the underlying cause seems clear: This is a physiological disorder.

2. *Is it appropriate to use drugs to treat disruptive behavior in children?* It is clear that drugs such as Ritalin are very effective for treating ADHD, and that bicyclic antidepressants can be effective for treating many cases of conduct disorder. However, some people are concerned about using drugs to treat children, and they are particularly alarmed by the dramatic increase in the use of Ritalin by children as young as 5; see Figure 13.5. There seem to be two reasons for the increased use: First, there is increasing recognition of ADHD as a disorder and of the fact that Ritalin is effective for treating it. Second, because more and younger children are being taken care of in day-care facilities, there may be more demands that children be under control. That is, day-care facilities will simply not take children who are suffering from ADHD, so more parents are turning to Ritalin. Given that there appears to be a need for Ritalin, the question arises as to whether the drug is safe for children as young as 5 or 6. At present we do not have an answer for that question because tests have not been conducted on children that young; we know that Ritalin is safe and does not have long-term side effects on older children (see the earlier discussion), but we just don't know about very young children.

FIGURE 13.5

There has been a great increase in the use of Ritalin.

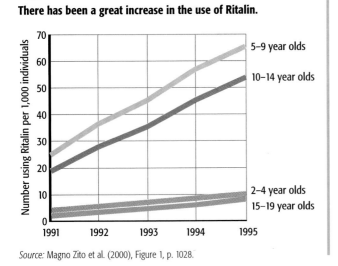

5–9 year olds

10–14 year olds

2–4 year olds

15–19 year olds

Source: Magno Zito et al. (2000), Figure 1, p. 1028.

Two other cautions should be noted: First, not all children who have problems with hyperactivity and attention are suffering from ADHD (some cases are due to bipolar disorder, and some are probably simple misbehavior), and therefore care must be taken to prescribe Ritalin only for those children who actually have ADHD. Although sometimes Ritalin is prescribed when it is not appropriate, it is unlikely that it will be used for long by those children because it will not reduce their symptoms; indeed, it can make their symptoms worse. That is, Ritalin only works when hyperactivity and problems with attention are due to brain underactivity.

The second concern revolves around the dosage level of Ritalin. Specifically, there is a dose-dependent relationship with Ritalin (higher doses have greater effects; see Chapter 15), so it is sometimes necessary to increase the dosage level until the maximum beneficial effect is achieved (Frankel et al., 1999; Pelham et al., 1985). However, dosage levels that are too high can push the inhibition of hyperactivity too far and the individual will respond to only a very limited range of stimuli, which can result in social withdrawal and repetitive or "mechanical" behaviors (Solanto & Conners, 1982; Wender, 1971). For example, after receiving a high dose of medication, one originally hyperactive child persisted in writing one homework assignment for 5 hours. In another case a previously talkative and sociable child withdrew to a corner, where he read the same story over and over and refused to interact with others. In other words, excessively high levels of the drugs will result in abnormal behavior that is the *opposite* of ADHD. The problems of overuse and excessively high doses are not unique to the drug treatment of ADHD, and potential problems associated with medication misuse should not be invoked as reasons for limiting the appropriate use of medication.

Evan is 5. He spends his days sitting cross-legged on the floor, rocking back and forth and staring into space. He is oblivious to what is going on around him. When he is touched or picked up, he is unresponsive and limp. This lack of response to others has been apparent since he was born; he just never cuddled like other infants. Evan has not developed any verbal behavior, but in a rather mechanical way, he will sometimes repeat words that are said to him. He is diagnosed as suffering from *autism*. What caused this disorder to set in so early in life, and is there a treatment?

Billy is fascinated by baseball and knows the important statistics about virtually every baseball team and every major league player. Apart from baseball he doesn't have any other particular interests. He isn't retarded–he just doesn't have interests. Furthermore, Billy doesn't seem interested in people. When you ask him about his family, you might as well be asking him about how things are on the moon. He just can't relate to people. Finally, Billy is very clumsy; he is always running into things. Billy's development is certainly limited. Does he have a developmental disorder?

The disruptive behavior disorders we discussed in the preceding section can be serious, but their symptoms are somewhat limited. That is, although they include problems with attention, hyperactivity, and aggressiveness, other aspects of the children's development are normal. In contrast, in **pervasive developmental disorders** virtually all aspects of development are disrupted. Indeed, children with these disorders may be unable to interact with other people, have severe problems with communication, have an extremely limited range of interests, and sometimes show serious repetitive behaviors such as head banging. Because of the extensive nature of these disorders, they can be devastating. In this chapter we will focus mostly on *autistic disorder*, but we will also consider three related disorders: *Asperger's, childhood disintegrative,* and *Rett's disorders.*

Autistic Disorder

The word *autism* means "self-centered" and "withdrawn from reality," and **autistic disorder** involves extreme problems with social interaction, a greatly reduced ability to communicate, and a very limited range of interests and activities. In other words, children with autism appear to be "in their own little worlds" and usually cannot be reached. Autism occurs four times more frequently in boys than girls, and it is thought to be relatively rare, occurring in about 1 of 2,000 children (Fombonne, 1999). However, in the past 10 years the rate has increased substantially (Gillberg & Wing, 1999; Fombonne, 1999; Rodier, 2000). Fortunately, the increase appears to be due to a greater awareness of the disorder and a greater willingness to use the diagnosis rather than to an actual increase in the incidence of the disorder. There are also regional variations in the incidence of autistic disorder; for example, it occurs more frequently in the United States than in most other countries (Gillberg & Wing, 1999; Howlin & Moore, 1997). However, this difference also appears to be due to differences in awareness of and willingness to use the diagnosis. Although some of the symptoms of autism are apparent shortly after birth, the disorder is usually not officially diagnosed until about age 6. That delay probably reflects a hesitancy to label a child as suffering from this very serious disorder. Finally, autism is a chronic disorder, but some individuals show a slight improvement over time (Popper & West, 1999). With this as background, let's consider the symptoms of autism in greater detail.

Symptoms

To be diagnosed as suffering from autistic disorder, a child must show the following three symptoms with at least one of them occurring before the age of 3:

1. *Impairments in social interactions.* Children who suffer from autism fail to show nonverbal interpersonal behaviors such as eye-to-eye contact or facial expressions, and they do not develop relationships with peers or seek out others. In many cases they even seem to be unaware of the presence of others. As infants they do not cry when left alone, do not smile at others, and do not vocalize in response to others. When picked up, they are stiff or limp and do not cuddle against their parents' bodies as normal infants do. Later in life they do not relate to others but neither do they get into conflicts with others. They are simply "on their own wavelength" and are unable to respond to other people.

2. *Impairments in communication.* Children with autism show a marked delay or total lack of development of spoken language. Indeed, many children with autism are essentially mute, or they make only meaningless sounds that are not used to communicate with others. The absence of language is a very important factor in determining a child's prognosis. Specifically, if the child does not have language skills by the age of 5, there is a 75% chance that he or she will never make an adequate personal or social adjustment (Gillberg, 1991).

Children with autism who do talk often show a variety of peculiar speech patterns. For example, they may simply repeat what is said to them; if you say, "Hello, Jimmy," the child may say, "Hello, Jimmy." This response pattern is referred to as **echolalia** (ek-o-LA-le-uh) because the child's response is like an echo coming back from a mountainside. In some cases echolalia is delayed, and the child repeats the phrase hours later, completely out of context and with no apparent stimulus. Another unusual speech pattern is *pronoun reversal,* whereby the child uses *he, she,* or *you* for *I* or *me.* For example, a boy with autism who wants a cookie may say, "You want a cookie" or "He want a cookie."

3. *Restricted, repetitive, and stereotyped behaviors.* Finally, children with autism may sit alone for hours with a fixed stare, or they may rock back and forth endlessly. In other cases they may repeat certain behaviors such as spinning a toy for hours, or they may repeatedly make unusual gestures with their fingers and hands. For example, for hours at a time they may move their fingers as if playing a piano. Often these children engage in self-mutilation behaviors such as scratching or hitting themselves. In one case a child who was not restrained banged his head 1,800 times in 8 days (Lovaas & Simmons, 1969).

Children with autism also seem to prefer sameness with regard to environmental stimuli. They rigidly keep things such as toys or clothing in careful order and become upset if there is any change in their daily routine.

The symptoms of autism appear *very early.* Indeed, parents who have some experience with infants and who know what to expect notice a problem with the child almost from birth.

Finally, it is important to recognize that although mental retardation is not technically part of the diagnosis, at least 80% of individuals with the disorder show seriously subnormal levels of intelligence (Fombonne, 1999; Kent et al., 1999). The presence of mental retardation often makes it difficult to decide between the diagnoses of autistic disorder and mental retardation (Vig & Jedrysek, 1999). In other words, it is sometimes difficult to determine whether

Children with autistic disorder show little response to other people, a reduced ability to communicate, and a restricted repertory of activities and interests.

a child's inability to interact with others, problems with communication, and limited range of behaviors are simply the result of mental retardation or whether they reflect autistic disorder.

Fortunately, some individuals with autistic disorder have symptoms that are less severe than those I have described and do not suffer from mental retardation. These individuals are generally referred to as **high-functioning individuals with autism** (Yirmiya & Sigman, 1991). In short, like almost all of the disorders we have considered, autism is not an either/or condition but instead differs in severity along a continuum from mild to severe.

In Case Study 13.2 (on pp. 384–385) you will find portions of an interview I had with the mother of a child who suffers from autistic disorder. In the interview she describes her child's behavior and her reactions.

Issues

Sociocultural Factors. The results of early studies suggested that autism was more likely to occur in upper than in middle or lower socioeconomic classes and that the parents of children with autistic disorder were likely to be professionals (Eisenberg & Kanner, 1956). However, subsequent and better studies have consistently indicated that autism is *not* related to social class (Gillberg & Schaumann, 1982; Tsai et al., 1982). The initial findings relating autism to upper-class status were probably due to the fact that the studies were conducted in prestigious and expensive hospitals, where the children of wealthy parents were more likely to be brought for treatment.

Intellectual Development and Savant Syndrome. Although many individuals with autistic disorder suffer from mental retardation, some of them also show extraordinary abilities in one particular area. For example, they may be able to play complex musical pieces after only hearing them once, or they may be able to tell on what day of the week a particular date falls even if the date is 50 years in the past or future. This condition is known as **savant** (sa-VANT) **syndrome.** Although savant syndrome is particularly striking in individuals with autism, it is not unique to those individuals. Indeed, it can occur in otherwise normal individuals. Importantly, the amazing ability of individuals with savant syndrome does not reflect strong abilities in closely related areas. For example, individuals who can quickly calculate the day of the week for a particular date years in the future do not show better than average abilities in memory or mathematics (Heavey, Pring, & Hermelin, 1999). I will discuss savant syndrome in greater detail later (see Chapter 17), but here I should point out that we do not yet understand what causes this syndrome.

Autism versus Schizophrenia in Childhood. For many years there was a controversy over whether autism was a separate disorder or simply a type of schizophrenia in childhood. However, it is now generally agreed that autism and schizophrenia in childhood are separate disorders. A variety of factors separate infantile autism from schizophrenia in childhood:

1. Individuals with autism rarely have a family history of schizophrenia, but individuals with schizophrenia often have a family history of schizophrenia.
2. Individuals with autism usually show a lack of intellectual development, but that is not the case with individuals who suffer from schizophrenia.
3. Individuals with autism have limited speech, whereas individuals with schizophrenia usually have normal speech ability but communicate bizarre ideas.
4. Autism is apparent almost at birth, whereas schizophrenia develops later.
5. Neuroleptic drugs are generally effective for treating individuals with schizophrenia but have relatively little effect on individuals with autistic disorder.

Overall, then, autism and schizophrenia in childhood are considered separate disorders, and you should not assume that the causes and treatments for one can be applied to the other.

Explanations

Autism is one of the major unsolved mysteries of abnormal psychology. However, since the disorder was first identified about 60 years ago, we have ruled out a number of erroneous explanations and are now developing a better understanding of what causes the disorder. Before discussing the new findings, we must give some attention to discredited explanations because they have become part of the folklore of psychology and still pop up occasionally.

Early psychodynamic explanations for autism were focused on the role of parents' personalities and their styles of child-rearing. For example, it was suggested that the parents of children with autism were cold, formal, humorless, detached, highly rational, and objective (Bettelheim, 1967; Kanner, 1943). Supposedly, such parents did not provide their children with interpersonal warmth and nurturing, and it was assumed that the children turned away from these "mechanical" parents and turned inward for comfort and stimulation. The psychodynamic explanations have lost most of their credibility and supporters because numerous investigations have revealed that the parents of

---

echolalia   A response pattern seen in autistic disorder that involves the repeating back of words or phrases, like an echo.

high-functioning individuals with autism   Individuals with autistic disorder whose symptoms are less severe than most other individuals with the disorder and who do not suffer from mental retardation.

savant syndrome   Condition characterized by the presence of one extraordinary ability in an autistic, mentally retarded, or normal individual.

A Mother Talks about Her 15-Year-Old Son, Who Was Diagnosed as Suffering from Autism

CASE STUDY 13.2

Holmes: Can you tell me when you first noticed that something was wrong with Tom?

Mother: In retrospect, I think I always felt there was something wrong, even as early as the pregnancy. The pregnancy was technically normal—tests didn't show any problems—but it just wasn't like my other two pregnancies. He was always moving and kicking, and I just thought he was unhappy in the womb. Then right after he was born, I noticed a couple of things that were different from my other children. Tom had difficulty sucking at the breast, and he never seemed to be comforted when he was picked up or cuddled. In fact, picking him up seemed to upset him more; his muscles would become rigid, and he would scream at the top of his lungs. This worried my husband and me; we thought we were doing something wrong in the bonding process.

Holmes: Can you tell me about his reactions to other people?

Mother: Well, at first he would scream and twist if touched by anyone, but as he got older, he stopped showing that extreme reaction, but he didn't react positively either. He was just neutral and limp. However, when he was picked up by an unfamiliar person, he would have a severe negative reaction, a real tantrum. Apart from that, he seemed to be in his own little world. When he was an infant, it was difficult to get his attention, and then it was impossible to hold it for more than a few seconds. He never played with other children or adults. Instead he would do activities like looking in mirrors or at shiny objects for hours at a time. He also liked to spin the lids from jars over and over. One of his favorite things was to sit in front of the washing machine and watch the clothes go round and round. Sometimes he would sit in a corner and rock back and forth, or he would flap his arms and sing "da da de la da" over and over. For a while we tried to force social interactions on him, hoping we could "break through." That never worked, and he would resist by banging his head on the floor and screaming. At around 8 or 9, he started interacting with others a little, and now he will sometimes initiate a conversation or an activity. I'm not sure whether we had an influence or he finally matured a little.

Holmes: How about developmental tasks—things like smiling, walking, and talking? Did he start doing those things on schedule?

Mother: Tom did everything much later than other children. He didn't roll over until 8 months, and he didn't walk until 26 months. When he finally did walk, he walked only on his toes until he was 5. He started talking at around 4, but even then he didn't talk, he just repeated what others were saying. We had a terrible time getting him toilet-trained. It wasn't until he was 5 that he could stay dry during the day, and he wet himself at night until he was 12.

Holmes: Did Tom show any unusual behaviors other than his lack of social interest and delayed development?

Mother: One thing that has been a real problem is that he just cannot deal with change. To keep peace in the house, everything in his room—which is where he stayed most of the time—had to be kept exactly the same all the time. One time I threw away an old beat-up wastebasket that had been in his room, and for 2 weeks he cried, demanding that it be returned. When he was moved from the 5th to the 6th grade, he refused to go to school for 3 weeks and became violent when we tried to drag him out

children with autism do not differ from the parents of normal children or from parents of children with other disorders (e.g., O'Hanrahan, Fitzgerald, & O'Regan, 1999).

Learning theorists explained autism by suggesting that behaviors such as head banging, uncooperativeness, tantrums, and mutism are often followed by rewards such as attention, food, and toys designed to distract the child and reduce the abnormal behaviors (Ferster, 1961; Lovaas & Smith, 1989). However, rather than reducing the abnormal behaviors, the rewards increase and strengthen them. In other words, learning theorists suggested that autistic behaviors are taught by parents who reward the wrong behaviors. This explanation for autism was tested indirectly with experiments in which attempts were made to eliminate autistic behaviors by not rewarding them and instead rewarding normal behaviors. In other words, it was assumed that if autistic symptoms were learned, they could be extinguished and normal behaviors could be learned in their place. These experiments will be discussed later in the section on treatment, but for now you should note that ignoring autistic behaviors and rewarding normal behaviors did not result in a reversal of autism. In view of that finding much of the interest in learning as the cause of autism waned.

It is now generally agreed that autism is due to problems with brain development, and although we do not yet completely understand the problems, an interesting pattern is beginning to emerge. Specifically, investigators are identifying links between particular problems in the brain and the symptoms of autism. For example, it has been found that *dominance of the right temporal lobe* over the left temporal lobe is related to the language/communication symptoms of autism (Mueller et al., 1999). (With regard to that finding you should note that for most people language abilities are controlled primarily by the *left* temporal lobe, so problems would be expected when the left lobe was underactive relative to the right lobe.) There is also evidence that increased size of the *amygdala,* which plays a role in rage and aggression, is linked to problems of temper and head banging (Abell et al., 1999). Next, increased size of the *basal ganglia,* which play a role in motor behavior, is associated with the abnormal motor behaviors and compulsions seen

of the house. As long as things were perfectly constant and no one tried to get into his little world, he would be all right. Well, I don't mean "all right," but he wouldn't become agitated or violent.

Holmes: You mentioned school. How's he been doing in school?

Mother: School has always been a struggle for us all. Just getting him to go has been tough, but on the whole Tom has done pretty well. Most of the time he has been in a special class for children with behavior disorders, so he gets more structure and more individualized instruction. Once he was "mainstreamed" into a regular typing class, but the change and additional stimulation were too much for him. He is now doing 10th-grade-level work, which is just about where he should be. For the past year he has been in a special occupational program where he earns school credit for working 3 hours a day. First, he worked in a veterinary clinic, where he did odd jobs. He loved being around the animals, but he couldn't handle the lack of structure—different chores all the time—so he started withdrawing and finally stopped going. Then he was switched to a fast-

food restaurant where he had a consistent assignment, but for some reason that didn't work out either. I think there was too much activity and pressure to keep up.

Holmes: When was Tom first diagnosed as suffering from autism?

Mother: (long pause; rubs her temples and slumps in her chair a little) All along we'd been very worried about Tom's development, and we'd taken him to a variety of specialists, but it was the language problem at age 4—the delay and the echolalia—that convinced everyone that Tom was autistic. *(pause)* I will never forget the day the diagnosis was finally made. The possibility that he was autistic had been mentioned earlier, but we had always avoided confronting it. We kept looking somewhere else for a "better" explanation—something that could be cured. When the social worker told us the diagnosis, it was like we had been hit by a truck. We had seen the truck coming, but we had intentionally looked the other way. We had a son who was autistic—what were we going to do? First, we got books and started reading about autism, but that made things worse because they said it was the parents' fault for being cold

and distant. We felt terrible, but then the psychologist explained that those were old theories and that now it is believed that autism is due to some genetic problem or a problem during pregnancy. That didn't make the problem less serious, but it helped relieve some of our guilt. *(pause)* We've come to accept the fact that Tom is different from other children. There are limits to what he can do and limits to what we can do for him. Autism isn't an either/or thing—there are degrees of it, and Tom's case isn't as severe as many others. He can live at home and function to some extent in the community. Someday, when we aren't around to take care of him, he will probably have to be moved to some sort of sheltered-living situation. I've grown to recognize that we have to accept people the way they are. We need to keep helping Tom, but we also need to accept him and his limitations. We think or hope he is happy, but a lot of the time it is hard to know what is going on in his world.

> As long as things were perfectly constant and no one tried to get into his little world, he would be all right.

in autism (Sears et al., 1999). Finally, an interesting recent finding is that when individuals with autism look at a face, the area of the brain that usually processes objects becomes active, rather than the area that processes faces (Schultz et al., 2000). That may explain why these individuals are generally uninterested in people and respond to them as objects. Admittedly, there are numerous other problems in the brains of individuals with autism that have not been linked to symptoms, but this approach is still new.

If autism is due to problems with brain development, the question then is, what causes these problems? There appear to be two answers, the first of which is *genetics* (Konstantareas & Homatidis, 1999; Trottier, Srivastava, & Walker, 1999). For example, there is an increased rate of autism in the siblings of individuals with autism (August, Stewart, & Tsai, 1981; Folstein, 1991; Hanson & Gottesman, 1976; Minton et al., 1982; Ritvo, Ritvo, & Brothers, 1982; Rutter, 1967). Furthermore, the "normal" siblings of individuals with autism are more likely to suffer from cognitive impairments, such as delayed speech development or reduced verbal abilities (Bartak, Rutter, & Cox, 1975; Fol-

stein & Rutter, 1977; Minton et al., 1982; Rutter, Bartak, & Newman, 1971; Vaillant, 1963). Indeed, delayed language development was found in 25% of the siblings of individuals with autism, thus suggesting that the siblings have mild symptoms of autism. Additional evidence for the role of genetics comes from studies of identical and nonidentical twins. The best study of this type found that in 36% of the identical twin pairs both twins suffered from autism, whereas in none of the nonidentical twin pairs did both twins suffer from autism (Folstein & Rutter, 1977). Finally, a disorder known as *fragile X syndrome* has been linked to autism (Turk & Graham, 1997). This syndrome involves a damaged X chromosome that can lead to mental retardation similar to that seen in many cases of autism. Fragile X syndrome is most likely to lead to symptoms in boys (who have an X and a Y sex chromosome) than in girls (who have two X chromosomes) because the second X chromosome in girls can offset the effects of a damaged X chromosome.

Genetic factors are important in autism, but they do not account for all cases; for example, there are cases of identical twins in which one suffers from autism, but the other does not. In view of that fact we must go on to consider a second factor, *problems during prenatal development* (Courchesne, 1997; Rapin & Katzman, 1998; Rodier, 2000; Trottier et al., 1999). For example, illness or drug use of the mother early in the prenatal period can cause fundamental problems in the brain that lead to autism. Although we cannot measure brain development early in pregnancy, we know that the problems in the brain develop early because they are linked to minor physical anomalies, such as ears that flop over slightly, that are known to develop early. That is, the physical anomalies provide "markers" indicating when the brain problems develop. These findings strongly suggest that the problems with brain development began between 20 and 24 days after conception, a time before many women know they are pregnant (Rodier, 2000).

Other evidence for the role of problems during prenatal development comes from the finding that mothers of children with autism experience more problems during pregnancy than mothers of normal children (Finegan & Quarrington, 1979; Kagan, 1981; Nelson, 1991; Torrey, Hersh, & McCabe, 1975). These problems include bleeding, infections, poisoning, and physical trauma. Consistent with the findings described in the preceding paragraph, these problems are most likely to be associated with autism when they occur during the first trimester of pregnancy.

There is also evidence that as many as 11% of individuals with autism suffer from rare diseases that could affect brain development and functioning (Ritvo et al., 1990). Finally, individuals with autism are more likely to have problems with their immune systems, and the reduced effectiveness of the immune system makes the individuals more vulnerable to infectious diseases that may disrupt brain development (Zimmerman et al., 1993; see also Chapter 14).

The fact that different factors can influence different parts of the brain explains why individuals with autism often show different patterns of symptoms (Szatmari, 1999). In that respect autism is similar to schizophrenia: Different causes or timing of causes can lead to differences in symptom patterns and severity (see Chapter 11). Our understanding of autism is far from complete, but we have come a long way in the past few years.

Treatments

There was a great deal of optimism about the treatment of autism in the mid-1960s when investigators began using behavior therapy. In these treatment programs children with autism were rewarded for appropriate behaviors and punished for inappropriate or self-destructive behaviors (Lovaas & Simmons, 1969; Lovaas et al., 1966; Wolf et al., 1967). The programs required a great deal of time and effort. For example, thousands of trials in which a child is given bits of food might be required in order to teach the child to say one word, and then it was unlikely that the child would know what the word means or be able to use it in a

sentence. However, the initial results were very encouraging, and a film documenting the progress made by children with autism was shown widely (Lovaas, 1969). At the end of that film children who were once mute, echolalic, self-destructive, and unable to interact with others were shown to be behaving much more normally. The implication was that behavior modification procedures are effective for treating autistic children.

Regrettably, that film and the related research reports implied and promised more than was actually accomplished. The results that were reported suffer from two serious problems that generally went unrecognized. The first is that the treatment effects did not last (Lovaas et al., 1973). Despite 6 hours of one-on-one treatment per day for a period of 14 months, the newly developed appropriate behaviors ceased almost immediately when the treatment was stopped, and the old inappropriate behaviors returned.

The second problem is that the treatment did not actually result in the hoped-for behavior, even during the treatment period. Behavior therapists suggested that the treatment increased social and affectionate behaviors, and as an example they pointed out that after treatment a previously withdrawn child with autism would run across the room with outstretched arms to his therapist in the hope of being picked up and hugged (Lovaas, 1969). However, what was not made clear in the film is that the child was barefoot and the behavior occurred in a room that had a shock-grid on the floor that would be used to administer punishment (Lovaas, Schaeffer, & Simmons, 1965). The child ran across the room to be picked up by the therapist to avoid getting shocks to his feet, not in an attempt to get or express affection! It is also noteworthy that the purportedly affectionate behavior did not generalize to another room that did not have a shock grid on the floor. Unfortunately, then, the responses achieved with the behavior modification program were not always what they appeared to be, and the improved behavior did not last or generalize to other situations. A sad footnote to this attempt at treatment is that the children in the film who were treated and for whom there were such high hopes were subsequently readmitted as full-time residents of psychiatric institutions.

The story did not end there, however, because the investigators tried again with a more extensive program (Lovaas, 1987, 1993). In this second investigation treatment was started earlier (at about 3 years of age), was more intensive (more than 40 hours per week of one-on-one treatment), and lasted longer (at least 2 years). Furthermore, parents were actively involved in the treatment. The notion was that the children needed more treatment and that other people in their lives should be involved so as to enhance the generalization and maintenance of the newly learned behaviors. Treatment involved ignoring or punishing inappropriate behaviors (aggression, self-stimulation, noncompliance with instructions) and rewarding appropriate behaviors (attempts to talk, prosocial activities, compliance with instructions).

The results indicated that 47% of the children in the treatment condition successfully passed through normal first grade in a public school and demonstrated a normal IQ, whereas none of the children in the control condition got through first grade or demonstrated a normal IQ (Lovaas, 1987). Symptoms of autism such as self-stimulation and abnormal speech were assessed before treatment began but not at the end of treatment, so we do not know the degree to which those behaviors were influenced.

These results are certainly positive, but the investigation came under severe criticism, and the results are surrounded in controversy (Lovaas, Smith, & McEachin, 1989; McEachin, Smith, & Lovaas, 1993; Schopler, Short, & Mesibov, 1989; Smith, McEachin, & Lovaas, 1993). For example, critics pointed out that (1) the children were not randomly assigned to the treatment and control conditions, (2) no data on behavior were reported, and (3) the children in the treatment condition may have been pushed through school because of staff pressure. At present it is hazardous to draw firm conclusions concerning this approach to treatment; the children in the treatment condition were more likely to complete first grade, but it is not clear how or why. Unfortunately, although this treatment continues to be popular, no new data supporting its effectiveness have been published, which may be telling. In the absence of good data, we must be careful neither to hold out false hopes nor to abandon hope. Indeed, today there is a strong movement to "mainstream" children with autism, that is, to try to have them go to school with otherwise normal children as much as possible (Connor, 1999).

Numerous drugs have been used in attempts to treat autism, but the results have been mixed at best (Bolman & Richmond, 1999; Feldman, Kolmen, & Gonzaga, 1999; Rossi, Posar, & Parmeggiani, 1999). For example, the neuroleptic Haldol (see Chapter 11) may help reduce the hyperactivity, outbursts of rage, and sleeplessness that are sometimes present in autism (Anderson et al., 1984; Gittelman & Kanner, 1986). However, although the drug may make children with autistic disorder somewhat easier to manage, it does not reduce the core symptoms of the disorder. It has also been found that the antidepressant drug that is effective for treating obsessive-compulsive disorder (clomipramine) is more effective than a placebo for eliminating the repetitive ritualized behaviors, such as object spinning and hand movements, that are often seen in autism (Gordon et al., 1993).

In view of the ineffectiveness of the treatments and the fact that in most cases autistic disorder does not diminish as the individual gets older, the prognosis for autistic children is poor. Fewer than 25% make a satisfactory adjustment by adolescence or adulthood, and many must live in institutions. Overall, autism represents one of the most conspicuous and most serious failures of psychology and psychiatry, and we can only hope for a breakthrough in the future. At present, however, the picture is bleak.

The prognosis for children suffering from autistic disorder is poor; fewer than 25% make a satisfactory adjustment by adolescence or adulthood. Dustin Hoffman (left) portrayed an autistic adult in the movie *Rain Man*.

 Asperger's and Other Developmental Disorders

An interesting disorder known as **Asperger's disorder** is similar to autism in that individuals have serious problems with social skills and very restricted interests and activities. However, unlike autism, Asperger's disorder does not involve problems with communication, and individuals with Asperger's do not show the mental retardation that often accompanies autism (American Psychiatric Association, 1994; Kugler, 1998; Tonge et al., 1999). Indeed, individuals with Asperger's often become very knowledgeable about specific topics in which they are interested. For example, I know a 6-year-old with Asperger's who is exceptionally knowledgeable concerning the geography of major cities, post-Impressionist art, and baseball statistics of

Asperger's disorder A pervasive developmental disorder that is similar to autism in that individuals have serious problems with social skills and very restricted interests and activities but that does not involve problems with communication or mental retardation.

major league players. When we talk, he tells me a great deal about these topics and discusses them in detail, but when I ask him simple questions about his family or school, he appears to draw a blank. After a vague and somewhat mechanical statement such as "Oh, fine," he launches into another discussion of one of his favorite topics. He just isn't "connected" to people the way he is connected to his favorite topics. It is not that such individuals have savant syndrome; instead they simply focus all of their attention on a limited set of topics. Because of their intense interest in limited topics and lack of social skills, they were originally characterized as "little professors."

Another symptom that is obvious in individuals with Asperger's disorder is a general *clumsiness* (Gillberg, 1993). The boy I described in the preceding paragraph simply cannot catch a ball, and he is usually stumbling and running into things. The same may be true of individuals with autism, but it is less noticeable because they do not play and have limited movements.

The cause of Asperger's disorder is unknown. However, it appears to be related to autism, the difference being that whatever damages the various areas in the brain and results in autism somehow missed the area responsible for communication skills in individuals with Asperger's. Like autism, Asperger's disorder has no effective treatment. However, individuals with Asperger's can build on their strengths and become experts in the areas in which they are interested. As the mother of the boy I described earlier commented to me one day, "He's probably going to be a happy and successful expert on some topic, but he's going to be a social nerd."

Finally, brief comments should be made concerning two other developmental disorders described in *DSM-IV.* First, in **childhood disintegrative disorder** children show normal development for at least 2 years, but then sometime between the ages of 2 and 10 their abilities begin to go through a period of rapid disintegration (Brown & Hoadley, 1999). Specifically, there is a dramatic decline in their language abilities, social skills, bladder and bowel control, and motor skills. Co-occurring with the decline in abilities is a decline in the growth of the head. Like autism, this disorder is most likely to occur in males. However, childhood disintegrative disorder differs from autism in that *its development is delayed;* that is, with autism the skills never develop, whereas with disintegrative disorder they develop and then disintegrate. The cause of this disorder is not known, but it may be that whatever causes autism is at work in this disorder but is delayed.

The other developmental disorder that merits mention is **Rett's disorder.** Rett's disorder is similar to childhood disintegrative disorder in that development begins normally. However, it differs from disintegrative disorder in that the decline in functioning begins at about 5 months rather than after 2 years. Furthermore, Rett's disorder occurs only in girls, whereas autism and childhood disintegrative disorder are more common in boys. The cause of Rett's disorder is unknown, but because it occurs only in females and because biological relatives sometimes also suffer from Rett's disorder, it is probably a sex-linked genetic problem (Schanen, 1999). The similarities and differences among autistic, Asperger's, childhood disintegrative, and Rett's disorders are summarized in Table 13.2.

TABLE 13.2

Comparisons of autistic, Asperger's, childhood disintegrative, and Rett's disorders

Disorder	Symptoms	Onset	Gender
Autistic disorder	Problems with social interactions and communication. Restricted interests and repetitive, often self-injurious behaviors. Mental retardation often present.	At birth	Primarily males
Asperger's disorder	Problems with social interactions. Limited interests. Clumsiness.	At birth	Primarily males
Childhood disintegrative disorder	Rapid loss of previously developed skills, such as language abilities, social skills, bladder and bowel control, and motor skills. Decline in growth of head.	Between 2 and 10 years of age	Primarily males
Rett's disorder	Same as childhood disintegrative disorder.	At about 5 months of age	Only females

Questions about Pervasive Developmental Disorders

1. *Are pervasive developmental disorders separate disorders, or are they a group of related disorders?* It appears that pervasive developmental disorders belong to a group of related disorders and can be organized on two dimensions (Eaves, Ho, & Eaves, 1994; Gillberg, 1999; Rodier, 2000; Szatmari, 1992). First, the disorders can be organized in terms of *how many symptoms are present.* Most notable in this regard is the link between Asperger's disorder and autistic disorder. Specifically, Asperger's appears to be autism without the communication problems. When the communication problems are added, the diagnosis becomes autism. The factor underlying this dimension seems to be the *number of sites in the brain that are disrupted* (more disrupted sites lead to more symptoms). With regard to the link between autism and Asperger's, it is interesting to note that the biological relatives of individuals with autism have a relatively high rate of Asperger's disorder. (Ehlers & Gillberg, 1993; Gillberg, Gillberg, & Steffenburg, 1992).

The second organizational dimension for these disorders revolves around *when the symptoms appear.* In cases of autistic and Asperger's disorders, symptoms are noticeable at birth or very shortly thereafter, whereas with childhood disintegrative and Rett's disorders, the symptoms do not develop until later (after 2 years or at about 5 months, respectively). Because the symptoms of childhood disintegrative and Rett's disorders are generally similar to those of autistic and Asperger's disorders, it appears that the underlying causes may be the same (problems with brain structures), but for reasons we do not yet understand, with disintegrative and Rett's disorders the problems in the brain develop later. The fact that the various developmental disorders are related to one another may turn out to be helpful because finding the cause and appropriate treatment for one disorder might then provide us with explanations and treatments for the other disorders.

2. *Is it appropriate to use punishment to control the self-injurious symptoms of autism?* Children with autism frequently engage in very serious self-injurious behaviors such as head banging, which they might do hundreds of times a day. One strategy that is effective for reducing these dangerous behaviors is *punishment,* which is often referred to as **aversive treatment** (Etzel et al., 1987; Guess et al., 1987; Kiernan, 1988; Lavigna & Donnellan, 1986; Wedell et al., 1987). Aversive treatment involves slapping children, giving them painful electrical shocks, or spraying noxious substances in their faces when they use dangerous behaviors. This type of treatment is effective for reducing the behaviors, but the question is, is it ethical to use aversive treatment on children who are not in a position to object? That is, does the end justify the means?

Some people have argued that aversive treatment is not justified, and they have taken steps to outlaw it. For example, a bill was introduced in Congress in 1987 to withhold funding from any agency that used aversive treatment. The bill died in committee and has not been reintroduced. In another case the state of Massachusetts attempted to suspend the operation of a treatment center where aversive treatment was used for children with autism (Fuller, 1986). Opponents of aversive treatment argued that the procedures constituted "officially sanctioned child abuse." In response the parents of a boy named Brendon filed a class-action suit in which they argued that by denying the use of aversive treatment, the state was denying Brendon and other children the right to an effective treatment in the absence of any good alternative. They pointed out that over a period of 15 years, Brendon had been discharged as "untreatable" from a number of prestigious institutions for autistic children, but he had shown remarkable improvement while being treated with aversive procedures at the Behavioral Research Institute. The judge found in favor of the parents and permitted the use of the aversive procedures. Since that decision there have been a number of other challenges to the use of aversive treatment, but they have all failed. Aversive treatment works, and although it seems harsh, the treatment is more humane than letting people do serious harm to themselves. The key to the effective and ethical use of aversive treatment is to limit its use to only the amount that is necessary to suppress the inappropriate behaviors and to institute a system of checks to ensure that the treatment is not misused.

Elimination, Tic, and Learning, Communication, and Motor Skills Disorders

Carolyn is 7 years old and is still wetting her bed at night. Recently, her parents bought a pad for her bed. When Carolyn urinates, the pad becomes damp and causes a bell to ring. That

---

childhood disintegrative disorder   A pervasive developmental disorder in which development is normal for at least 2 years, but then sometime between the ages of 2 and 10 previously developed abilities begin to disintegrate rapidly.

Rett's disorder   A pervasive developmental disorder that is similar to childhood disintegrative disorder in that development begins normally, but the decline in functioning begins at about 5 months of age and the disorder is limited to females.

aversive treatment   The use of punishment such as slapping children and giving them mildly painful shocks to stop self-injurious behaviors.

wakes Carolyn up, and she stops urinating. What causes Carolyn's bed-wetting, and will the "pad-and-bell" treatment work?

Tim is 14 and shows a variety of twitches and tics. His head sometimes jerks, and he often blinks and grimaces. Most surprising is that occasionally he blurts out "dirty" words. He does not mean to do it and is embarrassed by it, but he cannot control it. Why is Tim twitching and yelling dirty words? Can this behavior be brought under control?

Chris is a sophomore in college who is struggling to keep his grades up. The problem is that he has a great deal of difficulty reading, which slows his studying and poses problems on exams. Does Chris have a learning disability or a psychiatric disorder?

In this last section of the chapter we will consider three groups of disorders: *elimination disorders,* which involve problems with bowel and bladder control; *tic disorders,* which revolve around uncontrollable body movements; and a group of other disorders that revolve around problems with skills in reading, writing, mathematics, speaking, and motor movements.

Elimination Disorders

Let's begin with elimination disorders, in which children urinate or defecate at times or in places they shouldn't.

Symptoms

Children who voluntarily or involuntarily urinate into their clothing or beds after the age of 5 can be diagnosed as suffering from **enuresis** (en-yoo-RE-sis) (Kuh et al., 1999). (The term *enuresis* is based on a Greek word meaning "to urinate.") For the diagnosis to be made, the problem must occur at least twice a week for a period of 3 months; this requirement ensures that the urinations are not just "accidents." The disorder is thought to occur in about 7% of males and 3% of females.

In contrast, **encopresis** (en-kuh-PRE-sis) is the voluntary or involuntary passage of feces in inappropriate places, such as in clothing or onto the floor (Friman & Jones, 1998; Geffken & Monaco, 1996). To be diagnosed with encopresis, a child must be at least 4 years old, and the inappropriate bowel movements must occur at least once a month for a period of 3 months. This symptom is thought to occur in about 1% of 5-year-olds and is more likely to occur in boys than girls (American Psychiatric Association, 1994).

Explanations

In this discussion I will focus on enuresis because it is a more widespread problem and because more is known about it. When considering the causes of enuresis, we must first make a distinction between *primary* and *secondary* enuresis. A diagnosis of primary enuresis applies when the child *has never learned to control urination,* whereas secondary enuresis is said to occur *when a child begins wetting again, after bladder control has been learned.* That distinction is important because primary enuresis is thought to be due to physiological rather than psychological factors. For example, some children have low levels of a hormone (*antidiuretic hormone, ADH*) that helps concentrate urine during the night (it reduces the water level in the urine); when that hormone is low, children are more likely to have their bladder overfill during the night. In addition, children with primary enuresis have apparently not yet learned to recognize the physiological signals of a full bladder, so they do not wake up at night and may also have "accidents" during the day. Strong support for the physiological basis of primary enuresis comes from the findings that genetic factors play an important role (Bakwin, 1971). For example, if both parents suffered from enuresis, almost 80% of their offspring will also suffer from the disorder. Furthermore, the rate of co-occurrence in identical twins is much higher than in nonidentical twins (68% versus 36%). Finally, investigators have located a specific gene on the 13th chromosome that appears to be responsible for insensitivity to a full bladder (Eberg et al., 1995). Overall, then, it's clear that primary enuresis is a physiological rather than a psychological problem. However, because "wetting" can be very embarrassing for children, it can easily lead to psychological problems such as anxiety, shame, and withdrawal.

Unfortunately, the causes of secondary enuresis are less clear. It is possible that stress plays a role, though exactly how has not been specified. It is also possible that in a few cases urination may be voluntary, to get attention or as an act of obstinence. Finally, it is also possible that physiological problems like those discussed earlier develop and lead to relapses in the ability to control the bladder; for example, there may be a drop in ADH, the hormone that concentrates urine.

Treatments

The most popular treatment for enuresis is what is known as the **bell-and-pad procedure.** With this strategy an electrically wired pad is placed beneath the sheet of the child's bed, and when the child urinates, the fluid closes a circuit in the pad that immediately sounds a bell to awaken the child (Friman & Vollmer, 1995; Mowrer & Mowrer, 1938; Rajigah, 1996). We do not understand exactly why this strategy works, but apparently it helps the child learn to recognize the signs of a full bladder and wake up before it is "too late." The research indicates that the bell-and-pad procedure is effective with about 75% of children and that it is more effective than other approaches (Houts, Berman, & Abramson, 1994). There is a relapse rate of about 40%, but if the treatment procedure is reinstituted, about 30% of the individuals regain bladder control.

Finally, it should be noted that there is now a synthetic form of the hormone ADH (see the earlier discussion). The synthetic hormone is easily used in the form of a nasal spray before bedtime. About 70% of children who use this hormone treatment stop bed-wetting almost immediately, and another 10% show substantial reductions (Rappaport, 1993).

 ## Tic Disorders

Tics are simply *recurrent involuntary motor movements.* The movements range from small twitches of the mouth or eye blinks to large movements of major portions of the body such as arms or legs. Individuals with tics can consciously suppress the tics for short periods of time, but as soon as attention is turned away, the tics return. Because tics are generally not under voluntary control and can greatly disrupt life, they can lead to serious psychological and physical problems. When such problems occur, the individual is diagnosed as suffering from a **tic disorder.** The best known and most serious tic disorder is *Tourette's disorder,* which I'll describe in the following sections.

Symptoms and Issues

Tourette's disorder involves numerous motor tics such as blinking, facial grimaces, and movements of large parts of the body, but it also includes **vocal tics.** A vocal tic occurs when there is a sudden involuntary contraction of the muscles of the diaphragm; the contraction of the diaphragm forces air past the vocal cords, and consequently the individual grunts, yelps, barks, or says or yells words. Involuntary grunting and barking can be embarrassing, but what is more embarrassing is that individuals with Tourette's disorder often have verbal tics that involve the involuntary uttering or yelling of *obscenities.* That is, in the absence of any reason for doing so, an individual yells out words that most people find shocking. This syndrome, called **coprolalia** (kop-ruh-LA-le-uh), occurs in about 30% of the individuals with Tourette's and can obviously be very disruptive of psychosocial functioning (Comings, 1990).

In one interesting case a radio disk jockey suffered from a severe form of Tourette's disorder, but he was able to suppress his vocal outbursts during the 15- or 20-second periods he was on the air between records. However, as soon as the microphone was off, he would begin yelling things uncontrollably. He reported that he often yelled things he was thinking about but would not ordinarily say out loud. For example, at the beginning of our interview he yelled, "Get me a hamburger!" At that time he was hungry and thinking about lunch. He described the verbal outbursts as being like a cough that can be suppressed temporarily but eventually wells up and bursts through uncontrollably.

The symptoms of Tourette's disorder are made worse by stress, and a vicious circle can develop in which the symptoms result in social stress, which in turn increases the likelihood of the symptoms. Tourette's usually begins around age 7, is three times more likely to occur in males than females, and lasts throughout adulthood (Comings, 1990). Furthermore, individuals with Tourette's disorder often also show symptoms of ADHD and OCD (Comings & Comings, 1990).

In Case Study 13.3 (on p. 392) a student of mine describes her struggles with Tourette's disorder.

Explanations

It is now generally recognized that tics are caused by a physiological dysfunction of the brain (Hyde & Weinberger, 1995, Kerbeshian & Burd, 1994; McDougle, Goodman, & Price, 1994, Rogeness, Javors, & Pliszka, 1993). More specifically, tics are due to oversensitivity of the dopamine receptors in the basal ganglia (where motor behavior is controlled). That oversensitivity leads to excessive firing in the brain, which triggers the tics (Popper & West, 1999).

Evidence linking dopamine activity to Tourette's includes findings that drugs that increase dopamine activity increase tics, whereas drugs that reduce dopamine activity can be effective for treating tic disorders (see the later discussion). It has been suggested that coprolalia (yelling obscenities) can be explained by the fact that dopamine is also an important transmitter in the limbic system, which is responsible for emotion. The combination of elevated emotion with elevated tic behavior might result in the spontaneous utterance of obscenities (Messiha & Carlson, 1983).

A number of factors could contribute to the excessive dopamine activity, but primary among them is genetics (see Devor, 1990). For example, there is evidence that the incidence of Tourette's disorder is higher in family members with the disorder than it is in the general population (7.4% versus .05%, respectively), and there is a higher rate of co-occurrence of the disorder in identical than in non-identical twins (Messiha & Carlson, 1983; Pauls et al., 1984;

---

enuresis An elimination disorder in which the symptom is the failure to control urination.

encopresis An elimination disorder in which the symptom is the failure to control bowel movements.

bell-and-pad procedure An effective treatment for enuresis, involving an electrically wired pad that sounds a bell when wet.

tics Recurrent involuntary motor movements, which can be controlled briefly when attention is focused on them, but not otherwise.

tic disorders Disorders in which tics result in serious psychological and physical problems.

Tourette's disorder A tic disorder involving both motor and vocal tics.

vocal tics Involuntary grunts, yelps, barks, and words that result from sudden involuntary contractions of the muscles of the diaphragm.

coprolalia Syndrome that involves the involuntary uttering or yelling of obscenities.

Tourette's Disorder: My Daily Struggle

"I BEGAN TO DEVELOP the first signs of Tourette's when I was about 14, but, of course, at that time I didn't know what it was. It began with a hop; I'd just start hopping. It was embarrassing, and I'd try to hide it. When my parents caught me hopping, they would tell me to stop, but of course I couldn't, at least not for long. Soon I began meowing like a cat and swearing uncontrollably, sometimes without realizing that I was doing it. My parents would become annoyed when I meowed, but they really had trouble with the swearing. I would also often get in trouble at school for swearing.

> **I wanted badly for the twitching to go away and I tried everything I could to stop it . . .**

One thing I should point out is that stress brings on higher levels of the symptoms, so when I got a low grade on a test, which would upset me because I am somewhat of a perfectionist, I would swear obnoxiously. When other students saw me acting this way, they would laugh at me, and because I didn't realize they were laughing because of how stupidly I was acting, I thought they knew I had a low test grade. That added more stress, and therefore I had more outbursts of uncontrollable swearing.

"Eventually my mother called a neurologist, and after she described my symptoms, he concluded I had Tourette's disorder and prescribed some medication. However, when my mother learned about the bad side effects of the medication, she concluded (having my best interests at heart) that I should just go on without being treated. She naively thought that, like clothes, I would grow out of the symptoms. How wrong she was! Unfortunately, she didn't tell me about the diagnosis, so I still had no idea what was wrong.

"By the end of my sophomore year in high school, I was shaking my head and hands almost constantly and turning my whole body around every few minutes. The other kids in school nicknamed me 'Tremors,' and at work I was called 'the freak.' By the end of the year I was very depressed and would go home every night crying from embarrassment. I would dread going to school and would often fake being sick to get out of class. I wanted badly for the twitching to go away, and I tried everything I could to stop it, but it never went away. No one understood —not even me.

"Finally, in the middle of my junior year a person at work who saw me twitching asked me if I had Tourette's disorder, and when I said I didn't know what it was, he explained it to me. That night I ran home excited because I had some hope that maybe the twitching wasn't my fault—maybe I had a biological disorder! When I told my mother, she explained that I did have Tourette's, but the side effects of the medication were worse than the symptoms and nothing could be done. However, after pleading with her, we went to see a neurologist, who explained that there was some new medication that didn't have any side effects.

"I started taking the medication, and my symptoms started toning down. I still had some symptoms, and a few kids at school still called me 'Tremors,' but it was getting better, and when I explained the disorder, people became more understanding. As my symptoms lessened, my self-esteem improved dramatically. I also started taking Zoloft for my depression, and doing that helped. Some days I was better and some days I was worse, but I was slowly improving, and I finally felt good about myself; I had a *disorder*, I wasn't just *weird*.

"I'm in college now, and I still have some symptoms, such as gulping, swallowing my tongue, blinking my eyes rapidly, and sometimes I chirp or meow a little, but most of the time my tics are under control. In fact, one day I got up and talked about my disorder in Professor Holmes's abnormal psychology class; that was really stressful, but I didn't yell out any swear words. With the medication I've come a long way, but it's a daily struggle."

Shapiro & Shapiro, 1982). In some cases Tourette's appears to be related to an abnormal reaction of the immune system, stemming from infections (see Chapter 14), but exactly how that occurs is not clear (Popper & West, 1999).

Treatments

Because Tourette's is caused by high levels of dopamine activity, the key to treatment is the use of drugs that reduce dopamine activity (Hyde & Weinberger, 1995; Popper & West, 1999; Rapoport, 1994). In most cases the drugs used to treat Tourette's are the same ones that are used to reduce dopamine activity in the treatment of schizophrenia; widely used drugs include Haldol and the atypical neuroleptics, such as Risperidal and Zyprexa (see Chapter 11).

The effects of neuroleptic drugs were illustrated in an interesting case of a professional baseball player who suffered from Tourette's. After playing successfully for some years, his performance began to decline, and he was eventually dropped from the team. At that point he sought treatment for his disorder and was prescribed a neuroleptic drug that blocked dopamine activity. Taking the drug had two interesting effects: First, it reduced his Tourette's disorder, and second, it improved his general physical coordination to the extent that he was able to make a successful comeback in the major leagues. In this case it appears that the excessive dopamine activity had resulted in muscle problems, which led to both Tourette's and a reduced ability to play baseball; when the dopamine problem was corrected, both symptoms went away.

Learning, Communication, and Motor Skills Disorders

Before concluding our discussion of developmental disorders, we should give some attention to three relatively new sets of disorders called **learning, communication,** and **motor skills disorders.** These disorders are summarized in Table 13.3. As you can see from the brief descriptions given in the table, these disorders involve problems with skills in reading, writing, mathematics, language, and motor movements. These problems can lead to anxiety and depression and can greatly disrupt an individual's ability to function. For example, an otherwise normal individual who cannot read because of a reading disorder could become frustrated and depressed and withdraw in failure. The importance of diagnosing these disorders so that individuals are not erroneously classed as "dumb" or retarded cannot be overemphasized. A colleague of mine was initially unable to learn to read as a child, and school administrators classed him as retarded and recommended that he be taken out of regular school and sent to a "sheltered living environment." However, it turned out that he was actually suffering from a severe case of dyslexia (for example, he could not tell 3's from E's or 6's from 9's). When that was discovered and he was taught how to cope, he went on to do very well, graduating with honors and earning three graduate degrees.

TABLE 13.3

Learning, communication, and motor skills disorders

Disorder	Symptoms
Reading disorder	Reading ability is markedly below what would be expected on the basis of the child's intellectual ability.
Mathematics disorder	Mathematical ability is markedly below what would be expected on the basis of the child's intellectual ability.
Written expression disorder	Composition of written text is markedly below what would be expected on the basis of the child's intellectual ability (e.g., poor spelling, grammar).
Expressive language disorder	Use of language is markedly below what would be expected on the basis of the child's intellectual ability (e.g., poor vocabulary, overly simple sentences, use of only present tense).
Phonological disorder	Child fails consistently to use speech sounds as expected for age and dialect.
Stuttering disorder	Child fails consistently to speak without involuntary disruption or blocking.
Developmental coordination disorder	Performance in motor skills is markedly below what would be expected on the basis of the child's chronological age and intellectual ability.

Note: For all disorders the symptoms must interfere with achievement and activities for the diagnosis to apply.

Children with a phonological disorder consistently fail to use speech sounds as expected for their age and dialect. There is much debate over whether phonological disorder and the other learning, communication, and motor skills disorders are psychological or educational problems.

THINKING CRITICALLY

Questions about Elimination, Tic, and Learning, Communication, and Motor Skills Disorders

Are disorders such as primary enuresis and Tourette's disorder psychological or physiological disorders? It is clear that primary enuresis and Tourette's are caused by physiological factors and that their symptoms are physiological in nature (i.e., an inability to control urination or tics). Why then are these disorders considered psychiatric in nature and listed

learning disorders A set of developmental disorders consisting of reading, mathematics, and written expression disorders in which individuals have difficulty developing these skills despite normal intelligence.

communication disorders A set of developmental disorders consisting of expressive language, phonological, and stuttering disorders, in which individuals have difficulty with communication despite normal intelligence.

motor skills disorder Problems with motor skills despite normal intelligence.

in *DSM-IV*? The answer seems to be that the physiological symptoms lead to psychological symptoms such as anxiety and depression and also disrupt psychological functioning. In other words, the physiological symptoms lead to secondary symptoms that are psychological in nature. However, that is the case for many disorders that are not listed as psychiatric. For example, cancer certainly leads to anxiety and depression, but it is not considered a psychiatric disorder. Some critics have suggested that labeling disorders such as Tourette's as being psychiatric in nature reflects a psychological or psychiatric "imperialism," whereby mental health professionals are trying to gain control over problems that are beyond their traditional and appropriate scope. That expanded reach might be motivated by finan-

cial reasons; more disorders under the psychiatric umbrella result in more patients for mental health professionals. However, another and probably more accurate explanation lies in the fact that these disorders were originally thought to have psychological causes. In other words, their inclusion in *DSM-IV* is based on history rather than on what we now know about the disorders. If that is the case, might it be appropriate to drop them from *DSM*? That would not mean that mental health professionals would not treat individuals who were anxious or depressed because of the disorders; rather, the patients would be treated like other individuals whose anxiety or depression stems from some known factor.

Summary

Topic I: Disruptive Behavior Disorders

▶ Attention-deficit/hyperactivity disorder (ADHD) involves the inability to maintain attention and hyperactivity or impulsivity. ADHD can disrupt social and academic development and persist into adulthood. Diagnosis is based on clinical judgment and is often unreliable.

▶ ADHD is due to low levels of activity in the areas of the brain responsible for the control of attention and motor activity, primarily the prefrontal and premotor cortexes. The problems in the brain that lead to ADHD can be caused by environmental factors, such as disease and poisons, or by genetic factors.

▶ ADHD can be treated most effectively with stimulants such as Ritalin and Dexedrine.

▶ Conduct disorder involves persistent misbehaviors, such as aggression, destruction of property, deceitfulness, and other serious violations of rules.

▶ Psychodynamic theorists suggest that conduct disorder stems from overly indulgent or restrictive parenting, and learning theorists attribute it to imitation of and rewards for inappropriate behavior. Physiological explanations revolve around maternal smoking during pregnancy, which leads to problems with brain development; low levels of serotonin, which reduce inhibitions; and high levels of testosterone, which enhance aggression.

▶ Depending on the cause, effective treatment of conduct disorders may involve punishing inappropriate behaviors while rewarding appropriate behaviors or using antidepressant drugs that increase levels of serotonin.

▶ Symptoms of oppositional defiant disorder include problems with temper, arguing with adults, refusing to comply with the requests of adults, deliberately annoying people, and being angry, resentful, and spiteful. Little is known about this disorder.

▶ Concerns have been expressed about the use of Ritalin for treating ADHD in young children. It must be used only with children who actually have ADHD, and it should not be used in excessively high levels.

Topic II: Pervasive Developmental Disorders

▶ Autistic disorder involves (1) impairments in social interactions, (2) impairments in communication, and (3) unusual and stereotyped behaviors, such as head banging, repetitive finger movements, or gazing at objects for long periods of time. The symptoms appear shortly after birth and are more common in males than females.

▶ Contrary to what was once thought, autistic disorder is not more common in the upper class than in other socioeconomic classes. Autistic disorder often involves mental retardation, but retardation is not part of the formal definition of autism. Individuals with autism sometimes have savant syndrome. Autism is different from schizophrenia in childhood.

▶ It was once thought that autism was caused by cold and detached parents, but that explanation has been abandoned. Interest in the idea that the symptoms are learned has waned because treatment based on this approach was not effective. Evidence has accumulated that specific problems in the brain are linked to specific symptoms of autism. The problems in the brain can be caused by genetic factors and by problems during prenatal development (illness of the mother, poisoning, physical traumas), particularly during the first trimester.

▶ The treatment of autism by extinguishing symptoms and rewarding the use of normal behaviors has not received support from research. Furthermore, although drugs can be used to reduce the activity of children with autism and thereby make them more manageable, drugs have not been found to be effective for controlling the core symptoms.

- Asperger's disorder is similar to autism, but individuals with Asperger's do not have problems with communication and do not show mental retardation.

- Children with childhood disintegrative disorder show normal development until at least age 2, but sometime in the next few years they begin going through a period of rapid disintegration. Rett's disorder is similar to disintegrative disorder, but the deterioration begins at about 5 months and the disorder is limited to girls.

- Pervasive developmental disorders appear related in that they share some symptoms but the symptoms occur at different times.

- Concern has been expressed over the use of aversive treatment for self-injurious behaviors in children with autism. However, the treatment is effective, and the courts have upheld its use.

Topic III: Elimination, Tic, and Learning, Communication, and Motor Skills Disorders

- Enuresis is inappropriate urination after the age of 5, whereas encopresis is inappropriate bowel movements after the age of 4.

- Primary enuresis is due to physiological factors, such as a low level of the hormone that helps concentrate urine at night and insensitivity to signals that the bladder is filled. These problems have a strong genetic basis. The cause of secondary enuresis is less clear.

- The most effective treatment for enuresis is the bell-and-pad procedure. Administration of a synthetic form of the urine-concentrating hormone can also reduce enuresis.

- Tics are recurrent involuntary motor movements, which are made worse by stress.

- Tourette's disorder involves motor tics and vocal tics. Individuals with vocal tics sometimes yell obscenities, a problem known as coprolalia.

- Tics are caused by oversensitivity of the dopamine receptors in the basal ganglia. The increased sensitivity can be caused by genetic factors or an abnormal reaction of the immune system.

- Tics and Tourette's disorder can be treated by decreasing dopamine activity. This is usually done with neuroleptic drugs (the same ones used to treat schizophrenia).

- Learning, communication, and motor skills disorders involve problems with skills in reading, writing, mathematics, language, and motor movements. These problems can interfere with individuals' academic performance and thereby lead to anxiety, depression, and social withdrawal.

Questions for Making Connections

1. What disorders other than primary enuresis and Tourette's disorder might be considered to be physiological rather than psychological in nature? Should those disorders be dropped from *DSM*? If not, why? Justify your answer.

2. What are the similarities and differences between conduct disorder and antisocial personality disorder (which was discussed in Chapter 12)? Consider causes, symptoms, and treatments.

3. If you had a child who suffered from autism, what kind of care would you want for him or her? Would you care for your child at home, or would you place the child in an institution? Do you think it is appropriate to use aversive treatment to reduce self-injurious behaviors? Could you use that treatment on your child?

Key Terms and People

In reviewing and testing yourself, you should be able to discuss each of the following:

Asperger's disorder, p. 387
attention-deficit/hyperactivity
  disorder (ADHD), p. 372
autistic disorder, p. 381
aversive treatment, p. 389
bell-and-pad procedure, p. 390
childhood disintegrative disorder,
  p. 388
communication disorders, p. 393
conduct disorder, p. 377

coprolalia, p. 391
Dexedrine, p. 375
disruptive behavior disorders, p. 372
echolalia, p. 382
encopresis, p. 390
enuresis, p. 390
high-functioning individuals with
  autism, p. 383
learning disorders, p. 393
motor skills disorders, p. 393

oppositional defiant disorder, p. 380
pervasive developmental disorders,
  p. 381
Rett's disorder, p. 388
Ritalin, p. 375
savant syndrome, p. 383
tic disorders, p. 391
tics, p. 391
Tourette's disorder, p. 391
vocal tics, p. 391

14 Eating, Sleep, and Psychophysiological Disorders

HAVE YOU EVER known someone who suffered from a heart attack, arthritis, or cancer? If so, you probably assumed that the disorder had a physical cause. That may have been true, but it is also possible that the disorder was caused in part by a psychological factor such as stress. Indeed, stress plays a role in disorders ranging from colds to cancer. In this chapter we will examine a variety of physical disorders and consider their psychological as well as their physical causes.

At the outset I should distinguish between the disorders to be discussed here and the *somatoform disorders* that were discussed in Chapter 7. In somatoform disorders psychological factors cause symptoms of physical disorders, but there is no actual physical damage. For example, an individual with a conversion disorder may have a paralyzed arm, but there is no actual damage to the nerves, muscles, or bones of the arm. In contrast, in the disorders discussed in this chapter, *psychological factors cause real physical damage and disorders.* For example, prolonged psychological stress can lead to the buildup of plaque in the arteries and eventually to a heart attack.

This chapter is divided into three parts. In the first part I will deal with *eating disorders,* such as anorexia and bulimia; the second part is focused on *sleep disorders,* which range from insomnia to narcolepsy; and the third part

includes a variety of *psychophysiological disorders,* including heart attacks, headaches, arthritis, and cancer.

TOPIC I
Eating Disorders

Yolande is emaciated; she is 5 feet 4 inches tall but weighs only 89 pounds. Everyone thinks she looks like "just skin and bones," but she thinks she is fat and is afraid of gaining weight. She is also having some physical problems such as low blood pressure, slow heart rate, and low body temperature. She has not had a menstrual cycle in many months. Her condition is becoming life-threatening. Yolande is suffering from anorexia. Why is she refusing to keep her weight at a normal level, and can this process be reversed?

Ann is an attractive college freshman. She is bright and athletic and appears normal to her friends. What nobody knows, however, is that five or six times a week Ann goes on uncontrollable eating binges during which she stuffs herself with tremendous amounts of food in a short period of time. She does this by going to three or four different drive-through fast-food restaurants. To relieve the abdominal pain caused by the binge and to avoid gaining weight, Ann forces herself to vomit all that she ate during the binge. This behavior pattern is upsetting to Ann, and she is often depressed; but somehow she cannot stop it. Because the vomiting brings gastric acid into her mouth, Ann is developing sore spots in her throat, and the enamel on her teeth is beginning to deteriorate. Ann suffers from bulimia. Why does she have uncontrollable urges to binge eat?

Anorexia and Bulimia

Anorexia nervosa and *bulimia nervosa* are eating disorders that together may afflict as many as 4% of young women and in some cases can even cause death. Because these disorders are so widespread and serious, they deserve our very careful consideration.

Symptoms

Anorexia Nervosa. The major symptom of **anorexia nervosa** (an-uh-REK-se-uh nur-VO-suh) is an individual's *refusal to maintain body weight* above the minimal normal weight for the individual's age and height (American Psychiatric Association, 1994). (*Anorexia* comes from the Greek for "lack of appetite.") A body weight that is *15% or more below the expected minimum* leads to a diagnosis of anorexia.

Other symptoms of anorexia include an *intense fear of gaining weight* or becoming fat and a *distortion of body image*. In other words, regardless of how thin and emaciated the individuals become, they are still afraid of becoming fat, they "feel fat," and therefore they continue their

Regardless of how emaciated individuals with anorexia may be, they still feel fat and may continue to lose weight. Pictured here is gymnast Christy Heinrich with her boyfriend in 1993 (above) and on the balance beam in 1988 (right). She died in 1994 after a long battle with two eating disorders that had reduced her to just 60 pounds. Gymnasts and other professionals such as dancers and models are more vulnerable to eating disorders because of the emphasis their professions place on size.

---

anorexia nervosa An eating disorder in which an individual refuses to maintain body weight above the minimal normal weight for the individual's age and height; a body weight that is 15% or more below the expected minimum leads to a diagnosis of anorexia.

amenorrhea The absence of menstruation; missing at least three consecutive menstrual cycles is necessary for a diagnosis of anorexia in women.

bulimia nervosa An eating disorder in which the major symptoms are eating binges and inappropriate compensatory behavior such as purging, designed to prevent weight gain.

purging A strategy, such as vomiting or the use of laxatives, that is designed to prevent weight gain and often used following an eating binge.

---

attempts to lose weight. One student of mine became seriously anorexic, weighed only 85 pounds, thought she looked great, and could not understand why her boyfriend from home was repelled by her appearance when he came for a visit. The last major symptom of anorexia in females is the *absence of at least three consecutive menstrual cycles*. The absence of menstruation is known as **amenorrhea** (uh-men-uh-RE-uh). In some cases amenorrhea actually sets in before there is significant weight loss.

Secondary symptoms that stem from inappropriate diet and weight loss include slow heart rate (bradycardia), low blood pressure (hypotension), low body temperature (hypothermia), and other problems associated with disturbances in metabolism. One woman with anorexia had a heart rate of only 28 beats per minute and blood pressure so low it could not be measured with traditional methods (Brotman & Stern, 1983). Finally, most of the individuals who suffer from anorexia also suffer from serious depressions, obsessions, and compulsions (Thiel et al., 1995; Vitousek & Manke, 1994). Case Study 14.1 was written by a very bright student of mine who suffered from anorexia.

It is interesting to note that individuals with anorexia do not lose their interest in food and, in fact, will sometimes go to great lengths to prepare elaborate meals for others but

Anorexia in a High School Student: Her Story

"My PROBLEM BEGAN when I was 16 years old, a sophomore in high school. I had just experienced a growth spurt that was accompanied by a weight gain. I had also recently joined the swim team where, to my horror, one had to walk around in swimming suits. I had a gym class where we assessed our body fat percentages. Mine was 19.7%; too high for my liking. [*Note:* An individual must have a score of 26 to be considered "overweight."] Because we were supposed to reassess the percentage again at the end of the semester, I decided that it would be a wonderful time to diet and do something about what I perceived to be my repulsive-looking body.

"I began by starting a running program where I ran every morning for 45 minutes, regardless of the weather or the amount of sleep I had gotten the night before. I followed my run with a hot shower, because someone had told me this would increase my metabolism, thus precipitating my weight loss. I then had a slice of dry whole-wheat toast and a Diet Coke for breakfast. I scrutinized myself in front of the mirror as I dressed, and then proceeded to cover my body with the baggiest clothes I could find.

"At school I felt as if everyone was disgusted with the way I looked, and thus I walked through the halls without making any eye contact with anyone. In gym class I worked as hard as I could, and I changed my clothes in the bathroom stalls so nobody could ridicule me. After school, still not having eaten anything except my toast, I went to swim practice, where I completely exhausted myself. There I would again change my clothes in the bathroom stall. I came home for dinner and ate all my vegetables to please my parents, but since my family did not eat together, I put the majority of my dinner down the garbage disposal. After dinner I did an aerobic tape or two, followed by an extra 250 sit-ups. Then I took another hot shower.

"At night my control would diminish. I would binge on ice cream or any carbohydrates I could get my hands on. Sometimes, if I felt really guilty or my stomach hurt, I would make myself vomit with the water running so nobody could hear [see note below].

"It took about 4 months, a few blackouts, a cessation of menstruation, and many threats from my father for me to realize I had a problem. What many people did not realize was that my behavior was being reinforced. When I was losing weight, I was getting more compliments and a lot more attention. I suppose I thought that more weight loss would bring even more attention. I dropped down to about 7% body fat, and somewhere along the way my body could not take the abuse any more. Somehow I began to eat relatively normally again. Body-image perception, however, is still somewhat of a problem for me. Once, during my freshman year in college, I abused laxatives for about 2 months in an attempt to lose some weight, but for the most part my struggle is over."

CASE STUDY 14.1

At school, I felt as if everyone was disgusted with the way I looked. . . .

Note: The bingeing on carbohydrates followed by voluntary vomiting at first appears to suggest *bulimia,* a different eating disorder. However, carbohydrate craving and bingeing is a relatively normal response to prolonged exercise like that in which the student had just participated and is not necessarily a symptom of bulimia. Indeed, many athletes, such as distance runners, strongly crave carbohydrates after a strenuous workout and often consume large amounts. In contrast, however, self-induced vomiting is not a normal response and in this case appears to reflect the concern for weight associated with anorexia.

will not eat the meals themselves. One student of mine who suffered from anorexia frequently brought me rich and wonderful chocolate desserts but never ate any of them herself. She made the desserts for me after jogging a few miles, going to her aerobics class, and limiting her food intake for the day to a bowl of cereal and a few carrots.

Bulimia Nervosa. The first major symptom of **bulimia nervosa** (byoo-LEE-me-uh nur-VO-suh) is *eating binges.* (*Bulimia* comes from a Greek word meaning "great hunger.") During an eating binge the individual consumes huge amounts of food in a short period of time. Binges are usually carefully planned and carried out in secret. The eating binge is often accompanied by a feeling of lack of control over the eating behavior. The binge ends when the individual cannot eat any more and develops abdominal pains. Importantly, the binge is not the result of an actual need for food, as might be the case following a strenuous aerobic workout (see note in Case Study 14.1). For example, distance runners often experience a craving for ice cream following a workout and may consume large amounts, but those are not bulimic binges.

The second major symptom is *inappropriate compensatory behavior designed to prevent weight gain.* In other words, to relieve the pain that comes from eating too much and to avoid gaining weight, individuals use self-induced vomiting, laxatives, enemas, fasting, or excessive exercise to get rid of the food. The use of vomiting, laxatives, or enemas is often referred to as **purging.** Because purging is effective for helping the individual maintain a normal

After her separation from Prince Charles, Princess Diana admitted in a television interview that she had suffered from bulimia for several years. Without that admission, her disorder probably would have remained a secret, despite constant media attention.

sive-compulsive symptoms are often associated with bulimia. One woman's struggle with bulimia is presented in Case Study 14.2.

Issues

Historical Trends. It is widely believed that anorexia and bulimia are relatively new disorders, but that is not the case. Indeed, examples of these disorders can be found in the records of the ancient Greeks, while the modern history of "fasting girls" began with reports in 1873 (Vandereycken & Lowenkopf, 1990). Initially, eating disorders did not attract attention as a separate type of disorder because they were simply considered a phobia (*sitophobia*)—that is, fear of eating. A study of the incidence of anorexia over a 50-year period in Rochester, Minnesota, revealed a steady rate of the disorder over time, with perhaps a slight increase in the 1980s (Lucas et al., 1991). That increase may simply have reflected a greater willingness to admit to the disorder because of the attention and acceptance it began receiving. In fact, in some cases the mothers of daughters who are being treated for eating disorders admit somewhat sheepishly that they had similar problems when they were younger but that they never admitted the problems to anyone.

Gender and Age. Women are 10 times more likely than men to suffer from anorexia and bulimia, and the disorders have an earlier onset in women than in men, a difference that may be due to the fact that women mature earlier than men (Carlat & Camargo, 1991; Lucas et al., 1991).

Anorexia and bulimia are disorders primarily of late adolescence and early adulthood, with the most frequent age of onset being between 15 and 19; see Figure 14.1 (on p. 402). Fortunately, in most cases the disorder burns out within a few years, although the individuals may experience some lingering concerns about weight. That is, the more serious symptoms of eating disorders appear to be time-limited. However, about 30% of the individuals continue to have problems into adulthood (Keel et al., 1999).

Sociocultural Factors. It is also widely believed that eating disorders are more prevalent in the middle and upper classes, but that is not the case (Rogers et al., 1997). Indeed, if there are class differences, it appears that individuals with eating disorders are more likely to be in the lower classes (Pope et al., 1987). The original impression that middle- or upper-class individuals are more likely to have eating disorders was probably based on the observation that such individuals were more likely to seek treatment. However, who gets treated is not a good index of who has the disorder. Specifically, we know that lower-class individuals are less likely to come in for treatment when they need it and, when they do come in, are more likely to present their problems

weight, it helps hide the disorder. In this regard it is interesting to note that Diana, Princess of Wales, suffered from bulimia for years. Yet, despite constant public scrutiny she was able to conceal it with careful purging.

Unfortunately, frequent purging leads to a variety of other problems, such as sore throats, ulcers of the mouth and throat, swollen salivary glands, and destruction of tooth enamel. These symptoms occur because the vomit contains high levels of stomach acid, which destroys tissues and tooth enamel. Individuals with bulimia can also suffer from nutritional problems and dehydration because they are not getting any benefit from the food they consume. Finally, as is the case with anorexia, depression and obses-

A Student Talks about Her Bulimia and Her Desperation

THE FOLLOWING ACCOUNT was written by an honors student of mine who had suffered from anorexia in high school and from bulimia for approximately 2 years before writing this.

"If I were to use one word to describe how it feels to be bulimic, I would use *desperate.* I experience many feelings while bingeing, purging, and waiting for the next cycle, but the most noticeable is desperation.

"Once I've decided to binge, I can't think of anything else. The first thing I have to do is get off by myself. I will lie to my friends and skip classes to get away. I usually tell my friends that I'm going to class or to study. I even leave for class early or late so no one will walk with me.

"After I figure out how I'm going to get off by myself, I think about money. What I eat when I binge depends on how much money I have. If I have quite a bit, I'll binge on whatever I crave regardless of cost. If I have only a little, I buy the cheapest things I can. Even if I'm broke, I will find a way to binge. At the sorority house I will pack a big sack lunch. I've sold books for binge money, and I've borrowed from others. When all else fails, I'll even write a bad check.

"Next comes the actual binge. I usually eat at a number of places because I don't want anyone to know how much I actually eat. I almost always buy something I can carry out, and then I eat as I go from place to

place. I do that because I have an irrational belief that as long as I am in the process of eating, the food is not being digested, but when I stop eating, my stomach will start working double-time to get all the calories out of the food.

"This irrational belief leaves me feeling desperate to get rid of the food I've just eaten, and that leads to the purge. As soon as possible after eating, I travel from bathroom to bathroom, purging. I don't want to spend too much time in any one bathroom because I'm afraid someone might walk in. I'm also afraid of leaving a noticeable odor. I think that I know every public bathroom in town, and I know when most of them are likely to be empty.

"My bingeing will take on different tones, depending on why I am doing it. Sometimes it's just habit, and I can't think of an alternative. In that case I'm fairly calm, and my actions have a determined, inevitable quality. It's almost like I'm in a trance. I purposefully move from place to place, and I don't get anxious about little inconveniences.

"More often, however, a specific event or emotion triggers a binge. It can be just about anything—fear, anger, depression. Whatever the reason for bingeing, the procedure takes on a frantic quality. I need to binge, and I need to do it immediately! I still take precautions so nobody knows what

I'm doing, but I'm more likely to take some risks. The binge takes precedence over everything else. I eat faster, and I'm more likely to take laxatives if I don't think I've gotten rid of enough.

"Sometimes I feel relieved afterward, especially if it was an overwhelming or upsetting emotion that triggered the binge. If I'm bingeing out of habit, I usually feel depressed and might cry afterward, wondering why I'm doing this to myself. Often I go right into another binge.

"It's not only when I'm bingeing that I feel desperate. In between binges I am desperately searching for a strategy to stop the behavior. I've spent endless hours in the library and bookstores looking for an answer. I've read many diet books and tried their diets hoping that the structure of a diet will help me stop bingeing. I've read antidiet books, books on nutrition, and books on anorexia and bulimia. Ironically, I often read these books as I pig out. For me bingeing, purging, and the desperate struggle have become a way of life."

> **Whatever the reason for bingeing, the procedure takes on a frantic quality.**

as physical rather than psychological—thus, they do not get directed into the mental health system (see Chapter 4). The higher rate of eating disorders in the lower classes is interesting because there is a strong link between eating disorders and depression, and the rate of depression is also higher in the lower classes (see Chapter 8). The links among socioeconomic class, eating disorders, and depression may be due to a higher level of stress in the lower classes (see Chapter 8).

Do the rates of eating disorders differ across cultures? This is an interesting question because some cultures place

a high value on being slim, whereas in others being heavy is socially acceptable or even encouraged (Hoek et al., 1998). However, virtually all of the well-done cross-cultural investigations have revealed similar rates of anorexia across cultures (e.g., Hoek et al., 1998; Mangweth et al., 1996, 1997).

Strategic Eating Disorders. Finally, it will be helpful to make a distinction between what appear to be two types of eating disorders. On the one hand, there are individuals like the student in Case Study 14.2, in whom the behavior appears to be *out of control* and *involuntary.* Just as the individual

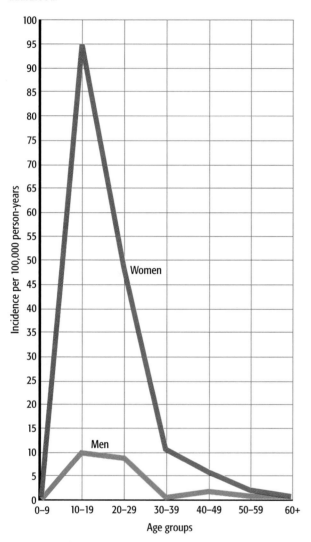

FIGURE 14.1

Anorexia occurs most frequently in adolescence and early adulthood.

Source: Lucas et al. (1991), Table 2, p. 919.

with schizophrenia cannot voluntarily stop hallucinating, so these individuals cannot control their inappropriate eating behaviors. On the other hand, there are also individuals who show many of the symptoms of anorexia or bulimia but who have the behavior *under voluntary control.* Many

strategic eating disorders   Eating disorders that are under voluntary control and that involve behaviors designed to achieve a specific goal, such as losing weight before an important social event.

people diet excessively, and numerous others abuse stimulants to curb appetite; I know of women students who keep bottles of ipecac syrup hidden in their dresser drawers to use occasionally for purging when they have eaten too much and have to get into a special dress for a particular occasion. (Ipecac is a nonprescription medication designed to induce vomiting in children who have swallowed poison.) In these cases, however, the behavior is *voluntary, controllable, and designed to achieve a specific goal.* These behaviors might be called **strategic eating disorders** to distinguish them from the other eating disorders, in which the behavior is out of control. The fact that some eating disorders are under control while others are not will be important later when we consider causes and treatments. Case Study 14.3 focuses on the eating behavior of actress Jane Fonda, who seems to have suffered from strategic anorexia and bulimia. Her experiences and behaviors are in sharp contrast to those of the young woman in Case Study 14.2, who described her behavior as uncontrolled and desperate.

Explanations

Psychodynamic Explanations. Initially it was believed that eating disorders were due to various psychodynamic conflicts. For example, it was suggested that by refusing to eat young girls were denying their emerging sexual urges—an explanation based on the fact that anorexia can limit the development of secondary sexual characteristics, reduce sexual drive, and lead to amenorrhea (Ross, 1977). This explanation has now been generally abandoned. It was also suggested that young women with anorexia were using their refusal to eat as a means of passively rebelling against overcontrolling mothers; that is, by not eating the young girls could at least take control of their own bodies (Bruch, 1982). This explanation has also been generally dismissed. Another widely accepted explanation was that anorexia and bulimia were related to childhood sexual abuse, but there is no evidence that individuals who suffer from anorexia have experienced more sexual abuse than other individuals— leaving this explanation without scientific support (Kinzl et al., 1994; Pope & Hudson, 1992; Pope et al., 1994; Rorty, Yager, & Rossotto, 1994; Welch & Fairburn, 1994). Why were these erroneous explanations developed? Therapists noted that some of their patients with eating disorders had overprotective mothers or had been abused, so they assumed those were the causes of the disorders. The problem was that the therapists were not also seeing normal individuals, so they did not realize that many normal individuals also have overprotective mothers and may also have been abused.

A more general psychodynamic explanation is that *stress leads to eating* and that extreme stress can lead to the binge eating seen in bulimia (Greeno & Wing, 1994). This

Jane Fonda: A Case of Strategic Anorexia and Bulimia

CASE STUDY **14.3**

IN THE INTRODUCTION to her first book on exercise, Jane Fonda (1981) talked about how for many years she binged, purged, and misused medication to control her weight. The bingeing apparently began at the age of 14, when she went away to boarding school. She and her classmates developed "a preoccupation with food," and she recalls bingeing on coffee ice cream by the gallon, pound cake by the pound, and brownies by the bagful.

For the young Fonda "eating binges were *de rigueur*" (required by fashion, etiquette, or custom). The routine of eating binges became firmly established and was broken only by an occasional crash diet to slim down for a dance or a weekend away from school. In other words, bingeing was an activity, not a compulsion, and it could be stopped when necessary—for example, when she needed to fit into a certain dress.

Fonda and her classmates discovered purging in a class on Roman civilization, in which they learned that during large feasts the Romans would go to a room called a *vomitorium*, vomit up what they had eaten, and then return to the feast and start all over again. This was a great discovery for Fonda and her friends because, as she put it, they thought, "Ah-ha, here's a way to *not* have our cake and eat it too!" (p. 14).

When she went to college, Fonda discovered another way to avoid gaining weight—taking stimulants to curb appetite. She used Dexedrine and reports becoming addicted to the drug. She then experienced "a terrible sense of fatigue and depression" when she stopped taking it. (That effect was probably poststimulant depression; see Chapter 8.)

After college, Fonda worked as a model to support her acting lessons. She was thin but still concerned about gaining weight. She wanted to lose more weight because at the time, the extremely thin and angular look was the "ideal." The answer was more pills. She writes, "In boarding school I had discovered vomiting, in college Dexedrine, and as a model I learned about diuretics" (p. 15). Diuretics have the effect of reducing fluids in the body and thereby reducing weight. With diuretics inches seemed to evaporate overnight, and Fonda took them for the next 20 years. Because her body adjusted to them (a process called *tolerance;* see Chapter 15), she had to keep increasing the dosage. The prescribed level was one pill every 3 days, but soon she was taking two or three pills a day. It wasn't until many years later that she learned that prolonged use of high levels of diuretics can be very dangerous unless the diuretics are accompanied by dietary supplements

to replace the vitamins and minerals flushed out of the body with the fluids.

Clearly, for a long time Fonda engaged in serious and potentially dangerous eating, dieting, and vomiting patterns that might qualify as an eating disorder. These patterns started in her early teens, lasted well into adulthood, and involved bingeing, purging, and the inappropriate use of medication to reduce appetite and weight. As Fonda describes it, however, her behavior seems to have been *goal-directed* and *voluntary*. She wanted to achieve a culturally valued look (lean and lovely) that was essential for social acceptance and her profession. She used inappropriate eating behaviors to achieve her goal until she realized the dangers and found alternatives. Her actions had been "strategic," that is, effective for gaining acceptance and a professional goal, and over a long period of time had become part of a lifestyle. Although the pattern of her behavior was serious, it was quite different from the irrational and uncontrolled starvation, bingeing, and purging seen in many individuals with eating disorders.

> **... for a long time, Fonda engaged in serious and potentially dangerous eating ...**

---

hypothesis was originally based on research with rats, in which it was found that when rats were stressed with a tail pinch or an electric shock, they showed dramatic increases in eating. To test the effects in humans, researchers induced stress with electric shocks, frightening films, or difficult tests and then measured the amount of food the individuals ate. The results indicated that women are more likely to eat during stress than men, and the women who are most likely to eat during stress are those trying to control their weight through procedures such as dieting (Cools, Schotte, & McNally, 1992; Heatherton, Herman, & Polivy, 1991; Schotte, Cools, & McNally, 1990). It appears, then, that

stress might contribute to bulimia in those individuals who are already struggling with weight problems.

Learning Explanation. A very different explanation was offered by learning theorists, who suggested that anorexia may be brought on by *rewards* from the environment. Specifically, because "slim is in," individuals who are losing weight may get rewarded for doing so, and this reinforces their inappropriate diet behavior. In women's dorms and sorority houses it is not unusual to see weight-loss programs and even contests between groups, with the women losing the most weight getting attention, praise, and even prizes. The student with anorexia who used to bring me desserts was particularly successful in this regard and was envied and consistently rewarded by her peers. Unfortunately, they did not realize that they were rewarding her for the symptoms of a potentially fatal disorder.

The emphasis on slimness comes in large part from attempts to imitate the ultraslim women identified as beautiful in Western culture. Indeed, the Duchess of Windsor was quoted as saying that one "can never be too rich or too thin," and Miss America pageant winners have become progressively thinner over the decades. Furthermore, we are constantly reminded of the importance of slimness by numerous advertisements for diets, low-calorie foods, and weight-loss programs.

Rewards for thinness can lead to reduced eating, but the problem with this explanation is that the reductions in eating used to get the rewards are under voluntary control, whereas in many cases of anorexia the reductions in eating are involuntary. That is, individuals with anorexia cannot bring themselves to eat, which is very different from not eating simply to get rewards. To overcome this problem with the learning explanation, we must take the explanation one step further. Specifically, it may be that not only do the individuals *want to be thin,* they may be *afraid of becoming fat,* and the fear of becoming fat leads to a *phobia for eating* (Crisp, 1967; Hsu & Lee, 1993). In other words, individuals may start out by losing a little weight and getting rewarded for doing so. Having done that, they may then become fearful about gaining the weight back, and if the fear of gaining weight is paired with eating, a *classically conditioned anxiety response* to eating will develop (see Chapter 2). Once that occurs, eating will automatically lead to anxiety; to reduce the anxiety the individuals must avoid eating. One woman told me that when she went through a cafeteria line, she would feel fine while in the salad section (nonfattening food) but would become increasingly anxious as she came closer and closer to the main course and dessert sections. She would therefore rush by those sections very quickly; her anxiety would subside when she got to the beverages, where she would only take water. The woman had developed a phobia for fattening foods, and she reduced her classically conditioned anxiety by avoiding them. This is identical to the case in which, for example, fear is paired with a spider so that the individual develops a classically conditioned uncontrollable fear (phobia) of spiders and therefore feels compelled to avoid spiders (see Chapter 5). Classical conditioning of fear provides a good explanation for anorexia because it accounts for the unrealistic fear of becoming fat and the uncontrollable nature of the avoidance of eating.

Cognitive Explanation. From a cognitive perspective it is assumed that individuals with anorexia have *incorrect beliefs* about their "weight problem" and that they exagger-

ate the consequences of gaining weight. The individual starts out thinking, "I'm a little overweight," is concerned that the weight might become a problem, and so embarks on a reasonable diet. However, as time goes by, the individual begins exaggerating the seriousness of the "weight problem," focusing on any information suggesting that there is a problem and ignoring information to the contrary. This selective attention leads to increasingly erroneous beliefs, severe dieting, and, ultimately, anorexia (Zotter & Crowther, 1991).

Physiological Explanations. The physiological explanations for anorexia and bulimia revolve around a suspected malfunction of the **hypothalamus,** which is a structure in the brain that is responsible for control of appetite. This explanation can be traced back to early experiments with rats and monkeys in which it was found that when lesions were made in the lateral (side) portions of the hypothalamus, the animals greatly reduced or ceased eating (Anand & Brobeck, 1951a, 1951b; Anand, Dua, & Schoenberg, 1955). It was also found that if the animals could be kept alive by forced feeding, many of them eventually recovered and

The ideal of slim female beauty promoted by the media sets a standard that many women cannot achieve without extreme measures.

began eating normally again, a pattern similar to that seen in humans with anorexia (Teitelbaum & Steller, 1954). In contrast, lesions made in the ventromedial (front center) portion of the hypothalamus resulted in excessive eating similar to that seen in bulimia (Duggan & Booth, 1986). Although it is possible that eating disorders in humans are due to structural problems in the hypothalamus, it seems more likely that the hypothalamus is not functioning properly because of low levels of **serotonin,** a crucial neurotransmitter in the hypothalamus. In other words, low levels of serotonin lead to a malfunction of the hypothalamus, which leads to eating disorders. The parallel between animal and human behavior is provocative, but it does not necessarily prove that anorexia in humans is due to problems in the hypothalamus. Let's go on to consider some other evidence.

Evidence for the role of serotonin in eating disorders in humans came from research in which investigators measured levels of serotonin in individuals who were suffering from eating disorders and in individuals who were not. For example, in one study the investigators measured serotonin levels in patients who had a high frequency of eating binges (a mean of 23 binges per week), patients who had a low frequency of binges (a mean of 10 binges per week), and individuals who did not have eating disorders (Jimerson et al., 1992). The results were clear: The more serious the eating disorder, the lower the level of serotonin.

Other interesting evidence came from studies in which women who were suffering from bulimia and women who were not were put on a diet low in **tryptophan** (TRIP-tuh-fan), and then changes in their eating and self-perceptions were determined (Smith, Fairburn, & Cowen, 1999; Weltzin et al., 1995). Tryptophan, a substance found in some foods, is relevant because it is converted into serotonin in the body; so a diet that is low in tryptophan leads to low levels of serotonin (see Chapter 8). The results indicated that among the women with bulimia, a low-tryptophan diet led to an increase in food intake and to increased feelings of "being fat"—that is, to an exacerbation of the symptoms of their eating disorder.

If low levels of serotonin cause eating disorders, correcting those levels with drugs should correct the disorders. In fact, as you will learn later when I discuss treatment of these disorders, drugs that increase serotonin levels are indeed effective for treating eating disorders.

Two other points should be made concerning the link between serotonin and eating disorders. First, it is important to note that low levels of serotonin also explain the depression and obsessive-compulsive symptoms that frequently accompany eating disorders (Thiel et al., 1995; Vitousek & Manke, 1994). Specifically, you will recall that many cases of depression and obsessive-compulsive disorder are due to low levels of serotonin (see Chapters 6 and 8). The fact that serotonin levels can account for eating dis-

orders and for other disorders that often co-occur with eating disorders adds considerable credibility to the serotonin explanation for eating disorders. Second, because low levels of serotonin are linked to impulsivity and decreases in inhibition (see Chapter 12), they can also explain the impulsive eating and purging seen in bulimia.

Low levels of serotonin provide a good explanation for eating disorders, but they provide only half of the explanation—we also need to know what causes the low levels of serotonin. There are two possibilities, the first of which is *genetic factors* (Gorwood et al., 1998). Supporting this possibility are the results of investigations of anorexia in identical (monozygotic) and nonidentical (dizygotic) twins. In two studies the concordance rate for the disorder was high in identical twin pairs (75% and 45%, respectively), whereas the concordance rate in nonidentical twin pairs was zero (Nowlin, 1983; Schepank, 1981). In a more recent study, it was found that if one twin had an eating disorder, the other twin was 2.6 times more likely to have the disorder than if the first twin did not have an eating disorder (Walters & Kendler, 1995).

The second possibility is that *prolonged stress* lowers the level of serotonin. Indeed, the results of numerous experiments have indicated that stress leads to reduced levels of serotonin (see Chapter 8), so prolonged psychological stress could trigger the physiological process that leads to an eating disorder.

Finally, I should point out that there is now also evidence that *problems during prenatal development and birth* can lead to eating disorders. In the most convincing of the studies, the birth records of women who did or did not have eating disorders were examined, and it was found that those with eating disorders were more likely to have been born prematurely, been small in size, and suffered from bleeding in the skull (Cnattingius et al., 1999). These findings lead to the conclusion that some cases of eating disorders may be the result of minor brain damage. These findings are particularly interesting in view of the effects of brain lesions on eating behaviors in rats and monkeys that I described earlier.

At present we have a number of good explanations for eating disorders, including social rewards for not eating, classically conditioned eating phobias, incorrect beliefs, low levels of serotonin, and brain damage. However, no one

---

hypothalamus   A structure in the brain that is responsible for the control of appetite.

serotonin   A neurotransmitter in the hypothalamus; low levels are linked to eating disorders.

tryptophan   A substance that is converted into serotonin in the body; in some individuals a diet low in tryptophan can trigger an eating disorder.

There is now evidence that problems during prenatal development and birth can lead to eating disorders. One study found that women with eating disorders were more likely to have been born prematurely, been small in size, and suffered from bleeding in the skull.

explanation accounts for all cases; that is, it is not the case that "one explanation fits all." Of course, different causes require different approaches to treatment, and in the next section I will describe the various treatments for eating disorders.

Treatments

Alarm over the prevalence and seriousness of anorexia and bulimia led to the development of eating disorder clinics, which are inpatient facilities that are usually part of a general hospital. In most of these clinics heavy reliance is placed on the external control of eating. For example, diets are carefully prepared, food intake is closely monitored, and opportunities for purging are eliminated by controlling access to bathrooms and other areas where an individual might vomit. These clinics are typically rather expensive ($1,000 per day), and clients generally stay for 30 days (the amount of time covered by health insurance). Of course, not all individuals with anorexia and bulimia require or can

afford this form of treatment, and so most are treated in outpatient clinics.

Psychodynamic Approaches. Psychodynamic treatments usually involve attempts to relieve depression and improve self-concept because those factors are believed to be the causes of anorexia and bulimia. There have been numerous claims for the effectiveness of psychodynamic treatment, but in most cases the investigations did not have adequate control conditions (Fairburn et al., 1993; Jones et al., 1993). In cases in which there were adequate controls, patients in treatment improved but not more so than those not in treatment (Eisler et al., 1997). That is, in many cases the improvements seen in traditional psychotherapy are due to the natural progression of the disorders or outside sources of support. However, insofar as eating disorders may be brought on by stress, which lowers the levels of neurotransmitters, psychotherapy may be effective because it can reduce stress. So far the evidence for that effectiveness is limited at best.

Learning Approaches. Therapists have also used the principles of learning and have provided rewards such as visitors, television, and tokens for appropriate eating and weight gains (Azerrad & Stafford, 1969; Geller et al., 1978; Halmi, Powers, & Cunningham, 1975; Mizes & Lohr, 1983). Unfortunately, the absence of controlled research makes it impossible to conclude that these techniques are effective.

Cognitive Approaches. There is now a substantial amount of research indicating that cognitive therapy can be effective for treating eating disorders (Peterson & Mitchell, 1999; Whital, Agras, & Gould, 1999; Wilson, 1999; Wilson & Fairburn, 1993; Wilson et al., 1999). For example, in one experiment 40 women who were suffering from bulimia were randomly assigned to either an immediate cognitive-behavioral treatment condition or a delayed cognitive-behavioral treatment condition (Telch et al., 1990). Women in the immediate treatment condition participated in one 90-minute group therapy session per week for a 10-week period and then were followed up after another 10 weeks. In contrast, women in the delayed treatment condition did not receive any treatment for the first 10-week period but then participated in the treatment program during the next 10-week period. In the treatment sessions the women were first taught how to identify the patterns of eating, thinking, and mood that triggered binge-eating episodes. They were then taught how to gradually develop alternative patterns that would lead to healthy, binge-free eating. Self-reports of binge eating were collected at the beginning of the project, after the first 10-week period (treatment or delay), and after the second 10-week period (treatment or followup). The results indicated that the women who were treated in the first 10-week period showed significant reductions in

FIGURE 14.2

Cognitive-behavior therapy was effective for reducing binge eating.

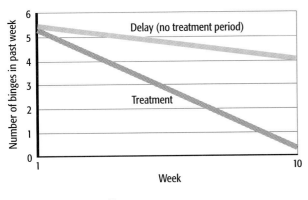

Source: Telch et al. (1990), Table 1, p. 632.

FIGURE 14.3

Prozac was effective for reducing vomiting in women with bulimia.

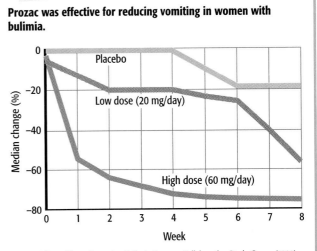

Source: Adapted from Fluoxetine Bulimia Nervosa Collaborative Study Group (1992), Figure 1, p. 142.

binges relative to the women whose treatment was delayed. Those results are presented in Figure 14.2. It was also found that the women who were treated in the second 10-week period showed reductions in binges like those shown earlier by the other group of women. Other research has indicated that about two-thirds of the individuals who benefit from cognitive therapy maintain their improvements for at least 6 months (Thackwray et al., 1993). Clearly, for some individuals cognitive therapy seems to be an effective treatment.

Physiological Approaches. The physiological approaches are founded on the notion that eating disorders stem from low levels of serotonin, and therefore treatment involves the use of antidepressant drugs that increase the levels of serotonin (see Chapter 8 for a discussion of these drugs).

Substantial evidence has accumulated indicating that antidepressant drugs are effective for treating many cases of anorexia and bulimia (Fairburn, Agras, & Wilson, 1992; Fluoxetine Bulimia Nervosa Collaborative Study Group, 1992; Freeman, 1998; Goldstein et al., 1999; Hudson, Carter, & Pope, 1996; Hudson et al., 1998; Hughes et al., 1986; Marcus et al., 1990; Mayer & Walsh, 1998; Mitchell & Groat, 1984; Peterson & Mitchell, 1999; Pope & Hudson, 1982, 1984; Pope et al., 1983, 1985; Walsh et al., 1982; Walsh et al., 1984; Walsh et al., 1991). For example, in one experiment almost 400 patients with bulimia were given either a relatively low level of Prozac (20 mg per day), a relatively high level of Prozac (60 mg per day), or a placebo (Fluoxetine Bulimia Nervosa Collaborative Study Group, 1992). Prozac was used because it blocks the reuptake of serotonin, thereby increasing the level of serotonin at the synapses. When

reductions in vomiting were assessed, the high dose of Prozac was most effective, followed by the low dose and then the placebo. The results are presented in Figure 14.3. Similar results were found when reductions in binge eating were considered.

In another experiment patients with bulimia were given either an antidepressant (Norpramin/desipramine) or a placebo for 6 weeks (Hughes et al., 1986). The patients taking the drug experienced a 91% decrease in binge eating and a 30% decrease in depression. In contrast, the patients taking the placebo showed only a 19% decrease in binge eating and a 5% decrease in depression. Later, when the patients who originally took the placebo were given the drug, they showed an 84% decrease in binge eating, thus offering additional support for the effects of the drug. Other evidence concerning the effectiveness of the antidepressant drugs comes from analyses of the levels of the drug found in the patients' blood. The drug levels in the blood of 10 patients were below the level that is thought to be necessary to be effective. Four of those patients had recovered, but the other six still had symptoms. When the dosage level was increased for the six patients who still had symptoms, four of them recovered completely—suggesting that when the drug did not work, in most cases it was probably due to an insufficient dose.

The research on antidepressants consistently indicates that they are fast-acting and effective for treating eating disorders, but note that no drug was effective for treating all patients. Therefore, it may be that there are subgroups of patients who are responsive to different types of drugs (just as different types of depressive patients respond to different types of drugs) or that eating disorders stem from different causes, only one of which is physiological. It is also noteworthy that antidepressants appear to be more effective for treating bulimia than anorexia. The reason for that is not yet clear, but it may be that the cessation of bingeing and purging can occur faster than eating can be returned to normal. We know that after a long period of starvation the digestive system cannot handle a sudden increase in food because, among other things, the stomach has shrunk. In other words, it may be that it takes the body longer to adjust to eating than to not bingeing.

In summary, cognitive therapy and drugs can be effective for treating eating disorders, and thus the outlook for individuals with those disorders is much more positive than it was just a few years ago.

Other Eating Disorders

Finally, two other eating disorders deserve mention. These are relatively rare and usually limited to infants or very young children. Although the symptom patterns have been described, little is known about the causes of these eating disorders.

Pica

The major symptom of **pica** (PI-kuh) is the *persistent eating of nonnutritive substances* such as paint, plaster, hair, cloth, sand, bugs, leaves, pebbles, and animal droppings. For reasons that are not yet understood, the individual prefers to eat nonnutritive substances over food. (The term *pica* comes from the Latin name for the magpie, a bird that is a "miscellaneous feeder"; that is, it eats random things off the ground. Like magpies, people with pica are miscellaneous feeders.) The symptom pattern of pica can result in serious weight loss, malnutrition, poisoning, and intestinal problems.

Although this eating disorder is usually found in children, it has a relatively high rate of occurrence in adults who suffer from mental retardation, and it is often linked to problems in the temporal lobe (Beecroft et al., 1998; Swift et al., 1999). In one interesting case a 75-year-old woman

pica A relatively rare eating disorder that is most common in children and is characterized by the persistent eating of nonnutritive substances.

rumination A relatively rare eating disorder that is most common in children and that involves the repeated regurgitation of food.

with a 20-year history of pica was found to have over 100 pounds of loose change in her stomach (Beecroft et al., 1998).

Rumination

In contrast, **rumination** (RU-ma-na-shun) is an eating disorder that involves the repeated regurgitation of food. Specifically, the individual brings partially digested food up into his or her mouth and either spits it out or rechews and reswallows it much as a cow chews its cud. (The word *rumination* comes from a Latin word meaning "to chew the cud.") It is noteworthy that the regurgitation associated with rumination does not involve unpleasant vomiting activity (retching, nausea, disgust) but instead seems to result in considerable pleasure and satisfaction. The disorder can be serious because if food is continually spit out, malnutrition and even death may result.

Although this eating disorder is most common in children, it is found in about 10% of individuals with severe mental retardation (Fredericks, Carr, & Williams, 1998). In some cases allowing individuals to eat unlimited amounts at and between meals can reduce rumination (Masalsky & Luiselli, 1998). Apparently the eating blocks rumination, but the additional eating can lead to excessive weight. Fortunately, spontaneous remissions are thought to be common (see Franco et al., 1993; Fullerton, Neff, & Carl, 1992).

THINKING CRITICALLY

Questions about Eating Disorders

What causes anorexia, and how can we determine the cause for any particular individual? Much of this section has been focused on understanding the causes of anorexia, but because of the importance and complexity of the issue, it may be helpful to step back and review. Here we will not consider "strategic" anorexia, for which the explanation is clear: The individual wants to achieve a specific weight reduction goal and therefore voluntarily reduces her or his intake of food. Instances of anorexia that are not under voluntary control are more difficult to explain but appear to be the result of one of two factors: First, many cases seem to be due to classical conditioning, or what cognitive theorists call incorrect beliefs. (Recall that classical conditioning can be interpreted as powerfully held expectations; see Chapter 2). Specifically, anxiety about becoming fat is paired with eating, so eventually eating and food elicit anxiety in the individual; to reduce the anxiety the individual avoids food and eating. Second, anorexia may be caused by a low level of serotonin, which disrupts the functioning of the hypothalamus, which controls appetite; consequently, the individual eats less. This explanation is interesting because it also accounts for the other disorders such as depression and OCD that often accompany anorexia (i.e., depression and OCD can also be due to low levels of serotonin).

The fact that there are two good explanations for anorexia leads to an interesting question: How can you tell which explanation is correct for a particular individual? Unfortunately, at present there isn't a good answer to that question. One possible approach is to determine whether there is a family history of the disorder and whether the individual also suffers from depression and possibly OCD. A family history could suggest a genetic basis for a low level of serotonin, and the presence of depression might also suggest a low level of the neurotransmitter. However, the same information can be used to argue for the cognitive explanation. That is, the classically conditioned response may have been learned vicariously by watching others in the family struggle with concerns about weight, and the individual may be depressed because of the eating disorder. There simply is not an easy answer to the question of why a particular individual suffers from anorexia, and that poses a problem in terms of deciding what treatment to use: That is, treatment must be based on overcoming the underlying cause, and without knowing the cause it is difficult to select a treatment.

There is no doubt that we have learned a great deal about anorexia in the past few years, but when it comes to individual cases of anorexia, we still have some important unanswered questions.

TOPIC II

Sleep Disorders

José has a great deal of difficulty getting to sleep at night, and even when he does get to sleep, he does not sleep soundly and often wakes up. As a result, José is constantly tired and drags through the day. José's problem is known as *primary insomnia*. To overcome his problem he is receiving relaxation training and taking a drug called a *hypnotic*. What causes insomnia, and will these treatments be effective?

Katia has a very different problem; she has uncontrollable attacks in which she suddenly falls sound asleep. Sometimes when that occurs, she collapses because all of her muscles go limp. She suffers from *narcolepsy*. What causes narcolepsy, and can it be treated?

Think about how badly you feel and how much trouble you have studying when you haven't gotten enough sleep for a couple of days. Now imagine what it would be like if you didn't get enough sleep for weeks, months, or even years. That's what some people with sleep disorders go through. In this section we will consider a variety of sleep disorders that range from insomnia to nightmares and sleepwalking.

The Nature of Sleep and Dreams

Before we discuss sleep disorders, it is essential that I explain why we sleep and dream. In other words, before you can understand sleep disorders, you must understand what normal sleep is.

Circadian Rhythms

We all go through a daily pattern of wakefulness and sleep called the **circadian** (sur-KA-de-in) **rhythm.** (*Circadian* is based on the Latin *circa,* which means "about," and *die,* which means "day," so the word means "about a day.") There are two important things to note concerning circadian rhythms: First, *they are controlled primarily by an internal "biological clock"* rather than by external factors such as light. You can "reset" your clock with light or by going to bed early, but the clock always runs at the same speed. Second, although there are wide differences among individuals as to the length of the circadian rhythm, *the average length is about 25 hours.* That is, most people have a cycle of wakefulness and sleep that lasts longer than the cycle of day and night, which is why most people tend to go to bed later and later until they get "out of synch" with the day–night cycle and have difficulty getting up on time in the morning. Eventually, of course, they must reset their biological clocks.

Stages and Cycles of Sleep

After you fall asleep, you go through four **stages of sleep** that become progressively deeper. For example, Stage 1

---

circadian rhythm   The daily pattern of wakefulness and sleep, which is controlled primarily by an internal "biological clock" and which has an average length of about 25 hours.

stages of sleep   Four progressively deeper levels of sleep that occur in cycles each night.

FIGURE 14.4

Stages of sleep, cycles of sleep, and rapid eye movement (REM) sleep

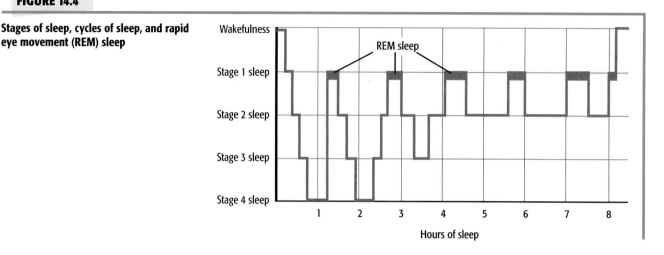

sleep is the light sleep you enter just after falling asleep and from which it is easy to awaken, whereas Stage 4 sleep is the very deep sleep that occurs later and from which it is difficult to awaken. After reaching Stage 4 sleep, you reverse the process and work your way back up to Stage 1 sleep. That **cycle of sleep** is repeated three or four times each night. Stages and cycles of sleep are illustrated in Figure 14.4.

REM (Rapid Eye Movement) Sleep and Dreams

During the Stage 1 sleep that occurs in the second and later cycles of sleep (i.e., not during the Stage 1 sleep that occurs when you are first going to sleep), your eyes begin moving very rapidly. This type of sleep is called **rapid eye movement sleep,** or **REM sleep** for short. The eye movements per se are not important, but they are of interest because they co-occur with dreams; that is, they usually signal the presence of a dream. You should note that the rapid eye movements do not occur because of the dream; that is, they do not occur because you are watching the action in the

cycle of sleep   The progress from Stage 1 sleep (light sleep) to Stage 4 sleep (deep sleep) and then back to Stage 1 sleep; this cycle occurs three or four times each night.

rapid eye movement sleep (REM sleep)   Sleep during which the eyes move rapidly; it occurs during Stage 1 sleep in the second and later cycles of sleep and is often associated with dreaming.

electroencephalogram (EEG)   A record of electrical activity in the brain, used to study sleep.

brain stem   A structure at the base of the brain where the electrical activity that is essential for wakefulness originates.

reticular activating system   A network of nerve tracts that carries electrical activity from the brain stem up to the cortex.

dream. Rather, rapid eye movements and dreams are separate effects that stem from the same underlying process. (I will discuss the underlying process shortly.)

Causes of Sleep

You go to sleep when the level of electrical activity in the cortex of your brain is lowered. Such electrical activity is measured by placing electrodes on the surface of the skull and then using the electrodes to detect the electrical impulses that are occurring inside the skull. The record of such electrical activity is called an **electroencephalogram,** or **EEG** for short (see Chapter 4). In general, sleep is associated with slower and more regular waves of electrical activity than are seen during wakefulness.

The electrical activity in the cortex of your brain originates in your **brain stem,** which is located at the base of the brain where it joins the spinal cord (see Chapter 3). The activity is then carried up to the cortex via a network of nerve tracts called the **reticular activating system.** In other words, if the brain stem is thought of as an electrical generating plant, the nerve tracts of the reticular activating system are the power lines carrying electricity to customers. Sleep sets in (the "lights" in the cortex dim) when the reticular activating system carries less stimulation (electricity) to the cortex.

The question is, why does less stimulation get to the cortex? Most people assume that they go to sleep simply because they run out of energy, or electrical stimulation, but that is not necessarily the case. Instead sleep is an active process; that is, rather than resulting from a depletion of energy, it is a process that begins when something stops stimulation from going up the reticular activating system to the cortex, and it is this inhibition of stimulation that brings on sleep. Specifically, at the base of the reticular activating system where it leaves the brain stem, there is a group of inhibitory neurons called the *raphe* (RA-fe] *nuclei*. When those neurons fire, they block impulses from traveling up the reticular activating system to the cortex, and sleep begins. These inhibitory neurons are activated by impulses from the hypothalamus, which is where the "biological clock" is located. To sum up, then, sleep occurs when the hypothalamus activates the inhibitory neurons (raphe nuclei), which block electrical stimulation from going up the reticular system to the cortex.

Causes of REM Sleep and Dreams

REM Sleep. Now that you have a basic understanding of sleep, I can turn to the questions of what causes REM sleep and dreams. While sleep is caused by a general decrease in the electrical activity in the cortex, the rapid eye movements that occur during sleep are caused by an increase in electrical activity in the area of the cortex that is responsible for eye movements. Specifically, there is a nerve tract called the *PGO system* that during Stage 1 sleep carries stimulation up to the part of the cortex where eye movements are controlled, and this stimulation is responsible for REM. *PGO* stands for *pons, geniculate,* and *occipital,* which are the structures in the brain through which the nerve tract passes; that is, it starts in the pons, which is in the brain stem; goes through a set of neurons in the thalamus known as the geniculate; and ends in the occipital lobe. This stimulation explains REM sleep, but what about dreams? We'll consider them next.

Dreams. Freud originally suggested that dreams occur when material that has been repressed and stored in the unconscious breaks through into consciousness. This breakthrough supposedly occurs because we are less vigilant during sleep. The strange nature of dreams was explained by suggesting that the contents are distorted as a way to protect us from their real meaning (see Chapter 2).

Freud's explanation was widely accepted, but there is now an intriguing alternative explanation that is based on what we know about brain physiology. Before describing this explanation, I should remind you that memories are stored in sets of neurons (called *cell assemblies*) in the brain and that memories can be activated by stimulating those neurons (Penfield & Perot, 1963; see Chapter 11). In view of the way memories are stored and activated, it was suggested that dreams occur when electrical impulses come up from the brain stem and stimulate those areas of the cortex in which various memories are stored; the brain then puts the memories together to form a dream (Hobson, 1988). The fact that stimulation of memories is generally *random* explains why the storyline of most dreams is so "weird"; that is, the brain is putting random memories together in order to make a story. Analogously, if I gave you 10 random pictures, you could make up a story to fit the pictures, but the story might be a little strange—and remember, with

dreams, your brain has to do it while you are asleep. The fact that dreams often involve parts of recent or important experiences is explained by the fact that recently or frequently used memories are more easily activated. This theory is referred to as the **activation-synthesis explanation for dreams**; that is, random memories are activated and then synthesized into a meaningful story (Hobson, 1988; Hobson & McCarley, 1977).

This explanation for dreams is consistent with the finding that hallucinations are the result of excessive and erratic firing of neurons in the brain, which stimulates images and thoughts (see Chapter 11). In view of this dreams might simply be considered *nocturnal hallucinations*. The activation-synthesis explanation of dreams is more consistent with what we know about brain physiology than Freud's explanation was, and its acceptance is growing.

In summary, sleep results when inhibitory neurons reduce the transmission of electrical activity through the reticular activating system to the cortex. However, during periods of Stage 1 sleep that occur after the first sleep cycle, a second system (the PGO system) carries stimulation up to the cortex, and this stimulation results in rapid eye movements and dreams. With this material as background, we can go on to consider sleep disorders.

Primary Sleep Disorders

Primary sleep disorders are due to *physiological problems associated with the process that leads to sleep*. These disorders are divided into two types: *dyssomnias* and *parasomnias*. A **dyssomnia** (dis-SOM-ne-uh) is a disorder that involves *problems with the amount, quality, or timing of sleep*. For example, individuals with dyssomnia sleep too much or too little, do not get good sleep, or cannot control when they fall asleep. (*Dys* means "abnormal," and *somnia* means "sleep," so *dyssomnia* means "abnormality of sleep.") In contrast, a **parasomnia** (par-uh-SOM-ne-uh) involves *an abnormal behavior that is associated with sleep*. For example, individuals with parasomnias may have nightmares or may

---

activation-synthesis explanation for dreams   A theory suggesting that dreams result from the activation and then synthesis of random memories stored in the cortex.

primary sleep disorders   Sleep disorders (e.g., primary insomnia, narcolepsy) caused by physiological problems associated with the process that leads to sleep.

dyssomnia   A type of primary sleep disorder that involves problems with the amount, quality, or timing of sleep.

parasomnia   A type of primary sleep disorder that involves an abnormal behavior that is associated with sleep (e.g., sleepwalking or sleep terrors).

TABLE 14.1

Primary sleep disorders and their symptoms

Disorder	Symptoms
Dyssomnias (problems of quantity or timing of sleep)	
Primary insomnia	Problems getting to sleep or staying asleep
Primary hypersomnia	Excessive sleepiness, prolonged sleep, daytime sleep
Narcolepsy	Irresistible attacks of sleep, loss of muscle tone, intrusions of REM
Breathing-related sleep disorder	Sleep disruption due to apnea or hypoventilation
Circadian rhythm sleep disorder	Sleep problems due to a mismatch between internal rhythms and external demands
Parasomnias (abnormal behavioral or physiological events occurring during sleep)	
Nightmare disorder	Repeated frightening dreams that disrupt sleep
Sleep terror disorder	Awakening with a panicky scream or cry
Sleepwalking disorder	Walking during sleep

Note: Secondary sleep disorders are due to *another mental disorder* (e.g., anxiety or depression), a *general medical condition,* or the *ingestion of substances* (e.g., drugs). They should not be confused with *primary* sleep disorders.

Source: Adapted from American Psychiatric Association (1994).

walk in their sleep. (*Para* is Latin for "alongside," so *parasomnia* refers to problems that happen along with sleep.) The various dyssomnias and parasomnias are summarized in Table 14.1. In the following sections I will describe the symptoms, explain the causes, and examine the treatments for each disorder. (*Note: Primary* sleep disorders should not be confused with *secondary* sleep disorders, which are caused by another psychological disorder such as anxiety or depression, a general medical condition, or the use of drugs.)

Dyssomnias

Primary Insomnia. The major symptoms of **primary insomnia** are difficulty getting to sleep, difficulty staying asleep long enough, and difficulty getting sleep that is restful. These problems with sleep can lead to tension, frustration, and anxiety, which are secondary symptoms and not causes of the sleep problems. Of course, tension and anxiety can lead to additional sleep problems. Primary insomnia is a relatively widespread disorder; it may occur in as much as 30–40% of the population. Older individuals, especially women, are most likely to suffer from primary insomnia.

This disorder is due to *excessive levels of internally generated neurological arousal;* in other words, the reticular acti-

vating system is carrying too much activity from the brain stem up to the cortex and therefore preventing sleep. At present we do not know exactly why or how the excessive arousal is generated, but we take two general approaches to reducing the arousal: physiological and psychological.

The physiological approach to reducing arousal often involves the use of drugs known as **hypnotics** (hip-NOT-iks). (The word *hypnotic* comes from a Greek word that means "to put to sleep.") Most hypnotics are in a class of drugs called *benzodiazepines,* the same class of drugs used to treat anxiety (see Chapter 5). In general, these drugs increase the activity of inhibitory neurons, and the increased activity of the inhibitory neurons serves to reduce general arousal, thus facilitating sleep. Commonly used hypnotics include Halcion (trizolam), Restoril (temazepam), and Dalamine (flurazepam).

The benzodiazepines used as hypnotics have a relatively short **half-life,** which is the amount of time it takes for half of a dose of a drug to be eliminated from the body. A short half-life is necessary so that the level of the drug is reduced below its effective level before morning. In other words, a short half-life is necessary to reduce "hangover" effects, which include drowsiness, cognitive confusion, and problems with muscle coordination the next day (Neylan, Reynolds, & Kupfer, 1994). Elderly individuals frequently suffer from primary insomnia and are often treated with hypnotics, but this poses a problem because elderly individuals eliminate the drugs from their bodies more slowly than younger people, thus increasing the likelihood of hangover effects (Greenblatt, Grosser, & Wechsler, 1991; Woodward, 1999). Indeed, older individuals taking drugs with long half-lives were found to be involved in 28% more automobile crashes than older individuals taking drugs with short half-lives or taking no drugs (Hemmelgarn et al., 1997). It should also be noted that if a drug's half-life is too short, the drug will be out of the individual's system before the night is over, and the individual will awaken early. Like so many other things, treating insomnia is a matter of timing.

Even if hangover effects are minimized by using a drug with an appropriate half-life, problems can develop because the individual may develop a *tolerance* for the drug and consequently require higher and higher levels to achieve the desired effect (see Chapter 15). Finally, concern has been expressed about a possible **rebound effect** when the individual stops taking the drug; that is, it is possible that the symptoms will be worse than they were before the drug was taken (Hajak et al., 1998; Lader, 1998). To some extent the rebound effect is simply the sudden return of symptoms that had been controlled with the drug. However, there is some evidence that rebound symptoms may be worse than they were originally if the individual has been on a high level of the drug and the drug is terminated quickly rather than being gradually phased out.

Sleep disorders, such as primary insomnia, can be extremely frustrating. Difficulty falling asleep or staying asleep can lead to anxiety and tension, which in turn can lead to additional sleep problems.

Finally, with regard to drug treatment it should be noted that in the past few years there has been a great increase in the use of *antidepressants* (e.g., Elavil/amitriptyline) for treating insomnia (Thase, 1998; Walsh & Scweitzer, 1999). Antidepressants are apparently effective because they increase levels of serotonin, and higher levels of serotonin are crucial for the functioning of the hypothalamus, which controls sleep cycles (see the earlier discussion).

Because of the possible side effects of drugs, in some cases psychological strategies are used to reduce arousal and aid in sleep (Morin, Mimeault, & Gagne, 1999; Murtagh & Greenwood, 1995). These strategies are (1) *cognitive therapy,* in which the individual's beliefs about sleep are changed (e.g., "I can get along with less than 8 hours of sleep") so that tension over the lack of sleep is reduced; (2) *relaxation training,* in which the individual is taught how to relax muscles and thereby reduce tension and arousal; (3) *stimulus control,* in which the individual goes to bed only when tired and does not use the bedroom for anything other than sleeping (no reading or sex) so that the stimuli of the bedroom become paired with sleep; and (4) *paradoxical intention,* in which the individual is instructed to try to stay awake, and that "permission" actually reduces the tension associated with staying awake and allows the individual to fall asleep. Research indicates that compared to various placebo treatments, all of these strategies are gener-

ally effective for decreasing the length of time required to get to sleep, increasing the total amount of sleep, reducing the number of awakenings, and enhancing the quality of sleep (Morin, Culbert, & Schwartz, 1994; Murtagh & Greenwood, 1995; Nowell et al., 1998).

Primary Hypersomnia. The major symptom of **primary hypersomnia** is *excessive sleepiness,* which can lead to long periods of sleep at night and the necessity of taking naps during the day. (*Hyper* means "excessive," so *hypersomnia* literally means "excessive sleep.") Unfortunately, the nighttime sleep and daytime naps do not relieve the sleepiness of primary hypersomnia, so the individual drags through the day and may become grouchy and ineffective. In some cases the sleepiness and the need for naps pose a danger—for example, when an individual is driving. It is important to note that many of us often become tired and have to get a good night's sleep or take a nap; what distinguishes this tiredness from primary hypersomnia is that the sleep or the nap refreshes us and we "snap back." That does not happen in cases of primary hypersomnia.

Primary hypersomnia is caused by *insufficient neurological arousal* being generated in the brain stem, a condition that can result from a wide variety of factors, including lesions in the hypothalamus. In other words, the cause of primary hypersomnia is the opposite of the cause of insomnia. The problem is usually treated with *stimulants,* just as you might take caffeine to increase alertness and stay awake. Frequently used stimulants include Ritalin (methylphenidate) and various amphetamines.

Narcolepsy. Individuals who suffer from **narcolepsy** (NAR-kuh-lep-se) have daily *irresistible attacks of sleep.* (The term comes from the Greek words *narco,* meaning "sleep," and *lepsy,* meaning "seizure"; individuals with the disorder are literally seized by sleep.)

---

primary insomnia   A sleep disorder (dyssomnia) in which the symptoms are difficulty getting to sleep, difficulty staying asleep long enough, and difficulty getting sleep that is restful.

hypnotics   Drugs that are used to reduce general arousal and thus facilitate sleep.

half-life   The amount of time it takes for half of a dose of a drug to be eliminated from the body.

rebound effect   The return of symptoms such as sleep problems, possibly in worse form, that can occur when an individual stops taking a drug used to treat the symptoms.

primary hypersomnia   A sleep disorder (dyssomnia) characterized by excessive sleepiness.

narcolepsy   A sleep disorder (dyssomnia) characterized by daily irresistible attacks of sleep.

We should note four characteristics of narcolepsy: First, the sleep is *irresistible;* the individual cannot simply fight off the sleep and stay awake. Second, the sleep is often associated with a sudden and complete *loss of muscle tone,* to the extent that the individual collapses. Third, there is usually evidence of *REM sleep* at the beginning or end of the sleep period, and the individual has *vivid dreams* that are sometimes described as hallucinations. In some cases the dreams or hallucinations are so vivid that the individuals confuse them with reality and believe that the events really happened. Indeed, there is some reason to believe that reports of being visited by space aliens may stem from narcoleptic dreams (Spanos et al., 1993). Fourth, the sleep is *temporarily refreshing;* the individual wakes up feeling good, but a few hours later he or she may have another sleep attack. The sleep attacks can be embarrassing and dangerous and often have a very disruptive effect on the individual's life (Rechtschaffen & Siegel, 1999; Siegel, 2000a). In some cases individuals experience *cataplexy* (a sudden loss of muscle tone), and they collapse but remain conscious of what is happening around them. Attacks like this are most likely to occur in response to a sudden emotion such as fear, joy, or surprise. One investigator described a young woman who fell to the floor completely unable to move after hearing a funny joke. She heard her parents explain to her friends that she would be all right in a few minutes, but she could not respond and was very embarrassed (Siegel, 2000b).

Like hypersomnia, narcolepsy is due to *insufficient neurological arousal.* Interestingly, the disorder also occurs in dogs (Doberman pinchers and Labrador retrievers), so they are often used for research on narcolepsy. Such research suggests that narcolepsy may stem from early brain damage that does not progress (symptoms of the disorder remain constant over the lifespan), but the exact location of the crucial damage is not yet clear (Guilleminault, Heinzer, et al., 1998; Mignot, 1998; Siegel, 2000b). Unfortunately, we do not have a satisfactory treatment for narcolepsy. Stimulants can be effective, but they lead to high heart rates, anxiety, and insomnia (Fry, 1998; Mitler & Hajdukovic, 1991; Portyansky, 1999).

Breathing-Related Sleep Disorder. Individuals with **breathing-related sleep disorder** have their *sleep frequently disrupted because of problems with breathing.* For example, an individual may suffer from **apnea** (AP-ne-uh), which is a *brief cessation of breathing* (*a* means "no," and *pnea* means "breath," so *apnea* means "no breath"), causing a reduction of oxygen intake that wakes the individual up. This occurs hundreds or even thousands of times during the night, so by morning the individual has had a poor night's sleep. Importantly, because individuals fall asleep quickly after each awakening, they are often unaware of the disruptions in their sleep and cannot figure out why they are always tired. The persistent lack of sleep can lead to a variety of

psychological problems, such as depression (Aikens, Caruana Montaldo, & Vanable, 1999; Aikens & Wallace, 1999).

Sleep apneas fall into two general types depending on their cause. The first type is **obstructive apnea,** which involves *obstruction of the airway to the lungs that causes the individual to be briefly deprived of oxygen.* The upper airway path at the top of the throat is flexible and can collapse, thus cutting off the air supply to the lungs. Normally, muscles hold the airway open when an individual inhales, but three factors can interfere with that process. First, in some cases the muscles that keep the airway open may not receive enough stimulation, and therefore they relax and allow the airway to collapse. This is most likely to occur during REM sleep because during that time stimulation to the muscles is generally decreased. It is also possible that insufficient stimulation of muscles can stem from the use of sedatives that cause low levels of general arousal. Second, obesity can lead to a narrowing of the airway, thus making it more likely that the airway will close. Third, the position in which an individual sleeps can increase the likelihood that the airway will collapse.

Behavioral treatments for obstructive apnea include avoiding sedatives so that the muscles will get more stimulation, losing weight so that the airway widens, and sleeping on the side or face down so that the airway does not fall closed (Cartwright et al., 1991). Drug treatment involves the use of antidepressants. Those drugs suppress REM sleep, which is the time when the brain provides the least amount of stimulation to the muscles that hold the airway open. Mechanical approaches to treatment include using a device that fits in the individual's mouth and holds the tongue down or repositions the jaw so that air can pass through the lower airway when the upper airway is blocked. In other cases a tube is placed in the individual's nose, a current of air is passed through it, and the air forces the pathway to remain open (Nakazawa et al., 1992). Finally, surgery can be used to increase the size of the airway.

The second general type of sleep apnea is **central apnea,** which stems from a problem in the brain that causes a brief interruption in breathing. This problem occurs most often in older individuals.

Circadian Rhythm Sleep Disorder. The **circadian rhythm sleep disorder** involves a *mismatch between the timing of an individual's natural sleep–wakefulness cycle and the demands made on the individual by the circumstances in which he or she lives.* For example, an individual's circadian rhythm may follow a 28-hour sleep–wakefulness cycle, while the rest of the world is running on a 24-hour cycle. In that case the individual would be "out of synch" with others, which can lead to conflict and stress. You may have seen mild forms of the disorder in "morning people," who are up and going long before anyone else (they have short cycles), or in

The circadian rhythm sleep disorder is an occupational hazard for many shift workers, for airline pilots and flight crews, and for others who must cope with irregular schedules or time zone changes.

"night people," who are still going long after everyone else has gone to bed (they have long cycles).

Circadian rhythms are controlled by the "biological clock," and because that clock can be reset by bright light, the circadian rhythm sleep disorder can be treated by exposing the individual to a bright light (Rosenthal et al., 1990). Specifically, light early in the morning will start a new phase when the problem is that the cycle is too long, and light in the evening will prolong an existing phase when the problem is that the cycle is too short (Neylan et al., 1994).

Parasomnias

We can now turn our attention to the parasomnias, which involve abnormal activities that occur during sleep.

Nightmare Disorder. Individuals who suffer from **nightmare disorder** repeatedly experience *frightening dreams (nightmares) that awaken them* (American Psychiatric Association, 1994; Bearden, 1994). After awakening, the individuals can remember the nightmare, but they are immediately oriented and alert, and they realize that the nightmare was "only a dream." However, they may find the experience frightening and have a lingering sense of fear or anxiety that can cause problems in getting back to sleep. Of course, the disruptions in sleep and problems getting back to sleep can lead to tiredness and problems with normal functioning.

Nightmares occur frequently in children, especially after some frightening event, but children should not be diag-

nosed as having nightmare disorder unless the nightmares are causing considerable distress and impairment. Fortunately, nightmares become less frequent after childhood, and most children with nightmare disorder outgrow it. The effects of nightmares can be greater in individuals who believe that dreams have spiritual or supernatural implications. For those people the nightmares are not "just dreams"; instead the nightmares may be interpreted as important messages from gods or others.

Sleep Terror Disorder. The major symptom of **sleep terror disorder** is the *abrupt awakening from sleep with a panicky scream.* The panicky scream is accompanied by feelings of intense fear and a very high heart rate. While in the state of panic or terror, the individual is disoriented and cannot be comforted by others. Indeed, the individual may resist being touched or held by others, probably because he or she is confused and is being self-protective. After calming down, the individual does not remember having had a nightmare that triggered the terror. In that regard it is noteworthy that the terrors usually occur during non-REM sleep, when the individual would not be expected to be dreaming. If the terrors are not caused by dreams, what does cause them? One interesting possibility is that the terrors may actually be the result of nocturnal panic attacks (see Chapter 5); that is, an individual has a panic attack while sleeping and wakes up terrified. The pattern of terrors fits with that of panic attacks in that both occur during deep, non-REM sleep. Fortunately, sleep terror disorder

breathing-related sleep disorder A sleep disorder (dyssomnia) in which sleep is frequently disrupted because of problems with breathing (e.g., apnea).

apnea A brief cessation of breathing that causes a reduction of oxygen intake that wakes a sleeping individual.

obstructive apnea A type of sleep apnea involving an obstruction of the airway to the lungs that causes the individual to be briefly deprived of oxygen.

central apnea A type of sleep apnea that stems from a problem in the brain (central nervous system) that causes a brief interruption in breathing.

circadian rhythm sleep disorder A sleep disorder (dyssomnia) in which there is a mismatch between the timing of an individual's natural sleep–wakefulness cycle and the demands made on the individual by the circumstances in which he or she lives.

nightmare disorder A sleep disorder (parasomnia) characterized by repeated awakenings caused by frightening dreams (nightmares).

sleep terror disorder A sleep disorder (parasomnia) characterized by the abrupt awakening from sleep with a panicky scream.

is relatively rare, suspected to occur in fewer than 6% of children and fewer than 1% of adults.

Sleepwalking Disorder. **Sleepwalking disorder** involves *rising from bed and walking while asleep.* Because the individual is asleep, he or she has a blank expression and is usually unresponsive to others. However, in some cases the individual may respond to simple commands, such as an order to go back to bed. If awakened while walking, the individual will be initially confused about where he or she is and will not have any memory of sleepwalking. It is noteworthy that sleepwalking occurs during periods of *non-REM sleep,* so it is unlikely that the individual's sleepwalking is in response to a dream. Sleepwalking is more frequent in children (between 10% and 30% have at least one episode) than in adults, among whom it is rather rare. Contrary to a widely held myth, an individual who is awakened during an episode of sleepwalking will not die.

It is interesting to note that some individuals engage in relatively complex activities, such as eating, while asleep. I have one student who cleans her apartment and another who washes her hair; they wake up in the morning surprised to find a clean apartment or wet hair. There are even cases of individuals who have committed violent acts such as murder while apparently sleepwalking (Broughton et al., 1994; Gilmore, 1991; Guilleminault, Leger, et al., 1998). Such cases raise difficult legal questions: Are people responsible for the acts they commit while asleep?

THINKING CRITICALLY

Questions about Sleep Disorders

1. *Is circadian rhythm disorder really a "disorder," or is it a cultural artifact?* Technically, the answer is that it is a disorder because it is listed in *DSM-IV* and because, as described in *DSM-IV,* the symptoms result in "significant distress or impairments in social, occupational, or other important areas of functioning" (American Psychiatric Association, 1994, p. 578). As I pointed out earlier, distress and disability are two important elements in the definition of what is abnormal (see Chapter 1). However, this may be a case in which distress and disability are due to artificial (and maybe even unrealistic) cultural definitions of what is appropriate. For example, why must everyone work on a nine-to-five schedule? If work schedules were more flexible, persons with circadian rhythms of different lengths would not be "out of synch." Indeed, because the circadian rhythm for *most* people is *not* 24 hours, the standard work schedule seems inappropriate, and that may explain why workers are

often unhappy and ineffective at the end of the week. In other words, if most people seem to be off-schedule, maybe it is the schedule that is wrong. In this regard, some companies allow employees to make their own work schedules, the crucial thing being not when they work but that they work well and get the job done. This is often the case for people who telecommute. As more people begin telecommuting and take control of their own schedules, will there be fewer cases of circadian rhythm disorder?

2. *Are primary sleep disorders psychological or physiological disorders?* By definition, primary sleep disorders are due to physiological problems that influence sleep. For example, primary insomnia, primary hypersomnia, and narcolepsy are caused by problems with arousal in the brain, and sleep apnea is due to problems with respiration. In view of that and the fact that the symptoms are primarily physical (too much or too little sleep), why are primary sleep disorders classified as psychiatric disorders? There is no good answer for that question, but it may be that they are included for historical reasons; that is, they were once thought to be psychological in nature, and despite new findings they remain classified as psychiatric disorders. Certainly these disorders have psychological implications, but so does cancer, so that is not a reason to consider them as psychiatric disorders. Is this a case of psychiatric imperialism? Should these disorders be declassified?

TOPIC III

Psychophysiological Disorders

Bill was an enthusiastic, aggressive, effective mid-level executive who was rapidly climbing the corporate ladder at a computer company. Bill always set high goals for himself, and while others complained about pressure, he sought it out. Because of the demands he placed on himself, Bill was always "on the run." He became impatient in meetings when others talked slowly or took time to state the obvious. When that happened he would jump in and finish their sentences for them so that the group could "get on with it." Bill's career progress was brought to an immediate halt when, at the age of 43, he had a serious heart attack. Stress contributed to the heart attack, but how does stress lead to a heart attack?

Helen has been under a lot of stress during the past 6 months. Her mother was seriously ill for a few months, and then she and her husband moved from Chicago to Los Angeles. Now she is struggling with the problems of establishing herself in her new job as well as looking after their 3-year-old son. Lately she has been sick a lot: colds, sore throats, the flu. Does stress reduce an individual's ability to fight off infections, and if it does, how does it do it?

sleepwalking disorder A sleep disorder (parasomnia) characterized by rising from bed and walking while asleep.

In this section we will consider how psychological stress can cause or contribute to physical disorders such as heart

FIGURE 14.5

Organization of the nervous system

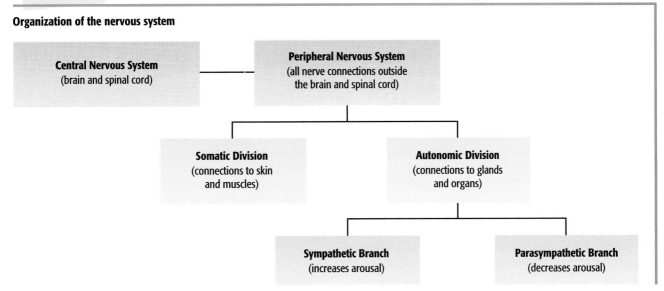

attacks, high blood pressure, strokes, headaches, joint pain, colds, and even cancer.

Stress and Physiological Responses

Because stress provides the basis for the disorders considered in this section, I will begin with a brief review of the concept of stress (see also Chapter 2). A **stressor** is a problem that places a great demand on an individual and leads to high levels of both *psychological arousal* (anxiety) and *physiological arousal* (increased heart rate or blood pressure). These increases in arousal result in what we call *stress.* The increase in physiological arousal is most important in this discussion because if physiological arousal is prolonged, it can result in a variety of physical disorders. For example, prolonged elevation of heart rate, blood pressure, and muscle tension can lead to physical disorders such as heart attacks, hypertension, and headaches.

To understand how stress affects physiological functioning it is essential to understand the organization of the nervous system; so let's consider that first. As shown in Figure 14.5, the nervous system is divided into two major parts: the **central nervous system** and the **peripheral nervous system.** The central nervous system consists of the *brain* and the *spinal cord,* and its major function is to *interpret information* and *initiate responses.* In contrast, the peripheral nervous system involves all of the nerves *not* in the brain and spinal cord, and its major function is to *carry information* to and from the central nervous system.

The peripheral nervous system is, in turn, broken into two divisions: The **somatic division** connects the central nervous system to the *muscles* and *skin,* and the **autonomic**

division connects the central nervous system to various *glands* and *organs.* The autonomic division is of most interest here because it controls organs such as the heart that play a crucial role in the physiology of stress.

Finally, the autonomic system is divided into the **sympathetic branch,** which is responsible for *increasing arousal,* and the **parasympathetic branch,** which is responsible for

stressor A problem that places a great demand on an individual and leads to high levels of both psychological arousal (anxiety) and physiological arousal (increased heart rate or blood pressure), which together result in stress.

central nervous system Part of the nervous system that consists of the brain and the spinal cord and whose function is to interpret information and initiate responses.

peripheral nervous system Part of the nervous system that consists of all of the nerve pathways outside the brain and spinal cord and whose function is to carry information to and from the central nervous system.

somatic division The part of the peripheral nervous system that connects the central nervous system to the muscles and skin.

autonomic division The part of the peripheral nervous system that connects the central nervous system to various glands and organs.

sympathetic branch The part of the autonomic division of the peripheral nervous system that is responsible for increasing arousal.

parasympathetic branch The portion of the autonomic division of the peripheral nervous system that is responsible for decreasing arousal.

decreasing arousal. The two branches are connected, however, so activity in one branch eventually leads to activity in the other branch; therefore, a balance in arousal is usually achieved. For example, when confronted with a stressor, the sympathetic branch is activated, so there is an increase in arousal (e.g., higher heart rate), but activation of the sympathetic branch also leads to the activation of the parasympathetic branch, which then decreases arousal (e.g., lower heart rate).

There are three important points to recognize concerning the organization and function of the nervous system. First, *stressors cause intense and prolonged stimulation of the sympathetic branch of the autonomic system,* thereby overwhelming the calming effect of the parasympathetic branch. As long as stressful stimulation is coming in, the sympathetic branch will be continually activated and you will remain in a high state of arousal.

Second, *the sympathetic branch responds as a unit,* so when it is activated, there is *general arousal.* Unfortunately, some components of that general arousal may be irrelevant for a particular stressor. For example, if confronted by an attacker, you would find it helpful to have an increased heart rate that supplies more blood to the muscles so that you could fight or run; however, an increased heart rate is irrelevant when what you are confronting is a difficult physics examination. The general physiological response to stressors may have been adaptive for our ancestors, whose survival depended on running away from wild animals, but it is maladaptive today, when most stressors are of the cognitive or intellectual type.

Third, *the autonomic division is not under voluntary control* (the autonomic division is *automatic*), so the arousal generated by the sympathetic branch cannot be voluntarily controlled. For example, when you are under stress, your heart beats faster and your blood pressure goes up, but under most circumstances you cannot do much to control

these responses. Overall, then, stressors lead to prolonged physiological arousal that is not under voluntary control, and the arousal leads to various disorders.

With this understanding of stress as background, we can begin our examination of some of the disorders that are linked to stress. I will discuss cardiovascular disorders, headaches, and illnesses related to the immune system because these disorders are widespread and reflect different processes. Although these disorders are relatively common, many people do not understand them. For example, the exact mechanisms of heart attacks and strokes are often misunderstood. Therefore, I will explain each disorder before discussing the role that psychological factors play in its development. The explanations will provide you with an understanding of the disorders and will enable you to see how physiological and psychological factors work together to cause the disorders.

Cardiovascular Disorders

First, we will consider two related cardiovascular disorders: *coronary artery disease* and *hypertension.* These disorders are leading causes of death because they contribute to heart attacks, strokes, kidney failure, and a wide variety of other serious problems.

Coronary Artery Disease

Coronary artery disease involves the buildup of fats (*cholesterol* and *triglycerides*) inside the arteries. This buildup results in a narrowing of the passages through which blood must flow, and that narrowing reduces blood flow. A reduction of blood flow can be very serious because blood delivers oxygen and nutrients to tissues throughout the body. If an artery becomes *occluded* (clogged and closed) because of the buildup of fats, blood flow to the tissues served by that artery will be reduced and the tissues may die. The buildup of fats in blood vessels is called **atherosclerosis** (ath-uh-ro-skluh-RO-sis). (This term is derived from the Greek words *athera,* meaning "gruel" or "porridge," and *sklerosis,* meaning "hardening," so the condition is a hardening of substances in the arteries.) Figure 14.6 shows a cross section of a coronary artery that is almost completely occluded because of atherosclerosis. Atherosclerosis often results in what is commonly called a *heart attack.* A heart attack occurs when the arteries that supply blood to the muscles of the heart become occluded; that occlusion deprives the muscles of blood, and so the muscles die. When the muscles die, the heart stops pumping, blood supply to the rest of the body is cut off, and the individual dies. The heart muscle is known as *myocardium,* and an area of tissue that

---

coronary artery disease A cardiovascular disorder involving a buildup of fats (cholesterol and triglycerides) inside the arteries, causing a narrowing of the arteries that reduces blood flow.

atherosclerosis The buildup of fats in blood vessels.

myocardial infarction (MI) The technical term for a heart attack, which means "death of heart muscles."

angina Sharp pain in the chest or in the left shoulder or arm that is due to insufficient blood supply to the heart muscle and can be a sign of an impending heart attack.

Type A behavior pattern A pattern of behavior that is characterized by intensity, competitiveness, aggressiveness, hostility, and a sense of time urgency and that has been linked to coronary artery disease and heart attacks.

FIGURE 14.6

This coronary artery is almost completely occluded by the buildup of fats (cholesterol and triglycerides).

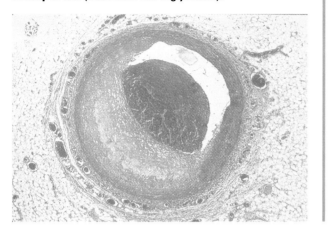

has died is called an *infarct;* therefore, the technical term for a heart attack is a **myocardial** (mi-o-KAR-de-ul) **infarction (MI)**—in other words, the death of heart muscles. A heart attack is most likely to occur during periods of exercise or stress because the heart must beat faster at those times and its muscles require more blood (Giri et al., 1999). (For an extended discussion of atherosclerosis and related problems, see Chapter 17.)

An early sign of insufficient blood to the heart muscle is a sharp pain in the chest or in the left shoulder or arm. This pain is called **angina** (an-JI-nuh), and it usually occurs with exercise. (*Note:* You should always take such pains seriously and have the cause determined. A physician/colleague of mine dismissed his pain as "heartburn" and the next day died of a massive heart attack—at the age of 52!) When individuals are diagnosed as suffering from angina, they usually take tablets containing *nitroglycerin* (ni-tro-GLIS-uh-rin), which causes the arteries to dilate temporarily and allow more blood through. Unfortunately, nitroglycerin tablets are only a short-term solution for the problem. With this description of coronary artery disease as background, I can go on to explain how psychological factors contribute to the disease.

Influence of Type A Behavior and Hostility

Numerous factors contribute to coronary artery disease, including genetics, diet (high intake of fats, cholesterol, triglycerides, and salt), carbon monoxide from cigarette smoking, personality, and stress. Many of these factors are related to lifestyle and thus are psychological in nature. However, the psychological factor that has received most attention is the **Type A behavior pattern,** so let's consider it first. The notion that behavior was linked to heart attacks

gained prominence in the late 1950s when two cardiologists noted that their patients who had heart attacks tended to be intense, competitive, concerned with achievement, aggressive, hostile, overcommitted, and driven by a sense of time urgency (Friedman & Rosenman, 1959, 1974). They termed this the *Type A* behavior pattern and contrasted it with the *Type B* pattern, which involves a more relaxed, leisurely, mellow approach to life that is not associated with coronary artery disease. Actually, the notion that behavior patterns are related to heart attacks goes back to 1892 when it was observed that the individual most likely to develop coronary artery disease was "vigorous in mind and body . . . keen and ambitious" and behaved as though his or her "engine is always at full speed ahead" (Osler, 1892).

An understanding of what makes up the Type A behavior pattern can be gained by examining how it is measured. One method of measurement involves a *structured interview,* in which the interviewer asks about a variety of behaviors that are related to the Type A behavior pattern—for example, "Do you often do two things at the same time?" "Do you eat and walk rapidly?" "Do you always feel in a hurry to get going and finish what you have to do?" (Rosenman, 1978). The answers to those questions help in making a diagnosis, but of most importance is the *way* the individual responds during the interview. Compared to individuals with Type B behavior, individuals with Type A behavior speak more vigorously, more rapidly, and louder; they also answer faster and give shorter answers that are more to the point. In addition, Type A individuals are more alert, tense, and hostile and are more likely to try to hurry the interviewer and jump in and finish a sentence if the interviewer pauses (Chesney, Eagleston, & Rosenman, 1981).

The Type A behavior pattern can also be measured with a paper-and-pencil questionnaire (Glass, 1977; Haynes et al., 1978). The questionnaire includes items like this:

When waiting for an elevator, I

(a) wait calmly until it arrives.

(b) push the button again even if it has already been pushed.

Type A Behavior Pattern and Cardiovascular Disease. The link between the Type A behavior pattern and coronary artery disease has been demonstrated in a number of major investigations. In the classic study a variety of risk factors such as smoking, blood pressure, cholesterol levels, amount of exercise, education, and personality were measured in more than 3,000 men between the ages of 39 and 59 (Rosenman et al., 1975, 1976). When the men were examined 8½ years later, it was found that those who originally showed the Type A behavior pattern were more than twice as likely to have developed coronary artery disease (i.e., have occluded arteries) and to have had a heart attack than were those with the Type B behavior pattern. Importantly, the relationship between the Type A behavior pattern and coronary artery disease existed even after the effects of other risk factors such as smoking, blood pressure, and diet were controlled, thus clearly indicating that something about the Type A behavior itself led to the coronary problems. Other large-scale studies have yielded similar findings (e.g., Akerblom et al., 1999; Matthews, 1988).

The Role of Hostility. Once investigators established the link between Type A behavior and cardiovascular disease, they began to speculate about whether one aspect of the overall Type A behavior pattern was more important than other aspects. As it turns out, the overall Type A behavior pattern has three components—*competitiveness, time urgency,* and *hostility*—and of these three **hostility** is the component that is the best predictor of coronary artery disease (Barefoot, Dahlstrom, & Williams, 1983; Chesney & Rosenman, 1985; Deary et al., 1994; Houston et al., 1992; MacDougal et al., 1985; Matthews et al., 1977; Meesters & Smulders, 1994; T. Q. Miller et al., 1996; Patel, 1994; Smith, 1992; Williams et al., 1980). For example, in one study of more than 400 individuals, it was found that among those with high hostility scores, 70% had an occlusion, whereas among those with low scores, only 48% had an occlusion (Williams et al., 1980). In another study the investigators followed up 255 physicians who had taken a test of hostility 25 years earlier when they were in medical school (Barefoot et al., 1983). The results indicated that physicians with hostility scores above the median were almost five times

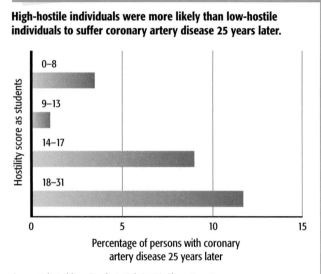

FIGURE 14.7

High-hostile individuals were more likely than low-hostile individuals to suffer coronary artery disease 25 years later.

Source: Adapted from Barefoot et al. (1983), Figure 1, p. 60.

more likely to have a heart attack than those with scores below the median; see Figure 14.7. (Note that high hostility scores were also related to higher rates of death due to other factors, such as cancer, accidents, suicide, and gastrointestinal problems, thus suggesting that hostility may play a very broad role in human health.) From these and other results we know that the Type A behavior pattern is related to coronary artery disease and that it is the hostility component that is responsible for the effect.

Processes Linking Type A Behavior or Hostility to Disease. Having determined that there is a link between Type A behavior and coronary artery disease, the question is, why does Type A behavior lead to coronary artery disease? To answer that question, we must turn first to laboratory research on how Type A individuals respond to stress. There are two findings of particular interest. The first is that Type A individuals show higher heart rates and higher blood pressure in stressful or challenging situations than do Type B individuals (see Glass, 1977; Holmes, 1983; Houston, 1983; Lyness, 1993; Matthews, 1982). For example, in one experiment college students worked on an intelligence test that was either easy or difficult while their blood pressure was monitored (Holmes, McGilley, & Houston, 1984). The results indicated that while working on the difficult test, Type A students showed higher systolic blood pressure than did Type B students.

The second notable finding is that Type A individuals set higher goals for themselves than do Type B individuals; therefore, they force themselves into more stressful or challenging situations. For example, in the experiment just

We all tend to "multitask" occasionally, but individuals with Type A behavior pattern are overcommitted, competitive, hurried, and often hostile. It now appears that the hostility component of the pattern is associated with increased risk of heart attack.

mentioned, when students were asked to indicate whether they would like to work on harder or easier tasks in a second part of the experiment, Type A students chose more difficult tasks than Type B students (Holmes et al., 1984). In another experiment in which Type A and Type B individuals ran on a treadmill, Type A individuals ran until they were closer to their actual limits of physical exhaustion before giving up than did Type B individuals (Carver, Coleman, & Glass, 1976).

The combination of increased arousal during challenges and greater challenge-seeking leads the Type A individuals to be more highly aroused more frequently than Type B individuals. The next question is, how does the arousal lead to the disease? Actually, there are four ways in which increased arousal can lead to cardiovascular disease:

1. *Arousal leads to the increased production of cholesterol.* In two studies it was found that students who were under high levels of stress had higher levels of cholesterol than did students under low stress, and the results of another study revealed higher levels of cholesterol in military veterans with PTSD (Coleman et al., 1999; Kagan et al., 1999; Schwartz et al., 1999). Both acute and chronic stress can increase cholesterol (Stoney et al., 1999). For example, corporate accountants who were under chronic stress had consistently high levels of cholesterol, whereas tax accountants showed high levels of cholesterol only when they were under pressure at tax return time (Friedman, Rosenman, & Carroll, 1958). Why does cholesterol go up during stress? It is a basic building block in the body, so an increase in its production is a defense against the deterioration that comes with stress.

2. *Arousal leads to greater clotting of cholesterol.* During stress certain hormones (e.g., epinephrine and norepinephrine) are secreted into the bloodstream, and they cause the particles of cholesterol that are floating in the blood to become sticky and form clots in the blood vessels or on the artery walls (Ardlie, Glew, & Schwartz, 1966). Those clots may then lead to occlusion of the arteries.

3. *Arousal leads to higher heart rates and hence to more rapid accumulation of cholesterol on the artery walls.* Stress leads to a higher heart rate, and there is evidence that a higher heart rate enhances the buildup of cholesterol on the artery walls. That effect was neatly demonstrated in an experiment in which the heart rates of six monkeys in an experimental group were artificially lowered by destroying part of the nerve node that controls heart rate (Beere, Glagov, & Zarins, 1984). Eight other monkeys in a control condition underwent the same operation, but the node was not destroyed; so the heart rates of those monkeys were not lowered. After the operation the monkeys in both conditions were fed a high-cholesterol diet for 6 months. Examination of the coronary arteries of the monkeys at the end of the 6-month period revealed that the monkeys whose heart rates had been lowered showed occlusions of about 20%, whereas the monkeys whose heart rates had not been lowered showed occlusions of 55%. In other words, the monkeys with slower heart rates had occlusions that were about 35% less extensive than did the monkeys with higher heart rates. It appears that higher heart rates lead to more extensive occlusion because the brief pause of blood flow that occurs between heartbeats provides an opportunity for cholesterol to become attached to the walls of the arteries. That is, more heartbeats lead to more pauses in blood flow, which in turn lead to more buildup on the artery walls.

4. *Arousal leads to high blood pressure, and the consequent stretching of the arteries causes their walls to become rough, making it easier for cholesterol to adhere.* This process enhances the buildup of cholesterol on the artery walls and leads to occlusions.

In summary, Type A (hostile) individuals have higher and more frequently elevated levels of arousal, which lead to the development of coronary artery disease because they increase (1) the production of cholesterol, (2) the clotting of cholesterol particles, (3) the accumulation of cholesterol on artery walls, and (4) the ease with which cholesterol can adhere to artery walls.

Hypertension

The other major cardiovascular disease is **hypertension** (hi-pur-TEN-shun), or *high blood pressure*. There are two types of hypertension: *essential* and *secondary*. **Essential hypertension** is high blood pressure *for which a physical cause has not been found,* and so it is assumed that the elevated pressure is due to psychological factors. (Essential hypertension is sometimes referred to as *primary hypertension.*) In contrast, **secondary hypertension** is high blood pressure that stems from a *known physiological cause* such as excessive salt in the diet, atherosclerosis, or kidney malfunction. It is called *secondary* because the elevated blood pressure is a side effect of some other physical disorder. In this section I will focus on essential hypertension.

---

hostility The component of the Type A behavior pattern that is the best predictor of coronary artery disease.

hypertension A cardiovascular disease involving high blood pressure, usually 140/90 or higher.

essential hypertension High blood pressure for which a physical cause has not been found and so it is assumed to be due to psychological factors; sometimes referred to as *primary hypertension.*

secondary hypertension High blood pressure that stems from a known physiological cause such as excessive salt in the diet or atherosclerosis.

Hypertension is a widespread and potentially serious disorder. Specifically, it has been estimated that 1 out of every 6 adults has hypertension and that 90% of those individuals suffer from essential hypertension. Many individuals are not aware that they have hypertension because it does not have any noticeable symptoms. The seriousness of hypertension is evidenced by its ability to increase the risk of coronary artery disease, heart attacks, strokes, and kidney failure.

There are two important measures of blood pressure: *systolic* and *diastolic.* **Systolic** (sis-TOL-ik) **blood pressure** is the high level of pressure that occurs immediately after each heartbeat, when blood is suddenly forced through the system. In contrast, **diastolic** (di-uh-STOL-ik) **blood pressure** is the low level of pressure that occurs just before each heartbeat. Blood pressure is measured in terms of the height of a column of mercury that could be supported by the pressure. Normal systolic pressure is about 120 mm Hg (millimeters of mercury), and normal diastolic pressure is generally considered to be 80 mm Hg. When talking about blood pressure, we give the systolic pressure first and then the diastolic pressure; thus we might say that an individual's pressure is "120 over 80" (written 120/80). Although 120/80 is considered "normal," blood pressure varies widely. Women generally have lower pressure, older individuals have higher pressure, and any one individual's pressure may go up and down during the day due to a variety of factors.

Individuals are usually diagnosed as suffering from hypertension if they have sustained blood pressure readings of 140/90 or higher. However, both figures need not be high for a problem to exist, and there is no agreement over whether elevation of systolic or diastolic pressure is more important. It might be noted that some individuals suffer from **hypotension** (hi-po-TEN-shun)—that is, *low blood pressure.* Hypotension is not a serious problem. However, when getting up quickly from a chair or a bed, an individual with hypotension can experience sudden dizziness because for a brief period there is not enough pressure to get blood to the brain.

The development of essential hypertension involves two steps: First, stress results in a temporary increase in blood pressure. Second, the increase in blood pressure causes the arteries to stretch, and the stretch is detected by a set of sensors called **baroreceptors** (bar-o-re-SEP-turz), which then send signals to the central nervous system to reduce blood pressure. Specifically, to reduce pressure the peripheral blood vessels are dilated, heart rate is reduced, and the strength of the heart's contraction is reduced. However, if pressure is high for a prolonged period of time, the baroreceptors adjust to the higher level of pressure and signal the central nervous system only when the pressure goes even higher. In other words, after an extended increase in pressure the baroreceptors reset themselves, and high pressure becomes "normal."

A review of the evidence concerning the role of personality factors in hypertension revealed three interesting findings (Jorgensen et al., 1996). First, high blood pressure is most likely to be associated with *negative emotions* such as *anger* (hostility) and with the *suppression of those emotions in interpersonal situations.* In other words, when dealing with other people, angry individuals, especially those who hold the anger in rather than expressing it, are most likely to experience high blood pressure. Second, these effects are *more likely to occur in African Americans than in European Americans.* This finding is consistent with the notion that African Americans are exposed to more stressors such as crime, poverty, and discrimination and may feel that they must suppress their outrage and anger to avoid retaliation. Third, the influence of personality on blood pressure becomes *stronger with increasing age,* an effect that probably reflects the accumulation of the effects over time and the body's reduced ability to adjust to the stress of the suppressed anger. Overall, then, there is solid evidence that psychological factors such as stress and personality contribute to hypertension.

Treatment

An individual whose coronary arteries are approaching the point of occlusion might undergo **coronary bypass surgery,** which involves grafting an unclogged piece of artery at the location of the occlusion so that blood can bypass the occluded area and hence get to the heart. Another operation called **angioplasty** (AN-je-o-plast-e) is

---

systolic blood pressure   The high level of blood pressure (normally 120 mm Hg) that occurs immediately after each heartbeat, when blood is suddenly forced through the system.

diastolic blood pressure   The low level of blood pressure (normally 80 mm Hg) that occurs just before each heartbeat.

hypotension   Low blood pressure.

baroreceptors   Sensors that detect an increase in blood pressure and then send signals to the central nervous system to reduce blood pressure.

coronary bypass surgery   A procedure that involves grafting an unclogged piece of artery at the location of an occlusion so that blood can bypass the occluded area and hence get to the heart.

angioplasty   A procedure in which a tiny flexible tube with an inflatable balloon on the end is inserted into an occluded artery, and the balloon is inflated at the point of the occlusion, thereby forcing the fatty material against the side of the artery and expanding the passageway in the artery.

frequently performed; it involves taking a tiny flexible tube with an inflatable balloon on the end and inserting it into the occluded artery. The balloon is then inflated at the point of the occlusion, forcing the fatty material against the side of the artery and expanding the passageway in the artery. A related procedure involves inserting a tube with a rotating knife blade on the end; when the blade spins, it chops up the obstructing material so that it can be carried away in the bloodstream. More recently, drugs referred to as "clot busters" have been developed. These drugs, if administered at the first sign of a heart attack or stroke, can dissolve clots and prevent further damage.

Stress on the cardiovascular system can also be reduced with drugs known as **beta** (BA-tuh) **blockers** (such as *propranolol,* sold under the trade name Inderol), which reduce heart rate (Kristal-Boneh et al., 1995). If heart rate is reduced, the heart's need for oxygen is reduced, and therefore the likelihood of heart attack is reduced. These drugs are called beta blockers because they block synaptic transmission at *beta receptors* at the synapses of the sympathetic nervous system.

One type of drug widely used to treat hypertension is **diuretics** (di-yuh-RET-iks). Diuretics reduce the amount of fluid in the body, and when the fluid level is lower, there is less pressure in the cardiovascular system. Hypertension is also treated with drugs called **vasodilators** (VA-zo-di-la-turz); these cause the blood vessels to dilate, making more room in the cardiovascular system and thereby reducing the pressure.

Prevention

Surgery and medication can be effective for treating cardiovascular disorders, but if the underlying problems are not solved, the symptoms will return. Indeed, it is not unusual for patients to have two or three angioplasties or bypass operations. Therefore, the key is *prevention.* In the following sections I will describe programs and strategies that are helpful in preventing cardiovascular disease and heart attacks.

Stress Management. Programs known as **stress management training** were originally designed to make Type A individuals more like Type B individuals. For example, in one investigation individuals who had experienced heart attacks were randomly assigned either to a condition in which they participated in a standard cardiac rehabilitation program where they received instructions concerning diet and exercise or to a condition in which they participated in the same rehabilitation program but also participated in group counseling sessions designed to reduce their Type A behavior (Friedman et al., 1984; Friedman & Ulmer, 1984). The results indicated that the individuals who received counseling to reduce Type A behavior showed reductions in

such behavior and were less than half as likely to have another heart attack as the individuals who participated in only the traditional rehabilitation program. These results suggest that it is possible to change the Type A behavior pattern. However, achieving such a change is very difficult, because most individuals do not want to give up the Type A behavior that has been essential to their achievement of success. Indeed, in Western society the Type A behavior pattern is generally admired and rewarded, and unless individuals face imminent death from another heart attack, they are resistant to changing their behavior.

Recently, stress management programs have focused more on education concerning diet and exercise and techniques for reducing stress. A review of the results of almost 40 studies in which such programs were evaluated revealed that they reduced deaths due to heart attacks by 34% and reduced second heart attacks by 29% (Dusseldorp et al., 1999).

Social Support. Another strategy for managing stress revolves around enhancing **social support.** There is consistent evidence that social support reduces stress and is associated with lower heart rate and blood pressure (Berkman, 1995; Bland et al., 1991; Dressler, 1991; Elizur & Hirsh, 1999; Gerin et al., 1992; Logsdon et al., 1998; Uchino, Cacioppo, Kiecolt-Glaser, 1996; Unden, Orth-Gomer, & Elofsson, 1991). For example, individuals who participate in more club activities and individuals who receive more social support at home or at work show lower cardiovascular arousal in social and work settings. Of course, it is possible that social support does not reduce arousal but that individuals who are less aroused attract more support (e.g., they may be less hostile). To determine whether social support actually leads to lower cardiovascular arousal, an experiment was conducted in which an accomplice of the experimenter argued with an individual while the individual's blood pressure was taken (Gerin et al., 1992). In a social-support condition a third person defended the individual, whereas in a no-social-support condition the third

---

beta blockers   Drugs used to reduce heart rate and thereby reduce the amount of oxygen needed by the heart.

diuretics   Drugs used to treat hypertension by reducing the amount of fluid in the body, thus lowering the pressure in the cardiovascular system.

vasodilators   Drugs used to treat hypertension by dilating blood vessels thereby making more room in the cardiovascular system.

stress management training   Programs designed to reduce stress, often by encouraging Type B rather than Type A behavior.

social support   The presence of others on whom an individual can rely for support, which reduces stress.

person did not come to the individual's defense. The results indicated that when individuals were given social support, they showed smaller increases in blood pressure and heart rate, thus confirming the link between social support and reduced cardiovascular arousal.

Positive Attitude. There is now evidence that a generally positive attitude (optimism, high self-esteem, hopefulness, sense of control) can enhance recovery from cardiovascular disorders and prevent their recurrence (Helgeson & Fritz, 1999; Khalid & Sial, 1998; King et al., 1998). Why? Individuals who are optimistic anticipate fewer problems and therefore are under less stress than those who expect a bad outcome; lower levels of stress enhance recovery and reduce the likelihood of another heart attack.

Aerobic Exercise. For many years rest was the treatment of choice for individuals who had had heart attacks. The notion was that the heart muscles had been weakened and

Aerobic exercise can help reduce the buildup of cholesterol in the arteries and serves to enlarge and strengthen the heart so that it can pump blood more efficiently. The relationship between aerobic fitness and improved cardiovascular responses during stress has been demonstrated in a number of studies.

should not be strained. However, it is now generally agreed that **aerobic exercise** can aid in the treatment and prevention of cardiac disorders in a number of ways. (Aerobic exercise includes jogging, swimming, cycling, and other activities that elevate heart rate to 70% of its maximum for at least 20 minutes. Your maximum heart rate is estimated by subtracting your age from 220.) For example, aerobic exercise can reduce the buildup of cholesterol in arteries. To understand how this works you must first recognize that there are two types of cholesterol, one "bad" and one "good." The bad type, known as **LDL** (low-density lipoproteins), comes from fat in the diet and builds up in the arteries. The good type, known as **HDL** (high-density lipoproteins), is produced when we exercise, and it carries away the LDL before it can build up. Therefore, by exercising we increase the production of HDL, which restricts the buildup of LDL.

Aerobic exercise also serves to enlarge and strengthen the heart so that it can pump more blood more efficiently (i.e., the volume of blood pumped with each beat is increased). The increased efficiency of the heart means that it won't have to work as hard (it will beat slower and require less oxygen) both under normal conditions and under stress.

The relationship between aerobic fitness and improved cardiovascular responses during stress has been demonstrated in a number of investigations (Holmes, 1993). For example, in one study the heart rate and blood pressure of students were measured while they rested and while they worked on a stressful intellectual task (subtracting by 7 as fast as possible from the number 3,584) (McGilley & Holmes, 1988). The results indicated that during stress the students who were in better aerobic condition had heart rates that were almost 30 beats per minute lower than the less fit students. Furthermore, during stress the students who were in better aerobic condition also had systolic blood pressures that averaged almost 14 mm Hg lower than those of the less fit students.

Exercise programs have also been demonstrated to be very effective for physiological and psychological rehabilitation of individuals after a heart attack or bypass surgery (Dunn et al., 1999; Gould et al., 1995; Higashi et al., 1999; Manson et al., 1999; Ornish et al., 1998; Roviaro et al., 1984). One experiment revealed that compared to patients who received routine medical care, patients who participated in an exercise program showed (1) lower heart rate, (2) lower blood pressure, (3) better performance on a treadmill, (4) better self-concept, (5) less employment-related stress, (6) more enjoyment of leisure time, and (7) greater sexual activity (Roviaro et al., 1984). Unfortunately, when the patients were reexamined 7 years later, those who had been in the routine-care condition were doing better than those who had been in the exercise condition (McGilley, Holmes, & Holmsten, 1993). The problem was that the patients in the exercise condition thought they were "cured" when the program was over, so they stopped exercising, but the patients who received routine care were still concerned about their health so they slowly began to increase the amount they exercised, and that exercise led to improvements in their physical and psychological health. Clearly, *exercise must be part of a change in lifestyle,* not just a temporary treatment.

The fact that changing one's lifestyle can stop, and even reverse, the process of cardiovascular disease was clearly demonstrated in an experiment in which some patients participated in an intense program that involved (1) a diet that was low in cholesterol, (2) aerobic exercise 3 hours per week, and (3) stress management practice for 1 hour per day. In contrast, patients in a control condition received only routine medical care (Gould et al., 1995; Ornish et al., 1998). Before the program was begun and again after 5 years, blood flow through the tissues of the heart muscles was measured with PET scans. It turned out that the patients in the control condition showed *decreases* in blood flow through the heart muscles; that is, despite medical treatment the disease was getting worse. In contrast, patients in the treatment condition showed *increases* in blood flow through the heart muscles. In other words, not only was the disease process stopped, it was reversed, and the improvements were achieved without drugs or surgery and with relatively little cost. Obviously, lifestyle changes can be very effective.

Biofeedback Training. Responses of the autonomic branch of the peripheral nervous system are generally not under voluntary control, making it difficult to control physiological responses to stress. For example, ordinarily we cannot voluntarily reduce our heart rate or blood pressure during periods of stress. However, some years ago it was suggested that our inability to control autonomic responses was due to the fact that we had not had sufficient opportunities to learn such control. Feedback about performance is essential to learning (e.g., you cannot learn to decrease your blood pressure unless you know when it is going up and down), and thus it could be that we do not learn to control autonomic responses because we do not ordinarily get enough feedback about them. That speculation led to the development of **biofeedback training,** procedures in which electronic equipment is used to provide individuals with immediate feedback about changes in their autonomic responses in an attempt to help them learn to control the responses.

Biofeedback training has been widely publicized as an effective treatment for hypertension, and a number of investigators have reported that hypertensive patients who received biofeedback training showed decreases in blood pressure of as much as 26 mm Hg. They also reported that after biofeedback training individuals could maintain nor-

mal blood pressure without the aid of medication (e.g., Mukhopadhyay & Turner, 1997; Nakao et al., 1997). However, in most of those studies the changes in blood pressure in patients receiving biofeedback training were not compared to the changes in patients who simply sat quietly for a time and did not receive biofeedback training (individuals who relaxed without the aid of biofeedback), so we cannot determine whether it was the biofeedback or sitting quietly that was resonsible for the decreases in blood pressure. To correct that problem a series of experiments was conducted in which some patients received blood pressure biofeedback training while others simply sat quietly for a comparable length of time. Surprisingly, the results of those experiments indicated that biofeedback training was no more effective than sitting quietly (see Holmes, 1981). Thus despite widespread publicity and extensive clinical use of biofeedback training for treating hypertension, questions remain concerning its effectiveness.

To sum up, cardiovascular disorders pose a variety of serious medical problems, and there is now substantial evidence that psychological factors contribute to cardiovascular disorders. The most important factor seems to be hostility. Hostility leads to cardiovascular disorders because it is associated with increased levels of arousal. Fortunately, cardiovascular disorders can be reduced with stress management, social support, a positive attitude, aerobic exercise, and medication (beta blockers).

Headaches

You've probably had a really bad headache at some time. Now imagine the pain being two or three times as bad and occurring often. That's the problem we will consider in this section. Indeed, headaches are among the most common causes of pain, and it is estimated that between 10% and

aerobic exercise   Exercise such as jogging or swimming that increases heart rate to at least 70% of its maximum rate for at least 20 minutes.

LDL (low-density lipoproteins)   The "bad" cholesterol that comes from fat in the diet and builds up in the arteries.

HDL (high-density lipoproteins)   The "good" type of cholesterol that results from exercise and carries away LDL.

biofeedback training   Procedures in which electronic equipment is used to provide individuals immediate feedback about changes in their autonomic responses in an attempt to help them learn to control the responses.

30% of Americans suffer from chronic headaches. Here I will focus on *migraine* and *tension headaches* because they pose the most serious and frequent problems.

Migraine Headaches

A **migraine headache** produces pain so severe that it can completely incapacitate an individual. Some patients describe the pain as a burning rod being driven through the brain. There are two types of migraine headaches: classic and common. The *classic* type afflicts about 2% of headache sufferers and consists of two phases. The first phase begins about 30 minutes before the actual headache starts, and the symptoms involve visual problems such as flashing lights and blind spots, dizziness, and sometimes abdominal pain. These are called *prodromal symptoms,* and they serve as a warning that a headache is about to begin. The actual headache begins in the second phase, and at first it involves a unilateral (one-sided) throbbing pain that usually occurs in the temporal or occipital area (side or back of the head). In addition to feeling pain the individual usually becomes nauseated and very sensitive to light and is most comfortable in a dark, cool place. As time goes on, the pain changes from throbbing to constant. The headache lasts for a few hours, usually less than 24.

The second type of migraine is the *common* type, and it afflicts about 12% of headache sufferers. The common migraine is not preceded by prodromal symptoms, and the pain is usually generalized rather than limited to one area of the head. However, the common migraine does involve the other symptoms of nausea and sensitivity to light and is just as painful as the classic type. The severity of the pain associated with migraine headaches cannot be understated.

The prodromal symptoms of the classic migraine are due to an extreme *constriction of the cranial arteries* (the arteries that supply blood to the head). The constriction limits the blood supply, causing the symptoms. As the process progresses, the cranial arteries change from a state of constriction to a state of *extreme dilatation.* When the arteries dilate and increase in size, they put pressure on the surrounding pain-sensitive nerves, and it is that pressure that results in the pain. The initial throbbing nature of the pain is due to the hydraulic pulsations of blood through the dilated arteries. As the attack continues, the arteries become inflamed and rigid in their dilated state, and therefore the pain changes from throbbing to steady.

We know that migraine pain is due to extreme dilatation of the cranial arteries, but we do not yet clearly understand the factors that cause the arteries to dilate. However, it appears that genetic factors play a role in predisposing individuals to migraine headaches and that the genetic link is stronger for women than men. It also appears that estrogen is somehow connected to migraine headaches because

the incidence of migraines in women drops sharply after menopause and because the incidence of migraines in women who are taking estrogen supplements drops sharply when those supplements are reduced (Lay & Newman, 1999). Finally, over the years there have been numerous speculations concerning the role of stress in precipitating migraine headaches, but as yet the effects of stress have not been demonstrated to be particularly important (Holm, Lokken, & Myers, 1997; Robbins, 1994; Solomon, 1994). Individuals often report that stress precedes the onset of migraines, but they ignore the fact that more often stress does not lead to migraines.

One medical approach to the treatment of migraines involves the administration of stimulants such as *ergotamine tartrate* and *caffeine.* Stimulants are effective for reducing the pain because they cause constriction of the dilated arteries, thus reducing the pressure on the surrounding pain-sensitive nerves. However, to be effective the stimulants must be taken during the very early stage of the headache, before the dilated arteries become rigid. If the attempt to constrict the arteries is made after they become rigid, the use of stimulants will not be effective, and the individual will have to endure the pain until the headache has run its course. Fairly recently, a drug named Imitrex (sumatriptan) was introduced; it is fast acting (pain is reduced in minutes) and effective for treating serious migraines by slowing the firing of specific serotonin receptors (Goadsby, 1998; Lipton, 1999; Lobo, Cooke, & Landy, 1999; Ueberall & Wenzel, 1999). Although this drug is expensive, its use is cost-effective because it reduces the number of work-hours lost to pain (Laloux et al., 1998). Finally, if migraines occur frequently, a variety of drugs (e.g., some antidepressants, beta blockers, and at least one antiseizure drug) can be taken to help prevent them.

The most widely publicized psychological treatment of migraine headaches involves *finger temperature biofeedback training,* in which the individual attempts to increase his or her finger temperature with the aid of biofeedback. Finger temperature increases when more blood flows to the area; the assumption is that if more blood is flowing to the hands, less blood will be flowing to the head, thus decreasing pressure and pain there. A variety of early case studies seemed to provide support for this treatment, and it quickly became very popular. Unfortunately, subsequent controlled research has not provided any support for the efficacy of biofeedback training for the treatment of migraine headaches (see Holmes, 1981; Holmes & Burish, 1984). For example, in one experiment the individuals were given either true biofeedback or false biofeedback that did not accurately reflect skin temperatures (Mullinix et al., 1978). The results indicated that the individuals in the true biofeedback condition were better able to increase their finger temperatures, but they showed no greater reductions in headaches or in medication usage than did the individuals who received the false biofeedback. In other words, the control of finger temperature (blood flow) was not related to headache activity. Even more devastating were the findings of another investigation in which it was demonstrated that individuals who were given biofeedback training could learn to relax and control blood flow but that the changes in blood flow to the hands were not related to changes in blood flow to the cranial arteries (Largen et al., 1978). Furthermore, it now appears that the dilatation of the cranial arteries is not due to changes in blood flow. Thus, finger temperature biofeedback training has not been found to be effective for treating migraine headaches and, for physiological reasons, probably cannot be effective. However, because of the publicity given to the results of the early case studies and the intuitive appeal of the approach, this biofeedback training is still widely advertised and used as a treatment for migraine headaches.

Tension Headaches

Tension headaches, sometimes called *muscle contraction headaches,* are very common (Silberstein, 1994). The pain is constant (nonpulsating), usually occurs on both sides of the head, and most frequently occurs primarily in the forehead and the back of the head just above the neck. The pain of tension headaches stems from the fact that the muscles in the afflicted area have been contracted for prolonged periods of time. Exactly how the pain is generated is not clear, but it is probably related to reduced blood flow and reduced energy stores that are associated with prolonged contractions of the muscles. The prolonged muscle contractions are generally believed to stem from bad posture or from psychological stress (Marcus et al., 1999; Myers, Wittrock, & Foreman, 1998;Wittrock & Myers, 1998). For example, individuals who are attempting to deal with stressors may frown persistently, thereby contracting the muscles in the forehead, or they may hold their heads rigidly for long periods of time, causing prolonged contraction of the muscles at the base of the skull. More generally, there is evidence that individuals with tension headaches are likely to be tense and depressed, to suffer from anxiety disorders, and to be in the lower socioeconomic classes where there is more stress (Cathcart & Pritchard, 1998; Jorge et al., 1999; Scher et al., 1998)

Treatment of tension headaches is focused on reducing muscle tension. In some cases the reduction is achieved with muscle-relaxing drugs, but a more frequently used approach involves teaching individuals how to relax. One method, called **progressive muscle relaxation training,** teaches individuals to tense and then relax different sets of muscles. The training allows them to become familiar with the sensations and techniques that are associated with mus-

cle relaxation, and with this increased awareness they become more effective at achieving relaxation (see Chapter 5 for an example of muscle relaxation training). When training is focused on muscles in the forehead and neck, progressive muscle relaxation training can be an effective way to treat tension headaches (Holmes & Burish, 1984; Holroyd & Penzien, 1994; Larsson & Carlsson, 1996). This strategy is relatively easy to learn, and it was even shown to be effective in a school-based program in which the school nurse taught relaxation techniques to 10- to 15-year-olds.

A second treatment approach for tension headaches involves **electromyographic** (e-lek-tro-mi-o-GRAF-ik) **(EMG) biofeedback training.** With this approach electrodes are used to detect muscle activity, and the individual is given immediate feedback about whether muscles are tensing or relaxing. A tone is usually used to provide the feedback; the tone gets higher when the muscles become tense and lower when they relax. By listening to the tone and trying to lower it, the individual can learn to relax specific sets of muscles. There is substantial evidence that EMG biofeedback training is more effective than no treatment for reducing muscle tension headaches (see Holmes & Burish, 1984). Those findings are encouraging, but it is important to note that in experiments in which the effects of EMG biofeedback training were compared to the effects of progressive muscle relaxation training, both techniques were *equally effective.* In other words, EMG biofeedback training is effective for reducing tension headaches but not more effective than the cheaper and easier progressive muscle relaxation training. Thus, muscle relaxation training is probably the treatment of choice.

In summary, at present there is no strong evidence linking psychological factors to migraine headaches and no evidence that psychological approaches such as biofeedback training are helpful for treating those headaches. However, stress that leads to prolonged muscle contractions does appear to provoke muscle tension headaches, which can

---

migraine headache   A severe type of headache caused by the dilatation of the cranial arteries.

tension headaches   Headaches caused by prolonged muscle contractions, usually in the forehead and the back of the head just above the neck.

progressive muscle relaxation training   A treatment approach for tension headaches in which an individual is taught how to tense and then relax different sets of muscles, usually beginning with the neck or shoulders and working down to the legs.

electromyographic (EMG) biofeedback training   A treatment approach for tension headaches that uses biofeedback training focused on relaxing specific sets of muscles.

then be treated effectively with either progressive muscle relaxation training or EMG biofeedback training.

 Immunological Disorders

You may not be aware of it, but you are constantly exposed to infectious and toxic agents such as bacteria, viruses, fungi, and parasites that can cause physical disorders ranging from colds to cancer. If that's the case, why aren't you sick more often? The answer is that your body has an **immune system** that fights the disease-causing agents. What is important here is that psychological factors play a role in the functioning of the immune system and therefore influence your general health. In this section I will explain how the immune system works, examine the role that psychological factors play in its functioning, and consider the role that psychological factors play in two disorders that are influenced by the immune system, rheumatoid arthritis and cancer.

Immune System Functioning

Disease-causing agents that enter the body are known as **antigens** (AN-ti-junz). The function of the immune system

---

immune system   A system of the body that fights disease-causing agents. (See *leukocytes* and *lymphocytes*.)

antigens   Disease-causing agents that enter the body.

white blood cells   Blood cells that are produced by the immune system to fight antigens; also called *leukocytes*.

leukocytes   Technical name for white blood cells.

lymphocytes   A type of leukocytes that are produced in the lymph nodes and are particularly effective for controlling antigens.

killer cells   A type of lymphocytes that kill antigens.

helper cells   A type of lymphocytes that identify antigens and signal the lymph nodes to produce more killer cells.

suppressor cells   A type of lymphocytes that signal the lymph nodes to reduce production of killer cells when the killer cells are no longer needed.

immunocompetence   The degree to which the immune system is active and effective in fighting antigens.

HIV (human immunodeficiency virus)   A virus that kills lymphocytes (helper cells) so that the body cannot recognize the presence of antigens and mount a defense against them, thus leading to disease. (See *AIDS*.)

AIDS (acquired immunodeficiency syndrome)   The consequence of an HIV infection, resulting from the absence of sufficient killer cells.

---

is to destroy antigens and thereby prevent diseases. The major combatants in the war against antigens are the **white blood cells** that circulate throughout the body in the bloodstream. White blood cells are technically called **leukocytes** (LOO-kuh-sits), from the Greek for "light-colored cells." Leukocytes are produced in the lymph nodes, bone marrow, spleen, and parts of the gastrointestinal tract.

There are a number of kinds of leukocytes, but most attention has been focused on **lymphocytes** (LIM-fuh-sits), which are produced in the lymph nodes and are particularly effective for controlling antigens. Some lymphocytes are called **killer cells** because they destroy antigens, while others are called **helper cells** because they identify antigens and signal the lymph nodes when it is necessary to produce more killer cells. Still others are called **suppressor cells** because they cause a reduction in the production of killer cells by signaling the lymph nodes when killer cells are no longer needed.

The degree to which the immune system is active and effective in fighting antigens is referred to as the individual's level of **immunocompetence**. High immunocompetence is characterized by high levels of killer and helper cells and a low level of suppressor cells. (It is because the number of white blood cells increases to fight infection that an individual's white blood cell count is checked to determine whether he or she has an infection.) There are wide individual differences in immunocompetence, and the less responsive an individual's immune system is, the more the individual will suffer from infections and diseases. Let's now take a look at the factors that influence immunocompetence.

Psychological Factors and Immune System Functioning

Decreases in Immunocompetence. Immunocompetence can be influenced by both physiological and psychological factors (Maier, Watkins, & Fleshner, 1994). A physiological factor that has attracted widespread attention is **HIV** (human immunodeficiency virus), which kills lymphocytes instead of being killed by them. Specifically, HIV kills the helper cells, and therefore the system is not stimulated to produce more killer cells when the body is invaded by antigens. In the absence of sufficient killer cells, the individual develops **AIDS** (*acquired immunodeficiency syndrome*) and usually dies of an infection-related disease such as pneumonia, which his or her body cannot fight off.

Of most importance for our discussion here is the fact that *psychological stress can cause a decrease in the functioning of the immune system,* which in turn can lead to physical illnesses (Andersen et al., 1994; Borella et al., 1999; Cohen et al., 1999; De Gucht, Fischler, & Demanet, 1999; Delahanty, 1998; Herbert & Cohen, 1993; Hiramoto et al., 1999; Kiecolt-Glaser, 1999; Peters et al., 1999; Segerstrom,

FIGURE 14.8

Men who experienced high life stress were more likely to get sick than men who experienced lower life stress.

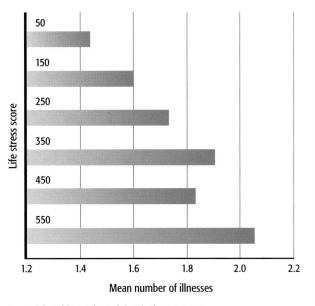

Source: Adapted from Rahe et al. (1970), Figure 1, p. 404.

Taylor, et al., 1998, 1999; Weisse, 1992). For example, in one of the early studies the investigators measured the levels of life stress (e.g., family or financial problems) in a group of seamen before they left for an extended cruise and then determined the number of illnesses the men experienced during the cruise (Rahe, Mahan, & Arthur, 1970). As indicated in Figure 14.8, the men who had experienced higher levels of life stress experienced more illnesses than those who had experienced lower levels of life stress.

In another investigation individuals in a stress condition worked on a challenging intellectual task for 30 minutes, while individuals in a control condition read magazines (Cohen et al., 1993). Measures of the levels of killer cells indicated that the levels were comparable before and during the tasks, but the individuals in the stress condition showed substantially lower levels 40 minutes later. It has also been found that stressful final examinations lead to lower immunocompetence among students, and the effect is greater among lonely students who lack social support (Kiecolt-Glaser et al., 1984). That finding explains why you are likely to become sick after final exams. The common cold has also been linked to stress (Divale, 1995; Stone et al., 1992). In one experiment stress was assessed in almost 400 individuals, who were then given nasal drops that contained a cold virus (Cohen et al., 1991). The results indicated that individuals who were under high stress were about twice as likely to develop a cold as those under low stress. Finally, it has also been demonstrated that individu-

als who are undergoing prolonged stress due to the death of a family member show lower levels of immunocompetence than do individuals who are not experiencing such stress (Bartrop et al., 1977; Denney et al., 1988; Kronfol et al., 1983; Linn, Linn, & Jensen, 1982; Schleifer et al., 1984). Overall, then, it is clear that psychological stress has the effect of reducing immunocompetence, which in turn can influence physical health.

Increases in Immunocompetence. If stress can decrease immunocompetence, can reducing stress increase immunocompetence? Yes; that effect was demonstrated in an experiment in which students participated in a series of stress reduction training sessions before taking an important examination (Kiecolt-Glaser et al., 1984). Levels of immunocompetence were assessed a month before the examination and again after the examination. The results revealed that students who had received the stress reduction training had higher levels of immunocompetence after the exams than did students who had not received the training. In another experiment it was found that elderly individuals who received relaxation training and social contact showed greater increases in immunocompetence than did elderly individuals who did not receive the training or contact (Kiecolt-Glaser et al., 1985). Overall, then, there is evidence that stress management techniques are effective for reducing the effects of stress on the immune system.

Another behavioral strategy that is effective for increasing immunocompetence is aerobic exercise. Ample evidence indicates that an acute bout of strenuous aerobic exercise increases the levels of various lymphocytes (LaPerriere et al., 1994; Mackinnon, 1994; Smith, 1995). Indeed, the results of one study suggest that aerobic exercise and fitness can serve to reduce illness (Roth & Holmes, 1985). In that study it was found that students who were under high levels of life stress but who had good aerobic fitness were less likely to get sick than students who were under high levels of life stress but did not have good aerobic fitness. In fact, the highly fit students who were under high stress showed illness levels that were comparable to those of the less fit students under low stress. In other words, aerobic fitness served to offset the effects of stress in the stress–illness relationship.

Finally, it is noteworthy that a recent study of students in law school found that those who were generally optimistic had higher levels of immunocompetence than those who were less optimistic (Segerstrom et al., 1999). Why should optimism be related to the functioning of the immune system? Optimistic people believe that they will be successful in dealing with problems, and therefore they are under less stress.

In sum, a wide variety of evidence links stress to reduced functioning of the immune system, and reduced immunocompetence leads to illness. In other words, the chain of events is

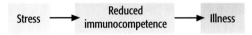

Stress → Reduced immunocompetence → Illness

Stress management and aerobic exercise programs have been shown to be effective for increasing immunocompetence, and a high level of optimism is also linked to enhanced immunocompetence. With this material as background, we can now go on to consider two of the many diseases that are related to the immune system and are influenced at least in part by psychological factors.

Rheumatoid Arthritis

Arthritis is a disease that involves *pain in the joints*. It is the second most prevalent disease in the United States, following coronary heart disease. Although arthritis is rarely fatal, it can be exceptionally painful and often results in severe crippling. You've probably seen people whose hands were so crippled by arthritis that they had great difficulty picking things up. There are three types of arthritis, but in this section I will focus on **rheumatoid arthritis** (ROOM-uh-toyd ar-THRI-tus), which occurs when the protective membrane that covers the joints is damaged. When this membrane is damaged, friction develops, which leads to pain.

Rheumatoid arthritis afflicts about 1% of the population, and females are three times more likely than males are to suffer from the disease. Most cases occur between the ages of 20 and 50, but a rare juvenile form occurs in young children. Rheumatoid arthritis usually affects the small joints in the hands, wrists, knees, and ankles.

Psychological Factors Contributing to Rheumatoid Arthritis. There is a growing body of evidence that psychological stress, arising from such things as financial problems and marital conflict, is related to the development of rheumatoid arthritis (Anderson et al., 1985; Chover-Gonzalez, 1999; Huyser & Parker, 1998; Stewart et al., 1994; Zautra et al., 1994, 1998, 1999). In one study interviews dealing with life events were conducted with a group of patients who were believed to be developing rheumatoid arthritis and

with a group of patients suffering from other general medical problems (Baker, 1982). The results indicated that 68% of the arthritic patients reported an important life stress in the year before the onset of their symptoms, whereas only 36% of the general medical patients reported such a stress.

Stress and Subtypes of Rheumatoid Arthritis. Stress is often but not always implicated in the development of rheumatoid arthritis, and it is important that we understand the inconsistency in the findings. One possible explanation for the inconsistency is that there are two forms of the disease, one stress-related and one non–stress-related (Rimon & Laakso, 1985; Stewart et al., 1994). The characteristics of the two forms are listed in Table 14.2. What is most noteworthy is the fact that in one form the symptoms are associated with stress and there is *not* a family history of the disease, whereas in the other form the symptoms are not related to stress but there *is* a family history of the disorder. In other words, rheumatoid arthritis may be related to stress *or* to genetics.

A 15-year followup of the patients who had stress-related or non–stress-related rheumatoid arthritis revealed that those in the stress-related group showed symptoms that got worse during periods of high stress and better during periods of low stress, whereas those in the non–stress-related group had symptoms that remained stable, regardless of stress levels (Rimon & Laakso, 1985). These findings refine our understanding of rheumatoid arthritis and suggest that stress plays an important role in the development of at least one form of the disease. The possible relationship between stress and rheumatoid arthritis is illustrated by the experience of the 34-year-old woman who describes her personal story in Case Study 14.4.

arthritis A disease that involves pain in the joints. (See *rheumatoid arthritis*.)

rheumatoid arthritis A type of arthritis that occurs when the protective membrane that covers the joints is damaged, allowing friction in the joints to develop, which leads to pain.

TABLE 14.2

Characteristics of stress-related and non–stress-related forms of rheumatoid arthritis

Stress-related form	Non–stress-related form
Rapid onset of symptoms	Slow, insidious onset of symptoms
Varying severity of symptoms	Fairly constant symptoms
Little or no family history of rheumatoid arthritis	High proportion of family members with rheumatoid arthritis
Onset of symptoms associated with stress	Onset of symptoms not associated with stress

Source: Adapted from Rimon and Laakso (1985).

Stress and Rheumatoid Arthritis in a Physically Active 34-Year-Old Woman: A Personal Account

"I HAVE ALWAYS BEEN HEALTHY, physically active, and interested in sports. I ride my horse a couple of times a week, play golf and tennis frequently, and play on a softball team. Because of my interest in sports, 4 years ago I took all of my savings, borrowed some money, and opened a sporting goods store. More about that later; first let me tell you about the physical problems that developed.

"One day about 3 years ago, I started having a pain and some swelling in my right wrist. It bothered me, but I didn't worry about it at first because I assumed that it stemmed from some tendinitis I had from a skiing accident a few years earlier. However, a few days later I also began to have pain in my other wrist, and my fingers began swelling. Then I noticed that my feet and ankles were swollen, and I started having trouble putting on my shoes. The problem got worse very fast, and soon I couldn't open a bottle or a car door, couldn't shift my car's gears, and couldn't bend my knees, which made fitting people for athletic shoes really tough. Things came to a head when I had to make a long drive and developed severe aches in all of my joints. My feet and knees hurt so badly that I had to stop every half hour to stretch and rest them. The next day I went to my physician, who took some blood tests and told me that I had rheumatoid arthritis. Arthritis? Me?

How could that be? Arthritis is for old people—how did I get it?

"I went to a rheumatologist for a second opinion, but she came to the same diagnosis. In talking with me, the rheumatologist asked whether anyone in my family suffered from arthritis and whether I was under stress. No, no one else in the family suffered from arthritis, but yes, I was definitely under a tremendous amount of stress. The stress was associated with my new business. The problem was that I had paid a contractor $75,000 to remodel my store in a mall, but the contractor left town without paying the subcontractors who had done the work. I was left responsible for paying the $75,000 again. The store was making money, but not enough to pay off the startup costs twice. I was trying to run the store, I was deep in debt, and I was being constantly harassed by creditors, lawyers, and vendors. I was struggling to keep my head above water, but I was slowly slipping under—and now I was rapidly developing a crippling case of rheumatoid arthritis.

"I was put on some expensive medication to reduce the inflammation in my joints, and my physical activities were restricted so that I would not hurt my inflamed joints and cause permanent damage. I also did simple exercises with a physical therapist so that my joints wouldn't freeze up.

"The medication held the symptoms in check, but I had to stay on it. And though the arthritis was under control, my business problems weren't, and finally I had to sell out and give up. It had been a terrible time; I was personally and financially devastated, but it was over and behind me. I decided to take a year off, come back to school, and try to figure out what to do next. I really enjoyed being back in school, and after a couple of months, I noticed that my joint pain was becoming less and less and I was getting more movement and flexibility. In consultation with my physician, I began slowly to reduce the amount of medication I was taking until I was completely off it. I have now been off the medication and *symptom-free* for a little over a year. I can't prove that the stress of the business failure caused the arthritis, but the arthritis came and went with the stress. I've got my fingers crossed that neither will come back—and the fact that I can cross my fingers tells you how well I'm doing!"

Given that psychological stress can lead to or exacerbate rheumatoid arthritis, the question is, can reducing stress reduce the symptoms? The experience of the woman in Case Study 14.4 would suggest that it can (her symptoms got better when she got away from the stress of her business), but there is also evidence from controlled experiments. For example, in one experiment individuals who suffered from rheumatoid arthritis were asked to write either about the most stressful experience they had ever undergone or about a neutral experience (Smith et al., 1999). (Previous research has shown that writing about stressful experiences reduces the stress; see Berry & Pennebaker, 1993.) The results were clear: Individuals who wrote about stressful experiences showed greater improvements in symptoms than did those who wrote about neutral experiences.

To sum up, there is a substantial amount of evidence that psychological stress is one of the factors that contributes to the development of rheumatoid arthritis. Most theorists assume that the effect of stress is mediated by the immune system, but we still do not understand the process. Fortunately, it also appears that reducing stress can provide symptom relief.

Cancer

Could something as serious as cancer be caused in part by psychological stress? As a start toward answering that question, let's first consider what cancer is and how it develops. In general, **cancer** involves the abnormal reproduction of cells; for example, if a cell begins reproducing itself when it should not, a tumor will develop. This can be dangerous because the tumor may invade and choke out crucial organs in the body, thus causing death. The abnormal reproduction of cells can be caused by foreign substances, such as some of the elements of tobacco smoke, and by genetic problems within the cells. However, the immune system plays an important role in the control of cancer in two ways: (1) Leukocytes can destroy the foreign substances before they cause a cancerous growth to occur, and (2) leukocytes can identify abnormal cancerous growths and destroy them, thus eliminating the tumor or at least holding it in check.

Unfortunately, if the individual is under high stress, the functioning of the immune system is reduced and that can enhance the likelihood of cancer (Eysenck, 1994; Kiecolt-Glaser & Glaser, 1995). In one study depression was assessed in more than 2,000 healthy males. When the men were followed up 17 years later, it was found that those who had had high levels of depression (which is stressful) were twice as likely to have developed cancer (Shekelle et al., 1981). Suppressing anger, which can lead to prolonged tension and stress, was linked to cancer in a study of women who were suspected of having breast cancer but who had not yet undergone tumor biopsies (Greer & Morris, 1978). Followup examinations of the women 5 years later revealed that those who suppressed anger were more likely to have cancerous tumors than those who expressed their anger. An important feature of these studies is that the stress was identified *before* the diagnoses of cancer were made, and therefore the higher levels of stress in the individuals with cancer cannot be attributed to the presence of the disease.

Because stress can play a role in the development of cancer, stress reduction may play a role in the treatment of some forms of cancer. In one dramatic test of that possibility patients who were suffering from skin cancer (*malignant melanoma*) were randomly assigned to either a treatment

or a control condition. Patients in both conditions received medical care, but the patients in the treatment condition also participated in a 6-week program in which they received education about cancer, stress management training, and emotional support. Followup examinations revealed that the patients in the treatment condition showed (1) greater reductions in depression, tension, and anger, (2) improved functioning of their immune systems, (3) reduced recurrence of the cancer, and (4) increased survival rate 6 years later (Fawzy et al., 1993; Fawzy, Cousins, et al., 1990; Fawzy, Kemeny, et al., 1990).

These findings are impressive, but two important qualifications should be noted: First, *psychological treatments should not be used as an alternative to medical treatment;* instead they should be used as an *additional* treatment. Second, although stress reduction appears to be an effective treatment for some forms of cancer, *there is no reliable evidence that treatments focused on imagining white blood cells destroying (eating) cancer cells are effective.* The imagination approach has attracted a great deal of attention in the popular press, and some dramatic case studies have been reported, but there is no controlled research demonstrating that the approach is effective.

THINKING CRITICALLY

Questions about Psychophysiological Disorders

How important are psychological factors in psychophysiological disorders? Psychological factors contribute to many physical disorders such as heart attacks, but they are rarely the sole cause. The question then is, how much do they contribute? That is often difficult to determine, but in the case of coronary artery disease it appears that the Type A behavior pattern accounts for only about 10% of the differences in the disease among individuals. This figure contrasts sharply with the many popular books and articles that suggest that Type A behavior is *the* cause of heart attacks. Does the 10% figure mean that the Type A behavior pattern is a "weak" variable? Yes and no; on the one hand, it is not a powerful variable in an absolute sense, but on the other hand its effect is not smaller than the effects of other variables. For example, smoking also accounts for only about 10% of the differences in coronary artery disease. The point here is that coronary artery disease is caused by many factors (e.g., genetics, diet, exercise, stress, smoking), which combine to result in the disease. The Type A behavior pattern is only one of these factors, but it appears to be as strong as any other. If we are going to be effective at controlling the disease, attention must be given to all of these factors.

cancer Any disease that involves the abnormal reproduction of cells.

Summary

Topic I: Eating Disorders

▶ The major symptom of anorexia nervosa is the refusal to maintain a normal body weight (weight that is 15% or more below the acceptable minimum leads to a diagnosis of anorexia). Other symptoms include an intense fear of gaining weight, distortion of body image, and amenorrhea in women.

▶ A major symptom of bulimia nervosa is eating binges. The other important symptom is inappropriate behavior such as purging that is designed to prevent weight gain. Depression and obsessive-compulsive symptoms often accompany anorexia and bulimia.

▶ Eating disorders are not new, are 10 times more likely to occur in women than in men, are not limited to middle- or upper-class individuals, and are more prevalent in late adolescence and early adulthood.

▶ Initially it was thought that these disorders stemmed from conflicts of sexuality, passive rebellion, attempts at control, or childhood sexual abuse, but there is no reliable evidence for those explanations. There is evidence that in some individuals stress can lead to excessive eating.

▶ Learning theorists suggest that eating disorders are due to receiving rewards for being slim and/or developing a classically conditioned fear of gaining weight.

▶ Cognitive theorists suggest that anorexia is due to incorrect beliefs about "weight problems," beliefs that are supported by selective attention.

▶ From a physiological perspective eating disorders are thought to stem from low levels of serotonin, which disrupt the functioning of the hypothalamus, the brain center responsible for eating behavior. The low levels of serotonin also explain the accompanying symptoms of depressions, obsessions, and compulsions. Low levels of serotonin could be due to genetic factors, prolonged stress, or problems during prenatal development and childbirth.

▶ Cognitive therapy that is focused on changing beliefs and the use of antidepressants to increase levels of serotonin can be effective for overcoming eating disorders.

▶ Other eating disorders include pica, which is persistent eating of nonnutritive substances, and rumination, which involves repeated regurgitation of food, sometimes accompanied by rechewing and swallowing of the food.

Topic II: Sleep Disorders

▶ The circadian rhythm is the daily pattern of sleep and wakefulness. It is driven by a "biological clock," and there are wide individual differences in the timing of sleep.

▶ We cycle up and down through four stages of sleep three or four times each night.

▶ Stage 1 sleep in the second and later sleep cycles involves rapid eye movements. It is during this REM sleep that dreams occur.

▶ Sleep occurs when stimulation generated in the brain stem is stopped from going to higher areas of the brain. The raphe nuclei inhibit impulses from moving up the reticular activating system.

▶ Rapid eye movements are due to stimulation that travels via the PGO (pons, geniculate, occipital) system. They occur with but are not caused by dreams. Freud suggested that dreams were the result of material breaking out of the unconscious, but it now appears that they occur when activation from the PGO system stimulates groups of neurons in which memories and thoughts are stored.

▶ There are two types of primary sleep disorders: dyssomnias, which are problems with too little, too much, poor-quality, or the timing of sleep, and parasomnias, which are abnormal behaviors that occur with sleep.

▶ There are five dyssomnias: (1) primary insomnia, (2) primary hypersomnia, (3) narcolepsy, (4) breathing-related sleep disorder, and (5) circadian rhythm sleep disorder.

▶ There are three parasomnias: (1) nightmare disorder, (2) sleep terror disorder, and (3) sleepwalking disorder.

Topic III: Psychophysiological Disorders

▶ Some physical disorders are caused in part by stress. Stressors stimulate activity in the sympathetic branch of the autonomic nervous system, thereby increasing general arousal, and prolonged physiological arousal leads to the disorders.

▶ Coronary artery disease involves the narrowing of arteries because of the buildup of fats (atherosclerosis); the narrowing then reduces the blood flow necessary to sustain life in tissues. Occlusions can result in myocardial infarctions (heart attacks).

▶ Individuals with the Type A behavior pattern, and particularly those who are hostile, are at greater risk for coronary artery disease. The Type A behavior and hostility lead to higher arousal, and arousal leads to increased production, clumping, and accumulation of cholesterol on artery walls.

▶ Essential hypertension is high blood pressure for which a physiological cause has not been found. Stress increases pressure, the baroreceptors that control pressure become adapted, and thus high pressure becomes "normal."

▶ Treatments for heart disease such as bypass surgery, angioplasty, "clot busters," diuretics, vasodilators, and beta blockers may not have long-term effects, so attention is focused on prevention through stress management, social support, facilitation of a positive attitude, aerobic exercise, and biofeedback training procedures.

▶ Migraine headaches are due to the dilatation of cranial arteries, which puts pressure on pain-sensitive nerves. The effects of stress on this process have not been reliably confirmed. Treatment usually revolves around stimulants that cause the arteries to constrict, but drugs that influence serotonin receptors are very effective for reducing the pain quickly.

▶ Tension headaches are due to prolonged muscle contractions stemming from bad posture or stress. Treatment involves muscle relaxation training or sometimes with EMG biofeedback training.

▶ The immune system is crucial for fighting diseases. White blood cells (leukocytes) known as lymphocytes play important roles in this. There are three types of lympho-cytes: killer cells destroy antigens (foreign bodies), helper cells identify antigens and signal the production of killer cells, and suppressor cells signal for the reduction of killer cells when antigens are no longer present. Stress can cause a decrease in immunocompetence, which can lead to increased rates of illness. Stress reduction (e.g., from social support) and aerobic exercise can increase immunocompetence and decrease illness.

▶ Rheumatoid arthritis occurs when the protective membrane covering the joints is damaged, resulting in painful friction. Stress contributes to some forms of rheumatoid arthritis.

▶ Cancer involves the abnormal reproduction of cells. The immune system plays a role in fighting cancer: It can destroy antigens that would otherwise stimulate abnormal cell reproduction and it can destroy tumors. Stress, which leads to lowered immunocompetence, can influence the development of cancer, and stress reduction can play a role in cancer treatment.

Questions for Making Connections

1. In this chapter you learned that physical health problems including colds, coronary artery disease, and cancer are caused in part by stress. Some of those are life-threatening disorders. What stressors in your life may be contributing to the development of these disorders? What can you do to reduce the stressors or at least offset their effects?

2. *Comorbidity* refers to the co-occurrence of two or more disorders in one individual. The comorbidity may occur because one disorder causes another disorder or because both disorders stem from a common cause. In this chapter you learned that people who suffer from eating disorders often also suffer from depression and OCD. What is the cause of the comorbidity in those cases? What would be the cause-and-effect relationship in an individual who suffered from both generalized anxiety disorder and coronary artery disease?

Key Terms and People

In reviewing and testing yourself, you should be able to discuss each of the following:

activation-synthesis explanation for dreams, p. 411
aerobic exercise, p. 424
AIDS, p. 428
amenorrhea, p. 398
angina, p. 419
angioplasty, p. 422
anorexia nervosa, p. 398
antigens, p. 428
apnea, p. 414
arthritis, p. 430
atherosclerosis, p. 418
autonomic division, p. 417

baroreceptors, p. 422
beta blockers, p. 423
biofeedback training, p. 425
brain stem, p. 410
breathing-related sleep disorder, p. 414
bulimia nervosa, p. 399
cancer, p. 432
central apnea, p. 414
central nervous system, p. 417
circadian rhythm, p. 409
circadian rhythm sleep disorder, p. 414
coronary artery disease, p. 418
coronary bypass surgery, p. 422

cycle of sleep, p. 410
diastolic blood pressure, p. 422
diuretics, p. 423
dyssomnia, p. 411
electroencephalogram (EEG), p. 410
electromyographic (EMG) biofeedback training, p. 427
essential hypertension, p. 421
half-life, p. 412
HDL, p. 424
helper cells, p. 428
HIV, p. 428
hostility, p. 420

15 Substance-Related Disorders

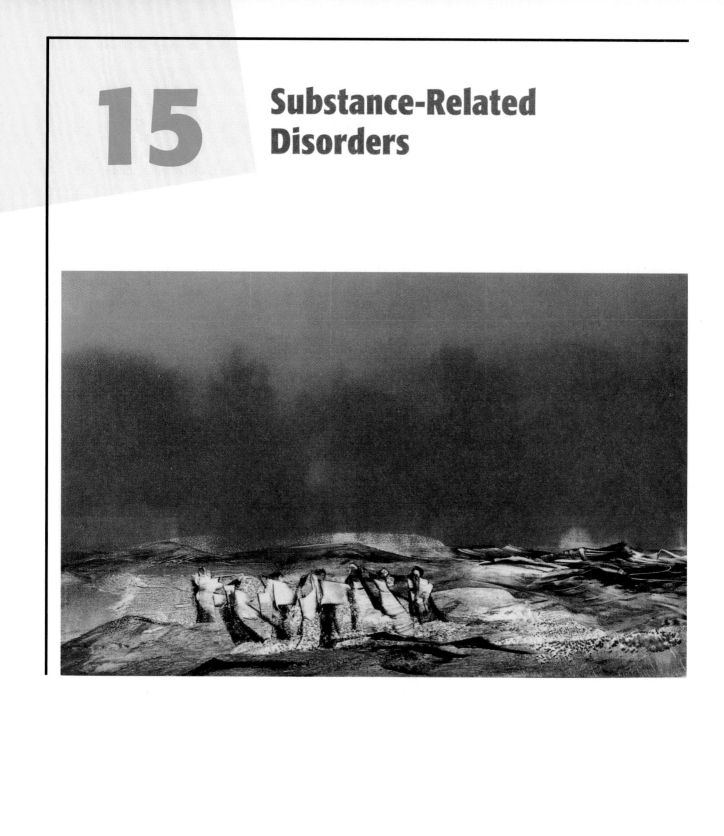

WE ARE CONSTANTLY BOMBARDED with stories documenting the fact that drug abuse is one of the most serious problems facing Western civilization today. For example, the cost of alcohol abuse alone is estimated to be over $100 billion a year, and that number does not take into account the terrible human costs such as broken families, destroyed careers, and personal misery. A good friend of mine was a successful artist and businessman until he lost his battle with drugs; he wound up frozen in an alley with rats nibbling on his toes. Alcohol is only one of the drugs that can pose problems; others are cocaine, "speed," heroin, LSD, and "designer" drugs such as *angel dust* and *ecstasy.* To these drugs we must also add nicotine and caffeine. Certainly, substance-related disorders pose a major challenge and require our thorough understanding.

The drugs I will discuss in this chapter are generally referred to as *psychoactive.* Stated simply, a **psychoactive drug** is any substance that *alters mood, awareness of the external environment, or awareness of the internal environment.* For example, after taking a psychoactive drug, an individual may feel elated, be unaware of the passage of time, and focus on fantasies rather than what is going on in the immediate environment.

Over the years the term *psychoactive* has taken on numerous negative connotations. For example, it conjures up images of a rock star sniffing coke or a disheveled heroin addict slumped in a doorway. However, the term itself does not imply good or bad, legal or illegal. Marijuana, cocaine, heroin, and LSD are all psychoactive drugs, but so are sugar, caffeine, nicotine, alcohol, and codeine. Furthermore, although psychoactive drugs are often abused and can lead to serious problems, they also have many important and valuable uses, such as the reduction of anxiety and the control of pain. In this chapter I will not take a moral stand concerning whether or not it is appropriate to use psychoactive drugs. Instead I will focus on helping you under-

psychoactive drug Any substance that alters mood, awareness of the external environment, or awareness of the internal environment.

stand the effects of the drugs and the reasons some individuals become dependent on them. Armed with that background you will be able to make your own informed judgments concerning what is and what is not appropriate.

It will be helpful if I give you an overview of how this chapter is organized before beginning our discussion of psychoactive drugs. In the first section I will describe the various types of psychoactive drugs. Next I will explain why people use and abuse these drugs, and finally I will describe drug-related disorders and their treatment.

TOPIC I
Types of Psychoactive Drugs

Len Bias was a talented college basketball player who had just signed a multimillion-dollar contract to play for the Boston Celtics. His future was bright, but one day he started shooting cocaine rather than free throws and died. Did the cocaine kill him, and if so, how?

The nicotine in cigarettes is a stimulant, so people often smoke to get a "lift." However, people also often have a cigarette to reduce tension. How can nicotine both increase arousal and decrease tension?

Cynthia used LSD occasionally with some of her friends, and the "trips" were usually pleasant and fun. However, twice she had really bad trips that were terrifying, and during one bad trip she tried to kill herself. Because of the bad trips, she has stopped using LSD, but now she is having "flashbacks" (trips that occur when she does not take the drug). She never knows when a flashback will occur, and she feels out of control. She is afraid to be alone because she does not know when she will need help. What causes flashbacks, and will they be a permanent problem for Cynthia?

A common problem in discussions of drugs is that distinctions are not made among different types of drugs. That omission leads to misunderstandings because there are important differences among drugs in terms of their effects and the dangers they pose. Therefore, to lay a foundation for our later discussions of drug problems and treatments, in this section I will describe the different types of drugs. However, let's first consider the factors that influence the effects of any one drug.

dose-dependent effect   The fact that the amount of a drug that is taken can influence the drug's effects.

tolerance   The fact that after repeated administrations of the same dosage of a drug, that dosage will have less of an effect than it did originally.

cross-tolerance   The fact that when a drug of one type is taken, tolerance can develop for other drugs of that type.

Factors That Influence the Effects of Drugs

Each drug tends to have a specific effect, but that effect can sometimes be influenced by a variety of factors, such as how much of the drug has been taken and what other drugs have been taken. Because understanding these factors is essential to understanding the effects of drugs, let's begin by considering them.

Dose-Dependent Effects

One of the first things to recognize is that *the amount of a drug that is taken can influence the effects of the drug.* This can occur in two ways: First, the amount of the drug taken can influence *how much* of an effect will occur. For example, a few beers can result in a slight slurring of speech, and a few more may cause the individual's speech to be unintelligible. Second, drug levels can influence the *type* of effects that will occur. For instance, small doses of nicotine act as a stimulant and produce physiological *arousal*, but larger doses result in physiological *sedation*. Indeed, the sedation from nicotine can be great enough to cause death. The fact that the amount taken can influence the effects of a drug is called the **dose-dependent effect.**

Tolerance and Cross-Tolerance

Tolerance refers to the fact that after repeated administrations of the same dosage of a drug, *that dosage will have less of an effect than it did originally.* Therefore, as tolerance for the drug develops, the individual must take greater amounts of the drug to achieve the same effect. In ancient Greece tolerance was used as a defensive strategy by individuals who thought that someone might attempt to poison them. Specifically, those individuals would take increasing amounts of the poison they thought an enemy might use so that they would eventually be immune to a dose given by the enemy. After developing tolerance, individuals must take increasing higher doses of the drugs to achieve the desired effects. Increasing the doses can have serious consequences, because at high doses the drugs may have dangerous side effects.

Cross-tolerance refers to the fact that when a drug of one type is taken, *tolerance can develop for other drugs of that type.* For example, alcohol and some antianxiety drugs are depressants, so individuals who have been drinking alcohol over a prolonged period of time may have to take higher than normal doses of antianxiety drugs before the medications will reduce anxiety.

Interaction Effects

The effects of a drug can be drastically altered if it is taken in combination with another drug. That is, when taken

When a drug is taken together with another drug—such as the combination of Valium and alcohol—the effects of the drugs can be drastically altered.

together, drugs often interact and produce an effect that is *greater than the sum of the two drugs taken separately*. For example, the combination of Valium (an antianxiety drug) and alcohol results in much greater levels of physiological sedation than would be the case if the effects of each drug were simply added together. Some individuals will intentionally take combinations of drugs to get stronger effects, but that can be dangerous because it is difficult to predict how potent the combination will be. For example, the singer Janis Joplin died because she took heroin after drinking heavily.

Individual Differences

The effects of many drugs are also influenced by differences within the individuals taking them. For example, the caffeine contained in about two cups of coffee can enable *extroverted* individuals to study better, but the same dose can interfere with the studying of *introverted* individuals (Revelle, Amaral, & Turriff, 1976). That result stems from the fact that extroverts are often neurologically underaroused, so the stimulating effect of the caffeine brings them up to an optimal level of arousal, whereas introverts are already at an optimal level of arousal, so the additional stimulation provided by the caffeine pushes them beyond the optimal level and causes their performance to decline.

Differences in previous experiences with drugs can also influence the effects of drugs. For instance, individuals who have not used marijuana (cannabis) before often do not report any effects of the drug even when physiological mea-

sures indicate that effects are occurring. In contrast, experienced users notice the effects right away.

The fact that genetic factors play a strong role in drug-related disorders such as alcoholism provides additional support for the role of individual differences (Franklin & Frances, 1999). In other words, individual genetic differences influence the effects that drugs have and thereby influence the likelihood that individuals will develop drug-related disorders.

Expectations

Finally, the effects of drugs are also influenced by what the individuals expect the effects to be (Aas et al., 1995; Downey & Kilbey, 1995; Evans & Dunn, 1995; Grube et al., 1995; Hittner, 1995; P. B. Johnson, 1994; Jones & McMahon, 1994; Kidorf, Sherman, & Johnson, 1995; Kushner et al., 1994; Tate et al., 1994). For example, when individuals who expected that alcohol would reduce their inhibitions drank a placebo that they thought contained alcohol, they showed reductions in inhibitions that were as great as those shown by individuals who actually drank alcohol (Cooper et al., 1992; Leigh, 1989; Wilson, 1987). In other research, individuals who thought that drinking alcohol would lead to poorer motor coordination showed poorer motor performance when they drank a placebo that they thought was alcohol (Fillmore & Vogel-Sprott, 1995). In other words, individuals can get "drunk" on nonalcoholic beer or wine.

Because of the factors discussed here, any one drug can have different effects at different times for the same individual and can have different effects for different individuals. Therefore, when attempting to explain the effects of a drug, we must understand the individual, the situation, the individual's history of drug use, and the drug itself. With this as background, let's go on to consider the effects of different types of drugs.

Types of Psychoactive Drugs

In general, psychoactive drugs can be classified into four types as a function of the effects they produce:

1. *Depressants,* which have a general *sedating* effect
2. *Opiates,* which have a *dulling* effect on sensory experiences
3. *Stimulants,* which have a general *arousing* effect
4. *Hallucinogens,* which have a *distorting* effect on sensory experiences

In the following sections I will discuss these four types of psychoactive drugs. Specifically, for each type I will provide examples of the drugs, and then for each drug I will describe its effects and the potential problems associated with its use. This information will enable you to compare

TABLE 15.1

Types of drugs, their effects, and their problems

Type	Examples	Effects	Problems
Depressants	Alcohol Barbiturates Benzodiazepines	Reduce physiological arousal and cause sedation. High levels can cause a "high."	Interfere with functioning, serious withdrawal symptoms, death due to overdose.
Opiates (narcotics)	Opium Morphine Codeine Heroin	Reduce physiological arousal and cause a dulling or numbing of senses. High levels can cause a "high."	Interfere with functioning, serious withdrawal symptoms, death due to overdose.
Stimulants	Amphetamines Cocaine Caffeine Nicotine	Increase physiological arousal and cause euphoria.	High levels of amphetamines and cocaine can interfere with functioning and cause a psychotic episode. Serious withdrawal symptoms. At high levels some cause death.
Hallucinogens	Cannabis (marijuana) LSD (lysergic acid) Psilocybin Mescaline	Distort sensory experience (process not understood). No evidence for enhanced creativity.	Dangerous behaviors because of changed reality. Possible gene damage. LSD flashbacks. No withdrawal symptoms but possible psychological dependence.

Note: Increases and decreases in arousal are due to increases and decreases in neurological transmission in the brain. At high levels most drugs increase activity in the pleasure center, thus causing a "high."

different types of drugs and will prepare you for our later discussion of the explanations and treatments for drug abuse. The drugs, their effects, and related problems are summarized in Table 15.1.

Depressants

Depressants *reduce physiological arousal and help individuals relax.* Because of their effects, they are frequently used to counteract the stress of daily living. Examples include an alcoholic drink at the end of the day, a sleeping pill, and an antianxiety drug. Although depressants usually reduce arousal, at high dosage levels they can cause a brief high, or "rush." There are three types of depressants: *alcohol, barbiturates,* and *benzodiazepines.*

Alcohol. You may be surprised that **alcohol** is a depressant because after a few drinks, many people become happier, more outgoing, and less inhibited. The uplifting effect of alcohol is due to two processes. First, alcohol activates the pleasure center of the brain, which causes the happiness (see the later discussion). Second, alcohol initially depresses *inhibitory* centers in the brain, causing the individual to become less inhibited and more expansive. However, as the level of intoxication increases, the areas of the brain

depressants   Psychoactive drugs that reduce physiological arousal and help individuals relax.

alcohol   A widely used depressant.

responsible for *arousal* are inhibited, and then sedation and sleep set in.

Alcohol also affects vision and balance and reduces muscle control. As a consequence, speech becomes slurred and coordination decreases. Concentration and judgment are also influenced, so individuals may make poor decisions. The combination of impaired vision, lessened muscle control, and impaired cognitive functioning can lead to disastrous consequences, especially in the case of driving.

The alcohol we drink (technically called *ethyl alcohol,* or *ethanol*) is produced by a process called *fermentation.* Fermentation occurs when sugar is dissolved in water, and then microorganisms called *yeasts* convert the sugar into alcohol and carbon dioxide. The carbon dioxide bubbles off, leaving the alcohol and water. Fermentation of sugar from different sources leads to different types of beverages; for example, fermentation of grapes leads to wine, and fermentation of grains leads to beer. Alcohol makes up between 3% and 12% of the volume of these beverages.

Because the yeasts that convert sugar into alcohol die in solutions that contain more than 10–15% alcohol, the fermentation process stops when the alcohol content is still relatively low. To produce beverages with alcohol content higher than 15%, the process of *distillation* is used. Distillation involves heating the liquid containing alcohol until the alcohol vaporizes, leaving the water behind. The vapor is then cooled and condensed to yield a liquid with a higher alcohol content. Distilling the alcohol from different sources leads to different drinks; for example, grapes produce brandy, grains yield whiskey, molasses produces rum, and potatoes make schnapps. (Gin and vodka are mixtures of alcohol, water, and flavoring.) Alcohol makes up between 40% and 50% of the volume of these drinks, so they are very potent.

Alcohol is usually drunk and then absorbed into the bloodstream from the digestive tract. Drinking alcohol just before or during a meal reduces the rate of absorption because most of the absorption occurs in the small intestine, and the alcohol will be diluted and delayed in getting there if it is mixed with food that is being digested in the stomach. Once alcohol is absorbed, it is widely distributed to tissues throughout the body and brain. Some alcohol goes to the lungs, where it is vaporized into the air. The Breathalyzer test that is used by police to determine the degree to which an individual is intoxicated simply measures the amount of alcohol in expired air, thus providing a measure of the amount of alcohol in the system.

Alcohol can also be consumed by inhalation. When inhaled, alcohol vapors are absorbed by the lungs, dissolved in the blood, and then distributed throughout the body. This process is much faster than absorption in the intestines and can cause a quick kick. The traditional brandy snifter is designed to facilitate the inhalation of alcohol vapors. The large base of the glass can be cupped in the hand so that heat from the hand aids vaporization; the small opening at the top of the glass concentrates the vapors so that they can be effectively inhaled. Brandy produces a substantial amount of vapor because it has a very high alcohol content.

Tolerance for alcohol develops rapidly, so within a few weeks dose levels must be increased by 30–50% to achieve the desired effect. Tolerance develops because drinking alcohol stimulates the body's production of substances that destroy alcohol; so, the more alcohol consumed, the more destroyed.

After a period of chronic consumption, cessation of alcohol intake leads to withdrawal symptoms that can be severe and may even lead to death. The first withdrawal symptoms include agitation and involuntary contraction of the muscles (the "shakes"). Next, the individual experiences muscle cramps, nausea, vomiting, and profuse sweating. In extreme cases withdrawal involves delirium (hallucinations) and seizures. This condition is referred to as **delirium tremens,** often abbreviated as **d.t.'s.** Withdrawal symptoms can be reduced quickly by giving the individual small amounts of other short-acting depressants such as Valium.

Barbiturates and Benzodiazepines. **Barbiturates** (bar-BICH-u-riz) were the first type of tranquilizers and they are very effective for reducing arousal. At low levels they result in relaxation, light-headedness, and a loss of motor coordination. Higher doses bring on slurred speech, increased reductions in motor control, mild euphoria, and then sleep. At very high doses they cause a brief high, or rush, which is followed by relaxation or sleep. **Benzodiazepines** (ben-zo-di-AZ-uh-pinz) are a more recent generation of tranquiliz-

ers. Well-known drugs of this type include Ativan, Librium, Valium, and Xanax (see Chapter 5).

Barbiturates and benzodiazepines are misused by two different groups of individuals. One group consists of individuals who use the drugs to reduce daily tensions and aid in sleep but then begin to use them too frequently or in excessively high doses, and thus unwittingly slip across the fine line that separates appropriate use from abuse. The other group of misusers consists of "street" drug users, who use these drugs to produce a rush, to achieve a state of relaxed euphoria, or to aid in "coming down" from a high caused by taking a stimulant.

Barbiturates are quickly absorbed into the bloodstream from the digestive system and then pass rapidly into the brain. However, after a very short period they are redistributed to fatty areas of the body and then slowly released from there. Because of this pattern of rapid absorption, storage, and then slow release, barbiturates have a quick effect (a high), but then the effects drop off and persist at a low level for some time. At low levels barbiturates reduce arousal by reducing neural transmission.

A serious problem associated with barbiturate use is death due to accidental overdose. Death occurs because barbiturates reduce respiration, and high doses may cause an individual to stop breathing completely. As is the case with alcohol, prolonged use of barbiturates results in serious withdrawal symptoms that can be dangerous and even lethal. When this happens, it may be necessary to give the individual a less potent depressant, such as phenobarbital or even alcohol, for which the dosage level can be controlled and slowly reduced.

In summary, depressants such as alcohol, barbiturates, and benzodiazepines reduce physiological arousal and thereby reduce tension. However, at high levels they can cause a brief high. The use of depressants can lead to serious withdrawal symptoms, which in some cases can lead to death.

Opiates (Narcotics)

Opiates (O-pe-its) are drugs that are derived from opium, and they include *opium, morphine, codeine,* and *heroin.* Opiates have the effect of *dulling or numbing the senses,* and they can produce a sleeplike state. However, when high

---

delirium tremens (d.t.'s)   Severe withdrawal symptoms suffered if alcohol intake stops after a period of chronic consumption; include hallucinations and seizures.

barbiturates   A type of depressant (tranquilizers) that is very effective for reducing arousal.

benzodiazepines   A type of depressant (tranquilizers).

opiates   Psychoactive drugs derived from opium that have the effect of dulling or numbing the senses; sometimes called *narcotics.*

doses are rapidly delivered to the brain, opiates can cause a sudden high or rush. There are also a number of synthetic (artificially produced) opiates, including Demerol (meperidine) and Darvon (propoxyphine), which are used to control pain. It should be noted that opiates are also referred to as **narcotics.** However, because the term *narcotic* is often used to refer to any illegal drug, in this discussion I will use the term *opiates.*

Opium. **Opium** (O-pe-um) is the sap of a poppy plant (the name *opium* comes from a Greek word that means "sap"). The sap of the opium poppy can be chewed, and it will produce a prolonged state of mellow relaxation, a strategy often used in Southeast Asian countries where the poppies are grown. Opium can also be inhaled by smoking it, which is an effective way to get greater quantities to the brain faster. One of the most notorious early uses of opium occurred in Chinese opium dens, where it was smoked in pipes and smokers would languish for days in a stuporous state. Ironically, the Chinese developed the technique of smoking opium in 1644, when the emperor forbade the smoking of tobacco. Opium was also used in Britain during the 19th century, when it was incorporated into pills, candies, and wines. One notable use was in Mrs. Winslow's Soothing Syrup, which was used to "dope" the children of working mothers while the mothers were away. Because of opium's widespread use, many individuals became addicted to it, including such literary notables as Lord Byron, Percy Shelley, John Keats, Sir Walter Scott, Elizabeth Barrett Browning, and Samuel Coleridge. In an attempt to break his addiction, Coleridge once hired a man to follow him and physically block his entry to any store in which he might buy opium. The use of opium reached epidemic proportions in Britain, and its nonprescription use was finally banned in 1868 under the Pharmacy Act. Opium was also used widely in the United States until 1914, when its nonmedical use was outlawed.

Smoking opium results in a stupor that can be maintained for hours. The Chinese developed the technique of smoking opium in 1644, when the emperor forbade smoking tobacco.

Morphine and Codeine. **Morphine** (MOR-fen) is one of the active ingredients in opium, and it is extracted from opium and used as a drug itself. It is dissolved in liquid and then injected into the bloodstream. After producing a brief high, it results in a mellow state of relaxation. (The name *morphine* comes from Morpheus, the Greek god of sleep.) The most widespread use of morphine is as an analgesic (painkiller) in hospitals. **Codeine** (CO-den) is another, less powerful ingredient of opium that is isolated and used by itself. It is widely used as an analgesic and is found in various prescription painkillers and cough medicines.

Heroin. **Heroin** (HAR-uh-win) is also derived from opium, but it is a semisynthetic drug that is produced by adding chemical structures to the morphine molecule. The chemical structures enable heroin to get to the brain faster; once in the brain it is changed back into morphine. The faster delivery makes heroin about three times more potent than morphine and ten times more potent than opium. Heroin was invented in 1898 by the chemist who had earlier invented aspirin, and it was initially advertised by the Bayer company as a superior type of aspirin.

Heroin is usually used in powdered form. It is mixed with tobacco and smoked, inhaled directly into the nostrils (an act known as "snorting"), dissolved and injected under the skin ("skin popping"), or dissolved and injected directly into the veins ("mainlining"). Heroin can cause a rush that users say is similar to orgasm. The rush lasts about 60 seconds and is followed by a 4- to 6-hour stuporous period of pleasant relaxation, reverie, and mild euphoria. However,

narcotics A term sometimes used for opiates.

opium An opiate in the sap of a poppy plant.

morphine An opiate that is one of the active ingredients in opium and is extracted from opium; used in hospitals as a painkiller.

codeine An opiate that is one of the active ingredients in opium but less powerful than morphine; used in prescription painkillers and cough medicines.

heroin A semisynthetic opiate that is produced by adding chemical structures to the morphine molecule, which speeds its delivery to the brain.

stimulants Psychoactive drugs that increase arousal and cause states of euphoria.

amphetamines A powerful type of stimulant.

after the period of relaxation very unpleasant symptoms of withdrawal begin setting in. With increased use tolerance for the drug develops, and larger and larger quantities are needed to achieve the effects. In those cases heroin "habits" become very expensive.

Opiates achieve their dulling or numbing effects by reducing neural transmission. The inhibition of neural transmission is also responsible for the pain-reducing effects of these drugs. Specifically, opiates stop pain-related nerve impulses from entering the spinal cord and going to the brain. Similarly, opiates are effective cough suppressants because they reduce activity in the cough center of the brain. (Codeine has been used in cough medicines for many years but is now often replaced with *dextromethorphan,* which is less addicting.) Opiates can also be used to treat diarrhea because they reduce the activity of the intestines, thus slowing the movement of digested materials. (A side effect of pain medications that contain opiates is constipation.)

The prolonged use of opiates leads to serious withdrawal symptoms that begin about 8 hours after the drug was last used. The individual has chills, hot flashes, and difficulty breathing. Some individuals then fall into a deep sleep, but others have prolonged insomnia. Next, the individual experiences a loss of motor control, resulting in twitching, shaking, and kicking, which may be accompanied by painful muscle cramps, diarrhea, vomiting, and extreme sweating. During withdrawal it is as though all of the systems that had been suppressed by the opiate are turned on full blast and going wild; tranquility has turned to terror, and heaven has turned to hell. The process of withdrawal usually takes about 3 days, but it can be stopped immediately by another dose of the drug. Therefore, when the early symptoms of withdrawal begin, users will do almost anything to get more opiates.

High doses of opiates can lead to death because they reduce activity in an area of the brain that is responsible for respiration; the individual simply stops breathing. In that regard it is noteworthy that many terminally ill individuals who are given high doses of morphine for pain do not die because of their illnesses; they die because the morphine causes them to stop breathing. Heroin overdose deaths "on the street" usually occur because individuals take too much heroin or use it in combination with other drugs such as alcohol that also reduce respiration. Finally, it should be noted that sharing syringes when injecting heroin leads to a substantial increase in the risk of contracting AIDS.

In summary, opiates such as opium, morphine, and heroin are derived from the poppy plant. At low levels they dull the senses and lead to a sleeplike state, but at high levels they can cause a rush. Their use can lead to serious withdrawal symptoms, and at high dosage levels they can cause death by stopping respiration.

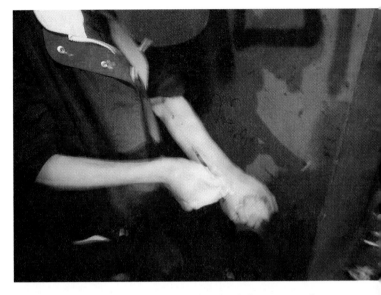

Heroin is a semisynthetic drug created by adding chemical structures to the morphine molecule. The resulting chemical structure enables heroin to get quickly to the brain, where it is changed back into morphine.

Stimulants

Stimulants *increase arousal and cause states of euphoria* that are generally referred to as highs. These effects result from increased activity in the area of the brain that is responsible for pleasure (see the later discussion). The two most powerful stimulants that are abused are *amphetamines* and *cocaine,* but attention must also be given to *caffeine* and *nicotine.*

Amphetamines.

When **amphetamines** (am-FET-uh-menz) are taken orally, they result in feelings of well-being, high spirits, high energy, vigor, elation, and reduced fatigue. Because amphetamines are absorbed slowly from the digestive system, when they are taken orally, the effects come on slowly but last between 3 and 6 hours. In contrast, when amphetamines are inhaled or injected into the bloodstream, they are delivered to the brain faster and in greater quantity and so produce a sudden high, or rush. Regardless of whether amphetamines are swallowed or injected, the high is followed by a "low" or depression.

When used appropriately, amphetamines have a number of beneficial effects such as reducing fatigue, dilating air passages in the lungs to relieve asthma attacks, and treating attention-deficit/hyperactivity disorder (see Chapter 13). During World War II amphetamines were given to GIs so that they could fight longer and harder. However, many people also use amphetamines to "get high."

Amphetamines increase arousal by stimulating the release of neurotransmitters, which in turn increases brain activity. For example, increased activity in the pleasure center results in a high and feelings of euphoria. However, when the stimulants wear off, the release of neurotransmitters falls below normal and so there is less activity in the brain. As a result, mood changes from euphoria to depression.

Apart from the problems of withdrawal, the use of amphetamines has three serious consequences: First, high doses cause dramatic increases in blood pressure that can result in strokes (breaking of blood vessels in the brain), which can lead to impaired intellectual functioning or death (see Chapter 17). Second, high doses of amphetamines can result in **amphetamine psychoses,** which involve delusions like those seen in paranoid schizophrenia. The psychotic behavior stems from the fact that amphetamines stimulate the production of the neurotransmitter dopamine, and high levels of dopamine are related to schizophrenia (see Chapter 11). Although amphetamine psychoses can be serious, they dissipate as the drug wears off and therefore do not usually have long-term consequences. The third serious effect of high levels of amphetamines is that they cause some individuals to become very aggressive or do foolish things that endanger their own lives or the lives of others. Some of these erratic and dangerous behaviors may be due to the amphetamine high or the delusions associated with amphetamine psychoses.

Cocaine.
Cocaine is the other major stimulant that is often abused. The effects of cocaine on mood are similar to those of amphetamines, but the rush is much more intense. Cocaine comes from the leaves of the coca plant of South America. When it was first shipped to Europe around the beginning of the 20th century, the young Sigmund Freud found its pleasure-producing effects to be helpful in dealing with his depression. In fact, Freud enjoyed cocaine so much that he gave some to his friends and his fiancée and encouraged them to use it. (Indeed, Freud may have been one of the first "pushers.")

Probably the most widespread use of cocaine occurred between 1886 and 1906 when coca leaves were used in the recipe for Coca-Cola. Coca leaves are still used in Coca-Cola, but the cocaine has been removed; the stimulant effect of Coca-Cola now comes from caffeine. In its original formula with the cocaine base Coca-Cola was thought to have health benefits and was therefore sold in drugstores, which is probably why soda fountains originally developed in drugstores.

---

amphetamine psychoses Brief periods of psychosis caused by high doses of amphetamines and characterized by delusions like those seen in paranoid schizophrenia.

cocaine A powerful type of stimulant.

caffeine A relatively weak stimulant that is one of the methylxanthines and is found in coffee and tea.

Cocaine can be processed and used in a number of ways. The simplest way to use it is to chew the coca leaves, as the Indians of South America still do. Like amphetamines, cocaine is absorbed slowly from the digestive system; therefore, taking it orally results in a prolonged mild euphoria.

Most of the cocaine used in the United States is in the form of a powdered white salt called *cocaine hydrochloride,* which has been diluted ("cut") with various substances. By inhaling ("sniffing" or "snorting") cocaine or dissolving it and injecting it into the bloodstream, an individual can deliver high doses to the brain quickly, producing a rush. The strength of the rush is determined by the degree to which the cocaine has been diluted with other substances, and consequently a number of processes have been developed to purify the drug so as to enhance the rush. One common procedure is to heat cocaine until it forms a vapor that is free of the impurities with which it was diluted, and then inhale the vapor. An even more refined and powerful form of cocaine can be obtained by chemically separating the cocaine molecule from the hydrochloride. Freed from its hydrochloride base, the cocaine can be burned, and the pure vapors inhaled. This practice is known as "freebasing." "Crack" is a highly concentrated form of cocaine.

The cocaine rush results from the fact that cocaine increases the level of dopamine in the pleasure center of the brain. Unfortunately, in some individuals the increase in dopamine also results in a period of schizophrenia that often involves paranoid delusions (recall from Chapter 11 that high levels of dopamine lead to schizophrenia; see also Gawin, 1991; Satel & Edell, 1991; Satel et al., 1991). In individuals who already suffer from schizophrenia, this episode may last for months; in others, it will dissipate as the drug wears off.

Cocaine also blocks the conduction of nerve impulses along axons, thereby reducing neurological activity. Because of this blocking effect, injections of cocaine can be used as a local anesthetic; that is, cocaine blocks the pain impulse. In fact, Novocain, which is often used as an anesthetic in dental procedures, is a synthetic form of cocaine that lacks the stimulant properties. (With regard to cocaine's anesthetic properties, it is interesting to note that inhalation of the drug is sometimes called "a freeze" because the cocaine anesthetizes the nose.) Unfortunately, the nerve-impulse-blocking action of cocaine can also have a lethal effect when it blocks the impulses that stimulate the beating of the heart. Indeed, it is suspected that many emergency room cases of heart failure for "unknown reasons" may actually be due to cocaine.

An unfortunate combination of the psychological and medical effects of cocaine occurred in a case in which police were summoned to a house where they found an irrational man who was brandishing a knife and threatening to kill the people around him. The police attempted to subdue him, but while they were doing so, he suddenly fell dead. An autopsy revealed high levels of cocaine in the man's system. Apparently the strange behavior that caused the police to be called was cocaine psychosis, and his sudden death was the result of cardiac arrest due to the cocaine.

Cocaine use is not generally thought to be "addictive," but this notion is controversial. However, there is no doubt that because of the extreme pleasure it can produce and because it can relieve the depression associated with withdrawal from its use, many individuals develop strong needs for cocaine and will do almost anything to get it. Indeed, it is estimated that as much as half of the violent crime in the United States may be cocaine-related.

Caffeine. **Caffeine** is the most prominent and strongest stimulant in a group of drugs called *methylxanthines* (meth-ul-ZAN-thenz). Caffeine occurs naturally in coffee and tea, and it is also added to many cola drinks and over-the-counter drugs. The levels of methylxanthines found in various preparations are listed in Table 15.2.

The discovery of caffeine in coffee is often attributed to a herd of goats that belonged to an Islamic monastery (Jacob, 1935). As the story goes, one day the goats wandered off and ate some berries from a *Coffea arabica* bush, and for the next 5 days they frolicked continuously without showing any signs of fatigue. Having observed this, the abbot of the monastery sampled the berries late one evening, the result being that he was still wide awake and invigorated when it came time for midnight prayers. As the saying goes, "The rest is history."

TABLE 15.2

Levels of methylxanthines in frequently used products

Product	Caffeine (mg)	Other Methylxanthines (mg)
One cup of coffee		
Decaffeinated	1–2	
Instant	29–117	
Perked	39–168	
Drip	56–176	
One cup of tea	30–75	
One cup of cocoa		75–150 total
Coca-Cola (12 oz.)	45	
Pepsi-cola (12 oz.)	30	
Chocolate bar		150–300 total
Analgesics (1 tablet)		
Anacin	22.7	
Dristan	16.2	
Excedrin	65.0	
Stimulants (1 tablet)		
No-Doz	100	
Vivarin	200	

Coffeehouses got their start in England at about the same time that opium dens were popular in China. In contrast to opium dens, in which customers were "doped" and lay semiconscious, in coffeehouses patrons were stimulated and participated in animated discussions late into the night. These discussions frequently revolved around politics, and because of concerns that coffeehouses were hotbeds of sedition and revolution, an attempt was made to outlaw them in 1675. The attempt failed, and the tradition of the coffeehouse continues to this day. Indeed, there has recently been a great resurgence of interest in coffee drinking and coffeehouses.

The arousing effect of caffeine is usually used for maintaining wakefulness. For example, two or three cups of coffee (about 300 milligrams of caffeine) more than doubles the amount of time an individual can stay awake and cuts sleeping time by about a quarter (Brenesova, Oswald, & Loudon, 1975). Caffeine also improves performance on simple tasks such as driving, but it has little or no effect on complex intellectual tasks such as solving mathematical problems or on tasks requiring fine motor coordination (Bovim et al., 1995; Muehlbach & Walsh, 1995). Furthermore, caffeine does not improve the performance of rested individuals. Instead it serves only to offset the effects of fatigue (Lorist et al., 1994).

Caffeine in coffee and tea is absorbed from the digestive system and reaches peak blood levels in 30–60 minutes.

The consumption of caffeine is woven into the social fabric of our society. Coffeehouses and coffee bars provide places to socialize as well as drink coffee.

Caffeine then remains active in the body for about $3\frac{1}{2}$ hours. It is interesting to note that smoking cigarettes speeds the elimination of caffeine from the body, and therefore the frequent pattern of smoking and drinking coffee actually reduces the effect of the coffee.

Ingestion of large amounts of caffeine (500–800 milligrams per day, the equivalent of 8 to 10 cups of coffee) results in agitation, tension, irritability, insomnia, loss of appetite, increased heart rate, and headaches. In short, it results in the symptoms of an anxiety disorder. At extremely high levels (1,800 milligrams per day, the equivalent of more than 20 cups of coffee), it can result in toxic psychosis, with symptoms revolving around mania that can lead to violence. High levels of caffeine can also exacerbate existing psychological problems because caffeine increases arousal and blocks the effects of antianxiety and antipsychotic drugs (benzodiazepines and neuroleptics) (Greden et al., 1978; Kulhanek, Linde, & Meisenberg, 1979; Paul et al., 1980).

Withdrawal symptoms occur even in individuals who drink as few as five cups of coffee a day. The symptoms usually include tension, agitation, and muscle tremors. As with other drugs, the symptoms of caffeine withdrawal can be terminated with a dose of caffeine. A mild form of withdrawal can be seen in individuals who are grouchy in the morning until they have their first cup of coffee. The withdrawal symptoms (e.g., tension, headache, agitation) these individuals are experiencing set in because they did not get any caffeine while sleeping during the night.

Nicotine. **Nicotine** is derived from tobacco, and most people get nicotine from smoking. People use nicotine for two reasons: (1) when they are sluggish and want to increase arousal, such as after a meal or sex, and (2) when they are tense and want to decrease arousal, such as during periods of stress. In other words, although nicotine is classed as a stimulant, it can act as *both a stimulant and a depressant.* I will explain nicotine's sometimes contradictory effects after reviewing its background.

Nicotine is naturally produced by the tobacco plant, which was originally cultivated and used by the native peoples of North America. In 1492, when Columbus arrived in what is now the Bahamas, the natives presented him with some "dry leaves" and showed him and his crew how to smoke them. At first the explorers did not understand the smoking behavior (they called it "drinking smoke") and found it repulsive. Furthermore, when one of the crew realized that smoking could be pleasurable and took up the habit, he was tried and imprisoned for his "devilish habit."

nicotine A stimulant derived from tobacco that can also act as a depressant.

This conflict between smokers and nonsmokers still goes on today, and although smokers are not imprisoned, numerous laws have been passed that limit where and when they may smoke.

Most people get nicotine from smoking cigarettes or cigars that consist of the dried (cured) leaves of the tobacco plant. When the tobacco is burned, nicotine vapors are absorbed by the lungs; the nicotine is then passed into the bloodstream, where it is carried first to the heart and then to the brain. Because this is a very direct route, absorbing nicotine from the lungs results in a relatively strong and fast effect. However, increasing numbers of people also get nicotine from chewing tobacco. Tobacco designed for chewing consists of the leaves of the tobacco plant that have been soaked in a solution of sugar and licorice and then dried. When the tobacco is chewed, nicotine is absorbed through the membranes of the mouth and passed to the bloodstream; the tobacco is spit out. Absorption from the mouth results in less effect than absorption from the lungs.

Once absorbed, nicotine influences both the central and the peripheral nervous systems. In the central nervous system nicotine stimulates numerous nerve centers and causes higher levels of neurological arousal. For example, nicotine stimulates the area of the brain that is responsible for respiration and thereby increases breathing rate. It also stimulates the area of the brain stem that is responsible for vomiting, which is why new smokers who have not yet developed a tolerance for nicotine get sick to their stomachs when they first try smoking. This is also why nonsmokers become nauseated when they are around smokers and must inhale tobacco smoke. With regard to the peripheral nervous system, nicotine stimulates the release of adrenaline into the bloodstream, which increases arousal. Specifically, nicotine results in muscle tremors, increases in heart rate, increases in blood pressure, and constriction of the blood vessels in the skin. The limitation of blood flow to the skin is responsible for the cold hands of smokers (skin temperature is determined by the amount of blood in the area) and for the fact that the skin of smokers wrinkles and ages faster than that of nonsmokers.

However, at high levels the effects of nicotine are *reversed,* and it blocks the stimulation of various nerves, thus serving as a depressant. The blocking of nerve transmission can be very serious because some of the nerves that are blocked are responsible for respiration. When those nerves are blocked, the individual can die of respiratory arrest. Unfortunately, each year a number of children die because they eat tobacco and get too much nicotine into their systems.

Probably the most notable problems associated with nicotine revolve around withdrawal, the symptoms of which include tension, irritability, inability to concentrate, dizziness, drowsiness, nausea, constipation, muscle tremors, headaches, insomnia, and an increase in appetite that

One of the reasons that people use nicotine is to reduce their anxiety level during stressful periods.

results in weight gain. The withdrawal symptoms usually last less than 6 months but can persist for years.

The physical symptoms of nicotine withdrawal are certainly not as severe as those of heroin withdrawal, but individuals who have used both report that it is psychologically as difficult to give up smoking as it is to give up heroin (McKim, 1986). In fact, there is a growing body of evidence that nicotine withdrawal can lead to a wide variety of psychiatric symptoms such as depression and anxiety disorders (Breslau, Kilbey, & Andreski, 1992, 1993; Leibenluft et al., 1993). These symptoms occur in many individuals but are seen most often in those with a history of depression or anxiety. One individual I know began having hallucinations when she stopped smoking, but she could quickly stop the hallucinations by having a cigarette. Because a cigarette will reduce the unpleasant withdrawal symptoms immediately and because cigarettes are readily available, it is often very difficult to give up smoking (Boyle et al., 1995; Fowler et al., 1996; Stolerman & Jarvis, 1995).

Before concluding our discussion of nicotine, I want to return to the paradox mentioned earlier concerning the fact that although nicotine is a stimulant, it can also serve as a depressant. Understanding this paradox can help you understand why and in what situations individuals use nicotine. There are three reasons why nicotine can act as a depressant. The first involves the *amount of nicotine* that is taken. As noted earlier, at low levels nicotine stimulates nerve activity, but at high levels it blocks that activity. However, dosage level cannot account for all of the contradictory effects, because the same dose (e.g., one cigarette) will serve to arouse at one time and relax at another time.

The second explanation revolves around the *reduction of withdrawal symptoms.* The symptoms of nicotine withdrawal involve unpleasant increases in tension, but those symptoms can be quickly reduced by another dose of nicotine. Therefore, for a smoker who is aroused by withdrawal symptoms, nicotine may result in arousal reduction.

The third explanation is strictly psychological. If an individual is tense, smoking a cigarette may be calming because it gives the individual something to do; that is, it serves as a temporary *distraction,* which reduces arousal.

Finally, a brief comment should be made concerning a drug commonly known as *ecstasy* (technically MDMA, which is short for *3,4-methylenedioxymethamphetamine*). This drug is now being used by a wide variety of individuals, often as a stimulant at all-night dance parties (Mammersley et al., 1999; Pedersen & Skrondal, 1999; van de Wijngaart et al., 1999). Although most users believe ecstasy is safe and has no long-term effects, recent evidence indicates that its use is linked to depression, paranoia, and memory loss. Furthermore, ecstasy can destroy ("burn out") neurons for which serotonin is the neurotransmitter, particularly those in the amygdala and the hippocampus (Obrocki et al., 1999; O'Shea et al., 1998). Clearly, contrary to the "word on the street," ecstasy can lead to serious problems.

In summary, stimulants include amphetamines, cocaine, caffeine, and nicotine, and they increase arousal, sometimes leading to states of euphoria. At high doses nicotine can also serve as a depressant. The use of stimulants can lead to serious symptoms of withdrawal and in some cases to periods of psychosis.

The effects of marijuana seem to be influenced to some degree by the mood of the other individuals with whom the drug is taken.

Hallucinogens

The effect of **hallucinogens** (huh-LOO-sin-uh-jinz) is to *distort sensory experiences*. In other words, while under the influence of hallucinogens, the things people see or hear are altered reality or not real at all. These distortions are called *hallucinations* (perceptual experiences that do not have a basis in reality), hence the term *hallucinogen*. It is important to note that a high dose of almost any drug can cause hallucinations; therefore, the term *hallucinogen* should be reserved for drugs that produce hallucinations even at low levels. The commonly used hallucinogens that we will discuss in this section are cannabis (marijuana), LSD, psilocybin, and mescaline.

Cannabis. **Cannabis** (KAN-uh-bis) comes from the hemp plant, *Cannabis sativa,* and is the active ingredient in **marijuana** (ma-ri-HWA-nuh), which is simply the dried leaves of the cannabis plant. Cannabis is usually inhaled by smoking the leaves in the form of a cigarette (a "joint," or "reefer"), but it can also be taken orally by grinding the leaves and baking them in cookies and candy ("Alice B. Toklas brownies"). More refined forms of cannabis are *hashish* (ha-SHESH), which is the dried resin from the top of the female hemp plant that is mixed with tobacco and smoked or baked in cookies and eaten, and *hash oil,* which is obtained by extracting the active ingredients from hashish and used by putting a drop on a normal cigarette

and then smoking it or by putting a drop on hot metal and inhaling the vapors.

Cannabis can affect mood, sensory experiences, and cognitive functioning, but its effects vary greatly from individual to individual and from one time to another. Probably the most common effect is mood swings that range from a placid dreaminess or a floating sensation called "getting off" to euphoric gaiety referred to as "a high." The high brought on by cannabis is very different from the high achieved with stimulants such as amphetamines or cocaine. Rather than a rush of excitement and arousal, the cannabis high involves mild euphoria and feelings of gaiety. During the high everything may seem funny or even hilarious. Cannabis usually results in a positive mood shift, but sometimes results in depression or negative experiences. The negative mood shifts are relatively rare and mild, and they should not be confused with the "bad trips" that will be discussed later in connection with LSD and other hallucinogens.

Cannabis also affects sensory perceptions; experiences seem richer, fuller, brighter, and more intense. Users describe the cannabis experience as similar to going from black-and-white to color TV, from mono to stereo sound, and from bland to spicy food. The sense of time is also distorted; time seems stretched out, so that a 5-minute period seems to last at least twice as long.

Finally, cannabis has a number of cognitive effects. The simplest things may seem very important, interesting, and profound. While under the influence of cannabis, individuals have what they think are great insights, and they believe themselves to be more creative. However, research has consistently shown that individuals who are using cannabis are not more insightful or creative; in fact, they are probably less so (Braden, Stillman, & Wyatt, 1974; Grinspoon, 1977). Other cognitive effects of cannabis include an increase in distractibility and a decline in short-term memory such that sometimes individuals start sentences

hallucinogens   Psychoactive drugs that distort sensory experiences.

cannabis   A hallucinogen that is the active ingredient in marijuana.

marijuana   The dried leaves of the cannabis plant.

but cannot finish them because they forget what they started to say.

The active ingredients in cannabis are substances called *cannabinoids* (KAN-uh-bin-oydz). When cannabis is inhaled, the cannabinoids are quickly absorbed through the lungs, and the effects are noticed within a few minutes, with the peak effect occurring in 30–60 minutes. The effects of smoking cannabis can be enhanced by taking a deep draw on the cannabis cigarette and then holding the smoke in the lungs for 15–20 seconds before exhaling, thus allowing more time for absorption. Absorption of cannabinoids from the digestive system is much slower, so the effects from eating cannabis do not peak for 3 hours, but once started, may last 5 hours or longer.

The chemical basis for the effects of cannabis is very complex and not well understood, in part because cannabis contains more than 80 different cannabinoids that may contribute to the effects in different ways. Furthermore, burning cannabis (as is done when it is smoked) changes some of the cannabinoids and creates other ones, and when cannabis is eaten (as in brownies), new cannabinoids are formed during digestion and metabolism.

While under the influence of cannabis, an individual's physical coordination and perceptual abilities are diminished, which can cause problems with driving (Kurzthaler et al., 1999). In this regard, cannabis is like alcohol. However, the problem is that many people do not realize cannabis has these effects so they drive or work while under its influence, which can be very dangerous.

LSD, Psilocybin, and Mescaline.
The remaining group of hallucinogens contains a wide variety of drugs, but probably the best known and most widely used are **LSD** (lysergic acid), which is a synthetic hallucinogen; **psilocybin** (su-luh-SI-bin), which is found in *Psilocybe mexicana* mushrooms; and **mescaline,** which comes from small, buttonlike growths on the peyote cactus of Mexico and the southwestern United States (Strassman, 1995).

These drugs come from very different sources and have very different modes of action; the effects of any one of them may differ from individual to individual and from time to time for a particular individual. However, hallucinogens generally result in periods of dramatically changed sensory experiences. Colors are brighter, sounds are more intense, and shapes are often distorted. Because everything is so different, it is like taking a trip to a different world, and for that reason the period of the drug effect is called a "trip." Trips usually last between 4 and 8 hours.

The changes in perception and the feelings of being transported lead to a variety of emotional experiences such as depersonalization and detachment. If the changed perceptions are pleasant, the trip can be enjoyable and exciting; if the changed perceptions are unpleasant, the trip can be terrifying and traumatic. Bad trips get the most attention because they can lead to dangerous acts or hospitaliza-

tion. However, even good trips can lead to serious consequences, as in the case of a young woman who thought she had supernatural powers and jumped out of a 12-story window in an attempt to fly. We do not understand what makes some trips enjoyable and others terrifying, but the individual's mood or expectations when beginning the trip appear to play some role.

In the 1960s it was thought that hallucinogens caused brief periods of schizophrenia and that hallucinogens and hallucinogenic experiences might be helpful for understanding schizophrenia. However, we now know that the causes and nature of hallucinogenic experiences are very different from those of schizophrenia; consequently, the use of hallucinogens to study schizophrenia has been abandoned. However, there is one very important exception: The drug phencyclidine (better known as PCP or "angel dust"), can lead to schizophrenia and therefore *is very dangerous* (Olney & Farber, 1995).

It was also once thought that hallucinogens might help people discover important personal insights about themselves, and therefore these drugs were sometimes used as an aid in psychotherapy. That notion also turned out to be erroneous. What seemed important to the individual while taking the drug turned out to be silly, meaningless, or wrong when the drug wore off.

Hallucinogens are taken orally, absorbed through the digestive tract, and then carried to the brain via the bloodstream. Because most hallucinogens are structurally similar to certain neurotransmitters in the brain (LSD and psilocybin are similar to serotonin, and mescaline is similar to norepinephrine), it is assumed that in the brain they stimulate the postsynaptic receptor sites that are normally stimulated by those neurotransmitters. The fact that hallucinogens generate such a wide variety of effects can probably be attributed to the fact that the nerves they stimulate are very basic and interconnect with and stimulate many other nerve networks, thereby setting in motion a cascade of complex neurological activity.

The use of LSD, psilocybin, and mescaline has a number of negative consequences. First, during a trip individuals may do things that are dangerous to themselves or others. An example of this is the woman who jumped out a window because she thought she could fly. Second, at least 5% of the individuals who use LSD experience **flashbacks,**

LSD   A hallucinogen that is synthetically produced.

psilocybin   A hallucinogen that is found in *Psilocybe mexicana* mushrooms.

mescaline   A hallucinogen that is derived from buttonlike growths on the peyote cactus.

flashbacks   Sudden and uncontrollable recurrences of perceptual distortions like those experienced during an LSD trip.

which are sudden and uncontrollable recurrences of perceptual distortions like those experienced during an LSD trip (Abraham & Aldridge, 1993; Smith & Seymour, 1994). Flashbacks are particularly frightening because the individual does not understand what is happening or why. After experiencing a flashback, individuals may become chronically anxious, worry about having another one, and worry about losing control in a potentially dangerous situation. We do not know why flashbacks occur, but it appears that when the drug is taken, some of it is stored somewhere in the body and then released at a later time, causing the delayed effect. A third negative consequence is that LSD can result in chromosomal damage, and thus its use poses serious problems for children born to individuals who have used hallucinogens. Finally, although hallucinogens are generally not physiologically addictive (they do not lead to withdrawal symptoms), some individuals become psychologically dependent on them as a means of escaping from the tedium of their everyday lives.

In summary, the major effect of hallucinogens such as cannabis (marijuana), LSD, psilocybin, and mescaline is to distort sensory experiences by interfering with neural transmission in the brain. These drugs are probably not physiologically addicting, but individuals can become psychologically dependent on them for pleasure and escape. The problems posed by the use of hallucinogens include foolish and dangerous behaviors, flashbacks, chromosomal damage, and the exacerbation of symptoms of schizophrenia. Hallucinogens are different from the other psychoactive drugs we have considered in that they do not produce a rush or a high. Instead, their use is motivated by the novelty or distraction they provide.

This concludes our discussion of psychoactive drugs. In the next section we'll examine the reasons why individuals use and abuse these drugs.

THINKING CRITICALLY

Questions about
Types of Psychoactive Drugs

Does using cannabis have long-term negative side effects? There is a great deal of controversy over this question, but a couple of findings have emerged. First, there is consistent evidence that using cannabis can exacerbate the symptoms of schizophrenia or trigger a relapse among individuals who have recovered from the disorder (Caspari, 1999; Linszen, Kingemans, & Lenior, 1994; Martinez-Arevalo, Calcedo-Ordonez, & Varo-Prieto, 1994). For example, in a followup study of individuals who had recovered from schizophrenia, it was found that the relapse rates were 61% for heavy users of cannabis, 18% for mild users, and 17% for nonusers. Those results are summarized in Figure 15.1. There were no other differences among the groups that

FIGURE 15.1

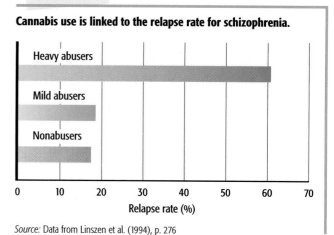

Cannabis use is linked to the relapse rate for schizophrenia.

Source: Data from Linszen et al. (1994), p. 276

could account for the differences in relapse rates, and the connection between the use of cannabis and relapse is strengthened by the fact that in most cases the symptoms of schizophrenia increased immediately after the cannabis was taken.

Why does cannabis increase the symptoms of schizophrenia? The answer lies in the fact that cannabis increases the activity of dopamine in the nerve tracts that lead to the frontal lobes of the cortex, and high levels of dopamine activity in those tracts is one of the causes of schizophrenia (Gardner & Lowinson, 1991; see also Chapter 11). The connection between cannabis use and the exacerbation of symptoms is clearly reflected in the comments of an individual with a history of a serious delusional disorder (the individual who was featured in Case Study 10.7). She is now functioning normally but made the following comments concerning the consequences of smoking cannabis:

> I do not smoke marijuana because when I do, all of my paranoid symptoms come back. I have never experienced a "nice high" like many of my friends have. In an attempt to understand what happens, I have smoked alone with a tape recorder so I could record what happens. However, it all happens so fast that I freak out and go into a paranoid panic. I check the house for bugs, and, of course, I turn the tape recorder off! All of the behaviors are present that I experienced during my rough moments without the drug—and that's no fun. I simply don't smoke marijuana anymore.

There is also evidence that chronic use of cannabis is associated with impaired cognitive functioning, such as problems with memory, attention, and the ability to organize and integrate information (Ehrenreich et al., 1999; Solowij, 1998). Furthermore, chronic cannabis use is linked to reduced brain activity, a factor that could explain the impaired cognitive functioning (Loeber & Yurgelun Todd, 1999). However, because the studies linking cannabis use to cognitive and brain functioning were correlational in nature, we cannot necessarily conclude from them that the use of cannabis caused the problems with cognitive and brain functioning. In other words, it is possible that problems with cognitive and brain functioning lead to the use of cannabis. To establish a cause-and-effect relationship researchers would have to conduct an experiment in which a randomly selected group of individuals used cannabis for a prolonged period of time, while another group of individuals did not. Differences between the two groups in terms of cognitive and brain functioning could then be compared. However, no researcher can do this experiment because it would be unethical to expose some individuals to a procedure (smoking cannabis) that was thought to result in long-term damage.

Overall, then, cannabis use can exacerbate the symptoms of schizophrenia and is correlated with cognitive and brain problems in otherwise normal individuals. However, the causal nature of its relationship to impaired cognitive functioning and reduced brain activity is not yet clear.

TOPIC II
Explanations for Drug Use

At low dosage levels depressants and opiates have a calming effect, but at high dosage levels they cause a rush or a high. Why do high doses of these drugs cause highs, and can highs be used to explain why people take the drugs?

Mike is generally more tense than most of his friends, and he really gets "wired" when under stress. Mike also drinks a lot of alcohol, usually beer, which helps him relax. Is his drinking related to a need to "come down"? Is Mike using alcohol as an antianxiety medication?

Lorie smokes about half of a pack of cigarettes a day; she has tried to stop smoking but can't. If she doesn't smoke for a while, she gets tense and irritable, and her hands tend to shake. However, if she then has a cigarette, she's fine. Does Lorie smoke for the pleasure of smoking or to relieve her withdrawal symptoms?

We can now turn to the important question of why individuals use and abuse psychoactive drugs. There are two related groups of explanations. The first group of explanations is based on physiology and is focused on the fact that most psychoactive drugs *produce powerful sensations of pleasure* or *reduce unpleasantly high levels of arousal*. The second group of explanations revolves around the psychological and sociocultural factors that lead individuals to use drugs to obtain pleasure or reduce arousal. For example, individuals who are under more stress are more likely to take drugs to relieve the stress, and some societies are more likely than others to condone the use of drugs for pleasure. It is essential to consider both the physiological and the psychological/sociocultural explanations because although physiological factors probably provide the primary reasons for taking drugs (e.g., pleasure), psychological/sociocultural factors help us understand why some individuals use drugs for pleasure, whereas others do not. Let's begin by examining the physiological explanations and then consider the psychological/sociocultural explanations.

Physiological Explanations

Pleasure Production

At high levels virtually all psychoactive drugs produce intense pleasure, and that pleasure provides a major explanation as to why people use the drugs. (*Note:* The one exception to the pleasure effect is hallucinogens.) To understand the pleasure effect you must understand how the **pleasure center** in the brain works.

The pleasure center was discovered when investigators were electrically stimulating different parts of the brains of animals in attempts to determine what the parts did. To their surprise they found that when one particular area was stimulated, the animal immediately experienced a high level of pleasure. Indeed, when rats were given electrical stimulation in their pleasure center each time they pressed a lever, the rats pressed the lever as frequently as 2,000 times per hour and did so until they collapsed with fatigue (Olds, 1958). In fact, when rats were given a choice between pressing a lever for either stimulation or food, the rats pressed the lever for stimulation even when they were near starvation. A pleasure center in humans was also found, and when it was stimulated, one woman said it was "almost orgasm." The pleasure center is located in a strip that runs through the middle of the *limbic system*. (The strip is technically called the *mesolimbic area; meso* means "middle.") The fact that the pleasure center is located in the limbic system is consistent with the fact that emotions are generated in the limbic system.

Two things should be noted with regard to drugs and the pleasure center: First, the major neurotransmitter in the pleasure center is *dopamine*. Second, the drugs that result in pleasure cause a sudden release of high levels of dopamine. In other words, when these drugs are taken, the pleasure center is flooded with dopamine, which results in high levels of neurological activity in the pleasure center, and this activity results in intense pleasure (Picciotto, 1998).

High levels of dopamine lead to pleasure, but different types of drugs increase dopamine levels in different ways.

pleasure center A strip that runs through the middle of the limbic system of the brain and that produces feelings of pleasure when dopamine is released.

Specifically, depressants (alcohol, barbiturates, benzodiazepines) and most stimulants (amphetamines, caffeine, nicotine) increase dopamine levels by increasing the *release* of dopamine, whereas cocaine increases dopamine levels by blocking its *reuptake.*

Arousal Reduction

A second physiological explanation for using psychoactive drugs is that some individuals have genetically determined high levels of physiological arousal that are unpleasant, and these individuals use drugs to reduce their arousal. Furthermore, for some individuals drugs may be more effective for reducing arousal; so these individuals are more likely to use drugs to reduce arousal. Research on alcoholism provides a good illustration of the links between genetics, high arousal, drug use, and arousal reduction. In some of this research investigators focused on the differences between children of individuals who suffered from alcoholism and children of those who did not (e.g., Pihl, Peterson, & Finn, 1990; Volavka et al., 1996). The logic behind this approach is as follows: (1) Alcoholism is in large part an inherited disorder; (2) parents who suffer from alcoholism pass on to their children the physiological factors that lead to alcoholism; and (3) comparing the children before they begin drinking makes it possible to identify differences that exist before the effects of drinking set in—that is, any differences that are found cannot be attributed to a history of drinking.

This type of research has revealed two important findings: First, before they begin drinking, the sons of parents who suffer from alcoholism have *higher levels of arousal,* as measured by brain activity and heart rate, than do the sons of parents who do not suffer from alcoholism. In other words, the offspring of parents with alcoholism are genetically predisposed to abuse alcohol because they have unpleasantly high levels of arousal that can be reduced with alcohol. The second finding is that sons of parents who suffer from alcoholism show *greater reductions in arousal after drinking alcohol* than do the sons of parents who do not suffer from alcoholism. That is, alcohol is uniquely effective for reducing arousal in individuals who are genetically predisposed to suffer from alcoholism. The two effects I described here are clearly illustrated in Figure 15.2 (Finn, Zeitouni, & Pihl, 1990).

Avoiding Withdrawal

Psychoactive drugs can produce pleasure and reduce arousal, but when individuals stop taking them, very unpleasant withdrawal symptoms occur. These symptoms range from mild depression to uncontrollable jerking of the body and even death. However, taking another dose of the

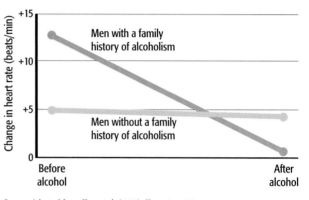

FIGURE 15.2

Men with a family history of alcoholism had higher heart rates and showed greater reductions in heart rate after drinking alcohol than did men without a family history of alcoholism.

Source: Adapted from Finn et al. (1990), Figure 2, p. 83.

drug will quickly eliminate the withdrawal symptoms, thereby providing another strong reason for use of the drug. In other words, apart from producing pleasure and reducing arousal, individuals use drugs because the drugs help them avoid withdrawal symptoms.

Increased Impulsivity

Finally, prolonged drug use can lead to changes in the brain that lead to impulsivity, and impulsivity can contribute to continued drug use because individuals will be less likely to inhibit inappropriate drug use. Specifically, there is now evidence that chronic drug use can reduce the functioning of the *prefrontal cortex* of the brain (Jentsch & Taylor, 1999). That finding is important because the prefrontal cortex is responsible for inhibition; when it is damaged, individuals become impulsive. The role of the prefrontal cortex in inhibition was originally illustrated in the case of Phineas Gage, a thoughtful, restrained, and responsible man who became impulsive and irresponsible after his prefrontal cortex was damaged in an accident (see Chapter 12). Indeed, among other things he began using alcohol inappropriately. More recently, a variety of other evidence has been found that links reduced size of the prefrontal cortex to impulsivity and antisocial behavior (Damasio, 2000; Raine et al., 2000). These findings are particularly interesting in view of other recent findings that prolonged use of alcohol results in a reduction of the size of the brain (Agartz et al., 1999).

Overall, then, the production of pleasure and reduction of arousal are powerful reasons for drug use. Once drugs are used, the avoidance of withdrawal symptoms and increases in impulsivity provide additional reasons for their continued use.

Psychological and Sociocultural Explanations

Taking psychoactive drugs leads to pleasure and arousal reduction in virtually everyone, so the question is, why are some individuals more likely than others to take psychoactive drugs? I already gave you one answer when I pointed out that some individuals have higher levels of arousal than others and therefore have a greater need to reduce arousal. However, differences in arousal levels are not sufficient to account fully for the differences between those who use drugs and those who do not. Thus, in this section we'll consider a number of other factors.

Exposure

Early theorists assumed that exposure to drugs would necessarily lead to the abuse of drugs. That orientation led early antidrug crusaders to predict that one puff on a marijuana cigarette would ultimately lead to opium dens and heroin addiction. Of course, an individual must be exposed to drugs before he or she can use them, but exposure is not sufficient to explain drug use. Convincing evidence for this comes from the fact that only 12% of the soldiers who used high levels of heroin while in Vietnam continued to use heroin after returning to the United States (Robins, Davis, & Nurco, 1974; Robins, Helzer, & Davis, 1975; see also Craig, 1995). The drug was available in the United States, but the life situations of most of the returning soldiers had changed, and so their pattern of drug usage changed.

Situational Factors

It is possible that situational factors such as stress or boredom might lead to drug abuse. For example, individuals in stressful jobs may drink too much or take excessive numbers of sleeping pills to escape the stress. Furthermore, individuals who have nothing to do and are bored may look for "kicks" with stimulants or take trips with hallucinogens. Also, individuals who feel trapped in poor living conditions may abuse drugs in an attempt to temporarily escape an intolerable situation.

The effects of situational factors on drug abuse were clearly demonstrated in experiments in which laboratory animals were given free access to drugs in their cages. Specifically, animals that were housed alone in small cages consumed 16 times more morphine than did animals that were housed with other animals in large cages (Alexander, Coambs, & Hadaway, 1978; Alexander et al., 1981; Hadaway et al., 1979). Apparently, the physical restriction and social isolation were stressful, and the animals' drug use was a response to the stressful situation. Similarly, the very high rate of drug abuse and dependence among soldiers serving in Vietnam may have been due to the high stress of that situation, and the lessening of stress upon returning to the United States may account for the substantial dropoff in drug use among the veterans.

From these results it appears that situational factors do contribute to drug use; however, situational factors do not account for all of the problems because many individuals who live in stressful, boring, or otherwise unpleasant situations do not turn to drugs. Why are only some individuals affected? Let's consider family characteristics and personality factors that might predispose individuals to drug abuse.

Situational factors, such as an intensely stressful job, may lead to drug abuse. For example, individuals may seek to escape workplace stress by drinking too much.

Family Characteristics

Theorists have long suspected that family characteristics during individuals' childhood years predispose the individuals to later drug abuse. Often-cited factors are poor role models, lack of discipline, and stress in the form of family disorganization (divorce, separation, inappropriate punishment) from which the child might want to escape through the use of drugs. To determine whether family characteristics are related to alcoholism, numerous investigations were conducted in which families were studied and then the children were later followed up as adults and examined for alcoholism. A review of the results of those investigations revealed that the children who went on to develop alcoholism (1) were raised in homes with more marital conflict, (2) received inadequate parenting, and (3) had parents who were more likely to be alcoholic, sexually deviant, or antisocial (Zucker & Gomberg, 1986).

These findings suggest that parents have an important influence on children's drug behavior, but the effects may be due to genetic rather than social factors. Specifically, the behaviors seen in the parents of many individuals who develop alcoholism are like those seen in individuals with antisocial personality disorder, and as I pointed out in Chapter 12, that disorder is due in large part to genetics. It may be, then, that the antisocial behavior of the parents and the antisocial behavior (drug abuse) of the children is due to shared genes.

Personality

In seeking an explanation for drug abuse, a considerable amount of early research was devoted to identifying an *addictive personality* (Nathan, 1988; Sutker & Allain, 1988). A unique addictive personality was not found, but further research did reveal two consistent findings: First, drug abuse in adulthood is related to *antisocial behavior and impulsivity* in childhood, adolescence, and adulthood (Disney et al., 1999; Molina, Smith, & Pelham, 1999; Sher & Trull, 1994). Specifically, it appears that many individuals who abuse drugs suffer from antisocial personality disorder or conduct disorder (see Chapters 12 and 13). The second personality factor consistently related to drug abuse is *depression* (Romach et al., 1999). However, there is some question about whether the depression is a cause or an effect of drug abuse. In some cases individuals use stimulants to relieve their depression (as Freud used cocaine); however, in other cases individuals become depressed because of the problems caused by their drug abuse (loss of jobs and friends).

At first the findings linking both antisocial behavior and depression to drug abuse seem inconsistent because antisocial behavior is not usually associated with depression. However, the explanation for the inconsistency lies in the possibility that drug abuse may be associated with antisocial behavior *or* depression, and that the two characteristics are associated with different types of drug abuse. For example, there is evidence that two types of alcoholism are associated with different personality characteristics (Cloninger, 1987; Gallant, 1990; Penick et al., 1990; Sullivan et al., 1990). One type is characterized by *persistent drinking* at moderate to heavy levels. In those cases, it appears that the individual does not have the ability to abstain from using alcohol regularly. This *persistent type of alcoholism* is associated with impulsivity, lack of anxiety, risk taking, novelty seeking, independence, distractibility, and antisocial behavior. In other words, individuals with the persistent type of alcoholism seem to suffer from antisocial personality disorder. The second type of alcoholism is characterized by *long periods of abstinence*, during which the individual is able to control the drinking. However, once drinking begins, the individual *cannot stop*, and the drinking takes the form of a binge. Individuals with this *binge type of alcoholism* are characterized as anxious, inhibited, shy, dependent, and, most importantly, depressed. Because depression is cyclical (see Chapter 8), it may be that alcohol bingeing varies with mood. (*Note:* The binge type of alcoholism should not be confused with "binge drinking," which is often engaged in by adolescents and college students. Binge drinking is under voluntary control and is very dangerous because the sudden consumption of a large amount of alcohol can cause respiration to stop, thus causing death.)

Anxiety Reduction

It has long been argued that the consumption of alcohol *reduces anxiety* and therefore leads to more consumption. This anxiety reduction explanation was originally based on research with laboratory animals in which it was found that stressors such as electrical shocks increased alcohol consumption and that the animals would come closer to a feared stimulus if they had been given alcohol (Conger, 1951; Freed, 1971; Wright, Pekanmaki, & Malin, 1971). Similar results have been reported with humans (Sher & Levenson, 1982). It appears that alcohol can reduce anxiety, but the question is why.

There are three reasons: First, alcohol reduces anxiety because it is a *physiological depressant,* and as such it can reduce the arousal we label anxiety (Finn, Zeitouni, & Pihl, 1990). The second explanation is that alcohol reduces anxiety because it *impairs cognitive functioning* (information processing), making individuals no longer aware of the problems that led to their stress (Steele & Josephs, 1988; Steele, Southwick, & Pagano, 1986). You may have noticed that individuals who have been drinking tend to focus on one or two ideas and ignore other ideas that may be more relevant or more important. If they do not attend to all of the relevant factors in their environment, they may not see or remember a problem that is anxiety-provoking. Third, alcohol may reduce anxiety because it *enhances positive feelings.* Indeed, I pointed out earlier that at high levels alcohol increases the release of dopamine, which stimulates pleasure in the brain, and that pleasure may overwhelm the anxiety.

In summary, alcohol can reduce anxiety through physiological sedation, cognitive distraction, and the production of pleasure. All three types of anxiety reduction are rewarding and could encourage drinking.

Conditioning

There is also good evidence that classical conditioning plays a role in drug craving and use (Robbins & Everitt, 1999; Self, 1998). Specifically, when individuals are exposed to situations similar to those in which they have taken drugs in the past or are exposed to drug paraphanalia similar to what they have used in the past, they experience a dramatic increase in the need for the drugs they have used. This is similar to the case in which Pavlov's dogs began salivating when they heard the bell that previously had been associated with food (see Chapter 2). The increased craving for drugs can then lead to greater use. This suggests that it will be easier for former drug users to remain drug-free if they avoid the situations, equipment, and friends that earlier were associated with drug use.

Expectations

Drug use can also be influenced by what individuals expect drugs will do for them (Aas et al., 1995; Downey & Kilbey, 1995; Evans & Dunn, 1995; Fillmore & Vogel Sprott, 1996; Grube et al., 1995; P. B. Johnson, 1994; Jones & McMahon, 1994; Kilbey, Downey, & Breslau, 1998; Kushner et al., 1994). For example, if individuals expect that a drug will help them get a lift, relax, or perform better, they are more likely to use the drug than if they do not have those expectations. Indeed, the expectations of college freshmen about the positive and negative effects of alcohol are good predictors of students' levels of drinking at the end of the year; positive expectations are linked to more drinking (Werner, Walker, & Greene, 1995). The recent resurgence in the popularity of LSD may be due to the fact that LSD is now perceived as "safer" than other drugs, and individuals do not expect negative outcomes from its use (Gold, 1994).

Sociocultural Factors

Finally, it is essential to consider the role of sociocultural factors in drug use. I left these factors for last not because they are unimportant but because their effects are mediated by factors such as exposure, situational variables, expectations, and physiological differences, which therefore needed to be addressed first.

The role of sociocultural factors is clearly apparent in cultural differences in drug use. For example, consider the high consumption of wine in France, the high consump-

Expectations can be a powerful force when it comes to substance abuse. Many college freshmen, for example, have positive expectations about drinking–they may believe that drinking will help them to have a good time and interact well with others.

tion of vodka in Russia, the high consumption of beer in Germany, and the low consumption of any form of alcohol in areas where there are many Muslims or Mormons. These differences are due to differences in the availability of various types of alcohol (wine, vodka, beer) and to differences in *religious prohibitions* concerning the use of alcohol.

Differences in drug use across groups can also be due to differences in levels of *stress*. For example, the greater level of stress experienced by members of lower socioeconomic classes may offer a partial explanation for why drug abuse is often higher in lower classes. Furthermore, the high level of drug use by some minority groups such as African Americans and Native Americans may not be linked to their ethnicity per se but rather to the fact that they are more likely to be members of a lower class, where stress is higher (Collins, 1993; D. Johnson, 1994).

It is also interesting to note that there are data indicating that dietary differences related to social class may also contribute to alcohol consumption (Adams, Kiefer, & Badia-Elder, 1995). For example, in studies of rats it was found that a low-tryptophan diet greatly increases alcohol consumption. Tryptophan is a protein found in dairy products, and if lower-class individuals consume fewer dairy products, that could lead to low levels of tryptophan and increased consumption of alcohol. (Low levels of tryptophan are probably linked to drinking because they result in low levels of serotonin, which contribute to impulsivity and increased drinking; see Chapters 9 and 12.)

Finally, it should be recognized that some ethnic differences in drug use may be due in part to genetic factors. For example, growing evidence indicates that one particular set of genes (e.g., ALDH$_2$) is associated with a more pleasant response to alcohol and a higher level of alcohol consumption. This is relevant because Asians are more likely to have this set of genes than are members of other ethnic groups, and it might explain their expectations concerning the effects of alcohol and their high level of alcohol consumption (O'Hare, 1995; Roberts, Fournet, & Penland, 1995; Thomasson & Li, 1993; Tu & Israel, 1995; Wall et al., 1992).

In summary, psychoactive drugs are taken because they produce pleasure, reduce withdrawal symptoms, and reduce unpleasant levels of arousal. Drug use also leads to problems in the prefrontal cortex, which then lead to impulsivity. Individual differences in the use of psychoactive drugs stem from situational factors, family characteristics, personality, conditioning, expectations, and sociocultural factors.

THINKING CRITICALLY

Questions about Explanations for Drug Use

1. *What are the implications of the findings that some individuals are physiologically predisposed to use drugs?* From the preceding discussion it should be clear that some individuals are predisposed to use psychoactive drugs. For example, children of parents who suffer from alcoholism often have uncomfortably high levels of arousal, making them more likely to use depressants (probably alcohol) to reduce that arousal. The fact that some people are physiologically predisposed to use drugs has two implications: First, it is harder for these individuals to resist using psychoactive drugs than it is for other people. Imagine a situation in which you have a bad headache and your friend does not. In this situation it will be harder for you to resist taking an aspirin than it will be for your friend. I am not suggesting that drug abuse should be ignored or condoned, but I am suggesting that we need to empathize with people who are struggling with a problem that led to drug abuse. Next time you are about to criticize someone for abusing drugs, think how you would feel if you had a terrible headache and someone told you not to take aspirin. The second implication is that people who abuse drugs are usually not "bad" people; instead, they got some bad genes that are causing problems. Again, I am not condoning drug abuse but simply suggesting that we consider the other person's situation and work to help him or her.

2. *Can the use of psychoactive drugs be considered a form of self-medication?* Each of us has an optimal level of arousal at which we are most comfortable or at which we

work most effectively. To get to or maintain that level, we often take psychoactive drugs. For example, students in my early morning class often come in with Cokes or mugs of coffee. Indeed, while working on this chapter, I began "running down" and so I had a cup of tea; the caffeine and sugar got me back "up" to where I could work better. This appears to be what many people are doing when they use strong forms of psychoactive drugs. For instance, individuals who are always drinking alcohol may be trying to reduce a high level of arousal.

The notion that people use drugs to adjust their own levels of arousal is referred to as the **self-medication explanation** for drug use (Corrigan et al., 1994; Geekie & Brown, 1995; Khantzian, 1985; Meisch, 1991; Schinka, Curtiss, & Mulloy, 1994). This practice is simply an extension of what is "normally" done with drugs, for example, when individuals with anxiety or schizophrenia are given medication to reduce arousal. The only difference in self-medication is that the individual writes his or her own prescription and in some cases may use drugs that are illegal.

TOPIC III

Disorders and Treatments

Stan suffers from alcoholism, and it seems that no matter how hard he tries, he cannot stop drinking. Recently, he began taking a drug called Antabuse that causes him to become extremely sick if he drinks any alcohol. Will the threat of becoming sick if he drinks be enough to stop his drinking?

Blake has become dependent on heroin. She originally took it to get high but now takes it to avoid the terrible withdrawal symptoms. To help her stop taking heroin she is taking a drug called *methadone*. Methadone stops her withdrawal symptoms but does not cause a high. Will ending the withdrawal symptoms be enough to enable her to stop using heroin?

To help him stop smoking Vincent is wearing a patch on his arm that slowly releases nicotine into his system through his skin. Is he simply substituting the nicotine from the patch for the nicotine he used to get from cigarettes? Will he get withdrawal symptoms when he stops using the patch?

Now that you understand why people take psychoactive drugs, we can go on to consider the disorders that stem from drug use and how the disorders can be treated.

Problems Related to Drug Use

You've probably taken a psychoactive drug recently; you may have had a cup of coffee or Coke containing caffeine to get a "lift," or possibly you've had an alcoholic drink. The question is, when does normal use of psychoactive drugs cross the line and become a substance-related disorder? According to *DSM-IV,* any one of the following four factors can lead to a diagnosis of substance-related disorder:

1. *Abuse.* **Drug abuse** is said to occur when *the use of a drug leads to clinically significant impairment or distress.* Examples include the failure to meet responsibilities at school, work, or home; engaging in hazardous behaviors such as driving while intoxicated; recurrent legal problems such as arrests for disorderly conduct; and social or interpersonal problems such as arguments or physical fights that result from taking drugs. In essence, when individuals begin wrecking their lives or the lives of others because of the effects of drugs, the individuals are abusing drugs.

2. *Intoxication.* **Intoxication** is defined as *reversible symptoms that stem from the recent use of a drug that influences the central nervous system.* Symptoms of intoxication include changes in mood, belligerence, impaired judgment, and problems with functioning. A key word in the definition of intoxication is *reversible;* that is, the symptoms go away when the drug wears off. A common example of intoxication is drunkenness from alcohol.

3. *Withdrawal.* **Withdrawal** refers to the *physiological symptoms that occur when an individual stops taking a drug or takes less of the drug than he or she took before.* In some cases withdrawal symptoms are relatively mild, such as the feelings of tension that occur when an individual stops drinking coffee. In other cases withdrawal symptoms are terrifying and can be fatal. Because the symptoms of withdrawal can be so severe, anticipation of the symptoms often produces psychological symptoms such as fear and anxiety.

4. *Dependence.* There are essentially three components of **dependence.** First, *drug tolerance develops,* and therefore the individual must take higher doses of the drug to achieve the desired effect. Second, *withdrawal symptoms occur,* so the drug must be taken to avoid those symptoms. Third, much of the *individual's life is devoted to obtaining or taking the drug.* For example, an individual spends a great deal of time getting the drug, using it, and recovering from the use (being "hungover"). A common word for dependence is *addiction.*

Abuse, intoxication, withdrawal, and dependence all provide bases for substance-related disorders. Does that mean that if you've been intoxicated (drunk) or had withdrawal symptoms after drinking too much coffee you've had a substance-related disorder? No, to have a substance-related disorder, abuse, intoxication, withdrawal, or dependence must lead you to experience *clinically significant impairments in functioning or personal distress.* In other words, your life must be persistently disrupted. Next we'll consider exactly what the substance-related disorders are.

Substance-Related Disorders

In *DSM-IV* substance-related disorders are organized in terms of the *drug that is causing the problem:*

Alcohol-related disorders

Amphetamine-related disorders

Caffeine-related disorders

Cannabis-related disorders

Cocaine-related disorders

Hallucinogen-related disorders (e.g., LSD)

Inhalant-related disorders (e.g., glue, paint thinner, spray propellants)

Nicotine-related disorders

Opioid-related disorders (e.g., morphine, heroin)

Phencyclidine-related disorders (e.g., PCP, or "angel dust")

Sedative-, hypnotic-, or anxiolytic-related disorders (e.g., tranquilizers such as barbiturates, sleeping pills, antianxiety drugs)

Polysubstance-related disorder (multiple drugs)

However, within each of the drug-based diagnoses there are subdiagnoses of *abuse, intoxication, withdrawal,* and *dependence.* For example, within the alcohol-related disorders there are subdiagnoses of *alcohol abuse, alcohol intoxication, alcohol withdrawal,* and *alcohol dependence,* and one or more can be applied to a given individual. With this diagnostic system we can specify what drug is causing the problem and the nature of the problem.

self-medication explanation   The notion that individuals use psychoactive drugs to adjust their own levels of arousal.

drug abuse   Clinically significant impairment or distress, such as failing to meet responsibilities and behaving dangerously, due to psychoactive drug use.

intoxication   Reversible symptoms, such as changes in mood, belligerence, impaired judgment, and impaired functioning, that stem from the recent ingestion of a drug that influences the central nervous system.

withdrawal   Physiological symptoms that occur when an individual stops taking a drug or takes less of the drug than he or she took before.

dependence   Condition in which an individual has developed drug tolerance, will suffer withdrawal symptoms if the drug is not taken, and devotes much of his or her life to obtaining and taking the drug; commonly called *addiction.*

Treatments

Drug problems can be very serious, so a great deal of effort has been focused on developing effective treatments. Unfortunately, in the past many of the treatments were ineffective, but the situation is changing and the future looks brighter. The treatment strategies that are used today can be divided into three major groups: First, physiological treatments are designed to *reduce the pleasurable effects of drugs.* The notion is that if the drugs no longer provide pleasure, individuals will stop taking them. The second treatment strategy involves *reducing the needs that lead to the use of psychoactive drugs.* For example, if stress is reduced, taking depressants to reduce stress may not be necessary. The third strategy involves *enhancing individuals' self-control so that they will be able to resist taking psychoactive drugs.* Let's consider these strategies and evaluate their effectiveness.

Reducing the Pleasure-Producing Effects of Drugs

Imagine that a candy you have enjoyed in the past no longer tastes good or even tastes bad. Would you continue eating it? Probably not, and that is the principle that underlies one of the major approaches to drug treatment: *Give individuals medication that reduces the pleasure-producing effects of psychoactive drugs.* In the following sections I'll describe three medications that can reduce the pleasure produced by psychoactive drugs.

Naltrexone. Earlier you learned that most psychoactive drugs produce pleasure because they increase the level of dopamine activity in the pleasure center of the brain. It follows, then, that if dopamine activity is reduced, the pleasure produced by psychoactive drugs will be reduced and therefore the drugs will be used less. The drug that is used most widely to block dopamine activity is **Naltrexone** (nal-TREX-own), which works by blocking receptor sites on the neurons in the pleasure center so that those neurons cannot be stimulated to produce pleasure.

There is a good deal of evidence that Naltrexone can reduce alcohol consumption (Anton et al., 1999; Davidson

et al., 1999; de Wit, Svenson, & York, 1999; Garbutt et al., 1999; Gatch & Lai, 1998; Landabaso et al., 1999; O'Malley et al., 1992, 1996; Swift et al., 1994; Swift, 1999; Volpicelli et al., 1992). For instance, among individuals who were suffering from alcoholism, those who took Naltrexone had more drink-free days, consumed less alcohol in general, were less likely to relapse, and had longer times between relapses than did individuals who took placebos. The individuals who took Naltrexone were also less likely to get "high" on alcohol and less likely to progress to heavy drinking. In one interesting experiment males who usually drank a lot of beer were given either Naltrexone or a placebo and then were allowed to drink as much as they wished during a 1½-hour period. The results indicated that after taking Naltrexone individuals had fewer urges to drink, drank less, took longer to finish each glass of beer, and quit drinking earlier (Davidson et al., 1999; see also Covey, Glassman, & Stetner, 1999). However, one problem associated with treatment with Naltrexone is that individuals often stop taking it because they miss the pleasure associated with use of the psychoactive drug (Swift, 1999).

Methadone. A drug that is widely used to block the pleasurable effects of heroin is **methadone (Dolopine)** (Jaffe, 1995; Rosenbaum, 1995). In addition to partially blocking the pleasure produced by heroin, methadone prevents the painful effects of heroin withdrawal. That effect is important because once a heroin habit is established, it is maintained largely in an attempt to avoid the terrible withdrawal symptoms. For many individuals, then, a treatment strategy called *methadone maintenance treatment,* in which methadone is substituted for heroin is effective. During methadone maintenance treatment individuals do not need to resort to illegal behavior to get drugs to avoid the feared withdrawal. Although heroin itself could be used in maintenance therapy (as is sometimes done in Great Britain), there are two advantages in using methadone: First, methadone can be taken orally, and therefore the problems associated with using needles, such as spreading HIV infections, are avoided. Second, methadone delays withdrawal symptoms for 24 hours (rather than 8 hours with heroin), so it needs to be taken only once a day. Although addicted individuals can be kept on methadone indefinitely, the goal is to wean them slowly from the drug. This is difficult, however, because eventually withdrawal symptoms set in.

The results of research concerning the effects of methadone maintenance are mixed. One explanation for the sometimes weak effects of this treatment strategy is that although methadone reduces withdrawal symptoms, it does not provide the pleasure that heroin does. Therefore, if heroin use is due even in part to the pleasure derived from the drug, the effectiveness of methadone will be reduced. A second explanation for treatment failures is that patients are sometimes not given high enough doses of methadone (Hartel et al., 1995; Maxwell & Shinderman,

---

Naltrexone   A medication used to treat psychoactive drug abuse by reducing the pleasure the drugs produce.

methadone (Dolopine)   A medication used to block the pleasurable effects of heroin and prevent the painful effects of heroin withdrawal.

Antabuse (disulfiram)   A medication used to control alcohol consumption by causing nausea and vomiting when alcohol is drunk.

1999; Ward, Mattick, & Hall, 1994). Indeed, there is consistent evidence that higher levels of methadone are related to higher levels of treatment success. Although the cost of methadone treatment is about $6,000 per year, it is cost-effective because this is less than the costs of other treatments and less than the costs of crime and imprisonment (Barnett, 1999).

Antabuse. There are also medications that can cause severe nausea and vomiting when psychoactive drugs are taken. In other words, rather than just reducing pleasure, these medications produce pain. This type of medication is used to control alcohol consumption, and the most widely used example is **Antabuse (disulfiram).** Here is how Antabuse works: When an individual consumes alcohol, it is first converted into a substance (acetaldehyde) that can cause flushing, rapid heart rate, nausea, and vomiting. In most cases this substance is quickly broken down, so it has little or no effect. However, Antabuse inhibits that breakdown, so the individual gets very sick rather than high. The notion is, then, if individuals are given Antabuse, they will not consume alcohol because they know it will make them sick.

The results of the research on the effectiveness of Antabuse are mixed (Besson et al, 1998; Carroll et al., 1998; Elkins, 1991; Garbutt et al., 1999; Gatch & Lai, 1998; Swift, 1999). However, what sometimes appears at first to be a treatment failure may subsequently be a success. For example, in one major experiment it was found that men who took Antabuse did not go longer without taking a drink than men who took a placebo, thus suggesting that the treatment did not work (Fuller et al., 1986). However, what should be noted is that after taking their first drink, the men who were taking Antabuse and got sick were less likely to drink again later than the men taking the placebo. It appears then that for Antabuse to be effective individuals must experience the sickening effects it can have, which requires that they have a drink. In other words, there must be a failure in abstinence before the drug can be effective. Interestingly, some individuals who know that the combination of Antabuse and alcohol will make them very sick take Antabuse only during high-risk periods in which it is likely that they will drink. That is, they take Antabuse only as needed.

Overall, then, we can use medication to (1) block the pleasure produced by psychoactive drugs, (2) reduce the symptoms of withdrawal, and (3) make the use of psychoactive drugs unpleasant. All of these strategies can be effective.

Reducing the Need for Pleasure-Producing Drugs

If an individual's need for the pleasure produced by psychoactive drugs is reduced, it follows that the use of the drugs will be reduced. In other words, just as you stop taking aspirin when you no longer have a headache or find a more effective drug, so individuals may stop taking psychoactive drugs if the drugs are not needed or if there is an acceptable substitute. Let's first consider the use of substitutes.

Common substitutes for cigarettes are patches, gum, and nasal sprays that contain nicotine. Patches and gum deliver a constant flow of nicotine to the bloodstream, whereas nasal sprays can be used to provide nicotine on an as-needed basis. Because the patches, gum, and sprays provide nicotine, there is no need to get nicotine from cigarettes. This approach can be very effective for reducing nicotine withdrawal symptoms and thus is helpful in smoking treatment programs (Cepeda-Benito, 1993; Fiore et al., 1992; Fortmann & Killen, 1995; Hatsukami et al., 1995; Hurt et al., 1998; Kornitzer et al., 1995). Indeed, a long-term followup study found that the combined use of nicotine patches and psychological treatments (e.g., a support group for stopping smoking) was more than 50% more effective than the psychological treatments alone. In addition to helping people stop smoking, nicotine patches can make them easier to live with during the withdrawal period. For example, in one experiment it was found that stopping smoking was associated with a general decrease in cooperative behavior, but use of a nicotine patch returned cooperation to normal levels (Spiga et al., 1998). However, eventually the individual must be weaned from the patch or the gum, and that event can result in withdrawal symptoms and relapse (Hatsukami et al., 1995; Hurt et al., 1995). In other words, substituting the patch or gum for cigarettes eliminates the use of cigarettes, but it does not eliminate the eventual problems of nicotine withdrawal. However, with patches and gum the doses of nicotine can be slowly and systematically reduced, thereby easing the individual through withdrawal.

Another drug-substitution strategy involves using a different drug that will provide pleasure, thereby making the pleasure-producing cigarettes unnecessary. The most common drug used for this purpose is Zyban (*bupropion*), which increases pleasure by increasing the production of dopamine. (It might be noted that Zyban is simply another name for Wellbutrin, which is marketed as an antidepressant; see Chapter 8. It is often pointed out in advertisements for Zyban that individuals who take Wellbutrin should not take Zyban. The reason for that is simple; if you are taking Wellbutrin, you are already taking Zyban.) The results of a variety of experiments have indicated that by increasing dopamine levels, Zyban can be effective for reducing smoking (Goldstein, 1998; Jorenby et al., 1999). Of course, as with the nicotine patch and gum, eventually the individual must be weaned from Zyban by slowly reducing the dosage level.

Finally, the last way to reduce a need for psychoactive drugs is to correct personal or situational problems that create the need (Acierno, Donohue, & Kogan, 1994). In other words, rather than satisfying a need with medication,

D.A.R.E. is one example of a drug abuse prevention program designed to increase self-control. The goal of this program is to educate children early about the dangers of substance abuse.

eliminate the need. Doing that may involve reducing stress by changing an entire lifestyle or by removing an individual from a stressful situation. Unfortunately, in many cases that may be very difficult or impossible to accomplish. Furthermore, the cost of therapy necessary to achieve the changes may be high relative to the cost of drugs, and so drug treatment is more likely to be used.

Increasing Self-Control

Alcoholics Anonymous. The oldest approach to treating drug abuse involves helping individuals develop enough self-control so that they can "just say no" to the use of drugs. The organization that is best known for using this strategy is **Alcoholics Anonymous (AA).** Members of AA begin their "12-step program" by acknowledging that they are powerless over alcohol and that their lives have become unmanageable. Next, they turn for help to a "power" greater than themselves (that is, God in whatever form they understand God to be). Specifically, they ask for help in removing their "shortcomings" so that they can cope more effectively. In essence, they acknowledge they have a problem but go on to develop the belief that with help from God and with the support of other members of AA they can overcome the problem. Some psychologists have suggested that in doing

this, members of AA are going through a form of cognitive therapy in which they develop new beliefs about themselves (Steigerwald & Stone, 1999). Another very important element of AA is that it is run by individuals who have suffered from and overcome problems with alcohol in the past. In other words, these are people who have "been there" and come back successfully, thus providing inspiration and good role models. In Case Study 15.1 a young man I know describes his experience with alcoholism and AA.

There is some dispute over the success of AA, but a recent review of 21 controlled experiments indicated AA was no better but no worse than many other treatments (Kownacki & Shadish, 1999). It is clear that AA is very successful for some individuals, but not for all. However, it is not clear what type of individual is most likely to be helped by AA (Kaskutas et al., 1999). The success of AA has lead to other, similar groups such as Nicotine Anonymous for smokers and Synanon for individuals who are addicted to opiates (Lichtenstein, 1999; McCrady, 1994).

D.A.R.E. A very popular approach designed to reduce drug abuse by educating young children about the problem is **D.A.R.E.,** which stands for *Drug Abuse Resistance Education.* This program is started in elementary school, and you have probably seen bumper stickers proclaiming membership in the D.A.R.E. program. Unfortunately, in sharp contrast to the attention the program receives and the large amount of money spent on it, controlled evaluations of it revealed that it has little or no long-term effects (Lisnov et al, 1998; Lynam et al., 1999; Rosenbaum & Hanson, 1998). For example, followup studies indicated that although students rated the program as successful, students who participated in the program did not differ in drug use, attitudes

Alcoholics Anonymous (AA) An organization that helps individuals develop enough self-control to overcome problems with alcohol abuse.

D.A.R.E. An educational program for school-age children that is designed to reduce drug abuse; the acronym stands for Drug Abuse Resistance Education.

A Young Man Talks about His Alcoholism and AA

MY USE OF ALCOHOL—and other drugs—began when I was just a teenager, but it became very serious when I was in my 20s. At the time I had a responsible job in New York City, but dark moods of depression began to claim more and more of my time. I found that alcohol had the effect of taking the edge off of my depression, and it helped bring sleep when my mind was racing into negative territory. As months and years passed, the comforting effect that I had felt with my first drink became harder to achieve. I drank more, and I drank daily.

My career began to crumble, so I decided to make a change. First I moved to a small fishing village in Mexico, where I thought I would write a screenplay. That didn't work out, so I moved to southern California, then back to New York, and next to a boat in the Caribbean to lead "the good life." The only constant in my life was the bottle. It was my career, my art, my mistress. A bottle of vodka a day was necessary to stop the shakes and give me hope—hope that the second bottle

would bring peace. Finally my money ran out. The next day, in pain from head to toe, I boarded a flight back to New York City. My hands shook so badly I couldn't lift a cup of coffee.

In New York I got a job and took an apartment in a once beautiful, now derelict, part of the city. I lay in bed for days at a time paralyzed by alcohol. Holding down food was impossible, and I would vomit pools of blood. One day while I was half conscious, three gun shots were fired through my door, intended for the drug dealer who had once lived there. I was upset only because they disturbed my attempt at sleep.

A few days later a friend, realizing my desperation, asked me if I wanted help. "Yes" was the hardest reply I have ever given. Attempts at therapy had never been successful; no one had been able to break through the fog of alcohol. Anyone who had not experienced the "dark place" was suspect. They could not possibly know the loneliness and desperation.

Now I found myself thrust into my first AA meeting. The faces were those

from "Park Avenue to park bench, from Yale to jail." My panic gave way to comfort in knowing that, for the first time, I was surrounded by people who did know this pain, and had refused to live with it any longer. They had found a key, and I wanted it.

The speaker that night was a man in his 30s. His story was different from mine, but exactly the same. His riches weren't measured in dollars, but in sober experience. As time went on, I would see many tragically broken lives transformed.

My drinking stopped. Slowly, one day at a time, my mind began to clear. The reasons for my depressions were more complex than I could have ever realized, masked by alcohol. Combing through the wreckage of a drunken past at times filled me with remorse, but AA gave me the balance between self-awareness and compassion. Today, through sobriety, I have a strong foundation on which to explore and build. AA gave me that foundation.

---

toward drugs, or self-esteem from students who did not participate in the program.

THINKING CRITICALLY

Questions about Disorders and Treatments

1. *What can be done to increase compliance with treatment programs?* It is clear that we have some treatments that are effective for reducing drug abuse. However, a problem in many cases is that individuals who start the treatment programs do not continue. For example, they will stop taking their methadone or Naltrexone. One strategy for overcoming this problem is to reward individuals for continuing the treatment. In some respects, taking methadone rewards individuals because methadone prevents withdrawal symptoms. However, taking the methadone only enables the individuals to avoid something negative but

does not provide something positive. To overcome this problem some investigators tried using monetary rewards (Piotrowski et al., 1999; Silverman et al., 1999). Payments were generally effective, and higher payments were more effective for getting individuals to take methadone; when the payments stopped, however, many individuals went back to using heroin.

In one interesting experiment investigators tested to determine whether rewards might be effective for keeping individuals off cocaine (Higgins et al., 1994). The individuals who participated in the experiment were cocaine-dependent adults in a treatment program for cocaine abuse, and they had urine specimens tested for cocaine three times per week. The individuals were randomly assigned to two groups: reward and no reward. For each individual in the reward group, the first urine specimen that tested negative for cocaine was worth $2.50, and each additional consecutive negative specimen was worth an additional $1.25, so, for example, the sixth consecutive negative specimen was worth $8.75. Furthermore, a bonus of

$10.00 was paid for every three consecutive negative specimens, so six consecutive negative specimens were worth a total of $53.75. The presence of a positive urine specimen caused the reward level to be reset at $2.50. The individuals in the no-reward group did not receive rewards for negative specimens. The results indicated that 70% of the individuals in the reward group were continuously cocaine-free for at least 5 weeks, whereas only 50% of the individuals in the no-reward group showed that level of improvement. The difference was even greater after 10 weeks. The results of this experiment are summarized in Figure 15.3.

These results clearly indicate that the use of rewards can be an effective strategy for reducing drug abuse, but the procedures raise an interesting question: Should individuals be given substantial monetary rewards for doing what they should be doing anyway? If someone is not taking cocaine now, should he or she be paid? That is an interesting ethical question, but the bottom line is that illegal and dangerous behavior can be brought under control with a system of rewards.

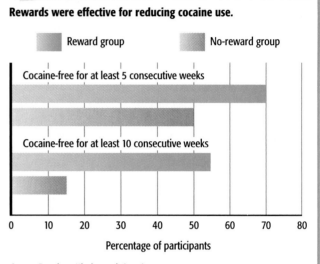

FIGURE 15.3

Rewards were effective for reducing cocaine use.

Source: Data from Higgins et al. (1994), p. 572.

Summary

Topic I: Types of Psychoactive Drugs

▶ A number of factors can influence the effects of a drug.

▶ Dose-dependent effects refer to the fact that drugs can have different effects at different dosage levels.

▶ Tolerance refers to the fact that increasing amounts of a drug may have to be taken to achieve a given effect, and cross-tolerance refers to the fact that taking a drug of one type will lead to tolerance for other drugs of that type.

▶ Drugs taken in combination can have a greater effect than the simple sum of their separate effects.

▶ Factors such as personality, previous experiences with drugs, and genetics can influence a drug's effects.

▶ Expectations about the effects of drugs will influence their effects.

▶ There are four types of psychoactive drugs: depressants, opiates, stimulants, and hallucinogens.

▶ Depressants include alcohol, barbiturates, and benzodiazepines. At low levels they reduce arousal, but at high levels they can produce a rush. Misuse can cause withdrawal symptoms and even death because respiration is stopped.

▶ Opiates include opium, morphine, codeine, and heroin, all of which are derived from the poppy plant. At low levels they dull or numb the senses and bring on a sleeplike state, but at high levels they can produce a rush. Misuse can cause withdrawal symptoms and even death because respiration is stopped.

▶ Stimulants include amphetamines, cocaine, caffeine, and nicotine. At low levels they increase arousal, and at high levels they produce a high. Misuse leads to withdrawal symptoms (e.g., depression, amphetamine psychoses), dangerous behavior, and possibly death. Nicotine can act as both a stimulant and a depressant.

▶ Hallucinogens include cannabis, LSD, psilocybin, and mescaline. They distort sensory experiences. Their use is not linked to withdrawal symptoms, but it can lead to dangerous behavior, flashbacks, chromosomal damage, and exacerbation or relapse of schizophrenia.

Topic II: Explanations for Drug Use

▶ Physiological explanations include the production of pleasure, the reduction of unpleasantly high levels of arousal, the avoidance of arousal, and increases in impulsivity because prolonged drug use reduces the functioning of the prefrontal cortex.

▶ Psychological and sociocultural explanations include exposure to drugs; situational factors such as boredom and stress; family characteristics such as poor role models, inadequate parenting, and shared genes; personality factors such as antisocial personality disorder and depression; anxiety reduction; classical conditioning of craving; expectations about the effects of drugs; and sociocultural factors such as availability of drugs, religious prohibitions, stress levels, dietary differences, and genetic factors linked to ethnic groups.

▶ Physiological factors that predispose individuals to drug abuse make it difficult for some individuals to resist drugs. Some drug use can be considered to be self-medication (adjustment of arousal levels).

Topic III: Disorders and Treatments

▶ Diagnoses of substance-based disorders are based on (1) abuse, which involves impairment or distress; (2) intoxication, which involves reversible symptoms such as changes in mood and impaired judgment that result from drug use; (3) withdrawal, which involves negative symptoms that occur when drug usage is stopped or decreased; and (4) dependence, which involves the development of drug tolerance, withdrawal symptoms, and spending large amounts of time in obtaining or using drugs. For a diagnosis to be made, these factors must result in clinically significant impairments in functioning or personal distress.

▶ Disorders are organized in terms of the drug that is used and the nature of the resulting problem (e.g., intoxication, withdrawal).

▶ There are three treatment strategies. The first involves the use of medications that reduce the pleasure-producing effects of drugs. Naltrexone blocks receptor sites on neurons in the pleasure center, methadone blocks pleasure from heroin and reduces withdrawal symptoms, and Antabuse causes nausea and vomiting when alcohol is consumed.

▶ The second treatment strategy involves reducing the need for pleasure-producing drugs. To reduce smoking an individual may use nicotine patches, gum, and nasal sprays that provide nicotine. Alternatively, Zyban can be used to increase dopamine and pleasure. Attempts are also made to correct the personal or situational problems that may create a need for drugs.

▶ The third treatment strategy involves increasing self-control. Notable programs are Alcoholics Anonymous, which appears to be successful in some cases, and D.A.R.E., which is not efffective.

Questions for Making Connections

1. What links are there between drug abuse and disorders such as major depressive disorder, generalized anxiety disorder, antisocial personality disorder, and conduct disorder? Specifically, does drug abuse cause these disorders, do these disorders cause drug abuse, or do drug abuse and these disorders stem from a common factor?

2. Compare the treatment of substance-related disorders to the treatment of major depressive disorder, schizophrenia, and generalized anxiety disorder.

Key Terms and People

In reviewing and testing yourself, you should be able to discuss each of the following:

alcohol, p. 440
Alcoholics Anonymous, p. 460
amphetamine psychoses, p. 444
amphetamines, p. 443
Antabuse (disulfiram), p. 459
barbiturates, p. 441
benzodiazepines, p. 441
caffeine, p. 445
cannabis, p. 448
cocaine, p. 444
codeine, p. 442
cross-tolerance, p. 438
D.A.R.E., p. 460

delirium tremens (d.t.'s), p. 441
dependence, p. 457
depressants, p. 440
dose-dependent effect, p. 438
drug abuse, p. 457
flashbacks, p. 449
hallucinogens, p. 448
heroin, p. 442
intoxication, p. 457
LSD, p. 449
marijuana, p. 448
mescaline, p. 449
methadone (Dolopine), p. 458

morphine, p. 442
Naltrexone, p. 458
narcotics, p. 442
nicotine, p. 446
opiates, p. 441
opium, p. 442
pleasure center, p. 451
psilocybin, p. 449
psychoactive drug, p. 437
self-medication explanation, p. 456
stimulants, p. 443
tolerance, p. 438
withdrawal, p. 457

16 Sexual and Gender Identity Disorders

SEX IS LINKED to a wide variety of disorders. For example, some individuals simply aren't interested in sex, others are interested but cannot become physically aroused, and still others can become aroused but only in unusual ways, such as by harming others or exposing themselves. In this chapter I will consider three types of disorders that are associated with sex. The first type is known as *sexual dysfunctions,* which involve insufficient sexual *desire,* insufficient sexual *arousal,* and problems with *orgasm.* The second type of disorders I will discuss are *paraphilias,* in which individuals achieve sexual arousal through *inappropriate means.* For example, individuals may gain sexual pleasure from dressing in the clothes of the opposite sex or hurting their sexual partners. The third type is called *gender identity disorder,* in which individuals have a *strong cross-gender identification that is accompanied by discomfort with their own physiologically determined sex.* For example, a male may believe that he would be more comfortable if he were a woman, or he may believe that he actually is a woman. The types of sexual and gender identity disorders are summarized in Table 16.1 (on p. 466).

When discussing sexual disorders, we must distinguish between *illegal* behaviors and *abnormal* behaviors. Illegal behaviors are not necessarily abnormal, and vice versa. For example, oral sex is illegal in many states, but it is not defined as abnormal in *DSM-IV.* In contrast, wearing clothes of the opposite sex to gain sexual pleasure is not illegal, but it is defined as abnormal. In this chapter our focus will be on abnormal behaviors.

It is also important to note that sociocultural factors play a key role in determining what is defined as abnormal. This point is clearly illustrated by the case of homosexuality. Until 1980 homosexuality was identified as a disorder in *DSM,* but as attitudes toward homosexuality changed, it was considered a disorder only if it made the individual anxious or uncomfortable. That is, the focus changed from the homosexual behavior itself to the feelings that it generated. Finally, as attitudes became even more tolerant, homosexuality was dropped as a disorder from *DSM* in 1987. Similarly, in China the very existence of lesbianism was denied until recently, but it has now been recognized and may someday be regarded as more acceptable (Ruan & Bullough, 1992). It is also interesting to note that in some Native American societies a clear distinction is not always made between "man" and "woman," and therefore in those societies behaviors such as homosexuality and transvestism (dressing in the clothes of the "opposite sex") are not necessarily seen as problematic (Schnarch, 1992). Clearly, when considering the normality or abnormality of sexual behavior, we must take the time and the culture into account.

TABLE 16.1

Sexual and gender identity disorders

Sexual Dysfunctions

▶ *Desire disorders*
Hypoactive sexual desire disorder
Sexual aversion disorder

▶ *Arousal disorders*
Female sexual arousal disorder
Male erectile disorder

▶ *Orgasmic disorders*
Female orgasmic disorder
Male orgasmic disorder
Premature ejaculation

Paraphilias

▶ Exhibitionism
▶ Fetishism
▶ Transvestic fetishism
▶ Frotteurism
▶ Pedophilia
▶ Sexual masochism
▶ Sexual sadism
▶ Voyeurism

Gender Identity Disorder

Note: DSM-IV also contains a category of "Sexual Pain Disorders" that includes dyspareunia (pain associated with intercourse) and vaginismus (involuntary contractions of the muscles of the vagina that interfere with sexual intercourse).

Sexual disorders are usually not as debilitating as other disorders such as anxiety, depression, and schizophrenia, and therefore they are often seen as less serious. Nonetheless, sexual disorders can be very serious because of the impact they can have on other people. This is particularly true when the disorders involve behaviors such as rape, sadism, or the sexual abuse of children. Because sexual disorders are very prevalent in our society and because some of them can pose a danger, it is important that we give them careful consideration.

TOPIC I

Sexual Dysfunctions

Ken is worried about his sex life—or more accurately, his lack of sex life. There are a lot of good-looking women around, and a few have "put a move on him," but he just isn't interested in sex. Good friendships with women are fine, but unlike most of the other guys his age, he has little or no sexual desire. He knows he is not gay, but he worries about his lack of interest in women. Ken suffers from a sexual dysfunction known as *desire disorder.* What causes this disorder? Can it be treated?

Alice is a 33-year-old woman who has always enjoyed sex. The problem is that during intercourse she cannot reach orgasm, regardless of how long the sexual activity is maintained. She is confused because she can achieve orgasm easily through masturbation. Alice does not blame her sexual partners and instead assumes that she has some "unconscious problem" about men, which is beginning to interfere with her relationships. Alice suffers from a very common sexual dysfunction known as *orgasmic disorder.* Is Alice correct in believing that she has an unconscious problem, or is there some other explanation? Is this disorder difficult to treat?

Sexual dysfunctions are disorders that involve the *absence or failure of the sexual response at some point during the sexual response cycle.* Three types of sexual dysfunction disorders have been identified, and each is associated with a different phase of the sexual response cycle:

1. *Desire disorders* are associated with the *appetitive phase,* in which the individual has fantasies about sexual activities and develops a desire for sex. These disorders involve a lack of sexual desire.

2. *Arousal disorders* are associated with the *excitement phase,* which consists of subjective sexual pleasure and physiological changes such as erections in males and vaginal lubrication in females. Arousal disorders involve insufficient physiological arousal, despite the presence of desire.

3. *Orgasmic disorders* are associated with the *orgasm phase,* which involves a peaking of subjective sexual pleasure with heightened physiological changes such as ejaculation in males and the contraction of the walls of the vagina in women. Orgasmic disorders involve either failure to achieve an orgasm, despite the presence of desire and arousal, or premature orgasm.

Desire Disorders

Desire disorders involve a *deficiency in or lack of desire for sexual activity.* Individuals with desire disorders lack sexual urges, have few sexual fantasies, and therefore may not seek sexual stimulation. However, if the individuals are sexually stimulated, they can become sexually aroused. Technically, there are two desire disorders, which generally reflect different degrees of the lack of desire. **Hypoactive sexual desire disorder** involves a *lack of sexual desire,* and **sexual aversion disorder** involves an extreme *aversion to sexual activities.* Desire disorders occur in up to 15% of males and up to 35% of females (Nathan, 1986).

Individuals differ greatly in the degree to which they are upset by desire disorders. Some individuals are not concerned about their lack of desire, and they simply do not miss the sexual activities in which they are not interested. However, others are very upset because they want the sexual pleasure they once experienced, see portrayed in the media, or read about. Furthermore, for some individuals the lack of desire is inconsistent with their cultural role (e.g., the "macho" male or the female "sex symbol"), and they become concerned about how they are perceived by others. In such cases desire disorders can lead to depression because the individuals think they are missing out on something or to anxiety because the individuals think they are not measuring up. Finally, lack of sexual desire can cause depression and anxiety for the individual's partner, who may assume that the lack of desire is a reflection on his or her sexual attractiveness.

Psychological Explanations and Treatments

There are two psychological explanations for desire disorders. The first is the *defensive suppression* of desire. The notion is that individuals who were raised to believe that sex is "bad" or "dirty" avoid the forbidden attraction by suppressing their desire.

Second, it has been suggested that lack of desire is due to *stress.* Individuals who are under stress must focus their attention and energy on coping with the stress, and that leaves little attention or energy available for sex. For example, in one study it was found that men who were under stress because of unemployment experienced more sexual difficulty than did men who were not under such stress (Morokoff & Gillilland, 1993).

Psychotherapy is a popular technique for treating desire disorders, but unfortunately there is no consistent evidence that this approach is particularly helpful (Becker & Kavoussi, 1994; Bergin & Garfield, 1994; O'Carroll, 1991).

Physiological Explanations and Treatments

The physiological explanation for desire disorders is based on *hormone imbalances,* and treatment revolves around restoring the balances. Before discussing this explanation and treatment, it will be helpful if I describe the physiological process that is responsible for normal desire.

The process begins in the **hypothalamus,** the structure in the brain that is responsible for arousal in general. In the male, when the hypothalamus is stimulated by some sex-related stimulus such as a visual image, a touch, or a scent, the hypothalamus secretes a **releasing hormone** that stimulates the **pituitary gland,** which in turn secretes hormones known as **gonadotropins** (guh-nad-uh-TRO-pinz). (*Gonad* refers to any reproductive gland, such as the testes or ovaries, and *tropin* means "alter or influence.") As the name implies, the gonadotropins stimulate the male's testes, which then produce **testosterone** (tes-TOS-tuh-ron), the hormone responsible for the arousal of desire in males.

Testosterone results in desire, but it also causes the hypothalamus to *reduce* production of the releasing hormone that started the process. In other words, there is a feedback loop in the system that helps keep the level of testosterone within a narrow range. If this were not the case, once stimulated, the system would run unchecked. The chemical process responsible for arousal in men is illustrated in Figure 16.1 (on p. 468).

The chain of events is similar in women but considerably more complex because the production of hormones varies greatly during a woman's menstrual cycle and because additional hormones are involved. In general, however, in women the gonadotropins stimulate the ovaries to produce **progesterone** (pro-JES-tuh-ron). Progesterone contributes to desire, and like testosterone in the male, it is involved in a negative-feedback loop that reduces hypothalamic production of the releasing hormone that started the process.

It is important to recognize that this system involves a number of different parts (hypothalamus, pituitary gland, sex organs), as well as a variety of hormones (releasing hormone, gonadotropins, testosterone or progesterone), and that all of the components must operate within narrow tolerances if the system is to work effectively. If any of the components of the system are thrown off by spontaneous fluctuations, damage, disease, or external factors, the individual will experience an altered level of sexual desire.

sexual dysfunctions Disorders that involve the absence or failure of the sexual response at some point during the sexual response cycle; include desire, arousal, and orgasmic disorders.

desire disorders Sexual dysfunctions that involve a deficiency in or lack of desire for sexual activity.

hypoactive sexual desire disorder A type of desire disorder that involves a lack of sexual desire.

sexual aversion disorder A type of desire disorder that involves an extreme aversion to sexual activities.

hypothalamus A structure in the brain that is responsible for arousal in general.

releasing hormone A hormone released by the hypothalamus that stimulates the pituitary gland during sexual arousal.

pituitary gland A structure in the brain that, among other functions, secretes hormones known as gonadotropins, which are essential for sexual arousal.

gonadotropins Hormones released by the pituitary gland that stimulate the gonads during sexual arousal.

testosterone The hormone responsible for the arousal of desire in males; released primarily by the testes.

progesterone The hormone responsible for the arousal of desire in females; released by the ovaries.

FIGURE 16.1

The physiological process responsible for sexual desire in males

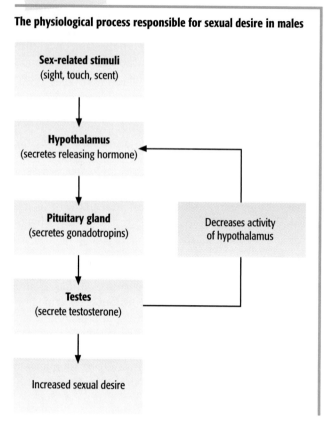

Support for the notion that hormone imbalances can result in desire disorders comes from two sets of research results. First, research has provided ample evidence that *low levels of sex hormones are associated with low sexual desire* (e.g., Bancroft, 1984a, 1984b; Lo Piccolo, 1983; Regan, 1999). For example, in one investigation the sexual responses (erections) of men with normal or low levels of testosterone were compared when the men engaged in erotic fantasy and when they were exposed to an erotic film (Bancroft, 1984a). The results indicated that men with low levels of testosterone showed much lower sexual arousal in response to fantasy but only slightly lower sexual arousal when stimulated by the erotic film. In other words, males with low hormone levels showed *less sexual desire* but *could be aroused by actual stimulation*. These results are presented in Figure 16.2. In a more recent longitudinal study, testosterone levels were measured once a month in the saliva of adolescent males, and it was found that during times when testosterone levels were elevated, the adolescent males initiated more sexual activity; that is, levels of testosterone were linked to levels of desire (Halpern, Udry, & Suchindran, 1998).

Related to the finding that low hormone levels are associated with low desire is the finding that as men grow older, their levels of testosterone decline, and so they experience diminishing sexual desire and arousal (Schiavi et al., 1990, 1991). However, once older men become stimulated and aroused, they report normal levels of desire, enjoyment, and satisfaction.

The second set of research findings supporting the hormone explanation for desire disorders consists of data indicating that *increasing the levels of the sex hormones increases sexual desire* (e.g., Bancroft, 1984a; Bancroft & Wu, 1983; Davidson, 1984; Davidson, Camargo, & Smith, 1979; Kwan et al., 1983). For example, in one investigation men with low levels of testosterone either were or were not injected with testosterone, and then the men's responses to sexual fantasy and erotic films were assessed (Bancroft, 1984a).

Because the treatment approaches differ, it is important to consult a physician to determine whether a sexual desire disorder stems from a psychological or physiological problem.

FIGURE 16.2

Men with low levels of testosterone showed low levels of desire in response to fantasy but normal levels in response to stimulation.

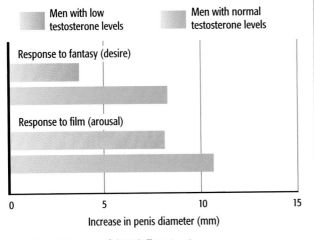

Source: Adapted from Bancroft (1984a), Figure 2, p. 6.

FIGURE 16.3

Testosterone replacement therapy increased men's desire response (erections).

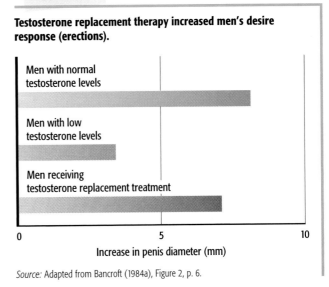

Source: Adapted from Bancroft (1984a), Figure 2, p. 6.

The results of this investigation indicated that the men who were injected with testosterone showed higher levels of arousal while fantasizing about sex than did the men who were not given testosterone. In fact, the men who were given the testosterone showed a level of arousal during fantasy that was almost as high as that of men with normal levels of testosterone. Those results are summarized in Figure 16.3.

It should be noted that there is some controversy over the question of whether hormone levels are linked to sexual desire in women (Schreiner-Engel et al., 1989; Zillmann, Schweitzer, & Mundorf, 1994). One study that supported the relationship showed that women were most likely to choose to view films with erotic content just prior to, during, and just after menses.

Now that you understand that low levels of sex hormones are related to low levels of sexual desire, at least in men, let's go on to examine possible causes for the low levels of the hormones. Hormone levels can be influenced by many factors, including disease, age, and genetic background, but external influences are of most interest here. For many years zoologists have known that subtle alterations in weather and amount of light can cause changes in the levels of gonadotropins produced in sheep, goats, and deer and that those changes in turn influence the animals' mating behavior. For humans turning the lights down low may not increase hormone levels, but recent evidence has clearly documented that *psychological stress can decrease hormone levels.* For example, when men who were under normal levels of stress were compared to men who were under high levels of stress, as in military training or combat, it was found that the men under higher stress produced

lower levels of testosterone (Rose et al., 1969). These findings are presented in Figure 16.4.

From the findings reported in this discussion, it is clear that physiological factors play an important role in determining sexual desire in humans but that psychological factors can influence the physiological factors. That is, psychological stress can lead to physiological changes, which then cause a desire disorder. It might be mentioned that drugs such as alcohol, antidepressants, and steroids can also reduce sexual desire (Becker, Johnson, & Kavoussi, 1999).

In considering treatments for desire disorders, we must determine whether a disorder stems from a physiological problem (disease, genetic factors) or a psychological problem (stress). If low levels of testosterone are due to low levels of hormone production because of a physiological

FIGURE 16.4

Men under stress showed lower levels of testosterone than did men not under stress.

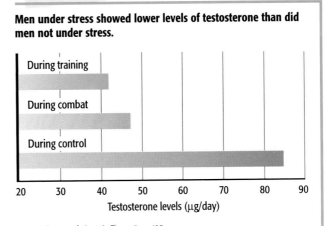

Source: Rose et al. (1969), Figure 3, p. 425.

problem, treatment for male patients may simply involve administering testosterone to bring the level up to normal, a procedure called **testosterone replacement therapy** (Bagatell & Bremner, 1996). This procedure can be very effective, as indicated by the results reported in Figure 16.3. When men with low levels of testosterone were given testosterone, their levels of sexual arousal became almost as high as those of men with normal levels of testosterone.

In contrast, if low levels of testosterone are due to the effects of stress, treatment can be directed at reducing stress. An interesting illustration of the effects of stress reduction on testosterone levels is provided by a study of men in officer candidate school (Kreuz, Rose, & Jennings, 1972). The testosterone levels of these men were measured during the first phase of the training, when stress was very high, and then again during the second phase of the training, when the men were "over the hump" and stress levels were greatly reduced. The men's levels of testosterone during the first and second phases of training are presented in Figure 16.5. Inspection of that figure reveals that testosterone levels went up when stress went down.

Let's now go on to consider arousal disorders.

Arousal Disorders

Individuals with **arousal disorders** desire sexual activity, but once the activity is initiated, they *cannot achieve an adequate level of physiological arousal or cannot maintain an adequate level of arousal.* In males the major symptom of an arousal disorder is the failure to achieve or maintain a complete erection. The prevalence of arousal disorders is estimated to be between 10% and 20% in males and between 10% and 50% in women (Laumann, 1999; Nathan, 1986). Case Study 16.1 is an excerpt from an interview with a young man who came to a clinic because of an arousal disorder.

Diagnostic Procedures

Arousal disorders can stem from either psychological or physiological causes. One approach to determining what is causing an arousal disorder is to determine whether the

> **testosterone replacement therapy** A treatment for desire disorders in males, involving bringing testosterone levels up to normal.
>
> **arousal disorder** Sexual dysfunctions in which individuals cannot achieve or maintain an adequate level of physiological arousal.
>
> **nocturnal penile tumescence** Erection of the penis during REM sleep.

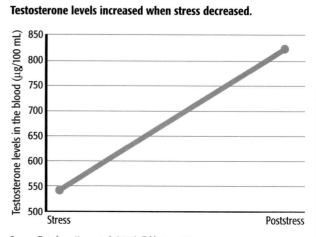

FIGURE 16.5

Testosterone levels increased when stress decreased.

Source: Data from Kreuz et al. (1972), Table 1, p. 480.

individual is physiologically capable of arousal. One technique for determining whether a male is capable of sexual arousal involves measuring **nocturnal penile tumescence** (tyoo-MES-ins). *Tumescence* refers to the state of erection, and in physiologically normal males erection occurs occasionally during periods of rapid eye movement (REM) sleep. If the individual has erections during sleep, it can be assumed that he is physiologically capable of sexual arousal and that his problems in achieving or maintaining arousal while awake must be due to psychological factors. (Note that the erections occur during REM sleep, which is associated with dreams, but the erections are not necessarily related to the nature of the dreams; rather, both the dreams and the erections are due to an increase in neurological arousal.)

Nocturnal penile tumescence is measured by placing a cuff on the penis. If erection occurs during sleep, the cuff expands, breaking a series of small seals. In the morning the seals are checked to determine whether erection occurred.

Psychological Explanations and Treatments

There is widespread agreement that *anxiety* is the major psychological cause of arousal disorders. The question is, how does anxiety reduce arousal? The answer is that individuals become distracted by whatever it is that is making them anxious, and the distraction reduces sexual arousal.

The role of distraction in reducing sexual arousal has been demonstrated in a variety of ways (Cerny, 1978; Geer & Fuhr, 1976; Henson & Rubin, 1971; Laws & Rubin, 1969). For example, it has been shown that individuals can voluntarily suppress sexual arousal while watching erotic films if they shift their attention to something else (i.e., watch the film but think about something else). Also, involuntary

Interview with a Man Complaining of an Arousal Disorder

CASE STUDY 16.1

THE CLIENT WAS A HANDSOME 34-year-old man. The early part of the interview did not offer any evidence of adjustment problems, and it was apparent that the client had an active and mature social life. The following discussion ensued when the interviewer turned the conversation to the problem that had brought the client to the clinic.

Client: Well, the problem is that—well, I just have a hard time getting an erection when I get physically involved with a woman. It's not that I don't want sex—I really do. But somehow when we get right down to it . . . when the time comes to begin making love, I can't get an erection. I'm just limp.

Interviewer: Hmmm. Can you tell me a little more about it? Can you describe a typical situation in which you have a problem?

Client: (pause) Well, let's say I've gone out with a woman for a while, and it comes to the point where one night things are getting physical. Everything goes great—I mean, I'm aroused and excited—and she is too, but then I just can't seem to go further. It's not that I don't stay excited; I'm really excited and enjoying what we're doing, but when it gets to the point at which I should have a good erection, it doesn't come.

Interviewer: Have you ever had an erection? For example, do you ever wake up in the morning with an erection, or can you get an erection with masturbation?

Client: Oh, yeah, I frequently wake up with an erection—that's normal—and I can masturbate. Sometimes it takes me a little while to get started, but I always get there.

Interviewer: How about with a woman? Do you ever get an erection with a woman?

Client: Yes. Sometimes when we just get started and we're just necking, I'll get an erection for a while, and then I think, "Great, this time we're going to make it," but then I lose it and can't get it back. It's really annoying.

Interviewer: Have you ever completed intercourse with a woman?

Client: Oh, sure. It didn't used to be a problem, but lately it just hasn't been working. It's a relatively recent problem. *(pause)* It gets kind of embarrassing. I get to a high point, and then I just can't go further. I usually hide what's happening—or not happening—and make up some excuse to, well, to bring things to an end. *(pause)* Not long ago, I dated a woman who caught on to what was going on, but she was pretty relaxed about the whole thing. She just laughed and said, "Don't worry. We'll get around

it," and we just kept making out. She kept playing with me and eventually I came around, at least for a while. She seemed to know what she was doing.

Interviewer: Has anything changed for you that might be associated with the problem? Have you had any physical or psychological problems?

Client: (sighs) No, nothing that I can think of. When the problem started, I did a little reading about it. The articles I read said that anxiety was the problem and that the trick was not to let yourself get distracted by upsetting thoughts, so I worked real hard to concentrate on what I was doing, how much I enjoyed the woman's body, and I tried not to think about the problem. *(sighs)* Great idea but tough to pull off. The problem is always there. Forcing yourself to concentrate on what you are doing is . . . well, by working to avoid the problem, you admit that there is a problem, and it doesn't seem to work for me. The work of concentrating is almost enough to wreck my arousal. *(sighs)* It's a mess—and it's frustrating as hell.

> It's not that I don't want sex— I really do.

reductions in sexual arousal occur when subjects hear erotic material in one ear but distracting material (e.g., math problems) in the other ear.

The distracting thoughts that are most common among individuals with arousal disorders involve concerns about sexual performance and failure. In other words, it is assumed that problems with arousal result because individuals worry about their sexual performance, these thoughts distract them, and then the distraction reduces arousal.

It is also worth noting that individuals with arousal disorders underestimate their levels of sexual arousal. This was demonstrated in an investigation in which males estimated their levels of sexual arousal while their actual levels of arousal were measured in terms of penile erection (Sakheim et al., 1984). The results indicated that males with psychologically based arousal disorders underestimated

their arousal more than normal males did and more than males with physiologically based arousal disorders did. Comparable results have been reported for females (Morokoff & Heinman, 1980). The tendency for individuals with arousal disorders to underestimate their arousal levels is important because their erroneous assumptions about their underarousal could contribute to their concerns and lead to additional distraction.

Treatment for psychologically based arousal disorders revolves around attempts to reduce anxiety by instilling more confidence in the individual and thereby reducing the cognitions that interfere with sexual arousal (Lo Piccolo & Stock, 1986). Therapists and clients usually report success with these techniques, but so far there is little adequately controlled research to document their long-term effectiveness (Bergin & Garfield, 1994).

Physiological Explanations and Treatments

It was once assumed that most arousal disorders were due to psychological problems, but we now know that the majority are actually due to various organic conditions. However, before discussing the physiological explanations for arousal disorders, I will comment briefly on the physiology of sexual arousal. Sexual arousal can be initiated either in the brain by sexual thoughts and desires or in the genital area by stimulation of the sex organs and the area around them. In both cases nerve impulses are sent to the lower portion (sacral section) of the spinal cord. From there parasympathetic nerve impulses are sent to the male's penis or to the female's clitoris. (The clitoris is the major site of arousal for the female, and it will be described and discussed in greater detail later, when we consider orgasmic disorders.) The parasympathetic impulses cause a dilation of the **erectile tissues** in the penis or clitoris. Erectile tissues consist of blood channels that are normally empty but, when stimulated, dilate tremendously and fill with blood. Considerable pressure builds up in erectile tissues because outgoing blood flow is restricted. Dilation and filling of the erectile tissues in the penis cause it to become enlarged and erect. In the female the dilation and filling of erectile tissues results in a swelling and firming of the clitoris. In the female the parasympathetic impulses also cause the secretion of mucus just inside the vaginal opening.

A number of physiological problems can reduce sexual arousal. For example, *neurological damage* to the hypothalamus, spinal cord, or connecting nerve pathways could result in the reduction or absence of the nerve stimulation that causes changes in blood flow. More commonly, reduced arousal stems from blockage of the arteries that supply blood to the penis or clitoris. If those arteries are blocked, the filling of the erectile tissues is limited, and therefore arousal will be reduced. This problem is more pronounced in older men, probably because men are more prone to the development of atherosclerosis during midlife (see Chapter 14).

There are two physiological treatments for arousal disorders. The first is the use of drugs that increase blood flow to the genital area. The best known of these drugs is Viagra (sildenafil) which has proven to be effective for both men and women (Derry et al., 1998; Glass et al., 1998; Goldenberg, 1998). The other treatment involves surgically implanting a prosthetic device in the penis (Metz & Mathiesen, 1979; Michal et al., 1977). This device consists of an inflatable balloon that is connected to a pump; when an erection is desired, the pump is turned on, the balloon is inflated, and the penis becomes erect.

erectile tissues   Tissues in the penis and clitoris that fill with blood during sexual arousal.

The recognition that sexual arousal disorder can be caused by various physiological conditions—rather than purely psychological problems—has led to an explosion in research on treatment methods. Pioneers in this world of sexual medicine include, from left, Jennifer Berman, urologist; Laura Berman, sex therapist; and Irwin Goldstein, urologist.

Finally, *anxiety* can lead to physiological effects that can reduce sexual arousal. Specifically, anxiety is associated with increased physiological arousal (e.g., heart rate, blood pressure) that is due to increased activity of the *sympathetic* branch of the autonomic nervous system, whereas sexual arousal is due to increased activity of the *parasympathetic* branch of the autonomic nervous system. What is important is that sympathetic activity and parasympathetic activity produce *competing* reactions. In particular, parasympathetic activity leads to the *dilation* and filling of the peripheral and erectile tissues crucial to sexual arousal, but sympathetic activity leads to *constriction* of these tissues and consequently to a drop in sexual arousal. Because sympathetic activity initially dominates parasympathetic activity, the sympathetic activity associated with anxiety can overwhelm the parasympathetic activity and reduce or elimi-nate sexual arousal. In this case a psychological factor (anxiety) causes a change in a physiological factor (reduced parasympathetic activity), which produces an arousal disorder.

The effects of chronic and acute stress (anxiety) on sexual arousal in males was demonstrated in a study of employed and unemployed men (Morokoff et al., 1987). In this study it was assumed that unemployed men were under chronic stress and that employed men were under less stress. To manipulate acute stress researchers told half of the men in each group that at the end of the laboratory session they would be asked to give a short talk about their sexual behavior to a group of students. The other half of the men were not led to believe that they would have to talk about their sexual behavior. During the laboratory session the men watched an erotic film of a heterosexual couple making love, and while they watched the film, their sexual arousal was measured by assessing changes in penis diameter (erection). The results indicated that among men who were under chronic stress, the addition of the acute stress (expecting to talk about their sex lives with students) resulted in a lower level of arousal in response to erotic stimulation than in the other men. In other words, the combination of chronic and acute stress resulted in a reduction in arousal.

 ## Orgasmic Disorders

Individuals with **orgasmic disorders** desire and participate in sexual activity, become aroused and maintain the arousal, but *they do not experience an orgasm or, in the case of males, experience orgasm too soon.* Orgasmic disorders pose problems because they deprive individuals of the pleasure they seek, and the disorders may lead to feelings of inadequacy. Indeed, at one time individuals who did not experience orgasm were referred to as sexually "inadequate" or "frigid." Those degrading labels have been abandoned, but it is still common to talk about the "failure to achieve orgasm," and that phrase reflects an underlying negative evaluation. Orgasmic disorders occur in both men and women, but they are more common in women.

Explanations and Treatments of Orgasmic Disorders in Women

In women, a distinction is sometimes made between **primary orgasmic disorder,** in which the woman has never experienced an orgasm through any means, and **secondary orgasmic disorder,** in which the woman can experience orgasm during masturbation but not during sexual intercourse. Together, these problems affect more than 24% of women (Laumann, 1994).

Traditionally, orgasmic disorders in women have been explained in terms of anxieties and unconscious conflicts associated with sex. For example, it was assumed that women who did not experience orgasm were unable to "let go" sexually. Their resistance was thought to be rooted in childhood experiences that led the women to believe that sex was dirty or harmful. If women with orgasmic disorders were not aware of such thoughts, it was assumed that they had *unconscious conflicts* about sexuality, probably revolving around unresolved attractions for their fathers or mothers.

For many years the concepts of anxiety and conflict were widely used to explain orgasmic disorders, but the popularity of those explanations has declined drastically. That

decline occurred because there was no evidence to support the effects of anxiety and conflict and because of the development of a simpler explanation that led to a very effective treatment. Specifically, it is now widely believed that most orgasmic disorders are due to the fact that women or their sexual partners *simply do not know what should be done to achieve maximal stimulation* or fail to do what they know should be done. In other words, the fact that a woman does not reach orgasm is probably due to a lack of knowledge or inadequate sexual technique rather than underlying conflicts. Support for this explanation comes from the finding that teaching women more about their bodies and educating sexual partners about what type of stimulation is most arousing are very effective methods for overcoming orgasmic disorders. To help you understand the problems that women may encounter in achieving orgasm, I will briefly discuss how stimulation does and does not occur during intercourse.

As the penis moves in the vagina during intercourse, the friction created by the penis rubbing against the walls of the vagina stimulates the sensitive penis, thereby maintaining the male's arousal and leading to his orgasm. In contrast, the movement of the penis in the vagina does not result in much direct sexual stimulation for the woman because the first two-thirds of the vagina has relatively few nerve endings and hence is not particularly sensitive to stimulation. Stated simply, intercourse is maximally effective for the attainment of the male's orgasm but is not particularly effective for achieving that goal for the female. (In that regard it is interesting to note that men and women require about the same amount of time to achieve orgasm through masturbation, but men experience orgasm much faster than women during intercourse; Offir, 1982.)

Some investigators believe that some women have a short, sexually sensitive area just inside the vagina known as the **G spot** and stimulation of that area may lead to arousal and orgasm (Addiego et al., 1981; Alzate & Hoch, 1986; Goldberg et al., 1983; Ladas, Whipple, & Perry, 1982; Perry & Whipple, 1981). However, the existence of the G spot is not well documented, and its importance is a matter of some controversy.

orgasmic disorders Sexual dysfunctions in which individuals become sexually aroused but do not experience an orgasm or, in the case of males, experience orgasm too soon.

primary orgasmic disorder An orgasmic disorder in which a woman has never experienced an orgasm through any means.

secondary orgasmic disorder An orgasmic disorder in which a woman can experience orgasm during masturbation but not during sexual intercourse.

G spot An area of the vagina that is allegedly very sensitive to sexual stimulation.

FIGURE 16.6

The clitoris is made up of erectile tissue and is the primary area of sexual stimulation for most women.

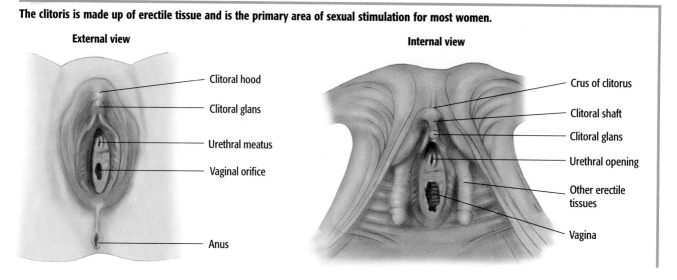

External view

- Clitoral hood
- Clitoral glans
- Urethral meatus
- Vaginal orifice
- Anus

Internal view

- Crus of clitorus
- Clitoral shaft
- Clitoral glans
- Urethral opening
- Other erectile tissues
- Vagina

The fact that the vagina is not particularly sensitive does not mean that intercourse is not pleasurable and cannot result in orgasm for women. Instead the pleasure, arousal, and orgasm experienced by women during intercourse appear to be due primarily to the stimulation of the **clitoris** (KLIT-uh-ris), which is a pea-sized structure located a small distance above the vaginal opening (see Figure 16.6). The clitoris is normally covered by a hood (a small flap of skin). Gently pulling the hood back reveals the tip of the clitoris, called the **glans.** In contrast to the vagina, the clitoris contains many nerve endings (probably more than the larger penis), and it is exceptionally sensitive to stimulation. In fact, it is so sensitive that some women do not want it touched directly and prefer that it be stimulated indirectly by caressing the area around it, which serves to move the hood and thereby stimulates the glans.

Because the clitoris is easily manipulated and its manipulation results in sexual arousal, the clitoris plays an important role in achieving orgasm through masturbation. The clitoris also plays an important role in sexual arousal and orgasm during intercourse because as the penis moves in and out of the vagina, it causes the tissues around the vaginal opening to move. That movement causes the hood over the clitoral glans to move, stimulating the glans and thereby providing pleasurable sensations and orgasm.

The clitoris is actually the end of the clitoral shaft, which extends back into the body and then divides into two leg-like structures (see Figure 16.6). The clitoral shaft contains erectile tissues like those in the penis, and during sexual excitement the erectile tissues of the clitoris fill with blood, causing a swelling such that the shaft doubles or triples in size. The pressure caused by the increase in size results in greater sensitivity, which contributes to increased arousal. Because of the size and importance of the underlying structures, the small clitoris and glans have been referred to as the "tip of an erogenous iceberg."

Treatment for orgasmic disorders using education entails a number of steps. First, it may be necessary for the woman to learn more about her body and what gives her pleasure. This may involve sitting down with a mirror and visually exploring her body, followed by gentle touching, fondling, or massaging of the genital area to discover where and what type of stimulation is most effective for achieving sexual arousal. Such exploration and self-stimulation may have previously been avoided or forbidden by traditional attitudes toward sexuality. In most cases manual stimulation is sufficient to achieve arousal and orgasm, but sometimes a device or vibrator is used as an aid. Essentially, the woman learns to achieve orgasm through masturbation. (This step is not needed with secondary orgasmic disorder, in which orgasm can be achieved through masturbation.)

The next step involves having the woman communicate to her partner what arouses her. Because it is sometimes difficult to talk about these things, some therapists suggest that the woman take her partner's hand and gently guide him and show him the kind of stimulation she wants. Once the couple is comfortable with this form of genital stimulation, it is suggested that they attempt intercourse. Many therapists suggest that the first intercourse should be done with the woman on top because that way she has the major responsibility for movement and can better control the nature of the stimulation. Once orgasm has been achieved in this position, the couple is encouraged to experiment with other positions.

Communication plays an important role in the treatment of sexual disorders. A woman who experiences an orgasmic disorder is encouraged to communicate to her partner what arouses her.

Education, self-exploration, self-stimulation, communication with the partner, and practice are all important steps in this therapy. However, couples must also develop attitudes of self-acceptance and responsibility for their own sexual pleasure. The woman must realize that *sex is not something that just happens or is done to her* but rather something in which *she actively participates and for which she shares control* with her partner.

This approach to the treatment of orgasmic disorders is very effective, with success rates usually reported to be greater than 75% (see reviews by Marks, 1981; Masters & Johnson, 1970; Offir, 1982; van Lankveld, 1998). The proportion of women with primary orgasmic disorder who are subsequently able to experience an orgasm with masturbation may be as high as 95%.

It should not be concluded that overcoming an orgasmic disorder is always a strictly mechanical or educational process. There is no doubt that anxiety about sex or interpersonal tensions with her partner can interfere with a woman's arousal and enjoyment of sex and can reduce the likelihood of an orgasm. However, it is now clear that anxiety is less important than it was once thought to be, and in many cases anxiety and interpersonal tension may be the *result* of problems with sex rather than their cause. For example, a woman who feels that her partner does not understand or is not sensitive to her needs may become tense or resentful in their sexual relationship, and that may disrupt her personal relationship with her partner. This disruption interferes with communication and reduces the likelihood that the sexual problem will be resolved, allowing a vicious cycle to develop. In such cases attention must be given to personal and interpersonal problems as well as to education and technique.

Explanations and Treatments of Orgasmic Disorders in Men

Fewer than 10% of males are unable to achieve orgasm, and consequently relatively little attention has been given to this problem (Spector & Carey, 1990). In contrast, an orgasmic disorder that occurs in almost 40% of males is **premature ejaculation** (Carver, 1998). As the term implies, this disorder involves reaching orgasm *too soon*. Specifically, ejaculation occurs after only minimal stimulation, before the male wishes it and before his partner has been sufficiently stimulated and satisfied.

Numerous explanations have been offered to account for premature ejaculation. For example, it has been attributed to supersensitivity of the penis, which leads to excessively high levels of stimulation, and to a lack of sexual activity, which results in a buildup that cannot be restrained. Unfortunately, there is no good evidence for any of the explanations that have been proposed, and we do not yet understand the cause of premature ejaculation.

However, despite the fact that we do not yet understand the cause of premature ejaculation, there are three effective treatments for the problem. The first is known as the

clitoris   A pea-sized body that is located a small distance above the vaginal opening and is extremely sensitive to sexual stimulation.

glans   The tip of the clitoris.

premature ejaculation   A type of orgasmic disorder in men that involves reaching orgasm too soon.

start–stop technique. It involves stimulation of the penis, as in masturbation, until a high level of arousal is achieved (the start phase). Then the stimulation is stopped before the level of arousal gets to the point of ejaculation. During the stop phase the arousal subsides, and then the procedure is repeated. This is done three or four times on any one day and is usually practiced two or three times per week. Gradually, the length of time between the start of stimulation and the point of ejaculation becomes longer. The prolongation of arousal before ejaculation achieved in the practice sessions appears to generalize well to sexual activity with a partner.

The second treatment is known as the **start–squeeze technique** (Masters & Johnson, 1970). The start–squeeze technique is very similar to the start–stop technique except that when arousal becomes high, instead of simply stopping the stimulation, the individual firmly squeezes the end of the penis. Doing so does not hurt, but it immediately reduces arousal and eliminates the urge to ejaculate. The squeeze seems to be a fast way to reduce arousal between periods of stimulation. Both the start–stop and start–squeeze techniques are very effective for treating premature ejaculation, and success rates as high as 90–98% have been reported (Kilmann & Auerbach, 1979). It is encouraging that these treatments are effective, but we still do not understand the cause of premature ejaculation or why these treatments are effective for overcoming this orgasmic disorder.

The third effective treatment for premature ejaculation involves the use of *antidepressant drugs,* such as Prozac and Zoloft. When I discussed these drugs in Chapter 8, I pointed out that one negative side effect was that they eliminated or greatly prolonged the time to orgasm or ejaculation (Nafziger et al., 1999; Rosen, Lane, & Menza, 1999). Prolonging the time to ejaculation may pose a problem for individuals who do not have problems with ejaculation, but it is exactly what individuals suffering from premature orgasm want. There is a substantial amount of evidence that antidepressants are very effective for treating premature ejaculation (Haensel et al., 1998; Strassberg et al., 1999). Indeed, in one study the use of an antidepressant increased the time to ejaculation from 30 seconds to 10 minutes (Waldinger, Hengeveld, & Zwinderman, 1994). Although the drugs work, in view of their cost and their side effects,

it seems wiser to try the start–stop or start–squeeze techniques first.

THINKING CRITICALLY

Questions about Sexual Dysfunctions

What is the role of depression in sexual dysfunctions? Depression can play a major role in sexual dysfunctions, particularly desire and arousal disorders. Specifically, depression is associated with reduced sexual desire and arousal (see Chapter 8). The link between depression and reduced sexual desire/arousal exists because depression is caused in part by reduced activity in the hypothalamus, which is also responsible for sexual activity. When depression causes a sexual dysfunction, the dysfunction is a *secondary effect* of the depression rather than a separate disorder. When a sexual dysfunction is a secondary effect of depression, the treatment must be focused on the depression, not on the sexual problem. Paradoxically, however, although the use of antidepressants can relieve depression and return sexual desire and arousal to normal levels, many of these drugs reduce the likelihood of orgasm and thereby cause an orgasmic disorder (see the discussion of side effects of antidepressants in Chapter 8). To avoid that problem, individuals may use one of the atypical antidepressants such as Wellbutrin, which reduces depression and increases sexual desire but apparently does not influence orgasm.

TOPIC II

Paraphilias

Annette and her husband love each other very much and would not think of hurting each other. However, for Annette to become sexually aroused, it is necessary for her husband to slap her face and twist her arm behind her back until it hurts. He does not like doing it, but Annette wants him to do it, because it is the only way she can become aroused. Thus, they have gone through this ritual every time they have had sex for the past 8 years. Annette suffers from *sexual masochism.* Why does pain lead to sexual arousal for Annette?

James has had sexual relationships with a couple of women, but his favorite way of achieving sexual gratification is to dress in women's clothing and then masturbate. Wearing women's clothing is very exciting for him, and he has three different outfits hidden in the bottom drawer of his dresser. This behavior is an example of *transvestic fetishism.* Is this related to homosexuality? Do all cross-dressers gain sexual arousal from the behavior?

---

start–stop technique   A treatment for premature ejaculation.

start–squeeze technique   A treatment for premature ejaculation.

paraphilias   A class of sexual disorders that revolve around abnormal means of achieving sexual arousal.

Paraphilias (par-uh-FIL-e-uz) are sexual disorders that revolve around *abnormal means of achieving sexual arousal*. The major symptoms of paraphilias are recurrent sexual urges, fantasies, and arousal that are associated with (1) nonhuman objects such as articles of clothing, (2) suffering or humiliation, or (3) nonconsenting individuals such as children. (The term *paraphilia* is derived from *para*, meaning "abnormal," and *philia*, meaning "attraction," so paraphilias are abnormal sexual attractions.)

We do not know how widespread paraphilias are because the behaviors are usually private and often occur either without a partner or with a partner who consents and therefore does not report the behavior. Furthermore, in some cases a sexual partner may not even be aware that the other individual's arousal stems from a paraphilia. For example, a woman having sex with a man may not realize that his arousal stems from her clothes or from fantasies about harming her rather than from her and her body.

Despite the fact that reports of paraphilias are relatively rare, it is believed that the prevalence of these disorders is high. This assumption is based in part on the fact that there are hundreds of catalogs for paraphiliac paraphernalia such as whips, chains, handcuffs, and leather sex suits, and there are numerous magazines devoted to things such as child pornography and transvestism (dressing in the clothes of the opposite sex). It is generally assumed that with the exception of sexual masochism, paraphilias are found primarily in men.

Because many or most individuals with paraphilias keep their behaviors private, our understanding of these disorders is based on a very limited and probably unrepresentative subset of individuals; we must therefore be very cautious in drawing conclusions from the existing data. For example, individuals with paraphilias are sometimes described as less intelligent and more likely to have other adjustment or legal problems, but it is probable that only more inept individuals have been caught engaging in these behaviors and then studied.

Before beginning our discussion of paraphilias, I should point out three qualifications: First, abnormal means of gaining sexual arousal are not diagnosed as paraphilias unless "the fantasies, urges, or sexual arousal cause clinically significant distress or impairment in social, occupational, or other important areas of functioning" (American Psychiatric Association, 1994, p. 523). For example, a man may find women's underwear arousing, but that is not considered abnormal unless the man is distressed by the arousal or it interferes with his functioning. Second, for a diagnosis of paraphilia to be made, the behavior must have resulted in "recurrent, intense sexual urges or behaviors" for a period of at least 6 months (American Psychiatric Association, 1994). In other words, occasional arousal or brief experimentation does not constitute a disorder and

should not be a source of alarm. Third, in many cases paraphilias such as fetishes (using objects of clothing as a part of the sex act) are relatively harmless when acted out with a consenting adult partner. In such cases, the major problem is that the partner may not share the paraphilia and will therefore not find the behavior pleasurable. However, paraphilias can be *very serious when they involve nonconsenting individuals or children*.

Eight paraphilias are identified in *DSM-IV*. I will briefly describe each and then go on to discuss their suspected causes and treatments. The symptoms of these paraphilias are summarized in Table 16.2.

TABLE 16.2

Paraphilias and their symptoms

Paraphilia	Symptoms
Exhibitionism	Sexually arousing fantasies, sexual urges, or behaviors involving exposure of the genitals to an unsuspecting stranger
Fetishism	Sexually arousing fantasies, sexual urges, or behaviors involving the use of nonliving objects
Transvestic fetishism	Sexually arousing fantasies, sexual urges, or behaviors involving cross-dressing by a heterosexual male
Frotteurism	Sexually arousing fantasies, sexual urges, or behaviors involving touching and rubbing against a nonconsenting person
Pedophilia	Sexually arousing fantasies, sexual urges, or behaviors involving a prepubescent child
Sexual masochism	Sexually arousing fantasies, sexual urges, or behaviors involving being humiliated or made to suffer
Sexual sadism	Sexually arousing fantasies, sexual urges, or behaviors in which the psychological or physical suffering of the victim is sexually exciting to the person
Voyeurism	Sexually arousing fantasies, sexual urges, or behaviors involving the act of observing an unsuspecting person who is naked, in the process of disrobing, or engaging in sexual activity

Note: To be considered a disorder, the fantasies, urges, or behaviors must have lasted for at least 6 months and must cause distress and impairment in functioning.

Source: Adapted from American Psychiatric Association (1994).

Types of Paraphilias

In the following sections I will describe the unique characteristics of each of the paraphilias.

Exhibitionism

Exhibitionism involves having fantasies about or actually *exposing the genitals to an unsuspecting stranger* in order to achieve sexual arousal. Exhibitionism does not lead to further sexual activity with the stranger, and therefore exhibitionists do not pose a physical danger to others. The classic example of an exhibitionist is the "flasher" who suddenly opens his coat to expose himself to an unsuspecting woman. Some years ago "streaking" (running nude in public places) was a frequent prank on college campuses, but it did not result in arousal (at least not for the streaker) and therefore would not be considered exhibitionism.

A variety of surveys suggest that about 60% of exhibitionists are married and that they do not differ from the general population in intelligence, educational level, or vocation. There is also evidence that they are no more likely to suffer from other forms of abnormal behavior than the general population (Blair & Lanyon, 1981). An example of exhibitionism is described in Case Study 16.2.

Fetishism

The major symptom of **fetishism** is the use of *nonliving objects (fetishes)* to obtain sexual arousal. The most common fetish objects are articles of women's clothing such as bras, underpants, stockings, shoes, and boots. The individual often masturbates while fondling, kissing, or smelling the fetish object. In some cases the individual's sexual partner wears the object during sexual encounters, thereby providing an arousing stimulus that enables the fetishist to participate in otherwise normal sexual behavior. The diagnosis of fetishism is not used when an individual gains sexual pleasure from the use of nonliving objects such as vibrators that are designed to stimulate sexual arousal.

Transvestic Fetishism

Heterosexual men who suffer from **transvestic fetishism** gain sexual pleasure from *dressing in women's clothing*, a behavior that is often referred to as *cross-dressing*. Cross-dressing can range from wearing only one article of women's clothing while alone to dressing completely in women's clothing and appearing that way in public. In some cases the cross-dressing is so effective that it is difficult to distinguish a cross-dressed transvestite from a woman. However, the goal of an individual with transvestic fetishism is not to "pass" as a woman but to achieve sexual

---

Exhibitionism in a 43-Year-Old Man

CASE STUDY 16.2

> He described "the chase" as a "very exciting part of the whole thing."

THE CLIENT WAS A MARRIED, college-educated, 43-year-old man of average appearance who was the manager of a small printing business. He was referred to the clinic by the court after his second arrest for exposing himself in public. On each occasion he had exposed himself to an attractive woman. In his initial interview he admitted that he had probably exposed himself as often as once a month for the past 20 years.

His acts of exhibitionism always occurred in public places such as busy streets, entrances to department stores, or subway platforms as the train pulled out. After exposing himself, he would run and quickly lose himself in the crowd.

The exposures were not spontaneous events but were instead carefully planned over a couple of days, and the planning was associated with increasing anticipation, excitement, and tension. Just before the exposure he would have an erection, and by slipping his hand through an opening in the bottom of his coat pocket, he would unzip his pants and pull his penis and testicles forward and out of his pants. Then when he was directly in front of the woman, he would open his coat and stand with his genitals exposed. After 2 or 3 seconds he would pull his coat closed and run away. He would usually run two or three blocks, often dodging through stores and across streets. He described "the chase" as a "very exciting part of the whole thing." After the chase he felt "exhausted but relaxed—you know, like you feel after good sex."

A psychological examination did not reveal anything particularly striking about the client. The only other unusual sexual behavior he reported involved going to a "male peep show" in the back of a porno bookstore a few times. His wife reported that he always seemed "completely normal." She commented that their sex life was "limited but OK." She repeatedly mused, "I can't figure this out. It just doesn't make sense." The patient's reaction was mixed. He seemed thoroughly ashamed and chagrined about being caught, but there was a tone of futility and hollowness in his promise that he would not do it again, an attitude shared by the clinic staff. To avoid prosecution the client agreed to treatment.

Men suffering from transvestic fetishism gain sexual pleasure from dressing in women's clothing.

Frotteurism usually takes place in crowded public places, such as the subway, where minor instances of rubbing can be attributed to simply bumping into the other person.

arousal. It is interesting to note that *DSM-IV* limits this disorder to *heterosexual men;* a homosexual male or a woman who dresses as a man would not be diagnosed as suffering from transvestic fetishism.

A man with transvestic fetishism will often masturbate while dressed in women's clothes and may fantasize about other men being attracted to him while he is so dressed. In a very limited number of cases, homosexual males may cross-dress to attract other men, but homosexual males who do so are not diagnosed as having transvestic fetishism because the cross-dressing is not used to gain sexual arousal. Similarly, female impersonators may cross-dress as part of a stage act, but unless they gain sexual pleasure from the cross-dressing itself, they are not diagnosed as having transvestic fetishism. Finally, it is important to recognize that the presence of transvestic fetishism does not necessarily preclude participation in normal sexual relationships, as illustrated in Case Study 16.3 (on p. 480).

Frotteurism

The diagnostic label **frotteurism** (fro-TUR-iz-um) is derived from the French word *frotter,* which means "to rub," and the disorder involves *rubbing against or touching a nonconsenting individual.* The rubbing is usually done in crowded public places such as stores or on public transportation where minor instances of rubbing can be attrib-

uted to simply bumping into the other person. In such situations a male might rub his genitals against the thighs or buttocks of a woman. In more overt cases the male may actually fondle the woman's genitalia or breasts and then flee when she realizes what is happening.

Pedophilia

Pedophilia (ped-uh-FIL-e-uh) refers to a *sexual attraction to children.* (*Pedo* comes from a Greek word that means "child.") In most cases of pedophilia the child is younger than 13 years old (prepuberty), and the molesting individual is a male aged 16 or older (postpuberty). Attraction to girls is reported to be twice as common as attraction to boys, but many individuals with pedophilia are attracted to both girls and boys.

exhibitionism   A paraphilia involving having fantasies about or actually exposing the genitals to an unsuspecting stranger in order to achieve sexual arousal.

fetishism   A paraphilia involving the use of nonliving objects (fetishes) to obtain sexual arousal.

transvestic fetishism   A paraphilia in which a heterosexual man gains sexual pleasure from dressing in women's clothing; often referred to as *cross-dressing.*

frotteurism   A paraphilia in which sexual arousal is obtained by rubbing against or touching a nonconsenting individual.

pedophilia   A paraphilia involving sexual attraction to children.

Transvestic Fetishism in a Happily Married Man: His Wife's Report

CASE STUDY 16.3

. . . dressing in women's clothes was something that was just "separate from everything else" . . .

"ALLAN AND I WERE MARRIED during the summer before our senior year in college. Married life was great. We had a cozy apartment close to campus, our classes and grades went well, and we really loved being married. It was wonderful—until one terrible afternoon in December. I had classes in the afternoon, but that day I didn't feel very well, so I cut my 2 o'clock chem lab and went home to the apartment. When I walked in, I got the shock of my life. *Allan was sitting on the bed dressed in my clothes—hose, skirt, blouse, and jewelry— the works!* He even had one of my bras under the blouse, but he couldn't snap it because it was too small. I couldn't believe it, and at first I just stood stock-still and stared.

"As soon as Allan saw me, he jumped up and started to 'explain.' I became so upset, I don't remember everything he said, but I know he tried to tell me that he had a multiple personality. He said that I married the 'straight' half and this was his 'other half.' He said that the half that married me didn't know about this and that everything was all right with that half. I didn't believe a word he was saying. I thought that he was making it up as an excuse. I didn't know what to think; I was in shock. There sat my husband dressed in my clothes—and he'd been doing it for months! I finally just broke down and cried; my neat little world was coming apart. Allan changed clothes and tried to comfort me, but I didn't want him to touch me. Finally, he went out for a walk so that I could be alone for a while.

"By the time he came back, I had settled down emotionally, but I still didn't know what to do. He sat down and explained that he was ashamed of what he had done and that the story about having a multiple personality was just an excuse. He admitted that he had been dressing in women's clothing secretly since he was 12 or 14 but that he didn't know how it all started. It just did, and it had been going on for a long time. He told me that sometimes he just sat in the clothes, and other times he masturbated. He seemed really ashamed of that. He said he never went out of the house dressed that way and that he never did it with anyone else. He told me he wasn't a homosexual. After a while he told me that he loved me, that our sex had always been really good for him, that dressing in women's clothes was something that was just 'separate from everything else,' and that he was sorry. My feelings were confused. I loved Allan, but I felt weird with him.

That night he slept on the couch. The next day we went to a counselor at the university clinic. I didn't know what would happen. I thought that maybe there was some form of drug therapy or that we should consider divorce. The counselor was pretty calm about the whole thing, but he really didn't have much to say, either. We saw him once a week for a couple of months. One thing that came from the sessions is that I learned that Allan's cross-dressing problem is a 'stand-alone' problem, and it does not mean that there is anything else wrong with Allan. I was relieved about that. The other thing that happened in our sessions was that we came to view Allan's cross-dressing as a 'mistake' or as an 'alternative sexual behavior.' The analogy was to an affair—it was an inappropriate indiscretion that could be stopped. You couldn't erase the past, but you could try to forget (forgive?) it and go on. That may be stretching the point a bit, but it is a way of thinking about it that helps us. It's been two years since that December afternoon. The topic of the cross-dressing is still a bit touchy, but usually I don't think about it, and Allan and I are very happy. Sometimes you just have to 'go with the flow' and take things one step at a time. Allan had kind of an unusual affair, but it's over and behind us now."

The activities undertaken by a child molester may include undressing the child and looking at the child's naked body, exposing himself to the child, masturbating in the presence of the child, fondling the child, engaging in oral sex with the child, and penetrating the child's vagina, mouth, or anus with fingers or penis. In many cases it is not necessary for the offending individual to use physical force because the child is not aware of the inappropriate nature of the activities, and the offender presents them as "games." However, force is used in some cases, and sometimes elaborate ruses or threats of punishment are employed to prevent the child from informing others about the activities.

Individuals who sexually molest children are often thought of as "marginal characters" or "dirty old men," but this is usually not the case. Child molestation is an abnormal act, reflecting a serious problem, but the typical child molester is an otherwise respectable, law-abiding individual who began the behavior while a teenager (Groth et al., 1982). Furthermore, most child molesters are not strangers to their victims; in many cases they are brothers, fathers, or uncles of the victims (Conte & Berliner, 1981). It is proba-

sexual masochism   A paraphilia in which an individual derives sexual pleasure from being abused or from suffering.

sexual sadism   A paraphilia in which an individual derives sexual pleasure from causing others to suffer.

bly because child molesters do not fit the stereotype that many of them go undetected; no one suspects these otherwise normal individuals of engaging in such behavior, and reports by the children may be disregarded.

An important distinction has been made between molesters who *have a preference for children* and molesters who *use children as substitutes for adult sexual partners* (Groth & Birnbaum, 1978; Groth et al., 1982; Howells, 1981). Those who prefer children to adults are usually unmarried, their victims are often males rather than females, and their offenses are generally planned and form a consistent part of their lives. In contrast, individuals who use children as substitutes are primarily attracted to adults as sexual partners, they have more or less normal sexual histories, and their abuse of children seems to be impulsive and associated with periods of life stress or rejection. As with most distinctions in psychology, this distinction between preference and substitution probably represents two ends of a continuum rather than a dichotomy. However, the distinction highlights the fact that it is difficult to impossible to generalize about individuals who suffer from pedophilia (Lanyon, 1986).

Sexual Masochism

The diagnosis of **sexual masochism** (MAS-uh-kiz-um) is used when an individual derives sexual pleasure from *being abused* or from *suffering.* The abuse may be verbal and involve humiliation, but it is more likely to be physical and involve being beaten, bound, or tortured. Masochistic activities may be used independently of other sexual acts, as when an individual gains sexual pleasure from simply being hurt by another person, or masochistic activities may be combined with sexual acts, as when an individual wants to be beaten during intercourse.

One woman client reported that she could become aroused only if her partner "treated me like a whore and pretended to rape me," and a male client could maintain arousal during intercourse only if his partner scratched or dug into his back with a sharp fork. For these individuals being humiliated or experiencing pain was the only way they could achieve or maintain sexual arousal. In some cases masochism is played out only in fantasies. The fantasies may involve being raped or being held or bound by others so that there is no possibility of escape. An otherwise well-adjusted individual suffering from sexual masochism is described in Case Study 16.4.

Sexual Sadism

Sexual sadism (SA-diz-um) is the flip side of sexual masochism in that an individual with this disorder derives sexual pleasure from *causing others to suffer.* Sadists may physically abuse their partners during sexual activity as a

Sexual Masochism in an Otherwise Normal Man

ONE 26-YEAR-OLD, middle-class, college-educated man routinely visited a prostitute who would remain dressed but undress him and then beat him with a rolled-up newspaper. The beating was only somewhat painful, but the slapping of the paper against his skin made a considerable amount of noise. Taking a beating like this resulted in intense sexual arousal, and as the beating became harder and faster, he would ejaculate.

The man's ability to attain sexual arousal in normal foreplay with a woman was very limited, and usually he became aroused only if he fantasized that after becoming aroused, he was going to be severely beaten by the woman. He never told his partners that his arousal was due to his fantasies. Because his normal sexual activities with women were relatively unsuccessful and because he did not want to tell

his partners what they would have to do to really "turn him on," he limited most of his sexual activities to the prostitute, whom he paid to "do what I needed."

The young man came to the clinic for a "checkup" to make sure that he did not have any other problem. He said that some years ago, he had come to terms with the fact that he "did things a little differently," but he wanted assurance that his "eccentricity" was not a sign of some other problem of which he was not aware. Despite a very thorough examination, no signs of any psychological disturbance other than sexual masochism could be found. The only relevant childhood experience he was able to recall was that he once became very upset when his older brother was severely spanked with a rolled-up newspaper. He was informed that no

other problems were apparent, and he was offered treatment for the masochism. He declined treatment, pointing out, "It's not causing me any other problems, I'm not hurting anyone, I'm not doing anything illegal, and I'm enjoying myself. What I do is a little different, but so what?" He mused that it might be easier if he enjoyed normal sex but indicated that he did not want "to fix what is working pretty well for me." A follow-up call made a year later by a member of the clinic staff did not reveal any evidence of change in the young man's sexual behavior, attitude, or general adjustment.

CASE STUDY 16.4

> . . . usually he became aroused only if he fantasized that after becoming aroused, he was going to be severely beaten by the woman.

Sexual Sadism in a 47-Year-Old Man

THE PATIENT WAS a 47-year-old man who was unable to obtain sexual satisfaction unless he hurt his wife. Throughout the 25 years of their marriage, the patient had frequently handcuffed his wife, shaved her head, stuck pins in her back, and hit her as a means of achieving ejaculation. Although his behaviors were often extreme, he never hurt his wife seriously enough for her to require medical attention, and because she never took legal action, the problem went undetected. In addition to the actual behavior, the patient was preoccupied with sadistic fantasies, which made it difficult for him to concentrate and work.

The patient was clearly aware of the inappropriate nature of his behavior, and after each occurrence, he was disgusted with himself and remorseful. To avoid the problem, when he felt the tension mounting, he would stay at the office late. Alternative means of obtaining sexual gratification were largely ineffective. Masturbation led to an erection, but he could achieve ejaculation only if he hurt his wife.

Source: Adapted from Berlin and Meinecke (1981), p. 605.

means of achieving arousal and satisfaction. An "ideal" couple might include a sadist and a masochist. Case Study 16.5 concerns a case of sexual sadism; we will return to this case later when we discuss treatment. In some cases sexual sadism becomes extremely brutal and bizarre, and the individuals known to be responsible for the behavior attract widespread publicity. Unfortunately, at present we know relatively little about these individuals, and their "profiles" do not distinguish them from many other individuals (Dietz, Hazelwood, & Warren, 1990).

Voyeurism

The disorder known as **voyeurism** (vwa-YUR-iz-um) involves gaining sexual pleasure from *observing an unsuspecting individual who is naked, disrobing, or engaging in sexual activity.* The "peeping Tom" who looks into a woman's window at night is the classic example of a voyeur. It is important to note that a voyeur does not seek contact or actual sexual activity with the individual he or she is watching. Instead the simple act of looking and fantasizing about being with the individual is sufficient to achieve sexual pleasure; in some cases the voyeur may masturbate while watching or later while recalling what was seen.

A huge industry is built on the needs of voyeurs. It includes pornographic magazines, movies, videotapes, strip shows, and "peep shows," where a man can sit alone in a small room and "peep" through a small window at a woman stripping. It should not be concluded that all viewing for sexual pleasure necessarily reflects a paraphilia. On the contrary, viewing is often an important component of normal sexual behavior, and it is considered a disorder only if it results in distress for the viewer.

Other Problems

Before concluding this section, I should point out that we now know that some individuals gain sexual arousal by *depriving themselves of oxygen* for brief periods of time, for example, by hanging themselves. Apparently, when they are deprived of oxygen and fighting for their lives, the individuals become very aroused and that arousal leads to sexual arousal. Unfortunately, in some cases the process goes too far, and the individuals die (Hucker & Blanchard, 1992; O'Halloran & Dietz, 1993; Tough, Butt, & Sanders, 1994). Using oxygen deprivation to gain sexual arousal is known as **autoerotic asphyxiation.** This behavior pattern fits within the definition of paraphilias, but it is not yet defined as a disorder. A related strategy for increasing sexual arousal involves inhaling substances (e.g., amyl nitrate) that reduce oxygen to the brain. The arousal induced by the oxygen deficit apparently spreads to sex and increases the intensity of the experience. This *inhalation masturbation* is less dangerous than hanging, but it can be very harmful; for example, it can lead to a heart attack.

A huge industry is built on the needs of voyeurs as well as normal individuals who experience sexual pleasure from observing.

Explanations and Treatments

With an understanding of the symptoms of paraphilias as background, we can now consider why these disorders occur and what can be done to treat them.

Psychodynamic Approaches

The psychodynamic explanation for sexual sadism is based on Freud's idea that sex and aggression are basic instincts and that *the arousal from those instincts is interchangeable.* In other words, the arousal that is associated with aggression can be transferred to (spill over to) sex, and in that way aggressive acts such as whipping or beating can lead to sexual arousal (Bieber, 1974; Freud, 1920/1955c). In contrast, the transfer of arousal from sex to aggression can be used to explain instances in which sadism occurs after the individual is sexually aroused and sex is in progress; in that case sexual arousal increases aggressive arousal. It is noteworthy that minor aggressive acts such as biting often occur at the height of normal sexual behavior and have been used as evidence for the sex-to-aggression transfer.

The explanation of masochism posed a problem for most psychodynamic theorists because Freud asserted that humans are driven by the pursuit of pleasure (see Chapter 2), but masochism involves the seeking of *pain* (Bieber, 1974; Freud, 1915/1955a, 1919/1955b, 1925/1955c). However, Freud (1920/1955d) suggested that there is another instinct, the *death instinct,* and masochism is a reflection of our unconscious wish to be hurt and die.

The traditional psychodynamic explanation for exhibitionism and transvestism is that they are attempts to deny the possibility of castration (Bak & Stewart, 1974). For example, with exhibitionism, a male who is concerned about castration can convince himself and others that he has not been castrated; with transvestic fetishism (cross-dressing), a male who is concerned about castration can deny that women have been castrated because beneath the women's clothing there is a penis. These psychodynamic explanations were once widely accepted, but there is no evidence for them; today they are largely ignored.

Learning Approaches

Learning theorists attribute paraphilias to *classical conditioning.* Specifically, they suggest that paraphilias develop when sexual arousal is paired with an object or activity so that later the object or activity elicits sexual arousal. For example, a young boy may happen to experience sexual arousal while being physically punished, and the pairing leads to an association between punishment and sexual arousal. Therefore, when the young man is punished in the future, he will experience sexual arousal. As a consequence he will seek punishment to achieve sexual arousal and thus develop sexual masochism.

Support for the classical conditioning explanation comes from laboratory research in which paraphilias were developed by pairing sexual arousal with previously neutral stimuli (Langevin & Martin, 1975; Plaud & Martini, 1999; Rackman, 1966; Rackman & Hodgson, 1968). For example, in one investigation 10 men were first shown a slide of a pair of women's boots (a neutral stimulus) while their sexual arousal was assessed. (Sexual arousal was assessed with a device that measured changes in penis size.) Next, in a series of trials the men were again shown the slide of the boots, but immediately after the boots were shown, the men were shown a slide of a scantily dressed woman (a source of sexual arousal). In other words, the boots were paired with sexual arousal. Finally, when the men were shown only the slide of the boots, every one of the men responded with sexual arousal! That is, after the boots were paired with sexual arousal, simply seeing the boots resulted in an erection. Furthermore, for some of the men the effects of the conditioning generalized to related objects, and the men showed sexual arousal when they were shown slides of a pair of high-heeled black shoes and a pair of gold sandals. In these experiments, then, paraphilias were developed in the laboratory through classical conditioning. It is interesting to note that in one study of individuals with foot fetishism, many reported that feet (shoes, socks, etc.) reminded them of a pleasurable (arousing) experience (Weinberg, Williams, & Colham, 1994).

With regard to this explanation, a question arises: How does sexual arousal originally get paired with nonsexual stimuli? In answering that question, it should first be noted that emotions such as anger, anxiety, and sexual desire *all result in similar patterns of physiological arousal.* Indeed, unless changes in the genital area are taken into account, it is usually impossible to determine what emotion an individual is experiencing by measuring only physiological arousal. One implication of the similarity of arousal across emotions is that *arousal generated by one emotion can be transferred and therefore can provide the basis for another emotion* (Schach-ter, 1964; Zillmann, 1983). The transfer usually happens through *relabeling* of the arousal. For example, an individual who is fearful will experience arousal, but the arousal may be labeled as sex rather than fear, and therefore the arousal will be *experienced* as sex

voyeurism A paraphilia in which an individual gains sexual pleasure from observing an unsuspecting individual who is naked, disrobing, or engaging in sexual activity

autoerotic asphyxiation Using oxygen deprivation (partial strangling) to gain sexual arousal.

rather than fear. The transfer of arousal across emotions is referred to as **arousal transference.**

Evidence that arousal from other emotions can be transferred and lead to sexual arousal has been provided by a number of interesting experiments (e.g., Berscheid & Walster, 1974; Dutton & Aron, 1974; Redmond, Kosten, & Peiser, 1982; Roviaro & Holmes, 1980). For example, males who had just been frightened by walking across a swaying suspension bridge showed more interest in a female experimenter and used more sexual themes in the stories they told in response to the Thematic Apperception Test than did males who had just walked across a stable bridge (Dutton & Aron, 1974). In another experiment male college students who rode a bicycle vigorously before meeting a woman rated the woman as more attractive than did men who did not ride a bicycle before meeting her (White et al., 1981). Indeed, men felt more romantically attracted to a woman after listening to a gruesome description of a man being mutilated by a mob than after listening to a description of the circulatory system of a frog. That is, the arousal generated by the exercise or gruesome story got transferred to sex.

Arousal transference involving sex is apparently frequent among adolescents, for whom sex is relatively new and not yet well defined. For example, studies of adolescent boys indicate that approximately 50% experience an erection from some type of nonsexual but exciting stimulus such as an accident, a fire, being chased, or being punished (Bancroft, 1970).

The notion that paraphilias are the result of classical conditioning has led to a treatment strategy known as **aversion therapy,** which involves pairing anxiety with the paraphiliac object or activity so that in the future the object or activity will elicit anxiety instead of sexual arousal (Barker, 1965; Cooper, 1964; Kushner, 1965; Marks & Gelder, 1967; Marks, Gelder, & Bancroft, 1970; Raymond & O'Keefe, 1965). In essence, the goal of aversion therapy is to develop a classically conditioned phobia for the paraphiliac object or activity. In one study of aversion therapy, individuals with transvestic fetishes participated in training sessions in which they wore electrodes through which they could be given painful shocks by remote control (Marks & Gelder, 1967). Shocks were administered whenever the individuals began putting on any article of women's clothing or when they indicated that they were fantasizing about women's clothing. The results indicated that as training progressed,

arousal transference The idea that arousal can be transferred across different emotions (e.g., from fear to sex).

aversion therapy A treatment strategy that involves pairing anxiety with a paraphiliac object or activity so that in the future the object or activity will elicit anxiety in addition to or instead of sexual arousal.

the clients became less and less likely to have erections while handling or thinking about women's clothing. It is noteworthy that the training procedures did not reduce the clients' sexual responsiveness to appropriate sexual stimuli (e.g., slides of nude women). In other words, aversion therapy reduced the response to women's clothing but not to women. The results of a followup study conducted 2 years later indicated that for most individuals the effects of the training were still apparent (Marks et al., 1970).

One individual in the study initially became sexually aroused when he fantasized about "being tied up" (a mild sexual masochism disorder). Treatment involved administering a mild electrical shock whenever he indicated that he was having one of his masochistic fantasies. The degree to which the individual experienced an erection while thinking about being tied up declined sharply with training and, by the end of the third session, was virtually eliminated. That finding is illustrated in Figure 16.7.

A potential problem with aversion therapy is that clients may become anxious about paraphiliac objects while in the therapist's office, where they know the objects will be paired with negative consequences (e.g., shock), but they may realize that the negative consequences will *not* occur when the objects are used in the privacy of their homes. In other words, clients may distinguish between situations, and the conditioned anxiety will not generalize.

A second learning explanation for paraphilias is also based on the concept of classical conditioning, but this explanation assumes that for some reason the appropriate sexual partner is *not available,* and therefore the individual achieves sexual arousal or pleasure from some object that is

FIGURE 16.7

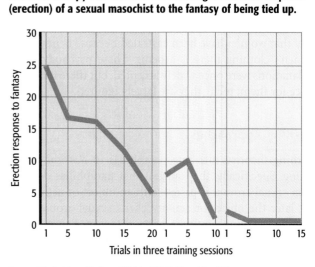

Aversion therapy was effective for reducing the arousal response (erection) of a sexual masochist to the fantasy of being tied up.

Source: Adapted from Marks and Gelder (1967), Figure 2, p. 715.

associated with the desired but absent partner. In this explanation the paraphilia is a *substitute*. For example, men find women arousing, and because articles of women's clothing are associated with women, those objects could give rise to arousal and pleasure through the process of *generalization*. Therefore, when a woman is not available, the man might use a woman-associated object as a substitute in order to achieve arousal and pleasure. Support for this explanation comes from the fact that most paraphiliac objects are associated with women; that is, men with paraphilias usually collect women's clothing, not garbage can covers, and when men with paraphilias dress inappropriately to gain sexual pleasure, they do so in women's clothing, not in animal costumes.

A crucial question concerning this explanation and the related approach to treatment is, why is a sexual partner not available? In many cases a partner is not available because members of the opposite sex and sexual relationships are perceived as threatening and hence are avoided. Indeed, some individuals with paraphilias are characterized as timid and lacking in social skills.

Treatment based on this explanation revolves around making members of the opposite sex more psychologically accessible, usually through some form of social skills training that will increase the likelihood of social success. Relaxation training is also used to reduce the anxiety associated with interacting with members of the opposite sex (Bond & Hutchinson, 1960; Wolpe, 1958). However, treatment based on social skills training and relaxation training may not be completely effective; even though the treatment may make members of the opposite sex seem more approachable, the paraphiliac behavior has a long history of reward (sexual gratification), and the individual may not wish to give it up.

Physiological Approaches

One popular explanation for paraphilias is that they result from *excessively high sex drive*. The underlying notion seems to be that a high level of sex drive somehow "spills over" into inappropriate sexual behavior or leads the individual to behave abnormally. This explanation underlies the image of the "oversexed pervert" widely held by the general public. However, the data supporting this explanation are very limited and inconsistent. For example, when men who had transvestic fetishes were compared with those who did not on a variety of sex-related hormones, no differences were found (Buhrich et al., 1979).

The notion that paraphilias are due to excessively high sex drive has led to the use of surgery (castration) or medication to reduce the sex drive of individuals with paraphilias. In some cases these treatments have been effective, but that result does not necessarily mean that the paraphilias are due to excessively high sex drive. Instead paraphilias may be due to *misdirected* sex drive; reducing the drive might decrease paraphilias by *reducing sexual behaviors in general*, not necessarily because the drive was too high.

Independent of whether or not paraphilias are due to excessively high sex drive, we must carefully examine the treatments designed to reduce sex drive because they have generated considerable controversy. The most drastic treatment is *castration* (surgical removal of the testicles), which removes the source of testosterone. The use of castration is limited to individuals such as rapists whose sexual behavior poses a serious danger to others. Castration does reduce sexual desire, but contrary to what many people believe, it does not necessarily eliminate sexual arousal and behavior. For example, rapists who had been castrated and released from jail reported that after castration they had greatly reduced frequencies of sexual thoughts, masturbation, and sexual intercourse, but 50% of the rapists reported that they were still able to have sexual intercourse (Heim, 1981). Overall, then, the main effect of castration may be to reduce the sexual desires that led to the inappropriate sexual behavior.

The second approach to lowering sex drive involves the use of *medication*. The drugs that are used to reduce sex drive in males are known as **antiandrogens** (an-ti-AN-druh-jenz) because the male hormones they inhibit belong to a class known as **androgens** (AN-druh-jenz). The most frequently used antiandrogen is widely known by its trade name, **Depo-Provera** (DEP-o-pro-VAR-uh; medroxyprogesterone acetate). Depo-Provera is injected into a muscle from which it is slowly released into the bloodstream. Because the drug is released slowly, patients undergoing treatment need to be given a shot only once or twice a week. Once Depo-Provera is in the bloodstream, it inhibits the release of sex-related hormones from the pituitary gland. That inhibition is important because the hormones from the pituitary gland ordinarily stimulate the testes and cause the release of testosterone, which is responsible for sexual arousal (see Figure 16.1). Depo-Provera thus reduces the male sex drive by reducing the release of sex-related hormones. It should be noted that the drug is not a "feminizing" medication, and men who take it do not develop female sex characteristics such as breasts. Furthermore, all of the effects of Depo-Provera are eliminated within about 10 days after its discontinuance; therefore, its use does not have long-term effects. The use of Depo-Provera is sometimes referred to as *chemical castration*, but unlike surgical castration, Depo-Provera's effects are reversible if the use of the drug ceases.

antiandrogens Drugs (e.g., Depo-Provera) that reduce sex drive in males by inhibiting the effects of androgens.

androgens A class of male hormones.

Depo-Provera An antiandrogen used to control sexual drive in men.

Depo-Provera has often been found to be effective for controlling inappropriate sexual behavior (e.g., Berlin & Meinecke, 1981; Gange, 1981; Kiersch, 1990; Wincze, Bansal, & Malamud, 1986). For example, in one study in which patients were followed for 5 to 15 years, it was found that only 15% of those who received Depo-Provera relapsed (Berlin & Meinecke, 1981). However, insofar as the drug does reduce inappropriate sexual behavior, its effects seem to be due primarily to the fact that it reduces subjective sexual *desire,* so the individual does not then pursue sexual activities (Langevin et al., 1979; Wincze et al., 1986). In other words, like castration, Depo-Provera appears to reduce the thoughts or desires that lead to sexual behavior; if the individual is properly stimulated, however, he can become sexually aroused and active. Case Study 16.6 describes the use of Depo-Provera for treating a case of sexual sadism. (As an aside, it might be noted that Depo-Provera can be effective in women for birth control.)

The use of antiandrogens to treat paraphilias is controversial, and some researchers have questioned whether the procedures are ethical (e.g., Berlin, 1989; Melella, Travin, & Cullen, 1989; Miller, 1998). Individuals such as sadists, rapists, and child molesters pose serious threats, and in the absence of other effective treatments for those individuals, the use of antiandrogens may be appropriate. Indeed, laws have been passed in four states requiring sex offenders to take sex-drive-reducing medication as a condition of parole, and a number of other states are considering such laws (Miller, 1998). However, concerns have been raised about the possibility of forcing medication on individuals whose abnormal sexual practices may be matters of preference or eccentricity and do not endanger others; in such cases medication may not be appropriate.

Finally, one other explanation and associated treatment for paraphilias merits attention. Could it be that some of these behaviors are *compulsions* that just happen to be sexual in nature? Their repetitive nature sometimes seem compulsive, but more important, there is some evidence suggesting that the drugs (antidepressants) that are effective for treating obsessive-compulsive disorder can also be effective for treating paraphilias (Abouesh & Clayton, 1999; Bradford, 1995; Clayton, 1993; Greenberg & Bradford, 1997; Greenberg et al., 1996; Kafka, 1994; Kafka & Prentky, 1992; see also Chapter 6). Placebo-controlled double-blind experiments are yet to be done, but this treatment is promising, especially in view of the fact that other treatments are not particularly effective.

THINKING CRITICALLY
Questions about Paraphilias

1. *What are the current laws concerning sexual predators?* One of the most distressing findings concerning the treatment of paraphilias is that the rate of recidivism (repeat offenses) among sexual criminals is high (Alexander, 1999; Doren, 1998; Firestone et al., 1998; Greenberg, 1998; Grossman, Martis, & Fichtner, 1999; Hanson & Bussiere, 1998; Petrosino & Petrosino, 1999). For example, in one sample of individuals who had been convicted of sexual offenses such as child molestation and rape, it was found that 31% were later convicted of a second sexual offense, and individuals who received treatment for their disorder were just as likely to be convicted of another offense as those who did not receive treatment (Rice, Quinsey, & Harris, 1991). Even this high rate of recidivism is probably an underestimate because sex crimes often go unreported and because the individuals had to actually be convicted of the second offense (such convictions are often difficult to obtain).

Because of the general ineffectiveness of traditional treatments for sexual offenders and because of the fear that

---

Use of Depo-Provera for Treating Sexual Sadism

CASE STUDY 16.6

THE PATIENT WAS a 47-year-old man who was obsessed with thoughts of sexual sadism and who had handcuffed, beaten, and stuck pins in his wife to achieve sexual satisfaction throughout their 25-year marriage. (This man's symptoms were described in greater detail in Case Study 16.5.) The patient voluntarily sought treatment when he became frightened that he might seriously harm or even kill his wife.

For 4 years the patient was given Depo-Provera, which maintained the testosterone in his blood at below-normal levels. During the treatment period the patient did not report a single instance of sexual sadism, did not have any extramarital sexual relationships, and reported that conventional sexual activities became a regular part of his marriage. In addition, the patient reported that his sexual sadistic urges and obsessions were greatly reduced. In this case, then, the medication was effective for reducing inappropriate sexual obsessions, urges, and behaviors.

Source: Adapted from Berlin and Meinecke (1981), p. 605.

As the family of Megan Kanka looked on, President Clinton signed the federal version of Megan's law in 1996. Megan was raped and murdered by a previously convicted sex offender.

these individuals engender in the public, **sexual predator laws** have been passed; these are designed to confine sexual offenders to prison for periods beyond their usual criminal sentences. Specifically, if a jury finds that an individual is likely to commit another sexual offense in the future, the individual can be confined for an indeterminate length of time. More specifically, the individual can be confined until he or she is judged to no longer pose a threat to society.

Other laws have been passed requiring that residents of a neighborhood be notified, often through newspaper announcements, when a convicted sex offender who has served a criminal sentence is being released and coming to the community. Indeed, in many communities the names, addresses, and pictures of individuals who were once convicted of sexual offenses are posted on Web sites. A law permitting the public identification of sexual offenders is often called **Megan's law** because the first one was passed in response to the case of a little girl named Megan, who was raped and murdered by a previously convicted sex offender (Petrosino & Petrosino, 1999). In general, then, sexual criminals can be confined longer—hopefully until they are no longer a threat—and when they are released, local residents are notified of their presence in the community.

2. *Are sexual predator laws and Megan's laws appropriate?* Concerns about the presence of a previous offender in the community may be justified, but these laws raise serious questions. For example, under all other laws individuals are imprisoned only *after it has been proven that they committed a crime,* but under sexual-predator laws individuals are kept in prison when it is only *suspected that they might commit another offense in the future.* This is comparable to putting individuals in prison because they might

commit a murder in the future. Is that appropriate? Other violent criminals such as murderers also have very high recidivism rates, but after these individuals have served their prison terms, they are not subject to additional confinement and their return to the community does not require public announcement (Cooper, 1999; Firestone et al., 1998). However, the U.S. Supreme Court ruled that the laws are constitutional *if the confinement is for the purpose of treatment rather than punishment.* That ruling was made in the case of a man who had been convicted and imprisoned five times for sexually molesting children and who, at the end of his most recent 10-year sentence, said that he could not guarantee that he would not molest children again. Given the man's own statement, the local court ruled that he would have to go back to prison for more treatment, and the Supreme Court concurred. Additional confinement for the purpose of treatment seems reasonable, but again there is a problem: If the original treatment that the individual received while in prison was not effective, is there any reason to believe that additional confinement and treatment will be effective? Clearly, we are in a quandary; society must be protected from dangerous sexual offenders, but as yet no effective treatments exist and it is unconstitu-

sexual predator laws   Laws permitting the confinement of convicted sexual offenders for periods beyond their criminal sentences if they are judged to be at high risk for repeating their crimes.

Megan's law   Any law permitting the public identification of convicted sexual offenders.

tional to keep people imprisoned once they have served their sentence for a crime. Apart from imposing extremely long initial sentences, the courts have not yet found a solution for this problem.

TOPIC III
Gender Identity Disorder

As long as Daniel can remember, he has wanted to be a girl. As a child he preferred to play with girls, and when they played house, he wanted to be the mother. When the other boys in the neighborhood called him a sissy, he didn't care; he thought boys were disgusting. In adolescence Daniel tried to "become a man," but it just didn't "feel right." Later he drifted between playing the traditional male role in public and, in private or with close friends, taking the more comfortable role of a woman. Now at age 30 he says he is tired of "fighting the battle of who I am," and he is being considered for sex reassignment surgery. He says, "On the outside I may have a penis, but inside I am a woman, and that's who I like being, so let's change the outside." Daniel has a *gender identity disorder*. What causes Daniel to feel he is a woman?

It will be helpful if I begin this discussion by making a distinction between *physiological sex identification*, which is the objective knowledge of whether an individual is male or female based on the individual's genitalia, and *psychological gender identity*, which is the subjective feeling of being a male or a female. Most individuals have a gender identity that is consistent with their physiological sex identification, but there are exceptions. For example, an individual may possess a penis, have all of the normal male secondary sex characteristics (e.g., deep voice, facial hair), and play a traditional male role in public but may feel that he is in fact a woman. When there is an inconsistency between an individual's physiological sex identification and his or her gender identity, the individual is diagnosed as suffering from **gender identity disorder.** This is sometimes also referred to as *gender dysphoria* (unhappiness over one's physiological gender), but that term is not a diagnostic label.

There are two major symptoms in gender identity disorder, the first of which is *persistent cross-sex identification*. That is, the individual wants to be or claims to be a member of the opposite sex. Second, the individual is *uncomfortable about his or her actual sex*. For example, a little girl

may reject typical feminine behavior and dress, believe that she will grow a penis and will not grow breasts or menstruate, and refuse to urinate in a sitting position. A young boy may reject masculine behavior and dress, believe that he will grow up to be a woman, and feel that his genitals are disgusting and that it would be better not to have a penis or testes. During adolescence and adulthood individuals with this disorder become more realistic and realize that their physiological sex identification will not change, but they are still very uncomfortable with it. Some individuals with gender identity disorder dress as members of the opposite sex, but they do so because they are more comfortable in those clothes, not because it gives them sexual gratification, as in the case of transvestic fetishism.

Individuals differ in the degree to which they experience an incongruence between their sex and gender identities. For some individuals the incongruence is relatively mild, and the individuals experience only "discomfort" with their physiological sex. In more severe cases the individuals have the sense of actually belonging to the opposite sex (e.g., "a woman trapped in a man's body"). These individuals are often preoccupied with actually changing their primary and secondary sexual characteristics to those of the opposite sex.

A phrase that is often used when discussing sexual practices or disorders is "sexual preference," and the phrase is usually taken to imply that the individual has voluntarily *chosen* one type of sexual partner or identity over another. For example, it is implied that an individual with gender identity disorder has *chosen* to identify with an opposite-sex role. However, individuals with gender identity disorder *do not feel that they have a choice about their sexual identity.* Indeed, individuals with gender identity disorder often initially fight the cross-sex identification, but they usually fail and eventually give up and accept the cross-sex identity as their "fate." For these individuals the expression "sexual imperative" is more appropriate than "sexual preference."

The consequences of fighting the cross-sex identification are reflected in the results of a survey that was conducted on male transvestites whose behaviors appeared to be part of gender identity disorder. About 70% of the individuals surveyed reported that at one time or another they had gone through a "purge" in which they had destroyed or given away all of their feminine clothing. However, the pressure to cross-dress had become too great, and at the time of the survey 99% had given up trying to stop cross-dressing and over 70% had decided to expand their activities and develop their feminine selves more fully (Prince & Bentler, 1972). It seems that just as individuals with anxiety cannot voluntarily reduce their arousal and individuals with schizophrenia cannot suppress their delusions, so persons with gender identity disorder may not be able to avoid or deny their cross-sex identification. One man's experience with gender identity disorder is reflected in a letter he wrote to me, which is reproduced in Case Study 16.7.

gender identity disorder   A disorder involving an inconsistency between an individual's physiological sex identification and his or her gender identity; sometimes referred to as *gender dysphoria*.

A Note from a Man with Gender Identity Disorder

"IT'S VERY DIFFICULT to talk about this with a male because it seems so 'shameful,' but I decided that I would risk more, be a little more 'myself.'"

"I have never done anything overt (e.g., dress up) because I didn't want to be ridiculous. (I did wear a skirt and blouse once but experienced nothing sexual from it but more a sense of 'yes, of course.') I've had one sexual relationship with a man but broke it off when I realized that part of his turn-on was that our lovemaking was 'homosexual,' which was not how I was experiencing it at all. My earliest memories include the awareness of a dichotomy between my physical gender and my 'self,' or soul. I NEVER told anyone because I thought that one day my penis would drop off and there would be a big party to celebrate my rite of passage into my true self. When I realized that wasn't going to happen, I concealed everything and managed to create a persona that could successfully negotiate my passage through the world.

"A few years ago after going through a deep depression, I went into counseling, where my situation came out. After batteries of tests and interviews, which eliminated multiple personality disorder, dissociative states, and schizophrenia, I was diagnosed with gender dysphoria, and treatment was recommended. I refused as I was married and had a son. Once my wife discovered my real 'inner' self, our marriage was essentially over, the divorce coming last year. I decided that, as I'm in the last third of my life, it would be nice to express myself just a little, and I shared myself with a couple of people, mostly with good response, but in a couple of circumstances, disaster. If it got out, my job could be in jeopardy, although I have tenure, and it would probably be difficult to dismiss me for being a woman.

"I have always experienced my femininity as a pretty pink world, a place of transcendent beauty, an inconsolable longing . . . so hard to put into words. C. P. Snow came close when he described being out on a moonlit night and all around you in the magical darkness the 'horns of elfland are blowing.' My physical self has been the locked gate at the entrance to this Eden. No, I do not imagine that being physically female would result in no problems. No, it's more a whispering promise of a coming together, of a wholeness, or remembering a forgotten melody from childhood.

"Well. Better stop; probably getting boring at this point. Please feel free to contact me. Maybe I can make some form of contribution to others who have had to suffer through this purgatory."

> My earliest memories include the awareness of a dichotomy between my physical gender and my 'self' or soul.

Explanations and Treatments

What causes gender identity disorder? As there have been for many of the disorders we have considered, there are two strongly opposing points of view: psychological and physiological. As you will see in the following sections, the path to the explanation for gender identity disorder has recently taken an interesting and dramatic turn.

Psychological Explanations

The traditional explanation is that gender identity disorder is learned in childhood when parents encourage cross-sex behaviors. Specifically, it was suggested that parents somehow foster the development of cross-sex behaviors, possibly because they want a child of the other sex. For example, the father who wants a son may treat his daughter like a son, taking her to football games or to the office, thereby teaching her to be "one of the boys." It has also been suggested that the disorder stems from the possibility that the child *identifies with the opposite-sex parent* because the same-sex parent is not available as a role model due to such factors as a broken home or hostility on the part of the same-sex parent. If a father is away much of the time or is so threatening that he cannot be approached, a young boy may spend most of his time with his mother and learn her gender role. The notion that gender roles develop in childhood seemed to gain support from early research, in which it was reported that individuals with gender identity disorder had shown cross-sex behaviors early in childhood (Green, 1974, 1976, 1985). That is, as children the males were described as "sissies" who preferred feminine activities and the females were described as "tomboys" who preferred masculine activities.

The learning explanation is appealing, but it has three problems that should be recognized. First, it is possible that parents respond to children in a cross-sex fashion because the children behave in a cross-sex manner. Fathers may get out and throw the football with their tomboy daughters because the daughters are good at it and enjoy it. In other words, the responses of the parents may be an *effect* rather than a *cause* of the children's behavior.

Second, for every case in which parents may have encouraged cross-sex behavior, there are many cases in which frustrated parents have done everything possible to *dis-*

courage the cross-sex behaviors. Fathers sometimes literally drag their feminine acting sons to sporting events to teach them to be men and, failing that, bring them to a clinic for help.

Third, a study of families in which there either was or was not an individual with gender identity disorder did not reveal differences on any social, family, or child-rearing variable that might be related to gender role development (Green, 1976).

However, the learning explanation gained strong support from a famous case study of a little boy who was surgically changed to a little girl shortly after birth and who, according to reports at the time, was then successfully raised as a girl. The case appeared to prove that gender identity was learned. However, as indicated in Case Study 16.8, more recent evidence concerning that case has drastically changed our views of what happened, and the case now leads to a very different conclusion.

Physiological Explanations

If differences in gender identity are not learned, what does cause them? A physiological explanation for which there is a considerable amount of evidence is that individuals with gender identity disorder were exposed to high levels of the hormones associated with the opposite sex during fetal development, and that those hormones influenced brain development and gender identity development (Collaer & Hines, 1995). There is strong evidence that exposing animals to opposite-sex hormones during prenatal development can influence, and even reverse, their physical sex characteristics and sexual behavior, but the question is, can early hormone exposure also influence the *social* behavior that is generally thought to be learned?

To test that possibility investigators exposed one group of female monkeys to androgens (male hormones) while they were in the womb but did not do so to another group of female monkeys; then the social behavior of all of the monkeys was monitored as they grew up (Young, Goy, & Phoenix, 1964). The results indicated that the female monkeys who were exposed to the androgens behaved more like male monkeys than did those who were not exposed to the androgens. For example, like male monkeys, the androgen-exposed females were more likely to threaten other monkeys, initiate play, and engage in more rough-and-tumble play patterns. Especially noteworthy was the fact that these masculine behaviors were strictly social and were not related to sexual behavior per se, thereby providing an

interesting parallel for the behavior seen in humans with gender identity disorder.

The results with animals are interesting, but it must be asked whether the same effects can be found in humans, for whom it is believed that social factors play an important role in psychosexual development. A number of studies are relevant when considering this question; three of them will be considered here. Two of the studies focused on girls whose mothers had been given high levels of androgens while pregnant in attempts to avoid complications during pregnancy (Ehrhardt, Epstein, & Money, 1968; Ehrhardt & Money, 1967). The results of both studies indicated that when compared to other girls, those who had been exposed in utero to the androgens were more likely to be described as "tomboys," participate in rough-and-tumble play, prefer boyish clothes, and aspire to culturally masculine ideals. The third study was conducted on a group of 16-year-old boys whose mothers had been given high levels of estrogens (female hormones) during pregnancy (Yalom, Green, & Fish, 1973). When compared to boys whose mothers had not taken high levels of estrogens during pregnancy, these boys were rated as generally less masculine. For example, they were more feminine when throwing and catching a ball, swinging a bat, and running; they were less aggressive; and they had fewer masculine interests.

As a footnote to this discussion, I should point out that there is also some recent evidence that prenatal exposure to *anticonvulsant* medications, such as phenobarbital (feen-o-BAR-bih-tol) and Dilantin (phenytoin; FEN-ih-toin), may also influence gender identity. Specifically, in a followup study of individuals whose mothers had or had not taken these drugs during pregnancy, it was found that those individuals who had been exposed to the drugs reported higher levels of cross-gender behavior and/or gender dysphoria (Dessens, Cohen-Kettenis, & Mellenbergh, 1999). From this finding it appears that a variety of biochemical factors may influence brain development and in turn influence gender.

Hormone Therapy and Sex Reassignment Surgery

In an attempt to cope with gender identity disorder, some individuals simply take on the gender role with which they feel more comfortable. In other words, they behave socially like opposite-sex individuals, and for some this provides an acceptable, albeit imperfect, solution. In some cases individuals may also begin taking hormones consistent with their desired gender (men take estrogens and women take androgens) so that they develop some of the secondary sex characteristics of the desired gender (Schlatterer et al., 1998). Other individuals seek a more drastic solution, **sex reassignment surgery,** or what is commonly called a *sex-change operation.* The first of the modern sex reassignment surgeries was the celebrated case of Christine Jorgensen in 1952 (Hamburger, Sturup, & Kahl-Iversen, 1953); since

---

sex reassignment surgery A procedure whereby the genitals of an individual are surgically altered so that they appear like those of the opposite sex; commonly called a *sex-change operation.*

The Boy Who Was Raised as a Girl

CASE STUDY 16.8

THIS CASE INVOLVES an individual who was born a boy (XY chromosomes), raised as a girl, and later reverted to living as a boy. When discussing the individual, I will use pseudonyms, "John" for the individual when he was living as a boy and "Joan" when the individual was living as a girl.

When John was 8 months old, his penis was accidentally destroyed during a surgical procedure. That posed a problem because at that time it was difficult or impossible to surgically construct a new penis, and therefore it was decided to construct a vagina and raise John as a girl. Raising John as a girl seemed reasonable because it was generally assumed that infants were sexually neutral and therefore John could be started down the path to being Joan.

Early descriptions of Joan's progress in becoming a girl were encouraging. For example, when Joan was 6, her mother reported that she could act quite feminine when she wanted to: "One thing that really amazes me is that she is so feminine. I've never seen a little girl so neat and tidy as she can be when she wants to be . . . ." (Money & Tucker, 1975, p. 119). In medical journals and the popular press, it was widely reported that the case provided strong support for the belief that patterns of masculine and feminine behavior were learned rather than caused by biological factors. The case soon became a "classic" that was always cited in debates over the basis of gender identity.

However, we now know that the reports were not accurate. Why the reports were inaccurate is not clear, but it may be that observers saw what they wanted to see and were reluctant to report findings that were contrary to the prevailing theory (see note below). In any event, insofar as there were early "feminine" behaviors, they were only random instances that would be expected in a young child or they were simply cases of acting: Joan's typical behavior was quite the opposite. Here are some examples: When pretty dresses were bought for Joan, she would refuse to wear them. Joan would usually mimic her father rather than her mother. In one instance, while her father was shaving and her mother was putting on makeup, Joan put shaving cream on her face and pretended to shave. When her mother attempted to correct her and suggested that she put on makeup, she said, "No, I don't want no makeup, I want to shave." With regard to toys and activities, Joan would usually reject dolls and girls' activities, and instead play with her brother's toys. In fact, when her brother refused to let her play with his trucks, she saved her allowance and bought one of her own. She also dressed in boys' clothing, played soldier, and participated in rough and tumble sports typical of little boys. Despite the lack of a penis, Joan often tried to urinate standing up. Doing that at school upset her female classmates and made a mess, so sometimes she would go into the boys' bathroom to urinate.

When Joan was 12, a program of estrogen supplements was begun to aid in her development of secondary sex characteristics such as breasts, but she rebelled against the treatment because she said it made her "feel funny" and she was upset about developing breasts. At age 14, when she was discussing her breast development with her physician, she said that she had suspected that she was a boy since the second grade, and shortly thereafter Joan simply gave up living like a girl and began living like a boy. Later, in a tearful episode Joan's father told her what had happened when she was an infant, and Joan recalled, "All of a sudden everything clicked. For the first time things made sense, and I understood who and what I was" (Diamond & Sigmundson, 1997, p. 300). Joan immediately requested a mastectomy to get rid of the unwanted breasts, and when that was accomplished, surgical procedures were undertaken to construct a new penis. (In the years since the botched operation, new procedures had been developed.) Testosterone treatment was then started to help reverse the other secondary sexual characteristics that had been produced by the estrogen treatment.

John adjusted well after the surgical procedures and began dating; he even bought a van with a bed and a bar! Girls who used to tease "Joan" about being masculine were now attracted to John. At age 25 John married a woman and adopted her children. Today John lives comfortably as a male. Contrary to the original reports, this case clearly does not provide evidence that gender identity is learned. Indeed, if anything, it indicates that gender identity is "in the wiring."

> "For the first time things made sense, and I understood who and what I was."

Note: For other examples of inaccurate reporting of famous case studies, see the discussion of Anna O in Chapter 2 and Case Study 2.3.

Source: Diamond & Sigmundson (1997). See Reiner (1997) for a discussion of the issues raised here.

then many such operations have been performed, but there is controversy over the procedure (Collyer, 1994; Olsson, Jansson, & Moller, 1995; Petersen & Dickey, 1995; Pfafflin, 1992).

Surgery can be effective in making individuals look like members of the opposite sex, but the operations are more than just cosmetic. In the case of the male-to-female change, it is possible to create an artificial vaginalike open-

Dr. Richard Raskind, an ophthalmologist and professional tennis player, became Renee Richards through sex reassignment surgery.

ing so that the individual can have intercourse and even experience orgasm (Lief & Hubscham, 1993). The female-to-male change is more difficult and less successful; although it is now possible to construct a penis, it has not been possible to reroute blood flow to enable the individual to have an erection. In addition to the surgery, in many cases the individuals take the hormones of their adopted sex (testosterone, estrogen). The hormones contribute to the physical characteristics (e.g., development of breasts) and behaviors of the reassigned sex (Asscheman & Gooren, 1992; Cohen-Kettenis & Gooren, 1992; Futterweit, 1998). Case Study 16.9 concerns a woman who applied for sex reassignment surgery.

Apart from appearance and sexual performance, the important question is, does sex reassignment surgery result in improved gender identity adjustment? Since 1975 there have been at least 14 studies in which data have been collected from individuals who underwent sex reassignment surgery, and they have generated three noteworthy findings (see Abramowitz, 1986). First, about two-thirds of the individuals who undergo sex reassignment surgery report improved adjustment after surgery. Second, although the

male-to-female operation is cosmetically more effective, it appears that the female-to-male surgery is psychologically more effective. The reasons for that are not clear. Third, about 7% of the operations result in bad or tragic outcomes, such as serious adjustment problems or suicide. Sometimes individuals request another operation to restore the original sex. One of the best predictors of success is whether the individual tried living the life of the other sex for a period of time before the operation (Pfafflin, 1992). That is, a real-life pretest may reveal to the individual that the change in sex roles does not solve all of his or her problems, so the surgery is not undertaken and disappointment is avoided.

A question that often arises is, does sex reassignment surgery result in a change in sexual orientation? For example, following a male-to-female operation, does an individual have an increased attraction to males? There is some controversy over this, but it is generally agreed that sexual orientation is established early by physiological factors and that changing genital structures and even hormones will not change the orientation (Daskalos, 1998).

Overall, there is a great deal of controversy and many unanswered questions with regard to sex reassignment surgery. We will have to wait for the results of more and better research before we will be able to draw conclusions about the psychological consequences of this procedure.

THINKING CRITICALLY

Questions about Gender Identity Disorder

Should gender identity disorder be considered a "disorder"? In Western society the definitions of sex-appropriate behaviors are changing dramatically. On the one hand, we have women executives, construction workers, and fighter pilots, on the other hand we have male secretaries and "stay-at-home dads." Women wear pants, and men wear earrings. Indeed, we consciously try to break down old gender-role stereotypes by giving little girls trucks and little boys dolls. Today androgyny is in. In view of this trend, is it appropriate to define as "abnormal" having feelings that one is the opposite sex? For example, if "feminine" feelings are appropriate for men, then men who have "feminine" feelings are not having abnormal feelings. In other words, the notion that an individual feels like a member of the opposite sex only exists if the feelings of the other sex are necessarily different. If women and men can have the same feelings, then the distinction between sexes on the basis of feelings disappears. Is gender identity disorder disappearing?

In *DSM*, one of the criteria for a diagnosis of gender identity disorder is that feelings about one's sexual identity

Marilyn: An Applicant for Sex Reassignment Surgery

MARILYN PRESENTED HERSELF as a tall, rugged-looking male with masculine voice quality, gait, and mannerisms. She is the fifth of six children. Her father died in an automobile accident 10 years ago at age 60. There is no family history of psychiatric contacts, alcoholism, or suicide. The family is described as deeply religious and supportive, apart from one sister who refers to the patient as a "queer."

As early as Marilyn can remember, she wanted to be like "other guys." In fact, as a young child she prayed for a penis. When she entered grade school, she became very upset when she wore dresses. Her family and school finally consented to her wearing overalls.

Marilyn preferred boys' games to girls' activities, which led her peers to dub her "half-boy, half-girl." Marilyn has lived as a male since she left school and currently manages a section of a large drugstore.

Marilyn reports a long-standing sexual attraction to females but disgust with her own genitals and breasts. At age 17 she attempted heterosexual intercourse, which she describes as a dismal failure. She had a brief romance some 20 years ago with another female who left her to marry a male; that woman divorced her husband recently and is now living with Marilyn. Marilyn sought out sex reassignment surgery approximately 15 years ago,

but she did not follow through on it because of the state of the surgical technology at that time.

Marilyn does not allow women to touch her breasts or vagina during sex play. She is adamant about not being a lesbian or interested in lesbian women. She feels that sex reassignment surgery will enhance her relationships with desired partners and enable her to live more comfortably as a male.

Source: Adapted from Roback and Lothstein (1986), pp. 407–408.

CASE STUDY 16.9

> As early as Marilyn can remember, she wanted to be like "other guys."

---

cause "clinically significant distress or impairment in social, occupational, or other important areas of functioning" (American Psychiatric Association, 1994, p. 538). However, the distress and impairment individuals experience may occur because the feelings they have are contrary to what is sanctioned by society. If the feelings were accepted and not defined as different or reflecting a disorder, then there would be no basis for the distress. In other words, given this criterion, the disorder appears to be a disorder only because it is defined as such.

Until a few years ago homosexuality was defined as a disorder. That was changed in 1987; might the same happen to gender identity disorder?

Summary

Topic I: Sexual Dysfunctions

▶ There are three types of sexual dysfunctions: (1) desire disorders, (2) arousal disorders, and (3) orgasmic disorders. All involve the absence or failure of sexual arousal at some time during the sexual response cycle.

▶ Desire disorders involve a deficiency in or lack of desire for sexual activity. This can be a simple lack of interest (hypoactive sexual desire disorder) or an active dislike and avoidance of sex (sexual aversion disorder).

▶ Psychological explanations for desire disorders revolve around defensive suppression and stress. The physiological explanation involves hormone imbalances (e.g., low levels of testosterone for males).

▶ There is little evidence for the effectiveness of psychotherapy in treating desire dirorders, but hormone replacement therapy can be effective.

▶ Arousal disorders involve the inability to achieve or maintain an adequate level of physiological arousal, although desire is present.

▶ Psychological explanations for arousal disorders are focused on anxiety and distraction, whereas physiological explanations involve neurological damage, blockage of the arteries that supply blood to the penis or clitoris, and stimulation of the sympathetic nervous system by anxiety.

▶ Psychological treatment of arousal disorders is focused on anxiety reduction, whereas physiological treatment involves enhancing blood supply or the implanting of a prosthetic device.

▶ Orgasmic disorders involve the inability to experience orgasm or, in the case of males, experiencing premature orgasm.

▶ Orgasmic disorders in women appear to be due to the fact that the women or their partners do not know what to do to achieve maximal sexual stimulation or fail to do what they know should be done. Treatment involves education. The cause for premature ejaculation is not yet understood, but it can be treated with the start–stop and the start–squeeze techniques, as well as with antidepressant drugs.

Topic II: Paraphilias

▶ Paraphilias involve the use of abnormal means for achieving sexual arousal. These disorders include exhibitionism, fetishism, transvestic fetishism, frotteurism, pedophilia, sexual masochism, sexual sadism, and voyeurism. Auto-erotic asphyxiation is another abnormal means of gaining arousal.

▶ Psychodynamic explanations revolve around the interchangeable nature of drives such as sex and aggression. The learning explanation is based on classical conditioning. It has also been suggested that paraphilias are due to excessively high sex drive, but there is little evidence for that, and it is probably that the drive is misdirected rather than excessive.

▶ Treatment of paraphilias based on learning often involves aversion therapy, in which anxiety is paired with the arousing stimuli so that they are avoided or the anxiety blocks the sexual arousal. Physiological treatments involve antiandrogens and castration, and they are effective because they reduce desire so that the individual is less inclined to act inappropriately.

▶ There is a very high rate of recidivism among sexual offenders, and this has led to the passage of sexual offender laws.

Topic III: Gender Identity Disorder

▶ Gender identity disorder involves a persistent cross-sex identification and discomfort with one's actual gender.

▶ The psychological explanation for gender identity disorder is that the individual was given inappropriate gender-role training as a child, but there is no support for that.

▶ The physiological explanation is that during fetal development, the individual was exposed to high levels of opposite-sex hormones. In extreme cases, treatment for gender identity disorder can involve sex reassignment surgery.

Questions for Making Connections

1. What is the connection between the development of phobias and the use of aversion therapy for paraphilias?

2. Sexual predator laws make it possible to imprison an individual if it is only suspected that he or she will commit another sexual crime, whereas other criminals such as murderers can only be imprisoned after being convicted of a crime. Is that "double standard" fair, or are sexual criminals more dangerous? Defend your answer.

3. Should rapists and individuals who sexually molest children be forced to take drugs (antiandrogens) that reduce their sexual desire, or, if they have already "served their time," is that an infringement on their civil rights?

4. Homosexuality is no longer considered a sexual disorder. Are there any sexual disorders you think should be dropped from the list in DSM?

Key Terms and People

In reviewing and testing yourself, you should be able to discuss each of the following:

androgens, p. 485
antiandrogens, p. 485
arousal disorder, p. 470
arousal transference, p. 484
autoerotic asphyxiation, p. 482
aversion therapy, p. 484
clitoris, p. 474
Depo-Provera, p. 485

desire disorders, p. 466
erectile tissues, p. 472
exhibitionism, p. 478
fetishism, p. 478
frotteurism, p. 479
G spot, p. 473
gender identity disorder, p. 488
glans, p. 474

gonadotropins, p. 467
hypoactive sexual desire disorder, p. 466
hypothalamus, p. 467
Megan's law, p. 487
nocturnal penile tumescence, p. 470
orgasmic disorders, p. 473
paraphilias, p. 477

17 Cognitive Disorders and Mental Retardation

IMAGINE THAT your mother has developed Alzheimer's disease. Her brain is slowly but surely deteriorating, and she is losing her memory. At first she cannot remember simple things such as phone numbers and appointments. As time goes by, however, her problem becomes severe: She does not remember who you are, and she loses the ability to talk and dress herself. What will you do? Now, imagine that even though you appear healthy, one day you suddenly lose a large portion of your memory; then a few weeks later the left side of your face and left arm become paralysed, and a month later you lose the ability to recognize simple objects such as a hammer. What's happening? Strokes are killing off portions of your brain, and as they do, you lose the abilities controlled by those areas. Can this process be stopped? Finally, imagine that you have a child who is mentally retarded; his intellectual ability will never be greater than that of a 4-year-old. What caused this, and what plans will you have to make for your child?

These are frightening possibilities, *but they are real.* For example, today more than 4 million people in the United States suffer from Alzheimer's disease, and the number is expected to *triple* in the next 20 years. In this chapter we will consider a number of serious disorders involving problems with cognitive functioning that occur independently of psychiatric disorders such as depression and schizophre-

nia. In most cases these disorders are the result of structural problems in the brain. We will first examine cognitive disorders that involve problems with memory and thinking and are caused by conditions such as Alzheimer's disease and strokes. We will then consider various types of mental retardation.

TOPIC I

Cognitive Disorders

When Anthony plays soccer, he often uses his head to hit the ball, a practice called "heading." Lately he has been having problems with memory, and it is sometimes difficult for him to pay attention in school. Could these problems be a result of heading? Might the heading be causing concussions that are disrupting the functioning of his brain?

Emma is 68 years old, and her daughter describes her as "slipping a lot lately." Most notable has been her loss of memory concerning recent events. For example, Emma can carry on a normal conversation, but 15 minutes later she will begin discussing the same topic again, as though it had not already been discussed. At other times she will go to get something in another room, but halfway there she will forget why she is going. Emma realizes that she is losing control, and it makes her very anxious. Is this just a normal aspect of aging, or is she suffering from some disorder? Is she suffering from Alzheimer's disease or strokes? Is there anything she can do about the problem?

In this section I will discuss three cognitive disorders: *amnesia, dementia,* and *delirium.* As the name implies, *cognitive* disorders involve problems with *thinking.* The most common problem is loss of memory, but other symptoms such as confusion, loss of language ability, and difficulty carrying out motor activities like dressing and walking can occur. The symptoms of the three cognitive disorders are listed in Table 17.1. In the following sections I will first explain how memory works and then go on to discuss the three cognitive disorders.

An Overview of Memory

Because problems with memory play a prominent role in each of the cognitive disorders, it will be helpful if I begin with a brief summary of how memory works and sometimes doesn't work. Understanding memory will help you understand the cognitive disorders.

How Memory Works

The process of memory begins when new information (sights, sounds, etc.) enter your *sensory memory,* where you select what is relevant from all that is coming in. For example, you may attend to the new term *sensory memory* and ignore the sound of a car driving by outside. Once you have selected what is relevant, you send that information from your sensory memory to your *short-term memory,* where you use it for thinking and also process it for storage in your *long-term memory* (see Chapter 3). Physiologically, the processing of information for long-term storage is done primarily in a small structure in your brain called the **hippocampus** (hip-uh-KAM-puhs). After a memory is

---

hippocampus   A small structure in the brain responsible for processing memories for long-term storage.

cell assembly   A group of neurons (cells) in the cortex of the brain in which a memory is stored.

aphasia   Condition characterized by the inability to remember or use words.

retrograde amnesia   The inability to recall previous experiences.

---

processed in the hippocampus, it is sent to the cortex of your brain, where it is stored in a group of neurons (cells) called a **cell assembly** (that is, an *assembly of cells;* Hebb, 1949). In the cortex the memories (in cell assemblies) are organized in networks of related memories; for example, there are networks of school-related memories, networks of sad memories, and networks of memories about psychology. The memories in each network are connected to one another by nerve pathways. Memories are usually retrieved by first activating the network in which they are stored, which then activates the particular cell assembly containing the memory. For example, when you are trying to remember the name of a friend from high school, you begin by thinking about high school, which activates your network of high school memories, including the specific cell assembly in which the name of your friend is stored, and the name comes to mind. Of course, if you happen to think of your friend's name first, that activates your network of high school memories, and other memories from high school come flooding back. (As an aside, I might mention that because memories are recalled when they are activated by related memories, when studying you should always link new information to other information or experiences rather than memorizing isolated facts. That is, putting information in networks will increase the likelihood that you will be able to recall the information later, because it can be activated by other bits of information.)

Why Memory Fails

There are three ways in which the memory system can break down. First, the nerve pathway to a cell assembly where a memory is held can somehow deteriorate so that the cell assembly cannot be activated. Fortunately, in most cases an alternative route to the cell assembly can be found. However, that route may not be as direct as the original route, so it may take longer to get to the specific memory. In other words, if one route to a memory does not work anymore, you can take a detour, but it may take longer. You've probably had the experience of knowing there was a word you wanted to use but you just couldn't pull it up, and then after a while it suddenly "popped into your head." In that case the delay may have occurred because for some reason you had to find a new route to the cell assembly in which the memory was stored. When problems remembering or using words become serious, the individual is said to be suffering from **aphasia** (uh-FA-zhuh). (The word *aphasia* is based on *a,* which means "no," and the Greek word *phasia,* which means "speech," so *aphasia* literally means "no speech.")

Second, in extreme cases all of the connections to a cell assembly or the cell assembly itself can be destroyed; in these cases the memory stored there is lost. The inability to recall previous experiences is called **retrograde amnesia** (RET-ro-grad am-NE-zhuh). (The word *amnesia* comes

TABLE 17.1

Cognitive disorders and their symptoms

Disorder	Symptoms
Amnesia	1. Loss of memory (primarily *retrograde amnesia* but sometimes *anterograde amnesia*) *Note:* Symptoms may be transient or chronic.

Dementia	1. Loss of memory (*retrograde* and *anterograde amnesia*)
	2. One or more of the following:
	   a. Language disturbance (*aphasia*)
	   b. Problems with motor behaviors (*apraxia*)
	   c. Difficulty recognizing objects (*agnosia*)
	   d. Problems with planning, organizing, etc.
	
	Note: Symptoms have a gradual onset, become progressively worse, and are chronic.

Delirium	1. Disturbance of consciousness (e.g., confusion about location, problems with attention) 2. Disruption in thought processes (loss of memory, confusion, language problems, hallucinations) *Note:* Symptoms develop over a short period of time, may fluctuate in severity, and are usually transient.

Note: For each disorder there must be evidence that the disorder is caused by a medical condition (e.g., concussion, Alzheimer's disease, drug abuse).

Source: Adapted from American Psychiatric Association (1994).

from a Greek word that means "forgetfulness"; also, *retro* means "back" or "backward," and *grade* means "progression," so *retrograde amnesia* refers to a loss of memory that progresses back in time.)

The third problem with memory involves the deterioration or destruction of the hippocampus, where memories are processed for storage. When that happens, new experiences cannot be put into memory. Individuals with problems in the hippocampus can recall information they stored in memory *before* the problems developed, but they are unable to recall information presented to them *after* the problems developed because they were not able to process it for storage. The hippocampus can be thought of as a file clerk; if the clerk is not working, new information cannot get stored in the files (cell assemblies) in the brain. This problem is illustrated in a man known as H. M., who at the age of 27 had to have a large portion of his hippocampus removed because of a life-threatening case of epilepsy (Hilts, 1995; Milner, 1970; Scoville & Milner, 1957). Following the operation H. M. could remember things that happened to him before the operation, but he now lacked a hippocampus so he could not store new information and could not remember anything that happened to him after the operation. For example, if you met and talked with H. M. and then left the room for a few minutes, when you returned, H. M. would have no memory of ever having met or talked with you. In essence, H. M. is trapped in the time before his operation. Indeed, when he is asked what date it is, he gives a date a few days before his operation, which

occurred many years ago. The inability to put new experiences into memory and recall them is called **anterograde amnesia** (AN-ti-ro-grad am-NE-zhuh).

The process by which memories are stored and the ways in which the storage and recall of memories can be disrupted are illustrated in Figure 17.1. Now that you understand how memories are stored and retrieved, we can go on to consider the three cognitive disorders.

Amnesia Disorders

The major symptom of **amnesia** (am-NE-zhuh) **disorders** is a serious problem with memory. Specifically, the individual either cannot recall previously known things (retrograde amnesia) or cannot put new information into memory (anterograde amnesia) (Kapur, 1999). Amnesia disorders can result from medical conditions, such as concussions and diseases, and also from the use of various drugs. In the following sections I will describe some of the most common causes of amnesia.

anterograde amnesia   The inability to put new experiences into memory and recall them.

amnesia disorders   Cognitive disorders in which the major symptom is a serious problem with memory.

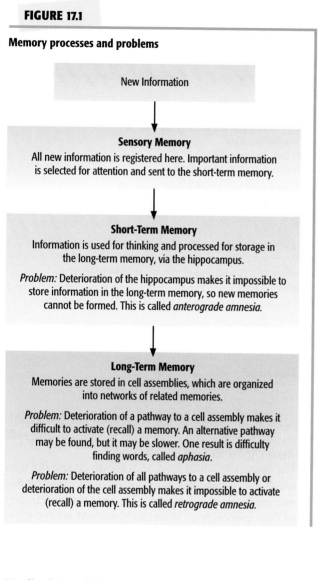

FIGURE 17.1

Memory processes and problems

New Information

Sensory Memory
All new information is registered here. Important information is selected for attention and sent to the short-term memory.

Short-Term Memory
Information is used for thinking and processed for storage in the long-term memory, via the hippocampus.

Problem: Deterioration of the hippocampus makes it impossible to store information in the long-term memory, so new memories cannot be formed. This is called *anterograde amnesia.*

Long-Term Memory
Memories are stored in cell assemblies, which are organized into networks of related memories.

Problem: Deterioration of a pathway to a cell assembly makes it difficult to activate (recall) a memory. An alternative pathway may be found, but it may be slower. One result is difficulty finding words, called *aphasia.*

Problem: Deterioration of all pathways to a cell assembly or deterioration of the cell assembly makes it impossible to activate (recall) a memory. This is called *retrograde amnesia.*

Medical Conditions as a Cause of Amnesia

One of the major causes of amnesia disorders is *head trauma;* specifically, a blow to the head causes violent shaking of the brain within the skull, which results in a loss of memory. The shaking of the brain is called a **concussion** (kun-KUSH-en). A concussion does not result in detectable brain damage, but it probably stretches or twists the axons in the brain, thereby disrupting the connections among the neurons (Wise et al., 1999). (Recall that axons are the armlike structures on neurons that make connections with other neurons.) Concussions can result in a brief loss of consciousness and dizziness, but they can also cause retrograde amnesia, which may extend back over a few hours or weeks depending on the severity of the blow. It is not clear exactly why more recent information is more likely to be lost than older information, but it is probably because the connections to new information are weaker

and fewer in number. In many cases much of the information that is lost comes back later, probably because new connections to it are made.

Concussions and amnesia often occur as a result of automobile accidents, but they can also be caused by blows to the head during sports such as football, rugby, soccer, karate, skiing, and boxing (Collins et al., 1999; Erlanger et al., 1999; Hinton-Bayre et al., 1999; Matser et al., 1999; Powell & Barber-Foss, 1999). Indeed, after a fall in a karate class in which he hit his head, one of my students was not able to recall anything from the previous 3 weeks of class. One blow to the head is sufficient to cause a concussion and amnesia, but the effects can become increasingly more severe and other serious symptoms can set in if an individual experiences repeated concussions (Erlanger et al., 1999). For this reason it is essential that athletes who have a concussion be benched, sometimes permanently. (I will discuss the other effects later when I discuss dementia.) Obviously, it is important to protect your brain from blows. In this regard it is interesting to note that skiers often pay hundreds of dollars for bindings to protect their knees, but rarely wear helmets to protect their brains.

Retrograde amnesia can also be caused by convulsions that result from epilepsy or electroconvulsive shock therapy (ECT; see Chapter 8). For example, individuals may not be able to remember what happened just before an epileptic seizure or just before a session of ECT. Fortunately, in many cases the loss of memory that stems from seizures is transient, and the memories come back later.

Another important cause of amnesia is a disruption of blood flow to the brain. Because neurons in the brain do not store energy, they must have a constant supply of blood to provide them with energy (glucose). If the supply is cut off, the affected neurons will cease functioning and eventually die, resulting in lost memories. Disruption of the blood supply can occur when blood vessels become blocked. The blockage is usually due to pieces of fatty material breaking off the interior wall of an artery and then flowing into and blocking a small blood vessel in the brain (see the later discussion and Chapter 14). Depending on what areas of the brain are affected, symptoms can include weakness in parts of the body, problems with vision or hearing, dizziness, slurred speech, and loss of memory. The symptoms generally last less than 30 minutes. Such an episode is called a **transient ischemic** (is-KE-mik) **attack** (sometimes abbreviated **TIA**). (*Transient* means "brief," and *ischemic* comes from a combination of two Greek words meaning "hold" and "blood," so a *transient ischemic attack* is a brief holding back of blood.) Between attacks the individual functions normally. However, because transient ischemic attacks can be frightening and because the individual never knows when they will recur, they can lead to other symptoms such as social withdrawal. An older woman I knew, who stayed in bed and was thought to be incontinent, was actually having frequent TIAs, during which she would become confused and not know where she was. As a protective strategy she stayed in bed, even when she needed to go to the bathroom. Over time the effects of TIAs can accumulate and result in more serious problems (see the later discussion of vascular dementia).

Finally, amnesia (particularly anterograde amnesia) can be caused by a prolonged deficiency of *vitamin B1 (thiamine)* in the diet (Squire et al., 1990). Specifically, if there is not enough vitamin B1, the neurons in the brain will shrink and eventually die; if this damage occurs in the hippocampus, the individual will develop anterograde amnesia. The deterioration of the hippocampus because of a lack of vitamin B1 is called **Korsakoff's syndrome,** and it is seen most often in individuals who are suffering from alcoholism, which causes them to have very poor diets.

Drugs as a Cause of Amnesia

Amnesia can also be caused by drugs such as alcohol, anesthetics, and benzodiazepines (Coenen & van Luijtelaar, 1997; Green, McElholm, & King, 1996). (Benzodiazepines include antianxiety drugs such as Valium and Ativan; see Chapter 5.) The amnesia occurs because the drugs reduce brain activity and thereby reduce the ability to retrieve information or to store new information. I experienced this when I was given a benzodiazepine as an anesthetic for a minor surgical procedure. I am told that when I regained consciousness, I asked the nurse about the outcome of the procedure and she explained it all. A few minutes later I asked again, and I asked again a few minutes after that. What happened was that I had regained consciousness before the drug had worn off completely, and because it was preventing me from putting information into storage (activity in my hippocampus was being blocked), I was experiencing anterograde amnesia. It is noteworthy that some of the drugs that are used in "date rape" have the effect of sedating the woman and also producing anterograde amnesia so that she does not remember what happened to her (Calhoun et al., 1996; Hindmarch & Brinkmann, 1999).

 ## Dementia Disorders

We now come to a much more serious set of cognitive disorders known as **dementia** (di-MEN-shuh) **disorders,** which, like the other cognitive disorders, are due to deterioration of the brain. (The word *dementia* is derived from the Latin *de,* which means "to reduce" or "to remove," and *ment,* which means "mind," so the word literally means a "reduction or removal of the mind.") In dementia disorders the problems with memory are much more severe than in

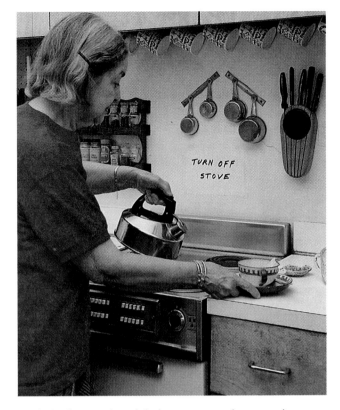

People develop strategies to help them compensate for memory loss. Reminder notes can help individuals function more competently, at least during the early stages of dementia.

amnesia disorders, and thus dementia disorders can seriously disrupt the ability to function. For example, some individuals suffering from these disorders may get lost in their own homes or forget how to dress themselves. Furthermore, the loss of memory can be so severe that it greatly reduces intellectual ability. Specifically, individuals in the advanced stages of dementia can lose their ability to plan activities, speak, and even use their muscles.

Dementia begins with relatively minor problems with memory. For example, individuals in the early stages may

---

concussion A shaking of the brain within the skull due to a head trauma; can cause amnesia.

transient ischemic attack (TIA) A brief interruption of blood flow to the brain that causes weakness in parts of the body, problems with vision or hearing, dizziness, slurred speech, and loss of memory.

Korsakoff's syndrome Deterioration of the hippocampus because of a lack of vitamin B1; often occurs with alcoholism and results in anterograde amnesia.

dementia disorders Cognitive disorders caused by deterioration of the brain that can seriously disrupt the ability to function. (See *Alzheimer's disease.*)

simply be unable to remember things such as names, phone numbers, directions, or unimportant events. During this stage individuals often develop coping strategies that allow them to compensate for their loss of memory. For instance, many people write notes reminding them of things they must do. One woman who was rapidly losing her memory took extensive notes while watching TV programs so that during commercial breaks she would not forget what had already happened in a program. She also left notes to herself all around the house: "Turn off the stove," "Lock the front door," "Feed the cat," and even "Put toothpaste on your brush."

During the early stages of a dementia disorder there can also be changes in personality. Specifically, as individuals begin to lose control, some become irritable and difficult to manage, whereas others essentially give up and become very compliant. Some individuals develop paranoid delusions. These delusions probably stem from the fact that these individuals are losing control and do not understand what is happening around them; so they make up explanations. In other words, instead of saying, "I can't find things because I am getting old and losing my memory," the individual might say, "I can't find things because other people are taking them or hiding them." Another symptom often associated with dementia is depression (Chen et al., 1999). In most cases the changes in personality are *secondary effects* of the dementia; for example, individuals get depressed because of their dementia. However, in some cases it may be that the brain deterioration causing the dementia is also causing the depression (see Chapter 8 for a discussion of how brain deterioration can cause depression).

Unfortunately, as the disorder progresses, the memory loss becomes more pervasive and serious. For example, individuals may not remember what they said only minutes earlier so they repeat themselves over and over; eventually they may not remember people whom they have known for many years. Indeed, individuals can "forget" their children

and even be unable to recognize themselves in a mirror. Furthermore, in some cases the problems can impair language functioning because the individuals cannot recall words or names (*aphasia*). In more advanced cases individuals who are shown a common object such as a shoe or a pencil are not even able to name the object or to say what it is used for. Such problems with recognition are called **agnosia** (ag-NO-zhe-ah). (This term is based on *a*, which means "no," and a Greek word meaning "to know," so the term means "not knowing.") In other cases the loss of memory can lead to problems with simple motor activities; for instance, individuals are not able to dress themselves or even walk. This inability to perform activities such as walking or dressing is called **apraxia** (a-PRAK-se-a). (This term is derived from *a*, which means "no," and *praxis*, which is a Greek word for "action," so the word literally means "no action.") It is not that the individuals' muscles don't work; rather the individuals simply do not remember how to use their muscles to carry out various behaviors. Finally, because of the loss of memory, the individual's abilities to think abstractly and make plans diminish. During the advanced stages of dementia, there are no effective coping strategies, and the disorder is frightening and devastating. Indeed, as the word *dementia* implies, *the mind is removed.* The symptoms necessary for a diagnosis of dementia are summarized in Table 17.1.

For most people the decline in functioning is slow and smoothly progressive because the underlying deterioration of the brain is slow and gradual. However, in cases due to strokes, declines may be sudden and steplike because each stroke suddenly destroys a part of the brain. Furthermore, when strokes are the cause, there may be differences from stroke to stroke in what functions are lost, because the strokes destroy different parts of the brain. For instance, an individual may show a steady level of functioning and then a sudden drop in memory performance, followed by another steady level of functioning, then the sudden loss of some motor ability. The nature of the decline (smooth versus steplike) is sometimes an important factor in determining the cause of the dementia.

If the decline in functioning begins before the age of 65, it is referred to as **presenile dementia;** if it begins after age 65, it is called **senile dementia.** The age of onset of dementia is important for the individual suffering from the disorder, but it is also important for family members: An early onset is associated with a greater likelihood that biological relatives will also suffer from the disorder (Li et al., 1995; Silverman et al., 1994).

Finally, it is important to distinguish between primary and secondary dementia. **Primary dementia** refers to a decline in intellectual functioning that is due to a *physiological problem in the brain,* whereas **secondary dementia** refers to a decline in intellectual functioning that is the result of *some other disorder.* For example, a decline in func-

---

agnosia   The inability to name an object or describe its use; a symptom of advanced dementia.

apraxia   The inability to perform activities such as walking or dressing because of a loss of memory as to how to perform the activities.

presenile dementia   Dementia that begins before the age of 65.

senile dementia   Dementia that begins after the age of 65.

primary dementia   A decline in intellectual functioning that is due to a physiological problem in the brain.

secondary dementia   A decline in intellectual functioning that is the result of some other disorder, such as depression or schizophrenia.

tioning due to Alzheimer's disease is primary dementia, whereas a decline in functioning associated with depression is an instance of secondary dementia. In one case it was thought that a woman with Alzheimer's disease had gone through a period of particularly rapid deterioration or had had a stroke because she became listless, disoriented, and almost mute. However, when she was given an antidepressant, those recently developed symptoms were eliminated. In her case, then, secondary dementia due to depression had been superimposed on primary dementia, and when her depression was lifted, so was the secondary dementia. Actually, it is often very difficult to distinguish between dementia that stems from mild Alzheimer's disease and the symptoms of depression. This poses a serious problem because almost 20% of the individuals admitted to nursing homes may suffer from severe undiagnosed depression (Rovner et al., 1991; Rubin et al., 1991). Obviously, if the basis for the dementia is misdiagnosed, treatment will be aimed at the wrong problem. Dementia disorders involve *primary* dementia, on which we'll focus here.

With this discussion of symptoms as background, we can turn to the causes of dementia. As I indicated earlier, dementia is due to a deterioration of the brain. However, a common misconception is that dementia is an inevitable consequence of the normal deterioration of the brain that occurs in all of us as we age. In fact, the brain begins to deteriorate in one's 20s, and by about age 50 the volume of the brain may be reduced by as much as 15% to 20% (Coffey et al., 1992; Strassburger et al., 1997). However, this process is *normal* and usually leads only to a *slowing* of brain activity rather than to the massive loss of memory and other symptoms seen in dementia. Instead, dementia is due to specific problems in the brain, such as diseases or strokes, and the underlying problem must be specified in any diagnosis of dementia. The various dementia disorders listed in DSM-IV are summarized in Table 17.2 (on p. 504) by their causes.

Dementia Caused by Alzheimer's Disease

Alzheimer's (OLTS-hi-murz) **disease** is probably the most common cause of dementia among elderly people, and it is three times more prevalent among women than men. In the early phase of this disease, the individual is generally forgetful and is most likely to forget recent events and experiences. That is, the problem is with *short-term memory*. In the middle phase problems with short-term memory increase and may become so severe that the individual is unable to hold a memory long enough to act on it. For example, an individual may go into a room to do something but once in the room may completely forget why he or she is there. (That happens to all of us at times, but in Alzheimer's disease it is a persistent problem.) This short-term memory problem is known as **cognitive abulia** (uh-

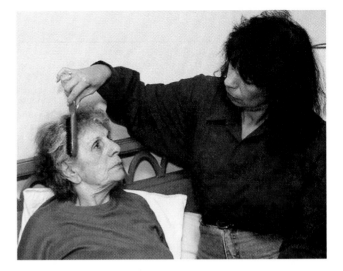

In the final stages of Alzheimer's disease, the memory loss may be so severe that a patient may be unable to carry out basic self-care.

BYOO-le-uh). (The word *abulia* refers to an abnormal lack of ability to act or make a decision.) In the middle phase individuals may also have problems with language because they cannot recall the words they need (aphasia).

In the final phase of Alzheimer's disease problems with short-term memory persist, and severe problems with long-term memory develop; for example, individuals may not be able to recognize family members including their own children. In this phase people suffering from Alzheimer's disease are disoriented and may not be able to take care of themselves.

Alzheimer's disease is most likely to occur after age 65 (Gao et al., 1998), but presenile cases do occur. One woman I knew was afflicted in her early 50s, and within 3 years the deterioration had reached a point where she had difficulty talking because she could no longer remember words. The age of onset of Alzheimer's disease is related to the probability that biological relatives will also suffer from the disorder. The earlier the onset, the greater the likelihood that the patient's children will also develop the disorder (Li et al., 1995; Silverman et al., 1994).

Autopsies of individuals who suffered from Alzheimer's disease have revealed three types of brain deterioration: First, the neurons in the brains of individuals with

---

Alzheimer's disease   A disorder that is probably the most common cause of dementia among elderly people.

cognitive abulia   A short-term memory problem that disrupts planned actions because of failure to remember the goal.

plaque   Accumulation of proteins on the neurons in the brains of individuals with Alzheimer's disease.

TABLE 17.2

Causes of dementia disorders

Cause of dementia disorder	Characteristics
Alzheimer's disease	The brain deterioration associated with Alzheimer's disease involves the development of plaque on the neurons, a tangling of the axons of neurons, and the presence of holes in the neurons. The dementia is slowly progressive.
Vascular disease	Dementia caused by vascular disease is due to the combined effects of numerous strokes (*cerebral infarctions*), which destroy the brain. Its course is often steplike rather than smooth, with a decline in intellectual functioning occurring after each stroke.
HIV infection (AIDS)	HIV (*human immunodeficiency virus*) infection leads to a reduction of the white blood cells that fight infections, and therefore the individual's ability to fight off other infections is reduced. The resulting condition is known as AIDS (*acquired immunodeficiency syndrome*). Uncontrolled brain infections can result in progressive deterioration of the brain and dementia.
Head trauma	Dementia can result from a blow (*trauma*) to the head. It will not be progressive unless there are additional blows, as often experienced by boxers and football players who sustain multiple blows. The long-term effects of one or more concussions constitute a *postconcussive disorder*.
Parkinson's disease	Parkinson's disease is due to the deterioration of neurons in the basal ganglia, which produce dopamine. Dopamine is essential for the control of motor movements, so the primary symptoms of Parkinson's disease involve problems with movement, such as tremors and rigidity. Dementia sets in later, is progressive in nature, and is due to further brain deterioration.
Huntington's disease	The early symptoms of Huntington's disease involve twitches (often in the face) but progress to a general jerking of the body, which is known as *Huntington's chorea* (*chorea* means "dance"). These symptoms are due to deterioration of the areas of the brain that control movements. As the deterioration progresses and involves other areas, dementia sets in and becomes progressively worse. The disease is due to a dominant gene (offspring of someone with the disease have a 50% chance of developing the disease) and usually results in death in about 15 years.
Pick's disease	Pick's disease is a very rare disease that is similar to Alzheimer's disease, except that it affects a smaller area of the brain (primarily the frontal and temporal lobes) and progresses more slowly.
Creutzfeld-Jakob disease	Creutzfeld-Jakob disease is rare. It is due to an infection of the brain and may be similar to mad cow disease. The infection causes deterioration of the brain that leads to dementia and to problems with reflexes, motor movements, and vision.
Substance abuse	In some cases drugs, such as alcohol, can result in brain deterioration and dementia. For a diagnosis of dementia to be made, the cognitive effects must be present after the effects of drug intoxication and withdrawal are no longer present. In other words, the cognitive effects are due to brain deterioration rather than to intoxication and withdrawal.

Source: Adapted from American Psychiatric Association (1994).

FIGURE 17.2

Compared to a normal brain (right), the brain of an individual with Alzheimer's disease (left) is characterized by deterioration.

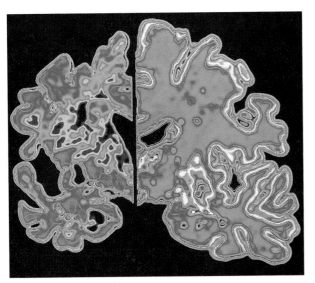

Alzheimer's disease are encrusted with patches of **plaque** (plak), consisting of accumulated proteins. The plaque inhibits the transmission of nerve impulses from one neuron to the next, and it may also poison and cause deterioration of the neurons. Second, there are small holes in the bodies of the neurons, which reflect general deterioration. Third, the axons of the neurons are tangled and in disarray, as though "all the wires got crossed." This condition is called **neurofibrillary** (nyoo-ro-FIB-ruh-ler-e) **tangling.** See Figure 17.2.

The deterioration can occur in almost any area of the brain, and where it occurs will determine the nature of the symptoms. Most notable is deterioration in the *hippocampus,* which plays a major role in processing memories for storage (see the earlier discussion). If memories cannot be put into storage, the individual will suffer from anterograde amnesia. Another crucial area is the *amygdala,* which controls the processing of emotional memories. If it is damaged, the memory loss will primarily affect memories that were particularly pleasant or unpleasant (Mori et al., 1999). As the deterioration becomes more widespread, connections among cell assemblies and the cell assemblies themselves are destroyed, thus obliterating long-term memories. Deterioration of other areas of the brain can cause additional symptoms such as involuntary motor movements (twitches or facial grimaces), slurring of speech, and the inability to control the bowel and the bladder.

The crucial question is, what causes the brain deterioration that leads to Alzheimer's disease? That question stumped investigators for many years, but recently a major part of it was answered (Sinha et al., 1999; Vassar et al.,

1999; Yan et al., 1999). Specifically, research revealed that there are strands of protein protruding from the neurons in the brain, and in cases of Alzheimer's disease an enzyme called a **protease** (PROT-e-az) **enzyme** cuts off these protein strands. The cutoff protein strands then accumulate and form the plaque that covers and poisons the neurons. This explanation is called the **protease theory of Alzheimer's disease.** As a rough analogy, you can think of grass being mowed, the clippings covering the grass beneath them, and killing that grass as they rot.

If Alzheimer's disease is caused by a protease enzyme, the next question is, why is the protease enzyme present in the brains of some people and not others? The answer is that the production of the enzyme is controlled by a specific gene and people differ with regard to that gene. However, although the enzyme is controlled primarily by a gene, it is possible that environmental toxins might also contribute to the problem. This possibility is still under investigation.

Finally, we must address the question of whether Alzheimer's disease can be treated. Thus far the treatments have usually involved drugs that increase the brain's levels of neurotransmitters associated with thinking and memory (Mayeux & Sano, 1999). Most attention has been focused on a neurotransmitter called **acetylcholine** (e-set-l-KO-len). The notion underlying this approach is that if portions of the brain have deteriorated and are not functioning effectively, increasing the level of acetylcholine may cause the remaining portions to function more effectively and thereby compensate for the damaged areas. Drugs can be used to restore the normal levels of acetylcholine. One widely used drug (*donepezil,* sold under the name Arcept) increases the level of acetylcholine by reducing the chemical breakdown of acetylcholine; that is, if less acetylcholine is broken down, more will be available at the synapses, and the brain will function more effectively. Unfortunately, in most cases these drugs are only marginally effective for improving memory (Burns et al., 1999; Joensson et al., 1999; Mayeux & Sano, 1999). Furthermore, the drugs do

neurofibrillary tangling   Tangling of the axons of neurons, which is characteristic of the brains of individuals with Alzheimer's disease.

protease enzyme   An enzyme that cuts protein strands from neurons in the brain and thus contributes to Alzheimer's disease.

protease theory of Alzheimer's disease   An explanation for Alzheimer's disease that suggests that a protease enzyme cuts protein strands from neurons in the brain and the strands then accumulate to form the plaque that covers and poisons the neurons.

acetylcholine   A neurotransmitter in the brain whose level is increased by some drugs used to treat Alzheimer's disease.

A Daughter Talks about Her Mother's Experience with Alzheimer's Disease and Her Concerns about Her Own Future

"MY MOTHER WAS ONCE an active, healthy, charming, independent, and very intelligent woman. When my father died, Mother took a position with a small importing company, and in a short time she became the company's executive manager. After she retired, she had a very active social life. She had lots of friends, traveled a lot, did volunteer work, gardened, and gave splendid parties. In short, she really 'had it together,' and she was fun to be around.

"Around age 68 or 69, however, Mother began to slow down. She stopped going out and ceased seeing friends. She spent most of her time at home reading or watching television. I really wasn't too concerned; after all, she was almost 70. After a while, however, her behavior seemed to deteriorate somewhat. She became very forgetful and sometimes seemed a little confused, although she covered it up well. I attributed most of these changes to the fact that she wasn't getting much social stimulation, and undoubtedly that did play a role. As time went on, however, her forgetfulness became very pervasive, and she had to leave notes for herself everywhere reminding her what to do (e.g., 'Be sure to lock the door,' 'Remember to turn the oven off,' 'Feed the cat'). Most noticeable was the fact that when she read books or watched television, she would take extensive notes. I soon realized that without the notes she would not be able to remember what had happened at that point in the story. As this got worse, I became concerned about her living alone, so I arranged for a woman who lived across the hall to look in on her a few times a day. Over the next year Mother got by on her own, but she was doing less and less well.

Because of my increasing concern, I made arrangements for her to have a complete checkup at the medical center.

"Four days after her examination, I was called in for a conference with the physician, neurologist, psychologist, and social worker who had seen her. The physician came right to the point and said that there were three things I needed to know. First, he said that Mother was in excellent physical condition (90th percentile for her age group on most measures) and that she would probably live another 15 years. Second, he said that it was their judgment that Mother was suffering from a serious and rapidly progressing case of Alzheimer's disease. He said—these are his words—that at the rate her disease was advancing, '*she will be a vegetable in 5 years.*' I had been prepared for bad news, but that really stunned me. He went on to point out that given Mother's life expectancy and the speed with which the Alzheimer's was progressing, she would need *total* care for an *extended* period of time, and therefore I was going to have to face a very substantial financial responsibility. I had barely taken that in when he made his third point. 'Finally, I have to tell you that Alzheimer's is inherited, and it is highly probable that you will develop the disease. You should take that into account in making financial plans for your own future.' Clearly, *I was facing serious problems.*

"The first thing I had to do was find a place for Mother to live. Because she could still take care of herself, she didn't need to live in a nursing home, and I was fortunate to find a 'minimal care' facility that was operated by the Catholic church. Originally, the building had been a college dormitory, but it had been converted to a home for

elderly persons when the college no longer needed it. Residents have individual rooms, which they furnish with their own furniture. The homelike rooms are good-sized and have washbasins, but like in many old dorms, the residents share bathroom facilities on each floor. Meals are provided in a dining room just as in a college dorm. Residents must be relatively healthy because there is no nursing care. However, the staff will remind residents to take medication as needed. All of the staff members are caring and wonderful, and the facility has been a godsend.

"Of course, Mother did not want to move out of her own home, and as she left, she said to her neighbor, 'I'll never have another happy day in my life. It's over.' I almost broke down and cried, but the move had to be made.

"Over the next 2 years Mother began showing a slow and progressive deterioration. After the first year she had almost no short-term memory. While talking with her on the phone one evening, for example, I asked her to check to make sure she had clean socks in her dresser drawer. She put down the phone to go to the dresser, but before she got there, she forgot what she was supposed to do, and then she forgot that she was on the phone, so she just went and sat in her chair, leaving the phone off the hook. I had to hang up, call the front desk, and have them send someone up to hang the phone up so I could call back.

"She also started having trouble with aphasia [loss of the ability to use certain words]. One evening on the phone, she said, 'It's broken.' I asked, 'What's broken, Mother?' but she couldn't tell me. She just couldn't find the word. Finally, in frustration she said, 'You know, the thing on the wall.' 'Where on the wall, Mother?' 'Next to

not stop the deterioration, and as the deterioration progresses, the drugs become less and less effective because they cannot compensate for large losses; that is, eventually there is simply not enough brain left with which to work.

However, a better treatment strategy was suggested by the discovery that the brain deterioration seen in Alzheimer's disease is due in large part to the presence of the protease enzyme that clips off protein strands. Specifically,

the window.' 'Do you mean the clock, Mother?' 'Yes, the clock's broken and not working.' Sometimes talking with Mother is like playing 20 questions because she just can't find the words she needs. She gets very frustrated and sometimes just gives up.

"As time went by, Mother became less and less aware of what was happening around her. On a number of occasions I noticed that Mother would become very confused for a couple of days, and when the confusion cleared up, she would not be functioning as well as she had before. I think she may be having little strokes. The Alzheimer's is causing the slow deterioration, and the strokes are probably responsible for the sudden drops in ability.

"As her level of functioning has declined, Mother has withdrawn and interacts less and less with other residents. She goes to meals and 'goes through the motions' of social interaction, but I don't think she really understands what is going on around her. Most of the time now she simply sits in her room, hunched forward, looking at the floor. Sometimes the television is on, but it doesn't make much difference because she really can't follow it anymore. The *TV Guide* that used to be heavily marked with reminders about what to watch now lies unopened on the floor.

"One of the saddest things is that at times Mother is aware of the fact that she has lost control. One day I told her that I thought she was looking good, and after a moment's pause she frowned and said in a weak little voice, 'Oh, maybe I look good, but I'm not really good. I get all mixed up about everything. I don't know what to do. I don't know what's happening.' Sometimes she seems absolutely terrified.

It tears me apart to see her like that. Sometimes I think it might be better if she lost that one last vestige of insight.

"I've heard that some people become hostile or paranoid as they go through this deterioration, but I'm very fortunate in that so far Mother has remained very sweet, affectionate, and considerate. She always says she is 'fine,' but I know that she is worried and very unhappy. The other day, she told one of the other residents that she wishes she were dead and would like to jump out of her window but can't open it.

"We've had a couple of crises recently. About 3 months ago I was called at my office and told that Mother had put all of her clothes in a pile outside her door, stating that she was leaving. When I got there 20 minutes later, I found Mother sitting on her bed weeping with her head in her hands. She knew that she had done something wrong, but she could not remember what it was, and she was frightened. I put the clothes away, and the incident passed. Two weeks ago I was called early in the morning and told that I had to come over right away. Mother had not come down for breakfast, and when the staff had gone to her room to check on her, they found her disoriented, mute, and incontinent. She had soiled herself and was wandering around half-dressed. After cleaning her up, I took her to the medical center. A checkup did not reveal any physical problem; indeed, she was pronounced 'physically very healthy.' When the tests were done that afternoon, some of the confusion had cleared up, so I took her back to her room. The crisis passed, but Mother's level of functioning did not return to what it had been. She is much more confused and less verbal, and for some reason she can't seem to

change clothes by herself anymore. Now every evening I have to stop by and help her get ready for bed and put out her clothes for the next day. With this help she can get by, but the woman who administers the home says that she doesn't think they will be able to keep Mother much longer. I have begun looking for a facility that can provide more care.

"I'm struggling with three rough problems. First, it's a terrible experience to watch Mother go through this. I love her, she has done so much for me, and now there's so little I can do for her as she slowly loses control. It's tearing me apart emotionally.

"Second, I'm not sure how I'm going to handle all of this financially. It's clear that soon Mother will have to be moved to a nursing home, but nursing home care is terribly expensive, it isn't covered by insurance, and Mother might need it for years and years. This could wipe me out financially. I'm not sure how I'm going to handle it, and if I can't, what will happen? What will happen to Mother when we can't afford the care she needs?

"Last, I worry about what is ultimately going to happen to me. Sometimes when I see Mother confused and slumped in her chair staring at the floor, I see myself 20 years from now. It's like looking into a horrible crystal ball. Is this going to happen to me? Is this my future I'm looking at, slumped alone in the chair? If it is, who is going to look after me when I lose control, become incontinent, and can't dress myself? Will I waste away like that— and be alone with no one to help? It's frightening. . . ."

> **As time went by, Mother became less and less aware of what was happening around her.**

---

if the protease enzyme can be inhibited, the brain deterioration will be arrested. Researchers are working to develop drugs that will inhibit the activity of the protease enzyme. There is reason to be cautiously optimistic about the devel-

opment of such drugs because earlier research developed a protease inhibitor that is effective for treating AIDS.

Case Study 17.1 reflects the early and middle phases of Alzheimer's disease as seen by a patient's daughter, who, because of the genetic basis of the disease, may also be at risk.

Dementia Caused by Vascular Disease (Strokes)

Blood provides the nourishment that the body's cells must have to survive, and if the supply of blood is cut off for even a relatively short period of time, the cells will die. For example, when the blood supply to a part of the brain is cut off, the neurons in that part of the brain die, and the individual is said to have had a **cerebral infarction.** The common term for a cerebral infarction is a *stroke.*

If the infarction affects a part of the brain that is essential to life, the individual will die. However, if the infarction affects a part of the brain responsible for language, the result will be an inability to use words; if the infarction is in an area of the brain responsible for motor activity, the result will be a paralysis (Leys & Pasquier, 1998). The case of a professor friend of mine provides a particularly poignant example of the language difficulties that can be caused by a cerebral infarction. After his first infarction the professor developed aphasia, which posed problems when he lectured. A nationally recognized expert on Shakespeare, he had not forgotten anything he knew about Shakespeare, but he could not remember Shakespeare's name when he was lecturing. His lectures began something like this: "Yesterday I began lecturing about the sonnets of . . . of . . . oh, you know, the chap who wrote *Hamlet.*" Over time he developed a list of important words that he could not bring to mind, and when he drew a blank during a lecture, he would quickly go down his "cheat sheet" to find the word he needed. Unfortunately, he suffered several more cerebral infarctions and lost almost all of his ability to talk and much of his memory. This increasing loss of cognitive abilities as the result of progressive destruction of the brain by

repeated infarctions is called **multi-infarct dementia;** that is, dementia that results from multiple small strokes. Cerebral infarctions are the second leading cause of dementia (De Deyn et al., 1999).

Because neurons in the central nervous system (brain and spinal cord) cannot replace themselves, once these neurons are dead, they are gone forever. Fortunately, however, other areas of the brain are able in some instances to take over the functions that were performed by the dead areas. Therefore, with time and retraining, approximately 20% of stroke victims regain their abilities (20% die, and 60% have some residual impairment).

The symptom pattern in multi-infarct dementia is different from that of other dementias in two ways: First, the decline in abilities is *uneven* rather than smoothly progressive. That is, there is a sudden loss of an ability following an infarction, followed by a plateau until the next infarction. The second distinguishing feature of multi-infarct dementia is that usually each infarction results in the loss of *a specific ability,* such as language, memory, or control of a specific body part, rather than a general deterioration of function. In other words, the loss of abilities is "patchy" rather than general. The patchy nature of the loss is due to the fact that specific areas of the brain are destroyed by the infarctions. However, over time many infarctions will result in a widespread loss of multiple functions, and the deterioration becomes general.

There are four factors that can interfere with blood flow in the brain and lead to cerebral infarctions. First, the blood vessels in the brain become blocked because of a buildup of fatty material on their walls, a process called **atherosclerosis** (ath-e-ro-skle-RO-ses). Second, infarctions occur because blood vessels lose their elasticity and rupture when blood pressure increases. When a rupture occurs, the blood flow to the area of the brain served by that artery is interrupted. This is the "hardening of the arteries" that is often mentioned when discussing cerebral problems in older individuals; it is technically called **arteriosclerosis** (ar-te-re-o-skle-RO-sis). The third cause of infarctions also involves a rupture of a blood vessel, but in this case the rupture occurs when the wall of the vessel develops a weak spot, swells, and finally breaks. Such a weak spot is called an **aneurysm** (AN-yur-iz-um). Fourth, a clump of atherosclerotic plaque may develop on the wall of a blood vessel, suddenly break off, flow downstream to a narrower part of the blood vessel, and clog the vessel and reduce blood flow. Such an obstruction of a blood vessel is known as an **embolism** (EM-bo-liz-em).

Until recently there was nothing that could be done once an artery was blocked by an embolism (clot), but now there are powerful drugs ("clot busters") that can break up the clot and restore blood flow. However, because neurons cannot live for long without blood, it is essential that the drugs be administered as soon as possible. *Do not hesitate to go to*

---

cerebral infarction   The death of neurons in a part of the brain, which can cause dementia; commonly called a *stroke.*

multi-infarct dementia   Increasing loss of cognitive abilities as the result of progressive destruction of the brain by repeated cerebral infarctions (strokes).

atherosclerosis   The process by which blood vessels become blocked by the buildup of fatty material on their walls.

arteriosclerosis   A process by which blood vessels lose their elasticity and rupture when blood pressure increases; commonly called "hardening of the arteries."

aneurysm   A weak spot in the wall of a blood vessel that swells and finally breaks.

embolism   An obstruction of a blood vessel, often by a clump of atherosclerotic plaque.

an emergency room if the early symptoms of a stroke (paralyses, numbness, dizziness) appear; any delay could result in serious dementia or death.

Although clot busters can sometimes provide emergency treatment, the most effective treatment strategy for vascular dementia is prevention. The keys to prevention are (1) a diet that lowers cholesterol so that the buildup of plaque in blood vessels will be minimized, and (2) control of blood pressure with aerobic exercise or medication so that it is less likely that blood vessels will rupture (see Chapter 14). The importance of controlling cholesterol was clearly illustrated in a study of over 1,000 75-year-old individuals who showed no sign of dementia. Over the next 8 years, 26% of them developed dementia, and 21% of those cases were due to strokes. Importantly, those individuals whose dementia was due to strokes were those who had high levels of cholesterol when the study was begun (Moroney et al., 1999). Reducing their cholesterol levels would have reduced the likelihood of cerebral infarctions and dementia.

Finally, although a distinction is made between dementia resulting from Alzheimer's disease and dementia due to cerebral infarctions, in fact, dementia in many individuals is a product of both Alzheimer's and infarctions, and the combination may be particularly devastating (Henon et al., 1998; Leys & Pasquie, 1998).

Dementia Due to Other Medical Conditions

Dementia can also stem from a variety of other medical conditions. Primary among these are HIV (*human immunodeficiency virus*) infection, trauma (blow) to the head, and diseases such as Parkinson's, Huntington's, Pick's, and Creutzfeldt-Jakob (Aarsland et al., 1999; Jordan, 1998; Kuzis et al., 1999; Neary, 1999; Thomas Ollivier et al., 1999; Wise et al., 1999). As an example, let's briefly consider the dementia related to HIV infection.

When considering the effects of HIV infection, we usually think about problems with the immune system, which lead to declines in physical health (see the discussion of AIDS in Chapter 14); however, HIV infection also brings on dementia (Grant, Marcotte, & Heaton, 1999; Portegies & Rosenberg, 1998). The nature and severity of **HIV-related dementia** varies widely from patient to patient, but it generally involves the *slowing* of cognitive functioning. For example, memory, thinking, and problem solving are slowed and require more effort. It appears that most of the brain damage from HIV infection occurs primarily in the subcortical areas of the brain, particularly in the white matter just beneath the gray matter of the cortex. The white matter is important because it provides chemicals such as neurotransmitters that are necessary for the functioning of the cortex; thus, if support from the white matter is diminished, activity and cognitive processing in the cortex is slowed down. Specifically, in cases of HIV-related dementia, there is evidence of reduced levels of dopamine, a neurotransmitter essential for maintaining activity in the brain (Lopez et al. 1999). Consistent with this evidence are findings that individuals with HIV-related dementia show lower levels of brain activity when trying to use their memories (Weisman et al., 1999). Unfortunately, as with cerebral infarcts there is very little that can be done once the brain is damaged by the infection.

Delirium Disorders

Delirium (di-LIR-e-um) **disorders** have two major symptoms, the first of which is a *disturbance in consciousness.* For example, individuals may have difficulty focusing attention, maintaining attention, or shifting attention when necessary. In other words, individuals with delirium disorders cannot concentrate. The second symptom is *problems with thinking* (cognition). That is, in addition to problems with attention, individuals' thoughts are disrupted, and they become confused about where they are, are incoherent in their speech, and have problems with memory. Some individuals also have visual hallucinations (i.e., see things that are not there). The symptoms of delirium usually develop quickly (over a few hours or a couple of days), and once they have developed, the symptoms may fluctuate in severity. In many respects individuals who are developing a delirium disorder show symptoms similar to those of individuals who are becoming progressively more drunk. Also like people who are drunk, individuals with delirium disorder respond differently to their condition; some become passive and withdrawn, whereas others become agitated and aggressive.

Delirium differs from dementia in two important ways: First, delirium develops rapidly and then goes away when the physiological problem causing the delirium is corrected, whereas dementia comes on slowly and is usually permanent (see the earlier discussions of Alzheimer's disease, cerebral infarctions, and HIV infection). Second, delirium results in behaviors that are more bizarre than those seen with dementia. Indeed, individuals suffering from delirium are sometimes incorrectly diagnosed at first as suffering from schizophrenia. In fact, the term *delirium* comes from a Latin word meaning "to leave the track" or, used figuratively, "to be crazy."

HIV-related dementia   Slowing of cognitive functioning caused by HIV (human immunodeficiency virus) infection, which damages subcortical (white matter) areas of the brain.

delirium disorders   Cognitive disorders characterized by a disturbance in consciousness and problems with thinking.

Delirium Caused by General Medical Conditions

Delirium disorders can be caused by a wide variety of medical conditions, ranging from simple problems such as dehydration (individuals who are lost in the desert without water often become delirious and show symptoms such as hallucinations) to life-threatening infections such as encephalitis and meningitis, which involve inflammation of the tissues surrounding the brain. In most cases the factor that causes the delirium is the *high fever* that accompanies the medical condition; specifically, the increased temperature causes a disruption in brain functioning. For example, brief periods of delirium are seen in children who are running very high fevers and in individuals who are suffering from "heat stroke" (*hyperthermia*). An important point here is that when the medical condition goes away, so will the delirium, and there will not be any long-term effects.

Delirium Caused by Substance Intoxication or Withdrawal

Delirium disorders can be brought on by a variety of drugs, including opiates such as morphine, hallucinogens such as LSD, and depressants such as barbiturates and alcohol (Hersh, Kranzler, & Meyer, 1997). Delirium can also be triggered by many poisons and allergic reactions. One of the most frequent causes of delirium disorders is a high level of blood alcohol; indeed, individuals who are very drunk might be considered to be suffering from a minor form of delirium in that they are not completely aware of what is going on around them, they have difficulty with attention, they have problems with memory and language, and they may even hallucinate. Furthermore, individuals who have been using alcohol heavily for long periods of time and whose bodies have adjusted to high blood levels of alcohol may experience a delirium disorder when the alcohol is withdrawn (Trevisan et al., 1998). This condition is referred to as **delirium tremens (d.t.'s)** because in addition to the cognitive symptoms of delirium, the individuals experience uncontrollable muscle tremors. (*Tremens* means "tremor," so *delirium tremens* is literally "delirium with tremors.") In some cases delirium can also be brought on by nicotine withdrawal (Gallagher, 1998). The substances that cause delirium do so by disrupting neurological activity in the brain, resulting in a disruption of cognitive functioning. Treatment usually involves using a drug that will offset the effects of the original drug and restore normal brain functioning. Because delirium disorders are usually triggered by acute infections, sudden changes in body temperature, or drugs, they typically have a rapid onset.

delirium tremens (d.t.'s)　Condition involving a combination of delirium and tremors associated with withdrawal from heavy use of alcohol.

Questions about Cognitive Disorders

1. *Have dementia disorders impaired national leaders and thereby altered world history?* Because national leaders are generally older, they are at increased risk for dementia disorders, and there are a number of cases of leaders who appear to have suffered from disorders that influenced their performance and may have changed history (Burke & Mitchell, 2000; Hachinski, 1999; Toole, 1999). For example, Woodrow Wilson had a serious cerebral infarction that completely incapacitated him for a number of years while he continued as president of the United States. President Franklin D. Roosevelt suffered from very high blood pressure, and it is suspected that it caused some multi-infarct dementia that impaired his ability to negotiate with the Russian leader, Joseph Stalin, over the division of Europe after World War II, a division that eventually led to the Cold War. Stalin also presents an interesting case. During his later years as Soviet Premier he became extremely paranoid and suspicious of everyone. He withdrew from personal and official functions and wandered around muttering to himself that it was time for another purge. In fact, it is reported that he was afraid of his shadow and did not even trust himself. Was he having TIAs? That's likely, because he suffered from very high blood pressure and died of a stroke. An autopsy revealed that he had had a series of strokes before the final one that killed him. We also now know that Ronald Reagan had Alzheimer's disease during the last few years of his presidency and that it greatly impaired his memory. Finally, concerns have been raised about the potential cognitive effects that Parkinson's disease may have on Pope John Paul II.

2. *Can dementia be slowed or reversed?* Some degree of dementia occurs in many of us as we age, so it is a widely held concern whether anything can be done to slow or reverse the process. One frequent suggestion is to continue using your cognitive abilities; the notion is "use it, and you won't lose it." Indeed, there is evidence from a number of countries that individuals who remain socially active show better cognitive functioning (memory, problem solving, learning) than do socially inactive individuals (Arbuckle et al., 1992; Deeg et al., 1992; Hultsch et al., 1993; Smits et al., 1995). Those findings are encouraging, but let's think about them for a minute: Does continued social functioning help maintain cognitive functioning, or do individuals who have better cognitive functioning maintain social functioning longer?

In one series of experiments designed to answer that question, older individuals were randomly assigned either to training conditions in which they were taught strategies that enhance problem solving and memory or to no-train-

It was announced after he left office that President Ronald Reagan was suffering from Alzheimer's disease. As his disease has progressed, he has made fewer and fewer public appearances. The former president is pictured here on his 89th birthday with his wife, Nancy.

ing control conditions (Baltes & Kliegl, 1992; Hayslip, 1989a, 1989b; Kliegl et al., 1989, 1990; Raykov, 1995; Verhaeghen et al., 1992). The results consistently indicated that the training led to increased abilities; that is, you can "teach an old dog new tricks." This truism was clearly demonstrated to me recently when, after taking a few months to "brush up," a 69-year-old student of mine scored above the 90th percentile on the test used to screen students for admission to graduate school!

Although these findings and the case of my older student are interesting, they really do not provide a complete answer to the question. They indicate that some older people can learn new facts (what psychologists call *crystallized* intelligence), but they do not indicate whether older people can be trained to come up with creative new ways to solve problems (what psychologists call *fluid* intelligence). It is fluid intelligence that shows the greatest decline as we age. Overall, then, we continue to learn new things as we grow older, but it appears that there may be a decline in our ability to solve new problems.

Another very important finding is that estrogen replacement therapy may prevent, or at least slow down, brain deterioration and dementia in women following menopause (Yaffe et al., 1998). In fact, the results of 10 studies suggest that women who received estrogen supplements following menopause showed a 30% reduction in the likelihood of developing dementia. Unfortunately, at present we do not understand exactly why estrogen is helpful in preventing dementia, and we do not know whether it would have similar effects in men.

TOPIC II
Mental Retardation

Michael suffers from a moderate level of mental retardation due to *Down syndrome*. His abilities are very limited, but he is a lovable, good-natured, and playful child. There is no treatment for Down syndrome. His parents worry about who will take care of him after they are gone. Is there a place for individuals with mental retardation in our high-tech society?

When she was pregnant with her daughter, Anna developed a mild case of German measles. Her only symptoms were a mild fever and skin rash. However, her daughter was born with a serious heart condition, has problems with vision, and suffers from mental retardation. Could these problems be the result of Anna's case of measles?

Mark and Mandy are twins and have grown up together. However, Mandy suffers from a unique form of mental retardation called *Turner's syndrome,* and as a result she cannot understand the relationships between forms; for example, she cannot put puzzles together. Why does Mandy suffer from this disorder while Mark does not?

It is estimated that there are well over 6 million people in the United States who have IQs in the retarded range (under 70). *That represents the number of people who live in Los Angeles and Chicago combined,* and it makes retardation one of our most widespread mental health problems. If individuals with borderline IQs (between 70 and 85) are included, the number of afflicted individuals rises to well over 40 million—*more than twice the combined populations of the 10 largest cities in the United States!* Stated in another way, one out of every six Americans suffers from mental retardation to some extent. The personal, social, and economic impact of mental retardation is especially great because it is usually a chronic and irreversible condition. Clearly, this is a problem to which we must give careful consideration.

DSM-IV sets out three criteria that must be met to reach a diagnosis of **mental retardation**:

1. The individual must have an IQ of 70 or below.
2. The individual must have problems with daily functioning that are due to low intelligence. For example, individuals may have problems taking care of themselves, supporting themselves, or getting along with others.

mental retardation A usually chronic and irreversible condition whose diagnosis is based on an IQ of 70 or below and problems with daily functioning that begin before the age of 18.

3. The disorder must set in before the age of 18. If an individual functions normally until the age of 18 and only thereafter shows a decline, the individual is diagnosed as suffering from some form of dementia rather than retardation.

The line between normal ability and retardation is not always clear or consistent because it is often difficult to measure IQ exactly. Also, what is demanded of an individual in terms of functioning varies widely from one situation to another. For example, the intellectual demands on a secretary in an urban office may be much higher than those on a farm laborer. Therefore, an individual may move back and forth across the line between normality and retardation, depending on the circumstances of testing and the demands of the individual's life situation.

There are three major causes of mental retardation: *genetic factors; physical factors* in the environment, such as problems during pregnancy and diet; and *psychosocial factors,* such as impoverished living conditions. In the following section I will discuss some of the difficult and controversial issues associated with mental retardation, and then I will examine the types of retardation that stem from genetic, physical, and psychosocial factors.

Issues Associated with Mental Retardation

Are there different levels of mental retardation? Can we measure mental retardation accurately? Is mental retardation due to an insurmountable defect, or is it simply a delay in development? These are some of the questions we will consider in this section.

Levels of Retardation

There are four *levels of retardation:* mild, moderate, severe, and profound. Just as the line between normality and retardation is not clear, the lines between the various levels of retardation are not clear, but for general descriptive purposes it is helpful to identify ranges of retardation. The four generally accepted ranges of retardation are described in Table 17.3.

William's syndrome   A disorder in which individuals suffer from serious retardation in most areas but show normal verbal and social skills.

savant syndrome   The presence of one extraordinary ability in a mentally retarded or normal individual.

Alfred Binet   A French physician who developed the first IQ test, designed to predict performance in school.

It is also important to note that an individual who suffers from mental retardation may not be retarded in all areas. One particularly interesting example of this is a disorder known as **William's syndrome.** Individuals with William's syndrome suffer from serious retardation in most areas but show *normal verbal and social skills* (Goldstein et al., 1999; Klein & Mervis, 1999; Lashkari, Smith, & Graham, 1999; Pezzini et al., 1999). One day in a local restaurant I had a very pleasant talk with a young woman with William's syndrome. She is a delightful and socially skilled young woman, who is very articulate. After answering numerous questions for me, she paused and then said, "Gee, David, we've spent a lot of time talking about me; let's talk about you for a while," and then she took charge of the interview. She showed few if any signs of retardation until I asked a couple of questions that tapped her cognitive abilities. For example, when I asked if she knew how to get home from the restaurant, she replied, "I'll call a cab." When I then asked if she could get home without a cab, she paused thoughtfully and said no. It turned out that although she lived only a few blocks away, she had no idea how to get home. Similarly, when the server brought the check, I put a $10 bill on the table and asked her if she knew how much change I should get back. She grinned at me and said, "I'm not good at numbers." She had no idea how to subtract.

There are also individuals who are generally retarded but show one extraordinary ability; this condition is known as **savant** (sa-VANT) **syndrome** (Cheatham et al., 1995; Hermelin et al., 1987, 1994; Horwitz et al., 1969; Moriarty et al., 1993; Mottron & Belleville, 1995; O'Connor & Hermelin, 1994; Pring et al., 1995; Treffert, 1988; Young & Nettelbeck, 1995). The word *savant* comes from a word meaning "wise," but these individuals are exceptionally wise in only one area. For example, one child had an IQ of only about 60 and could barely care for himself, but he could reproduce on the piano any piece he heard no matter how complex, and he could even improvise accompaniments for performances he heard. In another case a young man who was given a date within a 6,000-year range could state "in a flash" on what day of the week that date would fall. I once met a student who, after looking briefly at a table of thousands of random numbers, could recite the numbers starting at any point and going either forward or backward. (Note that although the savant syndrome occurs in otherwise retarded individuals, it can also occur in individuals of generally normal intelligence.)

Problems with Measuring Intelligence

IQ scores are usually the major factor in determining whether an individual is suffering from mental retardation. However, there are three potentially serious problems with using traditional IQ tests for measuring mental retardation.

TABLE 17.3

The four levels of mental retardation

Level	Education and training potential	Long-term outlook
Mild mental retardation (IQ of 50–70): This level is roughly equivalent to what was once called "educable." This group constitutes the largest segment of persons with mental retardation—about 85%.	People with mild retardation typically develop social and communication skills during preschool years and are often indistinguishable from normal children until a later age. They can acquire academic skills up to about the 6th-grade level.	During their adult years, individuals with mild retardation usually achieve minimal self-support. Virtually all can live successfully in the community, either independently or in supervised apartments or group homes.
Moderate mental retardation (IQ of 35–50): This level is roughly equivalent to what used to be referred to as "trainable." This group constitutes about 10% of individuals with mental retardation.	Individuals with moderate retardation can learn to communicate during the preschool years. They may profit from vocational training and with moderate supervision can take care of themselves. They can profit from social and occupational training but are unlikely to progress beyond the 2nd-grade level in academic subjects.	During adolescence moderate retardation may interfere with peer relationships. In adulthood individuals with moderate retardation may be able to contribute to their own support by performing unskilled or semi-skilled work under supervision in sheltered workshops or in the competitive job market. They adapt well to life in the community, usually in supervised group homes.
Severe mental retardation (IQ of 20–35): This group constitutes 3–4% of individuals with mental retardation.	During the preschool years individuals with severe retardation display poor motor development and acquire little or no communicative speech. During the school years they may learn to talk and can be trained in elementary hygiene skills. They profit to only a limited extent from training in such things as the alphabet and simple counting. They can be taught to sight-read words such as *men, women,* and *stop.*	In their adult years individuals with severe retardation may be able to perform simple tasks under close supervision. Most adapt well to life in the community, in either group homes or with their families.
Profound mental retardation (IQ below 20): This group constitutes 1–2% of individuals with mental retardation.	As children individuals with profound retardation display minimal capacity for sensorimotor functioning. A highly structured environment with constant aid and supervision by a caregiver is required for optimal development. Motor development and self-care and communication skills may improve if appropriate training is provided.	Individuals with profound retardation can perform simple tasks under close supervision.

Source: Adapted from American Psychiatric Association (1994).

Sociocultural Factors. The first problem with using traditional IQ tests for measuring retardation is the possibility that these tests are not always effective for measuring the abilities of children who come from poor or minority backgrounds; these children may be growing up in a cultural setting that is very different from that of the white middle-class children on whose cultural tradition the IQ tests are based. Evidence for this is provided by a study in which it was found that African American and white children showed comparable levels of functioning in their daily lives but the African-American children scored lower than the white children on traditional IQ tests (Adams, McIntosh, & Weade, 1973). In this study it appeared that traditional IQ tests did not adequately measure the intelligence of the African American students. Insofar as that is true, traditional measures of IQ may be irrelevant or invalid for diagnosing mental retardation in members of groups with different cultural backgrounds.

Measurement of Relevant Abilities. The second problem with traditional IQ tests is that they may not measure abilities that are relevant for the "real world," and therefore the abilities they measure may be limited to the schoolroom (Ginsberg, 1972). In this regard, it is interesting to note that when French physician **Alfred Binet** (be-NA) (1857–1911) developed the first widely used IQ test in 1905, the test was explicitly designed to predict how well students would do *in school.* Thus, an IQ test may indicate that an individual is retarded in terms of the types of tasks performed in school, but that does not necessarily mean that he or she is retarded with regard to tasks that may be important outside of school.

Given that children from poor or minority group backgrounds may have grown up in a cultural setting that is quite different from that of white middle-class children, traditional IQ tests may not always be effective for measuring the abilities of these children.

Physical and Emotional Factors. The third problem with using traditional IQ tests stems from the fact that in some cases individuals with mental retardation also suffer from a variety of physical and emotional problems, and these other problems may interfere with their performance on an IQ test and consequently distort the results. For example, a retarded child who also suffers from depression or dyslexia may receive a particularly low score on an IQ test. The level of performance that results from the combination of the retardation and other problems may reflect the individual's current *functional* level of ability (what he or she is able to do given all the problems), but it does not reflect what the individual would be able to do if his or her other problems were treated. In that sense, then, an IQ test may provide an unrealistically low estimate of the abilities of some individuals.

In summary, cultural bias, the measurement of irrelevant abilities, and physical and emotional problems can all serve to invalidate the results of IQ testing and lead to an erroneous diagnosis of mental retardation. Note, however, that in *DSM-IV* it is explicitly required that the assessment of IQ be based on one or more of the *individually administered* general intelligence tests (see Chapter 4) rather than on paper-and-pencil tests. Individually administered tests usually involve up to 2 hours of interaction between the

individual being tested and a highly trained test administrator, who should be able to recognize when a problem is interfering with the client's performance, so that allowances can be made or the test can be disregarded. Note also that the diagnosis of mental retardation requires that the individual perform poorly on an intelligence test and *also demonstrate an inability to function adequately.* Therefore, even if an IQ test provides a low but invalid measure of the individual's capacity, by itself it will not result in a diagnosis of mental retardation. Clearly, safeguards are built into the system, but the system is not perfect. Constant care must be taken to guard against misdiagnoses.

Mental Defect or Delayed Development?

There is no doubt that *severe* retardation is due to a *mental defect* such as brain damage. However, there is some controversy over the cause of *mild* retardation. On the one hand, some theorists believe that even mild retardation is due to mental defects, which have not yet been found because they are very small and subtle. On the other hand, other theorists believe that mild retardation is due to *delayed development* (Zigler, 1969; Zigler & Balla, 1982). These theorists suggest that individuals go through stages of cognitive development and that for some reason the intellectual development of some individuals is slowed or stopped at an early stage. (Note that the term *retarded* implies that there is a *delay* in development rather than a *defect*.) The delay could stem from (1) growing up in a culturally impoverished environment, (2) attitudes about achievement ("I can't do it, so I won't try"), (3) lack of motivation ("I don't care about doing it, so I won't try"), or (4) lack of parental encouragement ("You're dumb, so don't bother to try").

The answer to the question of whether mild mental retardation is due to a defect or delayed development has important implications in terms of treatment. If retardation is due to a mental defect, treatment should be focused on teaching individuals ways of *compensating* for the problem because it probably cannot be corrected. For example, individuals might be given vocational training designed to provide them with income-producing skills that do not require great intelligence. In contrast, if retardation is due to a delay in development, treatment should be focused on *correcting* the problem. For example, individuals might be placed in a program in which they are exposed to experiences that will enable them to grow intellectually and change their attitudes about themselves and their abilities.

The answer to the defect-or-delay question also has implications for the prevention of mild retardation. If it is assumed that retardation is due to mental defects, attention must be focused on things such as good prenatal care and the elimination of lead in the environment so that such impediments to brain development will be eliminated. In contrast, if mild retardation is due to delayed development, it is important that children be exposed to cultural opportunities and positive attitudes. Indeed, the Head Start program was founded on the assumption that mental retardation is due to delays in development, and the program was designed to prevent or offset those delays. Delayed development is certainly a more optimistic explanation because it suggests that with appropriate experiences mild retardation can be prevented or effectively treated.

A variety of attempts have been made to resolve the defect-or-delay debate. The results have been mixed, and it is probably safest to conclude that mild retardation can be due to either a defect or a delay in development and that attention should be given to both possibilities when considering prevention and treatment. The best approach at this point may be not to try to determine which explanation is correct in general, but rather to determine which explanation is correct for a particular individual.

With an understanding of these issues as background, we can go on to consider the causes and types of mental retardation. In the following sections I will describe types of retardation that result from genetic, physical, and psychosocial factors.

Retardation Due to Genetic Factors

Retardation due to genetic factors accounts for only about 25% of the cases of mental retardation, but this type of retardation is particularly important because it is often the most severe. In this section I will describe some of the most common genetic causes of mental retardation.

Down Syndrome: The Effect of an Extra Chromosome

Down syndrome results in a moderate to severe level of general retardation (IQs range from 35 to 49). Individuals suffering from Down syndrome are easily recognizable because they have almond-shaped eyes that slant upward, a small nose with a low bridge, and a furrowed tongue that protrudes because the mouth is small and has a low roof. Their hands are usually small with short stubby fingers, and as adults these individuals are often short and stocky. This syndrome occurs in about 1 of every 1,000 live births and is therefore one of the most common genetic causes of retardation.

In addition to their mental retardation, individuals with Down syndrome develop Alzheimer's disease relatively early in life (Dalton et al., 1999; Lai et al., 1999; Popper & West, 1999; Schupf et al., 1998). Indeed, one study found that 100% of the individuals with Down syndrome who lived to age 40 showed signs of Alzheimer's disease.

Down syndrome results in a moderate to severe level of retardation. The facial features associated with Down syndrome are almond-shaped eyes that slant upward, a small nose with a narrow bridge, and a tongue that protrudes because the mouth is small and has a low roof.

Down syndrome is due to the fact that the individual has an *extra chromosome 21*, a problem known as **trisomy** (TRI-so-me) **21** (Guthrie, Mast, & Engel, 1999). That is, individuals with Down syndrome have *three (tri-)* rather than two of the chromosome labeled 21.

One important finding concerning Down syndrome is that older women are more likely to give birth to infants with the disorder. In fact, the number of Down syndrome births per 1,000 live births increases from 0.58 for mothers who are 20 years old to 87.93 for mothers who are 49. Figure 17.3 (on p. 516) dramatizes this increase in the rate of Down syndrome births. Researchers do not yet understand why the mother's age is associated with the syndrome, but it is possible that because older women's ova (eggs) have been held in "storage" longer, they have been exposed to

Down syndrome A type of mental retardation that is due to the presence of an extra chromosome 21.

trisomy 21 The presence of a third chromosome 21, which causes Down syndrome.

A Mother Talks about Her 15-Year-Old Daughter, Who Has Down Syndrome

"I AM THE MOTHER of a 15-year-old daughter with Down syndrome. Kimberly is currently attending junior high school and is in the ninth grade, enjoying all the ordinary things that teenage girls enjoy. Her passions are rock music and movie stars. She is looking forward to being able to work next summer and earn some money (probably to buy more music tapes) and to eventually move into her own apartment, just like her brother did when he graduated from high school.

"When Kimberly was born, the city had numerous support programs for developmentally disabled children and their families, but the problem was finding the programs. The medical community and social service offices were not coordinated, and therefore new parents in the hospital with a disabled child could not get all the information they needed to help them adjust to this dramatic change in their lives. Trying to deal with the shock of having a child that was not 'normal' and not being able to find support services was traumatic for both my hus-

band and me. All our pediatrician told me was that I did not have to take her home if I didn't want to, that there were institutions available. I remember thinking that she is only a baby, and a baby only needs love and care and a family. There was no way that I was going to put her in an institution. Fortunately, my mother lived across the street from a family that had a son with Down syndrome, and she immediately brought as much information as she could to the hospital.

"Adequate support is critical at this time because the parents in this situation go through a grieving process—grieving for the normal child that they did not have. The hopes and dreams that you have for your children must be adjusted to encompass your special child, and this takes time. I believe that it is important to recognize this process, for it helps us to finally accept the situation and move positively toward the future.

"We found that at first we were able to plan ahead for only a short period of time, and we did not look too far down the road. When Kim was a baby,

for instance, my hopes were only that she be able to go to a preschool. When she was 3 years old, we started thinking about what would be available for her when she was 5. We also learned not to let our own thoughts and objectives create limits for Kim. When she was 3, it never occurred to me that she would ever be reading at the third- or fourth-grade level and that she would be interested in the things she is interested in today.

"We were fortunate to be in a school district in which she had the opportunity to be mainstreamed into some regular classrooms, and for many classes that was successful. In one case, however, I think Kim realized that she was not comfortable in a regular classroom, and she seemed much happier when we returned her to her special-education classroom. She is currently attending special-education classes but is mainstreamed into regular physical education, art, and music classes and enjoys participating in all of them. She is learning, in a somewhat structured environment, to participate in the real world.

FIGURE 17.3

Older mothers are more likely to give birth to children with Down syndrome.

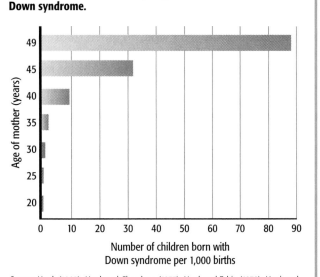

Source: Hook (1982), Hook and Chambers (1977), Hook and Fabia (1978), Hook and Lindsjo (1978).

more environmental agents or stressors that can negatively affect them. It is also possible that the hormonal changes that occur in women in midlife influence the process (Crowley, Hayden, & Gulitai, 1982).

There is also evidence that the father's age is related to the risk of Down syndrome in his offspring (Erickson & Bjerkedal, 1981; Regal et al., 1980). However, whereas the risk greatly increases after the mother passes her mid-30s, the risk from the father's side does not increase until he passes his mid-50s.

Fortunately, a variety of tests can now be used to determine early in a pregnancy whether the fetus is developing Down syndrome. Because of the serious long-term problems associated with Down syndrome, these tests are often recommended, especially for older pregnant women who are at highest risk for giving birth to a child with the syndrome.

Although individuals with Down syndrome are seriously retarded, they are usually good-natured, happy, affectionate, socially well adjusted, and playful. Unfortunately, as they age, they are more likely to suffer from Alzheimer's

"Kim's wants and desires are not very different from those of normal teenagers, but trying to meet those wants and desires is. As parents of a child with Down syndrome—or any disability, for that matter—we frequently have to go to bat for our child in order for her to have some of the experiences that ordinary children take for granted. It is normal for seventh and eighth graders to gather with their friends on Friday or Saturday night, and Kim wants to do the same thing, but she doesn't always have the capacity to handle the situation. We also have to be careful that other people do not take advantage of her. Fortunately, we have been able to work with the city's Parks and Recreation Department to develop some structured weekend activities in which Kim and her friends can participate successfully and safely.

"Kim wants to drive a car when she is 16, which is not too far away, and we haven't quite figured out how to deal with that. Our stock answer is that if she can pass the written driving test like everyone else, she can get her learner's permit. That's the same answer that we give to her younger sister. In essence, we are trying, and have always tried, to treat Kimberly as normally as possible and to expect the same responsibilities from her that we do from the other children. The hard part is to give her enough leeway to try so that she (and we) can learn her limits but to do so without being too lax and assuming that she can handle everything. When Kim was only 2 months old, a good friend told me that I shouldn't put limits on what I thought Kim was capable of becoming. I have never forgotten her advice, and I know that Kim has far exceeded anything that I could have imagined when she was only a few months old.

"As a parent of a disabled child who is soon to be an adult, I am learning that it is important for Kim to learn to cope with the real world. I want her to be able to go to the movies, go to the store, go on a date if she wants, and do ordinary things independently, without having people stare at her and think she is weird. I want her to learn to dress nicely, to keep her hair combed and her face washed. I want her to care that her clothes match and that she looks presentable. I want her to move out of the house when it is appropriate, just as I want my other children to do the same thing. Our hopes and dreams for Kim are the same as our hopes and dreams for our other children: that she will build a life for herself beyond the family; that she will have her own job, her own home, and some independence; that she can cope with the world around her and be happy. I want people around her to accept that she has the same rights to these goals and happiness that anyone else does. Our fears are that she will be rejected because of her disability, that there will not be anyone to watch out for her when we are gone, and that the necessary services for people with developmental disabilities will disappear."

> **Kim's wants and desires are not very different from those of normal teenagers. . . .**

disease and other disorders that add appreciably to the problems of their care.

It is important to recognize that some individuals with Down syndrome are only moderately retarded, and with careful guidance they can make a somewhat normal adjustment. In Case Study 17.2 a mother talks about her moderately retarded daughter who has Down syndrome.

Phenylketonuria (PKU): A Genetic Problem with Metabolism

Phenylketonuria (fe-nul-ke-tun-YOO-re-uh), usually abbreviated **PKU,** results in a severe level of mental retardation (IQ rarely higher than 40 or 50). Many individuals with this disorder are so retarded that they cannot walk or talk. They are also likely to be irritable, unpredictable, and hyperactive, and they are generally unresponsive to other persons (Robinson & Robinson, 1976; Sullivan & Chang, 1999). Furthermore, they often show aimless motor behavior such as arm waving, rocking, and unusual finger movements. This combination of emotional and motor symptoms is similar to the symptom pattern seen in children with autism (see Chapter 13), and therefore children with PKU are sometimes misdiagnosed as suffering from autism. Individuals who suffer from PKU are likely to have blond hair, blue eyes, and very fair skin. PKU occurs in approximately 1 of every 15,000 live births.

PKU results from a low level of an enzyme that is necessary to break down an amino acid called **phenylalanine** (fe-nul-AL-uh-nin). If the phenylalanine is not broken down, it forms **phenylpyruvic** (fe-nul-pi-ROO-vik) **acid,** which destroys the brain. In other words, when the enzyme level is

phenylketonuria (PKU)   A genetic disorder that results in a severe level of mental retardation due to high levels of phenylpyruvic acid, which destroy the brain.

phenylalanine   An amino acid that is converted into brain-destroying phenylpyruvic acid in individuals with PKU.

phenylpyruvic acid   An acid that is formed from phenylalanin and destroys the brain in individuals with PKU.

low, the acid level builds up and destroys the brain, resulting in mental retardation. The low level of the enzyme is due to a recessive gene that is carried by as many as 1 in 50 individuals. If two individuals with the gene give birth to a child, there is a 25% chance that the child will have PKU (Waisbren, 1999).

Although an infant with PKU is born with an inability to break down phenylalanine, at birth the acid levels have not had time to build up and begin destroying the brain. Therefore, if the disorder is diagnosed early and steps are taken to treat the problem, the effects of the disorder can be reduced or eliminated. Screening for PKU is done with a simple urine or blood test when the infant is only a few days old. Infants found to have PKU are put on a diet that is low in phenylalanine, thereby preventing the buildup of phenylpyruvic acid and preventing destruction of the brain. The sooner the low-phenylalanine diet is begun, the less severe the retardation will be. Indeed, if the diet is begun early in infancy and is maintained for at least 6 years, the retardation will be minimal (Tredgold & Soddy, 1970). There is one difficulty with a low-phenylalanine diet, however: Phenylalanine is found in almost all foods that contain protein. This means that there is very little that the child can eat without being deprived of protein, which is essential for growth. To get around the problem, the child must eat synthetically developed foods (Lofenalac, PKU-Aid, Phenylfree) that contain protein but not phenylalanine. Unfortunately, these foods are expensive, they usually do not taste good, and it is often difficult to get the child to eat them. In sum, PKU can and must be treated, but the process can be very difficult. Because the disorder can be corrected if the diet is begun early, it is especially tragic when it is misdiagnosed (usually as autism) and treatment is delayed. If the treatment is delayed more than a couple of years, severe and irreversible brain damage occurs.

Turner's syndrome   A genetic disorder that can cause mental retardation in women; the retardation involves problems with seeing relationships between objects and the inability to put things together.

Klinefelter's syndrome   A genetic disorder that can cause mental retardation in men and that results from the presence of one or more extra female chromosomes.

cretinism (hypothyroidism)   A genetic disorder that can involve mental retardation and whose symptoms are due to low levels of thyroxin, causing slowed metabolism and development.

fetal alcohol syndrome (FAS)   A pattern of symptoms, including mental retardation, caused by maternal consumption of alcohol during the prenatal period.

One more important fact concerning PKU should be mentioned: Women who had PKU as children but were effectively treated are likely to give birth to brain-damaged children. This occurs because the mothers still have high levels of phenylalanine, which can damage the fetus while it is developing in the womb. In fact, in one study it was found that 30% of the children of mothers who had had PKU developed intellectual and social problems (Wansbren et al., 2000). In view of the facts that women with PKU will pass the recessive gene on and that they will provide a dangerous fetal environment for their children, these women should give serious consideration to not having children.

Other Types of Retardation Due to Genetic Factors

Many other types of mental retardation stem from genetic problems, but most of those are rare. In Table 17.4 I have summarized the characteristics of three of the more notable of those genetic disorders: **Turner's syndrome, Klinefelter's syndrome,** and **cretinism.**

Retardation Due to Physical Factors in the Environment

Unfortunately, there are a number of environmental and physical factors, such as infections, drugs, exposure to lead, temperature, nutrition, and injuries, that can damage the brain and result in retardation. These factors are most likely to have their effects during pregnancy, the birth process, or the early years of life. Attention to such causes of retardation is important because in most cases they can be avoided.

Fetal Alcohol Syndrome: Effects of Maternal Drinking during Pregnancy

We now know that the consumption of alcohol by pregnant women can result in a particular set of problems in their offspring, and this pattern has come to be known as **fetal alcohol syndrome,** sometimes abbreviated **FAS.** One of the symptoms is mental retardation, which can range from mild to severe. Other cognitive symptoms can include attentional difficulties and hyperactivity (Kaemingk & Paquette, 1999; Korkman et al., 1998; Mattson & Riley, 1999; Mattson et al., 1999; Roebuck, Mattson, & Riley, 1999). Physical abnormalities include microencephaly (small brain), distortions of the face, and cardiac abnormalities. Not all of these symptoms are always present, and which ones occur depends on when during the prenatal period the mother was drinking. Because different parts of

TABLE 17.4

Characteristics of some genetic disorders that can lead to mental retardation

Disorder	Characteristics
Turner's syndrome	Limited to women and occurs when a women is missing one of the two female sex chromosomes (X instead of XX). Only sometimes causes retardation, which involves deficits in the ability to see relationships between objects and how to put things together. Physical characteristics consist of a lack of secondary sex characteristics, which can be corrected with hormones, but hormones do not correct deficits in cognitive abilities.
Klinefelter's syndrome	Limited to men and results from the presence of one or more extra female chromosomes; instead of an XY configuration, the individual will have an XXY or an XXXY configuration. Retardation occurs in about half of the cases, but the severity of the retardation increases as the number of extra X chromosomes increases.
Cretinism (hypothyroidism)	Frequently but not always associated with retardation. Physical characteristics usually include short stature ("dwarfism"), obesity, stubby fingers, dry skin, sparse hair, low heart rate, low temperature, and low respiration rate. Physical and cognitive symptoms are due to low levels of thyroxin, which is produced by the thyroid gland; specifically, low thyroxin levels lead to slowed metabolism and development. The low levels of thyroxin are caused by a recessive gene, by radiation (X-rays) during pregnancy that interferes with the normal development of the thyroid gland, or by an iodine deficiency in the mother during pregnancy (that cause has been largely eliminated in countries where iodine is added to table salt). If detected early and treated with thyroid medication (thyroxin obtained from animals), the problem can often be overcome or reduced. The treatment reverses the progression of the disease following birth but cannot repair any damage that might have occurred before birth.

the body develop at different times during the prenatal period, different parts are influenced depending on when the alcohol is present.

Fetal alcohol syndrome may affect as many as 1 in 750 live births, making alcohol one of the most common causes of physically based mental retardation. Furthermore, many victims of fetal alcohol syndrome grow up to abuse alcohol as adults, thereby producing another generation of sufferers. This serious and widespread form of mental retardation is all the more tragic because it can be so easily prevented.

Alcohol has a number of serious effects on fetal brain structure and functioning. Specifically, it can kill neurons in the brain, interfere with the movement of neurons in the brain during development, and disrupt the connections between parts of the brain. It may also cause problems with the production of neurotransmitters. Because alcohol can influence the development of the fetus at any time during pregnancy and because even small amounts may have effects, the best rule of thumb is *to avoid all alcohol consumption during pregnancy.* Is the brief pleasure of a couple of drinks worth the destruction of a child's brain? Recent research indicates that because of the publicity that fetal

Symptoms of children with fetal alcohol syndrome can include mental retardation, attentional difficulties, hyperactivity, small brain, facial distortions, and cardiac abnormalities.

alcohol syndrome has received, the dangers of drinking during pregnancy are now widely known. Unfortunately, however, among heavy drinkers the knowledge has had only a minimal effect on drinking during pregnancy (Murphy-Brennan & Oei, 1999).

Rubella (German Measles): Effects of Infection during Pregnancy

Earlier you learned that maternal infections during the prenatal period can lead to schizophrenia (see Chapter 11). The question here is, can a mother's illness during pregnancy influence the intelligence of her child? Yes. When a pregnant woman suffers from a case of **rubella** (roo-BEL-uh) (*German measles*), she experiences only a low-grade fever and a slight skin rash. However, her infection can cause an inflammation of the brain of the fetus, which in turn leads to a degeneration of the brain tissue. Different parts of the brain are destroyed depending on the stage of fetal development when the inflammation occurs, and thus the effects of rubella may differ from one child to another. Retardation may be mild or very severe, and there may also be defects in sight, hearing, and heart function. (Note that the pattern linking stage of development to symptoms is similar to what occurs with fetal alcohol syndrome.) The likelihood of mental retardation is 50% if the infection occurs in the first month of pregnancy but declines thereafter. As with most other forms of retardation, there is no treatment for retardation due to rubella once it occurs, but it can be effectively prevented by vaccination before pregnancy.

Lead Poisoning: Effects of Exposure during Pregnancy and Childhood

The use of lead-free gasoline and lead-free paint has been an important step in combating mental retardation. Why? Because lead is a poison and exposure to lead early in life can disrupt neurological development and cause mental retardation (Bryant & Maxwell, 1999). This form of retardation may be of only moderate severity, but it is very widespread and therefore a serious problem. Children develop lead poisoning when they eat chips of paint that contain lead, play in dirt in lead-contaminated areas, or inhale lead in the air (from automobile or industrial pollutants). The poisoning can also occur during fetal development if pregnant women are exposed to lead.

rubella (*German measles*)   A virus infection that, if present in a woman during pregnancy, can cause an inflammation of the brain of the fetus, which in turn can lead to mental retardation.

The effects on IQ of exposure to lead were demonstrated in the results of a study in which lead concentrations were assessed in pregnant women and later in their offspring (Baghurst et al., 1992). The individuals in the study lived in a city with a large lead-smelting plant, which caused high levels of lead in the air. IQ was measured when the children were 7 years old. The results of the study indicated that high and low levels of lead in the mothers were linked to differences in IQ in their children of almost 10 points (99.8 vs. 108.5, respectively) and that high and low levels of lead in the children were linked to differences in IQ of more than 10 points (98.7 vs. 109.6).

Diet: Effects on Brain Development and Energy

You may have heard the old saying "Breakfast is the most important meal of the day." There may be some truth to this, especially with regard to the effects of a good breakfast on intellectual development. What's the evidence? To test the effects of diet on intellectual development, investigators first identified children who were living in poverty-stricken villages in Guatemala and who were eating very poor diets. The children in two villages were then given a dietary supplement that was high in *protein* and *calories,* whereas the children in two other villages were given a supplement that did not contain protein and contained only about a third as many calories (Brown & Pollitt, 1996; Pollitt et al., 1993). When the children's intellectual performance was assessed some years later, two interesting findings emerged. First, the children who received the protein/calorie supplement scored generally higher on a wide variety of intelligence tests than did the other children. Second, the protein/calorie supplement was only effective for increasing the intellectual performance of children who *went to school.* Why only those children? It is probably the case that the protein contributed to brain development and the calories provided the children with energy so that they could take advantage of their intellectual opportunities. In other words, the dietary supplement enabled their brains to respond to educational stimulation, and the calories made it possible for the students to remain alert while in school. It's clear that diet is important, but primarily because it interacts with a psychosocial factor (schooling). In view of this finding, let's go on to consider some of the psychosocial factors that are important for intellectual development.

Retardation Due to Psychosocial Factors

Severe forms of mental retardation constitute only a small proportion of the cases of mental retardation; severe cases are found in equal proportions in all levels of society, and they stem from physiological problems. In contrast, moderate forms of mental retardation are much more prevalent; moderate cases are more likely to be found in the lower socioeconomic classes, and most are presumed to be due to social and psychological factors (Bryant & Maxwell, 1999). In this section we will briefly examine six psychosocial factors that can contribute to retardation. Understanding these factors is particularly important because unlike physiological factors such as genes, psychosocial factors can be changed relatively easily.

1. *Limited psychosocial environments.* Enriched social environments are thought to contribute to enhanced brain development and superior cognitive skills. Unfortunately, lower-class children have fewer toys to play with, and they are less likely to be taken on trips to places like museums or zoos. The effect of improving the psychosocial environment on IQ was clearly demonstrated in a series of studies on children from "disadvantaged" homes who were raised in "advantaged" homes. In a classic study of this type investigators found that disadvantaged children who had been adopted in the first year and raised in advantaged homes had IQ scores that averaged *20 points higher* than those of a similar group of children who had not been adopted and who had been raised in disadvantaged homes (Scarr & Weinberg, 1977, 1978). Importantly, a followup evaluation conducted 10 years later revealed that the difference in IQ scores had been maintained, thus indicating that the effect was not fleeting (Weinberg et al., 1992).

2. *Language habits.* Verbal behavior plays an important role both in the assessment of intelligence and in daily functioning; therefore, poor language habits are a crucial factor contributing to mental retardation. Some minority group members who speak English use a nonstandard form of English. Although this nonstandard English enables the individuals to communicate with other members of their group, it reduces their ability to communicate with or learn from individuals in the larger society or to perform well on tests of intelligence. Also, lower-class children often learn very restricted language patterns because the adults around them do not talk with them much or use very restricted language patterns when they do. In this way the limited language skills of the adults hamper the development of the children's thinking processes and problem-solving abilities.

3. *Child-rearing style.* A variety of studies have demonstrated that relative to middle-class mothers, lower-class mothers are more authoritarian and allow their children fewer opportunities for self-exploration. They are also less likely to explain things, are more critical, talk less with their children, and use shorter and less complex sentences with fewer abstract words. Such interactions do not foster critical thinking or academic abilities.

4. *Motivation.* Motivation is crucial for effective intellectual performance, but lower-class children are often not encouraged to do well in school and do not see school performance as relevant or important. In some cases lower-class individuals see themselves as locked into their situation and develop feelings of helplessness. In other words, they do not see themselves as being in control but rather as controlled by external factors, so they give up and do not try to improve their performance (Battle & Rotter, 1963). This view of control has been documented in children as young as 3 years old (Stephens & Delys, 1973).

5. *Schooling.* There are often important differences in the facilities available to students from different social classes or racial groups. Also important is the nature of the teaching and the interaction that go on in the classroom. Particularly important in this regard are the expectations that teachers have for their students. In a classic study of the effects of teachers' expectations, teachers were told at the beginning of the year that some of their students would probably "bloom" by the end of the year, but others would not (Rosenthal & Jacobson, 1968). At the end of the year all of the students were given an IQ test, and it was found that those students whom the teachers were led to believe would bloom had higher IQ scores, even though the students had been randomly assigned to the bloomer and nonbloomer groups. A related study revealed that children who were not expected to do well were generally ignored by the teacher, and such reduced attention could certainly result in lowered performance (Rist, 1970).

Because positive early educational experiences are important for getting individuals off to a good start, and because those experiences are most likely to be lacking in poor families, in 1965 the Head Start program was started to provide underprivileged children with a good preschool program. To evaluate the effects of the Head Start program, researchers tested children before, during, and after they left the program, and this testing revealed two important findings: First, children in the program showed immediate and often dramatic increases in intelligence, sometimes by as much as 10 IQ points in the first few weeks (Zigler & Muenchow, 1992; Zigler & Styfco, 1994). Second, however, these effects often faded after the children left the program and started elementary school (Cicirelli, 1969). Does that mean the program was not successful? No; the problem was that the program did not last long enough, and the children went on to substandard educational environments. Consider the case of vocabulary. The children in the Head Start program were exposed to more words and hence developed large vocabularies, but when they left the program and entered substandard schools, where they were no longer exposed to new words, their vocabulary development stopped. An analogy to athletic training may be appropriate here. A young child may receive good training and coaching in swimming at age 6 and show outstanding performance, but

The Contribution of Psychosocial Factors to a Boy's Mild Retardation

. . . he was passed along from grade to grade without having learned anything.

LESTER WAS RAISED in a tough, severely blighted urban ghetto. His father deserted the family soon after Lester was born, so he, his mother, and his two older sisters lived on welfare. Occasionally, his mother worked as a cleaning woman and was paid "under the table," but for the most part they had to subsist on public assistance. In the first eight years of Lester's life, the family moved six times because the buildings in which they were living were condemned, set on fire, or unheated in winter or because the family was evicted for not paying rent. Lester's diet during his early childhood consisted largely of soft drinks, donuts, and junk food. His major activities consisted of watching television and roaming the streets at all hours of the day and night.

Elementary school started badly. He was not prepared for the limitations it placed on him (despite his young age, he was used to doing what he wanted when he wanted), and he could not see any value in what he was supposed to learn. Even at age 6, in his world "street-wise" was better than "book-wise." He told his teacher, "Letters 'n them don't git ya nothin.'" Because of his lack of interest and the frequent disruptions he caused, he alienated his teacher. Within 3 months he and his teacher had implicitly arrived at a standoff: He came to school (or usually did) because he had to, but once there he did nothing; as long as he did not cause trouble, the teacher ignored him. He wasted away the days doodling, napping, or goofing off. Because he was not an overt troublemaker, he was not disliked, and he was passed along from grade to grade without learning anything.

His entrance into high school changed little except that when he did not feel like going to school, he simply "cut." Letters to his mother had no effect, and threats of suspension were empty because he did not want to be in school anyway. Lester was not alone in coming to and going from school as he wished; on a typical day almost half of the students would be absent from any one of his classes. The only class in which he showed any consistent interest and ability was auto shop, where he became adept at fine-tuning automobiles. Lester did not graduate, but it is not clear from the records whether he ever formally dropped out. Apparently, he just drifted out of school, and no one bothered to try to bring him back.

When he was 17, Lester was picked up by the police on suspicion of auto theft, and as part of the pretrial assessment, he was sent to a juvenile detention center, where he was given an individual intelligence test. The results revealed that his IQ was only 62. Followup was never done because he was released when the case was dropped.

Today Lester is functionally illiterate. He cannot effectively read or write, and his math skills are limited to simple addition and subtraction. Socially, he is pleasant and gets along well with just about anyone. He works as a "gofer" in a local automobile repair shop. When he is not running errands, he acts as a helper for one of the mechanics, who is teaching him the job. In this hands-on situation Lester is learning quickly, but ultimately his progress will be limited by the fact that he cannot read the repair manuals.

that does not mean that if the training and coaching stop, the individual will be likely to compete in the Olympics at age 18. Clearly, quality education is essential, but the quality must be consistent throughout the school experience.

6. *Poor physical or medical care.* Individuals in the lower classes often receive poorer prenatal and postnatal care than do individuals in the middle class, and these differences in care can lead to retardation. Strictly speaking,

normalization   The notion that individuals who suffer from mental retardation will be better able to develop more normal behavior patterns if they are exposed to normal living conditions.

infection, trauma, premature birth, and nutrition are not psychosocial factors, but they are associated with psychosocial factors (economic class) and therefore deserve mention in this context.

The effects of psychosocial factors were dramatically illustrated in the case of a child who was locked in an attic until she was 6 years old (Davis, 1947). When she was found, her IQ was estimated to be only 25, but within 3 years she was functioning at the appropriate level for her age. This child's retardation was more extreme than what is usually thought to stem from psychosocial factors, but, of course, the psychosocial factors to which she was exposed were more extreme than those most children experience. Case Study 17.3 focuses on an individual whose retardation stems from psychosocial factors.

Questions about Mental Retardation

1. *How are individuals who suffer from mental retardation treated and cared for today?* Until the 1970s most individuals who suffered from mental retardation were kept in large institutions where they were essentially "warehoused." The notion was that individuals who suffered from retardation could not care for themselves and needed protection. It also seems likely that many parents were ashamed of their retarded children and attempted to hide them. Since then, however, great strides have been taken to modify, if not reverse, that pattern and to bring retarded individuals into the mainstream of society. Indeed, today most retarded individuals live in the community.

This change in the treatment of retarded individuals was motivated by two factors: First, it was suggested that if retarded individuals were exposed to normal living conditions, they would be more likely to develop more normal behavior patterns than if they were left to languish in institutions. This notion is known as **normalization** (Landesman & Butterfield, 1987). Those who supported normalization did not deny that intellectual limitations influence the behavior of retarded individuals, but they suggested that intellectual limitations are only part of the problem. In an attempt to overcome the problems caused by experiential limitations, it was proposed that efforts be made to integrate retarded individuals into the mainstream of society.

The second factor in the deinstitutionalization of retarded individuals was economics. The average yearly cost per institutionalized individual is well over $40,000, and costs are rising sharply. The overall cost to federal and state governments is over $4 billion per year. In addition, there are the enormous costs of private hospitalization and many hidden costs associated with keeping retarded individuals at home (e.g., a potential wage earner has to stay home to care for the individual).

Both normalization and economic pressures led to deinstitutionalization, but deinstitutionalization has had mixed effects. In some cases retarded individuals were taken out of institutions only to be ignored and left alone in deplorable circumstances. In other cases specialized programs were developed to help individuals with mental retardation, and deinstitutionalization was very effective. Case Study 17.4 describes one effective program for helping retarded individuals in the community. In this case not only did the community help the retarded individuals, but the retarded individuals also made a meaningful contribution to the community.

2. *What role do individuals who suffer from mental retardation play in today's high-tech society?* At first you might think that retarded individuals have no role in today's high-tech society, but that is definitely *not* the case. They will not be computer programmers or rocket scientists, but the addition of new high-tech jobs has not eliminated all of the other jobs that require less skill but must be done. The people in the Cottonwood program described in Case Study 17.4 hold jobs in manufacturing, shipping, and restaurant and hotel services, among many others. Those jobs may not

The move toward deinstitutionalization of individuals with mental retardation has led to efforts to integrate them into mainstream society. Community-based programs that offer group homes and supervised work situations have been effective in many cases.

Cottonwood: A Community Program That Is "Good Business" and a Whole Lot More

CASE STUDY 17.4

Employing retarded persons is not charity.

COTTONWOOD, INC., IS a community-based program for individuals who suffer from mental retardation in Lawrence, Kansas, a university town of about 80,000 people. Cottonwood serves two major functions. Its first function is to provide supervised home living for its clients. It accomplishes this through 10 group homes that are scattered throughout the city. Rather than being "institutional," these homes are indistinguishable from other homes in the area. Most people are not even aware that the houses are group home facilities. Between four and six residents and a home supervisor live in each home. When the residents are not working, the supervisor provides training in nutrition, grocery shopping, cooking, grooming, hygiene, clothing care, housekeeping, home maintenance, money management, leisure skills, and social skills. Residents pay a monthly fee to cover rent, utilities, and food, and they are responsible for the care and maintenance of the homes. As residents develop the necessary skills, they progress to a semi-independent living arrangement in which they have their own apartments, but they are still given up to 5 hours a week of training and guidance, which is tailored to their particular needs.

Cottonwood's second major function is to provide occupational training and opportunities for its clients. There are three levels of training. First, approximately 30 clients work in the "sheltered workshop" program. In this program clients are brought to the Cottonwood administrative building, where, with close supervision and training, they work on projects involving light manufacturing, packaging, collating, and the preparation of bulk mailings. These are not meaningless or "make-work" projects. Instead Cottonwood has contracted for real work on a competitive basis with local businesses, and the clients are paid for their work. Because the projects are bid on a competitive basis and because Cottonwood clients may work somewhat more slowly than other people, the wages paid to the clients may be somewhat lower than those paid to others. The important point is that Cottonwood clients become productive, contributing members of society and are paid on a fair basis. Everyone wins.

The second level of job training and experience involves supervised group work in the community. For example, large companies often need a workforce to complete a particular project, and a group from Cottonwood will take on the job. In those cases Cottonwood transports its clients to and from the work site and provides on-site supervisors for them. This real-world work is an important experience for Cottonwood's clients because they can use their nonretarded coworkers as role models. In one case a client stopped carrying his Snoopy lunch box when he saw that everyone else was carrying a plain black lunch box. The clients want to fit in, and with normal role models available they quickly learn how. Having the clients on the production line is also an important experience for the other workers, who learn to overcome their stereotypes about persons with mental retardation and accept them as coworkers.

Some clients go on to normal independent and competitive community employment. Typical employment involves work in fast-food restaurants, janitorial services, housecleaning jobs (especially in hotels and motels), and some light industry.

Employing retarded persons is not charity. As one executive after another says, "*It's just good business.*" Indeed, the experiences of employers across the country consistently indicate that retarded workers are often more reliable, happier, and more likely to remain in the job than their nonretarded coworkers. Cottonwood clients find their jobs challenging and interesting, and that makes them good employees. With this approach everyone wins: Mentally retarded persons get meaningful jobs and a chance to grow, employers get excellent workers, and the economy is helped because people who were once consumers of tax dollars become producers of tax dollars. Cottonwood's logo is a "thumbs up" sign, and that is appropriate because the program is making things work for everyone. It's good business *and a whole lot more.*

be glamor jobs that get attention on the national news, but they must get done if the economy is going to function. The people from Cottonwood may be preparing for shipment the high-tech equipment needed at a scientific laboratory. Furthermore, in many cases they are doing jobs that other people might not be able to do well. That is, retarded individuals can do repetitive work that others might not do well because they would get bored and distracted. The point here is that to keep modern society running smoothly, a lot of people need to do a lot of different things, and persons who are mentally retarded do many essential things very well. Everyone contributes in his or her own way, and retarded individuals contribute in many important ways. We're a team, and they are essential players.

Summary

Topic I: Cognitive Disorders

▶ Cognitive disorders involve problems with thinking and are due to physiological factors such as brain deterioration. There are three types of cognitive disorders: (1) amnesia, (2) dementia, and (3) delirium.

▶ Relevant information coming into the sensory memory is sent to the short-term memory for thinking and processing for storage. Physiologically, the hippocampus processes information for storage in networks of cell assemblies in the cortex. Activating a network activates the memories in that network. Memory fails when (1) the nerve pathway to a cell assembly does not function, (2) all of the connections to a cell assembly or the cell assembly itself is destroyed, or (3) the hippocampus deteriorates or is destroyed. The inability to recall previously stored information is called retrograde amnesia and the inability to store new information is called anterograde amnesia.

▶ Amnesia disorders involve problems with memory. They can be due to medical conditions such as concussions, brief interruptions in blood flow (TIAs), and deterioration of the hippocampus due to a lack of vitamin B1 (Korsakoff's syndrome). They can also be caused by drugs such as anesthetics or alcohol.

▶ Dementia disorders also revolve around problems with memory, but the problems are more severe and can seriously disrupt cognitive functioning. Individuals may suffer from aphasia (loss of words), agnosia (loss of meaning), and apraxia (loss of ability to perform motor activities such as walking). Presenile dementia sets in before age 65, while senile dementia occurs after age 65. Primary dementia is due to physiological problems in the brain whereas secondary dementia is the result of some other disorder, such as depression. There are three causes of dementia disorders: (1) Alzheimer's disease, (2) vascular disease (strokes), and (3) other medical conditions, such as HIV infection or Parkinson's disease.

▶ Dementia in elderly people is often due to a progressive and general deterioration of the brain caused by Alzheimer's disease. Symptoms in the brain involve plaque on the neurons, holes in the neurons, and tangling of axons of the neurons. The primary cause of Alzheimer's disease, specifically of the plaque on neurons, is a protease enzyme that cuts protein strands off neurons; the protein strands then accumulate to form the plaque, which covers and poisons the neurons. This is the protease theory of Alzheimer's disease.

▶ Current treatment for Alzheimer's disease revolves around the use of drugs that increase levels of acetylcholine, a neurotransmitter that is involved in thinking and memory. Future treatment will be focused on protease inhibitors that will reduce the accumulation of the plaque.

▶ The vascular type of dementia is due to cerebral infarctions (strokes) that result in the death of an area of the brain. The infarctions occur when the blood supply to an area is cut off because of atherosclerosis (narrowing of the blood vessels), rupturing of vessels due to arteriosclerosis ("hardening of the arteries"), an aneurysm (weak spot in the vessel wall which breaks), or an embolism (clot in a blood vessel).

▶ Dementia due to a general medical condition can stem from HIV infection, a physical trauma to the head, Parkinson's disease, Huntington's disease, Crentzfeldt-Jakob disease, or drug use. HIV infection causes damage in subcortical areas and results primarily in a slowing of cognitive processing.

▶ Delirium disorders involve problems with consciousness (attention) and thinking (confusion) and sometimes involve hallucinations. Delirium disorders often occur in connection with conditions in which the individual has a high fever (e.g., meningitis, hyperthermia). They can also be caused by drugs such as opiates (morphine), hallucinogens (LSD), and depressants (alcohol) and by poisons and allergic reactions. The symptoms go away when the underlying cause (high body temperature, drug use) is eliminated.

▶ It seems likely that some older national leaders suffered dementia disorders that may have impaired their ability to function and thereby altered history. It is widely believed that keeping socially and intellectually active will reduce the development of dementia, but there is no hard evidence for that belief.

Topic II: Mental Retardation

▶ To be diagnosed as suffering from mental retardation, an individual must meet three criteria: (1) have an IQ of 70 or below, (2) experience problems in daily functioning (e.g., be unable to take care of himself or herself), and (3) show signs of the disorder before the age of 18.

▶ There are four levels of mental retardation: mild (IQ of 50–70), moderate (IQ of 35–50), severe (IQ of 20–35), and profound (IQ below 20).

▶ Problems with the measurement of intelligence revolve around sociocultural factors (e.g., poor individuals or those from ethnic minorities may have had different experiences from those on which the tests are based), the measurement of abilities that are relevant for functioning in the "real world," and the presence of physical or emotional problems that interfere with intellectual performance. However, many of these problems can be overcome with individually administered tests.

▶ It appears that severe retardation is due to mental defects, whereas mild retardation can be due to defects or delayed development. There is a controversy over whether mild retardation is due to mental defects or delayed development that stems from culturally impoverished environments, attitudes about achievement, lack of motivation, or lack of encouragement. This question is relevant for the treatment of individuals who suffer from mental retardation (i.e., compensation or correction).

▶ Retardation due to genetic factors is usually the most serious form of retardation. Major examples of genetic problems associated with retardation are Down syndrome, which is due to an extra chromosome 21 (trisomy 21) and is seen more often in the children of older women and sometimes older men; and phenylketonuria (PKU), which is caused by the inability to break down phenylalanine, which then forms phenylpyruvic acid, which destroys the brain.

▶ Retardation due to physical factors in the environment (e.g., infections, drugs, diet, injuries) can also be serious. Major examples of physical factors that lead to retardation are exposure to alcohol during fetal development, which causes fetal alcohol syndrome (FAS); (2) rubella (German measles), which when contracted during fetal development can destroy neurons in different parts of the developing brain; and (3) lead poisoning during infancy and early childhood, which disrupts brain development.

▶ Mental retardation due to psychosocial factors is less severe than retardation due to genetic or physical factors in the environment but is more widespread. In most cases it is caused by socioeconomic and cultural factors that limit a child's exposure to learning experiences and development (e.g., impoverished environments, limited language exposure, lack of encouragement and motivation, low-quality schooling).

▶ Many individuals who suffer from mental retardation can function effectively in the community if they are provided with sufficient support and structure. Mainstreaming of retarded individuals helps overcome problems that stem from their isolation in institutions and can also reduce the costs of caring for these individuals. Importantly, there are many jobs for which individuals with limited abilities are well suited and from which they can gain satisfaction.

Questions for Making Connections

1. What could you do to reduce the likelihood that you will develop a cognitive disorder (dementia or amnesia)?

2. How would you feel if one of your parents developed a dementia disorder? More importantly, what would you do with regard to treatment and care?

3. What could you do to reduce the likelihood that you would have a child who suffered from mental retardation?

4. If you had a child who suffered from mental retardation, what would you do for your child, and how do you see him or her fitting into today's high-tech world?

Key Terms and People

In reviewing and testing yourself, you should be able to identify and discuss each of the following:

acetylcholine, p. 505
agnosia, p. 502
Alzheimer's disease, p. 503
amnesia disorders, p. 499
aneurysm, p. 508
anterograde amnesia, p. 499
aphasia, p. 498
apraxia, p. 502
arteriosclerosis, p. 508

atherosclerosis, p. 508
Binet, Alfred, p. 513
cell assembly, p. 498
cerebral infarction, p. 508
cognitive abulia, p. 503
concussion, p. 500
cretinism (hypothyroidism), p. 518
delirium disorders, p. 509
delirium tremens (d.t.'s), p. 510

dementia disorders, p. 501
Down syndrome, p. 515
embolism, p. 508
fetal alcohol syndrome (FAS), p. 518
hippocampus, p. 498
HIV-related dementia, p. 509
Klinefelter's syndrome, p. 518
Korsakoff's syndrome, p. 501
mental retardation, p. 511

18 Legal Issues

SHOULD INDIVIDUALS BE HELD RESPONSIBLE for a crime they committed because they were suffering from a serious mental disorder? When can individuals be committed to a mental hospital against their will? Are mental patients dangerous, and if so, what protections does society have? These are some of the interesting legal questions I will discuss in this chapter. Apart from being interesting, these questions are important because they reflect the protection that is given to disturbed individuals and to other members of society who may be threatened by disturbed individuals. For example, in 1980 John W. Hinckley, Jr., attempted to assassinate the president of the United States. In his defense he claimed that he had a psychiatric disorder and therefore was not responsible for his act. Should he have been treated for his disorder and then released, or should he have been punished for his crime as another citizen would be punished? Joyce Brown lived next to a heat vent on a New York City street and sometimes burned money that was given to her by passersby. Should she have been committed to a hospital against her will, or should she have been allowed to continue living on the street as she wished?

TOPIC I

Incompetence and Insanity

Andrew was arrested for stealing a car, but before his trial it was discovered that he was suffering from a severe case of schizophrenia. Thus, he would not understand the legal proceedings and would not be able to testify accurately. Because of that, he probably couldn't get a fair trial. Should the trial go

on, or should it be postponed until Andrew has been treated and is able to understand what is going on and participate effectively?

Leslie believed that the man next door was building a nuclear device in his basement and that he was going to use it to blow up the Capitol. One night, while listening to a commercial on television, she received a "secret message from the president" that instructed her to kill the man next door and thereby save civilization. The next morning she shot the man with a .38 as he left for work. She knew that killing is wrong, but she said her act was "self-defense for the world—I had no choice." At her trial her attorney argued that Leslie's behavior was caused by a serious psychiatric disorder, and therefore she was not responsible for her behavior. Was Leslie "insane" and not responsible for killing her neighbor? How do the courts decide whether someone is insane? If it is decided that someone is insane, is the person simply let go? How can we be sure the individual won't do it again?

In this section we will consider the questions of whether individuals with serious psychiatric disorders can stand trial for crimes and whether they should be held responsible for crimes they did commit.

Incompetence to Stand Trial

Assume for a moment that you have been arrested for committing a crime and you are about to stand trial. Also assume that you are suffering from schizophrenia and are so confused that you do not understand what is happening and you cannot help your attorney with your defense. Would you get a fair trial under these circumstances?

It is important that individuals who are accused of crimes be given the best opportunity to defend themselves in court. However, individuals whose disorders result in such mental confusion that they *cannot understand the proceedings* or *cannot contribute to their defense* can be declared **incompetent to stand trial,** and their trial will be postponed (Appelbaum, 1993; Grisso, 1992; Philipsborn, 1990). For example, an individual with schizophrenia whose thought processes are so disturbed that he or she cannot understand what is being said or cannot respond appropriately will be declared incompetent to stand trial. The incompetence defense is an extension of the notion that an individual should not be tried in absentia. In other words, defendants must be physically and mentally present at their trials.

The decision concerning whether an individual is competent to stand trial is made by a judge based on recommendations from experts such as psychiatrists and psychologists (*Dusky* v. *United States,* 1960; *Pate* v. *Robinson,* 1966). The symptoms that are most likely to lead experts to recommend a judgment of incompetence are hallucinations, delusions, disturbed behavior, or seriously disturbed mood that would interfere with the ability to participate in a legal defense (Nicholson & Kugler, 1991; Slovenko, 1995).

It is important to note that *incompetence does not relieve the individual of responsibility for an illegal act.* Instead it simply allows the trial to be postponed until the individual can participate appropriately. During the postponement the defendant is confined in a hospital or a prison for the criminally insane. This confinement is for the purpose of treating the individual so that eventually he or she will be competent to stand trial.

There are three potential problems with the use of the incompetence defense. First, some individuals attempt to *fake* incompetence as a means of stalling the legal proceedings against them. Fortunately, experts are usually able to detect attempts to fake incompetence, and even if the attempts are successful, they only postpone the trial and do not relieve the individual of responsibility from the crime.

---

incompetent to stand trial   A court ruling that declares an individual is unable to stand trial because he or she cannot understand the proceedings or cannot contribute to his or her own defense and that postpones the trial until the person is judged to be competent.

insanity defense   A legal defense claiming that an individual cannot behave appropriately because of a mental disorder and should not be held responsible for or punished for illegal behavior.

The second problem is that it is possible for individuals to be *confined longer for the treatment of their incompetence than they would be confined if they stood trial for their crimes and were convicted.* For example, an individual might be confined in a hospital for treatment for 2 years when the crime itself carries a penalty of less than a year. To limit such unfairness the U.S. Supreme Court has ruled that the confinement must not be longer than what is necessary to treat the individual, and if it is likely that the individual will never become competent, he or she must either be committed to a hospital or released (*Jackson* v. *Indiana,* 1972). Of course, there is always the possibility that after a prolonged confinement for treatment, the individual will be found not guilty of the crime.

The third problem occurs when the system is *misused* by law enforcement officials. When dealing with individuals who are a nuisance but who do not commit serious crimes, law enforcement officials may arrest the individuals and then have them declared incompetent as a means of getting them off the streets for longer periods than are justified by their illegal acts (Appelbaum et al., 1993). In these cases what was originally developed as a defense becomes a tool for the prosecution. This type of confinement is particularly onerous because unlike other pretrial confinements, incarceration for incompetence does not permit release on bail.

In summary, the concept of incompetence to stand trial is used to protect disturbed individuals from unfair trials. However, the question that arises is whether disturbed individuals should be tried at all. For example, if their illegal acts were caused by their disorders, maybe they should not be held responsible for their illegal acts. We will consider that possibility in the next section.

The Insanity Defense

Assume that you committed a serious crime such as murder, but you killed the other person because you had a delusion that he was about to kill you. In other words, you honestly believed your life was in danger, so you acted in self-defense. Should you be punished—possibly executed—for the crime?

In our society it is generally agreed that individuals are in control of their behavior, and therefore they are responsible for their behavior and should be punished if they do something that is illegal. However, if for some reason individuals cannot control their behavior, then it is not appropriate to hold them responsible or punish them for their behavior. This line of reasoning led to the development of the **insanity defense.** Stated most broadly, the insanity defense asserts that *individuals who cannot behave appropriately because of mental disorders should not be held responsi-*

Two famous cases involving the insanity defense: John C. Salvi III (left), who went on a shooting rampage at two suburban abortion clinics, was found guilty of murder in 1996 and sentenced to life in prison without parole, despite his lawyers' attempts to prove him insane. Theodore Kaczynski, the Unabomber (right), refused to use the insanity defense, as he wanted to keep his mental state out of the trial.

ble for their behavior and should not be punished for their illegal behavior.

In most cases, if an individual is judged to be "not guilty by reason of insanity," he or she is committed to a hospital for treatment rather than to a prison for punishment. When authorities agree that the individual no longer suffers from the disorder that led to the criminal behavior, the individual is released and does not have to go to prison. The insanity plea is very controversial, and we must give it careful consideration because it has a variety of important implications.

Before discussing the rules that are used to determine whether or not an individual is insane, I should briefly mention three related issues: First, the term *insanity* is a *legal* term, not a psychological or medical one. This distinction is relevant because it means that whether or not an individual is judged insane is determined by the laws of a given state rather than by what is defined as abnormal in *DSM-IV*. For example, under some state laws an individual could be hallucinating, delusional, and diagnosed as suffering from schizophrenia and still be judged to be sane.

Second, different states employ different rules for determining insanity. In one state an individual might be declared not guilty by reason of insanity, whereas in another state the same individual would be judged guilty and punished.

Third, there are wide differences of opinion concerning how strict or lenient the rule for determining insanity should be. On the one hand, some critics argue that insanity should be defined very narrowly so that individuals who willfully commit crimes will not be able to slip through an "insanity loophole" and go unpunished. The most conservative position is that all humans are always responsible for their behavior, and the insanity defense should be abol-

ished. Indeed, it has been abolished in the states of Utah, Montana, and Idaho. On the other hand, some people contend that insanity should be defined broadly so as to avoid the possibility of punishing disturbed individuals who need treatment. The most liberal position is that anyone who commits an illegal act is suffering from some sort of problem and should be rehabilitated rather than punished. As you will soon learn, the rules for defining insanity differ widely. As you read about them, you should consider which rule you think is most appropriate. Indeed, because insanity is determined by law, someday you may be asked to vote to determine how insanity will be defined in your state.

Rules for Defining Insanity

At present there are two basic rules for defining insanity: the M'Naghten rule and the American Law Institute rule. I'll discuss them in chronological order so that you can see how rules for defining insanity are evolving.

The M'Naghten Rule: Knowledge of Right versus Wrong. This rule is named for Daniel M'Naghten, who in 1843 murdered the secretary of the British prime minister. M'Naghten actually meant to kill the prime minister but mistook the minister's male secretary for the minister. During the trial it was discovered that M'Naghten thought that the prime minister was plotting against him and furthermore that "the voice of God" had instructed him to kill the prime minister. Because M'Naghten's behavior resulted from delusions of persecution and hallucinations rather than evil intent, he was found not guilty by reason of insanity. Rather than being punished, he was committed to a mental hospital, where he remained for the rest of his life.

There was widespread public outrage over the fact that an individual who had willfully committed murder was not punished. Most important, Queen Victoria was infuriated by the insanity verdict because numerous attempts had been made on the lives of members of the royal family, and she thought that the failure to punish M'Naghten would encourage more such attempts. Therefore, the queen demanded that a tougher rule be developed for determining who is insane. The rule that was subsequently developed in the House of Lords holds that an individual can be declared insane if *at the time of the crime the individual did not know what he or she was doing or did not know that it was wrong.* This rule came to be known as the **M'Naghten** (mik-NOT-un) **rule.** Had this rule been in place when M'Naghten was tried, he would have been punished because he knew that killing another person was wrong.

M'Naghten rule   A legal rule for determining insanity based solely on the individual's knowledge of right versus wrong at the time the crime was committed.

In 1843 Daniel M'Naghten murdered a public official, but the British court ruled that he was not guilty by reason of insanity. Outrage over this verdict resulted in a new standard for determining insanity—the M'Naghten rule.

The M'Naghten rule has been severely criticized because it is based entirely on the individual's *knowledge of right versus wrong,* and therefore it ignores all of the other mental abnormalities that can contribute to behavior. For example, it does not take into consideration the possibility that the individual knew that the act was wrong but had to commit it because of hallucinations or delusions. An individual who suffers from schizophrenia might know that killing is wrong but believe that it must be done in self-defense because the other person is sending brain-killing X-ray waves. Furthermore, the rule does not take into consideration the possibility that the individual knew that the act was wrong but could not exercise control because of overpowering emotions ("crimes of passion" or "irresistible impulses"). The critics of the M'Naghten rule argue that symptoms such as hallucinations, delusions, and over-

whelming emotions are at least as important as the simple knowledge of right versus wrong, and hence they believe that the M'Naghten rule is too narrow.

In some states that employed the M'Naghten rule, an additional rule was introduced that takes into account the influence of an **irresistible impulse** (a sudden, overwhelming emotion) that can lead to illegal behavior (*Smith* v. *United States,* 1929). The rule concerning irresistible impulses is sometimes known as the **elbow rule** because it essentially asks, *would the individual have committed the crime if a police officer had been standing at his or her elbow, thereby ensuring that he or she would be caught?* The notion is that if a police officer were standing next to you so that you would certainly be caught and you still committed the illegal act, you must be out of control and should be judged to be insane.

Despite what many thought were serious problems with the M'Naghten rule, it stood unchallenged for over 100 years, and it is still used in some states today.

The American Law Institute Rule: Mental Disease or Defect.

Because of dissatisfaction with the M'Naghten rule, a number of alternatives were suggested, and in 1972 many courts adopted a new rule that was developed by the American Law Institute, called the **American Law Institute rule** (*United States* v. *Brawner,* 1972). The first part of the rule reads as follows:

> A person is not responsible for criminal conduct if at the time of such conduct as a result of mental disease or defect he [sic] lacks substantial capacity either to appreciate the criminality (wrongfulness) of his conduct or to conform his conduct to the requirements of law.

irresistible impulse   A sudden, overwhelming emotion that can lead to illegal behavior. (See *elbow rule.*)

elbow rule   A legal standard used to identify crimes that result from an irresistible impulse: Would the person have committed the crime if a police officer had been standing at his or her elbow?

American Law Institute rule   A legal rule for determining insanity by which the individual is judged insane if at the time of the criminal act the individual was suffering from a mental disease or defect that either interfered with the ability to understand right versus wrong or caused cognitive (hallucinations, delusions) or emotional problems (irresistible impulses) that led to the criminal act.

This rule greatly expanded the basis for insanity because in addition to using knowledge of right versus wrong (i.e., appreciate the wrongfulness of the conduct), the rule indicates that illegal behavior that results from a *mental disease or defect* can also be considered to be the product of insanity. For example, an individual who commits a murder because he or she has hallucinations or delusions can be found to be insane. (Interestingly, that was the basis on which Daniel M'Naghten was originally ruled insane.) It should also be noted that the American Law Institute rule defined *mental disease or defect* very broadly so as to include "any abnormal condition of the mind which substantially *affects mental or emotional processes* and substantially *impairs behavior controls*" (emphasis added). That is, mental diseases could lead to disturbed thoughts or disturbed emotions. This definition allows for "crimes of passion" in which the individuals lose emotional control. Clearly, the American Law Institute rule is much more liberal than the M'Naghten rule.

A second part of the American Law Institute rule reads:

> The terms "mental disease or defect" do not include an abnormality manifested only by repeated criminal or otherwise antisocial conduct.

This provision is important because it explicitly precludes habitual criminals from using their repeated criminal activities as evidence of a mental disease or defect. That is, a repeat offender cannot argue, "The fact that I repeatedly break the law is evidence that I have a mental disease and therefore I should be judged to be insane and not responsible for my acts."

To recap, under the M'Naghten rule insanity is defined very narrowly in terms of knowledge of right versus wrong, whereas under the American Law Institute rule insanity is defined broadly and includes both knowledge of right versus wrong and the effects of mental disease or defect.

Practical Problems with the Insanity Defense

Apart from the question of how broadly insanity should be defined, there are a number of practical problems associated with the insanity defense. One problem revolves around the fact that the decision concerning whether an individual is insane is determined by the vote of a jury. This can pose a problem because jurors may not have the technical knowledge or training that is necessary to make informed judgments concerning insanity. Leaving the decision concerning insanity to jurors might be like asking 12 individuals with no training in medicine to decide whether an individual who reports a pain on the right side has appendicitis or some other medical condition. After reading this book, you will probably be more knowledgeable about abnormal behavior than most jurors, but would you be comfortable judging whether an individual has a mental disease or defect, or would you rather leave that decision to

The decision concerning competence to stand trial is put in the hands of experts, but the more complex decision concerning insanity is left to untrained jurors.

an expert? It is interesting to note that the decision concerning *competence to stand trial* is put in the hands of experts (psychologists and psychiatrists), whereas the more complex decision concerning insanity is left to untrained jurors. Should the decision concerning insanity be left instead to a panel of independent experts?

Related to the fact that a jury makes the decision about insanity is the fact that in many cases the jury must rely on opinions of expert witnesses, who often disagree. What are juries to do when expert witnesses disagree?

Another problem revolves around the fact that in making a decision about insanity a jury must determine the nature of the individual's state of mind *at the time the act was committed*. It is difficult enough to determine an individual's present mental condition; it is almost impossible to determine what it was days, weeks, or even years earlier.

There is also the problem of what to do with an individual who was insane at the time of the criminal act but is sane now. Should the individual simply be set free? Will the public stand for that? What is to prevent the "temporary insanity" from coming back and leading the individual to commit another crime?

Still another problem is that individuals who are found not guilty by reason of insanity are incarcerated until they are "cured," but in many cases the resulting period of incarceration is longer than what would have occurred if they had been found to be sane and simply sent to prison. Is that appropriate?

Finally, in most cases the individual is presumed sane until proven insane. However, in the American judicial system the burden of proof is on the prosecution, and therefore perhaps the individual should be presumed to be insane until proven sane.

Some of the problems associated with judging insanity are illustrated in the case of John W. Hinckley, Jr., who attempted to assassinate President Ronald Reagan and then pleaded insanity; see Case Study 18.1.

Rule Changes in Response to the Hinckley Verdict

Like the M'Naghten case 200 years earlier, the decision that John Hinckley, Jr., was innocent on the basis of insanity caused an uproar. In some states the insanity defense was simply abolished. Two other changes that occurred in response to the Hinckley verdict are also noteworthy.

Return to M'Naghten. First, in response to the Hinckley decision the American Psychiatric Association recommended that the basis for insanity should no longer include mental disease or defect as an acceptable reason for not conforming behavior to the requirements of the law (Insanity Defense Work Group, 1983). In essence, that change returned the basis for insanity to the M'Naghten rule (knowledge of right versus wrong), and the change was accepted by the U.S. Congress, so it now applies in all U.S. federal courts. It was also adopted by about half of the state courts. Interestingly, although knowledge of right versus wrong is certainly a narrower definition of insanity, returning to that rule has not resulted in a dramatic decline in the use of the insanity defense or in its success (acquittal rate) (McGreevy, Steadman, & Callahan, 1991).

"Guilty but Mentally Ill" Rule. A second change that occurred involves what is known as the **"guilty but mentally ill" rule** for insanity. Under this rule the defendant is given two trials. The first is used to determine whether the defendant is guilty or innocent, and the second is used to determine whether the defendant is sane or insane. If found to be both guilty and insane, the individual is first sent to a mental hospital for treatment until judged to be sane; then the individual is sent to prison to be punished for the crime (Borum & Fulero, 1999; Bumby, 1993). This procedure was developed to satisfy both supporters and opponents of the insanity defense, but both cannot be satisfied without some logical contradiction. Specifically, how can you agree that

"guilty but mentally ill" rule   A court ruling under which a defendant who is found to be guilty and insane is treated, but when treatment is completed, the defendant is punished for the crime.

an individual was insane and not responsible for his or her behavior, and then punish him or her for the behavior for which he or she was judged to be not responsible?

Before concluding this discussion of insanity, I should note that in recent years a number of defendants have used multiple personality (dissociative personality) disorder as the basis for insanity pleas (Dawson, 1999; Serban, 1992). These defendants allege either that they are incompetent to stand trial because they do not know what their other personality did or that they are insane because they are not responsible for the actions of their other personality. A second currently popular defense involves posttraumatic stress disorder (Garrison, 1998; Weintraub, 1997). Defendants who use that defense allege that their crimes (usually shooting sprees) are defensive reactions that occur during a "flashback." These flashbacks are usually linked to military experiences in the Vietnam War, but some defendants have claimed that growing up in dangerous slums caused posttraumatic stress disorder, leading to flashbacks and hence to crimes. These defenses have been referred to as "trendy alibis," and although they receive a lot of attention, there is no evidence that they are particularly effective (Appelbaum et al., 1993).

In conclusion, many people believe that it is better to treat than to punish individuals whose illegal behavior is due to a mental disorder. However, it is exceptionally difficult to formulate a generally acceptable rule for determining who is insane. Furthermore, because the attitudes about

Chemical fortune heir John DuPont, who murdered Olympic wrestling champion David Schultz in 1995, was found "guilty but mentally ill" at his murder trial.

John W. Hinckley, Jr.: An Insanity Defense after an Attempt to Assassinate the President

JOHN HINCKLEY, JR., was the 25-year-old son of wealthy parents. After dropping out of college, Hinckley wandered around the country for a few years and was generally supported by his parents. During that time he sought treatment for a number of physical symptoms, and physicians prescribed an antihistamine, an antidepressant, and an antianxiety drug. At one point he took an overdose of the antidepressant, and consequently he was seen by a psychiatrist for 22 sessions. Around 1980 Hinckley became infatuated with Jodie Foster, a movie star who was then a student at Yale University, and he began leaving her notes, poems, and presents. He somehow became convinced that Foster was a "prisoner at Yale." One of his notes to her read, "Just wait. I'll rescue you very soon. Please cooperate." In another note he said, "I love you six trillion times. Don't you maybe like me just a little bit? (You must admit that I am different.) It would make all of this worthwhile."

On March 30, 1980, Hinckley wrote a love letter to Jodie Foster, in which he told her that he was going to kill the president of the United States in an attempt to "impress" her. He wrote:

> I will admit to you that the reason I'm going ahead with this attempt now is because I just cannot wait any longer to impress you. . . . By sacrificing my freedom and possibly my life, I hope to change your mind about me. This letter is being written before I leave for the Hilton Hotel [where President Reagan was scheduled to speak]. Jodie, I'm asking you to please look into your heart and at least give me the chance, with this historic deed, to gain your respect and love. I love you forever.

A few hours later, when the President left the hotel, John Hinckley opened fire.

At his trial Hinckley did not deny that he had attempted to assassinate the president. However, his defense attorneys argued that Hinckley was suffering from major depression and schizophrenia, and that at the time of the act he was insane and not responsible for his actions. To support this defense one expert testified that scans of Hinckley's brain showed deterioration characteristic of schizophrenia, and another expert testified that Hinckley had high scores on a test that is used to measure abnormal behavior (the MMPI). Furthermore, it was pointed out that Hinckley had seen the movie *Taxi Driver* 15 times. In that movie a lonely taxi driver named Travis meets a 12-year-old prostitute, who is played by Jodie Foster. When Travis attacks the prostitute's pimp and is shot, he is portrayed in the newspapers as a hero. Later, when Travis picks the prostitute up in his cab, she shows renewed interest in him because of what he did for her. The defense argued that Hinckley had identified with Travis, and because of Hinckley's disorder, the line between fantasy and reality had become blurred.

The prosecuting attorneys did not dispute the fact that Hinckley was a troubled young man, but they argued that his problems were not serious enough to explain his behavior. They argued that he was suffering from dysthymia (a mild type of depression) rather than major depression and from borderline personality disorder rather than schizophrenia. Furthermore, they argued that there was no evidence that he could not tell right from wrong. They concluded that rather than suffering from a serious mental disorder, Hinckley was a lazy, fame-seeking, spoiled loner. As evidence for his attention-seeking, they pointed out that after the shooting, Hinckley asked if reports of his assassination attempt would preempt the Academy Awards show that was scheduled for that night.

The trial went on for over a month, and when at the end the judge gave the jury its instructions, he told them that mental illness was "any abnormal condition of the mind" that "substantially affects mental or emotional processes and substantially impairs [an individual's] behavior control." The judge also told the jury that Hinckley must be *presumed insane until proven sane;* that is, it was the prosecution's responsibility to prove that Hinckley was sane. Given those instructions, would you have judged Hinckley to be sane or insane?

After 4½ days of deliberation, the jury returned its verdict: *not guilty by reason of insanity.* John W. Hinckley, Jr., was sent to a psychiatric hospital for treatment, where he remains to this day.

Source: Based on Caplan (1984).

In 1980 John W. Hinckley, Jr., attempted to assassinate President Ronald Reagan in an effort to impress actress Jodie Foster. He was judged not guilty by reason of insanity and sent to a hospital for treatment.

insanity change with the political climate and public events, the debate over the insanity defense will continue. It is important that you understand the issues and appreciate the implications of the various options so that you can make an informed decision if you must confront the question of insanity. What rule would you use for determining insanity, and whose responsibility do you think it should be to determine whether an individual is sane or insane?

Questions about Incompetence and Insanity

1. *Is the insanity plea used too frequently and is it a "ripoff" of the legal system?* The answer to both parts of that question is no. Although cases in which insanity pleas are used are often given a lot of attention in the media, the use of the insanity plea is really quite rare. Furthermore, when it is used, it is usually successful only in extreme and clearcut cases. Furthermore, even when it is successful and individuals are "let off," the individuals usually spend a considerable amount of time in confinement while they are being treated (Lymburner & Roesch, 1999).

2. *Is getting intoxicated a basis for an insanity plea?* In Chapter 15 you learned that drug intoxication is the basis for a substance-related disorder, so the question arises, if an individual does something illegal while intoxicated, can he or she plead insanity and avoid responsibility for the act? Most jurisdictions have clear laws regarding this, and in virtually every case intoxication is not a basis for insanity (Marlowe, Lambert, & Thompson, 1999).

TOPIC II

Hospitalization and the Rights of Patients

Lois is suffering from severe depression and is suicidal. Psychotherapy and drugs have not helped, so her psychiatrist has decided to try electroconvulsive therapy (ECT). However, Lois has refused the treatment. Can she be given ECT without her permission? That is, can treatments such as ECT be forced on patients against their will?

Craig signed himself into a psychiatric hospital voluntarily when he thought he was "losing control" of his thoughts. After being in the hospital a week, he felt better, but he did not like the hospital or the drugs he was being given, so he decided to sign himself out and go home. However, during the 2-day waiting period before he could leave, the hospital staff changed his admission status from "voluntary" to "involuntary" commitment, and therefore he could not leave. Is this fair? Medical patients can sign themselves out when they want to; why can't psychiatric patients do the same?

Imagine what it would be like if you were suddenly confined to a psychiatric hospital. Because hospitalizing an individual is often an important and drastic act, we must give very careful consideration to the type of hospitalization chosen and the rights of hospitalized patients.

Voluntary and Involuntary Hospitalization

It is widely believed that many psychological disorders can be treated effectively in a hospital and, furthermore, that many disturbed individuals must be confined in hospitals for their own safety and for the safety of others. Because of these beliefs, disturbed individuals are often hospitalized, many of them against their will. In the following sections I will consider the difficult question of who can be hospitalized voluntarily or involuntarily.

Voluntary Hospitalization

Anyone who feels that he or she needs help can apply for **voluntary admission** to a mental hospital. The individual is examined by an admitting psychiatrist or a psychologist, and if the symptoms are judged to be serious, the individual will be admitted at least for a period of evaluation. However, now that hospitals are facing serious economic cutbacks, individuals are not admitted unless it is really necessary, and the individuals may not stay as long as was once the case.

With regard to voluntary hospitalization it is important to realize that *voluntary admission does not guarantee voluntary release.* Specifically, an individual may sign into a hospital voluntarily and then later decide to sign out, but in most cases there is a waiting period (often up to 72 hours) before the individual can be discharged. During the waiting period, if the hospital staff believes the individual requires hospitalization, they can change the admission from voluntary to involuntary. Although this is done for the good of the patient, perhaps individuals who are about to sign into a mental hospital voluntarily should be given a warning: "Anything you say or do can and will be used against you, and you may be involuntarily committed." We protect suspected criminals in that way; why not potential mental patients? It is noteworthy that medical patients are allowed to leave hospitals "against medical advice," so why isn't the same right granted to psychiatric patients?

The U.S. Supreme Court raised concerns about the validity of some voluntary admissions when it ruled that *some individuals may not be legally competent to make the decision concerning admission.* That is, some individuals may be too disturbed to be able to consent to hospitalization (Cournos et al., 1993; Hoge, 1994). One case involved a man who was found walking along a highway, bruised, bloodied, disoriented, and thinking he was "in heaven." He was taken to a mental hospital, where he voluntarily signed himself in and then was held for 5 months. However, when he was released, he filed a suit alleging that he had been deprived of his liberty without due process; his argument was that when he agreed to the admission, he was highly disturbed and therefore not competent to give a valid informed consent (R. D. Miller, 1994; Winick, 1991; *Zinermon* v. *Burch*, 1990). This Supreme Court decision could mean that patients who want to admit themselves voluntarily would first have to be examined and judged to be competent. However, if they were found to be incompetent, they would have to be committed involuntarily. Let's go on to consider involuntary commitment.

Involuntary Hospitalization

Is it possible to be hospitalized against your will? Yes, and many individuals in mental hospitals have been hospitalized against their will by means of **involuntary commitment.** The act of committing individuals against their will must be done carefully because an involuntary commitment deprives an individual not only of civil liberties, but of freedom. There are two justifications for committing an individual to a mental hospital: the *protection of the individual* and the *protection of society*.

Protection of the Individual (*Parens Patriae*).

It is generally agreed that the state has the right and responsibility to protect and provide for the well-being of people within its jurisdiction. That doctrine is referred to as ***parens patriae*** (par-enz PA-tre; the term is Latin for "parent of the country"), which under English law held that the king was "the general guardian of all his infants, idiots, and lunatics." Under the doctrine of *parens patriae* there are three situations in which the state has the right to commit an individual to a mental hospital:

1. The individual *needs treatment.*
2. The individual is *dangerous to himself or herself.*
3. The individual *cannot take care of himself or herself.*

Most people agree that individuals meeting one or more of these requirements need hospitalization. For example, suicidal individuals are dangerous to themselves, need treatment, and in many cases should be hospitalized at least until the crisis has passed. However, problems arise when the disturbed individuals do not think they need treatment but the authorities think they do. For example, suicidal individuals usually think they know what is best for themselves and do not want to be hospitalized.

In court decisions it has been stressed that *individuals should not be committed to hospitals involuntarily if they are capable of making their own decisions on the matter* (*Lessard* v. *Schmidt*, 1972, 1974). The problem with this ruling is that if the authorities want to hospitalize an individual but the individual decides that he or she does not want to be hospitalized, the authorities can simply conclude that the individual is not able to make an appropriate decision and then hospitalize him or her involuntarily. In essence, the ability to make an appropriate decision about hospitalization is operationally defined as *agreeing with the authorities* on the decision. This places the potential patient in a Catch-22 situation: *The patient has the right to make the decision about hospitalization only as long as that decision is the same as that of the authorities.*

There is also a potential legal problem with committing individuals to mental hospitals under the doctrine of *parens patriae*. We do not involuntarily hospitalize individuals with medical disorders such as cancer, so if we involuntarily hospitalize individuals with mental disorders, we may be violating their **right to equal protection,** a right guaranteed by the 14th Amendment to the U.S. Constitution. In other words, individuals who suffer from mental disorders must not be treated differently from individuals who suffer from medical disorders. Because of this problem, the states of Pennsylvania, Michigan, Washington, Alabama, West Virginia, and Kentucky no longer permit involuntary hospitalization on the basis of *parens patriae*.

Protection of Society (Police Power of the State).

Involuntary commitment may also be justified under the **police power of the state** if the individual is considered dangerous to others (*Humphrey* v. *Cady*, 1972; *Jackson* v. *Indiana*, 1972). Most persons would probably agree that individuals who are dangerous to others should be confined. However, a problem arises because the results of numerous studies indicate that psychologists and psychiatrists are not particularly accurate at predicting who is dangerous (Diamond, 1974; Ennis & Litwack, 1974; Kozol, Boucher, & Garofalo, 1972; Monahan, 1973, 1976, 1978, 1984; Rofman, Askinazi, & Fant, 1980; Steadman, 1973; Steadman & Keveles, 1972,

voluntary admission   Self-admission to a mental hospital, which carries with it the right to leave after appropriate notice unless the admission status is changed to involuntary commitment.

involuntary commitment   Commitment to a mental hospital against the patient's will because the patient is considered a danger to self or to others. (See also *involuntary outpatient commitment*.)

parens patriae   The doctrine that the state has the right and responsibility to protect and provide for the well-being of people within its jurisdiction; used as the justification for involuntary hospitalization.

right to equal protection   Constitutional right under the 14th Amendment, which is sometimes violated in the case of mental patients when they are hospitalized involuntarily and thus denied rights allowed to medical patients.

police power of the state   The principle that the state has the right to protect citizens from individuals who are dangerous; used as a basis for the involuntary hospitalization of individuals believed to be dangerous to others.

Disturbed individuals are sometimes hospitalized against their will. The justifications for this include protection of the individual and protection of society. However, many observers have argued that involuntary commitment of homeless people has occurred because these individuals disturb other people, not because they are disturbed.

1978; A. A. Stone, 1975). If psychologists and psychiatrists cannot accurately predict who is dangerous, they may commit individuals who do not need to be committed and thereby unjustifiably deprive those individuals of their freedom.

In one study investigators followed up and determined the rate of dangerous acts of almost 1,000 criminally insane patients who had been released from prison hospitals (Steadman & Keveles, 1972). (The patients were released because of a change in the law rather than because they were judged to be "cured.") After 4 years only 2.7% of them had behaved dangerously and were back in a hospital or in prison. In other words, *97.3% of the individuals who had been incarcerated because they were supposedly dangerous did not commit dangerous acts when they were released!* That finding is particularly noteworthy because these individuals were originally hospitalized because they had committed a dangerous act, and therefore we might expect them to be more likely to commit another dangerous act.

There has been a recent movement toward requiring that the danger posed by the individual be "imminent" rather than occurring at some unspecified time in the future. Because we are probably better able to assess an individual's current mental and emotional state of mind than to predict what he or she will be like sometime in the future, we may be better able to predict imminent danger than danger in general.

Hospitalization of individuals who are only suspected of being dangerous may be violating their legal right to equal protection. Specifically, mentally ill individuals who are suspected of being dangerous are confined, but individuals who are not mentally ill and are suspected of being dangerous (e.g., a suspected "hit man") are not confined. Further-

more, mentally ill individuals who might be dangerous *in the future* are confined, but others who are not mentally ill cannot be locked up until it has been proved that they have *already* committed a dangerous act. In summary, it appears that in many cases mentally ill individuals are not treated equally under the law, and it must be asked whether it is fair to treat them more harshly than suspected criminals are treated.

In recent years questions about the appropriate use of involuntary commitment have arisen with regard to the treatment of homeless people. For example, in cities such as New York and Washington, police conducted sweeps, in which individuals who were living on the streets were picked up and taken to mental hospitals against their will. City officials justified the sweeps by saying that the commitments were for the good of the individuals involved, but critics argued that the homeless people were not a danger to anyone and were able to take care of themselves. In short, the critics argued that the street people were being taken off the street and committed to hospitals because they *disturbed other people* rather than because *they were disturbed.* This problem is illustrated in Case Study 18.2.

The case of Joyce Brown illustrates a number of the problems and issues we have discussed in this book. First, how do we define *abnormal?* From a personal perspective Brown was neither distressed nor disabled, but from a cultural perspective she was deviant. The case also illustrates the point that behavior must be considered in context. Burning or throwing money away certainly sounds "crazy," but doing so in an attempt to convince people who were forcing it on you that you have all you need and do not want more may not be crazy. More germane to the concerns of this chapter is the question of the protection of the

The Woman Who Burned Money

THE CASE OF THE WOMAN who burned money began when the *New York Times* carried a front-page story under the headline "Mentally Ill Homeless Taken Off New York Streets." The article explained how vans carrying a psychiatrist, a nurse, and a social worker had been dispatched to begin a "vigorous campaign to remove severely mentally ill homeless people from Manhattan streets, parks and byways" so that the city could "forcibly provide them with medical and psychiatric care."

The first person to be picked up and taken to the Bellevue Hospital Center was described as "a disheveled woman in her 40's who lived for nearly a year against the wall of a restaurant . . . and often defecated in her clothes." The woman was thought to be named Ann Smith, and she had been living on the sidewalk, where she kept warm by sitting in front of a heat vent from a restaurant. Local merchants and residents had shown sympathy for her and had often left her food or given her money. A florist had given her flowers. "She liked them," he said, "but was troubled that they die." The article went on to point out that one of the most confusing aspects of this "troubled person" was her vacillation between begging and belligerence, belligerence that often involved throwing away or burning money that she had been given. A woman from the restaurant reported, "She asks for a quarter and then when you give her three quarters, she is going to throw the other two away. . . . I don't know why. It's very strange. A lot of people were worried about her. . . . They stop and give her money, but sometimes she won't take it. 'I don't need your money,' she yelled." The florist reported that "around Christmas time, that's the only woman I know who rips up $100 and $50 bills. . . . She rips them up in teeny little pieces." His coworker added, "She likes to burn them."

At a news conference the next day the mayor called the roundup program a "breakthrough" that "should have

been started 5 years earlier." However, resistance was developing among individuals who believed that the rights of the people being picked up were being violated. A staff attorney with the New York Civil Liberties Union said that he had received a call from Smith, who wanted help getting out of the hospital. He said Smith was "lucid and extremely articulate and extremely angry. . . . She was aware of her rights and felt strongly that they had been violated."

The next development in the case occurred about 4 days later when in a telephone interview from the hospital Smith said, "I like the streets, and I am entitled to live the way I want to live. . . . I know that there are people and places I can go to if I don't choose to be on the streets. . . . In the United States of America, where everyone comes to be free, my rights are being violated." With regard to her burning of money, she said that she did it because she was sometimes insulted

Joyce Brown lived on the streets until she was hospitalized for 84 days against her will. In a court hearing she effectively argued that she was not disturbed but had an eccentric lifestyle. She later spoke about her case at Harvard Law School.

that people threw money at her. She was angry about a press release distributed by city hall describing her as "dirty, disheveled and malodorous, . . . delusional, withdrawn and unpredictable." In fact, her comments did not sound like those of the derelict described in the press release. Smith asked the reporter to visit her at the hospital but despite the fact that Smith was entitled to visitors, hospital officials barred the reporter and barred Smith from making additional phone calls. These restrictions were justified by suggesting that "the kind of media attention that is being requested by members of the press would be detrimental to her condition."

A few days later a hearing was conducted in a courtroom at Bellevue to determine whether the city had the right to take Smith off the street and treat her in a psychiatric ward against her will. Psychiatrists for the city testified that she was suffering from chronic schizophrenia, ran in front of cars, lived in her own feces, was so sick that she was completely unaware of her illness, and had to be hospitalized for her own good because she was a danger to herself and might be assaulted by others.

The defense attorneys denied these allegations and argued that Smith was only an "eccentric," who wanted to live on the streets and be left alone. They also pointed out that on five occasions during the past year Smith had been taken to other psychiatric hospitals, but she had not been admitted because there was no evidence that she was a danger to herself. On cross-examination city officials admitted that they had no evidence that Smith had ever harmed herself.

A particularly noteworthy fact about the hearing was that throughout the proceedings, Smith was well groomed and attentive, penciled notes to her lawyer during testimony, and was consistently articulate, lucid, and knowledgeable. She certainly did not

(continued)

Case Study 18.2 (cont.)

fit the stereotype of the disoriented homeless person or appear to be "so sick that she was completely unaware of her illness," as had been alleged earlier.

The next surprising turn of events occurred when three women identified Ann Smith as Joyce Brown and reported that for 10 years she had been a secretary for the Human Rights Commission in Elizabeth, New Jersey. The women were Brown's sisters, who went on to explain that Brown had been raised in a middle-class family in Livingston, New Jersey, had graduated from high school and business college, and then had worked as a secretary for 19 years. Over several years she had used cocaine and heroin and eventually lost her job. She then moved in with her family, but she became abusive and was asked to leave. Next she lived in shelters in Newark, but according to her sisters she was asked to leave the shelters when she became abusive.

On the third day of the hearing Brown defended her life on the street and her right to continue living there. She argued that she was a "profes-

> . . . I like the streets, and I am entitled to live the way I want to live. . . .

sional" homeless person, who was able to care for herself on the streets and was longing to get "back to the streets." She explained that she could live effectively on a budget of $7 a day and that she could easily panhandle between $8 and $10 per day. Local businesses allowed her to use their rest rooms and the air from the heating vent kept her warm, so all of her needs were taken care of. She described how she talked with passersby such as executives, lawyers, and doctors about movies, restaurants, current events, and their families. When asked if she could take care of herself, she replied, "That's what I have been doing all along, and I have done a good job. . . . My mental health is good, and my physical health is good." She explained that she used false names to help her evade her sisters, who were looking for her and wanted to put her in a hospital.

When asked about tearing up money, she replied that she only did it when people insisted on throwing money at her when she already had enough for the day. "If money is given to me and I don't want it, of course, I am going to destroy it. . . . I've heard people say: 'Take it, it will make you feel good.' But I say, 'I don't want it, I

don't need it.' It is not my job to make them feel good by taking their money."

In his closing argument Brown's defense attorney said that the city had not provided any evidence that Brown had hurt herself or was dangerous to others, and he added that she was skilled in living on the streets. The attorney for the city rebutted, "Decency and the law and common sense do not require us to wait until something happens to her. It is our duty to act before it is too late."

If you had been the judge, what would you have decided in this case? Was Brown disturbed, unable to care for herself, and a danger to others, or had she chosen an unconventional lifestyle in which she functioned effectively and posed no threat to others? Was she disturbed, or was she simply disturbing to others?

The judge ruled against Brown. She was involuntarily committed in the psychiatric ward at Bellevue Hospital Center for 84 days. Upon her release Harvard University invited her to speak. After her lecture at Harvard, she returned to the streets.

Source: Based on *New York Times* reports, October 29–November 7, 1987.

---

rights of individuals. Brown's right to live as she wishes must be protected, but at the same time we must be sensitive to the concerns of people visiting businesses and restaurants in the area who might be offended by her.

There is also the question of how to determine whether a person is a danger to self or others. Joyce Brown was forcibly taken off the streets purportedly for her own good, but in fact she was physically healthy and life on the streets was the life she preferred. She was also picked up because of concern that others would attack her, but our society usually incarcerates the *attackers,* not the *individuals they attack.* The case

of Joyce Brown illustrates all of these problems and questions, but it does not solve or answer any of them. What decision would you have made about Joyce Brown?

Finally, as with all case studies, it is important that you do not generalize from Brown to all homeless people. Many are not on the streets by choice, many have been literally thrown out of hospitals in which they would rather be living and getting treatment, and many are not able to function effectively; therefore, they desperately cling to—and sometimes fall from—a thin ledge of existence.

Before concluding this discussion of involuntary commitment, a comment should be made concerning a court judgment called **involuntary outpatient commitment** (Borum et al., 1999; Geller et al., 1998; Lefkovitch, Weiser, & Levy, 1993; McCafferty & Dooley, 1990; Mulvey, Geller, & Roth, 1987). Under such a judgment an individual is not confined to a hospital but is *required to attend outpatient*

involuntary outpatient commitment A court judgment whereby a person is required to participate in outpatient treatment as an alternative to involuntary hospitalization.

therapy. This is a middle-ground approach that does not deprive individuals of their basic freedom and saves the state the cost of hospitalization. At the same time it ensures that individuals receive the treatment and supervision they need. Involuntary outpatient commitment cannot be used with all patients (clearly, dangerous individuals would not be eligible), but it might be an appropriate and advantageous approach for many.

It should be clear from this discussion that attempts to help disturbed individuals and protect society through involuntary hospitalization are fraught with legal, logical, and practical problems. At best the system is an imperfect series of compromises, designed to protect the rights of all. As with other such compromises, sometimes the protection of one individual's rights infringes on the rights of another. We must be constantly sensitive to the needs of all and work to maintain the delicate balance between protection and infringement.

Procedures for Involuntary Hospitalization. Earlier you learned that the grounds for involuntary hospitalization are need for treatment, danger to self, inability to care for self, and danger to others. The question we must consider now is, what procedures are used to commit an individual to a hospital? Stated more personally, what would someone have to do to get you hospitalized against your will?

There are differences from state to state, but in most states the procedures for involuntary hospitalization are very simple. The process starts when a police officer, a mental health professional, or any citizen alleges to the police or a judge that an individual is dangerous to self or others. Note that no real evidence is necessary other than the opinion of the individual filing the complaint, and often that individual has no training, knowledge, or expertise concerning abnormal behavior.

Once the allegation has been made, the police take the individual to a mental hospital, where a brief examination is conducted by at least one physician. Often this examination lasts only a few minutes, and it may be conducted by a physician who is not necessarily a psychiatrist. The examination usually leads to **emergency (involuntary) hospitalization** so that additional observations and examinations can be conducted. The probability of emergency hospitalization is very high because physicians do not want to risk letting individuals go who might hurt themselves or others. Depending on the state, the period of emergency hospitalization can be as short as 24 hours (Texas) or as long as 20 days (New Jersey). In some states a preliminary hearing must be conducted within 48 hours to determine whether there is probable cause for continued detention of the individual. At the end of the emergency hospitalization period, the individual must (1) agree to voluntary hospitalization, (2) be committed for an indeterminate length of time, or (3) be released.

Clearly, it is quite easy to have an individual committed and detained for a considerable length of time. Indeed, in many cases an individual who is suspected of having committed a crime will be released from jail sooner than an individual who is suspected of suffering from a mental disorder will be released from a hospital.

Rights of Hospitalized Mental Patients

Now that you understand the principles and procedures that determine why and how individuals are hospitalized, we can go on to consider the rights that individuals have once they are hospitalized.

Right of the "Least Restrictive Alternative"

At one time treatment meant total hospitalization, but it is now recognized that there is a continuum of treatment options that differ in the degree to which the patient is confined. Those options include (1) total hospitalization in a closed ward; (2) hospitalization in an open ward, where patients have the right to leave and go to other parts of the hospital; (3) day hospitalization, in which patients spend the day in the hospital but spend the night at home; (4) night hospitalization, in which patients spend the evening and night in the hospital but spend the day at work or at home; and (5) outpatient care, in which patients live at home and come to a clinic only for treatment sessions. Recognition of these options is important because the courts have consistently ruled that if individuals are committed for treatment, they have the right to be treated by means of the **least restrictive alternative** that will serve the purpose of the treatment (*Lake* v. *Cameron,* 1966; *Lessard* v. *Schmidt,* 1974; *Shelton* v. *Tucker,* 1960; *Welsch* v. *Litkins,* 1974; *Wyatt* v. *Stickney,* 1971, 1972). Not only does this mean that patients should be treated outside of the hospital if that is feasible, but if they must be hospitalized, they must be treated in the least restrictive ward possible (*Covington* v. *Harris,* 1969).

emergency (involuntary) hospitalization A state-mandated hospitalization of a person thought to be a danger to self or to others so that additional observations and examinations can be conducted.

least restrictive alternative A legal standard requiring that mental patients not be subjected to more restrictive treatment than is absolutely necessary.

Right to Receive Treatment and Be Released

You may have assumed that individuals who were hospitalized against their will would at least be treated so that they could improve and someday be released. Unfortunately, that has not always been the case, and many patients languished in mental hospitals for years without being treated. However, four important legal decisions have been passed down concerning a patient's right to treatment and right to be released. Let's consider them.

The first case involved a man named Charles Rouse who was tried for carrying a dangerous weapon, was found not guilty by reason of insanity, and was involuntarily committed to a mental hospital. After 4 years in the hospital, during which he was not given any treatment, Rouse applied for a discharge. When his case was taken to court, the judge ruled that "the purpose of involuntary hospitalization is treatment, not punishment" and that if patients are not treated, a hospital is simply a "penitentiary" (*Rouse* v. *Cameron,* 1966). In other words, patients in hospitals have a right to be treated. However, that ruling did not indicate what constitutes appropriate treatment.

The question of appropriate treatment was first addressed in a class action suit in which it was charged that 8,000 involuntarily committed mental patients in Alabama were not receiving adequate treatment (*Wyatt* v. *Stickney,* 1971, 1972). There was good evidence to support the charge; for example, the Alabama state mental hospitals averaged one physician for every 2,000 patients! Even assuming that the physicians did nothing but see patients 8 hours a day, 52 weeks a year, each patient would receive approximately *1 minute of therapy a week!* In ruling on this case the judge specified the numbers and types of staff members who must be available to provide treatment. Specifically, he ruled that for every 250 patients there have to be at least 2 psychiatrists, 4 psychologists, 3 general physicians, 7 social workers, 12 registered nurses, and 90 attendants.

That ruling set standards for how much staff is required, but it skirted the question of what treatment is appropriate. However, that question was raised again in the case of Nicholas Romeo, a profoundly retarded 33-year-old man with an IQ between 8 and 10. His mother brought a lawsuit against the superintendent of the hospital in which Nicholas was a patient because Nicholas had injured himself at least 63 times in one 29-month period (one of his symptoms was self-mutilation). She argued that if Nicholas was injuring himself that frequently, he must not be receiving adequate treatment. The judge ruled that Nicholas did have a right to reasonable care and safety, but he went on to conclude that because judges are not trained in psychology or psychiatry, they are not in a position to determine what treatment is most effective for various patients. Therefore,

the judge ruled that decisions concerning what treatment is appropriate should be left to professionals (*Youngberg* v. *Romeo,* 1981). While this ruling seems reasonable, by allowing professionals to determine what is appropriate, the court opened the door to a wide variety and level of treatments because standards may differ from one professional or hospital to another.

The last case we'll consider here focused on the question of when patients must be released. This case involved Kenneth Donaldson who was committed to the Florida state hospital at Chattahoochee at the age of 49 when his father reported that he was delusional (Behnke, 1999). After a brief hearing before a county judge, Donaldson was found to be suffering from paranoid schizophrenia and was committed to the hospital. A progress note written in his hospital file shortly after he was hospitalized indicated that he was "in remission," which meant that he was no longer showing the symptoms of his disorder—but he was not released from the hospital. After Donaldson had been hospitalized against his will for almost 20 years, he petitioned for release. He argued that he should be released because (1) he was not dangerous or mentally ill, (2) he was not receiving treatment, and (3) there were people in the community who were willing to take him in and give him a job. In responding the U.S. Supreme Court ruled that a state cannot confine "a nondangerous individual who is capable of surviving safely in freedom by himself or with the help of willing and responsible family members or friends" (*O'Connor* v. *Donaldson,* 1974, 1975). In other words, the Supreme Court said that individuals who are not dangerous and who can live effectively outside of a hospital cannot be held in hospitals against their will.

What are the results of these decisions? It is now the law that (1) hospitalized mental patients have a right to treatment, (2) a minimum number of staff members must be available to treat patients, (3) it is the responsibility of professionals to determine what type and how much treatment is appropriate, and (4) nondangerous individuals cannot be confined if they are able to function independently outside of a hospital.

Right to Refuse Treatment

It is clear that patients have the right to be treated, but do they also have the right to refuse treatment? For example, if you were hospitalized, would you have the right to refuse electroconvulsive therapy or psychosurgery if it were recommended?

In our society individuals are generally free to decide what is best for them, which implies that patients have the right to refuse treatment if they do not think that the treatment is appropriate. However, there are three situations in which mental patients may *not* have the right to refuse treatment (Slovenko, 1992). First, they may not have the right to refuse treatment if they are declared *incompetent.* The notion is that an incompetent individual is unable to understand or evaluate what is going to be done and is therefore unable to make an informed judgment about whether the treatment is appropriate. If an individual is declared incompetent, the power to make the decision about treatment may be shifted to a parent or guardian. However, in most of those cases whoever is empowered to make the decision simply accepts the recommendation of the psychiatrist or psychologist in charge.

Second, individuals may not have the right to refuse treatment if they are *involuntarily committed* to a hospital for their own protection or for the protection of others. For example, suicidal individuals who have been committed may not have the right to refuse antidepressants, and paranoid individuals who have been committed because they are dangerous to others may not have the right to refuse neuroleptic (antipsychotic) drugs. In those cases the necessity to protect the individual or society takes precedence over the individual's right to refuse treatment.

Third, even a competent and voluntarily committed individual may not have the right to refuse treatment if the refusal results in *increased costs* for the community. For example, an individual may not have the right to refuse

group psychotherapy or medication if the only option is more expensive individual psychotherapy.

However, there are two situations in which patients do have the right to refuse treatment. First, patients have the right to refuse treatment if the treatment *violates their religious beliefs.* This was affirmed when a circuit court ruled in favor of a patient who objected to taking drugs because she was a Christian Scientist (*Winters* v. *Miller,* 1971). The ruling was based on the 1st Amendment, which guarantees U.S. citzens the right to free expression of religion.

Second, an individual has the right to refuse a particular treatment if another *equally effective but less intrusive treatment is available.* For example, if it could be demonstrated that for a given patient psychotherapy would be as effective as electroconvulsive therapy, the patient could refuse the electroconvulsive therapy.

To sum up, patients may not refuse treatment if (1) they are not competent to make the decision, (2) the refusal puts them or others at increased risk, or (3) the refusal increases the expenses of the state. However, these reasons can be set aside on religious grounds or if there is another equally effective treatment available.

Some of the problems posed by the courts' decisions to grant patients the right to refuse treatment are illustrated in Case Study 18.3. The case involves a patient with bipolar

Delay of Effective Treatment and Increased Cost of Care

CASE STUDY 18.3

Ms. A WAS a 55-year-old woman who was admitted for her fifth hospitalization to a private psychiatric hospital. She was diagnosed as suffering from a manic episode of bipolar disorder. Ms. A was held in an intensive treatment ward but was frequently placed in seclusion because of outbursts in which she hit others and burned herself with cigarettes. During the first week of hospitalization, Ms. A was started on lithium, but the treatment was discontinued because she refused it. No attempt was made to force her to take the medication because of potential legal implications, and consequently she remained unmedicated for 19 days. After 37 days in the hospital, a hearing was held in which the court authorized an involuntary commitment. Once Ms. A was involuntarily committed, she was no longer able to

refuse treatment, and so she was immediately given lithium. Within a month she showed significant improvement, and 2 weeks later she was discharged.

Ms. A's hospital bill was $25,137. Because of the delay in getting effective treatment started, it was estimated that the cost was $11,550 higher than it would have been if she had accepted the lithium immediately. (Because only 80% of Ms. A's hospital expenses were paid by an insurance company, some of the expense associated with her refusal to take medication was borne by the public.) The family also incurred additional costs of $1,017 for legal fees and the consultation of an independent psychiatrist. In addition to these financial costs there were also the costs to other patients of having a highly disturbed and disruptive patient

on the ward and the emotional cost to the family of the prolonged illness of a loved one.

Because of cases such as this, the hospital in which Ms. A was hospitalized established a policy whereby if a potentially dangerous patient refuses treatment and if, after outside legal consultation, the family concurs with the patient's decision, the patient is sent to a public mental hospital. In other words, this hospital will no longer take responsibility for patients who refuse effective treatments.

> . . . this hospital will no longer take responsibility for patients who refuse effective treatments.

Source: Adapted from Perr (1981).

The question of whether a patient should be forced to work in a hospital is difficult. Being involved in productive work can boost self-esteem. However, a patient who has been involuntarily committed and then forced to work is essentially being subjected to involuntary servitude, a violation of the 13th Amendment to the Constitution.

disorder who was in a private hospital and who refused medication. (For background on the treatment of the bipolar disorder, see Chapter 9.)

Other Rights of Patients

In addition to patients' rights to the least restrictive alternative and to receive and refuse treatment, hospitalized patients are guaranteed four other rights:

1. *Physical environment.* For each patient there should be at least 40 square feet of space in the dayroom and 10 square feet in the dining room or cafeteria. Patients must also be provided with curtains or screens in their sleeping quarters to ensure privacy. There must be at least one toilet for every eight patients (*Wyatt* v. *Stickney*, 1971, 1972).

2. *Personal clothing.* Each patient has the right to wear his or her own clothing unless the clothing is determined to be dangerous or otherwise inappropriate in terms of the treatment program. Patients who are likely to try to escape from an open ward may be required to wear hospital gowns so that they can be easily spotted if they try to leave, and patients who are suicidal may not be allowed to wear belts or other articles of clothing that they could use to hang themselves. A patient who thinks he is Superman would

probably not be allowed to go around the hospital in a red-and-blue cape because that would condone his delusion.

3. *Patient labor.* The question of whether patients should be required to work in the hospital is a difficult one. On the one hand, being involved in productive work can provide a much-needed boost in self-esteem, and work done in the hospital may reduce the cost of running the hospital. On the other hand, patients who are committed involuntarily and then compelled to work are essentially slaves, and slavery is prohibited by the 13th Amendment to the Constitution.

Two important decisions have been passed down by the courts in an attempt to strike a balance between work and slavery. First, it was ruled that mental patients may be required to do work that contributes to the operation of the institution *so long as the work has some therapeutic value.* The problem is in defining what work is therapeutic. It could be argued that forcing patients to scrub floors is inappropriate, but it can also be argued that scrubbing floors is a normal and necessary activity and that, in doing so, patients learn to take responsibility and may even develop a sense of accomplishment and pride.

Second, a more recent court decision placed a serious limitation on patient work programs by ruling that patients may not perform work "for which the hospital is under contract with an outside organization" (*Wyatt* v. *Stickney*, 1971, 1972). This means that if a hospital has contracted with an outside company to do maintenance work or prepare food, patients cannot participate in those activities, even if doing so is therapeutic. It appears that this ruling was designed for the economic benefit of commercial firms that do business with the hospital rather than the psychological benefit of the patients who are confined in the hospital. The ruling has had some unfortunate consequences. For example, in one hospital in a rural area, the patients grew all of their own food, a practice that filled their days, gave them considerable self-satisfaction, and substantially offset the expense of their hospitalization. However, a local grocery company brought considerable political pressure to bear and got a contract to supply the hospital with food. Today the patients sit idly on benches and watch others plow the fields, and hospital costs have soared. Clearly, numerous pressures and concerns must be weighed, and a delicate balance must be achieved if patient work is to be effective.

4. *Civil rights.* The protection of civil rights is very important in our society, and simply being hospitalized as a mental patient *cannot be used as grounds for the restriction of civil rights.* For example, patients have the right to manage their personal and financial affairs, make contracts, marry, divorce, vote, and make a will (*Wyatt* v. *Stickney*, 1971, 1972). However, those rights can be restricted if the individual is judged incompetent; in such cases a court-appointed guardian will take responsibility for looking after the welfare of the individual.

THINKING CRITICALLY

Questions about Hospitalization and the Rights of Patients

1. *Are court rulings enough to protect the rights of patients?* The court rulings I discussed here specify what should be done with regard to the hospitalization, treatment, and release of mental patients, but there is often a considerable difference between what the law requires and what, in fact, occurs. Unfortunately, most mental patients are not in a good position to defend their rights because they usually do not know what their rights are and therefore simply accept what seems to be their fate. In an attempt to make sure that patients know their rights with regard to treatment, the law now requires that a statement of patients' rights be posted prominently in hospitals. That statement is reproduced in Figure 18.1.

FIGURE 18.1

This notice of mental patients' rights must be posted in mental hospitals.

NOTICE TO PATIENTS

The United States Supreme Court recently ruled that a mental patient who has been involuntarily hospitalized, who is not dangerous to himself or others, who is receiving only custodial care, and who is capable of living safely in the community has a constitutional right to liberty—that is, has a right to be released from the hospital. The Supreme Court's opinion is available for patients to read.

If you think that the Supreme Court ruling may have a bearing on your present status, please feel free to discuss the matter with your hospital staff. In addition, if you wish to talk with an attorney about the meaning of the Supreme Court decision and how it may apply to you, the Superintendent has a list of legal organizations that may be of assistance. The staff will be glad to aid anyone who wishes to contact a lawyer.

Source: National Institute of Mental Health.

Posting a notice of patients' rights is a step in the right direction, but it is a small and rather passive step, and its impact is questionable. Patients may not see the notice, and even if they do, they may not understand it. It should also be noted that in many cases the hospital (or state) is not required to provide an attorney to help patients. In sharp contrast, prisoners are guaranteed legal counsel. In other words, convicted criminals are treated better than hospitalized mental patients. Furthermore, if patients believe that their rights are being violated and complain, there is often no one to listen; if people do listen, they do not take the patients seriously. Why should they? The patients are "crazy"—if they weren't crazy, they wouldn't be in the hospital, right? Unfortunately then, patients and their rights are often ignored.

2. *Can society afford to do what is required by the law with regard to treatment?* It is clear that we have moral and legal obligations to provide hospitalized mental patients with good care, but what if sufficient funds are not available? Indeed, the mandate to treat all hospitalized patients imposes an overwhelming financial burden on some states. When that occurs, two things happen: First, the mental health professionals who run the state hospitals must define as "adequate" whatever can be afforded, and therefore some hospitals are turned into little more than holding bins, human warehouses, or prisons. The second alternative is to discharge patients and let them fend for themselves outside the hospital, often on the streets. In other words, if the patients are no longer in the hospital, the hospital's legal responsibilities to them no longer exist. Obviously, neither of these are attractive alternatives, and in the next chapter we will consider other strategies for treating patients.

TOPIC III

Dangerousness and the Public's Right to Protection

Mick was hospitalized for the treatment of antisocial personality disorder, and Jake is in the hospital because he suffers from schizophrenia. Both Mick and Jake are about to be released from the hospital. Their friends and other people in the community to which Mick and Jake will be returning are a little nervous because they've heard that former mental patients are often dangerous, even after treatment. Is that true?

Tanya ignored and actively rejected the attention of a male student. Because of her rejection, the student became very upset and told his therapist about fantasies he had about killing Tanya. A few weeks later he stabbed Tanya to death. Should the therapist have warned Tanya? Is the therapist responsible in part for Tanya's death?

"FORMER MENTAL PATIENT KILLS WIFE." We've all seen headlines like that many times, and they give the impression that former mental patients are dangerous. In this last section we will consider the question of whether such individuals are indeed dangerous and what protections are available to the public.

Dangerousness of Mental Patients

Over the years there has been a great deal of controversy over whether mental patients are more dangerous than other people. Unfortunately, much of the early research was plagued by methodological problems. However, the results of a recent well-controlled, large-scale study provide us with some reliable answers concerning the dangerousness of former patients. In that study about 1,700 former mental patients in three major cities in the United States were followed up, and their rates of violence were compared to those of other people living in the same area (Steadman et al., 1998). The results indicate we should not draw conclusions about violence in mental patients in general, but rather consider three groups separately. Specifically, 1 year after being released, patients who suffered from *personality disorders* or who suffered from *drug-related disorders in addition to some other disorder* were, in fact, more likely than other people to be violent, but *other patients were not more likely to be violent*. The fact that patients with personality disorders and drug problems were more violent is consistent with other findings that these individuals are generally more aggressive (see Chapter 12). It is also very important to note that when former mental patients were violent, they were most likely to express their aggression against family members or close friends and not against strangers. Indeed, almost 90% of their violent acts were against family and friends, so it appears that we are not at risk of violence from patients we don't know.

Overall, then, with the notable exception of individuals with personality and drug-related problems, former mental patients are not more dangerous than other people. The popular image of former patients as being dangerous apparently comes from the fact that when they do commit violent acts, media reports draw attention to the individuals' history of hospitalization. In contrast, we do not see headlines such as "PERSON WITH NO HISTORY OF MENTAL ILLNESS COMMITS MURDER," although, in fact, that situation is more prevalent.

The Public's Right to Protection

Most of our attention in this chapter has been focused on the rights of mental patients, but other people's right to safety must not be ignored because *sometimes* they are at risk from patients. The right to safety was discussed briefly when I pointed out that one of the reasons for involuntary hospitalization of patients was the protection of others (police power of the state). However, the right to safety has been extended to include *the right to be protected from patients who are not hospitalized*. That right grew out of a case in California in which a young male student told his therapist about his fantasies about killing a young woman named Tanya Tarasoff, who had rejected his advances. The therapist was concerned, and he informed the campus police, who questioned the young man but then released him when he promised that he would stay away from Ms. Tarasoff. However, the therapist did not inform Ms. Tarasoff of the potential danger. A few weeks later the young man stabbed Tanya Tarasoff to death. Her parents filed suit, alleging that the therapist was negligent for not warning their daughter about the danger. In what has come to be known as the **Tarasoff ruling,** the Supreme Court of California concluded that when a therapist *knows* or *should know* that a patient presents a serious risk of violence, the therapist "incurs an obligation to use reasonable care to protect the intended victim against such danger" (*Tarasoff* v. *Regents of the University of California*, 1976, supra note 8; Davis, Davis, & Davis, 1999; Meyers, 1997). To discharge that obligation, the therapist must (1) warn the intended victim or others who are likely to warn the intended victim, (2) notify the police, or (3) take other reasonable steps to protect the intended victim. This is often called the *"duty to warn" principle,* but, in fact, the court ruled only that therapists must take reasonable care to protect individuals they know to be at risk, and reasonable care may or may not involve warning. Therefore, this is more accurately referred to as the **"duty to protect" principle.**

This principle continues to evolve as new cases are brought to the courts, and there are a number of ambiguities and inconsistencies from state to state. One inconsistency involves the question of whether the patient must name a specific person in the threat. For example, when John Hinckley, Jr., attempted to assassinate President Reagan, he seriously harmed some of the Secret Service people

Tarasoff ruling A legal decision that a therapist has an obligation to use reasonable care to protect an intended victim if the therapist knows or should know tht the client presents a serious risk of violence.

"duty to protect" principle A more common name for the Tarasoff ruling.

and the president's press secretary who were with the president at the time. Some of those injured sued Hinckley's therapist, alleging that he should have known that Hinckley was dangerous. However, their suits were dismissed because no specific threats were made against those persons. In contrast, in a case in which a former mental patient with a history of violent behavior began shooting people at random with a shotgun, a woman who was blinded in the attack and whose husband was killed filed suit against the man's therapist; the court ruled in her favor because the patient's history of violence supposedly made the future violence foreseeable, despite the fact that the patient did not make a specific threat.

The duty to protect usually does not extend to cases of suicide. For example, when a young woman named Tammy committed suicide and her parents sued her therapist for not doing something to protect Tammy from herself, the court ruled against the suit. However, there are cases in which the duty to protect has been extended to property. For example, in one case a patient told his therapist that he wanted to burn down his father's barn and then later did so. When the father filed suit, the court concluded that the therapist was liable because he had not warned the father. Obviously, there is a need for increased clarity and consistency in the application of the duty to protect.

THINKING CRITICALLY

Questions about Dangerousness and the Public's Right to Protection

Is there a conflict between the public's need for protection and patients' need for confidentiality with regard to treatment? Yes. To protect an individual who might be endangered by a patient, a therapist may have to inform the individual about what is said in therapy, and breaking the bond of confidentiality that ordinarily surrounds therapy may interfere with progress in therapy (Kagle & Kopels, 1994). For example, if patients are not assured of confidentiality, they might not feel free to talk openly with their therapists. Issues of confidentiality can also pose problems for therapists: They could be sued for breaches of confidentiality but could also be sued for failure to protect if they do not breach confidentiality (Monahan, 1993). In other words, therapists may be "damned if they do and damned if they don't" breach confidentiality. Court rulings have been inconsistent with regard to whether a patient has grounds for suit if a therapist discloses information about the threat the patient poses, but the code of ethics of the American Psychological Association is clear: *Protection of others takes precedence over the right to confidentiality.*

Summary

Topic I: Incompetence and Insanity

▸ An individual can be declared incompetent to stand trial if he or she cannot understand the legal proceedings and cannot participate in his or her defense. Being declared incompetent to stand trial does not relieve the individual of responsibility; it only postpones the trial until the individual is competent.

▸ The insanity defense is based on the notion that individuals who cannot control their behavior because of a mental disorder should not be held responsible for their behavior and therefore should not be punished. An individual who is found to be insane is not punished but is sent to a hospital for treatment.

▸ *Insanity* is a legal term, not a psychological or medical one. Different jurisdictions use different definitions of insanity, and there are differences of opinion concerning how insanity should be defined and whether there should even be an insanity defense.

▸ The M'Naghten rule is based on the knowledge of right versus wrong; that is, an individual is deemed insane if at the time of the criminal act the individual did not know that what he or she was doing was wrong. In some states

an irresistible impulse was also accepted as the basis for insanity ("elbow rule"). Critics argue that the M'Naghten rule does not make allowances for problems such as hallucinations or delusions as causes of illegal behavior.

▸ The American Law Institute rule says that an individual is insane if at the time of the criminal act the individual was suffering from a mental disease or defect that either interfered with the ability to understand right versus wrong or caused cognitive (hallucinations, delusions) or emotional problems (irresistible impulses) that led to the criminal act. This rule excludes repeated criminal behavior as evidence for a mental disease or defect, and it is more liberal than the M'Naghten rule.

▸ Practical problems with the insanity defense include the following: (1) Jurors must make decisions concerning insanity, but they may not have the necessary technical knowledge to make the decisions; (2) jurors must make decisions on subjects about which experts disagree; (3) decisions must be made about insanity at the time the criminal act was committed, but that may have been months or years earlier; (4) there is concern that an individual who is found to have been only temporarily insane and who is then released will become insane again and commit another crime; (5) individuals who are found to be insane may be incarcerated for treatment for a longer period of time than they would be imprisoned for the crime; and (6) in most states an individual is presumed sane until proven insane.

▶ After John Hinckley, Jr., attempted to assassinate President Reagan but was found to be insane, some states abolished the insanity defense. Other states gave up using the American Law Institute rule and returned to using the M'Naghten rule, and some states introduced the "guilty but mentally ill" rule.

Topic II: Hospitalization and the Rights of Patients

▶ With voluntary hospitalization an individual who feels in need of help signs into a hospital, but if the staff later concludes that the individual continues to need help, the individual may not be allowed to leave the hospital voluntarily.

▶ Individuals can be hospitalized involuntarily for their own protection (parens patriae) or for the protection of others (police power of the state). Concerns about equal treatment for mental patients arise because medical patients are not confined (hospitalized) for their protection nor are other individuals (suspected criminals) whom we suspect of being dangerous to others confined.

▶ Hospitalized patients have the right to (1) live in the least restrictive alternative; (2) receive treatment; and (3) refuse treatment unless they are judged to be incompetent, are involuntarily committed to the hospital, or their

refusal increases the cost of their treatment to the state. Those reasons may be set aside if the individual refuses on religious grounds or if an equally effective alternative treatment is available.

▶ Mental patients also have the right to (1) have a reasonable amount of living space; (2) wear their own clothes unless doing so is dangerous or inappropriate; (3) refuse to be forced to work (slavery) unless the work has some therapeutic value (they also cannot be made to perform work for which the hospital is under contract with an outside organization, even if the work is therapeutic); and (4) exercise their civil rights (e.g., make contracts, marry, divorce, vote) unless they have been declared incompetent.

Topic III: Dangerousness and the Public's Right to Protection

▶ According to one study, after release from a mental hospital only patients with personality disorders and drug problems are more likely than other people to be violent. This is consistent with findings that these individuals are generally more aggressive. They are most likely to express aggression against family members or close friends.

▶ Under the Tarasoff ruling, mental health workers have the duty to warn or otherwise protect individuals who may be endangered by individuals with mental disorders. If the duty to protect conflicts with a patient's right to confidentiality, the duty to protect takes precedence.

Questions for Making Connections

1. Based on what you know about psychiatric disorders, describe one or more patients who would be declared incompetent to stand trial and who would probably never be competent to stand trial. What should be done with these individuals?

2. If you committed a crime and pleaded insanity, would you rather be judged on the M'Naghten rule, the American Law Institute rule, or the "guilty but mentally ill" rule? Are there differences between the rule you would want to be judged on and the rule on which you would want others to be judged? In general, which rule seems best and why?

3. A person who suffers from schizophrenia commits a crime because his "voices" tell him to do it. Under what

rule would he be declared insane, and under what rule would he be declared sane? Which outcome do you think is most appropriate for this person, and why?

4. Imagine that you are suffering from serious depression, and a psychiatrist recommends that you receive electroconvulsive therapy (ECT). Under what conditions could you be forced to have ECT, and under what conditions could you refuse the treatment?

5. Compare the rights of psychiatric and medical patients with regard to involuntary hospitalization and the right to refuse treatment. Should mental patients have less control over their own treatment than medical patients do? If so, why?

Key Terms and People

In reviewing and testing yourself, you should be able to discuss each of the following:

American Law Institute rule, p. 532
"duty to protect" principle, p. 546
elbow rule, p. 532
emergency (involuntary) hospitalization, p. 541
"guilty but mentally ill" rule, p. 534
incompetent to stand trial, p. 530

insanity defense, p. 530
involuntary commitment, p. 537
involuntary outpatient commitment, p. 540
irresistible impulse, p. 532
least restrictive alternative, p. 541
M'Naghten rule, p. 531

parens patriae, p. 537
police power of the state, p. 537
right to equal protection, p. 537
Tarasoff ruling, p. 546
voluntary admission, p. 536

19 Hospitalization, Community Care, and Prevention

THERE IS A MAJOR REVOLUTION with regard to progress in mental hospitals. Put simply, hospitals are being closed, patients are being turned out, and other people who need help are being turned away. Where are the patients and other people going? Some are able to go to one of the remaining hospitals, and many are living in the community and can get help at various outpatient clinics. However, many former patients are living in deplorable conditions on the streets or in abandoned buildings. The movement of patients out of hospitals and into the community has important implications for the patients, their families, and other residents of the community. To explain the problems and promises of this revolution, I will begin by describing mental hospitals as they once existed and as they exist today. Then I will explain why hospitals are being closed and what alternatives are being offered. Finally, I will discuss the attempts being made to prevent the development of future psychiatric disorders.

TOPIC I

Mental Hospitals and Deinstitutionalization

Andrea is suffering from schizophrenia and is hospitalized in a psychiatric hospital. She spends most of her time in a large rather drab room with 15 or 20 other patients watching televi-sion or sleeping. She doesn't know many of the other patients, and they all seem wrapped up in their own problems. Her psychologist sees her for only about 2 hours each week, and the nurses talk to her only when they come to give her medication; so most of the time she is very lonely. The person she has gotten to know best is the woman who supervises the patients on the ward, but that woman is not really a therapist. Being hospitalized isn't very pleasant, and Andrea wonders whether it is doing her any good. Might she be better off taking her medication at home where she has family and friends?

The state legislature faced a dilemma: The costs of programs such as education were increasing, but revenues were decreasing because taxes had been cut. What could be done? One solution was to close the state mental hospital, where each patient was costing the state tens of thousands of dollars per year. Legislators denied that they were going to close the hospital for economic reasons and said that getting patients out of the hospital and treating them in the community was a step in the direction of "modern mental health practice." The bill authorizing the closing of the hospital passed. A month later the hospital was closed, and a patient who was suffering from chronic schizophrenia was discharged. As she stood on the steps of the hospital she asked, "But where do I go?" No one heard because the door to the hospital was tightly shut. Where did she go?

In this section we'll consider what mental hospitals are like and examine the reasons why they are being closed.

Mental Hospitals Then and Now

Until about 1950 the majority of mental hospitals were little more than human warehouses, sometimes holding thousands of patients in deplorable conditions for years. Psychological treatments were rarely used, and effective drugs had not yet been developed (see Chapter 1). As a consequence, most patients spent their days staring into space or struggling in the straightjackets that were used to control them during periods of mania. Not only did patients suffer from the symptoms that initially caused them to be hospitalized, but their hospitalization itself caused them to develop what was called the **institutionalization syndrome.** That is, they became totally dependent on the hospital staff, often ate with their hands, did not wash or dress properly, urinated in their clothes, and were afraid to leave the hospital. In short, even if their original symptoms diminished, many of the patients would not have been able to return to the community (Braginsky, Grosse, & Ring, 1966; Braginsky & Braginsky, 1967; Drake & Wallach, 1979; Goffman, 1961; Rosenblatt & Mayer, 1974; Shiloh, 1968). For the most part what I have described here is history, but in some economically deprived areas there are still hospitals that are not much better than those of 50 or 100 years ago. Fortunately, however, the vast majority of today's hospitals reflect a more modern approach, and in the next sections I'll describe their facilities, staff, and costs.

Hospitalized patients spend most of their waking time in a day room.

Physical Facilities

Today psychiatric inpatient treatment occurs either on a ward in a *psychiatric hospital* or, more likely, on a psychiatric ward within a *general medical hospital.* There are usually separate wards for children and adults, and in large hospitals there may be separate wards for patients with different types of disorders, such as those with eating disorders and those with schizophrenia. However, in small general hospitals there are usually not enough patients or facilities for specialized wards, so all patients are grouped together on one ward. The number of patients on a ward can range from 10 to 100.

Less disturbed patients and those who are not likely to escape or attempt suicide are often assigned to **open wards,** where the doors are not locked and the patients are free to go to other parts of the hospital. More disturbed patients are assigned to **closed wards,** where the doors are locked and may be guarded by an attendant.

An important part of any ward is the **day room** where patients spend most of their waking hours, usually sitting with nothing to do or watching endless hours of television. Unfortunately, day rooms are usually rather barren, drab, and utilitarian, with a minimum of furniture.

Another important part of the ward is the **nurses' station,** which is usually a glass-enclosed office where the nurses spend most of their time and where patients' medications and records are kept. The nurses supervise the patients from the station, and in some hospitals the nurses' station is comparable to the guard tower in a prison.

Most wards also have an **isolation room** (often referred to as the "quiet room") in which patients can be confined if they become agitated, destructive, or abusive. Most isolation rooms are cell-like and contain only a mattress so that patients will not have anything with which to hurt themselves. Patients are forcibly confined to the isolation room when they are being disruptive or self-destructive, but sometimes patients voluntarily use it as a retreat.

Adjoining the day room are the patients' sleeping rooms, each with from one to five beds. Patients are usually not allowed to go to their sleeping rooms during the day, so they often nap in the day room.

Other typical facilities are a cafeteria, a recreational area for exercise, and an area for art, music or occupational therapy. Finally, it is noteworthy that the offices of the psychologists, psychiatrists, and social workers who are responsible for the patients' treatment are not on the ward. That fact is unfortunate because it separates the treatment staff from

Most wards have an isolation room in which patients can be temporarily confined if they become agitated, destructive, or abusive.

contact with the outside world if they are not hospitalized 24 hours a day. Another advantage is that the hospital can serve twice as many patients, with less cost to each patient. Unfortunately, despite the fact that the use of day and night hospitalization is less expensive and at least as effective as full-time hospitalization, these options are not widely used.

Staff

Every psychiatric ward has a variety of staff members who have different responsibilities. Psychologists, psychiatrists, and social workers develop treatment plans for patients and are involved in individual and group therapy. Because psychiatrists are trained in medicine, they also take responsibility for various physiological treatments, such as drugs and electroconvulsive (shock) therapy. (For a discussion of the training of psychologists, psychiatrists, and social workers, see Chapter 1.)

Because psychologists, psychiatrists, and social workers spend most of their time in their offices, the day-to-day running of the ward is primarily in the hands of psychiatric nurses. Nurses are extremely important and powerful in patients' lives because it is often the nurses' reports about patients that determine what happens to the patients. For example, if a nurse reports that a patient is agitated, the patient may be given a sedative, sent to the isolation room, or confined to the ward. In contrast, positive reports from

the life of the patients, and it symbolically separates treatment from daily living.

The atmosphere on most psychiatric wards is bleak and lonely. The physical facilities are usually gloomy, and although there may be many patients, they are often emotionally isolated from one another and hence alone in the crowd. Furthermore, the limited contact between patients and staff leads to feeling of abandonment. Indeed, many staff members walk past patients as if they were inanimate objects rather than human beings who are overwhelmed with problems.

Most patients live in the hospital on a 24-hour-a-day basis, but there are two notable exceptions: First, some patients who have a supportive environment in which they can spend the night will come to the hospital in the morning, receive treatment during the day, and go home in the late afternoon or early evening. This pattern is referred to as **day hospitalization** (Hoge, Davidson, & Sledge, 1997; Russell et al., 1996). Second, there is **night hospitalization** for patients who have a place to go during the day, such as a job. These patients come to the hospital about dinnertime, receive treatment during the evening, spend the night, and leave in the morning. An advantage of day and night hospitalization lies in the fact that patients can maintain better

institutionalization syndrome The deterioration of personal behavior and the tendency to become dependent on the hospital as a consequence of long-term hospitalization.

open wards Psychiatric wards where patients who are less disturbed and not likely to escape or attempt suicide are assigned; the doors are not locked and patients are free to go to other parts of the hospital.

closed wards Psychiatric wards where patients who are suffering from serious disorders or are suicidal are assigned; the doors are locked and may be guarded.

day room A room in a psychiatric ward where patients spend most of their time, usually watching television.

nurses' station An office in a psychiatric ward, usually glass-enclosed, where nurses remain while not attending to patients and where medications and records are kept.

isolation room A room in a psychiatric ward in which disruptive or self-destructive patients can be confined or to which a patient may go for quiet.

day hospitalization A form of hospitalization in which patients stay in the hospital for treatment during the day but go home at night.

night hospitalization A form of hospitalization in which patients come to the hospital for treatment in the evening, stay the night, and go home in the morning.

Psychiatric nurses—such as those portrayed in the film *Girl, Interrupted*—are extremely important individuals in patients' lives. Their reports often determine what happens to the patients.

a nurse can result in movement to a better ward, home visits, and other privileges. There are numerous stories about head nurses, such as Nurse Ratched in the book and movie *One Flew over the Cuckoo's Nest* (Kesey, 1962), who rule their wards like monarchs rule kingdoms. There is a good deal of truth in these stories. However, the investment of power in nurses is not necessarily bad because nurses are probably in the best position to know and evaluate the patients. Psychologists, psychiatrists, and social workers may see patients in therapy for an hour or two each week, but the nurses must deal with the patients on a daily basis, when the patients are tired, hungry, frustrated, unable to sleep at night, and rejected by their peers and families.

Although nurses have more contact with the patients than do other professionals, that does not necessarily mean that they have a lot of contact. One study revealed that nurses came out of the nurses' station an average of only 11.5 times in an 8-hour shift, and the counts included the times they came out simply to leave the ward (Rosenhan, 1973). Furthermore, in that study it was impossible to determine how much time the nurses actually spent with the patients because their contacts were so brief.

The members of the hospital staff who have the most contact with the patients are the **psychological technicians** (formerly called *ward attendants*) who supervise the patients on the ward throughout the day. These "psych techs" spend a lot of time with patients and often provide patients with their only ongoing contacts with normal indi-

psychological technicians Nonprofessional staff members who work on wards supervising patients; formerly called *ward attendants*.

viduals. Also, because the technicians are not professional staff, the patients can often relate to them better and sometimes become friends with them. In some circumstances the contact between technicians and patients can be very intense. This is especially true if a patient is put on "suicide watch," which means that a technician must stay within 2–3 feet of the patient 24-hours-a-day regardless of what the patient is doing. Concerning the relationship between patients and technicians, one patient commented:

> Mike, the psych tech on my ward, is the only real friend I have left. He's the only guy I can talk to. The nurses, hell, they just come out to yell at me. The only time they know I'm alive is when I'm doing something wrong or when it's time to shove more medicine down me. The goddamned doctors just play useless word games in their offices and try to screw my head around. They don't know what's going on. How could they? They almost never see me. Mike knows me and keeps me straight.

Although the technicians are low on the staff hierarchy, they do have considerable power because their reports, like those of nurses, often provide the basis for the impressions that are formed by the psychologists and psychiatrists who ultimately make the decisions about the patients.

Finally, various activity therapists, including *occupational therapists, art therapists,* and *music therapists* often work with hospitalized patients. Activities such as knitting, painting, and listening to music do not by themselves provide effective treatments for psychiatric disorders, but the social interactions that go along with these activities provide opportunities to talk about problems, try out new social roles, and increase contact with reality. In other words, although the activities themselves are not treatments, they may provide a medium through which more normal behavior can be developed. Furthermore, the activities serve to enhance the quality of life and the self-esteem of hospitalized patients, which is very important.

Overall, then, in the war against mental illness, psychiatrists and psychologists are the generals, nurses are the lieutenants, and psychological technicians and activity therapists are the foot soldiers on the front line.

It should be clear that on the ward there is often very little informal contact between patients and professional staff members. The question then arises, what happens when such contact does occur? In one study individuals who were pretending to be patients (pseudopatients) approached staff members with questions like "Could you tell me when I will be eligible for grounds privileges?" and "Could you tell me when I am likely to be discharged?" (Rosenhan, 1973). The results indicated that the staff members responded to the patients *less than 5% of the time*. Indeed, 71% of the time psychiatrists simply looked away and walked past. Those results are summarized in Table 19.1.

TABLE 19.1

Psychiatric ward staff avoided responding to questions asked by pseudopatients

Type of response	Frequency of response (%)	
	Psychiatrist	Nurse or attendant
Moved on, head averted	71	88
Made eye contact	23	10
Paused to chat	2	2
Stopped to chat	4	<1

Source: Data from Rosenhan (1973), Table 1, p. 255.

Furthermore, when staff members did respond to the questions asked by patients, their answers were often not really answers—for example:

> *Pseudopatient:* Pardon me, Doctor. Could you tell me when I'm eligible for grounds privileges?
>
> *Physician:* Good morning, Dave. How are you today? (*moves off without waiting for a response*)

If a patient responded that way to a question from a staff member, the response would be considered "inappropriate" and taken as evidence that the patient was out of contact with reality and needed continued hospitalization!

The fact that the professional staff often avoids informal contact with patients is unfortunate. However, you should not conclude that their behavior reflects a lack of concern or commitment. Instead, in most cases the avoidance of contact stems from the fact that the staff is overworked. Furthermore, it is stressful to work with highly disturbed individuals on a daily basis. As the old saying goes, "There but for the grace of God go I," and that thought can be very threatening. It may be that the interpersonal distance that the staff maintains is a defensive strategy. Just as surgeons cover their patients' faces when they operate to separate "the person" from "the operation," so staff members in mental hospitals may place emotional screens between themselves and their patients.

In summary, today's hospitals are a great improvement over the warehouses of only 50 years ago, but in most cases they are not pleasant places. There are some private hospitals that are like posh resorts, but they are well beyond the financial reach of most patients. Case Study 19.1 (on p. 556) was written by a student of mine who was admitted to a psychiatric ward of a general medical hospital after she attempted suicide. Her comments are particularly interesting because they reflect changes in her attitudes about hospitalization and convey her ambivalence about the experience.

Costs

In most textbooks the costs of treatment are ignored, but in the "real world" costs are an important consideration, often determining what treatments are available to patients. Let's examine the costs of hospitalization. It's difficult to provide general cost figures because different disorders call for different treatment approaches that entail different costs, costs can vary with the quality of treatment, and there are regional differences in costs. However, the following figures will provide you with some rough estimates of costs.

The typical cost of hospitalization in a private hospital is often *at least $1,000 a day,* and in many cases that does not include "extras" such as psychotherapy, medication, other treatments such as ECT, physical exams, psychological tests, laboratory work, or the services of other professionals such as social workers. Those additional costs can easily add hundreds of dollars a day to the bill. The cost of psychiatric hospitalization is often comparable to the cost of medical or surgical hospitalization, but there is one very important difference: Whereas medical or surgical hospitalization usually lasts for a few days or a week, *psychiatric hospitalization can last for months.* Being in a psychiatric hospital for one month can easily cost well over $50,000; clearly, such costs can be overwhelming.

When attempting to understand the high costs of hospitalization, we need to recognize that private hospitals are usually run to make a profit and they have relatively little competition. Thus, there is little necessity to keep costs down and considerable incentive to keep them high. In some instances hospitalization is essential for the good of the patients and the community, but in many cases individuals are hospitalized to keep beds full and profits up. Indeed, one study revealed that about 75% of hospital admissions for substance abuse were unnecessary, and nearly 40% of days spent in mental hospitals by patients in general were not necessary (American Psychological Association, 1993). At one hospital I know of, patients who are being treated for eating disorders are usually discharged after 28 or 29 days. Why not earlier or later? The answer is that patients' insurance benefits run out after 30 days! In other words, it appears that in many cases the length of patients' hospital stay is a function of their *financial* condition rather than their *mental* condition. Such abuse is possible because patients and family members are frightened by psychiatric disorders and are not in a position to judge what treatment or how much treatment is necessary. Unfortunately, individuals rarely get second opinions concerning the treatment of psychiatric disorders.

Day hospitalization can cost $200–300 a day—still high, but representing a considerable savings compared to staying overnight (and little treatment is provided at night anyway). Of course, all of the extras such as psychotherapy must be added to that base figure. Outpatient treatment is

Psychiatric Hospitalization after a Suicide Attempt: A College Junior Talks about Her Experience

"THE FIRST THING I REMEMBER was being in the emergency room of the hospital. All I could do was lie there. I wanted to tell them that I was all right, that everything would be fine if they would just let me die, but Mom and Dad were talking to a nurse, and I couldn't make myself move. They told me later that I rocked back and forth and moaned a lot, but I don't remember.

"A few hours later a male nurse from the psychiatric ward came to my room and asked if I would sign a form to enter myself into the hospital voluntarily. I remember that it took me several minutes to figure out that I was supposed to sign my name—or at least it seemed like several minutes. My next thought was that later I was going to be really sorry that I signed myself in.

"When I awoke in the morning, I was in a hospital room in a regular medical ward, and they were getting ready to take me up to the psychiatric ward. When I realized what was going on, I pleaded with my parents to take me home. The thought of spending time on a psychiatric ward was scary!

> It's even harder for people to understand when a person admits that he has a problem.

"When the nurse took me up to the ward to show me around, I was really worried. I was worried that they would make me stay there, which they did. The psychiatric ward was different from the rest of the hospital. People walked around in street clothes, and adults sat in the lounge watching TV and playing games. I kept waiting for someone to start screaming or for someone to appear in a straitjacket.

"They assigned me to a room by myself, but first they took away everything I had. I found out later that they removed anything with which I could hurt myself. It took 2 days for me to get back my curling iron and my contact cooker. I wasn't allowed a razor, and they looked through everything that anyone brought me.

"They gave me a phone only on the condition that I promise not to try to hurt myself. They said that if I did try to hurt myself, they would put me in a hospital where they'd tie me down and keep me that way. I decided on the phone. I was so embarrassed when they told me that it would be a while before they would trust me to eat with the other patients in the cafeteria or to do anything by myself. Because I was a suicide risk, I was put on 'special observation,' which meant that someone sat right next to me *at all times.* Also, when I was in the bathroom, they knocked on the door every few seconds and made me answer.

"I told Mom not to tell my [college] roommates or anyone where I was. I was afraid they wouldn't want to know or, worse yet, wouldn't care. Mom told them anyway, but I was visited only twice by my roommates. I can understand that; it's hard to talk to someone who is not allowed to have sharp objects around and who you think is crazy. I suppose it was also frightening for them to be on the ward.

"The first few days were bad. I felt out of touch and like a person who was stuck someplace he wasn't supposed to be but couldn't convince anyone of it. When I was escorted around the halls for a walk, I looked at the other patients and wondered what it was like to be a psychiatric patient. It was scary and embarrassing to realize that I was one.

"My boyfriend came to visit me every day and always called. I don't think I could have maintained contact without him. He was the only person, except for the people on the floor, who saw me as an individual with problems, not as a *social disease.* My parents were uncomfortable at first. They stumbled when they talked and wouldn't look at me. I hated myself for putting them through it, but I blamed them for letting me live. Gradually, though, I was glad I was there. My mom was terrific. She was cheerful and optimistic. She told me not to worry about school, that I deserved a break. She sympa-

thized with me and made me feel like it was OK to admit I had problems. My dad didn't handle it as easily. He wouldn't come to see me alone because the one time he did, we had nothing to say. He wouldn't talk about what was wrong, why I was there, or what help I was getting. I think he kind of tried to see it as a normal hospital stay.

"I was on the ward for about a week when they finally took me off 'special observation' and put me in a double room and allowed me to eat with the others. They told me that I was expected to mingle and talk with others on the ward, in group meetings, and with my counselors. I didn't want to talk. I didn't see the use of telling my problems to people who were already mentally ill. What good was that going to do anyone? Also, I was ashamed. Normal people do not lose control. Every time I tried to talk in group therapy, all I could do was cry. I just lost control, and I hated myself and them for making me do it.

"After about 2 weeks in the hospital, I begged my doctor to let me out. He did on Thanksgiving Day. Sometimes I wish that he'd made me stay longer, but I can't ask to go back because asking to go in is worse than being put there because then you're admitting you have a problem. It's even harder for people to understand when a person admits that he has a problem. Then they say he's begging for attention. I'm not so sure that's wrong, either. I don't know.

"When I got back to school, I felt like everyone was looking at me, saying, 'Look, I can tell she's been in a mental hospital.' I was scared to come back. I didn't want to be put into a group of people who were singled out for the rest of their lives. I still get nervous every time someone says, 'What were you doing last semester?' I don't want to talk about it or think about it. I still wish it had never happened. I needed to go to the hospital and it helped, but I wish it had never happened."

probably the most cost-effective. Psychotherapy outside of the hospital usually costs between $75 and $125 an hour.

Case Study 19.2 (on p. 558) illustrates the very high cost of treatment for Betty, about whom you read earlier (see Case Study 10.3).

Deinstitutionalization

Some years ago the superintendent of a large state mental hospital told me that one of his major goals was to "build more flower gardens." When I looked surprised, he explained that the hospital had embarked on an ambitious program of returning patients to the community, and that as the hospital population became smaller, the buildings that had once housed patients were torn down. The foundations of the demolished buildings were then filled with earth and planted with flowers, trees, and shrubs. Indeed, when I looked out his office window, I saw a series of large rectangular gardens, each surrounded by a low wall formed by the top of the foundation of the original building. Where patients once languished, petunias now flourished. However, as you will see, in some cases the bulldozing of buildings and planting of petunias may have been premature.

The process of closing mental hospitals and sending patients to the community for treatment is called **deinstitutionalization,** and its recent effects have been dramatic. For example, in the 20 years between 1970 and 1990 only 14 state hospitals were closed, but in the next 10 years more than 40 were closed, and the number of patients in the remaining hospitals was reduced greatly (Dowdall, 1999; McGrew et al., 1999). Deinstitutionalization also had dramatic effects on the expenses of private insurance companies. For example, because fewer patients were hospitalized and because those who were hospitalized stayed for shorter periods, the costs for hospitalization dropped by over 30% in a 3-year period (Leslie & Rosenheck, 1999a, 1999b). Surprisingly, there were also drops of between 15% and 40% in *outpatient* costs. That decrease apparently occurred because fewer patients were initially admitted to a hospital and so fewer had to be followed up later. This suggests that when hospitals were closed, some people who needed help "fell through the cracks," a problem to which we will return later. The reduction of the number of patients in hospitals is certainly striking, but it is even more dramatic when you realize that the reduction occurred while the general population was increasing.

There are a number of reasons for the reduced number of patients in hospitals. One is that as more effective drugs are developed, the symptoms of more patients can be brought under control, and therefore fewer patients need to be hospitalized (Galvin et al., 1999). More importantly, however, is the belief that patients can be treated more

A key factor in the movement to deinstitutionalize patients is economics—mental hospitals are extremely expensive to operate.

effectively in the community than in hospitals. Yet another reason is that it is less expensive to treat patients in the community than it is in the hospital. Let's consider these reasons in a little more detail.

Hospital versus Community Treatment

For many years seriously ill psychiatric patients were treated in hospitals, so what led to the belief that they can be treated more effectively in the community? One reason hospitals lost favor can be summarized with the statement "You can't make a normal adjustment in an abnormal environment." The notion is that a major goal of treatment is to help individuals make a better adjustment, but it may be difficult for patients to make a normal adjustment while living with many others who have very serious problems. For example, it is unlikely that a patient will be able to learn to deal with his or her own problems while surrounded by individuals who think they are Napoleon, hear the voice of God in the bathroom, or believe they have radioactive saliva.

Furthermore, hospitalization is not conducive to normal adjustment because it fosters dependency and undermines self-confidence. These effects occur because in most hospitals things are done *to* or *for* patients rather than *by* patients. In other words, when we hospitalize people, we are telling them that they cannot take care of themselves, and in the hospital they learn the *role of patient.* In view of these reasons it seems wise to get patients out of hospitals.

deinstitutionalization A process by which patients are discharged from mental hospitals, which are often closed, and then are treated in the community.

The Cost of Betty's Drugs: $353 a Week

THIS CASE STUDY IS BASED on Betty, the woman who suffers from schizophrenia whom I discussed in Case Studies 11.2 and 13.4. You will recall that Betty has suffered from a very severe case of schizophrenia for about 20 years and that she has been hospitalized numerous times. However, Betty is now taking a number of drugs that are effective for reducing many of her symptoms. Those drugs, plus a good deal of social support from friends and the staff at a local mental health center, make it possible for Betty to live outside of the hospital.

Unfortunately, the drugs do not eliminate the symptoms, and she is still plagued by a variety of delusions (that the police are after her) and hallucinations (monks and demons telling her to kill herself, rats on the floor, people dissolving into blobs of blood). Struggling with her symptoms poses one serious problem for Betty, but she faces another—paying for her drugs. Here is a list of the drugs and treatments Betty must have, with their weekly costs:

Drug or treatment	Weekly cost ($)
Clozaril (antipsychotic)	220
Zoloft (antidepressant)	14
Oxybutynin chloride (antispasmodic for bladder control to counter a side effect of the other drugs)	7
Ativan (antianxiolytic)	13
Klonopin (antianxiolytic)	28
Chloral hydrate (sleeping pill)	1
Blood test for agranulocytosis	20
Psychiatric consultation (to monitor symptoms, drugs)	50
Total	**353**

The cost of Betty's treatment comes to $18,356 a year. How does Betty pay for this? Betty is a very bright woman with a graduate degree in library science who once had a career as a librarian; however, because of her symptoms she is unable to work. Therefore, Betty must live on Social Security disability benefits of $160 a week, which is *less than half of her weekly medical bill.* Fortunately, Betty qualifies for Medicaid assistance, which will pay her medical bills *after she pays the annual deductible of $2,321.* Spread over the year, the deductible comes to $45 a week, so Betty has $115 a week to cover *all* of her expenses (rent, utilities, food, clothing, etc.). Sometimes Betty is simply not able to pay the deductible fee for the drugs, in which case she cannot get the drugs. Usually her pharmacist will give her credit and let her go into debt, but there are limits. One time Betty had no money and was within 2 days of running out of Clozaril. Without the drug Betty's condition would immediately deteriorate, she would not be able to function in the community, and she would have to be placed in a state hospital (assuming that a space could be found). Hospitalization in the state hospital would cost the government about $40,000 per year, so the cost of the Clozaril is a bargain. With deficits mounting, however, the government may not be able to afford either. Then what will happen? Clearly, the cost of treatment can be an overwhelming financial burden both for the individuals and for the government. And remember, in many cases, this is a lifelong burden. What would you do if you faced this situation?

Note: The costs described here do not include those of the mental health service that provides a case manager who helps Betty deal with daily problems.

Although drugs tend to cost less than most other treatments, some drugs—such as Clozaril—can be very expensive.

In contrast, there are a number of reasons to believe that treatment in the community can be very effective. Most notable in this regard is that if individuals are treated in the community, they will not have to be separated from their friends, family, and coworkers—people from whom they can obtain valuable social support. Furthermore, while living in the community patients can work directly on overcoming the stressors in their lives rather than being isolated from them and only talking about them. Finally, if patients are treated in the community, they can avoid the difficult transition from the hospital back to the community. That transition can be frightening and stressful because patients are unsure about their ability to function in the outside world, which is after all where they "broke down." Overall, when contrasted with the negative aspects of hospitals, the positive aspects of communities tip the balance in favor of treatment in the community.

Economics

The other major factor behind the deinstitutionalization movement is simple economics. Mental hospitals are very expensive to operate, so closing them saves a great deal of money. If patients are treated in the community, there are still the direct costs of treatment, such as those for therapists and medication, but there is a savings of all of the indirect costs for things such as food, building maintenance, and extensive support staffs that include everyone from kitchen workers to groundskeepers.

However, you should note that the savings achieved by deinstitutionalization are not always as great as they appear at first. The main reason is that patients who are discharged from state hospitals often go to other facilities such as privately operated nursing homes. The costs of institutionalizing patients in those facilities are generally higher and are usually paid for by the federal government through the Medicare program. In other words, in some cases costs are not saved but simply *shifted* from state governments to the federal government.

Problems with Deinstitutionalization

The original factor favoring deinstitutionalization was improved care of patients. However, saving money became more important when it was necessary to cut budget deficits and appease voters with tax cuts. An unfortunate consequence of the need to save money was that the funds that were saved by closing hospitals were not reinvested in developing alternative treatments in the community. As a result, doors to hospitals were closed but doors in the community were not opened, and patients were left stranded without treatment. Here's a dramatic example: a man named Andrew Goldstein, who suffered from schizophrenia, killed a woman he didn't know by pushing her in front of a New York subway train. What's relevant here is that Mr. Goldstein knew he suffered from schizophrenia, knew he was dangerous, and on numerous occasions *pleaded* to be hospitalized. Unfortunately, because of deinstitutionalization and budget cutbacks, no hospital space was available and there weren't sufficient alternative treatments in the community.

Closing mental hospitals and discharging patients is usually presented as a "progressive, modern movement" toward more humane treatment of patients. However, if we do not make treatment available in the community, we are probably being more inhumane than humane. Indeed, in many cases deinstitutionalized patients end up living on the streets or in run-down areas of the cities that have become known as "psychiatric ghettos." The existence of psychiatric ghettos and of cases like that of Mr. Goldstein has occasionally caused a backlash against deinstitutionalization, and some efforts have made to reinstitutionalize some patients. An example of such an effort was the program in New York City that resulted in the institutionalization of Joyce Brown, the woman who burned money, described in Case Study 18.2. However, those programs have been tokens at best. Indeed, the program in New York City involved setting aside only 28 hospital beds for a city with nearly 9 million people!

In summary, the number of patients in hospitals is being drastically reduced because of (1) improved medications, (2) the belief that patients can be treated more effectively in the community, and (3) attempts to save money. Unfortunately, sometimes when hospitals are closed and patients are returned to the community, alternative sources of treatment are not provided. However, some interesting treatments in the community are available, and we'll consider them in the next section.

THINKING CRITICALLY

Questions about Mental Hospitals and Deinstitutionalization

1. *Is treatment in hospitals really less effective than treatment in the community?* Much of the movement toward deinstitutionalization is based on the assumption that treatment in hospitals is less effective than treatment in the community, but is that really the case? What's the evidence? To compare the effects of hospital and community treatment, 10 separate experiments were conducted in which patients were randomly assigned either to hospital treatment or to some alternative care—drugs with outpatient psychotherapy, day care, or simply adequate housing without any specific treatment (see reviews by Kiesler, 1982a, 1982b; Kiesler & Sibulkin, 1988). The results of these experiments were startling: *In no experiment was hospitalization found to be more effective than the alternative care, and in almost every case the alternative care had more positive effects.* For example, in one experiment patients suffering from schizophrenia were randomly assigned either to a good mental hospital, where they received traditional treatment including psychotherapy, drugs, occupational therapy, and ward meetings, or to a small, homelike facility run by a nonprofessional staff, where the patients and staff shared the responsibility for maintenance and food preparation (Mosher & Menn, 1978; Mosher, Menn, & Matthews, 1975). Followup evaluations of the patients after 2 years revealed that those who had been assigned to the homelike facility were suffering from fewer symptoms and were more likely to be employed. Among patients who had been discharged, those from the homelike facility were more likely to be living alone or with peers, whereas those from the hospital were more likely to be living with parents or relatives. Furthermore, the patients from the homelike facility were 20% less likely to be rehospitalized.

In another experiment patients with acute schizophrenia were assigned either to regular inpatient treatment or to outpatient treatment in which they received drug therapy and counseling (Levenson et al., 1977). There were no dramatic differences between the success rates of the two groups, but the patients who received the outpatient treatment tended to do better, and their treatment cost only *one-sixth* of what the inpatient treatment cost. In summary, the results of the 10 experiments indicated that alternative care outside a hospital was at least as effective as treatment in a hospital—and it cost less. This evidence certainly provides support for the notion of deinstitutionalization. It is interesting to note, however, that even though hospital treatment was found to be less effective than the alternatives, the bureaucracy responsible for operating the mental hospitals fought the movement to close the hospitals; jobs were apparently more important than the health of patients (Hunter, 1999; Pescosolido, Wright, & Kikuzawa, 1999).

2. *Are mental hospitals still needed?* Yes, hospitals are still needed. That answer may surprise you because the findings I just discussed consistently indicated that treatment in mental hospitals is less effective than treatment elsewhere. To understand why hospitals are still needed, it is helpful to remember the term originally used for mental hospitals—*asylums* (see Chapter 1). *Asylum* means "a place of refuge or protection," and there are times of overwhelming stress during which individuals need such a place. If individuals have no other place to go while in crisis, hospitals are necessary. Consider an individual who lives alone and who suddenly develops a severe case of schizophrenia; all of a sudden he or she is hallucinating, delusional, and terribly confused. Should we just give this individual some medication and send him or her home with instructions to take the medication and come back next week? That doesn't sound like a humane thing to do. Furthermore, it is unlikely to work because the individual will probably forget to take the medication or be confused about when to take it. A similar case can be made for an individual who is severely depressed and suicidal. Indeed, because medication and even electroconvulsive therapy require a while to take effect, it would be dangerous to send a suicidal person home. Clearly, sometimes individuals need a refuge—an asylum. I am not suggesting that individuals should be hospitalized for long periods, but short stays may sometimes be necessary until the storm of stress passes.

The alternative to hospitalization is community care, but what types of care are available in the community? Furthermore, are there things we can do in the community to prevent the development of psychiatric disorders, thereby reducing the need for treatment? These are the questions we will consider in this section.

Community Care

The notion that patients can be treated in the community can be traced back to the town of Gheel in Flanders (modern-day Belgium) in the 13th century (Earle, 1851/1994). As legend has it, in 600 A.D. a pagan king cut off the head of his beautiful daughter, Dymphna, when she refused to marry him. The townspeople thought that the king was mentally ill and that his behavior was the work of the Devil. Because Dymphna was able to resist her father, it was assumed that God had granted her special powers to fight the evil forces that led to mental illness. When her story spread, people who were struggling with mental disorders came to Gheel in the hope of being inspired to fight the Devil more effectively and be cured. A number of miraculous cures were documented, and Dymphna was made a saint by the

In 600 in the town of Gheel, in Flanders, a pagan king executed his daughter, Dymphna, for refusing to marry him. The townspeople thought that the king was mentally ill and that his behavior was the work of the Devil. Because his daughter had resisted the Devil, people thought that she had special powers to fight the evil forces that caused mental illness. Disturbed individuals flocked to the town of Gheel, and the community developed a tradition of caring for them.

Catholic church in 1247. (She is the patroness of individuals with epilepsy and mental illness.)

As a result of the publicity, hundreds of disturbed individuals began coming to Gheel seeking cures, and in 1430 a small hospital was built. However, because so many people came and because many who were not cured stayed on, the number of disturbed individuals quickly swelled beyond the capacity of the hospital. In an attempt to accommodate everyone, the townspeople began taking disturbed individuals into their homes. The church initially administered the program, but in 1852 the responsibility was shifted to the government of Belgium, which "certified" families as qualified to provide housing and care. Being certified became a matter of pride, social standing, and tradition that was handed down for generations.

For hundreds of years the people of Gheel have provided a model for how people in a community can accept mentally ill individuals and care for them. However, today community care has expanded to include *outpatient clinics, community mental health centers,* and *halfway houses* as well as *home care.*

Outpatient Clinics

Outpatient clinics are usually associated with large hospitals (they are often in the same buildings), and patients can be treated in such a clinic after being discharged from the hospital or as an alternative to being hospitalized. For example, after a hospitalized patient has improved enough to be discharged, his or her treatment can be continued in an outpatient clinic. However, the problem with outpatient clinics is that the hospitals with which they are affiliated usually serve very large areas, and so the clinics are not conveniently located for many patients. Unfortunately, if patients have to travel long distances to get to an outpatient clinic, they are unlikely to begin treatment, and if they do begin, they often drop out. Therefore, although outpatient clinics can play an important role in community care, their role is often limited by the practical problems posed by their location.

Community Mental Health Centers

Community mental health centers, or **CMHCs** as they are often called, were designed to overcome the problem of the inconvenient location of many hospital-based outpatient clinics. As the name implies, community mental health centers are small clinics that are conveniently located in the communities in which potential users live. However, community mental health centers were designed to be much

outpatient clinics Clinics that are usually associated with mental hospitals and that provide treatment to patients after they are discharged from the hospital or as an alternative to being hospitalized.

community mental health centers (CMHCs) Small clinics that are conveniently located in the communities in which potential users live and that provide outpatient therapy with day hospitalization, short-term inpatient hospitalization, 24-hour-a-day emergency services, and educational and consultation services.

Community mental health centers are usually effective for short-term inpatient treatment, outpatient care, and crisis intervention.

more than just convenient. Specifically, they were designed to provide four types of service:

1. *Outpatient therapy with day hospitalization.* First and foremost CMHCs were designed to provide convenient outpatient treatment for individuals in their local communities. When necessary the treatment can involve staying at the CMHC during the day (a form of day hospitalization). The hope was that making treatment readily available, near where the individuals lived, would make individuals more likely to come in for help before their problems became so serious that hospitalization was necessary.

2. *Short-term inpatient hospitalization in emergency cases.* In emergencies CMHCs can provide short-term hospitalization. In this way they can provide the refuge, or asylum, that some people need to ride out a storm (see the earlier discussion). Hospitalizing individuals near where they live rather than in a distant hospital allows social support from friends and relatives to be maintained and the difficult transition from the distant hospital back to the community can be avoided. CMHCs usually do not have their own inpatient facilities, so they use the facilities of local general hospitals.

3. *Round-the-clock emergency services.* In addition to providing regularly scheduled treatment, CMHCs provide immediate help through walk-in clinics and 24-hour-a-day "hot-lines." These emergency services are important: When an individual is in the middle of a crisis, it does not help much to say, "Well, we can see you a week from Tuesday at 2:30." People in crisis need help *immediately,* and early intervention may keep the problem from getting worse. Essentially, at CMHCs the concept of the medical emergency room is applied to the treatment of psychological problems.

4. *Educational and consultation services.* Finally, CMHCs work to prevent disorders from developing by providing consultation and seminars and lectures on topics such as stress management and the early identification of personal problems. Furthermore, staff members are quick to step in to provide help when potential problems arise. For example, when a firefighter in my community was killed while battling a fire, the staff of the CMHC immediately set up group and individual counseling sessions for the members of the fire department to help them deal with the stress associated with the death of their comrade.

Overall, the goals of CMHCs are summed up in their name: They provide help for individuals in their *community,* and they promote *mental health* by providing treatment, catching problems early, and working toward prevention.

Another potential value of CMHCs is that they may be more "culturally sensitive" than large, hospital-based treatment facilities (Rogler et al., 1987). Traditionally, the mental health services provided by large hospitals are aimed at the middle class and are based on a middle-class lifestyle. However, because CMHCs are located where the patients are, they are in a better position to be sensitive to the unique characteristics of the people they serve. That sensitivity may make CMHCs more attractive to members of minority groups, and therefore more effective than traditional facilities.

CMHCs have met with mixed success. On the positive side, the centers are located in the neighborhoods where their clients live, and they do make outpatient treatment, day hospitalization, short-term inpatient treatment, and 24-hour crisis intervention readily available to members of the community. On the negative side, however, their success has been limited because there are simply not enough of them to meet the need. When President Kennedy originally proposed such centeres in the 1960s, he suggested that there should be one center for every 100,000 persons. With today's population that would mean almost 3,000 centers, but only about 1,000 have been established. Furthermore, in many centers the staff is so busy treating people that they have very little time to devote to prevention. In other words, they are so busy bailing out the psychological boat that they do not have time to fix the cracks in the hull. Even so, CMHCS play a very important role in the delivery of mental health services, and there is no doubt that they will continue to do so in the future. They are effective—and cost-effective.

Halfway Houses

By now it should be clear that some patients need to be in a hospital and others do not. However, many patients fall between those extremes—they do not require the intensive care provided by hospitals, but they do need a semistructured environment in which to live. Other patients may need a supportive environment in which to live while making the transition from hospital to community life. As the name implies, **halfway houses** provide places for patients to live that are somewhere between hospitalization and independent life in the community.

Halfway houses are usually large older homes that have been converted into a number of small living units. Residents usually cook and eat together so that costs can be kept low, work can be shared, and residents do not become socially isolated. Halfway houses are usually staffed by paraprofessionals, often a married couple who manage the house and supervise the residents in exchange for rent and possibly a small wage. Like the other residents in the house, the managers usually have other jobs.

Most halfway houses are not designed for long-term use by residents. Rather, they serve as transitional care facilities while the residents are readjusting to life in the community. While living in the halfway house the residents get settled into jobs and social groups before moving out on their own. In the halfway house the residents can get support from the paraprofessionals and the other residents. Indeed, residents who have been out of the hospital longer serve as models for newer residents ("I did it and you can do it").

Home Care

All of the treatment programs we have considered so far require that patients go to the treatment facility, but many programs have been established in which caregivers go to the patients (Combs & Lasuzzo, 1995; Fitzgerald & Kulkarni, 1998; Knapp et al., 1998). Going to patients is sometimes necessary because they are too ill to come in for treatment. This approach is not unique to the care of psychiatric patients; indeed, for years visiting nurse programs have served medical patients who are not sick enough for full-time hospitalization but are too sick or are unable for some other reason to go to the hospital for outpatient care. Psychological "house calls" are more expensive than having patients come in for treatment, but they are cheaper than hospitalizing patients, which may be the only other way many patients could get treatment. Case Study 19.3 (on p. 564) highlights a program in Baltimore called COSTAR, in which psychiatric nurses work in the community providing psychological, medical, and social support for patients.

Public Acceptance of Patients in the Community

Most people agree that treating patients in the community is a good idea, but how do people respond when faced with the possibility of having mental patients live in *their* neighborhoods? Numerous surveys have indicated that most people have negative attitudes about mentally ill individuals and are afraid of them. Because of those attitudes and fears, residents often block the establishment of treatment facilities in their communities. In one city in New York the residents went so far as to pass a law making it illegal for mental patients to live within the city limits. (A mental patient was defined as anyone who was taking antipsychotic medication.) That law was later overturned by the court.

People oppose the presence of mentally ill individuals in their communities, but do many actually notice patients in their communities? To answer that question one group of investigators conducted a survey of individuals living in 12 residential neighborhoods in New York City (Rabkin, Muhlin, & Cohen, 1984). Six of the neighborhoods contained a treatment facility, such as a large outpatient clinic or halfway house, and the residents who were surveyed lived within one block of the treatment facility. The other six neighborhoods were comparable in all respects but did not contain a treatment facility; residents in those areas were used as controls.

The results revealed two interesting findings: First, when residents were asked to rate problems in their community, such as burglary, unemployment, and "crazy people in the street," there were no differences between the responses of residents in the treatment areas and the responses of residents in the control areas. In other words, the presence of patients in their neighborhood did not influence the residents' perception of the quality of life in the neighborhood. Second, when residents were asked about the presence of treatment facilities in their neighborhoods, 77% of the residents in the neighborhoods with a treatment facility did not even know that they lived within one block of such a facility. Of the residents living near a facility, 23% reported being aware of it—but 13% of the residents in the control areas *incorrectly* reported the presence of a treatment facility in their neighborhood. If 13% is taken as the error rate (the percentage of people who incorrectly believe that there is a facility in their neighborhood), it could be concluded that only 10% of the individuals living within one block of a psychiatric treatment facility were aware of its existence.

These results indicate that the presence of a psychiatric treatment facility does not have a negative impact on the quality of life in a community, and that only a very few people are even aware of the existence of such a facility. Unfortunately, facts like these do little to change people's emotionally based attitudes. Would you be in favor of having a facility for treating mental patients in your neighborhood?

halfway houses Small residential facilities in which individuals live while making the transition from hospitalization to independent life in the community.

Taking Help to the Homeless Mentally Ill: The Example of COSTAR

IN BALTIMORE it was recognized that many individuals are too disturbed to come in for treatment. One scenario runs as follows: A disturbed individual is hospitalized temporarily, put on a maintenance dosage of medication that enables him or her to function in the community, and is then released with the expectation that he or she will return to the hospital (or outpatient clinic) for medication as needed. However, for some reason the patient stops taking the medication and consequently relapses. Once relapsed, the patient becomes too disoriented to return to the hospital. Then the disturbed patient is likely to wind up on the street because he or she cannot pay the rent, is rejected by his or her family, or is so disoriented that he or she cannot coexist with others in a normal environment.

In an attempt to reach out and treat such individuals, the Johns Hopkins Hospital and the city of Baltimore established the Community Support, Treatment, and Rehabilitation (COSTAR) program, in which psychiatric nurses work with the patients in the community—on the streets and in their homes. This program differs from most other programs in that it relies primarily on psychiatric nurses rather than on social workers, and therefore patients can be given medical attention in addition to psychological treatment.

The case of a 41-year-old woman named Sinora provides a good example of the kinds of problems that the patients have and the kinds of treatments that are used. Sinora was diagnosed as suffering from chronic schizophrenia, and she must take antipsychotic medication every day or her condition will seriously deteriorate.

> *... psychiatric nurses work with the patients in the community— on the streets and in their homes.*

However, living on the streets as she did, she often forgot her medication, so she became very disoriented and eventually had to be rehospitalized. To circumvent this problem, every day Sinora is visited by a nurse who gives her the medication and makes sure she takes it, but that is not all the nurse does. When Sinora was first found, she was unable to take care of herself, and the nurse had to begin by helping her eat and even bathing her because Sinora frequently soiled herself. The nurse explains, "You start right where they are. . . . Often they'll stumble and go back down, but we all do. Everybody has the right to do that." Over the course of 2 years, the nurse has kept Sinora on her medication, helped her find housing, taught her good grooming and hygiene, taught her how to keep house and shop economically, and helped her budget her money, and she is now taking Sinora to a job-training center. This is real progress, progress that could not be made without daily contact. The nurse commented, "By seeing Sinora every morning for 15 or 20 minutes or maybe a half hour, she and I can sit down and plan her day, see what problems have come up, and solve them before they get to be big problems."

By seeing Sinora every day and doing things like having a meal with her in a fast-food restaurant, the nurse can consistently monitor Sinora's emotional state so that the medication can be adjusted if necessary. The nurse is also able to observe Sinora's behavior in the reality of day-to-day living so that real problems can be identified and solved. This is more effective than trying to work with a patient in the artificial environment of a hospital, where you can only talk about what goes on there.

COSTAR even handles Sinora's welfare checks, budgeting the funds carefully over each month. This can be difficult because initially the client may not trust the nurse or understand what is being done. However, with assisted budgeting, as with other aspects of the program, the clients are encouraged to participate in treatment; the treatment is not forced on them from the outside.

Is the COSTAR program successful? The answer depends on how you measure success. It is unlikely that clients like Sinora will ever be completely "normal," and they will probably always require a visit once a week or every other week, if not every day. However, their ability to function on their own has been greatly increased, and with some assistance many clients do very well. For example, recall that Sinora is now living in stable housing and is getting job training, so eventually she may be at least somewhat self-supporting. That is a long way from being a disoriented schizophrenic living on the street. An initial evaluation of the program revealed that in the year following admission to the COSTAR program, patients were much less likely to require hospitalization than they were in the preceding year when they were not in the program. Apart from the human benefit in terms of quality of life, keeping clients out of the hospital results in a substantial financial saving that more than offsets the costs of the labor-intensive visiting program.

Does Sinora think the program is successful? When asked about COSTAR, Sinora said, "I'm glad COSTAR found me so they could give me my right medicines. I don't never want to be put away no more, Mister. I'm tired of it."

Source: Giansante (1988).

It is interesting to note that some of the stigma associated with treatment facilities is related to the names we give these facilities. "Mental hospital" and "hospital for the criminally insane" certainly sound ominous to both the public and patients. One state mental hospital in which I worked was labeled a "mental health center," and nurses often threatened disruptive patients by saying, "If you keep acting that way, we are going to transfer you from this *men-*

tal health center to a *mental hospital!*" The patients quickly complied with whatever the nurse wanted! The effects of labels on the public's response to treatment facilities was documented when the name of one "mental hospital" was changed to "The Madison Center." Immediately after the name change, the local residents passed a bond issue to provide additional funding, and children began walking on the sidewalk in front of the building rather than crossing the street to avoid coming near it (Roberts & Roberts, 1985).

As was the case in Gheel centuries ago, economic necessity is once again giving birth to the community care of disturbed individuals. Unfortunately, unlike the people of Gheel, in many cases people today support community care grudgingly at best and often want the care to be given in someone else's community.

 ## Prevention of Abnormal Behavior

Most of our efforts with regard to the problem of abnormal behavior are focused on *treatment,* but we might be wise to devote additional attention to *prevention.* Indeed, it may be more efficient, cheaper, and more humane to prevent than to treat abnormal behavior. Therefore, in this final section I will describe some of the attempts being made to prevent the development of abnormal behaviors.

Before discussing specific prevention programs, we should take note of two obvious but often overlooked issues: First, when working to prevent abnormal behavior, we must concentrate on the factors that we think *cause* the abnormal behavior. That's obvious, but what is often missed is that for any one disorder there are usually a number of different potential causes, such as stress, learning, incorrect beliefs, and physiological problems. The question then is, on which suspected cause should we focus? So far most intervention programs have revolved around stress reduction. That approach may help in many cases, but when it doesn't, we should not assume that prevention doesn't work, only that the program was focusing on the wrong variable.

Second, regardless of what we think causes abnormal behavior, there are ethical and practical limits on what we can do to prevent the development of abnormal behavior. For example, we may believe that abnormal behavior is due to genetic problems, but it is not ethical to use selective mating to avoid "bad" genes, and it is not yet technically possible to surgically remove "bad" genes. Therefore, when we design intervention programs, we must focus on what is possible, and that narrower focus can greatly limit what we are able to do.

In summary, attempts at prevention are difficult because we do not always know what causes a disorder and because it may not be possible to devise an ethical and practical intervention.

There are three strategies for preventing abnormal behavior:

1. *Eliminate the causes of abnormal behavior.*
2. *Catch problems early before they become serious.*
3. *Take steps to reduce relapses in recovered patients.*

Let's examine the programs and problems associated with these three types of prevention.

Eliminating the Causes

Attempts to eliminate the causes of abnormal behavior include such things as improved prenatal and postnatal care, day care for children and the elderly, educational programs to reduce substance abuse, reductions in environmental poisons (e.g., lead in paint and exhaust fumes), improvements in diet, increases in exercise, prevention of head injuries with better athletic helmets and greater use of seat belts, improved housing that allows for privacy and reduces stress, and the reduction of poverty in an attempt to lessen the stress it brings. Sometimes these programs are not thought of as mental health programs because they have more immediate benefits in terms of physical health and safety. However, the programs have important "downstream" effects on mental health because they reduce the brain damage and stress that lead to abnormal behavior.

One noteworthy prevention program involved providing poor, unmarried, pregnant women with better prenatal care and preparation for motherhood. These women usually get very poor prenatal care and often give birth to babies who are underweight and suffer from neurological difficulties that lead to serious problems later. In addition, these women are more likely to neglect or abuse their babies, causing additional problems for the children. The intervention program involved having a nurse visit the women to teach them proper diet and to help them obtain medical and financial assistance available in the community. The nurse also helped the women establish relationships with others in the community so that they would have someone to turn to when problems arose. Visits by the nurse continued after the babies were born so that the mothers could be taught about infant development, care, and safety.

An evaluation of the effects of the program revealed that compared to mothers who were not visited, mothers who were visited made better use of community services, gave birth to heavier babies, were less likely to neglect or abuse their babies, and provided their babies with more appropriate playthings. In addition, the mothers who were visited were less likely to get pregnant again and were more likely to hold a job, and so were in a better financial position to care for their children (Olds, 1982). Clearly, this program got children off to a better start and avoided some of the problems linked to the later development of disorders.

The implementation of prevention programs that focus on problems such as air pollution, poverty, and safety often seems to be more a matter of politics than of psychology. For that reason a subfield of psychology known as **community psychology** was developed. Mental health professionals in this area work in governments rather than in clinics, and they try to change communities. The notion is that if you can change the community, you will prevent or solve the problems of many of the people who live there.

Unfortunately, many of the problems on which prevention programs have been focused have proved to be very difficult to solve, and consequently successes have been limited. For example, despite massive federal programs we have not been able to eliminate poverty. Also, although advances have been made on some problems, changes in budgetary priorities resulted in the cutting of funds, and the progress came to a halt. For example, prenatal and postnatal care is crucial for warding off brain damage and various behavior problems, but funds for that care were cut when Congress wanted to cut taxes. Advocates of prenatal and postnatal care argued that in the long run cutting the programs would lead to higher costs because the expense of supporting a mentally retarded individual for a lifetime is much higher than the cost of providing prenatal and postnatal care. In essence, they argued that we can pay *hundreds* of dollars for prenatal care now or pay *hundreds of thousands* of dollars for institutionalization later. However, most legislators saw small immediate savings as preferable to larger long-term savings, and the programs were cut. Much of the early optimism about eliminating the causes of abnormal behavior has faded. We cannot deny that great strides have been made, but the dream of a Camelot of mental health has turned out to be as elusive as the mythical kingdom itself.

Catching Problems Early

Because eliminating the causes of abnormal behavior has proved to be very difficult, we must often fall back to a second line of defense: *catching the problems in their early stages so that they will not lead to more serious problems.* There are a number of ways in which early correction can be done. One involves treating schoolchildren who show behavior problems (e.g., Durlak, 1980; Kirschenbaum et al., 1980; Yu et al., 1986). In one such project 1st, 2nd, and 3rd graders with school behavior problems were assigned to a condition in which they were given rewards for appropriate

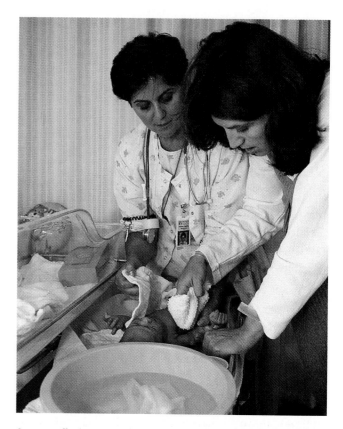

One very effective means of primary intervention is good postnatal care. The goal is to help improve the health of the newborn and provide support for the mother, thus reducing many of the physical complications and emotional stressors that can lead to abnormal behavior.

behaviors or to a control condition in which no rewards were used (Durlak, 1980). Before and after the 10-week program teachers rated the children on behaviors such as acting out and shyness or withdrawal. A comparison of the two sets of ratings indicated that the children who received rewards for appropriate behaviors showed substantial reductions in problem behaviors, whereas the children in the control condition showed no improvement. Findings like these indicate that we can intervene effectively with young children, and the assumption is that correcting the problems early will stop them from becoming serious later.

Another approach to catching problems early involves the use of **support groups** for individuals who are facing specific stressors that could lead to abnormal behavior. Support groups are small groups of people who share a common problem, such as being a single parent or dealing with a serious illness. The groups meet to discuss their experiences and to help one another deal with the problem. Case Study 19.4 reflects the experiences of people who are in a support group for individuals with muscular dystrophy.

Support groups are very popular today. In fact, in one university town of approximately 60,000 people there were almost 60 different active support groups, and it is esti-

community psychology A subfield of psychology in which mental health professionals work in governments to change communities in order to prevent and solve problems associated with abnormal behaviors.

support groups Small groups of individuals who share a common problem and meet to provide one another with emotional support and to exchange information and coping strategies.

Support groups are often helpful to individuals who face specific stressful situations. Participants can benefit by sharing their experiences with others who face similar problems.

mated that nationally 12 million people participate in roughly 500,000 support groups. Name your problem, and there is probably a group for you; in fact, there is a national self-help clearinghouse to help you find an appropriate group. Probably the best known of the support groups is Alcoholics Anonymous (see Chapter 15).

Support groups seem to derive their value from three factors: First, support groups provide *emotional support.*

A Support Group for Individuals with Muscular Dystrophy: Comments of Group Members

MUSCULAR DYSTROPHY (MD) IS an inherited disease that involves the progressive deterioration of the muscles. During the early phases individuals with this disease may lose the ability to walk and have to rely on a wheelchair. Later they may lose all muscle control and even go blind. Because the consequences of MD are so dire and because there is no treatment for it, having this disease can be very stressful.

In my community there is a support group for individuals with MD. Eight or 10 people get together once a week at the home of one of them. The group was originally organized by a professor who has MD, but everyone shares in the leadership. Members include students, professionals, and blue-collar workers. Here are some responses members gave when I asked what the group meant to them:

For me, the most important thing the group does is let me feel and express really strong emotions that I couldn't express anywhere else. Knowing that

you've got MD and knowing what might happen to you can be really frightening. It can also make you angry—why me? In the group it's OK to have strong feelings and to express them. Others do it too. It's good to get those feelings out, especially with other people who understand what you are going through. Our support group is strong because we cry together—and because we curse together!

The group helps me maintain my self-esteem. It's really hard to maintain your self-esteem when you are losing control of your body, have to live in a wheelchair, and may be going blind. It's easy to see yourself as "one down," not as good as others, or not having a future. But group members constantly tell you, "You're important to us," "We need you," "We care about you," "You're important in our lives," and "You have a contribution to make." With that boost from the group, I get the guts to go on. Without the group I would have given up on myself long ago.

We don't share only bad things. It's important to get the bad things out, but it's also important to share some laughs. We have a thing we call "Laugh Together." Group members videotape or tape-record things that make them laugh and feel really good, and then we play the tapes at the meetings. We also share "take-home laugh tapes." You have to balance the crying with a little laughing, and we share and help each other with both.

I learn a lot from the people in the group. I learn what to expect if my disease progresses, and I learn practical ways of dealing with the problems. People with MD can tell you more about the disease and how to cope than your doctor can. They're living with it on a daily basis. With the tips they give me and with them showing me that they can live with this thing, I think I'll make it.

CASE STUDY 19.4

The group helps me maintain my self-esteem.

An Undergraduate Talks about Her Experiences Working at a Crisis Center

"WHEN MOST PEOPLE THINK about a phone-in crisis center, they probably think immediately about suicide calls, but that is only a very small part of what goes on. The crises come in all shapes and sizes and at all times of the day and night. Sometimes the work at our center is pretty intense, but at other times it can be fairly laid-back. People call to talk about relationships, loneliness, frustrations at work, and just about everything else. Our job is not to tell them how to handle these problems; we give them information and help them sort things out. The idea is to enable them to help themselves.

"The center in which I work as a volunteer is in a large, old, three-story house that's located between the university campus and the downtown area of the city. The first floor of the house has a room with three phones and two old couches, and it is here that the volunteers spend most of their time. Most night shifts are busy until about 2 or 3 in the morning, and then those couches come in really handy to crash on. Of course, there are some nights when you can kiss sleep good-bye completely. There are rooms on both the first and second floors where we can go with people who come in and want to talk. The second and third floors have sleeping accommodations for 10 or 12 people, but those are used only for emergencies, not for long-term stays.

"People volunteer to work at the center for a lot of different reasons. Some have had crises and want to return the help they received during those times, and others, like me, are just interested in what goes on at such a center. Regardless of what originally

drew us to the center, we all share one motivation: We care about people and want to be able to express that in an active way.

"Before starting work, the 15 people in my training group took part in over 60 hours of training. We were taught about community services and resources so that we could make effective referrals, and we were given a lot of training in counseling skills. Most of that involved role playing and watching experienced staff members while they worked. We also spent a lot of time hashing through information and our own feelings about issues such as drug use, sexuality, suicide, and rape. Through those discussions I learned a lot about the topics and myself. As for my skills as a counselor, I'm certainly no professional, but I know a lot more about how to find and give help than I did before.

"Nights in the center can be really hectic. One night not long ago, I came in the back door at about 20 before midnight and found the two staff members on the phone and the front doorbell ringing. I answered the door and found a family of five who'd just driven into town from Texas. They'd been driving all day and, having no money, needed a place to stay for a few days. I explained that we offer only emergency housing and that they would have to start looking for other accommodations the next day. (We don't encourage or allow people to stay for more than a few days. Independence is the goal, not dependence.) After explaining a few guidelines—smoking is permitted only on the first floor, short cleanup chores were expected in the morning in exchange for staying—I showed them to a bedroom.

"When I got downstairs, one of the phones was ringing. The caller was a young woman wanting to know the effects of some pills she'd found. I looked up the drug in one of the reference books we have and told her that the drug was an antihistamine with slight sedative effects. She thanked me and then went on to tell me that she'd found the pills on her roommate's dresser. She wanted to know what they were because her roommate had been acting funny lately, and she was worried about her. We talked for another half hour or so about her relationship with her roommate and the frustration and sadness connected with the whole situation. She'd called for the drug info, but I think that the real issue was something different. It often seems to work that way.

"I had only a few minutes to record the call in the log, say hello to my shift partner, and say good-bye to the two departing staffers from the previous shift before the next call came in. It was from a man who started off by saying, 'Life's really slowing down for me.' His sleepy voice seemed to echo his sentiments, and he told me that he'd now been unemployed for about 3 months and he and his wife had separated. He missed his kids. I recognized this caller as someone who'd called before, depressed. We talked for a few minutes about his feelings of loneliness and worthlessness, and then I ventured a question about his sleepy voice. He admitted that he'd been drinking heavily and that he'd taken a few pills too. I told him that I was concerned about the effects of both the alcohol and the pills, and he replied that he thought it was okay, especially because he wouldn't mind not waking up in the morning. We then talked about his suicidal

During a crisis someone is there to hold you, figuratively and sometimes literally. Parents whose child has just died unexpectedly are likely to be emotionally devastated, but others in a support group who have had similar experiences can provide much-needed emotional support during the

crisis. Similarly, a member of Alcoholics Anonymous who is struggling to stop drinking can be helped greatly by other members who sit through the night with the individual.

Second, support groups demonstrate to members that *it is possible to survive the problem.* For example, seeing

feelings, and he expressed a lot of his hurt and depression, but at the same time he said he didn't really want to die. Because he was sounding sleepier and sleepier, I asked him if he would feel comfortable calling a friend to take him to the emergency room to make sure the alcohol and pills weren't doing permanent damage. He was fairly open to both my concern and his ambivalence about suicide and agreed to call a friend. I encouraged him to call back the next day and let us know how he was doing. It's rare that we do a 'crisis outreach' (driving to the person), even for suicide calls. This call is an example of how we encourage people to use their own resources such as friends to help them.

"Our next caller was a police officer requesting that we send a rape counselor to the hospital. Paul, my shift partner, called one of the staffers who is specially trained in rape counseling and asked her to go to the hospital.

"The call immediately following that was from a woman at the Women's Transition Center, a shelter mainly for abused women. She was calling to let us know that one of their volunteers was coming to meet a woman who'd been beaten up by her husband earlier in the evening. Our place serves as a neutral meeting ground for the shelter's volunteers to meet with women in transition (leaving an abusive situation, divorce, etc.) before taking them to the shelter's secret location. (The location of the Women's Transition Center is kept under wraps so that angry husbands and others cannot find the women.)

"While we were waiting for the staff member from the shelter, Paul got a call from a 'regular' (a person who calls us a lot). Some of these folks are trying

to work through frustrating situations, but usually the reason they call is loneliness. While Paul talked with the regular, I took a call from a person wanting to know where he could get a free blood test. It turned out that the blood test he really wanted was for HIV antibodies, so I looked up the information in our files under 'AIDS' and recommended that he contact the Health Department for the cheapest, most confidential setting. Then we talked for a while about some of the AIDS myths that are floating around and about the pressures he felt because he is gay.

"It was then about 2:30, and as I was finishing up the call about AIDS, Paul answered a knock at the front door. He expected it to be the volunteer from the women's shelter, but it turned out to be two men and a woman, all rather inebriated. When I arrived in the entry hall, our late-night visitors were trying to convince Paul to let the woman spend the night at the center to 'sleep it off.' Paul was explaining to them that we generally don't serve as a flophouse, but they were in an argumentative mood and couldn't understand why we were refusing them a place to stay. While this was going on, the woman who had been beaten up by her husband arrived to meet the person from the women's shelter. It was a bit tricky for a moment because the woman was kind of skittish, having just left a violent situation. Walking in on a group of drunk people who were talking angrily couldn't have helped her much, so I took her off to another part of the house. Paul soon convinced the three drunken characters to leave, and as they were going out the front door, there was a knock at the back door. It was a relief to find it was just

the staff member from the women's shelter.

"Paul and I spent the next hour talking about the various calls and visitors and writing up our log reports. Talking over what goes on with my shift partner helps me work through contacts that were disturbing or that I feel I didn't handle well. It also gives me a chance to offer support for what my partner is doing. Because everything is kept confidential within the center, we really rely on each other for encouragement and support.

"The two women left for the women's shelter around 3:45, and then Paul and I slept on the couches until about 7:30, when I was awakened by a phone call. The caller wanted to talk about what she was going to do that day and needed a listening ear and some support as she made plans to continue her job search and write some letters. I recognized this woman as someone who'd recently been released from the state hospital and who was reentering community life. She apologized for waking me up, and we laughed a little about her escapades earlier in the kitchen as she'd tried to make an omelet. I told her before she hung up that it was good to talk with her, and I meant it. Working at this center has given me a real sense of what's important when working with people: Whatever type of crisis they're in—whether it's suicide or a burned omelet—let them know that they're understood and that someone cares. It's that kind of human contact that makes this work so fulfilling."

> **The idea is to enable them to help themselves.**

other members of Alcoholics Anonymous who have been able to stay "in recovery" for years can be helpful to a new member who is struggling to stop drinking. The operative message is "If they can do it, with their help I can do it also."

Third, support groups provide *information.* Members tell one another about other sources of help and how to cope with various problems. They also warn one another about what to expect in the future so as not to be caught offguard by a new phase of the problem.

Most support groups do not involve professionals or even paraprofessionals. Professionals such as physicians, psychologists, social workers, and child care specialists might be called on occasionally to talk to a group about a particular problem, but for the most part support groups involve *peers helping peers*. That is important because not only do peers provide good role models, but reliance on peers also greatly reduces the cost of support groups. Indeed, support groups usually operate free of charge. Sometimes support groups are referred to as "self-help groups," but in many respects that is a misnomer because the individuals in such a group help one another. Probably a better name would be *mutual-help groups* or *help and information groups*. Whatever they are called, these groups provide emotional support for the present, a sense of belonging, hope for the future, role models, and valuable information. Thus, these groups probably do a lot to reduce stress and limit the development of abnormal behavior.

Most support groups are designed to provide prolonged help for relatively chronic problems. However, there are sometimes acute crises that require immediate short-term help. Examples of such crises include the death of a loved one, rape, suicide attempts, and financial problems. In those situations, many individuals turn to **crisis intervention centers,** which provide services such as 24-hour-a-day telephone hot-lines and walk-in counseling.

A typical crisis center is reflected in Case Study 19.5 (on pp. 568–569), which was written by an undergraduate student of mine who is a volunteer in the center.

> **crisis intervention centers**   Facilities that provide services such as telephone hot-lines and walk-in counseling, designed to reduce stress during crises and thereby prevent the development of abnormal behaviors.

Preventing Relapses

Unfortunately, we are often unable to eliminate the causes of abnormal behavior before they have their effects, and we are sometimes not successful in treating problems in their early stages to prevent their becoming more serious. When those preventive strategies fail, individuals develop disorders that must be treated. This necessity gives rise to the third line of defense against abnormal behavior: *preventing relapses*. However, in most cases the strategies for preventing relapses are no different from the strategies used to treat the disorders. In other words, the factors that originally caused the problem are probably the same ones that trigger the relapse, so attention must be focused on eliminating or controlling those factors. Note that in most cases we do not *cure* abnormal behavior, we *treat* it, and the treatment must be maintained. For example, stress must be maintained at low levels or neurotransmitters must be kept at appropriate levels (Herz et al., 2000). That's simple and straightforward; the problem is that after a disorder is effectively treated and the symptoms are gone or at least under control, many individuals think that treatment is no longer necessary and therefore go back to their old lifestyles or stop taking their medication. That is often a recipe for relapse.

In many respects the treatment of alcoholism provides a good model for the treatment of psychiatric disorders in general. Specifically, persons who suffer from alcoholism never say that they are "cured" but instead say that they are "in recovery" and continue to work on their recovery. As you have learned throughout this book, we have some very effective treatments for abnormal behaviors, but in using them we must continually emphasize to patients that to avoid relapses in most cases the treatments must be continued. In summary, the treatment of abnormal behavior is "a work in progress."

Summary

Topic I: Mental Hospitals and Deinstitutionalization

▸ Until about 50 years ago mental hospitals offered little in terms of effective treatments, and because patients often spent many years in hospitals, they were likely to develop institutionalization syndrome.

▸ Today patients are hospitalized on psychiatric wards in psychiatric hospitals or general medical hospitals. Patients on open wards are free to go to other parts of the hospital, whereas those on closed wards are confined to that ward.

▸ Most wards have a day room, a nurses' station, an isolation room, sleeping rooms, and areas for recreation and activity therapy.

▸ Either day or night hospitalization enables patients to stay in touch with their communities and is less expensive than 24-hour-a-day hospitalization.

▸ The staff of a psychiatric ward includes psychologists, psychiatrists, and social workers who provide treatment, psychiatric nurses who oversee the patients on a daily basis, psychological technicians (ward attendants) who supervise the patients on the ward, and activity therapists such as occupational, art, and music therapists.

▸ There is often little informal contact between patients and professional staff members.

▸ Hospitalization is expensive, often costing more than $1,000 a day.

- Deinstitutionalization involves discharging patients from hospitals and treating them in the community. Deinstitutionalization was originally undertaken because it was believed that patients could be treated more effectively in the community than in hospitals and because of the development of more effective drugs. Today deinstitutionalization is often motivated by attempts to reduce costs. Deinstitutionalization poses problems because sometimes treatment in the community is not available to the patients who are discharged from hospitals.

- Although treatment in hospitals is not particularly effective, hospitals are still needed to provide refuge and protection during times of crisis.

- There is consistent evidence that treatment in hospitals is less effective than alternative treatments in the community, some of which simply involve providing individuals with supported living conditions.

Topic II: Community Care and Prevention

- The notion of community care dates back to the 13th century, when mental patients were cared for by the residents of Gheel, a town in Flanders.

- Today community care is provided in (1) outpatient clinics associated with hospitals, (2) community mental health centers that are conveniently located, (3) halfway houses that aid in the transition from hospital to community living, and (4) home care programs that allow professionals such as nurses and social workers to treat individuals wherever they live.

- The public has negative attitudes about mentally ill individuals, and people often oppose having mentally ill individuals live in their community.

- Attempts at preventing the development of abnormal behavior are hampered by our lack of understanding of what causes some disorders and by ethical and practical problems that can limit what we are able to do.

- There are three prevention strategies: (1) eliminate the causes of abnormal behavior, (2) treat problems early before they become serious, and (3) reduce relapses in recovered patients.

Questions for Making Connections

1. Assume that you are the director of mental health for your state and that the legislature just passed a bill mandating deinstitutionalization of mental patients. What community treatment options would you develop? What questions or concerns do you think the public would have, and how would you answer them?

2. Based on what you know about disorders, are there some patients for whom deinstitutionalization is not appropriate? If so, which ones, and why?

3. Based on what you now know about psychiatric disorders, what might be done to prevent their development? For example, what would you do to prevent schizophrenia? What would you do to prevent depression? Describe cases in which it might not be possible to prevent the development of these disorders.

Key Terms and People

In reviewing and testing yourself, you should be able to discuss each of the following:

closed wards, p. 552
community mental health centers (CMHCs), p. 561
community psychology, p. 566
crisis intervention centers, p. 570
day hospitalization, p. 553

day room, p. 552
deinstitutionalization, p. 557
halfway houses, p. 563
institutionalization syndrome, p. 552
isolation room, p. 552
night hospitalization, p. 553

nurses' station, p. 552
open wards, p. 552
outpatient clinics, p. 561
psychological technicians, p. 554
support groups, p. 566

References

Aarsland, D., Larsen, J. P., Cummings, J. L., & Laake, K. (1999). Prevalence and clinical correlates of psychotic symptoms in Parkinson disease: A community-based study. *Archives of Neurology, 56*(5), 595–601.

Aas, H., Klepp, K. I., Laberg, J. C. & Edvard, L. (1995). Predicting adolescents' intentions to drink alcohol: Outcome expectancies and self-efficacy. *Journal of Studies on Alcohol, 156*, 193–199.

Abel, K. M., O'Keane, V., Murray, R. M., & Cleare, A. J. (1997). Serotonergic function and negative and depressive symptomatology in schizophrenia and major. *Psychoneuroendocrinology, 22*(7), 539–548.

Abell, F., Krams, M., Ashburner, J., Passingham, R., Friston, K., Frackowiak, R., Happe, F., Frith, C., & Frith, U. (1999). The neuroanatomy of autism: A voxel-based whole brain analysis of structural scans. *Neuroreport: For Rapid Communication of Neuroscience Research, 10*(8), 1647–1651.

Abi Dargham, A., Laruelle, M., Aghajanian, G. K., & Charney, D. (1997). The role of serotonin in the pathophysiology and treatment of schizophrenia. *Journal of Neuropsychiatry and Clinical Neurosciences, 9*(1), 1–17.

Abi-Saab, W. M., D'Souza, D. C., Moghaddam, B., & Krystal, J. H. (1998). The NMDA antagonist model for schizophrenia: Promise and pitfalls. *Pharmacopsychiatry, 31*(Suppl. 2), 104–109.

Abouesh, A., & Clayton, A. (1999). Compulsive voyeurism and exhibitionism: A clinical response to paroxetine. *Archives of Sexual Behavior, 28*(1), 23–30.

Abou-Saleh, M. T., & Ghubash, R. (1997). The prevalence of early postpartum psychiatric morbidity in Dubai: A transcultural. *Acta Psychiatrica Scandinavica, 95*(5), 428–432.

Abraham, H. D., & Aldridge, A. M. (1993). Adverse consequences of lysergic acid diethylamide. *Addiction, 88*, 1327–1334.

Abramowitz, J. S. (1996). Variants of exposure and response prevention in the treatment of obsessive-compulsive disorder: A meta-analysis. *Behavior Therapy, 27*(4), 583–600.

Abramowitz, J. S. (1997). Effectiveness of psychological and pharmacological treatments for obsessive-compulsive. *Journal of Consulting and Clinical Psychology, 65*(1), 44–52.

Abramowitz, S. I. (1986). Psychosocial outcomes of sex reassignment surgery. *Journal of Consulting and Clinical Psychology, 54*, 183–189.

Abramson, L. Y., Seligman, M. E. P., & Teasdale, J. D. (1978). Learned helplessness in humans: Critique and reformulation. *Journal of Abnormal Psychology, 87*, 49–74.

Acierno, R., Donohue, B., & Kogan, E. (1994). Psychological intervention for drug abuse: A critique and summation of controlled studies. *Clinical Psychology Review, 14*, 417–442.

Ackerson, J., Scogin, F., McKendree Smith, N., & Lyman, R. D. (1998). Cognitive bibliotherapy for mild and moderate adolescent depressive symptomatology. *Journal of Consulting and Clinical Psychology, 66*(4), 685–690.

Acocella, J. (1998, April 6). The politics of hysteria. *New Yorker,* 64–79.

Adams, J., McIntosh, E., & Weade, B. L. (1973). Ethnic background, measured intelligence, and adaptive behavior scores in mentally retarded children. *American Journal of Mental Deficiency, 78*, 1–6.

Adams, W. R., Kiefer, S. W., and Badia-Elder, N. (1995). Tryptophan deficiency and alcohol consumption in rats as a model for disadvantaged human populations: A preliminary study. *Medical Anthropology, 16*, 175–191.

Addiego, F., Belzer, E. G., Comolli, J., Moger, W., Perry, J. D., & Wipple, B. (1981). Female ejaculation: A case study. *Journal of Sex Research, 17*, 13–21.

Addonizio, G. (1991). The pharmacologic basis of neuroleptic malignant syndrome. *Psychiatric Annals, 21*, 152–156.

Agency for Health Care Policy and Research (1993). *Depression in primary care: Vol 1. Detection and diagnosis.* Bethesda, MD: Department of Health and Human Services.

Agras, W. S., & Berkowitz, R. I. (1999). Behavior therapies. In R. E. Hales, S. C. Yudofsky, & J. A. Talbot (Eds.), *Textbook of psychiatry* (pp. 1185–1204). Washington, DC: American Psychiatric Press.

Agren, H. (1982). Depressive symptom patterns and urinary MHPG excretion. *Psychiatry and Research, 6*, 185–196.

Ai, A. L., Dunkle, R. E., Peterson, C., & Bolling, S. F. (1998). The role of private prayer in psychological recovery among midlife and aged patients following. *Gerontologist, 38*(5), 591–601.

Aikens, J. E., Caruana Montaldo, B., & Vanable, P. A. (1999). MMPI correlates of sleep and respiratory disturbance in obstructive sleep apnea. *Sleep, 22*(3), 362–369.

Aikens, J. E., & Mendelson, W. B. (1999). A matched comparison of MMPI responses in patients with primary snoring or obstructive sleep. *Sleep, 22*(3), 355–359.

Akbarian, S., Bunney, W. E., Jr., Potkin, S. G., Wigal, S. B., Hagman, J. O., Sandman, C. A., & Jones, E. G. (1993). Altered distribution of nicotinamide-adenine dinucleotide phosphate-diaphorase cells in frontal lobe schizophrenics implies disturbances of cortical development. *Archives of General Psychiatry, 50*, 169–177.

Akbarian, S., Vinuela, A., Kim, J. J., Potkin, S. G., Bunney, W. E., Jr., & Jones, E. G. (1993). Distorted distribution of nicotinamide-adenine dinucleotide phosphate-diaphorase neurons in temporal lobe of schizophrenics implies anomalous cortical development. *Archives of General Psychiatry, 50,* 178–187.

Akerblom, H. K., Viikari, J., Raitakari, O. T., & Uhari, M. (1999). Cardiovascular risk in young Finns study: General outline and recent developments. *Annals of Medicine, 31*(Suppl. 1), 45–54.

Albertini, R. S., & Phillips, K. A. (1999). Thirty-three cases of body dysmorphic disorder in children and adolescents. *Journal of the American Academy of Child and Adolescent Psychiatry.*

Alexander, B. K., Beyerstein, B. L., Hadaway, P. F., & Coambs, R. B. (1981). The effect of early and later colony housing on oral ingestion of morphine in rats. *Pharmacology, Biochemistry, and Behavior, 15,* 571–576.

Alexander, B. K., Coambs, R. B., & Hadaway, P. F. (1978). The effect of housing and gender on morphine self-administration in rats. *Psychopharmacology, 58,* 175–179.

Alexander, J., Holtzworth-Monroe, A., & Jameson, P. (1994). Process and outcome of marital and family therapy: Research review and evaluation. In A. E. Bergin & S. L. Garfield (Eds.), *Handbook of psychotherapy and behavior change* (4th ed.). New York: Wiley.

Alexander, M. A. (1999). Sexual offender treatment efficacy revisited. Sexual Abuse: *Journal of Research and Treatment, 11*(2), 101–116.

Allison, R. B. (1984). Difficulties diagnosing the multiple personality syndrome in a death penalty case. *International Journal of Clinical and Experimental Hypnosis, 32,* 102–117.

Allison, R. B., & Schwartz, T. (1980). *Minds in many pieces: The making of a very special doctor.* New York: Rawson, Wade.

Alloy, L. B., Abramson, L. Y., Whitehouse, W. G., & Hogan, M. E. (1999). Depressogenic cognitive styles: Predictive validity, information processing and personality. *Behaviour Research and Therapy, 37*(6), 503–531.

Alonso, J. C. L., & Jarabo, G. G. (1998). Differential responses to stress in panic disorders. *European Journal of Psychiatry, 12*(3), 133–138.

Altamura, A. C., Percudani, M., Guercetti, G., & Invernizzi, G. (1989). Efficacy and tolerability of fluoxetine in the elderly: A double-blind study versus amitryptiline. *International Journal of Psychopharmacology, 4,* 103–106.

Altshuler, L., Bartzokis, G., Grieder, T., Curran, J., & Mintz, J. (1998). Amygdala enlargement in bipolar disorder and hippocampal reduction in schizophrenia: An MRI. *Archives of General Psychiatry, 55*(7), 663–664.

Alzate, H., & Hoch, Z. (1986). The "G spot" and "female ejaculation": A current appraisal. *Journal of Sex and Marital Therapy, 12,* 211–220.

Amenson, C. S., & Lewinsohn, P. M. (1981). An investigation into the observed sex differences in prevalence of unipolar depression. *Journal of Abnormal Psychology, 90,* 1–13.

American Psychiatric Association. (1980). *Diagnostic and statistical manual of mental disorders* (3rd ed.). Washington, DC: Author.

American Psychiatric Association. (1987). *Diagnostic and statistical manual of mental disorders* (3rd ed., rev.). Washington, DC: Author.

American Psychiatric Association. (1994). *Diagnostic and statistical manual of mental disorders* (4th ed.). Washington, DC: Author.

American Psychological Association. (1993). Evidence grows of abuse by psychiatric hospitals. *APA Monitor, 24*(1), 20.

Amsterdam, J. D., Garcia-Espana, F., Fawcett, J., & Quitkin, F. M. (1998). Efficacy and safety of fluoxetine in treating bipolar II major depressive episode. *Journal of Clinical Psychopharmacology, 18*(6), 435–440.

Anand, B. K., & Brobeck, J. R. (1951a). Hypothalamic control of food intake in rats and cats. *Yale Journal of Biology and Medicine, 24,* 123.

Anand, B. K., & Brobeck, J. R. (1951b). Localization of a feeding center in the hypothalamus of the rat. *Proceedings of the Society for Experimental Biology and Medicine, 77,* 323–324.

Anand, B. K., Dua, S., & Schoenberg, K. (1955). Hypothalamic control of food intake in rats and monkeys. *Journal of Physiology (London), 127,* 143–152.

Andersen, B. L., Kiecolt-Glaser, J. K., & Glaser, R. (1994). A biobehavioral model of cancer stress and disease course. *American Psychologist, 49,* 389–404.

Anderson, K. O., Bradley, L. D., Young, L. D., & McDaniel, L. K. (1985). Rheumatoid arthritis: Review of psychological factors related to etiology, effects, and treatment. *Psychological Bulletin, 98,* 358–387.

Anderson, L. T., Campbell, M., Grega, D. M., Perry, R., Small, A. M., & Green, W. H. (1984). Haloperidol in the treatment of infantile autism: Effects on learning and behavior symptoms. *American Journal of Psychiatry, 141,* 1195–1202.

Anderson, S., & Rizzo, M. (1994). Hallucinations following occipital lobe damage: The pathological activation of visual representations. *Journal of Clinical and Experimental Neuropsychology, 16,* 651–663.

Andreasen, N. C. (1982). Negative symptoms in schizophrenia: Definition and reliability. *Archives of General Psychiatry, 39,* 784–788.

Andreasen, N. C. (1987). Creativity and mental illness: Prevalence rate in writers and their first-degree relatives. *American Journal of Psychiatry, 144,* 1288–1292.

Andreasen, N. C. (1988). Brain imaging: Applications in psychiatry. *Science, 239,* 1381–1388.

Andreasen, N. C. (1997). The role of the thalamus in schizophrenia. *Canadian Journal of Psychiatry, 42*(1), 27–33.

Andreasen, N. C., Arndt, S. V., Alliger, R., Miller, D., & Flaum, M. (1995). Symptoms of schizophrenia. *Archives of General Psychiatry, 52,* 341–551.

Andreasen, N. C., & Hoenk, P. R. (1982). The predictive value of adjustment disorders: A follow-up study. *American Journal of Psychiatry, 139*(5), 584–590.

Andreasen, N. C., & Olsen, S. C. (1982). Negative v. positive schizophrenia: Definition and validation. *Archives of General Psychiatry, 39,* 789–794.

Andreasen, N. C., Rezai, K., Alliger, R., Swayze, V. W., Flaum, M., Kirchner, P., Cohen, G., & O'Leary, D. S. (1992). Hypofrontality in neuroleptic-naive patients and in patients with chronic schizophrenia: Assessment with xenon 133 single-photon emission computed tomography and the Tower of London. *Archives of General Psychiatry, 49,* 943–958.

Angst, J., Angst, F., & Stassen, H. H. (1999). Suicide risk in patients with major depressive disorder. *Journal of Clinical Psychiatry, 60*(Suppl. 2), 57–62.

Anisman, H. (1978). Aversively motivated behavior as a tool in psychopharmacological analysis. In H. Anisman & G. Binami (Eds.), *Psychopharmacology of aversively motivated behavior*. New York: Plenum.

Ansbacher, H. L., & Ansbacher, R. R. (1956). *The individual-psychology of Alfred Adler*. New York: Basic Books.

Antelman, S. M., Caggiula, A. R., Kucinski, B. J., & Fowler, H. (1998). The effects of lithium on a potential cycling model of bipolar disorder. *Progress in Neuro Psychopharmacology and Biological Psychiatry, 22, 3.*

Anton, R. F., Moak, D. H., Waid, R., & Latham, P. K. (1999). Naltrexone and cognitive behavioral therapy for the treatment of outpatient alcoholics. *American Journal of Psychiatry, 156*(11), 1758–1764.

APA Monitor. (1997). WWII veterans provide evidence for repressed memories. *APA Monitor*, August, 8–9.

Appelbaum, P. S., Jick, R. Z., Grisso, T., Givelber, D., Silver, E., & Steadman, H. J. (1993). Use of posttraumatic stress disorder to support an insanity defense. *American Journal of Psychiatry, 150*, 229–234.

Appleby, I. L., Klein, D. F., Schar, E. J., & Levitt, M. (1981). Biochemical indices of lactate-induced panic: A preliminary report. In D. F. Klein & K. Rabkin (Eds.), *Anxiety: New research and changing concepts*. New York: Raven Press.

Appleby, L., Mortensen, P. B., & Faragher, E. B. (1998). Suicide and other causes of mortality after post-partum psychiatric admission. *British Journal of Psychiatry, 173*, 209–211.

Arbisi, P. A., & Ben-Porath, Y. S. (1998). The ability of Minnesota Multiphasic Personality Inventory—2 validity scales to detect. *Psychological Assessment, 10*(3), 221–228.

Arbuckle, T. Y., Gold, D. P., Andres, D., Schwartzman, A., et al. (1992). The role of psychosocial context, age, and intelligence in memory performance of older men. *Psychology and Aging, 7*(1), 25–36.

Ardlie, N. G., Glew, G., & Schwartz, C. J. (1966). Influence of catecholamines on nucleotide-induced platelet aggregation. *Nature, 212*, 415–417.

Arita, A. A., & Baer, R. A. (1998). Validity of selected MMPI-A content scales. *Psychological Assessment, 10*(1), 59–63.

Armony, J. L., & LeDoux, J. E. (1997). How the brain processes emotional information. In R. Yehuda, A. C. McFarlane, et al. (Eds.), *Psychobiology of*

Arndt, S. V., Andreasen, N. C., Flaum, M., Miller, D., & Nopoulos, P. (1995). A longitudinal study of symptom dimensions in schizophrenia. *Archives of General Psychiatry, 52*, 352–360.

Arnold, S. E., Franz, B. R., Gur, R. C., Gur, R. E., Shapiro, R. M., Moberg, P. J., & Trojanowski, J. Q. (1995). Smaller neuron size in schizophrenia in hippocampal subfields that mediate cortical hippocampal interactions. *American Journal of Psychiatry, 152*, 738–748.

Aromaeki, A. S., Lindman, R. E., & Eriksson, C. J. P. (1999). Testosterone, aggressiveness, and antisocial personality. *Aggressive Behavior, 25*(2), 113–123.

Asscheman, H., & Gooren, L. J. (1992). Hormone treatment in transsexuals. *Journal of Psychology and Human Sexuality, 5*, 39–54.

Associated Press (1998, Dec. 22). Historian: Famous psychiatric patient might be former Minnesotan.

August, G. J., Stewart, M. A., & Tsai, L. (1981). The incidence of cognitive disabilities in the siblings of autistic children. *British Journal of Psychiatry, 138*, 416–422.

Austin, M. P., Mitchell, P., Wilhelm, K., Parker, G., Hickie, I., Brodaty, H., & Chan, J. (1999). Cognitive function in depression: A distinct pattern of frontal impairment in melancholia? *Psychological Medicine, 29*(1), 73–85.

Avasthi, A., Sharma, A., Malhotra, S., Gupta, N., & Kulhara, P. (1999). Rapid cycling affective disorder: A descriptive study from North India. *Journal of Affective Disorders, 54*(1–2), 67–73.

Avery, D. H., Bolte, M. A., Dager, S. R., Wilson, L. G., Weyer, M., Cox, G. B., & Dunner, D. L. (1993). Dawn simulation treatment of winter depression: A controlled study. *American Journal of Psychiatry, 150*, 113–117.

Avery, D. H., Bolte, M. A., & Ries, R. (1998). Dawn simulation treatment of abstinent alcoholics with winter depression. *Journal of Clinical Psychiatry, 59*(1), 36–42.

Ayllon, T. (1963). Intensive treatment of psychotic behavior by stimulus satiation and food reinforcement. *Behaviour Research and Therapy, 1*, 53–61.

Aytaclar, S., Tarter, R. E., Kirisci, L., & Lu, S. (1999). Association between hyperactivity and executive cognitive functioning in childhood and. *Journal of the American Academy of Child and Adolescent Psychiatry.*

Azerrad, J., & Stafford, R. L. (1969). Restorative eating behavior in anorexia nervosa through operant conditioning and environmental manipulation. *Behaviour Research and Therapy, 7*, 165–171.

Backman, L., & Forsell, Y. (1994). Episodic memory functioning in a community-based sample of older adults with major depression: Utilization of cognitive support. *Journal of Abnornal Psychology, 103*, 361–370.

Baer, L., Rauch, S. L., Ballantine, T., Martuza, R., Cosgrove, R., Cassem, E., Girunas, I., Manzo, P. A., Dimino, C., & Jenike, M. A. (1995). Cingulotomy for intractable obsessive-compulsive disorder: Prospective long-term follow-up of 18 patients. *Archives of General Psychiatry, 52*, 384–392.

Bagatell, C. J., & Bremner, W. J. (1996). Androgens in men: Issues and abuses. *New England Journal of Medicine, 334*, 707–714.

Bagby, R. M., Rogers, R., Nicholson, R. A., Buis, T., & Seeman, M. V. (1997). Effectiveness of the MMPI-2 validity indicators in the detection of defensive responding in. *Psychological Assessment, 9*(4), 406–413.

Bak, R. C., & Stewart, W. A. (1974). Fetishism, transvestism, and voyeurism: A psychoanalytic approach. In S. Arieti (Ed.), *American handbook of psychiatry* (Vol. 3). New York: Basic Books.

Baker, F. M. (1991). Cocaine psychosis. *Journal of the National Medical Association, 81*, 987–1000.

Baker, G. H. (1982). Life events before the onset of rheumatoid arthritis. *Psychotherapy and Psychosomatics, 38*, 173–177.

Bakker, A., van Balkom, A. J. L. M., & Spinhoven, P. (1998). Follow-up on the treatment of panic disorder with or without agoraphobia: A quantitative. *Journal of Nervous and Mental Disease, 186*(7), 414–419.

Baldessarini, R. J., Kando, J. C., & Centorrino, F. (1995). Hospital use of antipsychotic agents in 1989 and 1993: Stable dosing with decreased length of stay. *American Journal of Psychiatry, 152*, 1038–1044.

Baldessarini, R. J., Tondo, L., & Hennen, J. (1999). Effects of lithium treatment and its discontinuation on suicidal behavior in bipolar. *Journal of Clinical Psychiatry, 60*(Suppl. 2), 77–84.

Baldwin, D. S., & Birtwistle, J. (1998). The side effect burden associated with drug treatment of panic disorder. *Journal of Clinical Psychiatry, 59*(8), 39–44.

Ballard, X., & Davies, R. (1996). Postnatal depression in fathers. *International Review of Psychiatry, 8*(1), 65–71.

Baltes, P. B., & Kliegl, R. (1992). Further testing of limits of cognitive plasticity: Negative age differences in a mnemonic skill. *Developmental Psychology, 28*(1), 121–125.

Bancroft, J. (1970). Disorders of sexual potency. In O. Hill (Ed.), *Modern trends in psychosomatic medicine.* Norwalk, CT: Appleton & Lange.

Bancroft, J. (1984a). Hormones and human sexual behavior. *Journal of Sex and Marital Therapy, 10,* 3–22.

Bancroft, J. (1984b). Testosterone therapy for low sexual interest and erectile dysfunction in men: A controlled study. *British Journal of Psychiatry, 14,* 146–151.

Bancroft, J., & Wu, F. C. (1983). Changes in erectile responsiveness during androgen therapy. *Archives of Sexual Behavior, 12,* 59–66.

Bandura, A. (1969). *Principles of behavior modification.* New York: Holt, Rinehart and Winston.

Bandura, A. (1983). Psychosocial mechanisms of aggression. In R. G. Geen & E. I. Donnerstein (Eds.), *Aggression: Theoretical and empirical reviews, Vol. 1: Theoretical and methodological issues.* New York: Academic Press.

Bandura, A., & Walters, R. H. (1963). *Social learning and personality development.* New York: Ronald Press.

Barbee, E. L. (1992). African-American women and depression: A review and critique of the literature. *Archives of Psychiatric Nursing, 6,* 257–265.

Barbini, B., Scherillo, P., Benedetti, F., Crespi, G., Colombo, C., & Smeraldi, E. (1997). Response to clozapine in acute mania is more rapid than that of chlorpromazine. *International Clinical Psychopharmacology, 12*(2), 109–112.

Barefoot, J. C., Dahlstrom, W. G., & Williams, R. B. (1983). Hostility, CHD incidence, and total mortality: A 25-year follow-up study of 255 physicians. *Psychosomatic Medicine, 45,* 59–63.

Barker, J. C. (1965). Behavior therapy for transvestism: A comparison of pharmacological and electrical aversion techniques. *British Medical Journal, 111,* 268–276.

Barksy, A. J., Fama, J. M., Bailey, E. D., & Ahern, D. K. (1998). A prospective 4- to 5-year study of *DSM-III-R* hypochondriasis. *Archives of General Psychiatry, 55*(8), 737–744.

Barlow, D. H. (1986). Causes of sexual dysfunction: The role of anxiety and cognitive interference. *Journal of Consulting and Clinical Psychology, 54,* 140–148.

Barlow, D. H. (1988). *Anxiety and its disorders: The nature and treatment of anxiety and panic.* New York: Guilford Press.

Barlow, D. H., Esler, J. L., & Vitali, A. E. (1998). Psychosocial treatments for panic disorders, phobias, and generalized anxiety disorder. In P. E. Nathan & J. M. Gorman (Eds.), *A guide to treatments that work* (pp. 288–318). New York: Oxford University Press.

Barnett, P. A., & Gotlib, I. H. (1988). Psychosocial functioning and depression: Distinguishing among antecedents, concomitants and consequences. *Psychological Bulletin, 104,* 97–126.

Barnett, P. G. (1999). The cost-effectiveness of methadone maintenance as a health care intervention. *Addiction, 94*(4), 479–488.

Barr, C. E., Mednick, S. A., & Munk-Jorgensen, P. (1990). Exposure to influenza epidemics during gestation and adult schizophrenia. *Archives of General Psychiatry, 47,* 869–874.

Barsky, A. J. (1992). Psychiatric comorbidity in *DSM-III-R* hypochondriasis. *Archives of General Psychiatry, 49,* 101–108.

Barsky, A. J. (1993). The diagnosis and management of hypochondriachal concerns in the elderly. *Journal of Geriatric Psychiatry, 26,* 129–141.

Barsky, A. J., Orav, J. E., Delamater, B. A., & Clancy, S. A. (1998). Cardiorespiratory symptoms in response to physiological arousal. *Psychosomatic Medicine, 60*(5), 604–609.

Bartak, L., Rutter, M., & Cox, A. (1975). A comparative study of infantile autism and specific developmental receptive language disorders: 1. The children. *British Journal of Psychiatry, 126,* 127–145.

Barthlow, D. L., Graham, J. R., Ben Porath, Y. S., & McNulty, J. L. (1999). Incremental validity of the MMPI-2 content scales in an outpatient mental health setting. *Psychological Assessment, 11*(1), 39–47.

Bartrop, R., Luckhurst, E., Lazarus, L., Kiloh, L., & Penney, R. (1977). Depressed lymphocyte function after bereavement. *Lancet, 1,* 834–836.

Basco, M. R., & Rush, A. J. (1996). *Cognitive-behavioral therapy for bipolar disorder.*

Basoglu, M., Paker, M., Ozmen, E., Tasdemir, O., & Sahin, D. (1994). Factors related to long-term traumatic stress responses in survivors of torture in Turkey. *Journal of the American Medical Association, 272,* 357–363.

Battaglia, M., Fossati, A., Torgersen, S., Bertella, S., & Bajo, S. (1999). A psychometric-genetic study of schizotypal disorder. *Schizophrenia Research, 37*(1), 53–64.

Battle, E. S., & Rotter, J. B. (1963). Children's feelings of personal control as related to social class and ethnic group. *Journal of Personality, 31,* 482–490.

Bauer, M. S., Calabrese, J. R., Dunner, P. L., & Post, R. (1994). Multisite data reanalysis of the validity of rapid cycling as a course modifier for bipolar disorder in *DSM-IV. American Journal of Psychiatry, 151,* 506–515.

Bauer, M. S., Kurtz, J. W., Rubin, L. B., & Marcus, J. G. (1994). Mood and behavioral effects of four-week light treatment in winter depressives and controls. *Journal of Psychiatric Research, 28,* 135–145.

Baum. A., & Fleming, I. (1993). Implications of psychological research on stress technological accidents. *American Psychologist, 48,* 665–672.

Baum, A., Gatchel, R. J., & Schaeffer, M. A. (1983). Emotional, behavioral, and physiological effects of chronic stress at Three Mile Island. *Journal of Consulting and Clinical Psychology, 51,* 565–572.

Baving, L., Laucht, M., & Schmidt, M. H. (1999). Atypical frontal brain activation in ADHD: Preschool and elementary school boys and girls. *Journal of the American Academy of Child and Adolescent Psychiatry, 38*(11), 1363–1371.

Baxter, L. R., Phelps, M. E., Mazziotta, J. C., Guze, B. H., Schwartz, J. M., & Selin, C. E. (1987). Local cerebral glucose metabolic rates in obsessive-compulsive disorder. *Archives of General Psychiatry, 44,* 211–218.

Baxter, L. R., Phelps, M. E., Mazziotta, J. C., Schwartz, J. M., Gerner, R. H., Selin, C. E., & Sumida, R. M. (1985). Cerebral metabolic rates for glucose in mood disorders. *Archives of General Psychiatry, 42,* 441–447.

Baxter, L. R., Schwartz, J. M., Bergman, K. S., Szuba, M. P., Guze, B. H., Mazziotta, J. C., Alazraki, A., Selin, C. E., Ferng, H. K., Munford, P., & Phelps, M. E. (1992). Caudate glucose metabolic rate changes with both drug and behavior therapy for obsessive-compulsive disorder. *Archives of General Psychiatry, 49,* 681–689.

Beale, M. D., Bernstein, H. J., & Kellner, C. H. (1996). Maintenance electroconvulsive therapy for geriatric depression: A one year follow-up. *Clinical Gerontologist, 16*(4), 86–90.

Bearden, C. (1994). The nightmare: Biological and psychological origins. *Dreaming, 4,* 139–152.

Beasley, C. M. (1997). Efficacy of olanzapine: An overview of pivotal clinical trials. *Journal of Clinical Psychiatry Monograph Series, 15*(2), 16–18.

Beasley, C. M., Dornseif, B. E., Bosomworth, J. C., Sayler, M. E., Rampey, A. H., Heiligenstein, J. H., Thompson, V. L., Murphy, D. J., & Masica, D. N. (1991). Fluoxetine and suicide: A meta-analysis of controlled trials of treatment for depression. *British Medical Journal, 303,* 685–692.

Beasley, C. M., Jr., Tollefson, G. D., & Tran, P. V. (1997). Efficacy of Olanzapine: An overview of pivotal clinical trials. *Journal of Clinical Psychiatry, 58*(Suppl. 10), 7–12.

Beautrais, A. L., Joyce, P. R., & Mulder, R. T. (1999). Personality traits and cognitive styles as risk factors for serious suicide attempts among. *Suicide and Life Threatening Behavior, 29*(1), 37–47.

Bechara, A., Damasio, H., Tranel, D., & Damasio, A. R. (1997). Deciding advantageously before knowing the advantageous strategy. *Science, 275,* 1293–1294.

Beck, A. T. (1967). *Depression: Clinical, experimental, and theoretical aspects.* New York: Harper & Row.

Beck, A. T. (1976). *Cognitive therapy and the emotional disorders.* New York: International Universities Press.

Beck, A. T., Brown, G., Berchick, R. J., Stewart, B. L., & Steer, R. (1990). Relationship between hopelessness and ultimate suicide: A replication with psychiatric outpatients. *American Journal of Psychiatry, 147,* 190–195.

Beck, A. T., & Emery, G. (1985). *Anxiety disorders and phobias: A cognitive perspective.* New York: Basic Books.

Beck, A. T., Rush, A. J., Shaw, B. F., & Emery, G. (1979). *Cognitive therapy of depression.* New York: Guilford Press.

Beck, A. T., Steer, R., Kovacs, M., & Garrison, B. (1985). Hopelessness and eventual suicide: A 10-year prospective study of patients hospitalized with suicidal ideation. *American Journal of Psychiatry, 142,* 559–563.

Beck, A. T., Ward, C. H., Mendelson, M., Mock, J. E., & Erbaugh, J. K. (1961). An inventory for measuring depression. *Archives of General Psychology, 4,* 561–571.

Beck, A. T., Ward, C. H., Mendelson, M., Mock, J. E., & Erbaugh, J. K. (1962). Reliability of psychiatric diagnosis: 2. A study of consistency of clinical judgments and ratings. *American Journal of Psychiatry, 119,* 351–357.

Beck, A. T., Weissman, A., Lester, D., & Trexler, L. (1974). The measurement of pessimism: The Hopelessness Scale. *Journal of Consulting and Clinical Psychology, 42,* 861–865.

Beck, C. T. (1998). The effects of postpartum depression on child development: A meta-analysis. *Archives of Psychiatric Nursing, 12*(1), 12–20.

Becker, E. S., Rinck, M., Roth, W. T., & Margraf, J. (1998). Don't worry and beware of white bears: Thought suppression in anxiety patients. *Journal of Anxiety Disorders, 12*(1), 39–55.

Becker, J. V., Johnson, B. R., & Kavoussi, R. J. (1999). Sexual and gender identity disorders. In R. E. Hales, S. C. Yudofsky, & J. A. Talbot (Eds.), *Textbook of psychiatry* (pp. 739–758). Washington, DC: American Psychiatric Press.

Becker, J. V., & Kavoussi, R. J. (1994). Sexual and gender identity disorders. In R. E. Hales, S. C. Yudofsky, & J. A. Talbott (Eds.), *American Psychiatric Press textbook of psychiatry* (2nd ed.). Washington, DC: American Psychiatric Press.

Becker, T., Becker, G., Seufert, J., Hoffmann, E., & Lange, K. W. (1997). Parkinson's disease and depression: Evidence for an alteration of the basal limbic system. *Journal of Neurology, Neurosurgery and Psychiatry, 63*(5), 590–596.

Beckman, H., & Goodwin, F. K. (1980). Urinary MHPG in subgroups of depressed patients and normal controls. *Neuropsychobiology, 6,* 91–100.

Bedau, H. A., & Radelet, M. L. (1987). Miscarriages of justice in potentially capital cases. *Stanford Law Review, 40,* 21–179.

Bednar, R., & Kaul, T. (1994). Experimental group research. In A. E. Bergin & S. L. Garfield (Eds.), *Handbook of psychotherapy and behavior change* (4th ed.). New York: Wiley.

Beecroft, N., Bach, L., Tunstall, N., & Howard, R. (1998). An unusual case of pica. *International Journal of Geriatric Psychiatry, 13*(9), 638–641.

Beere, P. A., Glagov, S., & Zarins, C. K. (1984). Retarding effect of lowered heart rate on coronary atherosclerosis. *Science, 226,* 180–182.

Behnke, S. H. (1999). O'Connor v. Donaldson: Retelling a classic and finding some revisionist history. Journal of the *American Academy of Psychiatry and the Law, 27*(1), 115–126.

Bell, I. R. (1994). Somatization disorder: Health care costs in the decade of the brain. *Biological Psychiatry, 35,* 81–83.

Bell, R. A. (1968). A reinterpretation of the direction of effects in studies of socialization. *Psychological Review, 75,* 81–95.

Bellak, L. (1954). *The Thematic Apperception Test and the Children's Apperception Test in clinical use.* Philadelphia: Grune & Stratton.

Belsher, G., & Costello, C. G. (1991). Do confidants of depressed women provide less social support than confidants of nondepressed women? *Journal of Abnormal Psychology, 100,* 516–525.

Benkelfat, C., Ellenbogen M. A., Dean, P., Palmour, R. M., & Young, S. N. (1994). Mood-lowering effect of tryptophan depletion: Enhanced susceptibility in young men at genetic risk for major affective disorder. *Archives of General Psychiatry, 51,* 687–697.

Bennett, D., & Holmes, D. S. (1975). Influence of denial (situation redefinition) and projection on anxiety associated with threat to self-esteem. *Journal of Personality and Social Psychology, 32,* 915–921.

Bennett, D., Holmes, D. S., & Frost, R. O. (1978). Effects of instructions, biofeedback, cognitive mediation, and reward on the control of heart rate and the application of that control in a stressful situation. *Journal of Research in Personality, 12,* 416–430.

Benson, H. (1975). *The relaxation response.* New York: Morrow.

Bergant, A. M., Heim, K., Ulmer, H., & Illmensee, K. (1999). Early postnatal depressive mood: Associations with obstetric and psychosocial factors. *Journal of Psychosomatic Research, 46*(4), 391–394.

Bergin, A. E., & Garfield, S. L. (1994). *Handbook of psychotherapy and behavior change* (4th ed.). New York: Wiley.

Berlin, F. S. (1989). The paraphilias and Depo-Provera: Some medical, ethical, and legal considerations. *Bulletin of the American Academy of Psychiatry and the Law, 17,* 233–239.

Berlin, F. S., & Krout, E. (1986). Pedophilia: Diagnostic concepts, treatment, and ethical considerations. *American Journal of Forensic Psychiatry, 7,* 13–30.

Berlin, F. S., & Meinecke, C. (1981). Treatment of sex offenders with antiandrogenic medication: Conceptualization, review of treatment modalities, and preliminary findings. *American Journal of Psychiatry, 138,* 601–607.

Berman, K. F., Torrey, E. F., Daniel, D. G., & Weinberger, D. R. (1992). Regional cerebral blood flow in monozygotic twins discordant and concordant for schizophrenia. *Archives of General Psychiatry, 49,* 927–934.

Berman, R. M., Narasimhan, M., Miller, H. L., Anand, A., Cappiello, A., Oren, D. A., Heninger, G. R, & Charney, D. S. (1999). Transient depressive relapse induced by catecholamine depletion. *Archives of General Psychiatry, 56,* 395–403.

Bernstein, H. J., Beale, M. D., Burns, C., & Kellner, C. H. (1998). Patient attitudes about ECT after treatment. *Psychiatric Annals, 28*(9), 524–527.

Berry, H. K., Sutherland, B. S., Umbarger, B., & O'Grady, D. (1967). Treatment of phenylketonuria. *American Journal of Diseases of Childhood, 113,* 2–5.

Berscheid, E., & Walster, E. (1974). A little bit about love. In T. Huston (Ed.), *Foundations of interpersonal attraction.* New York: Academic Press.

Bertelsen, A., Havald, B., & Hauge, M. (1977). A Danish twin study of manic-depressive disorders. *British Journal of Psychiatry, 130,* 330–351.

Berthier, M. L., Kulisevsky, J., Gironell, A., & Heras, J. A. (1996). Obsessive-compulsive disorder associated with brain lesions: Clinical phenomenology, cognitive function, and anatomic correlates. *Neurology, 47*(2), 353–361.

Besson, J., Aeby, F., Kasas, A., Lehert, P., & Potgieter, A. (1998). Combined efficacy of acamprosate and disulfiram in the treatment of alcoholism: A controlled. *Alcoholism: Clinical and Experimental Research, 22*(3), 573–579.

Bettelheim, B. (1967). *The empty fortress.* New York: Free Press.

Bexton, W. H., Heron, W., & Scott, T. (1954). Effects of decreased variation in sensory environment. *Canadian Journal of Psychology, 8,* 70–77.

Bianchi, G. N. (1973). Patterns of hypochondriasis: A principal components analysis. *British Journal of Psychiatry, 122,* 541–548.

Biber, B., & Alkin, T. (1999). Panic disorder subtypes: Differential responses to CO_2 challenge. *American Journal of Psychiatry, 156*(5), 739–744.

Biby, E. L. (1998). The relation between body dysmorphic disorder and depression, self-esteem, somatization. *Journal of Clinical Psychology, 54*(4), 489–499.

Bieber, I. (1974). Sadism and masochism: Phenomenology and psychodynamics. In S. Arieti (Ed.), *American handbook of psychiatry* (Vol. 3). New York: Basic Books.

Biederman, J., Faraone, S. V., Mick, E., Spencer, T., Wilens, T., Kiely, K., Guite, J., Ablon, J. S., Reed, E., & Warburton, R. (1995). High risk for attention-deficit hyperactivity disorder among children of parents with childhood onset of the disorder: A pilot study. *American Journal of Psychiatry, 152,* 431–435.

Biederman, J., & Spencer, T. (1999). Attention-deficit/hyperactivity disorder (ADHD) as a noradrenergic disorder. *Biological Psychiatry, 46*(9), 1234–1242.

Biggam, F. H., & Power, K. G. (1999). Suicidality and the state-trait debate on problem solving deficits: A re-examination with. *Archives of Suicide Research, 5*(1), 27–42.

Bihari, K., Pato, M. T., Hill, J. L., & Murphy, D. L. (1991). Neurologic soft signs in obsessive-compulsive disorder. *Archives of General Psychiatry, 48,* 278.

Billings, A. G., Cronkite, R. C., & Moos, R. H. (1983). Social-environmental factors in unipolar depression: Comparisons of depressed patients and nondepressed controls. *Journal of Abnormal Psychology, 92,* 119–133.

Billings, A. G., & Moos, R. H. (1981). The role of coping responses and social resources in attenuating the impact of stressful life events. *Journal of Behavioral Medicine, 4,* 139–157.

Binzer, M., Anderson, P. M., & Kullgren, G. (1997). Clinical characteristics of patients with motor disability due to conversion disorder. *Journal of Neurology, Neurosurgery and Psychiatry, 63*(1), 83–88.

Binzer, M., & Kullgren, G. (1998). Motor conversion disorder: A prospective 2- to 5-year follow-up study. *Psychosomatics, 39*(6), 519–527.

Black, D. W. (1988). Recognition and treatment of obsessive-compulsive spectrum disorders. In R. P. Swinson, M. M. Antony, et al. (Eds.), *Obsessive compulsive.*

Black, D. W., & Andreasen, N. C. (1999). Schizophrenia, schizophreniform disorder, and delusional (paranoid) disorders. In R. E. Hales, S. C. Yudofsky, & J. A. Talbot (Eds.), *Textbook of psychiatry* (pp. 425–478). Washington, DC: American Psychiatric Press.

Black, D. W., Goldstein, R. B., Noyes, R., & Blum, N. (1994). Compulsive behaviors and obsessive-compulsive disorder (OCD): Lack of a relationship between OCD, eating disorders, and gambling. *Comprehensive Psychiatry, 35*(2), 145–148.

Black, D. W., & Moyer, T. (1998). Clinical features and psychiatric comorbidity of subjects with pathological gambling behavior. *Psychiatric Services, 49*(11), 1434–1439.

Blair, C. D., & Lanyon, R. I. (1981). Exhibitionism: Etiology and treatment. *Psychological Bulletin, 89,* 439–463.

Bland, S. H., Krogh, V., Winkelstein, W., & Trevisan, M. (1991). Social network and blood pressure: A population study. *Psychosomatic Medicine, 53,* 598–607.

Blaney, P. H. (1977). Contemporary theories of depression. *Journal of Abnormal Psychology, 86,* 203–233.

Blaney, P. H. (1986). Affect and memory: A review. *Psychological Bulletin, 99,* 229–246.

Blaszczynski, A. (1999). Pathological gambling and obsessive-compulsive spectrum disorders. *Psychological Reports, 84*(1), 107–113.

Blaszczynski, A., & Steel, Z. (1998). Personality disorders among pathological gamblers. *Journal of Gambling Studies, 14*(1), 51–71.

Blazer, D. (1999). Geriatric psychiatry. In R. E. Hales, S. C. Yudofsky, & J. A. Talbot (Eds.), *Textbook of psychiatry* (pp. 1447–1462). Washington, DC: American Psychiatric Press.

Blazer, D. G., Kessler, R. C., & Swartz, M. S. (1998). Epidemiology of recurrent major and minor depression with a seasonal pattern: The National. *British Journal of Psychiatry, 172,* 164–167.

Bleuler, E. (1936). *Textbook of psychiatry* (A. Brill, Trans.). New York: Macmillan.

Bleuler, E. (1950). *Dementia praecox* (J. Zinkin, Trans.). New York: International Universities Press.

Blier, P., & de Montigny, C. (1998). Possible serotonergic mechanisms underlying the antidepressant and anti-obsessive-compulsive disorder responses. *Biological Psychiatry, 44*(5), 313–323.

Bliss, E. L. (1980). Multiple personality. *Archives of General Psychiatry, 37,* 1388–1397.

Bliss, E. L. (1984). A symptom profile of patients with multiple personalities, including MMPI results. *Journal of Nervous and Mental Disease, 171,* 197–202.

Bloom, B. L. (1992). Computer-assisted psychological intervention: A review and commentary. *Clinical Psychology Review, 12,* 169–197.

Bloom, F. E. (1993). Advancing a neurodevelopmental origin of schizophrenia. *Archives of General Psychiatry, 50,* 224–227.

Bloom, L., Houston, B. K., Holmes, D. S., & Burish, T. G. (1977). The effectiveness of attentional diversion and situation redefinition for reducing stress due to a nonambiguous threat. *Journal of Personality and Social Psychology, 11,* 83–94.

Boath, E. H., Pryce, A. J., & Cox, J. L. (1998). Postnatal depression: The impact on the family. Journal of Reproductive and *Infant Psychology, 16*(2–3), 199–203.

Bocola, V., Trecco, M. D., Fabbrini, G., Paladini, C., Sollecito, A., & Martucci, N. (1998). Antipanic effect of fluoxetine measured by CO_2 challenge test. *Biological Psychiatry, 43*(8), 612–615.

Bollen, K. A., & Phillips, D. P. (1981). Suicidal motor vehicle fatalities in Detroit: A replication. *American Journal of Sociology, 81,* 404–412.

Bollen, K. A., & Phillips, D. P. (1982). Imitative suicides: A national study of the effects of television news stories. *American Sociological Review, 47,* 802–809.

Bolman, W. M., & Richmond, J. A. (1999). A double-blind, placebo-controlled, crossover pilot trial of low doses dimethylglycine in patients with autistic disorder. *Journal of Autism and Developmental Disorders, 29*(3), 191–194.

Bond, I. K., & Hutchinson, H. C. (1960). Application of reciprocal inhibition therapy to exhibitionism. *Canadian Medical Association Journal, 83,* 23–25.

Bond, P. A., Jenner, J. A., & Sampson, D. A. (1972). Daily variation of the urine content of 3-methoxy-4-hydroxyphenylglycol in two manic-depressive patients. *Psychological Medicine, 2,* 81–85.

Borch-Jacobsen, M. (1997, April 24). Sybil—The making of a disease: An interview with Dr. Herbert Spiegel. *New York Review of Books,* 60–64.

Borch-Jacobsen, M. (1998). Anna O.: The first tall tale. In F. C. Crews (Ed.), *Unauthorized Freud.* New York: Viking.

Borella, P., Bargellini, A., Rovesti, S., Pinelli, M., & Vivoli, R. (1999). Emotional stability, anxiety, and natural killer activity under examination stress. *Psychoneuroendocrinology, 24*(6), 613–627.

Borison, R. L. (1995). Clinical efficacy of serotonin-dopamine antagonists relative to classic neuroleptics. *Journal of Clinical Psychopharmacology, 15,* 24S–29S.

Borison, R. L., Pathiraja, A. P., Diamond, B. I., & Meibach, R. C. (1992). Risperidone: Clinical safety and efficacy in schizophrenia. *Psychopharmacology Bulletin, 28,* 213–217.

Borum, R., & Fulero, S. M. (1999). Empirical research on the insanity defense and attempted reforms: Evidence toward informed. *Law and Human Behavior, 23*(1), 117–135.

Borum, R., Swartz, M., Riley, S., Swanson, J., & Hiday, V. A. (1999). Consumer perceptions of involuntary outpatient commitment. *Psychiatric Services, 50*(11), 1489–1491.

Borus, J. F., & Sledge, W. H. (1999). Psychiatric education. In R. E. Hales, S. C. Yudofsky, & J. A. Talbot (Eds.), *Textbook of psychiatry* (pp. 1575–1598). Washington, DC: American Psychiatric Press.

Bostock, T., & Williams, C. L. (1975). Attempted suicide: An operant formulation. *Australian and New Zealand Journal of Psychiatry, 9,* 107–110.

Boston, P. F., Dursun, S. M., & Reveley, M. A. (1996). Cholesterol and mental disorder. *British Journal of Psychiatry, 169*(6), 682–689.

Bouchard, T. J., Jr., McGue, M., Hur, Y. M., & Horn, J. M. (1998). A genetic and environmental analysis of the California Psychological Inventory using adult. *European Journal of Personality, 12*(5), 307–320.

Bovim, G., Naess, P., Helle, J., & Sand, T. (1995). Caffeine influence on the motor steadiness battery in neuropsychological tests. *Journal of Clinical and Experimental Neuropsychology, 17,* 472–476.

Bower, G. H. (1981). Mood and memory. *American Psychologist, 36,* 129–148.

Bower, G. H. (1987). Commentary on mood and memory. *Behaviour Research and Therapy, 25,* 443–455.

Boyd, J. D. (1997). Clinical hypnosis for rapid recovery from dissociative identity disorder. *American Journal of Clinical Hypnosis, 40*(2), 97–110.

Boyle, R. G., Jensen, J., Hatsukami, D. K., & Severson, H. H. (1995). Measuring dependence in smokeless tobacco users. *Addictive Behaviors, 20,* 443–450.

Bradbury, T. N., & Miller, G. A. (1985). Season of birth in schizophrenia: A review of evidence, methodology, and etiology. *Psychological Bulletin, 98,* 569–594.

Braden, W., Stillman, R. C., & Wyatt, R. J. (1974). Effects of marijuana on contingent negative variation and reaction times. *Archives of General Psychiatry, 31,* 537–541.

Bradford, J. M. W. (1995). Pharmacological treatment of the paraphilias. *American Psychiatric Press Review of Psychiatry, 14,* 755–777.

Brady, E. U., & Kendall, P. C. (1992). Comorbidity of anxiety and depression in children. *Psychological Bulletin, 111,* 244–255.

Braginsky, B. M., & Braginsky, D. D. (1967). Schizophrenic patients in the psychiatric interview: An experimental study of their effectiveness at manipulation. *Journal of Consulting Psychology, 21,* 543–547.

Braginsky, B. M., Grosse, M., & Ring, K. (1966). Controlling outcomes through impression management: An experimental study of the manipulative tactics of mental patients. *Journal of Consulting Psychology, 30,* 295–300.

Bramel, D., Bell, J., & Margulis, S. (1965). Attributing danger as a means of explaining one's fear. *Journal of Experimental Social Psychology, 1,* 267–281.

Brancato, V., Barbini, B., Regazzetti, M. G., Colombo, C., et al. (1994). Negative symptoms in schizophrenia: An open study of placebo-fluvoxamine treatment added to neuroleptics. *New Trends in Experimental and Clinical Psychiatry, 10,* 21–24.

Brandsma, J. M., & Ludwig, A. M. (1974). A case of multiple personality: Diagnosis and treatment. *International Journal of Clinical and Experimental Hypnosis, 22,* 216–233.

Braun, B. G. (1983a). Neurophysiologic changes in multiple personality due to integration: A preliminary report. *American Journal of Clinical Hypnosis, 26,* 84–92.

Braun, B. G. (1983b). Psychophysiologic phenomena in multiple personality and hypnosis. *American Journal of Clinical Hypnosis, 26,* 124–137.

Braun, B. G. (1984). Hypnosis creates multiple personality: Myth or reality? *International Journal of Clinical and Experimental Hypnosis, 32,* 191–197.

Brawman-Mintzer, O., & Lydiard, R. B. (1997). Biological basis of generalized anxiety disorder. *Journal of Clinical Psychiatry, 58*(Suppl. 3), 16–26.

Breen, R. B., & Zuckerman, M. (1999). "Chasing" in gambling behavior: Personality and cognitive determinants. *Personality and Individual Differences, 27*(6), 1097–1111.

Breier, A. (1995). Serotonin, schizophrenia, and antipsychotic drug action. *Schizophrenia Research, 14,* 187–202.

Breier, A., Buchanan, R. W., Elkashef, A., Munson, R. C., Kirkpatrick, B., & Gellad, F. (1992). Brain morphology and schizophrenia: A magnetic resonance imaging study of limbic, prefrontal cortex, and caudate structures. *Archives of General Psychiatry, 49,* 921–926.

Breier, A., Buchanan, R. W., Kirkpatrick, B., Davis, O. R., Irish, D., Summerfelt, A., & Carpenter, W. T. (1994). Effects of clozapine on positive and negative symptoms in outpatients with schizophrenia. *American Journal of Psychiatry, 151,* 20–26.

Breier, A. F., Malhotra, A. K., Su, T. P., Pinals, D. A., & Elman, I. (1999). Clozapine and risperidone in chronic schizophrenia: Effects on symptoms, parkinsonian side. *American Journal of Psychiatry, 156*(2), 294–298.

Breitholtz, E., Westling, B. E., & Oest, L. G. (1998). Cognitions in generalized anxiety disorder and panic disorder patients. *Journal of Anxiety Disorders, 12*(6), 567–577.

Bremner, J. D., Southwick, S. M., Johnson, D. R., Yehuda, R., et al. (1993). Childhood physical abuse and combat-related posttraumatic stress disorder in Vietnam veterans. *American Journal of Psychiatry, 150*(2), 235–239.

Brennan, P. A., Grekin, E. R., & Mednick, S. A. (1999). Maternal smoking during pregnancy and adult male criminal outcomes. *Archives of General Psychiatry, 56*(3), 215–219.

Brennan, P. A., & Mednick S. A. (1994). Learning theory approach to the deterrence of criminal recidivism. *Journal of Abnormal Psychology, 103,* 430–440.

Breslau, N., Davis, G. C., Andreski, P., & Peterson, E. (1991). Traumatic events and posttraumatic stress disorder in an urban population of young adults. *Archives of General Psychiatry, 48,* 216–222.

Breslau, N., Davis, G. C., Andreski, P., Peterson, E. L., & Schultz, L. R. (1997). Sex differences in posttraumatic stress disorder. *Archives of General Psychiatry, 54*(11), 1044–1048.

Breslau, N., Kilbey, M. M., & Andreski, P. (1992). Nicotine withdrawal symptoms and psychiatric disorders: Findings from an epidemiological study of young adults. *American Journal of Psychiatry, 149,* 464–469.

Breslau, N., Kilbey, M. M., & Andreski, P. (1993). Nicotine dependence and major depression: New evidence from a prospective investigation. *Archives of General Psychiatry, 50,* 31–35.

Bromberg, W. (1959). *The mind of man: A history of psychotherapy and psychoanalysis.* New York: Harper Collins.

Broocks, A., Bandelow, B., Pekrun, G., George, A., & Meyer, T. (1998). Comparison of aerobic exercise, clomipramine, and placebo in the treatment of panic. *American Journal of Psychiatry, 155*(5), 603–609.

Brooks-Gunn, J., & Petersen, A. C. (1991). Studying the emergence of depression and depressive symptoms during adolescence. *Journal of Youth and Adolescence, 20,* 115–119.

Brosse, A. L., Craighead, L. W., & Craighead, W. E. (1999). Testing the mood-state hypothesis among previously depressed and never-depressed individuals. *Behavior Therapy, 30*(1), 97–115.

Broughton, R. J., Billings, R., Cartwright, R., Doucette, D., Orchard, B., Hill, R., & Turnell, G. Edmeads, J., Edwards, M., Ervin, F., (1994). Homicidal somnambulism: A case report. *Sleep, 17,* 253–264.

Brown, C., Shear, M. K., Schulberg, H. C., & Madonia, M. J. (1999). Anxiety disorders among African-American and White primary medical care patients. *Psychiatric Services, 50*(3), 407–409.

Brown, D. R., Ahmed, F., Gary, L. E., & Milburn, N. G. (1995). Major depression in a community sample of African Americans. *American Journal of Psychiatry, 152,* 373–378.

Brown, G. W., & Birley, J. L. T. (1968). Crises and life changes and the onset of schizophrenia. *Journal of Health and Social Behavior, 9,* 203–214.

Brown, J. L., & Pollitt, E. (1996). Malnutrition, poverty and intellectual development. *Scientific American, 274,* 38–43.

Brown, R. T., & Hoadley, S. L. (1999). Rett syndrome. In S. Goldstein & C. R. Reynolds (Eds.), *Handbook of neurodevelopmental and genetic disorders in children* (pp. 459–477).

Brown, T. A. (1998). The relationship between obsessive-compulsive disorder and other anxiety-based disorders. In R. P. Swinson, M. M. Antony, et al. (Eds.), *Obsessive compulsive.*

Bruce, T. J., Spiegel, D. A., & Hegel, M. T. (1999). Cognitive-behavioral therapy helps prevent relapse and recurrence of panic disorder following alprazolam discontinuation: A long-term follow-up of the Peoria and Dartmouth studies. *Journal of Consulting and Clinical Psychology, 67*(1), 151–156.

Bruch, H. (1982). Anorexia nervosa: Therapy and theory. *American Journal of Psychiatry, 139,* 1531–1538.

Bryant, D. M., & Maxwell, K. L. (1999). The environment and mental retardation. *International Review of Psychiatry, 11*(1), 56–67.

Bryant, N. L., Buchanan, R. W., Vladar, K., Breier, A., & Rothman, M. (1999). Gender differences in temporal lobe structures of patients with schizophrenia: A volumetric MRI. *American Journal of Psychiatry, 156*(4), 603–609.

Bryant, R. A., Barnier, A. J., Mallard, D., & Tibbits, R. (1999). Posthypnotic amnesia for material learned before hypnosis. *International Journal of Clinical and Experimental Hypnosis, 47*(1), 46–64.

Bryant, R. A., Harvey, A. G., Dang, S. T., & Sackville, T. (1998). Assessing acute stress disorder: Psychometric properties of a structured clinical interview. *Psychological Assessment, 10*(3), 215–220.

Bryant, R. A., Harvey, A. G., Dang, S. T., Sackville, T., & Basten, C. (1998). Treatment of acute stress disorder: A comparison of cognitive-behavioral therapy and. *Journal of Consulting and Clinical Psychology, 66*(5), 862–866.

Buchanan, C. M., Becker, J. B., & Eccles, J. S. (1992). Are adolescents the victims of ranging hormones? Evidence for activational effects of hormones on mood and behavior in adolescence. *Psychological Bulletin, 111,* 62–107.

Buchanan, R. W., Vlader, K., Barta, P. E., & Pearlson, G. D. (1998). Structural evaluation of the prefrontal cortex in schizophrenia. *American Journal of Psychiatry, 155*(8), 1049–1055.

Buchsbaum, M. S., Haier, R. J., Potkin, S. G., Nuechterlein, K., Bracha, H. S., Katz, M., Lohr, J., Wu, J., Lottengerg, S., Jerabek, P. A., Trenary, M., Tafalla, R., Reynolds, C., & Bunney, W. E., Jr. (1992). Frontostriatal disorder of cerebral metabolism in never-medicated schizophrenics. *Archives of General Psychiatry, 49,* 935–942.

Buchsbaum, M. S., Someya, T., Teng, C. Y., & Abel, L. (1996). PET and MRI of the thalamus in never-medicated patients with schizophrenia. *American Journal of Psychiatry, 153*(2), 191–199.

Buchsbaum, M. S., Yang, S., Hazlett, E., & Siegel, B. V., Jr. (1997). Ventricular volume and asymmetry in schizotypal personality disorder and schizophrenia. *Schizophrenia Research, 27*(1), 45–53

Buck, J. N. (1948). The H-P-T test. *Journal of Clinical Psychology, 4,* 151–158.

Buhrich, N., Theile, H., Yaw, A., & Crawford, A. (1979). Plasma testosterone, serum FSH, and serum LH levels in transvestism. *Archives of Sexual Behavior, 8,* 49–53.

Bull, D. L., Ellason, J. W., & Ross, C. A. (1998). Exorcism revisited: Positive outcomes with dissociative identity disorder. *Journal of Psychology and Theology, 26*(2), 188–196.

Bumby, K. M. (1993). Reviewing the guilty but mentally ill alternative: A case of the blind "pleading" the blind. *Journal of Psychiatry and Law, 21,* 191–220.

Burgess, E. S., & Haaga, D. A. F. (1998). Appraisals, coping responses, and attributions as predictors of individual differences in. *Cognitive Therapy and Research, 22*(5), 547–573.

Burke, J. D., Jr., & Regier, D. A. (1999). Epidemiology of mental disorders. In R. E. Hales, S. C. Yudofsky, & J. A. Talbot (Eds.), *Textbook of psychiatry* (pp. 83–108). Washington, DC: American Psychiatric Press.

Burns, A., Rossor, M., Hecker, J., Gauthier, S., Petit, H., Moeller, H. J., Rogers, S. L., & Friedhoff, L. T. (1999). The effects of donepezil in Alzheimer's disease—results from a multinational trial. *Dementia and Geriatric Cognitive Disorders, 10*(3), 237–244.

Burns, A., Russell, E., & Page, S. (1999). New drugs for Alzheimer's disease. *British Journal of Psychiatry, 174,* 476–479.

Burt, D. B., Zembar, M. J., & Niedershe, G. (1995). Depression and memory impairment: A meta-analysis of the association, its pattern, and specificity. *Psychological Bulletin, 117,* 285–305.

Burt, V. K., & Hendrick, V. (1999). Psychiatric assessment of female patients. In R. E. Hales, S. C. Yudofsky, & J. A. Talbot (Eds.), *Textbook of psychiatry* (pp. 1429–1446). Washington, DC: American Psychiatric Press.

Busatto, G. F., & Kerwin, R. W. (1997). Schizophrenia, psychosis, and the basal ganglia. *Psychiatric Clinics of North America, 20*(4), 897–910.

Buss, A. H., & Lang, P. J. (1965). Psychological deficit in schizophrenia: 1. Affect, reinforcement, and concept attainment. *Journal of Abnormal Psychology, 70,* 2–24.

Busto, U., Sellers, E. M., Naranjo, C. A., Cappell, H., Sanchez-Craig, M., & Sykora, K. (1986). Withdrawal reaction after long-term therapeutic use of benzodiazepines. *New England Journal of Medicine, 315,* 854–859.

Butcher, J. N. (1999). Introduction to the Special Section on Assessment in Psychology Treatment: A necessary step for effective intervention. *Psychological Assessment, 9,* 331–333.

Butler, S. F., Newman, F. L., Cacciola, J. S., & Frank, A. (1998). Predicting Addiction Severity Index (ASI) interviewer severity ratings for a. *Psychological Assessment, 10*(4), 399–407.

Butzlaff, R. L., & Hooley, J. M. (1998). Expressed emotion and psychiatric relapse. *Archives of General Psychiatry, 55*(6), 547–552.

Bystritsky, A., & Waikar, S. (1994). Inert placebo versus active medication: Patient blindability in clinical pharmacological trials. *Journal of Nervous and Mental Disease, 182,* 475–485.

Cade, J. F. (1949). Lithium salts in the treatment of psychotic excitement. *Medical Journal of Australia, 2,* 349–352.

Cadenhead, K. S., Perry, W., Shafer, K., & Braff, D. L. (1999). Cognitive functions in schizotypal personality disorder. *Schizophrenia Research, 37*(2), 123–132.

Cadoret, R. J. (1978). Evidence of genetic inheritance of primary affective disorder in adoptees. *American Journal of Psychiatry, 135,* 463–466.

Calabrese, J. R., Bowden, C. L., Sachs, G. S., & Ascher, J. A. (1999). A double-blind placebo-controlled study of lamotrigine monotherapy in outpatients with. *Journal of Clinical Psychiatry, 60*(2), 79–88.

Calev, A., Nigal, D., Shapira, B., Tubi, N., Chazan, S., Ben-Yehuda, Y., Kugelmass, S., & Lerer, B. (1991). Early and long-term effects of electroconvulsive therapy and depression on memory and other cognitive functions. *Journal of Nervous and Mental Disease, 179,* 526–533.

Calhoun, S. R., Wesson, D. R., Galloway, G. P., & Smith, D. E. (1996). Abuse of flunitrazepam (rohypnol) and other benzodiazepines in Austin and South Texas. *Journal of Psychoactive Drugs, 28*(2), 183–189.

Callahan, J. (1996). Negative effects of a school suicide postvention program—a case example. *Crisis, 17*(3), 108–115.

Callicott, J. H., Egan, M. F., Bertolino, A., & Mattay, V. S. (1999). Hippocampal N-acetyl aspartate in unaffected siblings of patients with schizophrenia. *Biological Psychiatry, 45*(2), 245.

Campbell, F., & Lester, D. (1999). The impact of gambling opportunities on compulsive gambling. *Journal of Social Psychology, 139*(1), 126–127.

Canivez, G. L., & Watkins, M. W. (1998). Long-term stability of the Wechsler Intelligence Scale for Children—Third Edition. *Psychological Assessment, 10*(3), 285–291.

Cannon, T. D., Mednick, S. A., Parnas, J., Schulsinger, F., Praestholm, J., & Vestergaard, A. (1993). Developmental brain abnormalities in the offspring of schizophrenic mothers. *Archives of General Psychiatry, 50,* 551–564.

Cannon, T. D., Mednick, S. A., Parnas, J., Schulsinger, F., Praestholm, J., & Vestergaard, A. (1995). Developmental brain abnormalities in the offspring of schizophrenic mothers: 2. Structural brain characteristics of schizophrenia and schizotypal personality disorder. *Archives of General Psychiatry, 51,* 955–962.

Cantor Graae, E., McNeil, T. F., Sjostrom, K., & Nordstrom, L. G. (1997). Maternal demographic correlates of increased history of obstetric complications in. *Journal of Psychiatric Research, 31*(3), 347–357.

Caplan, L. (1984). *The insanity defense and the trial of John W. Hinckley, Jr.* Boston: Godine.

Carey, G., & Di Lalla, D. L. (1994). Personality and psychopathology: Genetic perspectives. *Journal of Abnormal Psychology, 103,* 32–43.

Carlat, D. J., & Camargo, C. A. (1991). Review of bulimia nervosa in males. *American Journal of Psychiatry, 148,* 831–843.

Carlin, A. S., Hoffman, H. G., & Weghorst, S. (1997). Virtual reality and tactile augmentation in the treatment of spider phobia: A case report. *Behaviour Research and Therapy, 35*(2), 153–158.

Carlson, J. G. (1996). Behavioral interventions for posttraumatic stress disorder. In C. D. Spielberger, I. G. Sarason, et al. (Eds.), *Stress and emotion.*

Caroff, S. N., Man, S. C., Lazarus, A., Sullivan, K., & MacFadden, W. (1991). Neuroleptic malignant syndrome: Diagnostic issues. *Psychiatric Annals, 21,* 147.

Carpenter, W. T. (1995). Serotonin-dopamine antagonists and treatment of negative symptoms. *Journal of Clinical Psychopharmacology, 15,* 30S–35S.

Carpenter, W. T., Buchanan, R. W., Kirkpatrick, B., & Breier, A. F. (1999). Diazepam treatment of early signs of exacerbation in schizophrenia. *American Journal of Psychiatry, 156*(2), 299–303.

Carpenter, W. T., & Tamminga, C. A. (1995). Why neuroleptic withdrawal in schizophrenia? *Archives of General Psychiatry, 52,* 192–193.

Carrasco, J. L., Saiz-Ruiz, J., Hollander, E., Cesar, J., et al. (1994). Low platelet monoamine oxidase activity in pathological gambling. *Acta Psychiatrica Scandinavica, 90,* 427–431.

Carrington, P. J., & Moyer, S. (1994). Gun availability and suicide in Canada: Testing the displacement hypothesis. *Studies on Crime and Crime Prevention, 3,* 168–178.

Carroll, K. M., Nich, C., Ball, S. A., & McCance, E. (1998). Treatment of cocaine and alcohol dependence with psychotherapy and disulfiram. *Addiction, 93*(5), 713–727.

Carter, C. S., Perlstein, W., Ganguli, R., Brar, J., & Mintun, M. (1998). Functional hypofrontality and working memory dysfunction in schizophrenia. *American Journal of Psychiatry, 155*(9), 1285–1287.

Carter, M. M., Hollon, S. D., Carson, R., & Shelton, R. C. (1995). Effects of a safe person on induced distress following a biological challenge in panic disorder with agoraphobia. *Journal of Abnormal Psychology, 104,* 156–163.

Cartwright, R. D., Ristanovic, R., Diaz, F., Caldarelli, D., & Adler, G. (1991). A comparative study of treatments for positional sleep apnea. *Sleep, 14,* 546–522.

Carver, C. (1998). Premature ejaculation: A common and treatable concern. *Journal of the American Psychiatric Nurses Association, 4*(6), 199–204.

Carver, C. S., Coleman, A. E., & Glass, D. C. (1976). The coronary-prone behavior pattern and the suppression of fatigue on a treadmill test. *Journal of Personality and Social Psychology, 33,* 460–466.

Casacalenda, N., & Boulenger, J. P. (1998). Pharmacologic treatments effective in both generalized anxiety disorder and major depressive. *Canadian Journal of Psychiatry, 43*(7), 722–730.

Caspari, D. (1999). Cannabis and schizophrenia: Results of a follow-up study. *European Archives of Psychiatry and Clinical Neuroscience, 249*(1), 45–49.

Cassady, S. L., Adami, H., Moran, M., Kunkel, R., & Thaker, G. K. (1998). Spontaneous dyskinesia in subjects with schizophrenia spectrum personality. *American Journal of Psychiatry, 155*(1), 70–75.

Castle, D., & Murray, R. (1991). The neurodevelopmental basis of sex differences in schizophrenia. *Psychological Medicine, 21,* 565–575.

Cathcart, S., & Pritchard, D. (1998). Relationships between arousal-related moods and episodic tension-type headache. *Headache, 38*(3), 214–221.

Ceci, S. J., Huffman, M. L. C., and Smith, E. (1995). Repeatedly thinking about a non-event: Source misattributions among preschoolers. The recovered memory/false memory debate [Special issue]. *Consciousness and Cognition: An International Journal, 3,* 388–407.

Centers for Disease Control. (1986). *Youth suicide surveillance.* Washington, DC: U.S. Public Health Service.

Cepeda-Benito, A. (1993). Meta-analytical review of the efficacy of nicotine chewing gum in smoking treatment programs. *Journal of Consulting and Clinical Psychology, 61,* 822–830.

Cerletti, U., & Bini, L. (1938). L'elettroshock. *Archivio Generale di Neurologia Psichiatria e Psicoanalisi, 19,* 266–268.

Cerny, J. A. (1978). Biofeedback and the voluntary control of sexual arousal in women. *Behavior Therapy, 9,* 847–855.

Chapman, L. J., Chapman, J. P., & Miller, G. A. (1964). A theory of verbal behavior in schizophrenia. In B. A. Maher (Ed.), *Progress in experimental personality research* (Vol. 1). New York: Academic Press.

Chapman, L. J., Chapman, J. P., & Miller, G. A. (1984). A theory of verbal behavior in schizophrenia: Postscript. In B. A. Maher (Ed.), *Contributions to the psychopathology of schizophrenia.* New York: Academic Press.

Charney, D. S., Deutch, A. Y., Krystal, J. H., Southwick, S. M., & David, M. (1993). Psychobiologic mechanisms of posttraumatic stress disorder. *Archives of General Psychiatry, 50,* 294–305.

Chaturvedi, S. K. (1993). Neurosis across cultures. International *Review of Psychiatry, 5,* 179–191.

Cheatham, S. K., Rucker, H. N., Polloway, E. A., Smith, J. D., et al. (1995). Savant syndrome: Case studies, hypotheses, and implications for special education. *Education and Training in Mental Retardation and Developmental Disabilities.*

Chen, P., Ganguli, M., Mulsant, B. H., & DeKosky, S. T. (1999). The temporal relationship between depressive symptoms and dementia: A community-based. *Archives of General Psychiatry, 56*(3), 261–266.

Chen, W. J., Liu, S. K., Chang, C. J., Lien, Y. J., & Chang, Y. H. (1998). Sustained attention deficit and schizotypal personality features in nonpsychotic relatives of. *American Journal of Psychiatry, 155*(9), 1214–1220.

Chen, W. J., Yeh, L. L., Chang, C. J., Lin, L. C., Rin, H., & Hwu, H. G. (1996). Month of birth and schizophrenia in Taiwan: Effect of gender, family history and age at onset. *Schizophrenia Research, 20*(1–2), 133–143.

Cherek, D. R., & Lane, S. D. (1999). Effects of d,1-fenfluramine on aggressive and impulsive responding in adult males with history of conduct disorder. *Psychopharmacology, 146* (4), 473–481.

Chesney, M. A., Eagleston, J. R., & Rosenman, R. H. (1981). Type A behavior: Assessment and interventions. In C. K. Prokop & L. A. Bradley (Eds.), *Medical psychology: Contributions to behavioral medicine.* New York: Academic Press.

Chesney, M. A., & Rosenman, R. H. (1985). *Anger and hostility in cardiovascular and behavioral disorders.* Washington, DC: Hemisphere.

Cheung, F. M., & Ho, R. M. (1997). Standardization of the Chinese MMPI-A in Hong Kong: A preliminary study. *Psychological Assessment, 9*(4), 499–502.

Chew, P. K., Phoon, W. H., & Mae-Lim, H. A. (1976). Epidemic hysteria among some factory workers in Singapore. *Singapore Medical Journal, 17,* 10–15.

Chorpita, B. F., & Barlow, D. H. (1998). The development of anxiety: The role of control in the early environment. *Psychological Bulletin, 124*(1), 3–21.

Chouinard, G., Saxena, B., Belanger, M. C., Ravidran, A., & Bakish, D. (1999). A Canadian multicenter, double-blind study of paroxetine and fluoxetine in major depressive. *Journal of Affective Disorders, 54*(1–2), 39–48.

Chover Gonzalez, A. J., Harbuz, M. S., & Tejedor Real, P. (1999). Effects of stress on susceptibility and severity of inflammation in adjuvant-induced arthritis. In M. Cutolo & A. T. Masi (Eds.), *Neuroendocrine immune basis of the rheumatic.*

Christensen, H., Jorm, A. F., Mackinnon, A. J., Korten, A. E., & Jacomb, P. A. (1999). Age differences in depression and anxiety symptoms: A structural equation modelling analysis. *Psychological Medicine, 29*(2), 325–339.

Chua, S. E., & Murray, R. M. (1996). The neurodevelopmental theory of schizophrenia: Evidence concerning structure and. *Annals of Medicine, 28*(6), 547–555.

Clark, D. M., & Teasdale, J. D. (1985). Constraints on the effects of mood on memory. *Journal of Personality and Social Psychology, 48,* 1595–1608.

Clarke, R. V., & Lester, D. (1989). *Suicide: Closing the exits.* New York: Springer.

Clarkin, J. F., Carpenter, D., Hull, J., Wilner, P., & Glick, I. (1998). Effects of psychoeducational intervention for married patients with bipolar disorder and their. *Psychiatric Services, 49*(4), 531–533.

Clarkin, J. F., Hurt, S. W., & Mattis, S. (1999). Psychological and neuropsychological assessment. In R. E. Hales, S. C. Yudof-

sky, & J. A. Talbot (Eds.), *Textbook of psychiatry* (pp. 253–280). Washington, DC: American Psychiatric Press.

Classen, C., Koopman, C., Hales, R., & Spiegel, D. (1998). Acute stress disorder as a predictor of posttraumatic stress symptoms. *American Journal of Psychiatry, 155*(5), 620–624.

Clayton, A. H. (1993). Fetishism and clomipramine. American *Journal of Psychiatry, 150*(4), 673–674.

Clomipramine Collaborative Study Group. (1991). Clomipramine in the treatment of patients with obsessive-compulsive disorder. *Archives of General Psychiatry, 48,* 730–738.

Cloninger, C. R. (1987). Neurogenetic adaptive mechanisms in alcoholism. *Science, 236,* 410–416.

Cloud, J. (2000, March 13). It's all the rave. *Time Magazine,* 64–65.

Clum, G. A., Clum, G. A., & Surls, R. (1993). A meta-analysis of treatments for panic disorder. *Journal of Consulting and Clinical Psychology, 61,* 317–326.

Cnattingius, S., Hultman, C. M., Dahl, M., & Sparen, P. (1999). Very preterm birth, birth trauma, and the risk of anorexia nervosa among girls. *Archives of General Psychiatry, 56*(7), 634–638.

Coburn, K. L., Shillcutt, S. D., Tucker, K. A., & Estes, K. M. (1998). P300 delay and attenuation in schizophrenia: Reversal by neuroleptic medication. *Biological Psychiatry, 44*(6), 466–474.

Coccaro, E. F. (1998). Clinical outcome of psychopharmacologic treatment of borderline and schizotypal personality. *Journal of Clinical Psychiatry, 59*(Suppl. 1), 30–35.

Coccaro, E. F., & Kavoussi, R. J. (1997). Fluoxetine and impulsive aggressive behavior in personality-disordered subjects. *Archives of General Psychiatry, 54*(12), 1081–1088.

Coccaro, E. F., Kavoussi, R. J., Sheline, Y. I., Lish, J. D., & Csernansky, J. G. (1996). Impulsive aggression in personality disorder correlates with tritiated paroxetine binding in the platelet. *Archives of General Psychiatry, 53,* 531–536.

Cochrane, R., & Robertson, A. (1975). Stress in the lives of parasuicides. *Social Psychiatry, 10,* 161–172.

Coenen, A. M. L., & van Luijtelaar, E. L. J. M. (1997). Effects of benzodiazepines, sleep and sleep deprivation on vigilance and memory. *Acta Neurologica Belgica, 97*(2), 123–129.

Cohen, A. (1999). A curse of cliques. *Time* (May 3) 44–45.

Cohen, A., Barlow, D. H., & Blanchard, E. (1985). Psychophysiology of relaxation-associated panic attacks. *Journal of Abnormal Psychology, 94,* 96–101.

Cohen, F., Kearney, K. A., Zegans, L. S., & Kemeny, M. E. (1999). Differential immune system changes with acute and persistent stress for optimists vs pessimists. *Brain, Behavior and Immunity, 13*(2), 155–174.

Cohen, L., Delahanty, D. L., Schmitz, J. B., Jenkins, F. J., & Baum, A. (1993). The effects of stress on natural killer cell activity in healthy men. *Journal of Applied Biobehavioral Research, 1,* 120–132.

Cohen, R. Z., Seeman, M. V., Gotowiec, A., & Kopala, L. (1999). Earlier puberty as a predictor of later onset of schizophrenia in women. *American Journal of Psychiatry, 156*(7), 1059–1064.

Cohen, S., Tyrrell, D. A., & Smith, A. P. (1991). Psychological stress and susceptibility to the common cold. *New England Journal of Medicine, 325,* 606–616.

Cohen, S. L., & Fiedler, J. E. (1974). Content analysis of multiple messages in suicide notes. *Suicide and Life-Threatening Behavior, 4,* 75–95.

Cohen-Kettenis, P. T., & Gooren, L. J. (l992). The influence of hormone treatment on psychological functioning of transsexuals. *Journal of Psychology and Human Sexuality, 5,* 55–67.

Cole, D. A., Martin, J. M., Peeke, L., Henderson, A., & Harwell, J. (1998). Validation of depression and anxiety measures in White and Black youths. *Psychological Assessment, 10*(3), 261–276.

Cole, J. O., Goldberg, S. C., & Davis, J. M. (1966). Drugs in the treatment of psychosis: Controlled studies. In P. Solomon (Ed.), *Psychiatric drugs.* Philadelphia: Grune & Stratton.

Cole, J. O., Goldberg, S. C., & Klerman, G. L. (1964). Phenothiazine treatment in acute schizophrenia. *Archives of General Psychiatry, 10,* 246–261.

Coleman, C. A., Friedman, A. G., & Burright, R. G. (1998). The relationship of daily stress and health-related behaviors to adolescents' cholesterol levels. *Adolescence, 33*(130), 447–460.

Collaer, M. L., & Hines, M. (1995). Human behavioral sex differences: A role of gonadal hormones during early development? *Psychological Bulletin, 118,* 55–107.

Colligan, M. J., Pennebaker, J. W., & Murphy, L. R. (1982). *Mass psychogenic illness: A social psychological analysis.* Hillsdale, NJ: Erlbaum.

Collins, A. M., & Loftus, E. F. (1975). A spreading-activation theory of semantic processing. *Psychological Bulletin, 82,* 407–428.

Collins, M. W., Grindel, S. H., Lovell, M. R., Dede, D. E., Moser, D. J., Phalin, B. R., & Nogle, S. (1999). Relationship between concussion and neuropsychological performance in college football. *Journal of the American Medical Association, 282*(10), 964–70.

Collins, R. L. (1993). Sociocultural aspects of alcohol use and abuse: Ethnicity and gender. *Drugs and Society, 8,* 89–116.

Collyer, F. (1994). Sex-change surgery: An "unacceptable innovation?" *Australian and New Zealand Journal of Sociology, 30,* 3–19.

Colvin, C. R., & Block, J. (1994). Do positive illusions foster mental health? An examination of the Taylor and Brown formulation. *Psychological Bulletin, 116,* 3–20.

Combs, P., & Lasuzzo, S. (1995). Homebased therapy: Historical perspectives & practical applications. *Journal of Psychological Practice, 1*(1), 19–29.

Comings, D. E. (1990). *Tourette's syndrome and human behavior.* Duarte, CA: Hope Press.

Comings, D. E., & Comings, B. G. (1990). A controlled family history study of Tourette's syndrome: 1. Attention-deficit hyperactivity disorder and learning disorders. *Journal of Clinical Psychiatry, 51,* 275–280.

Congdon, M. H., Hain, J., & Stevenson, I. (1961). A case of multiple personality illustrating the transition from role playing. *Journal of Nervous and Mental Disease, 132,* 497–504.

Conger, J. J. (1951). The effects of alcohol on conflict between behavior in the albino rat. *Quarterly Journal of Studies on Alcohol, 12,* 1–29.

Conners, C. K., (1980). *Food additives and hyperactive children.* New York: Plenum.

Connor, D. F., Fletcher, K. E., & Swanson, J. M. (1999). A meta-analysis of clonidine for symptoms of attention-deficit hyperactivity disorder. *Journal of the American Academy of Child and Adolescent Psychiatry, 38*(12), 1551–1559.

Connor, M. (1999). Children on the autistic spectrum: Guidelines for mainstream practice. *Support for Learning, 14*(2), 80–86.

Conte, H. R. (1986). Multivariate assessment of sexual dysfunction. *Journal of Consulting and Clinical Psychology, 54,* 149–157.

Conte, J. R., & Berliner, L. (1981). Sexual abuse of children: Implications for practice. *Social Casework, 62,* 601–606.

Cook, M., Mineka, S., Wolkenstein, B., & Laitsch, K. (1985). Observational conditioning of snake fear in unrelated rhesus monkeys. *Journal of Abnormal Psychology, 94,* 591–610.

Cook, T. D., & Campbell, D. T. (1979). *Quasi-experimentation: Design and analysis issues for field settings.* Chicago: Rand McNally.

Cools, J., Schotte, D. E., & McNally, R. J. (1992). Emotional arousal and overeating in restrained eaters. *Journal of Abnormal Psychology, 101,* 348–351.

Coons, P. M. (1988). Psychophysiological aspects of multiple personality disorder. *Dissociation, 1,* 47–53.

Coons, P. M., Milstein, V., & Marley, C. (1982). EEG studies of two multiple personalities and a control. *Archives of General Psychiatry, 39,* 823–825.

Cooper, A. J. (1964). A case of fetishism and impotence treated by behavior therapy. *British Journal of Psychiatry, 109,* 649–652.

Cooper, A. J. (1999). Re: Sexual recidivism in sex offenders. *Canadian Journal of Psychiatry, 44*(1), 94.

Cooper, M. L., Russell, M., Skinner, J. B., Frone, M. R., & Mudar, P. (1992). Stress and alcohol use: Moderating effects of gender, coping, and alcohol expectancies. *Journal of Abnormal Psychology, 101,* 139–152.

Coppen, A., & Farmer, R. (1998). Suicide mortality in patients on lithium maintenance therapy. *Journal of Affective Disorders, 50*(2–3), 261–267.

Corrigan, P. W., Wallace, C. J., Schade, M. L., & Green, M. F. (1994). Learning medication self-management skills in schizophrenia: Relationships with cognitive deficits and psychiatric symptoms. *Behavior Therapy, 25,* 5–15.

Coryell, W., Endicott, J., & Keller, M. (1991). Major depression in a nonclinical sample. *Archives of General Psychiatry, 49,* 117–125.

Coryell, W., Endicott, J., & Keller, M. (1992). Rapidly cycling affective disorder: Demographics, diagnosis, family history, and course. *Archives of General Psychiatry, 49,* 126–131.

Coryell, W., Endicott, J., Winokur, G., Akiskal, H., Solomon, D., Leon, A., Mueller, T., & Shea, T. (1995). Characteristics and significance of untreated major depressive disorder. *American Journal of Psychiatry, 152,* 1124–1129.

Coryell, W., Turvey, C., Endicott, J., Leon, A. C., & Mueller, T. (1998). Bipolar I affective disorder: Predictors of outcome after 15 years. *Journal of Affective Disorders, 50*(2–3), 109–116.

Costello, C. G. (1982). Fears and phobias in women: A community study. *Journal of Abnormal Psychology, 91,* 280–286.

Courchesne, E. (1997). Brainstem, cerebellar and limbic neuroanatomical abnormalities in autism. *Current Opinion in Neurobiology, 7*(2), 269–278.

Courchesne, E., Mueller, R.A., & Saitch, O. (1999). Brain weight in autism: Normal in the majority of cases, megalencephalic in rare cases. *Neurology, 52*(5), 1057–1059.

Cournos, F. Faulkner, L. R., Fitzgerald, L., Griffith, E. Muntez, M. R., & Winick, B. (1993). Report of the Task Force on Consent to Voluntary Hospitalization. *Bulletin of the American Academy of Psychiatry and the Law, 21,* 293–307.

Covey, L. S., Glassman, A. H., & Stetner, F. (1999). Naltrexone effects on short-term and long-term smoking cessation. *Journal of Addictive Diseases, 18*(1), 31–40.

Covington v. *Harris,* 419 F.2d 617 (D.C. Cir. 1969).

Coward, D. M., Imperato, A., Urwyler, S., & White, T. G. (1989). Biochemical and behavioral properties of clozapine. *Psychopharmacology, 99,* S6–S12.

Cox, J. L. (1992). Depression after childbirth. In E. S. Paykel (Ed.), *Handbook of affective disorders* (2nd ed.). New York: Guilford Press.

Coyle, J. T., & Hyman, S. E. (1999). The neuroscientific foundations of psychiatry. In R. E. Hales, S. C. Yudofsky, & J. A. Talbot (Eds.), *Textbook of psychiatry* (pp. 3–34). Washington, DC: American Psychiatric Press.

Coyne, J. C., Aldwin, C., & Lazarus, R. S. (1981). Depression and coping in stressful episodes. *Journal of Abnormal Psychology, 90,* 439–447.

Coyne, J. C., Pepper, C. M., & Flynn, H. (1999). Significance of prior episodes of depression in two patient populations. *Journal of Consulting and Clinical Psychology, 67*(1), 76–81.

Coyne, J. C., & Whiffen, V. E. (1995). Issues in personality as diathesis for depression: The case of sociotropy-dependency and autonomy–self-criticism. *Psychological Bulletin, 118,* 358–376.

Craig, R. J. (1995). The role of personality in understanding substance abuse. *Alcoholism Treatment Quarterly, 13,* 17–27.

Craighead, W. E., Craighead, L. W., & Ilardi, S. S. (1998). Psychosocial treatments for major depressive disorder. In P. E. Nathan & J. M. Gorman (Eds.), *A guide to treatments that work* (pp. 226–239). New York: Oxford University Press.

Craighead, W. E., Miklowitz, D. J., Vajk, F. C., & Frank, E. (1998). Psychosocial treatments for bipolar disorder. In P. E. Nathan & J. M. Gorman (Eds.), *A guide to treatments that work* (pp. 240–248). New York: Oxford University Press.

Craske, M. G., & Barlow, D. H. (1989). Nocturnal panic. *Journal of Nervous and Mental Disease, 177,* 160–167.

Creese, I. (1985). Dopamine and antipsychotic medications. In R. E. Hales & A. J. Frances (Eds.), *Psychiatry update: The American Psychiatric Association annual review* (Vol. 4). Washington, DC: American Psychiatric Press.

Crews, F. C. (1998). *Unauthorized Freud: Doubters Confront a Legend.* New York: Viking.

Crisp, A. H. (1967). The possible significance of some behavioral correlates of weight and carbohydrate intake. *Journal of Psychosomatic Research, 11,* 117–131.

Crits-Christoph, P. (1998). Psychosocial treatments for personality disorders. In P. E. Nathan & J. M. Gorman (Eds.), *A guide to treatments that work* (pp. 544–553). New York: Oxford University Press.

Crosby, A. E., Cheltenham, M. P., & Sacks, J. J. (1999). Incidence of suicidal ideation and behavior in the United States, 1994. *Suicide and Life Threatening Behavior, 29*(2), 131–140.

Crowe, R. R., Noyes, R., Pauls, D. L., et al. (1983). A family study of panic disorder. *Archives of General Psychiatry, 40,* 1065–1069.

Crowley, P. H., Hayden, T. L., & Gulitai, D. K. (1982). Etiology of Down syndrome. In S. M. Pueschel & J. E. Rynders (Eds.), *Down syndrome: Advances in biomedicine and the behavioral sciences.* Cambridge, MA: Ware Press.

Cueller, I. (1998). Cross-cultural clinical psychological assessment of Hispanic Americans. *Journal of Personality Assessment, 70*(1), 71–86.

Culbertson, F. M. (1997). Depression and gender. *American Psychologist, 52,* 25–31.

Cummings, J. L., Trimble, M. R., & Hales, R. E. (1999). Clinical neuropsychiatry. In R. E. Hales, S. C. Yudofsky, & J. A. Talbot (Eds.), *Textbook of psychiatry* (pp. 1667–1692). Washington, DC: American Psychiatric Press.

Curtis, V. A., Bullmore, E. T., Brammer, M. J., & Wright, I. C. (1998). Attenuated frontal activation during a verbal fluency task in patients with schizophrenia. *American Journal of Psychiatry, 155*(8), 1056–1063.

Dabbs, J. M., Jr., & Hargrove, M. F. (1997). Age, testosterone, and behavior among female prison inmates. *Psychosomatic Medicine, 59*(5), 477–480.

Da Costa, J. M. (1871). On irritable heart. American Journal of Medical Science, 61, 17–52.

Dager, S. R., Saai, A. K., Comess, K. A., & Dunner, D. L. (1988). Mitral valve prolapse and the anxiety disorders. *Hospital and Community Psychiatry, 39,* 517–527.

Dager, S. R., Strauss, W. L., Marro, K. I., Richards, T. L., Metzger, G. D., & Artru, A. A. (1995). Proton magnetic resonance spectroscopy investigation of hyperventilation in subjects with panic disorder and comparison subjects. *American Journal of Psychiatry, 152,* 666–672.

Dalman, C., Allebeck, P., Cullberg, J., Grunewald, C., & Koester, M. (1999). Obstetric complications and the risk of schizophrenia: A longitudinal study of a national birth. *Archives of General Psychiatry, 56*(3), 234–240.

Dalton, A. J., Mehta, P. D., Fedor, B. L., & Patti, P. J. (1999). Cognitive changes in memory precede those in praxis in aging persons with Down Syndrome. *Journal of Intellectual and Developmental Disability, 24*(2), 169–187.

Damasio, A. R. (1994). *Descartes' error: Emotion, reason, and the human brain.* New York: Putnam.

Damasio, A. R. (1997). Toward a neuropathology of emotion and mood. *Nature, 386,* 769–770.

Damasio, A. R. (2000). A neural basis for sociopathy. *Archives of General Psychiatry, 57*(2), 128–129.

Danion, J. M., Rizzo, L., & Bruant, A. (1999). Functional mechanisms underlying impaired recognition memory and conscious awareness in. *Archives of General Psychiatry, 56*(7), 639–644.

Daskalos, C. T. (1998). Changes in the sexual orientation of six heterosexual male-to-female transsexuals. *Archives of Sexual Behavior, 27*(6), 605–614.

Davey, G. C. (1987). Integrating human and animal theories of conditioning. *Journal of Psychophysiology, 1*(2), 105–108.

David, A. S., Woodruff, P. W. R., Howard, R., Mellers, J. D. C., et al. (1996). Auditory hallucinations inhibit exogenous activation of auditory association cortex.

David, O. J., Clark, J., & Voeller, K. (1979). Lead and hyperactivity. *Lancet, 2,* 900–903.

Davidson, D., Palfai, T., Bird, C., & Swift, R. (1999). Effects of naltrexone on alcohol self-administration in heavy drinkers. *Alcoholism: Clinical and Experimental Research, 23*(2), 195–203.

Davidson, G. N. S., & Horvath, A. O. (1997). Three sessions of brief couples therapy: A clinical trial. *Journal of Family Psychology, 11*(4), 422–435.

Davidson, J. M. (1984). Response to "Hormones and human sexual behavior" by John Bancroft, MD. *Journal of Sex and Marital Therapy, 10,* 23–27.

Davidson, J. M., Camargo, C. A., & Smith, E. R. (1979). Effects of androgens on sexual behavior in hypogonadal men. *Journal of Clinical Endocrinology and Metabolism, 48,* 955–958.

Davidson, J. R., Hughes, D. C., George, L. K., & Blazer, D. G. (1994). The boundary of social phobia: Exploring the threshold. *Archives of General Psychiatry, 51,* 975–983.

Davidson, J. R. T. (1998). The long-term treatment of panic disorder. *Journal of Clinical Psychiatry, 59*(8), 17–21.

Davidson, J. R. T., Tupler, I. A., & Potts, N. I. S., (1994). Treatment of social phobia with benzodiazepines. *Journal of Clinical Psychiatry, 55*(Suppl. 6), 28–32.

Davidson, J. R. T., Tupler, L. A., Wilson, W. H., & Connor, K. M. (1998). A family study of chronic posttraumatic stress disorder following rape trauma. *Journal of Psychiatric Research, 32*(5), 301–309.

Davidson, J. R. T., Weisler, R. H., Malik, M. L., & Connor, K. M. (1998). Treatment of posttraumatic stress disorder with nefazodone. *International Clinical Psychopharmacology, 13*(3), 111–113.

Davidson, M., Harvey, P. D., Powchik, P., Parrella, M., White, L., Knobler, H. Y., Losonczy, M. F., Keefe, R. S., Katz, S., & Frecska, E. (1995). Severity of symptoms in chronically institutionalized geriatric schizophrenic patients. *American Journal of Psychiatry, 152,* 197–207.

Davidson, M. H., Hauptman, J., DiGirolamo, M., Forety, J. P., Halsted, C. H., Heber, D., Heimburger, D. C., Lucas, C. P., Robbins, D. C., Chung, J., & Heymsfield, S. B. (1999). Weight control and risk factor reduction in obese subjects treated for 2 years with Orlistat. *Journal of the American Medical Association, 20,* 235–242.

Davis, D. L., Davis, H. L., & Davis, T. L. (1999). The further perils of psychotherapy practice: Ohio expands the duty to warn. *American Journal of Forensic Psychology, 17*(2), 25–39.

Davis, J. M., Schaffer, C. B., Killian, G. A., Kinard, C., & Chan, C. (1980). Important issues in the drug treatment of schizophrenia. *Schizophrenia Bulletin, 6,* 70–87.

Davis, K. (1947). Final note on a case of extreme isolation. *American Journal of Sociology, 57,* 432–457.

Dawes, R. M. (1994). *House of cards.* New York: Free Press.

Dawes, R. M., Faust, D., & Meehl, P. E. (1989). Clinical versus actuarial judgment. *Science, 243,* 1668–1674.

Dawson, J. (1999). The alter as agent: Multiple personality and the insanity defence. *Psychiatry, Psychology and Law, 6*(2), 203–206.

Deary, I. J., Fowkes, F. G. R., Donnan, P. T., & Housle, E. (1994). Hostile personality and risks of peripheral arterial disease in the general population. *Psychosomatic Medicine, 56,* 197–202.

de Beurs, E., van Balkom, A. J., Lange, A., Koele, P., & van Dyck, R. (1995). Treatment of panic disorder with agoraphobia: Comparison of fluvoxamine, placebo, and psychological panic management combined with exposure and of exposure in vivo alone. *American Journal of Psychiatry, 152,* 683–691.

DeCaria, C. M., Hollander, E., Grossman, R., & Wong, C. M. (1996). Diagnosis, neurobiology, and treatment of pathological gambling. *Journal of Clinical Psychiatry, 57*(Suppl. 8), 80–84.

De Deyn, P. P., Goeman, J., Engelborghs, S., Hauben, U., D'Hooge, R., & Baro, F. (1999). From neuronal and vascular impairment to dementia. *Pharmacopsychiatry, 32*(Suppl. 1), 17–24.

Deeg, D. J., Haga, H., Yasumura, S., Suzuki, T., et al. (1992). Predictors of 10-year change in physical, cognitive and social function in Japanese elderly. *Archives of Gerontology and Geriatrics, 15*(2), 163–179.

De Gucht, V., Fischler, B., & Demanet, C. (1999). Immune dysfunction associated with chronic professional stress in nurses. *Psychiatry Research, 85*(1), 105–111.

Delahanty, D. L. (1998). The influence of an experimental hassle on natural killer cell reactivity to acute stress. *Dissertation Abstracts International: Section B: The Sciences and Engineering.*

DeLeon, P. H., & Wiggins, J. G. (1996). Prescription privileges for psychologists. *American Psychologist, 51,* 225–229.

DeLeon-Jones, F., Maas, J. W., Dekirmenjian, H., & Sanchez, J. (1975). Diagnostic subgroups of affective disorders and their urinary excretion of catecholamine metabolites. *American Journal of Psychiatry, 132,* 1141–1148.

Delgado, P. L., & Moreno, F. A. (1998). Different roles for serotonin in anti-obsessional drug action and the pathophysiology of. *British Journal of Psychiatry, 173*(Suppl. 35), 21–25.

Delgado, P. L., Price, L. H., Heninger, G. R., & Charney, D. S. (1992). Neurochemistry. In E. S. Paykel (Ed.), *Handbook of affective disorders* (2nd ed.). New York: Guilford Press.

Delgado, P. L., Price, L. H., Miller, H. L., Salomon, R. M., Aghajanian, G. K., Heninger, G. R., & Charney, D. S. (1994). Serotonin and the neurobiology of depression: Effects of tryptophan depletion in drug-free depressed patients. *Archives of General Psychiatry, 51,* 865–874.

DeLisi, L. E., Sakuma, M., Tew, W., Kushner, M., & Hoff, A. L. (1997). Schizophrenia as a chronic active brain process: A study of progressive brain structural. *Psychiatry Research: Neuroimaging, 74*(3), 129–140.

De Man, A. F. (1999). Correlates of suicide ideation in high school students: The importance of depression. *Journal of Genetic Psychology, 160*(1), 105–114.

den Boer, J. A., & Slaap, B. R. (1998). Review of current treatment in panic disorder. *International Clinical Psychopharmacology, 13*(Suppl. 4), S25–S30.

DeNelsky, G. Y. (1996). The case against prescription privileges for psychologists. *American Psychologist, 51,* 207–212.

Denney, D. R., Stephenson, L. A., Penick, E., & Weller, R. (1988). Lymphocyte subclasses and depression. *Journal of Abnormal Psychology, 97,* 499–502.

Derby, K. M., Fisher, W. W., Piazza, C. C., Wilke, A. E., & Johnson, W. (1998). The effects of noncontingent and contingent attention for self-injury, manding, and collateral responses. *Behavior Modification, 22*(4), 474–484.

Derogatis, L. R. (1993). *The symptom checklist series.* Minneapolis: NSC Assessments.

Derry, F. A., Dinsmore, W. W., Fraser, M., Gardner, B. P., Glass, C. A., Maytom, M. C., & Smith, M. D. (1998). Efficacy and safety of oral sidenafil (Viagra) in men with erectile dysfunction caused by spinal cord injury. *Neurology, 51*(6), 1629–1633.

DeRubeis, R. J., Gelfand, L. A., Tang, T. Z., & Simons, A. D. (1999). Medications versus cognitive behavior therapy for severely depressed outpatients. *American Journal of Psychiatry, 156*(7), 1007–1013.

DeSmet, P. A., & Nolen, W. A. (1996). St. John's wort as an antidepressant. *British Journal of Medicine, 313,* 241–242.

Desmond, D. W., & Tatemichi, T. K. (1998). Vascular dementia. In M. F. Folstein et al. (Eds.), *Neurobiology of primary dementia* (pp. 167–190).

Dessens, A. B., Cohen Kettenis, P. T., & Mellenbergh, G. J. (1999). Prenatal exposure to anticonvulsants and psychosexual development. *Archives of Sexual Behavior, 28*(1), 31–44.

Devanand, D. P., Dwork, A. J., Hutchingson, E. R., Bolwig, T. G., & Sackeim. H. A. (1994). Does ECT alter brain structure? *American Journal of Psychiatry, 151,* 957–970.

Devanand, D. P., Verma, A. K., Tirumalasetti, F., & Sackeim, H. A. (1991). Absence of cognitive impairment after more than 100 lifetime ECT treatments. *American Journal of Psychiatry, 148,* 929–932.

Devor, E. J. (1990). Untying the Gordian knot: The genetics of Tourette's syndrome. *Journal of Nervous and Mental Disease, 178,* 669–679.

de Wit, H., Svenson, J., & York, A. (1999). Non-specific effect of naltrexone on ethanol consumption in social drinkers. *Psychopharmacology, 146*(1), 33–41.

Diamond, B. L. (1974). Psychiatric prediction of dangerousness. *University of Pennsylvania Law Review, 123,* 439–452.

Diamond, M., & Sigmundson, K. (1997). Sex reassignment at birth: Long-term review and clinical implications. *Archives of Pediatric and Adolescent Medicine, 151,* 298–304.

Dickey, C. C., McCarley, R. W., & Voglmaier, M. M. (1999). Schizotypal personality disorder and MRI abnormalities of temporal lobe gray matter. *Biological Psychiatry, 45*(11), 1392–1402.

Diekstra, R. F. (1990). Suicide and attempted suicide: An international perspective. *Acta Psychiatrica Scandinavica, 80,* Suppl. 354, 1–24.

Dietz, P. E., Hazelwood, R. R., & Warren, J. (1990). The sexually sadistic criminal and his offenses. *Bulletin of the American Academy of Psychiatry and the Law, 18,* 163–178.

Di Mascio, A., Weissman, M. M., Prusoff, B. A., Neu, C., Zwilling, M., & Klerman, G. L. (1979). Differential symptom reduction by drugs and psychotherapy in acute depression. *Archives of General Psychiatry, 36,* 1450–1456.

Disney, E. R., Elkins, I. J., McGue, M., & Iacono, W. G. (1999). Effects of ADHD, conduct disorder, and gender of substance use and abuse in adolescence. *American Journal of Psychiatry, 156* (10), 1515–1521.

Docherty, N. M. (1994). Cognitive characteristics of the parents of schizophrenic patients. *Journal of Nervous and Mental Disease, 182,* 443–451.

Dodge, K. A., & Somberg, D. R. (1987). Hostile attributional biases among aggressive boys are exacerbated under conditions of threats to the self. *Child Development, 58,* 213–224.

Dohrenwend, B. S., & Dohrenwend, B. P. (1974). *Stressful life events.* New York: Wiley.

Dollard, J., & Miller, N. (1950). *Personality and psychotherapy.* New York: McGraw-Hill.

Domino, G., & Takahashi, Y. (1991). Attitudes toward suicide in Japanese and American medical students. *Suicide and Life-Threatening Behavior, 21,* 345–359.

Doogan, D. P., & Caillard, V. (1992). Sertraline in the prevention of depression. *British Journal of Psychiatry, 160,* 217–222.

Doren, D. M. (1998). Recidivism base rates, predictions of sex offender recidivism, and the "Sexual Predator." *Behavioral Sciences and the Law, 16*(1), 97–114.

Douglas, N. J. (1998). The psychosocial aspects of narcolepsy. *Neurology, 50*(2, Suppl. 1), S27–S30

Dowdall, G. W. (1999). Mental hospitals and deinstitutionalization. In C. S. Aneshensel, J. C. Phelan, et al. (Eds.), *Handbook of sociology of.*

Downey, K. K., & Kilbey, M. M. (1995). Relationship between nicotine and alcohol expectancies and substance dependence. *Experimental and Clinical Psychopharmacology, 3,* 174–182.

Drake, R. E., & Wallach, M. A. (1979). Will mental patients stay in the community? A social psychological perspective. *Journal of Consulting and Clinical Psychology, 47,* 285–294.

Dressler, W. W. (1991). Social support, lifestyle incongruity, and arterial blood pressure in a southern black community. *Psychosomatic Medicine, 53,* 608–620.

Drevets, W. C., Price, J. L., Simpson, J. R., Todd, R. D., Reich, T., Vannier, M., & Ralchle, M. (1997). Subgenual prefrontal cortex abnormalities in mood disorders. *Nature, 386,* 824–827.

Drew, B. L. (1999). No-suicide contracts to prevent suicidal behavior in inpatient psychiatric settings. *Journal of the American Psychiatric Nurses Association, 5*(1), 23–28.

Dubovsky, S. L., & Buzan, R. (1999). Mood disorders. In R. E. Hales, S. C. Yudofsky, & J. A. Talbot (Eds.), *Textbook of psychiatry* (pp. 479–566). Washington, DC: American Psychiatric Press.

Duckworth, J. C., & Anderson, W. P. (1995). *MMPI-1 and MMPI-2 interpretation manual for counselors and clinicians* (4th ed.). Bristol, PA: Accelerated Development.

Dugas, M. J., Freeston, M. H., Ladouceur, R., & Rheaume, J. (1998). Worry themes in primary GAD, secondary GAD, and other anxiety disorders. *Journal of Anxiety Disorders, 12*(3), 253–261.

Duggan, J. P., & Booth, D. A. (1986). Obesity, overeating, and rapid gastric emptying in rats with ventromedial hypothalamic lesions. *Science, 231,* 609–611.

Dulit, R. A., Fyer, M. R., Lenon, A. C., Brodsky, B. S., & Frances, A. J. (1994). Clinical correlates of self-mutilation in borderline personality disorder. *American Journal of Psychiatry, 151,* 1305–1311.

Dunn, A. L., Marcus, B. H., Kampert, J. B., Garcia, M. E., Kohl, H. W., 3rd, & Blair, S. N. (1999). Comparison of lifestyle and structured interventions to increase physical activity and. *Journal of the American Medical Association, 281*(4), 327–334.

DuPaul, G. J., Power, T. J., Anastopoulos, A. D., & Reid, R. (1997). Teacher ratings of attention deficit hyperactivity disorder symptoms: Factor structure and. *Psychological Assessment, 9*(4), 436–444.

Durham, R. C., Fisher, P. L., Treliving, L. R., Hau, C. M., Richard, K., & Stewart, J. B. (1999). One year follow-up of cognitive therapy, analytic psychotherapy and anxiety management training for generalized anxiety disorder: Symptom change, medication usage and attitudes to treatment. *Behavioural and Cognitive Psychotherapy, 27*(1), 19–35.

Durkheim, E. (1951). *Suicide* (J. A. Spaulding & G. Simpson, Trans.). New York: Free Press. (Originally published 1897)

Durlak, J. A. (1980). Comparative effectiveness of behavioral and relationship group treatment in the secondary prevention of school maladjustment. *American Journal of Community Psychology, 8,* 327–339.

Dusky v. *United States,* 362 U.S. 402 (1960).

Dusseldorp, E., van Elderen, T., Maes, S., Meulman, J., & Kraaij, V. (1999). A meta-analysis of psychoeducational programs for coronary heart disease patients. *Health Psychology, 18*(5), 506–519.

Dutton, D. G., & Aron, A. P. (1974). Some evidence for heightened sexual attraction under conditions of high anxiety. *Journal of Personality and Social Psychology, 30,* 510–517.

Dyck, M. J. (1991). Positive and negative attitudes mediating suicide ideation. *Suicide and Life-Threatening Behavior, 21,* 360–373.

Dyer, A. R. (1999). Ethics and psychiatry. In R. E. Hales, S. C. Yudofsky, & J. A. Talbot (Eds.), *Textbook of psychiatry* (pp. 1599–1616). Washington, DC: American Psychiatric Press.

D'Zurilla, T. J., Chang, E. C., Nottingham, E. J. I. V., & Faccini, L. (1998). Social problem-solving deficits and hopelessness, depression, and suicidal risk in college. *Journal of Clinical Psychology, 54*(8), 1091–1107.

Earle, P. (1994). Gheel. *American Journal of Psychiatry, 151,* 16–19. (Originally published 1851)

Easton, W. W., Thara, R., Federman, B., Melton, B., & Liang, K. (1995). Structure and course of positive and negative symptoms in schizophrenia. *Archives of General Psychiatry, 52,* 127–134.

Eaves, G., & Rehm, A. J. (1984). Cognitive patterns in symptomatic and remitted unipolar major depression. *Journal of Abnormal Psychology, 93,* 31–40.

Eaves, L. C., Ho, H. H., & Eaves, D. M. (1994). Subtypes of autism by cluster analysis. *Journal of Autism and Developmental Disorders, 24,* 3–22.

Ebrahim, S. H., Floyd, R. L., Merritt, R. K., II, Decoufle, P., & Holtzman, D. (2000). Trends in pregnancy-related smoking rates in the US, 1987–1996. *Journal of the American Medical Association, 283*(3), 266–381.

Ebstein, R. P., Novick, O., Umansky, R., Priel, B., Osher, Y., Blaine, D., Bennett, E. R., Nemanov, L., Katz, M., & Belmaker, R. H. (1996). Dopamine D4 receptor (D4DR) exon III polymorphism associated with the human personality of novelty seeking. *Nature Genetics, 12,* 78–80.

Echeburua, E., Baez, C., & Fernandez-Montalvo, J. (1996). Comparative effectiveness of three therapeutic modalities in the psychological treatment of. *Behavioural and Cognitive Psychotherapy, 24*(1), 51–72.

Edelbrock, C. (no date). The child attention/activity profile. Unpublished manuscript, Pennsylvania State University.

Edelson, S. M., Edelson, M. G., Kerr, D. C. R., & Grandin, T. (1999). Behavioral and physiological effects of deep pressure on children with autism: A pilot study evaluating the efficacy of Grandin's Hug Machine. *American Journal of Occupational Therapy, 53*(2), 145–152.

Edgerton, R. B., & Cohen, A. (1994). Culture and schizophrenia: The DOSM challenge. *British Journal of Psychiatry, 164,* 222–231.

Ehlers, S., & Gillberg, C. (1993). The epidemiology of Asperger syndrome: A total population study. *Journal of Child Psychology and Psychiatry and Allied Disciplines, 34,* 1327–1350.

Ehrenreich, H., Rinn, T., Kunert, H. J., & Moeller, M. R. (1999). Specific attentional dysfunction in adults following early start of cannabis use. *Psychopharmacology, 142*(3), 295–301.

Ehrhardt, A., Epstein, R., & Money, J. (1968). Fetal androgens and female gender identity in the early-treated andrenogenital syndrome. *Johns Hopkins Medical Journal, 122,* 160–167.

Ehrhardt, A., & Money, J. (1967). Progestin-induced hermaphroditism: IQ and psychosexual identity in a study of ten girls. *Journal of Sex Research, 3,* 53–100.

Eiberg, H., Berendt, I., & Mohr, J. (1995). Assignment of dominant inherited nocturnal enuresis (ENUR1) to chrormosome 13q. *Nature Genetics, 10,* 354–356.

Eisen, S. A., Lin, N., Lyons, M. J., Scherrer, J. F., & Griffith, K. (1998). Familial influences on gambling behavior: An analysis of 3359 twin pairs. *Addiction, 93*(9), 1375–1384.

Eisenberg, L., & Kanner, L. (1956). Early infantile autism, 1943–1955. *American Journal of Orthopsychiatry, 26,* 556–566.

Eisendrath, S. J., & Valan, M. N. (1994). Psychiatric predictors of pseudoepileptic seizures in patients with refractory seizures. *Journal of Neuropsychiatry and Clinical Neurosciences, 6,* 257–260.

Eisler, I., Dare, C., Russell, G. F. M., & Szmukler, G. (1997). Family and individual therapy in anorexia nervosa: A 5-year follow-up. *Archives of General Psychiatry, 54*(11), 1025–1030.

El-Islam, M. (1991). Transcultural aspects of schizophrenia and ICD–10. *Psychiatria Danubina, 3,* 485–494.

Elizur, Y., & Hirsh, E. (1999). Psychosocial adjustment and mental health two months after coronary artery bypass surgery. *Journal of Behavioral Medicine, 22*(2), 157–177.

Elkin, I., Shea, M. T., Watkins, J. T., Imber, S. D., Sotsky, S. M., Collins, J. F., Glass, D. R., Pilkonis, P. A., Leber, W. R., Kocherty, J. P., Fiester, S. J., & Parloff, M. B. (1989). National Institute of Mental Health Treatment of Depression Collaborative Research Program. *Archives of General Psychiatry, 46,* 971–982.

Elkins, R. (1991). An appraisal of chemical aversion (emetic therapy) approaches to alcoholism treatment. *Behaviour Research and Therapy, 29,* 387–411.

Ellicott, A., Hammen, C., Gitlin, M., Brown, G., & Jamison, K. (1990). Life events and the course of bipolar disorder. *American Journal of Psychiatry, 147,* 1194–1198.

Elliott, R., Baker, S. C., Rogers, R. D., O'Leary, D. A., et al. (1997). Prefrontal dysfunction in depressed patients performing a complex planning task: A study. *Psychological Medicine, 27*(4), 931–942.

Elliott, R., Sahakian, B. J., Michael, A., Paykel, E. S., & Dolan, R. J. (1998). Abnormal neural response to feedback on planning and guessing tasks in patients with. *Psychological Medicine, 28*(3), 559–571.

Ellis, A. (1962). *Reason and emotion in psychotherapy.* Secaucus, NJ: Lyle Stuart.

Ellis, A., & Grieger, R. (1977). *Handbook of rational emotive therapy* (Vol. 1). New York: Springer.

Ellis, A., & Grieger, R. (1986). *Handbook of rational emotive therapy* (Vol. 2). New York: Springer.

Ennis, B. J., & Litwack, T. R. (1974). *Psychiatry and the presumption of expertise: Flipping coins in the courtroom.* California Law Review, 62, 693–752.

Epperson, C. N., Fasula, D., Wasylink, S., & Price, L. H. (1999). Risperidone addition in serotonin reuptake inhibitor-resistant trichotillomania: Three cases. *Journal of Child and Adolescent Psychopharmacology, 9*(1), 43–49.

Erickson, J. D., & Bjerkedal, T. O. (1981). Down syndrome associated with father's age in Norway. *Journal of Medical Genetics, 18,* 22–28.

Eriksson, E., & Humble, M. (1990). Serotonin and psychiatric pathophysiology: A review of data from experimental and clinical research. In R. Pohl & S. Gershon (Eds.), *The biological basis of psychiatric treatment: Progress in basic and clinical pharmacology.* Basel, Switzerland: Karger.

Erlanger, D. M., Kutner, K. C., Barth, J. T., & Barnes, R. (1999). Neuropsychology of sports-related head injury: Dementia pugilistica to post concussion. *Clinical Neuropsychologist, 13*(2), 193–209.

Erlenmeyer Kimling, L., Adamo, U. H., Rock, D., & Roberts, S. A. (1997). The New York High Risk Project: Prevalence and comorbidity of Axis I disorders in. *Archives of General Psychiatry, 54*(12), 1096–1102.

Escobar, J. I. (1996). Pharmacological treatment of somatization/hypochondriasis. *Psychopharmacology Bulletin, 32*(4), 589–596.

Eslinger, P. J., & Damasio, A. R. (1985). Severe disturbance of higher cognition after bilateral frontal lobe ablation: Patient EVR. *Neurology, 35,* 1731–1741.

Estes, W. K. (1991). Cognitive architectures from the standpoint of an experimental psychologist. *Annual Review of Psychology, 42,* 1–28.

Etzel, B. C., Hineline, P. N., Iwata, B. A., Johnston, J. M., Lindsley, O. R., McGrale, J. E., Morris, E. K., & Pennypacker, H. S. (1987). The ABA Humanitarian Awards for outstanding achievement in pursuit of the right to effective treatment. *Behavior Analyst, 10,* 235–237.

Etzersdorfer, E., Sonneck, G., & Nagel-Fuess, S. (1992). Newspaper reports and suicide. *New England Journal of Medicine, 327,* 502–550.

Evans, D. M. & Dunn, N. J. (1995). Alcohol expectancies, coping responses, and self-efficacy judgments: A replication and extension of Cooper et al.'s 1988 study in a college sample. *Journal of Studies on Alcohol, 56,* 186–193.

Evans, K., Tyrer, P., Catalan, J., Schmidt, U., Davidson, K., Dent, J., & Tata, P. (1999). Manual-assisted cognitive-behaviour therapy (MACT): A randomized controlled trial of a. *Psychological Medicine, 29*(1), 19–25.

Evans, R. L. (1981). New drug evaluations: Alprazolam. *Drug Intelligence and Clinical Pharmacy, 15,* 633–637.

Exner, J. E. (1993). *The Rorschach: A comprehensive system (Vol. 1. Basic foundations)* (3rd ed.). New York: Wiley.

Exner, J. E., & Weiner, I. B. (1994). *The Rorschach: A comprehensive system (Vol 3. Assessment of children and adolescents)* (2nd ed.). New York: Wiley.

Fahy, T. A. (1988). The diagnosis of multiple personality disorder: A critical review. *British Journal of Psychiatry, 153,* 597–606.

Fairburn, C. G., Agras, W. S., & Wilson, G. T. (1992). The research on the treatment of bulimia nervosa: Practical and theoretical implications. In G. Anderson & S. Kennedy (Eds.), *Biology of feast and famine: Relevance to eating disorders.* New York: Academic Press.

Fairburn, C. G., Jones, R., Peveler, R. C., Hope, R. A., & O'Connor, M. (1993). Psychotherapy and bulimia nervosa: Longer-term effects of interpersonal psychotherapy, behavior therapy, and cognitive therapy. *Archives of General Psychiatry, 50,* 419–428.

Falconer, D. S. (1960). *Introduction to quantitative genetics.* New York: Ronald Press.

Falk, B., Hersen, M., & Van Hasselt, V. B. (1994). Assessment of posttraumatic stress disorder in older adults: A critical review. *Clinical Psychology Review, 14,* 359–381.

Fallon, B. A., Klein, B. W., & Liebowitz, M. R. (1993). Hypochondriasis: Treatment strategies. *Psychiatric Annals, 23,* 374–381.

Fallon, B. A., Liebowitz, M. R., Campeas, R., & Schneier, F. R. (1998). Intravenous clomipramine for obsessive-compulsive disorder refractory to oral clomipramine. *Archives of General Psychiatry, 55*(10), 918–924.

Falloon, I. R., Boyd, J. L., McGill, C. W., Williamson, M., Razani, J., Moss, H. B., Gilderman, A. M., & Simpson, G. M. (1985). Family management in the prevention of morbidity of schizophrenia. *Archives of General Psychiatry, 42,* 887–896.

Faraone, S. V., & Biederman, J. (1998). Neurobiology of attention-deficit hyperactivity disorder. *Biological Psychiatry, 44*(10), 951–958.

Faraone, S. V., Chen, W. J., Goldstein, J. M., & Tsuang, M. T. (1994). Gender differences in age at onset of schizophrenia. *British Journal of Psychiatry, 164,* 625–629.

Farberow, N. L., & Shneidman, E. S. (1961). *The cry for help.* New York: McGraw-Hill.

Farberow, N. L., & Simon, M. D. (1975). Suicide in Los Angeles and Vienna. In N. L. Farberow (Ed.), *Suicide in different cultures.* Baltimore: University Park Press.

Farde, L., Wiesel, F., Halldin, C., & Sedvall, G. (1988). Central D2 dopamine receptor occupancy in schizophrenic patients treated with antipsychotic drugs. *Archives of General Psychiatry, 45,* 71–76.

Fava, G. A., Rafanelli, C., Grandi, S., & Canestrari, R. (1998). Six-year outcome for cognitive behavioral treatment of residual symptoms in major. *American Journal of Psychiatry, 155*(10), 1443–1445.

Fava, M., & Rosenbaum, J. F. (1991). Suicidality and fluoxetine: Is there a relationship? *Journal of Clinical Psychiatry, 52,* 108–111.

Fava, M., Rosenbaum, J. F., McGrath, P. J., Stewart, J. W., Amsterdam, J. D., & Quitkin, F. M. (1994). Lithium and tricyclic augmentation of fluoxetine treatment for resistant major depression: A double-blind controlled study. *American Journal of Psychiatry, 151,* 1372–1373.

Fawzy, F. I., Cousins, N., Fawzy, N. W., Kemeny, M. E., et al. (1990). A structured psychiatric intervention for cancer patients: I. Changes over time in methods of. *Archives of General Psychiatry, 47*(8), 720–725.

Fawzy, F. I., Kemeny, M. E., Fawzy, N. W., Elashoff, R., et al. (1990). A structured psychiatric intervention for cancer patients: II. Changes over time in. *Archives of General Psychiatry, 47*(8), 729–735.

Feingold, B. F. (1975). *Why your child is hyperactive.* New York: Random House.

Feingold, B. F. (1976). Hyperkinesis and learning disabilities linked to the ingestion of artificial food colors and flavors. *Journal of Learning Disabilities, 9,* 551–559.

Feldman, H. M., Kolmen, B. K., & Gonzaga, A. M. (1999). Naltrexone and communication skills in young children with autism. *Journal of the American Academy of Child and Adolescent Psychiatry, 38*(5), 587–593.

Femina, D. D., Yeager, C. A., & Lewis, D. O. (1990). Child abuse: Adolescent records v. adult recall. *Child Abuse and Neglect, 145,* 227–231.

Fenichel, O. (1945). *The psychoanalytic theory of neuroses.* New York: Norton.

Fenton, W., Wyatt, R. J., & McGlashan, T. H. (1994). Risk factors for spontaneous dyskinesia in schizophrenia. *Archives of General Psychiatry, 51,* 643–650.

Ferdinand, R. F., & Verhulst, F. C. (1995). Psychopathology from adolescence into young adulthood: An 8-year follow-up study. *American Journal of Psychiatry, 152,* 1586–1594.

Ferster, C. B. (1961). Positive reinforcement and behavioral deficits of autistic children. *Child Development, 32,* 437–456.

Figiel, G. S., Epstein, C., McDonald, W. M., & Amazon Leece, J. (1998). The use of rapid-rate transcranial magnetic stimulation (rTMS) in refractory depressed. *Journal of Neuropsychiatry and Clinical Neurosciences, 10*(1), 20–25.

Fillmore, M. T., & Vogel-Sprott, M. (1995). Expectancies about alcohol-induced motor impairment predict individual differences in responses to alcohol and placebo. *Journal of Studies on Alcohol, 56,* 90–98.

Fillmore, M. T., & Vogel-Sprott, M. (1996). Social drinking history, behavioral tolerance and the expectation of alcohol. *Psychopharmacology, 127*(4), 359–364.

Finegan, J., & Quarrington, B. (1979). Pre-, peri-, and neonatal factors and infantile autism. *Journal of Child Psychology and Psychiatry, 20,* 119–128.

Fink, M. (1999). *Electroshock: Restoring the mind.* Oxford University Press.

Finn, P. R., Young, S. N., Pihl, R. O., & Ervin, F. R. (1998). The effects of acute plasma tryptophan manipulation on hostile mood: The influence of trait. *Aggressive Behavior, 24*(3), 173–185.

Finn, P. R., Zeitouni, N. C., & Pihl, R. O. (1990). Effects of alcohol on psychophysiological hyperreactivity to nonaversive and aversive stimuli in men at high risk for alcoholism. *Journal of Abnormal Psychology, 99,* 79–85.

Finney, J. W., & Moos, R. H. (1998). Psychosocial treatments for alcohol use disorders. In P. E. Nathan & J. M. Gorman. (Eds.), *A guide to treatments that work* (pp. 156–166). New York: Oxford University Press.

Fiore, M. C., Jorenby, D. E., Baker, T. B., & Kenford, S. L. (1992). Tobacco dependence and the nicotine patch. *Journal of the American Medical Association, 268,* 2687–2694.

Firestone, P., Bradford, J. M., McCoy, M., Greenberg, D. M., & Curry, S. (1998). Recidivism in convicted rapists. *Journal of*

the *American Academy of Psychiatry and the Law, 26*(2), 185–200.

Fischbach, R. L., & Herbert, B. (1997). Domestic violence and mental health: Correlates and conundrums within and across cultures. *Social Science and Medicine, 45*(8), 1161–1176.

Fischer, M., Barkley, R. A., Edelbrock, C. S., & Smallish, L. (1990). The adolescent outcome of hyperactive children diagnosed by research criteria: 2. Academic, attentional, and neuropsychological status. *Journal of Consulting and Clinical Psychology, 58,* 580–588.

Fishbain, D. A. (1991). "Koro: Proposed classification for *DSM-IV*": Comment. *American Journal of Psychiatry, 148,* 1765–1766.

Fishbain, D. A., Cutler, R. B., Rosomoff, H. L., & Rosomoff, R. S. (1998). Do antidepressants have an analgesic effect in psychogenic pain and somatoform pain? *Psychosomatic Medicine, 60*(4), 503–509.

Fisher, S. (1994). Identifying video game addiction in children and adolescents. *Addictive Behaviors, 19,* 545–553.

Fitzgerald, P., & Kulkarni, J. (1998). Home-oriented management programme for people with early psychosis. *British Journal of Psychiatry, 172*(Suppl. 33), 39–44.

Flaum, M., Swayze, V. W., O'Leary, D. S., Yuh, W. T., Ehrhardt, J. C., Arndt, S. V., & Andreasen, N. C. (1995). Effects of diagnosis, laterality, and gender on brain morphology in schizophrenia. *American Journal of Psychiatry, 152,* 704–714.

Fluoxetine Bulimia Nervosa Collaborative Study Group. (1992). Fluoxetine in the treatment of bulimia nervosa. *Archives of General Psychiatry, 49,* 139–147.

Foa, E. B., Hearst Ikeda, D., & Perry, K. J. (1995). Evaluation of a brief cognitive-behavioral program for the prevention of chronic PTSD in. *Journal of Consulting and Clinical Psychology, 63*(6), 948–955.

Foa, E. B., Rothbaum, B. O., Riggs, D. S., & Murdock, T. B. (1991). Treatment of posttraumatic stress disorder in rape victims: A comparison between. *Journal of Consulting and Clinical Psychology.*

Folkerts, H. W., Michael, N., Toelle, R., Schonauer, K., & Muecke, S. (1997). Electroconvulsive therapy vs. paroxetine in treatment-resistant depression: A randomized. *Acta Psychiatrica Scandinavica, 96*(5), 334–342.

Folkman, S., & Lazarus, R. S. (1980). Coping in an adequately functioning middle-aged population. *Journal of Health and Social Behavior, 19,* 219–239.

Folland, S. S. (1975). *Suspected toluene exposure at a boot factory.* Internal report. Nashville: Tennessee Department of Health.

Folstein, S. E. (1991). Etiology of autism: Genetic influences. *Journal of Child Psychology and Psychiatry, 31,* 99–119.

Folstein, S. E., & Rutter, M. (1977). Infantile autism: A genetic study of 21 twin pairs. *Journal of Child Psychology and Psychiatry, 18,* 297–321.

Fombonne, E. (1999). The epidemiology of autism: A review. *Psychological Medicine, 29*(4), 769–786.

Fombonne, E., Roge, B., Claverie, J., Courty, S., & Fremolle, J. (1999). Microcephaly and macrocephaly in autism. *Journal of Autism and Developmental Disorders, 29*(3), 235–248.

Fonda, J. (1981). *Jane Fonda's workout book.* New York: Simon & Schuster.

Fortmann, S. P., & Killen, J. D. (1995). Nicotine gum and self-help behavioral treatment for smoking relapse prevention:

Results from a trial using population-based recruitment. *Journal of Consulting and Clinical Psychology, 63,* 460–468.

Fountain, J., Bartlett, H., Griffiths, P., Gossop, M., & Boys, A. (1999). Why say no? Reasons given by young people for not using drugs. *Addiction Research, 7*(4), 339–353.

Fowler, J. S., Volkow, N. D., Wang, G. J., Pappas, N., Logan, J., MacGregor, R., Alexoff, D., Shea, C., Schyler, D., Wolf, A. P., Warner, D. Zezulkova, I., & Cilento, R. (1996). Inhibition of monoamine oxidase B in the brains of smokers. *Nature, 379,* 733–736.

Franco, K. S., Campbell, N. Tamburrion, M. B., and Evans, C. (1993). Rumination: The eating disorder of infancy. *Child Psychiatry and Human Development, 24,* 91–97.

Frank, E. (1991). Interpersonal psychotherapy as a maintenance treatment for patients with recurrent depression. *Psychotherapy, 28,* 259–266.

Frank, E., Kupfer, D. J., & Perel, J. M. (1989). Early recurrence in unipolar depression. *Archives of General Psychiatry, 46,* 771–775.

Frank, E., Kupfer, D. J., Perel, J. M., Cornes, C. L., Jarrett, D. J., Mallinger, A., Tase, M. E., McEachran, A. B., & Grochocini, V. J. (1990). Three-year outcomes for maintenance therapies in recurrent depression. *Archives of General Psychiatry, 47,* 1093–1099.

Frank, E., Kupfer, D. J., Wanger, E. F., McEachran, A. B., & Cornes, C. L. (1991). Efficacy in interpersonal psychotherapy as a maintenance treatment for recurrent depression: Contribution factors. *Archives of General Psychiatry, 48,* 1053–1059.

Frank, E., & Spanier, C. (1995). Interpersonal psychotherapy for depression: Overview, clinical efficacy, and future directions. *Clinical Psychology Science and Practice, 2,* 349–369.

Frank, J. D. (1982). Therapeutic components shared by all psychotherapies. In J. H. Harvey & M. M. Parks (Eds.), *Psychotherapy research and behavior change* (Vol. 1). Washington, DC: American Psychological Association.

Franklin, J. E., Jr., & Frances, R. J. (1999). Alcohol and other psychoactive substance use disorders. In R. E. Hales, S. C. Yudofsky, & J. A. Talbot (Eds.), *Textbook of psychiatry* (pp. 363–424). Washington, DC: American Psychiatric Press.

Franklin, M. E., & Foa, E. B. (1998). Cognitive-behavioral treatments for obsessive-compulsive disorder. In P. E. Nathan & J. M. Gorman (Eds.), *A guide to treatments that work* (pp. 339–357). New York: Oxford University Press.

Frazier, J. A., Giedd, J. N., Hamburger, S. D., Albus, K. E., et al. (1996). Brain anatomic magnetic resonance imaging in childhood-onset schizophrenia. *Archives of General Psychiatry, 53*(7), 617–624.

Frederick, B. P., & Olmi, D. J. (1994). Children with attention-deficit hyperactivity disorder: A review of the literature on social skills deficits. *Psychology in the Schools, 31,* 288–296.

Fredericks, D. W., Carr, J. E., & Williams, W. L. (1998). Overview of the treatment of rumination disorder for adults in a residential setting. *Journal of Behavior Therapy and Experimental Psychiatry, 29* (1), 31–40.

Fredrikson, M., Annas, P., Fischer, H., & Wik, G. (1996). Gender and age differences in the prevalence of specific fears and phobias. *Behaviour Research and Therapy, 34*(1), 33–39.

Freed, E. X. (1971). Anxiety and conflict: Role of drug-dependent learning in the rat. *Quarterly Journal of Studies on Alcohol, 32,* 13–29.

Freeman, C. (1998). Drug treatment for bulimia nervosa. *Neuropsychobiology, 37* (2), 72–79.

Freeman, H. (1994). Schizophrenia and city residence. British *Journal of Psychiatry, 164,* 39–50.

Freeman, T. (1971). Observations on mania. *International Journal of Psychoanalysis, 52,* 479–486.

Freinkel, A., Koopman, C., & Spiegel, D. (1994). Dissociative symptoms in media eyewitnesses of an execution. *American Journal of Psychiatry, 151,* 1335–1339.

Freud, S. (1955a). Beyond the pleasure principle. In J. Strachey & A. Freud (Eds.), *The standard edition of the complete psychological works of Sigmund Freud* (Vol. 18). London: Hogarth Press. (Originally published 1920)

Freud, S. (1955b). A child is being beaten. In J. Strachey & A. Freud (Eds.), *The standard edition of the complete psychological works of Sigmund Freud* (Vol. 17). London: Hogarth Press. (Originally published 1919)

Freud, S. (1955c). The economic problems of masochism. In J. Strachey & A. Freud (Eds.), *The standard edition of the complete psychological works of Sigmund Freud* (Vol. 19). London: Hogarth Press. (Originally published 1925)

Freud, S. (1955d). Instincts and their vicissitudes. In J. Strachey & A. Freud (Eds.), *The standard edition of the complete psychological work of Sigmund Freud* (Vol. 14). London: Hogarth Press. (Originally published 1915)

Freud, S. (1955e). Mourning and melancholia. In J. Strachey & A. Freud (Eds.), *The standard edition of the complete psychological works of Sigmund Freud* (Vol. 14). London: Hogarth Press. (Originally published 1911)

Freud, S. (1957). The interpretation of dreams. In J. Strachey & A. Freud (Eds.), *The standard edition of the complete psychological works of Sigmund Freud* (Vol. 4). London: Hogarth Press. (Originally published 1900)

Frick, P. J., Lahey, B. B., Loeber, R., Stouthamer-Lober, M., Christ, M. A., & Hanson, K. (1992). Familial risk factors to oppositional defiant disorder and conduct disorder: Parental psychopathology and maternal parenting. *Journal of Consulting and Clinical Psychology, 60,* 49–55.

Friedman, M., & Rosenman, R. H. (1959). Association of specific overt behavior pattern with blood and cardiovascular findings: Blood cholesterol level, blood clotting time, incidence of arcus senilis and clinical coronary artery disease. *Journal of the American Medical Association, 169,* 1286–1296.

Friedman, M., & Rosenman, R. H. (1974). *Type A behavior and your heart.* New York: Knopf.

Friedman, M., Rosenman, R. H., & Carroll, V. (1958). Changes in the serum cholesterol and blood clotting time in men subjected to cyclic variation of occupational stress. *Circulation, 17,* 852–861.

Friedman, M., Thoresen, C. E., Gill, J. J., Powell, L. H., Ulmer, D., Thompson, L., Price, V. A., Rabin, D. D., Breall, W. S., Dixon, T., Levy, R., & Bourg, E. (1984). Alteration of Type A behavior and reduction in cardiac recurrences in postmyocardial infarction patients. *American Heart Journal, 108,* 237–248.

Friedman, M., & Ulmer, D. (1984). *Treating Type A behavior and your heart.* New York: Knopf.

Friedman, S., Hatch, M., Paradis, C. M., Poplin, M., & Shalita, A. R. (1993). Obsessive-compulsive disorder in two black ethnic groups: Incidence in an urban dermatology clinic. *Journal of Anxiety Disorders, 7,* 343–348.

Friman, P. C., & Vollmer, D. (1995). Successful use of the nocturnal urine alarm for diurnal enuresis. *Journal of Applied Behavior Analysis, 28,* 89–90.

Frost, R. O., & Green, M. (1982). Velten Mood Induction Procedure effects: Duration and post-experimental removal. *Personality and Social Psychology Bulletin, 8,* 341–348.

Fry, J. M. (1998). Treatment modalities for narcolepsy. *Neurology, 50*(2, Suppl. 1), S43–S48.

Frye, M. A., Ketter, T. A., Altshuler, L. L., Denicoff, K., & Dunn, R. T. (1998). Clozapine in bipolar disorder: Treatment implications for other atypical antipsychotics. *Journal of Affective Disorders, 48*(2–3), 91–104.

Fukuzako, H., Yamada, K., Kodama, S., & Yonezawa, T. (1997). Hippocampal volume asymmetry and age at illness onset in males with schizophrenia. *European Archives of Psychiatry and Clinical Neuroscience, 247*(5), 248–251.

Fuller, B. (1986, August 7). Parents sue agency head for $15 million [Press release]. United Press International.

Fuller, R. K., Branchey, L., Brightwell, D. R., Derman, R. M., Emrick, C. D., Iber, F. L., James, K. E., Laacoursiere, R. B., & Lowensstam, I. (1986). Disulfiram treatment of alcoholism. A Veterans Administration cooperative study. *Journal of the American Medical Association, 256,* 1449–1455.

Fullerton, D. T., Neff, S. and Carl, J. (1992). Persistent functional vomiting. *International Journal of Eating Disorders, 12,* 229–233.

Furst, S. S., & Ostow, M. (1979). The psychodynamics of suicide. In L. D. Hankoff & B. Einsidler (Eds.), *Suicide: Theory and clinical aspects.* Acton, MA: Publishing Sciences Group.

Futterweit, W. (1998). Endocrine therapy of transsexualism and potential complications of long-term treatment. *Arch. Sex. Behav., 27*(2), 209–226.

Gadow, K. D., Sverd, J., Sprafkin, J. Molan, E. E., & Grossman, S. (1999). Long-term methylphenidate therapy in children with comorbid attention deficit hyperactivity disorder and chronic multiple tic disorder. *Archives of General Psychiatry, 56*(4), 330–336.

Galin, D., Diamond, R., & Braff, D. (1977). Lateralization of conversion symptoms: More frequent on the left. *American Journal of Psychiatry, 134,* 578–580.

Gallagher, M., & Millar, R. (1998). Gender and age differences in the concerns of adolescents in Northern Ireland. *Adolescence, 33*(132), 863–876.

Gallagher, R. (1998). Nicotine withdrawal as an etiologic factor in delirium. *Journal of Pain and Symptom Management, 16*(2), 76–77.

Gallant, D. M. (1990). The Type 2 primary alcoholic? *Alcoholism Clinical and Experimental Research, 14,* 631.

Galvin, P. M., Knezek, L. D., Rush, A. J., & Toprac, M. G. (1999). Clinical and economic impact of newer versus older antipsychotic medications in a. *Clinical Therapeutics: The International Journal of Drug Therapy, 21,* 6.

Gange, P. (1981). Treatment of sex offenders with MPA. *American Journal of Psychiatry, 138,* 644–646.

Ganzini, L., McFarland, B. H., & Cutler, D. (1990). Prevalence of mental disorders after catastrophic financial loss. *Journal of Nervous and Mental Disease, 178,* 680–685.

Gao, S., Hendrie, H. C., Hall, K. S., & Hui, S. (1998). The relationships between age, sex, and the incidence of dementia and Alzheimer disease. *Archives of General Psychiatry, 55*(9), 809–815.

Garb, H. N. (1985). The incremental validity of information used in personality assessment. *Clinical Psychology Review, 4,* 641–655.

Garb, H. N. (1997). Race bias, social class bias, and gender bias in clinical judgment. *Clinical Psychology: Science and Practice, 4*(2), 99–120.

Garb, H. N., Florio, C. M., & Grove, W. M. (1998). The validity of the Rorschach and the Minnesota Multiphasic Personality Inventory: Results. *Psychological Science, 9*(5), 402–404.

Garbutt, J. C., West, S. L., Carey, T. S., & Lohr, K. N. (1999). Pharmacological treatment of alcohol dependence: A review of the evidence. *Journal of the American Medical Association, 281*(14), 1318–1325.

Gardner, D. L., & Cowdry, R. W. (1985). Alprazolam-induced dyscontrol in borderline personality disorder. *American Journal of Psychiatry, 142,* 98–100.

Gardner, E. L. (1999). The neurobiology and genetics of addiction: Implications of the "reward deficiency." In J. Elster et al. (Eds.), *Addiction: Entries and exits* (pp. 57–119). New York.

Gardner, E. L., & Lowinson, J. H. (1991). Marijuana's interaction with brain reward systems: Update 1991. *Pharmacology Biochemistry, and Behavior, 40,* 571–580.

Garland, A. F., & Zigler, E. (1993). Adolescent suicide prevention: Current research and social policy implications. *American Psychologist, 48,* 169–182.

Garretson, D. J. (1993). Psychological misdiagnosis of African Americans. *Journal of Multicultural Counseling and Development, 21,* 119–126.

Garrison, A. H. (1998). The history of the M'Naghten insanity defense and the use of posttraumatic stress disorder as. *American Journal of Forensic Psychology, 16*(4), 39–88.

Gatch, M. B., & Lai, H. (1998). Pharmacological treatment of alcoholism. *Progress in Neuro Psychopharmacology and Biological Psychiatry, 22,* 6.

Gaw, A. C., & Bernstein, R. L. (1992). Classification of amok in DSM-IV. Hospital and Community Psychiatry, 43, 789–793.

Gawin, F. H. (1991). Cocaine addiction: Psychology and neurophysiology. *Science, 251,* 1580–1586.

Geddes, J. R., & Lawrie, S. (1995). Obstetric complications and schizophrenia: A meta-analysis. *British Journal of Psychiatry, 167*(6), 786–793.

Geekie, K. M., & Brown, H. P. (1995). Treating substance abuse in the multidisabled: An overview. *Alcoholism Treatment Quarterly, 12,* 87–95.

Geer, J. H., & Fuhr, R. (1976). Cognitive factors in sexual arousal: The role of distraction. *Journal of Consulting and Clinical Psychology, 44,* 238–243.

Geffken, G.R., & Monaco, L. (1996). Assessment and treatment of encopresis. *Journal of Psychological Practice, 2*(3), 22–30.

Geller, J., Grudzinskas, A. J., Jr., McDermeit, M., & Fisher, W. H. (1998). The efficacy of involuntary outpatient treatment in Massachusetts. *Administration and Policy in Mental Health, 25*(3), 271–285.

Geller, M. I., Kelly, J. A., Traxler, W. T., & Marone, I. J. (1978). Behavioral treatment of an adolescent female's bulimic anorexia: Modification of immediate consequences and antecedent conditions. *Journal of Clinical Child Psychology, 14,* 138–141.

George, M. S. (1998). Why would you ever want to?: Toward understanding the antidepressant effect of prefrontal.

Human Psychopharmacology Clinical and Experimental, 13(5), 307–313.

George, M. S., Huggins, T., McDermut, W., Parekh, P. I., & Rubinow, D. (1998). Abnormal facial emotion recognition in depression: Serial testing in an ultra-rapid-cycling. *Behavior Modification, 22*(2), 192–204.

George, M. S., Ketter, T. A., Parekh, P. I., Herscovitch, P., et al. (1996). Gender differences in regional cerebral blood flow during transient self-induced sadness or. *Biological Psychiatry, 40*(9), 859–871.

George, M. S., Ketter, T. A., Parekh, P. I., Horwitz, B., Herscovitch, P., & Post, R. M. (1995). Brain activity during transient sadness and happiness in healthy women. *American Journal of Psychiatry, 152,* 341–351.

George, M. S., Ketter, T. A., & Post, R. M. (1994). Activation studies in mood disorders. *Psychiatric Annals, 24*(12), 648–652.

George, M. S., Lisanby, S. H., & Sackeim, H. A. (1999). Transcranial magnetic stimulation: Applications in neuropsychiatry. *Archives of General Psychiatry, 56*(4), 300–311.

George, M. S., Wassermann, E. M., Kimbrell, T. A., & Little, J. T. (1997). Mood improvement following daily left prefrontal repetitive transcranial magnetic stimulation. *American Journal of Psychiatry, 154*(12), 1752–1756.

George, M. S., Wassermann, E. M., & Post, R. M. (1996). Transcranial magnetic stimulation: A neuropsychiatric tool for the 21st century. *Journal of Neuropsychiatry and Clinical Neurosciences, 8*(4), 373–382.

George, M. S., Wassermann, E. M., Williams, W. A., Callahan, A., et al. (1995). Daily repetitive transcranial magnetic stimulation (rTMS) improves mood in depression.

Gerardi, R. J., Kean, T. M., Cahoon, B. J., & Wlauminzer, G. W. (1994). An in vivo assessment of physiological arousal in posttraumatic stress disorder. *Journal of Abnormal Psychology, 103,* 825–827.

Gerin, W., Pieper, C., Levy, R., & Pickering, T. G. (1992). Social support in social interaction: A moderator of cardiovascular reactivity. *Psychosomatic Medicine, 54,* 324–336.

Ghaemi, S. N., & Sachs, G. S. (1997). Long-term risperidone treatment in bipolar disorder: 6-month follow up. *International Clinical Psychopharmacology, 12*(6), 333–338.

Ghaziuddin, N., & Alessi, N. E. (1992). An open clinical trial of trazodone in aggressive children. *Journal of Child and Adolescent Psychopharmacology, 2,* 291–297.

Ghosh, T. B., & Victor, B. S. (1999). Suicide. In R. E. Hales, S. C. Yudofsky, & J. A. Talbot (Eds.), *Textbook of psychiatry* (pp. 1383–1404). Washington, DC: American Psychiatric Press.

Giansante, L. (1988, February 5). *The Morning Show,* National Public Radio.

Gibbs, N. (1999). Just a routine school shooting. *Time* (May 31), 34–38.

Giglio, J. C. (1998). A comment on World War II repression. *Professional Psychology: Research and Practice, 29*(5), 470.

Gilbert, P. L., Harris, M. J., McAdams, L. A., & Jeste, D. V. (1995). Neuroleptic withdrawal in schizophrenic patients. *Archives of General Psychiatry, 52,* 173–188.

Gillberg, C. (1991). Outcome in autism and autistic-like conditions. *Journal of the American Academy of Child and Adolescent Psychiatry, 30,* 375–382.

Gillberg, C. (1993). Asperger syndrome and clumsiness. *Journal of Autism and Developmental Disorders, 23,* 686–687.

Gillberg, C. (1999). Neurodevelopmental processes and psychological functioning in autism. *Development and Psychopathology, 11*(3), 567–587.

Gillberg, C., Gillberg, I. C. & Steffenburg, S. (1992). Siblings and parents of children with autism: A controlled population-based study. *Developmental Medicine and Child Neurology, 34,* 389–398.

Gillberg, C., & Schaumann, H. (1982). Social class and infantile autism. *Journal of Autism and Developmental Disorders, 12,* 223–228.

Gillberg, G., & Wing, L. (1999). Autism: Not an extremely rare disorder. *Acta Psychiatrica Scandinavica, 99*(6), 399–406.

Gilmore, J. H., Sikich, L., & Lieberman, J. A. (1997). Neuroimaging, neurodevelopment, and schizophrenia. *Child and Adolescent Psychiatric Clinics of North America, 6*(2), 325–341.

Gilmore, J. V. (1991). Murdering while asleep: Clinical and forensic issues. *Forensic Reports, 4,* 455–459.

Ginsberg, H. (1972). *The myth of the deprived child.* Englewood Cliffs, NJ: Prentice Hall.

Ginsburg, G. S., & Silverman, W. K. (1996). Phobic and anxiety disorders in Hispanic and Caucasian youth. *Journal of Anxiety Disorders, 10*(6), 517–528.

Giri, S., Thompson, P. D., Kiernan, F. J., Clive, J., Fram, D. B., Mitchel, J. F., Hirst, J. A., & McKay, R. G. (1999). Clinical and angiographic characteristics of exertion-related acute myocardial infarction. *Journal of the American Medical Association, 282*(18), 1731–1736.

Gist, R., & Welch, Q. B. (1989). Certification change versus actual behavior change in teenage suicide rates, 1955–1979. *Suicide and Life-Threatening Behavior, 19,* 277–288.

Gitlin, M. J., Swendsen, J., Heller, T. L., & Mammenen, C. (1995). Relapse and impairment in bipolar disorder. *American Journal of Psychiatry, 152,* 1635–1640.

Gittelman, R., & Kanner, A. (1986). Psychopharmacotherapy. In H. C. Quay & J. S. Werry (Eds.), *Psychopathological disorders of childhood* (3rd ed.) New York: Wiley.

Gladis, M. M., Levinson, D. F., & Mowry, B. J. (1994). Delusions in schizophrenia spectrum disorders: Diagnostic issues. *Schizophrenic Bulletin, 20,* 747–754.

Glantz, K., Durlach, N. I., Barnett, R. C., & Aviles, W. A. (1996). Virtual reality (VR) for psychotherapy: From the physical to the social environment. *Psychotherapy, 33*(3), 464–473.

Glass, D. C. (1977). *Behavior patterns, stress, and coronary disease.* Hillsdale, NJ: Erlbaum.

Glassman, A. H., & Shapiro, P. A. (1998). Depression and the course of coronary artery disease. *American Journal of Psychiatry, 155*(1), 4–11.

Glazer, H. I., & Weiss, J. M. (1976). Long-term interference effect: An alternative to "learned helplessness." *Journal of Experimental Psychology: Animal Behavioral Processes, 2,* 202–213.

Goadsby, P. J. (1998). Serotonin 5-HT$_{1B/1D}$ receptor agonists in migraine: Comparative. *CNS Drugs, 10*(4), 271–286.

Goetz, K., & Price, T. R. (1994). The case of koro: Treatment response and implications for diagnostic classification. *Journal of Nervous and Mental Disease, 182,* 590–591.

Goff, D. C., & Evins, A. E. (1998). Negative symptoms in schizophrenia: Neurobiological models and treatment response. *Harvard Review of Psychiatry, 6*(2), 59–77.

Goffinet, S., Seghers, A., Bol, A., Melin, J., & Cassiers, L. (1997). Cerebral glucose metabolism in retarded depression. *New Trends in Experimental and Clinical Psychiatry, 13*(2), 111–115.

Goffman, E. (1961). *Asylums: Essays on the social situation of mental patients and other inmates.* Garden City, NY: Doubleday.

Golan, H. P. (1997). The use of hypnosis in the treatment of psychogenic oral pain. *American Journal of Clinical Hypnosis, 40*(2), 89–96.

Gold, M. S. (1994). The epidemiology, attitudes, and pharmacology of LSD use in the 1990s. *Psychiatric Annals, 24,* 124–126.

Goldberg, C. (1998). Cognitive-behavioral therapy for panic: Effectiveness and limitations. *Psychiatric Quarterly, 69*(1), 23–44.

Goldberg, D. C., Whipple, B., Fishkin, R. E., Waxman, H., & Fink, P. J. (1983). The Grafenberg spot and female ejaculation: A review of initial hypotheses. *Journal of Sex and Marital Therapy, 9,* 27–37.

Goldberg, J., Szatmari, P., & Nahmias, C. (1999). Imaging of autism: Lessons from the past to guide studies in the future. *Canadian Journal of Psychiatry, 44*(8), 793–801.

Goldberg, J. F., Harrow, M., & Grossman, L. S. (1995). Course and outcome in bipolar affective disorder: A longitudinal follow-up study. *American Journal of Psychiatry, 152,* 379–384.

Goldenberg, M. M. (1998). Safety and efficacy of sildenafil citrate in the treatment of male erectile dysfunction. *Clinical Therapeutics: The International Journal of Drug Therapy, 20*(6), 1033–1048.

Golding, J. M., Smith, R., & Kashner, M. (1991). Does somatization disorder occur in men? *Archives of General Psychiatry, 48,* 321–325.

Goldman, M. J. (1992). Kleptomania: An overview. *Psychiatric Annals, 22,* 68–71.

Goldney, R. D. (1998). Suicide prevention is possible: A review of recent studies. *Archives of Suicide Research, 4*(4), 329–339.

Goldstein, D. J., Wilson, M. C., Ascroft, R. C., & Al-Banna, M. (1999). Effectiveness of fluoxetine therapy in bulimia nervosa regardless of comorbid depression. *International Journal of Eating Disorders, 25*(1), 19–27.

Goldstein, E. B. (1998). *Sensation and perception.* Belmont, CA: Wadsworth.

Goldstein, J. M., Goodman, J. M., Seidman, L. J., & Kennedy, D. N. (1999). Cortical abnormalities in schizophrenia identified by structural magnetic resonance imaging. *Archives of General Psychiatry, 57*(6), 537–547.

Goldstein, M. G. (1998). Bupropion sustained release and smoking cessation. *Journal of Clinical Psychiatry, 59*(Suppl. 4), 66–72.

Goldstein, M. J. (1980). Family therapy during the aftercare treatment of acute schizophrenia. In J. S. Strauss, M. Bowers, T. W. Dowey, S. Fleck, S. Jackson, & I. Levine (Eds.), *The psychotherapy of schizophrenia.* New York: Plenum.

Goldstein, R. B., Weissman, M. M., Adams, P. B., Horwath, E., Lish, J. D., Charney, D. S., Woods, S. W., Sobin, C., & Wickramaratne, P. J. (1994). Psychiatric disorders in relatives of probands with panic disorder and/or major depression. *Archives of General Psychiatry, 51,* 383–394.

Golomb, M., Fava, M., Abraham, M., & Rosenbaum, J. F. (1995). Gender differences in personality disorders. *American Journal of Psychiatry, 152,* 579–582.

Good, B. J. (1992). Culture, diagnosis, and comorbidity. *Culture, Medicine and Psychiatry, 16,* 427–446.

Goodman, S. H., & Emory, E. K. (1992). Perinatal complications in births to low socioeconomic status schizophrenic and depressed women. *Journal of Abnormal Psychology, 101,* 225–229.

Goodwin, A., & Williams, J. (1982). Mood-induction research: Its implications for clinical depression. *Behaviour Research and Therapy, 20,* 373–382.

Goodwin, F. K. (1999). Anticonvulsant therapy and suicide risk in affective disorders. *Journal of Clinical Psychiatry, 60*(Suppl. 2), 89–93.

Goodwin, J. (1980). The etiology of combat-related post-traumatic stress disorders. In T. Williams (Ed.), *Post-traumatic stress disorders of the Vietnam veteran.* Cincinnati, OH: Disabled American Veterans.

Gordon, C. T., State, R. C., Nelson, J. E., Hamburger, S. D., & Rapoport, J. (1993). A double-blind comparison of clomipramine, desipramine, and placebo in the treatment of autistic disorder. *Archives of General Psychiatry, 50,* 441–447.

Gorman, J. M. (1984). The biology of anxiety. In L. Grinspoon (Ed.), *Psychiatry update: The American Psychiatric Association annual review* (Vol. 3). Washington, DC: American Psychiatric Association.

Gorman, J. M., Goetz, R. R., Fyer, M., King, D. L., Fyer, A. J., Liebowitz, M. R., & Klein, D. F. (1988). The mitral valve prolapse–panic disorder connection. *Psychosomatic Medicine, 50,* 114–122.

Gorman, J. M., Papp, L. A., Coplan, J. D., Martinez, J. M., Lennon, S., Goetz, R. R., Ross, D., & Klein, D. F. (1994). Anxiogenic effects of CO2 and hyperventilation in patients with panic disorder. *American Journal of Psychiatry, 151,* 547–553.

Gormley, N., Cullen, C., Walters, L., Philpot, M., & Lawlor, B. (1998). The safety and efficacy of electroconvulsive therapy in patients over age 75. *International Journal of Geriatric Psychiatry, 13*(12), 871–874.

Gorwood, P., Bouvard, M., Mouren-Simeoni, M. C., Kipman, A., & Ades, J. (1998). Genetics and anorexia nervosa: a review of candidate genes. *Psychiatric Genetics, 8*(1), 1–12.

Gorwood, P., Leboyer, M., Jay, M., Payan, C., & Feingold, J. (1995). Gender and age at onset in schizophrenia: Impact of family history. *American Journal of Psychiatry, 152,* 208–212.

Goswami, M. (1998). The influence of clinical symptoms on quality of life in patients with narcolepsy. *Neurology, 50*(2, Suppl. 1), S31–S36.

Gotlib, I. H., & Krasnoperova, E. (1998). Biased information processing as a vulnerability factor for depression. *Behavior Therapy, 29*(4), 603–617.

Gotlib, I. H., Ranganath, C., & Rosenfeld, J. P. (1998). Frontal EEG alpha asymmetry, depression, and cognitive functioning. *Cognition and Emotion, 12*(3), 449–478.

Gotlib, I. H., Whiffen, V. E., Wallace, P. M., & Mount, J. H. (1991). Prospective investigation of postpartum depression: Factors involved in onset and recovery. *Journal of Abnormal Psychology, 100,* 122–132.

Gottesman, I. I. (1991). *Schizophrenia genesis.* New York: Freeman.

Gottesman, I. I., & Shields, J. (1972). *Schizophrenia and genetics: A twin study vantage point.* New York: Academic Press.

Gould, K. L., Ornish, D., Scherwitz, L., Brown, S., Edens, P., Hess, M. J., Mullani, N., Bolomey, L., Dobbs, F., Armstrong, W. T., Meritt, T., Ports, T., Sparler, S., & Billings, J. (1995). Changes in myocardial perfusion abnormalities by positron emission tomography after long-term, intense, risk factor modification. *Journal of the American Medical Association, 274,* 894–901.

Gould, M. S., Wallenstein, S., & Davidson, L. (1989). Suicide clusters: A critical review. *Suicide and Life-Threatening Behaviors, 19,* 17–29.

Gould, R. A., Otto, M. W., Pollack, M. H., & Yap, L. (1997). Cognitive behavioral and pharmacological treatment of generalized anxiety disorder: A preliminary meta-analyis. *Behavior Therapy, 28*(2), 285–305.

Govoni, R., Frisch, G. R., Rupcich, N., & Getty, H. (1998). First year impacts of casino gambling in a community. *Journal of Gambling Studies, 14*(4), 347–358.

Graham, J. R. (1990). *MMPI-2: Assessing personality and psychopathology.* New York: Oxford University Press.

Grant, I., Marcotte, T. D., & Heaton, R. K. (1999). Neurocognitive complications of HIV disease. *Psychological Science, 10*(3), 191–195.

Gray, P. (1988). *Freud: A life for our time.* New York: Norton.

Gray, P. (1989). *The Freud reader.* New York: W.W. Norton.

Greden, J. F., Fontaine, P., Lubetsky, M., & Chamberlin, K. (1978). Anxiety and depression associated with caffeinism among psychiatric inpatients. *American Journal of Psychiatry, 135,* 963–966.

Greden, J. F., & Tandon, R. (1995). Long-term treatment for lifetime disorders? *Archives of General Psychiatry, 52,* 197–200.

Green, J. F., McElholm, A., & King, D. J. (1996). A comparison of the sedative and amnestic effects of chlorpromazine and lorazepam. *Psychopharmacology, 128*(1), 67–73.

Green, R. (1974). *Sexual identity conflict in children and adults.* New York: Basic Books.

Green, R. (1976). One hundred ten feminine and masculine boys: Behavioral contrasts and demographic similarities. *Archives of Sexual Behavior, 5,* 425–446.

Green, R. (1985). Gender identity in childhood and later sexual orientation: Follow-up of 78 males. *American Journal of Psychiatry, 142,* 339–341.

Greenberg, D. M. (1998). Sexual recidivism in sex offenders. *Canadian Journal of Psychiatry, 43*(5), 459–465.

Greenberg, D. M., & Bradford, J. M. W. (1997). Treatment of the paraphilic disorders: A review of the role of the selective serotonin reuptake. *Sexual Abuse: Journal of Research and Treatment, 9*(4), 349–360.

Greenberg, D. M., Bradford, J. M. W., Curry, S., & O'Rourke, A. (1996). A comparison of treatment of paraphilias with three serotonin reuptake inhibitors. *Bulletin of the American Academy of Psychiatry and the Law, 24*(4), 525–532.

Greenblatt, D. J., & Shader, R. I. (1974). *Benzodiazepines in clinical practice.* New York: Raven Press.

Greenblatt, D. J., & Shader, R. I. (1978). Pharmacotherapy of anxiety with benzodiazepines and B-adrenergic blockers. In M. Lipton, A. Di Mascio, & K. Killam (Eds.), *Psychopharmacology: A generation of progress.* New York: Raven Press.

Greenblatt, M., Grosser, G. H., & Wechsler, H. (1964). Differential response of hospitalized depressed patients to somatic therapy. *American Journal of Psychiatry, 120,* 935–943.

Greenfield, S. F., & O'Leary, G. (1999). Sex differences in marijuana use in the United States. *Harvard Review of Psychiatry, 6*(6), 297–303.

Greenhill, L. (1998). Childhood attention deficit hyperactivity disorder: Pharmacological treatments. In P. E. Nathan & J. M. Gorman (Eds.), *A guide to treatments that work* (pp. 42–64). New York: Oxford University Press.

Greeno, C. G., & Wing, R. R. (1994). Stress-induced eating. *Psychological Bulletin, 115,* 444–464.

Greer, S., & Morris, T. (1978). The study of psychological factors in breast cancer: Problems of method. *Social Science and Medicine, 12*(3-A), 129–134.

Greil, W., Kleindienst, N., Erazo, N., & Mueller-Oerlinghausen, B. (1998). Differential response to lithium and carbamazepine in the prophylaxis of bipolar disorder. *Journal of Clinical Psychopharmacology, 18*(6), 455–460.

Greist, J. H., & Jefferson, J. W. (1998). Pharmacotherapy for obsessive-compulsive disorder. *British Journal of Psychiatry, 173*(Suppl. 35), 64–70.

Greist, J. H., Jefferson, J. W., Kobak, K. A., Katzelnick, D. J., & Serlin, R. C. (1995). Efficacy and tolerability of serotonin transport inhibitors in obsessive-compulsive disorder: A meta-analysis. *Archives of General Psychiatry, 52,* 53–60.

Griffith, E. E., & Gonzales, C. A. (1994). Essentials of cultural psychiatry. In R. Hales, S. Yudofsky, & J. Talbott (Eds.), *American Psychiatric Press textbook of psychiatry.* Washington, DC: American Psychiatric Press.

Griffith, E. E. H., Gonzalez, C. A., & Blue, H. C. (1999). The basics of cultural psychiatry. In R. E. Hales, S. C. Yudofsky, & J. A. Talbot (Eds.), *Textbook of psychiatry* (pp. 1463–1492). Washington, DC: American Psychiatric Press.

Grinspoon, L. (1977). *Marijuana reconsidered.* Cambridge, MA: Harvard University Press.

Grinspoon, L., Ewalt, J., & Shader, R. I. (1968). Psychotherapy and pharmacotherapy in chronic schizophrenia. *American Journal of Psychiatry, 124,* 67–75.

Grinspoon, L., Ewalt, J., & Shader, R. I. (1972). *Schizophrenia: Pharmacotherapy and psychotherapy.* Baltimore: Williams & Wilkins.

Grisaru, N., Chudakov, B., Yaroslavsky, Y., & Belmaker, R. H. (1998). Transcranial magnetic stimulation in mania: A controlled study. *American Journal of Psychiatry, 155*(11), 1608–1610.

Grisso, T. (1992). Five-year research update (1986–1990): Evaluations for competence to stand trial. *Behavioral Sciences and the Law, 10,* 353–369.

Gross, M. (1979). Pseudoepilepsy: A study in adolescent hysteria. *American Journal of Psychiatry, 136,* 210–213.

Gross, M. D. (1995). Origin of stimulant use for treatment of attention deficit disorder. *American Journal of Psychiatry, 152,* 298–299.

Grossman, L. S., Martis, B., & Fichtner, C. G. (1999). Are sex offenders treatable? A research overview. *Psychiatric Services, 50*(3), 349–361.

Groth, A. N., & Birnbaum, H. J. (1978). Adult sexual orientation and attraction to underage persons. *Archives of Sexual Behavior, 7,* 175–181.

Groth, A. N., Hobson, W. F., & Gary, T. S. (1982). The child molester: Clinical observations. In J. Conte & D. A. Shore (Eds.), *Social work and child sexual abuse.* New York: Haworth Press.

Grube, J. W., Chen, M. J., Madden, P., & Morgan, M. (1995). Predicting adolescent drinking from alcohol expectancy values: A comparison of addictive, interactive, and nonlinear models. *Journal of Applied Social Psycholgy, 25,* 839–857.

Gruber, A. J., Pope, H. G., & Oliva, P. (1997). Very long-term users of marijuana in the United States: A pilot study. *Substance Use and Misuse, 32*(3), 249–264.

Gruenewald, D. (1971). Hypnotic techniques without hypnosis in the treatment of a dual personality. *Journal of Nervous and Mental Disease, 153,* 41–46.

Gualtieri, T., Adams, A., Shen, D., & Loiselle, D. (1982). Minor physical anomalies in alcoholic and schizophrenic adults and hyperactive and autistic children. *American Journal of Psychiatry, 139,* 640–642.

Guerguerian, R., & Lewine, R. R. J. (1998). Brain torque and sex differences in schizophrenia. *Schizophrenia Research, 30*(2), 175–181.

Guess, D., Hemstetter, E., Turnbull, H. R., & Knowlton, S. (1987). Use of aversive procedures with persons who are disabled: A historical review and critical analysis. *Monograph for the Association for Persons with Severe Handicaps* (Whole No. 2).

Guilleminault, C., Heinzer, R., Mignot, E., & Black, J. (1998). Investigations into the neurologic basis of narcolepsy. *Neurology, 50*(2, Suppl. 1), S8–S15.

Guilleminault, C., Leger, D., Philip, P., & Ohayon, M. M. (1998). Nocturnal wandering and violence: Review of a sleep clinic population. *Journal of Forensic Sciences, 43*(1), 158–163.

Gupta, R., & Derevensky, J. L. (1998). Adolescent gambling behavior: A prevalence study and examination of the correlates. *Journal of Gambling Studies, 14*(4), 319–345.

Gur, R. E., Cowell, P., Turetsky, B. I., Gallacher, F., & Cannon, T. (1998). A follow-up magnetic resonance imaging study of schizophrenia: Relationship of. *Archives of General Psychiatry, 55*(2), 145–152.

Gur, R. E., Maany, V., Mozley, D., Swanson, C., & Bilker, W. (1998). Subcortical MRI volumes in neuroleptic-naive and treated patients with schizophrenia. *American Journal of Psychiatry, 155*(12), 1711–1717.

Gur, R. E., Turetsky, B. I., Bilker, W. B., & Gur, R. C. (1999). Reduced gray matter volume in schizophrenia. *Archives of General Psychiatry, 56*(10), 905–911.

Gureje, O., Uestuen, T. B., & Simon, G. E. (1997). The syndrome of hypochondriasis: A cross-national study in primary care. *Psychological Medicine, 27*(5), 1001–1010.

Guthrie, E., Mast, J., & Engel, M. (1999). Diagnosing genetic anomalies by inspection. *Child and Adolescent Psychiatric Clinics of North America, 8*(4), 777–790.

Guttmacher, L. B., Murphy, D. L., & Insel, T. R. (1983). Pharmacologic models of anxiety. *Comprehensive Psychiatry, 24,* 312–326.

Hachinski, V. (1999). Stalin's last years: Delusions or dementia? *European Journal of Neurology, 6*(2), 129–132.

Hadaway, P. F., Alexander, B. K., Coambs, R. B., & Beyerstein, B. (1979). The effect of housing and gender on preference for morphine-sucrose solutions in rats. *Psychopharmacology, 66,* 87–91.

Haddad, G. G., Mazza, N. M., Defendini, R., Blanc, W. A., Driscoll, J. M., Epstein, M A., Epstein, R. A., & Mellins, R. B. (1978). Congenital failure of automatic control of ventilation, gastrointestinal motility, and heart rate. *Medicine, 57,* 517–526.

Haensel, S. M., Klem, T. M. A. L., Hop, W. C. J., & Slob, A. K. (1998). Fluoxetine and premature ejaculation: A double-blind, crossover, placebo-controlled study. *Journal of Clinical Psychopharmacology, 18*(1), 72–77.

Hafner, H., & an der Heiden, W. (1997). Epidemiology of schizophrenia. *Canadian Journal of Psychiatry, 42,* 139–151.

Hajak, G., Clarenbach, P., Fischer, W., Rodenbeck, A., Bandelow, B., Broocks, A., & Ruether, E. (1998). Rebound insomnia after hypnotic withdrawal in insomniac outpatients. *European Archives of Psychiatry and Clinical Neuroscience, 248*(3), 148–156.

Hakim, A. A., Petrovitch, H., Burchiel, C. M., Ross, W., Rodriguez, B. L., White, L. R., Yano, K., Curb, J. D., & Abbott, R. D. (1998). Effects of walking on mortality among nonsmoking retired men. *New England Journal of Medicine, 338,* 94–99.

Haley, R. W., Kurt, T. L., & Hom, J. (1997). Is there a Gulf War syndrome? Searching for syndromes by factor analysis of symptoms. *Journal of the American Medical Association, 277*(3), 215–222.

Halford, W. K., & Hayes, R. (1991). Psychological rehabilitation of chronic schizophrenic patients: Recent findings on social skills training and family psychoeducation. *Clinical Psychology Review, 11,* 23–44.

Hall, G. C. N., Bansal, A., & Lopez, I. R. (1999). Ethnicity and psychopathology: A meta-analytic review of 31 years of comparative. *Psychological Assessment, 11*(2), 186–197.

Halmi, K. A. (1999). Eating disorders: Anorexia nervosa, bulimia nervosa, and obesity. In R. E. Hales, S. C. Yudofsky, & J. A. Talbot (Eds.), *Textbook of psychiatry* (pp. 983–1002). Washington, DC: American Psychiatric Press.

Halpern, C. T., Udry, J. R., & Suchindran, C. (1998). Monthly measures of salivary testosterone predict sexual activity in adolescent males. *Arch Sex Behav, 27*(5), 445–465.

Hambrecht, M., Riecher-Rossler, A., Fatkenheuer, B., Louza, M. R., & Hafner, H. (1994). Higher morbidity risk for schizophrenia in males: Fact or fiction? *Comprehensive Psychiatry, 35,* 39–49.

Hamburger, C., Sturup, G. K., & Kahl-Iversen, E. (1953). Transvestism: Hormonal, psychiatric, and surgical treatment. *Journal of the American Medical Association, 152,* 391–396.

Hamilton, E. W., & Abramson, L. Y. (1983). Cognitive patterns and major depressive disorder: A longitudinal study in a hospital setting. *Journal of Abnormal Psychology, 92,* 173–184.

Hammen, C., & Gitlin, M. (1997). Stress reactivity in bipolar patients and its relation to prior history of disorder. *American Journal of Psychiatry, 154*(6), 856–857.

Hammersley, R., Ditton, J., Smith, I., & Short, E. (1999). Patterns of ecstasy use by drug users. *British Journal of Criminology, 39*(4), 625–647.

Hanback, J. W., & Revelle, W. (1978). Arousal and perceptual sensitivity in hypochondriacs. *Journal of Abnormal Psychology, 87,* 523–530.

Handwerk, M. L., Larzelere, R. E., Soper, S. H., & Friman, P. C. (1999). Parent and child discrepancies in reporting severity of problem behaviors in three. *Psychological Assessment, 11*(1), 14–23.

Hanksworth, H., & Schwarz, T. (1977). *The five of me.* New York: Pocket Books.

Hanley, W., Levy, H. L., Shifrin, H., Allred, E., Azen, C., Chang, P., Schmidty, S., Cruz, F., Hall, R., Matalon, R., Nanson, J., Rouse, G., Trefz, F., & Rouse, R. (2000). Outcome at age 4 years in offspring of women with maternal phenyl-ketonuria. *Journal of the American Medical Association, 283,* 756–662.

Hanna, G. L. (1997). Trichotillomania and related disorders in children and adolescents. *Child Psychiatry and Human Development, 27*(4), 255–268.

Hans, S. L., Marcus, J., Nuechterlein, K. H., & Asarnow, R. F. (1999). Neurobehavioral deficits at adolescence in children at risk for schizophrenia: The Jerusalem. *Archives of General Psychiatry, 56*(8), 741–748.

Hanson, D. R., & Gottesman, I. I. (1976). The genetics, if any, of infantile autism and childhood schizophrenia. *Journal of Autism and Childhood Schizophrenia, 6,* 209–234.

Hanson, R. K., & Bussiere, M. T. (1998). Predicting relapse: A meta-analysis of sexual offender recidivism studies. *Journal of Consulting and Clinical Psychology, 66*(2), 348–362.

Hare, R. D. (1965). Acquisition and generalization of a conditioned-fear response in psychopathic and non-psychopathic criminals. *Journal of Psychology, 59,* 367–370.

Hare, R. D., & Craigen, D. (1974). Psychopathy and physiological activity in a mixed-motive game situation. *Psychophysiology, 11,* 197–203.

Hare, R. D., McPherson, L. M., & Forth, A. E. (1988). Male psychopaths and their criminal careers. *Journal of Consulting and Clinical Psychology, 56,* 710–714.

Hare, R. D., & Quinn, M. J. (1971). Psychopathy and autonomic conditioning. *Journal of Abnormal Psychology, 77,* 223–235.

Harlow, H. F. (1959). Love in infant monkeys. *Scientific American, 54,* 244–272.

Harris, B. (1979). Whatever happened to Little Albert? *American Psychologist, 34,* 151–160.

Harris, J. A., Rushton, J. P., Hampson, E., & Jackson, D. N. (1996). Salivary testosterone and self-report aggressive and pro-social personality characteristics in. *Aggressive Behavior, 22*(5), 321–331.

Harris, J. A., Vernon, P. A., & Boomsma, D. I. (1998). The heritability of testosterone: A study of Dutch adolescent twins and their parents. *Behavior Genetics, 28*(3), 165–171.

Hartel, D. M., Schoenbaum, E. E., Selwyn, P. A., Kline, J., & Friedland, G. H. (1995). Heroin use during methadone maintenance treatment: The importance of methadone dose and cocaine use. *American Journal of Public Health, 85,* 83–88.

Hartl, T. L., & Frost, R. O. (1999). Cognitive-behavioral treatment of compulsive hoarding: A multiple baseline experimental case study. *Behaviour Research and Therapy, 37*(5), 451–461.

Hatsukami, D., Skoog, K., Allen, S., & Bliss, R. (1995). Gender and the effects of different doses of nicotine gum on tobacco withdrawal symptoms. *Experimental and Clinical Psychopharmacology, 3,* 163–173.

Hawton, K. (1992). Suicide and attempted suicide. In E. S. Paykel (Ed.), *Handbook of affective disorders,* (2nd ed.) New York: Guilford Press.

Hay, P., Sachdev, P., Cumming, S., Smith, J. S., Lee, T., Kitchener, P., & Matheson, J. (1993). Treatment of obsessive-compulsive disorder by psychosurgery. *Acta Psychiatrica Scandinavica, 87,* 197–207.

Hayes, S. C. & Heibly, E. (1996). Psychology's drug problem: Do we need a fix or should we just say no? *American Psychologist, 51,* 198–206.

Haynes, S. G., Levine, S., Scotch, N., Feinleib, M., & Kannel, W. B. (1978). The relationship of psychosocial factors to coronary heart disease in the Framingham Study: 1. Methods and risk factors. *American Journal of Epidemiology, 107,* 362–383.

Hayslip, B. (1989). Alternative mechanisms for improvements in fluid ability performance among older adults. *Psychology and Aging, 4*(1), 122–124.

Hazlett, E. A., Buchbaum, M. S., Byne, W., & Wei, T. C. (1999). Three-dimensional analysis with MRI and PET of the size, shape, and function of the. *American Journal of Psychiatry, 156*(8), 1190–1199.

Heatherton, T. F., Herman, C. P., & Polivy, J. (1991). Effects of physical threat and ego threat on eating behavior. *Journal of Personality and Social Psychology, 60,* 138–143.

Heaton, R., Paulsen, J. S., McAdams, L., Kuck, J., Zissok, S., Braff, D., Harris, M. J., & Jeste, D. V. (1994). Neuropsychological deficits in schizophrenics. *Archives of General Psychiatry, 51,* 469–476.

Heavey, L., Pring, L., & Hermelin, B. (1999). A date to remember: The nature of memory in savant calendrical calculators. *Psychological Medicine, 29*(1), 145–160.

Hebb, D. O. (1949). *Organization of behavior.* New York: Wiley.

Hecker, J. E., Fink, C. M., Vogeltanz, N. D., & Thorpe, G. L. (1998). Cognitive restructuring and interoceptive exposure in the treatment of panic disorder. *Behavioural and Cognitive Psychotherapy, 26*(2), 115–131.

Hefez, A. (1985). The role of the press and the medical community in the epidemic of "mysterious gas poisoning" in the Jordan West Bank. *American Journal of Psychiatry, 142,* 833–837.

Heiligenstein, J. H., Coccaro, E. F., Potvin, J. H., Beasley, C. M., Dornseif, B. E., & Mascia, D. N. (1992). Fluoxetine not associated with increased violence or aggression in controlled clinical trials.

Heim, N. (1981). Sexual behavior of castrated sex offenders. *Archives of Sexual Behavior, 10,* 11–19.

Heimberg, R. G., Dodge, C. S., Hope, D. A., Kennedy, C. R., & Zollo, L. J. (1990). Cognitive behavioral group treatment for social phobia: Comparison with a credible placebo control. *Cognitive Therapy and Research, 14,* 1–23.

Helgeson, V. S., & Fritz, H. L. (1999). Cognitive adaptation as a predictor of new coronary events after percutaneous transluminal. *Psychosomatic Medicine, 61*(4), 488–495.

Helmes, E., & Reddon, J. R. (1993). A perspective on developments in assessing psychopathology: A critical review of the MMPI and MMPI-2. *Psychological Bulletin, 113,* 453–471.

Helzer, J. E., Robin, L. N., & McEvoy, L. (1987). Posttraumatic stress disorder in the general population: Findings from the Epidemiological Catchment Area Survey. *New England Journal of Medicine, 317,* 1630–1634.

Hemmelgarn, B., Suissa, S., Huang, A., Boivin, J., & Pinard, G. (1997). Benzodiazepine use and the risk of motor vehicle crash in the elderly. *Journal of the American Medical Association, 278,* 27–31.

Henderson, J. L., & Moore, M. M. (1944). The psychoneuroses of war. *New England Journal of Medicine, 230,* 273–278.

Hendin, H. (1999). Suicide, assisted suicide, and medical illness. *Journal of Clinical Psychiatry, 60*(Suppl. 2), 46–50.

Hendrick, V., Altshuler, L. L., & Burt, V. K. (1996). Course of psychiatric disorders across the menstrual cycle. *Harvard Review of Psychiatry, 4*(4), 200–207.

Hendrick, V., Altshuler, L. L., & Suri, R. (1998). Hormonal changes in the postpartum and implications for postpartum depression. *Psychosomatics, 39*(2), 93–101.

Henon, H., Pasquier, F., Durieu, I., Pruvo, J. P., & Leys, D. (1998). Medial temporal lobe atrophy in stroke patients: Relation to pre-existing dementia. *Journal of Neurology, Neurosurgery and Psychiatry, 65*(5), 641–647.

Henson, D. E., & Rubin, H. B. (1971). Voluntary control of eroticism. *Journal of Applied Behavior Analysis, 4,* 37–44.

Herbert, T. B., & Cohen, S. (1993). Depression and immunity: A meta-analytic review. *Psychological Bulletin, 113,* 472–486.

Hermelin, B., O'Connor, N., & Lee, S. (1987). Musical inventiveness of five idiots-savants. *Psychological Medicine, 17*(3), 685–694.

Herrington, R. N., & Lader, M. H. (1981). Lithium. In H. Van Praag, M. H. Lader, O. Rafaelsen, & E. Sachar (Eds.), *Handbook of biological psychiatry: Vol. 5., Drug treatment in psychiatry: Psychotropic drugs.* New York: Dekker.

Hersh, D., Kranzler, H. R., & Meyer, R. E. (1997). Persistent delirium following cessation of heavy alcohol consumption: Diagnostic and treatment implications. *American Journal of Psychiatry, 154*(6), 846–851.

Hersh, D., Van Kirk, J. R., & Kranzler, H. R. (1998). Naltrexone treatment of comorbid alcohol and cocaine use disorders. *Psychopharmacology, 139*(1–2), 44–52.

Herz, M. I., Lamberti, J. S., Mintz, J., Scott, R., & O'Dell. (2000). A program for relapse prevention in schizophrenia: A controlled study. *Archives of General Psychiatry, 57*(3), 277–283.

Heston, L. L. (1966). Psychiatric disorders in foster-home-reared children of schizophrenic mothers. *British Journal of Psychiatry, 112,* 819–825.

Hewitt, P. L., Norton, R., Flett, G. L., Callander, L., & Cowan, T. (1998). Dimensions of perfectionism, hopelessness, and attempted suicide in a sample of alcoholics. *Suicide and Life Threatening Behavior, 28*(4), 395–406.

Hietala, J., Syvalahti, E., Vuorio, K., Nagren, K., Lehikoinen, P., Ruotsalainen, U., Rakkolaien, V., Lehtinen, V., & Wegelius, U. (1994). Striatal D2 dopamine receptor characteristics in neuroleptic-naive schizophrenic patients studied with positron emission tomography. *Archives of General Psychiatry, 51,* 116–123.

Higashi, Y., Sasaki, S., Kurisu, S., Yoshimizu, A., Sasaki, N., Matsuura, H., & Kajiyama, G. (1999). Regular aerobic exercise augments endothelium-dependent vascular relaxation in. *Circulation, 100*(11), 1194–2002.

Higgins, S. T., Budney, A. J., Bickel, W. K., Foerg, F. E., Donham, R., & Badger, G. J. (1994). Incentives improve outcome in outpatient behavioral treatment of cocaine dependence. *Archives of General Psychiatry, 51,* 568–576.

Highley, J. R., Esiri, M. M., McDonald, B., Cooper, S. J., & Crow, T. J. (1998). Temporal-lobe length is reduced, and gyral folding is increased in schizophrenia. *Schizophrenia Research, 34*(1–2), 1–12.

Highley, J. R., Esiri, M. M., McDonald, B., Cortina Borja, M., & Cooper, S. J. (1998). Anomalies of cerebral asymmetry in schizophrenia interact with gender and age of onset. *Schizophrenia Research, 34*(1–2), 13–25.

Higley, J. D., Thompson, W. W., Champoux, M., Goldman, D., Hasert, M. F., Kraemer, G. W., Scanlan, J. M., Suomi, S. J., & Linnoila, M. (1993). Parental and maternal genetic and environmental contributions to cerebrospinal fluid monoamine metabolites in rhesus monkeys (Macaca mulatta). *Archives of General Psychiatry, 50,* 615–623.

Hilgard, E. R., & Marquis, D. G. (1961). *Conditioning and learning* (rev. ed.). Norwalk, CT: Appleton & Lange.

Hilts, P. (1995). *Memory's ghost.* New York: Simon & Schuster.

Hilty, D. M., & Servis, M. E. (1999). Psychiatry and primary care. In R. E. Hales, S. C. Yudofsky, & J. A. Talbot (Eds.), *Textbook of psychiatry* (pp. 1617–1644). Washington, DC: American Psychiatric Press.

Hindmarch, I., & Brinkmann, R. (1999). Trends in the use of alcohol and other drugs in cases of sexual assault. *Human Psychopharmacology Clinical and Experimental, 14*(4), 225–231.

Hinshaw, S. P. (1991). Stimulant medication and the treatment of aggression in children with attention deficits. *Journal of Clinical Child Psychology, 20,* 301–312.

Hinshaw, S. P., Heller, T., & McHale, J. P. (1992). Covert antisocial behavior in boys with attention-deficit hyperactivity disorder: Validation and effects of methylphenidate. *Journal of Consulting and Clinical Psychology, 60,* 274–281.

Hinshaw, S. P., Klein, R. G., & Abikoff, H. (1998). Childhood attention deficit hyperactivity disorder: Nonpharmacological and combination treatments. In P. E. Nathan & J. M. Gorman (Eds.), *A guide to treatments that work* (pp. 26–41). New York: Oxford University Press.

Hinton-Bayre, A. D., Geffen, G. M., Geffen, L. B., & McFarland, K. A. (1999). Concussion in contact sports: Reliable change indices of impairment and recovery. *Journal of Clinical and Experimental Neuropsychology, 21*(1), 70–86.

Hiramoto, R. N., Solvason, H. B., Hsueh, C. M., & Rogers, C. F. (1999). Psychoneuroendocrine immunology: Perception of stress can alter body temperature and natural. *International Journal of Neuroscience, 98*(1–2), 95–129.

Hirayasu, Y., Shenton, M. E., Salisbury, D. F., & Dickey, C. C. (1998). Lower left temporal lobe MRI volumes in patients with first-episode schizophrenia compared. *American Journal of Psychiatry, 155*(10), 1384–1391.

Hiroto, D. S. (1974). Locus of control and learned helplessness. *Journal of Experimental Psychology, 102,* 187–193.

Hiroto, D. S., & Seligman, M. E. P. (1975). Generality of learned helplessness in man. *Journal of Personality and Social Psychology, 31,* 311–327.

Hitchcock, P. B. & Mathews, A. (1992). Interpretation of bodily symptoms in hypochondriasis. *Behaviour Research and Therapy, 31,* 223–234.

Hittner, J. B. (1995). Tension-reduction expectancies and alcoholic beverage preferences revisited: Associations to drinking frequency and gender. *International Journal of the Addictions, 30,* 323–336.

Hobson, J. A. (1988). *The dreaming brain.* New York: Basic Books.

Hobson, J. A., & McCarley, R. W. (1977). The brain as a dream state generator: An activation-synthesis hypothesis of the dream process. *American Journal of Psychiatry, 134,* 1335–1348.

Hochman, J., & Pope, H. G., Jr. (1997). Debating dissociative diagnoses. American Journal of Psychiatry, 154(6), 887–888.

Hoek, H. W., Susser, E., Buck, K. A., & Lumey, L. H. (1996). Schizoid personality disorder after prenatal exposure to famine. *American Journal of Psychiatry, 153*(12), 1637–1639.

Hoek, H. W., van Harten, P. N., van Hoeken, D., & Susser, E. (1998). Lack of relation between culture and anorexia nervosa: results of an incidence study on Curacao. *New England Journal of Medicine, 338* (17), 1231–1232.

Hoffman, R. E., & McGlashan, T. H. (1997). Synaptic elimination, neurodevelopment, and the mechanism of hallucinated "voices" in. *American Journal of Psychiatry, 154*(12), 1683–1689.

Hogarty, G. E., Anderson, C. M., Reiss, D. J., Kornblith, S. J., Greenwald, D. P., Javna, C. D., & Madonia, M. J. (1986). Family psychoeducation, social skills training, and maintenance chemotherapy in the aftercare treatment of schizophrenia. *Archives of General Psychiatry, 43,* 633–642.

Hogarty, G. E., Anderson, C. M., Reiss, D. J., Kornblith, S. J., Greenwald, D. P., Ulrich, R. F., & Carter, M. (1991). Family psychoeducation, social skills training, and maintenance chemotherapy in the aftercare treatment of schizophrenia: 2. Two-year effects of a controlled study on relapse and adjustment. *Archives of General Psychiatry, 48,* 340–347.

Hogarty, G. E., Greenwald, D., Ulrich, R. F., & Kornblith, S. J. (1997). Three-year trials of personal therapy among schizophrenic patients living with or independent. *American Journal of Psychiatry, 154*(11), 1514–1524.

Hoge, M. A., Davidson, L., & Sledge, W. H. (1997). Alternatives to acute hospitalization. In K. Minkoff, D. Pollack, et al. (Eds.), *Managed mental health care in.*

Hoge, S. K. (1994). On being "too crazy" to sign into a mental hospital: The issue of consent to psychiatric hospitalization. *Bulletin of the American Academy of Psychiatry and the Law, 22,* 431–451.

Hohagen, F., Winkelmann, G., Rasche Raeuchle, H., & Hand, I. (1998). Combination of behaviour therapy with fluvoxamine in comparison with behaviour therapy. *British Journal of Psychiatry, 173*(Suppl. 35), 71–78.

Holahan, C. K., Holahan, C. J., & Belk, S. S. (1984). Adjustment in aging: The roles of life stress, hassles, and self-efficacy. *Health Psychology, 3,* 315–328.

Hollander, E. (1998). Treatment of obsessive-compulsive spectrum disorders with SSRIs. *British Journal of Psychiatry, 173*(Suppl. 35), 7–12.

Hollander, E., Allen, A., Kwon, J., Aronowitz, B., Schmeidler, J., Wong, C., & Simeon, D. (1999). Clommipramine vs. desipramine crossover trial in body dysmorphic disorder. *Archives of General Psyeniatry, 56,* 1033–1039.

Hollander, E., & Benzaquen, S. (1997). The obsessive-compulsive spectrum disorders. *International Review of Psychiatry, 9*(1), 99–110.

Hollander, E., DeCaria, C. M., Mari, E., & Wong, C. M. (1998). Short-term single-blind fluvoxamine treatment of patholog-

ical gambling. *American Journal of Psychiatry, 155*(12), 1781–1783.

Hollander, E., DeCaria, C. M., Nitescu, A., Gully, R., Suckow, R., Cooper, T. B., Gorman, J., Klein, D. F., & Liebowitz, M. (1994). Serotonergic function in obsessive-compulsive disorder: Behavioral and neuroendocrine responses to oral m-chlorophenylpiperazine and flenluramine in patients and healthy volunteers. *Archives of General Psychiatry, 49,* 21–28.

Hollander, E., Schiffman, E., Cohen, B., Rivera-Stein, M. A., Rosen, W., Gorman, J. M., Fyer, A. J., Papp, L., & Liebowitz, M. R. (1990). Signs of central nervous system dysfunction in obsessive-compulsive disorder. *Archives of General Psychiatry, 47,* 27–32.

Hollander, E., Simeon, D., & Gorman, J. M. (1999). Anxiety disorders. In R. E. Hales, S. C. Yudofsky, & J. A. Talbot (Eds.), *Textbook of psychiatry* (pp. 567–634). Washington, DC: American Psychiatric Press.

Hollingshead, A. B., & Redlich, F. C. (1958). *Social class and mental illness.* New York: Wiley.

Hollister, J. M., Mednick, S. A., Brennan, P., & Cannon, T. D. (1994). Impaired autonomic nervous system habituation in those at genetic risk for schizophrenia. *Archives of General Psychiatry, 51,* 552–558.

Hollon, S. D., & Beck, A. T. (1979). Cognitive therapy of depression. In P. C. Kendall & S. D. Hollon (Eds.), *Cognitive-behavioral interventions: Theory, research, and procedures.* New York: Academic Press.

Holm, J. E., Lokken, C., & Myers, T. C. (1997). Migraine and stress: A daily examination of temporal relationships in women migraineurs. *Headache, 37*(9), 553–558.

Holmes, D. S. (1967). Verbal conditioning or problem solving and cooperation? *Journal of Experimental Research in Personality, 2,* 289–295.

Holmes, D. S. (1968). Dimensions of projection. *Psychological Bulletin, 69,* 248–268.

Holmes, D. S. (1971). The conscious self-appraisal of achievement motivation: The self-peer rank method revisited. *Journal of Consulting and Clinical Psychology, 36,* 23–26.

Holmes, D. S. (1974). Investigations of repression: Differential recall of material experimentally or naturally associated with ego threat. *Psychological Bulletin, 81,* 632–653.

Holmes, D. S. (1981). Existence of classical projection and the stress-reducing function of attributive projection: A reply to Sherwood. *Psychological Bulletin, 90,* 460–466.

Holmes, D. S. (1983). An alternative perspective concerning the differential physiological responsivity of persons with Type A and Type B behavior patterns. *Journal of Research in Personality, 17,* 40–47.

Holmes, D. S. (1984). Meditation and somatic arousal: A review of the experimental evidence. *American Psychologist, 39,* 1–10.

Holmes, D. S. (1985). Self-control of somatic arousal: An examination of meditation and biofeedback. *American Behavioral Scientist, 28,* 486–496.

Holmes, D. S. (1987). The influence of meditation versus rest on physiological arousal: A second examination. In M. A. West (Ed.), *The psychology of meditation.* Oxford: Oxford University Press.

Holmes, D. S. (1990). The evidence for repression: An examination of sixty years of research. In J. L. Singer (Ed.), *Repression and dissociation.* Chicago: University of Chicago Press.

Holmes, D. S. (1993). Aerobic fitness and the response to psychological stress. In P. Seraganian (Ed.), *Exercise psychology: The influence of physical exercise on psychological processes.* New York: Wiley.

Holmes, D. S., & Burish, T. G. (1984). Effectiveness of biofeedback for treating migraine and tension headaches: A review of the evidence. *Journal of Psychosomatic Research, 27,* 515–532.

Holmes, D. S., & Houston, B. K. (1974). Effectiveness of situation redefinition and affective isolation for reducing stress. *Journal of Personality and Social Psychology, 29,* 212–218.

Holmes, D. S., & McGilley, B. M. (1987). Influence of a brief aerobic training program on heart rate and subjective response to stress. *Psychosomatic Medicine, 49,* 366–374.

Holmes, D. S., McGilley, B. M., & Houston, B. K. (1984). Task-related arousal of Type A and Type B persons: Level of challenge and response specificity. *Journal of Personality and Social Psychology, 46,* 1322–1327.

Holmes, D. S., & Roth, D. L. (1985). Association of aerobic fitness with pulse rate and subjective responses to psychological stress. *Psychophysiology, 22,* 525–529.

Holroyd, K. A., and Penzien, D. B. (1994). Psychosocial interventions in the management of recurrent headache disorders: 1. Overview and effectiveness. *Behavioral Medicine, 20,* 53–63.

Honigfeld, G., & Patin, J. (1990). A two-year clinical and economic follow-up of patients on clozapine. *Hospital and Community Psychiatry, 41,* 882–885.

Hook, E. B. (1982). Epidemiology of Down syndrome. In S. M. Pueschel & J. E. Rynders (Eds.), *Down syndrome: Advances in biomedicine and the behavioral sciences.* Cambridge, MA: Ware Press.

Hook, E. B., & Chambers, G. M. (1977). Estimated rates of Down's syndrome in live births by one-year maternal age intervals for mothers aged 20 to 49 in a New York State study. In D. Bergsma, R. B. Lowry, B. K. Trimble, & M. Feingold (Eds.), *Numerical taxonomy of birth defects and polygenic disorders* (pp. 123–141). New York: Liss.

Hook, E. B., & Fabia, J. J. (1978). Frequency of Down syndrome by single-year maternal age interval: Results of a Massachusetts study. *Teratology, 17,* 223–228.

Hook, E. B., & Lindsjo, A. (1978). Down syndrome in live births by single-year maternal age interval in a Swedish study: Comparison with results from a New York study. *American Journal of Human Genetics, 30,* 19–27.

Hook, M. K., & Cleveland, J. L. (1999). To tell or not to tell: Breaching confidentiality with clients with HIV and AIDS. *Ethics and Behavior, 9*(4), 365–381.

Hopkins, J., Marcus, M., & Campbell, S. B. (1984). Postpartum depression: A critical review. *Psychological Bulletin, 95,* 498–515.

Horney, K. (1937). *Neurotic personality of our times.* New York: Norton.

Horney, K. (1939). *New ways in psychoanalysis.* New York: Norton.

Horney, K. (1945). *Our inner conflicts.* New York: Norton.

Horney, K. (1967). *Feminine psychology.* New York: Norton.

Horwitz, W. A., Deming, W. E., & Winter, R. F. (1969). A further account of the idiots savants, experts with the calendar. *American Journal of Psychiatry, 126*(3), 412–415.

Houston, B. K. (1983). Psychophysiological responsivity and the Type A behavior pattern. *Journal of Research in Personality, 17,* 22–39.

Houston, B. K., Chesney, M. A., Black, G. W., Cates, D. S., & Hecker, M. H. (1992). Behavioral clusters and coronary heart disease risk. *Psychosomatic Medicine, 54,* 447–461.

Houston, B. K., & Holmes, D. S. (1974). Effectiveness of avoidant thinking and reappraisal in coping with threat involving temporal uncertainty. *Journal of Personality and Social Psychology, 30,* 382–388.

Howells, K. (1981). Adult sexual interest in children: Considerations relevant to theories of etiology. In M. Cook & K. Howells (Eds.), *Adult sexual interest in children.* London: Academic Press.

Howlin, P., & Moore, A. (1997). Diagnosis in autism: A survey of over 1200 patients in the UK. *Autism, 1*(2), 135–162.

Howsepian, A. A. (1998). Post-traumatic stress disorder following needle-stick contaminated with suspected. *General Hospital Psychiatry, 20*(2), 123–124.

Hucker, S. J., & Blanchard, R. (1992). Death scene characteristics in 118 fatal cases of autoerotic asphyxia compared with suicidal asphyxia. *Behavioral Sciences and the Law, 10,* 509–523.

Hudson, J. I., Carter, W. P., & Pope, H. G., Jr. (1996). Antidepressant treatment of binge-eating disorder: Research findings and clinical guidelines. *Journal of Clinical Psychiatry, 57*(Suppl. 8), 73–79.

Hudson, J. I., McElroy, S. L., Raymond, N. C., Crow, S., & Keck, P. E., Jr. (1998). Fluvoxamine in the treatment of binge-eating disorder: A multicenter placebo-controlled. *American Journal of Psychiatry, 155*(12), 1756–1762.

Huff, C. O. (1999). Source, recency, and degree of stress in adolescence and suicide ideation. *Adolescence, 34*(133), 81–89.

Hughes, P. L., Wells, L. A., Cunningham, C. J., & Ilstrup, D. M. (1986). Treating bulimia with desipramine. *Archives of General Psychiatry, 43,* 182–186.

Hultsch, D. F., Hammer, M., & Small, B. J. (1993). Age differences in cognitive performance in later life: Relationships to self-reported health. *Journals of Gerontology, 48*(1), 1.

Humphrey v. *Cady,* 405 U.S. 504 (1972).

Hunsley, J., & Bailey, J. M. (1999). The clinical utility of the Rorschach: Unfulfilled promises and an uncertain future. *Psychological Assessment, 11*(3), 266–277.

Hunter, R. H. (1999). Public policy and state psychiatric hospitals. In W. D. Spaulding et al. (Eds.), *The role of the state hospital in the twenty first.*

Hurt, R. D., Offord, K. P., Croghan, I. T., Croghan, G. A., & Gomez Dahl, L. C. (1998). Temporal effects of nicotine nasal spray and gum on nicotine withdrawal symptoms. *Psychopharmacology, 140*(1), 98–104.

Hutchinson, G., Daisley, H., Simeon, D., & Simmonds, V. (1999). High rates of paraquat-induced suicide in southern Trinidad. *Suicide and Life Threatening Behavior, 29*(2), 186–191.

Huttunen, M. O. (1995). The evolution of the serotonin-dopamine antagonist concept. *Journal of Clinical Psychopharmacology, 15,* 4S–10S.

Huyser, B., & Parker, J. C. (1998). Stress and rheumatoid arthritis: An integrative review. *Arthritis Care and Research, 11*(2), 135–145.

Hyde, T. M., & Weinberger, D. R. (1995). Tourette's syndrome: A model neuropsychiatric disorder. *Journal of the American Medical Association, 273,* 498–501.

Hyman, I., Husband, T. H., & Billings, F. J. (1995). False memories of childhood experiences. *Applied Cognitive Psychology, 9,* 181–187.

Iacono, W. G., & Beiser, M. (1992). Are males more likely than females to develop schizophrenia? *American Journal of Psychiatry, 149,* 1070–1074.

Iga, M. (1993). Japanese suicide. In A. A. Leenaars (Ed.), *Suicidology.* Northvale, NJ: Aronson.

Ilardi, S. S., & Craighead, W. E. (1994). The role of nonspecific factors in cognitive-behavior therapy for depression. *Clinical Psychology: Science and Practice, 1*(2), 138–156.

Imber, S. D., Pilkonis, P. A., Sotsky, S. M., Elkin, I., Watkins, J. T., Collins, J. F., Shea, M. T., Leber, W. R., & Glass, D. R. (1990). Mode-specific effects among three treatments for depression. *Journal of Consulting and Clinical Psychology, 58,* 352–359.

Ingram, R. E. (1984). Toward an information-processing analysis of depression. *Cognitive Therapy and Research, 8,* 443–478.

Insanity Defense Work Group. (1983). American Psychiatric Association statement on the insanity defense. *American Journal of Psychiatry, 140,* 681–688.

Insel, T. R. (1993). Toward a neuroanatomy of obsessive-compulsive disorder. *Archives of General Psychiatry, 49,* 739–744.

Ironside, R., & Batchelor, I. R. (1945). The ocular manifestations of hysteria in relation to flying. *British Journal of Ophthalmology, 29,* 88–98.

Isaacs, M. L. (1997). The duty to warn and protect: Tarasoff and the elementary school counselor. *Elementary School Guidance and Counseling, 31*(4), 326–342.

Isen, A., & Gorgoglione, J. (1983). Some specific effects of four affect-induction procedures. *Personality and Social Psychology Bulletin, 9,* 136–143.

Isometsae, E. T., & Loennqvist, J. K. (1998). Suicide attempts preceding completed suicide. *British Journal of Psychiatry, 173,* 531–535.

Ivanoff, A., & Jang, S. J. (1991). The role of hopelessness and social desirability in predicting suicidal behavior: A study of prison inmates. *Journal of Consulting and Clinical Psychology, 59,* 394–399.

Jablensky, A., & Cole, S. W. (1997). Is the earlier age at onset of schizophrenia in males a confounded finding? *British Journal of Psychiatry, 170,* 234–240.

Jackson v. *Indiana,* 406 U.S. 715 (1972).

Jacob, H. E. (1935). *Coffee: The epic of a commodity.* New York: Viking Penguin.

Jacobsen, C. F., Wolfe, J. B., & Jackson, T. A. (1935). An experimental analysis of the functions of the frontal association areas in primates. *Journal of Nervous and Mental Disease, 82,* 1–14.

Jacobson, E. (1938). *Progressive relaxation.* Chicago: University of Chicago Press.

Jacobson, N. S. (Ed.). (1988). Defining clinically significant change [Special issue]. *Behavioral Assessment, 10*(2).

Jacobson, N. S., & Hollon, S. D. (1996). Cognitive-behavior therapy versus pharmacotherapy: Now that the jury's returned its verdict, it's time to present the rest of the evidence. *Journal of Consulting and Clinical Psychology, 64*(1), 74–80.

Jacobson, N. S., & Truax, P. (1991). Clinical significance: A statistical approach to defining meaningful change in psychotherapy. *Journal of Consulting and Clinical Psychology, 59,* 12–19.

Jaffe, J. H. (1995). Pharmacological treatment of opioid dependence: Current techniques and new findings. *Psychiatric Annals, 25,* 369–375.

James, D. (1998). Multiple personality disorder in the courts: A review of the North American experience. *Journal of Forensic Psychiatry, 9*(2), 339–361.

James, D., & Schramm, M. (1998). "Multiple personality disorder" presenting to the English courts: A case-study. *Journal of Forensic Psychiatry, 9*(3), 615–628.

Jamison, K. K. (1992). Suicide and manic-depressive illness in artists and writers. *National Forum, 73,* 28–30.

Jamison, K. K., & Akiskal, H. S. (1983). Medication compliance in patients with bipolar disorder. *Psychiatric Clinics of North America, 6,* 175–192.

Jamison, K. R. (1995). *An Unquiet Mind.* New York: Knopf.

Jamison, K. R. (1996). Mood disorders, creativity and the artistic temperament. In J. J. Schildkraut, A. Otero, et al. (Eds.), *Depression and the spiritual.*

Jamison, K. R., & Baldessarini, R. J. (1999). Effects of medical interventions on suicidal behavior. *Journal of Clinical Psychiatry, 60*(Suppl. 2), 4–6.

Janca, A., Isaac, M., Bennett, L. A., & Tacchini, G. (1995). Somatoform disorders in different cultures: A mail questionnaire survey. *Social Psychiatry and Psychiatric Epidemiology, 30,* 44–48.

Janicak, P. G., & Levy, N. A. (1998). Rational copharmacy for acute mania. *Psychiatric Annals, 28*(4), 204–212.

Jarey, M. L., & Stewart, M. A. (1985). Psychiatric disorder in the parents of adopted children with aggressive conduct disorder. *Neuropsychobiology, 13,* 7–11.

Jarrett, R. B., Schaffer, M., McIntire, D., Witt Browder, A., Kraft, D., & Risser, R. C. (1999). Treatment of atypical depression with cognitive therapy or phenelzine: A double-blind, placebo-controlled trial. *Archives of General Psychiatry, 56*(5), 431–437.

Jeans, R. F. (1976). Independently validated case of multiple personality. *Journal of Abnormal Psychology, 85,* 249–255.

Jenike, M. A. (1998). Neurosurgical treatment of obsessive-compulsive disorder. *British Journal of Psychiatry, 173*(Suppl. 35), 79–90.

Jenike, M. A., Baer, L., Ballantine, H. T., Martuza, R. L., Tynes, S., Giriunas, I., Buttolph, M. L., & Cassem, N. H. (1991). Cingulotomy for refractory obsessive-compulsive disorder: A long-term follow-up of 33 patients. *Archives of General Psychiatry, 48,* 548–555.

Jennings, K. D., Ross, S., Popper, S., & Elmore, M. (1999). Thoughts of harming infants in depressed and nondepressed mothers. *Journal of Affective Disorders, 54*(1–2), 21–28.

Jentsch, J. D., Redmond, D. E., Elsworth, J. D., Taylor, J. R., Yungren, K. D., & Roth, R. H. (1997). Enduring cognitive deficits and cortical dopamine dysfunction in monkeys after long-term administration of phencyclidine. *Science, 277,* 953–955.

Jentsch, J. D., & Roth, R. H. (1999). The neuropsychopharmacology of phencyclidine: From NMDA receptor hypofunction to the. *Neuropsychopharmacology, 20*(3), 201–225.

Jentsch, J. D., & Taylor, J. R. (1999). Impulsivity resulting from frontostriatal dysfunction in drug abuse: Implications for the. *Psychopharmacology, 146*(4), 373–390.

Jessen, G., Andersen, K., Arensman, E., Bille Brahe, U., Crepet, P., & De Leo, D. (1999). Temporal fluctuations and seasonality in attempted suicide in Europe. *Archives of Suicide Research, 5*(1), 57–69.

Jeste, D. V., Gilbert, P. L., McAdams, L. A., & Harris, M. J. (1995). Considering neuroleptic maintenance and taper on a continuum: Need for individual rather than dogmatic approach. *Archives of General Psychiatry, 52,* 209–212.

Jimerson, D. C., Lesem, M. D., Kay, W. H., & Brewerton, T. D. (1992). Low serotonin and dopamine metabolite concentrations in cerebrospinal fluid from bulimic patients with frequent binge episodes. *Archives of General Psychiatry, 49,* 132–138.

Jobes, D. A., & Mann, R. E. (1999). Reasons for living versus reasons for dying: Examining the internal debate of suicide. *Suicide and Life Threatening Behavior, 29*(2), 97–104.

Joensson, L., Lindgren, P., Wimo, A., Joensson, B., & Winblad, B. (1999). The cost-effectiveness of donepezil therapy in Swedish patients with Alzheimer's disease: A Markov Model. *Clinical Therapeutics: The International Journal of Drug Therapy, 21*(7), 1230–1240.

Joffe, R. T., Singer, W., Levitt, A. J., & MacDonald, C. (1993). A placebo-controlled comparison of lithium and triiodothyronine augmentation of tricyclic antidepressants in unipolar refractory depression. *Archives of General Psychiatry, 50,* 387–393.

Johnson, D. (1994). Stress, depression, substance abuse, and racism. *American-Indian and Alaska Native Mental Health Research, 6,* 29–33.

Johnson, J. G., & Bornstein, R. F. (1991). Does daily stress independently predict psychopathology? *Journal of Social and Clinical Psychology, 10,* 58–74.

Johnson, M. H., & Magaro, P. A. (1987). Effects of mood and severity on memory processes in depression and mania. *Psychological Bulletin, 101,* 28–40.

Johnson, P. B. (1994). Alcohol expectancies and reaction expectancies: Their impact on student drinking. *Journal of Alcohol and Drug Education, 40,* 57–68.

Johnson, S. L., & Roberts, J. E. (1995). Life events and bipolar disorder: Implications from biological theories. *Psychological Bulletin, 117,* 434–449.

Jones, B. T., & McMahon, J. (1994). Negative alcohol expectancy predicts posttreatment abstinence survivorship: The whether, when, and why of relapse to a first drink. *Addiction, 89,* 1653–1665.

Jones, E. G. (1997). Cortical development and thalamic pathology in schizophrenia. *Schizophrenia Bulletin, 23*(3), 483–501.

Jones, F. D., Maas, F. J., Dekirmenjian, H., & Fawcett, J. A. (1973). Urinary catecholamine metabolites during behavioral changes in a patient with manic-depressive cycles. *Science, 179,* 300–302.

Jones, H., Curtis, V. A., Wright, P., & Lucey, J. V. (1998). Neuroendocrine evidence that clozapine's serotonergic antago-

nism is relevant to its efficacy in. *American Journal of Psychiatry, 155*(6), 838–840.

Jones, M. C. (1924). The elimination of children's fears. *Journal of Experimental Psychology, 7,* 382–390.

Jones, R., Peveler, R. C., Hope, R. A., & Fairburn, C. G. (1993). Changes during treatment for bulimia nervosa: A comparison of three psychological treatments. *Behaviour Research and Therapy, 31,* 479–485.

Jones, S. H., Gray, J. A., & Hemsley, D. R. (1990). The Kamin blocking effect, incidental learning and psychoticism. *British Journal of Psychology, 81,* 95–109.

Jones, S. H., Gray, J. A., & Hemsley, D. R. (1992). Loss of the Kamin blocking effect in acute but not chronic schizophrenics. *Biological Psychiatry, 32,* 739–755.

Jones, T. F., Craig, A. S., Hoy, D., Gunter, E. W., Ashley, D. L., Barr, D. B., Brock, J. W., & Schaffner, W. (2000). Mass psychogenic illness attributed to toxic exposure at a high school. *New England Journal of Medicine, 342,* 96–100.

Jordan, B. D. (1998). Dementia pugilistica. *Neurobiology of primary dementia,* pp. 191–203.

Jorenby, D. E., Leischow, S. J., Nides, M. A., & Rennard, S. I. (1999). A controlled trial of sustained-release bupropion, a nicotine patch, or both for smoking. *New England Journal of Medicine, 340*(9), 685–691.

Jorge, R. E., Leston, J. E., Arndt, S., & Robinson, R. G. (1999). Cluster headaches: Association with anxiety disorders and memory deficits. *Neurology, 53*(3), 543–547.

Judd, L. L., McAdams, L., Budnick, B., & Braff, D. L. (1992). Sensory gating deficits in schizophrenia. *American Journal of Psychiatry, 149,* 488–493.

Jung, C. G. (1963). *Memories, dreames, reflections.* New York: Pantheon.

Jung, C. G. (1964). *Man and his symbols.* Garden City, NY: Doubleday.

Kadis, L. B., & McClendon, R. (1999). Marital and family therapy. In R. E. Hales, S. C. Yudofsky, & J. A. Talbot (Eds.), *Textbook of psychiatry* (pp. 1313–1330). Washington, DC: American Psychiatric Press.

Kaemingk, K., & Paquette, A. (1999). Effects of prenatal alcohol exposure on neuropsychological functioning. *Developmental Neuropsychology, 15*(1), 111–140.

Kafka, M. P. (1994). Sertraline pharmacotherapy for paraphilias and paraphilia-related disorders: An open trial. *Annals of Clinical Psychiatry, 6*(3), 189–195.

Kafka, M. P., & Prentky, R. (1992). Fluoxetine treatment of nonparaphilic sexual addictions and paraphilias in men. *Journal of Clinical Psychiatry, 53*(10), 351–358.

Kagan, B. L., Leskin, G., Haas, B., Wilkins, J., & Foy, D. (1999). Elevated lipid levels in Vietnam veterans with chronic posttraumatic stress disorder. *Biological Psychiatry, 45*(3), 374–377.

Kagan, J. (1996). Three pleasing ideas. *American Psychologist, 51*(9), 901–908.

Kagan, J., Reznik, J. S., & Snidman, N. (1999). Biological basis of childhood shyness. In A. Slater, D. Muir, et al. (Eds.), *The Blackwell reader in development.*

Kagan, V. (1981). Nonprocess autism in children: A comparative etiopathogenic study. *Soviet Neurology and Psychiatry, 14,* 25–30.

Kagle, J. D., & Kopels, S. (1994). Confidentiality after Tarasoff. *Health and Social Work, 19,* 217–222.

Kalafat, J., & Ryerson, D. M. (1999). The implementation and institutionalization of a school-based youth suicide prevention. *Journal of Primary Prevention, 19*(3), 157–175.

Kamin, L. J. (1969). Predictability, surprise, attention, and conditioning. In B. A. Campbell & R. M. Church (Eds.), *Punishment and aversive behavior.* New York: Appleton-Century-Crofts.

Kane, J. M., Honigfeld, G., Singer, J., & Meltzer, H. (1988). Clozapine for the treatment-resistant schizophrenic. *Archives of General Psychiatry, 45,* 789–796.

Kane, J. M., Honigfeld, G., Singer, J., & Meltzer, H. (1989). Clozapine for the treatment-resistant schizophrenic: Results of a U.S. multicenter trial. *Psychopharmacology, 99,* S60–S63.

Kanner, A. D., Coyne, J. C., Schaefer, C., & Lazarus, R. S. (1981). Comparison of two modes of stress management: Daily hassles and uplifts versus major life events. *Journal of Behavioral Medicine, 4,* 1–40.

Kanner, L. (1943). Autistic disturbances of affective content. *Nervous Child, 2,* 217–240.

Kanofsky, J. D., Sandyk, R., & Kay, S. R. (1990). Anatomical abnormalities in the brains of monozygotic twins discordant for schizophrenia. *New England Journal of Medicine, 323,* 547.

Kaplan, H. S. (1981). *The new sex therapy: Active treatment of sexual dysfunctions.* New York: Brunner/Mazel.

Kaplan, J. R., Manuck, S. B., & Shively, C. A. (1991). The effects of cholesterol on social behavior in monkeys. *Psychosomatic Medicine, 53,* 634–642.

Kapur, N. (1999). Syndromes of retrograde amnesia: A conceptual and empirical synthesis. *Psychological Bulletin, 125*(6), 800–825.

Kapur, S., Zipursky, R. B., & Remington, G. (1999). Clinical and theoretical implications of 5-HT2 and D2 receptor occupancy of. *American Journal of Psychiatry, 156*(2), 286–293.

Karlsson, J. L. (1966). *The biologic basis of schizophrenia.* Springfield, IL: Thomas.

Kaskutas, L. A., Weisner, C., Lee, M., & Humphreys, K. (1999). Alcoholics Anonymous affiliation at treatment intake among White and Black Americans. *Journal of Studies on Alcohol, 60*(6), 810–816.

Kassin, S. M., & Kiechel, K. L. (1996). The social psychology of false confessions: Compliance, internalization, and confabulation. *Psychological Science, 7*(3), 125–128.

Kazdin, A. (1998). Psychosocial treatments for conduct disorder in children. In P. E. Nathan & J. M. Gorman (Eds.), *A guide to treatments that work* (pp. 65–89). New York: Oxford University Press.

Keane, T. M. (1998). Psychological and behavioral treatments for post-traumatic stress disorder. In P. E. Nathan & J. M. Gorman (Eds.), *A guide to treatments that work* (pp. 398–407). New York: Oxford University Press.

Keck, P. E., McElroy, S. L., & Pope, H. G. (1991). Epidemiology of neuroleptic malignant syndrome. *Psychiatric Annals, 21,* 148–151.

Keck, P. F., Jr., & McElroy, S. L. (1998). Pharmacological treatments of bipolar disorders. In P. E. Nathan & J. M. Gorman (Eds.), *A guide to treatments that work* (pp. 249–269). New York: Oxford University Press.

Keel, P. K., Mitchell, J. E., Miller, K. B., Davis, T. L., & Crow, S. J. (1999). Long-term outcome of bulimia nervosa. *Archives of General Psychiatry, 56*(1), 63–69.

Kegeles, L. S., Humaran, T. J., & Mann, J. J. (1998). In vivo neurochemistry of the brain in schizophrenia as revealed by magnetic resonance. *Biological Psychiatry, 44*(6), 382–398.

Kellermann, A. L., Rivara, F. P., Somes, G., Reay, D. T., Francisco, J., Banton, J. B., Prodzinski, J., Fligner, C., & Hackman, B. B. (1992). Suicide in the home in relation to gun ownership. *New England Journal of Medicine, 327,* 467–472.

Kellner, R. (1992). The case for reassurance. *International Review of Psychiatry, 4,* 71–75.

Kellner, R., Uhlenhuth, E. H., & Glass, R. (1978). Clinical evaluation of antianxiety agents: Subject-own-control designs. In M. Lipton, A. Di Mascio, & K. Killam (Eds.), *Psychopharmacology: A generation of progress.* New York: Raven Press.

Kendall, P. C. (Ed.). (1992). Comorbidity and treatment implications. *Journal of Consulting and Clinical Psychology, 60,* 833–908.

Kendell, R. E., Chalmers. J. C., & Platz, D. (1987). Epidemiology and puerperal psychosis. *British Journal of Psychiatry, 150,* 662–673.

Kendler, K. S. (1993). Twin studies of psychiatric illness. *Archives of General Psychiatry, 50,* 905–915.

Kendler, K. S., Gallagher, T. J., Abelson, J. M., & Kessler, R. C. (1996). Lifetime prevalence, demographic risk factors, and diagnostic validity of nonaffective psychosis as assessed in a US community sample. *Archives of General Psychiatry, 53,* 1022–1031.

Kendler, K. S., Gruenberg, A. M., & Strauss, J. S. (1982). An independent analysis of the Copenhagen sample of the Danish adoption study of schizophrenia: The relationship between childhood withdrawal and adult schizophrenia. *Archives of General Psychiatry, 39,* 1257–1261.

Kendler, K. S., Heath, A. C., Neale, M. C., Kessler, R. C., & Eaves, L. J. (1992). A population-based twin study of alcoholism in women. *Journal of the American Medical Association, 268,* 1877–1882.

Kendler, K. S., McGuire, M., Gruenberg, A. M., O'Hare, A., Spellman, M., & Walsh, D. (1993a). The Roscommon Family Study: 3. Schizophrenia-related personality disorders in relatives. *Archives of General Psychiatry, 50,* 781–788.

Kendler, K. S., McGuire, M., Gruenberg, A. M., O'Hare, A., Spellman, M., & Walsh, D. (1993b). The Roscommon Family Study: 4. Affective illness, anxiety disorders, and alcoholism in relatives. *Archives of General Psychiatry, 50,* 952–960.

Kendler, K. S., Neale, M. C., Kessler, R. C., Heath, A. C., & Eaves, L. J. (1992a). Generalized anxiety disorder in women: A population-based twin study. *Archives of General Psychiatry, 49,* 267–272.

Kendler, K. S., Neale, M. C., Kessler, R. C., Heath, A. C., & Eaves, L. J. (1992b). A population-based twin study of major depression in women. *Archives of General Psychiatry, 49,* 257–266.

Kendler, K. S., Neale, M. C., Kessler, R. C., Heath, A. C., & Eaves, L. J. (1993a). The lifetime history of major depression in women: Reliability of diagnosis and heritability. *Archives of General Psychiatry, 50,* 863–870.

Kendler, K. S., Neale, M. C., Kessler, R. C., Heath, A. C., & Eaves, L. J. (1993b). A longitudinal twin study of 1-year prevalence of major depression in women. *Archives of General Psychiatry, 50,* 843–852.

Kendler, K. S., Neale, M. C., Kessler, R. C., Heath, A. C., & Eaves, L. J. (1993c). A twin study of recent life events and difficulties. *Archives of General Psychiatry, 50,* 789–796.

Kendler, K. S., Neale, M. C., MacLean, C. J., Heath, A. C., Eaves, L. J., & Kessler, R. C. (1993d). Smoking and major depression. *Archives of General Psychiatry, 50,* 36–43.

Kendler, K. S., Pedersen, N., Johnson, L., Neale, M. C., & Mathe, A. S. (1993). A pilot Swedish twin study of affective illness, including hospital- and population-ascertained samples. *Archives of General Psychiatry, 50,* 699–706.

Kendler, K. S., Walters, E. E., Truett, K. R., Heath, A. C., Neale, M. C., Martin, N. G., & Eaves, L. J. (1994). Sources of individual differences in depressive symptoms: Analysis of two samples of twins and their families. *American Journal of Psychiatry, 151,* 1605–1614.

Kent, L., Evans, J., Paul, M., & Sharp, M. (1999). Comorbidity of autistic spectrum disorders in children with Down Syndrome. *Developmental Medicine and Child Neurology, 41*(3), 153–158.

Kerbeshian, J., & Burd, L., (1994). Tourette's syndrome: A developmental psychobiologic view. *Journal of Developmental and Physical Disabilities, 6,* 203–218.

Kesey, K. (1962). *One flew over the cuckoo's nest.* New York: Viking Penguin.

Keshavan, M. S., Rosenberg, D., Sweeney, J. A., & Pettegrew, J. W. (1998). Decreased caudate volume in neuroleptic-naive patients. *American Journal of Psychiatry, 155*(6), 774–778.

Kessler, R. C., Borges, G., & Walters, E. E. (1999). Prevalence of and risk factors for lifetime suicide attempts in the National Comorbidity Survey. *Archives of General Psychiatry, 56*(7), 617–626.

Kessler, R. C., Foster, C. L., Saunder, W. B., & Stang, P. E. (1995). Social consequences of psychiatric disorders: 1. Educational attainment. *American Journal of Psychiatry, 152,* 1026–1032.

Kessler, R. C., McGonagle, K. A., Zhao, S., Nelson, C. B., Hughes, M., Eshleman, S., Wittchen, H., & Kendler, K. S. (1994). Lifetime and 12-month prevalence of DSM-III-R psychiatric disorders in the United States. *Archives of General Psychiatry, 51,* 8–19.

Kessler, R. C., Stang, P. E., Wittchen, H. U., & Ustun, T. B. (1998). Lifetime panic-depression comorbidity in the National Comorbidity Survey. *Archives of General Psychiatry, 55*(9), 801–808.

Kety, S. (1986). Genetic factors in suicide. In A. Roy (Ed.), *Suicide.* Baltimore, MD: Williams & Witkins.

Kety, S. S., Rosenthal, D., Wender, P. H., Schulsinger, F., & Jacobsen, B. (1975). Mental illness in the biological and adoptive families of adopted individuals who have become schizophrenic: A preliminary report based on psychiatric interviews. In R. R. Fieve, D. Rosenthal, & H. Brill (Eds.), *Genetic research in psychiatry.* Baltimore: Johns Hopkins University Press.

Kety, S. S., Wender, P. H., Jacobsen, B., Ingraham, L., Jansson, L., Faber, B., & Kinney, D. K. (1994). Mental illness in the biological and adoptive relatives of schizophrenic adoptees. *Archives of General Psychiatry, 51,* 442–455.

Keuthen, N. J., O'Sullivan, R. L., Goodchild, P., & Rodriguez, D. (1998). Retrospective review of treatment outcome for 63 patients with trichotillomania. *American Journal of Psychiatry, 155*(4), 560–561.

Keuthen, N. J., O'Sullivan, R. L., & Sprich Buckminster, S. (1998). Trichotillomania: Current issues in conceptualization and treatment. *Psychotherapy and Psychosomatics, 67*(4–5), 202–213.

Keyes, D. (1981). *The minds of Billy Milligan.* New York: Bantam, Books.

Khalid, R., & Sial, S. (1998). Personality factors and the recovery rate of heart patients after coronary artery bypass surgery. *Journal of Behavioural Sciences, 9*(1–2), 37–54.

Khantzian, E. J. (1985). Self-medication hypothesis of addictive disorders. *American Journal of Psychiatry, 142,* 1259–1263.

Kidorf, M., Sherman, M. F., & Johnson, J. G. (1995). Alcohol expectancies and changes in beer consumption of first-year college students. *Addictive Behaviors, 20,* 225–231.

Kiecolt-Glaser, J. K. (1999). Stress, personal relationships, and immune function: Health implications. *Brain, Behavior and Immunity, 13*(1), 61–72.

Kiecolt-Glaser, J. K., Garner, W., Speicher, C., Penn, G. M., Holliday, J., & Glaser, R. (1984). Psychosocial modifiers of immunocompetence in medical students. *Psychosomatic Medicine, 46,* 7–14.

Kiecolt-Glaser, J. K., Glaser, R., Williger, D., Stout, J., Messick, G., Sheppard, S., Ricker, D., Romisher, S. C., Briner, W., Bonnell, G., & Donnerberg, R. (1985). Psychosocial enhancement of immunocompetence in a geriatric population. *Health Psychology, 4,* 25–41.

Kiernan, C. (1988). Child abuse: A case of change? *British Journal of Special Education, 15,* 140–142.

Kiersch, T. A. (1990). Treatment of sex offenders with Depo-Provera. *Bulletin of the American Academy of Psychiatry and the Law, 18,* 179–187.

Kiesler, C. A. (1982). Public and professional myths about mental hospitalization: An empirical. *American Psychologist, 37*(12), 1323–1339.

Kiesler, C. A., & Sibulkin, A. E. (1987). *Mental hosptialization: Myths and facts about a national crisis.* Ann Arbor, MI: Books-on-Demand.

Kilbey, M. M., Downey, K., & Breslau, N. (1998). Predicting the emergence and persistence of alcohol dependence in young adults: The role of. *Experimental and Clinical Psychopharmacology, 6*(2), 149–156.

Kilmann, P. R., & Auerbach, R. (1979). Treatments of premature ejaculation and psychogenic impotence: A critical review of the literature. *Archives of Sexual Behavior, 8,* 81–100.

Kimbrell, T. A., George, M. S., Parekh, P. I., & Ketter, T. A. (1999). Regional brain activity during transient self-induced anxiety and anger in healthy adults. *Biological Psychiatry, 46*(4), 454–465.

King, K. B., Rowe, M. A., Kimble, L. P., & Zerwic, J. J. (1998). Optimism, coping and longterm recovery from coronary artery surgery in women. *Research in Nursing and Health, 21*(1), 15–26.

King, S. A. (1999). Pain disorders. In R. E. Hales, S. C. Yudofsky, & J. A. Talbot (Eds.), *Textbook of psychiatry* (pp. 1003–1024). Washington, DC: American Psychiatric Press.

Kinney, D. K., Yurgelun Todd, D. A., Levy, D. L., Medoff, D., et al. (1993). Obstetrical complications in patients with bipolar disorder and their siblings. *Psychiatry Research, 48*(1), 47–56.

Kinney, D. K., Yurgelun Todd, D. A., Tohen, M., & Tramer, S. (1998). Pre- and perinatal complications and risk for bipolar disorder: A retrospective study. *Journal of Affective Disorders, 50*(2–3), 117–124.

Kinzl, J. F., Traweger, C., Guenther, V., & Biebl, W. (1994). Family background and sexual abuse associated with eating disorders. *American Journal of Psychiatry, 151*, 1127–1131.

Kirkpatrick, B., Ram, R., Amador, X. F., & Buchanan, R. W. (1998). Summer birth and the deficit syndrome of schizophrenia. *American Journal of Psychiatry, 155*(9), 1221–1226.

Kirmayer, L. J., & Young, A. (1998). Culture and somatization: Clinical, epidemiological, and ethnographic perspectives. *Psychosomatic Medicine, 60*(4), 420–430.

Kirov, G., Owen, M. J., Jones, I., McCandless, F., & Craddock, N. (1999). Trytophan hydroxylase gene and manic-depressive illness. *Archives of General Psychiatry, 56*(1), 98–99.

Kirschenbaum, D. S., De Voge, J. B., Marsh, M. E., & Steffen, J. J. (1980). Multimodal evaluation of therapy versus consultation components in a large inner-city intervention program. *American Journal of Community Psychology, 8*, 587–692.

Klein, B. P., & Mervis, C. B. (1999). Contrasting patterns of cognitive abilties of 9- and 10-year-olds with Williams Syndrome or Down Syndrome. *Developmental Neuropsychology, 16*(2), 177–196.

Klein, D. F. (1982). Medication in the treatment of panic attacks and phobic states. *Psychopharmacology Bulletin, 18*, 85–90.

Klein, D. F. (1993) False suffocation alarms, spontaneous panics, and related conditions: An integrative hypothesis. *Archives of General Psychiatry, 50*, 306–317.

Klein, D. F. (1994). "Klein's suffocation theory of panic": Reply. *Archives of General Psychiatry, 51*, 506.

Klein, D. F. (1996). Preventing hung juries about therapy studies. *Journal of Consulting and Clinical Psychology, 64*(1), 81–87.

Klein, E., Kreinin, I., Chistyakov, A., Koren, D., & Mecz, L. (1999). Therapeutic efficacy of right prefrontal slow repetitive transcranial magnetic stimulation in. *Archives of General Psychiatry, 56*(4), 315–320.

Klein, R. G. (1996). Comments on expanding the clinical role of psychologists. *American Psychologist, 51*, 216–218.

Klein, R. G., Landa, B., Mattes, J. A., & Klein, D. F. (1988). Methylphenidate and growth in hyperactive children: A controlled withdrawal study. *Archives of General Psychiatry, 45*, 1127–1130.

Klerman, G. L. (1990). Treatment of recurrent unipolar major depressive disorder. *Archives of General Psychiatry, 47*, 1158–1162.

Klerman, G. L., Di Mascio, A., Weissman, M., Prusoff, B. A. & Paykel, E. S. (1974). Treatment of depression by drugs and psychotherapy. *American Journal of Psychiatry, 131*, 186–191.

Klerman, G. L., & Schechter, G. (1982). Drugs and psychotherapy. In E. S. Paykel (Ed.), *Handbook of affective disorders.* New York: Guilford Press.

Kliegl, R., Smith, J., & Baltes, P. B. (1989). Testing-the-limits and the study of adult age differences in cognitive plasticity of a mnemonic. *Developmental Psychology, 25*(2), 247–256.

Kliegl, R., Smith, J., & Baltes, P. B. (1990). On the locus and process of magnification of age differences during mnemonic training. *Developmental Psychology, 26*(6), 894–904.

Klorman, R., Brumaghim, J. T., Fitzpatrick, P. A., Borgstedt, A. D., & Strauss, J. (1994). Clinical and cognitive effects of methylphenidate on children with attention deficit disorder as a function of aggression/oppositionality and age. *Journal of Abnormal Psychology, 103*, 206–221.

Klosko, J. S., Barlow, D., Tassinari, R., & Cerny, J. A. (1990). A comparison of of alprazolam and behavior therapy in treatment of panic disorder. *Journal of Consulting and Clinical Psychology, 58*, 77–84.

Kluft, R. P. (1982). Varieties of hypnotic interventions in the treatment of multiple personality. *American Journal of Clinical Hypnosis, 24*, 230–240.

Kluft, R. P. (1993). The treatment of dissociative disorder patients: An overview of discoveries, successes, and failures. *Dissociation Progress in the Dissociative Disorders, 6*, 87–101.

Knapp, M., Scott, S., & Davies, J. (1999). The cost of antisocial behaviour in younger children. *Clinical Child Psychology and Psychiatry, 4*(4), 457–473.

Knapp, M. R. J., Marks, I. M., Wolstenholme, J., & Beecham, J. K. (1998). Home-based versus hospital-based care for serious mental illness: *Controlled. British Journal of Psychiatry, 172*(6), 506–512.

Knowles, J. A., Kaufmann, C. A., & Rieder, R. O. (1999). Genetics. In R. E. Hales, S. C. Yudofsky, & J. A. Talbot (Eds.), *Textbook of psychiatry* (pp. 35–82). Washington, DC: American Psychiatric Press.

Koch, J. L. (1891). *Die psychopathischen Minderwertigkeiten.* Ravensburg, Germany: Maier.

Kocsis, J. H., & Stokes, P. (1979). Lithium maintenance: Factors affecting outcome. *American Journal of Psychiatry, 136*, 563–566.

Kohn, M. L. (1973). Social class and schizophrenia: A critical review and reformation. *Schizophrenia Bulletin, 1*, 60–79.

Konstantareas, M. M., & Homatidis, S. (1999). Chromosomal abnormalities in a series of children with autistic disorder. *Journal of Autism and Developmental Disorders, 29*(4), 275–285.

Kopelowicz, A., & Liberman, R. P. (1998). Psychosocial treatments for schizophrenia. In P. E. Nathan & J. M. Gorman (Eds.), *A guide to treatments that work* (pp. 190–211). New York: Oxford University Press.

Korkman, M., Autti Raemoe, I., Koivulehto, H., & Granstroem, M. L. (1998). Neuropsychological effects at early school age of fetal alcohol exposure of varying duration. *Child Neuropsychology, 4*(3), 199–212.

Kornfeld, A. D. (1989). Mary Cover Jones and the Peter case: Social learning versus conditioning. *Journal of Anxiety Disorders, 3*, 187–195.

Kornitzer, M., Boutsen, M., Dramaix, M., Thijs, J., & Gustavsson, G. (1995). Combined use of nicotine patch and gum in smoking cessation: A placebo-controlled clinical trial. *Preventive Medicine, 24*, 41–47.

Koss, M., & Shiang, J. (1994). Research on brief psychotherapy. In A. E. Bergin & S. L. Garfield (Eds.), *Handbook of psychotherapy and behavior change* (4th ed.). New York: Wiley.

Kovacs, M., Akiskal, H. S., Gatsonis, C., & Parrone, P. L. (1994). Childhood-onset dysthymic disorder. *Archives of General Psychiatry, 51*, 365–374.

Kownacki, R. J., & Shadish, W. R. (1999). Does Alcoholics Anonymous work? The results from a meta-analysis of controlled. *Substance Use and Misuse, 34*(13), 1897–1916.

Kozol, H., Boucher, R., & Garofalo, R. (1972). The diagnosis and treatment of dangerousness. *Crime and Delinquency, 18,* 371–392.

Kramer, B. A. (1985). Use of ECT in California. *American Journal of Psychiatry, 142,* 1190–1192.

Kramer, M. A. (1957). A discussion of the concepts of incidence and prevalence as related to epidemiologic studies of mental disorders. *American Journal of Public Health, 47,* 826–840.

Krasucki, C., Howard, R., & Mann, A. (1998). The relationship between anxiety disorders and age. *International Journal of Geriatric Psychiatry, 13*(2), 79–99.

Kremen, W. S., Faraone, S. V., Toomey, R., Seidman, L. J., & Tsuang, M. T. (1998). Sex differences in self-reported schizotypal traits in relatives of schizophrenic probands. *Schizophrenia Research, 34*(1–2), 27–37.

Krener, P., Simmons, M. K., Hansen, R. L., & Treat, J. N. (1989). Effect of pregnancy on psychosis: Life circumstances and psychiatric symptoms. *International Journal of Psychiatry and Medicine, 19,* 65–84.

Kreuz, L. E., Rose, R. M., & Jennings, J. R. (1972). Suppression of plasma testosterone levels and psychological stress: A longitudinal study of young men in officer candidate school. *Archives of General Psychiatry, 26,* 479–482.

Kristal-Boneh, E., Melamed, S., Bernheim, J., Peled, I., & Green, M. S. (1995). Reduced ambulatory heart rate response to physical work and complaints of fatigue among hypertensive males treated with beta-blockers. *Journal of Behavioral Medicine, 18,* 113–126.

Kronfol, Z., Silva, J., Greden, J., Deminski, S., Gardner, R., & Carroll, B. (1983). Impaired lymphocyte function in depressive illness. *Life Sciences, 33,* 241–247.

Kruesi, M. J., Hibbs, E. D., Zahn, T. P., Keysor, C. S., Hamburger, S. D., Bartko, J. J., & Rapoport, J. L. (1992). A 2-year prospective follow-up study of children and adolescents with disruptive behavior disorders. *Archives of General Psychiatry, 49,* 429–435.

Kugler, B. (1998). The differentiation between autism and Asperger syndrome. *Autism, 2*(1), 11–32.

Kuh, D., Cardozo, L., & Hardy, R. (1999). Urinary incontinence in middle aged women: Childhood enuresis and other lifetime risk. *Journal of Epidemiology and Community Health, 53*(8), 453–458.

Kulhanek, F., Linde, O. K., & Meisenberg, G. (1979). Precipitation of antipsychotic drugs in interaction with coffee or tea. *Lancet, 2,* 1130.

Kulhara, P., Basu, D., Mattoo, S. K., Sharan, P., & Chopra, R. (1999). Lithium prophylaxis of recurrent bipolar affective disorder: Long-term outcome and its. *Journal of Affective Disorders, 54*(1–2), 87–96.

Kulisevsky, J., Berthier, M. L., Avila, A., & Gironell, A. (1998). Unrecognized Tourette syndrome in adult patients referred for psychogenic tremor. *Archives of Neurology, 55*(3), 409–414.

Kumari, V., Soni, W., & Sharma, T. (1999). Normalization of information processing deficits in schizophrenia with clozapine. *American Journal of Psychiatry, 156*(7), 1046–1051.

Kunugi, H., Takei, N., Aoki, H., & Nanko, S. (1997). Low serum cholesterol in suicide attempters. *Biological Psychiatry, 41*(2), 196–200.

Kurzthaler, I., Hummer, M., Miller, C., & Sperner Unterweger, B. (1999). Effect of cannabis use on cognitive functions and driving ability. *Journal of Clinical Psychiatry, 60*(6), 395–399.

Kushner, M. (1965). The reduction of a long-standing fetish by means of aversive conditioning. In L. P. Ulmann & L. Krasner (Eds.), *Case studies in behavior modification.* New York: Holt, Rinehart and Winston.

Kushner, M. G., Sher, K. J., Wood, M. D., & Wood, P. K. (1994). Anxiety and drinking behavior: Moderating effects of tension-reduction alcohol outcome expectancies. *Alcoholism Clinical and Experimental Research, 18,* 852–860.

Kuzis, G., Sabe, L., Tiberti, C., Merello, M., & Leiguarda, R. (1999). Explicit and implicit learning in patients with Alzheimer disease and Parkinson Disease. *Neuropsychiatry, Neuropsychology, and Behavioral Neurology, 12,* 4.

Kwan, M., Greenleaf, W. J., Mann, J., Crapo, L., & Davidson, J. M. (1983). The nature of androgen action on male sexuality: A combined laboratory–self-report study on hypogonadal men. *Journal of Clinical Endocrinology and Metabolism, 57,* 557–562.

Kwon, J. S., McCarley, R. W., Hirayasu, Y., & Anderson, J. E. (1999). Left planum temporale volume reduction in schizophrenia. *Archives of General Psychiatry, 56*(2), 142–148.

Kwon, S., & Oel, T. P. S. (1992). Differential causal roles of dysfunctional attitudes and automatic thoughts in depression. *Cognitive Therapy and Research, 16,* 309–328.

Labbate, L. A., Grimes, J. B., & Arana, G. W. (1998). Serotonin reuptake antidepressant effects on sexual function in patients with anxiety. *Biological Psychiatry, 43*(12), 904–907.

Lacey, J. I. (1950). Individual differences in somatic response patterns. *Journal of Comparative and Physiological Psychology, 43,* 599–604.

Lacey, J. I. (1967). Somatic response patterning and stress: Some revisions of activation theory. In M. H. Appley & R. Trumball (Eds.), *Psychological stress.* New York: McGraw-Hill.

Lackner, J. M., Carosella, A. M., & Feuerstein, M. (1996). Pain expectancies, pain, and functional self-efficacy expectancies as determinants of disability. *Journal of Consulting and Clinical Psychology, 64*(1), 212–220.

Ladas, A. K., Whipple, B., & Perry, J. D. (1982). *The G spot.* New York: Holt, Rinehart and Winston.

Lader, M. (1998). Withdrawal reactions after stopping hypnotics in patients with insomnia. *CNS Drugs, 10*(6), 425–440.

Lader, M., & Scotto, J. C. (1998). A multicentre double-blind comparison of hydroxyzine, buspirone and placebo in patients with generalized anxiety disorder. *Psychopharmacology, 139*(4), 402–406.

Lahey, B. B., Hart, E. L., Pliszka, S., Applegate, B., & McBurnett, K. (1993). Neurophysiological correlates of conduct disorder: A rational and a review of research. *Journal of Clinical Child Psychology, 22,* 141–153.

Lahey, B. B., Loeber, R., Hart, E., L., Frick, P. J., Applegate, B., Zhang, Q., Green, S. M., & Russo, M. F. (1995). Four-year longitudinal study of conduct disorder in boys: Patterns and predictors of persistence. *Journal of Abnormal Psychology, 104,* 83–93.

Lai, F., Kammann, E., Rebeck, G. W., Anderson, A., Chen, Y., & Nixon, R. A. (1999). APOE genotype and gender effects on Alzheimer disease in 100 adults with Down. *Neurology, 53*(2), 331–336.

Laing, R. D. (1964). Is schizophrenia a disease? *International Journal of Social Psychiatry, 10,* 184–193.

Lake v. *Cameron,* 364 F.2d 657 (D.C. Cir. 1966).

Laloux, P., Vakaet, A., Monseu, G., Jacquy, J., Bourgeois, P., & Van Der Linden, C. (1998). Subcutaneous sumatriptan compared with usual acute treatments for migraine: Clinical and. *Acta Neurologica Belgica, 98*(4), 332–341.

Lam, Raymond W. (1994). Morning light therapy for winter depression: Predictors of response. *Acta Psychiatrica Scandinavica, 89,* 97–101.

Lamb, H. R. (1999). Public psychiatry and prevention. In R. E. Hales, S. C. Yudofsky, & J. A. Talbot (Eds.), *Textbook of psychiatry* (pp. 1535–1556). Washington, DC: American Psychiatric Press.

Lamberg, L. (1998). Dawn's early light to twilight's last gleaming. *Journal of the American Medical Association, 280*(18), 1556–1558.

Lambert, M. J., & Bergin, A. E. (1994). The effectiveness of psychotherapy. In A. E. Bergin & S. L. Garfield (Eds.), *Handbook of psychotherapy and behavior change* (4th ed.). New York: Wiley.

Land, W., & Salzman, C. (1994). Risperidone: A novel antipsychotic medication. *Hospital and Community Psychiatry, 45,* 434–435.

Landabaso, M. A., Iraurgi, I., Sanz, J., Calle, R., & Ruiz de Apodaka, J. (1999). Naltrexone in the treatment of alcoholism. Two-year follow up results. *European Journal of Psychiatry, 13*(2), 97–105.

Lander, E. S., & Schork, N. J. (1994). Genetic dissection of complex traits. *Science, 265,* 2037–2048.

Landesman, S., & Butterfield, E. C. (1987). Normalization and deinstitutionalization of mentally retarded individuals. *American Psychologist, 42,* 809–816.

Lang, P. J., & Buss, A. H. (1965). Psychological deficit in schizophrenia: 2. Interference and activation. *Journal of Abnormal Psychology, 70,* 77–106.

Langevin, R., Paitich, D., Hucker, S. J., Newman, S., Ramsay, G., Pope, S., Geller, G., & Anderson, C. (1979). The effect of assertiveness training, Provera, and sex of therapist in the treatment of genital exhibitionism. *Journal of Behavioral and Experimental Psychiatry, 10,* 275–282.

Langewisch, M. W. J., & Frisch, G. R. (1998). Gambling behavior and pathology in relation to impulsivity, sensation seeking, and risk. *Journal of Gambling Studies, 14*(3), 245–262.

Langhinrichsen-Rohling, J., Lewinsohn, P., Rohde, P., & Seeley, J. (1998). Gender differences in the suicide-related behaviors of adolescents and young adults. *Sex Roles, 39*(11–12), 839–854.

Lanyon, R. I. (1986). Theory and treatment of child molestation. *Journal of Consulting and Clinical Psychology, 54,* 176–182.

Largen, J. W., Mathew, R. J., Dobbins, K., Meyer, J. S., & Claghorn, J. L. (1978). Skin temperature self-regulation and noninvasive regional cerebral blood flow. *Headache, 18,* 203–210.

Larmore, K., Ludwig, A. M., & Cain, R. L. (1977). Multiple personality: An objective case study. *British Journal of Psychiatry, 131,* 35–40.

Larsson, B., & Carlsson, J. (1996). A school-based, nurse-administered relaxation training for children with chronic tension-type. *Journal of Pediatric Psychology, 21*(5), 603–614.

Lashkari, A., Smith, A. K., & Graham, J. M. (1999). Williams-Beuren syndrome: An update and review for the primary physician. *Clinical Pediatrics, 38*(4), 189–208.

Laumann, E. O., Paik, A., & Rosen, R. C. (1999). Sexual dysfunction in the United States: Prevalence and predictors. *Journal of the American Medical Association, 281*(6), 537–544.

Lavigna, G., & Donnellan, A. (1986). *Alternatives to punishment: Solving behavior problems with nonaversive strategies.* New York: Irvington.

Laws, D. R., & Rubin, H. B. (1969). Instructional control of an autonomic sexual response. *Journal of Applied Behavioral Analysis, 2,* 93–99.

Lawson, J. S., McGhie, A., & Chapman, J. (1967). Distractibility in schizophrenia and organic cerebral disease. *British Journal of Psychiatry, 113,* 527–535.

Lay, C. L., & Newman, L. C. (1999). Menstrual migraine: Approaches to management. *CNS Drugs, 12*(3), 189–195.

Lazarus, R. S. (1999). Stress and emotion: A new synthesis.

Lazarus, R. S., & Folkman, S. (1984). *Stress, appraisal, and coping.* New York: Springer.

Leamon, M. H., & Plewes, J. (1999). Factitious disorders and malingering. In R. E. Hales, S. C. Yudofsky, & J. A. Talbot (Eds.), *Textbook of psychiatry* (pp. 695–710). Washington, DC: American Psychiatric Press.

Lecomte, D., & Fornes, P. (1998). Suicide among youth and young adults, 15 through 24 years of age: A report of 392 cases. *Journal of Forensic Sciences, 43*(5), 964–968.

Le Doux, J. (1998). Fear and the brain: Where have we been, and where are we going? *Biological Psychiatry, 44*(12), 1229–1238.

Le Doux, J. E. (1992). Brain mechanisms of emotion and emotional learning. *Current Opinion in Neurobiology, 2,* 191–197.

Le Doux, J. E. (1994). Emotion, memory, and the brain. *Scientific American, 270* (6), 50–57.

Leff, J. P. (1992). Transcultural aspects. In E. S. Paykel (Ed.), *Handbook of affective disorders,* (2nd ed.). New York: Guilford Press.

Lefkovitch, Y., Weiser, M., & Levy, A. (1993). Involuntary outpatient commitment: Ethics and problems. *Medicine and Law, 12,* 213–220.

Leibenluft, E., Fiero, P. L., Bartko, J. J., Moul, D. E., & Rosenthal, N. E. (1993). Depressive symptoms and the self-reported use of alcohol, caffeine, and carbohydrates in normal volunteers and four groups of psychiatric outpatients. *American Journal of Psychiatry, 150,* 294–301.

Leigh, B. C. (1989). In search of the Seven Dwarves: Issues of measurement and meaning in alcohol expectancy research. *Psychological Bulletin, 105,* 361–373.

Lemelin, S., & Baruch, P. (1998). Clinical psychomotor retardation and attention in depression. *Journal of Psychiatric Research, 32*(2), 81–88.

Lenzenweger, M. F. (1999). Stability and change in personality disorder features: The Longitudinal Study of Personality. *Archives of General Psychiatry, 56*(11), 1009–1015.

Leon, A. C., Keller, M. B., Warshaw, M. G., & Mueller, T. I. (1999). A prospective study of fluoxetine treatment and suicidal behavior in affectively ill subjects. *American Journal of Psychiatry, 156*(2), 195–201.

Leppig, M., Bosch, B., Naber, D., & Hippius, H. (1989). Clozapine in the treatment of 121 out-patients. *Psychopharmacology, 99*, 77–79.

Lerer, B., Weiner, R. D., & Belmaker, R. (1984). *ECT: Basic mechanisms.* Washington, DC: American Psychiatric Association.

Lerman, C., Caporaso, N., Main, D., Audrain, J., & Boyd, N. R. (1998). Depression and self-medication with nicotine: The modifying influence of the dopamine D4. *Health Psychology, 17*(1), 56–62.

Lesage, A., Boyer, R., Grunberg, F., Vanier, C., Morissette, R., Menard-Buteau, C., & Loyer, M. (1994). Suicide and mental disorders: A case-control study of young men. *American Journal of Psychiatry, 151*, 1063–1068.

Leslie, D. L., & Rosenheck, R. (1999a). Shifting to outpatient care? Mental health care use and cost under private insurance. *American Journal of Psychiatry, 156*(8), 1250–1257.

Leslie, D. L., & Rosenheck, R. (1999b). Changes in inpatient mental health utilization and costs in a privately insured population. *Medical Care, 37*(5), 457–468.

Lessard v. *Schmidt,* 349 F. Supp. 1078 (E.D. Wis. 1972); 94 S.Ct. 713 (1974).

Lester, D. (1989). Can we prevent suicide? New York: AMS Press.

Lester, D. (1990). The effects of the detoxification of domestic gas in Switzerland on the suicide rate. *Acta Psychiatrica Scandinavica, 82*, 383–384.

Lester, D. (1991a). Do suicide prevention centers prevent suicide? *Homeostasis in Health and Disease, 33*, 190–194.

Lester, D. (1991b). Suicide across the life span: A look at international trends. In A. A. Leenaars (Ed.), *Life span perspectives of suicide.* New York: Plenum.

Lester, D. (1992). State initiatives in addressing youth suicide: Evidence for their effectiveness. *Social Psychiatry and Psychiatric Epidemiology, 27*, 75–77.

Lester, D. (1993). The effectiveness of suicide prevention centers. *Suicide and Life-Threatening Behavior, 23*, 263–267.

Lester, D. (1995). The concentration of neurotransmitter metabolites in the cerebrospinal fluid of suicidal individuals: A meta-analysis. *Pharmacopsychiatry, 28*, 45–50.

Lester, D. (1997a). Menninger's motives for suicide in suicide notes from America and Germany. *Perceptual and Motor Skills, 85*(3, Pt. 2).

Lester, D. (1997b). Suicide in America: A nation of immigrants. *Suicide and Life Threatening Behavior, 27*(1), 50–59.

Lester, D. (1998). Differences in content of suicide notes by age and method. *Perceptual and Motor Skills, 87*(2), 530.

Lester, D., & Akande, A. (1998). Attitudes about suicide in Zambian and Nigerian students. *Perceptual and Motor Skills, 87*(2), 690.

Lester, D., & Linn, M. (1997). Sex differences in suicide notes. *Psychological Reports, 80*(3, Pt. 2).

Lester, D., & Saito, Y. (1998). The reasons for suicide in Japan. *Omega: Journal of Death and Dying, 38*(1), 65–68.

Levenson, A. J., Lord, C. J., Sermas, C. E., Thornby, J. I., Sullender, W., & Comstock, B. A. (1977). Acute schizophrenia: An efficacious outpatient treatment approach as an alternative to full-time hospitalization. *Diseases of the Nervous System, 38*, 242–245.

Levenson, H., & Butler, S. F. (1999). Brief dynamic individual psychotherapy. In R. E. Hales, S. C. Yudofsky, & J. A. Talbot (Eds.), *Textbook of psychiatry* (pp. 1133–1156). Washington, DC: American Psychiatric Press.

Levenson, J. L., McDaniel, S., Moran, M. G., & Stoudemeire, A. (1999). Psychological factors affecting medical conditions. In R. E. Hales, S. C. Yudofsky, & J. A. Talbot (Eds.), *Textbook of psychiatry* (pp. 635–662). Washington, DC: American Psychiatric Press.

Levin, A. P., Schneier, F. R., & Liebowitz, M. R. (1989). Social phobia: Biology and pharmacology. *Clinical Psychology Review, 9*, 129–140.

Levitt, J. J., McCarley, R. W., Nestor, P. G., & Petrescu, C. (1999). Quantitative volumetric MRI study of the cerebellum and vermis in schizophrenia: Clinical. *American Journal of Psychiatry, 156*(7), 1105–1107.

Levy, F., Barr, C., & Sunohara, G. (1998). Directions of aetiologic research on attention deficit hyperactivity disorder. *Australian and New Zealand Journal of Psychiatry, 32*(1), 97–103.

Levy, K. N., Becker, D. F., Grilo, C. M., & Mattanah, J. J. F. (1999). Concurrent and predictive validity of the personality disorder diagnosis in adolescent patients. *American Journal of Psychiatry, 156*(10), 1522–1528.

Lewin, B. (1951). *The psycho-analysis of elation.* London: Hogarth.

Lewine, R. J., & Seeman, M. V. (1995). Gender, brain, and schizophrenia: Anatomy of differences/differences in anatomy. In M. V. Seeman (Ed.), *Gender and psychopathology.* Washington, DC: American Psychiatric Press.

Lewinsohn, P. M., Mischel, W., Chaplin, W., & Barton, R. (1980). Social competence and depression: The role of illusory self-perceptions. *Journal of Abnormal Psychology, 89*, 203–212.

Lewinsohn, P. M., Roberts, R. E., Seeley, J. R., Rohde, P. D. Gotlib, I. H., & Hops, H. (1994). Adolescent psychopathology: 2. Psychosocial risk factors for depression. *Journal of Abnormal Psychology, 103*, 302–315.

Lewinsohn, P. M., Rohde, P. D., Seeley, J. R., & Fischer, S. A. (1993). Age-cohort changes in the lifetime occurrence of depression and other mental disorders. *Journal of Abnormal Psychology, 102*, 110–120.

Lewinsohn, P. M., Rohde, P. D., Seeley, J. R., & Hops, H. (1991). Comorbidity of unipolar depression: 1. Major depression with dysthymia. *Journal of Abnormal Psychology, 100*, 205–213.

Lewinsohn, P. M., Steinmetz, J. L., Larson, D. W., & Franklin, J. (1981). Depression-related cognitions: Antecedent or consequence? *Journal of Abnormal Psychology, 90*, 213–219.

Lewis, D. A. (1997). Development of the prefrontal cortex during adolescence: Insights into vulnerable neural circuits in schizophrenia. *Neuropsychopharmacology, 16*, 385–398.

Leys, D., Henon, H., & Pasquier, F. (1998). White matter changes and poststroke dementia. *Dementia and Geriatric Cognitive Disorders, 9*(Suppl. 1), 25–29.

Leys, D., & Pasquier, F. (1998). Subcortical vascular dementia: Epidemiology and risk factors. *Archives of Gerontology and Geriatrics, 6,* 281–294.

Li, G., Silverman, J. M., Smith, C. J., Zaccario, M. L., Schmeidler, J., Mohs, R. C., & Davis, K. L. (1995). Age at onset and familial risk in Alzheimer's disease. *American Journal of Psychiatry, 152,* 424–430.

Lichtenstein, E. (1999). Nicotine Anonymous: Community resource and research implications. *Psychology of Addictive Behaviors, 13*(1), 60–68.

Lidren, D. M., Watkins, P. L., Gould, R. A., Clum, G. A., Asterino, M., & Tulloch, H. (1994). A comparison of bibliotherapy and group therapy in the treatment of panic disorder. *Journal of Consulting and Clinical Psychology, 62,* 865–869.

Lieberman, J. A., Safferman, A. Z., Pollack, S., Szymanski, S., Johns, C., Howard, A., Kronig, M., Bookstein, P., & Kane, J. M. (1994). Clinical effects of clozapine in chronic schizophrenia: Responses to treatment and predictors of outcome. *American Journal of Psychiatry, 151,* 1744–1752.

Lief, H., & Hubscham, L. (1993). Orgasm in the postoperative transsexual. *Archives of Sexual Behavior, 22,* 145–155.

Lilienfeld, S. O., Kirsch, I., Sarbin, T. R., & Lynn, S. J. (1999). Dissociative identity disorder and the sociocognitive model: Recalling the lessons of the past. *Psychological Bulletin, 125*(5), 507–523.

Lilienfeld, S. O., & Loftus, E. F. (1999). A step backward in the recovered memory debate. *Professional Psychology: Research and Practice, 30*(6), 623.

Lilienfeld, S. O., & Waldman, I. D. (1990). The relation between childhood attention-deficit hyperactivity disorder and adult antisocial behavior reexamined: The problem of heterogeneity. *Clinical Psychology Review, 10,* 699–725.

Lim, K. O., Hedehus, M., Moseley, M., & de Crespigny, A. (1999). Compromised white matter tract integrity in schizophrenia inferred from diffusion tensor. *Archives of General Psychiatry, 56*(4), 367–374.

Linde, K., Ramirez, G., Mulrow, D. C., Pauls, A., Weidenhammer, W., & Melchart, D. (1996). St. John's wort for depression—an overview and meta-analysis of randomized clinical trials. *British Journal of Medicine, 313,* 253–258.

Lindsay, M., Crino, R., & Andrews, G. (1997). Controlled trial of exposure and response prevention in obsessive-compulsive disorder. *British Journal of Psychiatry, 171,* 135–139.

Lindstrom, L. H. (1989). A retrospective study on the long-term efficacy of clozapine in 96 schizophrenic and schizoaffective patients during a 13-year period. *Psychopharmacology, 99,* 84–86.

Linehan, M. M., Goodstein, J. L., Nielsen, S. L., & Chiles, J. A. (1983). Reasons for staying alive when you are thinking of killing yourself: The Reasons for Living Inventory. *Journal of Consulting and Clinical Psychology, 51,* 276–286.

Linn, B., Linn, M., & Jensen, J. (1982). Degree of depression and immune responsiveness. *Psychosomatic Medicine, 44,* 128–129.

Linszen, D. H., Kingemans, P. M., & Lenior, M. E. (1994). Cannabis abuse and the course of recent-onset schizophrenic disorders. *Archives of General Psychiatry, 51,* 273–279.

Lipinski, J. F., Mallya, G., Zimmerman, P., & Pope, H. (1989). Fluoxetine-induced akathisias: Clinical and theoretical implications. *Journal of Clinical Psychiatry, 50,* 339–342.

Lipton, R. B. (1999). Pharmacologic profile and clinical efficacy of rizatriptan. *Headache, 39*(Suppl. 1), S9–S15.

Lisnov, L., Harding, C. G., Safer, L. A., & Kavanagh, J. (1998). Adolescents perceptions of substance abuse prevention strategies. *Adolescence, 33*(130), 301–311.

Litz, B. T. (1992). Emotional numbing in combat-related post-traumatic stress disorder: A critical review and reformulation. *Clinical Psychology Review, 12,* 417–432.

Livingston, R. (1993). Children of people with somatization disorder. *Journal of the American Academy of Child and Adolescent Psychiatry, 32,* 536–544.

Livingston, R., Witt, A., & Smith, G. R. (1995). Families who somatize. *Journal of Developmental and Behavioral Pediatrics, 16,* 42–46.

Lobo, B. L., Cooke, S. C., & Landy, S. H. (1999). Symptomatic pharmacotherapy of migraine. *Clinical Therapeutics: The International Journal of Drug Therapy, 21*(7), 1118–1130.

Loeb, J., & Mednick, S. A. (1976). Asocial behavior and electrodermal response patterns. In K. O. Christiansen & S. A. Mednick (Eds.), *Crime, society, and biology: A new look.* New York: Gardner Press.

Loeber, R. T., & Yurgelun Todd, D. A. (1999). Human neuroimaging of acute and chronic marijuana use: Implications for frontocerebellar. *Human Psychopharmacology Clinical and Experimental, 14*(5), 291–304.

Loehlin, J. C., & Nichols, R. C. (1976). *Heredity, environment, and personality.* Austin: University of Texas Press.

Loewenstein, R. J. (1994). Diagnosis, epidemiology, clinical course, treatment, and cost effectiveness of treatment for dissociative disorders and MPD: Report submitted to the Clinton Administration Task Force on Health Care Financing Reform. *Dissociation Progress in the Dissociative Disorders, 7,* 3–11.

Loftus, E. F. (1992). *The reality of repressed memories.* Psi Chi Lowell Lewis Distinguished Lecture, American Psychological Association, Washington, DC.

Loftus, E. F., & Palmer, J. C. (1974). Reconstruction of automobile destruction: An example of the interaction between language and memory. *Journal of Verbal Learning and Verbal Behavior, 13,* 585–589.

Loftus, E. F., & Polage, D. C. (1999). Repressed memories: When are they real? When are they false? *Forensic Psychiatry, 22,* 61–70.

Logsdon, M. C., Usui, W. M., Cronin, S. N., & Miracle, V. A. (1998). Social support and adjustment in women following coronary artery bypass surgery. *Health Care for Women International, 19*(1), 61–70.

Londborg, P. D., Wolkow, R., Smith, W. T., DuBoff, E., & England, D. (1998). Sertraline in the treatment of panic disorder: A multi-site, double-blind, placebo-controlled. *British Journal of Psychiatry, 173,* 54–60.

Lopez, O. L., Smith, G., Meltzer, C. C., & Becker, J. T. (1999). Dopamine systems in human immunodeficiency virus-associated dementia. *Neuropsychiatry, Neuropsychology, and Behavioral Neurology, 12,* 3.

Lo Piccolo, J. (1983). The prevention of sexual problems in men. In G. Albee, S. Gordon, & H. Leitenberg (Eds.), *Promoting sexual responsibility and preventing sexual problems.* Burlington, VT: University Press of New England.

Lo Piccolo, J., & Stock, W. E. (1986). Treatment of sexual dysfunction. *Journal of Consulting and Clinical Psychology, 54,* 158–167.

Loranger, A. W. (1984). Sex difference in age at onset of schizophrenia. *Archives of General Psychiatry, 41*, 157–161.

Lorion, R. P. (1996). Applying our medicine to the psychopharmacology debate. *American Psychologist, 51*, 219–224.

Lorist, M. M., Snel, J., Kok, A., & Mulder, G. (1994). Influence of caffeine on selective attention in well-rested and fatigued subjects. *Psychophysiology, 31*, 525–534.

Lovaas, O. I. (1969). *Behavior modification: Teaching language to psychotic children* [Film]. Norwalk, CT: Appleton & Lange.

Lovaas, O. I. (1987). Behavioral treatment and normal educational and intellectual functioning in young autistic children. *Journal of Consulting and Clinical Psychology, 55*, 3–9.

Lovaas, O. I. (1993). The development of a treatment-research project for developmentally disabled and autistic children. *Journal of Applied Behavior Analysis, 26*, 617–630.

Lovaas, O. I., Berberich, J. P., Perloff, B. F., & Schaeffer, B. (1966). Acquisition of imitative speech in schizophrenic children. *Science, 151*, 705–707.

Lovaas, O. I., Schaeffer, B., & Simmons, J. Q. (1965). Experimental studies in childhood schizophrenia: Building social behaviors by use of electric shock. *Journal of Experimental Studies in Personality, 1*, 99–109.

Lovaas, O. I., & Simmons, J. Q. (1969). Manipulation of self-destruction in three retarded children. *Journal of Applied Behavior Analysis, 2*, 143–157.

Lovaas, O. I., & Smith, T. (1989). A comprehensive behavioral theory of autistic children: Paradigm for research and treatment. *Journal of Behavior Therapy and Experimental Psychiatry, 20*, 17–29.

Lovaas, O. I., Smith, T., & McEachin, J. J. (1989). Clarifying comments on the Young Autism Study: Reply to Schopler, Short, and Mesibov. *Journal of Consulting and Clinical Psychology, 57*, 165–167.

Lucas, A. R., Beard, C. M., O'Fallon, W. M., & Kurland, L. T. (1991). 50-year trends in the incidence of anorexia nervosa in Rochester, Minn.: A population-based study. *American Journal of Psychiatry, 148*, 917–922.

Lucio, E., Reyes-Lagunes, I., & Scott, R. (1994). MMPI-2 for Mexico: Translation and adaptation. *Journal of Personality Assessment, 63*, 105–116.

Ludwig, A. M. (1994). Mental illness and creative activity in female writers. *American Journal of Psychiatry, 151*, 1650–1656.

Ludwig, A. M., Brandsma, J. M., Wilbur, C. B., Benfeldt, F., & Jameson, D. H. (1972). The objective study of a multiple personality, or are four heads better than one? *Archives of General Psychiatry, 26*, 298–310.

Lydiard, R. B., Steiner, M., Burnham, D., & Gergel, I. (1998). Efficacy studies of paroxetine in panic disorder. *Psychopharmacology Bulletin, 34*(2), 175–182.

Lykken, D. T. (1957). A study of anxiety in the sociopathic personality. *Journal of Abnormal and Social Psychology, 55*, 6–10.

Lykken, D. T., Bouchard, T. J., McGue, M., & Tellegen, A. (1993). Heritability of interests: A twin study. *Journal of Applied Psychology, 78*, 649–661.

Lymburner, J. A., & Roesch, R. (1999). The insanity defense: Five years of research (1993–1997). *International Journal of Law and Psychiatry, 22*(3–4), 213–240.

Lynam, D. R., Milich, R., Zimmerman, R., Novak, S. P., & Logan, T. K. (1999). Project DARE: No effects at 10-year follow-up.

Journal of Consulting and Clinical Psychology, 67(4), 590–593.

Lyness, S. A. (l993). Predictors of differences between Type A and B individuals in heart rate and blood pressure reactivity. *Psychological Bulletin, 114*, 266–295.

Lyons, J. A., & Adams, C. (1999). Posttraumatic stress disorder. In A. J. Goreczny, M. Hersen, et al. (Eds.), *Handbook of pediatric and.*

Lyons, M. J., Eisen, S. A., Goldberg, J., True, W., Lin, N., Meyer, J., Toomey, R., Varaone, S. V., Merla-Ramos, M., & Tsuany, M. T. (1998). A registry-based twin study of depression in men. *Archives of General Psychiatry, 55*, 486–472.

Maas, J. W. (1975). Catecholamines and depression: A further specification of the catecholamine hypothesis of the affective disorders. In A. J. Friedhoff (Ed.), *Catecholamines and behavior.* New York: Plenum.

Maas, J. W., Fawcett, J. A., & Dekirmenjian, H. (1972). Catecholamine metabolism, depressive illness, and drug response. *Archives of General Psychiatry, 26*, 246–262.

MacDougal, J. M., Dembroski, T. M., Dimsdale, J. E., & Hackett, T. P. (1985). Components of Type A, hostility, and anger-in: Further relationships to angiographic findings. *Health Psychology, 4*, 137–152.

Machon, R. A., Mednick, S., & Huttunen, M. O. (1997). Adult major affective disorder after

Machover, K. (1949). *Personality projection in the drawing of the human figure.* Springfield, IL: Thomas.

Macleod, A. D. (1999). Posttraumatic stress disorder, dissociative fugue and a locator beacon. *Australian and New Zealand Journal of Psychiatry, 33*(1), 102–104.

MacLeod, A. K., Tata, P., Evans, K., Tyrer, P., & Schmidt, U. (1998). Recovery of positive future thinking within a high-risk parasuicide group: Results from a pilot. *British Journal of Clinical Psychology, 37*(4), 371–379.

Madge, N., & Harvey, J. G. (1999). Suicide among the young: The size of the problem. *Journal of Adolescence, 22*(1), 145–155.

Maes, M., Smith, R., Christophe, A., Vandoolaeghe, E., Van Gastel, A., & Neels, H. (1997). Lower serum high-density lipoprotein cholesterol (HDL-C) in major depression and in. *Acta Psychiatrica Scandinavica, 95*(3), 212–221.

Magee, W. J., Eaton, W. W., Wittchen, H. U., & McGonagle, K. A. (1996). Agoraphobia, simple phobia, and social phobia in the national comorbidity survey. *Archives of General Psychiatry, 53*(2), 159–168.

Magno Zito, J., Safer, D., dosReis, S., Gardner, J., Boles, M., & Lynch, F. (2000). Trends in the prescribing of psychotropic medications to preschoolers. *Journal of the American Medical Association, 283*(8), 1028.

Mago, R., & Crits-Christoph, P. (1999). Prevention of recurrent depression with cognitive behavioral therapy. *Archives of General Psychiatry, 56*(5), 479.

Maher, B. A. (1968). The shattered language of schizophrenia. *Psychology Today.* pp. 30–33, 60.

Maher, B. A. (1972). The language of schizophrenia: A review and interpretation. *British Journal of Psychiatry, 120*, 4–17.

Maher, B. A. (1983). A tentative theory of schizophrenic utterance. In B. A. Maher & W. Maher (Eds.), *Progress in experimental personality research* (Vol. 12). New York: Academic Press.

Maher, B. A. (1988a). Anomalous experience and delusional thinking: The logic of explanations. In T. F. Oltmanns & B. A. Maher (Eds.), *Delusional beliefs.* New York: Wiley.

Maher, B. A. (1988b). Delusions as the product of normal cognitions. In T. F. Oltmanns & B. A. Maher (Eds.), *Delusional beliefs.* New York: Wiley.

Maher, B. A., Manschreck, T. C., Yurgelum Todd, D. A., & Tsuang, M. T. (1998). Hemispheric asymmetry of frontal and temporal gray matter and age of onset in. *Biological Psychiatry, 44*(6), 413–417.

Maher, W. B., & Maher, B. A. (1985). Psychopathology: I. From ancient times to the eighteenth century. In G. A. Kimble and K. Schlesinger (Eds.), *Topics in the history of psychology* (Vol. 2). Hillsdale, NJ: Erlbaum.

Mahesh Yogi, M. (1963). *The science of being and art of living.* London: Allen & Unwin.

Maier, S. F., & Seligman, M. E. P. (1976). Learned helplessness: Theory and evidence. *Journal of Experimental Psychology: General, 103,* 3–46.

Maier, S. F., Seligman, M. E. P., & Solomon, R. (1969). Pavlovian fear conditioning and learned helplessness: Effects on escape and avoidance behavior of the CS-US contingency and voluntary responding. In B. Campbell & R. Church (Eds.), *Punishment and aversive behavior.* Norwalk, CT: Appleton & Lange.

Maier, S. F., Watkins, L. R., & Fleshner, M. (1994). Psychoneuroimmunology; The interface between behavior, brain, and immunity. *American Psychologist, 49,* 1004–1017.

Maier, W., Lichtermann, D., Minges, J., & Heun, R. (1994). Personality disorders among the relatives of schizophrenia patients. *Schizophrenia Bulletin, 20,* 481–493.

Maldonado, G., & Kraus, J. F. (1991). Variation in suicide occurrence by time of day, day of week, and lunar phase. *Suicide and Life-Threatening Behavior, 21,* 174–187.

Maldonado, J. R., Butler, L. D., & Soegel, D. (1998). Treatments for dissociative disorders. In P. E. Nathan & J. M. Gorman (Eds.), *A guide to treatments that work* (pp. 423–446). New York: Oxford University Press.

Males, M. (1991a). Reply to Kim Smith, PhD, on "Teen suicide and changing cause-of-death certification, 1953–1987." *Suicide and Life-Threatening Behavior, 21,* 402–405.

Males, M. (1991b). Teen suicide and changing cause-of-death certification, 1953–1987. *Suicide and Life-Threatening Behavior, 21,* 245–259.

Maletzky, B. M. (1998). The paraphilias, research and treatment. In P. E. Nathan & J. M. Gorman (Eds.), *A guide to treatments that work* (pp. 472–500). New York: Oxford University Press.

Malgady, R. G., & Costantino, G. (1998). Symptom severity in bilingual Hispanics as a function of clinician ethnicity and language of. *Psychological Assessment, 10*(2), 120–127.

Malkoff-Schwartz, S., Frank, E., Anderson, B., Sherrill, J. T., Siegel, L., Patterson, D., & Kupfer, D. J. (1998). Stressful life events and social rhythm disruption in the onset of manic and depressive bipolar episodes. *Archives of General Psychiatry, 55*(8), 702–707.

Malmquist, C. P. (1986). Children who witness parental murder: Posttraumatic aspects. *Journal of the American Academy of Child Psychiatry, 25,* 320–325.

Manela, M., Katona, C., & Livingston, G. (1996). How common are the anxiety disorders in old age? *International Journal of Geriatric Psychiatry, 11*(1), 65–70.

Manford, M., & Andermann, F. (1998). Complex and visual hallucinations: Clinical and neurobiological insights. *Brain, 121*(10), 1819–1840.

Mangweth, B., Pope, H. G., Hudson, J. I., & Biebl, W. (1996). Bulimia nervosa in Austria and the United States: A controlled cross-cultural study. *International Journal of Eating Disorders, 20*(3), 263–270.

Mangweth, B., Pope, H. G., Jr., Hudson, J. I., & Olivardia, R. (1997). Eating disorders in Austrian men: An intracultural and crosscultural comparison study. *Psychotherapy and Psychosomatics, 66*(4), 214–221.

Mann, J. J., & Kapur, S. (1991). The emergence of suicidal ideation and behavior during antidepressant pharmacotherapy. *Archives of General Psychiatry, 48,* 1027–1033.

Mann, J. J., Oquendo, M., Underwood, M. D., & Arango, V. (1999). The neurobiology of suicide risk: A review for the clinician. *Journal of Clinical Psychiatry, 60*(Suppl. 2), 7–11.

Mannuzza, S., Klein, R. G., Bessler, A., Malloy, P., & La Padula, M. (1993). Adult outcome of hyperactive boys. *Archives of General Psychiatry, 50,* 565–576.

Mannuzza, S., Klein, R. G., Bonagura, N., Malloy, P., Giampino, T. L., & Adilli, K. A. (1991). Hyperactive boys almost grown up. *Archives of General Psychiatry, 48,* 77–83.

Manoach, D. S., Press, D. Z., Thangaraj, V., & Searl, M. M. (1999). Schizophrenic subjects activate dorsolateral prefrontal cortex during a working memory task. *Biological Psychiatry, 45*(9), 1128–1137.

Manson, J. E., Hu, F. B., Rich Edwards, J. W., Colditz, G. A., Stampfer, M. J., & Willett, W. C. (1999). A prospective study of walking as compared with vigorous exercise in the prevention of. *New England Journal of Medicine, 341*(9), 650–658

Marangell, L. B., Silver, J. M., & Yudofsky, S. C. (1999). Psychopharmacology and electroconvulsive therapy. In R. E. Hales, S. C. Yudofsky, & J. A. Talbot (Eds.), *Textbook of psychiatry* (pp. 1025–1132). Washington, DC: American Psychiatric Press.

Marcotte, D. (1998). Use of topiramate, a new anti-epileptic as a mood stabilizer. *Journal of Affective Disorders, 50*(2–3), 245–251.

Marcus, D. A., Scharff, L., Mercer, S., & Turk, D. C. (1999). Musculoskeletal abnormalities in chronic headache: A controlled comparison of headache. *Headache, 39*(1), 21–27.

Marcus, M. D., Wing, R. R., Ewing, L., Kern, E., McDermott, M., & Gooding, W. (1990). A double-blind, placebo-controlled trial of fluoxetine plus behavior modification in the treatment of obese binge-eaters and non-binge-eaters. *American Journal of Psychiatry, 147,* 876–881.

Marder, S. R., & Meibach, R. C. (1994). Risperidone in the treatment of schizophrenia. *American Journal of Psychiatry, 151,* 825–835.

Marder, S. R., Wirshing, W. C., Van Putten, T., Mintz, J., McKenzie, J., Johnston-Cronk, K., Labell, M., & Liberman, R. P. (1994). Fluphenazine vs placebo supplementation for prodromal signs of relapse in schizophrenia. *Archives of General Psychiatry, 51,* 280–287.

Margraf, J., Barlow, D. H., Clark, D. M., & Telch, M. J. (1993). Psychological treatment of panic: Work in progress on outcome, active ingredients, and follow-up. *Behaviour Research and Therapy, 31*(1), 1–8.

Margraf, J., Ehlers, A., & Roth, W. T. (1988). Mitral valve prolapse and panic disorder: A review of their relationship. *Psychosomatic Medicine, 50,* 93–113.

Maris, R. W. (1997). Social and familial risk factors in suicidal behavior. *Psychiatric Clinics of North America, 20*(3), 519–550.

Markowitz, J., Brown, R., Sweeney, J., & Mann, J. J. (1987). Reduced length and cost of hospital stay for major depression in patients treated with ECT. *American Journal of Psychiatry, 144,* 1025–1029.

Marks, I. M. (1981). Review of behavioral psychotherapy: 2. Sexual disorders. *American Journal of Psychiatry, 138,* 750–756.

Marks, I. M., & Gelder, M. G. (1967). Transvestism and fetishism: Clinical and psychological changes during faradic aversion. *British Journal of Psychiatry, 113,* 711–729.

Marks, I. M., Gelder, M. G., & Bancroft, J. (1970). Sexual deviants two years after electric aversion. *British Journal of Psychiatry, 117,* 173–185.

Marks, I., Lovell, K., Noshirvani, H., Livanou, M., & Thrasher, S. (1998). Treatment of posttraumatic stress disorder by exposure and/or cognitive restructuring: A controlled study. *Archives of General Psychiatry, 55*(4), 317–325.

Markus, C. R., Panhuysen, G., Tuiten, A., Koppeschaar, H., Fekkes, D., & Peters, M. L. (1998). Does carbohydrate-rich, protein-poor food prevent a deterioration of mood and cognitive. *Appetite, 31*(1), 49–65.

Marlowe, D. B., Lambert, J. B., & Thompson, R. G. (1999). Voluntary intoxication and criminal responsibility. *Behavioral Sciences and the Law, 17*(2), 195–217.

Marlowe, M., Cossairt, A., Moon, C., Errera, J., McNeel, A., Peak, R., Ray, J., & Schroeder, C. (1985). Main and interaction effects of metallic toxins on classroom behavior. *Journal of Abnormal Child Psychology, 13,* 185–198.

Marmer, S. S. (1999). Theories of the mind and psychopathology. In R. E. Hales, S. C. Yudofsky, & J. A. Talbot (Eds.), *Textbook of psychiatry* (pp. 147–192). Washington, DC: American Psychiatric Press.

Marsh, L., Harris, D., Lim, K. O., Beal, M., Hoff, A. L., Minn, K., Csernansky, J. G., DeMent, S., Faustman, W. O., Sullivan, E. V., & Pfefferbaum, A. (1997). Structural magnetic resonance imaging abnormalities in men with severe chronic schizophrenia and an early age at clinical onset. *Archives of General Psychiatry, 54*(12), 1104–1112.

Marsh, L., Lim, K. O., Hoff, A. L., Harris, D., Beal, M., & Minn, K. (1999). Severity of schizophrenia and magnetic resonance imaging abnormalities: A comparison of state. *Biological Psychiatry, 45*(1), 49–61.

Marshall, P. (1989). Attention deficit disorder and allergy: A neurochemical model of the relation between the illnesses. *Psychological Bulletin, 106,* 434–446.

Martin, A. (1923). History of dancing mania. *American Journal of Clinical Medicine, 30,* 265–271.

Martin, R. L., & Yutzy, S. H. (1994). Somatoform disorders. In R. E. Hales, S. C. Yudofsky, & J. A. Talbott (Eds.), *American Psychiatric Press textbook of psychiatry* (2nd ed.). Washington, DC: American Psychiatric Press.

Martin, R. L., & Yutzy, S. H. (1999). Somatoform disorders. In R. E. Hales, S. C. Yudofsky, & J. A. Talbot (Eds.), *Textbook of psychiatry* (pp. 663–694). Washington, DC: American Psychiatric Press.

Martinez-Arevalo, M. J., Calcedo-Ordonez, A., & Varo-Prieto, J. R. (1994). Cannabis consumption as a prognostic factor in schizophrenia. *British Journal of Psychiatry, 164,* 679–681.

Marx, E. M., Williams, J. M. G., & Claridge, G. C. (1992). Depression and social problem solving. *Journal of Abnormal Psychology, 101,* 78–86.

Marzuk, P. M., Leon, A. C., Tardiff, K., Morgan, E. B., Stajic, M., & Mann, J. J. (1992). The effect of access to lethal methods of injury on suicide rates. *Archives of General Psychiatry, 49,* 451–458.

Masalsky, C. J., & Luiselli, J. K. (1998). Effects of supplemental feedings of white bread on chronic rumination. *Behavioral Interventions, 13*(4), 227–233.

Maslow, A. H. (1970). *Motivation and personality.* New York: Harper & Row.

Mason, M. A., & Gibbs, J. T. (1992). Patterns of adolescent psychiatric hospitalization: Implications for social policy. *American Journal of Orthopsychiatry, 62,* 447–457.

Masson, J. M. (1984). *The assault on truth: Freud's suppression of the seduction theory.* Harmondsworth, England: Penguin.

Masten, A. S., & Coatsworth, J. D. (1998). The development of competence in favorable and unfavorable environments: Lessons from. *American Psychologist, 53*(2), 205–220.

Masters, W., & Johnson, V. (1970). *Human sexual inadequacy.* Boston: Little, Brown.

Matarazzo, J. D. (1986). Computerized clinical psychological test interpretations. *American Psychologist, 41,* 14–24.

Mathiesen, K. S., Tambs, K., & Dalgard, O. S. (1999). The influence of social class, strain and social support on symptoms of anxiety and depression. *Social Psychiatry and Psychiatric Epidemiology, 34*(2), 61–72.

Matser, E. J. T., Kessels, A. G. H., Jordan, B. D., Lezak, M. D., & Troost, J. (1998). Chronic traumatic brain injury in professional soccer players. *Neurology, 51*(3), 791–796.

Matser, E. J. T., Kessels, A. G., Lezak, M. D., Jordan, B. D., & Troost, J. (1999). Neuropsychological impairment in amateur soccer players. *Journal of the American Medical Association, 282*(10), 971–973.

Matt, G. E., Vazquez, C., & Campbell, W. K. (1992). Mood-congruent recall of affectively toned stimuli: A meta-analytic review. *Clinical Psychology Review, 12*(2), 227–255.

Matthews, G. R., & Antes, J. R. (1992). Visual attention and depression: Cognitive biases in the eye fixations of dysphoric and the nondepressed. *Cognitive Therapy and Research, 16,* 359–371.

Matthews, K. A. (1982). Psychological perspectives on the Type A behavior pattern. *Psychological Bulletin, 91,* 293–323.

Matthews, K. A. (1988). Coronary heart disease and Type A behaviors: Update on and alternative to the Booth-Kewley and Friedman (1987) quantitative review. *Psychological Bulletin, 104,* 373–380.

Matthews, K. A., Batson, C. D., Horn, J., & Rosenman, R. H. (1981). "Principles in his nature which interest him in the fortune of others . . .": The heritability of empathic concern for others. *Journal of Personality, 49,* 237–247.

Matthews, K. A., Glass, D. C., Rosenman, R. H., & Bortner, R. W. (1977). Competitive drive, pattern A, and coronary heart disease: A further analysis of some data from the Western Collaborative Group Study. *Journal of Chronic Diseases, 30,* 489–498.

Mattick, R. P., Andrews, G., Hadzi-Pavlovic, D., & Christensen, H. (1990). Treatment of panic and agoraphobia: An integrative review. *Journal of Nervous and Mental Disease, 178,* 567–576.

Mattson, S. N., Goodman, A. M., Caine, C., Delis, D. C., & Riley, E. P. (1999). Executive functioning in children with heavy prenatal alcohol exposure. *Alcoholism: Clinical and Experimental Research, 23*(11), 1808–1815.

Mattson, S. N., & Riley, E. P. (1999). Implicit and explicit memory functioning in children with heavy prenatal alcohol exposure. *Journal of the International Neuropsychological Society, 5*(5), 462–471.

Mavissakalian, M. R., & Perel, J. M. (1989). Imipramine dose-response relationship in panic disorder with agoraphobia. *Archives of General Psychiatry, 46,* 127–131.

Mavissakalian, M. R., & Perel, J. M. (1992a). Clinical experiments in maintenance and discontinuation of imipramine therapy in panic disorder with agoraphobia. *Archives of General Psychiatry, 49,* 318–323.

Mavissakalian, M. R., & Perel, J. M. (1992b). Protective effects of imipramine maintenance treatment in panic disorder with agoraphobia. *American Journal of Psychiatry, 149,* 1053–1057.

Mavissakalian, M. R., & Perel, J. M. (1995). Imipramine treatment of panic disorder with agrophobia: Dose ranging and plasma level-response relationships. *American Journal of Psychiatry, 152,* 673–682.

Mavissakalian, M. R., & Perel, J. M. (1996). The relationship of plasma imipramine and N-desmethylimipramine to response in panic. *Psychopharmacology Bulletin, 32*(1), 143–147.

Maxwell, S., & Shinderman, M. (1999). Optimizing response to methadone maintenance treatment: Use of higher-dose methadone. *Journal of Psychoactive Drugs, 31*(2), 95–102.

May, P. R. (1968). *Treatment of schizophrenia.* New York: Science House.

Mayer, L. E. S., & Walsh, B. T. (1998). The use of selective serotonin reuptake inhibitors in eating disorders. *Journal of Clinical Psychiatry, 59*(Suppl. 15), 28–34.

Mayes, S. D., Crites, D. L., Bixler, E. O., Humphrey, F. J., & Mattison, R. E. (1994). Methylphenidate and ADHD: Influence of age, IQ and neurodevelopmental status. *Developmental Medicine and Child Neurology, 36,* 1099–1107.

Mayeux, R., & Sano, M. (1999). Treatment of Alzheimer's disease. *New England Journal of Medicine, 341*(22), 1670–1679.

Mazure, C. M. (1998). Life stressors as risk factors in depression. *Clinical Psychology: Science and Practice, 5*(3), 291–313.

Mazza, J. J., & Reynolds, W. M. (1998). A longitudinal investigation of depression, hopelessness, social support, and major and minor. *Suicide and Life Threatening Behavior, 28*(4), 358–374.

McCabe, R. E. (1999). Implicit and explicit memory for threat words in high- and low-anxiety-sensitive participants. *Cognitive Therapy and Research, 23*(1), 21–38.

McCafferty, G., & Dooley, J. (1990). Involuntary outpatient commitment: An update. *Mental and Physical Disability Law Reporter, 14,* 277–287.

McCann, I. L., & Holmes, D. S. (1984). Influence of aerobic exercise on depression. *Journal of Personality and Social Psychology, 46,* 1142–1147.

McCarley, R. W., Shenton, M. E., O'Donnell, B. F., & Nestor, P. G. (1994). Neural circuits in schizophrenia. *Archives of General Psychiatry, 51,* 515.

McCarley, R. W., Wible, C. G., Frumin, M., Hirayasu, Y., & Levitt, J. J. (1999). MRI anatomy of schizophrenia. *Biological Psychiatry, 45*(9), 1099–1119.

McCrady, B. S. (1994). Alcoholics Anonymous and behavior therapy: Can habits be treated as diseases? Can diseases be treated as habits? *Journal of Consulting and Clinical Psychology, 62,* 1159–1166.

McCue, J. D., & Cohen, L. M. (1999). Freud's physician-assisted death. *Archives of Internal Medicine, 159,* 1521–1522.

McDougle, C. J., Goodman, W. K., & Price, L. H. (1994). Dopamine antagonists in tic-related and psychotic spectrum obsessive compulsive disorder. *Journal of Clinical Psychiatry, 55,* 24–31.

McEachin, J. J., Smith, T., & Lovaas, O. I. (1993). Long-term outcome for children with autism who received early intensive behavioral treatment. *American Journal on Mental Retardation, 97,* 359–372.

McElroy, S. L., Hudson, J. I., Pope, H. G., Keck, P. E., & Aizley, H. G., (1992). The *DSM-III-R* impulse control disorders not elsewhere classified: Clinical characteristics and relationship to other psychiatric disorders. *American Journal of Psychiatry, 149,* 318–327.

McElroy, S. L., Keck, P. E., Pope, H., G. & Hudson, J. I. (1989). Pharmacological treatment of kleptomania and bulimia nervosa. *Journal of Clinical Psychopharmacology, 9,* 358–360.

McElroy, S. L., Soutullo, C. A., Beckman, D. A., & Taylor, P., Jr. (1998). *DSM-IV* intermittent explosive disorder: A report of 27 cases. *Journal of Clinical Psychiatry, 59*(4), 203–210.

McFarlane, W. R., Lukens, E., Link, B., Dushay, R., et al. (1995). Multiple-family groups and psychoeducation in the treatment of schizophrenia. *Archives of General Psychiatry, 52*(8), 679–687.

McGaugh, J. L. (1989). Involvement of hormonal and neuromodulatory systems in the regulation of memory storage. *Annual Review of Neuroscience, 2,* 255–287.

McGaugh, J. L. (1990). Significance and remembrance: The role of neuromodulatory systems. *Psychological Science, 1,* 15–25.

McGhie, A., & Chapman, J. (1961). Disorders of attention and perception in early schizophrenia. *British Journal of Medical Psychology, 34,* 103–116.

McGilley, B. M., & Holmes, D. S. (1988). Aerobic fitness and response to psychological stress. *Journal of Research in Personality, 22,* 129–139.

McGilley, B. M., Holmes, D. S., & Holmsten, R. D. (1993). Influence of exercise rehabilitation on coronary patients: A six-year follow-up. Unpublished manuscript. University of Kansas at Lawrence.

McGlashan, T. H., & Fenton, W. S. (1992). The positive-negative distinction in schizophrenia. *Archives of General Psychiatry, 49,* 63–72.

McGrath, E., Keita, G. P., Strickland, B., & Russo, N. F. (1990). *Women and depression: Risk factors and treatment issues.* Washington, DC: American Psychological Association.

McGreevy, M. A., Steadman, H. J., & Callahan, L. A. (1991). The negligible effects of California's 1982 reform of the insanity defense test. *American Journal of Psychiatry, 148,* 744–750.

McGrew, J. H., Wright, E. R., Pescosolido, B. A., & McDonel, E. C. (1999). The closing of Central State Hospital: Long-term outcomes for persons with severe mental. *Journal of Behavioral Health Services and Research, 26*(3), 246–261.

McGue, M., & Lykken, D. T. (1992). Genetic influence on risk of divorce. *Psychological Science, 3,* 368–373.

McGue, M., Bacon, S., & Lykken, D. T. (1993). Personality stability and change in early adulthood: A behavioral genetic analysis. *Developmental Psychology, 29*(1), 96–109.

McGuire, P. K., Quested, D. J., Spence, S. A., & Murray, R. M. (1998). Pathophysiology of "positive" thought disorder in schizophrenia. *British Journal of Psychiatry, 173,* 231–235.

McHugh, P. R., & Goodell, H. (1971). Suicidal behavior: A distinction in patients with sedative poisoning seen in a general hospital. *Archives of General Psychiatry, 25,* 456–464.

McIntosh, J. L. (1992). Epidemiology of suicide in the elderly. *Suicide and Life-Threatening Behavior, 22,* 15–35.

McKay, D. (1997). A maintenance program for obsessive-compulsive disorder using exposure with response prevention: 2-year follow-up. *Behaviour Research and Therapy, 35*(4), 367–369.

McKim, W. A. (1986). *Drugs and behavior.* Englewood Cliffs, NJ: Prentice Hall.

McNeil, D. W., Kee, M., & Zvolensky, M. J. (1999). Culturally related anxiety and ethnic identity in Navajo college students. *Cultural Diversity and Ethnic Minority Psychology, 5*(1), 56–64.

McNulty, J. L., Graham, J. R., Ben Porath, Y. S., & Stein, L. A. R. (1997). Comparative validity of MMPI-2 scores of African American and Caucasian mental health. *Psychological Assessment, 9*(4), 464–470.

Mednick, S. A., Gabrielli, W. F., & Hutchings, B. (1984). Genetic influences in criminal convictions: Evidence from an adoption cohort. *Science, 224,* 891–894.

Mednick, S. A., Machon, R. A., Huttunen, M. O., & Bonett, D. (1988). Adult schizophrenia following prenatal exposure to an influenza epidemic. *Archives of General Psychiatry, 45,* 189–192.

Mednick, S. A., Parnas, J., & Schulsinger, F. A. (1987). The Copenhagen High-Risk Project, 1962–86. *Schizophrenia Bulletin, 13,* 485–495.

Meduna, L. von. (1935). Die Konvolsionstherapie der Schizophrenie. *Psychiatrisch-Neurologische Wochenschrift, 37,* 317–319.

Meehan, P., Lamb, J. A., Saltzman, L. E., & O'Carroll, P. W. (1992). Attempted suicide among young adults: Progress toward a meaningful estimate of prevalence. *American Journal of Psychiatry, 149,* 41–44.

Meehl, P. E. (1954). Clinical versus statistical prediction: A theoretical analysis and a review of the evidence.

Meesters, C. M. G., & Smulders, J. (1994). Hostility and myocardial infarction in men. *Journal of Psychosomatic Research, 38,* 727–734.

Mehlum, L., Friis, S., Vaglum, P., & Karterud, S. (1994). The longitudinal pattern of suicidal behaviour in borderline personality disorder: A prospective follow-up study. *Acta Psychiatrica Scandinavica, 90,* 124–130.

Meisch, R. A. (1991). Studies of drug self-administration. *Psychiatric Annals, 21,* 196–205.

Melella, J. T., Travin, S., & Cullen, K. (1989). Legal and ethical issues in the use of antiandrogens in treating sexual offenders. *Bulletin of the American Academy of Psychiatry and the Law, 17,* 223–232.

Mellman, T. A., & Uhde, T. W. (1989). Electroencephalographic sleep in panic disorder. *Archives of General Psychiatry, 46,* 178–184.

Meltzer, H. Y. (1995a). Neuroleptic withdrawal in schizophrenic patients: An idea whose time has come. *Archives of General Psychiatry, 52,* 200–202.

Meltzer, H. Y. (1995b). The role of serotonin in schizophrenia and the place of serotonin-dopamine antagonist antipsychotics. *Journal of Clinical Psychopharmacology, 15* 2S–3S.

Meltzer, H. Y., Bastani, B., Ramirez, L. F., & Matsubara, S. (1989). Clozapine: New research on efficacy and mechanism of action. *European Archives of Psychiatry and Neurological Sciences, 238,* 332–339.

Meltzer, H. Y., & Okayli, G. (1995). Reduction of suicidality during clozapine treatment of neuroleptic-resistant schizophrenia: Impact on risk-benefit assessment. *American Journal of Psychiatry, 152,* 183–190.

Mendlewicz, J., & Rainer, J. D. (1977). Adoption study supporting genetic transmission in manic-depressive illness. *Nature, 268,* 327–329.

Messiha, F. S., & Carlson, J. C. (1983). Behavioral and clinical profiles of Tourette's disease: A comprehensive overview. *Brain Research Bulletin, 11,* 195–204.

Metalsky, G., Joiner, T. E., Hardin, T. S., & Abramson, L. Y. (1993). Depressive reactions to failure in a naturalistic setting: A test of the hopelessness and self-esteem theories of depression. *Journal of Abnormal Psychology, 102,* 101–109.

Mete, L., Schnurr, P. P., Rosenberg, S. D., & Oxman, T. E. (1993). Language content and schizophrenia in acute phase Turkish patients. *Social Psychiatry and Psychiatric Epidemiology, 28,* 275–280.

Metha, A., Weber, B., & Webb, L. D. (1998). Youth suicide prevention: A survey and analysis of policies and efforts in the 50 states. *Suicide and Life Threatening Behavior, 28*(2), 150–164.

Metz, P., & Mathiesen, F. R. (1979). External iliac "steal syndrome" leading to a defect in penile erection and impotence. *Vascular Surgery, 13,* 70–72.

Meyer, J., & Reter, D. (1979). Sex reassignment: Follow-up. *Archives of General Psychiatry, 36,* 1010–1015.

Meyers, C. J. (1997). Expanding Tarasoff: Protecting patients and the public by keeping subsequent caregivers. *Journal of Psychiatry and Law, 25*(3), 365–375.

Michal, V., Kramar, R., Pospichal, J., & Hejhal, L. (1977). Arterial epigastricocavernous anastomosis for the treatment of sexual impotence. *World Journal of Surgery, 1,* 515–524.

Michelson, L. K., & Marchione, K. (1991). Behavioral, cognitive, and pharmacological treatments of panic disorder with agoraphobia: Critique and synthesis. *Journal of Consulting and Clinical Psychology, 59,* 100–114.

Michelson, L. K., Marchione, K., Greenwald, M., Glanz, L., Testa, S., & Marchione, N. (1990). Panic disorder; Cognitive-behavioral treatment. *Behaviour Research and Therapy, 28,* 141–153.

Mignot, E. (1998). Genetic and familial aspects of narcolepsy. *Neurology, 50*(2, Suppl. 1), S16–S22.

Miguel, E. C., Rauch, S. L., & Jenike, M. A. (1997). Obsessive-compulsive disorder. *Psychiatric Clinics of North America, 20*(4), 863–883.

Mikkelsen, M., & Stene, J. (1970). Genetic counseling in Down's syndrome. *Human Heredity, 20,* 457–464.

Miklowitz, D. J. (1996). Psychotherapy in combination with drug treatment for bipolar disorder. *Journal of Clinical Psychopharmacology, 16*(Suppl. 1), 56S–66S.

Miles, J. E., McLean, P. D., & Maurice, W. L. (1976). The medical student therapist: Treatment outcome. *Canadian Psychiatric Association Journal, 21,* 467–472.

Milgram, N. A. (1969). The rational and irrational in Zigler's motivational approach to mental retardation. *American Journal of Mental Deficiency, 73,* 527–532.

Millberger, S., Biederman, J., Faraone, S. V., & Jones, J. (1998). Further evidence of an association between maternal smoking during pregnancy and attention. *Journal of Clinical Child Psychology, 27*(3), 352–358.

Miller, B. L., & Cummings, J. L. (1999). The human frontal lobes: Functions and disorders.

Miller, D. D., Perry, P. J., Cadoret, R. J., & Andreasen, N. C. (1994). Clozapine's effect on negative symptoms in treatment-refractory schizophrenics. *Comprehensive Psychiatry, 35,* 8–15.

Miller, I. W., & Norman, W. H. (1979). Learned helplessness in humans: A review and attributional theory model. *Psychological Bulletin, 86,* 93–118.

Miller, I. W., Norman, W. H., Keitner, G. I., Bishop, S. B., et al. (1989). Cognitive-behavioral treatment of depressed inpatients. *Behavior Therapy, 20*(1), 25–47.

Miller, M., & Kantrowitz, B. (1999, Jan 25). Unmasking Sybil: A re-examination of the most famous psychiatric patient in history. *Time,* 66–68.

Miller, R. D. (1994). The U.S. Supreme Court looks at voluntariness and consent. *International Journal of Law and Psychiatry, 17,* 239–252.

Miller, R. D. (1998). Forced administration of sex-drive reducing medications to sex offenders: Treatment or. *Psychology, Public Policy, and Law, 4*(1–2), 175–199.

Miller, S. D., & Triggiano, P. J. (1992). The psychophysiological investigation of multiple personality disorder: Review and update. *American Journal of Clinical Hypnosis, 35,* 47–61.

Miller, T. Q., Smith, T. W., Turner, C. W., Guijarro, M. L., & Hallet, A. J. (1996). A meta-analytic review of research on hostility and physical health. *Psychological Bulletin, 119,* 322–348.

Milner, B. R. (1970). Memory and medial temporal regions of the brain. In K. H. Pribram & D. E. Broadbent (Eds.), *Biology of memory.* New York: Academic Press.

Min, S. K., & Lee, B. O. (1997). Laterality in somatization. *Psychosomatic Medicine, 59*(3), 236–240.

Mineka, S., Davidson, M., Cook, M., & Keir, R. (1984). Observational conditioning of snake fear in rhesus monkeys. *Journal of Abnormal Psychology, 93,* 355–372.

Mineka, S., & Zinbarg, R. (1998). Experimental approaches to the anxiety and mood disorders. In J. G. Adair, D. Belanger, et al. (Eds.), *Advances in psychological science.*

Miniszek, N. A. (1983). Development of Alzheimer's disease in Down syndrome individuals. *American Journal of Mental Deficiency, 87,* 377–385.

Minton, J., Campbell, M., Green, W., Jennings, S., & Samit, C. (1982). Cognitive assessment of siblings of autistic children. *Journal of the American Academy of Child Psychiatry, 21,* 256–261.

Mischel, W. (1990). Personality dispositions revisited and revised: A view after three decades. In L. A. Pervin (Ed.), *Handbook of personality: Theory and research.* New York: Guilford Press.

Mitchell, J. E., & Groat, R. (1984). A placebo-controlled, double-blind trial of amitriptyline in bulimia. *Journal of Clinical Psychopharmacology, 4,* 186–193.

Mitler, M. M., & Hajdukovic, R. (1991). Relative efficacy of drugs for the treatment of sleepiness in narcolepsy. *Sleep, 14,* 218–220.

Mizes, J. S., & Lohr, J. M. (1983). The treatment of bulimia (binge-eating and self-induced vomiting): A quasi-experimental investigation of the effects of stimulus narrowing, self-reinforcement and self-control relaxation. *International Journal of Eating Disorders, 2,* 59–65.

Mohamed, S., Paulsen, J. S., O'Leary, D., Arndt, S., & Andreasen, N. (1999). Generalized cognitive deficits in schizophrenia: A study of first-episode patients. *Archives of General Psychiatry, 56*(8), 749–754.

Molina, B. S. G., Smith, B. H., & Pelham, W. E. (1999). Interactive effects of attention deficit hyperactivity disorder and adolescent substance use. *Psychology of Addictive Behaviors, 13* (4), 348–358.

Monahan, J. (1973). The psychiatrization of criminal behavior. *Hospital and Community Psychiatry, 24,* 105–107.

Monahan, J. (1976). The prevention of violence. In J. Monahan (Ed.), *Community mental health and the criminal justice system.* Elmsford, NY: Pergamon Press.

Monahan, J. (1978). Prediction research and the emergency commitment of dangerous mentally ill persons: A reconsideration. *American Journal of Psychiatry, 135,* 198–201.

Monahan, J. (1984). The prediction of violent behavior: Toward a second generation of theory and policy. *American Journal of Psychiatry, 141,* 10–15.

Monahan, J. (1993). Limiting therapist exposure to Tarasoff liability. *American Psychologist, 48,* 242–250.

Money, J., & Tucker, P. (1975). *Sexual signatures: On being a man or woman.* Boston: Little Brown.

Monroe, S. M., Imhoff, D. F., Wise, B. D., & Harris, J. E. (1983). Prediction of psychosocial symptoms under high-risk psychosocial circumstances: Life events, social support, and symptom specificity. *Journal of Abnormal Psychology, 92,* 338–350.

Monroe, S. M., & Simons, A. D. (1991). Diathesis-stress theories in the context of life stress research: Implications for the depressive disorders. *Psychological Bulletin, 110,* 406–425.

Montgomery, S. A., Dufour, H., Brion, S., & Gailledreau, J. (1988). The prophylactic efficacy of fluoxetine in unipolar disorder. *British Journal of Psychiatry, 153*(Suppl. 3), 69–76.

Montgomery, S. A., & Dunbar, G. (1993). Paroxetine is better than placebo in relapse prevention and the prophylaxis of recurrent. *International Clinical Psychopharmacology, 8*(3), 189–195.

Morens, D. M. (1999). Death of a President. *New England Journal of Medicine, 341,* 1845–1849.

Morgan, W. P. (1993). Hypnosis and sport psychology. In J. W. Rhue, S. J. Lynn, et al. (Eds.), *Handbook of clinical hypnosis.*

Mori, E., Ikeda, M., Hirono, N., Kitagaki, H., & Imamura, T. (1999). Amygdalar volume and emotional memory in Alzheimer's disease. *American Journal of Psychiatry, 156*(2), 216–222.

Moriarty, J., Ring, H. A., & Robertson, M. M. (1993). An idiot savant calendrical calculator with Gilles de la Tourette syndrome: Implications for an. *Psychological Medicine, 23*(4), 1019–1021.

Morihisa, J. M., Rosse, R. B., Cross, C. D., Balkoski, V., & Ingraham, C. A. (1999). Laboratory and other diagnostic tests in psychiatry. In R. E. Hales, S. C. Yudofsky, & J. A. Talbot (Eds.), *Textbook of psychiatry* (pp. 281–316). Washington, DC: American Psychiatric Press.

Morin, C. M., Culbert, J. P., & Schwartz, S. M. (1994). Nonpharmacological interventions for insomnia: A meta-analysis of treatment efficacy. *American Journal of Psychiatry, 151,* 1172–1180.

Morin, C. M., Mimeault, V., & Gagne, A. (1999). Nonpharmacological treatment of late-life insomnia. *Journal of Psychosomatic Research, 46*(2), 103–116.

Morokoff, P. J., Baum, A., McKinnon, W. R., & Gillilland, R. (1987). Effects of chronic unemployment and acute psychological stress on sexual arousal in men. *Health Psychology, 6,* 545–560.

Morokoff, P. J., & Gillilland, R. (1993). Stress, sexual functioning, and marital satisfaction. *Journal of Sex Research, 30,* 43–53.

Morokoff, P. J., & Heinman, J. R. (1980). Effects of erotic stimuli on sexually functional and dysfunctional women: Multiple measures before and after therapy. *Behaviour Research and Therapy, 18,* 127–137.

Moroney, J. T., Tang, M. X., Berglund, L., Small, S., & Merchant, C. (1999). Low-density lipoprotein cholesterol and the risk of dementia with stroke. *Journal of the American Medical Association, 282*(3), 254–260.

Morris, C. A., & Mervis, C. B. (1999). Williams syndrome. In S. Goldstein, C. R. Reynolds, et al. (Eds.), *Handbook of neurodevelopmental and genetic disorders in children* (pp. 555–590).

Morris, P. L. P., Robinson, R. G., Raphael, B., & Hopwood, M. J. (1996). Lesion location and poststroke depression. *Journal of Neuropsychiatry and Clinical Neurosciences, 8*(4), 399–403.

Mosher, L. R., & Keith, S. J. (1980). Psychosocial treatment: Individual, family, and community support approaches. *Schizophrenia Bulletin, 6,* 10–41.

Mosher, L. R., & Menn, A. Z. (1978). Community residential treatment for schizophrenia: Two-year follow-up. *Hospital and Community Psychiatry, 29,* 715–723.

Mosher, L. R., Menn, A. Z., & Matthews, S. M. (1975). Soteria: Evaluation of a home-based treatment for schizophrenia. *American Journal of Orthopsychiatry, 45,* 455–467.

Mottron, L., & Belleville, S. (1995) Perspective production in a savant autistic draughtsman. *Psychological Medicine, 25*(3), 639–648.

Mouton, S. G., & Stanley, M. A. (1996). Habit reversal training for trichotillomania: A group approach. *Cognitive and Behavioral Practice, 3*(1), 159–182.

Mowrer, O. H., & Mowrer, W. A. (1938). Enuresis: A method for its study and treatment. *American Journal of Orthopsychiatry, 8,* 436–447.

Muehlbach, M. J., & Walsh, J. K. (1995). The effects of caffeine on simulated night-shift work and subsequent daytime sleep. *Sleep, 18,* 22–29.

Mueller, R. A., Behen, M. E., Rothermel, R. D., Chugani, D. C., Muzik, O., Mangner, T. J., & Chugani, H. T. (1999). Brain mapping of language and auditory perception in high-functioning autistic adults: A PET study. *Journal of Autism and Developmental Disorders, 29*(1), 19–31.

Mueller-Oerlinghausen, B., & Berghoefer, A. (1999). Antidepressants and suicidal risk. *Journal of Clinical Psychiatry, 60*(Suppl. 2), 94–99.

Muijen, M., Silverstone, T., Mehmet, A., & Christie, M. (1988). A comparative clinical trial of fluoxetine, mianserin and placebo in depressed outpatients. *Acta Psychiatrica Scandinavica, 78,* 384–390.

Mukherjee, S. (1993). ECT-lithium combination. *Convulsive Therapy, 9,* 274–284.

Mukherjee, S., Sackeim, H. A., & Schnur, D. B. (1994). Electroconvulsive therapy of acute manic episodes: A review of 50 years' experience. *American Journal of Psychiatry, 151,* 169–176.

Mukhopadhyay, P., & Turner, R. M. (1997). Biofeedback treatment of essential hypertension: Review and enhancements. *Social Science International, 13*(1–2), 1–9.

Mulder, R. T., Beautrais, A. L., Joyce, P. R., & Fergusson, D. M. (1998). Relationship between dissociation, childhood sexual abuse, childhood physical abuse, and. *American Journal of Psychiatry, 155*(6), 806–811.

Muldoon, M. F., Manuck, S. B., & Mann, J. J. (1992). Effects of a low-fat diet on brain serotoninergic responsivity in cynomolgus monkeys. *Biological Psychiatry, 31,* 739–742.

Mullinix, J. M., Norton, B. J., Hack, S., & Fishman, M. (1978). Skin temperature biofeedback and migraine. *Headache, 17,* 242–244.

Mulvey, E. P., Geller, J. L., & Roth, L. H. (1987). The promise and peril of involuntary outpatient commitment. *American Psychologist, 42,* 571–584.

Muntaner, C., Eaton, W. W., Diala, C., Kessler, R. C., & Sorlie, P. D. (1998). Social class, assets, organizational control and the prevalence of common groups of psychiatric disorders. *Social Science and Medicine, 47*(12), 2043–2053.

Murphy, D. G. M., Murphy, D. M., Abbas, M., Palazidou, E., Binnie, C., Arendt, J., Costa, D., & Checkley, S. (1993). Seasonal affective disorder: Response to light as measured by electroencephalogram, melatonin suppression, and cerebral blood flow. *British Journal of Psychiatry, 163,* 327–331.

Murphy, E., & Macdonald, A. (1992). Affective disorders in old age. In E. S. Paykel (Ed.), *Handbook of affective disorders* (2nd ed.). New York: Guilford Press.

Murphy, J. (1976). Psychiatric labeling in cross-cultural perspective. *Science, 191,* 1019–1028.

Murphy, L. J., & Mitchell, D. L. (1998). When writing helps to heal: E-mail as therapy. *British Journal of Guidance and Counselling, 26*(1), 21–32.

Murphy-Brennan, M. G., & Oei, T. P. S. (1999). Is there evidence to show that fetal alcohol syndrome can be prevented? *Journal of Drug Education, 29*(1), 5–24.

Murray, H. A. (1943). *Thematic Apperception Test.* Cambridge, MA: Harvard University Press.

Murray, J. B. (1992). Kleptomania: A review of the research. *Journal of Psychology, 126*, 131–137.

Murray, J. B. (1998). Psychophysiological aspects of amphetamine-methamphetamine abuse. *Journal of Psychology, 132*(2), 227–237.

Murray, L., & Cooper, P. J. (1996). The impact of postpartum depression on child development. *International Review of Psychiatry, 8*(1), 55–63.

Murray, L. A., Whitehouse, W. G., & Alloy, L. B. (1999). Mood congruence and depressive deficits in memory: A forced-recall analysis. *Memory, 7*(2), 175–196.

Murray, R. M. (1998). Predictors of outcome in schizophrenia. *Journal of Clinical Psychopharmacology, 18*(2, Suppl. 1), 2S–4S.

Murtagh, D. R., & Greenwood, K. M. (1995). Identifying effective psychological treatments for insomnia: A meta-analysis. *Journal of Consulting and Clinical Psychology, 63*, 79–89.

Muscettola, G., Potter, W. Z., Pickar, D., & Goodwin, F. (1984). Urinary 3-methoxy-4-hydroxyphenylglycol and affective disorders. *Archives of General Psychiatry, 41*, 337–342.

Musselman, D. L., Evans, D. L., & Nemeroff, C. B. (1998). The relationship of depression to cardiovascular disease: Epidemiology, biology, and. *Archives of General Psychiatry, 55*(7), 580–592.

Myers, T. C., Wittrock, D. A., & Foreman, G. W. (1998). Appraisal of subjective stress in individuals with tension-type headache: The influence of baseline measures. *Journal of Behavioral Medicine, 21*(5), 469–484.

Myerson, A. (1940). Review of mental disorders in urban areas: An ecological study of schizophrenia and other psychoses. *American Journal of Psychiatry, 96*, 995–997.

Nafziger, A. N., Bertino, J. S., Jr., Goss Bley, A. I., & Kashuba, A. D. M. (1999). Incidence of sexual dysfunction in healthy volunteers on fluvoxamine therapy. *Journal of Clinical Psychiatry, 60*(3), 187–190.

Nakao, M., Nomura, S., Shimosawa, T., & Yoshiuchi, K. (1997). Clinical effects of blood pressure biofeedback treatment on hypertension by auto-shaping. *Psychosomatic Medicine, 59*(3), 331–338.

Nakazawa, Y., Sakamoto, T., Yasutake, R., Yamaga, K., Kotorii, T., Miyahara, Y., Ariyoshi, Y., & Kameyama, T. (1992). Treatment of sleep apnea with prosthetic mandibular advancement (PMA). *Sleep, 15*, 499–504.

Nankai, M., Yamada, S., Muneoka, K., & Toru, M. (1995). Increased 5-ht2 receptor-mediated behavior 11 days after shock in learned helpless rats. *European Journal of Pharmacology, 28*, 123–130.

Nardi, A. E., Valenca, A. M., Zin, W. A., & Figueira, I. (1997). Short term clonazepam treatment in carbon dioxide induced panic attacks. *Jornal Brasileiro de Psiquiatria, 46*(11), 611–614.

Nathan, P. E. (1988). The addictive personality is the behavior of the addict. *Journal of Consulting and Clinical Psychology, 56*, 183–188.

Nathan, P. E., & Gorman, J. M. (1998). Treatments that work—and what convinces us they do. In P. E. Nathan & J. M. Gorman (Eds.), *A guide to treatments that work* (pp. 3–25). New York: Oxford University Press.

Nathan, P. E., & Langenbucher, J. W. (1999). Psychopathology: Description and classification. *Annual Review of Psychology, 50*, 79–197.

Nathan, S. G. (1986). The epidemiology of the *DSM-III* psychosexual dysfunctions. *Journal of Sex and Marital Therapy, 12*, 267–281.

Neale, J. M., & Oltmanns, T. F. (1980). *Schizophrenia.* New York: Wiley.

Neary, D. (1999). Classification of the dementias. *Reviews in Clinical Gerontology, 9*(1), 55–64.

Needleman, H. L., Gunnoe, C., Leviton, A., Reed, R., Peresie, H., Maher, C., & Barrett, P. (1979). Deficits in psychologic and classroom performance of children with elevated dentine lead levels. *New England Journal of Medicine, 300*, 689–695.

Nehlig, A. (1999). Are we dependent upon coffee and caffeine? A review on human and animal data. *Neuroscience and Biobehavioral Reviews, 23*(4), 563–576.

Neimeyer, R. A. & Pfeiffer, A. M. (1994). Evaluation of suicide intervention effectiveness. *Death Studies, 18*, 131–166.

Nelson, K. B. (1991). Prenatal and perinatal factors in the etiology of autism. *Pediatrics, 87*, 761–766.

Nelson, L. D., & Adams, K. M. (1997). Challenges for neuropsychology in the treatment and rehabilitation of brain-injured patients. *Psychological Assessment, 9*(4), 368–373.

Nelson, M. D., Saykin, A. J., Flashman, L. A., & Riordan, H. J. (1998). Hippocampal volume reduction in schizophrenia as assessed by magnetic resonance imaging. *Archives of General Psychiatry, 55*(5), 433–440.

Nemeroff, C. B. (1998). The neurobiology of depression. *Scientific American*, 42–49.

Nemeroff, C. B., & Schatzberg, A. F. (1998). Pharmacological treatment of unipolar depression. In P. E. Nathan & J. M. Gorman (Eds.), *A guide to treatments that work* (pp. 212–225). New York: Oxford University Press.

Neylan, T. C., Reynolds, C. F., III, & Kupfer, D. J. (1999). Sleep disorders. In R. E. Hales, S. C. Yudofsky, & J. A. Talbot (Eds.), *Textbook of psychiatry* (pp. 955–982). Washington, DC: American Psychiatric Press.

Nicholson, R. A., & Kugler, K. E. (1991). Competent and incompetent criminal defendants: A quantitative review of comparative research. *Psychological Bulletin, 109*, 355–370.

Niederehe, G., & Schneider, L. (1998). Treatments for depression and anxiety in the aged. In P. E. Nathan & J. M. Gorman (Eds.), *A guide to treatments that work* (pp. 270–287). New York: Oxford University Press.

Nielsen, D. A., Goldman, D., Virkkunnen, M., Tokola, R., Rawlings, R., & Linnoila, M. (1994). Suicidality and 5-hydroxyindoleacetic acid concentrations associated with a tryptophan hydroxylase polymorphism. *Archives of General Psychiatry, 51*, 34–38.

Nielsen, D. A., Virkkunen, M., Lappalainen, J., & Eggert, M. (1998). A tryptophan hydroxylase gene marker for suicidality and alcoholism. *Archives of General Psychiatry, 55*(7), 593–602.

Nigg, J. T., & Goldsmith, H. H. (1994). Genetics of personality disorders: Perspectives from personality and psychopathology research. *Psychological Bulletin, 115*, 346–380.

Nilsson, A. (1999). Lithium therapy and suicide risk. *Journal of Clinical Psychiatry, 60*(Suppl. 2), 85–88.

Ninan, P. T., Knight, B., Kirk, L., Rothbaum, B. O., & Kelsey, J. (1998). A controlled trial of venlafaxine in trichotillomania: Interim Phase I results. *Psychopharmacology Bulletin, 34*(2), 221–224.

Niznikiewicz, M. A., Voglmaier, M., Shenton, M. E., & Seidman, L. J. (1999). Electrophysiological correlates of language processing in schizotypal personality disorder. *American Journal of Psychiatry, 156*(7), 1052–1058.

Nobler, M. S., Sackheim, H. A., Prohovik, I., Moeller, J. R., Mukherjee, S., Schnur, D. B., Prudic, J., & Devanand, D. P. (1994). Regional cerebral blood flow in mood disorders: 3. Treatment and clinical response. *Archives of General Psychiatry, 51*, 884–897.

Nolen-Hoeksema, S. (1990). *Sex differences in depression.* Stanford, CA: Stanford University Press.

Nolen-Hoeksema, S. (1991). Responses to depression and their effects on the duration of depressive episodes. *Journal of Abnormal Psychology, 100*, 569–582.

Nolen-Hoeksema, S., & Girgus, J. S. (1994). The emergence of gender differences in depression during adolescence. *Psychological Bulletin, 115*, 424–443.

Nopoulos, P., Flaum, M., & Andreasen, N. C. (1997). Sex differences in brain morphology in schizophrenia. *American Journal of Psychiatry, 154*, 1648–1654.

North, C., Nixon, S., Shariat, S., Mallonee, S., McMillen, H. J., Spitznagel, E., & Smith, E. (1999). Psychiatric disorders among survivors of the Oklahoma City bombing. *Journal of the American Medical Association, 282*, 755–762.

Nottelmann, E. D., & Jensen, P. S. (1998). Current issues in childhood bipolarity. *Journal of Affective Disorders, 51*(2), 77–80.

Nowell, P. D., Buysse, D. J., Morin, C. M., Reynolds, C. F., III, & Kupfer, D. J. (1998). Effective treatments for selected sleep disorders. In P. E. Nathan & J. M. Gorman (Eds.), *A guide to treatments that work* (pp. 531–543). New York: Oxford University Press.

Nowlin, N. S. (1983). Anorexia nervosa in twins: Case report and review. *Journal of Clinical Psychiatry, 44*, 101–105.

Noyes, R., Clarkson, C., Crowe, R. R., Yates, W. R., & McChesney, C. M. (1987). A family study of generalized anxiety disorder. *American Journal of Psychiatry, 144*, 1019–1024.

Noyes, R., Jr., Happel, R. L., Muller, B. A., & Holt, C. S. (1998). Fluvoxamine for somatoform disorders: An open trial. *General Hospital Psychiatry, 20*(6), 339–344.

Noyes, R., Kathol, R. G., Fisher, M. M., Phillips, B. M., Suelzer, M. T., & Woodman, C. L. (1994). Psychiatric comorbidity among patients with hypochondriasis. *General Hospital Psychiatry, 16*, 78–87.

Nurnberg, H. G., Hensley, P. L., Lauriello, J., Parker, L. M., & Keith, S. J. (1999). Sildenafil for women patients with antidepressant-induced sexual dysfunction. *Psychiatric Services, 50*(8), 1076–1078.

Nurnberger, J. I., & Gershon, E. S. (1992). Genetics. In E. S. Paykel (Ed.), *Handbook of affective disorders* (2nd ed.) New York: Guilford Press.

O'Brien, C. P., & McKay, J. (1998). Psychopharmacological treatments of substance use disorders. In P. E. Nathan & J. M. Gorman (Eds.), *A guide to treatments that work* (pp. 127–155). New York: Oxford University Press.

Obrocki, J., Buchert, R., Vaeterlein, O., Thomasius, R., & Beyer, W. (1999). Ecstasy—Long term effects on the human central nervous system revealed by positron. *British Journal of Psychiatry, 175*, 186–188.

O'Carroll, R. (1991). Sexual desire disorders: A review of controlled treatment studies. *Journal of Sexual Research, 28*, 607–624.

O'Connor v. Donaldson, 493 F.2d 507 (5th Cir. 1974); 422 U.S. 563 (1975).

O'Connor, F. L. (1998). The role of serotonin and dopamine in schizophrenia. *Journal of the American Psychiatric Nurses Association, 4*(4), S30–S34.

O'Connor, N., & Hermelin, B. (1994). Two autistic savant readers. *Journal of Autism and Developmental Disorders, 24*(4), 501–515.

Offir, C. W. (1982). *Human sexuality.* New York: Harcourt Brace.

Ofshe, R., & Watters, E. (1994). *Making monsters: False memories, psychotherapy, and sexual hysteria.* New York: Scribner.

Ogles, B. M., Lambert, M. J., & Sawyer, J. D. (1995). Clinical significance of the National Institute of Mental Health Treatment of Depression Collaborative Research Program data. *Journal of Consulting and Clinical Psychology, 63*, 321–326.

O'Halloran, R. L., & Dietz, P. E. (1993). Autoerotic fatalities with power hydraulics. *Journal of Forensic Sciences, 38*, 359–364.

O'Hanrahan, S., Fitzgerald, M., & O'Regan, M. (1999). Personality traits in parents of people with autism. *Irish Journal of Psychological Medicine, 16*(2), 59–60.

O'Hara, M. W., Schlechte, J. A., Lewis, D. A., & Varner, M. W. (1991). Controlled prospective study of postpartum mood disorders: Psychological, environmental, and hormonal variables. *Journal of Abnormal Psychology, 100*, 63–73.

O'Hara, M. W., Schlechte, J. A., Lewis, D. A., & Wright, E. J. (1991). Prospective study of postpartum blues. *Archives of General Psychiatry, 48*, 801–806.

O'Hara, M. W., & Swain, A. M. (1996). Rates and risk of postpartum depression—a meta-analysis. *International Review of Psychiatry, 8*(1), 37–54.

O'Hare, T. (1995). Differences in Asian and White drinking: Consumption level, drinking contexts, and expectancies. *Addictive Behaviors, 20*, 261–266.

Olds, D. (1982). The Prenatal/Early Infancy Project: An ecological approach to prevention of developmental difficulties. In J. Belsky (Ed.), *In the beginning.* New York: Columbia University Press.

Olds, D., Pettitt, L. M., Robinson, J., Henderson, C., Jr., & Eckenrode, J. (1998). Reducing risks for antisocial behavior with a program of prenatal and early childhood home. *Journal of Community Psychology, 26*(1), 65–83.

Olds, J. (1958). Hypothalamic substrates of reward. *Physiological Reviews, 42*, 554–604.

Olinger, L. J., Kuiper, N. A., & Shaw, B. F. (1987). Dysfunctional attitudes and stressful life events: An interactive model of depression. *Cognitive Therapy and Research, 11*, 25–40.

Olney, J. W., & Farber, N. B. (1995). Glutamate receptor dysfunction and schizophrenia. *Archives of General Psychiatry, 52*, 998–1007.

Olsson, S., Jansson, I., & Moller, A. (1995). A critical view on male-to-female sex reassignment surgical and hormonal treatment: An analysis of follow-up studies. *Norkisk-Sexologi, 13*, 14–35.

Oltmanns, T. F., & Maher, B. A. (1988). *Delusional beliefs.* New York: Wiley.

O'Malley, S., Jaffe, A. J., Chang, G., & Schottenfeld, R. S. (1996). Six-month follow-up of Naltrexone and psychotherapy for alcohol dependence. *Archives of General Psychiatry, 53,* 217–224.

O'Malley, S. S., Jaffee, A. J., Chang, G., Schottenfeld, R. S., Meyer, R. E., & Rounsaville, B. (1992). Naltrexone and coping skills therapy for alcohol dependence: A controlled study. *Archives of General Psychiatry, 49,* 881–887.

Oquendo, M. A., Malone, K. M., Ellis, S. P., & Sackeim, H. A. (1999). Inadequacy of antidepressant treatment for patients with major depression who are at risk for. *American Journal of Psychiatry, 156*(2), 190–194.

Orbach, I., Bar-Joseph, H., & Dror, N. (1990). Styles of problem solving in suicidal individuals. *Suicide and Life-Threatening Behavior, 20,* 56–64.

Oren, D. A., Moul, D. E., Schwartz, P. J., Brown, C., Yamada, E. M., & Rosenthal, N. E. (1994). Exposure to ambient light in patients with seasonal affective disorder. *American Journal of Psychiatry, 151,* 591–592.

Orne, M. T. (1962). On the social psychology of the psychological experiment: With particular reference to demand characteristics and their implications. *American Psychologist, 17,* 776–783.

Orne, M. T., Dinges, D. F., & Orne, E. C. (1984). On the differential diagnosis of multiple personality in the forensic context. *International Journal of Clinical and Experimental Hypnosis, 32,* 118–169.

Orne, M. T., & Scheibe, K. E. (1964). The contribution of non-deprivation factors in the production of sensory deprivation effects: The psychology of the panic button. *Journal of Abnormal and Social Psychology, 68,* 3–12.

Ornish, D., Scherwitz, L. W., Billings, J. H., Gould, K. L., Merritt, T. A., Sparler, S., & Armstrong, W. T. (1998). Intensive lifestyle changes for reversal of coronary heart disease. *Journal of the American Medical Association, 280*(23), 2001–2007.

Osgood, C. E., & Luria, Z. (1954). A blind analysis of a case of multiple personality using the semantic differential. *Journal of Abnormal and Social Psychology, 49,* 579–591.

Osgood, C. E., Luria, Z., & Smith, S. W. (1976). A blind analysis of another case of multiple personality using the semantic differential technique. *Journal of Abnormal Psychology, 85,* 256–270.

O'Shea, E., Granados, R., Esteban, B., Colado, M. I., & Green, A. R. (1998). The relationship between the degree of neurodegeneration of rat brain 5-HT nerve terminals. *Neuropharmacology, 37*(7), 919–926.

Osler, W. (1892). *Lectures on angina and allied states.* Norwalk, CT: Appleton & Lange.

Osowiecki, D., & Compas, B. E. (1998). Psychological adjustment to cancer: Control beliefs and coping in adult cancer patients. *Cognitive Therapy and Research, 22*(5), 483–499.

Overholser, J., Evans, S., & Spirito, A. (1990). Sex differences and their relevance to primary prevention of adolescent suicide. *Death Studies, 14,* 391–402.

Pachman, J. S. (1996). The dawn of a revolution in mental health. *American Psychologist, 51,* 213–215.

Paige, S. R. (1997). Current perspectives on posttraumatic stress disorder from the clinic and the laboratory. *Integrative Physiological and Behavioral Science, 32*(1), 5–8.

Pallanti, S., Quercioli, L., Pazzagli, A., & Rossi, A. (1999). Awareness of illness and subjective experience of cognitive complaints in patients with. *American Journal of Psychiatry, 156*(7), 1094–1096.

Palmer, D. D., Henter, I. D., & Wyatt, R. J. (1999). Do antipsychotic medications decrease the risk of suicide in patients with schizophrenia? *Journal of Clinical Psychiatry, 60*(Suppl. 2), 100–103.

Panzarino, P. J., Jr. (1998). The costs of depression: Direct and indirect; treatment versus nontreatment. *Journal of Clinical Psychiatry, 59*(Suppl. 20), 11–14.

Papassotiropoulos, A., Hawellek, B., Frahnert, C., & Rao, G. S. (1999). The risk of acute suicidality in psychiatric inpatients increases with low plasma cholesterol. *Pharmacopsychiatry, 32*(1), 1–4.

Papp, L. A., Martinez, J. M., Klein, D. F., Coplan, J. D., Norman, R. G., Cole, R., de Jesus, M. J., Ross, D., Goetz, R., & Groman, J. M. (1997). Respiratory psychophysiology of panic disorder: Three respiratory challenges in 98 subjects. *American Journal of Psychiatry, 154,* 1557–1565.

Paradis, C. M., Hatch, M., & Friedman, S. (1994). Anxiety disorders in African Americans: An update. *Journal of the National Medical Association, 86,* 609–612.

Paradiso, S., & Robinson, R. G. (1998). Gender differences in poststroke depression. *Journal of Neuropsychiatry and Clinical Neurosciences, 10*(1), 41–47.

Pardo, J. V., Pardo, P. J., & Raichle, M. E. (1993). Neural correlates of self-induced dysphoria. *American Journal of Psychiatry, 150*(5), 713–719.

Parellada, E., Catafau, A. M., Bernardo, M., & Lomena, F. (1998). The resting and activation issue of hypofrontality: A single photon emission computed. *Biological Psychiatry, 44*(8), 787–790.

Paris, J. (1992). Dhat: The semen loss anxiety syndrome. *Transcultural Psychiatric Research Review, 29,* 109–118.

Park, S., Holzman, P. S., & Goldman–Rakic, P. S. (1995). Spatial working memory deficits in the relatives of schizophrenic patients. *Archives of General Psychiatry, 52,* 821–828.

Parry, R., & Killick, S. (1998). An evaluation of the impact of an individually administered videotape for people with panic. *Behavioural and Cognitive Psychotherapy, 26*(2), 153–161.

Pascual-Leone, A., Catala, M. D., & Pascual, A. P. (1996). Lateralized effect of rapid-rate transcranial magnetic stimulation of the preforntal cortex on mood. *Neurology, 46,* 499–502.

Pascual-Leone, A., Gomez-Tortosa, E., Grafman, J., Alway, D., Nichelli, P., & Hallett, M. (1994). Induction of visual extinction by rapid-rate transcranial magnetic stimulation of parietal lobe. *Neurology, 44,* 494–498.

Pascual-Leone, A., Rubio, B., Pallardo, F., & Catala, M. D. (1996). Rapid-rate transcrainal magnetic stimulation of left dorsolateral prefrontal cortex in drug-resistant depression. *Lancet, 347,* 233–237.

Pascual-Leone, A., Valls-Sole, J., Wassermann, E., Brasil, N. J., Cohen, L., & Hallett, M. (1992). Effects of focial transcranial magnetic stimulation on simple reaction time to acoustic, visual and somatosensory stimuli. *Brain, 115,* 1045–1059.

Pate v. *Robinson,* 384 U.S. 375 (1966).

Patel, C. (1994). Identifying psychosocial and other risk factors in Whitehall II study. [2nd International Congress of Behavioral Medicine CIANS-ISBM satellite conference]. *Homeostasis in Health and Disease, 35,* 71–83.

Paul, G. L., & Lentz, R. J. (1977). *Psychosocial treatment of chronic mental patients.* Cambridge, MA: Harvard University Press.

Paul, S. M., Marangos, P. J., Goodwin, F. K., & Slotnick, P. (1980). Brain-specific benzodiazepine receptors and putative endogenous benzodiazepine-like compounds. *Biological Psychiatry, 15,* 407–428.

Pauls, D. L., Kruger, S. D., Leckman, J. F., Cohen, D. J., & Kidd, K. K. (1984). The risk of Tourette's syndrome and chronic multiple tics among relatives of Tourette's syndrome patients obtained by direct interview. *Journal of the American Academy of Child Psychiatry, 23,* 134–137.

Paykel, E. S., & Cooper, Z. (1992). Life events and social stress. In E. S. Paykel (Ed.), *Handbook of affective disorders* (2nd ed.). New York: Guilford Press.

Paykel, E. S., Prusoff, B. A., & Myers, J. K. (1975). Suicide attempts and recent life events: A controlled comparison. *Archives of General Psychiatry, 32,* 327–333.

Pearlin, L., & Schooler, C. (1978). The structure of coping. *Journal of Health and Social Behavior, 19,* 2–21.

Pearlson, G. D. (1997). Superior temporal gyrus and planum temporale in schizophrenia: A selective review. *Progress in Neuro Psychopharmacology and Biological Psychiatry, 21,* 8.

Pedersen, W., & Skrondal, A. (1999). Ecstasy and new patterns of drug use: A normal population study. *Addiction, 94*(11), 1695–1706.

Pelham, W. E., Bender, M. E., Caddel, J., Booth, S., & Moorer, S. H. (1985). Methylphenidate and children with attention deficit disorder. *Archives of General Psychiatry, 42,* 948–952.

Penava, S. J., Otto, M. W., Maki, K. M., & Pollack, M. H. (1998). Rate of improvement during cognitive-behavioral group treatment for panic disorder. *Behaviour Research and Therapy, 36*(7–8), 665–673.

Penfield, W. (1955). The permanent record of the stream of consciousness. *Acta Psychologica, 11,* 47–69.

Penfield, W., & Perot, P. (1963). The brain's record of auditory and visual experience. *Brain, 86,* 595–696.

Penick, E. C., Powell, B. J., Nickel, E. J., Read, M. R., et al. (1990). Examination of Cloninger's Type I and Type II alcoholism with a sample of men alcoholics in treatment. *Alcoholism Clinical and Experimental Research, 14,* 623–629.

Pennebaker, J. W. (1982). *The psychology of physical symptoms.* New York: Springer-Verlag.

Pennebaker, J. W. (1990). *Opening up: The healing power of confiding in others.* New York: Morrow.

Pennebaker, J. W. (1993). Nonverbal and verbal emotional expression and health. *Psychotherapy and Psychosomatics, 59,* 11–19.

Pennebaker, J. W. (1997). Writing about emotional experiences as a therapeutic process. *Psychological Science, 8*(3), 162–166.

People v. *Buono,* Calif. 81-A354231 (1983).

Perez, J., Tardito, D., Mori, S., Racagni, G., & Smeraldi, E. (1999). Abnormalities of cyclic adenosine monophosphate signaling in platelets from untreated. *Archives of General Psychiatry, 56*(3), 248–253.

Perna, G., Bertani, A., Arancio, C., Ronchi, P., & Bellodi, L. (1995). Laboratory response of patients with panic and obsessive–compulsive disorder to 35% CO_2 challenges. *American Journal of Psychiatry, 152,* 85–89.

Perna, G., Bertani, A., Caldirola, D., & Bellodi, L. (1996). Family history of panic disorder and hypersensitivity to CO_2 in patients with panic disorder. *American Journal of Psychiatry, 153*(8), 1060–1064.

Perna, G., Caldirola, D., Arancio, C., & Bellodi, L. (1997). Panic attacks: A twin study. *Psychiatry Research, 66*(1), 69–71.

Perna, G., Cocchi, S., Bertani, A., Arancio, C., & Bellodi, L. (1995). Sensitivity to 35% CO_2 in healthy first-degree relatives of patients with panic disorder. *American Journal of Psychiatry, 152,* 623–625.

Perr, I. N. (1981). Effects of the Rennie decision on private hospitalization in New Jersey: Two case reports. *American Journal of Psychiatry, 138,* 774–778.

Perry, J. D., & Whipple, B. (1981). Pelvic muscle strength of female ejaculators: Evidence in support of a new theory of orgasm. *Journal of Sex Research, 17,* 22–39.

Perry, W., Geyer, M. A., & Braff, D. L. (1999). Sensorimotor gating and thought disturbance measured in close temporal proximity in. *Archives of General Psychiatry, 56*(3), 277–281.

Person, J. B., & Miranda, J. (1992). Cognitive theories of vulnerability to depression: Reconciling negative evidence. *Cognitive Therapy and Research, 16,* 485–502.

Perugi, G., Akiskal, H. S., Giannotti, D., Frare, F., & Di Vaio, S. (1997). Gender-related differences in body dysmorphic disorder (dysmorphophobia). *Journal of Nervous and Mental Disease, 185*(9), 578–582.

Perugi, G., Giannotti, D., Di Vaio, S., Frare, F., Saettoni, M., & Cassano, G. B. (1996). Fluvoxamine in the treatment of body dysmorphic disorder (dysmorphophobia). *International Clinical Psychopharmacology, 11*(4), 247–254.

Pescosolido, B. A., Wright, E. R., & Kikuzawa, S. (1999). "Stakeholder" attitudes over time toward the closing of a state hospital. *Journal of Behavioral Health Services and Research, 26*(3), 318–328.

Peters, M. L., Godaert, G. L. R., Ballieux, R. E., & Brosschot, J. F. (1999). Immune responses to experimental stress: Effects of mental effort and uncontrollability. *Psychosomatic Medicine, 61*(4), 513–524.

Petersen, M. E., & Dickey, R. (1995). Surgical sex reassignment: A comparative survey of international centers. *Archives of Sexual Behavior, 24,* 135–156.

Peterson, C. B., & Seligman, M. E. P. (1984). Causal explanations as a risk factor for depression: Theory and evidence. *Psychological Review, 91,* 347–374.

Peterson, C. B., & Mitchell, J. E. (1999). Psychosocial and pharmacological treatment of eating disorders: A review of research findings. *Journal of Clinical Psychology, 55*(6), 685–697.

Petrides, G. (1998). Continuation ECT: A review. *Psychiatric Annals, 28*(9), 517–523.

Petrosino, A. J., & Petrosino, C. (1999). The public safety potential of Megan's law in Massachusetts: An assessment from a sample of. *Crime and Delinquency, 45*(1), 140–158.

Petry, N. M., & Armentano, C. (1999). Prevalence, assessment, and treatment of pathological gambling: A review. *Psychiatric Services, 50*(8), 1021–1027.

Pezzini, G., Vicari, S., Volterra, V., Milani, L., & Ossella, M. T. (1999). Children with Williams Syndrome: Is there a single neuropsychological profile? *Developmental Neuropsychology, 15*(1), 141–155.

Pfafflin, F. (1992). Regrets after sex reassignment surgery. *Journal of Psychology and Human Sexuality, 5,* 69–85.

Philipsborn, J. T. (1990). Assessing competence to stand trial: Rethinking roles and definitions. *American Journal of Forensic Psychology, 8,* 47–59.

Phillips, D. P. (1977). Motor vehicle fatalities increase just after publicized suicide stories. *Science, 196,* 1464–1465.

Phillips, D. P. (1979). Suicide, motor vehicle fatalities, and the mass media: Evidence toward a theory of suggestion. *American Journal of Sociology, 84,* 1150–1174.

Phillips, D. P., Christenfeld, N., Glynn, L. M., & Steinberg, A. (1999). The influence of medical and legal authorities on deaths facilitated by physicians. *Suicide and Life Threatening Behavior, 29*(1), 48–57.

Phillips, K. A., Dwight, M. M., & McElroy, S. L. (1998). Efficacy and safety of fluvoxamine in body dysmorphic disorder. *Journal of Clinical Psychiatry, 59*(4), 165–171.

Phillips, K. A., & Gunderson, J. G. (1999). Personality disorders. In R. E. Hales, S. C. Yudofsky, & J. A. Talbot (Eds.), *Textbook of psychiatry* (pp. 795–824). Washington, DC: American Psychiatric Press.

Phillips, K. A., Gunderson, C. G., Mallya, G., & McElroy, S. L. (1998). A comparison study of body dysmorphic disorder and obsessive-compulsive disorder. *Journal of Clinical Psychiatry, 59*(11), 568–575.

Piazza, L. A., Markowitz, J. C., Kocsis, J. H., Leon, A. C., & Portera, L. (1997). Sexual functioning in chronically depressed patients treated with SSRI antidepressants. *American Journal of Psychiatry, 154*(12), 1757–1759.

Picciotto, M. R. (1998). Common aspects of the action of nicotine and other drugs of abuse. *Drug and Alcohol Dependence, 51*(1–2), 165–172.

Pickar, D., Owen, R. R., Litman, R. E., Konicki, E., Gutierrez, R., & Rapaport, M. H. (1992). Clinical and biologic response to clozapine in patients with schizophrenia. *Archives of General Psychiatry, 49,* 345–353.

Pigott, T., Pato, M. T., Bernstein, S. E., Grover, G. N., Hill, J. L., Tolliver, T. J., & Murphy, D. L. (1990). Controlled comparisons of clomipramine and fluoxetine and the treatment of obsessive–compulsive disorder. *Archives of General Psychiatry, 47,* 926–932.

Pihl, R. O., Peterson, J., & Finn, P. (1990). Inherited predisposition to alcoholism: Characteristics of sons of male alcoholics. *Journal of Abnormal Psychology, 99,* 291–301.

Pine, D. S., Cohen, E., Cohen, P., & Brook, J. (1999). Adolescent depressive symptoms as predictors of adult depression: Moodiness or mood. *American Journal of Psychiatry, 156*(1), 133–135.

Piotrowski, N. A., Tusel, D. J., Sees, K. L., Reilly, P. M., & Banys, P. (1999). Contingency contracting with monetary reinforcers for abstinence from multiple drugs in a. *Experimental and Clinical Psychopharmacology, 7*(4), 399–411.

Piper, A., Jr. (1999). A skeptic considers, then responds to Cheit. *Ethics and Behavior, 9*(4), 277–293.

Piper, A., Pope, H. G., & Borowiecke, J. J. (2000). Custer's last stand: Brown, Scheflin, and Whitfield's latest attempt to salvage "dissociative amnesia." *Psychiatry and the Law,* in press.

Pitman, R. K. (1989). Posttraumatic stress disorder, hormones, and memory. *Biological Psychiatry, 26,* 221–223.

Plante, T. G., Boccaccini, M., & Andersen, E. (1998). Attitudes concerning professional issues impacting psychotherapy practice among members. *Psychotherapy, 35*(1), 34–42.

Plaud, J. J., & Martini, J. R. (1999). The respondent conditioning of male sexual arousal. *Behavior Modification, 23*(2), 254–268.

Plomin, R., De Fries, J. C., & McClearn, G. E. (1990). *Behavioral genetics: A primer.* New York: Freeman.

Plomin, R., Lichtenstein, P., Pedersen, N., McClearn, G. E., & Nesselroade, J. R. (1990). Genetic influences on life events during the last half of the life span. *Psychology of Aging, 5,* 25–30.

Pohl, R. B., Wolkow, R. M., & Clary, C. M. (1998). Sertraline in the treatment of panic disorder: A double-blind multicenter trial. *American Journal of Psychiatry, 155*(9), 1189–1195.

Pollack, M. H., Worthington, J. J., Manfro, G. G., Otto, M. W., & Zucker, B. G. (1997). Abecarnil for the treatment of generalized anxiety disorder: A placebo-controlled comparison of two dosage ranges of abecarnil and buspirone. *Journal of Clinical Psychiatry, 58*(Suppl. 11), 19–23.

Pollitt, E. (1993). The relationship between undernutrition and behavioral development in children. *Journal of Nutrition, 125,* Suppl. to no 8S.

Pollitt, E., Gorman, K. S., Engle, P. L., Martorell, R., et al. (1993). Early supplementary feeding and cognition: Effects over two decades. *Monographs of the Society for Research in Child Development, 58*(7), v–99.

Pollock, L. R., & Williams, J. M. G. (1998). Problem solving and suicidal behavior. *Suicide and Life Threatening Behavior, 28*(4), 375–387.

Pope, H. G., Aizley, H. G., Keck, P. E., & McElroy, S. L. (1991). Neuroleptic malignant syndrome: Long-term follow-up of 20 cases. *Journal of Clinical Psychiatry, 52,* 208–212.

Pope, H. G., Champoux, R. F., & Hudson, J. I. (1987). Eating disorders and socioeconomic class: Anorexia nervosa and bulimia in nine communities. *Journal of Nervous and Mental Disease, 175,* 620–623.

Pope, H. G., & Hudson, J. I. (1982). Treatment of bulimia with antidepressants. *Psychopharmacology, 78,* 176–179.

Pope, H. G., & Hudson, J. I. (1984). *New hope for binge eaters: Advances in the understanding and treatment of bulimia.* New York: Harper & Row.

Pope, H. G., & Hudson, J. I. (1992). Is childhood sexual abuse a risk factor for bulimia nervosa? *American Journal of Psychiatry, 149,* 455–463.

Pope, H. G., Hudson, J. I., Jonas, J. M., & Yurgelun-Todd, D. (1983). Bulimia treated with imipramine: A placebo-controlled double-blind study. *American Journal of Psychiatry, 140,* 554–558.

Pope, H. G., Hudson, J. I., Jonas, J. M., & Yurgelun-Todd, D. (1985). Antidepressant treatment of bulimia: A two-year follow-up study. *Journal of Clinical Psychopharmacology, 5,* 320–327.

Pope, H. G., Mangweth, B., Negrao, A., B., Hudson, J. I., et al (1994). Childhood sexual abuse and bulimia nervosa: A comparison of American, Austrian, and Brazilian women. *American Journal of Psychiatry, 151,* 732–737.

Pope, H. G., Jr., & Hudson, J. I. (1996). "Recovered memory" therapy for eating disorders: Implications of the Ramona verdict. *International Journal of Eating Disorders, 19*(2), 139–145.

Pope, H. G., Jr., Hudson, J. I., Bodkin, J. A., & Oliva, P. (1998). Questionable validity of "dissociative amnesia" in trauma victims: Evidence from prospective studies. *British Journal of Psychiatry, 172,* 210–215.

Pope, H. G., Jr., Jacobs, A., Mialet, J. P., & Yurgelun-Todd, D. (1997). Evidence for a sex-specific residual effect of cannabis on visuospatial memory. *Psychotherapy and Psychosomatics, 66*(4), 179–184.

Pope, H. G., Jr., Kouri, E. M., & Hudson, J. I. (2000). Effects of supraphysiologic doses of testosterone on mood and aggression in normal men. *Archives of General Psychiatry, 57*(2), 133–140.

Pope, H. G., Jr., Oliva, P. S., Hudson, J. I., Bodkin, J. A., & Gruber, A. J. (1999). Attitudes toward DSM-IV dissociative disorders diagnoses among board-certified American psychiatrists. *American Journal of Psychiatry, 156*(2), 321–323.

Pope, H. G., Jr., & Yurgelun-Todd, D. (1996). The residual cognitive effects of heavy marijuana use in college students. *Journal of the American Medical Association, 275*(7), 521–527.

Popper, C., & West, S. A. (1999). Disorders usually first diagnosed in infancy, childhood, or adolescence. In R. E. Hales, S. C. Yudofsky, & J. A. Talbot (Eds.), *Textbook of psychiatry* (pp. 825–954). Washington, DC: American Psychiatric Press.

Portas, C. M., Goldstein, J. M., Shenton, M. E., & Hokama, H. H. (1998). Volumetric evaluation of the thalamus in schizophrenic male patients using magnetic. *Biological Psychiatry, 43*(9), 649–659.

Portegies, P., & Rosenberg, N. R. (1998). AIDS dementia complex: Diagnosis and drug treatment options. *CNS Drugs, 9*(1), 31–40.

Post, F. (1996). Verbal creativity, depression and alcoholism: An investigation of one hundred American and. *British Journal of Psychiatry, 168*(5), 545–555.

Post, L. L. (1994). Sexual side effects of psychiatric medications in women. *American Journal of Psychiatry, 151,* 1247.

Potenza, M. N., Wasylink, S., Longhurst, J. G., & Epperson, C. N. (1998). Olanzapine augmentation of fluoxetine in the treatment of refractory obsessive-compulsive. *Journal of Clinical Psychopharmacology, 18*(5), 423–424.

Powell, J., Hardoon, K., Derevensky, J. L., & Gupta, R. (1999). Gambling and risk-taking behavior among university students. *Substance Use and Misuse, 34*(8), 1167–1184.

Powell, J. W., & Barber-Foss, K. D. (1999). Traumatic brain injury in high school athletes [see comments]. *Journal of the American Medical Association, 282*(10), 958–963.

Power, T. J., Andrews, T. J., Eiraldi, R. B., & Doherty, B. J. (1998). Evaluating attention deficit hyperactivity disorder using multiple informants: The incremental. *Psychological Assessment, 10*(3), 250–260.

Pressman, J. D. (1998). *Last resort: Psychosurgery and the limits of medicine.*

Price, L. H., & Heninger, G. R. (1994). Lithium in the treatment of mood disorders. *New England Journal of Medicine, 331,* 591–598.

Price, L. H., Malison, R. T., McDougle, C. J., & Pelton, G. H. (1998). The neurobiology of tryptophan depletion in depression: Effects of intravenous tryptophan. *Biological Psychiatry, 43*(5), 339–347.

Prigerson, H. G., & Slimack, M. J. (1999). Gender differences in clinical correlates of suicidality among young adults. *Journal of Nervous and Mental Disease, 187*(1), 23–31.

Prince, M. (1908). *The dissociation of personality.* New York: Longman.

Prince, V., & Bentler, P. M. (1972). Survey of 504 cases of transvestism. *Psychological Reports, 31,* 903–917.

Pring, L., Hermelin, B., & Heavey, L. (1995). Savants, segments, art and autism. *Journal of Child Psychology and Psychiatry and Allied Disciplines, 36,* 6.

Prudic, J., & Sackeim, H. A. (1999). Electroconvulsive therapy and suicide risk. *Journal of Clinical Psychiatry, 60*(Suppl. 2), 104–110.

Purcell, D., Thrush, C. R. N., & Blanchette, P. L. (1999). Suicide among the elderly in Honolulu county: A multiethnic comparative study (1987–1992). *International Psychogeriatrics, 11*(1), 57–66.

Purcell, R., Maruff, P., Kyrios, M., & Pantelis, C. (1998a). Cognitive deficits in obsessive-compulsive disorder on tests of frontal-striatal function. *Biological Psychiatry, 43*(5), 348–357.

Purcell, R., Maruff, P., Kyrios, M., & Pantelis, C. (1998b). Neuropsychological deficits in obsessive-compulsive disorder: A comparison with unipolar depression, panic disorder, and normal controls. *Archives of General Psychiatry, 55*(5), 415–423.

Putnam, F. W. (1989). *Diagnosis and treatment of multiple personality disorder.* New York: Guilford Press.

Putnam, F. W., Guroff, J. J., Silberman, E. K., Barban, L., & Post, R. M. (1986). The clinical phenomenology of multiple personality disorder: Review of 100 recent cases. *Journal of Clinical Psychiatry, 47,* 285–293.

Pynoos, R. S., Ritzmann, R. F., Steinberg, A. M., & Goenjian, A. (1996). A behavioral animal model of posttraumatic stress disorder featuring repeated exposure to. *Biological Psychiatry, 39*(2), 129–134.

Quay, H. C. (1986). Conduct disorders. In H. C. Quay & J. S. Werry (Eds.), *Psychopathological disorders of childhood* (3rd ed.). New York: Wiley.

Quitkin, F. M. (1999). Placebos, drug effects, and study design: A clinician's guide. *American Journal of Psychiatry, 156*(6), 829–836.

Rabheru, K., & Persad, E. (1997). A review of continuation and maintenance electroconvulsive therapy. *Canadian Journal of Psychiatry, 42*(5), 476–484.

Rabkin, J. G., Muhlin, G., & Cohen, P. W. (1984). What neighbors think: Community attitudes toward local psychiatric facilities. *Community Mental Health Journal, 20,* 304–312.

Rachlin, S., & Keill, S. L. (1999). Administrative psychiatry. In R. E. Hales, S. C. Yudofsky, & J. A. Talbot (Eds.), *Textbook of psychiatry* (pp. 1557–1576). Washington, DC: American Psychiatric Press.

Rackman, S. (1966). Sexual fetishism: An experimental analogue. *Psychological Record, 16,* 293–296.

Rackman, S., & Hodgson, S. (1968). Experimentally induced "sexual fetishism": Replication and development. *Psychological Record, 18,* 25–27.

Radloff, L. S., & Rae, D. S. (1979). Susceptibility and precipitating factors in depression: Sex differences and similarities. *Journal of Abnormal Psychology, 88,* 174–181.

Radomsky, E. D., Haas, G. L., Mann, J. J., & Sweeney, J. A. (1999). Suicidal behavior in patients with schizophrenia and other psychotic disorders. *American Journal of Psychiatry, 156*(10), 1590–1595.

Raesaenen, P., Hakko, H., Isohanni, M., & Hodgins, S. (1999). Maternal smoking during pregnancy and risk of criminal behavior among adult male offspring. *American Journal of Psychiatry, 156*(6), 857–862.

Raesaenen, P., Hakko, H., Visuri, S., Paanila, J., Kapanen, P., Suomela, T., & Tiihonen, J. (1999). Serum testosterone levels, mental disorders and criminal behaviour. *Acta Psychiatrica Scandinavica, 99*(5), 348–352.

Ragland, J. D., Gur, R. C., Glahn, D. C., Censits, D. M., & Smith, R. J. (1998). Frontotemporal cerebral blood flow change during executive and declarative memory tasks in. *Neuropsychology, 12*(3), 399–413.

Rahe, R. H., Mahan, J. L., & Arthur, R. J. (1970). Prediction of near–future health change from subjects' preceding life changes. *Journal of Psychosomatic Research, 14,* 401–406.

Raine, A., Lencz, T., Bihrle, S., LaCasse, L., & Colletti, P. (2000). Reduced prefrontal gray matter volume and reduced autonomic activity in antisocial. *Archives of General Psychiatry, 57*(2), 119–127.

Raleigh, M. J., McGuire, M. T., Brammer, G. L., & Yuwiler, A. (1984). Social and environmental influences on blood serotonin concentrations in monkeys. *Archives of General Psychiatry, 47,* 405–410.

Randolph, J. J., & Dykman, B. M. (1998). Perceptions of parenting and depression-proneness in the offspring: Dysfunctional attitudes as a mediating mechanism. *Cognitive Therapy and Research, 22*(4), 377–400.

Rapoport, J. L. (1994). Clozapine and child psychiatry. *Journal of Child and Adolescent Psychopharmacology, 4,* 1–3.

Rapoport, J. L., Giedd, J. N., Blumenthal, J., & Hamburger, S. (1999). Progressive cortical change during adolescence in childhood-onset schizophrenia. *Archives of General Psychiatry, 56*(7), 649–654.

Rapoport, J. L., Ryland, D. H., & Kriete, M. (1992). Drug treatment of canine acral lick: An animal model of obsessive–compulsive disorder. *Archives of General Psychiatry, 49,* 517–521.

Rappaport, L. (1993). The treatment of nocturnal enuresis: Where are we now? *Pediatrics, 92,* 465–466.

Rasmusson, A. M., & Charney, D. S. (1997). Animal models of relevance to PTSD. In R. Yehuda, A. C. McFarlane, et al. (Eds.), *Psychobiology of.*

Ratna, L., & Barbenel, D. (1997). The pharmacotherapy of posttraumatic stress disorder. A literature review and case report of. *International Journal of Psychiatry in Clinical Practice, 1*(3), 169–177.

Rauch, S. L., & Jenike, M. A. (1998a). Pharmacological treatment of obsessive compulsive disorder. In P. E. Nathan & J. M. Gorman (Eds.), *A guide to treatments that work.* New York: Oxford University Press.

Rauch, S. L., & Jenike, M. A. (1998b). Pharmacological treatments of post-traumatic stress disorder. In P. E. Nathan & J. M. Gorman (Eds.), *A guide to treatments that work* (pp. 358–376). New York: Oxford University Press.

Raykov, T. (1995). Multivariate structural modeling of plasticity in fluid intelligence of. *Multivariate Behavioral Research, 30*(2), 255–287.

Raymond, M. J., & O'Keefe, K. (1965). A case of pin-up fetishism treated by aversion conditioning. *British Journal of Psychiatry, 111,* 579–581.

Rechtschaffen, A., & Siegel, J. M. (1999). Sleep and dreaming. In E. Kandel, J. Schwartz, & T. Jessel (Eds.), *Principles of neuroscience.* New York: McGraw-Hill.

Redmond, D., Kosten, T., & Peiser, M. (1982). Spontaneous ejaculation associated with anxiety: Psychophysiological considerations. *American Journal of Psychiatry, 140,* 1163–1166.

Regal, R. R., Cross, P. K., Lamson, S. H., & Hook, E. B. (1980). A search for evidence for a paternal age effect independent of a maternal age in birth certificate reports of Down's syndrome in New York State. *American Journal of Epidemiology, 112,* 650–655.

Regan, P. C. (1999). Hormonal correlates and causes of sexual desire: A review. *Canadian Journal of Human Sexuality, 8*(1), 1–16.

Regier, D. A., Kaelber, C. T., Rae, D. S., & Farmer, M. E. (1998). Limitations of diagnostic criteria and assessment instruments for mental disorders. *Archives of General Psychiatry, 55*(2), 109–115.

Reid, P. D., Shajahan, P. M., Glabus, M. F., & Ebmeier, K. P. (1998). Transcranial magnetic stimulation in depression. *British Journal of Psychiatry, 173,* 449–452.

Reid, W. H. (1999). New vs. old antipsychotics: The Texas experience. *Journal of Clinical Psychiatry, 60*(Suppl. 1), 23–25.

Reid, W. H., Keller, S., Leatherman, M., & Mason, M. (1998). ECT in Texas: 19 months of mandatory reporting. *Journal of Clinical Psychiatry, 59*(1), 8–13.

Reiner, W. (1997). To be male or female—that is the question. *Archives of Pediatric and Adolescent Medicine, 151,* 224–225.

Reiss, D., Plomin, R., & Hetherington, M. (1991). Genetics and psychiatry: An unheralded window on the environment. *American Journal of Psychiatry, 148,* 283–291.

Renvoise, E. B., & Beveridge, A. W. (1989). Mental illness and the late Victorians: A study of patients admitted to three asylums in York, 1880–1884. *Psychological Medicine, 19,* 19–28.

Rescorla, R. A. (1988). Pavlovian conditioning: It's not what you think it is. *American Psychologist, 43,* 151–160.

Revelle, W., Amaral, P., & Turriff, S. (1976). Introversion/extroversion, time stress, and caffeine: Effect on verbal performance. *Science, 192,* 149–150.

Rhee, S. H., Waldman, I. D., Hay, D. A., & Levy, F. (1999). Sex differences in genetic and environmental influences on DSM-III-R. *Journal of Abnormal Psychology, 108*(1), 24–41.

Rice, E. H., Sombrotto, L., B., Markowitz, J. C., & Leon, A. C. (1994). Cardiovasuclar morbidity in high–risk patients during ECT. *American Journal of Psychiatry, 15,* 1637–1641.

Rice, M. E., Quinsey, V. L., & Harris, G. T. (1991). Sexual recidivism among child molesters released from a maximum security psychiatric institution. *Journal of Consulting and Clinical Psychology, 59,* 381–386.

Rickels, K., Case, W. G., Schweizer, E., Garcia–Espana, F., & Fridman, R. (1991). Long–term benzodiazepine users 3 years after participation in a discontinuation program. *American Journal of Psychiatry, 148,* 757–761.

Rieber, R. W. (1999). Hypnosis, false memory and multiple personality: A trinity of affinity. *History of Psychiatry, 10*(37, Pt. 1), 3–11.

Riecher-Rossler, A., & Hafner, H. (1993). Schizophrenia and estrogens—is there an association? *European Archives of Psychiatry and Clinical Neuroscience, 242,* 322–328.

Riedel, W. J., Klaassen, T., Deutz, N. E. P., & van Someren, A. (1999). Tryptophan depletion in normal volunteers produces selective impairment in memory. *Psychopharmacology, 141*(4), 362–369.

Rieder, R. O., Kaufmann, C. A., & Knowles, J. A. (1994). Genetics. In R. E. Hales, S. C. Yudofsky, & J. A. Talbott (Eds.), *American Psychiatric Press textbook of psychiatry* (2nd ed.) Washington, DC: American Psychiatric Press.

Rief, W., Shaw, R., & Fichter, M. M. (1998). Elevated levels of psychophysiological arousal and cortisol in patients with somatization. *Psychosomatic Medicine, 60*(2), 198–203.

Rifai, A. H. George, C. J. Stack, J. A., Mann, J. J., & Reynolds, C. F. (1994). Hopelessness in suicide attempters after acute treatment of major depression in late life. *American Journal of Psychiatry, 151,* 1687–1690.

Rifkin, A., Klein, D. F., Dillon, D., & Levitt, M. (1981). Blockade by imipramine or desipramine of panic induced by sodium lactate. *American Journal of Psychiatry, 138,* 676–677.

Righetti Veltema, M., Conne Perreard, E., Bousquet, A., & Manzano, J. (1998). Risk factors and predictive signs of postpartum depression. *Journal of Affective Disorders, 49*(3), 167–180.

Rimon, R., & Laakso, R. (1985). Life stress and rheumatoid arthritis. *Psychotherapy and Psychosomatics, 43,* 38–43.

Rind, B., Tromovitch, P., & Bauserman, R. (1998). A meta-analytic examination of assumed properties of child sexual abuse using college. *Psychological Bulletin, 124*(1), 22–53.

Rist, R. C. (1970). Student social class and teacher expectations: The self-fulfilling prophecy in ghetto education. *Harvard Educational Review, 40,* 411–451.

Ritter, E., & Holmes, D. S. (1968). Behavioral contagion: Its occurrence as a function of differential restraint reduction. *Journal of Experimental Research in Personality, 3,* 242–246.

Ritvo, E. R., Mason-Brothers, A., Freeman, B. J., Pingree, C., Jenson, W. R., McMahon, W. M., Petersen, P. B., Jorde, L. B., Mo, A., & Ritvo, A. (1990). The UCLA–University of Utah epidemiologic survey of autism: The etiologic role of rare diseases. *American Journal of Psychiatry, 147,* 1614–1621.

Ritvo, E. R., Ritvo, A., & Brothers, A. (1982). Genetic and immunohematologic factors in autism. *Journal of Autism and Developmental Disorders, 12,* 109–114.

Roback, H. B., & Lothstein, L. M. (1986). The female midlife sex change applicant: A comparison with younger transsexuals and older male sex change applicants. *Archives of Sexual Behavior, 15,* 401–415.

Robb, J. C., Young, L. T., Cooke, R. G., & Joffe, R. T. (1998). Gender differences in patients with bipolar disorder influence outcome in the medical. *Journal of Affective Disorders, 49*(3), 189–193.

Robbins, L. (1994). Precipitating factors in migraine: A retrospective review of 494 patients. *Headache, 34,* 214–216.

Robbins, T. W., & Everitt, B. J. (1999). Interaction of the dopaminergic system with mechanisms of associative learning and. *Psychological Science, 10*(3), 199–202.

Roberts, A. H. (1985). Biofeedback: Research, training, and clinical roles. *American Psychologist, 40,* 938–941.

Roberts, J., & Roberts, T. (1985). Taking the center to market. *Community Mental Health Journal, 21,* 264–281.

Roberts, T. G., Fournet, G. P., and Penland, E. (1995). A comparison of the attitudes toward alcohol and drug use and school support by grade level, gender, and ethnicity. *Journal of Alcohol and Drug Education, 40,* 112–127.

Robins, C. J., & Block, P. (1989). Cognitive theories of depression viewed from a diathesis-stress perspective: Evaluations of the models of Beck and of Abramson, Seligman, and Teasdale. *Cognitive Therapy and Research, 13,* 297–313.

Robins, E., & Guze, S. B. (1972). Classification of affective disorders: The primary-secondary, the endogenous-reactive, and the neurotic-psychotic concepts. In T. A. Williams, M. M. Katz, & J. A. Shields (Eds.), *Recent advances in the psychobiology of the depressive illnesses.* Washington, DC: U.S. Government Printing Office.

Robins, L. N., Davis, D. H., & Nurco, D. N. (1974). How permanent was Viet Nam drug addiction? In M. H. Green & R. L. Du Pont (Eds.), *The epidemiology of drug abuse* (NIDA Journal Suppl., Pt. N, Vol. 64). Washington, DC: U.S. Government Printing Office.

Robins, L. N., Helzer, J. E., & Davis, D. H. (1975). Narcotic use in Southeast Asia and afterwards. *Archives of General Psychiatry, 32,* 955–961.

Robins, L. N., Helzer, J. E., Weissman, M. M., Orvaschel, H., Gruenberg, E., Burke, J. D., & Reigier, D. A. (1984). Lifetime prevalence of specific psychiatric disorders in three sites. *Archives of General Psychiatry, 41,* 949–958.

Robinson, D., Woerner, M. G., Alvir, J. M. J., & Bilder, R. (1999). Predictors of relapse following response from a first episode of schizophrenia or. *Archives of General Psychiatry, 56*(3), 241–247.

Robinson, D., Wu, H., Munne, R. A., Ashtari, M., Alvir, M. J., Lerner, G., Koreen, A., Cole, K., & Bogerts, B. (1995). Reduced caudate nucleus volume in obsessive-compulsive disorder. *Archives of General Psychiatry, 52,* 393–398.

Robinson, N. M., & Robinson, H. B. (1976). *The mentally retarded child.* New York: McGraw-Hill.

Rodier, P. M. (2000). The early origins of autism. *Scientific American, 282,* 56–63.

Roebuck, T. M., Mattson, S. N., & Riley, E. P. (1999). Behavioral and psychosocial profiles of alcohol-exposed children. *Alcoholism: Clinical and Experimental Research, 23*(6), 1070–1076.

Roediger, H. L., III, & Bergman, E. T. (1998). The controversy over recovered memories. *Psychology, Public Policy, and Law, 4*(4), 1091–1109.

Roemer, L., Litz, B. T., Orsillo, S. M., & Ehlich, P. J. (1998). Increases in retrospective accounts of war-zone exposure over time: The role of PTSD. *Journal of Traumatic Stress, 11*(3), 597–605.

Rofman, E. S., Askinazi, C., & Fant, E. (1980). The prediction of dangerous behavior in emergency commitment. *American Journal of Psychiatry, 137,* 1061–1064.

Rogeness, G., Javors, M., & Pliszka, S. (1993). Neurochemistry and child and adolescent psychiatry. *Annual Progress in Child Psychiatry and Child Development,* 305–343.

Rogeness, G. A., Javors, M. A., & Pliska, S. R. (1992). Neurochemistry and child and adolescent psychiatry. *Journal of the American Academy of Child and Adolescent Psychiatry, 31,* 765–781.

Rogers, C. R. (1951). *Client-centered therapy.* Boston: Houghton Mifflin.

Rogers, L., Resnick, M. D., Mitchell, J. E., & Blum, R. W. (1997). The relationship between socioeconomic status and eating-disordered behaviors in a. *International Journal of Eating Disorders, 22*(1), 15–23.

Rogler, L. H., Malgady, R. G., Costantino, G., & Blumenthal, R. (1987). What do culturally sensitive mental health services mean? *American Psychologist, 42,* 565–570.

Rokeach, M. (1964). *The three Christs of Ypsilanti.* New York: Knopf.

Romach, M. K., Sproule, B. A., Sellers, E. M., & Somer, G. (1999). Long-term codeine use is associated with depressive symptoms. *Journal of Clinical Psychopharmacology, 19*(4), 373–376.

Rorschach, H. (1942). *Psychodiagnostics: A diagnostic test based on perception* (P. Lemkau & B. Kronenberg, Trans.). Philadelphia: Grune & Stratton.

Rorty, M., Yager, J., & Rossotto, E. (1994). Childhood sexual, physical, and psychological abuse in bulimia nervosa. *American Journal of Psychiatry, 151,* 1122–1126.

Rose, R. J., Bourne, P. G., Poe, R. O., Mougey, E. H., Collins, D. R., & Mason, J. W. (1969). Androgen responses to stress: 2. Excretion of testosterone, epitestosterone, androsterone, and etiochoanolone during basic combat training and under threat of attack. *Psychosomatic Medicine, 31,* 418–436.

Rosen, R. C., Lane, R. M., & Menza, M. (1999). Effects of SSRIs on sexual function: A critical review. *Journal of Clinical Psychopharmacology, 19*(1), 67–85.

Rosenbach, M. L., Hermann, R. C., & Dorwart, R. A. (1997). Use of electroconvulsive therapy in the Medicare population between 1987 and 1992. *Psychiatric Services, 48*(12), 1537–1548.

Rosenbaum, D. P., & Hanson, G. S. (1998). Assessing the effects of school-based drug education: A six-year multilevel analysis of Project. *Journal of Research in Crime and Delinquency, 35*(4), 381–412.

Rosenbaum, M. (1980). The role of the term schizophrenia in the decline of diagnoses of multiple personality. *Archives of General Psychiatry, 37,* 1383–1385.

Rosenbaum, M. (1995). The demedicalization of methadone maintenance. *Journal of Psychoactive Drugs, 27,* 145–149.

Rosenberg, D., & Leland, J. (1995, July 10). "Generation depressed": Suicide attempts rock a New England town. *Newsweek,* p. 63.

Rosenblatt, A., & Mayer, J. E. (1974). Patients who return: A consideration of some neglected influences. *Journal of the Bronx State Hospital, 2,* 71–81.

Rosenblum, A., Magura, S., Palij, M., & Foote, J. (1999). Enhanced treatment outcomes for cocaine-using methadone patients. *Drug and Alcohol Dependence, 54*(3), 207–218.

Rosenhan, D. L. (1973). On being sane in insane places. *Science, 179,* 250–258.

Rosenheck, R., Cramer, J., Xu, W., Thomas, J., & Henderson, W. (1997). A comparison of clozapine and haloperidol in hospitalized patients with refractory. *New England Journal of Medicine, 337*(12), 809–815.

Rosenheck, R., Dunn, L., Peszke, M., Cramer, J., & Xu, W. (1999). Impact of clozapine on negative symptoms and on the deficit syndrome in refractory. *American Journal of Psychiatry, 156*(1), 88–93.

Rosenheck, R., Tekell, J., Peters, J., Cramer, J., & Fontana, A. (1998). Does participation in psychosocial treatment augment the benefit of clozapine? *Archives of General Psychiatry, 55*(7), 618–625.

Rosenman, R. H. (1978). The interview method of assessment of the coronary-prone behavior pattern. In T. M. Dembroski, S. M. Weiss, J. L. Shields, S. G. Haynes, & M. Feinleib (Eds.), *Coronary-prone behavior.* New York: Springer.

Rosenman, R. H., Brand, R. J., Jenkins, C. D., Friedman, M., Straus, R., & Wurm, M. (1975). Coronary heart disease in the Western Collaborative Group Study: Final follow-up experience of $8\frac{1}{2}$ years. *Journal of the American Medical Association, 233,* 872–877.

Rosenman, R. H., Brand, R. J., Sholtz, R. I., & Friedman, M. (1976). Multivariate prediction of coronary heart disease during 8.5-year follow-up in the Western Collaborative Group Study. *American Journal of Cardiology, 37,* 903–910.

Rosenthal, D., Wender, P. H., Kety, S. S., Schulsinger, F. A., Weiner, J., & Ostergaard, L. (1968). Schizophrenics' offspring reared in adoptive homes. In D. Rosenthal & S. S. Kety (Eds.), *The transmission of schizophrenia.* Elmsford, NY: Pergamon.

Rosenthal, D., Wender, P. H., Kety, S. S., Welner, J., & Schulsinger, F. A. (1971). The adopted-away offspring of schizophrenics. *American Journal of Psychiatry, 128,* 307–311.

Rosenthal, N. E., Joseph-Vanderpool, J. R., Levendosky, A. A., Johnston, S. H., Allen, R., Kelley, K., Souetre, E., Schultz, P., & Starz, K. (1990). Phase-shifting effects of bright morning light as treatment for delayed sleep phase syndrome. *Sleep, 13,* 354–361.

Rosenthal, N. E., Sack, D. A., Gillin, J. C., Lewy, A. J., Goodwin, F. K., Davenport, Y., Mueller, P. S., Newsome, D. A., & Wehr, T. A. (1984). Seasonal affective disorder: A description of the syndrome and preliminary findings with light therapy. *Archives of General Psychiatry, 41,* 72–80.

Rosenthal, R., & Jacobson, L. (1968). *Pygmalion in the classroom.* New York: Holt, Rinehart and Winston.

Ross, C. A. (1989). *Multiple personality disorder: Diagnosis, clinical features, and treatment.* New York: Wiley.

Ross, C. A., Joshi, S., & Currie, R. (1990). Dissociative experiences in the general population. *American Journal of Psychiatry, 147,* 1547–1552.

Ross, C. A., Miller, S. D., Reagor, P., Bjornson, L., Fraser, G. A., & Anderson, G. (1990). Structured interview data on 102 cases of multiple personality disorder from four centers. *American Journal of Psychiatry, 147,* 596–601.

Ross, C. A., Norton R., & Wozney, K. (1989). Multiple personality disorder: An analysis of 236 cases. *Canadian Journal of Psychiatry, 34,* 413–418.

Ross, J. L. (1977). Anorexia nervosa: An overview. *Bulletin of the Menninger Clinic, 41,* 418–436.

Rossi, P. G., Posar, A., & Parmeggiani, A. (1999). Niaprazine in the treatment of autistic disorder. *Journal of Child Neurology, 14*(8), 547–550.

Roth, D. L., & Holmes, D. S. (1985). Influence of physical fitness in determining the impact of stressful life events on physical and psychological health. *Psychosomatic Medicine, 47,* 164–173.

Roth, D. L., & Holmes, D. S. (1987). Influence of aerobic exercise training and relaxation training on physical and psychological health following stressful life events. *Psychosomatic Medicine, 49,* 355–365.

Roth, S. (1979). A revised model of learned helplessness in humans. *Journal of Personality, 48,* 103–133.

Rothchild, E. (1997). E-mail therapy. *American Journal of Psychiatry, 154*(10), 1476–1477.

Rotter, J. B., & Rafferty, J. E. (1950). *Manual for the Rotter Incomplete Sentences Blank, College Form.* New York: Psychological Corporation.

Rouillon, F., Phillips, R., Serrurier, D., Ansart, E., & Gérard, M. J. (1989). Rechutes de dépression unipolaire et efficacité de la maprotiline. *Encéphale, 15,* 527–534.

Rouse v. Cameron, 373 F.2d 451 (D.C. Cir. 1966).

Roviaro, S., & Holmes, D. S. (1980). Arousal transference: The influence of fear arousal on subsequent sexual arousal for subjects with high and low sex guilt. *Journal of Research in Personality, 14,* 307–320.

Roviaro, S., Holmes, D. S., & Holmsten, D. (1984). Influence of a cardiac rehabilitation program on the cardiovascular, psychological, and social functioning of cardiac patients. *Journal of Behavioral Medicine, 7,* 61–81.

Rovner, B. W., German, P. S., Brant, L. J., Clark, R., Burton, L., & Folstein, M. F. (1991). Depression and mortality in nursing homes. *Journal of the American Medical Association, 265,* 993–996.

Roy, A. (1983). Family history of suicide. *Archives of General Psychiatry, 40,* 971–974.

Roy, A. (1996). Aetiology of secondary depression in male alcoholics. *British Journal of Psychiatry, 169*(6), 753–757.

Roy, A., Nielsen, D., Rylander, G., Sarchiapone, M., & Segal, N. (1999). Genetics of suicide in depression. *Journal of Clinical Psychiatry, 60*(Suppl. 2), 12–17.

Roy, A., Segal, N., Centerwall, B., & Robinette, D. (1991). Suicide in twins. *Archives of General Psychiatry, 48,* 29–32.

Roy, A., Segal, N. L., & Sarchiapone, M. (1995). Attempted suicide among living co-twins of twin suicide victims. *American Journal of Psychiatry, 152*(7), 1075–1076.

Roy-Byrne, P. P., & Cowley, D. S. (1998). Pharmacological treatments of panic, generalized anxiety, and phobic disorders. In P. E. Nathan & J. M. Gorman (Eds.), *A guide to treatments that work* (pp. 319–338). New York: Oxford University Press.

Ruan, F., & Bullough, V. L. (1992). Lesbianism in China. *Academy of Chinese Culture and Health Sciences, 21,* 217–226.

Rubin, E. H., Kincherf, D. A., Grant, E. A., & Storandt, M. (1991). The influence of major depression on clinical psychometric assessment of senile dementia of the Alzheimer type. *American Journal of Psychiatry, 148,* 1164–1171.

Rubin, R. T., Ananth, J., Villanueva Meyer, J., Trajmar, P. G., et al. (1995). Regional 2-3-3 xenon cerebral blood flow and cerebral-^{99m}Tc-HMPAO uptake in patients with obsessive compulsive disorder before and during treatment. *Biological Psychiatry, 38*(7), 429–437.

Rudestam, K. E. (1971). Stockholm and Los Angeles: A cross–cultural study of the communication of suicidal intent. *Journal of Consulting and Clinical Psychology, 36,* 82–90.

Ruff, G. A. (1985). Premature ejaculation: Past research progress, future directions. *Clinical Psychology Review, 5,* 627–639.

Rush, A. J., Beck, A. T., Kovacs, M., & Hollon, S. D. (1977). Comparative efficacy of cognitive therapy and imipramine in the treatment of depressed patients. *Cognitive Therapy and Research, 1,* 17–37.

Rushton, J. P., Fulker, D. W., Neale, M. C., Nias, D. K. B., & Eysenck, H. J. (l986). Altruism and aggression: The heritability of individual differences. *Journal of Personality and Social Psychology, 50,* 1192–1198.

Russell, V., Mai, F., Busby, K., & Attwood, D. (1996). Acute day hospitalization as an alternative to inpatient treatment. *Canadian Journal of Psychiatry, 41*(10), 629–637.

Rusting, C. L. (1998). Personality, mood, and cognitive processing of emotional information: Three conceptual frameworks. *Psychological Bulletin, 124*(2), 165–196.

Rutter, M. (1967). Psychotic disorders in early childhood. *British Journal of Psychiatry* (Special Publ. No. 1), 133–158.

Rutter, M., Bartak, L., & Newman, S. (1971). Autism: A central disorder of cognition and language? In M. Rutter (Ed.), *Infantile autism: Concepts, characteristics and treatment.* London: Churchill–Livingstone.

Rutter, M., Silberg, J., O'Connor, T., & Siminoff, E. (1999). Genetics and child psychiatry: II. Empirical research findings. *Journal of Child Psychology and Psychiatry and Allied Disciplines, 40,* 1.

Sabshin, M. (1999). The future of psychiatry. In R. E. Hales, S. C. Yudofsky, & J. A. Talbot (Eds.), *Textbook of psychiatry* (pp. 1693–1702). Washington, DC: American Psychiatric Press.

Sacchetti, E., Vita, A., Guarneri, L., & Cornarcchia, M. (1991). The effectiveness of fluoxetine, clomipramine, nortriptyline and desipramine in major depressives with suicidal behavior: Preliminary findings. In G. Cassano & H. S. Akiskal (Eds.), *Serotonin-related psychiatric syndromes: Clinical and therapeutic links.* London: Royal Society of Medicine Services.

Sachdev, P., & Kruk, J. (1994). Clinical characterisitcs and predisposing factors in acute drug-induced akathisia. *Archives of General Psychiatry, 51,* 963–974.

Sackeim, H. A. (1985, June), The case for ECT. *Psychology Today,* pp. 37–40.

Salaberria, K., & Echeburua, E. (1998). Long-term outcome of cognitive therapy's contribution to self-exposure in vivo to the. *Behavior Modification, 22*(3), 262–284.

Salama, S. A., & Salama, A. A. A. (1999). New behavioral approach to trichotillomania. *American Journal of Psychiatry, 156*(9), 1469–1470.

Saltzman, C., Wolfson, A. N., Schatzberg, A., Looper, J., Henke, R., Schwartz, J., & Miyakaki, E. (1995). Effect of fluoxetine on anger in symptomatic volunteers with borderline personality disorder. *Journal of Clinical Psychopharmacology, 15,* 23–29.

Sammons, M. T., Sexton, J. L., & Meredith, J. M. (1996). Basic science training in psychopharmacology. *American Psychologist, 51,* 230–234.

Sanderson, W. C., Di Nardo, P. A., Rapee, R. M., & Barlow, D. H. (1990). Syndrome comorbidity in patients diagnosed with a *DSM-III-R* anxiety disorder. *Journal of Abnormal Psychology, 99,* 308–312.

Sandmann, J., Bernd, L., Bandelow, B., Haertter, S., Winter, P., & Hiemke, C. (1998). Fluvoxamine or placebo in the treatment of panic disorder and relationship to blood. *Pharmacopsychiatry, 31*(4), 117–121.

Sanger, D. J., & Blackman, D. E. (1981). Rate dependence and the effects of benzodiazepines. In T. Thompson, P. Dews, & W. A. McKim (Eds.), *Advances in behavioral pharmacology* (Vol. 3). New York: Academic Press.

Sanger, T. M., Lieberman, J. A., Tohen, M., Grundy, S., & Beasley, C. (1999). Olanzapine versus haloperidol treatment in first-episode psychosis. *American Journal of Psychiatry, 156*(1), 79–87.

Sanyal, S., Chattopadhyay, P. K., & Bishwas, D. (1998). Electrodermal arousal and self-appraisal in patients with somatization disorder. *Indian Journal of Clinical Psychology, 25*(2), 144–148.

Sarbin, T. R. (1997). Multiple personality disorder: Fact or artifact? *Current Opinion in Psychiatry, 10*, 136–140.

Satel, S., & Edell, W. S. (1991). Cocaine–induced paranoia and psychosis proneness. *American Journal of Psychiatry, 148*, 1708–1711.

Satel, S., Southwick, S. M., & Gawin, F. H. (1991). Clinical features of cocaine-induced paranoia. *American Journal of Psychiatry, 148*, 495–498.

Sattler, D. N., Sattler, J. M., Kaiser, C., Hamby, B. A., Adams, M. G., Love, L., Winkler, J., Abu-Ukkaz, C., Watts, B., & Beatty, A. (1995). Hurricane Andrew: Psychological distress among shelter victims. *International Journal of Stress Management, 2*, 133–143.

Saxena, S., Brody, A. L., Schwartz, J. M., & Baxter, L. R. (1998). Neuroimaging and frontal-subcortical circuitry in obsessive-compulsive disorder. *British Journal of Psychiatry, 173*(Suppl. 35), 26–37.

Scarr, S., & Weinberg, R. A. (1977). Intellectual similarities within families of both adopted and biological. *Intelligence, 1*(2), 170–191.

Scarr, S., & Weinberg, R. A. (1978a). The influence of "family background" on intellectual attainment. *American Sociological Review, 43*(5), 674–692.

Scarr, S., & Weinberg, R. A. (1978b). The rights and responsibilities of the social scientist. *American Psychologist, 33*(10), 955–957.

Schachter, S. (1964). The interaction of cognitive and physiological determinants of emotional state. In L. Berkowitz (Ed.), *Advances in experimental social psychology* (Vol. 1). New York: Academic Press.

Schachter, S., & Latané, B. (1964). Crime, cognition and the autonomic nervous system. In M. R. Jones (Ed.), *Nebraska symposium on motivation.* Lincoln: University of Nebraska Press.

Schachter, S., & Singer, J. E. (1962). Cognitive, psychological, and physiological determinants of emotional state. *Psychological Review, 69*, 379–399.

Schafer, R. B., Wickrama, K. A. S., & Keith, P. M. (1998). Stress in marital interaction and change in depression: A longitudinal analysis. *Journal of Family Issues, 19*(5), 578–594.

Schanen, N. C. (1999). Molecular approaches to the Rett syndrome gene. *Journal of Child Neurology, 14*(12), 806–814.

Scheiber, S. C. (1999). The psychiatric interview, psychiatric history, and mental status examination. In R. E. Hales, S. C. Yudofsky, & J. A. Talbot (Eds.), *Textbook of psychiatry* (pp. 193–226). Washington, DC: American Psychiatric Press.

Schepank, H. G. (1981). Anorexia nervosa: Zwillings Kasuistik über ein seltens Krankheitsbild. In A. Heigl-Evers & H. G. Schepank (Eds.), *Ursprunge seelisch bedingter Krankheiten* (Vol. 2.). Göttingen, Germany: Verlag für Medizinische Psychologie/Vandenhoeck und Ruprecht.

Scher, A. I., Stewart, W. F., Liberman, J., & Lipton, R. B. (1998). Prevalence of frequent headache in a population sample. *Headache, 38*(7), 497–506.

Schiavi, R. C., Schreiner–Engel, P., Mandeli, J., Schanzer, H., & Cohen, E. (1990). Healthy aging and male sexual function. *American Journal of Psychiatry, 147*, 766–771.

Schiavi, R. C., Schreiner–Engel, P., White, B. S., & Mandeli, J. (1991). The relationship between pituitary-gonadal function and sexual behavior in healthy aging men. *Psychosomatic Medicine, 53*, 363–374.

Schildkraut, J. J., Hirshfeld, A., Murphy, J. M. (1994). Mind and mood in modern art: II. Depressive disorders, spirituality, and early deaths in the abstract expressionist artists of the New York School. *American Journal of Psychiatry, 151*, 482–488.

Schildkraut, J. J., Keeler, B. A., Grab, E. L., Kantrowich, J., & Hartmann, E. (1973). MHPG excretion and clinical classification in depressive disorders. *Lancet, 1*, 1251–1252.

Schildkraut, J. J., Orsulak, P. J., Schatzberg, A. F., Gudeman, J. E., Cole, J. O., Rohde, W. A., & La Brie, R. A. (1978). Toward a biochemical classification of depressive disorders: 1. Differences in urinary excretion of MHPG and other catecholamine metabolites in clinically defined subtypes of depression. *Archives of General Psychiatry, 35*, 1427–1433.

Schlatterer, K., Yassouridis, A., von Werder, K., Poland, D., Kemper, J., & Stalla, G. K. (1998). A follow-up study for estimating the effectiveness of a cross-gender hormone substitution. *Arch. Sex. Behav., 27*(5), 475–492.

Schleifer, S. J., Keller, S. E., Meyerson, A. T., Raskin, M. J., Davis, K. L., & Stein, M. (1984). Lymphocyte function in major depressive disorder. *Archives of General Psychiatry, 41*, 484–486.

Schmidt, A. J. M., Wolfs-Takens, D. J., Oosterlaan, J. & van den Hout, M. A. (1994). Psychological mechanisms in hypochondriasis: Attention-induced physical symptoms without sensory stimulation. *Psychotherapy and Psychosomatics, 61*, 117–120.

Schmidt, N. B., Staab, J. P., Trakowski, J. H., Jr., & Sammons, M. (1997). Efficacy of a brief psychosocial treatment for panic disorder in an active duty sample. *Military Medicine, 162*(2), 123–129.

Schnarch, B. (1992). Neither man nor woman: Berdache—a case for non-dichotomous gender construction. *Anthropologica, 34*, 105–121.

Schneider, F., Weiss, U., Kessler, C., Salloum, J. B., Posse, S., & Grodd, W. (1998). Differential amygdala activation in schizophrenia during sadness. *Schizophrenia Research, 34*(3), 133–142.

Schofield, W. (1964). *Psychotherapy: The purchase of friendship.* Engelwood Cliffs, NJ: Prentice Hall.

Schopler, E., Short, A., & Mesibov, G. (1989). Relation of behavioral treatment to "normal functioning": Comments on Lovaas. *Journal of Consulting and Clinical Psychology, 57*, 162–164.

Schotte, D. E., & Clum, G. (1987). Problem-solving skills in suicidal psychiatric patients. *Journal of Consulting and Clinical Psychology, 55,* 49–54.

Schotte, D. E., Cools, J., & McNally, R. J. (1990). Film-induced negative affect triggers overeating in restrained eaters. *Journal of Abnormal Psychology, 99,* 317–320.

Schotte, D. E., Cools, J., & Payvar, S. (1990). Problem-solving deficits in suicidal patients: Trait vulnerability or state phenomenon? *Journal of Consulting and Clinical Psychology, 58,* 562–564.

Schou, M. (1998). Has the time come to abandon prophylactic lithium treatment? A review for clinicians. *Pharmacopsychiatry, 31*(6), 210–215.

Schreiber, F. R. (1973). *Sybil.* New York: Warner Books.

Schreier, H. A. (1998). Auditory hallucinations in nonpsychotic children with affective syndromes and migraines: Report. *Journal of Child Neurology, 13*(8), 377–382.

Schreiner-Engel, P., Schiavi, R. C., White, D., & Ghizzani, A. (1989). Low sexual desire in women: The role of reproductive hormones. *Hormones and Behavior, 23,* 221–234.

Schulsinger, F. A., Kety, S. S., Rosenthal, D., & Wender, P. H. (1979). A family study of suicide. In M. Schou & E. Stromgren (Eds.), *Origin, prevention and treatment of affective disorders.* London: Academic Press.

Schultz, R., Braun, B. G., & Kluft, R. P. (1989). Multiple personality disorder: Phenomenology of selected variables in comparison to major depression. *Dissociation, 2,* 45–51.

Schultz, R. T., Gauthier, I., Klin, A., Fullbright, R. K., Anderson, A. W., Volkmar, F., Skudlarski, P., Laccadie, C., Cohen, D. J., & Gore, J. C. (2000). Abnormal ventral temporal cortical activity during face discrimination among individuals with autism and Asperger syndrome. *Archives of General Psychiatry, 57,* 331–340.

Schupf, N., Kapell, D., Nightingale, B., Rodriguez, A., Tycko, B., & Mayeux, R. (1998). Earlier onset of Alzheimer's disease in men with Down syndrome. *Neurology, 50*(4), 991–995.

Schwartz, J. M. (1998). Neuroanatomical aspects of cognitive-behavioural therapy response in obsessive-compulsive disorder: An evolving perspective on brain and behaviour. *British Journal of Psychiatry, 173*(Suppl. 35), 38–44.

Schwartz, J. M., Stoessel, P. W., Baxter, L. R., Martin, K. M., & Phelps, M. E. (1996). Systematic changes in cerebral glucose metabolic rate after successful behavior modification treatment of obsessive-compulsive disorder. *Archives of General Psychiatry, 53*(2), 109–113.

Schwartz, S. M., Gramling, S. E. & Mancini, T. (1994). The influence of life stress, personality, and learning history on illness behavior. *Journal of Behavior Therapy and Experimental Psychiatry, 25,* 135–142.

Schwartz, S. M., Schmitt, E. P., Ketterer, M. W., & Trask, P. C. (1999). Lipid levels and emotional distress among healthy male college students. *Stress Medicine, 15*(3), 159–165.

Scott, J. (1996). Cognitive therapy for clients with bipolar disorder. *Cognitive and Behavioral Practice, 3*(1), 29–51.

Scott, T., Bexton, W. H., & Doane, B. (1959). Cognitive effects of perceptual isolation. *Canadian Journal of Psychology, 13,* 200–209.

Scoville, W. B., & Milner, B. R. (1957). Loss of recent memory after bilateral hippocampal lesions. *Journal of Neurology, Neurosurgery, and Psychiatry, 20,* 11–21.

Sears, L. L., Vest, C., Mohamed, S., Bailey, J., Ranson, B. J., & Piven, J. (1999). An MRI study of the basal ganglia in autism. *Progress in Neuro-Psychopharacology and Biological Psychiatry, 23*(4), 613–624.

Sears, R. R., Maccoby, E. E., & Levin, H. (1957). *Patterns of child rearing.* Evanston, IL: Row & Peterson.

Sechrest, L., Stickle, T. R., & Stewart, M. (1998). The role of assessment in clinical psychology. In A. Bellack, M. Hersen, & C. R. Reynolds (Eds.), *Comprehensive clinical psychology: Vol. 4.*

Seeman, M. V. (1995). Sex differences in predicting neuroleptic response. In G. W. Awad & A. G. Vienna (Eds.), *The prediction of neuroleptic response.* New York: Springer-Verlag.

Seeman, M. V. (1997). Psychopathology in women and men: Focus on female hormones. *American Journal of Psychiatry, 154,* 1641–1647.

Seeman, M. V., & Lang, M. (1990). The role of estrogens in schizophrenia gender differences. *Schizophrenia Bulletin, 16,* 185–194.

Segal, J., Berk, M., & Brook, S. (1998). Risperidone compared with both lithium and haloperidol in mania: A double-blind. *Clinical Neuropharmacology, 21*(3), 176–180.

Segal, Z. V., & Ingram, R. E. (1994). Mood priming and construct activation in tests of cognitive vulnerability to unipolar. *Clinical Psychology Review, 14*(7), 663–695.

Segal, Z. V., Shaw, B. F., Vella, D. D., & Katz, R. (1992). Cognitive and life stress predictors of relapse in remitted unipolar depressed patients: A test of the congruency hypothesis. *Journal of Abnormal Psychology, 101,* 26–36.

Segerstrom, S. C., Glover, D. A., Craske, M. G., & Fahey, J. L. (1999). Worry affects the immune response to phobic fear. *Brain, Behavior and Immunity, 13*(2), 80–92.

Segerstrom, S. C., Solomon, G. F., Kemeny, M. E., & Fahey, J. L. (1998). Relationship of worry to immune sequelae of the Northridge earthquake. *Journal of Behavioral Medicine, 21*(5), 433–450.

Segerstrom, S. C., Taylor, S. E., Kemeny, M. E., & Fahey, J. L. (1998). Optimism is associated with mood, coping and immune change in response to stress. *Journal of Personality and Social Psychology, 74*(6), 1646–1655.

Segraves, R. T., & Althof, S. (1998). Psychotherapy and pharmacotherapy of sexual dysfunctions. In P. E. Nathan & J. M. Gorman (Eds.), *A guide to treatments that work* (pp. 447–471). New York: Oxford University Press.

Selemon, L. D., Rajkowska, G., & Goldman-Rakic, P. S. (1995). Abnormally high neuronal density in the schizophrenic cortex. *Archives of General Psychiatry, 52,* 805–818.

Self, D. W. (1998). Neural substrates of drug craving and relapse in drug addiction. *Annals of Medicine, 30*(4), 379–389.

Seligman, M. E. P. (1975). *Helplessness: On depression, development, and death.* New York: Freeman.

Seligman, M. E. P. (1995). *What you can change and what you can't.* New York: Ballantine.

Semba, J. I., Mataki, C., Yamada, S., Nankai, M., & Toru, M. (1998). Antidepressantlike effects of chronic nicotine on learned helplessness paradigm in rats. *Biological Psychiatry, 43*(5), 388–391.

Serban, G. (1992). Multiple personality: An issue for forensic psychiatry. *American Journal of Psychotherapy, 46,* 269–280.

Serretti, A., Rietschel, M., Lattuada, E., Krauss, H., & Held, T. (1999). Factor analysis of mania: Commentary. *Archives of General Psychiatry, 56*(7), 671–672.

Severus, W. E., Ahrens, B., Stoll, A. L., & Nemeroff, C. B. (1999). Omega-3 fatty acids—the missing link? *Archives of General Psychiatry, 56*(4), 380–381.

Shadish, W. R., Montgomery, L. M., Wilson, P., Wilson, M. R., Bright, I., & Okwumabua, T. (1993). Effects of family and marital psychotherapies: A meta-analysis. *Journal of Consulting and Clinical Psychology, 61*, 992–1002.

Shaffer, D. (1994). Attention-deficit hyperactivity disorder in adults. *American Journal of Psychiatry, 151*, 633–638.

Shaffer, D., & Craft, L. (1999). Methods of adolescent suicide prevention. *Journal of Clinical Psychiatry, 60*(Suppl. 2), 70–74.

Shapiro, A. (1980). A contribution to a history of the placebo effect. *Behavioral Science, 5*, 109–131.

Shapiro, A. K., & Shapiro, E. S. (1997). *The powerful placebo: From ancient priest to modern physician.* Baltimore, MD: Johns Hopkins University Press.

Shapiro, D. A., & Shapiro, D. (1982). Meta-analysis of comparative therapy outcome studies: A replication and refinement. *Psychological Bulletin, 92*, 581–604.

Shapiro, D. E., & Schulman, C. E. (1996). Ethic and legal issues in e-mail therapy. *Ethics and Behavior, 6*(2), 107–124.

Shapiro, D. H. (1980). *Meditation.* Chicago: Aldine.

Shapiro, T., & Hertzig, M. E. (1999). Normal child and adolescent development. In R. E. Hales, S. C. Yudofsky, & J. A. Talbot (Eds.), *Textbook of psychiatry* (pp. 109–146). Washington, DC: American Psychiatric Press.

Sharma, R. P., Shapiro, L. E., Kamath, S. K., & Soll, E. A. (1997). Acute dietary tryptophan depletion: Effects on schizophrenic positive and negative symptoms. *Neuropsychobiology, 35*(1), 5–10.

Shaw, E. D., Stokes, P. E., Mann, J. J., & Manevitz, A. Z. (1987). Effects of lithium carbonate on the memory and motor speed of bipolar outpatients. *Journal of Abnormal Psychology, 96*, 64–69.

Shea, M. T., Widiger, T. A., & Klein, M. H. (1992). Comorbidity of personality disorders and depression: Implications for treatment. *Journal of Consulting and Clinical Psychology, 60*, 857–868.

Shear, M. K., Fyer, A. J., Ball, G., Josephson, S., Fitzpatrick, M., Gorman, J., Liebowitz, M., Klein, D. F., & Francis, A. J. (1991). Vulnerability to sodium lactate in panic disorder patients given cognitive-behavior therapy. *American Journal of Psychiatry, 148*, 795–797.

Shear, M. K., Pilkonis, P. A., Cloitre, M., & Leon, A. C. (1994). Cognitive behavioral treatment compared with nonprescriptive treatment of panic disorder. *Archives of General Psychiatry, 51*, 395–401.

Shearer, S. L. (1994). Phenomenology of self-injury among inpatient women with borderline personality disorder. *Journal of Nervous and Mental Disease, 182*, 524–526.

Sheitman, B. B., Kinon, B. J., Ridgway, B. A., & Lieberman, J. A. (1998). Pharmacological treatments of schizophrenia. In P. E. Nathan & J. M. Gorman. (Eds.), *A guide to treatments that work* (pp. 167–189). New York: Oxford University Press.

Shekelle, R. B., et al. (1981). Psychological depression and 17-year risk of death from cancer. *Psychosomatic Medicine, 43*(2), 117–125.

Shelton v. Tucker, 364 U.S. 479 (1960).

Sher, K. J., & Levenson, R. W. (1982). Risk for alcoholism and individual differences in the stress-response-dampening effect of alcohol. *Journal of Abnormal Psychology, 91*, 350–367.

Sher, K. J., & Trull, T. J. (1994). Personality and disinhibitory psychopathology: Alcoholism and antisocial personality disorder. *Journal of Abnormal Psychology, 103*, 92–102.

Sher, L., Goldman, D., Ozaki, N., & Rosenthal, N. E. (1999). The role of genetic factors in the etiology of seasonal affective disorder and seasonality. *Journal of Affective Disorders, 53*(3), 203–210.

Sherman, A. D., Sacquitne, J. L., & Petty, F. (1982). Specificity of the learned helplessness model of depression. *Pharmacology, Biochemistry and Behavior, 16*, 449–454.

Shiloh, A. (1968). Sanctuary or prison? Responses to life in a mental hospital. *Trans-Action, 6*, 28.

Shioiri, T., Nishimura, A., Nushida, H., & Tatsuno, Y. (1999). The Kobe earthquake and reduced suicide rate in Japanese males. *Archives of General Psychiatry, 56*(3), 282–283.

Shorter, E. (1992). *From paralysis to fatigue: A history of psychosomatic medicine in the modern era.* New York: Free Press.

Siegel, J. M. (2000a). Brainstem mechanisms generating REM sleep. In M. Kryger, T. Roth, & W. Dement (Eds.), *Principles and practice of sleep medicine.* New York: Saunders.

Siegel, J. M. (2000b). Narcolepsy. *Scientific American, 282*, 76–81.

Siever, L. J., Silverman, J. M., Horvath, T. B., & Klar, H. M. (1990). Increased morbid risk for schizophrenia-related disorders in relatives of schizotypal personality disordered patients. *Archive of General Psychiatry, 47*, 634–640.

Silberstein, S. D. (1994). Tension-type headaches. *Headache, 34*, S2–S7.

Silbersweig, D. A., Stern, E., Frith, C., Cahill, C., et al. (1995). A functional neuroanatomy of hallucinations in schizophrenia. *Nature, 378*(6553), 176–179.

Silver, H., & Shmugliakov, N. (1998). Augmentation with fluvoxamine but not maprotiline improves negative symptoms in treated. *Journal of Clinical Psychopharmacology, 18*(3), 208–211.

Silver, J. M., Yudofsky, S. C., & Hurowitz, G. I. (1994). Psychopharmacology and electroconvulsive therapy. In R. E. Hales, S. C. Yudofsky, & J. A. Talbott (Eds.), *American Psychiatric Press textbook of psychiatry* (2d ed.). Washington, DC: American Psychiatric Press.

Silverman, J. M., Li, G., Zaccario, M. L., Smith, C. J., Schmeidler, J., Mohs, R. C., & Davis, K. L. (1994). Patterns of risk in first-degree relatives of patients with Alzheimer's disease. *Archives of General Psychiatry, 51*, 577–586.

Silverman, K., Chutuape, M. A., Bigelow, G. E., & Stitzer, M. L. (1999). Voucher-based reinforcement of cocaine abstinence in treatment-resistant methadone. *Psychopharmacology, 146*(2), 128–138.

Silverstone, T., & Hunt, N. (1992). Symptoms and assessment of mania. In E. S. Paykel (Ed.), *Handbook of affective disorders* (2nd ed.) New York: Guilford Press.

Simeon, D., Gross, S., Guralnik, O., Stein, D. J., et al. (1997). Feeling unreal: 30 cases of *DSM-III-R* depersonalization disorder. *American Journal of Psychiatry, 154*(8), 1107–1113.

Simeon, D., Stein, D. J., & Hollander, E. (1998). Treatment of depersonalization disorder with clomipramine. *Biological Psychiatry, 44*(4), 302–303.

Simon, G. E. (1998). Management of somatoform and factitious disorders. In P. E. Nathan & J. M. Gorman (Eds.), *A guide to treatments that work* (pp. 408–422). New York: Oxford University Press.

Simon, G. E., Katon, W. J., & Sparks, P. J. (1990). Allergic to life: Psychological factors in environmental illness. *American Journal of Psychiatry 147,* 901–906.

Simon, R. I. (1999). The law and psychiatry. In R. E. Hales, S. C. Yudofsky, & J. A. Talbot (Eds.), *Textbook of psychiatry* (pp. 1493–1534). Washington, DC: American Psychiatric Press.

Simonoff, E., Pickles, A., Meyer, J., Silberg, J., & Maes, H. (1998). Genetic and environmental influences on subtypes of conduct disorder behavior in boys. *Journal of Abnormal Child Psychology, 26* (6), 495–509.

Simons, A. D., Garfield, S. L., & Murphy, G. E. (1984). The processes of change in cognitive therapy and pharmacotherapy for depression: *Changes in mood and cognition. Archives of General Psychiatry, 41,* 45–51.

Simpson, S. G., & Jamison, K. R. (1999). The risk of suicide in patients with bipolar disorders. *Journal of Clinical Psychiatry, 60*(Suppl. 2), 53–56.

Sinclair, D., & Murray, L. (1998). Effects of postnatal depression on children's adjustment in school. *British Journal of Psychiatry, 172,* 58–63.

Singer, J. L. (1990). *Repression and dissociation.* Chicago: University of Chicago Press.

Singh, A., Herrmann, N., & Black, S. E. (1998). The importance of lesion location in poststroke depression: A critical review. *Canadian Journal of Psychiatry, 43*(9), 921–927.

Singh, A. N. (1996). Mitral valve prolapse syndrome. *International Medical Journal, 3*(2), 101–106.

Sinha, S., Anderson, J. P., Barbour, R., Basi, G. S., Caccavello, R., Davis, D., Doan, M., & Dovey, H. F. (1999). Purification and cloning of amyloid precursor protein beta-secretase from human brain. *Nature, 402*(6761), 537–540.

Sinyor, D., Schwartz, S. G., Peronnet, F., Brisson, G., & Seraganian, P. (1983). Aerobic fitness level and reactivity to psychosocial stress: Physiological, biochemical, and subjective measures. *Psychosomatic Medicine, 45,* 205–217.

Sirois, F. (1982). Perspectives in epidemic hysteria. In M. J. Colligan, J. W. Pennebaker, & L. R. Murphy (Eds.), *Mass psychogenic illness.* Hillsdale, NJ: Erlbaum.

Sizemore, C. C., & Pittillo, E. S. (1977). *I'm Eve.* Garden City, NY: Doubleday.

Skinner, B. F. (1953). *Science and human behavior.* New York: Macmillan.

Skoog, G., & Skoog, I. (1999). A 40-year follow-up of patients with obsessive-compulsive disorder. *Archives of General Psychiatry, 56*(2), 121–127.

Slater, E., & Glithero, E. (1965). A follow-up of patients diagnosed as suffering from hysteria. *Journal of Psychosomatic Research, 9,* 9–13.

Slater, J., & Depue, R. A. (1981). The contribution of environmental events and social support to serious suicide attempts in primary depressive disorder. *Journal of Abnormal Psychology, 90,* 275–285.

Slovenko, R. (1992). The right of the mentally ill to refuse treatment revisited. *Journal of Psychiatry and Law, 20,* 407–434.

Slovenko, R. (1995). Assessing competency to stand trial. *Psychiatric Annals, 25,* 392–397.

Slovenko, R. (1997). Multiple personality and criminal law. *Security Journal, 9,* 205–207.

Small, G. W., & Nicholi, A. (1982). Mass hysteria among schoolchildren. *Archives of General Psychiatry, 39,* 721–724.

Small, G. W., Propper, M. W., Randolph, E. T., & Spencer, E. (1991). Mass hysteria among student performers: Social relationship as a symptom predictor. *American Journal of Psychiatry, 148,* 1200–1205.

Smith v. United States, 148 F.2d 665 (1929).

Smith, A., & Weissman, M. M. (1992). Epidemiology. In E. S. Paykel (Ed.), *Handbook of affective disorders* (2nd ed.). New York: Guilford Press.

Smith, D. E., & Seymour, R. B. (1994). LSD: History and toxicity. *Psychiatric Annals, 24,* 145–147.

Smith, D. W., & Wilson, A. A. (1973). *The child with Down's syndrome (mongolism).* Philadelphia: Saunders.

Smith, G. R. (1994). The course of somatization and its effects on utilization of health care resources. Special series: Consultation-liaison outcome studies. *Psychomatics, 35,* 263–267.

Smith, G. R., Rost, K., & Kashner, T. M. (1995). A trial of the effect of a standardized psychiatric consultation on health outcomes and costs in somatizing patients. *Archives of General Psychiatry, 52,* 238–243.

Smith, J. C. (1976). Psychotherapeutic effects of transcendental meditation with controls for expectation of relief and daily sitting. *Journal of Consulting and Clinical Psychology, 44,* 630–637.

Smith, K. A., Fairburn, C. G., & Cowen, P. J. (1999). Symptomatic relapse in bulimia nervosa following acute tryptophan depletion. *Arch. Gen. Psychiatry, 56*(2), 171–176.

Smith, T., McEachin, J. J., & Lovaas, O. I. (1993). Comments on replication and evaluation of outcome. *American Journal on Mental Retardation, 97,* 385–391.

Smith, T. W. (1992). Hostility and health: Current status of a psychosomatic hypothesis. *Health Psychology, 11,* 139–150.

Smits, C. H. M., van Rijsselt, R. J. T., & Jonker, C. (1995). Social participation and cognitive functioning in older adults. *International Journal of Geriatric Psychiatry, 10*(4), 325–331.

Smolowe, J. (1990, Nov. 12). The 21 faces of Sarah. *Time,* 87.

Smyth, J. M., Stone, A. A., Hurewitz, A., & Kaell, A. (1999). Effects of writing about stressful experiences on symptom reduction in patients with asthma or. *Journal of the American Medical Association, 281*(14), 1304–1309.

Snaith, P., Tarsh, M., & Reid, R. W. (1993). Sex reassignment surgery: A study of 141 Dutch transsexuals. *British Journal of Psychiatry, 162,* 681–685.

Snyder, S. H. (1976). The dopamine hypothesis of schizophrenia. *American Journal of Psychiatry, 133,* 197–202.

Soares, J. C., Mallinger, A. G., Dippold, C. S., Frank, E., & Kupfer, D. J. (1999). Platelet membrane phospholipids in euthymic bipolar disorder patients: Are they affected by. *Biological Psychiatry, 45*(4), 453–457.

Soares, J. C., & Mann, J. J. (1997). The anatomy of mood disorders: Review of structural neuroimaging studies. *Biological Psychiatry, 41*(1), 86–106.

Sobin, C., & Sackeim, H. A. (1997). Psychomotor symptoms of depression. *American Journal of Psychiatry, 154*(1), 4–17.

Solanto, M. V., & Conners, C. K. (1982). A dose-response and time-action analysis of autonomic and behavioral effects of methylphenidate in attention deficit disorder with hyperactivity. *Psychophysiology, 19,* 658–667.

Soliday, E., McCluskey Fawcett, K., & O'Brien, M. (1999). Postpartum affect and depressive symptoms in mothers and fathers. *American Journal of Orthopsychiatry, 69*(1), 30–38.

Soloff, P. H., George, A., Nathan, R. S., Schulz, P. M., & Perel, J. M. (1987). Behavioral dyscontrol in borderline patients treated with amitriptyline. *Psychopharmacological Bulletin, 23,* 177–181.

Soloff, P. H., Lis, J. A., Kelly, T., Cornelius, J., & Ulrich, R. (1994). Risk factors for suicidal behavior in borderline personality disorder. *American Journal of Psychiatry, 151,* 1316–1323.

Solomon, D. A., Keller, M. B., Leon, A. C., & Mueller, T. I. (1997). Recovery from major depression: A 10-year prospective follow-up across multiple episodes. *Archives of General Psychiatry, 54*(11), 1001–1006.

Solomon, S. (1994). Migraine diagnosis and clinical symptomatology. *Headache, 34,* S8–S12.

Solowij, N. (1998). Cannabis and cognitive functioning.

Soubie, P. (1986). Reconciling the role of central serotonin neurons in human and animal behavior. *Behavioral and Brain Sciences, 9,* 319–364.

Southwick, S. M., Krystal, J. H., Morgan, C. A., Johnson, D., Nagy, L. M., Nicolaou, A. L., Heninger, G. R., & Charney, D. S. (1993). Abnormal noradrenergic function in posttraumatic stress disorder. *Archives of General Psychiatry, 50,* 266–274.

Southwick, S. M., Morgan, C. A., Darnell, A., Bremner, D., Nicolaou, A. L., Nagy, L. M., & Charney, D. S. (1995). Trauma-related symptoms in veterans of Operation Desert Storm: A 2-year follow-up. *American Journal of Psychiatry, 152,* 1150–1155.

Southwick, S. M., Morgan, C. A., III, Nicolaou, A. L., & Charney, D. S. (1997). Consistency of memory for combat-related traumatic events in veterans of Operation Desert Storm. *American Journal of Psychiatry, 154*(2), 173–177.

Spanos, N. P. (1986). Hypnosis, nonvolitional responding, and multiple personality: A social psychological perspective. In B. A. Maher & W. Maher (Eds.), *Progress in experimental personality research* (Vol. 14). New York: Academic Press.

Spanos, N. P. (1994). Multiple identity enactments and multiple personality disorder: A sociocognitive perspective. *Psychological Bulletin, 116,* 143–165.

Spanos, N. P., Cross, P. A., Dickson, K., & Dubreuil, S. C. (1993). Close encounters: An examination of UFO experiences. *Journal of Abnormal Psychology, 102,* 624–632.

Spanos, N. P., Weekes, J. R., & Bertrand, L. D. (1985). Multiple personality: A social psychological perspective. *Journal of Abnormal Psychology, 94,* 362–367.

Spector, I. P., & Carey, M. P. (1990). Incidence and prevalence of the sexual dysfunctions: A critical review of the empirical literature. *Archives of Sexual Behavior, 19,* 389–408.

Speer, D. C. (1992). Clinically significant change: Jacobson and Truax (1991) revisited. *Journal of Consulting and Clinical Psychology, 60,* 402–408.

Spence, S. A., Hirsch, S. R., Brooks, D. J., & Grasby, P. M. (1998). Prefrontal cortex activity in people with schizophrenia and control subjects: Evidence from. *British Journal of Psychiatry, 172,* 316–323.

Spencer, T., Wilens, T., Biederman, J., Faraone, S. V., Ablon, S., & Lapey, K. (1995). A double-blind, crossover comparison of methylphenidate and placebo in adults with childhood-onset attention-deficit hyperactivity disorder. *Archives of General Psychiatry, 52,* 434–443.

Spiegel, D. (1998). Consistency of memory among veterans of Operation Desert Storm. *American Journal of Psychiatry, 155*(9).

Spiegel, D., & Maldonado, J. R. (1999a). Dissociative disorders. In R. E. Hales, S. C. Yudofsky, & J. A. Talbot (Eds.), *Textbook of psychiatry* (pp. 711–738). Washington, DC: American Psychiatric Press.

Spiegel, D., & Maldonado, J. R. (1999b). Hypnosis. In R. E. Hales, S. C. Yudofsky, & J. A. Talbot (Eds.), *Textbook of psychiatry* (pp. 1243–1274). Washington, DC: American Psychiatric Press.

Spiegel, D. A. (1994). Dissociative disorders. In R. E. Hales, S. C. Yudofsky, & J. A. Talbott (Eds.), *American Psychiatric Press handbook of psychiatry* (2nd ed). Washington, DC: American Psychiatric Press.

Spiegel, D. A. (1998). Efficacy studies of alprazolam in panic disorder. *Psychopharmacology Bulletin, 34*(2), 191–195.

Spiga, R., Day, J. D., III, Schmitz, J. M., Broitman, M., & Elk, R. (1998). Context modulated effects of nicotine abstinence on human cooperative responding. *Experimental and Clinical Psychopharmacology, 6*(4), 390–398.

Spirito, A. (1997). Individual therapy techniques with adolescent suicide attempters. *Crisis, 18*(2), 62–64.

Spoont, M. R. (1992). Modulatory role of serotonin in neural information processing: Implications for human psychopathology. *Psychological Bulletin, 112,* 330–350.

Spranger, M., Spranger, S., Schwab, S., Benninger, C., & Dichgans, M. (1999). Familial hemiplegic migraine with cerebellar ataxia and paroxysmal psychosis. *European Neurology, 41*(3), 150–152.

Squire, L. R. (1986). Mechanisms of memory. *Science, 232,* 1612–1619.

Squire, L. R. (1992). Memory and the hippocampus: A synthesis from findings with rats, monkeys, and humans. *Psychological Review, 99,* 195–231.

Squire, L. R., & Butters, N. (1992). *Neuropsychology of memory* (2nd ed.).

Staal, W. G., Hulshoff Pol, H. E., & Kahn, R. S. (1999). Outcome of schizophrenia in relation to brain abnormalities. *Schizophrenia Bulletin, 25*(2), 337–348.

Staal, W. G., Pol, H. E. H., Schnack, H., & van der Schot, A. C. (1998). Partial volume decrease of the thalamus in relatives of patients with schizophrenia. *American Journal of Psychiatry, 155*(12), 1784–1786.

Stack, S. (1990). Media impacts on suicide. In D. Lester (Ed.), *Current concepts of suicide.* Philadelphia: Charles Press.

Stack, S. (1998). The relationship between culture and suicide: An analysis of African Americans. *Transcultural Psychiatry, 35*(2), 253–269.

Stahl, S. M., & Lebedun, M. (1974). Mystery gas: An analysis of mass hysteria. *Journal of Health and Social Behavior, 15,* 44–50.

Stanley, M. A., Beck, J. G., & Glassco, J. D. (1996). Treatment of generalized anxiety in older adults: A preliminary comparison of cognitive-behavioral and supportive approaches. *Behavior Therapy, 27*(4), 565–581.

Stanley, M. A., Breckenridge, J. K., Swann, A. C., Freeman, E. B., & Reich, L. (1997). Fluvoxamine treatment of trichotillomania. *Journal of Clinical Psychopharmacology, 17*(4), 278–283.

Stanley, M. A., Hannay, H. J., & Breckenridge, J. K. (1997). The neuropsychology of trichotillomania. *Journal of Anxiety Disorders, 11*(5), 473–488.

Statham, D. J., Heath, A. C., Madden, P. A. F., Bucholz, K. K., Bierut, L., Dinwiddie, S. H., Slutske, W. S., Dunne, M. P., & Martin, N. G. (1998). Suicidal behaviour: An epidemiological and genetic study. *Psychological Medicine, 28*(4), 839–855.

Steadman, H. J. (1973). Follow-up on Baxstrom patients returned to hospitals for the criminally insane. *American Journal of Psychiatry, 3,* 317–319.

Steadman, H. J., & Keveles, G. (1972). The community adjustment and criminal activity of Baxstrom patients, 1966–1970. *American Journal of Psychiatry, 129,* 304–310.

Steadman, H. J., & Keveles, G. (1978). The community adjustment and criminal activity of Baxstrom patients. *American Journal of Psychiatry, 135,* 1218–1220.

Steadman, H. J., Mulvey, E. P., Monahan, J., & Robbins, P. C. (1998). Violence by people discharged from acute psychiatric inpatient facilities and by others in the. *Archives of General Psychiatry, 55*(5), 393–401.

Steele, C. M., & Josephs, R. A. (1988). Drinking your troubles away: 2. An attention-allocation model of alcohol's effect on psychological stress. *Journal of Abnormal Psychology, 95,* 196–205.

Steele, C. M., Southwick, L., & Pagano, R. (1986). Drinking your troubles away: The role of activity in mediating alcohol's reduction of psychological stress. *Journal of Abnormal Psychology, 95,* 173–180.

Steffens, D. C., Hays, J. C., & Krishnan, K. R. R. (1999). Disability in geriatric depression. *American Journal of Geriatric Psychiatry, 7*(1), 34–40.

Steigerwald, F., & Stone, D. (1999). Cognitive restructuring and the 12-step program of Alcoholics Anonymous. *Journal of Substance Abuse Treatment, 16*(4), 321–327.

Stein, D. J., Bouwer, C., Hawkridge, S., & Emsley, R. A. (1997). Risperidone augmentation of serotonin reuptake inhibitors in obsessive-compulsive and. *Journal of Clinical Psychiatry, 58*(3), 119–122.

Stein, D. J., Bouwer, C., & Mand, C. M. (1997). Use of the selective serotonin reuptake inhibitor citalopram in treatment of trichotillomania. *European Archives of Psychiatry and Clinical Neuroscience, 247*(4), 234–236.

Stein, D. J., Hollander, E., & Liebowitz, M. R. (1993). Neurobiology of impulsivity and the impulse control disorders. *Journal of Neuropsychiatry and Clinical Neurosciences, 5,* 9–17.

Stein, D. J., Hollander, E., Mullen, L. S., DeCaria, C. M., et al. (1992). Comparison of clomipramine, alprazolam and placebo in the treatment of. *Human Psychopharmacology Clinical and Experimental, 7*(6), 389–395.

Stein, M. B., Millar, T. W., Larsen, D. K., & Kryger, M. H. (1995). Irregular breathing during sleep in patients with panic disorder. *American Journal of Psychiatry, 152*(8), 1168–1173.

Steinberg, M., Bancroft, J., & Buchanan, J. (1993). Multiple personality disorder in criminal law. *Bulletin of the American Academy of Psychiatry and the Law, 21,* 345–356.

Stephens, J. H., & Kamp, M. (1962). On some aspects of hysteria: A clinical study. *Journal of Nervous and Mental Disease, 134,* 305–315.

Stephens, M. W., & Delys, P. (1973). External control expectancies among disadvantaged children at preschool age. *Child Development, 44,* 670–674.

Stern, D. B. (1977). Handedness and the lateral distribution of conversion reactions. *Journal of Nervous and Mental Disease, 164,* 122–128.

Stevenson, W., Maton, K. I., & Teti, D. M. (1999). Social support, relationship quality, and well-being among pregnant adolescents. *Journal of Adolescence, 22*(1), 109–121.

Stewart, M. W., Knight, R. G., Palmer, D. G., & Highton, J. (1994). Differential relationships between stress and disease activity for immunologically distinct subgroups of people with rheumatoid arthritis. *Journal of Abnormal Psychology, 103,* 251–258.

Stewart, S. H., Karp, J., Pihl, R. O., & Peterson, R. A. (1997). Anxiety sensitivity and self-reported reasons for drug use. *Journal of Substance Abuse, 9,* 223–240.

Stice, E., Neuberg-Schupak, E., Shaw, H. E., & Stein, R. I. (1994). Relation of media exposure to eating disorder symptomatology: An examination of mediating mechanisms. *Journal of Abnormal Psychology, 103,* 836–840.

Stine, J. J. (1994). Psychosocial and psychodynamic issues affecting noncompliance with psychostimulant treatment. *Journal of Child and Adolescent Psychopharmacology, 4,* 75–86.

Stolerman, I. P., & Jarvis, M. J. (1995). The scientific case that nicotine is addictive. *Psychopharmacology, 117,* 2–10.

Stoll, A. L., Tohen, M., & Baldessarini, R. J. (1992). Increasing frequency of the diagnosis of obsessive-compulsive disorder. *American Journal of Psychiatry, 149,* 638–640.

Stone, A. A. (1975). *Mental health and law: A system in transition.* Rockville, MD: Center for Studies of Crime and Delinquency, National Institute of Mental Health.

Stone, E. A. (1975). Stress and catecholamines. In A. J. Friedhoff (Ed.), *Catecholamines and behavior.* New York: Plenum.

Stoney, C. M., Niaura, R., Bausserman, L., & Matacin, M. (1999). Lipid reactivity to stress: I. Comparison of chronic and acute stress responses in middle-aged. *Health Psychology, 18*(3), 241–250.

Stoudemire, A., Hill, C. D., Marquardt, M., & Dalton, S. (1998). Recovery and relapse in geriatric depression after treatment with antidepressants and ECT in. *General Hospital Psychiatry, 20*(3), 170–174.

Strain, J. J., Newcorn, J., Fulop, G., & Sokolyanskaya, M. (1999). Adjustment disorder. In R. E. Hales, S. C. Yudofsky, & J. A. Talbot (Eds.), *Textbook of psychiatry* (pp. 759–772). Washington, DC: American Psychiatric Press.

Strakowski, S. M., DelBello, M. P., Sax, K. W., & Zimmerman, M. E. (1999). Brain magnetic resonance imaging of structural abnormalities in bipolar disorder. *Archives of General Psychiatry, 56*(3), 254–260.

Strakowski, S. M., Keck, P. E., Jr., Sax, K. W., & McElroy, S. L. (1999). Twelve-month outcome of patients with DSM-III-R schizoaffective disorder: Comparisons to. *Schizophrenia Research, 35*(2), 167–174.

Strassberg, D. S., de Gouveia Brazao, C. A., Rowland, D. L., & Tan, P. (1999). Clomipramine in the treatment of rapid (premature) ejaculation. *Journal of Sex and Marital Therapy, 25*(2), 89–101.

Strassburger, T. L., Lee, H., Daly, E. M., Szczepanik, J., Krauski, J. S., Mentis, M. J., Salerno, J. A., DeCarli, C., Schapiro, M. B.,

& Alexander, G. E. (1997). Interactive effects of age and hypertension on volumes of brain structures. *Stroke, 28,* 1410–1417.

Strassman, R. J. (1995). Hallucinogenic drugs in psychiatric research and treatment: Perspectives and prospects. *Journal of Nervous and Mental Disease, 183,* 127–138.

Strauss, J. S., Kokes, F. R., Ritzler, B. A., Harder, D. W., & Van Ord, A. (1978). Patterns of disorder in first-admission psychiatric patients. *Journal of Nervous and Mental Disease, 166,* 611–623.

Strom, A., Refsum, S. B., Eitinger, L., Gronvik, O., Lonnum, A., Engeset, A., & Rogan, B. (1962). Examination of Norwegian ex–concentration camp prisoners. *Journal of Neuropsychiatry, 4,* 43–62.

Strupp, H. H. (1998). The Vanderbilt I Study revisited. *Psychotherapy Research, 8*(1), 17–29.

Suhail, K., & Cochrane, R. (1998). Seasonal variations in hospital admissions for affective disorders by gender and ethnicity. *Social Psychiatry and Psychiatric Epidemiology, 33*(5), 211–217.

Sullivan, J. E., & Chang, P. (1999). Review: Emotional and behavioral functioning in phenylketonuria. *Journal of Pediatric Psychology, 24*(3), 281–299.

Sullivan, J. L., Baenziger, J. C., Wagner, D. L., Rauscher, F. P., Nurnberger, J. I., & Holmes, J. S. (1990). Platelet MAO in subtypes of alcoholism. *Biological Psychiatry, 27,* 911–922.

Summerfeldt, L. J., & Endler, N. S. (1998). Examining the evidence for anxiety-related cognitive biases in obsessive-compulsive disorder. *Journal of Anxiety Disorders, 12*(6), 579–598.

Suppes, T., Baldessarini, R. J., Faedda, G. L., & Tohen, M. (1991). Risk of recurrence following discontinuation of lithium treatment in bipolar disorder. *Archives of General Psychiatry, 48,* 1082–1088.

Suryani, L., & Jensen, G. (1992). Psychiatrist, traditional healer, and culture integrated in clinical practice in Bali. *Medical Anthropology, 13,* 301–314.

Susser, E. S., & Lin, S. P. (1992). Schizophrenia after prenatal exposure to the Dutch hunger winter of 1944–1945. *Archives of General Psychiatry, 49,* 983–989.

Sutker, P. B., & Allain, A. N. (1988). Issues in personality conceptualization of addictive behaviors. *Journal of Consulting and Clinical Psychology, 56,* 172–182.

Sutker, P. B., Allain, A. N., & Johnson, J. L. (1993). Clinical assessment of long-term cognitive and emotional sequelae to World War II. *Psychological Assessment, 5*(1), 3–10.

Suvisaari, J., Haukka, J., Tanskanen, A., Hovi, T., & Loennqvist, J. (1999). Association between prenatal exposure to poliovirus infection and adult schizophrenia. *American Journal of Psychiatry, 156*(7), 1100–1102.

Suyemoto, K. L. (1998). The functions of self-mutilation. *Clinical Psychology Review, 18*(5), 531–554.

Swanson, J., Castellanos, F. X., Murias, M., & LaHoste, G. (1998). Cognitive neuroscience of attention deficit hyperactivity disorder and hyperkinetic disorder. *Current Opinion in Neurobiology, 8*(2), 263–271.

Swedo, S. E., Leonard, H. L., Kruesi, M. J. P., Rettew, D. C., Listwak, S. J., Berrettini, W., Sipetic, M., Hamburger, S., Gold, P. W., Potter, W. Z., & Rapoport, J. L. (1992). Cerebrospinal fluid neurochemistry in children and adolescents with obsessive-compulsive disorder. *Archives of General Psychiatry, 49,* 29–36.

Sweet, R. A., Mulsant, B. H., Gupta, B., Fifai, A. H., Pasternak, R. E., McEachran, A., & Zubenko, G. S. (1995). Duration of neuroleptic treatment and prevalence of tardive dyskinesia in late life. *Archives of General Psychiatry, 52,* 478–486.

Swift, I., Paquette, D., Davison, K., & Saeed, H. (1999). Pica and trace metal deficiencies in adults with developmental disabilities. *British Journal of Developmental Disabilities, 45*(89, Pt. 2), 111–117.

Swift, R. M. (1999). Medications and alcohol craving. *Alcohol Research and Health, 23*(3), 207–213.

Swift, R. M., Whilihan, W., Kuznetsov, O., Buongiorno, G., & Husing, H. (1994). Naltrexone-induced alterations in human ethanol intoxication. *American Journal of Psychiatry, 151,* 1463–1467.

Swinson, R. P., Antony, M. M., & Rachman, S. Obsessive-compulsive disorder: Theory, research, and treatment.

Sylvain, C., Ladouceur, R., & Boisvert, J. M. (1997). Cognitive and behavioral treatment of pathological gambling: A controlled study. *Journal of Consulting and Clinical Psychology, 65*(5), 727–732.

Szasz, T. S. (1961). *The myth of mental illness.* New York: HarperCollins.

Szasz, T. S. (1970). *The manufacture of madness.* New York: Macmillan.

Szatmari, P. (1992). The validity of autistic spectrum disorders: A literature review. *Journal of Autism and Developmental Disorders, 22,* 583–600.

Szeszko, P. R., Robinson, D., Alvir, J. M. J., Bilder, R. M., & Lencz, T. (1999). Orbital frontal and amygdala volume reductions in obsessive-compulsive disorder. *Archives of General Psychiatry, 56*(10), 913–919.

Szymanski, S., Lieberman, J. A., Alvir, J. M., Mayerhoff, D., Loebel, A., Geisler, S., Chakos, M., Koreen, A., Jody, D., Kane, J., Woener, M., & Cooper, T. (1995). Gender differences in onset of illness, treatment response, course, and biologic indexes in first-episode schizophrenic patients. *American Journal of Psychiatry, 152,* 698–703.

Takei, N., Sham, P., O'Callaghan, E., Murray, G. K., Glover, G., & Murray, R. M. (1994). Prenatal exposure to influenza and the development of schizophrenia: Is the effect confined to females? *American Journal of Psychiatry, 151,* 117–119.

Takemura, Y., Kikuchi, S., Takagi, H., & Inaba, Y. (1998). A cross-sectional study on the relationship between depression and left ventricular. *Preventive Medicine: An International Devoted to Practice and Theory,* Nov.–Dec.

Tamminga, C. A. (1998). Serotonin and schizophrenia. *Biological Psychiatry, 44*(11), 1079–1080.

Tamminga, C. A. (1999). Images in neuroscience: Brain development, IX. *American Journal of Psychiatry, 156* (January).

Tarasoff v. *Regents of the University of California,* 551 P.2d 334 (1976).

Tardiff, K. (1999). Violence. In R. E. Hales, S. C. Yudofsky, & J. A. Talbot (Eds.), *Textbook of psychiatry* (pp. 1405–1428). Washington, DC: American Psychiatric Press.

Tarrier, N., Pilgrim, H., Sommerfield, C., Faragher, B., & Reynolds, M. (1999). A randomized trial of cognitive therapy and imaginal exposure in the treatment of chronic. *Journal of Consulting and Clinical Psychology, 67*(1), 13–18.

Tate, J. C., Stanton, A. L, Green, S. B., Schmitz, J. M., et al. (1994). Experimental analysis of the role of expectancy in nicotine withdrawal. *Psychology of Addictive Behaviors, 8,* 169–178.

Taylor, S. (1994). Klein's suffocation theory of panic. *Archives of General Psychiatry, 51,* 505–506.

Taylor, S. E., & Brown, J. D. (1988). Illusion and well-being: A social psychological perspective on mental health. *Psychological Bulletin, 103,* 193–210.

Taylor, S. E., & Brown, J. D. (1994). Positive illusions and well-being revisited: Separating fact from fiction. *Psychological Bulletin, 116,* 21–27.

Teasdale, J. D., Howard, R. J., Cox, S. G., Ha, Y., & Brammer, M. J. (1999). Functional MRI study of the cognitive generation of affect. *American Journal of Psychiatry, 156*(2), 209–215.

Teicher, M. H., Gold, C. A., & Cole, J. O. (1990). Emergence of intense suicidal preoccupation during fluoxetine treatment. *American Journal of Psychiatry, 147,* 207–210.

Teicher, M. H., Gold, C. A., Oren, D. A., Schwartz, P. J., Luetke, C., Brown, C., & Rosenthal, N. E. (1995). The phototherapy light visor: More to it than meets the eye. *American Journal of Psychiatry, 152,* 1197–1202.

Teitelbaum, P., & Steller, E. (1954). Recovery from the failure to eat produced by hypothalamic lesions. *Science, 120,* 894–895.

Telch, C. F., Agras, W. S., Rossiter, E. M., Wilfrey, D., & Kenardy, J. (1990). Group cognitive-behavioral treatment for the non-purging bulimic: An initial evaluation. *Journal of Consulting and Clinical Psychology, 58,* 629–635.

Tellegen, A., Lykken, D. T., Bouchard, T. J., Wilcox, K., Segal, N., & Rich, S. (1988). Personality similarity in twins reared apart and together. *Journal of Personality and Social Psychology, 54,* 1031–1039.

Termal, M., Termal, J. S., Quitkin, F. M., McGrath, P. J., et al. (1989). Light therapy for seasonal affective disorder: A review of efficacy. *Neuropsychopharmacology, 2,* 1–22.

Terr, L. C. (1979). Children of Chowchilla. *Psychoanalytic Study of the Child, 34,* 547–623.

Terr, L. C. (1983). Chowchilla revisited: The effects of psychic trauma four years after a school-bus kidnapping. *American Journal of Psychiatry, 140,* 1543–1550.

Terr, L. C. (1994). *Unchained memories.* New York: Harper-Collins.

Thackwray, D. E., Smith, M. C., Bodfish, J. W., & Meyers, A. W. (1993). A comparison of behavioral and cognitive-behavioral interventions for bulimia nervosa. *Journal of Consulting and Clinical Psychology, 61,* 639–645.

Thapar, A., Holmes, J., Poulton, K., & Harrington, R. (1999). Genetic basis of attention deficit and hyperactivity. *British Journal of Psychiatry, 174,* 105–111.

Thase, M. E. (1998). Depression, sleep, and antidepressants. *Journal of Clinical Psychiatry, 59*(Suppl. 4), 55–65.

Thase, M. E., & Friedman, E. S. (1999). Is psychotherapy an effective treatment for melancholia and other severe depressive states? *Journal of Affective Disorders, 54*(1–2), 1–19.

Thase, M. E., Greenhouse, J. B., Frank, E., & Reynolds, C. F., III. (1997). Treatment of major depression with psychotherapy or psychotherapy–pharmacotherapy. *Archives of General Psychiatry, 54*(11), 1009–1015.

Thase, M. E., & Howland, R. H. (1994). Refractory depression: Relevance of psychosocial factors and therapies. *Psychiatric Annals, 24,* 232–239.

Thase, M. E., Reynolds, C. F., Frank, E., Simons, A. D., et al. (1994). Response to cognitive-behavioral therapy in chronic depression. *Journal of Psychotherapy Practice and Research, 3*(3), 204–214.

Thase, M. E., Simons, A. D., Cahalane, J., & McGeary, J. (1991). Cognitive behavior therapy of andogenous depression. *Behavior Therapy, 22,* 457–467.

Thiel, A., Broocks, A., Ohlmeier, M., Jacoby, G. E., & Schubler, G. (1995). Obsessive-compulsive disorder among patients with anorexia nervosa and bulimia. *American Journal of Psychiatry, 152,* 72–75.

Thigpen, C. H., & Cleckley, H. M. (1954). A case of multiple personality. *Journal of Abnormal and Social Psychology, 49,* 139–151.

Thigpen, C. H., & Cleckley, H. M. (1957). *The three faces of Eve.* New York: Fawcett.

Thomas Ollivier, V., Reymann, J. M., Le Moal, S., Schueck, S., Lieury, A., & Allain, H. (1999). Procedural memory in recent-onset Parkinson's disease. *Dementia and Geriatric Cognitive Disorders, 10*(2), 172–180.

Thomasson, H. R., and Li, T. K. (1993). How alcohol and aldehyde dehydrogenase genes modify alcohol drinking, alcohol flushing, and the risk for alcoholism. *Alcohol Health and Research World, 17,* 167–172.

Thompson, J., Weiner, R. D., & Myers, C. P. (1994). Use of ECT in the United States in 1975, 1980, and 1986. *American Journal of Psychiatry, 151,* 1657–1661.

Thompson, M. P., Kaslow, N. J., Kingree, J. B., & Puett, R. (1999). Partner abuse and posttraumatic stress disorder as risk factors for suicide attempts in a. *Journal of Traumatic Stress, 12*(1), 59–72.

Thorson, J. A., Powell, F. C., & Samuel, V. T. (1998). African- and Euro-American samples differ little in scores on death anxiety. *Psychological Reports, 83*(2), 623–626.

Tiihonen, J., Katila, H., Pekkonen, E., & Jaeaeskelaeinen, I. P. (1998). Reversal of cerebral asymmetry in schizophrenia measured with magnetoencephalography. *Schizophrenia Research, 30*(3), 209–219.

Timbrook, R. E., & Graham, J. R. (1994). Ethnic differences on the MMPI-2. *Psychological Assessment, 6,* 212–217.

Tohen, M., & Grundy, S. (1999). Management of acute mania. *Journal of Clinical Psychiatry, 60*(Suppl. 5), 31–34.

Tohen, M., Sanger, T. M., McElroy, S. L., & Tollefson, G. D. (1999). Olanzapine versus placebo in the treatment of acute mania. *American Journal of Psychiatry, 156*(5), 702–709.

Tollefson, G. D., Rampey, A. H., Potvin, J. H., Jenike, M. A., Rush, A. J., Dominguez, R. A., Koran, L. M., Shear, M. K., Goodman, W., & Genuso, L. A. (1994). A multicenter investigation of fixed-dose fluoxetine in the treatment of obsessive-compulsive disorder. *Archives of General Psychiatry, 51,* 559–567.

Tomarken, A. J., & Keener, A. D. (1998). Frontal brain asymmetry and depression: A self-regulatory perspective. *Cognition and Emotion, 12*(3), 387–420.

Tompson, M. C., Asarnow, J. R., Hamilton, E. B., & Newell, L. E. (1997). Children with schizophrenia-spectrum disorders: Thought disorder and communication. *Journal of Child Psychology and Psychiatry and Allied Disciplines, 38,* 4.

Tondo, L., & Baldessarini, R. J. (1998). Rapid cycling in women and men with bipolar manic-depressive disorders. *American Journal of Psychiatry, 155*(10), 1434–1436.

Toneatto, T., Blitz Miller, T., Calderwood, K., & Dragonetti, R. (1997). Cognitive distortions in heavy gambling. *Journal of Gambling Studies, 13*(3), 253–266.

Tonge, B. J., Brereton, A. V., Gray, K. M., & Einfeld, S. L. (1999). Behavioural and emotional disturbance in high-functioning autism and Asperger syndrome. *Autism, 3*(2), 117–130.

Toole, J. F. (1999). Dementia in world leaders and its effects upon international events: The examples of Franklin. *European Journal of Neurology, 6*(2), 115–119.

Toran-Allerand, C. D. (1996). The estrogen/neurotrophin connection during neural development: Is co-localization of estrogen receptors with neurotrophins and their receptors biologically relevant? *Developmental Neuroscience, 18,* 36–41.

Torgersen, S. (1983). Genetic factors in anxiety disorders. *Archives of General Psychiatry, 40,* 1085–1089.

Torrey, E. F., Hersh, S. P., & McCabe, K. D. (1975). Early childhood psychosis and bleeding during pregnancy. *Journal of Autism and Childhood Schizophrenia, 5,* 287–297.

Torrey, E. F., Miller, J., Rawlings, R., & Yolken, R. H. (1997). Seasonality of births in schizophrenia and bipolar disorder: A review of the literature. *Schizophrenia Research, 28*(1), 1–38.

Torrey, E. F., Rawlings, R., & Waldman, I. N. (1988). Schizophrenic births and viral diseases in two states. *Schizophrenia Research, 1,* 73–77.

Toufexis, A. (1988, June 20). Why mothers kill their babies. *Time,* pp. 81–82.

Tough, S., Butt, J. C., & Sanders, G. L. (1994). Autoerotic asphyxial deaths: Analysis of nineteen fatalities in Alberta, 1978–1989. *Canadian Journal of Psychiatry, 39,* 157–160.

Towbin, A. (1978). Cerebral dysfunctions related to perinatal organic damage: Clinical-neuropathologic correlates. *Journal of Abnormal Psychology, 87,* 617–635.

Tredgold, A. F., & Soddy, K. (1970). *Tredgold's mental retardation.* Baltimore: Williams & Wilkins.

Treffert, D. A. (1988). The idiot savant: A review of the syndrome. *American Journal of Psychiatry, 145*(5), 563–572.

Trestman, R. L., Horvath, T., Kalus, O., Peterson, A. E., et al. (1996). Event-related potentials in schizotypal personality disorder. *Journal of Neuropsychiatry and Clinical Neurosciences, 8*(1), 33–40.

Trevisan, L. A., Boutros, N., Petrakis, I. L., & Krystal, J. H. (1998). Complications of alcohol withdrawal: Pathophysiological insights. *Alcohol Health and Research World, 22*(1), 61–66.

Trottier, G., Srivastava, L., & Walker, C. D. (1999). Etiology of infantile autism: A review of recent advances in genetic and neurobiological research. *Journal of Psychiatry and Neuroscience, 24*(2), 103–115.

Trudeau, D. L., Anderson, J., Hansen, L. M., & Shagalov, D. N. (1998). Findings of mild traumatic brain injury in combat veterans with PTSD and a history of blast. *Journal of Neuropsychiatry and Clinical Neurosciences, 10*(3), 308–313.

True, W. R., & Pitman, R. (1999). Genetics and posttraumatic stress disorder. In P. A. Saigh, J. D. Bremner, et al. (Eds.), *Posttraumatic stress disorder: A comprehensive text* (pp. 144–159). Boston: Allyn & Bacon.

True, W. R., Rice, J., Eisen, S. A., Heath, A. C., Goldberg, J., Lyons, M. J., & Nowak, J. (1993). A twin study of genetic and environmental contributions to liability for posttraumatic stress symptoms. *Archives of General Psychiatry, 50,* 257–264.

Trull, T. J., Widiger, T. A., Useda, J. D., Holcomb, J., & Doan, B. T. (1998). A structured interview for the assessment of the Five-Factor Model of Personality. *Psychological Assessment, 10*(3), 229–240.

Tsai, L., Stewart, M., Faust, M., & Shook, S. (1982). Social class distribution of fathers of children enrolled in the Iowa Autistic Program. *Journal of Autism and Developmental Disorders, 12,* 211–221.

Tu, G. C., & Israel, Y. (1995). Alcohol consumption by Orientals in North America is predicted largely by a single gene. *Behavior Genetics, 25,* 59–65.

Tune, L. (1998). Treatments for dementia. In P. E. Nathan & J. M. Gorman (Eds.), *A guide to treatments that work* (pp. 90–126). New York: Oxford University Press.

Turk, J., & Graham, P. (1997). Fragile X syndrome, autism and autistic features. *Autism, 1*(2), 175–197.

Turner, R. J., & Wagonfeld, M. O. (1967). Occupational mobility and schizophrenia: An assessment of the social causation and social selection hypothesis. *American Sociological Review, 32,* 104–113.

Turvey, C. L., Carney, C., Arndt, S., & Wallace, R. B. (1999). Conjugal loss and syndromal depression in a sample of elders aged 70 years and older. *American Journal of Psychiatry, 156*(10), 1596–1601.

Uchino, B. N., Cacioppo, J. T., & Kiecolt-Glaser, J. K. (1996). The relationship between social support and physiological processes: A review with emphasis. *Psychological Bulletin, 119*(3), 488–531.

Ueberall, M. A., & Wenzel, D. (1999). Intranasal sumatriptan for the acute treatment of migraine in children. *Neurology, 52*(7), 1507–1510.

Uesugi, H., Onuma, T., Shimizu, H., & Maehara, T. (1997). Schizophrenia-like psychosis following temporal lobectomy in patients with epilepsy. *Journal of Epilepsy, 10*(4), 194–197.

Ullman, L. P., & Krasner, L. (1969). *A psychological approach to abnormal behavior.* Englewood Cliffs, NJ: Prentice Hall.

Unden, A., Orth-Gomer, K., & Elofsson, S. (1991). Cardiovascular effects of social support in the workplace: Twenty-four-hour ECG monitoring of men and women. *Psychosomatic Medicine, 53,* 50–60.

United States v. *Brawner,* 471 F.2d 969 (D.C. 1972).

Ursano, R. J., & Silberman, E. K. (1999). Psychoanalysis, psychoanalytic psychotherapy, and supportive psychotherapy. In R. E. Hales, S. C. Yudofsky, & J. A. Talbot (Eds.), *Textbook of psychiatry* (1157–1184). Washington, DC: American Psychiatric Press.

Vaernik, A. (1998). Suicide in the former republics of the USSR. *Psychiatria Fennica, 29,* 150–162.

Vaillant, G. E. (1963). Twins discordant for early infantile autism. *Archives of General Psychiatry, 9,* 163–167.

Valenstein, E. S. (Ed.). (1980). *The psychosurgery debate.* New York: Freeman.

van Balkom, A. J. L. M., de Haan, E., van Oppen, P., & Spinhoven, P. (1998). Cognitive and behavioral therapies alone versus in combination with fluvoxamine in the. *Journal of Nervous and Mental Disease, 186*(8), 492–499.

Vandereycken, W., & Lowenkopf, E. L. (1990). Anorexia nervosa in 19th-century America. *Journal of Nervous and Mental Disease, 178,* 531–535.

van der Hart, O., Brown, P., & Graafland, M. (1999). Trauma-induced dissociative amnesia in World War I combat soldiers. *Australian and New Zealand Journal of Psychiatry, 33*(1), 37–46.

van der Kolk, B. A., Dreyfuss, D., Michaels, M., Shera, D., et al. (1994). Fluoxetine in posttraumatic stress disorder. *Journal of Clinical Psychiatry, 55*(12), 517–522.

van de Wijngaart, G. F., Braam, R., de Bruin, D., & Fris, M. (1999). Ecstasy use at large-scale dance events in the Netherlands. *Journal of Drug Issues, 29*(3), 679–702.

van Lankveld, J. J. D. M. (1998). Bibliotherapy in the treatment of sexual dysfunctions: A meta-analysis. *Journal of Consulting and Clinical Psychology, 66*(4), 702–708.

van Os, J., & Selten, J. P. (1998). Prenatal exposure to maternal stress and subsequent schizophrenia: The May 1940 invasion. *British Journal of Psychiatry, 172,* 324–326.

Van Putten, T. (1975). Why do patients with manic-depressive illness stop their lithium? *Comprehensive Psychiatry, 16,* 179–183.

Vassar, R., Bennett, B. D., Babu Khan, S., Kahn, S., Mendiaz, E. A., Denis, P., & Teplow, D. B. (1999). Beta-secretase cleavage of Alzheimer's amyloid precursor protein by the transmembrane. *Science, 286*(5440), 735–741.

Veith, I. (1965). *Hysteria: The history of a disease.* Chicago: University of Chicago Press.

Velakoulis, D., Pantelis, C., McGorry, P. D., & Dudgeon, P. (1999). Hippocampal volume in first-episode psychoses and chronic schizophrenia: A high resolution. *Archives of General Psychiatry, 56*(2), 133–141.

Vera, G. H. (1998). Prevalence of seasonal affective disorder. *British Journal of Psychiatry, 173,* 270.

Verburg, K., Pols, H., de Leeuw, M., & Griez, E. (1998). Reliability of the 35% carbon dioxide panic provocation challenge. *Psychiatry Research, 78*(3), 207–214.

Verhaeghen, P., Marcoen, A., & Goossens, L. (1992). Improving memory performance in the aged through mnemonic training: A meta-analytic. *Psychology and Aging, 7*(2), 242–251.

Vieta, E., Gasto, C., Colom, F., Martinez, A., Otero, A., & Vallejo, J. (1998). Treatment of refractory rapid cycling bipolar disorder with risperidone. *Journal of Clinical Psychopharmacology, 18*(2), 172–174.

Viets, V. C. L., & Miller, W. R. (1997). Treatment approaches for pathological gamblers. *Clinical Psychology Review, 17*(7), 689–702.

Vig, S., & Jedrysek, E. (1999). Autistic features in young children with significant cognitive impairment: Autism or mental retardation? *Journal of Autism and Developmental Disorders, 29*(3), 235–248.

Vinogradov, S., Cox, P. D., & Yalom, I. D. (1999). Group therapy. In R. E. Hales, S. C. Yudofsky, & J. A. Talbot (Eds.), *Textbook of psychiatry* (pp. 1275–1312). Washington, DC: American Psychiatric Press.

Virkkunen, M., De Jong, J., Barthko, J., Goodwin, F. K., & Linnoila, M. (1989). Relationship of psychobiological variables to recidivism in violent offenders and impulsive fire setters: A follow-up study. *Archives of General Psychiatry, 46,* 600–603.

Virkkunen, M., Rawling, R., Tokola, R., Poland, R. E., Guidotti, A., Nemeroff, C., Biessette, G., Kologeras, K., Karen, S., & Linnoila, M. (1994). CSF biochemistries, glucose metabo-lism, and diurnal activity rhythms in alcoholics, violent offenders, fire setters, and healthy volunteers. *Archives of General Psychiatry, 51,* 20–27.

Visser, S., & Bouman, T. K. (1992). Cognitive-behavioural approaches in the treatment of hypochondriasis: Six single case cross-over studies. *Behaviour Research and Therapy, 30,* 301–306.

Vitousek, K., & Manke, F. (1994). Personality variables and disorders in anorexia nervosa and bulimia nervosa. *Journal of Abnormal Psychology, 103,* 137–147.

Volavka, J., Cooper, T., Czobor, P., Bitter, I., Meisner, M., Laska, E., Gastanaga, P., Krakowski, M., Chow, J., Growner, M., & Douyon, R. (1992). Haloperidol blood levels and clinical effects. *Archives of General Psychiatry, 49,* 354–361.

Volkow, N. J., Ding, Y., Fowler, J. S., Wang, G., Logan, J., Gatley, J. S., Dewey, S., Ashby, C., Liebermann, J., Hitzemann, R., & Wolf, A. P. (1995). Is methylphenidate like cocaine? *Archives of General Psychiatry, 52,* 456–463.

Volpicelli, J. R., Alterman, A. I., Hayashida, M., & O'Brien, C. P. (1992). Naltrexone in the treatment of alcohol dependence. *Archives of General Psychiatry, 49,* 876–880.

Volz, H. P., Gaser, C., Haeger, F., Rzanny, R., Poenisch, J., & Mentzel, H. J. (1999). Decreased frontal activation in schizophrenics during stimulation with the Continuous. *European Psychiatry, 14*(1), 17–24.

Vonnegut, M. (1975). *The Eden express.* New York: Praeger.

Vuksic-Mihaljevic, Z., Mandic, N., Barkic, J., & Mrdenovic, S. (1998). A current psychodynamic understanding of panic disorder. *British Journal of Medical Psychology, 71*(1), 27–45.

Waddington, J. L., Weller, M. P. I., Crow, T. J., & Hirsch, S. R. (1992). Schizophrenia, genetic retrenchment, and epidemiologic renaissance. *Archives of General Psychiatry, 49,* 990–994.

Wagner, E. E., & Heise, M. R. (1974). A comparison of Rorschach records of three multiple personalities. *Journal of Personality Assessment, 38,* 308–331.

Wahlbeck, K., Cheine, M., Essali, A., & Adams, C. (1999). Evidence of clozapine's effectiveness in schizophrenia: A systematic review and meta-analysis. *American Journal of Psychiatry, 156*(7), 990–999.

Waisbren, S. E. (1999). Phenylketonuria. In S. Goldstein, C. R. Reynolds et al. (Eds.), *Handbook of neurodevelopmental and genetic disorders.*

Waldinger, M. D., Hengeveld, M. W., & Zwinderman, A. H. (1994). Paroxetine treatment of premature ejaculation: A double-blind, randomized, placebo-controlled study. *American Journal of Psychiatry, 151,* 1377–1379.

Waldinger, M. D., Hengeveld, M. W., Zwinderman, A. H., & Olivier, B. (1998). Effect of SSRI antidepressants on ejaculation: A double-blind, randomized. *Journal of Clinical Psychopharmacology, 18*(4), 274–281.

Walker, E., Lewis, N., Loewy, R., & Palyo, S. (1999). Motor dysfunction and risk for schizophrenia. *Development and Psychopathology, 11*(3), 509–523.

Walker, E. F., Logan, C. B., & Walder, D. (1999). Indicators of neurodevelopmental abnormality in schizotypal personality disorder. *Psychiatric Annals, 29*(3), 132–136.

Wall, T. L., Thomasson, H. R., Schuckit, M. A., & Ehlers, C. L. (1992). Subjective feelings of alcohol intoxication in Asians with genetic variations of ALDH 2 alleles. *Alcoholism Clinical and Experimental Research, 16,* 991–995.

Walsh, B. T., Hadigan, C. M., Devlin, M. J., Gladis, M., & Roose, S. P. (1991). Long-term outcome of antidepressant treatment for bulimia nervosa. *American Journal of Psychiatry, 148,* 1206–1212.

Walsh, B. T., Stewart, J. W., Roose, S. P., Gladis, M., & Glassman, A. H. (1984). Treatment of bulimia with phenelzine. *Archives of General Psychiatry, 41,* 1105–1109.

Walsh, B. T., Stewart, J. W., Wright, L., Harrison, W., Roose, S. P., & Glassman, A. H. (1982). Treatment of bulimia with monoamine oxidase inhibitors. *American Journal of Psychiatry, 139,* 1629–1630.

Walsh, B. T., Wilson, G. T., Loeb, K. L., Devlin, M. J., et al. (1997). Medication and psychotherapy in the treatment of bulimia nervosa. *American Journal of Psychiatry, 154*(4), 523–531.

Walsh, J. K., & Scweitzer, P. K. (1999). Ten-year trends in the pharmacological treatment of insomnia. *Sleep, 22*(3), 371–375.

Walters, E. E., & Kendler, K. S. (1995). Anorexia nervosa and anorexia-like syndromes in a population-based female twin sample. *American Jounal of Psychiatry, 152,* 64–71.

Wampold, B. E., Mondin, G. W., Moody, M., & Stich, F. (1997). A meta-analysis of outcome studies comparing bona fide psychotherapies. *Psychological Bulletin, 122*(3), 203–215.

Ward, C. H., Beck, A. T., Mendelson, M., Mock, J. E., & Erbaugh, J. K. (1962). The psychiatric nomenclature: Reasons for diagnostic disagreement. *Archives of General Psychiatry, 7,* 198–205.

Ward, J., Mattick, R. P., & Hall, W. (1994). The effectiveness of methadone maintenance treatment: An overview. *Drug and Alcohol Review, 13,* 327–336.

Wassermann, E. M. (1998). Risk and safety of repetitive transcranial magnetic stimulation: Report and suggested. *Electroencephalography and Clinical Neurophysiology: Evoked Potentials.*

Wassink, T. H., Andreasen, N. C., Nopoulos, P., & Flaum, M. (1999). Cerebellar morphology as a predictor of symptom and psychosocial outcome in schizophrenia. *Biological Psychiatry, 45*(1), 41–48.

Watkins, J. G. (1984). The Bianchi (L.A. Hillside Strangler) case: Sociopath or multiple personality? *International Journal of Clinical and Experimental Hypnosis, 32,* 67–101.

Watson, C. G., Tilleskjor, C., Kucala, T., & Jacobs, L. (1984). The birth seasonality effect in nonschizophrenic psychiatric patients. *Journal of Clinical Psychology, 40,* 884–888.

Watson, J. B., & Rayner, R. (1920). Conditioned emotional reactions. *Journal of Experimental Psychology, 3,* 1–14.

Webb, C. T., & Levinson, D. F. (1993). Schizotypal and paranoid personality disorder in the relatives of patients with schizophrenia and affective disorders: A review. *Schizophrenia Research, 11,* 81–92.

Wedell, K., Welton, J., Evans, B., & Goacher, A. (1987). Policy and provision under the 1981 act. *British Journal of Special Education, 14,* 50–53.

Wehr, T. A., & Rosenthal, N. E. (1989). Seasonality and affective illness. *American Journal of Psychiatry, 146,* 829–839.

Weinberg, M. S., Williams, C. J., & Calham, C. (1994). Homosexual foot fetishism. *Archives of Sexual Behavior, 23,* 611–620.

Weinberg, R. A., Scarr, S., & Waldman, I. D. (1992). The Minnesota Transracial Adoption Study: A follow-up of IQ test performance at. *Intelligence, 16*(1), 117–135.

Weinberger, D. R. (1996). On the plausibility of "the neurodevelopmental hypothesis" of schizophrenia. *Neuropsychopharmacology, 14,* 1S–11S.

Weinberger, J. (1993). Common factors in psychotherapy. In J. Gold & G. Stricker (Eds.), *Handbook of psychotherapy integration.* New York: Plenum.

Weinberger, J. (1995). Common factors aren't so common: The common factors dilemma. *Clinical Psychology: Science and Practice, 2,* 45–69.

Weinstein, D. D., Diforio, D., Schiffman, J., Walker, E., & Bonsall, R. (1999). Minor physical anomalies, dermatoglyphic asymmetries, and cortisol levels in adolescents. *American Journal of Psychiatry, 156*(4), 617–623.

Weintraub, L. (1997). Inner-city post-traumatic stress disorder. *Journal of Psychiatry and Law, 25*(2), 249–286.

Weiss, J. M., Glazer, H. I., & Pohoresky, L. A. (1976). Coping behavior and neurochemical change in rats: An alternative explanation for the original "learned helplessness" experiments. In G. Serban & A. King (Eds.), *Animal models in human psychobiology.* New York: Plenum.

Weisse, C. S. (1992). Depression and immunocompetence: A review of the literature. *Psychological Bulletin, 111,* 475–489.

Weissman, M. M., (1974). The epidemiology of suicide attempts, 1969–1971. *Archives of General Psychiatry, 30,* 737–746.

Weissman, M. M. (1979). The psychological treatment of depression: Research evidence for the efficacy of psychotherapy alone, in comparison and in combination with pharmacotherapy. *Archives of General Psychiatry, 36,* 1261–1269.

Weissman, M. M., Bruce, M. L., Leaf, P. J., Florio, L. P. & Holzer, C. (1991). Affective disorders. In L. Robins and K. Regier (Eds.), *The Epidemiologic Catchment Area Study.*

Weissman, M. M., & Markowitz, J. C. (1998). An overview of interpersonal psychotherapy. In J. C. Markowitz et al. (Eds.), *Interpersonal psychotherapy. Review of psychiatry.*

Weissman, M. M., Prusoff, B. A., Di Mascio, A., Neu, C., Goklaney, M., & Klerman, G. L. (1979). The efficacy of drugs and psychotherapy in the treatment of acute depressive episodes. *American Journal of Psychiatry, 136,* 555–558.

Weissman, M. M., Warner, V., Wickramaratne, P. J., & Kandel, D. B. (1999). Maternal smoking during pregnancy and psychopathology in offspring followed to adulthood. *Journal of the American Academy of Child and Adolescent Psychiatry, 38* (7), 892–899.

Wekstein, L. (1979). *Handbook of suicidology: Principles, problems, and practice.* New York: Brunner/Mazel.

Welch, S. L., & Fairburn, C. G. (1994). Sexual abuse and bulimia nervosa: Three integrated case control comparisons. *American Journal of Psychiatry, 151,* 402–407.

Welsch v. *Litkins,* 373 F. Supp. 487 (D. Minn. 1974).

Weltzin, T. E., Fernstrom, M. H., Fernstrom, J. D., Neuberger, S. K., & Kaye, W. H. (1995). Acute tryptophan depletion and increased food intake and irritability in bulimia nervosa. *American Journal of Psychiatry, 152,* 1668–1671.

Wender, P. H. (1971). *Minimal brain dysfunction in children.* New York: Wiley-Interscience.

Wender, P. H., Rosenthal, D., Kety, S. S., Schulsinger, F. A., & Weiner, J. (1974). Cross-fostering: A research strategy for clarifying the role of genetic and experiential factors in the etiology of schizophrenia. *Archives of General Psychiatry, 30,* 121–128.

Werner, M. J., Walker, L. S., & Greene, J. W. (1995). Relationship of alcohol expectancies to problem drinking among college women. *Journal of Adolescent Health, 16,* 191–199.

Werth, J. L., Jr. (1999). Contemporary perspectives on rational suicide.

West, M. A. (1987). *The psychology of meditation.* Oxford: Oxford University Press.

West, S. A., McElroy, S. L., Strakowski, S. M., Keck, P. E., & McConville, B. J. (1995). Attention-deficit hyperactivity disorder in adolescent mania. *American Journal of Psychiatry, 152,* 271–273.

Westermeyer, J. F., Harrow, M., & Marengo, J. T. (1991). Risk of suicide in schizophrenia and other psychotic and nonpsychotic disorders. *Journal of Nervous and Mental Disease, 179,* 259–266.

Westrin, A., Ekman, R., & Traeskman-Bendz, L. (1999). Alterations of corticotropin releasing hormone (CRH) and neuropeptide Y (NPY) plasma. *European Neuropsychopharmacology, 9*(3), 205–211.

Wetter, M. W., Baer, R. A., Berry, D. T., & Reynolds, S. K. (1994). The effect of symptom information on faking on the MMPI-2. *Assessment, 1,* 199–207.

Whaley, A. L. (1997). Ethnicity/race, paranoia, and psychiatric diagnoses: Clinician bias versus sociocultural. *Journal of Psychopathology and Behavioral Assessment, 19*(1), 1–20.

Wheeler, L. (1966). Toward a theory of behavioral contagion. *Psychological Review, 73,* 179–192.

Whiffen, V. E. (1992). Is postpartum depression a distinct diagnosis? *Clinical Psychology Review, 12,* 485–508.

White, G. L., Fishbein, S., & Rutstein, J. (1981). Passionate love: The misattribution of arousal. *Journal of Personality and Social Psychology, 41,* 56–62.

White, J. L., Moffitt, T. E., Caspi, A., Bartusch, D. J., Needles, D. J., & Loeber-Stouthamer, M. (1994). Measuring impulsivity and examining its relationship to delinquency. *Journal of Abnormal Psychology, 103,* 192–205.

White, M. S., Maher, B. A., & Manschreck, T. C. (1998). Hemispheric specialization in schizophrenics with perceptual aberration. *Schizophrenia Research, 32*(3), 161–170.

Whitlock, F. A. (1967). The aetiology of hysteria. *Acta Psychiatrica Scandinavica, 43,* 144–162.

Whittal, M. L., Agras, W. S., & Gould, R. A. (1999). Bulimia nervosa: A meta-analysis of psychosocial and pharmacological treatments. *Behavior Therapy, 30*(1), 117–135.

Whitworth, A. B., Honeder, M., Kremser, C., & Kemmler, G. (1998). Hippocampal volume reduction in male schizophrenic patients. *Schizophrenia Research, 31*(2–3), 73–81.

Wiedemann, G. (1998). Kleptomania: Characteristics of 12 cases. *European Psychiatry, 13*(2), 67–77.

Wilcox, J. A., & Nasrallah, H. A. (1987a). Perinatal distress and prognosis of psychotic illness. *Neuropsychobiology, 17,* 173–175.

Wilcox, J. A., & Nasrallah, H. A. (1987b). Perinatal insult as a risk factor in paranoid and nonparanoid schizophrenia. *Psychopathology, 20,* 285–287.

Wilhelm, S., Otto, M. W., Zucker, B. G., & Pollack, M. H. (1997). Prevalence of body dysmorphic disorder in patients with anxiety disorders. *Journal of Anxiety Disorders, 11*(5), 499–502.

Wilkinson, A. (1999). Notes left behind. *New Yorker* (Feb. 15), 44–49.

Willcutt, E. G., Pennington, B. F., Chabildas, N. A., Friedman, M. C., & Alexander, J. (1999). Psychiatry comorbidity associated with DSM-IV ADHD in a nonreferred sample of twins. *Journal of the American Academy of Child and Adolescent Psychiatry, 38*(11), 1355–1362.

Williams, C., & House, A. (1994). Reducing the costs of chronic somatisation. *Irish Journal of Psychological Medicine, 11,* 79–82.

Williams, C. D. (1959). The elimination of tantrum behavior by extinction procedures. *Journal of Abnormal and Social Psychology, 59,* 269.

Williams, J. B. W. (1999). Psychiatric classification. In R. E. Hales, S. C. Yudofsky, & J. A. Talbot (Eds.), *Textbook of psychiatry* (pp. 227–252). Washington, DC: American Psychiatric Press.

Williams, L. M. (1992). Adult memories of child sexual abuse: Preliminary findings from a longitudinal study. *American Journal for Prevention of Child Abuse Advisor, 5,* 19–20.

Williams, L. M. (1994). Recall of childhood trauma: A prospective study of women's memories of child sexual abuse. *Journal of Consulting and Clinical Psychology, 62,* 1167–1176.

Williams, R. B., Haney, T. L., Lee, K. L., Kong, Y., Blumenthal, J. A., & Whalen, R. E. (1980). Type A behavior, hostility, and coronary atherosclerosis. *Psychosomatic Medicine, 42,* 539–549.

Williams, S. L., & Rappoport, A. (1983). Cognitive treatment in the natural environment for agoraphobics. *Behavior Therapy, 14,* 299–313.

Williamson, D. E., Birmaher, B., Frank, E., & Anderson, B. P. (1998). Nature of life events and difficulties in depressed adolescents. *Journal of the American Academy of Child and Adolescent Psychiatry.*

Wilson, A. A. (1903). A case of double consciousness. *Journal of Mental Service, 49,* 640–658.

Wilson, E. F., Davis, J. H., Bloom, J. D., & Batten, P. J. (1998). Homicide or suicide: The killing of suicidal persons by law enforcement officers. *Journal of Forensic Sciences, 43*(1), 46–52.

Wilson, G. T. (1987). Cognitive studies in alcoholism. *Journal of Consulting and Clinical Psychology, 55,* 325–331.

Wilson, G. T. (1999). Cognitive behavior therapy for eating disorders: Progress and problems. *Behaviour Research and Therapy, 37*(1), S79–S95.

Wilson, G. T., & Fairburn, C. G. (1993). Cognitive treatments for eating disorders. *Journal of Consulting and Clinical Psychology, 61,* 261–269.

Wilson, G. T., & Fairburn, C. G. (1998). Treatments for eating disorders. In P. E. Nathan & J. M. Gorman (Eds.), *A guide to treatments that work* (pp. 501–530). New York: Oxford University Press.

Wilson, G. T., Loeb, K. L., Walsh, B. T., Labouvie, E., & Petkova, E. (1999). Psychological versus pharmacological treatments of bulimia nervosa: Predictors and processes. *Journal of Consulting and Clinical Psychology, 67*(4), 451–459.

Wilson, J. J., & Gil, K. M. (1996). The efficacy of psychological and pharmacological interventions for the treatment of chronic. *Clinical Psychology Review, 16*(6), 573–597.

Wilson, K. D. (1998). Issues surrounding the cognitive neuroscience of obsessive-compulsive disorder. *Psychonomic Bulletin and Review, 5*(2), 161–172.

Winchel, R. M., & Stanley, M. A. (1991). Self-injurious behavior: A review of the behavior and biology of self-mutilation. *American Journal of Psychiatry, 148,* 306–317.

Winchester, S. (1999). *The professor and the madman.* New York: Harper Perennial.

Wincze, J., Bansal, S., & Malamud, M. (1986). Effects of MPA on subjective arousal, arousal to erotic stimulation, and nocturnal penile tumescence in male sex offenders. *Archives of Sexual Behavior, 15,* 293–305.

Winefield, H. R. (1987). Psychotherapy and social support: Parallels and differences in the helping process. *Clinical Psychology Review, 7,* 631–644.

Winick, B. J. (1991). Voluntary hospitalization after *Zinermon* v. *Burch. Psychiatric Annals, 21,* 584–589.

Winterowd, C. L., Street, V. L., & Boswell, D. L. (1998). Perceived social support, disability status, and affect in college students. *Journal of College Student Psychotherapy, 13*(2), 53–70.

Winters v. *Miller,* 446 F.2d 65, 71 (2d Cir. 1971).

Winters, K. C., & Rich, T. (1998). A twin study of adult gambling behavior. *Journal of Gambling Studies, 14*(3), 213–225.

Wirz-Justice, A., Graw, P., Krauchi, K., Gisin, B., Jochum, A., Arendt, J., Fisch, H., Buddeberg, C., & Poldinger, W. (1993). Light therapy in seasonal affective disorder is independent of time of day or circadian phase. *Archives of General Psychiatry, 50,* 929–936.

Wise, M. G., Gray, K. F., & Seltzer, B. (1999). Delirium, dementia, and amnestic disorders. In R. E. Hales, S. C. Yudofsky, & J. A. Talbot (Eds.), *Textbook of psychiatry* (pp. 317–362). Washington, DC: American Psychiatric Press.

Wise, M. G., & Tierney, J. G. (1999). Impulse control disorders not elsewhere classified. In R. E. Hales, S. C. Yudofsky, & J. A. Talbot (Eds.), *Textbook of psychiatry* (pp. 773–794). Washington, DC: American Psychiatric Press.

Wiseman, M. B., Sanchez, J. A., Buechel, C., & Mintun, M. A. (1999). Patterns of relative cerebral blood flow in minor cognitive motor disorder in human. *Journal of Neuropsychiatry and Clinical Neurosciences, 11*(2), 222–233.

Wisner, K. L., Gelenberg, A. J., Leonard, H., Zarin, D., & Frank, E. (1999). Pharmacologic treatment of depression during pregnancy. *Journal of the American Medical Association, 282*(13), 1264–1269.

Wittchen, H., Zhoa, S., Kessler, R. C., & Eaton, W. W. (1994). DSM-III-R generalized anxiety disorder in the National Comorbidity Survey. *Archives of General Psychiatry, 51,* 355–364.

Wittenborn, J. R. (1951). Symptom patterns in a group of mental hospital patients. *Journal of Consulting Psychology, 15,* 290–302.

Wittenborn, J. R. (1962). The dimensions of psychosis. *Journal of Nervous and Mental Disease, 134,* 117–128.

Wittrock, D. A., & Myers, T. C. (1998). The comparison of individuals with recurrent tension-type headache and headache-free controls. *Annals of Behavioral Medicine, 20*(2), 118–134.

Wolf, M., Risley, T., Johnston, M., Harris, F., & Allen, E. (1967). Application of operant conditioning procedures to the behaviour problems of an autistic child: A follow-up and extension. *Behaviour Research and Therapy, 5,* 103–112.

Wolf, T. M., Elston, R. C., & Kissling, G. E. (1989). Relationship of hassles, uplifts, and life events to psychological well-being of freshman medical students. *Behavioral Medicine, 15,* 37–45.

Wolkin, A., Sanfilipo, M., Wolf, A. P., Angrist, B., Brodie, J. D., & Rotrosen, J. (1992). Negative symptoms and hypofrontality in chronic schizophrenia. *Archives of General Psychiatry, 49,* 959–965.

Wolpe, J. (1958). *Psychotherapy by reciprocal inhibition.* Stanford, CA: Stanford University Press.

Wolpert, E. A., Goldberg, J. F., & Harrow, M. (1990). Rapid cycling in unipolar and bipolar affective disorders. *American Journal of Psychiatry, 147,* 725–728.

Wong, D. F., Wagner, H. N., Dannals, R. F., Links, J. M., Frost, J. J., Ravert, H. T., Wilson, A. A., Rosenbaum, A. E., Gjedde, A., Douglass, K. H., Petronis, J. D., Folstein, M. F., Toung, J. K. T., Burns, H. D., & Kuhar, M. J. (1984). Effects of age on dopamine and serotonin receptors measured by positron tomography in the living human brain. *Science, 226,* 1393–1396.

Wong, D. F., Wagner, H. N., Tune, L. E., Dannals, R. F., Pearlson, G. D., Links, J. M., Tamminga, C. A., Broussolle, E. P., Ravert, H. T., Wilson A. A., Toung, J. K. T., Malat, J., Williams, J. A., O'Tuma, L. A., Snyder, S. H., Kuhar, M. J., & Gjedde, A. (1986). Positron emission tomography reveals elevated D2 dopamine receptors in drug-naive schizophrenics. *Science, 234,* 1558–1563.

Woo-Ming, A. M., & Siever, L. J. (1998). Psychopharmalogical treatment of personality disorders. In P. E. Nathan & J. M. Gorman (Eds.), *A guide to treatments that work* (pp. 554–567). New York: Oxford University Press.

Wood, J. M., Nezworski, M. T., & Stejskal, W. J. (1996a). Thinking critically about the comprehensive system for the Rorschach: A reply to Exner. *Psychological Science, 7*(1), 14–17.

Wood, J. M., Nezworski, M. T., & Stejskal, W. J. (1996b). The comprehensive system for the Rorschach: A critical examination. *Psychological Science, 7*(1), 3–10.

Wood, J. M., Nezworski, M. T., & Stejskal, W. J. (1997). The reliability of the Comprehensive System for the Rorschach: A comment on Meyer. *Psychological Assessment, 9*(4), 490–494.

Woodruff, P. W. R., Wright, I. C., Bullmore, E. T., & Brammer, M. (1997). Auditory hallucinations and the temporal cortical response to speech in schizophrenia. *American Journal of Psychiatry, 154*(12), 1676–1682.

Woodward, M. (1999). Hypnosedatives in the elderly: A guide to appropriate use. *CNS Drugs, 11*(4), 263–279.

Wright, I. C., Ellison, Z. R., Sharma, T., Friston, K. J., Murray, R. M., & McGuire, P. K. (1999). Mapping of grey matter changes in schizophrenia. *Schizophrenia Research, 35*(1), 1–14.

Wright, J. H., & Beck, A. T. (1999). Cognitive therapy. In R. E. Hales, S. C. Yudofsky, & J. A. Talbot (Eds.), *Textbook of psychiatry* (pp. 1205–1242). Washington, DC: American Psychiatric Press.

Wright, P., Takei, N., Rifkin, L., & Murray, R. M. (1995). Maternal influenza, obstetric complications, and schizophrenia. *American Journal of Psychiatry, 152*(12), 1714–1720.

Wrightsman, L., Nietzel, M., & Fortune, W. (1998). *Psychology and the legal system.* Pacific Grove, CA: Brooks/Cole.

Wulsin, L. R., Vaillant, G. E., & Wells, V. E. (1999). A systematic review of the mortality of depression. *Psychosomatic Medicine, 61*(1), 6–17.

Wyatt v. *Stickney,* 325 F. Supp. 781 (M.D. Ala. 1971); 344 F. Supp. 343 (M.D. Ala. 1972).

Wynchank, D., & Berk, M. (1998). Behavioural changes in dogs with acral lick dermatitis during a 2 month extension phase of. *Human Psychopharmacology Clinical and Experimental, 13*(6), 435–438.

Xavier, F. A., Flaum, M., Andreasen, N. C., Strauss, D. H., Yale, S. A., Clark, S. C., & Gorman, J. M. (1994). Awareness of illness in schizophrenia and schizoaffective and mood disorders. *Archives of General Psychiatry, 51,* 826–836.

Yaffe, K., Sawaya, G., Lieberburg, I., & Grady, D. (1998). Estrogen therapy in postmenopausal women: Effects on cognitive function and dementia. *Journal of the American Medical Association, 279*(9), 688–695.

Yalom, I. D., Green, R., & Fish, N. (1973). Prenatal exposure to female hormones. *Archives of General Psychiatry, 28,* 554–561.

Yan, R., Bienkowski, M. J., Shuck, M. E., Miao, H., Tory, M. C., Pauley, A. M., & Brashier, J. R. (1999). Membrane-anchored aspartyl protease with Alzheimer's disease beta-secretase activity. *Nature, 402*(6761), 533–537.

Yehuda, R. (1998). Psychoneuroendocrinology of post-traumatic stress disorder. *Psychiatric Clinics of North America, 21*(2), 359–379.

Yehuda, R. (1999). Biological factors associated with susceptibility to posttraumatic stress disorder. *Canadian Journal of Psychiatry, 44*(1), 34–39.

Yehuda, R., Marshall, R., & Giller, E. L., Jr. (1998). Psychopharmalogical treatment of post-traumatic stress disorder. In P. E. Nathan & J. M. Gorman (Eds.), *A guide to treatments that work* (pp. 377–397). New York: Oxford University Press.

Yirmiya, N., & Sigman, M., (1991). High-functioning individuals with autism: Diagnosis, empirical findings, and theoretical issues. *Clinical Psychology Review, 11,* 669–683.

Yoder, K. A. (1999). Comparing suicide attempters, suicide ideators and nonsuicidal homeless and runaway. *Suicide and Life Threatening Behavior, 29*(1), 25–36.

Yonker, K. A., Kando, J. C., Cole, J. O., & Blumenthal, S. (1992). Gender differences in pharmacokinetics and pharmacodynamics of psychotropic medication. *American Journal of Psychiatry, 149,* 587–595.

Yonkers, K. A., Zlotnick, C., Allsworth, J., & Warshaw, M. (1998). Is the course of panic disorder the same in women and men? *American Journal of Psychiatry, 155*(5), 596–602.

Yoshikawa, H. (1994). Prevention as cumulative protection: Effects of early family support and education on chronic delinquency and its risks. *Psychological Bulletin, 115,* 28–54.

Young, R. L., & Nettelbeck, T. (1995). The abilities of a musical savant and his family. *Journal of Autism and Developmental Disorders, 25*(3), 231–248.

Young, W. C., Goy, R. W., & Phoenix, C. H. (1964). Hormones and sexual behavior. *Science, 143,* 212–218.

Youngberg v. *Romeo,* 457 U.S. 307 (1981).

Yu, P., Harris, G. E., Solovitz, B. L., & Franklin, J. L. (1986). A social problem-solving intervention for children at high risk for later psychopathology. *Journal of Clinical Child Psychology, 15,* 30–40.

Zald, D. H., & Kim, S. W. (1996a). Anatomy and function of the orbital frontal cortex: I. Anatomy, neurocircuitry, and obsessive-compulsive disorder. *Journal of Neuropsychiatry and Clinical Neurosciences, 8*(2), 125–138.

Zald, D. H., & Kim, S. W. (1996b). Anatomy and function of the orbital frontal cortex: II. Function and relevance to. *Journal of Neuropsychiatry and Clinical Neurosciences, 8*(3), 249–261.

Zametkin, A. J., Nordahl, T. E., Gross, M., King, A. C., Stemple, W. E., Rumsey, J., Hamburger, S., & Cohen, R. M. (1990). Cerebral glucose metabolism in adults with hyperactivity of childhood onset. *New England Journal of Medicine, 323,* 1361–1366.

Zamula, E. (1988). Taming Tourette's tics and twitches. *FDA Consumer Report, 22,* 104–110.

Zanarini, M. C., Gunderson, J. G., & Frankenburg, F. R. (1990). Cognitive features of the borderline personality disorder. *American Journal of Psychiatry, 147,* 57–63.

Zanarini, M. C., Gunderson, J. G., Frankenburg, F. R., & Chauncey, D. L. (1990). Discriminating borderline personality disorder from other Axis II disorders. *American Journal of Psychiatry, 147,* 161–167.

Zarin, D. A., McIntyre, J. S., Pincus, H. A., & Seigle, L. (1999). Practice guidelines in psychiatry and a psychiatric practice research network. In R. E. Hales, S. C. Yudofsky, & J. A. Talbot (Eds.), *Textbook of psychiatry* (pp. 1655–1666). Washington, DC: American Psychiatric Press.

Zatzick, D. (1999). In R. E. Hales, S. C. Yudofsky, & J. A. Talbot (Eds.), *Textbook of psychiatry* (pp. 1645–1654). Washington, DC: American Psychiatric Press.

Zautra, A. J., Burleson, M. H., Matt, K. S., Roth, S., & Burrows, L. (1994). Interpersonal stress, depression, and disease activity in rheumatoid arthritis and osteoarthritis patients. *Health Psychology, 13,* 139–148.

Zautra, A. J., Hamilton, N. A., Potter, P., & Smith, B. (1999). Field research on the relationship between stress and disease activity in rheumatoid arthritis. In M. Cutolo, A. T. Masi, et al. (Eds.), *Neuroendocrine immune basis of the rheumatic.*

Zelkowitz, P., & Milet, T. H. (1997). Stress and support as related to postpartum paternal mental health and perceptions of the. *Infant Mental Health Journal, 18*(4), 424–435.

Zigler, E. (1969). Development versus difference theories of mental retardation and the problem of motivation. *American Journal of Mental Deficiency, 73,* 536–555.

Zigler, E., & Balla, D. (1982). *Mental retardation: The developmental-difference controversy.* Hillsdale, NJ: Erlbaum.

Zigler, E., Glick, M., & Marsh, A. (1979). Premorbid social competence and outcome among schizophrenic and nonschizophrenic patients. *Journal of Nervous and Mental Diseases, 167,* 478–483.

Zigler, E., & Phillips, L. (1961). Psychiatric diagnosis: A critique. *Journal of Abnormal and Social Psychology, 3,* 607–618.

Zigler, E., & Styfco, S. J. (1994). Head Start: Criticisms in a constructive context. *American Psychologist, 49*(2), 127–132.

Zigler, E. F., & Muenchow, S. (1992). Head Start: The inside story of America's most successful educational.

Zillmann, D. (1983). Transfer of excitation in emotional behavior. In J. T. Cacioppo & R. E. Petty (Eds.), *Social psychophysiology: A sourcebook.* New York: Guilford Press.

Zillmann, D., & Bryant, J. (1974). Effect of residual excitation on the emotional response to provocation and delayed aggressive behavior. *Journal of Personality and Social Psychology, 30,* 782–791.

Zillmann, D., Schweitzer, K. J., & Mundorf, N. (1994). Menstrual cycle variation of women's interest in erotica. *Archives of Sexual Behavior, 23,* 579–594.

Zimmerman, A., Frye, V., & Potter, N. (1993). Immunological aspects of autism. *International Pediatrics, 8,* 199–204.

Zimmerman, M., & Mattia, J. I. (1999). The reliability and validity of a screening questionnaire for 13 DSM-IV Axis I disorders. *Journal of Clinical Psychiatry, 60*(10), 677–683.

Zinermon v. *Burch,* 110 S.Ct. 975 (1990).

Zipfel, S., Loewe, B., Paschke, T., Immel, B., Lange, R., & Zimmerman, R. (1998). Psychological distress in patients awaiting heart transplantation. *Journal of Psychosomatic Research, 45*(5), 465–470.

Zipursky, R. B., Lambe, E. K., Kapur, S., & Mikulis, D. J. (1998). Cerebral gray matter volume deficits in first episode psychosis. *Archives of General Psychiatry, 55*(6), 540–546.

Zotter, D. L., & Crowther, J. H. (1991). The role of cognitions in bulimia nervosa. *Cognitive Therapy and Research, 15,* 413–426.

Zubieta, J. K., & Alessi, N. E. (1993). Is there a role of serotonin in the disruptive behavior disorders? A literature review. *Journal of Child and Adolescent Psychopharmacology, 3,* 11–35.

Zucker, R., & Gomberg, E. (1986). Etiology of alcoholism reconsidered: The case for a biopsychosocial process. *American Psychologist, 41,* 783–793.

Zullino, D., Bondolfi, G., & Baumann, P. (1998). The serotonin paradox: Negative symptoms and SSRI augmentation. *International Journal of Psychiatry in Clinical Practice, 2*(1), 19–26.

Credits

Text Credits

Figure 3.3, p. 65: From Robin B. Jarrett, Martin Schaffer, Donald McIntire, Amy Witt-Browder, Dolores Kraft, and Richard C. Risser, "Treatment of Atypical Depression with Cognitive Therapy or Phenelzine: A Double-Blind, Placebo-Controlled Trial," from *Archives of General Psychiatry,* Vol. 56, May 1999, p. 435, Figure 1 and Table 2. Reprinted with permission of the American Medical Association. **Case Study 3.2, p. 81:** From Carl R. Rogers, *Client-Centered Therapy.* Copyright © 1951 by Houghton Mifflin Company. Reprinted with permission. **Figure 4.1, p. 89:** Reprinted with permission from the *Diagnostic and Statistical Manual of Mental Disorders,* Fourth Edition. Copyright © 1994 American Psychiatric Association. **Figure 4.3, p. 95:** Minnesota Multiphasic Personality Inventory-2 (MMPI-2) Profile for Basic Scales. Copyright © 1989 the Regents of the University of Minnesota. All rights reserved. "MMPI-2" and "Minnesota Multiphasic Personality Inventory-2" are trademarks owned by the University of Minnesota. **Figure 4.7, p. 101:** Scott Carnazine/Photo Researchers. **Case Study 4.1, pp. 116–117:** From David Holmes, "Aerobic Fitness and the Response to Psychological Stress," from *Exercise Psychology: The Influence of Physical Exercise on Psychological Processes,* edited by P. Seraganian. Copyright © 1993 by John Wiley & Sons, Inc. Reprinted by permission of John Wiley & Sons, Inc. **Figure in Case Study 4.1, p. 117:** From I. L. McCann and D. Holmes, "Influence of Aerobic Exercise on Depression," from *Journal of Personality and Social Psychology,* Vol. 46, p. 1145, Figure 1. Copyright © 1984 by the American Psychological Association. Reprinted with permission. **Table 5.1, p. 124:** Reprinted with permission from the *Diagnostic and Statistical Manual of Mental Disorders,* Fourth Edition. Copyright © 1994 American Psychiatric Association. **Figure 5.3, p. 138:** Reprinted from the *Journal of Anxiety Disorders,* Vol. 12, E. S. Becker, M. Rinck, W. T. Roth, and J. Margraf, "Don't Worry and Beware of White Bears: Thought Suppression in Anxiety Patients," p. 47, copyright © 1998, with permission from Elsevier Science. **Figure 6.3, p. 164:** From M. Lindsay, R. Crino, and G. Andrews, "Controlled Trial of Exposure and Response Prevention in Obsessive-Compulsive Disorder," from the *British Journal of Psychiatry,* Vol. 171, p. 137, Figure 1. Copyright © 1997 Royal College of Psychiatrists. Reprinted by permission of the Royal College of Psychiatrists. **Table 8.1, p. 215:** Reprinted with permission from the *Diagnostic and Statistical Manual of Mental Disorders,* Fourth Edition. Copyright © 1994 American Psychiatric Association. **Figure 8.4, p. 223:** Reprinted from *Clinical Psychology Review,* Vol. 12, No. 2, G. E. Matt, C. Vazquez, and W. K. Campbell, "Mood-Congruent Recall of Affectively Toned Stimuli: A Meta-Analytic Review," p. 248, copyright © 1992, with permission from Elsevier Science. **Figure 8.13, p. 235:** From Giovanni A. Fava, Chiara Rafanelli, Silvana Grandi, Sandra Conti, and Piera Belluardo, "Prevention of Recurrent Depression with Cognitive Behavioral Therapy: Preliminary Findings," from *Archives of General Psychiatry,* Vol. 55, September 1998, p. 819. Reprinted with permission of the American Medical Association. **Table 9.1, p. 251:** Reprinted with permission from the *Diagnostic and Statistical Manual of Mental Disorders,* Fourth Edition. Copyright © 1994 American Psy-

chiatric Association. **Figure 9.1, p. 255:** From "Cerebral Metabolic Rates for Glucose in Mood Disorders" by L.R. Baxter et al., in *Archives of General Psychiatry,* Vol. 42, May 1985. Reprinted by permission of the American Medical Association. **Case Study 9.3, p. 260:** Excerpt from *An Unquiet Mind* by Kay Redfield Jamison. Copyright © 1995 by Kay Redfield Jamison. Re-printed by permission of Alfred A. Knopf, a division of Random House, Inc. **Table 10.1, p. 285:** Reprinted with permission from the *Diagnostic and Statistical Manual of Mental Disorders,* Fourth Edition. Copyright © 1994 American Psychiatric Association. **Figure 10.3, p. 296:** From A. W. Loranger, "Sex Differences in Age at Onset of Schizophrenia," from *Archives of General Psychiatry,* Vol. 41, February 1984. Reprinted with permission of the American Medical Association. **Figure 11.8, p. 320:** Reprinted with permission from Andreasen. Brain Imaging: Applications in Psychiatry. *Science.* © 1988 American Association for the Advancement of Science. **Figure 11.9, p. 321:** From "Frontostriatal Disorder of Cerebral Metabolism in Never-Medicated Schizophrenia" by M. S. Buchsbaum et al., in *Archives of General Psychiatry,* Vol. 49, December 1992. Reprinted by permission of the Amercian Medical Society. **Figure 11.12, p. 331:** From J. M. Kane et al., "Clozapine for the Treatment-Resistant Scizophrenic," from *Archives of General Psychiatry,* Vol. 45, September 1998. Reprinted with permission of the American Medical Association. **Figure 11.15, p. 335:** I. R. Falloon et al., "Family Management in the Prevention of Morbidity of Schizophrenia," from *Archives of General Psychiatry,* Vol. 42, September 1985. Reprinted with permission of the American Medical Association. **Table 12.1, p. 346:** Reprinted with permission from the *Diagnostic and Statistical Manual of Mental Disorders,* Fourth Edition. Copyright © 1994 American Psychiatric Association. **Table 12.2, p. 347:** Reprinted with permission from the *Diagnostic and Statistical Manual of Mental Disorders,* Fourth Edition. Copyright © 1994 American Psychiatric Association. **Table 12.3, p. 355:** Reprinted with permission from the *Diagnostic and Statistical Manual of Mental Disorders,* Fourth Edition. Copyright © 1994 American Psychiatric Association. **Figure 13.1, p. 374:** From "Cerebral Glucose Metabolism in Adults with Hyperactivity of Childhood Onset" by A. J. Zametkin et al., in the *New England Journal of Medicine,* November 15, 1990. Copyright © 1990 Massachusetts Medical Society. Reprinted by permission of The New England Journal of Medicine. **Figure 13.5, p. 381:** From Julie Magno Zito, Daniel J. Safer, Susan dos-Reis, James F. Gardner, Myde Boles, and Frances Lynch, "Trends in the Prescribing of Psychotropic Medications to Preschoolers," from *JAMA,* Vol. 283, No. 8, February 2000, p. 1028, Figure 1. Reprinted with permission of the American Medical Association. **Figure 14.5, p. 419:** Biophoto Associates/Photo Researchers. **Figure 17.2, p. 505:** Alfred Pasieka/Science Photo Lab/Photo Researchers.

Photo Credits

Page 4, Jim Pickerell/Tony Stone Images; **p. 9,** Katsuyoshi Tanaka/ Woodfin Camp & Associates; **p. 10,** (top) Corbis-Bettmann, (bottom) Hulton Getty Picture Library/Tony Stone Images; **p. 11,** (left) Bettmann/Corbis, (right) Corbis-Bettmann; **p. 12,** (top) Benelux/Photo

DSM-IV CLASSIFICATION *(continued)*

AXIS I *(continued)*

Dissociative Disorders

Dissociative Amnesia

Dissociative Fugue

Dissociative Identity Disorder

Depersonalization Disorder

Sexual and Gender Identity Disorders

Sexual Dysfunctions

Sexual Desire Disorders:

Hypoactive Sexual Desire Disorder

Sexual Aversion Disorder

Sexual Arousal Disorders:

Female Sexual Arousal Disorder

Male Erectile Disorder

Orgasmic Disorders:

Female Orgasmic Disorder

Male Orgasmic Disorder

Premature Ejaculation

Sexual Pain Disorders:

Dyspareunia

Vaginismus

Sexual Dysfunction Due to a General
Medical Condition

Substance-Induced Sexual Dysfunction

Paraphilias

Exhibitionism

Fetishism

Frotteurism

Pedophilia

Sexual Masochism

Sexual Sadism

Transvestic Fetishism

Voyeurism

Gender Identity Disorders

In Children

In Adolescents or Adults

Eating Disorders

Anorexia Nervosa

Bulimia Nervosa

Sleep Disorders

Primary Sleep Disorders

Dyssomnias:

Primary Insomnia

Primary Hypersomnia

Narcolepsy

Breathing-Related Sleep Disorder

Circadian Rhythm Sleep Disorder

Parasomnias:

Nightmare Disorder

Sleep Terror Disorder

Sleepwalking Disorder

**Sleep Disorders Related to
Another Mental Disorder**

**Sleep Disorder Due to a General
Medical Condition**

*Substance-Induced Sleep
Disorder*

Impulse-Control Disorders Not
Elsewhere Classified

Intermittent Explosive Disorder

Kleptomania